EAST ASIA

Railroads

Railroads recently built
or projected

A HISTORY OF EAST ASIAN
CIVILIZATION · VOLUME TWO

East Asia

The Modern Transformation

A HISTORY OF EAST ASIAN

CIVILIZATION · VOLUME TWO

East Asia
The Modern Transformation

John K. Fairbank · Edwin O. Reischauer · Albert M. Craig

HOUGHTON MIFFLIN COMPANY · BOSTON

For

Alfred Kaiming Chiu

Custodian of the Chinese and Japanese Works

in the Harvard College Library

1927–1929

Librarian, 1929–

of the

Chinese-Japanese Library

of the Harvard-Yenching Institute

at Harvard University

Acknowledgments

This book, like its predecessor, *East Asia: The Great Tradition*, has grown out of our collaboration in a lecture course begun in 1939 and offered since 1947 under the Harvard Program in General Education. The initial responsibility for chapters in this volume has similarly reflected the division of lecturing assignments in the course. Accordingly, just as the early history of East Asia in Volume One was primarily the work of E. O. Reischauer, so most of the present volume on modern times is by J. K. Fairbank. Specifically, Chapters 1 and 2, 5 and 6, 8, 9, and part of 10 are primarily the work of the latter, while Chapters 3 and 4 and a small part of Chapter 7 were drafted by the former in 1960. These two authors are greatly indebted to their colleague, Albert M. Craig, who generously consented to take responsibility for writing Chapter 7 and part of Chapter 10 on recent Japanese history after Mr. Reischauer's appointment early in 1961 as Ambassador to Japan.

As in Volume One, the present three authors have benefited from each other's suggestions and criticisms, and we are indebted to one another in more ways than could be enumerated. Yet the pressure of official duties since going to Tōkyō has made it impossible for one of us, Mr. Reischauer, to assume any responsibility for the later chapters or to participate in the completion and production of this volume. As a consequence, the authors in Cambridge, Massachusetts, take the final responsibility for the book as produced.

Our debts to others are even more numerous than for Volume One. As teachers we have been in touch during the years with the work of other scholars, both pre-doctoral and post-doctoral, at Harvard and elsewhere, concerning the greater part of the subject matter dealt with in this volume. Although our debt is primarily to published works, or in some cases to manuscripts still in process of development, we are also indebted for specific textual comments to a great number of specialists who read portions of this volume in manuscript. Our sense of creative authorship has been at all times tempered by the realization that historical knowledge and understanding are a common fund and that we each get from this fund much more than we give. We should like to think that in writing this survey our function has been merely to transmit; yet the

Acknowledgments

necessity to select and organize our understanding of events has obliged us, like all historians, to exercise ultimate judgment as individuals.

As before, we are indebted to Wilma C. Fairbank for help in selecting illustrative materials. The following persons who have helped us concretely, in greater or less degree, represent the more obvious part of our indebtedness: Dr. William Ayers, Professor Robert N. Bellah of Harvard University, Professor Harry J. Benda of Yale University, Professor John Cady of Ohio University, Professor Hsin-pao Chang of the University of Iowa, Dr. Peter Chen, Professor Ying-wan Cheng of Adelphi Suffolk College (especially in connection with the map of "The Ch'ing Mounted Courier System"), Dr. Ching-young Choe, Dr. Kee-il Choi, Professor Tse-tsung Chow of the University of Wisconsin, Father Horacio de la Costa of the Ateneo de Manila University, Mrs. Teruko Craig, Peter Duus, Professor Lloyd Eastman of Connecticut College, Professor Rupert Emerson of Harvard University, Professor Shinkichi Etō of Tōkyō University, Professor David Farquhar of the University of Maryland, Professor Albert Feuerwerker of the University of Michigan, Joseph Fletcher, Edward Friedman, Professor Norton Ginsburg of the University of Chicago, Professor Frank Golay of Cornell University, Walter Gourlay, Professor Jerome Grieder of Ohio State University, Ikuhiko Hata, Dr. Stephen Hay, Professor Howard Hibbett of Harvard University, Professor Ping-ti Ho of the University of Chicago, Winston Hsieh, Dr. Akira Iriye of Harvard University, Professor John Israel of Claremont Men's College, Professor Marius Jansen of Princeton University, Harold L. Kahn of the University of London, Philip Kuhn of the University of Chicago, Mrs. Sally Kuhn, Professor Donald Lach of the University of Chicago, Dr. John M. H. Lindbeck of Harvard University, Professor Kwang-Ching Liu of the University of California at Davis, Professor James T. C. Liu of Stanford University, Dr. Mark Mancall of Harvard University, Professor Masao Maruyama of Tōkyō University, Professor Maurice Meisner of the University of Virginia, Thomas A. Metzger, Professor Esther Morrison of Howard University, Tetsuo Najita, Professor John L. Rawlinson of Hofstra College, Professor David Roy of Princeton University, Professor Robert Sakai of the University of Nebraska, Professor Harold Schiffrin of the Hebrew University, Jerusalem, Professor Benjamin I. Schwartz of Harvard University, Professor R. Lauriston Sharp and Professor G. William Skinner of Cornell University, Professor Ssu-yu Teng of the University of Indiana, Dr. James C. Thomson, Dr. Frank Trager of New York University, Professor Edward Wagner of Harvard University, Professor C. Martin Wilbur of Columbia University, Professor Mary C. Wright of Yale University, Professor Tatsuro Yamamoto of Tōkyō University, Professor Takeshi Ishida of Tōkyō University, Professor Lien-sheng Yang of Harvard University, Ernest Young.

Acknowledgments

We are also indebted to Mrs. Virginia Briggs, Mrs. Bertha Ezell, Mrs. Elizabeth Matheson, Miss Elizabeth Russell, Miss Pat Clark, and other members of the staff of the East Asian Research Center at Harvard University.

The dedication of this volume to Dr. Kaiming Chiu, finally, is intended to express in some small measure the thanks of several generations of scholars for his work in building up the Chinese-Japanese Library at Harvard.

JOHN K. FAIRBANK
EDWIN O. REISCHAUER
ALBERT M. CRAIG

July 1964
Cambridge, Massachusetts

A Note on Romanization   We have followed in this volume the same standard systems used in Volume One (*infra*, pp. 885–887) but with a similar omission of certain diacritical marks. Such marks, though desirable for scholarly accuracy, are normally omitted in English-language publications, especially in the modern press and periodicals. These omissions include, for example, the circumflex in Chinese transliterations, the aspirate sign used to separate syllables in Korean and Japanese, most of the diacritics in Vietnamese, and the ś in Sanskrit. We have followed the literature on China in using the older form Moslem instead of Muslim.

Contents

CHAPTER ONE

The Coming of the Europeans   3

The Modernization of East Asia · The Dynamics of European
Expansion · The Portuguese Empire · International Rivalries in
East Asia · The Christian Century in Japan · The Jesuit Success
in China · Sino-Russian Relations · The Jesuits between China
and Europe · The Decline of Sino-European Relations · The East
India Companies · The Rise of the Canton Trade

CHAPTER TWO

Invasion and Rebellion in China   80

Traditional China on the Eve of Change · China's Premodern
Economy · The Inertia of the Ch'ing Administration · The
Spread of Corruption · The Decline of Ch'ing Power · Trends
in Scholarship and Thought · The Collapse of the Canton System
· The Opium War · Western Influence through the Early Treaty
Ports · The Rise of Rebellion · The Second Treaty Settlement ·
The Restoration of the Ch'ing Government

CHAPTER THREE

Japan's Response to the West   179

Japanese Responsiveness · Japan's Capacity to Modernize · Early
Contacts with the West · The First Treaties · The Commercial
Treaties and Their Consequences · The Emergence of Satsuma

and Chōshū · The Fall of the Shogunate · The Creation of the
New Government · Consolidating the New Regime · The End
of Feudal Society

CHAPTER FOUR

The Development of Meiji Japan 244

Early Industrialization · The Development of the Business Community · The Growth of the Economy · The Transformation
of Society · Thought and Religion · Education · The Introduction of Representative Institutions · The Clamor for Parliamentary Government · Preparations for the Constitution · The Early
Years of Constitutional Government · The Fulfillment of the
Meiji Dream

CHAPTER FIVE

China's Response to the West 313

Early Westernization in Self-Defense · The Restoration of Confucian Government · Christian Missions and Their Repercussions
in the 1860's · Economic Developments under the Treaty System
· Early Industrialization · The Slow Progress of Modernization
in the 1870's and 1880's · Foreign Encroachment and Chinese
Resistance · The Failure of "Self-Strengthening" against Japan
· The Reform Movement · The Boxer Rising · China's Response
in Historical Perspective

CHAPTER SIX

East and Southeast Asia
in the Age of Imperialism 408

The Expansion of Europe in the Late Nineteenth Century ·
Southeast Asia before the Colonial Era · Burma and Siam in

Early Modern Times · The Development of Vietnam · The British Empire in Southeast Asia · The French Establishment of Indo-China · Modernization in Siam · Korea's Response to the Outside World · Power Politics over China, 1894–1901 · The Russo-Japanese Rivalry in Northeast Asia · Colonialism in Retrospect

CHAPTER SEVEN

*Imperial Japan:
From Triumph to Tragedy* 488

The Second Phase of Modernization · The Maturing of the Economy · Social Structure and Social Change · Currents of Thought · Politics from 1900 to 1918 · The Years of Party Government: 1918–1931 · The Rise of Militarism in the 1930's · Japan at War

CHAPTER EIGHT

The Rise of the Chinese Republic 613

The Late Ch'ing Reform Movement · The Republican Revolution of 1911 · The Republic's Decline into Warlordism · The Revolution in Thought and Culture · Background of the Nationalist Revolution · The Kuomintang's Rise to Power · The Decade of the Nanking Government · Japan's Aggression on China

CHAPTER NINE

*Colonialism and Nationalism
in the Peripheral Areas* 718

The Peripheral Areas in Modern East Asian History · Varieties of Experience under Colonialism: Indonesia and the Philippines · Colonial Development in Continental Southeast Asia · Japanese

Contents

Colonialism: Taiwan and Korea • Southeast Asia in World War
II • The Emergence of Independent Nations in Southeast Asia •
China's Inner Asian Frontiers: Mongolia and Sinkiang • Britain
and China in Tibet • Problems of Modernization among China's
Neighbors

CHAPTER TEN

East Asia in the New International World   804

The Pacific War • The Occupation of Japan • Japan's Years of
Prosperity and Change • The Division of Korea • The Chinese
Communists' Rise to Power • The Chinese Communists' Consolidation of Power • The Chinese Effort at "Socialist Transformation" • China in the World Scene

THE PRONUNCIATION OF CHINESE, KOREAN, AND JAPANESE   885

BIBLIOGRAPHICAL SUGGESTIONS   888

ILLUSTRATION ACKNOWLEDGMENTS   895

INDEX   899

Maps, Charts, and Tables

MAPS AND CHARTS

East Asia	*front endpaper*
Early European Expansion Toward the Far East (16th to 18th Centuries)	16–17
The Portuguese Stronghold at Malacca	23
Macao in the 1840's	23
Ortelius' Map of "Tartary or the Kingdom of the Great Khan"	40
The Linschoten Map	41
Early Russian-Chinese Contact	47
Chinese Kinship	83
A Simplified Chart of the Ch'ing Examination System	86
Administrative Areas under the Ch'ing Dynasty	94–95
Yamen of the Shanghai District Magistrate	100
The Ch'ing Mounted Courier System	105
Salt Producing-and-Distributing Zones under the Ch'ing	113
The Canton Estuary and Outer Waters (19th Century)	133
China's Premodern View of World Geography	148–149
Courses of the Yellow River	156
The Taiping and Nien Rebellions	160
The Yangtze Delta	176
Major Daimyo Domains around 1865	186–187
The Approaches to Edo (Early 19th Century)	201
The Political System under the Meiji Constitution	297
Foreign Encroachment on China	339
The Growth of Shanghai	341
Central Asia (19th Century)	367
The Approaches to Peking	399
Peking in 1900	401
The Legation Quarter (Peking)	401
Colonialism in Southeast Asia, at 60-Year Intervals	410
Early Kingdoms of Southeast Asia	419
Burma and Siam	428
French Indo-China	435
Malaya in the British Period	444
Korea in Recent Times	465
Organization of the Mitsui Combine	507
Percentage of School Age Children Attending Primary Schools in Japan	523
Growth of Japan's Empire	564
International Rivalry in Korea and Manchuria	585

Maps, Charts, and Tables

The China-Burma-India Theater in World War II 715
Taiwan 757
Sino-Russian Frontier Areas 785
Tibet and Environs 798
World War II in Greater East Asia 809
Modern Japan 824–825
The Rise of the Chinese Communists 853
East and Southeast Asia *back endpaper*

TABLES

Early European Envoys to the Court of Peking 53
Regular Ch'ing Tributaries and Their Ports of Entry 72
The "Opening" of East Asia: Principal Treaties in the
   "Unequal" Treaty System, 1842–1943 145
Major Events in Japan, 1853–1869 207
Prime Ministers and Diet Elections in Japan, 1885–1913 302
Estimates of Central Government Revenues Expected at Peking 327
Selected Governors-General in the Late Ch'ing Period 353
Principal Regimes in Vietnam, 1009–1802 436
European Rivalry in China, 1895–1898 472
The Growth of the Tenant Movement in Japan, 1917–1941 518
The Growth of Higher Education in Japan, 1900–1940 522
The Rise of Labor Unions in Japan, 1914–1920 527
Prices and Wages in Japan, 1912–1919 527
Labor Disputes in Japan, 1912–1920 527
Union Membership in Japan, 1922–1942 528
Parties and Prime Ministers in Japan, 1918–1932 573
Growth of the Japanese Electorate 576
Japanese Cabinets, 1929–1945 581
Population Growth in East and Southeast Asia 740–742
Overseas Chinese in Southeast Asia (1961 estimates) 782
Rise in Per Capita Real Income in Japan, 1934–1962 821
Economic Growth of Japan, 1955–1960 822
Japanese Exports and Imports, 1951–1961 823
Distribution of Votes for the Japanese House of
   Representatives, 1946–1963 839

East Asia
The Modern Transformation

1

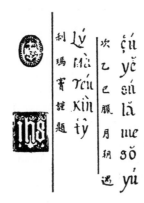

The Coming of the Europeans

THE MODERNIZATION OF EAST ASIA

During the last century and a half, East Asia and the West have grown ever nearer in space and travel time, yet they remain still far apart in many aspects of culture and politics. Clipper ships that could round the globe to reach London from Canton in ninety days have been supplanted by jet planes that need only a few hours. But the growth of contact made possible by modern technology seems to have increased rather than diminished international friction. This ironic and unhappy paradox — that the overcoming of geographical distance seems to intensify cultural and national differences — reflects in part the fact that, among all the great civilizations arising in the Old World, the East Asian was the most isolated and distinctive. This divisive difference in cultural traditions has underlain the political problems of our relations with East Asia during the last hundred and fifty years.

By the early nineteenth century, the great civilization of East Asia had evolved over the course of three millennia and had spread outward geographically from its ancient point of origin in North China, developing in the process distinctive variants in China, Japan, Korea, and Vietnam. This East Asian zone, then as now, contained between a quarter and a third of the world's population, the largest single segment of mankind. Until the nineteenth century its development had been largely

INSCRIPTION signed by Ricci at end of text written in Chinese and romanization. Right-hand column gives date (early 1606).

self-contained and evolutionary. Despite sharp differences among the countries of the area, all had remained within the bounds of the East Asian cultural tradition, little affected by outside influences.

In the nineteenth century, however, a profound transformation began. Contacts with the expanding Western world became much closer, and partly because of these contacts East Asia began to experience rapid and drastic changes which were often more revolutionary than evolutionary. This transformation, needless to say, is still going on, and in fact seems to be accelerating. The past century or so thus clearly constitutes the beginning of a new phase in the history of East Asian civilization.

The story of the gradual evolution of East Asia up to the early nineteenth century has been told in the preceding volume, *East Asia: The Great Tradition.* The present volume considers the great transformation that has occurred since then. This has been paralleled by similar changes in Southeast Asia, and that area has become more and more closely involved with China and Japan. We have therefore included in this volume a survey of the recent history of the various countries of Southeast Asia, together with some background on their traditional cultures.

Historical Viewpoints. The great transformation of East Asia is, of course, an extremely complex story, and there is no generally accepted interpretation of what essentially has been happening there during the past century and a half. The "facts" of history do not speak for themselves, revealing their own pattern and meaning. As presented in speech or writing, the "facts" can be no more than a tiny selection of supposedly significant data drawn from the vast sea of human experience. Behind this selection inevitably lie assumptions in the form of generalizations and abstractions, whether or not the historian himself is conscious of them. Moreover, general ideas about history may be at various levels of abstraction: at a high level, there are comprehensive schemes relating to the whole sweep of history in all times and places; at a lower level, more limited concepts relating to patterns or uniformities visible in certain types of structure or process. We feel that many of the comprehensive schemes that have been applied by both Western and Asian scholars to the history of East Asia have been based more on the particulars of Western experience than on those of East Asia. They have derived primarily from theorists of Occidental background whose views of the modern world have inevitably been influenced by a dominant interest in analyzing the transition from medieval to modern times in the West. When one attempts to make such broad, Western-inspired schemes universal and apply them equally to East Asia, they may suggest valuable insights, but they are not likely to fit very well.

Our own rather skeptical view is that the highest-level generalizations are likely to be the least useful in understanding history, which consists after all of a vast number of concrete and particular events. We doubt that any single scheme can meaningfully interpret all history. Human experience has been too rich and diverse for that. It seems to us that a better understanding can be achieved by looking at the manifold facts of history from a variety of points of view, each of which may reveal significant configurations. Thus each of the academic disciplines — such as economics, political science, or sociology — offers a different approach to the historical scene. Each has its special concepts and terms, which the historian may find useful in his own analysis.

Our attempt to sift the facts of recent East Asian history reveals no single grand pattern but rather a great deal of diversity. A variety of concepts seem helpful in interpretation. One is the concept of "change within tradition." The "Great Tradition" described in Volume One was not a unified entity but included many diverse elements within its overall pattern in each East Asian country. Yet the major traditional forms of thought and action, once established, had an inertial momentum, a tendency to continue in accepted ways. As long as their environment remained without direct Western contact, they underwent only "change within tradition," not transformation.

A second concept is that East Asia, once it came into closer contact with the West, began to "respond" to Western stimuli. While one may sometimes speak of a Western "impact" on East Asia, we believe the more significant element in such situations of challenge-and-response was the way in which the local people reacted to the foreign stimuli. For example, the challenge of foreign warships led some East Asians to try to exclude the foreigner and others to try to learn from him in self-defense: the stimuli (warships) were similar, the responses more various.

Another concept is that East Asia, once it had been stimulated to respond in some fashion to Western contact, began to undergo changes in some degree comparable to the changes that have transformed the Western world in the last few centuries. These changes in both West and East we call "modernization," but this term means little except as it is specifically defined and concretely applied. On the material plane, for example, East Asia appears to have been moving from a preindustrial, prescientific technological level to one characterized by the conscious use of scientific knowledge and the growing utilization of inanimate sources of energy and mechanical devices, just as the West has been making this same technological shift over a somewhat longer period and in considerably different circumstances. Thus the most obvious form of modernization has been "technological."

Another concept, or assumption, is that this great technological transformation in East Asia has been accompanied by many of the same institutional and intellectual changes as in the West. Thus there has been not only rapid economic development, through industrialization, mechanization of transportation, and scientific improvement of agriculture, but also broad political and social change. With improvements in transportation and in the dissemination of the written and spoken word, units of social and political organization have tended to grow in size and efficiency. Factories have in large part replaced the cottage industries, national educational systems the private tutor, and nationwide social organizations the village community. In the field of political ideas and institutions, East Asian countries have followed the Western example in developing mass movements of modern nationalism. Industrialization and nationalism have been accompanied by still other transformations — in family life, social structure, values, and ideologies. As in the West, these have in general tended toward the elimination of social distinctions between individuals and the equalization of status, at least for the masses, under the authority of the state.

Here again we may speak not only of "economic development" but also of "social and political modernization" as occurring both in the West and in East Asia, provided of course that we refer to concrete changes and avoid thinking of "modernization" as an independent force separate from the responses and efforts of human beings themselves.

Finally, since modernization in East Asia, as in other parts of the non-Western world, seems to have been initially stimulated by the West and to have been guided in part by prior Western experience, this fact alone has made it a very different process in East Asia than in the West. For it has been in large part a revolutionary response to a foreign challenge.

These various concepts — of the inertial force of "tradition," of "response" to foreign stimuli, and of modernization both technological and otherwise — have their limitations. Much has evolved quite naturally from within East Asian civilization, not as a response to external stimuli. Many other generalizations and points of view are useful in attempting to grasp the complex picture of East Asia in modern times. We have felt, however, that the best central theme around which to organize the complicated, many-channeled story presented in this volume is the modernization of the East Asian tradition, primarily as a response to Western stimuli.

Modernization and Westernization. There seems to be little question that increased contact with the technologically more advanced Occident gave the major initial impetus to the great changes in East Asia that started in the nineteenth century. The countries of the West, through their development of scientific technology, proved to have vastly superior physical power in almost every form — greater military and naval strength, more efficient transportation, cheaper production through the use of mechanically powered machines, and in general greater command over the resources of nature.

This physical power, however, was only one aspect of Western strength in this period. The application of science was part of a more general social development which included more efficient and powerful forms of economic and political organization. The Western lead in all these respects had been mounting for some time and by the nineteenth century had become overwhelming. As a result the countries of East Asia suddenly found their defenses crumbling, their economies disrupted, their governments threatened, and even their social systems undermined. Only by responding with revolutionary vigor could they hope for national and cultural survival. The ongoing evolution of traditional ways was interrupted. The whole tradition was challenged.

The adoption of Western technology was a major aspect of the East Asian response to this challenge. Thus at first glance, the rapid transformation of East Asia that followed might be viewed as "Westernization." This it undoubtedly has been in many ways. Much has come to East Asia, such as styles of clothing and types of music as well as weapons and machines, which can only be considered direct imitation of Western culture. But if we look more closely at the profound changes of the past century or so, we will see that it is generally the more modern elements in Western civilization which have had the deeper influence on East Asian civilization. Many things that characterized the West before recent times have not become as significant in modern Asia as they have remained in the West. For example, Christianity has not become dominant in countries where Confucian philosophy, Buddhism, or Islam was already established.

The most obvious evidence of fundamental change in East Asia has been in modern developments such as industrialization. Technological changes have been accompanied by the introduction less of traditional Western social and political institutions than of more modern ones — such as the modern national state and the spirit of nationalism that accompanies it, modern draft armies, universal education, the modern techniques of political organization, ranging from national electorates to national police systems, and the large modern units of economic activity, whether organized privately or by governments.

In short, the major impact of the West on East Asian civilization seems to have been in modern technology and modern forms of organization. Western values such as the importance of the individual have had at best a secondary role. In the sense that modern means have been accepted more readily than traditional Western ends, the great transformation of East Asia can be better described as "modernization" than as "Westernization."

The Process of Modernization. We can discern a general sequence of phases in this process of modernization. The first and most immediate reaction was on the material and tangible level of ships, goods, and fire-arms. Finding themselves threatened by the superior power of the West, East Asians sought to learn its secrets and acquire its military technology. This effort at self-defense led them into a broader second phase, in which they tried to secure the material means of building up their own railroads, factories, and scientific technology in general. This need in turn led them to a third phase of acquiring Western learning and new institutional methods of conducting government, business, and education. At the same time, Western ideals and social and religious values were studied and sometimes adopted. These successive phases overlapped and sometimes coincided, yet they are analytically distinct.

The process of borrowing Western techniques, institutions, and ideas was not simple. They naturally had to be adapted to local conditions and so were often greatly modified. Once established in an East Asian country, they also became in time integral, dynamic components of the evolving local culture, changing character in the process from "foreign" to "native." Thus, for example, educational or military systems originally of Western design became in time the Chinese and Japanese systems, molding future generations of Chinese and Japanese.

East Asians in their response to the West generally made a distinction between techniques and values, or, broadly speaking, between means and ends. Western ways of doing things might seem necessary, even if distasteful, but the people of East Asia for the most part intended to maintain their own traditional values. Yet the distinction between foreign ways and native values inevitably became blurred. For example, the anti-Western patriot who was ostensibly reviving native tradition might turn out to be in fact the exponent of a new and very modern form of nationalism.

Techniques and values, means and ends, interact closely. Initially, values may determine whether new techniques are adopted or how they are used. But sooner or later, the manner of life is likely to affect its aims. To put it another way, cultural values are likely to be transformed by technological changes. New scientific techniques may require new methods of social organization, such as universal education or the creation of large-scale factories, and these in turn will undoubtedly influence the attitudes and aims of the people whose way of life has been changed by them. New ends are implicit in the use of new means.

The Role of Tradition. Interaction and conflict between modernization and tradition are of course implicit in the definitions of these terms. Yet we need not become prisoners of these abstractions to recognize that the use of modern technology and of new forms of organization has been profoundly influenced by inherited cultural values, both in East Asia and in the West. The difference is that modernization has been more gradual and evolutionary in the West, going on over a longer period and much of it indeed arising from within Western civilization. In East Asia the shorter duration of modernization and the external origin of many of the stimuli for it have resulted in a more precipitous rate of change and a tendency toward modifications of traditional culture and society that are sudden and revolutionary rather than slow and evolutionary. This more rapid and revolutionary rate of change in East Asia does not mean that earlier traditions have had any less influence on the process and on the results in East Asia than in the Occident. In fact, the shorter time span may mean a greater survival of what is traditional.

Moreover, the peoples of East Asia have been highly selective in their borrowings from the West, clinging to those patterns within their ancient and mature cultures that are not definitely inconsistent with the modernizing trend. Only some among the Western techniques, institutions, and ideas produced an impact on them and were borrowed out of fear or admiration. Others were despised or ignored. And even the techniques, institutions, and ideas that were borrowed did not necessarily produce parallel results in East Asia and the West. Sharp differences in ways of life, and still more in attitudes and ideals, have persisted despite parallel technological changes. There is, therefore, no reason to suppose that a thoroughly modernized East Asia will be merely a reflection of the modernized West either in its superficial cultural patterns or in its more fundamental ideals and values.

So all-pervasive has been the influence of tradition that the whole story of East Asian modernization during the past century is not really intelligible without an understanding of the traditional civilization of that area. Only this cultural background can give us perspective and save us from mistaking some spectacular but transitory phase of recent history for a lasting characteristic.

In fact, to understand East Asia's modern history one must grasp not only East Asian civilization as a whole but also the distinctive variants within it. Only these explain why Japan responded more quickly and successfully to the Western challenge than did its neighbors, why China slowly disintegrated into temporary chaos, and why Korea was swallowed whole for a while into the Japanese empire. Without this historical perspective it would also be difficult to comprehend the subsequent metamorphosis of a weak and disorganized China into a disciplined, centralized political machine, the comparable transformation of the Korean people from seemingly meek colonials into fervent nationalists, and the even more sudden change of the Japanese from fanatical warrior-nationalists into peace-loving internationalists.

Thus we discern two major factors that have shaped recent East Asian

9

history — the forces of modernization, originally introduced in large part from the West, and the native traditions. The latter have been treated in detail in the preceding volume, and only their salient features will be summarized where appropriate in the pages that follow. We start with the impact of the West on East Asia, or rather with the expansion of Western activity which had by the nineteenth century made this impact unavoidable.

THE DYNAMICS OF EUROPEAN EXPANSION

The idea of Westernization is a modern anomaly, for the main flow of influence over the long course of history has been from East Asia *toward* the West, not the other way round. In 1500 an observer might more logically have looked forward to the "Asianization" of Europe. One has only to think of the ancient silk trade from China across Central Asia to Rome; or the great series of inventions emanating from China — paper, printing, the wheelbarrow, the crossbow, canal lock-gates, the stern-post rudder, the compass, gunpowder, porcelain, and all the rest; or the terrifying Mongol invasions in the thirteenth century of Persia, Russia, and Eastern Europe. To none of these early influences were there comparable movements in the opposite direction. China under the Sung was a far greater civilization, in both size and accomplishment, than its contemporary, medieval Europe. Marco Polo's incredible tale of the splendor of Cathay under the Yüan was true.

Paradoxically, the superiority of China over medieval Europe seems to have contributed to the dynamism of Europe's expansion in the post-medieval period. There was a long tradition of Europeans seeking contact with Asia. In Roman times ships voyaged through the Red Sea to India, and merchants from the Roman East reached China by sea as early as A.D. 166. Maritime commerce around the coasts of Asia was contemporary with the Roman Empire; under Arab leadership it grew to large proportions after the eighth century. During the Mongol domination of Asia in the thirteenth and fourteenth centuries, the wealth and power of China drew Christian missionaries and merchants like Marco Polo all the way thither. Finally, in the closing years of the fifteenth century, Europeans broke into the flow of trade around the southern shores of Asia, with profound results for both the European and the Asian peoples.

Since it was the Europeans who initiated this direct contact by sea, it is not surprising that they at first received the greater stimulus from it. They had made the effort to reach Asia and therefore responded to the strange peoples and places they found. Theirs was the novel experience. Moreover, the European countries were comparatively smaller. The trade and influences resulting from these early maritime contacts had proportionally a much greater impact on the limited populations of Europe than on the huge masses of people and relatively stable societies of the major countries of Asia.

Americans tend to see Columbus' discovery of the New World as the great feat that ushered in the age of European expansion. At the time, however, it had less immediate importance, commercially and politically, than Vasco da Gama's voyage around Africa to India in 1498. In his own lifetime Columbus' claim to fame was that he had reached the fabled Indies. Da Gama's successors who went around Africa actually did so. Where Columbus found a few savages on barren shores, da Gama and his successors began direct sea trade with the storied and populous empires and markets of the East — India, the Spice Islands of modern Indonesia, China, and Japan. In the sixteenth century the Spanish conquests of Mexico and Peru began to pour gold and silver into Europe, raising prices and stimulating the growth of capitalism. Yet much of this precious metal subsequently flowed eastward to balance the growing trade between Europe and Asia, for the New World produced no trade goods to compare with the finely wrought wares and valuable spices of Asia.

This overseas contact, both westward to the Americas and eastward to Asia, roused the young nations of the Occident to great activity. In the four centuries after 1500 modern Europe and America rose to political and economic domination of the world. Christian missions were also stimulated by the new contact with the Asian peoples. In the sixteenth and seventeenth centuries India, China, and Japan became the principal targets of Christian evangelism, since these countries even then contained nearly half of mankind.

The Commercial Motive. Many causes contributed to the sudden expansion of the Europeans over the globe in early modern times. One was that foreign trade was more important to Europe than to the major countries of Asia. Europe is, after all, only a peninsula of the Eurasian land mass, a small area with a rather narrow span of latitude (from 35 to 55 degrees north) and hence not rich in cotton, sugar, rice, spices, and other products of the Orient. The countries of Asia, particularly China, were not only larger and covered a wider range of latitude; they also had more varied products and were more self-sufficient. Consequently, trade between Europe and Asia was from the first more important to the West than to the East.

The rise of towns in medieval Europe, the growth of an independent merchant class and of commerce under law, all had their ancient background in the Greco-Roman trading civilization of the Mediterranean. When the ancient West sought trade with the East, the balance of trade had generally been in Asia's favor. When the Romans got silks and spices, they paid for them in gold and silver. Venice and Genoa traded with the eastern Mediterranean to get spices, especially pepper, from the

Arabs, who in turn had got them from still farther east. Eventually the Portuguese rounded Africa for the same purpose, lured by a trade which had not equally moved Orientals to voyage west.

Evangelism. From medieval times Europe had also been concerned about the ancient home of Christianity in the Holy Land. In the Crusades were combined religious, commercial, military, and political motives. At this same time the Papacy, with religious zeal and diplomatic acumen, had dispatched its first missions to Asia. Europeans developed the habit of looking to the East not only for commerce but also for a field of Christian proselytism.

The continuing European hope to convert the non-Christian world was paralleled by an inherited fear of invasion from the East. The Huns of the fifth century had been followed by the Arabs, who penetrated to France in the eighth century, and the Mongols, who penetrated to Hungary and the Dalmatian coast, almost to Venice, in the thirteenth. The Turkish capture of Constantinople in 1453 and the subsequent domination of southeastern Europe by the Ottoman Empire kept alive this infidel threat. The Spanish and Portuguese, after their long crusade had finally driven the Moors from Spain in 1492, carried religious fanaticism with them on their voyages overseas. European expansion eastward thus was regarded as the expansion of Christendom against the infidel. It derived a concrete strategic aim from the belief, inherited from medieval times, that a Christian ruler, the legendary "Prester John," still reigned in Asia as a possible ally against Islam.

Nationalism and Individualism. One unique factor in European expansion was the modern nation-state, a new institution unlike either the Greco-Roman city-state, which could govern itself by a meeting of all its citizens, or the ancient empires which embraced vast populations under a theocratic potentate. The nation-state of the West, originating in a fusion of ideas derived from Roman law and Germanic tribal customs, conceived of the corporation as a legal individual, and through this concept could bring together in an estates general or a parliament the representatives of the realm in its various corporate aspects. In this way, large segments of European populations came to identify themselves with their governments, which in turn became greatly strengthened. A combination of strong monarchy and representative institutions, in which commercial interests were well represented, replaced the old feudal order with much more efficiently organized and stronger nation-states.

As the new nations of Europe arose, patriotic rivalries spurred them on. Their trade was stimulated by the need of revenue for national warfare and of luxuries for royal courts and rich city merchants. Vigorous kings and adventurous merchants carried national rivalries into competition for trade and for territory in Asia and the Americas.

European society at the time of the early nation-states produced a type of rugged individualism that played a large role in European expansion. Acquisitiveness, evangelism, and patriotic competition abroad were necessarily expressed through individual persons, the hardy and adventurous few who voyaged overseas. Time after time the history of the sixteenth and seventeenth centuries records the exploits of Europeans whose almost unbelievable achievements were animated by a peculiar independence and vigor of spirit. The craving for adventure, geographical curiosity, evangelical faith, sheer greed, and patriotic fervor were as important as national policies. Great numbers of dynamic Western individuals went to the East. They were a group of men self-selected by their own outstanding qualities, both good and bad — including wily opportunists, dedicated evangelists, wastrels, and statesmen in great variety.

Technology. The most obvious factor in Europe's capacity for expansion was technological superiority over Asia, particularly in ships and guns. From the sixteenth down to the twentieth centuries, Western "superiority" was manifested in the weapons and skills of warfare. The lead, apparent already in the sixteenth century, steadily lengthened. Eventually it became clear that this superiority in military technology was merely one phase of a general superiority in scientific and industrial technology. The use of violence could be most easily commanded by those who excelled also in the arts of peace. In time, the economic imperialism made possible by superior machine production became as important as the military imperialism of superior weapons.

In the early centuries of maritime contact, however, the West had little or no industrial superiority, and its technological advantages were largely military. It is no accident that Europeans burst upon Asia in the same era that saw the final triumph of firearms. The crossbow disappeared from European warfare in the 1520's, yielding to an arquebus which could kill at about 400 yards, even though firing it required two hands and, at first, a lighted fuse. Carbines and pistols were developed thereafter, and eventually the musket. All these firearms were new to Asia when first used there by Europeans.

Shipboard artillery naturally revolutionized naval warfare and naval architecture. A two-ton culverin of 4½-inch caliber had a point-blank range of 460 yards, or 2650 yards at 10 degrees elevation. The round-ship, with broader beam and broadside firepower, began to supplant the war galley, except in the Mediterranean. The galley's sails and oars fitted it to close with and board an enemy, but its artillery fore and aft could not equal the broadside of a round-ship. A new vessel which emerged in the middle of the sixteenth century was the galleon, a sailing ship that could use oars in an emergency but was higher and bigger than a galley, with cannon firing fore and aft as well as broadside.

The naval superiority of the Europeans in the sixteenth century did not depend merely on superior artillery. Because of the difficulty of seafaring in the stormy North Atlantic, they had been obliged to develop sturdy ships. By combining the traditional European square-rigged sails with a lateen-rig adapted from the Arabs, they made ships more capable of sailing against the wind. As a result, they could outmaneuver in combat the ships of monsoon Asia, which were accustomed to sail downwind. Heavier construction permitted them to carry more guns, which were likely to be bigger than those on Asian vessels. Thus even in the sixteenth century European ships, though very few in Asian waters, generally outclassed in maneuverability and firepower any vessels that the states and traders of Asia could send against them.

For navigation in the open sea the Europeans of the sixteenth century now had not only the compass but a method of estimating latitude — in the northern hemisphere, by observing the altitude of the Pole Star, and in the southern, by observing the height of the sun at midday, for comparison with tables showing the sun's declination every day in the year. Speed was calculated by dropping overboard a log of wood tied to a knotted cord, and noting with a sand-glass how rapidly the knots on the cord ran out. Eventually, out of the Western invention of clockwork was produced in the eighteenth century the chronometer, which could be used to calculate longitude. Important as they were, these developments in armament, ships, and navigation were only aspects of the great revolution in scientific technology.

Historical Patterns of Contact. The countries of Asia reacted to early European expansion in very different ways. In fact, Asia after 1500 was almost like a laboratory of intercultural relations, in which Westerners might meet strikingly different responses in the successive countries they visited. Portuguese captains in the 1550's might find themselves obeyed as overlords in the East Indies, hired to fight as mercenaries in Burma and Siam, quickly welcomed to trade in Japan, and stubbornly excluded from China, depending upon the political situation in each local society.

On the other hand, there were well-marked phases in the European approach to Asia. The early Portuguese and Spanish explorers, merchants, and missionaries of the pioneer sixteenth century were not well coordinated. They reached far places but sometimes left no trace. The East India companies of the Dutch and British in the seventeenth and eighteenth centuries were more powerfully organized and were interested in trade more than in exploration or evangelism. The growth of trade was followed by the scramble for colonial territories by a number of Western powers in the nineteenth century.

Another pattern of importance was the fluctuation of central power in China and Japan. In both countries the central power was in decline during the sixteenth century. Late Ming China was beginning to expe-

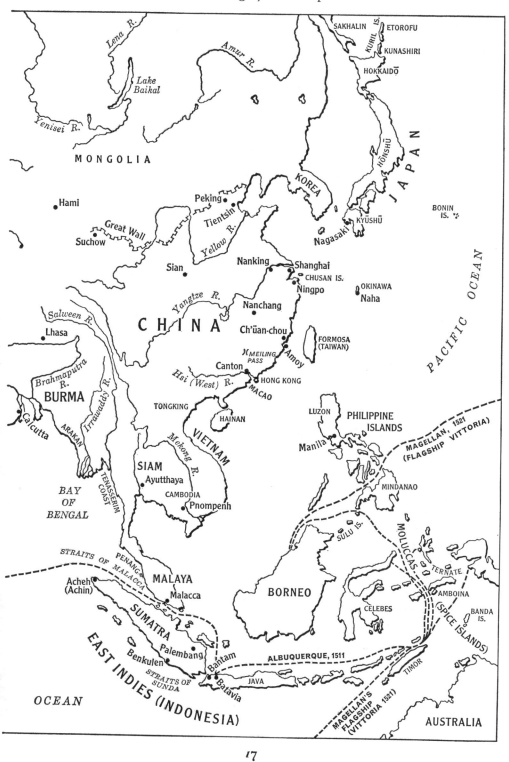

He was moved both by religious zeal and by commercial and scientific interests. After the Portuguese passed Cape Verde on the west coast of Africa in 1445, gold and the slave trade began to play a role in their ventures. By the time Bartolomeu Dias rounded the Cape of Good Hope in 1488, the Portuguese had behind them in their conquest of the oceans two generations of invaluable experience in shipbuilding, seamanship, navigation, and cartography. Their national expansion was directed by a king who soon came to style himself "Lord of the Conquest, Navigation, and Commerce of Ethiopia, Arabia, Persia, and India."

The Establishment of Bases in Asia. The chief target of the Portuguese was the rich commerce of the Moslem infidel. After establishing themselves in Brazil and Africa, they showed less desire for territory except in the form of bases from which to fight the Arabs and gain control of the carrying trade of the Eastern seas. Their particular object was the trade in spices, which had high value in small bulk. While spices were important ingredients for drugs and were also used for incense and as aphrodisiacs, they were particularly in demand to season and preserve the salted meat of the European winter diet in the era before refrigeration.

After da Gama reached the southwest (Malabar) coast of India in 1498, the Portuguese soon seized the rich emporium of Hormuz on the Persian Gulf and secured a degree of strategic control over the trade routes at the mouth of the Red Sea. For this purpose they defeated the Arab fleets, although they were never able to maintain control over the key port of Aden. Under Afonso d' Albuquerque they secured in 1510 a base on the small island of Goa on the west coast of India and made it their capital. This gave them some control of the western end of the ancient spice route from the Indies. From Goa, Albuquerque in 1511 went east to seize another base at Malacca on the west coast of Malaya. Here were built a factory (i.e., "factor's" or agent's residence and warehouse), a fortress, and a church. Thence the Portuguese pushed on to the Moluccas or "Spice Islands." They reached China in 1514, and Japan apparently in 1543.

Several circumstances facilitated this rapid expansion. The valuable spice trade originated in certain small centers of production — cloves grew in the Moluccas, nutmeg and mace in the Banda Islands to the south, and the principal commodity, pepper, though produced in several areas of Malaya and also on the Malabar coast of India, was for the most part funneled through the port of Bantam. The spice trade across the Indian Ocean was governed by the monsoon, which blew from the southwest in summer and the northeast in winter. The western end of the trade route had been controlled by the Arab merchants of Malabar and especially of the Gujarat Peninsula on the northwest coast of India. By accidents of geography there were two significant bottlenecks on the route: whoever dominated the narrow Straits of Malacca (between Malaya and Sumatra) and the Straits of Sunda (between Sumatra and Java) could control sea contact between South and East Asia. Once the Portuguese had defeated the Arab fleets in the Arabian Sea and had established control of one bottleneck through their base at Malacca, they could try to dominate the spice route. The hostility of newly converted Islamic states on Java prevented the creation of a Portuguese spice monopoly, but they got bases in the Moluccas, held Malacca from 1511 to 1641, and traded at Bantam during the latter half of the sixteenth century.

Although the Arabs and other Moslem merchants of Persia, India, and Malaya had for several centuries dominated the trade route from the Red Sea and Gulf of Persia around to China, the rise of Malacca dated only from about 1400. It had been founded as a new state by a prince of the Sailendra dynasty from the older commercial center of Palembang on Sumatra. Malacca had early developed tributary ties with China, in the period of the great Ming voyages after 1403, while its Arab merchants maintained close contact with their trading center of Gujarat in northwest India. From Malacca, as a center of sea power, piracy, and trade, the Islamic religion had spread not only over Malaya and Sumatra but also to the eastern and central coasts of Java, and thence in the late fifteenth century to the Moluccas. This process continued after the Portuguese seized Malacca in 1511.

Thus the Portuguese intruders at Malacca once again found themselves in competition and conflict with their traditional enemies, the Moslems. The Christian crusade against Islam proved to be as bitter in the Straits of Malacca as it had been in the Straits of Gibraltar. The Moslem enemy was still strong and vigorous. In their long conflict with Acheh (Achin), which lay across the straits in northern Sumatra, for example, the Portuguese faced at one time as many as 300 warboats and 15,000 troops, aided by 400 Turkish artillerymen. Moslem strength in Java often forced them to avoid Javanese waters and follow the route north of Borneo to the Moluccas. There they made trade agreements with local rulers and established posts ("factories") on islands such as Ternate and Amboina, in the homeland of the clove tree, allspice, and nutmeg.

The Nature of Portuguese Expansion. This early Portuguese expansion was a loosely organized combination of exploration, trade, piracy, and conquest. In addition to the domination of the spice trade of the East, it included the colonization of Brazil in the sixteenth century and the development of a slave trade on the African coast. In the early decades the king himself outfitted the expeditions, with the aid of foreign capital. He sent them as royal ventures, and until 1550 monopolized the main products. Thus he provided initial direction and unity, while his captains set up a strategic network of fortress bases to support the fleets.

The Portuguese crown, under its obligation to be the patron of Christianity (the *padroado*) in return for papal grants of territory and trade rights, naturally supported the expansion of the Church. At each outpost, such as Malacca, the representative of the Church was an important figure, in no way overshadowed by his lay colleagues with their individual prerogatives and personal ambitions — the captain of the fortress, the captain of the ships, the manager of the trade, the royal judge, and the governor of the natives.

Within the framework of royal control and monopoly, there soon grew up evils of corruption, smuggling, and personal rivalry. The king's administration failed to keep up with the actual expansion in far places. No imperial civil service was created, and all unity of leadership depended upon the crown, which was at a great distance. National interests therefore tended to become subordinated to local or individual interests. Each fortress colony usually developed its own elected municipal council, or "Senate," and its own hospital, or "House of Mercy." Private trade and profit soon began to exceed those of the king.

The early Portuguese forays into East Asia were far from being centrally organized and disciplined expeditions. The leaders were adventurers who seized whatever opportunities they found. They followed the ancient sailing routes to the established centers of commerce. Coming in minuscule numbers, the Portuguese had to ally themselves with local Asian rulers and factions. They fitted into local circumstances and gained profit or power by any means available. They entered into the politics and wars of Burma, Siam, and other Southeast Asian kingdoms and sultanates, acting by turns as mercenaries or as independent pirates. When the Siamese fought off the Burmese invaders at Ayutthaya (Ayuthia) in 1548, for example, Portuguese mercenaries were fighting on both sides. An adventurer named Felipe de Brito became a ruler in southern Burma for fourteen years (1599–1613). Others established fortified posts on the northeast coast of India and plied a slave trade by seizing and selling native people until the 1660's.

In the end, the Portuguese were too few, too disorganized, and too uncompromising in their crusading religious zeal to gain effective control of Asian lands and peoples. As the power of Islam expanded in both India and the Indies, the Portuguese attempt to create a commercial empire faltered for lack of personnel, diplomatic tact, capital, and fiscal administration. Aided by Egypt, the Arab traders regained a good share of the spice trade and continued to supply Cairo and Venice during most of the sixteenth century. Locally the Portuguese followed a practice of intermarriage and produced in their outposts a Eurasian population and culture. They were served by slaves and lived luxuriously when possible, but they were rather soon worn out by the life of the tropics. Lisbon, as the new terminus of the spice route, became rich; but by 1580, when

Portugal accepted the rule of the Spanish crown, the Portuguese expansion had spent itself. When Portugal again became independent in 1640, its power in the East had already been eclipsed by the more single-minded and better-organized Dutch and British.

The Portuguese in China. The early contact of the Portuguese with Ming China was merely an extension of their contact with Southeast Asia. They were known in China as the Fo-lang-chi, which was derived from the Arabic Feringhi, a name inherited from the Franks of the era of the Crusades (see page 127). Their inauspicious opening of contact with China largely set the tone for Sino-European relations to follow.

Appearing on the southeast coast as sea-"barbarians" at the back door, while Chinese military and political concern was still focused on the land frontiers of Inner Asia, these Europeans were a strategic novelty. Only pirates, like those from Japan, had previously caused trouble on these coasts. Never before had the Chinese been in direct contact with a people so radically different in culture and so unaware of Chinese concepts of international relations. The Portuguese were not inclined to accept the traditional Chinese pretensions to being the unique land of civilization, or the Chinese theory that all foreign trade should be subordinate to the exchange of tribute from "barbarian" rulers for gifts from the benevolent Chinese emperor. Nor were the Chinese for their part likely to tolerate the Western assumption of equality — especially when the early European voyagers, unaccustomed to daily bathing at home, commonly emerged from their cramped and fetid ships' quarters not only with more body hair than Asians but also with more body odor.

As a Chinese interpreter is said to have explained when the first Portuguese reached Japan in 1543: "They understand to a certain degree the distinction between Superior and Inferior, but I do not know whether they have a proper system of ceremonial etiquette. They eat with their fingers instead of with chopsticks. . . . They show their feelings without any self-control. They cannot understand the meaning of written characters. They are a people who spend their lives roving hither and yon. They have no fixed abode and barter things which they have for those they do not, but withal they are a harmless sort of people."

The new era of direct Sino-Western contact began in 1514 when the first Portuguese explorer (who had set out late in 1513) reached Lintin Island in the bay outside the entrance to the river that leads up to Canton. Others followed, usually in Chinese junks with Chinese pilots. In 1517 the Portuguese sent an embassy from the "King of Portugal" to the "King of China." On reaching Canton the mission fired a salute of cannon in proper Western style, which outraged the Chinese sense of etiquette and required an immediate apology. Landing to a blast of trumpets, the ambassador (Tomé Pires) unloaded his presents for the emperor, which naturally looked like tribute. He was housed in the office of the Superintendent of Trading Ships, like any tributary envoy, and in due course received permission to go to Peking in the usual manner.

Meanwhile, however, other Portuguese had descended upon the trading center at Lintin Island and built a fortress and mounted cannon in their usual fashion. Hindering trade and flouting Chinese law, these semi-pirates were accused of robbery and blackmail and of buying Chinese children stolen and marketed by Chinese kidnapers. Portuguese and Chinese sources both confirm this — evidently the children were sought as slaves, but the official *Ming History* says further that the Portuguese cooked and ate them. It became a part of Chinese folklore that the Portuguese loved to eat small children; Chinese writings of the early sixteenth century describe in vivid detail how they were boiled or roasted and consumed.

Thus the Pires embassy of 1517, which had gone north over the inland canal route via the Meiling Pass to Peking, began with a poor press. Chinese censors urged that the embassy be excluded. The king of Malacca had also complained to his suzerain in Peking, and about this time there occurred a series of Portuguese-Chinese naval battles. The Portuguese were expelled from Canton in 1522, and it is not surprising that Pires, the first Portuguese envoy, died in a Cantonese prison.

During the next three decades the Portuguese traded at a series of impermanent coastal centers. To the north they maintained a fortress post at Chin-hai near Ningpo, which was a center of the Chinese junk trade. In Fukien they traded at "Chinchew" (their name for Ch'üan-chou, the Arab Zayton). But their chief market was in the region of Canton. Here they used in succession several places off the Canton delta — Lintin Island, then another island south of Macao called St. Jean or "Sancian" (in Chinese Shang-ch'uan, where St. Francis Xavier died in 1552), and subsequently "Lampacau" nearby. Finally, they got local Chinese permission to base their trade on the small peninsula of Macao south of Canton and concentrated their activities there after 1557. The peninsula was walled off by the Chinese authorities, who continued until 1887 to assert China's sovereignty and to collect land and customs taxes while allowing the Portuguese to maintain their own form of self-government, much as the Arabs had done at Zayton under the Sung. Macao remains the oldest European base in East Asia, a survival of early Western colonialism with a mixed population.

After its first rapid establishment of bases at Goa, at Malacca, in the Indies, at Macao, and (from 1571) at Nagasaki in Japan, the Portuguese crown supported its empire not only by the spice trade to Europe but also by trading within Asia, particularly between China and Japan. The annually appointed "Captain General of the Voyage of China and Japan," securing his opportunity from the king, might sail in his carrack from "Golden Goa" in the spring with a miscellaneous cargo, winter at Macao

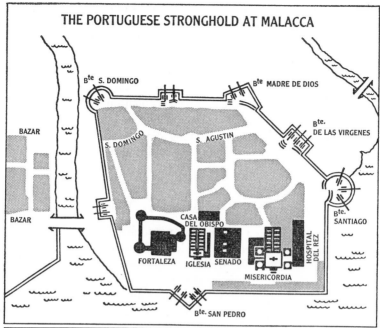

THE PORTUGUESE STRONGHOLD AT MALACCA

B^te S. DOMINGO

B^te MADRE DE DIOS

B^te. DE LAS VIRGENES

BAZAR

S. DOMINGO

S. AGUSTIN

BAZAR

CASA DEL OBISPO

B^te. SANTIAGO

FORTALEZA

IGLESIA

SENADO

MISERICORDIA

HOSPITAL DEL REZ

B^te. SAN PEDRO

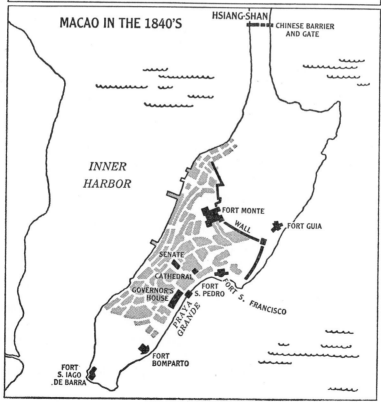

MACAO IN THE 1840'S

HSIANG-SHAN

CHINESE BARRIER AND GATE

INNER HARBOR

FORT MONTE

WALL

FORT GUIA

SENATE

CATHEDRAL

GOVERNOR'S HOUSE

FORT S. PEDRO

FORT S. FRANCISCO

PRAYA GRANDE

FORT BOMPARTO

FORT S. IAGO DE BARRA

buying principally Chinese silks, silk floss, and gold, and reach Nagasaki in the second summer. Exchanging his cargo for at least double its cost and usually much more, he would return to Macao with silver to invest again in silk.

Portuguese superiority in this local Asian carrying trade was due partly to the size and armament of their 1200- to 1600-ton carracks as protection against pirates and partly to their skill in navigation. For the latter they relied not only on the compass and astrolabe (to measure the altitude of sun and stars) but also on written sailing directions (Port. *roteiros*, Eng. "rutters"), which were far more detailed and useful than the early Portuguese charts.

INTERNATIONAL RIVALRIES IN EAST ASIA

The Portuguese were a disturbing new element among the Arab, Chinese, Japanese, and other local traders and adventurers already active in East Asian waters, and the arrival of Spaniards, Hollanders, and Englishmen further complicated the situation. The century from about 1540 to 1640 was one of rapidly expanding contact between Europeans and East Asians, mainly in international trade. Merchants, priests, and fighting men from the various European countries met and competed on the other side of the world.

Spain in the Philippines. The initial maritime and colonial rivalry of Portugal and Spain had been settled in 1494 by the Treaty of Tordesillas, which set a line of global demarcation 370 leagues west of the Azores. In this division of the globe, Portugal secured claims to Brazil and all non-Christian areas halfway round the earth to the east, while Spain secured claims extending westward to include, as it turned out, the rest of the Americas, the Pacific, the Philippines, and the Moluccas. Both powers assumed, along with these rights, obligations to bring Christianity to the native peoples.

Ferdinand Magellan, a Portuguese navigator who had participated in the first Portuguese attack on Malacca, set out in 1519 in the service of Spain to find a westward route to the Spice Islands. After sailing around South America, through the Straits of Magellan, and across the Pacific, he found the Portuguese already installed in the Moluccas, but he was able to claim the Philippines for Spain. After Magellan's death there at the hands of the natives, one surviving captain (del Cano) in the *Vittoria* completed the first circumnavigation of the earth. His return to Spain in 1522 precipitated an effort to oust the Portuguese from the Moluccas, but to no avail. In 1529 Spain sold Portugal her claims to the Moluccas by the Treaty of Saragossa.

Another generation passed before Legaspi, sailing from Mexico in

1565, again claimed the Philippines for Spain and founded Manila in 1571. It was also in 1565 that Spanish navigators learned how to sail eastward from the Philippines to Mexico by going far north to the latitudes of the westerly trade winds.

For the next 250 years, until Mexico became independent in 1821, the Philippines remained a trans-Pacific appendage of the viceroyalty of New Spain, governed in effect from Mexico. Spanish colonial institutions were transplanted. In 1583 Manila was given in the usual fashion an *audiencia*, a judicial court and council with wide executive powers. The *audiencia* was generally staffed by officials from Spain who represented the royal interest in absolutist government and economic monopolies, and who could keep some rein on the captain-general and other local officials.

Another Spanish institution imported into the Philippines was the semi-feudal *encomienda*, which was a village or group of villages "commended" to the care of an individual Spaniard. The latter had the duty of protecting the village people and maintaining missionary clergy for their welfare. He also had the right, in place of the crown, to collect a royal tribute in goods or labor service from the native people, even though they remained in theory free men and owners of their land. The general result was forced labor and exploitation.

Spanish oppression in the Philippines, as in the New World, was ameliorated by the Church. By 1601 there were some 400 missionaries at work. The various missionary orders, facing no competition in the Philippines from Buddhism, Islam, or other established Oriental religions, made rapid progress. The Filipinos thus became the only Christian people of East Asia. There was opposition only in the south, in the Sulu archipelago, where Islam had penetrated and the people, who were consequently called "Moors" or Moros, refused Christianity.

Lacking easily exportable riches, the Philippines remained a subordinate outpost of Spanish America and did not become a base for aggressive expansion in Asia, despite some early Spanish hopes and efforts in that direction. Manila was the exchange point of a limited Sino-American trade. Until 1815, the famous Manila galleons maintained annual contact with Acapulco on the west coast of Mexico. These vessels, like the Portuguese carracks, carried crews of 60 to 100 men and ranged in size from several hundred up to 1600 or even 2000 tons. So well established became their trade routes and operations that they crossed the Pacific for two centuries, passing westward on the south and eastward on the north of the Hawaiian Islands, without ever discovering them. Each year some thirty to fifty junks came to Manila from China, supplying silks for the galleon. Acting as middlemen, the Spanish community in Manila shared the profits and relied heavily on the sustenance of the galleon trade. Yet it remained limited by the restrictive principles of mercantilism, and the merchants of Seville jealously kept it from flowing directly to Europe. Thus Manila, like Macao, served mainly as an entrepot or funnel for Chinese exports of silk and imports of silver — so much so that the Spanish or "Mexican" dollar brought west in the cargoes of the Manila galleons eventually became the principal silver currency of the China coast.

Meanwhile a crowded community of tens of thousands of Chinese grew up at Manila, dominating retail trade and services and endangering Spanish control. Bloody affrays sometimes resulted, as in 1603, when a Chinese rising and Spanish reprisals were said to have cost 23,000 lives. A truculent, though smaller, Japanese community also grew up. As early as 1574 a Chinese pirate, Limahong (Lin Feng in Chinese), had attacked Manila, and for some years the small Spanish colony lived in fear of further attacks from the China coast.

The Spanish response to these dangers in the early decades was still that of the *conquistadores* of Mexico and Peru. Manila hatched several early schemes for the conquest of China, whose people were deemed "so cowardly that no one rides on horseback." During the first century in the Philippines, Spanish expeditions fought and traded in the Moluccas and on the coasts of Cambodia, Siam, and Vietnam, often accompanied by Dominican and Franciscan friars. The latter made several vain attempts to begin mission work in China and also joined actively in the Spanish contact with Japan after 1592.

Japanese Adventurers. The Japanese were by no means the least energetic or fearsome among the merchants and pirates in East Asian waters. After the decline of centralized power in Japan in the early fourteenth century, warrior-traders from West Japan had become more and more active as pirates on the China coast. Tributary trade had been carried on officially with China during the first century and a half of Ming rule (until 1549). But piracy had continued as an alternative form of intercourse, and by the 1550's it had reached a high point. Japanese freebooters, joined by Chinese pirates and local bandits (useful as guides), raided cities on the coast and as far inland as Nanking. When Chinese imperial forces were mobilized to defend Chekiang, the raiders harassed Kwangtung.

In the same period Japanese adventurers, like their Portuguese counterparts from whom they learned Western techniques of navigation and the making of firearms, roamed the trade routes as far as Malaya and fought in Burma and Siam. Japanese mercenaries, for example, assisted the Spanish expedition of 1595 to Cambodia, which reached Pnompenh and killed the king before withdrawing down the Mekong. When Hideyoshi, who succeeded in reunifying Japan in 1590, began licensing Japan's overseas shipping, it was recorded as going mainly to the area of Vietnam and secondarily to Siam and to Manila. Thus the beginning of the seventeenth century found the Japanese participating more and more in the Far Eastern maritime-trading community, and Japan's naval strength was such that the centralized regime of the Tokugawa, which came to power in 1600, could seriously contemplate the conquest of the Philippines.

The Arrival of the Dutch and the English. During the early seventeenth century, the seafaring powers of northwestern Europe — Holland and England — supplanted those of the Iberian Peninsula as leaders of Europe's commercial expansion, but with a different spirit. The Protestant powers were more effectively organized to pursue trade through trading companies but much less concerned for the spread of Christianity in foreign lands.

In this period the Dutch were ahead of the British as the commercial leaders of Western Europe, and their chief port of Amsterdam was a more important financial center than London. Through the development of their fishing fleets in the North Sea and of their shipping trade around the coast of northwestern Europe, the Netherlands had produced hardy seafarers of great nautical skill. The early export of woolens from the Low Countries contributed to their foreign trade, from which fluid capital was accumulated. Meanwhile the rise of the Dutch nation, in its long fight from 1568 to 1648 against Spanish control, combined with the spirit of the Protestant Reformation to stimulate a vigorous Dutch expansion.

The Dutch, beginning to penetrate Asia by sea at the same time as the British, were at first the more powerful. The problem was to break the Portuguese semi-monopoly of the spice trade routes, which Portugal had tried to keep secret from other European navigators. A powerful stimulus was applied when Spain, the mortal enemy of Holland, took over the crown of Portugal (1580–1640) and in 1594 legally excluded Dutch and British merchants from the Lisbon spice market. Just at this time a young Hollander, J. H. van Linschoten, returned from a decade of service under the Portuguese (including five years at Goa) with full details of the spice trade and the trade routes. The maps and particularly the sailing directions that he published aided the first Dutch expedition of 1595, which reached Java successfully. (See page 41.) The subsequent Dutch activity was spectacular: in 1598, twenty-two ships (in contrast to the four or five carracks a year from Lisbon) sailed in five expeditions to all parts of the Far East — to Java, the Moluccas, Manila, Canton, and even Japan. In 1601 there were 65 ships in 15 separate fleets, sent by various merchant groups of the Dutch cities. The need for unity of action in Asian markets and against the Portuguese tended to consolidate these competing enterprises.

The English, also finding their way to Asia, were not yet important rivals. As early as 1580 Sir Francis Drake had returned from his voyage around the world with cloves from Ternate, and, after the defeat of the Spanish Armada in 1588, London merchants had actually got ahead of the Dutch, sending an expedition to Sumatra in 1591–94.

In 1600, Queen Elizabeth granted a monopoly of trade between the Cape of Good Hope and the Straits of Magellan (that is, throughout the Indian and Pacific oceans) to a joint-stock company, "The Governor and Merchants of London Trading into the East Indies," which eventually developed into the British East India Company. This example was followed by the creation of the Dutch East India Company (Vereenigde Oostindische Compagnie) in 1602. By this time, however, the Dutch Company, with ten times the original capital of its British counterpart, represented six cities and already had half a dozen factories — trading posts — in the Indies. In 1609 the Dutch made a twelve years' truce with Spain and set up a governor-general of the Indies and a council to control the Company's activities so as to make every effort to secure the monopoly of the spice trade.

The first Dutch ship to reach Japan, where it was wrecked in 1600, brought as pilot Will Adams, an Englishman who eventually became the chief interpreter and adviser to the first Tokugawa shogun, Ieyasu, in his foreign contacts. In 1609, regular Dutch trade began at the isolated port of Hirado on an island off the western extremity of Japan, and the English too traded there from 1613 to 1623.

Thus the Dutch and British companies first sent their vessels into the eastern seas for trade rather than conquest. They shared an enmity for their Catholic rivals, Spain and Portugal, but often fought each other fiercely for the outposts and opportunities of commerce. In this struggle the Hollanders retained the upper hand.

The Dutch aim, under the leadership of ruthless organizers like Jan Pieterszoon Coen, who founded Batavia on Java in 1619, was at first merely to monopolize the spice trade by further developing the system of key bases and controlled sea routes. Accordingly, the Dutch Company maintained a broad network of factory posts: on the southeast (or Coromandel) coast of India, in Ceylon, on both the Arakan and the Tenasserim coasts of Burma, in Siam at the capital (Ayutthaya), in Cambodia, and in Vietnam. In 1641 the Dutch finally seized Malacca from the Portuguese. Meanwhile, as we shall see, they had become the only Europeans to continue trading with Japan.

The efforts of the Dutch to trade with Ming China, however, were rebuffed. They fortified a small island in the Pescadores between Taiwan and the mainland, but were soon driven out by a Ming fleet. In the same year, 1624, they established fortified posts on Taiwan (Formosa, the "beautiful" island, as the Portuguese had christened it). Here they carried on trade until 1661, when they were ousted by the Ming supporter "Koxinga" (Cheng Ch'eng-kung), whose fleets then held island strongholds like Quemoy, in Amoy harbor, on China's southeast coast. A Dutch fleet retaliated by aiding the new Ch'ing, or Manchu, dynasty in 1663–64. The Ch'ing finally conquered Taiwan in 1683 and made it part of Fukien province. Meanwhile the Dutch, through missions to Peking in 1656 and later, earned a place on the list of Ch'ing tributaries (see tables, pages 53 and 72), but still without securing a regular trade.

In the face of this powerful and widespread Dutch activity in tapping the routes of Far Eastern commerce, the British came off second best. In the early seventeenth century they set up factories side by side with the Dutch in India, Siam, and Japan, and at ten or a dozen centers in the Indies — on Sumatra, Java, Borneo, and the Moluccas — but this proved an expensive dispersion of meager resources. Under attacks by Coen, they began in 1623 to withdraw from the Indies, as well as from Japan. After 1684 they finally left the Dutch to their hard-won monopoly of the Indonesian archipelago and its spice trade.

The Overseas Chinese. All these early intrusions of European merchant-adventurers into Far Eastern waters had one common feature — contact with Chinese merchants. Except for the spice trade, the great continental empire was the principal source of trade goods such as silk, porcelain, and lacquer for the rest of Asia as well as for Europe, and Chinese trading junks were the principal carriers in the international commerce of East Asia. Communities of resident merchants, or "Overseas Chinese," were found by the Europeans at established ports like Malacca. Similar Chinese communities soon grew up at new ports like Manila and Batavia. The record of Western expansion has been more fully studied, but the fact is that it interpenetrated and was accompanied by an equally important Chinese expansion. The latter had begun centuries earlier, and it has lasted longer, even though — or perhaps because — it has been limited mainly to commerce and has seldom been aided by naval or political action by the Chinese government.

The Overseas Chinese communities in the seventeenth century were generally organized under a Chinese captain or headman, who was locally selected. There was a Chinese quarter in each port city, as at Batavia, Amboina, and Bantam in the Indies, at Manila under the Spaniards, at Hirado and Nagasaki in Japan, and later at Bangkok in Siam. Chinese merchants often became tax-farmers for the local authorities, as they did for the kings of Siam. Their thriving communities were far more important than the "Chinatowns" that grew up in Western cities in the nineteenth century.

Because of the anticommercial policies of the late Ming and early Ch'ing dynasties and their long-continued bans on foreign intercourse, these early Overseas Chinese were often renegades and pirates as well as merchants. Organized in antidynastic secret societies, they were a chief component of the early international community of lawless trader-adventurers. In the "Japanese pirate" raids on Ming China, for example (see Vol. I, p. 331), Chinese desperadoes were a major element, as they were also in the Dutch smuggling trade which centered on Formosa. The "China Captain" or chief of the community at Hirado became a principal commercial ally of the English and Dutch there. He extracted large sums from the English on the promise of opening a China trade for them and mediated between the Dutch and the Ming authorities.

Western merchants, attracted by the rich prospect of trade with China, found it expedient from the first to do business with Overseas Chinese, who maintained a useful contact with their native places, particularly Amoy and the Canton-Macao region. This alliance between Western and Chinese merchant-adventurers became a regular feature of Sino-Western contact. In the eyes of Peking it remained an illicit collusion of "barbarians" and "Chinese traitors."

THE CHRISTIAN CENTURY IN JAPAN[1]

Missionaries, as we have seen, were an integral part of Spanish and Portuguese expansion. Their role was no less adventurous and aggressive than that of the early explorers, traders, and pirates. For Portugal, the traditional enemy was Islam, and the gateway to Asia was India, where the administrative institutions and patterns of West-East contact were first worked out. These included such features as white supremacy, native slavery, and forced conversion to Christianity.

At Goa, as elsewhere in his empire, the Portuguese king, in return for political and commercial powers granted him by the Pope under the *padroado,* financed and supported the church establishment and its missions. The Franciscans set up headquarters at Goa in 1517 and thence spread eastward. But the lead in missionary penetration of East Asia was soon taken by a new order.

The Jesuits. The founder of the Society of Jesus, Ignatius de Loyola (1491–1556), made it from the first a highly educated group of men, international in background. Inspired by his *Spiritual Exercises,* they became thoroughly self-disciplined, non-monastic in aim, and trained for active accomplishment in the world. Offering their services to the Pope, they were made an order in 1540.

The quasi-military organization of the Jesuits, disciplined to absolute obedience under a "general" appointed with full powers for life, was combined with a constant concern for learning and education. This combination made the Jesuits a formidable cultural striking force. These "soldiers

1 This phase of history is told from the Japanese point of view on pages 581–583, 588–589, and 595–601 in the preceding volume, *East Asia: The Great Tradition.*

of the Cross" received many years of rigorous training, not only in grammar, logic, and theology, but also in the science, philosophy, and general higher learning of the Renaissance. Only a few, through careful selection, were admitted to the top grade of membership. Prepared to go anywhere, as "cavalry of the Church," the Jesuits also served incidentally as the first technical experts from the West to Asia.

One of the half dozen founding fathers was a Spaniard known to history as St. Francis Xavier (1506–1552). He came East soon after 1540, established a training center at Goa, and thence pushed on to Ceylon, Malacca, the Moluccas, and Japan, in travels which made him the first "Apostle of the Indies." In 1549, not long after the first recorded Portuguese contact with Japan in 1543, Xavier arrived at Kagoshima in Satsuma in southern Kyūshū on a Chinese pirate junk from Malacca. He was accompanied by Japanese converts from Southeast Asia, who helped him to communicate his Christian faith in Japanese.

Not unnaturally, certain major aspects of Christianity had to be described in Buddhist terminology, "religion" itself being translated as *Buppō*, the "law of Buddha." At first, Christianity appeared to the Japanese almost like a new variety of Buddhism, since both religions in their ritual used altars, candles, incense, images, rosaries, and processions, and many of the major tenets of Christianity were similar to those of the more popular sects of Buddhism.

Xavier was immediately delighted with the Japanese as the best heathen "who have as yet been discovered . . . a people of very good manners . . . a poor people in general but their poverty . . . is not considered a shame. . . . They esteem honor more than riches. . . . Never yet did I see a people so honest in not thieving." He found many Japanese to be literate, "very desirous of knowledge," and curious about Christianity. This enthusiasm for the Japanese was shared by many other Europeans in this early period of contact. In part it can be attributed to the similarity of attitudes and values between feudal Japanese society and the countries of early modern Europe, which were themselves just emerging from a comparable feudal experience.

Xavier at first went to the capital, Kyōto, in the mendicant manner, following the rule of poverty and therefore appearing almost as a beggar. But he soon found that more could be achieved if he put on a display of pomp, presented letters and gifts, and sought out the local daimyo, who were the territorial lords in a highly stratified feudal society. Within a decade Xavier's successors were accepted at Kyōto, where they soon had several churches and 500 converts. Further support now accrued to Christianity as Oda Nobunaga, rising to power in bitter conflict with the petty lords and powerful Buddhist monasteries of the capital region, gave patronage and protection to the Jesuits. By 1582, before their brothers at Macao could even get into China, the Jesuits in Japan had

75 priests at work and some 150,000 converts. There is no greater contrast in the responses of China and Japan to Western contact, nor a more interesting phenomenon to explore in its political, economic, and cultural ramifications.

The Christian Movement in Japan. The Japanese interest in Christianity came at the end of a century of severe domestic disorder. Despite the successive efforts after 1568 of Nobunaga, Hideyoshi, and Tokugawa Ieyasu, the feudal fiefs were not brought fully under a central power until 1600. Independent daimyo, particularly in Kyūshū, were thus able to follow the dictates of personal curiosity, political rivalry, and economic interest in their dealings with Portuguese merchants and Jesuit missionaries.

Among these Europeans, the merchants paid great deference to the priests, who in turn relied upon the Macao-Japan trade for almost half the financial support of their mission. The great Jesuit vicar-general of the Orient, the Italian Alessandro Valignano (1539–1606), spent a dozen years in Japan during three visits after 1579 and very early arranged for the Jesuit mission to receive a fixed allotment of Chinese silk in the annual carrack from Macao. Some daimyo adopted Christianity for themselves and their people in the hope that this would attract the Portuguese trade to their realms. Christian daimyo pressed the Jesuits to act as their brokers in the very profitable silk trade, while the central authorities of Japan tolerated Christianity partly to ensure the continuance of the profitable commercial contact. In 1579 the petty Christian daimyo of the region around Nagasaki, which after 1571 had become the chief Portuguese port of call, gave the village to the Jesuits as a sort of sub-fief. Thus their connection with the Portuguese trade gave them not only funds but influence.

Though Christianity and foreign trade grew side by side, reinforcing each other, the appeal of the Jesuits to their converts at Kyōto and among the daimyo of western Japan was also genuinely spiritual. They accommodated themselves in every material way to Japanese customs, dressing like Zen Buddhist monks and seeking out the upper class. Partly because Buddhism was beginning to lose its intellectual appeal in Japan and was also under severe political and military attack in this period of turmoil, the new religion was not only tolerated but gained devoted adherents. As early as 1555 a Japanese convert named "Bernardo" had reached Rome and entered the Society of Jesus. In 1582 Valignano was able to send a first embassy from the Christian daimyo to Rome. Accoutered as the "sons of kings," the four young Japanese samurai on this mission voyaged to Macao and Goa and on to Lisbon. They were feted by Philip II at Madrid. In Rome, accompanied to the Vatican by cavalry squadrons, they were received by the Pope, his face bathed in tears. In Venice, Tintoretto painted them. They returned to Japan in 1590.

Seizing the opportunity, the Jesuits began to create a vigorous indigenous church. Valignano was cordially received in succession by Nobunaga and Hideyoshi, the unifiers of Japan. He set up training centers for Japanese novitiates, which eventually began to produce a native priesthood, deemed essential because foreigners, it was felt, could never really master Japanese. "We who come hither from Europe," wrote Valignano, "find ourselves as veritable children who have to learn how to eat, sit, converse, dress, act politely, and so on." Like Xavier, he esteemed the Japanese. With all their apparent contradictions, they were still "all white, courteous and highly civilized . . . most warlike and bellicose . . . most affable . . . [yet] most false and treacherous. . . . When they are most determined to do evil to someone, the more outward compliments they pay him. . . . It is a marvel to see how despite so much poverty they can keep such cleanliness and good breeding." In his view, Japan produced "the finest Christianity in all the East."

By 1614, indeed, there were 300,000 or more converts and an establishment of 116 Jesuits, 24 residences, and 250 native catechists. The mission press had printed many translations into Japanese as well as linguistic aids and adaptations of native works romanized (i.e., written in the Latin alphabet) for European students. The spread of Christianity had been accompanied by an acceptance of Portuguese words, firearms, maritime technology, and art motifs. Japan seemed well launched upon a process of Westernization. She was being rapidly drawn into an international community in which Japanese came into increasing contact with Portuguese, Spaniards, Dutchmen, and Englishmen as well as with the peoples of East Asia.

The Seclusion of Japan. Several factors contributed to the drastic effort by which the early Tokugawa shoguns, who came into control of Japan in 1600, stopped Japan's maritime expansion and thus altered the course of East Asian history. One was the tendency of newly established centralized regimes in East Asia to turn their backs on commerce and rely on agricultural taxes for their support. Another more specific reason was the fear that the Europeans might interfere in domestic politics and that Christianity might become the basis for collusion between converted daimyo and European powers against the central government. This fear induced the central authorities to attack Christianity directly. Indeed, as early as 1587 Hideyoshi had issued a decree to banish the Jesuits, evidently fearful lest they support his rivals, but at first had not enforced it.

As long as Japan's European relations remained a Macao-Jesuit monopoly, as Valignano earnestly advocated, all went fairly well. But the arrival of Dominicans and Franciscans from Manila after 1592 opened up both the promise of alternative trade with the Philippines and also the fear that Spanish power would expand into Japan through the Christian community as a fifth column loyal to a foreign potentate. In 1597

Hideyoshi suddenly enforced his anti-Christian decrees, executing six European missionaries and twenty Japanese believers. The Dutch and British on their arrival were violently anti-Catholic and spread tales against both Spain and Portugal. They also demonstrated that trade with Europeans need not be accompanied by missionary activity. Thus the competing nations, priests, and faiths of the West undermined one another's prestige in Japan.

Even though some Christian daimyo fought against Ieyasu in 1600 when he won control over Japan (see Vol. I, p. 591), he was at first much interested in the promotion of foreign trade and a merchant marine and continued to have friendly relations with the missionaries. As late as 1613, the great Date daimyo of northern Honshū sent a mission of some sixty samurai across the Pacific by way of Acapulco to Seville, Madrid, and Rome. Long before the return of this mission in 1620, however, the Tokugawa had begun the liquidation of the Christian church and the cutting of Western relations.

Ieyasu too had come to fear the growing Christian influence within Japan and to suspect the Europeans of imperialistic designs. He officially proscribed Christianity in 1606, and in 1614 made a determined effort to drive all missionaries out of Japan. In 1623 the English voluntarily abandoned their trading post at Hirado, and the next year all Spaniards were expelled from Japan and further contact with Manila was prohibited. In the 1630's Japanese were forbidden to go abroad or to return thence, or to build ships big enough for long voyages.

Meanwhile Christians, both European and Japanese, were steadily ferreted out, despite their protection by an underground of the faithful. Many suffered martyrdom after slow burning, crucifixion, hanging upside down, and other tortures as effective as anything devised in Europe. The vitality of Japanese Christianity is indicated by the fact that out of more than three thousand martyrs in the period from 1597 to 1660, fewer than seventy were European clerics. The climax came with the rebellion and subsequent slaughter of some 37,000 Christians at Shimabara near Nagasaki in 1637–38. The Portuguese were expelled for suspected complicity in this uprising, and the members of a large embassy which arrived in 1640 to reopen relations were executed.

The Dutch East India Company's trading agents were moved in 1641 from Hirado to the little artificial island of Deshima in Nagasaki harbor, where they lived in virtual imprisonment. Dutch vessels continued to come annually to Nagasaki, along with a limited number of Chinese vessels, thus maintaining a strictly limited commerce between Japan and the rest of the world. The head of the Dutch factory made annual visits to Edo, the capital of the Tokugawa shogunate, and he and his colleagues remained an important source of information about the outside world. But this small window on the West was largely a defensive device, and was not adequate to keep Japan actively within the international community. (For a drawing of Deshima, see Plate 19.)

Thus after a century of rapidly increasing contact between the seafaring nations at the opposite ends of the Eurasian continent, the most active of the Asian peoples voluntarily and defensively withdrew from contact with Europe and the rest of East Asia and so left East Asian waters to the aggressive Westerners. The Tokugawa seclusion established in the 1630's was surely a turning point in world history, perhaps comparable to Ming China's cessation of the great voyages of exploration in the 1430's. In both instances the East Asian rulers turned away from overseas expansion for which they had the capacity but not the motivation.

Today we may conclude that the result was disastrous for both the Chinese and the Japanese peoples of a later age, since isolation resulted in fewer stimuli to change and in a slackened pace of growth that left Japan and China technologically far behind Europe by the nineteenth century. Yet at the time, this eschewing of overseas expansion and trade in each case reflected a relative self-sufficiency and a strong social order at home. A carefully controlled trade seemed adequate to the Japanese and Chinese, who felt no need for precious metals and slaves from abroad, nor for crusades against the infidel and the saving of heathen souls. Here it is Western conduct, not Eastern, that calls for explanation.

The Japanese suppression of Christianity and of free contact with the West had an accidental result of great significance — it removed Japan from the European horizon at the very moment when Europe was beginning to remake its view of the world. The discovery of ancient non-Christian societies in Asia was creating an intellectual revolution in Christendom. Between 1545 and 1619, at least a hundred works about Japan had been published in France alone. Stimulated by the two embassies of Christian daimyo, an idealized admiration for the Japanese and an enthusiasm for their conversion were developing in the West. But just as this trend set in, the Tokugawa exclusion and persecution abruptly cut it short. Thereafter China, not Japan, became the focus of European interest in the Far East.

The Jesuit Success in China

China's response to the Jesuits was slower than Japan's but went through somewhat similar phases. Because the Europeans were identified by the Chinese authorities as "barbarians" associated with "traitorous" and piratical Overseas Chinese, they met a less auspicious beginning in China than in Japan. After a slow start, however, Jesuit missionaries achieved a degree of success at Peking, in a period of political transition under the late Ming and early Ch'ing rulers. But after the Manchu emperors had established a strong central government, they became alarmed over the papal claims of spiritual superiority and turned against Christianity. This sequence of events in the seventeenth and eighteenth centuries appears to have been somewhat synchronous with the dynastic cycle. It was to have a later echo in the Christian success during the decline of the Ch'ing in the nineteenth century and the warlord interregnum of the early twentieth century, followed in recent years by the rise of the strongly centralized Communist power and its expulsion of missionaries and manipulation of the Chinese Christian church for its own ends.

St. Francis Xavier, impressed by the great prestige of Chinese culture in East Asia, had decided that the Chinese emperor must be the primary target of his mission, but had been unable even to enter the Middle Kingdom. After Xavier died off the South China coast in 1552, Jesuit priests made three attempts to enter the country, but could not get much further than the Portuguese trading settlement at Macao, where they, like all other Westerners, were effectively quarantined against Chinese contact. Augustinians from the Philippines reached Fukien, but were expelled. This Spanish competition, however, led the Pope in 1576 to create the diocese of Macao under the patronage of Portugal.

The Career of Matteo Ricci. The successful Jesuit approach to China began when Valignano, convinced that missionaries must master the language and culture of the ruling class, established in 1580 a training center at Macao. When the first priest assigned to study Chinese found it all but impossible, the way was prepared for the greatest of the Jesuit pioneers, Matteo Ricci (Chinese name, Li Ma-tou; 1552–1610). He had reached Goa in 1578 and was assigned to China in 1582, the ninth member of the order to be sent there.

Ricci was an Italian of impressive personality and attainments, a tall and vigorous man with a curly beard, blue eyes, and a voice like a great bell. By the age of thirty, he had studied jurisprudence as well as theology and much of the science of his day and had been trained in mathematics by Clavius, the leader in the Gregorian reform of the Julian calendar promulgated in 1582. Ricci knew the geometry of Euclid, some physics and the Ptolemaic system of astronomy (Copernicus' work published in 1543 was not yet accepted), as well as map-making and simple mechanics. Possessed also of a powerful photographic memory, Ricci made rapid progress in written and spoken Chinese.

When a local mandarin, or official, offered to let Ricci and a colleague reside at the important city of Shiuhing (Chao-ch'ing) on the West River about sixty miles west of Canton, he was ready to exploit the opportunity. One of Ricci's first successes was in making a large one-handed clock and a map of the world. The latter was of interest to many Chinese scholars and was republished in eight editions during Ricci's lifetime. Notes in

Chinese told the reader that thirty European countries embraced Catholicism and had "high regard for the 'five relationships' " of Confucian ethics.

Following Xavier's principles, derived from contact with the highly sophisticated and culturally stable societies of India and Japan, the Jesuits believed in adapting their message to the Asian scene. In China as in Japan they worked from the top down. To get the support of the court at Peking, they needed access to the ruling class of scholar-officials. Boring from within, they adopted Chinese forms as far as possible, avoiding all open connection with the Portuguese traders at Macao. They gave up their first, European-style house for one in the Chinese style, and later abandoned the Buddhist monk's costume for the Confucian scholar's gown. Instead of preaching to street crowds in the Western way, which could only seem upsetting to Chinese law and order, they held conversations with Chinese scholars, arousing their curiosity with demonstrations of prisms, clocks, and geographic knowledge. Above all they became fluent in Mandarin, or standard North Chinese, and literate in the Chinese Classics, quoting from them for Christian purposes. This approach enabled Ricci to represent Christianity as a system of wisdom and ethics compatible with Confucianism.

Through these indefatigable labors in the service of their faith, not the least arduous of which was some degree of mastery of the Chinese Classics, Ricci and his colleagues eventually reached their goal at Peking. But it took thirteen years — until 1595 — to get even as far as the Yangtze Valley at Nanchang. In 1598 Ricci was allowed to spend two months at Peking, but not until 1601 was he able to establish his residence there.

When Matteo Ricci began his ten-year sojourn in the Ming capital, the Wan-li Emperor, an archetype of incompetence and gluttony, had been twenty-eight years on the throne. Corruption and bureaucratic faction were rife, and Ricci had to maneuver among intriguing eunuchs and dogmatic scholars. His first success came when he presented two clocks and a clavichord, which caught the emperor's fancy. He and his colleagues were brought into the Forbidden City, the emperor's palace, to show how these mechanisms operated, and Ricci composed edifying madrigals to be sung to His Majesty. The Jesuits suffered many vicissitudes but were greatly aided by personal friendships with high officials. Ricci finally got himself out of the category of tribute-bearer and was given an imperial stipend and tacit permission to reside in Peking as a scholar. Within a few years he and his colleagues had made some two hundred Christian converts, including even ministers of state. When Ricci died in 1610, there were about 2500 Christians in the empire. He was buried at Peking in a plot granted by the emperor.

The Jesuit Role at Peking. Ricci's successors found that, though they could attract the emperor's interest with clocks, they could make themselves most useful to him by applying their Western knowledge of astronomy to the revision of the Chinese calendar. By his position at the top of the Chinese scheme of things, the Son of Heaven had a special responsibility to maintain a calendar which would accurately foretell the positions of the heavenly bodies and the timing of the seasons. This was an essential function in China's agricultural society, yet it was never simple: the sun and moon maintain no fixed relationship, and the orbits of the planets, being elliptical, seem constantly to change. The astronomical bureau under the Board of Rites at Peking had taken over the Moslem system of astronomy, which had come in through Arabic influence in the time of the Mongol dynasty. The Jesuits were surprised to find that the metal globes and other instruments of that period (still preserved at Peking) were almost as good as anything then used in Europe. However, the Moslem astronomers at the Chinese capital, as well as the old-style Chinese astronomers with whom they competed, were somewhat behind the times. In 1610 they predicted an eclipse several hours wrong. Such errors gave the Jesuits their opportunity, and they were asked in 1629 to undertake the reform of the imperial calendar. Ricci had been able to offer only the ancient Ptolemaic system, with its nine concentric spheres and other intricacies, but his great successor, the German Jesuit, Johannes Adam Schall von Bell (Chinese name, T'ang Jo-wang; 1591–1666), who came to China in 1622, was a trained astronomer. Coming from Rome in the time of Galileo, he succeeded in establishing the pre-eminence of Western astronomy at Peking, even though forbidden by his superiors to use the Copernican system openly. Schall got a position in the palace, where he first celebrated mass in 1632.

The position of Christianity was strengthened about this time by the unearthing of the famous Nestorian stone tablet or stele at Sian, erected in 781. It bore witness to the introduction of Nestorian Christianity into T'ang China almost a thousand years earlier (see Vol. I, p. 177).

By the last years of the Ming, the Jesuits had made numerous converts among the members of the imperial family, as well as among the eunuchs and ladies of the court, and the emperor was gradually coming under Christian influence. After the collapse of the Ming in 1644, refugees of the Ming house were baptized by Jesuits in South China in 1650. They even sent an unavailing embassy (under Father Michael Boym) to ask aid of the Pope.

By 1620 the Jesuit mission had brought to Peking a Western library of some 7000 volumes on which to base their writings in Chinese. By the end of the century they had produced a total of some 380 such works. The larger part concerned Christianity, but there were 83 publications in astronomy, 15 in mathematics, and others in geography, medicine, ethics, and linguistics. With the aid of devoted Chinese scholars and through their own scholarly competence, the missionaries produced Chinese treatises on such varied subjects as earthquakes, meteorology, mechanics, pharmacology, anatomy, zoology, logic, and European government and education. The influence of these works on Chinese learning still remains to be assessed.

Chinese Converts. The drama of the personal stories of Matteo Ricci and Adam Schall should not blind us to the favorable context of the times at Peking. The decay of the Ming regime made the dynasty, for many scholars, no longer a worthy focus of their loyalty; in this period of turmoil there were a number of conversions to the foreign faith, which the government was too weak to prevent or suppress. Another trend was less a product of the dynastic situation and rested on an intellectual more than a spiritual need — the Chinese scholar's interest in Western science and its applications. This interest attracted a wider group of scholars than did the Christian doctrine. Together, science and Christianity made a number of outstanding converts — a group of Chinese capable of collaborating with the equally select band of Jesuit fathers in truly bicultural endeavors.

An early collaborator was Li Chih-tsao (Christian name, Leo Li; d. 1630), a metropolitan graduate (or *chin-shih*, holder of the highest examination degree; see page 86), whose interest in geography led him to study Western science with Ricci. He wrote prefaces to several of Ricci's Chinese publications explaining Christian doctrine; and he himself composed, from Ricci's dictation, treatises on geometry and arithmetic and, in later collaboration with other Jesuits, works on logic and European astronomy.

The most famous of all converts was Hsü Kuang-ch'i (Christian name, Paul Hsü; 1562–1633), who became a Christian even before he passed the highest examination and entered the Hanlin Academy in 1604. With Ricci he completed the translation of the first six books of Euclid's geometry and wrote several works on trigonometry. With other Jesuits he produced works on hydraulics and on the soul and, still later, works of his own on astronomy, on agricultural technology, and against Buddhism. Hsü was made a Grand Secretary, at the top of the Ming administration, in 1632 not long before his death. For three decades his aid to the Jesuits had been invaluable, giving the missionaries an entrée into high official circles, protecting them in times of attack, and helping them to present Christianity through Chinese writings that had literary polish and avoided offense to traditional scholars. In modern times the chief Roman Catholic establishment in China has been in the suburbs of Shanghai at Zikawei (Hsü-chia-hui, "Hsü Family Village"), on the site of Paul Hsü's patrimonial estate.

ORTELIUS' MAP OF "TARTARY OR THE
KINGDOM OF THE GREAT KHAN"

This portion of a map of 1570 mixes medieval lore of "Cathay" with early modern
knowledge of "China," as separate countries.
Thus the captions follow the Marco Polo
tradition — "Cambalu [i.e. Peking], chief
city of Cathay, 28 miles in circumference";
"a marble bridge 300 paces long"; "mountains from which stones [i.e. coal] are dug
out for fuel"; "a kingdom of Christians in
Asia under Prester John." From early modern voyages come "China," Formosa ("Isola
Fermosa"), Ningpo, Kyōto or Miyako
("Meaco," chief city of Japan). Conflict
between these two sources puts one port in
two places: Chincheu ("Chincheo," below
30° parallel) is modern name for medieval
Ch'üan-chou ("Zaiton," just above 40°
parallel).

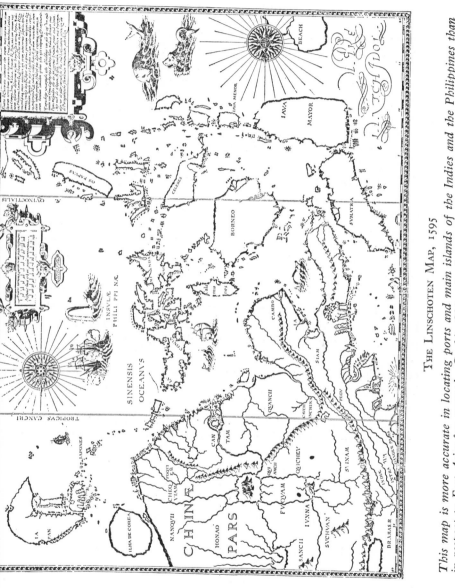

THE LINSCHOTEN MAP, 1595

This map is more accurate in locating ports and main islands of the Indies and the Philippines than in respect to East Asia: for example, Cochin China is shown as west of Kwangsi ("Qvancii"), and Korea as an island. (This reproduction omits the many detailed place names along the coasts.)

The Jesuits under the Early Ch'ing. Both Paul Hsü and Adam Schall, in addition to taking charge of calendar reform, helped the Ming court to obtain Western arms. To fight off the Manchus, Hsü procured cannon and Portuguese gunners from Macao in 1629. In 1636 Schall set up a foundry and cast some twenty big guns. Western science and the technology of the modern world, in short, gained acceptance more readily than Western religion. The Jesuit mission, on its part, hoping to make conversions, provided its technical services to whoever held power.

After the conquest of 1644, the Manchu regent, Dorgon, kept Schall in the post of chief astronomer. His successor as head of the mission, a Belgian Jesuit, Ferdinand Verbiest (Chinese name, Nan Huai-jen; 1623–1688), who came to Peking in 1659, succeeded to this post in 1669. Verbiest later superintended the casting of some 300 cannon, each named for a saint, for K'ang-hsi to use in suppressing the Rebellion of the Three Feudatories in 1673–81.

The young Shun-chih Emperor (1638–1661), although he ascended the Manchu throne in 1643, actually ruled only from 1651, after the death of the regent Dorgon. For several years Shun-chih saw much of Father Schall, whom he called "grandpa" (*ma-fa*) and consulted on many matters. He permitted the building of a Christian church at Peking and gave Schall high honors, but eventually came under the influence of the palace eunuchs and was won over to Buddhism.

During the middle decades of the long reign of K'ang-hsi (1662–1722), the Jesuit mission at Peking reached the height of its influence. Verbiest and his colleagues at certain periods enjoyed intimate contact with the emperor, seeing him sometimes almost daily. They explained Euclidian geometry to him, once gave him a new drug, "Jesuit's bark" or quinine, to cure an imperial fever, and were commissioned to survey and map the Chinese empire (1708–1721), using Western methods of astronomical observation and measurement. Brilliant French Jesuits like Jean-François Gerbillon (1654–1707), who came to China in 1685, and Dominique Parennin (1665–1741), a gifted linguist who came in 1698, succeeded to the influential position of Verbiest.

The position of the Jesuits was essentially that of courtiers with high official rank in the entourage of the emperor. Maintaining such status by one's personal conduct required great skill and self-control — performing the kotow with complete servility like other officials, displaying knowledge with finesse, presenting gifts and making friends with discrimination, and constantly preserving one's prestige. The Jesuit position depended upon the imperial favor.

Coming at the end of the great age of exploration, the Jesuits made a principal scientific contribution in geography. Ricci's map of the world had given the Chinese a number of geographical names, like *Ou-lo-pa* for "Europe" and *Ya-hsi-ya* for "Asia," which became part of the language. It introduced the use of meridians and of the equator and defined the five zones and five continents. Some versions were most remarkable, in Oriental eyes, for depicting China in the east of Asia and not the center of the world.

At the same time the Jesuits added to Western geographical knowledge when they finally demonstrated that the China which the Portuguese had reached by sea was identical with the medieval Cathay which Marco Polo and others had reached by land. This had long been a disputed question, but in 1603–1606 an intrepid Portuguese lay brother, Benedict de Goez, succeeded after many hardships in crossing Central Asia on the caravan route from India over the Pamirs and through the oases — Yarkand, Kucha, Hami, etc. — to western China. Disguised as a merchant, speaking only Persian, Goez survived the rigors of travel and the dangers of robbery and assassination and finally reached Suchow, within the Great Wall, whence he succeeded in getting a letter to Ricci at Peking. Ricci's reply, sent by a Chinese Christian, reached Goez at Suchow shortly before he died of illness and exhaustion.

In China, as in Japan, the early success of the Jesuits was eventually undone by the arrival of other Europeans and the raising of issues of power politics. In short, international rivalries within Europe complicated Western relations with East Asia in the seventeenth century, as they were later to do in the nineteenth. As we shall see, Franciscans, Dominicans, and Augustinians attacked the Jesuit position in China, France became Portugal's rival as would-be patron of the mission, while Dutch and British fleets endangered the sea route from Lisbon to Goa to Macao. Meanwhile Russian expansion created a new channel of European contact with Cathay.

SINO-RUSSIAN RELATIONS

The modern contact of Western Europe with East Asia came about wholly by sea and was profoundly conditioned by that fact. Early voyagers to the East were always able to follow customary routes on which Arab, Indian, and Chinese sailors had preceded them and along which were traditional ports of call, as well established as the oases on the ancient Central Asian silk route. Once embarked on these well-traveled routes, European merchant-adventurers could expect to find pilots and provisions all the way to the Far East.

Moreover, voyagers on these sea routes might increase rather than use up their resources on the way. The ports of call were not isolated way-stations in the desert but often were points of entrance to populous communities and kingdoms — centers of local commerce as well as entrepots in the international carrying trade of the Indian Ocean. In this way, during the age of sail before the railway and other modern forms of land and air transport, the Westerners had the advantage that their ships could bring them to Malacca or Canton in full force, almost direct from Lisbon or London, self-sufficient, mobile, with their own armament and accoutrement, and without the necessity of passing through foreign peoples and kingdoms. A British naval descent upon Macao or Manila, for example, demonstrating the potentialities of sea power, could bring great force to bear suddenly and unannounced. Maritime trade in the carracks of the Portuguese or the East Indiamen of the Dutch and English could handle more weight of goods than many camel caravans. Thus the approach to the East by sea was far more efficient than that by land, and far more powerful.

This logistic factor helps to explain the comparative slowness of the rise of Russian power in the Far East. After an initial burst of speed in crossing and exploring Siberia in the seventeenth century, the empire of the tsars waited another two centuries before penetrating northern Manchuria.

The Russian Advance across Siberia. Characteristically, the Russian colonizing expansion toward the Pacific, across the endless stretches of the Siberian tundra, was gradual but also relatively permanent. The Siberian climate and terrain were not hospitable, there were no great centers of population and production, nor were communications easy. Even though the Russians reached the Pacific almost as early as the English founded New England and more than 150 years before the crossing of the American continent, their penetration of the great countries of East Asia subsequently lagged far behind that of the Westerners who came by sea. Yet despite its slowness, Russia's expansion across the continent consisted of a steady and seemingly irreversible absorption of territory and native tribes, which became part of the Russian imperial administration. While British fleets might descend upon the East Asian coasts in irresistible force, their forays were still hit-and-run. If they came like an avalanche, the Russians advanced like a glacier.

As we pursue this subject we may well keep in mind that the American people today have inherited the Western European tradition of contact with the Far East by sea, and face there a Russian influence which has inherited a tradition of contact by land. The two traditions are very different.

In their long contact with China, the Russians have combined the qualities of northern "barbarians" with those of modern Europeans. They first appeared in Chinese history on the Inner Asian frontier and so inherited the status and treatment accorded to Mongol and other nomadic tribes.

In their rapid early advance across Siberia, beginning with the penetration of the Ob River basin about 1580 by the Cossack leader Yermak, the Russians traversed the closely adjoining upper waters of the great rivers that flow northward to the Arctic — the Ob, the Yenisei, and the Lena. There they found no great commercial opportunities and could do little more than lay down a communication network of fortified outposts (*ostrog*). The great stimulus to their expansion lay in the fur trade, especially in sables, promoted by merchant families like the Stroganov and supported by the tsar. By 1632, a dozen years after the Pilgrims first settled in New England, the Russians had established Yakutsk on the upper waters of the Lena River, and by 1637 they had reached the eastern edge of the continent at the Sea of Okhotsk. The North American continent, though less broad, was not similarly traversed until more than a century and a half later.

The administration of this vast region set up by officials from Moscow was parasitic, collecting its tribute (*yasak*) of furs and skins from the local Mongol, Tungusic, or other tribes through a network of out-stations joined by post routes. Fur was about all that could then be derived from Siberia. The food supply was precarious, and the Russian explorers felt a constant need to reach a grain-growing area, as well as the Pacific Ocean with its access to the populous countries of East Asian trade.

Inevitably the Russians were attracted to the Amur River, on which barges in summer and sledges in winter could reach more productive country and, eventually, the sea. After 1643, Cossack raiding parties from Yakutsk began to go down the Amur, fighting the local tribes and establishing fortified posts. Under energetic and ruthless leaders like Poiarkov (1643–1646), Khabarov (1649–1653), and Stepanov (1654–1658), these raiders terrorized the local tribes. Other Cossack expeditions, coming from Yeniseisk by way of Lake Baikal, founded in 1656 a post at Nerchinsk on the Shilka, the main tributary of the Amur. A permanent outpost and a fortress were established to the east at Albazin in 1665, at the top of the northernmost bend of the Amur.

Early Sino-Russian Contact. These posts within the Amur watershed brought the Russians into conflict with the Ch'ing empire. From the point of view of the Ch'ing, as well as the northern tribes, this Russian expansion had little more to commend it than had the early Portuguese forays on the Chinese coast. As Khabarov recorded of one incident, "With God's help, we burned them, we knocked them on the head, and counting big and little we killed six hundred sixty-one," in addition to acquiring 243 women and girls and 237 horses. Not unnaturally the local tribes of northern Manchuria appealed against these incursions to their overlords of the new Manchu (Ch'ing) dynasty at Peking. The latter sent troops, armed often with cannon and matchlocks, to fight off the Russians.

Ch'ing concern was heightened when a Tungus tribal chieftain on the Amur frontier, Ghantimur, after joining in the attack on the Russians, shifted his allegiance to them in the late 1660's. He became a Christian, a Russian noble, and a commander of forces at Nerchinsk, defying repeated Ch'ing demands for his extradition as a disloyal subject. This case posed concretely the problem of retaining Ch'ing control over the tribal leadership as well as the territory and strategic routes of the Amur area.

During the first generation of Manchu-Russian relations, from about 1651 to 1682, the Ch'ing rulers were not in a strong position. Their conquest of China was not completed until the suppression of the Revolt of the Three Feudatories (1673–1681). Meanwhile the Ch'ing hegemony over the Mongols was formidably challenged by the rise of the Dzungar tribe under Galdan in the far northwestern Ili region. Western Mongol tribes had already been in contact with the Russians on their north in Siberia, and Eastern Mongols as well as Tungus tribes were already trading with the Russians at Nerchinsk. The K'ang-hsi Emperor's aim, therefore, was not only to eject the Russians from the Amur but also, and primarily, to forestall the growth of their influence among the Tungus tribes and the Mongols. (On Ch'ing relations with the Western Mongols, see Vol. I, pp. 356–360.)

Diplomatic relations had begun informally between Russia and China as early as 1619, when Russian envoys from the governor of Tobolsk reached Peking, then still under Ming rule. Having brought no tribute, they were not received in audience. A more formal attempt was made in 1654 when Tsar Alexis sent an envoy, Baikov, to Peking, now under the Ch'ing, with a letter to the emperor of China. The resulting contretemps illustrates the different attitudes of the two powers. When he reached the Ch'ing capital in 1656, Baikov's chief aim was to facilitate trade without acknowledging Chinese suzerainty. He therefore refused to deliver the tsar's letter except to the emperor directly, and he also refused to perform the three kneelings and nine prostrations of the kotow. On their part the officials of the Mongolian Superintendency (*Li-fan yüan*), who were in charge of him, were not interested in trade but were much concerned to demonstrate that the emperor was the superior of the Russians, just as he claimed to be of the Mongols. The Russian envoy's stubborn demand for the European type of inter-state equality threatened the ideological basis of Ch'ing power over East Asia, and he was sent away without being received at court. Another Russian mission, which reached Peking in 1660, was similarly sent back.

Still another Russian envoy was the colorful N. G. Spathar-Milescu ("Spathar" was actually a title), an intellectual Greek educated in Constantinople who had had wide experience in Western Europe. After traversing Siberia, on which he became an authority, he reached Peking

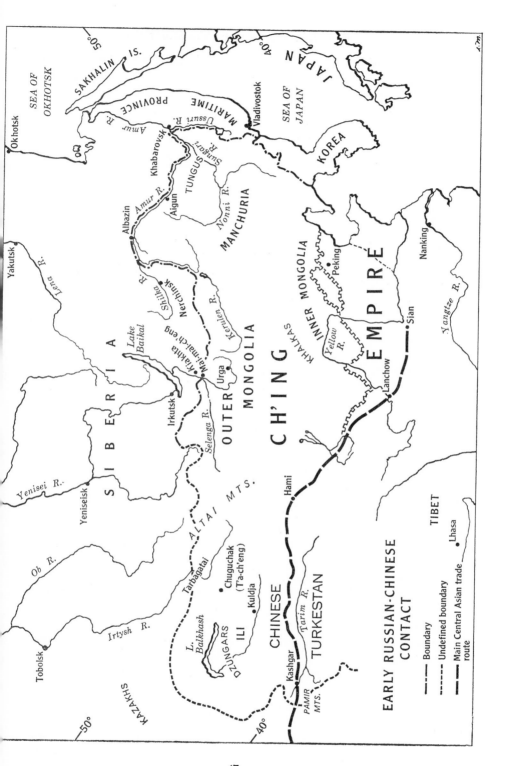

EARLY RUSSIAN-CHINESE
CONTACT

Boundary
Undefined boundary
Main Central Asian trade
route

in 1676 bearing credentials for the first time in Latin. He got Father Verbiest to serve as interpreter in his negotiations. Spathar-Milescu succeeded in avoiding the ceremonial of the kotow but asked in vain for commercial and diplomatic relations on an equal basis. He was sent away for refusing to kneel when receiving the emperor's presents for the tsar. K'ang-hsi thereupon again demanded the extradition of the renegade Tungus chieftain (Ghantimur) and decreed that all future relations must be in the tributary form.

After the consolidation of their rule within China in the early 1680's, the Manchus proceeded systematically to establish their military control of the Amur region. They developed post routes by land and water from South Manchuria to this area, setting up stations, building vessels, establishing granaries and military colonies, and creating a naval force to operate on the Manchurian river system. The Russians were soon ejected from their outposts on the Lower Amur. In 1685 and again in 1686 a superior Ch'ing army laid siege to the one remaining small fortress of Albazin.

The Treaty of Nerchinsk. Under this pressure the Russian court decided to negotiate and in 1686 sent an ambassador, F. A. Golovin, to Nerchinsk for this purpose. The time was favorable, for just at this point the Ch'ing position was weakened by the rising power of the Western Mongols. The Dzungar chieftain, Galdan, moved eastward in 1688 and defeated the Manchus' allies, the Eastern or Khalka Mongols. This made it necessary to postpone the negotiations with Russia, but it also made K'ang-hsi more ready for a settlement.

Following the precedent of Verbiest's interpreting for Spathar-Milescu, K'ang-hsi deputed two Jesuits — a Portuguese (Pereyra) and a Frenchman (Gerbillon) — to act as interpreters and advisers in negotiating with the Russians. The Ch'ing negotiators, including an uncle of the emperor, reached Nerchinsk overland, while a fleet of ninety boats bearing a thousand soldiers and forty cannon arrived on the river as military support for their diplomacy. The Manchu envoys, together with their servants and auxiliaries, other troops that came by land, and local tribes loyal to them, had on the spot a force great enough to overawe any native tribal chieftain. Golovin, nothing daunted, put on a show of pomp with flutes and trumpets and rich attire. He negotiated while seated on a yellow damask chair behind a gilded writing table, flanked by a tall clock and with all his retinue standing, whereas the Ch'ing envoys had to improvise rough benches, to avoid standing or sitting on the floor. In the end, however, Golovin had to yield more than the Chinese.

After much confusion, suspicion, and bargaining, during which the two Jesuits crossed the river repeatedly between the rival camps, an agreement was reached, and the Jesuits drew up official copies of a treaty in

P. MATTHÆVS RICCIVS MACERAT.
of the Society of Iesus, the first propagator
of the Christian Religion in the Kingdom of China.

LY PAVLVS GREAT COLAVS OF
the Chinese propagator of Christian Law.

THE JESUITS IN PEKING AS DEPICTED IN EUROPE

PLATE 1. Ricci and his chief convert. *Left:* "Fr. Matteo Ricci of Macerata, of the Society of Jesus, the first propagator of the Christian Religion in the Kingdom of China." *Right:* "Paul Li [error for Hsü], Great Colao [i.e. Grand Secretary] of the Chinese, propagator of the Christian Law." Chinese characters, miscopied by the Western artist, and romanizations give, left, Ricci's Chinese name: "Li Matou, with the courtesy name Hsit'ai [i.e. great scholar from the West]," and right: "Hsü Kuangch'i Pao-lu, with the literary name Hsuan-hu [i.e. profound scholar of Shanghai]." Illustration published in London in 1673.

P. AD'AM SCHALIGER A GERMAN, MANDARIN OF Y FIRST ORDER.

PLATE 2. Fr. Adam Schall with his astronomical instruments. Director of the Imperial Board of Astronomy, he wears on his cap the colored button and on his gown the "mandarin square" of a Ch'ing civil official. His rank was actually 5A, not "of the first order." His map of the world (on wall) bears Latin names. Illustration published in 1673.

PLATE 3. Jesuit architecture at Ch'ien-lung's Summer Palace. This European engraving (c. 1786) of the Hall of Peaceful Seas (Hai Yen T'ang) shows Chinese-style tile roof surmounting pilasters and "Chinese rococo" details, combined with Western perspective and staircases reminiscent of an Italian villa.

PLATE 4. *Chinoiserie:* European craftsmen use "Chinese" motifs. Wooden bed japanned in red and gilt, c. 1750–54, by Chippendale.

PLATE 5. Emperor Ch'ien-lung receives Mongol horses. Painted by the Jesuit lay brother G. Castiglione (Chinese name: Lang Shih-ning, 1688–1766), who reached Peking in 1715 and was court painter to three emperors.

CONQUESTS OF THE EMPEROR OF CHINA

PLATE 6. To celebrate the conquest of Ili and Chinese Turkestan, Emperor Ch'ien-lung had sixteen drawings by Catholic
missionaries at Peking sent to Paris for copperplate engraving.
This one (1772) shows a Manchu army camp in 1758. In the
central pavilion the commander, with his officers on either side,
receives a kneeling delegation, while wrestlers, lancers, and
archers perform.

PLATE 7. The great Manchu commander, Fu-k'ang-an, pacifies
the Taiwan rebels, 1787, in an amphibious assault. In his auto-
graphed poem, Emperor Ch'ien-lung celebrates the victory.
Engraved by Chinese artists, 1790.

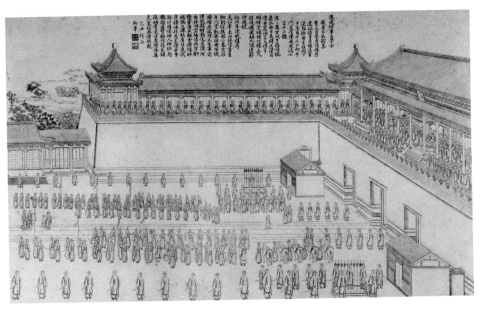

PLATE 8. The Khoja rebel Jehangir, captured in 1828 after his invasion of Kashgaria, was brought to Peking where the Tao-kuang Emperor imitated his grandfather, Ch'ien-lung, by performing special ceremonies for receiving a captive and presenting him to the ancestors before he was cut in pieces. This Chinese engraving of about 1830 shows the emperor enthroned (right) above the front gate (Wu Men) of the palace. Below, an official kneels to present Jehangir, who kneels (far left) between guards. Inscription by the emperor.

PLATE 9. Emperor Tao-kuang, enthroned above the palace gate, reviews troops. In this British engraving, roof-dragons and other architectural fancies have been invented, though details of Manchu dress and armament derive from Western observation.

Latin, while other copies were made in Manchu, Chinese, Mongolian, and Russian. The treaty was in terms of equality between the two rulers. It checked the Russian advance into the Amur region but gave Russia a stable basis for trade relations. The Russians agreed to destroy Albazin and withdraw from the Amur watershed. The treaty delimited the North Manchurian boundary but left its western end, between Mongolia and Siberia, uncertain. It also provided for extradition of future criminals and fugitives from either side and for mutual trade and travel under passport.

The Ch'ing envoys returned to find the emperor waiting, on a hunting expedition, eight days from Peking. K'ang-hsi received the two Jesuits in his quarters with great satisfaction, saying, "I know that it was through your ability and effort that this peace was concluded." In 1692 the emperor issued an edict of toleration for the Christian religion in China, and the next year gave land within the Imperial City for a church which remained in use until 1827. These events inaugurated the most successful two decades of the Jesuit mission.

The Development of Ch'ing Policy toward Russia. By the Treaty of Nerchinsk, K'ang-hsi had forestalled Russian aid to the Eastern Mongols. In the decade after 1689 he achieved the final defeat of Galdan (d. 1697) and began to assert and intensify his control over the Western Mongol tribes, employing and further developing all the methods for this purpose inherited from the Ming.

Russian trade caravans now crossed Mongolia via Urga to Peking under official passports, usually accompanied by envoys with a semi-commercial, semi-diplomatic status. Several of these official trading missions left written accounts — in particular, those of Izbrandt Ides (in Peking 1693–94), Lorentz Lange (1716–17, 1721–22), and the ambassadors L. V. Izmailov (1720–21) and Sava Vladislavich ("Raguzinski," 1726–27). In general, this early caravan trade fitted into the Chinese tributary pattern. Russian relations were handled by the Mongolian Superintendency. The missions were nominally limited to 200 persons, and eventually were conducted under a system of numbered tallies as in earlier tributary relations between the Chinese and the "barbarians." At Peking they were kept under guard in a Russian Hostel similar to the Hostel for Tributary Envoys. The Russian envoys performed the kotow.

There were new features, however. The Jesuits acted as official interpreters, using Latin as the official language. And Sino-Russian relations became important in the complex Ch'ing strategy for the control of Central Asia. This fact put the Russians in quite a different category from the European traders who came by sea.

In the early eighteenth century the Manchus had still not been able to subdue the Western Mongols, led by the Dzungar tribe of the Ili region under Galdan's nephew and successor, Tsewang Araptan (1643–1727). The Dzungars' intervention in Tibet in 1717 precipitated the successful Ch'ing counter-intervention at Lhasa in 1720. (See Vol. I, pp. 360–363) Meanwhile the Dzungars fought, traded, and negotiated with the Russians, who under Peter the Great were encroaching steadily on their western frontier. Consequently Peking tried by every means to secure Russian neutrality toward the Dzungars and the rest of the Western Mongols.

One spectacular attempt was made by the mission of the Manchu Tulisen, who traveled through Siberia to the Volga (1712–15) to establish contact with the Torguts, a Western Mongol tribe that in 1630 had migrated 2000 miles west to avoid the rising Dzungar pressure and so had come under Russian suzerainty. (The Russians called them Kalmuks.) Tulisen's exploratory mission had no immediate result. In 1770–71, however, the Torgut tribe, some 169,000 strong, fearing Russian domination and preferring Lamaism to Christianity, migrated with great difficulty back to Ili and were there allotted grazing lands by a gratified Son of Heaven.

After the death of K'ang-hsi in 1722, his successor, Yung-cheng, bent every effort both to prevent a Russian-Dzungar alliance in the west and to eliminate Russian influence among the Eastern Mongols. For this purpose he sought to delimit the Siberian-Mongolian boundary.

On their part the Russians tried to secure a permanent commercial-diplomatic foothold in Peking, with its own interpreters, independent of the Roman Catholic mission founded by the Jesuits. This effort eventually resulted in a Russian Orthodox ecclesiastical mission, whose ostensible purpose was to minister to the spiritual needs of a small Russian emigré community at the Ch'ing capital. This community had consisted originally of about a hundred Russian persons, prisoners or deserters. Many Cossacks on the Amur had gone there as fugitives from justice, with no desire to return to Russian jurisdiction, and so had entered the Ch'ing service. In 1684, even before the fall of Albazin, these men had been formed into a military company under the Manchu banner forces, the professional core of Ch'ing military power. In the 1690's Moscow began to use them as a pretext for sending Russian Orthodox priests to Peking along with the trading caravans. The Yung-cheng Emperor probably welcomed the establishment of the Russian ecclesiastical mission to offset that of the Jesuits, whom he suspected of plotting against him, as he did most people.

The Treaty of the Frontier. These various Russian commercial interests and Manchu strategic interests finally produced another important settlement in 1727. The Russian ambassador on this occasion, Sava Vladislavich, was supplied with 1500 troops and a retinue of 100 persons, including interpreters, commercial agents, surveyors, cartographers and other scientists, priests, and language students, together with numerous clocks, mirrors, pistols, and other presents, as well as private merchandise. The total outlay was 100,000 rubles (then equal to about £100,000), some of which was used for bribes. During six months in Peking in 1726–27 Vladislavich had some thirty conferences with Tulisen and the other negotiators. He finally withdrew to Kiakhta on the Mongol-Siberian border north of Urga. The Treaty of the Frontier was signed there and ratified in 1727.

By this treaty the boundary between Russia and the Ch'ing empire was finally delimited, and Russia was definitely excluded from Mongolia. Fugitives from either side were to be sent back. In return the Russians gained the right to trade regularly on the frontier at Kiakhta, much as the maritime powers did on the opposite frontier at Canton. Chinese devices for the control of foreigners at Kiakhta and at Canton, through licensed merchants and numerous regulations, make an interesting comparison.

Unlike the Westerners at Canton, the Russians were allowed to send official caravans triennially to Peking and to maintain there a Russian Orthodox ecclesiastic-diplomatic mission, building their own church and sending language students. As it turned out, however, this Russian access to Peking remained minimal, achieving little in trade and less in diplomacy. Whereas a score of Russian missions had reached Peking in the century before 1730, only half a dozen came in the century following. Although the Russians in Siberia were often tempted to fish in the troubled waters of Mongol politics, the imperial government in St. Petersburg consistently restrained them.

Where Russian policy preferred stable trade contact, instead of territorial expansion and warfare, Ch'ing policy aimed wholly at political stability through isolation. After the treaties of 1689 and 1727, Peking tried to seal off North Manchuria and Outer Mongolia, forbidding Chinese migration there and limiting contact from the Russian side as much as possible.

The realism of Ch'ing policy was illustrated in the two embassies sent at this time to secure Russia's friendly neutrality toward the Western Mongols and also preserve contact with the Torgut tribe on the Volga. The first Ch'ing mission spent two months in Moscow in 1731. It entered the city in nine carriages, received a 31-gun salute, and presented gifts. When received in audience, the envoys performed the short kotow, kneeling and bowing three times to the ground. The second mission in 1732 was similarly received at St. Petersburg. Thus in dealing with its powerful though distant neighbor on the northwest, the Manchu court under Yung-cheng seems to have been quite prepared to have its representatives perform the ceremonial kotow (which the Russian court expected of Oriental envoys), just as it expected Russian envoys to perform the kotow in Peking. This was tantamount to admitting that the supremacy of the Son of Heaven was not world-wide, but was confined to the area of the empire of East Asia. On the other hand, this realistic Ch'ing diplomacy was successful in excluding the Russians from that area. By 1760, Ch'ing power had been firmly established over Tibet, the Western Mongol menace had been destroyed in Turkestan, and Russian expansion was being held in check on distant frontiers.

THE JESUITS BETWEEN CHINA AND EUROPE

By the latter half of the seventeenth century the expansion of the European powers had created an increasing sense of national rivalry in Asia and a growing interest in contact with China. As indicated on the accompanying chart (opposite), two Portuguese, three Dutch, and three Russian missions reached Peking in this period. Except for two Russians (Baikov and Golovin), all these Western envoys performed the kotow in the fashion of Asian tribute-bearers at the Chinese court. None of them, with the possible exception of the Russians, achieved any modification of the tribute system or any permanent diplomatic relations. The Jesuits continued to be the sole channel of established contact with Peking. Consequently they felt themselves to be, and indeed they were, in a strategic position to advance their missionary cause in dealing with the various powers — particularly Portugal, Russia, and France.

Rivalries in the Missionary Movement. Portugal, as the patron and protector of Christian missions in East Asia, had tried hard to maintain its early monopoly of Christian contact with China. Even after Portuguese power declined and access by sea to Macao was sometimes interrupted by the Dutch and the English, the Portuguese crown saw to it that few subjects of rival maritime powers were included among the missionaries to China. Thus Italian, Portuguese, Belgian, and Central European Jesuits reached Peking, but few did so from Spain or France. In 1622 the Papacy set up the Propaganda (the Congregation of the Propagation of the Faith) to broaden and unify missionary activity. Subsequently the Jesuits sought to break the Portuguese monopoly by opening up alternatives to the Lisbon-Goa-Macao route.

Since Dutch sea power increasingly threatened the one established point of access to China at Macao, the Papacy and the Jesuit order, together with the French and with other supporters in Central Europe, tried to develop an overland road to China, free of the dangers and uncertainties of the sea route. Out of 323 ships that had left Lisbon for Goa in the 60 years from 1580 to 1640, 70 had been lost. In 1690 it was estimated that more than 600 Jesuits had been dispatched to China but that only 100 had arrived.

EARLY EUROPEAN ENVOYS TO THE COURT OF PEKING

Portugal	Holland	Russia	Papacy	Britain
1520–21 Tomé Pires sent by Emmanuel	1656 Pieter van Goyer and Jacob van Keyser	1656 Fedor Isakovich Baikov by Alexis I		
	(1663 J. van Kampen and C. Nobel to Fukien)			
1670 Manoel de Saldanha by Afonso VI	1667 Pieter van Hoorn	1676 Nikolai G. Spathar-Milescu by Alexis I		
1678 Bento Pereyra de Faria	1686 Vincent van Paets	1689 Fedor Alexeevich Golovin by regent Sophia (to Nerchinsk)		
		1692–94 Izbrandt Ides by Peter I	1705 Patr. T. Maillard de Tournon by Clement XI	
		1716–17 Lorentz Lange	1720–21 Patriarch Mezzabarba by Clement XI	
		1720–21 Lev Vasilevich Iznailov by Peter I		
1727 A. Metello de Sousa y Menezas by John V		1726–27 Sava Vladis-lavich ("Raguzinski") by Catherine I	1725 PP. Gottard and Ildefonso by Benedict XIII	
1753 F. X. Assis Pacheco Sampayo by Joseph I		1767 Commissioner Kropotov by Catherine II		1793 Lord Macartney by George III
	1795 Isaac Tithsing	1805–1806 Count Golovkin by Alexander I (turned back at Urga)		(1816 Lord Amherst not received)

Jesuit explorers in the early 1660's traversed a pioneer route from Peking overland via Lhasa to India, but it proved to be prohibitively difficult. Finally Father Verbiest in Peking decided to see if the Jesuits could use the Siberian route developed by the Russians. In 1676 he therefore gave help to the Russian envoy Spathar-Milescu, who subsequently published a map of Siberia and remained in touch with the Jesuits. In the 1680's a Jesuit residence was established in Moscow. Some of the early French Jesuits sent to China went first to Moscow in a vain effort to cross Siberia. The help that the Jesuits had given the Ch'ing court, both in cannon-making and in preparing diplomatic documents, did not commend them to the Russians, who refused passage.

The dominant role of France in Europe under Louis XIV (1643–1715) was naturally reflected in French support of Catholic missions abroad. The Société des Missions Étrangères, founded in 1658, began its work in Southeast Asia at the Siamese capital, Ayutthaya, in 1662, and soon thereafter in Cambodia and Vietnam (see pages 437 ff.). Partly to assist in this expansion the French East India Company was established in 1664 and secured its base at Pondichéry on the southeast coast of India a decade later. By the 1680's Louis XIV was deeply involved in an adventurous effort to take over the kingdom of Siam. Consequently, when Father Verbiest at Peking appealed for French support in men and money, Louis XIV was ready to respond. In 1685 he sent to China five French Jesuits trained in mathematics, astronomy, and other sciences. To avoid the jealous obstruction of the Portuguese at Macao, they landed at Ningpo in 1687 en route to Peking. This began the French interest in Catholic missions to China, in defiance of the claims of the Portuguese *padroado*.

The international context of Christian missions in China was now becoming complex, and to Chinese eyes confusing. Rivalry and competition became rife. The Jesuits in China had already been joined by friars of the mendicant orders, Dominicans and Franciscans, from the Philippines, who had Spanish support and became established in Fukien in the 1630's. Augustinians arrived in 1680 and French Jesuits in 1687. By an accord of 1696 the three dioceses, at Macao, Peking, and Nanking, remained under the patronage of Portugal, while five vicariates in major provinces were under the Propaganda at Rome. In 1701 there were in China 59 Jesuits, 29 Franciscans, 18 Dominicans, 15 secular priests, mainly from the French Society for Foreign Missions, and 6 Augustinians. The Jesuits alone had 70 mission residences and 208 churches or chapels. The total Christian community was estimated at 300,000.

The Peking missionaries, in addition to their relations with Portugal, Russia, and France, were in touch with princes and savants in Poland, Austria, Brandenburg, and other parts of Europe. In the Russian negotiations with the Ch'ing court, the Jesuits acted as interpreters until the establishment of the Russian Orthodox mission at Peking in 1727. At that time the Russian court finally professed itself willing to open the Siberian route to the Jesuits, but their fortunes at Peking, as we shall see, were already declining, and the plan was never realized.

The Jesuit Image of China. The rivalries of power and ideology which eventually destroyed the Jesuit position at Peking were no doubt unavoidable, for the fathers were pioneers in contact between two cultures, facing two ways and so suffering attack on both fronts. It is significant, however, that the main attack came from the competitive and aggressive Europeans, on whom the missionaries at Peking had much more influence than they had on China.

In the end it appeared that the early Jesuit success had been achieved by a policy of systematic compromise, in which Christianity was presented to China as compatible with Confucianism, while Confucianism was represented to Europe as compatible with Christianity. Closer contact eventually revealed to uncompromising conservatives on both sides that this was not true. Where the brilliant Jesuit intermediation had at first created mutual, though distant, respect and even admiration between China and Europe, neither side liked what it found on closer inspection. Familiarity produced distrust if not contempt. Area specialists who interpret one culture to another today may well be edified by this early chapter in the history of cultural contact.

The first effort to survey Chinese civilization was actually published in 1585 by an Augustinian (Gonzales de Mendoza) and was based on information he got at second-hand from friars who had visited China from the Philippines. But thereafter Jesuit writings based on first-hand experience became the main source for the European image of China. Marco Polo had been the first important European to write about Cathay. Matteo Ricci became the second. During the six months before his death in 1610, Ricci put together from his diaries a copious account of his twenty-eight years of missionary work and of the society of the late Ming period in which it was carried on. Translated from Italian into Latin, with additions by Father N. Trigault, this account was published in 1615 as a "History of the Christian Expedition to China." Editions soon followed in French, German, Spanish, Italian, and English. The learned world of Europe was given a systematic, comprehensive view of China's geography, products, crafts, customs, learning, government, ethics, and religious thought, in addition to the dramatic success-story of the Peking mission.

In this presentation, Ricci's treatment of Chinese religion for a Western audience was in keeping with his treatment of Christianity in his Chinese writings. His major doctrinal work in Chinese, among a score of products, had been a catechism, *T'ien-chu shih-i* or *A True Disputation about the Lord of Heaven* (preface 1607), in the form of a dialogue between a

Chinese and a Western scholar. This work, invoking many classical quotations, summarized Christian dogma, condemned Buddhism as a misleading aberration, and decried certain features of Neo-Confucianism but avoided any head-on collision with classical Confucianism. The Jesuit position in China, as phrased by the famous convert Hsü Kuang-ch'i (Paul Hsü), was that Christianity "does away with Buddhism and completes Confucianism." Christian faith could be added to Confucian practice. The cornerstones of this position were the acceptance of the Confucian canon in its textual form in the Classics as "ancient wisdom"; the rejection of much of the great corpus of Chinese interpretation and comment upon the Classics, constituting principally what we now call Neo-Confucianism, as unsound and misguided; and an attack upon Taoism and Buddhism as idolatry.

Similarly, Trigault's publication of 1615 for a European audience stated that Confucius "was never venerated with religious rites, as they venerate a god." Again, "The Chinese honor the great philosopher as a Master, and not as a deity." Confucianism was thus introduced to Europe as a system of ethics and political morality compatible with Christian faith, and the Jesuit mission embarked on its historic role as interpreter of East to West as well as West to East. Like the Protestant missionaries of a later age, the Jesuits had two constituencies — their converts in China and their supporters at home. They stood between these two worlds and explained each to the other.

The long Jesuit letters home, beginning with those of Xavier, were often monographs designed for the public. They were circulated to the Jesuit colleges and to private individuals in manuscript form, even when not used in publications. Books on China based on these writings appeared with increasing frequency in the late seventeenth and early eighteenth centuries. The engravings in Kircher's *China Illustrata* of 1667 portrayed in realistic detail the Jesuit fathers, the K'ang-hsi Emperor, and his court and subjects. In 1687 appeared *Confucius Sinarum Philosophus*, a Jesuit summary in Latin of the sage's teachings, with a translation of some texts ascribed to him. The famous *Lettres édifiantes et curieuses*, appearing at intervals between 1702 and 1776, with many later editions, published a great series of writings from China. The encyclopedic content of the earlier writings was systematically summed up in the four volumes of Father du Halde's *Description . . . de l'Empire de la Chine* of 1735, a vastly influential survey work with 42 maps, which had been preceded by a score of others less comprehensive in scope and detail. Later in the century appeared Father de Mailla's 13-volume *Histoire générale de la Chine*, a translation of the basic twelfth-century summary of Chinese history by Chu Hsi, *T'ung-chien kang-mu* or *The Outline and Details of the Comprehensive Mirror (for Aid in Government)*. Published in 1777–85, this formed an early milestone in Western Sinology.

Father du Halde and other members of the order in Europe who were engaged in the support and defense of the Peking mission received from it a great deal more than they published. By selecting and editing, they in fact suppressed or recast materials which might injure the Jesuit cause. Thus the summary of Confucianism, *Confucius Sinarum Philosophus*, was revised to suggest that the ancient Chinese had believed in one God and the immortality of the soul. In the *Lettres édifiantes et curieuses*, references to superstitions and other undesirable aspects of Chinese life were regularly cut out. Thus a double filtering occurred — the fathers in Peking did not stress unpleasant facts, and du Halde in Paris, who had never seen China, catered still more to the European public in revising the missionary writings in support of a worthy cause.

The personal correspondence of Verbiest, Grimaldi, and others at Peking with savants like the German philosopher Leibniz (1646–1716) also had great influence in the European learned world. Leibniz's publication of his *Novissima Sinica* or *Latest News of China* in 1697 put together diverse materials, mainly by Jesuits, which he had collected over a decade. His hope of achieving universal harmony through a sort of spiritual cosmopolitanism gave him an ardent interest in the Confucian teachings as interpreted by the Jesuits. "Now the Chinese Empire, which challenges Europe in cultivated area and certainly surpasses her in population," wrote Leibniz, "vies with us in many other ways in almost equal combat, so that now they win, now we. . . . All the laws of the Chinese, in contrast to those of other peoples, are directed to the achievement of public tranquillity and the establishment of social order." He therefore proposed an exchange of Christian doctrine and Western science for China's practical philosophy and principles of social order.

In this fashion the Jesuit picture of the Chinese empire was injected into European thought as one of the intellectual ingredients of the Enlightenment, as new evidence that could be cited in arguments over the reform of Christendom. For example, China figured prominently in the type of utopian literature known as "the imaginary voyage," in which the author's reformist ideals were expressed in his account of distant peoples and their institutions. Most important, the Middle Kingdom appeared upon the European horizon as a major new fact bearing upon the great question of the age, the relationship between morality and revealed religion.

The Jesuit publications depicted a society with a system of morals very like Christian morality. Yet it was an ancient society, which in fact antedated Christian revelation. Evidently the Chinese had a natural morality, independent of revealed religion, based upon and preserved by their own experience and adapted to their own character as a people. The ethical teaching of Confucius was not dogmatic but rational, acquired not from religion but from practical life; yet the Chinese were not atheists. Moreover, there was no gap in China between private morality and public policy: morals and politics were a unified whole, the ruler was genuinely

a father to his people. All this helped to account for the remarkable longevity of the Chinese empire.

This picture gave graphic support in Europe to the cult of Deism. European thinkers who now advocated a Religion of Nature, as an alternative to traditional Christian theology, cited China as evidence. So did the
leading Cartesian philosophers, Spinoza, Leibniz, and Malebranche.

The attack upon Christian orthodoxy was also aided unwittingly by
the theories of a minority group of Jesuits (known as "Figurists") in
China. Confronted with the fact that the chronology of Chinese history
went far back into the past, certain fathers decided that the Chinese were
descended from Noah and had originally had the Ancient Law of the
Hebrew tradition. They therefore saw in the Chinese classical texts
"figurative" meanings through which these ancient books had prophetically announced the basic truths of Christianity which, although visible
now to Christian eyes, had remained invisible to Chinese scholars. In this
theory certain Jesuits professed to see gratifying proof of the universality
of Catholicism. This heterodox idea was refused publication in Jesuit
channels but had influence through correspondence.

Thus the European debate over morality and religion came to a focus
on China: did the Chinese demonstrate that morality was possible without
the revealed religion of Christianity? In the Jesuit image of China, Confucianism was a system of morality. The Jesuits tried to show that the
Chinese had also had an idea of God the Creator. Their numerous enemies
and attackers, on the other hand, asserted that the Chinese were atheists
and hence lacked morality. The freethinkers of the early Enlightenment
meanwhile proved to their own satisfaction, citing the Jesuit writings, that
the Chinese were atheists to be sure, but also had a system of morality
which did not depend upon religion.

In its final effect, the Jesuit position would eventually lend support to
Voltaire and the Deists of the Enlightenment. Meanwhile, it was embroiled in the religious politics of the Catholic Church and the court of
Louis XIV. In 1700, in a great theological furor at Paris, the Jesuit position was condemned by the theological faculty of the Sorbonne as "false,
scandalous, and injurious." Thus began a more intense phase in a great
controversy over the Confucian rites that had already agitated missionary
circles in China for a century past.

The Rites Controversy. The early Jesuit accommodation of Christianity to Confucianism had never gone unchallenged by missionaries in the
field. Some of Ricci's successors, as well as the missionaries of rival orders,
began quite early to raise doubts concerning his theology as expressed in
Chinese. There were from the beginning, of course, many problems of
translation of the sort that later were to plague Protestant missionaries too.
Could the idea of "God" be found expressed in Chinese? How should

"God" be rendered in Chinese? Could the classical term *Shang-ti*, "Lord on High," or the classical word for "Heaven," *T'ien*, be considered equivalents of the Western "God"? The Jesuits said yes, the Dominicans no.

Even more important was the "rites question." Should the ritual performed in veneration of ancestors before the family altar and tablets be regarded merely as a "civil rite" and therefore permissible to Christians, or was it really "pagan worship," which could not be allowed? These were extremely practical problems, because the Jesuits' success in China had been based on doctrinal compromises not unlike the contemporary efforts of Jesuits in India to reconcile Christianity and Hinduism.

To many later theologians it seemed plain that these compromises went too far, that in making Christianity acceptable to Chinese classical scholars the early Jesuits had destroyed its essential monotheistic articles of faith. Ricci had argued that his writings "made every endeavor to draw over to our side the leader of the sect of the learned, that is Confucius, by interpreting in our sense some things that he presented in an ambiguous form." Ricci also pointed out that Confucianism avoided idolatry as well as questions of the creation and the afterlife. On the other hand, Jesuit and other scholars of today seem to agree that the state cult of Confucius, like ancestor rites in general, was of a religious nature, and the Chinese tradition to which the early Jesuit mission sought to adjust its teaching was one of syncretism in which all faiths could exist in some degree side by side. Such syncretism, involving coexistence of more than one faith in the individual mind and heart, was contrary to the Christian ideal.

Ricci's approach had also been called into question in Japan. There the early missionaries had broken away from the first description of their religion in terms of Japanese Buddhism by leaving their key words in Latin or Portuguese and publishing their religious tracts in romanized Japanese, that is, in the Latin alphabet. This had at first fitted into the current Japanese craze for Western things. Later, however, Neo-Confucianism had been promoted by Ieyasu in order to buttress his regime ideologically. In arguing with such Neo-Confucians as Hayashi Razan (1583–1657), the Japanese Jesuits had followed Ricci in relying upon the Classics, quoting them and reinterpreting them as a basis for Christianity, but they had soon lost the argument to the Neo-Confucians. Many leading converts renounced their Christian faith, and the Jesuits in Japan began to doubt the advisability of using classical terms to express Christian meanings. It was argued that since the pagan world, after all, had no idea of the true God, as a spiritual substance, its classical expressions could not be used to describe Him without the greatest ambiguity and confusion.

The complete expulsion of the Jesuits from Japan in 1614 made the controversy academic there, but it continued to agitate the Roman Catholic missionaries in China. These had to draw a fine line, for example, in deciding whether the cult of the imperial tablet was superstitious (they concluded it was merely political) and whether the prayers of magistrates in time of drought were licit (they were held to be illicit). Since the religious lore and practice of China were every bit as complex and varied as the intricacies and distinctions of seventeenth-century Christian theology and ritual, such decisions were difficult and complicated.

By the 1640's the controversy over the rites to be permitted and the terms to be used had been referred to Rome by mendicant friars of the Dominican and Franciscan orders, who had finally become established in Fukien province by way of the Philippines and felt sincerely concerned over the theological questions involved. The friars, coming principally from a Spanish background in the New World and the Philippines, had an utterly different approach to mission work than the Jesuits, who had learned how to spread the gospel in the more sophisticated societies of India, Japan, and China. The Dominicans and Franciscans in general based their approach to China on their experience in less culturally resistant lands like Mexico and the Philippines, where there were no powerful local rulers and bureaucracies to prevent a direct and uncompromising evangelical appeal to the masses. Consequently they followed the order of poverty and preached in the streets, thus disregarding most of the lessons the Jesuits had learned in China.

The "Rites Controversy" lasted a full century (ca. 1640–1742) and was carried on both within and between the various orders and missions in China and their supporters in Europe. It even became an item of dispute between the Pope and the Ch'ing emperor. It was also complicated by other difficulties which now beset Christian evangelism — particularly the jealousy of Chinese scholars and officials who had grown suspicious of missionary efforts to proselytize the emperor, feeling that their own interests were threatened by the foreigners at court. Persecution of Christianity as a heterodox sect, which had occurred twice during the turmoil of the late Ming period, in 1616 and 1622, was also prompted by the growing number of converts, their private organization, like that of a secret cult, and their foreign connections.

THE DECLINE OF SINO-EUROPEAN RELATIONS

In the politics of the Manchu court the Jesuit fathers had commended themselves to the emperor not only by their abilities but also by the fact that they depended entirely upon his favor. In this respect their position was like that of eunuchs or imperial relatives by marriage, who depended upon the emperor's person. The Manchu conquerors' use of Jesuit advisers in the government of China was also in the tradition of the Mongols, who had made similar use of Marco Polo and other foreigners. Yet the Manchu Son of Heaven had to function primarily as patron of the Chinese scholar class and therefore to maintain Confucianism. In the end he went along with the Confucian scholars' hostility to Christianity.

This hostility was based on several points of view — rational skepticism about such doctrines as original sin, the virgin birth, and the divinity of Jesus; a culturalistic defense of Taoism, Buddhism, and the Confucian rites of ancestor reverence; and a positive aversion to such alleged Christian practices as sexual promiscuity, kidnaping of children, and extraction of the eyes and hearts of the dead. Below the superficial level of polite toleration for the new Jesuit teachings, there finally emerged a hard antiheterodox conviction.

The leading Chinese opponent of Christianity, Yang Kuang-hsien (1597–1669), got his opportunity after the death of the Shun-chih Emperor in 1661. Yang was a highly emotional but articulate xenophobe. Appealing to Chinese pride, he cited Jesuit writings which depicted the Chinese as minor descendants of the Hebrews who had anciently worshiped God as *T'ien* or *Shang-ti* but had lost the true way until Ricci's arrival. Aided by disgruntled Chinese astronomers, he also accused Father Schall of having cast evil spells on the Shun-chih Emperor. This alarmed the Manchu court, which had an inherited belief in the spells of shamans. Schall and others were sentenced to death. Schall was saved by a providential earthquake, which seemed indicative of cosmic disapproval of the sentence, but five Chinese Christian astronomers were executed. Yang was made chief astronomer for a time (1665–1669), until his incompetence led to his disgrace and the installation of Father Verbiest. Thereafter Jesuits remained in charge of the calendar until the early nineteenth century. But the accusations of Yang Kuang-hsien outlived the Jesuit influence at Peking and were still circulating at the end of the nineteenth century.

Peking's Rejection of Christianity. Under K'ang-hsi, as we have seen, the Jesuits and other orders had their heyday in China. Their eclipse resulted from action in Europe. During the furor of 1700 at Paris, the Jesuits at Peking in self-defense secured a rescript from K'ang-hsi which supported their view of the Chinese rites honoring Confucius, the ancestors, and Heaven. This threw the fat in the fire, for K'ang-hsi had now been brought to pronounce on theology, which was the prerogative of the Pope. In 1704 the Inquisition at Rome moved the Pope to condemn Christian participation in the Chinese rites and to declare against the use of *T'ien* and *Shang-ti* for "God" and in favor of *T'ien-chu*, "Lord of Heaven," as had long been advocated by the Jesuits' adversaries in China. Thus the issue was joined.

The young and fervent but sickly papal legate, Maillard de Tournon, who was now sent out to settle the controversy, spent five years in China (1705–1710) in the midst of constant argument, bickering, intrigue, and disputation. The Christian priests, Jesuit and anti-Jesuit, representing the rival interests of Portugal and France, or of Pope and Emperor, now began to destroy the hard-won Christian position at Peking.

K'ang-hsi at first received de Tournon with great pomp and cordiality but found him uncompromising and, under pressure, disrespectful. The emperor naturally favored the *status quo* which the Jesuits had worked out. There ensued a trial of strength between Emperor and Pope, with the Jesuits largely on the side of the emperor. K'ang-hsi in 1706 commanded the missionaries under pain of eviction to promise to follow the usage of Matteo Ricci and to remain in China for life, as prerequisite to receiving imperial certificates permitting them to remain. De Tournon in the Pope's name forbade this. As a result some fathers sought and received certificates, some did not and were expelled. De Tournon, defeated by the Peking Jesuits and expelled to Macao, fell foul of the Portuguese, who abused him as an enemy of the *padroado,* and he died there in confinement. Meantime K'ang-hsi sent Jesuits to Rome with sixty-nine documents to lay before the Pope. But the Pope responded with the bull *Ex Illa Die* of 1715 reaffirming the anti-Jesuit position.

In a second attempt to assert the papal claims, another and more tactful legate, Mezzabarba, spent three months in Peking in 1720–21. The aged emperor received him politely but was enraged by the bull *Ex Illa Die.* Mezzabarba modified the Pope's strict injunctions, but to no avail. The Jesuit compromise with Chinese practice had been accepted at the court of Peking for over a century, and K'ang-hsi had found the missionaries useful and reliable throughout his sixty years on the throne. The papal attack on the Jesuits came now as an affront, difficult to believe, impossible to accept. K'ang-hsi sent a Jesuit emissary to Rome via Russia, but the only papal reply was a heightened denunciation of the Jesuit position.

The Yung-cheng Emperor came to the throne in 1722. Although an able administrator, he was consumed with violent suspicion and hostility toward those whom he regarded as his rivals among his many brothers. He also turned against the missionaries, who had been unable to avoid involvement in palace politics. A third mission from the Pope in 1725, performed by two Carmelites (Gottard Plaskowitz and Ildefonso), achieved no further result, and Yung-cheng began an active suppression of Christianity in China. Many churches were seized and used for civil purposes, and missionaries were forced into hiding. One Jesuit was executed. From that time on, persecution was sporadic, principally outside the capital; although the Jesuits and other orders continued to play a role at Peking, they remained there on sufferance. In 1724 Yung-cheng had a commentary added to his father's *Sacred Edict* (which was supposed to be read aloud to the populace twice a month) to the effect that Christianity was a heterodox sect. This was a very serious charge but it was a reasoned decision and remained the Ch'ing policy for over a century. Yung-cheng gave a polite reception to the sumptuous Portuguese mission of Metello in 1727 but only on condition that Christianity not be discussed.

The Coming of the Europeans

In 1742 the bull *Ex Quo Singulari* settled the Rites Controversy for the next two centuries. It required (until 1938) a strict oath by Catholic missionaries to forbid all Christian practice of "the Rites and Ceremonies of China." Thus in the early 1700's the dissension over the rites and the resulting persecution of Christianity formed a tragic denouement to a brilliant century of early cultural contact.

The Decline of Christian Influence in China. Under the Ch'ien-lung Emperor (1736–1795) the missionaries outside the Peking area suffered continued persecution. They were driven from some provinces and in certain cases cruelly executed — for example, Dominicans in Fukien and Jesuits at Nanking in 1747. While persecution stimulated faith, congregations shrank to perhaps half the total of some 300,000 claimed under K'ang-hsi. Missionaries were obliged to live and travel in disguise and to keep out of cities. Worst of all, the anti-Christian folklore became implanted in the popular mind — that priests, nuns, and converts practiced sexual immorality, and that they bewitched and killed little children and used their hearts and eyes in particular to make medicines and aphrodisiacs. As political restiveness increased in the late Ch'ien-lung period, Christianity suffered sporadic persecution by local officials and gentry as a secret society not only inimical to Chinese culture but dangerous politically.

At Peking, on the other hand, the missionaries continued to serve the court of Ch'ien-lung as astronomers, interpreters, cartographers, painters, engravers, architects, and even engineers. At the Yüan Ming Yüan — the old Summer Palace northwest of Peking, which was to be destroyed by the Anglo-French forces as a reprisal in 1860 — G. Castiglione laid out a miniature Versailles. He designed European baroque buildings and elaborate banks of fountains. These Western-style buildings housed Western clocks ("sing-songs"), pier glasses in a hall of mirrors, and Gobelin tapestries. As court painter from 1715 to 1766, Castiglione painted courtiers of three reigns, including the emperor's favorite concubine in the costume of Madame de Pompadour. But such things remained superficial adornments of the Ch'ing court. (See Plate 5.)

It is more significant that the Hanlin scholars who compiled an imperial encyclopedia in 1747 indicted Ricci's description of the five continents as a "wild fabulous story," and that the official history of the Ming, completed about 1750, remarked that Holland might possibly be near Portugal, which was near Malacca, yet Cheng Ho had sailed west seven times and never found it! The orthodox Chinese view of the world, in short, apparently remained impervious to Western ideas. Even one of the great early Ch'ing scholars, Ku Yen-wu (1613–1682), recorded that Portugal was "south of Java . . . It sent an envoy . . . for the purpose of buying small children to cook and eat." Superficially it would seem that Roman Catholic evangelism in its second period in China had achieved little more than in the medieval age of John of Montecorvino.

Following the dissolution of the Jesuit order in 1773, their work at Peking was resumed after 1784 by the Lazarists, but on a diminishing scale of activity and security. During more than two centuries the Society of Jesus had sent or recruited into the work of their China mission 463 men of all nationalities including Chinese. Their lasting influence on Chinese thought and culture, though it still remains to be appraised, seems to have been rather slight — far less than their influence on the European image of China in the eighteenth century.

The Chinese Influence on Europe. The Jesuits had no real competitors as interpreters of China to Europe. Until their day, the medieval European interest in Cathay had been kept alive by the wondrous tales of travelers like Polo and Friar Odoric and even more by romancers like Sir John Mandeville, whose *Travels*, written in 1371 and circulated in many manuscript copies in the mid-fifteenth century, drew heavily on Odoric and the other medieval travelers. With the great explorations and early maps came a more realistic view of Asian geography. The early trade brought greater quantities of porcelain, lacquer, cloisonné, textiles, and other handicraft products, from which in turn came the vogue for things in Chinese style, that is, *chinoiserie.* Eventually trading ventures produced first-hand accounts, like the *Travels* of Peter Mundy, who accompanied Captain John Weddell on the first English expedition to fight and trade at Canton in 1637. Diplomatic missions also left valuable accounts. But all such contact was superficial and sporadic compared with the inside knowledge, the translations and learned monographs sent back by Ricci and his successors. Consequently the scholars of the Enlightenment, as we have seen, based their view of the Middle Kingdom largely on the corpus of Jesuit writings.

In the aftermath of the Rites Controversy after 1742, China figured not only as a model society which had attained morality without organized religion but even more as a model of government. In developing this theme, Sinophile writers followed the Jesuits in extolling the Confucian Classics even above the Greco-Roman classics. China seemed to provide an alternative to the great Western traditions both of Christian orthodoxy and of classical learning. A notable series of writers stressed the ideal Confucian view of the sage-emperor as a man of letters who ruled by virtue. They praised the Chinese system of education and the examinations, the dominance of scholar over soldier, the customs of politeness and pacifism, the stability and long continuance of China's institutions. This idealized picture of Chinese government as the rule of virtue and reason was taken up with great enthusiasm. The Chinese ruler, as a philosopher-king and benevolent, paternalistic despot devoted to the public weal and the fostering of public works, fitted very neatly the current interest of European political philosophers. For example, Montesquieu's influential work, *The Spirit of the Laws* (1748), with its admiration for China's cosmopolitanism, gave that country top rank as a subject worthy of institutional study.

Sinophilism reached its height in the third quarter of the eighteenth century. The high priest of the cult was Voltaire, whose *Essay on Morals* (1756) depicted Ch'ien-lung as a philosopher-king and praised, most of all, the Chinese example of tolerance. He saw the highest achievements of China as "morality and law." Chinese officials were benevolent guardians over the people, the whole kingdom was one family. He pointed to the concern of Chinese officials for public works, roads, canals, and similar projects fostering prosperity. The laws not only punished crime but also recompensed virtue, as when the emperor honored virtuous persons.

Finally, the Physiocrats, seeking the reform of economic administration in France and other countries, also drew inspiration from China as a model for Europe. Prophets of the industrial revolution and the rise of the middle class, the Physiocrats demanded the inviolability of private property. They argued that the individual should be able to accumulate wealth without government supervision, and the state should foster and protect the natural right of private property. The leader of the Physiocrats, Dr. Quesnay, known as the "Confucius of Europe," published *The Despotism of China* in 1767. He pictured the Son of Heaven as an "Enlightened Despot" ruling over a government founded on wise laws, which the ruler himself also observed. The Chinese despot, in short, as an absolute monarch, ruled within the framework of natural law. Chinese society approached Quesnay's idea of perfection, for there was no hereditary nobility and a son succeeded to his father's goods but could succeed to his father's dignity only by study and self-improvement. China seemed a Deistic society which worshipped the Supreme Being. Property rights, it was assumed, were well assured. Taxes were regulated by the emperor, and no lands except temples were exempt. Commerce, to be sure, was not sufficiently encouraged, and corruption among the officials and the despotism of the ruler were only partly tempered by fear of rebellion. But on the whole, Quesnay's estimate was a very favorable one and marked the high point of Western adulation.

By the latter part of the eighteenth century, however, Western writers were becoming more skeptical of the superiority of Chinese ways. By the time of the French Revolution, few thought any longer of China as a model for Europe.

The vogue of *chinoiserie*, on the other hand, had found wide expression in European art and architecture. Chinese aesthetic influence in the work of Chippendale and other craftsmen had become part of the Western heritage, while blue-and-white Ming porcelain and its European imitations, wallpaper and latticework in the Chinese style, and Chinese *objets d'art* graced the mansions of the well-to-do. The Chinese vogue reached its height in England just after mid-century, exemplified by the ten-story pagoda in Kew Gardens (1763).

A few Chinese had reached Europe in the preceding centuries, and a Jesuit college for Chinese students had been set up at Naples in 1732. At least two Chinese of literate capacity came to England on vessels returning from Canton and were presented to the king. But they were regarded with interest as quaint specimens and did not acquire at the Court of St. James the status that K'ang-hsi had accorded Father Verbiest. The real English interest was in trade.

THE EAST INDIA COMPANIES

As we have seen, the early combination of exploration, fortified posts, freebooting, Christian evangelism, and the carrying trade developed by the Portuguese and Spanish gradually gave way in the seventeenth century to a new, more purely commercial and more powerfully organized advance under the British and Dutch East India companies. These bodies evolved into a new type of capitalistic mechanism for commercial expansion overseas. As joint-stock companies, like those created for the settlement of Virginia or Massachusetts Bay in America, they were private associations which brought together extensive capital resources under a central control. Yet by receiving royal charters for operations in new lands and places, the companies acquired wide powers of government abroad. After beginning as rather loose-knit organizations, they eventually monopolized their national trade within the areas and terms of their charters. They built and armed their outpost forts and factories, exercised a governmental type of jurisdiction over their countrymen there, developed navies as well as carrying fleets, and had in fact many of the prerogatives of government. Eventually they grew into full-fledged governments in India and the East Indies. This was indeed a very powerful type of trading organization — unashamedly aiming at profit, acting like a mere merchant concern whenever expedient, and yet capable of coordinating widespread activities, pursuing long-term policies, and mobilizing powerful military and financial resources like a sovereign power when necessary.

The Dutch in Indonesia. The main achievement of the people of Holland overseas during the seventeenth century, when their commercial empire reached its height, was their establishment of domination over the spice trade of the Indies. Jan Pieterszoon Coen, the empire-builder who founded Batavia, had an able successor in Antonie van Diemen, who was

66

governor-general of the Indies from 1636 to 1645. Having expanded its trade with Burma, Siam, and Vietnam, the Dutch Company finally ousted the Portuguese from Malacca in 1641 and at the same time sent out explorers like Tasman, who discovered the Kuril Islands north of Japan and subsequently Tasmania and New Zealand.

By the latter part of the seventeenth century, the Dutch East India Company, with its outposts on the coasts of India and Ceylon, at Malacca and throughout the Indies, on Formosa (until 1661), and at Nagasaki, was the principal European trader within Asia and from Asia to Europe. It had effectively pre-empted the ancient trade route from the Persian Gulf and northwest India (Gujarat and Surat) to the East. The Company's vessels sailed in big fleets, making Batavia from Amsterdam in about nine months and taking two years for the round trip. Dutch navigators learned how to sail from the Cape of Good Hope, which was colonized in 1652, with the westerly winds of the "roaring forties" direct to the Straits of Sunda, without having to rely upon Indian ports of call. Batavia, though appallingly unhealthy, was built up in European style as an administrative center. The spice monopoly was strengthened by destroying clove trees except on Amboina and by similarly confining nutmeg and other products to certain islands — measures which incidentally impoverished the local inhabitants.

A Dutch East Indiaman about the year 1700 might be of 350 or 400 tons burden and carry 40 cannon and 100 sailors, with gunners, officers, and merchants making a total of 150 persons. For ballast she might bring home Japanese copper, Siamese tin, red East Indian sapan-wood, black pepper, and saltpeter. Above this might be stowed a cargo of white pepper, spices (nutmeg, cloves, cinnamon), sugar, Chinese silks, and the new Indian cotton textiles (calico, chintz, muslin, "painted, dyed or printed or stained") which became the rage in Europe. Everyone aboard would also have a small "privilege" cargo of his own. A returning fleet, having escaped disaster from nature or the English, would be unloaded at the Zuider Zee with much excitement and many precautions against smuggling. Soon its cargo would go on sale, partly by prearranged contracts or at fixed prices, but increasingly, as time went on, at auction. Powerful special interests constantly tried to dominate the market in certain lines of goods. From Amsterdam the products of Asia would be spread over Europe. Meanwhile from that port also the silver coins and bullion obtained from the New World would flow out to the East.

Yet imperceptibly the Dutch position changed, and the Spice Islands lost their commanding position in the supply of Europe. Britain and France outdid the Dutch in India, and Amsterdam yielded to London. In the Indies the Dutch administration, like that of Britain in India a bit later, gradually became a territorial government as well as a trading company. In self-defense the Dutch Company felt obliged to intervene in nearby local wars on Java. Once involved, its forces became the chief support of native allies and intervened still further — for example, in three successive Javanese wars of succession (1704–1707, 1719–1723, and 1749–1757). From this it was only a step to the beginning of indirect rule, Dutch "residents" at each court dominating the Javanese potentates or "regents" through treaty relations that required them to pay tributes in kind — pepper, rice, or other products — but otherwise left them to rule their states. By the 1770's Java was completely under Dutch control and had no foreign trade or shipping except under the Company.

Meanwhile, in its economic policy during the eighteenth century, the Company remained bent upon commercial profit but paid its Dutch officials too little to deter them from corrupt private trading. It accumulated huge debts in order to pay annual dividends of 20 to 40 per cent and tried to increase its profits by requiring forced deliveries from the impoverished native cultivators at fixed prices. After coffee was introduced into Java from Mocha in Arabia as a new crop about 1700, it became a major export to Europe. Coffee and tea now took precedence over pepper, and the volume and value of the trade continued to increase.

But corruption, smuggling, piracy, and the constant squeezing of the peasantry, together with the costs of suppressing rebellions, fighting local wars, and maintaining an administration, left the Company financially exhausted. After 1780 the rising sea power of Britain menaced the Netherlands' trade at home and throughout the East, and eventually broke the Dutch monopoly system. The French Revolutionary wars, aligning Holland against Britain, led the British to seize the Dutch posts in India. In 1799 the Company and its debts were finally taken over by the Dutch government.

The British in India. Britain surpassed Holland, as Holland had eclipsed Portugal, by developing a larger home economy, and consequently bigger fleets and greater resources. The British made the subcontinent of India their main base. During their first century of trade there, the East India Company very gradually established early positions at Madras (1639), Bombay (1661), and Calcutta (founded 1690). As the central power of the Mogul empire in India declined, these posts developed during the eighteenth century into centers of British administrative and territorial expansion. After defeating the rival French East India Company in the Seven Years' War ending in 1763, the British Company began direct rule over Bengal in northeast India. Soon there were some 5000 Britishers and other Europeans at the three major centers, together with about 20,000 British troops in the Company's service — a tiny but potent sprinkling on the fringes of the subcontinent. Britain's expanding trade with the rest of Asia was based on this position in India. This expansive activity was superficial, if measured in numbers, being conducted by a few thousand individuals acting under the overall authority of the Honorable Company; but in the long run it had a deep influence on Asian life.

The commercial spirit remained dominant in the Company, even though, from 1784 until the end of its charter in 1858, it was under the control of the British crown as well as of its own Court of Directors. The latter was a self-perpetuating body of twenty-four persons, who acted for fewer than two thousand voting stockholders. The profits were fixed usually at eight per cent, but the Company paid more through various forms of patronage. For example, it long rented its vessels at high rates from shipowners who were also stockholders and who gave themselves a hereditary right to build and lease new vessels to replace those that wore out. In addition to this custom of "hereditary bottoms," it also became the practice for ship captains to bequeath or sell their positions. Directors had the right to appoint officers in rotation for an unofficial price. Officers in turn received large commissions and enjoyed a generous "privilege" of shipping private trade goods on their personal account. Decade after decade, among the directors at India House in London and among the Company's servants whom they appointed abroad, appeared the surnames of great English families, many of whose stately homes were built from the profits of the India trade.

Because the Company's business, including its "privileges" and patronage, was administered for private rather than public profit, it retained its peculiarly commercial spirit even after it began to supplant the crumbling Mogul empire as the actual government of India. The Company's servants sent out from England gradually became administrators in a nascent civil service. But they continued to be primarily entrepreneurs who used their Company posts as opportunities for all manner of private trading ventures. In a country where capital was scarce, they could lend money at usurious rates of interest. They could sell European arms and luxuries at fancy prices to Indian rulers and get secret commissions on purchases of native supplies for the Company, lending money to both and making profits at every turn. Such funds could then be further invested in trade or remitted to Europe under the cover afforded by the other European East India companies — Dutch, French, Danish, and the like. Through the channels of these former rivals, now in decline, many servants of the British Company could even flout its monopoly by trading to Europe secretly through Amsterdam, Antwerp, Copenhagen, Ostend, or Lisbon.

The "Country" Trade. Private enterprise had from the first been an indispensable support and extension of the operations of the various East India companies, necessary to connect them with the local Asian sources of trade and revenue. This took the form of the so-called "country" trade, that is, trade conducted by private individuals within the commercial domain of the various companies' charters, which usually included all the Indian Ocean and Asia from the Cape of Good Hope eastward.

This "country" trade grew up first within and around India. For instance, private entrepreneurs shipped Bengal raw silk, sugar, and textiles westward around the coast to Bombay and Surat, to be exchanged there for raw cotton. European private traders, captains, and ships, with crews of "lascars" (East Indian sailors) thus entered the ancient channels of local Indian trade. By the late eighteenth century an enterprising young English or Scottish captain might soon command a vessel of 1000 tons with a crew of 150 and 12 or 16 guns. The British Company sold bills of exchange, payable in Calcutta or London, to the "country" traders and so were able to use the traders' profits as a means of making Company remittances. Company officials also invested privately, and the "country" trade rapidly expanded, mainly from India toward the east.

The "country" trade expanded eastward in response to greater opportunities for profit. The supply of Bengal opium, for example, was monopolized by the Company, sold by it at auction, bought by European "country" traders, and exported by them mainly, at first, to the Straits of Malacca and Indonesia. Soon the Chinese market for opium drew this trade more and more to Canton, where raw cotton from Bombay was also in great demand. As the "country" trade to Southeast and East Asia grew, it gradually superseded that between Bengal and West India. Sugar from Dutch Java, for instance, began to supply West India, in place of sugar from Bengal. At the same time raw cotton from Bombay and Surat began to go to China more than to Bengal. Thus trade between India and East Asia grew rapidly. The "country" trade from Bengal, expanding to the east, went increasingly to China, taking at first silver bullion and then more and more opium.

The "country" trade was facilitated by private firms of Englishmen and Scotsmen, who formed "agency houses" which not only invested in shipments themselves, but also handled cargoes, ships, warehouses, insurance, and sales for other parties on a commission basis. To these Western enterprisers were added the vigorous Parsee merchants of the Bombay region. The Parsees had originally been Persians of the Zoroastrian faith who, under Moslem persecution, had migrated to northwest India. Over and above these private firms, and licensing their activities, stood the East India Company, still enjoying its monopoly of trade with Britain while expanding its rule over India.

As British trade expanded eastward, it sought a foothold within the Dutch preserve in Indonesia. However, the British Company's one outpost there, at Benkulen on the west coast of Sumatra, was remote from the main routes of trade in this area. In 1786 the Company secured an advanced base at Penang, on the west coast of Malaya above the Straits of

Malacca, to serve as a competitive center for local trade as well as a naval base and a port of call (for supplies) on the way to China (see page 441). Meanwhile the China trade was developing another dynamic in the British demand for tea from Canton. Thus England, India, and China were becoming joined in a triangular trade of growing importance and great potentiality, while the revenue of British India was becoming partially dependent on commerce at Canton.

THE RISE OF THE CANTON TRADE

The early British merchants in Japan, before their withdrawal in 1623, had continually sought trade with China, and in 1637 the first British vessels, under Captain Weddell as an "interloper" (infringing the Company's monopoly), went to Canton. But these early beginnings were not followed by the establishment of a regular Anglo-Chinese trade. The English overseas were fully occupied during the seventeenth century in North America and India. Occasional vessels traded at Chinese ports and nearby in Tongking (North Vietnam) but without continuity, until the Company ship *Macclesfield* finally established an English factory or trading post at Canton in 1699. During the next sixty years the Anglo-Chinese trade gradually became institutionalized into what we may call the Canton system.

Two main features marked the evolution of this system. One was that, after trading at Chusan Island outside Ningpo and especially at Amoy — both centers of the Chinese junk trade — the English finally concentrated all their business at Canton, the largest and oldest of the southern ports and the one which connected most easily from the southeast coast with the trade routes of the interior. The second feature was that, after first dealing in all the variety of exports carried in the traditional junk trade between China and Southeast Asia — silk, tea, copper, zinc ("tutenague"), sugar, rhubarb, musk, camphor, chinaware, and other handicraft products, such as fans, tea-tables, and lacquer ware — the English export trade finally came to concentrate on teas and silks. In the eighteenth century tea became the national drink of the English. Tea exports from Canton increased to the point where they produced the greatest part of the Company's commercial profits and important revenues for the British crown in London. Thus the China trade became a staple trade based on one port, Canton, and one principal export.

During the eighteenth century, the tea trade became a great vested interest which stimulated further developments in both England and China — the British effort to monopolize it at home and to finance it abroad through the "country" trade from India to China, and the Ch'ing effort to regulate it and profit from it. Canton became a meeting point between China's activity in trade to the south and European expansion by sea to the Far East. In this commercial growth at Canton, three elements must be distinguished — the Chinese or "native" trade with Southeast Asia (*nan-yang*, "the southern ocean"), the "country" trade of Europeans who invaded this "native" trade, and the "China trade" direct with Europe.

Chinese Trade with Southeast Asia. Under the Ming, countries that traded with China had regularly been enrolled as tributaries, which was considered a small price to pay for their contact with the Middle Kingdom, especially when the emperor's gifts to tribute-bearers and the profits of tributary trade, both at the port of entry and at Peking, were so rewarding. The Ch'ing continued this system, and tribute missions came regularly, though often at long intervals, from Central Asia through the channels supervised by the Mongolian Superintendency and also from countries in East and Southeast Asia. The tributaries may be tabulated as follows for the eighteenth century:

REGULAR CH'ING TRIBUTARIES AND THEIR PORTS OF ENTRY

Country	Frequency of Missions	Port of Entry
Korea	every year	by land via Mukden and Shanhaikuan
Ryūkyū (Liu-ch'iu)	2 years	Foochow
Vietnam (Annam)	3 years	by land via Kwangsi
Siam	3 years	Canton
Sulu	5 years	Amoy
Holland	8 or 5 years	Fukien or Canton
"Western Ocean" (Portugal, etc.)	not fixed	Macao
Burma	10 years	by land via Yunnan
Laos	10 years	by land via Yunnan

Foreign trade by sea, however, increased greatly during the Ch'ing period and burst the framework of the tribute system, even though the outward forms of it were preserved, at least in Chinese thinking and writing. By the middle of the eighteenth century two great commercial interests had grown up outside the system — the trade of Chinese merchants with Southeast Asia and the trade with Europeans. Since the Chinese traders led the way in expanding beyond the tribute system and the Westerners merely moved into channels they had created, we shall look first at the Chinese "junk" trade, as the Europeans called it, "junk" being derived from a Malay word for "ship."

Chinese vessels in this trade compared in size with their European counterparts and far outnumbered them. The biggest junks might be of 1000 tons burden, carrying a crew of 180 men. An average-sized junk of 150 tons, high-sterned, with lateen sails held out by battens to take a following wind, was most efficient when sailing with the monsoon. It could make six or even eight knots in the open sea. This compared well with the East Indiamen, which seldom averaged more than fifty miles a day.

Hundreds if not thousands of these sturdy merchantmen plied annually between Amoy or Canton and the Straits of Malacca, south in winter and north in summer. They followed detailed sailing directions through numerous ports of call. The so-called "western" route led along the coasts of Vietnam, Siam, and the Malay Peninsula — to Ligor, Sungora (Songkhla), Pattani, Trengganu, Pahang, Johore (see map, page 444). Many of these places had sent tribute to the Ming. Now they no longer did so and the trade with them was entirely in Chinese hands. The "eastern" route took vessels to Manila, the Moluccas, and Java.

Since this trade with Southeast Asia was carried in Chinese vessels, it could not be regulated under the old forms of tribute. Instead, the Ch'ing officials used a traditional device. They appointed merchant firms (*hang*, anglicized as "hong") to be licensed brokers (*ya-hang*) responsible for the conduct of the trade. At least three groups of these merchants were licensed at Canton, under the general name of "merchants in oceanic trade" (*yang-hang*). One group handled the junk trade along the Chinese coast to the north, another handled that with Southeast Asia just mentioned (to Siam and beyond), and a third handled the trade with Europeans.

Trade with the West. The group of Chinese merchants that handled trade with the Europeans gradually became organized into the merchant guild called by Westerners the Cohong (a transliteration of the term *kung-hang*, meaning "officially authorized merchants"). It consisted of roughly half-a-dozen to a dozen firms which were made responsible for all Western trade and given a monopoly over it. Through this merchant guild the Chinese state applied to the European traders the same type of regulatory mechanism that it used for merchants in China — a guild monopoly, licensed by and responsible to the officials. The essence of this system was monopoly coupled with responsibility, with little room left for free private enterprise.

At the top of the Canton scene were the local governor-general, whom Europeans generally called the "Viceroy," and the governor. With but just below them stood (after 1685) the official in charge of foreign trade, the superintendent of customs for Kwangtung province. This was a high officer specially deputed from Peking, whom the foreigners called the "Hoppo." Below these officials stood the Cohong as the licensed guild of Chinese merchant firms engaged in European trade, whose members were known as the hong merchants.

The hong merchants, in the usual Chinese fashion, paid large fees to the authorities, both publicly and privately, and bore responsibility for the foreign ships and traders. Every ship entering Canton would be guaranteed or "secured" by one of them acting as its "security merchant." On the foreign side, the British East India Company's Canton committee played its role by taking responsibility for all British vessels and persons. In this way the British trade, which gradually became dominant over that of its European rivals, was brought under a Chinese system of responsibility and control.

The foreign merchants were restricted by numerous regulations (not to bring in foreign wives, not to ride in sedan chairs, not to enter the city gates, etc.). As part of this system of restriction, they were obliged in the early days to spend the off season in Macao and always they were kept outside the city walls of Canton and confined to the riverbank area known as the "Thirteen Factories." More important, their trade dealings in tea and silk were legally confined to the licensed Cohong monopolists. Meanwhile, all foreigners remained subject to the procedures of Chinese criminal law. These gave the individual few civil rights and might subject him to arbitrary imprisonment and torture, practices which had come to be antithetic to Anglo-Saxon legal concepts but which were in accordance with Chinese custom and the Chinese doctrine of responsibility. Under the Canton system, China truly called the tune. In the eighteenth century, which was still dominated by mercantilist concepts, most Western merchants and sailors accepted the system readily enough.

But the system did not keep foreign merchants from waging a constant battle to maintain and improve their bargaining position and thwart the monopolists arrayed against them. East India Company supercargoes year after year demurred at the multitude of large and small charges, percentages, fees, "presents," duties, and miscellaneous payments that tended to accumulate and become "old custom." On the Chinese side, the Hoppo and Cohong and their hangers-on tried to keep foreigners ignorant of actual market conditions and prevent their trading elsewhere. Generally, however, this conflict of foreign and Chinese interests was outweighed by the common interest of the two sides in maintaining a trade so profitable to them both.

The chief effort to break the early trend toward a Canton monopoly was made by a colorful young Englishman, James Flint, who was in China between 1736 and 1762 and became one of the first Western merchants to learn the Chinese language. With him as interpreter, the Company tried in three successive years (1755–1757) to resume trade at Ningpo, but this resulted only in an imperial confirmation of the Canton monopoly, which was already a powerful vested interest. In desperation Flint sailed up the coast to Tientsin in 1759 and presented a petition, in the inveterate hope that, if only the emperor knew the facts of the corrupt exactions at Canton, he would curb them. The Ch'ien-lung Emperor did indeed take notice. He executed Flint's Chinese translator, imprisoned Flint at Macao for three years, and then expelled him. After 1760 the Canton monopoly system became confirmed and unassailable, restricting Western trade to the port farthest from Peking.

The Heyday of the Canton System. The picturesque life and trade at Canton have become a legend, well documented from the records of the East India Company. To offset the annoyances of restrictive regulations and a tropical climate, there was the exotic bustle on the Pearl River at the anchorage at Whampoa, where a score of 1200-ton East Indiamen and a couple of thousand British seamen might spend the winter months, to say nothing of other ships and nationals from Europe and India. For the mercantile representatives ensconced in the Thirteen Factories, there was the prospect of large profits and occasional contact with famous hong merchants. The concentration on trade made it hardly necessary to speak more than pidgin (i.e., "business") English, a patois with a limited vocabulary, obeying Chinese grammatical rules. This was a commercial lingua franca that can still be heard in Hong Kong. Young men quickly made fortunes, if they did not die of the ague, but they learned little of the Chinese language or higher culture.

Early Anglo-Chinese relations at Canton were relatively easy, because they were handled by a trading company, not a sovereign government. The Company's servants at Canton received good salaries and valuable perquisites: the head of the committee might make a fortune. The Company at Canton could carry on large capital transactions, control fleets of ships and their crews, and make its commercial contracts with a high degree of responsibility and regularity; yet it was able to do all these things in the status of a merchant firm without raising the touchy question of official equality between sovereign states. It would have been hard to devise a more effective institution to fit under the wing of the ancient Chinese tributary system. European mercantilism, in its East Asian manifestation, suited the Chinese tradition remarkably well.

As the tea exports to England mounted to twenty million pounds a year in the late eighteenth century, the British Company finally succeeded in monopolizing them. Company teas had been heavily taxed by the British government, at rates up to 100 per cent or more (the Boston Tea Party of 1773 was a protest against such taxes). More important, in proportion as the British crown imposed a high import duty, the rival East India companies of France, Holland, Denmark, and Sweden had provided stiff competition by bringing back teas for the vigorous smuggling trade across the English Channel. Sometimes more than half the

British tea supply came in illegally from the Continent. In 1784, however, the Commutation Act lowered the tea duties to 12½ per cent, the smugglers were ruined, and within a few more years the wars of the French Revolution eliminated the competition of the various East India companies on the Continent. The tea duties were raised again, and the Company became all the more a supporter of the Canton system.

The Company with its teas for London, however, was only one side of British trade at Canton. The other side consisted of private merchants in the "country" trade from India, which became the chief source of imports to pay for the teas and silks. How to balance the Canton trade was a constant problem. The Company's traditional exports of woolens from England were a drug on the market in tropical Canton, while silver bullion could be shipped to the East in the mercantilist era only with great regret. Hence silver and goods from India were used, to make one part of Britain's Asian trade pay for the other. Until well into the nineteenth century, the chief Indian export to China in private "country" vessels was raw cotton from Bombay, with Bengal opium second in value. Selling their imports at Canton, the private traders paid the proceeds to the Company, buying its bills of exchange payable in London. Thus the India-China "country" trade, handled by a growing number of private merchants, became the chief means of laying down funds in Canton to finance the valuable trade in tea.

The Macartney Embassy. Canton thus had been drawn into a worldwide process of commercial development, which spread from England to India, Southeast Asia, and beyond, even though the Chinese empire remained intellectually unaware of this far-reaching trade and politically cut off from the Western world. The gap between the theory of tribute relations and the reality of a growing trade set the stage for the first British attempt at diplomatic contact.

Early Ch'ing foreign policy had concentrated on the stabilizing of Inner Asian relations and had paid little attention to China's maritime trade. Tribute missions to Peking had grown more frequent as the great Ch'ing campaigns of the eighteenth century spread the dynasty's influence in Inner Asia and as maritime trade to the south continued to expand. In the century from 1662 to 1762, Peking had received at least 216 embassies from abroad. In the following century, from 1762 to 1860, there were 254. The increase was greatest in tribute embassies from the Ryūkyūs and Siam, which were symptomatic of an increase in trade. Trade in fact expanded faster than tribute relations. When the Ch'ing statutes in 1818 listed certain trading countries of Southeast Asia as outside the tribute system, it was a significant concession to reality. Nevertheless the façade of tribute relations was jealously preserved at Peking.

The idea of breaking down the traditional Chinese indifference to trade expansion seemed less urgent to the East India Company Court of Directors in London, who were conservatively concerned for their current profits, than to leaders in the British government. Influenced by the Industrial Revolution and the new production of textiles, the government now sought outlets for British manufactures. Already free trade was being advocated in place of the old mercantilist system. After 1785, enterprising young Americans began to compete in the Canton market. British exports of cotton goods were rapidly increasing, and private traders were agitating for access to the Indian market and the abolition of the Company's monopoly.

Against this background, the Earl of Macartney was sent on an embassy to the court of Ch'ien-lung in 1793. Though paid for by the East India Company, this was an embassy from the King of England and came in a ship of war to Tientsin. Macartney, who had been an envoy to Russia and governor of Madras, was accompanied by a suite of some 95 persons, including as interpreters two Chinese Catholic priests from Naples who could speak Latin and Italian, and an artillery guard of 50 redcoats. His object was to ask permission for trade at Ningpo, Tientsin, and other northern places, one or more island depots where British goods might be stored and ships re-fitted, and a promise that no duties or fees would be collected except as authorized by the emperor — in other words, a printed and regular tariff instead of the Chinese system of personal presents or "squeeze" in addition to more formal fees.

Almost from the beginning, however, the Macartney embassy struck the problem of fitting into the tribute system. It brought magnificent presents in 600 packages, which were finally carried into Peking by 90 wagons, 40 barrows, 200 horses, and 3000 coolies. The Chinese officials labeled these "tribute presents." They also urged Macartney to practice performance of the kotow. This he stoutly refused to do, and he only went down on one knee before Ch'ien-lung, as he would have done to his own sovereign. The emperor issued an edict commending King George III for his "respectful spirit of submission" but pointing out that "our celestial empire possesses all things in prolific abundance"; the Canton trade was a boon benevolently granted to the Europeans, but could not be expanded.

From this direct contact the embassy gained some knowledge of China but no change in the Canton system.[1] The dogma of tribute was confirmed in the Chinese records, which consistently treat the embassy as a tribute mission. A Dutch embassy of 1795 reinforced this idea, for the Dutch envoys found themselves lined up with those of the outlying

[1] Macartney's conclusion was: "The Empire of China is an old, crazy first-rate Man of War. . . . She may, perhaps, not sink outright; she may drift some time as a wreck, and will then be dashed to pieces on the shore; but she can never be rebuilt on the old bottom. . . ."

dominions at the Chinese New Year, and performed the kotow on numerous occasions.

Behind the failure of the Macartney embassy one may discern the vested interests of the merchants and officials of Canton, whose monopoly of commercial profits was being threatened. So strong was this interest in the early nineteenth century, and so cautious did the Honorable Company become in its last years, that the Canton system continued unchanged by any diplomatic effort until warfare finally washed it away. The embassy of Lord Amherst in 1816 was less well prepared than Macartney's and had the misfortune that the British were just then fighting with Nepal, a Chinese tributary. Amherst when he reached Peking was misrepresented by his Chinese escorts and querulously ordered away by the emperor without even an audience. Both the hong merchants and the East India Company directors in London thereafter opposed efforts at change which might provoke a stoppage of trade.

Thus during the first three decades of the nineteenth century the now-antiquated Canton system remained in force, giving China's rulers the erroneous impression that relations with the Western nations could still be handled within the traditional framework of tributary trade. On their part, the British had found no opportunity for expanded sales of manufactured goods to China, but their revenue in England had become more dependent on tea imports, and in India, on opium exports, on which the tea trade in turn depended (see page 130).

Even a brief survey of the early contact of Europe and the Far East from 1500 to 1800 draws a startling picture. The less numerous Western peoples, stimulated partly by their discovery of the American hemisphere, put forth great expansive efforts in the eastern seas, developed a trade which became much more important to them than to the Asian peoples, and underwent as a result great economic, political, and intellectual changes in their own societies. The aggressors, in short, received the principal shock of contact. After 1500 the West went through a continuous series of revolutionary changes, generated partly from within the European scene, partly from the New World, but also (in greater part than is sometimes recognized) from the economic and intellectual stimulus of relations with the ancient societies of Asia.

In marked contrast with this dynamism, the more populous and in some ways more sophisticated societies of Japan and China responded by going on the defensive. Although Japan had been expanding into the international scene in the sixteenth century, she withdrew into seclusion. And China, even under the powerful Ch'ing dynasty, maintained her tributary defenses. Both rejected Christianity.

By 1800, when European expansion was about to take on a new and overwhelming vigor, the West had even less contact with Edo and Peking than in 1600. Outside of Indonesia, the Philippines, Macao, and the Canton factories, almost the only Europeans in East Asia were a handful of Russians in the ecclesiastical mission at Peking and a few Hollanders on an island in Nagasaki harbor. Staple trades in Javanese coffee and Canton teas had been added to the early European imports of spices from the Moluccas and Chinese silks from Macao and Manila, but there was still little East Asian demand for Western products other than silver and curiosities like clockworks. The silver, cotton, and opium that were in greater demand in China were supplied from India rather than the West. Europe and even North America had achieved contact with China and Japan, but the first three centuries of this contact had ended in temporary stalemate.

2

Invasion and Rebellion in China

TRADITIONAL CHINA ON THE EVE OF CHANGE

In the nineteenth century China slipped into the downward phase of a dynastic cycle, that oft-repeated pattern of initial vigor, subsequent stability, slow deterioration, and eventual collapse which had characterized the administrative and political history of most regimes. By 1800, institutions of government that had functioned with remarkable stability since the Manchu conquest and establishment of the Ch'ing dynasty in the seventeenth century were seriously degenerating. At the same time the expanding Western powers began to beat upon the gates and demand the opening of the empire to Western diplomatic contact, trade, and evangelism, all of which were subversive of the old Chinese scheme of things.

Western Impact and Dynastic Cycle. These two domestic and foreign developments went hand in hand, as the nineteenth century advanced, each abetting the other, until by mid-century the dynasty was in dire peril from the ancient twin evils of "internal disorder and external aggression," which had proved the undoing of so many dynasties before. The chief problem for the student of this period is to discern the complex interaction between these two processes, the rise of rebellion within

CH'ING ARTILLERY with muskets attacking rebels. Detail from late eighteenth-century engraving.

China and the impact of the Western invasion from without. How far one process "caused" the other is an all-but-meaningless question, inasmuch as both went on in one form or another for an entire century, with constant give-and-take between them. Surely this is a case of multiple causes mutually interacting from moment to moment. Yet certain preliminary assumptions must be made, if we are to analyze China's modern transformation.

Our first assumption is that China's center of gravity at the beginning of the nineteenth century lay within — that the inertia of the Chinese way of life, its persistence in traditional patterns, made it resistant to outside influences and comparatively unresponsive to the challenge of the West. The old order was crumbling and yet not easily changed. No new order, as it turned out, was able to arise and supplant it.

By way of contrast, in Japan an economic and social ferment was already beginning bit by bit to transform the country in the early nineteenth century, even before its opening in 1854, and would thereafter develop into a full-scale political and social transformation. No similar developments of comparable intensity during the first half of the century have as yet been discerned within the Ch'ing empire. On the contrary, it presents us with a remarkable picture of conservative absorption in traditional ways inherited from a glorious and ancient past.

Our present assumption concerning China's remarkable inertia in the early nineteenth century is somewhat similar to the traditional Chinese view of the time, that foreign aggression was made possible only by the weakening of dynastic leadership and efficiency, whereas a strong dynasty in its prime could normally control the outside "barbarians." Whether we call it, in modern terms, unresponsiveness to the Western challenge, or in traditional terms, lack of virtue and vigor in the dynasty, the fact remains that the Ch'ing rulers, unlike the Japanese, proved unable to hold their own against the Western impact. From either point of view one might assume that, if by some chance the Opium War of 1840 had been thrust upon a new dynasty in its heyday — a regime like the early Ming under an emperor like Yung-lo (1403–1424) or the Ch'ing empire under K'ang-hsi — the outcome would have been very different. Historical conclusions cannot be attempted on the basis of might-have-beens. But certainly the government at Peking had seen better days than those of the 1830's. The dynastic cycle, in short, affected China's performance in the nineteenth as in certain previous centuries. Had the dynastic leadership and, with it, the official class been more vigorous, the whole Western impact might have had a very different outcome.

A discussion of might-have-beens is not entirely sterile, for it underlines the fact that at the end of the eighteenth century China's domestic developments were still autonomous and largely self-contained, occurring in a separate area that was not yet intimately bound up with the rest of world history. It was an unlucky accident that the heightened Western impact from abroad in the nineteenth century coincided with the accelerated decline of the Ch'ing regime at home.

This generalization may be qualified by future studies showing an interrelation, not yet perceived by us, of Chinese and European developments in the eighteenth century. In any case, to understand China's modern response to the West, we must begin by surveying the internal condition of the Ch'ing empire in 1800 and after. This may serve both to remind us of the traditional institutions of the Confucian state (more fully described in Volume One) and to appraise their condition at the beginning of the modern period.

The Traditional Chinese Image of China. Our perspective will be aided if we first note the traditional view that the Chinese held of themselves and of the cosmos — the self-image that was so violently shattered in the course of the nineteenth century. This was the psychological starting point for the long series of unexpected defeats and bitter humiliations brought by Western contact.

In her own tradition, China was and had always been in the center of the civilized world, surrounded by peoples of lesser culture who invariably acknowledged the cultural superiority of *Chung-kuo* (literally, "the Central Country," the Chinese name for China).

China's superiority was ascribed to her success in approximating, more closely than "barbarian" lands, the natural order of the cosmos. This was manifest in the order and harmony enjoined by the Confucian Classics — for example, the Five Relationships or Bonds that connected and subordinated subject to ruler, wife to husband, son to father, and younger to elder brother, and related friend to friend; or the distinction between the superior men who labor with their minds and the small men who labor with their muscles; or the hierarchy of classes which ranked them in the order of scholar-official, farmer, artisan, and merchant.

Proper conduct in daily life, according to the classical teachings, would maintain this social order of status and hierarchy. Conduct was molded by the family system. The individual was at all times subordinate to his family, which encompassed all members within five generations, including even third cousins (see chart, opposite). This extended family system provided economic support, social contact and recreation, education, and a religious focus in the reverence solemnly paid to the ancestors. It bore legal and political responsibility for all its members. Moreover it functioned as part of the larger common descent group or clan, which might promote the welfare of families composing it. Within this ramified kinship and clan structure the individual was taught filial piety as the highest virtue. He found that kinship imposed strong obligations. As a result he was motivated by a "particularistic" ethic which committed him to meet

GRANDFATHER
Tsu fu
=
GRANDMOTHER
Tsu mu

FATHER
Fu
=
MOTHER
Mu

UNCLE
Po fu
Shu fu
=
AUNT
Po mu
Shu mu

COUSIN (M)
T'ang hsiung
T'ang ti
=
COUSIN'S
WIFE

COUSIN (F)
T'ang chieh
T'ang mei
=
COUSIN'S
HUSBAND

EGO
=
WIFE
Ch'i

BROTHER
Pao hsiung
Pao ti
=
SISTER-IN-LAW
Pao sao
Pao ti fu

NEPHEW
Chih
=
NEPHEW'S WIFE
Chih fu

NIECE
Chih nü
=
NIECE'S HUSBAND
Chih hsü

GRANDNEPHEW
Chih sun
=
GRD. NEPHEW'S WIFE
Chih sun fu

GRANDNIECE
Chih sun nü
=
GRD. NIECE'S HUSBAND
Chih sun hsü

SON
Tzu
=
DAUGHTER-IN-LAW
Tzu fu

GRANDSON
Sun
=
GRD. DAU.-IN-LAW
Sun fu

DAUGHTER
Nü
=
SON-IN-LAW
Nü hsü

GRANDDAUGHTER
Sun nü
=
GRD. SON-IN-LAW
Sun hsü

AUNT
Ku mu
=
UNCLE
Ku fu

COUSIN (M)
Piao sao
Piao ti fu
=
COUSIN'S WIFE
Piao ti

COUSIN (F)
Piao chieh
Piao mei
=
COUSIN'S HUSB.
Piao chieh fu
Piao mei fu

SISTER
Pao chieh
Pao mei
=
BRO-IN-LAW
Pao chieh fu
Pao mei fu

The dotted lines enclose four male generations ideally to be kept in one household. Romanizations indicate specialized kinship terms. When two terms are given, the upper is for the elder, e.g., *hsiung* "elder brother," *ti* "younger brother," *chieh* "elder sister," *mei* "younger sister." The two characters for "husband" and for "wife" are both romanized *fu.*

83

the specific and particular demands of kinship rather than the more "universalistic" demands of legal regulations, religious principles, or market prices.

This social order, though based on the premise that individuals are not equally endowed, offered opportunity for the able and ambitious man. His advancement could come through self-cultivation, especially through learning based on study of the Classics, which would enable him to act like and to be a superior man and, through the government examination system, to become a degree-holder and even an official. In the early nineteenth century, local district examinations, held in two years out of every three, provided each time a total of about 25,000 degree-holders at the lowest regular level, who might thereafter compete in a ramified series of higher examinations to qualify for official posts.

The principles of the Confucian order, handed down through the Classics and inculcated by the family and the examinations, were also maintained from day to day by the benevolent rule of the emperor. As Son of Heaven he stood at the apex of the human scene and by his virtuous conduct set the example for mankind. The emperor's power was believed to be exerted primarily through this example. His virtuous conduct of itself moved others, including even outer "barbarians," to act correctly, and thus the social order was kept intact and in tune with the whole natural order of which it was a part. Rewards and punishments were necessary to control small men but were secondary to the power of right conduct which influenced superior men. The emperor therefore admonished his people as to the norms of proper conduct. The *Sacred Edict* of K'ang-hsi was for this purpose.

This summary, though brief, may indicate how closely the Chinese government was tied up with the tradition of learning. The Confucian world-view had been stated for all time in the Classics and in the lasting, orthodox interpretation of them by the Sung Neo-Confucian scholars of the twelfth century. It provided the ideological basis for the emperor's rule, for his selection and control of officials, and for the operation of the imperial bureaucracy. More important, qualification for high official posts was demonstrated by mastery of this classical philosophic and literary tradition, as demonstrated through examinations. As a result the state was coterminous with the culture. Political life was motivated by loyalty to the cultural order, by culturalism, rather than by nationalism. This was the basis for local government by a rather small number of officials with the cooperation of the so-called gentry class.

The Gentry as Perpetuators of Tradition. Strictly speaking, the gentry were the holders of official degrees gained through examination or purchase (see the discussion in Vol. I, pp. 309–313). Even a simplified

Invasion and Rebellion in China

THE SACRED EDICT (Sheng Yü)

Developed from the six maxims put out by his predecessor in 1652, this was issued by the K'ang-hsi Emperor in 1670, to be read and expounded to the populace in each locality on the first and fifteenth days of every month. Each of the 16 maxims is written in seven characters. (See Vol. I, pp. 312, 370). K'ang-hsi's successor, Yung-cheng, put out a greatly amplified exposition in 1724. Note that the 16 maxims deal with the social order (numbers 1–3, 9), education (6, 7, 11), livelihood (4, 5, 10), and keeping the peace (8, 12–16).

1. Perform with sincerity filial and fraternal duties in order to give due importance to social relations.

2. Behave with generosity to your kindred to demonstrate harmony and affection.

3. Cultivate peace and concord in your neighborhoods in order to prevent quarrels and litigations.

4. Recognize the importance of husbandry and the culture of mulberry trees in order to insure a sufficiency of food and clothing.

5. Hold economy in estimation in order to conserve money and goods.

6. Extend the schools of instruction in order to make correct the practice of scholars.

7. Reject false doctrines in order to honor learning.

8. Explain the laws in order to warn the ignorant and obstinate.

9. Manifest propriety and courtesy in order to make manners and customs good.

10. Work diligently at your proper calling in order to give settlement to the aims of the people.

11. Instruct your sons and younger brothers in order to guard them from evil-doing.

12. Put a stop to false accusations in order to protect the innocent and good.

13. Abstain from the concealment of fugitives in order to avoid being involved in their punishment.

14. Pay your taxes fully in order to dispense with official urging.

15. Combine in the *pao-chia** in order to suppress thieves and robbers.

16. Resolve animosities in order to value your lives duly.

* Mutual guaranty groupings of 100 (*chia*) and 1000 (*pao*) households.

A SIMPLIFIED CHART OF THE CH'ING EXAMINATION SYSTEM

Examinations	Degrees by examination	Degrees by purchase
Preliminary "qualifying" examinations		
Hsien-k'ao: In district seat (hsien)		
Fu-k'ao: Prefectural		
Yüan-k'ao: In prefectural capital, under provincial director of education; Quota for each district on number who could succeed	*Sheng-yüan* (government student) Popularly called *hsiu-ts'ai* (cultivated talent); English rendering: bachelor, licentiate; avenue to membership in *shen-shih* (officials-and-scholars, "gentry," literati)	*Chien-sheng* (student of the Imperial Academy, Kuo Tzu Chien). Irregular avenue to "gentry" membership.
For retention of status		
Sui-k'ao ("annual" examinations): Triennial, in prefectural capital, under provincial director of education; Had to be taken regularly by all *sheng-yüan* who were thus divided into:	*Ling-sheng* (*sheng-yüan* on stipend), *Tseng-sheng* (additional *sheng-yüan*), and *Fu-sheng* (supplementary *sheng-yüan*)	
K'o-k'ao: Triennial, in prefectural capital; Preliminary to:		
Provincial examination (Higher degrees)		
Hsiang-shih (the provincial examination): Triennial, in provincial capital, under examiner sent from the central government; Quotas for districts	*Chü-jen* (recommended man)	*Kung-sheng* (tribute student), of the Imperial Academy. Of several types — some awarded by purchase, some in other ways. Qualified for appointment to office. Limited number.
Metropolitan examinations		
Hui-shih (metropolitan examination): Triennial, in the imperial capital, under the Board of Rites; Examiner appointed by the emperor; Provincial quotas		
Tien-shih (palace examination under supervision of emperor)	*Chin-shih* (presented scholar)	
Ch'ao-k'ao: Further examination by the emperor	Specific official appointment	

chart of the various types of examinations makes a very complex picture full of detail. But in general there were usually about 1400 successful provincial graduates (*chü-jen*) in the triennial examinations at provincial capitals, and something over 200 successful metropolitan graduates (*chin-shih*) in the subsequent tests at Peking. The latter, normally in their mid-thirties, were the pick of the land, bearers of a title 1200 years old, and fit for appointment as district magistrates. As such they would be at the seventh level from the top among the nine classes into which the 40,000 officials of all kinds (military and educational as well as civil administrative) were divided.

As our simplified chart indicates, the lower level of degree-holders, not yet qualified for appointment to office, were of two types: the great majority were genuine scholars (*sheng-yüan*) who had passed the preliminary examinations, but about a third were usually degree-holders by purchase, whose "contributions" had been rewarded by degree status (*chien-sheng*). A few degrees were also acquired by inheritance or by recommendation. As of 1800 this lower level totaled something more than a million persons and formed a reservoir from which emerged the upper stratum of degree-holders and officials.

The upper level, consisting of persons qualified for appointment to office, included degree-holders by examination (*chü-jen* and *chin-shih*) and a small number of degree-holders by purchase (one type of *kung-sheng*). These higher degree-holders together with officials in office and in retirement totaled somewhere around 125,000 persons and had special privileges which set them apart from the lower level.

Thus the examination system was flexible, permitting upward mobility into the ruling class for people who could pay their way, and yet ensuring in normal times that the scholars, being the great majority especially at the higher levels, would predominate among the actual holders of power.

The gentry who were not in official posts performed a great variety of functions in local administration. They took the lead in maintaining the local Confucian temples, supporting schools and academies, arbitrating disputes, and generally sustaining the Confucian moral order — for example, by seeing that the *Sacred Edict* was expounded to the populace. They also arranged for upkeep of dikes, bridges, walls, granaries, and other public works, often under official leadership, and for maintenance of public order by organizing and leading militia when necessary. In these and other ways the gentry served as a local elite, beneath the officials and above the farming class.

Their elitist position, while symbolized by their semi-official status as degree-holders, was naturally many-sided. On the material side they were frequently, though not necessarily, connected with wealthy families, particularly landowning families. These families usually sought gentry status for their sons by educating them for the examinations. Either wealth or a strong tradition of scholarship in the family was essential to enable a youth to secure a classical education and succeed in the examinations. Talented boys from poor families might be educated in clan schools maintained by charitable estates bequeathed for this purpose.

Thus the extended family and clan system provided the social basis of the gentry class, while degree status conferred by the government examination system was the essential criterion that determined one's membership in the local gentry elite. Though buttressed by family wealth, social prestige, and political connections, the status of the local elite was dependent to an important extent on the cultural qualifications of scholarship, which by its orthodox content made them ideologically devoted to the established order. As bearers of the cultural tradition, the gentry were the principal preservers of the Chinese self-image sketched above. Their role as the local supporters of the Confucian order accounted for its vitality as the grand design of the Chinese state-and-society. Conversely, the alienation or demoralization of the gentry class, their loss of faith in the emperor as their patron and in the dynasty as the holder of Heaven's Mandate, could destroy the regime in power.

This necessary unity of state and culture, symbolized in the bond between emperor and scholar, had been as clearly recognized by the great Ch'ien-lung Emperor (1736–1795) as by his illustrious grandfather, K'ang-hsi (1661–1722). Ch'ien-lung's literary projects, winnowing the entire corpus of Chinese learning, employed thousands of scholars year after year. The 36,000 volumes of his *Four Treasuries* collection (see Vol. I, p. 381) were only one example of this imperial patronage of learning, which was not confined to officials but tried to embrace learned men all over the vast empire. In short, the Son of Heaven functioned at the pinnacle of education and the examination system to keep alive the great tradition of China's cultural superiority as the center of civilization from ancient times.

Their world-view gave the leaders of China during most of the nineteenth century an utterly different perspective from that of the West. They venerated tradition and had no idea of progress. Economic growth and the forms of individualism espoused by Western merchants and missionaries left them unimpressed. Most of all they assumed the superiority of Chinese ways over foreign ways and saw no need for change. On one point their perspective was like that of many Chinese patriots in modern times: both have viewed the Western impact on China as an almost unmitigated evil.

CHINA'S PREMODERN ECONOMY

Western contact came earliest in the form of commerce; trade was accepted long before diplomatic relations or Western ideas. Yet the

Chinese economy was slow to respond to the stimulus of foreign trade. It proved singularly unprepared for modernization and economic growth and did not achieve in the late nineteenth century a process of self-sustained industrialization, such as Japan achieved.

To answer the key question, why did China under the late Ch'ing fail to industrialize, one must look first at the nature of the premodern society and economy and then, as we shall in later sections, at the economic impact of the West and China's response to it. Several of the factors associated with industrialization in Western countries were present in China by 1800 — for example, increases of population and of foreign trade — but other key factors were missing.

The Growth of Population. Official estimates of cultivated land area and size of population can be found in abundance in Chinese records, but their true significance is not easy to assess. The early Ming recorded a cultivated area of 134 million acres in 1398, but the early Ch'ing recorded only half as much (67 million) in 1645, and in the early nineteenth century the estimates were only around 130 million acres. These figures cannot be taken literally because they were tax quotas, often produced by a complex process of converting actual acreage into a smaller amount of taxable acres, while in the meantime a good deal of land was kept unreported. In fact we know that during the first two centuries of the Ch'ing period the area of cultivated land had been increased both by colonization on the frontier of Mongolia and Manchuria and by opening new land to cultivation, especially in western and southern provinces within the Wall.

It is doubtful, however, that the increase of cultivated area had kept pace with the growth of population. The official Ch'ing estimates of the totals of households and able-bodied males present a startling picture — in fact too startling to be true. From a population estimate of about 60 million in 1651, the annual reports mount continually and sometimes by leaps and bounds to a total of some 430 million by 1850. Such an increase might be possible in a new country where immigration and industrialization were both at work, but in an ancient and thickly populated agricultural state like early modern China such figures can hardly be believed.

The ritualistic, rather than statistical, nature of the Ch'ing population figures seems evident from the way they were compiled and reported. From 1741 this was done by the *pao-chia* headmen in the villages at the three successive levels of the neighborhood collective-guaranty system — specifically, the respective headmen (*chang*) responsible for a *p'ai* of ten households, a *chia* of one hundred households, and a *pao* of one thousand households (see Vol. I, pp. 159, 374). Since these men had to report on local irregularities of all sorts — such as burglary, gambling, harboring criminals, illegal coinage or sale of salt, gang activities, or the presence of strangers — population figures recorded on the door placards of each household were only one of their concerns. Moreover, procedures were neither uniform nor reliable for reporting births, deaths, females, children, non-Han minority peoples, and migrants. Premodern China did not, in short, achieve a modern census. On the contrary, annual reporting of population figures became routinized and ritualized. Provinces reported regular increases year after year, often a fixed percentage, say 0.3 or 0.5 per cent, over the previous year. As Ch'ien-lung remarked, "The number increases the same year after year. This is absurd."

The literary nature of the Ch'ing figures suggests that the steep curve of increase should be flattened out. The Chinese population was greater at the beginning and probably less at the end of the Ch'ing period than the figures indicate. For example, the totals of population estimated in the Ming period do not exceed 60 million, the figure reached by the Han dynasty some 1500 years earlier. We may guess that the Ming population actually approached 150 million by 1600 and this total was inherited by the Ch'ing. In the early eighteenth century came an important administrative change that combined the head tax and the land tax and decreed that the quotas of these taxes to be collected in the provinces should remain fixed forever at the levels of 1711. This may have reversed the incentives in the estimating of population totals. Where formerly an official in charge of an area might have held his estimates down to avoid raising his tax quota, normally set according to population and land totals, now he might aim to please the throne by reporting a prosperous increase of the people under his care. Imperial demands for careful reporting called forth great increases. By 1800 the total population may have been about 300 million, rather than the 350 million reported to the emperor.

Even so, this was an extraordinary growth in an ancient farming country where industrialization had not yet commenced. Historians thus far have accounted for it mainly by citing the domestic peace and order of the eighteenth century and the increase of food supply through cultivating more land, using new crops from America like corn, sweet potatoes, and peanuts, which could grow in marginal soils, and planting faster-ripening types of rice. In ancient times, after transplanting from nursery beds into paddy fields, rice had required about 150 days to reach maturity. Importation and development of earlier-ripening varieties from Champa (in what is now South Vietnam) had gradually reduced this growing time to 100, then to 60, 40 and, in the nineteenth century, even 30 days. This made possible double- and even triple-cropping.

Yet population began eventually to press upon the increased food supply. By 1800, despite a considerable growth of the Chinese economy, living standards seem to have begun to decline. Nor do there seem to have been any significant technological advances, aside from the gradual spread of new crops and some expansion of trade. Unlike the economy of Europe, which had been making great strides forward, the Chinese economy was expanding within the limits set by geography and the inherited technology but was not rising to new levels of efficiency.

The Stationary State of the Rural Economy. All this may be seen if we look at the characteristics of the traditional Chinese economy, which made it so different from that of the expanding West. These may be briefly summarized at three levels, in ascending order: rural, commercial, and governmental.

At the rural level in 1800 lived three-quarters of the population. Their capital wealth consisted chiefly of the land itself as improved over the centuries by an arduous investment of labor. The earth in most of the cultivated area had been formed into paddy fields with embankments and irrigation channels and made into terraces even in the Northwest, where irrigation was often impossible. All sorts of waterways had been built, both for transport and for irrigation, with dikes and sluiceways and the equipment of foot-treadles, buckets, and wheels for moving water onto the soil. Also, many fields were planted to permanent crops, such as the mulberry trees and tea bushes cultivated by hand labor for silk and tea production. This farm economy represented a great investment of past labor and presupposed a continued heavy application of manpower to keep it working. By contrast, the accumulation of other types of capital equipment — tools, buildings, draft animals — was rather meager.

Unexploited natural resources available for development by the Chinese economy, assuming no revolution in technology, were limited: forests had already been largely used up; fisheries had already been rather fully developed; coal and iron extraction was on a local scale only; copper, tin, and lead mines in the Southwest had reached diminishing returns. Labor resources, on the other hand, were plentiful. Rapid population growth in the eighteenth century had put a high proportion of the populace in the younger age brackets, available for employment in the labor-intensive processes of farm-gardening and manpower transport, as well as in the tea, silk, cotton, and other subsidiary handicraft industries of the farm household. Thus land was limited and capital scarce, while labor was plentiful and generally skilled in the traditional methods of production. There was little means or incentive for labor-saving innovation in farm technology.

Innovation was also inhibited by two other social factors. One was the difficulty of saving in a society where a big family was the social ideal and where there was no primogeniture. A family's patrimony was customarily distributed in fragments among the sons, in a continual parceling out of landholdings. The other factor was the sharp functional distinction between hand-workers and brain-workers, who lived their separate lives at different social levels. Farmers and artisans remained generally illiterate, while men of learning seldom came up against the practical, mechanical problems of field and shop. Neither the scholar class nor the working class was in a position to combine theory and practice so as to produce inventions. Similarly, neither was prepared to borrow inventions from abroad.

The Commercial and Governmental Levels. On the commercial level of the old Chinese economy, merchants and middlemen performed distribution and exchange activities which overlay the rural level and connected it with the governmental. Local trade centered in the market towns, of which there were several score in each province. Most of them maintained periodic markets, which functioned at fixed intervals, generally every three or four days. At these were collected products from an area roughly within a day's foot-transport distance by beast, barrow, or carrying-pole or within a similar distance by sampan on a waterway. Peddlers and traveling merchants (*k'o-shang*, "guest merchants") brought the peasant those few essential commodities which he could not produce himself, primarily salt, metals, and paper, also simple luxury goods, textiles, pottery, tea, and the produce of city craftsmen or of other regions. Usually this trade was under the supervision of officially licensed brokers (*ya-hang*), who levied taxes on behalf of officialdom. In exchange, the local community shipped out its own special products or farm surpluses, if any, in addition to its unrequited export of tax grains to the government.

On this cellular pattern of local trade within market areas was superimposed a certain amount of interregional trade between provinces or larger areas. This trade was in special regional products such as copper, porcelain, furs, silk, or timber. China's international trade was an offshoot of this type of interregional exchange.

Water transport was the great facility on which the interregional trade depended. Brick tea (tea formed into bricks for transport) went up the Yangtze and its tributary the Han River and thence by caravan to Mongolia. North China and the Yangtze delta exchanged commodities by way of the Grand Canal as well as the coastal route. The teas of Fukien and the silks of Anhwei went to Canton by the Kan River route through Kiangsi. All manner of Szechwan products came down the Yangtze, while the junk fleets plying along the coast, especially from Ningpo northward all the way to Manchuria and from Amoy down to Southeast Asia, formed another extensive transport network. They took soybeans and beancake out of Manchuria and brought subtropical products to the north. This carrying trade on China's water routes was to prove the Westerner's main point of ingress into the Chinese economy in the nineteenth century, for here the introduction of the steamship could quickly alter the inherited technology.

On the other hand, even foreign contact could not easily change the pattern of the domestic economy. The great export commodities, tea and silk, were products of traditional labor-intensive farm handicrafts, not susceptible to quick modernization. Both the demand of the local population for imported goods and the supply of capital for trade remained rather limited. There was little creation of credit and only a limited supply of currency in the form of copper cash and silver bullion. Merchants were dominated by officials, on whom they depended for protection, or else they became semi-officials themselves, showing the spirit of monopolistic tax-gatherers rather than of risk-taking investors in productive enterprise. The classical doctrines of the state gave little thought to economic growth and stressed the frugal use of agrarian taxes rather than the creation of new wealth.

Thus on the governmental level there was no leadership in the direction of economic development. Government services were minimal — chiefly the maintenance of order and of waterworks, together with granaries, in order to receive the farmer's payment of taxes and to feed him in time of famine. Next to its own security, efficiency of tax collection was the regime's main aim, though it was always frustrated to greater or lesser degree by customary forms of corruption. Since an increase in the national wealth was not expected, any increase in taxes might seem to mean only that the government had grown harsher. It was commonly assumed that there was a fixed volume of trade. Customs taxes were levied on exports at the same rates as on imports. There was no Chinese equivalent of the contemporary European mercantilist concept of maximizing the national wealth through exports. Official monopolies and license systems were substituted for commercial competition. All in all, it would have been hard to find a greater contrast than that between the Ch'ing government, wedded to the idea of a fixed income from agricultural taxes, and the British, enamored of laissez faire and commerical expansion.

In sum, the Chinese economy around the year 1800 was not only at a different stage of development than the European economy; it was also differently constructed and was thought of in entirely different terms. First, in respect of commercial policy, whereas the leading countries of mercantilist Europe were much concerned about their foreign trade, China regarded herself as — and in fact was — a rather self-sufficient economic entity. Trade, both foreign and domestic, was still disesteemed in the orthodox value system. The interregional and local trade was neither formally encouraged nor heavily taxed. Second, in respect of technology, China had not yet institutionalized science and invention, as Europe was in the process of doing, and so this foundation for economic development was negligible. Third, lacking the stimuli of both foreign trade and new technology and thwarted by the whole nature of the society and government, the type of entrepreneurship so important in Britain's industrialization was quite impossible in the Middle Kingdom. Capital accumulation

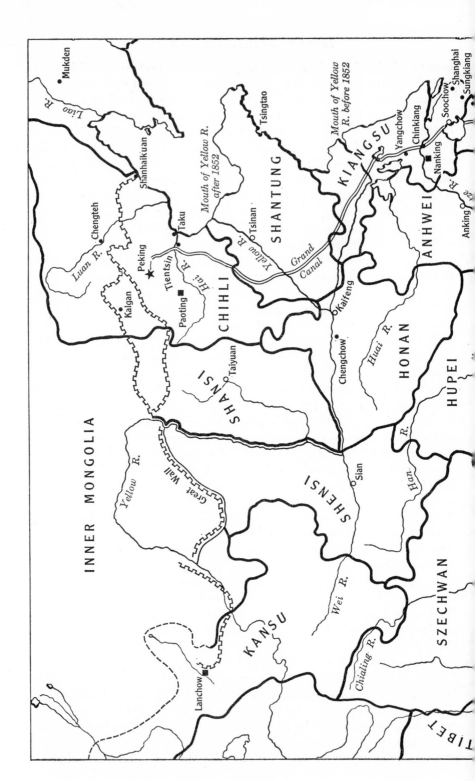

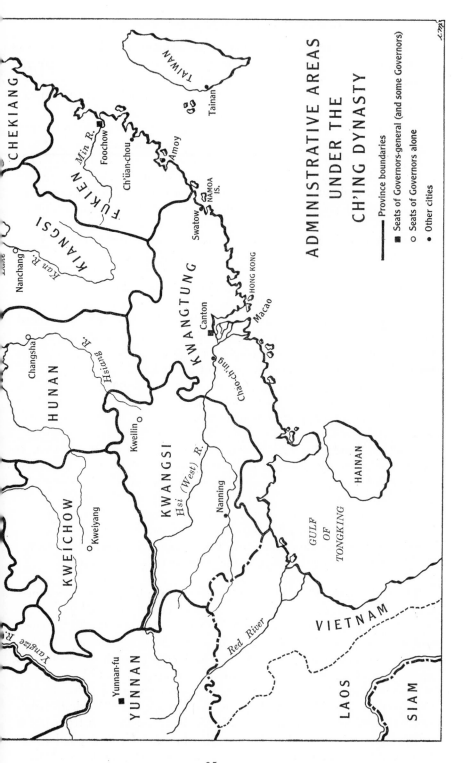

ADMINISTRATIVE AREAS
UNDER THE
CH'ING DYNASTY

Province boundaries
■ Seats of Governors-general (and some Governors)
○ Seats of Governors alone
• Other cities

was precarious except under the wing of officialdom. Legal safeguards, an investment market, and the forms of the joint-stock company were all lacking.

China's economic peculiarities were by no means all negative. On the contrary, the economy had certain points of strength, such as its self-sufficiency, which made it all the more unlikely to follow the European example of economic growth. The use of water had been developed to a high point of efficiency. Irrigation made possible a rice economy, which in turn made possible the world's largest population. The water transport network throughout Central and South China was remarkably service-able and well developed. In general, the methods for the application of abundant manpower to all the processes of the economy — irrigation, rice culture, transport, handicraft production of consumer goods, and the like — had been thoroughly worked out within the limits set by the inherited prescientific technology.

In this sense, we may speak of the Chinese economy of 1800 as "mature," in that it had realized most of the potentialities inherent in its traditional technology, within the given framework of social and political institutions and the intellectual values of the time. In other words, the Chinese economic process had reached a high degree of efficiency in the use of its resources at a stationary level of technology.

In this stationary situation, population pressed upon food resources, and we may assume that many forms of production faced diminishing returns — increased applications of manpower, as on small plots of land, would get less and less result — so that by 1800 both per capita productiv-ity and the standard of living were probably declining. Production, in short, was generally absorbed completely in consumption, in an endless circular flow just to keep people alive, so that net saving and investment were all but impossible. The Chinese economy on the whole merely reproduced and maintained itself without developing any further produc-tive capacity. A considerable effort would be needed for it to break out of this preindustrial stationary state. Consequently it could not be imme-diately or massively responsive to the stimulus of Western trade.

The Role of the Early Foreign Trade. As we have seen, Westerners such as the Portuguese had from the sixteenth century entered the ancient channels of China's overseas trade, carrying silk from Macao to Japan and returning with silver. The flow of silver into China through channels of foreign trade stimulated and made possible the growth of the modern money economy. Something like the following quantities of silver seem to have been imported during the 250 years down to about 1830: through Chinese traders at Manila perhaps 100,000,000 Spanish ("Mexican") dol-lars' worth of silver from the mines in Mexico; a similar sum from Japan, in the limited Chinese and Dutch trade at Nagasaki; through the East India companies at Canton, at least 60,000,000 or 70,000,000 Mexican dollars' worth of silver; through American merchants from 1784 until the 1820's, some 50,000,000 Mexican dollars' worth. Unknown amounts found their way to China from other Western sources as well as from Siam, Vietnam, and other parts of Asia. Thus by the early nineteenth century something on the order of 350,000,000 Mexican dollars' worth of bullion had entered the Middle Kingdom. Throughout the period there had also been a production of silver from Chinese mines, chiefly in Yunnan province.

Another effect of foreign trade was to provide an added demand for tea and for silk and cotton textiles, mainly produced by handicraft industries on the farms of Central and South China. Silk and porcelain, the traditional specialties of Cathay, were eclipsed by the export of tea, which by 1800 had risen to more than 20 million pounds a year through Canton. Cotton textiles went chiefly in the form of "nankeens," named for Nanking, because the main center of the Chinese cotton textile industry was in the nearby region of Soochow and Sungkiang. These exports for the West were taken from the total Chinese domestic production, for which the principal market remained the Chinese consuming public. So vast was this Chinese market that until well into the nineteenth century the chief import of the "country" trade from India was raw cotton to supply the textile industry. The European and American demand for Chinese goods through the Canton trade could be no more than a small fraction of the domestic demand.

Despite its comparatively small volume, however, the Canton trade was important as a center of growth, both in the accumulation of capital and in the creation of commercial mechanisms and an articulate commercial interest. The hong merchants served as funnels through which flowed out consignments of tea and silk collected by traveling merchants in the producing regions of Central China. The transport route by barge and by coolie carrier through Kiangsi to Canton was greatly developed. The "Canton interest," in the person of merchant firms and imperial officials who profited from the Canton monopoly of Western trade, sought vigorously to preserve itself. All these mechanisms and interests could become involved equally in an import trade, once a foreign product could be found for which a Chinese demand existed. Until the 1830's, however, China remained on the whole uninterested in Western goods. There was little demand for opium before 1800.

The Rise of the Shansi Banks. In the nineteenth century the use of paper credit instruments began to supplement or supplant the cumbersome official transfer of silver bullion. China had had a brilliant early development of paper money and credit in the ninth to fourteenth centuries, but thereafter, for reasons not fully explored, there had been a return to the use of bullion (see Vol. I, pp. 219, 279, 303). The new growth of private banking in the nineteenth century began in chains of money shops centered in the coastal region of Ningpo and also, curiously enough, in certain cities of Shansi in the landlocked Northwest. Of these two main groups, the Shansi banks were the more active and have been more fully studied. The date of their origin is disputed, but their operations became prominent in the second quarter of the nineteenth century.

Several factors accounted for their rise — first of all, geography. Shansi in recent times has been on the northwest periphery of China proper, but before the modern period it had long been a strategic center of imperial control and a crossroads of trade routes, between Mongolia and Szechwan and between North China and Central Asia. In general, Shansi was a transfer area between the camel caravan routes of Inner Asia and the canal transport of North and Central China. The province was also a chief center of iron (and coal) production and distribution.

As a result, merchants of this region already had widespread branches and connections. They had acquired a broad influence in the pawnshop business in provinces connected with Shansi by trade routes. Lending money against the security of goods was already a specialty. Some firms had also begun to guarantee silver shipments by employing private mounted troops to convoy them. After 1800 the spread of disorder and banditry increased the difficulty of shipping silver bullion. Whether the funds to be transferred were public or private, shippers began to use banking facilities rather than send silver under armed guard. After all, silver became useless as capital during the period of its transportation.

The pioneer Shansi banker about the turn of the century is said to have been a dye-store merchant (in the city of P'ing-yao, Shansi) who had a shop in Tientsin, set up an office to obtain materials in Chungking, and so got into the business of remitting funds. After this first banking chain began operation, the number of chains eventually grew to between twenty and thirty, organized in three main groups (centered at P'ing-yao, T'ai-ku, and Chi-hsien) in central Shansi, where the major firms developed a body of trained personnel. The banks became useful in the transfer of official and unofficial funds between the capital and the provinces.

They also extended their operations to meet the needs of the Canton trade for transfers of funds by draft to facilitate the purchase of teas and silks in Central China and remittances to Canton for opium. Where an armed convoy of silver bullion would cost two or three per cent of its value, these private banks charged a rate of only three-tenths of one per cent for drafts. Similar banking establishments grew up in other provinces, but the Shansi firms maintained an ascendancy until the end of the nineteenth century.

The original capital of these banking shops appears to have been usually well below 100,000 taels, although many eventually accumulated as much as 200,000 taels. The owners had an unlimited liability and kept their business organization on a simple and personal basis, the capital being put in the charge of a manager who took complete responsibility for its use. The general manager exercised undisputed authority over his staff of assistants and his branch offices. Behind him usually stood a number of partners who, like him, had invested both their funds and their reputations.

One secret of the phenomenal rise of the Shansi banks, aside from the growth of trade, undoubtedly lies in their relation to officialdom. For one thing, all banks had to be licensed by the Board of Revenue at Peking, which required a guarantee from other banks already in the business. This made it easy for the Shansi firms to maintain almost a banking monopoly by withholding their guarantee from extra-provincial capitalists.

Except for the need of licensing, the banks were nominally free of government control. But in actual fact they existed only by maintaining close personal relations with leading officials. Since the high provincial authorities were some of the greatest shippers of funds in the empire, they had the greatest need of banking assistance. More than that, the high officials, who normally accumulated their personal fortunes through the institution of "squeeze," came to rely upon these private bankers in many personal and unofficial ways. The banks not only transmitted their official funds for them to Peking, but became specialists in dealing with the various greedy functionaries who lined the route from the provincial treasuries to the Board of Revenue. The banks cultivated Board presidents and secretaries, gatemen and treasury guards. They were lavish in giving New Year's presents, on an appropriately graduated basis, and in entertaining high officials. The latter could use them in return as a source of loans or to effect necessary bribery or to secure private contributions or "squeeze" from official funds. The banks would advance funds to officials expecting lucrative appointments, assisting them to travel to their new posts. In maintaining their official connections, the bankers would affect sumptuous dress and often purchase semi-official status.

In short, these nineteenth-century bankers became established appendages of the official class, but for that very reason they were in no position to act as risk-taking entrepreneurs in imitation of foreign merchants. They were part of an economy which remained unresponsive to Western economic ideas and methods.

The Inertia of the Ch'ing Administration

A similar unresponsiveness to foreign stimuli characterized the Ch'ing government. In the background of this inertia we can distinguish several factors: the superficial, passive, and yet repressive role of local government in Chinese society (in such contrast with the sweeping prerogatives of its centralized state!), the bureaucratic checks and balances, and the nature of the administrative process, as well as the ideas and attitudes of the officials. Since political innovation was the function of the official class, and if exercised by others might almost constitute rebellion, this persistence of officialdom in traditional patterns of behavior inhibited change throughout the society.

The Superficiality of Local Government. In the first place, the official class was passive at the local level because it was spread so thin. Within the 1500 or so administrative districts, or *hsien*, which made up the eighteen provinces, a district magistrate was likely to have charge of an area of three hundred square miles and a population of a quarter of a million people. He was thus a very minor official in the government but faced a very large administrative task. He was in no position to coerce a defiant populace or the local gentry, or initiate new policies, nor would his philosophy of government have permitted him to attempt such things.

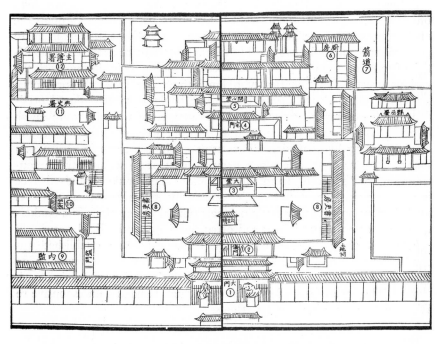

YAMEN OF THE SHANGHAI DISTRICT MAGISTRATE
(from the Shanghai gazetteer of 1871)

On the main axis, reading upward, are the (1) main entrance, (2) ceremonial gate, (3) main hall, (4) residence gate (to the magistrate's personal quarters), and his (5) meditation hall, and (6) kitchen (right top), adjoining (7) an archery butt. Right and left of the main hall are (8) clerk's offices. Far right is the small yamen of the assistant district magistrate. At left, reading upward, are the (9) jail, (10) "ever-normal" granary, (11) jail warden's office, and (12) registrar's office.

The local magistrate had his residence, audience hall, court, jail, treasury, and other offices all in one big walled establishment or *ya-men*. Here in his conduct of local administration the magistrate was aided by and entirely dependent upon a varied retinue of personal and semi-official assistants. These included private secretaries or advisers whom the official brought with him and paid himself. They were usually senior men of scholar-official background, who aided their patron and employer in legal and fiscal matters. The magistrate also brought his personal servants, who performed numerous assigned duties like the collection of customary fees (*lou-kuei*, or in English parlance "squeeze"), the supervision of his appointment schedule, the processing of documents, and other parts of the administrative routine. From the local scene came a staff of semi-permanent government clerks, who kept records and accounts and drafted and copied documents; and finally, an assortment of underlings — runners, jailers, police, and miscellaneous attendants.

Taken together, the clerks and yamen underlings formed a sort of permanent local civil service, whose power was increased by the fact that their superiors, the imperial officials, by the "law of avoidance" were supposed never to be native sons of the province in which they served and were usually transferred triennially. In a district magistrate's yamen there might be scores of clerks and perhaps two hundred underlings and servants of all kinds. But these subordinates, supposing they totaled a million or two, or even more, throughout the empire, were essentially local functionaries, like the village elders and headmen. They were of the people, and formed one link between them and the imperial administration.

The magistrate was also caught up in a web of responsibility which circumscribed and controlled his conduct. In the typical case, he bore immediate responsibility for all aspects of government within his area of jurisdiction and held together in his yamen all the various strands of government activity — fiscal, judicial, military, and the rest. His jurisdiction was territorial and complete rather than functional and specialized. From his study of the Classics, he was presumed to have derived the omnicompetence of the scholar. Knowledge supposedly was difficult, action easy. The man who knew the right thing to do presumably had the power that came from being morally correct. Since he in theory assumed responsibility for the whole government of his area, except for a few special services like the salt tax or the grain tribute, the magistrate's personal burden was without limit. The position of the lowliest territorial administrator was that of the emperor writ small. He was to blame or praise, almost in a ritual manner, for all that took place within his jurisdiction, just as was the emperor within the empire.

This doctrine of what we might call ritual responsibility made officials, or "mandarins," as Westerners called them, seek by all means to avoid the appearance of trouble. To have to suppress disorder and so acknowledge its existence might be more disastrous to one's personal career than to have it continue unreported. Better perhaps to buy off bandits by enlisting them in the local militia than to have to fight them publicly. The result was a deeply ingrained tendency to compromise. The avoidance of issues became a fine art. The bureaucracy learned how to harmonize the elements of the local scene, not how to change them. The spirit of Chinese official life was therefore passive. Officials waited for things to happen, hoping that they would not. They devised stratagems with which to meet all eventualities. They took negative measures to prevent things from happening, not positive measures to achieve objectives. They were constantly on their guard and particularly alarmed at innovators and newcomers.

The Control System. Officials were passive partly because they too were caught up in the complex of institutions by which the dynasty maintained control over the vast Chinese populace. These institutions included the ancient *pao-chia* system of mutual responsibility and the parallel *li-chia* system for levy of taxes and labor service (for details see Vol. I, pp. 374 and 337). Since control was by no means a merely physical effort, there were also the widespread network of official granaries, to control famine; the academies (*shu-yüan*) and other types of local schools to inculcate classical learning; the system of official honors to be paid to the aged and virtuous; the official sacrifices to local spirits; and finally the official lecturers (*hsiang-yüeh*) who expounded the *Sacred Edict* in the villages as a means of moral exhortation. All this added up to a comprehensive and watchful paternalism which tried to suppress evildoers, secure taxes, feed bodies, and indoctrinate minds. Police control was no more important than ideological control, at least in theory.

In practice this popular control system, largely dependent on the energetic cooperation of gentry and local officials, became increasingly ineffective. Its aims were mainly negative, to prevent revolt. It tended to stultify political initiative among the common people, or any sense of civic responsibility. By 1800 its various structures, except perhaps the *pao-chia* system, showed signs of serious decay.

Control of officials, on the other hand, was built into the governmental structure. There were ramified safeguards against any official's acquiring autonomous power. The main principle of these checks was to prevent the allocation of power to any one man. By the "law of avoidance" no official might serve in his native province, nor did he often stay more than three years, or perhaps six, in one post. The magistrate's personal advisers and servants, owing loyalty to him directly, were balanced against the local clerks and yamen underlings, who had their roots in the local scene. Similarly the magistrate had to balance the orders or demands received from his superiors against the interests represented by the local gentry, who might total a thousand persons, including not only the scholars, retired officials, and younger aspirants for office but also the big land-owners and big merchants of the region.

At a higher level, the governor of a province could seldom take serious action without the cooperation of the governor-general, but the latter was responsible also for the affairs of another province. Each of these officials also had the status of censor (see Vol. I, p. 297) to facilitate their reporting upon the provincial hierarchy, including each other. In general, one man would be appointed to many offices but have sole responsibility for no one function. Many men would be appointed to perform a single function; sometimes, indeed, several offices performed the same function. The president of a Board, or Ministry, at the capital was checked by the senior and junior vice-presidents, and all officials from top to bottom were checked by the Censorate, which spent its time doing nothing else.

This system of plural offices and mutual responsibilities was admirably suited to prevent upsetting changes, but it also deadened initiative and thwarted ambition. Initiative might also be restrained simply by the enervating formality of administration. A slip of one character in a memorial was sufficient excuse for castigation, and the intricate minutiae of the regulations and precedents could be counted on to absorb a good deal of attention. Merely by the exercise of these cumbersome rules, jealous superiors could prevent any inferior from gaining decisive authority, even when they did not have it themselves. The real significance of this bureaucratic discouragement of leadership is evident when we note that the initiative in the administrative process was expected to come from below.

The Administrative Process. The conduct of administration itself fostered inertia, for the personal rule of the emperor was passive. His function was to serve as a glorified clearing house rather than to initiate policy, for the empire was too large to admit of a personal administration emanating from one source. Rather, the administration flowed toward the emperor. Even a strong ruler had to accept the forms of this process. Business was initiated in memorials addressed to the emperor; business was concluded by edicts issued from him. The volume of business became so great that the emperor was forced more and more into the position of a transmitter and selector of proposals rather than a maker of them. This must be regarded as one chief reason for the inadaptability of the Chinese state to rapid change when confronted by the challenge of the West. Leadership was stultified below and worn out at the top. Officials on the spot in the provinces could not easily innovate, while the emperor in Peking was much too busy to do so.

The foregoing generalities concerning the dead weight of the Chinese ship of state can be illustrated most graphically by a study of the flow of official documents. Suppose we take as an example the probable steps in the transaction of official business concerning a port like Shanghai, where foreign relations were at times to become focused. What was the control of the central government at Peking over affairs in this commercial city at the mouth of the Yangtze?

Shanghai was the chief city of a district (*hsien*) under the administration of a district magistrate. The district was part of a prefecture (*fu*), the prefect of which had his official quarters or yamen inland at Sungkiang. Above these local officials was the taotai (a term anglicized from *tao-t'ai*) or intendant of circuit, who had charge of a circuit (*tao*), which included the prefectures of Soochow and Sungkiang and the independent department (*chou*) of T'ai-ts'ang. The taotai, in class 4A, was the lowest authority in the province who was privileged to memorialize the emperor directly. It was a privilege seldom used, but in foreign relations the taotai became important as the highest official on the spot. Business concerning Shanghai, therefore, normally came up from the district magistrate or the prefect to the Su-Sung-T'ai taotai, that is, the taotai of Soochow (Su-chou), Sungkiang, and T'ai-ts'ang. He reported it to the governor of Kiangsu and the governor-general of the Liang-Kiang provinces (Kiangsu, Anhwei, and Kiangsi), who were stationed respectively at Soochow and Nanking.

When it came to selecting local business for report to superior officers, there were of course routine matters concerning taxes, judicial cases, public works, and the like which were reported in a regular fashion to the appropriate provincial officers and by them to the appropriate Board at Peking. Extraordinary and important matters, like local uprisings, famines, foreign relations, or proposals for new action of any kind, were reported at the discretion of the responsible officials, who had to balance their chances of trouble from reporting disagreeable tidings against their chances of trouble from withholding such news until others reported it. Self-confident officials sometimes took long chances in suppressing the report of grave events, but the usual practice seems to have been to err on the active side and announce even very slight matters. By so doing, an official could get his own version on record for the future and, by having his superiors accept and transmit his report, he could involve them in responsibility for whatever might thereafter occur. The same choice confronted the governor and governor-general in turn in their memorials to the emperor. They had to select and set before the Son of Heaven all facts that, if not reported, might later be used against them. On the other hand, once a case or an incident had been reported in a memorial, it was likely to be raised again from Peking. A memorialist must always be ready to supply further evidence or self-justification on any matter made known to the court.

A report concerning Shanghai, having reached the provincial authorities, could be embodied by them in a memorial to the throne and dispatched by the official post to Peking. This long-established service consisted of two networks. The first, for routine government communication, had some 15,000 post-stations throughout the empire. It was maintained generally by foot couriers who traveled along lines of posts which were placed between ten and thirty *li* (three to ten miles) apart and were kept up by the local authorities. Routine reports were usually sent in this way. By statute those from Nanking to Peking (2300 *li*, roughly 766 miles) were supposed to take 23 days for delivery. The statutory times on other routes were comparable, 56 days by foot from Canton, 48 days from Chengtu in Szechwan, each time limit being calculated at the rate of 100 *li* (about 33 miles) a day.

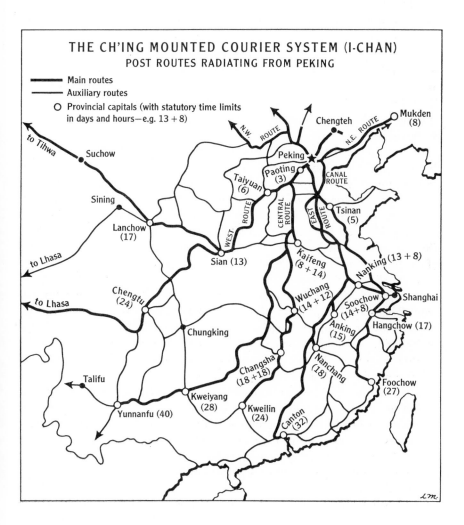

THE CH'ING MOUNTED COURIER SYSTEM (I-CHAN)
POST ROUTES RADIATING FROM PEKING

Important memorials, however, including those on foreign affairs, were sent by a second network of stations which supplied horses or boats and handled the transport of officials, tribute missions, and public goods, as well as urgent correspondence. It maintained some 1600 post-stations throughout the empire, staffed according to statute by 70,000 men and supplied with 40,000 horses, on five main routes which spread out from the capital. Kiangsu was on the eastern route which came through Shantung and then split into two sections to serve Kiangsu, Chekiang, and Fukien as one unit and Anhwei, Kiangsi, and Kwangtung as the other (see map, page 105).

The horse-post had stations set about 100 *li* apart and was capable of relatively high speed. The number of stations in each province was considerable, 40 in Kiangsu and as many as 139 in Shantung, while the number of horses required by statute at a center like Nanking totaled 359 for the civil authorities and 5726 under the military. The use of these postal facilities was regulated by a system of official tallies that were given to the mounted couriers who took documents over the route. When a high official traveled on government business, he would be accompanied by a great retinue including chair-bearers and porters as well as servants and secretaries, all of whom had to be fed and lodged by the local authorities at each stop.

In case of need this postal service could be speeded up considerably. If a document was sent by horse at express speed, it was expected to travel at the rate of 300 *li* (100 miles) a day, but in crises a memorialist might specify transmission at the rates of 400, 500, 600, or even 800 *li* a day. The rate of 800 *li* (about 266 miles), though not mentioned in the *Statutes*, is found occasionally in nineteenth-century documents and was the top limit of the service. It was attainable only on the flat dry land of the north.

Decision-making at Peking. On its arrival at Peking a routine memorial from Kiangsu would be processed bureaucratically — searched for ir-regularities of form, summarized in Chinese and Manchu, copied and considered. Possible endorsements would be drafted for the emperor to choose from when he met his Grand Secretariat (*Nei-ko*), the top of the routine administration inherited from the Ming.

This whole routine was supposed to take about four days. It was plainly as secure a system as one could ask for. Each draft endorsement was written out in the two languages by two persons who signed their names, and it was approved by their superiors and recopied by another office. The imperial decision was proposed by the Grand Secretariat but obtained through the Board of Censors. It was recorded by two offices, one in each language, and was placed in two different archives, in neither of which it had been previously seen. No one could tamper with either the original memorial or the imperial decision and not be discovered. On the other hand, admiration for this self-checking mechanism and gratitude for the wealth of archives it bequeathed to history cannot blind us to the fact that it put a premium upon inaction or the stereotyped treatment of business. The initiative, if any, rested with minor officers, who were the last people likely to dare to innovate.

If a memorial dealt with foreign affairs it was probably an urgent one carried by horse-post and was considered by the Grand Council (*Chün-chi-ch'u*). This had become the actual top of the administration, after its creation as an informal executive body in 1729. The emperor customarily saw his Grand Council in audience at dawn. For urgent matters under the Grand Council, the procedure was somewhat speedier — an important memorial from Kiangsu about Shanghai, after somewhere between five and thirteen days on the road, would be seen by the emperor before it was seen by his ministers. It was strictly forbidden to send even the Grand Council a duplicate of an important memorial of this type submitted to His Majesty. The emperor was expected to rule as well as reign, and he occupied part of nearly every day with a perusal of memorials (i.e., dispatches), on which he made his own comments and indications. After he had looked them over, the newly received important memorials were sent down to be dealt with by the staff of the Grand Council, whose secretaries classified, recorded, and distributed them, took action as indicated, and drafted endorsements or perhaps separate edicts in preparation for the next morning's audience. At that time further decisions would be taken by the emperor and his Council *in camera*. The whole procedure might take three days. If necessary it could be cut to a few hours.

The different treatment of routine and important matters, as just outlined, was an ingenious invention on the part of the Manchus and helps to account for their success in keeping the Chinese leviathan under way for as long as they did. Plainly, the pedestrian reports and accounts of the Grand Secretariat must have received only nominal surveillance from the emperor, while the important documents reached him directly and were limited in number.

In the conduct of administration, however, the emperor was obliged to hold the balance between "central" and "outer" echelons, between the bureaucracy at the capital and the bureaucracy in the provinces. This was because the top provincial officials memorialized him directly, not through the Six Boards at the capital. Except on routine matters, the provinces and the capital were in parallel harness under the emperor and he guided them both. The Grand Secretariat and Grand Council only advised and assisted him.

Unfortunately, as one might expect, only a superman could really hold the helm of the Chinese state, and after the time of Ch'ien-lung (1736–

1795) supermen appeared no more in the Manchu line. Nor could any-one substitute for the emperor. The administrative machine was com-pletely subordinated to the personal rule of the Manchu autocrat, who inevitably became a bottleneck at the very top of the bureaucracy. The empire and its problems focused upon the decision of the One Man in the imperial palace in Peking.

The favor of the emperor remained the essential basis of an official's authority, and any favorite who met difficulties might expect to be sum-marily degraded, if necessary on some ritualistic pretext. The personality of the monarch therefore counted for much. Chia-ch'ing (1796–1820) had a bad fright in 1813 when he was in danger of assassination, and he evidently became somewhat embittered. Tao-kuang (1821–1850) was chiefly known for his parsimony, no doubt accentuated by the gradual depletion of the imperial coffers that he witnessed. His successor, Hsien-feng (1851–1861), has generally been excoriated as an incompetent non-entity.

It would be extremism to argue that the institutional forms of imperial administration alone made the Chinese government unable to meet its modern problems. Like the Chinese writing system, the administrative institutions were capable of being developed and applied to new situations. Yet it seems plain that they contributed their share to the overall pattern of Chinese inertia. The broad responsibilities of the bureaucracy were not matched by a capacity for local initiative and innovation; the heavy centralized burden of imperial decision absorbed the emperor's energy; the cumbersome checks and safeguards which preserved the imperial power robbed it of adaptability to new circumstances.

THE SPREAD OF CORRUPTION

The rather static economy and administration described above were further handicapped, in their early-nineteenth-century contact with the West, by that chief symptom of dynastic decline, corruption among officials. The human tendency to put private interest above public wel-fare is of course the particular vice of all bureaucracies, but in the Chinese empire the term "corruption" must be understood in a special sense as the carrying to excess of practices that, when not excessive, were a normal and recognized part of government.

In brief, Ch'ing officials of the nineteenth century, as in previous eras, were expected to maintain both their public offices and their private estab-lishments out of the perquisites or unofficial revenues secured through their official positions. A local magistrate, for example, would ordinarily use the tax funds that he collected in three different ways — to meet statutory quotas of official payments to his superiors, to maintain his own official establishment, and to benefit his private interest. This confusion of public and private funds, as it would be considered today, reflected the very personal nature of the official's administration and responsibility, and also the fact that his revenues were not collected entirely in money (some being in kind or in labor), were not accounted for in a system of budgeting and auditing, and were produced by the infinitely complex interplay of personal relationships, haggling, and bargaining that characterized the old China on all levels. Just as market prices and wages were subjects of *ad hoc* negotiation from day to day, so the actual amounts of tax payments were not fixed but resulted in each case from an interplay of interests, including those of the taxpayer, the tax collector and his superiors, as well as the state.

Since the whole government apparatus from top to bottom was supported out of its unofficial or informal revenues more than from its inadequate official salaries, the custom of receiving unofficial fees or "squeeze" was well established and fully recognized. In this system genuine "corruption" appeared only when the customary limits of squeeze were exceeded by officials or underlings who were not restrained by the traditional sense of balance and proportion in such matters.

Land Tax Administration. When we try to study the finances of the Chinese empire, we find that the central government revenues recorded in the imperial archives give us only the most superficial view of the national economy. According to the statutes, the revenue of the Peking administration amounted in the middle period of the dynasty to about 40 million taels a year, which in the mid-nineteenth century would be the rough equivalent of about $65 million in United States money or perhaps double that number of Mexican dollars. This total was made up from the land tax and grain tribute (about 30 million taels), the salt tax (5 or 6 million taels) and customs collections (4 million taels; see table, p. 327). These totals, however, were derived by tax-farming in each province — that is, by the establishment of quotas that the provincial tax collectors were expected to meet, after which any further collection remained in their hands. This system of tax-farming on a massive scale was in fact, as it was in name, a sort of "tribute" collection from the provinces by the imperial regime.

The imperial land tax quotas due to Peking were perhaps only a fifth and certainly no more than a third of the total land tax revenues collected at the lowest level by the agents of the district magistrate. The other four-fifths or two-thirds of the collection went to maintain the local and provincial establishments of officials and their retinues. Alongside the official collections, unofficial extortion and exactions could redound to the local tax collectors. In short, the officially recorded quotas and reports made to Peking were a façade behind which the struggle between the officials and the populace went on without ceasing. It was here that a dynasty stood to lose or retain the Mandate of Heaven. For the tendency of the local officialdom was constantly to increase its private exactions. If unchecked this would make the dynasty responsible for ever-increasing burdens upon the populace, with inevitable results.

The operation of this process in the early nineteenth century has been studied particularly in the lower Yangtze Valley, a chief area of surplus rice production. The land tax in this area included chiefly two items. First was the fixed land-and-capitation tax (*ti-ting*), which was a combination of a tax on acreage and a tax originally levied on males between 16 and 60, but which had become since the early 1700's purely a fiscal quota of revenue to be collected from each administrative area. The second item, also to be collected by quota from certain particularly fertile rice-producing areas, was the grain tribute (*ts'ao-liang*). While the former was to be collected in fixed amounts of money, the latter was collected either in kind or in money. In any case, the collecting officers not only added to the established quotas a number of further charges, but also found ways to profit through the process of collection. In general this profit was achieved by bold-faced methods of discount, whereby several pecks might be discounted, i.e., "squeezed," from each bushel of rice; or silver payments substituted for the rice might be demanded at higher than the current market price; or copper payments in lieu of silver might be demanded at more than the current copper-silver exchange rate.

The operation of this graft can easily be illustrated. Officials in Kiangsu might first demand a discount of a seventh or an eighth, collect it twice over, and then add a porterage fee and other charges, with the result that it would take two and a half Chinese bushels to count as one bushel of tax payment. If the market price of rice was two thousand cash per bushel, the tax collectors might demand eight or ten thousand cash in payment of each bushel due. In order to effect the payment of one tael of tax in silver, the peasant might have to give up silver worth anywhere from 1.5 to 1.8 taels. On many occasions the extra charges and discounts would total ten times the stated tax.

These personal takings of the tax collectors usually had to be split both with certain local gentry who cooperated in the system and with the higher officials. Collectors, gentry, and higher officials formed a triangular corporation, living on the "sweat and blood" of the farmer. Much of this graft was also absorbed by the mass of official underlings and clerks. These ubiquitous hangers-on got their squeeze by manipulating a variety of charges for porterage, inspection, stamping, gate money, and the like. This whole intricate and highly organized system was thoroughly institutionalized, on a customary rather than a legal basis. In each yamen there were "establishment costs," "customary annual payments," and so on, totaling hundreds if not thousands of taels. These multifarious accumu-

lated charges were nominally connected with birthday ceremonies, contributions on taking office, holiday celebrations, contributions for public
notices, charges for torches, for official tents, or for the upkeep of official
horses, all in endless profusion.

The most significant aspect of this system whereby the official class
battened upon the populace was the alliance between the officials and the
"big households." In general, the big landlords, who usually had gentry
status, paid their taxes at lower rates than the middle and poor peasants.
This made the tax system "regressive," bearing more heavily on the poor,
rather than "progressive," like a modern income tax. The wealthier a
man was, the better arrangement he could make with the officials. Big
households might even pay less than their nominal due. As a result, it
would take the extra charges on the small households to offset the short
payments from the big households. Gentry degree-holders in the community, even if they were not landlords, through their access to officialdom could similarly oblige the tax collectors to give them favorable
arrangements. That the well-to-do paid at lower rates than the poor can
be documented in each province. Where a big house might pay four
thousand cash to discharge a tax of one bushel, a small village household
might have to pay twenty thousand. Where a well-to-do peasant might
pay only two bushels to count as one of tax, the small peasant would pay
four.

One consequence was that the poorer households sought the protection
of the bigger, so as to make their payments on the latter's more favorable
terms. On their part, the big gentry households were happy to make
these payments on behalf of their smaller neighbors and take a profit on
the transaction. These big establishments which paid taxes for others
were known as "tax-farming households." Thus the landlord gentry
got their middlemen's profit, the state was defrauded of revenue, and the
little people were defenseless against the dominant landlord-official class.

The Grand Canal and the Yellow River. Similar tendencies appeared
in the ancient services which supplied the so-called "tribute" grain to feed
the officials and the Manchu garrisons at the capital. For thirteen centuries, ever since the revival of central government under the Sui and
T'ang, the Grand Canal administration and the Yellow River conservancy,
which was closely related to it, had gone through repeated cycles of
innovation, deterioration, revival, and reform. After 1800 they both saw
increasing corruption and inefficiency.

During most of the Ch'ing period the Grand Canal and lower Yellow
River were under the special charge of three directors-general, stationed
respectively in Kiangsu, Honan-Shantung, and Chihli provinces. Since
the canal route north from Hangchow to Peking crossed the alluvial
flood plains of both the Yangtze and the Yellow rivers, its maintenance

was no easy task. At the crossing of the Yellow River, which until 1852 entered the sea south of the Shantung peninsula through the old mouth of the Huai River, flood waters almost every year tended to invade and destroy the canal system. Constant repair work was necessary to maintain the canal dikes and keep the channel free of silt. (See map, page 156.)

The grain transport service, under another director-general, used in the early nineteenth century some 6000 grain junks (canal barges), which averaged 80 feet in length and carried about 45 tons of grain and 10 men apiece. About 70,000 bargemen were required, drawn from hereditary tenants of imperial lands. Every year they sailed, poled, dragged, and pushed their grain junks in fleets of ten through the canal and back again, contending with low water, unloading their grain into shallow-draft lighters when their junks grounded, or even transporting it by carts on land in an emergency.

The yearly quota of tribute-rice collections, from the most fertile areas of the lower Yangtze provinces, totaled about 400,000 tons, a good share of which was used to meet costs of collection and losses in transit. About 275,000 tons of tribute rice were due at the Peking granaries. The canal also carried an important commercial traffic, and the bargemen were legally allowed to carry private cargo up to one-fifth the weight of tribute grain.

This grain transport service illustrated the land-minded, bureaucratic tradition of Chinese government. It shunned the difficulties of the sea route from the Yangtze to Tientsin, with its uncontrollable storms around the Shantung promontory (and in earlier times its dangers of piracy at the hands of Chinese, Koreans, and Japanese), in favor of a highly organized system of sinecures and quotas kept under control over the land route. During the nineteenth century the development of steamships made the canal junks technologically obsolete as carriers to North China, but the junk men and all the officials connected with the venerable institution had strong vested interests, and it continued, albeit in a vestigial form, until 1901.

The nature of these vested interests, which included customary perquisites and opportunities for corruption, can be seen more vividly in the case of the Yellow River conservancy, which gradually built up a staff of about 400 officials, with 20,000 troops, and an increasing cost of maintenance. Until the effort being made today to dam its headwaters, the Yellow River in flood was throughout Chinese history an unsolved technical problem, but one that gave continued opportunity for official activity and peculation. The fixed appropriation for conservancy, which had been about 3 million taels a year in the early Ch'ing, rose by the early nineteenth century to 4.5 million, more than a tenth of the central government's regular expenditures. In emergencies much larger sums were required, but contemporary critics estimated that the greater part of all funds went into the pockets of officials, who even employed a recognized class of experts to falsify their accounts and engineer dike repairs that would be just adequate to require subsequent repairs.

The Salt Monopoly. Another branch of revenue service requiring continual attention was the ancient salt monopoly, which was based on the dietary fact that the Chinese masses lived on cereals and therefore, more than meat eaters, required salt to maintain health. From the Sung period down to the 1850's China was officially divided into ten major salt producing-and-distributing zones (shown on the map below): first, a series of zones in which salt was produced on the seacoast for distribution inland — the Ch'ang-lu region (production area south of Tientsin); Shantung; the Liang-Huai region (really two zones, northern and southern, in which salt was produced on the coast north of the Yangtze and on either side of the mouth of the Huai River); and the coastal regions of Chekiang, Fukien, and Kwangtung. All these zones produced their salt from sea water in flat earthen areas called "pans," either by solar evapora-

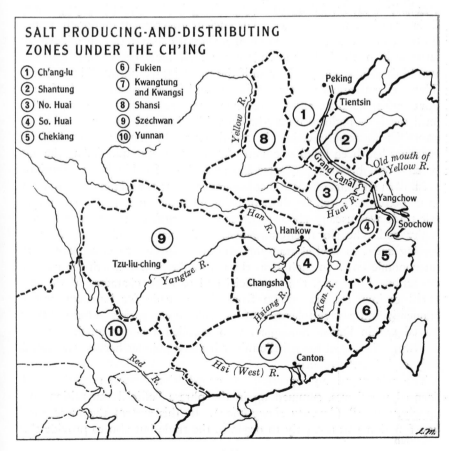

SALT PRODUCING-AND-DISTRIBUTING
ZONES UNDER THE CH'ING

① Ch'ang-lu ⑥ Fukien
② Shantung ⑦ Kwangtung and Kwangsi
③ No. Huai ⑧ Shansi
④ So. Huai ⑨ Szechwan
⑤ Chekiang ⑩ Yunnan

tion alone, in the north, or by evaporation followed by boiling in kettles, in the more humid south. In Shansi (within the great bend of the Yellow River) and in the northwest along the Mongolian frontier, salt was derived by evaporation from natural salt lakes. In southern Szechwan at the main producing center of Tzu-liu-ching a dense salt brine was drawn in long bamboo tubes from a great number of wells, which had been sunk by iron-headed bamboo drilling equipment, in some cases reportedly to a depth of three thousand feet. A total of 8832 salt wells was listed for Szechwan at the end of the nineteenth century. In Yunnan some salt was produced from mines and salt springs. Administration of these various producing centers necessitated a great variety of detailed regulations together with a widespread network of salt controllers and salt taotais with their staffs.

From the producing districts salt was distributed as a necessity of life to the teeming Chinese populace, whose needs created certainly one of the largest inelastic demands in existence before modern times. Salt from the Liang-Huai district on the seacoast north of Shanghai, for example, regularly went far inland to supply Kiangsi, Hunan, and Hupei, where little or no salt was produced. The ancient government monopoly rested on the fact that salt was a staple of universal consumption, produced by large-scale methods in known areas, which local or regional interests would distribute and profit from if the central government did not do so. Thus salt smugglers were a traditional and indeed normal kind of anti-government banditti, and salt revenues were customarily pre-empted by local rebels or regional power-holders. The imperial government had to assert its monopoly claims in self-defense. In some periods half its revenues had been listed as coming from salt. In the mid-Ch'ing the salt revenue was between a quarter and an eighth of Peking's total receipts.

Modern students estimate that the government salt administration, even in its better days, fell far short of being an actual monopoly. The illegal salt trade was usually about as great as the legal, partly because topography and other local circumstances made many producing and consuming areas, as well as transport routes, impossible to police except at uneconomic cost. In such areas the tax might be not worth the cost of collection. Moreover, the superficial and parasitic character of the imperial regime, reaching down from above, made for bureaucratic inefficiency and passive tolerance of local illegal enterprises as long as they stayed within limits. Smugglers who supplied a better quality of salt at lower prices than the gabelle might become popular heroes who could defy or bribe the officials.

The salt monopoly operated by cooperation between officials and licensed merchants, summed up in the phrase "official supervision and merchant sales" (*kuan-tu shang-hsiao*). In this system the merchants' key function was not only to organize the trade but also to provide the large investment of capital required for moving the salt supply, which was far beyond the means of the government treasuries.

For some eight hundred years the salt monopoly had been administered through the *yin* system, the *yin* being a certificate allowing the holder to buy and/or transport salt and giving him in effect a monopoly privilege. (The term *yin* also meant a measure of 266 pounds or more.) From about 1618 the essential principle was that the government did not itself handle salt shipments but gave to certain merchants the monopoly right of buying salt from the salt makers, and to others the rights of transporting it and selling it. The monopoly certificates (or *yin*) for both kinds of merchants were issued annually by the Board of Revenue at the request of the salt taotais. Each merchant paid a tax on each certificate he received, declared where he would buy his salt, and at the appointed time went there and procured it. The salt makers, buyers, and shippers were all registered with the authorities. Each monopolist was required to use his full allotment of certificates and pay accordingly year by year. (Until the late Ming period he generally obtained salt from the government, which procured the salt supply from the producers and sold it to the transport merchants; but from about 1618 the buying merchants dealt directly with the producers.)

Thus the salt monopolist was in a strong position to maintain his rights from year to year by passing on part of his profits as squeeze to the officials. Since quotas of production and sale were set up in each zone, the allotment of certificates readily came to be perpetuated in the monopolist's family. These allotments became vested interests and were accordingly protected by bribery of the officials, who profited from the fact that the salt monopolist, as an entrepreneur, was interested in maintaining his sales and profits but at the same time, as a Chinese merchant, was dependent upon official support to maintain his monopoly. This was a classic example of the profitable combination of merchant and official in the operation of a state monopoly at the expense of the populace.

A large part of the profits of the monopoly merchant were milked from him in various ways — either officially, by requiring him to make "contributions" to the government revenue, or privately by squeeze. One abuse of the system was that the quotas and allotments, once registered and handed down from generation to generation, allowed the monopolistic families to profit without labor by demanding fees from the active salt merchants who actually purchased their allotments and transported their salt for sale. Consequently it is not surprising that salt monopolists became known for their wealth and were pressed most frequently to make "contributions" to the public funds. These donations were usually requited by honorary titles or degrees. In the Ch'ang-lu region below Tientsin, for example, 600,000 taels were collected from salt merchants for military purposes in 1773, and 396,000 taels in 1799 to suppress the White Lotus

Rebellion in Szechwan. The merchants of the Liang-Huai region centered at Yangchow in North Kiangsu were the wealthiest. From the Liang-Huai region the contributions collected in 1773 totaled 4,000,000 taels and 4,000,000 taels again in 1792. Between 1724 and 1804 there were thirteen years in which the contributions of the Liang-Huai merchants totaled 1,000,000 taels or more.

The wealth of the salt merchants is also indicated by the degree to which they were involved in the bribery of officials. The Ch'ang-lu merchants were said to have such high official connections that they knew the forthcoming decisions of the court before the provincial governors and governors-general did. There is a story that on one occasion a censor secretly denounced the Ch'ang-lu salt merchants, and the emperor commanded him to investigate. When he tried to do so, he was able to journey only six miles in three days because of a multitude of sudden obstructions. He was offered a bribe of 600,000 taels and finally forced to abandon his effort. As another indication, we know that the emperors on their journeys through the provinces received large gifts from the Liang-Huai merchants.

THE DECLINE OF CH'ING POWER

In addition to the spread of corruption in the civil administration, the other classic harbinger of dynastic decline was the rise of rebellion, which was stimulated by official exactions and at the same time became difficult to suppress because of corruption in the military forces.

The Manchus had conquered China originally as a nation-in-arms enrolled in military units known by their various flags as the Eight Banners. Their Mongol and early Chinese allies were enrolled in similar units, to make twenty-four banners in all. Within China the Manchus also took over Ming and other local forces and established the Chinese "Army of the Green Standard" (*Lü-ying*), a larger but less mobile sort of constabulary. In peacetime both had deteriorated.

In the last decades of the sixty-year reign of Ch'ien-lung there were still on the rolls of the Manchu banners about 160,000 fighting men, roughly the same number as in 1644. But corruption had invaded this military establishment as it had the civil service. Officers and troops were both under the pressure of rising prices, in the decades before and after 1800. Impoverished bannermen who tried to subsist on rice stipends in their garrisons were forced to become artisans, petty traders, or evildoers to eke out a living. After more than a century of comparative peace within China, the deterioration of the Manchu military machine was startlingly exposed in a big peasant rebellion.

The White Lotus Rebellion. This rising occurred in the years 1796–1804 in the mountainous border region bounded by Hupei, Szechwan, and Shensi, the relatively inaccessible area between the upper waters of the Han River and the Yangtze gorges. Here a migration of poor settlers from the crowded lowlands had created new communities on infertile mountain soil, on the margin of subsistence. Though encouraged by the government, this immigration had not been accompanied by an equal extension of civil administration, communications, or military control.

The expression of discontent, evidently aroused by the exactions of petty tax collectors, was led by men who claimed the mantle of the ancient White Lotus Society (*Pai-lien chiao;* see Vol. I, p. 392). This religious cult, which had been active in the late Yüan and Ming periods, now promised its followers the advent of the Buddha, the restoration of the Ming, and personal salvation from suffering in this world and the next. This set of rather vague beliefs, like the Taoist folklore sometimes used by earlier rebels, provided enough of a common bond between leaders and followers to form an initial rebel organization. Once started, the rebellion became violently anti-Manchu, but it achieved no further ideological development. In 1796 the rebels were able to take over local self-defense corps that had been set up and armed against possible incursions of aboriginal Miao tribesmen who had revolted south of the Yangtze. But the White Lotus Rebellion, though it continued for nine years, remained a congeries of roving bands and did not create a government administration or claim a dynastic title as a rival of the Ch'ing.

During its early years the rising was an inconclusive contest between the ill-organized bands of rebels and the inefficient imperial forces sent to suppress them. The two sides struggled for control of the mountain villages and thus of the sinews of local military power — the supplies of men and food. For several years, however, the corrupt administration dominated by the imperial favorite Ho-shen (see Vol. I, p. 392), who held power behind the scenes until the retired and senile Ch'ien-lung Emperor died early in 1799, hamstrung the military effort. Forces went in and suppressed one outbreak after another, but could not keep the movement from spreading. The small rebel bands used guerrilla tactics, striking and disappearing in the mountainous terrain.

The suppression of the rebellion, after both sides had harassed the local scene for several years, showed many classic features. The first requirement was to restore discipline and morale to the banner forces. This became possible after the Chia-ch'ing Emperor came into effective power in 1799 and supported more vigorous Manchu commanders, like General E-le-teng-pao, a fighter from Manchuria who knew no Chinese and shared his troops' hardships in the field. A systematic program was also pursued of "strengthening the walls and clearing the countryside," that is, collecting the farming populace in hundreds of walled or stockaded villages and removing all food supplies from the open fields. The local manpower, thus concentrated, was organized into garrisons of self-defense corps paid and fed partly by the government. Recruitment of this militia was made easier by the devastation and poverty that the rebellion had brought. Some militia were also trained as a striking force to pursue the rebels. With its campaign of pursuit and extermination, the government combined a policy of conciliation, trying to split followers from leaders by offering amnesty to the rank and file who surrendered and putting a price on the heads of rebel commanders.

The Ch'ing program of suppression thus was many-sided, starving the rebels of food and new recruits, controlling and organizing military strength among the villages, and encouraging desertion from the rebel ranks, in addition to actual military operations. This program was eventually effective, and the banner forces, after their initial failure, somewhat redeemed themselves. But the Manchu fighting man had lost his reputation for invincibility. The government's victory, such as it was, was really due to its use of some 300,000 local militia, whom the government subsequently had to try to disarm. The small militia striking force which had been specially selected and trained became a particularly serious problem, for its offensive power was a double-edged sword capable of turning against the regime. After 1800 the door was plainly open for other rebels.

The Chinese Navy and Piracy. The decline of Ch'ing power was even more evident on the sea than on the land. The Ming navy after the fifteenth century had not maintained the reputation of the Southern Sung and Yüan fleets. With their semi-nomadic continental background, the Manchus were even more land-minded, as was evidenced in their eventual conquest of Taiwan.

Chinese migrants from Fukien during the late Ming period had begun to take over most of Taiwan from the primitive Malay-type tribesmen, who still live in the mountainous eastern half of the island. When the Ming loyalist and pirate leader Cheng Ch'eng-kung (1624–1662, the "Koxinga" of Western accounts) based his sea power on Taiwan, the Ch'ing conquerors' first tactic to subdue him was to try to starve the island of mainland supplies by moving the mainland population inland from China's southeast coast and forbidding sea contact. When the Ch'ing, subjugating all South China, finally conquered the island in 1683, they had no idea of making it a naval base. Similarly, the Ch'ing launched no far-ranging overseas expeditions comparable to those of the Mongols or the early Ming. There was in fact no naval tradition, no concept of a mobile striking force constantly in being and capable of applying sea power.

Instead, fleets were created to meet emergencies on an *ad hoc* basis, after crises had arisen. This followed the land army tradition of the Manchus, by which each striking force was created anew, as a composite of many contingents from separate commands, so as to forestall any rise of independent military power. Each coastal province maintained local flotillas of war junks responsible for suppressing disorder in certain assigned areas of coastal waters. These flotillas were under separate provincial commands but were expected to coordinate their efforts and also to follow directives from distant Peking. The "water forces" were trained neither for deep-water cruising nor for joint maneuvers as a national fleet. Partly this reflected the fact that the Chinese "water forces" had no national mission but were instead a sort of water-borne constabulary charged with suppressing piracy in the same way that the small garrison units in the provinces suppressed banditry. Pirates could therefore save themselves by using the same tactic as bandits — fleeing across jurisdictional boundaries, so that the province they had victimized would be unable to pursue them and the province they entered would have as yet no reason to do so.

In the absence of incentive to build a true navy, Chinese naval vessels remained generally small — about 300 tons burden and 100 feet in length, with 100 men aboard and half a dozen cannon — in a period when trading junks might carry 1000 tons. Regulations were issued, without avail, forbidding the construction of large commercial vessels, in the hope that the traditional fighting ships would not be outclassed by a growth of naval architecture.

In the late eighteenth century piracy had increased on the southeast coast. Some pirate fleets were based in Vietnam, where rivals for local power used them as a source of revenue (see page 437). Other pirates used traditional island lairs on the coasts of Kwangtung, Fukien, and Chekiang. Official efforts at pirate-hunting were impeded by each pirate's chameleon-like capacity to pose as an innocent fishing vessel or as a convoy ship allegedly "hired" by fishing or merchant fleets to "protect" them against piracy. Actually, plunder and blackmail were equally useful sources of livelihood. Pirate leaders of the decades before and after 1800 also used bigger vessels than the government could send against them. They grew so strong that in 1806, for example, they attacked Taiwan with more than 100 ships and 10,000 men. To Western observers it was plain that the imperial "water forces," with their divided commands and antiquated naval technology, were in no condition to defend China against a modern navy.

Secret Societies: The Triads. As the Ch'ing power grew less effective, opposition was organized by secret societies. In general, these bodies have been called *chiao*, meaning a religious sect or doctrine, in North China, and *hui*, meaning a society or association, in the South. Offshoots of the White Lotus Society (and forerunners of the Boxers of 1900) appeared in North China under the names of the Eight Trigrams Society

(*Pa-kua chiao*) and the Heavenly Reason Society (*T'ien-li chiao*). The latter staged risings in Honan, Shantung, and Chihli in 1813 and frightened the court by conniving with eunuchs and actually attempting to seize the Forbidden City in Peking. These outbreaks near the center of Manchu power in the north were quickly suppressed, but it was less easy to control dissidence in South China.

Here the main vehicle of unrest was the Triad Society (*San-ho hui* or *San-tien hui*), also known as the Heaven and Earth Society (*T'ien-ti hui*) or Hung League (*Hung-meng* or *Hung-men*) and by several other names. According to legend, this society was founded in 1674 by fighting Buddhist monks of a monastery near Foochow in Fukien who had been victimized by corrupt officials. Under the slogan "Overthrow the Ch'ing and restore the Ming," it developed an elaborate secret ritual replete with symbolism and traditional lore. It became a blood brotherhood whose members were sworn on pain of death to absolute loyalty to the society. Its principal idea was to exterminate Manchu rule. The day-to-day function of the Triad Society was more peaceful and prosaic, however. Like the Masonic orders of the West, with which it has been compared, it was a fraternal organization pledged to high moral principles and mutual help among its members. This made it particularly useful for persons who moved from place to place — traveling merchants, boatmen, transport coolies, petty officials, smugglers, and others bent on evil or merely on livelihood. Use of the secret Triad signs, esoteric characters, and passwords could secure one protection in strange places away from home, in cities, on the routes of trade, or overseas. While the White Lotus was prominent in North China, the Triad's secret structure was under five main lodges and strongest in the southern provinces, where foreign and domestic trade were expanding more rapidly. It early became known to Western observers by its prominence in the Overseas Chinese communities that grew up, along with the growth of Western activity, in Southeast Asian centers like Singapore and Batavia.

From year to year the Triad Society and its many offshoots were the vehicle for all sorts of illegality or, in modern parlance, rackets and underworld gangsterism. For anyone with unlawful purposes, it formed a natural means, ready at hand. Open rebellion was its ideological shibboleth rather than its normal activity, but racketeering, when threatened by officialdom, could often expand into armed revolt. This seems to have happened in Taiwan in the 1780's, as well as later on, and more than once in South China during the early nineteenth century.

Christianity as a Heterodox Cult. After the Yung-cheng Emperor (1723–1735) proscribed Christianity as heterodox or, in modern terms, "subversive," it had perforce taken on more of the attributes of a secret society, and it remained in this legal category for more than a century, until 1844. In view of the threats raised by rebels and pirates on land and sea after 1796, we can understand why persecution of Christianity, which under Ch'ien-lung had continued only sporadically, became more intense under his successors.

As of 1800 there were in China some 300,000 converts, according to the Roman Catholic count, and 198 priests, of whom 89 were Chinese and about 70 were at Macao. French Lazarist fathers had taken the Jesuits' place at Peking, after the dissolution of the Jesuit order in 1773. Franciscans and Dominicans continued active in Fukien, and Szechwan was a major center with 6 missionaries, 13 Chinese priests, and 40,000 Christians. On the other hand, the church organization at Nanking had been all but wiped out.

Under Chia-ch'ing (1796–1820) persecution became more vigorous in 1805 and after 1811, especially in Szechwan where the French vicar apostolic was executed along with several Chinese priests. While leaving the missionaries untouched at Peking, the Ch'ing government tried with some success to suppress Christianity. The last Franciscans were expelled. From 1801 to 1829 not a single new missionary was able to enter the country, except for the first Protestant pioneer, Robert Morrison, who reached Canton in 1807 under the wing of the East India Company.

Missionaries who were not seized and expelled had to live on the move, in hiding from the authorities, constantly traveling, sometimes in the guise of peddlers, to reach communicants who had purposely dispersed — in Szechwan, for example, into 577 separate places. All this made the Christian movement to all intents and purposes a subversive secret society, and it was so regarded and dealt with. The government's principal aims were to eliminate the leaders, scare away waverers, and send the die-hards into slavery. Thus in 1805 the seizure of a convert carrying a European letter led to the arrest of 29 persons in Peking, of whom 11 proved themselves to be nonbelievers, 5 were pressured (with 100 blows of the bamboo) to renounce the faith, and 13 who refused to do so were sentenced to be transported to slavery in Ili in Central Asia. In Kweichow in 1811 and later, out of 59 Christians seized, 34 renounced the faith and 25 did not. In Szechwan in 1815, eight hundred Christians were arrested, two leaders were strangled and eleven were sentenced to wear the cangue (a broad neck-board) for life.

The Christian community was a picked group, including many merchants who handled Western goods and sons of scholarly families who had inherited a Christian affiliation. There was little mass following among farmers or city artisans. In 1805 the emperor was particularly concerned to find that a number of Manchu bannermen and even two members of the imperial clan were Christians.

Under the Tao-kuang Emperor after 1821, there was no immediate let-up in the official policy of extermination. In 1827 the government confiscated and sold as a private residence the old Catholic cathedral (Pei-t'ang, or North Church) in Peking, which had been granted to the Jesuits by K'ang-hsi and had been used for 135 years. Christianity had reached a low point in its fortunes in China.

TRENDS IN SCHOLARSHIP AND THOUGHT

The symptoms of dynastic decline were not lost upon the Chinese scholar-official class, who were from their training particularly aware of, and believers in, the operation of a dynastic cycle. Corruption had shortened the life span of earlier dynasties. How could the Ch'ing escape?

Yet the very scholars who saw this danger were in the grip of a tradition that they could not easily shake off and that inhibited every effort to change the trend of political events. In their long training for the examinations, the scholars had made themselves masters of the "eight-legged essay" (*pa-ku wen*) style, which thereafter affected not only their writing but their manner of thought itself.

To cite an example of this style — the Ming examinations of 1487 had set as a topic a six-character quotation from the *Mencius: Lo t'ien che, pao t'ien-hsia*. The standard translation (of Legge) reads: "He who delights in Heaven, will affect with his love and protection the whole empire." (A literal translation would be "Love Heaven person, protect Heaven-below.") In his eight-legged essay the candidate would be expected to proceed as follows — make a preliminary statement (three sentences), treat the first half ("Love Heaven person") in four "legs" or sections, make a transition (four sentences), treat the second half ("protect Heaven-below") in four "legs," make a recapitulation (four sentences), and reach a grand conclusion. Within each four-legged section, his expressions should be in antithetic pairs, such as con and pro, false and true, shallow and profound, each half of each antithesis balancing the other in length, diction, imagery, and rhythm.

This comparatively straightforward and systematic Ming type of treatment was further refined under the Ch'ing, with many variations of form. To avoid repetition, classical quotations might be chopped up and parts juxtaposed out of context (as if we should set as a topic from *Hamlet:* "To be or not to be, perchance to dream"). The eight-legged style, in effect, called for playing a game with classical phrases. It stressed memory and detail without substance. Indeed, in stressing antithesis, it did violence to substance. As time passed, many critics inveighed against this system, but it was not abolished.

The "New Text" Movement. The Ch'ing school of "empirical research" (*k'ao-cheng hsüeh;* lit., "studies examining evidence") which had developed during the seventeenth and eighteenth centuries, had been in part a reaction against the Neo-Confucian orthodoxy of the Sung and

Ming. This reaction took the form of reinterpretation of the Classics and reappraisal of antiquity. It became known as the "Han Learning" and stressed the use of textual evidence. With the passage of time, however, the Han Learning had become firmly established as a new orthodoxy, devoted to its own methods of "no belief without evidence" and the pursuit of concrete facts, but all within the restricted sphere of classical studies.

In the nineteenth century two new trends became important. One was a continuation of the "new text" (*chin-wen*) school of classical criticism, which at the end of the century was to become a vehicle for the reform of China's traditional institutions through radical reinterpretation of the Classics. We shall note here only the early stages of this movement.

The first stage had already been reached in the late seventeenth century, when the scholar Yen Jo-chü, building on researches from previous centuries, spectacularly proved that the so-called "ancient text" of the *Shu ching* or *Classic of Documents* (also known as the *Book of History*), venerated and memorized for over a thousand years, had been a forgery. The orthodox Han Learning, as its name implies, studied texts of the Later Han period, when the "ancient text" (*ku-wen*) versions of the Classics had become accepted and established as orthodox. The "new text" school espoused the superiority of earlier versions of the Classics which had been recovered and accepted in the Earlier Han. Gradually their movement reached a second stage, in the eighteenth and early nineteenth centuries, when bold and vigorous scholars (like Chuang Ts'un-yü, 1719–1788, and his grandson Liu Feng-lu, 1776–1829) began to question other "ancient text" versions of the Classics and found in them further proofs of forgery or editorial tampering. Thus the "new text" movement, paradoxically, espoused certain texts which were, it alleged, older and more authentic than the orthodox "ancient texts" established in the Later Han period. At the same time it found in these "new text" versions of the Classics, especially in the *Kung-yang Commentary* on the *Spring and Autumn Annals* (*Ch'un-ch'iu*), radically new meanings which had implications for the hitherto taboo subject of politics and seemed relevant to the course of events in the nineteenth century. In brief, the concept of change in the *Kung-yang Commentary* could be used as a basis for advocating institutional reform.

This prepared the way for a third stage at the end of the century, when a wholesale attack upon the classical tradition would open the door for reform and indeed revolution at the very center of the tradition itself. Until the 1890's, however, the "new text" movement was still gradually gathering momentum. (For its later history, see page 388.)

The School of "Statecraft." The other new trend of the early nineteenth century was likewise a revival of an earlier approach. This was the school of "statecraft" (*ching-shih*), which aimed at the application of scholarship to the problems of government administration in reaction against intuitive knowledge, speculative philosophy, and formalism. This revival of concern with the policies and processes of administration was stimulated by the evidences of dynastic decline — such as corruption, rebellion, natural calamities, and foreign aggression — which were signposts well known to all students of earlier dynastic periods. The dominant tradition of Ch'ing scholarship, confined to the study of classical antiquity and especially philology, had provided detailed information on the imperial institutions including the sacrifices, funeral dress, conveyances, and even the styles of headgear of earlier eras, but it offered little wisdom on how to meet the pressing problems of government in the late Ch'ing period. As the portents of decline became more obvious, reflective minds began again, as they had during the disorder of the Ming-Ch'ing change-over in the seventeenth century, to blame the impracticality of the scholars and their absorption in dry-as-dust and useless book-learning. The writings of Ku Yen-wu (1613–1682), for example, provided a stimulus. The slogan of the new movement was "learning of practical use to society," which is a rough translation of the phrase *ching-shih chih yung*. Its leaders set themselves the task of studying how to maintain the economic and political institutions of the empire.

The efforts of the school of "statecraft" are illustrated in the career of Wei Yüan (1794–1857), a wide-ranging and practical-minded scholar-administrator from Hunan. He had studied the Neo-Confucianism of the Sung and the Han Learning at Peking, and his criticism of these orthodox traditions contributed to the rise of the "new text" movement. He also became a leading advocate of the application of the scholar's talents to the urgent practical problems of administration. When the Grand Canal became blocked, Wei Yüan in 1825 wrote a treatise advocating the transport of rice to Peking by sea. His admirer, the reforming governor of Kiangsu, T'ao Chu, put this plan into effect in 1826, for one year only, sending 1500 shiploads to Tientsin. A later treatise by Wei Yüan on sea transport was similarly admired by the governor of Shantung. During the 1830's Wei helped T'ao Chu in his reform of the North Huai salt monopoly, which abolished the traditional certificate (*yin*) system and instituted a system of tickets (*p'iao*). Later, in 1850, Wei himself administered part of this salt region, with exemplary results. Thus he was a scholar with practical experience.

In 1826 Wei Yüan was invited to edit a work called *Collected Essays on Statecraft under the Reigning Dynasty* (*Huang-ch'ao ching-shih wen-pien*), in which were reprinted over two thousand essays on economic and other administrative topics. This became the prototype for an entire genre of such collections, of which more than a dozen continuations or supplements later appeared, trying to make readily accessible the ideas of scholar-officials concerned with governmental problems. Wei Yüan next secured a post under the Grand Secretariat at Peking, with access to the archives, where he saw the vast sea of unpublished proposals, studies, reports, and decisions accumulated under the Ch'ing administration. He began to compile a large work of recent history on the campaigns of the Ch'ing period, the *Record of Imperial Military Exploits* (*Sheng wu chi*), in which he set forth the impressive record of Ch'ing subjugation of China, Mongolia, Tibet, Sinkiang, and Taiwan and defeat of the Russians, Burmese, Vietnamese, and the White Lotus rebels. He completed this work in 1842, which, as we shall see later, was the very moment of an unprecedented disaster at the hands of the British.

There were others like Wei Yüan concerned with current policy, but unfortunately they were a small leaven in a large mass. The Ch'ing dynasty's consistent policy of wooing the scholars, while at the same time suppressing dissent and forbidding scholarly discussion of official policy outside government channels, had diverted the early vigor of political thought, manifested in the period of the Manchu conquest, into orthodox textual research or fact-gathering for its own sake. Skepticism and criticism had been largely confined to matters of etymology and exegesis of the Classics. Thus, despite the efforts of some vigorous minds, Chinese scholarship of the early nineteenth century showed on the whole a sterile inability to respond to the immediate problems of Chinese society, partly, it seemed, because the scholarly talent of the day was absorbed in narrow bibliographical or purely classical literary activities.

This may be illustrated in the case of Juan Yüan (1764–1849), a famous bibliophile and promoter of scholarly enterprises, who served as governor-general at Canton in the crucial decade from 1817 to 1826. Juan Yüan had been several times a governor and governor-general, had founded several libraries and academies, and had published at least a dozen large works — catalogues of art objects, anthologies of poets, dictionaries and commentaries on the Thirteen Classics, collections of rare works, and the like. During his decade at Canton, when the disastrous conflict with Britain was taking shape there, Juan Yüan established another academy, edited the provincial gazetteer, printed in 366 volumes a collection of 180 works of classical commentary, published some fifty chapters of his own poems, prose, and bibliographical notes, and brought out an anthology of Kiangsu poets in 183 chapters. He also made important contributions to the study of Chinese painting, mathematics, and ancient inscriptions on stone and bronze. All this time he was the top official in charge of China's relations with the West. Small wonder that his policy toward the Westerners at Canton was generally one of compromise and passivity.

The Chinese Image of the Western World. With scholar-officials like the orthodox and assiduous Juan Yüan setting the example, there was little opportunity or incentive for trained minds to pursue a curious interest in the overseas peoples. There were of course writings on these peoples. But this literature produced by Ch'ing scholarship gave one no idea of what the West was actually like.

In the absence of closer contact and more precise information, Chinese observers of the early nineteenth century applied to the Europeans and Americans many of the stereotypes that had been developed during millennia of contact with neighboring peoples in Asia. Western ways seemed changeable and unsystematic, and consequently opportunistic and materialistic. Just as the pastoral tribes of the Inner Asian steppe constantly waxed and waned, changing their names and locations from generation to generation, so the Western peoples whose traders came to Canton, as recorded in Chinese writings, shifted about and changed identity like phantoms. Their names had become thoroughly confused. Since the heyday of the Jesuit mission in the seventeenth century, when Matteo Ricci's map of the world received attention, Chinese cartography concerning the West had made little progress and outside places remained shadowy and uncertain. The inherited lore of the Ming era, when Cheng Ho sailed west and Europeans first came to China, was laboriously copied out — errors, garbles, and all — and set forth as information about the Europeans of 1800, one outdated source being copied into another in endless succession. Aside from this lore, the only other source of information was the Westerners themselves who came to Canton; but they were few in number and more accessible to merchants than to scholars. Ch'ing scholars had of course added to the lore of overseas countries. But the decline of official contact in the eighteenth century had left even this knowledge out of date. A small systematic work, *Record of Things Seen and Heard about the Overseas Countries (Hai-kuo wen-chien lu)*, written about 1730, remained a standard reference for a century afterward (see the map from this work on page 148).

The superficiality of the early-nineteenth-century view of the West is evident in the score or more of Chinese works then available which described the overseas countries. We may take as one example the new edition of the Kwangtung provincial gazetteer, which was edited under Juan Yüan in 1819–22 and based in part on local archives. This work, produced at Canton, the single center of Western contact, boasted that its first edition of 1731 had provided rare and authoritative information, and implied that the new edition did too. In fact it offered an undigested, cut-and-paste series of summaries inherited from the Ming and early Ch'ing with no attempt to identify, locate, or differentiate the obscure places and peoples mentioned. The account of the Spaniards in the Philippines was sandwiched in between Quilon (in southern India) and the Moluccas, and dealt with the Ming period only. Portugal was stated to be near Malacca. England was another name for Holland, or alternatively was a dependency of Holland. France was originally Buddhist, and later became Catholic (it had become a common belief in China that

Christianity was an offshoot of Buddhism). Finally, France was said to be the same as Portugal.

This last error exemplifies the Chinese compilers' problem of names. From the medieval Franks in the time of the Crusades, the Arabs had carried eastward the name Feringhi, which in China became (as we now transliterate it) *Fo-lang-chi*. Coming from Europe subsequently, the early Portuguese were identified as *Fo-lang-chi*. When Spain (*Hsi-pan-ya*) took over the rule of Portugal, Spain became *Fo-lang-chi*, and when the French arrived from *Fa-lan-hsi*, they were soon being called *Fo-lang-hsi* as a variant of *Fo-lang-chi*. Meanwhile the Jesuits from Italy, by using Portuguese Macao as a base, got Italy (*I-ta-li-ya*) identified also as *Fo-lang-chi*. When a Portuguese envoy arrived in 1670 he identified his country, in evident desperation, as *Po-erh-tu-chia-li-ya*. But the Portuguese envoy of 1727 spelled it out as *Po-erh-tu-ka-erh*, which was officially recorded as still another country! Since Spain had once ruled Holland, whose king later had taken the throne of England, which had once possessed America, the circle of confusion was almost complete — especially when bits of information accumulated over several centuries were indiscriminately jumbled together in a single account. While some Western countries were thought to be in the southwestern sea, most were known to be in the "Great Western Ocean," which was also, however, one of the commonest names for tiny Portugal.

Aside from occasional references to the big ships and cannon and different costumes of Western peoples, there is little to distinguish them in this literature from the peoples of the small states of the Malay Peninsula, like Sungora (Songkhla), Pattani, Trengganu, Pahang, and Johore. One difference that should have been very striking was that Chinese traders went to these places in Southeast Asia whereas the Western traders took the initiative in coming to Canton. Nevertheless, Juan Yüan's listing for discussion in the Kwangtung gazetteer was in this sequence: Johore, Trengganu, Portugal, Holland, Calicut, Cochin, Quilon (these last three all in southern India), Hormuz (in Persia), Italy, Holland (listed a second time in different characters), Siam, etc. Since Chinese contact with southern India, to say nothing of Hormuz, had ceased by 1450, it is evident that this guidebook was a purely literary compilation unconnected with the facts of international trade in the nineteenth century.

The same pattern of confusion appears in another "authoritative" work, the gazetteer of Amoy (*Hsia-men chih*), completed in 1832. Here the countries of the Southwestern Ocean are listed in the sequence: Pattani, Cambodia, Holland, England, Spain, Johore, Pahang, France, and Achin (in northern Sumatra).

From the Chinese merchants themselves, little information seems to have been obtained. One exception was a small book, *A Maritime Record* (*Hai lu*), compiled about 1820 by a scholar (Yang Ping-nan) from the reminiscences of an interpreter (Hsieh Ch'ing-kao) who had traveled widely in Southeast Asia in the late eighteenth century. He describes the English as making their living by overseas trade and the establishment of bases abroad. Evidently as hearsay from sailors, he describes the three bridges of London, the city water supply through pipes, the many prostitutes; and how officers wear red and mourners black instead of white as in China, while the women wear narrow-waisted dresses, tight above and full below. So excellent is the English administration that it requires its ships to succor other seamen in distress. West of England, says this work, on an isolated island is America, whose people make ships containing a fire-box which turns paddle wheels without human effort. Though sparse and second- or third-hand, this account has a contemporary quality lacking in the more literary compilations of the period.

One is left with the impression that the scholars were not interested in learning about the West. When exceptional men like Wei Yüan sought to do so, they had to seek translations of Western writings. The facts were not to be found in China.

The Collapse of the Canton System

Both the institutional inertia of the traditional economy and administration and the worsening circumstances of corruption and rebellion kept the Ch'ing government's attention focused on its internal problems. When the crisis with Britain arose at Canton in the 1830's, it found China intellectually unprepared and practically unequipped to meet a novel and portentous situation. The expansive West caught China by surprise, and ways of handling foreign relations which had worked reasonably well for four centuries suddenly became useless.

The Canton system by this time was based on the outworn theory that foreign states could have relations with China only as tributaries. No tribute had come from Japan for several centuries, nor from Cambodia and the small states of Malaya in the Ch'ing period, though trade continued to come in Chinese ships. As Chinese traders went farther abroad, tribute from distant foreign states could no longer accompany China's overseas trade.

The European countries, when fitted into this system, illustrated the split within it. Holland, Portugal, the Papacy, and Britain, having at some time sent envoys in the approved fashion, were listed in 1818 as regular tributaries but without fixed periods. As for Britain, the official records stated that Lord Macartney in 1793 had presented tribute and performed the proper ritual, although actually he presented "gifts" and knelt on one knee only. To the list of "trading countries," on the other hand, were added Spain (in the Philippines), Java (under the Dutch), Portugal (under another of its names), France, Sweden, and Denmark. The Americans had not yet been noticed officially.

OLD PEKING: THE K'ANG-HSI EMPEROR'S SIXTIETH BIRTHDAY

PLATES 10 AND 11. Above, left: Peking street scene, before the imperial procession; note barrows, one-man and two-man carrying poles, Peking carts, shop lanterns and pennants. Right: Imperial procession; bystanders kneel as sixteen bearers carry the emperor past in his dragon-decorated palanquin.

A PEKING HOUSEHOLD

PLATE 12. Peking official (c. 1872) seated in his garden courtyard with his son; ladies, children, and servants above.

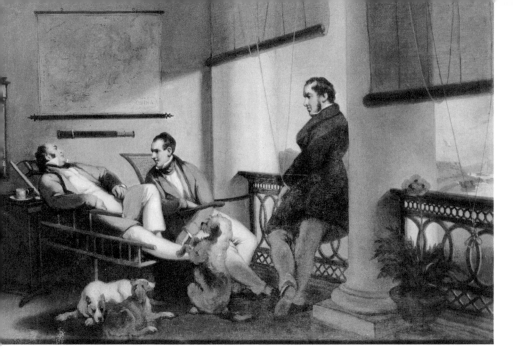

PLATE 13. Dent's Verandah, Macao, c. 1840. This painting by G. Chinnery (1774–1852), owned by the Jardine firm, shows "private traders" of the rival firm of Dent and Company relaxing within sight of the anchorage, with spyglass and barometer at hand.

PLATE 14. Tea production at a glance. Picked on the hillside (top left), tea leaves are dried, sorted, roasted, trampled, packed, weighed, and otherwise processed through successive stages until purchased by the three foreigners in top hats and tail coats (bottom left) and conveyed to their vessels (far right).

PLATE 15. The fate of China's traditional water forces. Supported by boats from British warships, the East India Company's iron-hulled, paddle-wheel steamer *Nemesis* — 184 feet long, 120 horsepower, with two 32-pounders on pivots fore and aft, but drawing only 6 feet of water — attacks a Chinese fleet in shallow water near Chuenpi on January 7, 1841. A Congreve rocket has just exploded a war junk's magazine.

PLATE 16. Canton factories, c. 1854. The 15-man fast-boat (foreground) seems to be vying with two Westerners out for exercise in a shell (center). The American side-wheeler *Riverbird* lies off the open space in front of the factories, each of which has its own flagstaff. (Oil painting by a Chinese artist)

The Growth of Hong Kong

PLATE 17. Harbor, city of Victoria, and Peak seen from Kowloon; a painting of 1856.

PLATE 18. Hong Kong in 1963. Big hotels and banks (upper right) dominate the waterfront of Victoria below the Peak. At lower left is a park on reclaimed land, fronted by low-cost housing blocks; and above, on the mountain roads, luxury apartments. At right are sampans of boat-dwellers, with private yachts in a basin beyond, and, farther out, warships at anchor.

"Illustrations of tributaries" for the Ch'ien-lung Emperor: "A 'Barbarian' from Sweden" (left) and "An Englishman" (from Huang-Ch'ing chih-kung t'u, Palace edition, 1761).

Thus the traditional Chinese world order of surrounding states, which benefited from trade with China's superior civilization while acknowledging its superiority with tribute missions, was already falling apart. The British dominated the Canton trade, with the Americans second, but they made no pretense of sending tribute to Peking.

The "Country" Trade and the Private Traders. This crack in China's ideological armor was steadily widened by new developments at Canton, centering on the growth of the "country" trade from India. This was the cutting edge of the commercial, financial, and industrial expansion of the Western states, with Britain in the lead. It represented the growing world order of the modern international economy.

The private traders were a new element at Canton. To avoid the control of the British East India Company, enterprising British subjects as early as the 1780's began to remain at Canton as nominal representatives of other European governments. This became an established custom — in 1823, for example, James Matheson was Danish consul and Thomas Dent was Sardinian consul. These private merchants carried on at Canton the more modern kind of enterprise pursued by the "agency houses," acting primarily as agents for merchants in London or India, from whom they received cargoes on consignment to be sold on a commission basis. While an agency house in the China trade might also buy and sell with its own funds, it acted mainly as a middleman, providing all the necessary services of buying and selling goods on behalf of its correspondents, chartering vessels, handling freight, insuring cargoes, remitting funds, recovering debts, and all the time charging a commission or fee for every service. To succeed in this kind of business required little capital but a great deal of enterprise and ingenuity. Thus Dent, Matheson, and the other "private English" at Canton soon began to acquire fleets, set up insurance companies, and carry on banking operations. Their new world of "free trade" was growing up within the outdated framework of the old Canton system and Company monopoly.

This private trade had a great capacity for growth. The private traders were the Far Eastern correspondents, friends, and often relatives of merchants in the similar but bigger agency houses in India, which had become well established after the Company ceased to monopolize British trade in India in 1813. These houses in turn, like those at Canton, dealt with the hub of Britain's world-wide economic expansion in London. In this expansion, the "country" trade between India and China played an increasingly crucial role, with a strategic importance out of proportion to its size. In brief, by providing (after about 1817) three-quarters of the British imports at Canton, it accomplished two things at once: it gave an outlet for Indian produce, remitting profits to India, and it continued to finance the Company's purchase of China's teas, which were as usual profitably taxed by the British government in London. It remained the channel by which the Company in India could remit surplus revenues from India via Canton to meet payments due in England.

In the growth of this triangular India-China-England trade, the dynamic factors had been, first, as we have noted, the British demand for tea and, second, the Chinese demand for Indian produce — mainly raw cotton and, increasingly, opium. The textiles of Lancashire had invaded the Indian market after 1813 but found little sale in China: the Industrial Revolution, in short, supplied the spirit and indirectly the financing of free enterprise and expansion at Canton rather than the actual trading goods. In this way by the 1830's the Canton trade had changed character. The private traders had become the dominant element in it, ready to exploit every commercial opportunity. Their increasing concentration on the import of opium bespoke opportunism and the search for profit.

Behind the growth of the opium trade lay the basic fact that British India had become dependent upon it for 5 to 10 per cent of its revenues. In Bengal opium was cultivated under Company control and sold officially to private traders at auctions in Calcutta. Opium in western India, grown not under Company control, at first competed with the Bengal product, but by the 1830's the Company had got control of the ports of shipment, like Bombay, which enabled it to levy a transit tax and profit accordingly. In the meantime, the competition between Bengal and western India had stimulated the production of more opium at lower prices.

The Growth of the Opium Trade. The origin of the opium trade lay partly in the growth of opium-smoking in China. Because opium-smoking used a habit-forming narcotic, harmful to the human system, it was a social evil even more serious than the gin that was considered an evil in contemporary Britain. The opium poppy had long been known in China and its product used as a drug, but the smoking of opium began only after tobacco-smoking had spread to China from America by way of Manila in the seventeenth century. During the late eighteenth century, about a thousand chests of opium a year were being imported from India to China. From 1800 to 1821, the average was about 4500 chests a year, but the annual total grew by 1838 to some 40,000 chests. (A chest usually contained 133 pounds.)

This increase in consumption, reflecting the spread of the smoking habit to a larger market, can no doubt be connected by the social historian with the other trends noted in preceding sections — toward population pressure, a probable lowering of living standards, and the increase of corruption in government and of rebelliousness among the Chinese people. The spirit of the age, in short, was one of demoralization. Opium-smoking as a visible symptom of this frame of mind spread particularly among the yamen underlings — runners, clerks, and petty officials — and among soldiers, the two groups who represented the government at the lower level of contact with the populace. Significantly, opium addicts were found even among imperial clansmen, eunuchs, and bodyguards at the palace in Peking. Being costly, opium was a luxury vice, to be indulged in by persons on the upper quite as much as the lower levels of society.

Foreign traders could make big profits, as prices fluctuated according to supply. A chest might sell for 1000 or even 2000 Mexican dollars before 1821, and for 700 to 1000 in the period of increased supply thereafter. Chinese smugglers likewise made profits, since addicts created a strong market. This speculative trade created intense competition. Merchants began to use the earliest type of clipper ships to get ahead of their rivals. They delivered cargoes to "receiving ships," floating warehouses which were heavily armed to ward off attackers.

The Chinese counterparts of the foreign opium traders were organized in brokerage houses (*yao-k'ou*), usually composed in each case of a score or more of partners, whose funds made up the capital for investment. Their smuggling boats, well armed and manned by sixty or seventy oarsmen (which gave them their Chinese names of "scrambling dragons" or "fast crabs") would normally take delivery of opium chests from the foreigners at the receiving ships. By the 1830's one to two hundred such Chinese boats were taking deliveries from about twenty-five foreign receiving ships in the waters outside Canton. At first the domestic distribution of opium was along the routes of inland trade to the west and especially to the north of Canton, toward Central China, but eventually a new phase began with distribution by foreign ships on the coast of China northeast of Canton.

The incapacity of the Chinese government to stop the trade was illustrated by the opposite courses followed in Ch'ing policy and official practice. Selling and smoking opium had been prohibited by imperial edict in 1729, its importation or domestic production in 1796, and after 1800 these bans were frequently repeated. But official connivance had grown as the trade had grown. Opium paid its way, becoming a new source of corruption in an era when corruption, above and beyond the customary levels of squeeze, was already debilitating all aspects of Ch'ing administration. To greed was added the motive of fear, for the opium distributors were tied in with the secret societies, and their armed bands could oppose with force those officials who would not accept bribes. The result was that the higher officials issued edicts of prohibition, while the lower officials connived at the trade, in most cases passing some of their ill-gotten gains on to their superiors, probably even to court officials. This created a widespread vested interest, a system that no one official could break.

Yet the higher authorities became more vulnerable to exposure, blackmail, or censure as the growth of the trade made their connivance, whether tacit or active, constantly greater. They found it the safest course to drive the contraband trade out of their immediate jurisdiction. This was attempted in 1821 when Governor-General Juan Yüan forced the receiving ships to leave the river anchorage below Canton. Thenceforward they anchored outside at Lintin Island. As a result the foreign traders began to seek outlets on the coast to the northeast, where Namoa Island and Chinchew (Ch'üan-chou) became important smuggling centers. This "coast trade," even less controllable than that in the Canton delta, began during the 1830's to import as much as Canton. When an East India Company ship (the *Lord Amherst*) voyaged up the coast in 1832 on a market survey, without opium, it found opium everywhere in demand.

The tragedy of the opium trade was a dual one. For not only had Britain's commercial expansion become dependent on opium; the trade had become entrenched in China as a powerfully organized smuggling system which corrupted the government increasingly as the number of addicts grew. By the early 1830's there were somewhere between two and ten million habitual smokers, many of them government personnel, yet the Ch'ing government had made no real effort to check the evil. The court at Peking had been accustomed for over a century to drawing revenue, officially or unofficially, from the Canton trade. Opium had merely increased the unofficial revenue and also strengthened the "Canton interest." Similarly, the British opium interest was a recent addition to the long-continued British desire for commercial expansion in China. It gave further impetus to British demands that had long been in process of formulation.

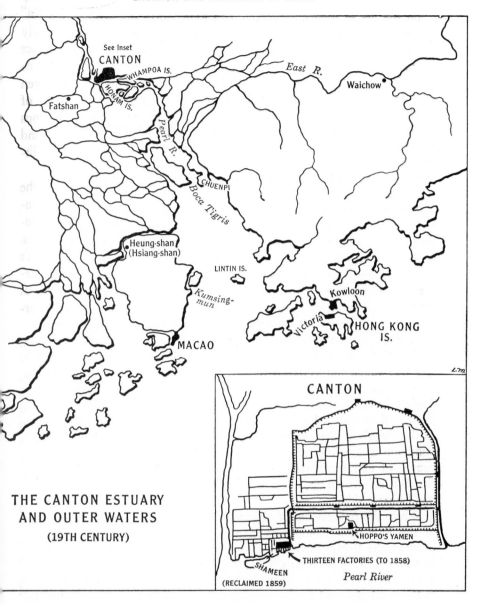

THE CANTON ESTUARY
AND OUTER WATERS
(19TH CENTURY)

CANTON

HOPPO'S YAMEN

THIRTEEN FACTORIES (TO 1858)

SHAMEEN
(RECLAIMED 1859)

Pearl River

Britain's Demand for Diplomatic Equality and Commercial Opportunity. As early as 1754, Company officials had wanted to trade at other ports, to have their own warehouses, and to station a representative at Peking. Macartney in 1793 had asked for island depots near Canton and near Chusan Island, not far from Shanghai, as well as for a fixed and printed tariff to take the place of the various fees, charges, presents, and exactions customarily levied at Canton.

To the list of British grievances had been added the increasing inadequacy of the hong merchants. These individuals, usually heading family firms, were known to foreigners by names customarily ending in "qua" (for *kuan*, "official"). The most famous was the head of the Wu family firm, Howqua (abbreviated from Wu Hao-kuan). There were in fact four Howquas in the Cohong in succession from about 1784 until its abolition in 1842. The second made a great fortune, trading and even investing abroad through his American friends of the Boston firm of Russell and Company. The fourth Howqua passed the lower examinations and purchased a higher degree. He inherited a famous garden and patronized the publication of four large collections (*ts'ung-shu*) of literary works.

But the success of the Howqua firm was exceptional. Most of the hong merchants, constantly pressed for "contributions" to the government, fell into financial difficulties. Short of capital themselves, they regularly went into debt to the East India Company or to private traders. The Company usually advanced the capital to buy up the next season's teas and silks, while the private traders tried to profit from the high interest rates at Canton and often invested in risky speculations. There was no legal machinery, however, for collecting debts owed to foreign merchants, and so the unpaid hong merchant debts accumulated.

To this inadequacy of Chinese economic institutions and commercial law was added the Western repugnance at the arbitrary arrest and torture of accused persons, as practiced under Chinese criminal law. Antithetic assumptions concerning the rights and responsibilities of the individual underlay the Anglo-Saxon and the Chinese legal traditions, and so the British at Canton had refused to submit to Chinese jurisdiction in homicide cases after 1784, and the Americans after 1821. In practice a degree of extraterritoriality (foreign legal jurisdiction over foreign nationals) had grown up, but it was not explicitly assured or admitted from the Chinese side.

When the proponents of reform and free trade secured the abolition of the East India Company's monopoly of British trade with China as of 1834, the British government sent an official Superintendent of Trade to Canton. This Scotsman, Lord Napier, had fought under Nelson as a naval officer and subsequently had become an enterprising sheep-farmer in Scotland, devoted to the agrarian reforms of the day. But he had had no experience in diplomacy, nor any contact with Asia, and he was sent by the Foreign Secretary, Lord Palmerston, without adequate instructions, preparation, or support to attempt an all but impossible task: the opening of equal relations between Britain and China, which would bring to an end the ancient Chinese tribute system.

The full import of this mission was perceived neither by Napier nor by Palmerston, who casually instructed him, "Announce your arrival by letter to the Viceroy." When Napier reached Canton in July 1834, the local officials predictably refused his demand for correspondence between them as equals. Soon they stopped the British trade which Napier had come to promote, trade stoppage being their usual device for curbing recalcitrant foreign merchants. Napier then circulated handbills in Chinese denouncing the Ch'ing officials' disregard for trade and its benefits. The officials in return cut off all supplies to the British factory on the riverbank at Canton. Lord Napier's two frigates, ordered to come up to the Whampoa anchorage below Canton, forced their way through the principal mouth of the river, the Bogue or Boca Tigris (a corruption of the Portuguese *Boca Tigre*, Chinese *Hu-men*, meaning Tiger Gate), and exchanged cannon fire with the Chinese forts.

Napier's aim was to enforce compliance with his demands, which seemed to him only right and proper. As he wrote at the time, "What can an army of bows, arrows, and pikes, and shields do against a handful of British veterans? . . . The batteries at the Bogue are contemptible." However, the governor-general, Lu K'un, was also a man of military experience, who had helped subjugate Moslem rebels in Sinkiang and rebellious Yao tribesmen in Hunan. He soon had the river effectually blocked against the English rebels. Lord Napier sent to India for armed support. The emperor ordered that the English be made to submit or be expelled by force.

This wrathful confrontation of the two governments was now somewhat palliated by the merchants who stood between them. The hong merchants on one side and the British free traders on the other, who together conducted most of the Canton trade, pressed for a compromise. Napier retired to Macao, where he died of illness in October 1834, and trade was resumed. He had raised the issue of diplomatic equality but had not settled it.

For the next four years Napier's successors in China pursued what has aptly been called a "quiescent policy." A majority group of merchants, headed by the enterprising firm of Jardine, Matheson and Company (a successor of earlier firms, which has retained this name since 1832), demanded that a British naval force repair the insults to Lord Napier and secure the opening of more ports. The rival group of merchants headed by Dent and Company preferred to reap the profits of trade quietly rather than aggressively. The Canton officials for their part demanded that England appoint a chief merchant (*tai-pan*, anglicized as taipan), not an official, to take responsibility for control of the British trade and traders. Meanwhile Lord Palmerston in London sent no instructions.

By 1836 the Canton system had thus fallen apart. Trade was no longer confined to Canton, the Cohong no longer monopolized the Chinese side of it (in particular, the opium imports), the hong merchants were frequently insolvent, the Company monopoly had given way to competing private traders and its function of controlling the British merchants had been assumed by an official who objected to taking orders from the hong merchants. The volume of trade and its lawlessness were increasing. Diplomacy was stalemated. The Canton situation was out of control.

THE OPIUM WAR

No episode in modern history has provided more occasion for the charge of "imperialist aggression" than the First Anglo-Chinese War of 1839–42 — a war that was precipitated by the Chinese government's effort to suppress a pernicious contraband trade in opium, concluded by the superior firepower of British warships, and followed by humiliating treaties that gave Westerners special privileges in China. As patriotic Chinese of all camps have reviewed the story in recent times, it has given substance to their feeling of grievance at the forceful intrusion of the West and the subjection of China to "semi-colonial" status for almost a century thereafter.

In addition to looking at the Opium War from this point of view, it is also necessary to see it in the context of certain major trends of modern world history.

By the nineteenth century, the Chinese position on foreign relations, like the contemporary seclusion policy of Japan, was out of date and no longer supportable. Sooner or later it would have had to give way, not only because of China's relative military weakness, but also because of the currents of ideas — concepts of scientific learning, of individual freedom, and of economic growth, for example — which were beginning to sweep over the modern world. In demanding diplomatic equality and commercial opportunity, Britain represented all the Western states, which would sooner or later have demanded the same things if Britain had not. It was an accident of history that the dynamic British commercial interest in the China trade centered not only on tea but also on opium. If the main Chinese demand had continued to be for Indian raw cotton, let us say, or at any rate if there had been no market for opium in late-Ch'ing China, as there had been none earlier, then there would have been no "opium war." Yet there is little doubt that some kind of Sino-foreign war would have come, given the irresistible vigor of Western expansion and the immovable inertia of Chinese institutions.

The Anti-Opium Movement. The British resort to warfare was precipitated when the Ch'ing court finally faced the opium-trade menace to its vital interests and strove, too late, to catch up with the situation at

Canton. The anti-opium movement was a moral crusade, though, as often happens in such cases, its righteous moral tone coincided with concrete material interests.

Until the 1830's, neither the growth of addiction among yamen underlings and soldiers, nor the increase of barefaced smuggling and official connivance in it, had roused the lethargic regime at Peking to a vigorous and sustained effort at suppression. But meanwhile another problem had arisen in a different sector. The exchange rate began to rise between the copper cash used in everyday transactions and the silver bullion (in the unit of weight and fineness known as the tael), which was chiefly used in remitting taxes and in government fiscal operations. Silver became dearer in terms of copper. Instead of 800 or 1000 cash to meet a statutory tax of one silver tael, which had been the usual rate for centuries, it began to take 1200, 1600, or even 2000 cash. This imposed hardship at all levels of the government's financial activities — peasants had to pay more coppers to meet taxes, salt merchants had to charge more copper cash for their sales, official tax collectors meeting their quotas in silver had less copper cash left over as private squeeze.

Several factors lay behind this situation. For one thing, there had been a debasement of the copper coinage. In the early eighteenth century China had depended heavily on copper imports from Japan, but these were supplanted at mid-century by increased production from mines in Yunnan. By the 1820's, however, Yunnan production was declining. Meanwhile the size and weight of the copper cash turned out by the various provincial mints had been reduced by somewhere around one-third, while the volume of cash minted every year was increased. Counterfeiting added to the volume of the cheap cash. Also, as the value of silver increased in terms of copper cash, silver seems to have been hoarded and so taken out of circulation.

To this trend was added a more spectacular one, an outflow or "drain" of silver beginning sometime after 1821. Until then, China had consistently been a net recipient of silver in foreign trade — from Japan, Manila, England, the United States, India, and elsewhere. As opium imports increased after 1821 and especially in the 1830's, China for almost the first time began to suffer a net loss of silver, mainly taken out to India as bullion to pay for opium. An apparent drain of this sort was noted long before the balance actually shifted. Chinese observers saw that silver was paid out for opium but did not see its subsequent return to pay for tea exports. This apparent outflow of silver in general foreign trade had long been deplored. When the balance really shifted, about 1830, it was all the more a cause of alarm. In 1825 a censor connected this outflow specifically with the opium inflow. Soon it was generally accepted that the fiscal crisis caused by the shift in the copper-silver exchange rate was due to a drain of silver caused by the opium trade.

As we can see now, there were several other factors involved besides opium imports, but the latter became the focus of concern. Added to the concern about opium addiction, this fiscal situation produced among Ch'ing officials a feeling of extreme crisis and urgency. Some were soon exaggerating the menace, estimating that the silver outflow was as much as 20 or 30 million taels a year, equal to half or more of the revenues received at Peking. Actually, when one allows for silver brought by Americans and others, the net outflow in the early 1830's was probably closer to 2 or 3 million; even so, this was an undesirably large annual loss.

So great was the opium evil by this time, both in its hold on the growing market of opium-smokers and in the expanding network of distributors who profited from it, that extirpation seemed an immensely formidable task. Some realists, especially a group of scholar-administrators connected with the academy (*Hsüeh-hai t'ang*) that Juan Yüan had founded at Canton in 1820, counseled a policy of compromise: to continue to oppose smoking by scholars, officials, and soldiers, but legalize the opium import trade under a tariff so as to discourage smuggling with all its disorderly evils and at the same time prevent the outflow of silver. Once legalized, opium imports would, according to this scheme, be purchased only by bartering Chinese goods, not silver. In May 1836, while Juan Yüan was a grand secretary in Peking, a proposal to this effect was presented to the emperor, referred to the Canton officials, and soon became known to the foreign traders.

While the leaders in the British smuggling trade on the coast were not enthusiastic about legalization, the idea took firm root among the general foreign community, which for some time anticipated that legalization would occur. In this they were encouraged by the fact that the Canton authorities in September 1836 gave their support to the proposal.

In Peking, however, the argument had meantime gone the other way. Memorialists argued that the drain of silver could not be stopped by requiring the barter of goods for opium, while on the other hand the spread of opium ought to be stopped within China. The emperor so ordered, and the legalization movement was dead within four months after it started.

In 1837–38 suppression was attempted more vigorously than ever before against the Chinese part of the trade at Canton. The effort made substantial progress locally, but smuggling continued to flourish on the coast, and though prices declined, imports reached a new peak. In the latter half of 1838 a great debate, consisting of memorials requested from high officials all over the empire, proved inconclusive. But the Taokuang Emperor at the end of 1838 finally decided on a root-and-branch attack upon the evil all along the line: against cultivators, distributors, and consumers, all of whom would be subject to the death penalty. This comprehensive statute, when issued in 1839, also provided the death penalty for foreign importers of opium. By this time the anti-opium campaign at Canton had destroyed opium dens, executed dealers, and depressed the trade, which for a time in the winter of 1838–39 was almost at a standstill. But this success at Canton seems in the long run to have stimulated the coast trade and induced the foreign importers to take a more active and forceful role in armed smuggling operations than they had ever had to take before. The position of the British government meantime was, as Palmerston put it, that it could not interfere "either by aiding or restraining the pursuits of the smugglers." Suppression would have to be effected by the Ch'ing government.

In the confused events of this period, one point stands out — that the Chinese government was attempting to do two things at once: suppress the opium evil and maintain the tribute system of foreign relations. The Canton authorities refused time after time to communicate with the Superintendent of British Trade, Captain Charles Elliot (1801–1875), except through the hong merchants, and demanded that the character "petition" (*ping*) head his letters, as from an inferior to a superior. Any kind of trade agreement or cooperative effort between the two governments thus remained impossible. Two worlds stood in opposition. The Chinese struggle against the opium trade went forward in the context of the equally determined British struggle against the tribute system.

Commissioner Lin at Canton. The man selected to exterminate the opium evil was Lin Tse-hsü (1785–1850), a leading official who had had thirty-five years of administrative experience in many branches of government and had been a close friend of Wei Yüan and other reform-minded scholars who were also opponents of the opium evil. Lin was both a proponent and a practitioner of the school of "statecraft" and had a great reputation as an incorrupt and effective administrator, devoted to the welfare of state and populace. Having offered vigorous and practical proposals in the debate on opium policy, he was given the special powers of an imperial commissioner. After two months' travel, averaging 20 miles a day by palanquin and canal boat to cover the 5600 *li* (more than 1200 miles) from Peking, he reached Canton on March 10, 1839.

Once arrived on the scene, Lin Tse-hsü became a vigorous pioneer in obtaining translations from Western books and newspapers. At Canton he organized his own intelligence service, headed by a translator who had been taught Latin by Roman Catholic missionaries at Penang in Malaya and English at the Anglo-Chinese College founded by English Protestants at Malacca. There was also a Chinese boy who had studied English under American missionaries at Macao. Through these assistants Lin got translations from Vattel's *Law of Nations* concerning a nation's right to control its foreign trade, and he addressed two eloquent letters to Queen Victoria:

> Though not making use of [opium] oneself, to venture nevertheless to manufacture and sell it, and with it to seduce the simple folk of this land, is to seek one's own livelihood by exposing others to death. . . .

> Suppose there were people from another country who carried opium for sale to England and seduced your people into buying and smoking it; certainly [you] would deeply hate it and be bitterly aroused. . . .

Lin's use of this kind of broad moral appeal to a foreign ruler, while in a traditional tone, foreshadowed China's eventual use of international law as an effective diplomatic weapon.

Commissioner Lin's program at Canton was to break up and wipe out the local network of Chinese opium importers and distributors, and this he practically accomplished. It was not his original aim to use force against the foreign traders, much less start a war with the British. But he soon found it necessary to coerce them into surrendering their opium stocks, and for this purpose he was finally obliged on March 24 to confine the foreign community of about 350 men in the Thirteen Factories, including the queen's representative, Captain Elliot. Deprived of their Chinese servants but not of necessary supplies, the foreigners spent six weeks in this detention. After applying in this way the Chinese principle of collective responsibility, Lin Tse-hsü released them when the British merchants delivered up their opium stocks, which he then proceeded to have publicly and spectacularly destroyed.

Unfortunately for Lin Tse-hsü's anti-opium campaign, he was handicapped by ignorance and made serious miscalculations which eventually led to disaster. He had accepted, for example, the ancient dictum that exports of Chinese tea and rhubarb were essential to the Westerners' well-being. Later Lin realized that rhubarb was unimportant at Canton. (Actually it was exported mainly from Central Asia to Russia.) Lin also failed to realize the magnitude of the British interests involved in the opium trade, or the vital concern of the British government in the continuance of the Canton trade as a whole.

By confining the foreign community, Lin secured delivery of some 20,000 chests of British opium. But two things made this a hollow victory: first, the opium market had collapsed, while the supply on hand in China or in prospect from India had risen to some 50,000 chests, so that the merchants' interest lay in getting whatever price they could; and second, Captain Elliot took personal responsibility for the surrender of the opium on behalf of the British government. As Matheson put it to Jardine at the time, "The Chinese have fallen into the snare of rendering themselves directly liable to the British Crown." Commissioner Lin's high-handed coercion of British subjects and officials was entirely in keeping with the unequal nature of the traditional tribute system; but from the viewpoint of the modern international world it gave the British government a strong *casus belli*.

The traditional order in China's foreign relations was further brought into question in July 1839 when drunken English sailors killed a Chinese villager (named Lin Wei-hsi), who became a symbol in the dispute over legal jurisdiction. The Chinese authorities demanded that a culprit be delivered up. Elliot followed the long-established British practice and refused to admit Chinese criminal jurisdiction over British subjects. He was also unable in a trial of his own to ascertain the actual offender. This was only the most prominent of many Sino-British incidents of this period involving the very different legal institutions of the two sides. As the dispute widened, it highlighted the Sino-Western conflict over diplomatic relations and legal jurisdiction as well as over the opium trade.

Under pressure from Lin the British community retreated successively from Canton to Macao and then to the outer islands. There they congregated in August 1839 at Hong Kong, a largely uninhabited island about thirty square miles in area, between which and the mainland peninsula of Kowloon lay one of the world's best deep-water harbors. Open to the sea at either end but protected against typhoons by the 1800-foot peak on the island, this harbor was to become the chief port of call for European vessels reaching China. From this island warehouse, trade goods could be carried ninety miles westward to Canton or up the coast to other ports. In 1839 it became the base for the British community of some fifty vessels and several thousand sailors as well as merchants and officials. Commissioner Lin tried to cut off provisions from the mainland but without success.

Hostilities began gradually, in small affrays intermixed with negotiations. The first pitched battle was in November 1839, between a Chinese fleet which was still demanding delivery of the man who had killed Lin Wei-hsi and two British warships which were trying to keep British merchantmen from trading at Canton on China's terms. It was typical of the Canton trade, however, that it survived even during the sporadic hostilities of wartime. In the legal trade, American firms like Russell and Company, working closely with their hong merchant friend, Howqua, handled the season's tea exports under the American flag on behalf of the British, for a price. Meanwhile the coast trade in opium continued, well armed, beyond the reach of Commissioner Lin.

When a British expeditionary force arrived in the summer of 1840, seized Chusan Island south of Shanghai, and then negotiated at the river mouth below Tientsin close to the capital, it was evident that Lin Tse-hsü had not succeeded in his twin efforts to suppress the opium evil and maintain the Canton system. In September the emperor recalled him in disgrace.

War and Negotiation. The Ch'ing dynasty's defeat was due both to the technological backwardness of its armed forces and to the decay of military administration. Aside from the now effete Manchu banners, the principal force was the Chinese constabulary, the so-called Army of the Green Standard, which was scattered throughout the provinces and supposedly totaled about 600,000 men. These Chinese troops, living dispersed in the cities and towns and along the highways, had come to be less and less distinguishable from traders and commoners. The impotence of this scattered and unwarlike standing army was assured by a system of administration that prevented the development of large units as striking forces with high morale and continuous leadership. To make up a force against bandits or rebels, small detachments would be transferred from a number of different garrisons and battalions. The contingents thus collected might come from several different provinces. In action, one detachment might stand by and laugh at another's difficulties. In case of victory, they would all join in looting the populace; but in case of defeat, melt away.

The malpractices of this Chinese army became a byword. Officers would fail to report vacancies, keep nonexistent persons on the rolls in order to get their rations, and hire temporary substitutes at times of inspection. They even enrolled their cooks and servants as troops so as to receive their rations also — the rolls might be full but the ranks empty. Sometimes the army existed mainly on paper. Its training stressed form without content, a meaningless posturing with swords and spears, like play-acting. As one patriot (Tso Tsung-t'ang) put it, the land troops could neither ride nor shoot and the water troops could not sail or fire a cannon. The officers could only keep the accounts.

Given these evils, discipline was very poor. Troops were commonly rebellious and refused to obey orders. Without training or discipline, they lacked skill and courage in the field and would run before the enemy could arrive, being fearless only toward the helpless common people. Officers treated their troops like slaves. The troops took up opium-smoking and petty robbery and became a menace to the populace.

To chastise the Ch'ing government in 1840–42, Britain sent a small mobile force of a few thousand men equipped with the latest devices of warfare, such as flat-bottomed, shallow-draft iron steamers that could defy wind, tide, fire-rafts, and fortresses. The Chinese war junks with their archers, antiquated cannon, and stink-pots (the forerunners of gas bombs) proved as ineffective as the coastal batteries with their fixed emplacements and poor gunnery. The British reduction of Chinese strong points all along the coast from Canton to Shanghai was not difficult (see Plate 15).

The real difficulty was how to capitalize on this naval and military superiority so as to create a new order in China's foreign relations. Britain had no territorial ambitions except for a commercial base, which was supplied by the island of Hong Kong with its fine harbor. Neither was it her aim to attack the Chinese populace, who, except at Canton, generally remained passive spectators of the fighting and supplied a coolie corps to work for the invaders' wages. The basic problem was how to make the Son of Heaven agree to a new status for the Westerners and their activities in China. Since this meant the end of an age-old set of beliefs and institutional practices — in short, the destruction of the tribute system — it was not a quick or easy process.

In the first phase of the war in 1840–41, Captain Elliot as plenipotentiary negotiated outside Tientsin, as we have noted, and later at Canton with Lin's successor, a wealthy Manchu grandee, Ch'i-shan (d. 1854). Together in January 1841 they signed the abortive Chuenpi (Ch'uan-pi) Convention, which would have ceded Hong Kong, given diplomatic equality and an indemnity to Britain, and reopened Canton. But both governments spurned this attempted settlement. Although he had saved Canton from attack, Ch'i-shan was cashiered in disgrace, while Elliot, who had disregarded instructions calling for greater gains, was recalled.

Up to this time, left largely without instructions, Captain Elliot had for several years combined negotiation with warlike action in a mixture always designed to keep trade moving. In May 1841, after the season's teas had been shipped, he had a small British force of 2400 troops attack Canton; but it withdrew from outside the city walls after Elliot secured a "ransom" of six million dollars. Since local militia, mobilized under gentry leadership at official instigation, were threatening the British when they withdrew, this incident (at the village of San-yüan-li) was hailed as a victory of the Cantonese populace over the British forces. Some recent historians have viewed it as the first evidence of a modern spirit of nationalism among the Chinese masses. At any rate, it inaugurated a tradition of strong antiforeignism at Canton, the oldest center of Western contact.

In the second phase of the war in 1841–42, the new plenipotentiary, Sir Henry Pottinger, negotiated, as Palmerston had instructed him, only after the British attack had forced the Ch'ing court to consent to an entire new deal in Anglo-Chinese relations. In the autumn of 1841 the British seized positions and left garrisons all along the coast, in Amoy harbor, on Chusan Island (which they had evacuated), and at Ningpo, before settling down for the winter. Reinforced from India in the spring of 1842, they seized Chapu in Hangchow Bay, occupied Shanghai, took Chinkiang, where the Grand Canal crosses the Yangtze, and advanced to the outskirts of Nanking, having defeated every form of Ch'ing resistance.

This resistance had had many aspects — the stoppage of British (but not other) trade, the mobilization of militia at Canton, the blocking of harbors and river-mouths with stakes, rocks, and chains, the building of war junks, the casting of cannon, and the assembling of contingents of troops from many provinces. In March 1842 a Chinese surprise attack was made, without success, on the British-held city of Ningpo. The logistic difficulties of provisioning the attacking force in the face of popular noncooperation and of transporting its antiquated arms were exceeded only by the staff problems of securing accurate intelligence in place of rumor and coordinating the various ill-assorted contingents. This Chinese military offensive in the traditional style was ineffective in command, organization, and armament alike. In defense, on the other hand, the garrisons of Manchu bannermen at Chapu and Chinkiang resisted the British with hopeless courage. By the time the British were prepared to attack Nanking, it was evident that they were irresistible.

The Manchu dynasty capitulated in order to preserve itself. As descendants of alien conquerors, the Manchu rulers at Peking were sensitive to the collaboration which so many "Chinese traitors" were giving to the invaders. Secret societies were active both in opium smuggling and among the Chinese who flocked to the new British base at Hong Kong. Wherever the imperial forces were defeated, local mobs rose and looted. Continued defeat by British arms would deal a blow to the dynasty's prestige that would weaken its hold on China even further. It had to give up its claim of superiority over foreigners in order to maintain its rule over the Chinese people. It was no accident that after the Chinese reformer Lin Tse-hsü had failed to suppress the opium evil, Manchu grandees like Ch'i-shan and, in 1842, his successor Ch'i-ying (d. 1858) were sent to appease the British with concessions.

The First Treaty Settlement. Ch'i-ying as imperial commissioner signed the Treaty of Nanking with Pottinger on August 29, 1842. This initial document prepared the way for the new order in China's foreign relations by abolishing the Cohong monopoly of foreign trade at Canton, promising a "fair and regular tariff," ceding Hong Kong to Britain, and opening five ports to British residence and trade — Canton, Amoy, Foochow, Ningpo, and Shanghai. An indemnity of 21 million Mexican dollars was given Britain to cover hong merchant debts to British merchants, pay for the opium confiscated by Lin Tse-hsü, and reimburse the British Indian government for the cost of the war.

The Treaty of Nanking was only the first step in creating the new legal structure of the treaty system. Three further treaties were necessary in 1843–44 to complete the first settlement: the British Supplementary Treaty of the Bogue (October 8, 1843), amplified by the American Treaty of Wang-hsia (July 3, 1844) and by the French Treaty of Whampoa (October 24, 1844). Because of the "most-favored-nation" clause — a promise to each power that it would receive whatever privileges might later be given another — these treaties reinforced one another to form a

THE "OPENING" OF EAST ASIA:
PRINCIPAL TREATIES IN THE "UNEQUAL" TREATY SYSTEM, 1842–1943

Characteristic features: treaty ports, extraterritoriality,
most-favored-nation clause, tariff fixed by treaty.

Beginning	Development	Termination
CHINA		
Nanking (British) 1842, plus Suppl. Treaty of Hu-men-chai ("The Bogue") 1843	Wanghia (American) 1844, Whampoa (French) 1844	Germany, Austria-Hungary 1919, USSR 1924
	Tientsin (Br., Fr., Am., Russian) 1858	Tariff autonomy 1930 (ff. Washington treaties 1922, recognition treaties 1928)
	Chefoo Convention (Br.) 1876, ratified 1885	
	Boxer protocol 1901	New equal treaties (Am. and Br.) 1943
JAPAN		
Kanagawa, Perry (Am.) 1854 (Br. 1854, Russian 1855)	Harris (Am.) 1858	Brit. revision treaty 1894; extrality ended 1899; tariff autonomy 1911
SIAM		
Bowring (Br.) 1855 (earlier Br. 1826, Am. 1833)	French 1907, Br. 1909, extrality relaxed	Ger., Aust. 1919, USA 1920, end extrality Tariff autonomy 1927 Extrality fully ended 1938–39 (ff. Sayre treaties 1925–27)
VIETNAM		
Saigon (Fr.) 1874 (earlier Fr. 1862)	Hué (Fr.) 1883, protectorate confirmed (1885 China recognizes French protectorate)	"Freedom within French Union" 1946, independence of Repub. of Vietnam 1954
KOREA		
Kanghwa (Jap.) 1876	Shufeldt (Am.) 1882	(Japanese protectorate 1905, annexation 1910)
		Repub. of (So. Korea) 1948

(For a list of treaties, see Morse and MacNair, *Far Eastern International Relations*, pp. 840-842, or Clyde, *The Far East*.)

single system of treaty law. Since China did most of the giving of privileges, the system has properly been called "unequal" and, by some, "semi-colonial." It was not created in a day, however, and actually took eighteen years of continued trade, diplomacy, and eventually warfare to become established. The lead in trading, negotiating, and fighting was taken throughout this period by Britain, while the United States, France, Russia, and smaller European nations followed suit in varying degree.

The first settlement was thus only an entering wedge. It placed British consuls in five ports, of which four were newly "opened" in 1843–44. British residents were under the protection of their consul's legal jurisdiction, that is, they had the right known as extraterritoriality. Nationals of other treaty powers soon had similar protection even though their "consuls" might be merchants who were given consular papers, as was the United States consul until 1854. The protection offered by Western legal procedures covered not only the persons of merchants and missionaries but also their goods and property. It was sometimes extended in practice to their Chinese servants and assistants and so created in the treaty ports a Western type of community in which the enterprises of both Western and Chinese businessmen were relatively secure from the arbitrary exactions of officials.

Foreign trade was now further facilitated by a fixed and printed treaty tariff based on the rates of the old imperial tariff, which ranged, very roughly, between 4 and 10 per cent ad valorem. Chinese trade monopolies or guilds, like the old Canton Cohong, were forbidden in the name of free trade.

The American treaty, negotiated by Caleb Cushing and Ch'i-ying in 1844, improved upon the British treaties in certain matters like the provisions for extraterritoriality and gave Americans without a struggle all the privileges that Britain had fought for. On this point there was a happy coincidence of British, Chinese, and American views. Britain, confident of her own competitive strength, sought equal conditions of free trade for all countries. China, intent on playing one "barbarian" against another, aimed to treat all the Western nations equally; thus all would be beholden to the emperor's generosity directly and would not get the benefits of China's trade through the generosity of the British. Meanwhile the American interest was already formulated as the desire for most-favored-nation treatment — to trade on as good terms as anyone else.

Western Influence through the Early Treaty Ports

China's antiforeignism was expressed in negative policies of noncooperation and avoidance of Western contact for almost two decades after the Opium War. Since this period saw the opening of Japan and the rapid advance of technology and national power in the West, China's lethargy in responding to the Western challenge in these years was disastrous. But the empire was not only too self-contained but also too much absorbed in domestic difficulties to make a vigorous response in these middle decades of the century. Consequently Western contact, with its inevitable undermining of the traditional order, proceeded by stages from the first war and subsequent treaties, in 1840–44, to a second set of wars and treaties in 1856–60. During this period the Ch'ing statesmen, whether Manchu or Chinese, found out too late what they were dealing with. Since few of them ever had any direct contact with the Western "barbarians," China and the Western powers were not yet really in the same universe of discourse.

The Beginning of Western Studies. Perhaps because of the rule enforced by the Ch'ing emperors, that mere scholars who were not in official positions should not be encouraged to discuss questions of official policy, the lead in learning about the Western invaders had to be taken by persons of the official class. The chief product of Commissioner Lin's inquiries at Canton had been a body of translations dealing with the Western countries. In 1841 he turned them over to his friend, the scholar-official Wei Yüan. From them Wei produced in 1844 his *Illustrated Gazetteer of the Countries Overseas (Hai-kuo t'u-chih)*, which was enlarged in later editions of 1847 and 1852 and widely read. This book was a collection of materials on world geography and Western conditions and also contained a discussion of how to handle the "barbarian" problem. Handicapped by sheer ignorance of such complexities as the British parliamentary system of government, Wei patched his compilation together as best he could, with bits of old Chinese lore about the West mixed in with his half-understood new translations from Western sources. Merely to use the latter was of course a great innovation.

Wei Yüan's studies, far from making him pro-Western, seem to have confirmed his hostility. In appraising Western religion, for example, he follows the Jesuits' early antagonists in attacking Christianity for its inherently irrational claims, its conflict with Chinese ways, and its "despicable practices," under this latter head accepting much of the scurrilous folklore enshrined in Chinese literature.

Wei Yüan's strategic thinking was similarly a mixture of old and new. He combined the ancient theme of "using barbarians to control barbarians" (e.g., the French and Americans to control the British) with the new concept of "learning their superior technology in order to control them." In his mind the superior techniques of the "barbarians" were evident in their warships, firearms, and methods of maintaining and training soldiers. From this concept was to come later in the century the whole movement for the strengthening (*tzu-ch'iang*, literally "self-strengthening") of the Chinese state by borrowing Western devices and

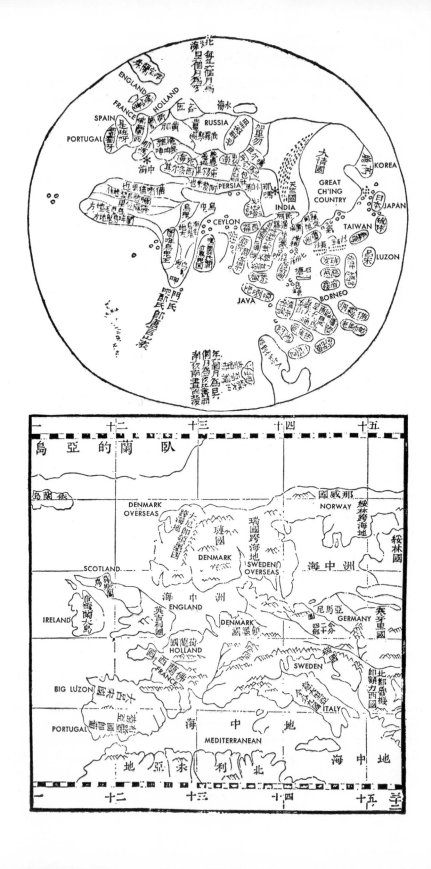

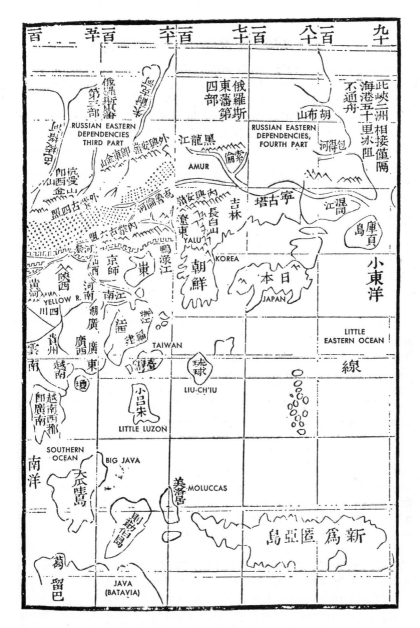

CHINA'S PREMODERN VIEW OF WORLD GEOGRAPHY
(We have superimposed the English captions.)

Round map (top left) is "A General Sketch of the Four Seas," from the widely used Hai-kuo wen-chien lu, *c. 1730. Among many anomalies, the Black Sea is labeled "Dead Sea," the Indian Ocean almost disappears, and both places marked * are labeled* No-ma *("Rome").*

Bottom left is Wei Yüan's map of Europe from Hai-kuo t'u-chih, 1844. *In it, Germany is "now divided into 24 parts," Italy into "9 countries." England is large and Denmark expanded. "Sweden"* (Shui-tien) *and "Switzerland"* (Shui-shih) *are confused, both being simply "Shui country."*

Above is Wei Yüan's map of East Asia (1844), from 140° to 190° longitude (counting eastward only, from the coast of Brazil). Chinese provinces bear Ming names. Russia in Asia is clearly marked.

Such maps, which deserve further study, gave Commissioner Lin his view of East and West.

technology. This was a direct application, to the problem of Western aggression, of those ideas of "statecraft" which Wei Yüan and others had already advocated in dealing with domestic problems.

The first phase of this movement in the 1840's was on the simplest level of military mechanisms. The period of the Opium War saw many efforts to copy such Western devices as cannon, explosive shells, copper-bottomed gunboats, and paddle-wheel ships (the Chinese imitations, however, substituted manpower for steam engines). Such efforts could be sanctioned by seventeenth-century precedent, when cannon had been secured from the Portuguese and the Dutch. The desire for knowledge of the West and its technology could be justified by quoting the Chou dynasty classic on the art of war, the *Sun-tzu:* "Know yourself, know your opponent; in a hundred battles, win a hundred victories."

Unfortunately this desire was felt by only a small minority of Ch'ing officials. The governor of Fukien, Hsü Chi-yü, obtained Western atlases and the assistance of a missionary and other foreigners, and in 1850 published a world geography, *A Brief Survey of the Maritime Circuit (Ying-huan chih-lueh).* This book broke new ground by presenting not bits and pieces of translations but an up-to-date, synthesized account of each Western country with rather accurate modern-style maps. It became a standard work. Yet in the very next year the author was denounced and recalled because of his intimacy with foreigners, even though his writings evidenced a considerable degree of xenophobia.

China was too big a country, with too many tradition-bound scholars annually moving into official life from the great reservoir of inland provinces like Szechwan, Honan, or Hunan, to be easily stirred by a marginal sea-frontier contact with foreign ideas. As a consequence, the stimulus of the Western example was largely confined to Hong Kong and the treaty ports, where the impetus for Westernization gradually accumulated during the 1840's and 1850's.

Trade under the Treaties. While the Western way of living and doing business was protected within the treaty ports, it had not been possible in the first treaties to get the opium trade legalized. The British requests for legalization were refused by Peking, but the India-China opium trade continued and expanded along the coast as far north as Shanghai without being mentioned in the treaties as either legal or illegal. Outside the five treaty ports there grew up double that number of "receiving stations," centers of unadvertised but regular and generally peaceable trade between the foreign opium importers and the Chinese opium distributors. These stations were left alone by both governments, and the opium evil went on making its inroads, without official protection from Britain or effective suppression by China. British consuls were instructed to take no legal cognizance of it.

Opium addiction increased. In the 1850's the import rose to 50,000 and even 60,000 chests a year, double the figure of the early 1830's at Canton. American opium merchants like Russell and Company, who had competed with the Indian supply at Canton by bringing opium from Turkey, now could compete directly with Jardine and Dent by acting as agents for shipments from India. American as well as Chinese, English, Scottish, and Parsee fortunes were made from the trade. Cultivation of the poppy increased rapidly within China, foreshadowing the eventual supplanting of the Indian import. But during the mid-century decades, the few big importing firms, with their fast clippers, well-armed receiving ships, accumulated capital, and superior facilities, maintained an oligopoly. Together they froze out small-scale competitors and kept the trade within limits south of the Yangtze — steady, lucrative, self-protected, and relatively uneventful.

In the interests of commerce in general, the British government began to protect the carrying trade in legal goods on the China coast against the growing menace of piracy. British subjects at Hong Kong were licensed to fly the union jack on their coastwise vessels. British merchants soon were hiring out their armed vessels to convoy Chinese merchant junks or fishing fleets and protect them against pirates. The British navy also moved in to substitute for the impotent Chinese water-forces and actively suppress the fleets of pirates along the coast.

The treaty-port communities throve meanwhile on trade conducted under treaty law. Tea exports rose above 100 million pounds, silk increased similarly, but both were paid for mainly by the funds received for opium imports. The Chinese market for textiles and other British manufactures remained disappointingly limited. Foreigners suspected that distribution was checked by inland taxes on goods in transit, but the chief impediment seems actually to have been the self-sufficiency and poverty of the Chinese peasantry, who still made their own textiles and had little money for purchases. This was not realized by the foreign merchants, perched on the rim of a vast subcontinent, and they continued to expect a great market, in the faith that the mills of Lancashire could be kept busy for a generation if only each "Chinaman" would add one inch to his shirt-tail.

The various activities in the new ports, particularly in Shanghai, represented an aggressive and highly dynamic new order based on organized competition. Western nationals and the consular officers who led them formed competing groups — Shanghai soon had special areas of British, French, and American settlement. Some two hundred firms, mainly British and American, though united in chambers of commerce at Shanghai and Canton, lived or died by competing in all aspects of trade. Yet for practical purposes the five ports and Hong Kong formed a single community, protected by gunboats, mainly British, and inhabited by a young and mobile population of merchants who, like the consular officers, were frequently transferred from one port to another.

The Missionary Movement. A similar degree of organized competition and a similarly expansive hope for the conversion of the "heathen" masses of China animated the early treaty-port missionaries, and often met with similar frustrations because of the slowness of the Chinese response.

Protestant missions had come out of that spiritual accompaniment of the rigors of industrialization, the evangelical movement in late-eighteenth-century Britain and parallel developments in New England. The pioneer Protestant missionary, Robert Morrison, sent by the London Missionary Society to Canton in 1807, had succeeded in studying Chinese and translating the Bible. To avoid hostility at Canton, his colleagues opened the Anglo-Chinese College at Malacca in 1818. Like the Jesuits before them, the Protestants found from the beginning that hard study, both for missionaries and for their converts, was prerequisite to evangelism.

The first American Protestants, who reached Canton in 1830, were sent by the American Board of Commissioners for Foreign Missions, an agency founded in 1810 by several denominations but which eventually represented the Congregational churches. At Canton the American Protestants founded an important monthly journal, *The Chinese Repository* (1832–1851). One of the editors, S. Wells Williams, compiled both a dictionary and an influential general account of China, *The Middle Kingdom* (1848). Another American pioneer, Peter Parker, inaugurated medical missions by opening an eye hospital at Canton. In 1839 Commissioner Lin got from him a truss to alleviate his hernia. Both Williams and Parker later served their government in diplomacy, just as Morrison and other British missionaries aided theirs.

Within the larger treaty-port communities, which by mid-century had grown at Canton to about 300 foreigners and at Shanghai to about 200, the missionaries formed a small minority (about 75 persons) in a dominantly commercial scene. But they also opened missions at the smaller ports, Amoy, Foochow, and Ningpo, where at first their chief or only fellow-residents were the British consuls and sometimes the opium captains. From the treaty ports Protestant missionaries ventured into the surrounding countryside, sometimes beyond the established port limits of half a day's journey (the regulations required foreigners to return by nightfall and so "reside" at the ports).

Though obliged at times to travel on the running vessels of the opium fleet, which provided the chief transportation link, the missionaries almost universally deplored and opposed the opium trade. They strove through Christian evangelism as well as through translations of the gospel, medical dispensaries, and schools to give the Chinese people the spiritual, intellectual, and material benefits of modern Western civilization. At first, however, their chief concentration was on spreading the word of the gospel in Chinese, particularly through tracts such as those written by the first convert, Liang A-fa (1789–1855). Yet for a long time converts remained very few, measured in tens rather than hundreds. Among their arduous preparations for the conversion of the Chinese, Protestant missionaries intent on making the gospel available began to experiment with systems of romanization (or transliteration, i.e., writing the sounds of Chinese in the Roman alphabet).

Meantime the revival of Roman Catholic missions went on both at the ports and in the interior, building on broader foundations two centuries old. The Catholic revival in Europe after the Napoleonic wars had been signalized by the re-establishment of the Office of the Propaganda at Rome and in 1822 by the creation in France of the Society for the Propagation of the Faith. As the modern patron of Catholic missions, the French government in negotiating its treaty of 1844 secured the issuance of imperial edicts of toleration, in 1844 and 1846, which removed Christianity from the category of a heterodox sect (or subversive secret society) and restored certain churches.

Missionaries like all other Westerners were still forbidden to reside outside the five treaty ports, but by working through its native hierarchy of Chinese priests and communicants, the Catholic Church was able to achieve a widespread growth from the 1840's on. The Society of Jesus, having been restored in 1814, became very active and set up its main center at Zikawei (the ancestral home of Ricci's great convert, Paul Hsü) in the suburbs of Shanghai. The Jesuit, Lazarist, Dominican, and other European missionaries, with their Chinese colleagues, vigorously revived the Catholic communities in nearly every province, setting up schools by the score and baptizing converts by the thousand.

This still illegal but extensive Catholic activity in the interior was little known in the treaty ports and continued to meet sporadic persecution. It was far more massive and better organized than the Protestant missionary effort, in point of numbers, and yet represented a less acute cultural challenge to Chinese society. The Catholic priests dressed and lived in Chinese style, and their schools did not teach European languages, whereas the Protestant missionaries brought more of their material culture along with them and attacked Buddhist and Taoist "idols" and Chinese religious and social customs more directly.

Thus Catholic missions penetrated much further among the Chinese population, yet in the end the Protestants had the more revolutionary impact, because they presented a sharper and broader challenge to the Chinese way of life. It was typical of this early contrast that while the Rev. W. H. Medhurst, Sr., of the London Missionary Society, was adventurously traveling inland from Shanghai in disguise for seven weeks in 1845, two French Lazarists, Huc and Gabet, in the years 1844–46 traversed China from south to north, Inner Mongolia from east to west, and Tibet as far as Lhasa, before being expelled to the coast. Their remarkable journey remained an isolated feat, whereas the region surveyed by Medhurst became more and more caught up in the new growth of Shanghai, as a focal point of Sino-Western contact.

Protestantism was soon represented by a dozen major societies. Efforts at cooperation among them were only partly successful and produced, for example, two versions of the Scriptures and continued disputation over the "term question": for the Chinese translation of "God" the British generally preferred *Shang-ti* ("Lord on high") and the Americans, *Shen* ("Divine spirit"). The Catholic orders, quite separate from the Protestants, similarly competed among themselves within their framework of cooperation; but all used the term *T'ien-chu* ("Lord of Heaven").

Chinese Participation in the Western Impact. The Western influence at the new ports was felt most directly through the Cantonese who assisted their Western employers or patrons in their contact with Chinese life. Household servants, Chinese merchants in foreign legal trade, Chinese opium distributors, and even some Christian colporteurs (distributors of religious writings), all came at first from the regions of longest contact in the South, particularly Canton but also Malaya. Speaking a strange "dialect" (actually a different language) and organized in their own secret societies or regional guilds, the community of Cantonese who accompanied foreign merchants to Shanghai or Amoy, for example, constituted in themselves an unassimilable foreign element, often in competition with the local people. If they had established residence in Singapore or Hong Kong, they might carry certificates giving them the status of British subjects. If so, or if they were part of the foreign merchant "establishments" permitted at the ports by treaty, they could claim foreign protection under the principle of extraterritoriality. Often they wore Western-style clothes to advertise their privileged position. While some became the modernizers of China, others used their privileged status to pursue all sorts of skulduggery on the China coast.

In the late 1840's these Chinese in contact with foreign merchants helped to develop still another social evil in the form of the coolie trade, which shipped male laborers under contract, mainly from Amoy but also from Macao and other ports, to meet the demand for cheap labor in newly developing areas overseas such as Cuba, Peru, Hawaii, Sumatra, or Malaya. Chinese emigration to Southeast Asia had been going on for centuries, but several factors now combined to speed it up and widen the area it reached. One was the world-wide effort to abolish slavery, which had created a demand for contract labor as a substitute; another was the introduction of foreign shipping, both sail and eventually steam, which could land a cargo of coolies at Havana as quickly as a junk could land them at Palembang. In this new trade under foreign flags, Chinese "crimps" (procurers of laborers) inevitably committed excesses while recruiting and keeping in depots (barracoons) the human cargoes for shipment, just as some foreign vessels, aptly called "floating hells," came near to duplicating the crowded and horrible conditions of the earlier African-American slave trade. Efforts of the British and other governments to prevent abuses, by laws and by consular inspection of ships, lagged behind the growth of these evils. Here again the Ch'ing government's policy was to maintain the traditional ban on emigration, while doing nothing to enforce it. Discoveries of gold in California in 1848 and Australia in 1851 stimulated Chinese emigration to those places, but on a free basis, not as contract labor.

The repercussions of the new foreign trade on China's domestic handicraft economy are difficult to assess, but it seems plain that until much later in the century Western textile imports were unable to find much market in competition with China's domestic production of cotton goods. At mid-century British textiles found less sale in China than they did, for example, in the West Indies. On the other hand, the mounting exports of tea and silk stimulated these subsidiary farm handicraft industries in Central and South China.

The abolition of the Cohong monopoly at Canton, required by treaty, led to the growth of new institutions. The hong merchants were now supplanted by a new type of Chinese merchant, the comprador, who was employed on contract to handle the Chinese side of a foreign firm's activities. The comprador hired and guaranteed an entire Chinese staff of shroffs (specialists in the exchange and handling of money), servants, linguists, watchmen, and coolies. He also conducted the foreign firm's business with the Chinese mercantile community, securing commercial intelligence and buying and selling. All this trained him, in time, to become a modern entrepreneur in the new Chinese business class which began to grow up within the protection of the treaty ports and to extend its contact into the producing regions and markets of the interior. Thus the Chinese from the first participated in the modern economy of international trade that began to take shape on the coastal fringe of the Chinese empire.

THE RISE OF REBELLION

After 1850, peasant-based rebellions covered much of the eighteen provinces for the greater part of two decades. Considering the restricted scope of the Western impact before 1850, one can hardly conclude that it was the chief cause of these vast disorders. China's center of gravity still lay within, affected mainly by traditional influences. Yet the foreigners played a part in this era of rebellion, usually minor but sometimes of strategic importance.

Background Elements. By the late 1840's the general condition of China was plainly conducive to rebellion. Population, if we accept the trend of the official estimates, had continued to increase. Administration, judging by selected cases, had continued to deteriorate under the pressure of widespread official self-seeking in the face of ever-mounting administrative problems. Thus, for example, the accumulation of silt in the Yellow River and Grand Canal was not offset by the maintenance of dikes. The canal became less usable for grain transport. In 1852 the Yellow River finally broke loose with great damage and began a long, disastrous process of

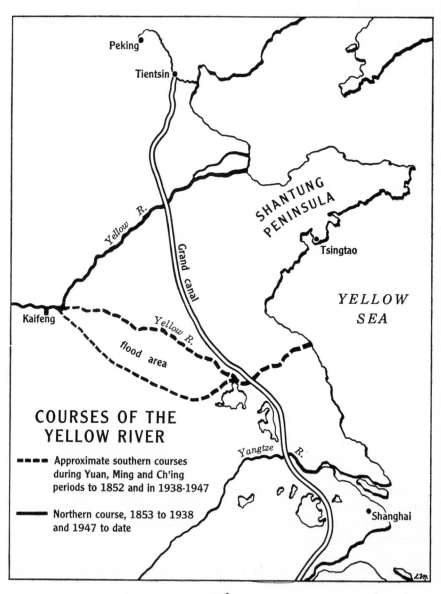

COURSES OF THE YELLOW RIVER

■■■■ Approximate southern courses
during Yuan, Ming and Ch'ing
periods to 1852 and in 1938-1947

━━━ Northern course, 1853 to 1938
and 1947 to date

shifting its main stream from the south to the north of the Shantung peninsula, the first such shift since 1194. Pressure of numbers, flood, famine, poverty, corruption and the resulting ineffectiveness of government were demonstrated in the increase of banditry, riots, and minor outbreaks in many areas. In varying degree secret societies were at work fomenting or capitalizing upon these disorders.

Disorder became most widespread in the late 1840's in South China — Kwangtung, Kwangsi, and southern Hunan. Imperial control of this region was diminished by two factors — first, it was the part of China conquered last and least dominated by the Ch'ing dynasty, farthest from Peking and garrisoned by Manchu bannermen only at Canton. Second, it included the Canton region, which had been longest subjected to the disturbing influences of foreign trade and Western contact, culminating in the opium traffic and the war with Britain.

As later events were to prove, Canton was the seedbed of modern Chinese nationalism, the focal point most stimulated by the Western example of patriotism and nationalistic interests. As the British invaders roused resentment by enforcing the "ransom" of Canton in 1841, the Manchu dynasty lost prestige by being unable to prevent it. When it became evident that this new alien power could make Peking dance to its tune, the dynasty seemed to many to be entering upon that irreversible process of political decline in which loss of moral prestige and the tacit consent of the populace lead a government to rule by ruthlessness toward the weak and appeasement of the strong, until everyone despises it and unites in destroying it. The Cantonese militia had been armed to repel the British, and felt in 1841 that they had done so single-handed. Although they were later dispersed by the Ch'ing government, they retained some military spirit and still harbored resentment against both the British and the Manchu appeasers of the British. The generally accepted theory of the Mandate of Heaven, which was supposed to sanction a regime as long as the people acquiesced in it, certainly eased the task of a strong government. But after unrest had reached a certain level, the same theory multiplied the difficulties of a weak government.

Economic factors were added to this political syndrome. The upsetting influence of foreign trade brought opportunity to some and both stimulus and frustration to others. On the long transport routes from Kiangsi and Hunan, over which thousands of coolies and boatmen carried the tea and silk export crops, secret societies could make themselves useful and powerful, while their members became dependent upon the steady flow of trade. However, because Shanghai was much closer to the districts of tea and silk production, its opening in 1843 had thrown transport gangs out of work on the routes to Canton. Finally, when the British navy began a program of pirate-suppression in 1849, its success forced pirate gangs to move inland from the coast, up the West River and into Kwangsi province, thus adding a further element of lawlessness to threaten this artery of trade.

The Founding of the Taiping Kingdom. As had been the case in most popular rebellions throughout Chinese history, a religious cult provided the fanatical basis of organization for the rebel movement that finally emerged in Kwangsi. The founder, Hung Hsiu-ch'üan (1814–1864), and his chief collaborators were Hakkas (in Peking pronunciation, *k'o-chia,* meaning "guest"), that is, members of a distinct linguistic group descended from North Chinese migrants who had settled many centuries earlier in large communities in South China and still retained their cultural identity. They were not fully assimilated and sometimes became involved in local friction with the "native" population. Hung was also a frustrated scholar, who had failed more than once in the Canton examinations. He was, finally, a mystic or, as his enemies put it, a madman — at any rate, an unstable personality — whose illness and religious experience convinced him that he was called upon to be a new messiah, a concept he picked up from Christianity.

It was largely an accident of history that Hung's religious cult was based nominally on the Protestant Bible, which reached him first in 1836 in the form of Chinese tracts written by the early convert Liang A-fa. Hung had a long delirium and saw visions. Subsequent reading of these tracts gave him the explanation: he had seen God and his own Elder Brother, Jesus Christ, for whom as the Heavenly Younger Brother he must now save mankind from the devil. Hung had some brief contact with Protestant missionaries at Canton (particularly the American, Issachar Jacox Roberts, who in 1847 refused to baptize him), but he put together his own religion, borrowing chiefly the militant teachings of the Old Testament rather than the loving-kindness of the New. The Ten Commandments, for example, were taken intact, but not the Sermon on the Mount.

The military organization of Hung's followers, after he had spent several years preaching his new faith, was actually carried out by one of his earliest disciples (Feng Yun-shan, 1822–1852) in conditions that were typical of the period. As the imperial officials lost their power to suppress bandits and settle disputes, local militia corps were commonly organized to maintain order. Usually they were sponsored, paid, and led by members of the gentry as the natural local leaders, but they could also be formed by secret societies or religious cults, who could develop similar sources of revenue from forced contributions, taxes, or rackets. The continued decline of central authority, however, soon set these local forces in competition. In addition to fighting off bandits, they fought local feuds against one another. Somewhat like the tribes of the steppe before the rise of a Chinggis Khan, these disparate militia units were susceptible of being swept up into a great expanding "horde." The unit into which Hung's disciple organized his followers in the late 1840's was called the "God Worshippers Society" (*Pai Shang-ti hui*). That this group was able to attract all manner of disaffected persons — Hakkas, Triad Society members, pirates, and homeless peasants — was a tribute to the faith and vigor of its leaders.

Hung and his young lieutenants began their armed resistance to imperial troops in July 1850 at the village of Chin-t'ien near their base, which was not far from Kuei-p'ing-hsien on the West River in Kwangsi. Expanding rapidly, in September 1851 they captured the departmental city of Yung-an to the north and there raised the banner of dynastic revolt. Hung took the title of Heavenly King (*T'ien-wang*)[1] of the "Heavenly Kingdom of Great Peace" (*T'ai-p'ing t'ien-kuo*). The term "Great Peace" (*T'ai-p'ing*) had been used in the Classics, by earlier rebels, and as a reign title in several Chinese dynasties, in addition to its new use to translate a Biblical phrase. The new dynasty issued its own calendar, different from both the Chinese lunar and the Western solar calendars.

By this time another leader had emerged in the person of a former charcoal dealer, Yang Hsiu-ch'ing (d. 1856). Yang became the Eastern King (*Tung-wang*) and commander-in-chief, while others became the Northern, Western, Southern, and Assistant Kings.

Besieged at Yung-an by imperial forces, the Taipings broke out in April 1852 and went north, acquiring cohorts as they went. Lacking artillery, they failed to take the provincial capitals of Kwangsi (Kweilin) and Hunan (Changsha) but seized the capital of Hupei (Wuchang) early in 1853 and descended the Yangtze in a great flotilla to Nanking, the second city of the empire, which they captured by assault in March 1853.

This remarkable success story was followed by a mixed record of ups and downs. Inadequate forces were sent toward Peking. Forced westward, they failed to take the capital of Honan (Kaifeng), went through Shansi into Chihli, but, harassed by the unaccustomed cold of the North China winter, were turned back near Tientsin late in 1853.

The Taipings had not set up administrative control over all the regions they traversed from Kwangsi northward. They lacked qualified personnel to install as officials in the local magistracies. First and last, their forces entered 16 of the 18 provinces and captured some 600 walled cities. But they could not administer what they conquered. Leaving both South and North China as secondary areas, they established themselves in the rich productive heartland along the Yangtze, pillaging city and countryside alike. They set up the traditional Six Boards or Ministries of central government at their capital, Nanking, but their regime seems to have been little more than a military administration in practice in the countryside.

1 *Wang*, the ancient term for king, had come to be used at Peking for imperial princes, as well as foreign rulers. In English the Taiping "kings" are sometimes called "princes."

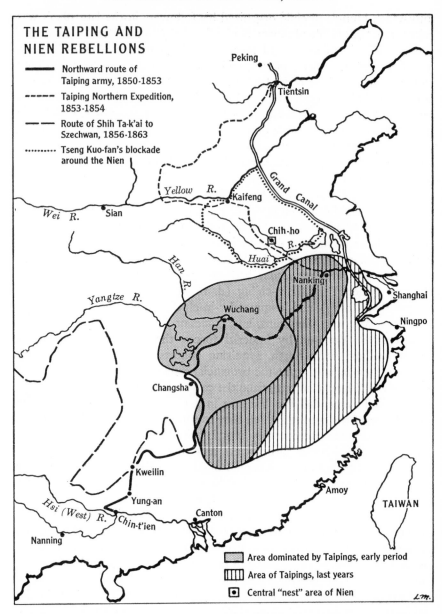

THE TAIPING AND NIEN REBELLIONS

— Northward route of Taiping army, 1850-1853

----- Taiping Northern Expedition, 1853-1854

— — Route of Shih Ta-k'ai to Szechwan, 1856-1863

.... Tseng Kuo-fan's blockade around the Nien

Area dominated by Taipings, early period

Area of Taipings, last years

Central "nest" area of Nien

The Taiping New Order. At Nanking the rebel regime was increasingly dominated by Yang Hsiu-ch'ing as prime minister and commander-in-chief, while Hung remained ensconced in the palace. Observers reported that Yang established strict discipline among the rebel horde and maintained for a time an egalitarian military-religious society. During this early period, men and women were strictly segregated and lived in separate barracks. Chastity was prescribed for the rank and file of both sexes under threat of execution. Women were organized into labor and even military battalions. Equality of the sexes was manifest in the abolition of foot-binding and the appointment of women as officers and administrators. The Taipings' puritanical zeal also set them against slavery, adultery, witchcraft, gambling, alcohol, opium, and tobacco. In defiance of the Manchu requirement that Chinese wear the queue and shave the forward part of their heads, they let their hair grow and so were called the "long-haired rebels." Their violent ethnic attack on the Manchus as non-Chinese released racial resentments which the Ch'ing rulers had tried for two centuries to keep suppressed.

Judging by the sacred books, hymns, proclamations, and other propaganda which they published, the Taipings' religion and ideology were a fascinating mixture of Christian and Chinese elements. God's second son, Hung, was hailed as a new Son of Heaven, appointed by the Mandate of Heaven. His followers preached to crowds and offered sacrifices to God; they destroyed idols and temples, Taoist, Buddhist, and Confucian; and their first moral precept was reverence for God, Jesus, and Hung. But their second moral precept was filial piety. The doctrine of the brotherhood of men, egalitarianism, was combined, paradoxically, with a society of hierarchy and status, in which the *li* or ancient principles of proper conduct were invoked to put everyone in his place by title, form of address, occupational class, and social relationships.

Much if not most of the Taiping system and credo came in fact from Chinese tradition. Since the Bible did not provide a detailed blueprint for the new society, Hung and Yang found their models in ancient Chinese works such as the classic *Rituals of Chou (Chou-li)*, a work compiled around the second century B.C. and representative of an early utopian strain in Chinese political thought. For example, the *Chou-li* had been cited by radical reformers like Wang Mang (in power A.D. 9–23) and Wang An-shih (1069–1074). This Chinese utopian tradition was reflected, along with certain Christian ideals, in the many regulations which the Taipings published in the early 1850's. Their ideal of brotherhood was expressed in a system of primitive economic communism. All persons were to contribute their possessions and services to a common treasury and receive their support from it. Both land and people were to be redistributed. Land holdings were to be classified in nine grades according to productivity, and farming households were to have equally productive allotments according to the number of household members. For this purpose every twenty-five families were to form a unit with a church and a public treasury under an officer, who was in charge of payments into and out of the common treasury, the religious devotions of the community, education of the youth, the judgment of disputes, and the military organization. Ideally every farmer was also a soldier and the government hierarchy was at once both civil and military. Equal land holdings, the groupings of families into mutually dependent units, and a peasant-militia were of course all old Chinese institutions.

Since in fact the Taipings did not set up a widespread territorial administration in the countryside, it is uncertain how far their program for equalization of land use was carried out in practice. Their blueprint for a new society was given effect mainly in the early years at Nanking and other cities of the Lower Yangtze region. From the beginning the egalitarian ideal was limited in operation, for each king built up his own palace, harem, administration, and military forces.

The mixture of Christian and Chinese concepts in the Taiping ideology is still being unraveled. Its Christian egalitarianism was confined within a hierarchic Chinese structure of authority and power. Yet Hung stressed the role of a personal and transcendent deity and so envisioned something quite different from the traditional Chinese state, with its rather rational claim to be based on the immanent order of nature. When an examination system was set up, for example, it used the classics of Taiping Christianity, including a Christian variant of the popular Confucian primer, the *Three-Character Classic (San-tzu ching;* see Vol. I, p. 307). This Taiping version, instead of commencing with the statement "At men's beginning, their nature is basically good," starts out with the declaration that "Almighty God created heaven and earth."

There is an obvious opportunity for comparison of the Taipings' new order with that inaugurated just a century later by the Chinese Communists. In addition to the zeal, vigor, and puritanical discipline so often found in new political movements, they shared certain traditional Chinese interests, such as propagating and maintaining doctrinal orthodoxy, recruiting an elite of talent, realizing a utopian social order, and developing military power based on farmer-soldiers. Furthermore, both made use of foreign ideologies which required translation into Chinese with inevitable modifications in the process. The fact that the differences are perhaps more numerous than the similarities should make comparison of the Taipings and Communists all the more interesting.

Strategic Weaknesses. The Taipings' general ignorance and genuine religious zeal gave them fanatical vigor but reduced the breadth of their appeal. Their anti-Manchu attack, which might have united many elements, was combined with attacks on Confucianism and the whole social order of the day. They repelled the conservative scholar-gentry class, yet failed to achieve an alliance with the rebellious Triad Society.

One of the Triad leaders (named, confusingly, Hung Ta-ch'üan but no relative of Hung Hsiu-ch'üan) seems to have been in their counsels, in the early days when the Taipings borrowed some Triad terminology; and many Triads joined the ranks. But the Taipings at Nanking did not succeed in helping Triads who engineered local rebellions at Amoy and Shanghai in 1853. A Triad offshoot, the Small Sword Society (*Hsiao-tao hui*) led by Cantonese and Fukienese at Shanghai, seized the walled Chinese city there in September and issued proclamations in the name of the Ming and also of the Taipings. But after seventeen months they were suppressed by imperial forces. Nanking had lent them no real support. In retrospect, the Taiping leaders seem to have underestimated the potential value of Shanghai as a source of foreign aid and made little effort to establish relations with Western governments or take advantage of foreign trade.

Meanwhile, jealousy among the kings who had been the original founders of the movement proved its undoing. The Machiavellian Yang Hsiu-ch'ing had from the first gained his power partly by going into trances and receiving visitations from God. Since the less devious Hung Hsiu-ch'üan, though he claimed to be the son of God, did not claim to receive similar communications, the word of God received through Yang was a potent force in the leaders' councils. At length Yang Hsiu-ch'ing, having brilliantly outmaneuvered the imperial forces outside Nanking, challenged Hung's superiority.

This produced a bloody purge in September 1856, when Hung got the Northern King (Wei Ch'ang-hui) to assassinate Yang. Seizing his chance, Wei went further and killed Yang's family and thousands of his followers. Hung soon felt obliged to have Wei assassinated in turn. Thereupon the one remaining original leader, the Assistant King (Shih Ta-k'ai), broke away with many followers on a long independent expedition (through areas in South and Southwest China later to be traversed by the Chinese Communists on their Long March in 1934–35). Hoping to set up a separate rebel kingdom in Szechwan, Shih Ta-k'ai finally was killed there in 1863.

His original lieutenants having all been removed, Hung now appointed mediocre relatives to govern his kingdom. The movement lost its spark, its early austerity gave way to profligacy and corruption, and it was saved only by the emergence of a new military genius in the person of Li Hsiu-ch'eng, who was given the title of Loyal King in 1859 and commanded the Taiping forces in their last years in the Lower Yangtze region (see page 174).

Confucian Support of the Ch'ing. It is amazing that, with rebellion arising in every province in the 1850's, the Ch'ing dynasty was able to survive and reassert itself. It was able to do so because it continued to monopolize the trained administrative talent, the men who knew how to govern, on the far-flung bureaucratic lines necessary in the Chinese empire. The loyalty of these men in turn was a tribute to the long-ingrained tradition of Chinese scholar government and to the achievement of the

K'ang-hsi Emperor and his successors in forging the unity of state and culture. The scholar class preferred Manchu rule on traditional lines to Chinese rule by heterodox rebels.

The military strategy against the Taipings was to hem them in, from both the Upper Yangtze (Hunan-Hupei) and the Lower Yangtze provinces. Imperial forces, mobilized on traditional lines from many sources, set up a Great Camp below Nanking and kept the rebels from controlling the coastal region. In the end, however, the Taipings were suppressed by new Chinese armies under Chinese scholar-official leadership, notably from Hunan province. The principal leader was Tseng Kuo-fan (1811–1872), whose career illustrates the whole process.

Tseng became a metropolitan graduate (*chin-shih*) in 1838, entered the top-ranking center of classical learning, the Hanlin Academy, and spent the next decade in high official and scholarly circles at Peking. In 1852 he was given the task of organizing a militia army to defend Hunan, his native province, incorporating militia corps that had already prevented the Taiping capture of the capital, Changsha. Tseng's success in this has been generally attributed, in rather Confucian terms, to his ethical vigor and his skill in training talented subordinates. He built his Hunan Army on Confucian principles, to defend China's traditional society and culture. Tseng had been an eclectic scholar, a student of both the Neo-Confucianism of the Sung and the newer Han Learning and an advocate of practical "statecraft" in administration. Not brilliant, but persistent, he first enlisted local gentry as officers personally loyal to himself. Then by discipline, training, and paternalism he built up the morale of their troops, inculcating as cardinal virtues (1) respect for superiors, (2) concern for the common people, and (3) cultivation of good habits.

The Hunan Army developed through several stages. First, it grew from a defensive into an offensive force when sent to save situations in other provinces. Second, it built and trained a naval arm for use on the Central China waterways. (Already imperialists and Taipings were competing to hire foreign steamers from Shanghai.) Third, Tseng refused to move out of Hunan prematurely, until in 1854 his forces recaptured Wuchang. Yet even at this date there was still no unity of command among the imperial forces and rebellion was still spreading.

The Rise of the Nien and Moslem Rebellions. Stimulated by the Taiping invasion of the Yangtze Valley in 1853 and its northern expedition toward Peking, a separate rebellion emerged in that year in the area west of the Grand Canal between the Huai and Yellow rivers (then in flood) in the southern part of the North China Plain. This region on the borders of four provinces (Kiangsu, Anhwei, Honan, and Shantung — see map) had long harbored secret-society bandit gangs called simply *nien* ("bands"), whose genealogy can be traced back to the White Lotus

Society in the late eighteenth century. Lacking major cities but with easy access in all directions, the area had been frequented by salt smugglers from the Ch'ang-lu district who competed with the government salt distribution from the Liang-Huai districts. Local clan and village feuds continually erupted, often involving a sizable and bellicose local minority of Chinese Moslems. In the early 1850's the whole region was beset by flood and therefore famine and refugees.

The *nien* bands had gradually accumulated and grown more active as the imperial power declined, and they finally achieved a degree of co-ordination after 1853 by selecting a top leader (Chang Lo-hsing). Several hundred local groups, based on their fortified, earth-walled villages, under local clan and village leaders, including some gentry degree-holders, thus supplanted the central government hierarchy of officials over a wide area. Following the custom of creating local militia corps for self-defense in times of disorder, they accumulated arms and horses, levied their own taxes, took care of the local food supply, and soon began to make cavalry raids to plunder adjoining regions.

The Nien movement was further organized in 1855 as an alliance of five main bands under yellow, white, blue, black, and red banners. Additional banner forces were soon added, to make a military structure reminiscent of the Manchu banner system. The leaders assumed titles (such as "Great Han Heavenly-mandated King" for Chang Lo-hsing), which suggested dynastic pretensions. They used secret symbols, esoteric terminology, blood oaths, and elaborate rituals in the secret society fashion. They also imitated the Taipings in wearing their hair long and in other aspects of terminology and organization. Nien and Taiping forces co-operated on many occasions. Yet the movement remained decentralized and never attempted to expand and take over big cities or set up a rival dynastic government. After the first large-scale outbreak in 1853, it developed only slowly and did not create an effective army, mainly cavalry, until early 1856. By degrees, however, the Nien leadership succeeded in establishing firm control, first over the local militia bands and then over the population and the food supply, in an area of perhaps 100,000 square miles. They also developed their contact with the Taipings, and by 1860 confronted the imperial government with still another region out of control, and the danger that the Nien and Taiping movements might join together.

An even more long-continued revolt against the Ch'ing central power arose in the most distant province of Yunnan. Islam had been firmly rooted in both Northwest and Southwest China ever since the Mongol period, and the Chinese Moslem minority in Yunnan still formed a distinct religious community and not infrequently fought with their non-Moslem neighbors. Friction was particularly rife in mining areas, where the dwindling resources of copper, tin, lead, and precious metals extractable by premodern mining methods were a bone of contention. The Ch'ing officials in this faraway mountain plateau were few and impotent. They proved quite unable to check disorders which began in 1855 under the leadership of the chief priest, or imam, Ma Te-hsin (the surname Ma, meaning "horse," was common among Chinese followers of Mohammed [Mahomet], the first syllable of whose name is transcribed with the same character). This devout and learned man had made his pilgrimage to Mecca, and even lived two years in Constantinople; he saw the Islamic faith as compatible with Confucian social teachings. In 1861 he was induced to return to an uncertain allegiance to the Ch'ing, together with many followers in eastern Yunnan.

In the western part of Yunnan, however, the revolt continued for another dozen years under a vigorous fighter, Tu Wen-hsiu. In 1856 he had made Tali (once capital of the medieval kingdom of Nan-chao) the capital of his new Islamic kingdom, which he called P'ing-nan ("Pacification of the South"), taking for himself the title of Sultan Suleiman. His rebel regime managed to get some arms through Burma (it is sometimes called the Panthay Rebellion, using a Burmese term meaning Moslem), and in 1872 even sent a vain mission to London seeking British help. Meantime another violent Moslem rising, beginning in 1862, had convulsed Northwest China (see page 323), while Miao tribesmen in the mountains of western Kweichow had been in rebellion ever since 1854.

Although these smaller movements — Nien, Moslem, and Miao — all lacked the size of the Taiping kingdom, they were a similar index to the collapse of the central power. The Ch'ing dynasty was now caught between the twin forces of "internal rebellion and foreign aggression" which had been the undoing of so many earlier regimes. While these inland rebels were proving unable to create institutions capable of supplanting the traditional system, the Westerners in the treaty ports were energetically seizing the opportunity to create a new order on the coast.

The Second Treaty Settlement

Compared with the fratricidal slaughter of millions and the wholesale destruction of cities and farming capital — such as the mulberry trees essential for silk culture — which attended the great rebellions, the Opium War with its few thousands of casualties had been a very small affair indeed. It was important more for what it represented, an alien challenge to the established traditional order, than for its concrete impact. Similarly the opium trade, the missionary movement, and the early treaty ports all began on a rather small scale. They did not directly affect the lives of ordinary Chinese, but by calling the old order into question they began the long-term process of undermining the institutions of Chinese society.

Yet in the short term the foreign diplomatic influence was not always revolutionary. On the contrary, one of the great issues of China's modern history is the question how far the Western powers after 1860 may have inhibited political change by propping up the faltering Ch'ing dynasty. In the decade from the rise of rebellion in 1851 to 1860, the Western powers moved from a policy of negotiation to one of coercion and then, having secured the Second Treaty Settlement, from coercion to cooperation with the dynasty.

The Growth of Shanghai. During the 1850's the disintegration of the central government's control of the local scene, in the treaty ports as in the provinces of the vast interior, led to the rise of local power-holders. In the case of the ports, however, the foreign consuls, instead of creating Chinese-type administrative agencies of the kind set up by the various rebel regimes or the gentry leaders of the interior, created new Western-type agencies of their own (see map, page 341).

At Shanghai the foreign settled areas, outside the walled district (*hsien*) city, were flooded with refugees after the Taipings took Nanking in March 1853. In the following September when the Small Sword Society seized the walled city, the imperial custom house was put out of action and the imperial officials, from the taotai on down, were ousted from Shanghai. The adjoining foreign settlement organized its own local militia of Western merchants, the Shanghai Volunteer Corps, and with its gunboats close at hand in the Whangpu River became an armed camp in self-defense. In July 1854 the foreign consuls of Britain, the United States, and France joined in getting the taotai's consent to new regulations which set up a degree of self-government and formed the basis for the later growth of the International Settlement and French Concession, with their own powers of local taxation and upkeep of roads and municipal police. Thus the future center of China's modernization at the entrance to the Yangtze Valley became a semi-foreign city run by the local foreign land-renters under the protection of their treaty rights of extraterritoriality.

This was not the only institutional innovation. In the absence of the imperial custom house, the British consul, Rutherford Alcock, had felt obliged in 1853 to maintain the collection of duties due by treaty, so as to forestall the Chinese collection of duties on foreign trade in the interior beyond foreign view. The whole idea of a treaty tariff, known to all and equally enforced, had proved generally unworkable in the face of corrupt collusion between Chinese customs collectors and competing foreign merchants. Yet without equal terms of taxation, the Western principle of free trade and the secure growth of legal commerce would be jeopardized if not nullified. Alcock and his American and French colleagues therefore arranged that their nominees should serve the taotai as his customs collectors, seeing to it that the foreign merchants were impartially assessed and also ensuring that the taotai would receive the revenue. This was agreed to in July 1854 by the Shanghai taotai Wu Chien-chang, who was actually the former Canton hong merchant Samqua and had a great reputation as an "expert on the barbarians." From this beginning grew the Foreign Inspectorate of Customs, under which after 1855 an Englishman (Horatio Nelson Lay) was employed by the Chinese government, as a private individual unconnected with any foreign government, to assess the customs duties due from China's foreign trade.

Neither the International Settlement nor the Foreign Inspectorate, we may imagine, would have been created in more normal times of strong Chinese administration. Under pressure of a crisis, they were a joint product of the British instinct for local *ad hoc* arrangements and Chinese resilience in cooperating with powerful aliens on the frontier.

Origins of the Anglo-French War with China. China's foreign trade in tea, silk, and opium continued even as rebellion spread more widely. Teas from Central China formerly exported through Canton were now sent out through Shanghai and, from 1854, through Foochow. As Canton lost its pre-eminence in foreign trade, antiforeign feeling mounted. The Ch'ing attitude toward Western relations also hardened, following the example of the popular hostility led by the gentry at Canton. Westerners were still excluded from the walled city there, and this became a bone of contention, an issue of "face," between Britain and China.

In 1847 the British tried coercion. Their local forces in a sudden raid fought their way up-river to the Canton factories outside the walls and before withdrawing secured a promise of future entrance to the city. This accomplished nothing, however, except to damage both the prestige of the British when they withdrew and that of the chief negotiator of the treaties, the Manchu Ch'i-ying, who was recalled in 1848. The new Hsien-feng Emperor, who ascended the throne in 1850, opposed Western contact and was in any case absorbed in meeting the spread of revolt. The fact of revolt also deterred Lord Palmerston in London. In 1851 he was ready to coerce China again to gain broader trading privileges. But he recognized that foreign aggression might add to domestic disorder and so hinder foreign trade rather than help it, and in any case the Crimean War absorbed Britain's energies until 1856.

The Christian aspect of the Taiping movement at first inspired missionary observers with the hope that the "servants of God" were going to take over China. When a scholarly British intelligence officer (Thomas Taylor Meadows) saw the Northern King (Wei Ch'ang-hui) in 1853 and recited the Ten Commandments to him, Wei "laid his hand on my shoulder in a friendly way and exclaimed 'The same as ourselves! the same as ourselves!'" But further foreign inquiries revealed that the Taiping religion was a far cry from Christianity. It also appeared unlikely that the Taiping rule would foster Western contact and trade any more than the Ch'ing, and the Western powers therefore maintained neutrality toward the civil conflict.

In 1854 Britain, the United States, and France tried to negotiate treaty revisions with Peking, on grounds that illustrate the working of the most-favored-nation clause: the American treaty of 1844 called for revision in twelve years (i.e., 1856), the second British treaty of 1843 promised Britain equally favorable treatment, the first British treaty of 1842 should therefore be revised in 1854, and so therefore should the American treaty of 1844. This legalism availed nothing, in pourparlers at Canton, Shanghai, and off Tientsin. Negotiation was refused or evaded, while occasional popular attacks on Western nationals raised the issue of foreign prestige. This revived the old question: which mode of Sino-foreign relations was to prevail, the Chinese or the Western?

During these years the selfsame Western diplomats and naval officers who were active in China were busy opening Japan, under a similar treaty system. Commodore Perry's squadron wintered at Hong Kong in 1853–54 (see Chapter 3). His treaty with Japan in 1854 and the second American treaty of 1858 were in each case followed by Japanese treaties with the other powers — Britain, Russia, and the Netherlands, and (in 1858 only) France. The Western nations were in a mood to press their claims for further contact with China on Western terms.

Convinced that the treaty system would deteriorate in China if not reaffirmed and extended, Palmerston finally found a *casus belli* in 1856, when the contumelious governor-general at Canton (Yeh Ming-ch'en) refused to give Consul Harry Parkes redress for an insult to a British flag lowered by Chinese police from a Chinese-owned vessel registered at Hong Kong, the lorcha *Arrow*. (A lorcha was a vessel with Western hull and Chinese rig, widely used on the China coast.) In the same year a French missionary (Chapdelaine), seized as a foreign subversive out of bounds in an area of rebellion, was judicially tortured and killed in Kwangsi. The government of Napoleon III found in this a basis for French cooperation with Britain to coerce the Chinese empire.

The Anglo-French expedition nominally originated in these rather small incidents, in which the rights of the matter were certainly debatable. Nevertheless the underlying issue was clear-cut. It was a conflict of wills as to whether the Western invasion of the ancient Middle Kingdom should continue along the lines already set by the first treaties. In the 1850's the mood of China's hard-pressed rulers was to answer "No." They were unable even to consider the one feasible alternative to the treaty system, that they should themselves undertake a radical remaking and modernization of Chinese life in all its aspects. As the first move in such a revolution, they would have had to scrap much of the political and intellectual tradition of two thousand years.

Hostilities and Negotiations, 1856–1860. Consul Parkes and his colleagues knew what they wanted — the capitulation of the Son of Heaven at Peking — but it took them four years to get it. Parkes began in October 1856 by having the British navy fight its way up to Canton, as it had done several times before, and bombard Governor-General Yeh Ming-ch'en's yamen with one gun at ten-minute intervals, but to no avail.[1] The expeditionary force from England was delayed by the Sepoy Mutiny, which broke out in India in May 1857, and Canton was not seized, along with Yeh Ming-ch'en, until the beginning of 1858. Yeh was shipped to Calcutta, while Parkes installed the Chinese governor of Kwangtung as his puppet to govern the city under an allied commission.

Aiming at the emperor, the Anglo-French negotiators (Lord Elgin and Baron Gros) took their forces direct to Tientsin and there in June 1858 secured their treaties, which provided that their ministers could reside at Peking on terms of diplomatic equality. The American and Russian plenipotentiaries went along with them as "neutrals" and secured almost identical treaties covering nearly every point the Western powers demanded.

Permanent Western legations at Peking would end the ancient tradition of China's superiority. After the Western fleets and diplomats had gone away, the Ch'ing court became increasingly determined not to concede this point, even though it had been accepted by the Ch'ing negotiators at Tientsin. When the British and French ministers arrived off Tientsin a year later, in June 1859, to go to Peking and exchange treaty ratifications, they were refused passage. Trying to force a passage up the river at Taku, they were repulsed by the Taku forts. Four British gunboats were unexpectedly sunk with many casualties.

Elgin and Gros therefore had to return again in 1860 with stronger forces. For this final showdown the British brought to North China 41 warships, 143 troop transports, 10,500 troops (including Sikh cavalry and other Indian forces), and a coolie corps of 2500 Cantonese. The French brought 6300 troops and more than 60 ships but lacked horses for transport. Advancing on Peking, the allies defeated much larger imperial forces under the Mongol commander-in-chief, Prince Senggerinchin (Seng-ko-lin-ch'in) and entered Peking in October, the emperor having fled beyond the Wall to Jehol.

The settlement at Peking was attended by many complications. Anglo-French rivalry and friction were intense in European diplomacy at this time and were not diminished by the French thirst for national glory, in the absence of any commercial interest in China. Lord Elgin, coming out from England, was also trying to restrain the expansionist demands of the "old China hands" like Consul Harry Parkes. A serious complication arose when Parkes was seized while under a flag of truce for negotiating.

[1] As a Cantonese jingle later described the obdurate Yeh Ming-ch'en: "He would not fight, he would not make peace, and he would not make a defense. He would not die, he would not surrender, and he would not run away."

Some twenty men in his party were executed before Parkes was released three weeks later. Elgin consequently took reprisal against the emperor personally by destroying his summer palace of some two hundred buildings northwest of Peking (the Yüan Ming Yüan), which had already been looted by the invading forces and by Chinese villagers.

Short of ammunition and faced with the onset of winter, the allies had to get a quick settlement and withdraw their forces. Elgin and Gros exchanged ratifications of the 1858 treaties and signed new conventions with the emperor's brother, Prince Kung, who now represented the dynasty. These documents confirmed the treaties of 1858, increased their indemnities, and added certain other concessions. Thus Britain secured the Kowloon Peninsula opposite Hong Kong. France obtained by a subterfuge the right for Catholic missions to hold property in the interior, as well as the restitution of all properties formerly confiscated.

The second treaty settlement of 1858–60, combined with tariff negotiations concluded at Shanghai in 1858, had the general effect of opening the whole Chinese empire to Western contact. Without introducing any radically new principles, it enlarged the scope and character of the foreign privileges that had been developed under British leadership at the five early treaty ports. By the most-favored-nation principle, Russia also secured these privileges, but meanwhile her envoys had also been active elsewhere.

The Russian Advance in Manchuria. Five days after the British and French envoys left Peking in November 1860, a skillful Russian negotiator secured there the territorial cession of the east coast of Manchuria. This diplomatic triumph, unexpected by the Western powers, came as the climax of a decade of energetic Russian expansion in Northeast Asia, but this activity had been preceded by a long period of inaction during the late eighteenth and early nineteenth centuries.

In the Sino-Russian treaties of 1689 and 1727 the Ch'ing emperors had succeeded in keeping the Russians out of the Amur watershed and on the far outer frontier of Mongolia. This achievement had diverted Russian expansion to other parts of Asia. In the early eighteenth century under Peter the Great, the Russians had continued their explorations of Siberia and the founding of trading posts. Vitus Bering discovered Alaska in 1741, Russian posts were established on Kamchatka and in the Aleutian Islands, and Russian contact began with Japan. In 1799 the Russian-American Company was chartered to keep up with the British East India Company by monopolizing and expanding Russian trade in the Pacific; from 1812 to 1839 it even maintained an outpost in California, not far north of the Spaniards at San Francisco. Meanwhile, from 1727 until after 1860, a regular Sino-Russian trade was carried on at the Chinese border town of Mai-mai-ch'eng in Outer Mongolia opposite the Russian town of Kiakhta, not far from Lake Baikal. As we have noted (page 51), this was a controlled and licensed trade, in many ways not unlike that at Canton, though conducted on the distant opposite border of the empire.

Although trading missions ceased going to Peking, the Russian ecclesiastical mission had continued there with four priests and half a dozen language students. This mission became an important center of Chinese studies. The early Russian sinologue, the Archimandrite Palladius (1817–1878), arrived in Peking under its auspices in 1840. The mission was also a point of semi-official contact, and continued to maintain a quiet existence down to 1860. Sino-Russian trade, however, remained inhibited by the great distance across Siberia and the lack of any nearby Russian economic base.

The opening of the treaty ports had coincided with a continued Russian advance into Central Asia west of the Pamirs, in the area soon to be known as Russian Turkestan (as opposed to Chinese Turkestan east of the Pamir massif). During the eighteenth century the Russians had steadily advanced into this area under Peter and Catherine the Great and their successors, setting up fortified lines of outposts against the mobile Kirghiz and Kazakh tribes of the steppe. These outposts soon extended from the Caspian Sea north to Orenburg and thence east along the Irtysh River in a broad arc. By degrees this arc was steadily pushed southward. On this frontier Russian trade developed with Chinese Turkestan as well as with the khanates of Khiva, Bokhara, and Samarkand (see map on page 16).

In 1851 a Sino-Russian treaty was signed at Kuldja, the main city of the Ili region, to regulate trade there on the lines already established at the more easterly mart at Kiakhta. In brief, the Russian trading caravans and merchants were to be carefully regulated as to routes, seasons, factories, residences, etc., but were to be under the control of their own consul at Kuldja. The agreement was in general on terms of equality and reciprocity, such as seem to have characterized the contact between the Ch'ing and Russian empires, particularly on this far frontier where both were conquering powers and had some community of interest against the warlike local tribes.

Against this background of expansion elsewhere and stimulated by the British success in China, the Russians began a second invasion of the Amur watershed, from which they had had to withdraw in the seventeenth century. This new move was led by a vigorous proconsul, Nikolai Muraviev, who was appointed governor-general of Eastern Siberia in 1847. After some preliminary exploration and establishment of posts on the Pacific coast of Manchuria, he sent Russian flotillas of barges down the Amur in 1854 and the years following, founding posts on the north bank all the way down to Khabarovsk, where the Ussuri River enters the Amur. Russian troops and settlers soon created a position of strength with which the local Ch'ing officials could not contend. On May 16, 1858, even before the Anglo-French treaties of that year were concluded at Tientsin, Muraviev secured a treaty at Aigun, on the middle course of the Amur, which ceded to Russia the north bank of that river and left China and Russia in joint possession of the territory between the Ussuri and the sea, pending its further disposition. Thus Muraviev's program of occupying sparsely populated frontier areas to achieve a *fait accompli* gained its first success and won support also from his own, hitherto reluctant, government in St. Petersburg (see map, page 47).

The Russian Treaty of Tientsin in June 1858, though it gained all the Western trading privileges, had left the question of the east coast of Manchuria unsettled. It remained for a clever diplomat, General Nikolai Ignatiev, to consolidate Russia's Far Eastern gains in 1860. This was all the more necessary after Peking decided in 1859 to reject the Treaty of Aigun.

In his negotiations Ignatiev used several stratagems. Reaching Peking on June 27, 1859, just after the Ch'ing victory over the British gunboats and landing party at Taku, he took up residence at the Russian ecclesiastical mission and negotiated fruitlessly for several months. On the approach of the Anglo-French expedition of 1860, he went to Shanghai and by his knowledge of Peking ingratiated himself with the other Western plenipotentiaries.

By the time the allies had fought their way to the capital, with Ignatiev in their train, he was in a position to mediate, to Russia's advantage, between them and the Ch'ing court. The Sino-Russian Treaty of Peking of November 1860, signed after the British and French had departed, was his reward for mediating as well as a confirmation of the Russian *fait accompli*. It confirmed the Treaty of Aigun and in addition gave Russia the Maritime Province between the Ussuri and the Pacific, where Muraviev had already founded Vladivostok (meaning in Russian "Rule of the East") in July 1860.

Thus the Ch'ing empire had barely been opened to trade and evangelism by the Western powers when Russia began the process of its territorial dismemberment.

THE RESTORATION OF THE CH'ING GOVERNMENT

To overcome the evils of domestic disorder and foreign invasion, the Chinese state required strong leadership at the top, but for this exacting task the Taiping rebels had early proved unprepared and ineffective — Heaven's Mandate never really came within their reach. The only hope of re-establishing peace and order remained at Peking.

Here a genuine "restoration" occurred, a revival of dynastic leadership such as had taken place before in Chinese history after devastating rebellions, notably in the founding of the Eastern Han (A.D. 25–57) and at the time of the An Lu-shan rebellion in the middle T'ang (see pages 327 ff.; also Vol. I, pp. 123 and 193).

This revival of imperial leadership coincided with several turning points in the struggles of the time — first of all, in the campaign against the rebels. In 1860 the imperial forces' Great Camp below Nanking was destroyed for a second time, by the vigorous Taiping commander Li Hsiu-ch'eng, and this disaster forced the Ch'ing court finally to give Tseng Kuo-fan unified command over the whole campaign of suppression. In August 1860 he was appointed governor-general and imperial commissioner with top military and civil authority over the middle and lower Yangtze provinces. He installed able subordinates as governors of key provinces (Hu Lin-i in Hupei, Tso Tsung-t'ang in Chekiang, and Li Hung-chang in Kiangsu), and with this new, better-organized effort finally began to hem in the rebel forces.

Meanwhile another corner was turned in the autumn of 1860 when the Anglo-French capture of Peking broke the back of the die-hard war party within the Ch'ing court, and the emperor's brother, Prince Kung, emerged to conclude the treaty settlement. Warfare having failed, appeasement of the foreign invaders by accepting the treaty system was now acknowledged to be the only possible way to save the dynasty.

Finally, the antiforeign Hsien-feng Emperor died in August 1861, and by a *coup d'état* his brother, Prince Kung, and the young Empress Dowager, Tz'u-hsi, mother of the new boy-emperor, came into power (see page 321). Executing rival princes who had been more antiforeign, they gave the new reign strong Manchu leadership along two main lines: in foreign affairs, to cooperate warily in the working of the treaty system; in domestic affairs, to continue to give full confidence and support to Tseng Kuo-fan and his lieutenants in the suppression of rebellion. As Prince Kung put it, the rebels were a disease in China's vitals, the barbarians an affliction only of the limbs. It was more important to put down the rebellion than to keep out the foreigners. The new reign was called *T'ung-chih*, meaning (from a passage in the *Classic of Documents*) "Union for Order."

Foreign Aid and the End of the Taiping Kingdom. To assist the Hunan Army, Tseng assigned to his able young disciple Li Hung-chang (1823–1901) the task of building up as a counterpart the Anhwei Army, a similar regionally-based gentry-led striking force. Whereas the Hunan Army was already declining in power, because of its long-continued losses and inadequate financial support, Li succeeded in moving his new Anhwei Army, on foreign-rented steamers and with gentry-merchant support, into Shanghai in April 1862. Confirmed as governor of Kiangsu, he gradually entrenched himself in the Yangtze delta rice-basket. Here, in addition to the tribute grain collections, he was able by degrees to get some control over the Maritime Customs revenues and to collect taxes on the commerce of the whole Shanghai area, including Liang-Huai salt. Thus financed, he purchased foreign arms and built his Anhwei Army up to 70,000 men, the most powerful force in China. Meantime he and Tseng set up arsenals to make Western guns and steamships, thus inaugurating the movement for "self-strengthening" (*tzu-ch'iang*), to make China strong by borrowing Western technology, which was to be the main slogan of Chinese foreign policy for the next thirty years. In the process first of suppressing rebels and second of "self-strengthening," Tseng and Li got their own men into power and built up a personal bureaucratic machine entrenched in the Yangtze provinces.

One impetus for the borrowing of Western arms was given by the example of a foreign-officered mercenary force at Shanghai. This began as a sort of local corps made up of foreign adventurers, paid for by Chinese merchants in foreign trade (who now represented large economic interests) and led by Frederick Townsend Ward of Salem, Massachusetts. When Ward achieved his first success against the Taipings in mid-1860, the Western powers were still maintaining neutrality, officially opposed to the use of Western arms, steamships, or adventurers by either side. The last great outbreak of the rebellion, however, brought Taiping forces to the outskirts of Shanghai early in 1862. Abandoning neutrality, Britain and France now cooperated with the Ch'ing military in defense of the area around the treaty ports of Shanghai and Ningpo. Instead of a foreign legion, Ward now trained a small Chinese force of about 4000 men, whose Western arms, high morale, and use of amphibious tactics of maneuver on the waterways of the Yangtze delta won more than a hundred engagements and brought them the name of "Ever-Victorious Army."

After Ward's death in 1862, Major Charles George Gordon, lent from the British army, eventually succeeded to the command, receiving, like Ward, Chinese military rank under Governor Li Hung-chang. "Chinese" Gordon and his small Sino-foreign army helped capture Soochow late in 1863. A similar Franco-Chinese force helped Tso Tsung-t'ang recapture Hangchow.

Finally, in July 1864, Nanking was taken by Tseng Kuo-fan's younger brother (Tseng Kuo-ch'üan), with no foreign assistance, after desperate fighting and much use of siege works, tunnels, mines, and explosive shells. Thus the rebel kingdom came to a bloody end. This massive movement, with all its early vigor and idealism, had lacked adequate leadership and had stumbled blindly into dissension, corruption, and final defeat. Hung Hsiu-ch'üan died before Nanking was taken, and Li Hsiu-ch'eng, the Loyal King, who had fought so well for a lost cause, was executed.

Some have concluded that the Ch'ing dynasty, after it agreed to the treaty settlement of 1860, was saved from defeat only by Western aid.

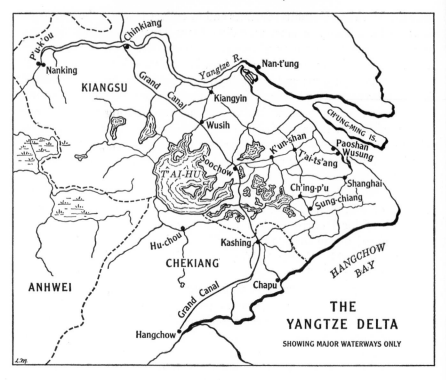

THE
YANGTZE DELTA
SHOWING MAJOR WATERWAYS ONLY

This view gained credence originally because in the final years of the rebellion the fighting near the treaty ports by British and French forces, as well as the exploits further inland of foreign-officered Chinese contingents like the spectacular "Ever-Victorious Army," were well publicized and loomed large in the Western view. At the same time, the military leadership of the Loyal King, his ability in conciliating the populace and organizing the Taipings' final bid for victory, seemed to put the outcome of the war much in doubt.

This raises a large question that cannot yet be answered, as to Western influence upon the whole course of the rebellion. Perhaps, if it had not had its own peculiar version of Christianity, the rebel cause might have been more successful in recruiting Chinese support. In this respect the Western influence of Christianity was a negative factor. At any rate, for several years the Taipings had the opportunity to enlist foreign aid while the Western powers were, part of the time, actually at war with the Ch'ing government; yet the opportunity was never taken. In the end it was the large Chinese armies mobilized under Tseng that did the great bulk of the fighting against the rebels. Chinese use of foreign forces was kept carefully limited. As an imperial edict put it in 1862, "For the time being, we have to make use of foreigners to train our soldiers, as a scheme for self-strengthening. . . . It would be better to select our own officers and order them to learn the military methods of foreign countries."

On balance, the real Western aid to the Ch'ing cause seems to have come less through the intervention of foreigners than through the Chinese leaders' own use of foreign trade revenues and of Western guns, ships, and training, in the spirit of "self-strengthening." We may conclude that the Manchu dynasty was saved by Chinese scholar-officials who were loyal to it as part of the Confucian order, and who found Western aid increasingly useful for their own purposes in the final years of their long-continued effort. It is noteworthy in this connection that the other mid-century rebellions — of the Nien (1853–1868) and of the Moslems in the Southwest (1855–1873) and in the Northwest (1862–1873) — were all suppressed without Western participation but with some use of modern arms (see Chapter 5).

The Opening of China. The suppression of the Taiping Rebellion followed soon after China's acceptance of the second treaty settlement. Together, these events gave the Western powers a stake in the established order in China, for they were now part of it. In the early 1860's they moved quickly to develop the opportunities they had acquired.

To facilitate trade, eleven more treaty ports were eventually opened, including places in North China and Manchuria, on Taiwan, and up the Yangtze as far as Hankow. Foreign vessels continued to participate in the domestic carrying trade among Chinese coastal and river ports, a right denied foreigners in most countries. The import of opium was legalized on payment of a moderate duty. Foreign imports of all kinds were allowed to pass freely in the interior on payment of a further transit duty of 2½ per cent ad valorem, which was half the import tariff duty. Thus they could compete with native products. The regulating of foreign trade was handled by an extension of the Shanghai Foreign Inspectorate system, which created the Chinese Imperial Maritime Customs Service as a foreign-staffed arm of the Peking government.

Travel in the interior under passport, permitted to all treaty-power nationals, now gave the missionaries access to the entire population. Both Catholics and Protestants soon began to acquire and use new property in the interior. Christian converts came more and more under foreign protection.

Behind all these opportunities for merchant and missionary expansion stood the established power of the Western nations, led by Britain. Their ministers at Peking, backed by gunboats in the ports, had the primary function of enforcing treaty rights. The long-term result was a great intensification of the Western challenge to the Chinese scheme of things. The new "barbarians" were now truly within the gates. The old Chinese civilization was grievously threatened.

China, however, had not yet responded to this threat in nationalistic terms. The tribute system had been destroyed but the treaty system constructed in its place was only a part-way step toward modern international relations. In some ways it was curiously reminiscent of the Chinese empire's traditional polity — under extraterritoriality, treaty-power nationals were added to, but did not displace, the privileged Manchu-Chinese ruling class. The traditional Chinese state and social order, which had accommodated alien rulers so often before, remained intact. In the long view of Chinese history, the very competitiveness of the Europeans seemed to give the dynasty an opportunity for manipulating these aggressors against one another. None of them could rule China directly. After 1864 the Ch'ing dynasty thus had a reprieve and China an opportunity to modernize in self-defense with Western help.

3

Japan's Response to the West

JAPANESE RESPONSIVENESS

The uninterrupted interest of Europeans, ever since the late Ming dynasty, in trade and missionary activity in China was not paralleled by a similar interest in Japan. In 1639 Japan adopted a policy of strictly limited contact with the outside world, and thereafter all but dropped out of the consciousness of Occidentals. Even the Catholic missionaries eventually gave up their fruitless attempts to re-enter the country, and few Western ships reached Japanese waters. The only important exception was the annual Dutch vessel from Indonesia to the Dutch trading post on the island of Deshima in Nagasaki harbor. This Dutch trade, some carefully controlled commerce with Chinese merchants at Nagasaki, and a restricted flow of trade by way of the island of Tsushima to Korea and through the Ryūkyūs to China, formed the only contact between Japan and the outside world. Europeans simply accepted the inaccessibility of the islands as a fact of political geography. Absorbed in their expansion into other, much larger areas in Asia, they came to regard Japan as a small, poor country of little interest.

But in the closing years of the eighteenth century and the first half of the nineteenth, the increased activity in China was reflected in a sharp

DAIMYO WITH SAMURAI. Detail from a contemporary engraving.

increase in Western pressures on Japan. Now, after a century and a half of Japanese isolation, Western ships began to appear in Japanese waters. Soon the nations of the West were demanding that the Japanese follow China and open their country to commercial and diplomatic relations. This was eventually achieved through the establishment of much the same unequal-treaty system as had been imposed on China. Commodore Perry of the United States led the way by facing the Japanese with unchallengeable naval power in 1853 and extracting from them the next year a treaty of friendship and limited trade relations. Then in 1858 the American consul, Townsend Harris, concluded a treaty opening Japan fully to trade. Both of these American treaties were followed by similar ones with the other interested Western nations.

As compared with the Chinese experience, however, the initial impact of the West on Japan in the middle of the nineteenth century was gentle. No wars were fought, no smuggling trade developed, no territory was forfeited. Not a single man was killed on either side during Perry's expedition to Japan, and the commercial treaties were negotiated amicably around a table. And yet Japan's response was far quicker and greater than that of China. Within a decade of the signing of the Harris treaty, the Japanese government had fallen, to be replaced by a regime of a radically different sort. Within another decade the whole feudal system of seven centuries' standing had been swept into the discard, and Japan was well launched on a series of astonishing reforms that were soon to make it a modern power.

This startling paradox — that Japan's greater response followed a less violent impact than in China — has posed difficult questions of historical interpretation. What forces at work in Japan produced so great a ferment? Obviously Japan in the mid-nineteenth century, even though it had derived a large part of its higher culture from China, was a very different country, capable of very different responses to the Western challenge.

Predisposing Factors. Insularity had from early times made the Japanese very much aware of their cultural and technological borrowings from the continent, even though the sum of such borrowings was probably no greater and possibly considerably less than in other countries of comparable size. Having early sent missions overseas to borrow from T'ang China, the Japanese were aware that useful things could be learned from abroad, and so found it easy to accept the idea of learning from the West. The Chinese normally assumed the opposite, and therefore were slow to appreciate what might be learned from the "barbarian" Occident.

The geographical isolation of Japan, as well as its distinctive language and feudal society, had also made the Japanese acutely aware that despite their heavy cultural debt to China they were a separate ethnic and political entity. In short, they already had a strong sense of separate identity which amounted to a feeling of nationalism. They assumed a plurality of countries in the world and made no claim to universal rule. In the nineteenth century, while the Chinese found the multi-state, international system of Europe wholly unacceptable, the Japanese could quickly understand and accept it, and begin to act accordingly.

The organization of their society also gave the Japanese a greater propensity to respond to Western influences. The hierarchical, feudal society of Japan was bound by vertical ties of loyalty. These reached from shogun to daimyo to samurai, and even in a sense to peasants who felt obligated to their superiors for benefits received. The actual social ties were reinforced by the Confucian ethic prescribing duties according to status and by the Japanese emphasis on reciprocal obligations. This pyramidal structure of loyalties had created a unifying, centripetal political tendency, visible since the sixteenth century, that was held in check only by the Tokugawa decentralization of power within the system of feudal fiefs, or *han*.

In China, by contrast, though the top level of administrative organization under the emperor was more centralized, loyalties even within the bureaucracy were more diffuse: obligations to family or to local community competed with duty to emperor and to society. The Chinese commitment to their traditional way of life, their "culturalism," served less well than Japanese feudal loyalty (even in the less centralized Tokugawa state) to produce the unity necessary for a modern nation.

The feudal character of Japanese society also led to a different appreciation of Confucianism than in China. The Japanese accepted the metaphysical and ethical system of Sung China, Chu Hsi's Neo-Confucianism. But China since the Sung dynasty had interpreted the Confucian Classics in such a way as to reconcile them with bureaucratic government. Japan rejected this interpretation and emphasized the "feudal" character of the ideal society depicted by the sages. This they saw as very similar to their own Tokugawa society. Thus the Classics were put to different uses in the two countries.

In Japanese feudal society, status depended overwhelmingly on birth, and yet the Confucian political and social doctrines which permeated Japanese thinking asserted the moral potential inherent in all men. The contrast between hierarchic feudalism and some of the egalitarian doctrines of Buddhism was even greater. Thus there was not the same unity of theory and practice as in China and hence perhaps less stability. Ambitious men, if denied high status, would seek distinction through achievement. The energies that such stirrings produced were all the more dynamic because they were channeled within and subordinated to the ends of the group. In sociological terms, the Japanese can be called goal-oriented, the Chinese status-oriented. This is one reason why, in the face of the Western menace in the nineteenth century, many Chinese tried to control the situation by playing traditional roles, while the Japanese generally reacted by seeking specific objectives.

Another difference was evidenced in the greater diversity and pragmatism of Japanese thought. Feudal class divisions and fragmentation of political authority presumably fostered these tendencies. In any case, despite the adoption in the early seventeenth century of Neo-Confucianism as the official philosophy of the Tokugawa shogunate, Japan produced a great variety of intellectual leaders in the eighteenth and early nineteenth centuries, and some quite original thinkers.

This greater pragmatism, as well as the different attitude toward the outside world, helps to explain Japan's active interest in the West and its science. While Chinese intellectuals generally excluded the West from their thinking, their Japanese counterparts were often avid for Western learning. Fear of Christianity had contributed to isolation in the seventeenth century; but once this threat had passed, the Japanese again became extremely curious about the West. In 1720 the ban was lifted on books about the Occident, so long as they did not deal with Christianity. Chinese books acquired through the Chinese merchants in Nagasaki were one source of information. Dutch traders were another. In fact, the Dutch language proved so important a source of learning about the West that the whole of Occidental scientific knowledge came to be known as "Dutch learning" (*Rangaku*).

Not only were the Japanese leaders much better informed than the Chinese about Western science; as feudal military men they had a more realistic understanding of military technology than did the scholar-gentry leadership of China. The Japanese did not have to be humiliated in bitter defeat before they could recognize their own military inferiority. At least some of them could see clearly, from the displacement of Western ships, the size and range of Western guns, and the strength of Western forces in the wars in China, that Japan was no match for the intruders.

Another underlying reason for the speed of the Japanese reaction was the relative smallness and accessibility of the islands and the close contacts maintained among all parts of the country. Perry's ships sailed within sight of Edo, the capital of the feudal government, and most of the other large cities were equally vulnerable from the sea. Although the country was divided into many autonomous feudal domains, the control system required the various lords and a large number of their retainers to spend alternate years in Edo (the *sankin kōtai* system). This brought the leadership into much closer contact than was afforded in China by the dispatch of officials from the capital to the provinces, even though the political structure of China was more highly centralized. Within a few weeks of Perry's arrival the whole country knew of this momentous event. Within four or five years, vigorous responses were coming from many areas, not merely from a few harried officials in a large bureaucracy or from residents of some port city remote from the capital.

An 1854 woodblock print giving a "true image" of Commodore Perry of the "North American Republican State."

The Diversity of Responses. Japan's responsiveness to Western contact seems actually to have been a variety of responses, only some of which proved successful and emerged as the new trend. Just because of this greater diversity, Japan was better able than China to find and pursue lines of action that proved meaningful and effective.

The feudal system itself made for this greater variety of response. The Tokugawa political structure, unlike that of China, was composed of units of various degrees of autonomy. After 1600 the Tokugawa shoguns had established their supremacy as feudal lords over the whole country, ruling a great central domain and indirectly controlling the rest of the land from Edo. But by the middle of the nineteenth century the emperor's court at Kyōto, as the theoretical source of the shogun's authority, was beginning to show signs of intellectual independence, though the shogunate still supported and controlled it. The bulk of the country was divided into about 265 *han*, or feudal domains, some of which showed even greater intellectual independence than the court.

The daimyo or lords of these *han* were divided into three categories. The majority were *fudai*, or "hereditary" vassals, descendants of men who had accepted the Tokugawa as overlords before the latter won control over Japan in 1600. The "hereditary" lords, together with the lesser direct retainers of the shogun — the "bannermen" and "honorable housemen" — supplied the officials of the shogunate and thus played an important role in the Tokugawa government. But they held small *han*, many having only the minimal domain needed to qualify as a daimyo — namely, a *han* with an officially assessed rice yield of 10,000 *koku* (a *koku* is 4.96 bushels). Only one of these, Ii of Hikone not far from Kyōto, who had a *han* of 350,000 *koku*, ranked as a large daimyo. Most depended entirely on their bureaucratic positions within the shogunate for whatever political power they exercised and thus were not politically separate sources of authority.

The other two categories of daimyo were much more independent of the shogunate. The "collateral" branches of the Tokugawa family, known as *shimpan* ("related *han*"), though usually excluded from direct participation in the shogunal government, had relatively large domains. For example, the so-called "Three Houses" had domains of between 350,000 and 619,500 *koku*, strategically located at Mito east of Edo, Wakayama (Kii) south of Ōsaka, and Nagoya (Owari) midway between. The domains of the "collateral" lords together with the shogun's own large area and the *han* of the many "hereditary" daimyo covered almost the whole of central Japan, including the large Kantō Plain around Edo in the east and the old capital region around Kyōto in the west.

The third category of lords, the *tozama*, or "outer" daimyo, were the descendants of men who had acknowledged Tokugawa suzerainty only after 1600. They were located for the most part in large domains on the periphery — in North Honshū or in Southwest Japan. Because of the size of their *han* and their distance from the center of Tokugawa power, they could afford to show some independence of the shogunate, but there were great differences among them in this respect. The Maeda, the greatest of the daimyo, with a *han* of 1,027,000 *koku*, located at Kanazawa (Kaga) on the west coast north of Kyōto, were traditionally friendly to the Tokugawa, as befitted the descendants of an early ally. On the other hand, the Mōri of Chōshū (369,000 *koku*) in West Honshū and the Shimazu of Satsuma (770,800 *koku*) in South Kyūshū carefully nurtured a traditional hostility toward the shogunate.

The division of political authority meant that, under Western pressure, reactions varied. The responses at the imperial court, the shogunal capital, and the many castle towns of the major daimyo ran the gamut from intransigent opposition to open-minded acceptance of foreign intercourse.

Even the class divisions contributed to this diversity of response. In theory, there were four classes: the samurai or warrior class of soldiers, administrators, and intellectuals at the top; then the peasants, artisans, and merchants, in that order. But actually there were only two main classes, samurai and commoners, though each was divided into many strata. Samurai and commoners were kept strictly apart both socially and in their functions in society. Men raised as peasants or townsmen had no chance of political and social eminence, and so developed somewhat different concepts of economic enterprise and service than did most samurai. Their responses to Western stimuli often differed from those of the ruling class.

The wide diffusion of education also made for a diversity of responses. The samurai class, constituting some five or six per cent of the population, was roughly five times the proportional size of the degree-holding gentry class in China. It was no narrow feudal aristocracy of the European type but a rather broad upper class of education and traditions of leadership. While the political hierarchy was rigidly fixed and in theory all powers were determined by heredity, in actuality the various *han* governments had developed into widely based bureaucracies. Just as the shogun's chief administrators were drawn from the "hereditary" daimyo, so the chief administrators under each daimyo were drawn from his major hereditary vassals, usually called "family elders" (*karō*). But most of the daimyo, like the shoguns, were little more than figureheads, and only rarely did their chief officers take political initiative. Lower officers, often of rather humble origin inside the samurai class, were not infrequently the chief formulators of policy, which they carried into effect by winning formal approval from the daimyo and "family elders." *Han* bureaucracies at times became divided into rival factions clustering around statesmen of this type, and "reform" and "conservative" parties might alternate in power.

Given this sort of bureaucratic politics within the *han*, it is not surprising that large numbers of samurai reacted strongly to the Western challenge, struggling with one another to determine the response of their respective *han* governments. Many, when unable to prevail within their own *han*, slipped away without their lord's approval and as *rōnin*, or masterless samurai, proceeded to Kyōto, Edo, or other *han* capitals to attempt to achieve whatever ends they had espoused — often by strong-arm methods. Men of this latter type became known as *shishi*, or "men of determination."

The potential leadership was not limited to the samurai class. A high percentage of the urban merchant class was well educated as were also the richer peasants, who often represented long traditions of local leadership. Japanese literacy rates in the first half of the nineteenth century probably compared favorably with those of Western countries. Though little political leadership could be expected from the non-samurai elements, which had been strictly denied it by the whole Tokugawa system, a few individuals of peasant background and even some groups of peasants did have the temerity to join in the political controversies that resulted from the Western challenge. More important, the high educational level and experience in economic leadership of the urban merchants and rich peasants prepared them to seize opportunities in a time of upheaval.

Behind the various responses to Western contact we can discern a pervasive concern for the fate of the nation. The Japanese were determined to preserve their independence, and the concept of national interest, though variously understood, was a basis on which some responses were sorted out as more meaningful or effective than others, and accordingly

MAJOR DAIMYO DOMAI

1 – TSUGARU

2 – SATAKE

3 – NAMBU

4 – SAKAI

5 – DATE

6 – UESUGI

7 – HOSHINA (MATSUDAIRA)

8 – TOKUGAWA (MITO)

9 – MAEDA (KAGA)

10 – TOKUGAWA (OWARI)

11 – MATSUDAIRA (ECHIZEN)

12 – II (HIKONE)

13 – TŌDŌ

14 – TOKUGAWA (KII)

15 – SAKAKIBARA

16 – HACHISUKA

17 – YAMANOUCHI (TOSA)

18 – IKEDA

19 – IKEDA

20 – ASANO

21 – MŌRI (CHŌSHŪ)

22 – KURODA

23 – ARIMA

24 – HOSOKAWA

25 – NABESHIMA (HIZEN)

26 – SHIMAZU (SATSUMA)

27 – SŌ

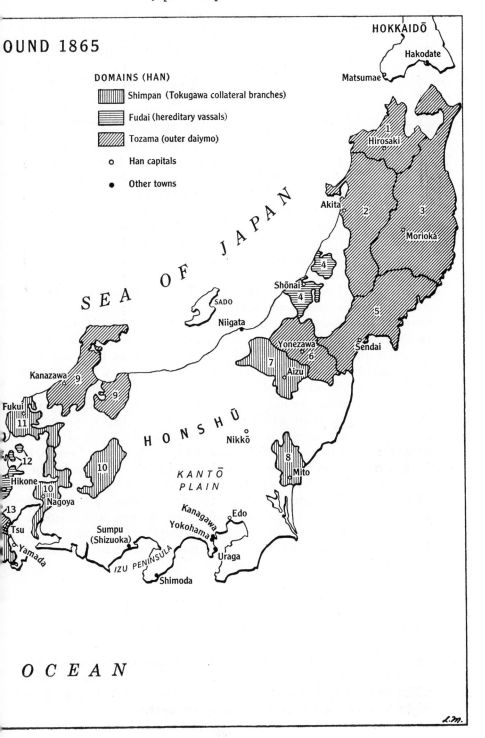

OUND 1865

DOMAINS (HAN)

Shimpan (Tokugawa collateral branches)

Fudai (hereditary vassals)

Tozama (outer daiymo)

o   Han capitals

•   Other towns

HOKKAIDŌ

Hakodate

Matsumae

SEA OF JAPAN

SADO

Niigata

Akita

Hirosaki

1

2

3

Morioka

4

Shōnai

4

5

Sendai

Yonezawa

6

7

Aizu

HONSHŪ

Kanazawa

9

9

Fukui

11

12

Hikone

10

10

Nagoya

13

Tsu

Yamada

Nikkō

KANTŌ
PLAIN

8

Mito

Sumpu
(Shizuoka)

Kanagawa

Yokohama

Edo

Uraga

IZU PENINSULA

Shimoda

OCEAN

found greater support and shaped national policy. Certain reactions to Western technological superiority and military might did not work, whereas other efforts were highly successful and catapulted their advocates to positions of power.

For example, attempts to fight off Western ships with antiquated weapons were doomed to failure, but adoption of Western techniques was likely to get results. And in the Westernizing process, those who were willing to accompany technology by substantial political and social changes were apt to be more successful than those who refused to tolerate such changes. The *shishi* who killed a foreigner and brought down retribution on his lord was likely to disappear from history after his one glorious moment; but the daring young samurai who went abroad to study might return to rise quickly by his new knowledge. Some restless samurai, disillusioned by their inability to drive out the foreigners, switched to advocate the development of national strength through further foreign intercourse, and by this new approach developed into prominent leaders.

To survive, Japan had to modernize its defenses and economy and achieve a more efficient and centralized political organization. Persons who had an anti-shogunate background could afford to be radical and revolutionary, since they had less reason to cling to the *status quo*. Among samurai with anti-Tokugawa backgrounds, those from large and effectively united *han* could win strong political and military backing, while those from small and divided or insolvent *han* could get little such support. An interesting anomaly was that the large anti-Tokugawa *han* of Southwest Japan, from which the new leadership largely came, were economically and socially backward compared with much of the area under the direct rule of the Tokugawa and their "hereditary" vassals, but for this very reason were more cohesive feudal units and therefore more able to act effectively. Thus the overthrow of the shogunate and the subsequent modernization of Japan presents the strange picture of men with a relatively old-fashioned background leading a revolutionary change, while those from more advanced parts of the country meekly followed their lead. The result was a certain conservative-radical ambivalence in the whole movement.

JAPAN'S CAPACITY TO MODERNIZE

Once Japan was launched on the course of modernization, certain underlying conditions made possible rapid progress, though most of these conditions had existed for at least a century without seriously affecting the Tokugawa regime. Without pressure from the West, which revealed its military and political weakness, the Tokugawa system might have continued another century or more.

It is useful to distinguish here, as with China, between long-range domestic trends and immediate foreign stimuli. The startling difference between Japan's response and that of China lies precisely in the domestic conditions in the two countries before their "opening" to more extensive Western contact. Some of these conditions in Japan had been developing over a long period. The tradition of "Dutch learning," for example, not only contributed to Japan's responsiveness to the West but also gave Japan a head start with the Western science and technological modernization that most Asian countries lacked. Another example was the long-term trend toward more centralized government. Although *han* administration was in theory autonomous, actually a high degree of central control had evolved. Similarly, within the shogunate and the various *han*, the ruling class, though of feudal warrior origin, had developed the kind of bureaucratic experience and tradition required in modern government.

Why Japan alone among Asian countries in the nineteenth century responded to the West with a clear sense of nationalism is an interesting question. One major reason was the peculiar relationship of Japan to China. As a sub-unit within East Asian civilization, Japan early realized its smallness compared to the whole cultural unit and perhaps in compensation began to emphasize its "uniqueness" and "superiority."

Nationalistic attitudes of this sort appeared as early as the thirteenth century, and by the nineteenth were widespread. Indeed, Japan's response to the West was so completely nationalistic that most Western observers took it for granted, not realizing that responses elsewhere in Asia were not the same. Despite the mutual hostility between Japanese political units, no *han* and few if any individual Japanese ever thought of making common cause with the foreigners against the rest of Japan. Inter-*han* rivalries dominated the domestic politics of these decades and were to remain important for the next half century, but the national interest took precedence over *han* loyalties or personal and family interests. Having the key ingredient of nationalist sentiment, the Japanese were well on the way to becoming a modern nation-state.

Economic Conditions. The relative advancement of the Japanese economy in the early nineteenth century also helps to explain the speed of subsequent modernization. The complete peace established by the Tokugawa in the seventeenth century had resulted in a tremendous growth of agriculture, trade, and industry. The shogunate and *han*, true to their feudal origins, were based on agricultural production, which was heavily over-taxed. As a result, other economic enterprises were under-taxed, and therefore were able to grow more freely. Moreover, the compulsory residence of the daimyo and their retinues in alternate years in Edo forced the feudal class to exchange much of its tax income, received largely in rice, for money to spend in travel and at the shogun's capital. For this and other reasons large national rice markets, dealing in futures, developed at Ōsaka and Edo, the whole nation became essentially a single market, and there was a great increase in the use of currency and credit. Edo, Ōsaka, and Kyōto became large cities, the former reaching a million in the early nineteenth century, and towns sprang up all over Japan, notably at the capitals of the larger *han*. The wholesale merchants and entrepreneurs of the big cities prospered enormously in the seventeenth century. For example, the house of Mitsui, which later grew into a commercial and industrial giant, then got its start as a provincial *sake* brewery, which branched successfully into dry goods and banking in the large cities.

Economic growth in the seventeenth century was paralleled by a growth in the population, which approached thirty million by the early 1700's. Thereafter it leveled off until the time of Perry, probably because of the lack of new arable land, the restrictions on foreign trade, and a slowing down of commercial expansion in the cities after the government authorities in 1721 began to transform the self-protective merchants' associations into restrictive monopolies.

But economic expansion continued in rural areas, and Japanese farmers were gradually becoming the most efficient producers in the world. Farming became increasingly commercialized, which led to an emphasis on specialized money crops, such as cotton and sugar cane. Rich farmers invested their surplus in the processing and merchandising of silk and other local products. Small-scale factories began to appear, especially in silk-producing areas in central Honshū, where some towns had dozens of small weaving establishments, employing hundreds of workers. By the nineteenth century small but aggressive rural entrepreneurs were invading the city markets, formerly the preserve of the big city merchants.

The commercial and industrial growth resulted in a general rise in standards of living, especially among town merchants and rich villagers, and apparently in an even greater rise in economic expectations. But the ruling class, tied economically to rice production, which developed more slowly than the rest of the economy, benefited less than other groups. The heavy expenses of alternate years in Edo had strained the finances of most *han* from the start, and by the beginning of the eighteenth century the military class was in financial trouble. Most daimyo and many of their samurai were heavily in debt to merchants and bankers, and it had become common practice to cut samurai stipends, sometimes by as much as 50 per cent, in the guise of loans to *han* treasuries.

This economic undermining of Tokugawa feudalism has often been cited as the cause of its eventual collapse, but the situation had already become serious by the early eighteenth century and was actually not much worse by the middle of the nineteenth. Moreover, the shogunate itself was on the whole better off than most of the *han*. It could debase the currency to its own advantage; it could assign the costs of special enterprises to its vassals; and it controlled all the great cities and most of the economically advanced parts of the country. It would be hard to argue that the shogunate fell from economic difficulties, though such troubles in the feudal system as a whole made its abolition all the easier.

But the other face of the coin is the more significant. The great economic development of the Tokugawa period made economic modernization easier. Feudalism, far from having retarded this growth, seems to have been a major cause of it. Townsmen and peasants, barred from political power by the feudal class system, did not dissipate their energies in political and social efforts, but devoted themselves to economic advancement. Furthermore, they were better protected by feudal custom and the disdain of the ruling class for economic activities than was true in the rest of Asia, where autocratic rulers had few compunctions about taking over lucrative commercial undertakings. As a result, Japanese merchants were able to make long-range investments with greater security than were their counterparts in most of Asia. Rich Japanese peasants, instead of investing in more land, the only relatively safe investment in most of Asia, put their wealth into trade and industry, which brought larger profits.

Actually the Japanese capacity for saving and investment was to prove unique in the modern world. Wide familiarity with long-range economic investment, the goal-oriented nature of the society, and a tradition of frugality and pride in simple living may account for this phenomenon. In any case, no other people in the past century have, without government compulsion, consistently saved and invested so high a percentage of the national income.

Thus by the nineteenth century the Japanese probably had the most advanced and thoroughly monetized economy in Asia and were well prepared for further economic development. They had little trouble understanding and adopting the commercial and industrial patterns of the West — and here again they had a running start at modernization.

Social Conditions. By the nineteenth century the feudal class structure had become outmoded and could be discarded with relative ease. Two centuries of peace had eroded the martial spirit and the bonds of loyalty on which it depended. The samurai had been transformed from feudal warriors into a salaried class of professional soldiers and administrators, arrogant by tradition but frustrated by poverty. Power and status were still determined largely by birth, but the more able and ambitious of the lesser samurai chafed under the system and often sought to escape its limitations by abandoning their hereditary duties for less restricted careers as scholars — sometimes of "Dutch learning" — or as military experts. The ambition of certain samurai of humble birth was the force most subversive to feudalism in the turmoil that followed Perry.

The strict social line between samurai and commoners was blurring. Poorer samurai frequently eked out their stipends with cottage industries, such as the plaiting of straw sandals. Some abandoned respectable feudal poverty for more lucrative and exciting careers as commoners; others escaped debt by flouting Tokugawa law and marrying their children to those of their creditors; and rich merchants who vied with the daimyo in wealth achieved samurai status as bankers or business managers for feudal domains.

Such conditions prepared Japanese society for great change. The more enterprising samurai were psychologically ready for a quick shift from the status of hereditary feudal retainers to that of modern professional businessmen. The prosperity of the cities and their complex economic development had produced literate urban populations prepared for a modern social and political system.

In some rural areas large extended families which earlier had formed cooperative farming groups had been replaced by the modern agricultural system of Japan, in which most farming units are of a size to be operated by a small, nuclear family — father, mother, and children. Rich peasants, often men of considerable education, usually farmed only their personal holding, renting the rest of their lands to tenants. Thus able to devote their surplus energy and resources to commerce and industry, they developed entrepreneurial attitudes and skills, and after the coming of Perry contributed many of the businessmen who were to modernize the Japanese economy. At the other end of the rural scale, tenant farmers and landless villagers had become accustomed to working for wages in local industries and to sending the excess members of their families to work in the cities. Therefore it was easy for them to adapt to the new demands for labor as Japan industrialized, and they became the reservoir for the industrial labor force.

Economic and social conditions thus contributed immensely to Japan's modernization, but they were not the immediate cause of the revolutionary changes that followed Perry's arrival. Most samurai were staunch defenders of the *status quo*. Neither townsmen nor peasantry showed any clear desire for political change or even awareness that society and government could be modified. Large-scale peasant riots had been increasing since the early eighteenth century, and similar riots sometimes occurred in the cities. But with the exception of an outburst led by an idealistic former police officer in Ōsaka in 1837, these riots lacked political motivation. The urban outbreaks were usually protests against food shortages, and those among the peasants were invariably directed toward the cancellation of debts, the reduction of crushing taxes, or the correction of obvious cases of misgovernment. They probably reflected tax pressures from debt-ridden feudal lords, loss of security by poor peasants no longer in close economic association with richer ones, and a general rise in economic expectations. But the riots did not represent a conscious desire for participation in government by the peasantry. Peasant riots were no more a threat to Tokugawa rule after Perry than they had been a century or more before.

Those few peasants who took part in the stirring political events of the post-Perry period were exceptions to the general peasant apathy. Usually men of education, they assumed the airs and prerogatives of samurai, instead of acting as spokesmen for their class. Political apathy in the towns was even greater. Rich merchants sought the favor of likely winners in the political free-for-all, but did not themselves attempt to influence the outcome. In short, these long-range economic and social changes facilitated but did not precipitate modernization.

The Imperial System. A final factor that speeded modernization was the peculiar status of the imperial institution. Whereas the Chinese eventually had to rationalize modernization by accepting strange foreign ideologies, the Japanese could justify it as strengthening a venerable native institution understood by all. The myth that change was merely part of the restoration of the direct rule of the emperors, after more than seven centuries of aberration, made it easier to sweep aside a regime that had ruled successfully for two and a half centuries and a political and social system of even longer duration. Only this myth made many otherwise distasteful features of modernization tolerable.

The myth could develop and become useful only because of the existing attitude toward the emperors. Obscured during the incessant wars of the fifteenth and sixteenth centuries, the imperial line had been restored to symbolic dignity and modest economic security by the unifiers of Japan in the late sixteenth century. The emphasis placed by the Tokugawa on Neo-Confucian philosophy further added to imperial prestige, because Confucianism stressed the imperial institution of China and also historical studies, which revealed that emperors rather than feudal lords had once been the rightful rulers of Japan. The second daimyo of the collateral Tokugawa line of Mito started a great historical project (*Dai Nihon shi*, or *The History of Great Japan*), which eventually turned his *han* into a hotbed of loyalist sentiment for the emperors. The imperial court and other groups also became imbued with these ideas, and some daring intellects even came to doubt the right of the shoguns to rule. Occasionally, during the last century of rule, the shogunate had to suppress pro-emperor enthusiasts who became openly subversive in their pronouncements.

The position of the emperors was also enhanced during the Tokugawa period by the expression of the growing nationalistic consciousness through imperialist symbols. Some argued that the "unbroken line of divine emperors" was the real reason for Japan's "uniqueness" and "superiority." The nationalistic use of Shintō symbols also contributed to imperial prestige. Shintō was originally a simple and direct nature worship, but since antiquity the cults of the imperial family, centering in the worship of the Sun Goddess as the family progenitress, had been the central cult of Shintō, and the emperors were the high priests of the religion. Shintō and the emperors, therefore, seemed indissolubly linked.

A marked rise of interest in Shintō in intellectual circles in the seventeenth century gave rise in the eighteenth to a movement known as National Learning (*Kokugaku*), which sought to return to early mythology and classical native literature to find the pure Japanese spirit, unsullied by continental influences. Many scholars of the National Learning were fanatic nationalists, strongly oriented toward the imperial line, not toward the feudal ruling class. In the nineteenth century, the growing interest in Shintō also gave rise to several popular religious movements, some with nationalistic overtones.

The increased prestige of the imperial institution made possible in the nineteenth century a theoretical return to direct imperial rule, after eight centuries of feudal military domination. This was undoubtedly an important feature of the Japanese response to the mid-nineteenth-century crisis, and traditional Japanese historians, reflecting the official ideology of the new government, have made it a central theme. In fact, the whole early course of Japan's modernization is commonly called the Meiji Restoration (*Meiji ishin*), in reference to the assumption of titular control of government by the young Meiji Emperor in 1868.

But the imperial "restoration" was not a basic cause of Japan's modernization. Pro-imperial sentiment existed long before Perry came to Japan, and it flourished after 1853 only through the selective process already described. Furnishing an understandable ideological basis for radical change, it proved a successful response to the crisis, and its adherents rose rapidly. Actually there was no "restoration" in the sense of recreating the imperial system of antiquity. The role of the emperors remained almost purely symbolic, and the political institutions that developed were those which fitted nineteenth-century conditions. In short, the "restoration" was the biggest revolutionary change Japan has ever experienced.

EARLY CONTACTS WITH THE WEST

In both China and Japan antecedent domestic conditions helped shape the response to foreign stimuli. But the actual opening of each country was brought about mainly by the application of Western power or the threat of it. In Japan as in China, it took the impact of Western military strength to crack the framework of the old system and reveal its inability to cope with the new situation.

Russian and British Pressures. The Russians were the first to press upon Japan's closed doors. By the middle of the seventeenth century they were established on the Sea of Okhotsk, and during the eighteenth century Russian and Japanese explorers and traders sometimes had encounters in the Kuril Islands and Sakhalin, north of Japan's northern island of Hokkaidō. Vitus Bering, the man for whom the famous straits are named, became interested in establishing the whereabouts of Japan, and at his instigation a Russian expedition under Spanberg discovered a route to Japan in 1739 by following the Kuril Islands southward from Kamchatka to Hokkaidō and Honshū.

In 1792 the Russians made a more serious but unsuccessful effort to open relations. The young Russian representative, Lieutenant Laxman, was courteously treated in Hokkaidō, where he had gone to negotiate, but was firmly told that Nagasaki was the only port foreigners were allowed to enter. Laxman was given a permit for a Russian vessel to enter Nagasaki harbor, and the next envoy, Rezanov, accordingly went there in 1804. The Japanese authorities were courteous but informed him that Japan had no need for foreign trade.

Rezanov was so piqued that he induced two young naval officers to raid the Japanese trading posts and garrisons in Sakhalin and the Kurils in 1806 and 1807. These raids added to the mounting concern in Japan over the danger of Russian aggression. To strengthen its northern defenses, the shogunate for a while took over control of Hokkaidō from the local feudal domain of Matsumae, and in 1811 the Japanese forces in the southern Kurils by trickery seized a Russian naval officer, Golovnin, and some of his companions. At first the Russians were treated severely, but they and their compatriots who came to seek their release eventually persuaded the Japanese that the earlier raids had not been authorized by the Russian government, and the Russian prisoners were released in 1813 with cordial expressions of good will on both sides. Golovnin on his return to Russia published a very fair account of his captivity, together with a realistic appraisal of Japanese capabilities.

Meanwhile the British too were beginning to frequent Japanese waters. Captain Cook, at the time of his death in the Hawaiian Islands in 1778, had orders to explore the coasts of Japan. The Macartney mission to Peking in 1793 had credentials to Japan but made no attempt to go there. An English vessel, however, did visit Hokkaidō as early as 1797. Then in 1808 the British frigate *Phaeton* entered Nagasaki harbor in search of Dutch ships (a repercussion of the distant Napoleonic wars) and, by threatening bombardment, obtained supplies. In 1818 a British trading ship even entered Edo Bay (the present Tōkyō Bay) on the approaches to the shogun's capital. And an armed clash occurred in 1824 between English sailors and the inhabitants of a small island south of Kyūshū.

American Interest in Japan. By the middle of the nineteenth century, the United States had replaced both England and Russia as the nation most interested in opening Japan. Large numbers of whaling vessels from

New England frequented the North Pacific, and the great circle route across the Pacific brought American clipper ships close to the shores of Japan on their way to and from Canton. As early as 1791 two American ships, probably carrying furs from the northwest coast of North America, had entered Japanese waters. In 1797 the *Eliza* visited Nagasaki, the first of several foreign ships chartered by the Dutch authorities in Batavia to replace their own vessels, which had been cut off from them by the Napoleonic wars.

The crews of both whalers and clippers were naturally interested in obtaining permission to enter the many good harbors of Japan to escape storms or to take on provisions and water after the long Pacific crossing or during the interminable months the whalers spent on the open seas. There was also concern over the cruel treatment of shipwrecked seamen by the hostile and suspicious Japanese. Since American ships frequented Japanese waters much more than did those of other Western nations, this problem loomed especially large in American minds. Toward the middle of the century, as steam came into use, there was also a mounting interest in finding coaling stations in Japan.

For all these reasons, opening the ports of Japan became increasingly important to Americans in the 1840's, just at the time westward expansion to the Pacific was further heightening American interest. The "manifest destiny" which had taken Americans so far overland beckoned them on across the sea. To American minds, transoceanic activities westward in countries technologically behind the United States seemed more attractive and less dangerous than similar activities among the more powerful countries of Europe.

In 1837 an American businessman in Canton sent a small ship, the *Morrison*, to repatriate seven Japanese castaways and, through this act of good will, to open relations with Japan; but the unarmed vessel was fired upon in Edo Bay and again in the harbor of Kagoshima on the southern tip of Kyūshū. An American whaler which returned other castaways in 1845 was treated more civilly, but no Americans were allowed ashore.

Meanwhile the United States government had become interested in opening the island kingdom. In 1835 and twice again in the next ten years, American diplomats were authorized to open negotiations, and in 1846 Commodore Biddle actually arrived for this purpose in Edo Bay in command of two ships. To appear friendly, he tolerated indignities by Japanese who surrounded his ships and swarmed over them, but received a curt refusal for his pains. His failure induced Commander Glynn to assume a stiffer attitude when he came to Nagasaki in 1849 to pick up fifteen stranded American seamen. He was successful in this mission; but despite authorization from Washington to negotiate further, he made no attempt to do so.

The Strengthening of Isolationist Sentiment. The Japanese reacted sharply to this invasion of their cherished isolation. It had long been the policy that foreign ships could come only to Nagasaki, and that even there only the privileged Chinese and Dutch could trade. Following Rezanov's visit, a shogunal decree in 1806 instructed local authorities to drive off foreign ships from any other port, and in 1825, after the clash with the English sailors, the government issued a "No Second Thought" order: local authorities were to destroy without hesitation all foreign ships and crews that approached Japan.

The obvious impracticality of this order forced the government in 1842 to permit local authorities to provide foreign ships with needed supplies, but most of the leaders in both the shogunate and the local *han* remained violently opposed to relaxing the policy of isolation. They were indignant at what seemed to them Western affronts to Japan's national dignity. The only honorable course seemed to be to deal with the "barbarians" as firmly as in the seventeenth century.

This view was expressed with particular vigor by men from the "collateral" Tokugawa domain of Mito, which had long been a center of strong nationalist sentiment with pro-emperor overtones. In 1825 Aizawa Yasushi (or Seishisai; 1782–1863), in a document called *New Proposals (Shinron)*, stressed Japan's rightful supremacy because of its direct heritage from the Sun Goddess and urged the shogunate to "smash the barbarians whenever they come in sight." He argued that foreign trade was economically injurious to Japan, that foreign contacts would undermine Japanese morale, and that the only sound defense was to build national strength through greater unity and the judicious use of Western techniques, while excluding Westerners themselves. This general position was subsequently developed further by Fujita Tōko (1806–1855), an even more influential Mito intellectual.

In 1830 Tokugawa Nariaki (1800–1860), the daimyo of Mito, called for political reform, emphasizing these Mito views. A great feudal lord and a leading member of the Tokugawa family, Nariaki was no revolutionary. In the traditional Confucian manner, he envisaged political reform through moral reawakening. But the expression of his views was in itself an act of insubordination, because the "collateral" daimyo were not normally included in Tokugawa government councils. And he clearly placed national considerations ahead of Tokugawa dynastic interests in his emphasis on the shogun's stewardship of national affairs in behalf of the emperor. Specifically he argued that, in the face of grave national peril, the shogunate should relax the controls which had kept the daimyo militarily weak and financially impotent. Thus he advocated continued isolation backed up by greater national consolidation and military reform.

Nariaki failed to influence shogunate policy, but he started, with the aid of Aizawa and Fujita, vigorous reforms within his own domain. He put *han* finances in order, carried out extensive public works, and borrowed Western military techniques to strengthen the *han* army, even taking his retainers on maneuvers under the guise of hunting expeditions. In 1844, however, he was temporarily forced to abdicate as daimyo for having broken the shogunate's prohibition against increasing *han* armaments.

Meanwhile reform movements (known from the "year period" as the "Tempō reforms") had spread through the shogunate and many of the *han*. These reforms were only partly a response to the foreign menace. They were brought on primarily by bad harvests in the 1830's, and were modeled on previous reform movements in the early eighteenth century and around 1790. The shogunate efforts, carried out between 1841 and 1843 by Mizuno Tadakuni, to restore the economic position of the shogunate and its retainers, were largely unsuccessful. Reforms in some of the individual domains, however, did restore *han* finances and samurai morale, giving these particular *han* a sound foundation during the turmoil of the post-Perry period.

When Mizuno, the would-be conservative reformer, fell from power in 1843, he was replaced as leading figure among the Elders (*Rōjū*), the supreme shogunate body, by Abe Masahiro. Abe was a twenty-five-year-old "hereditary" lord, and he remained a dominant figure in the shogunate until shortly before his death in 1857. Sympathizing with the ideas of Nariaki, the lord of Mito, for maintaining isolation through strength, Abe took him out of retirement and made him a military adviser. He also relaxed the restrictions on *han* military establishments and built up coastal defenses. He even took the unprecedented step of seeking advice from certain great "outer" and "collateral" lords, who before had been jealously excluded from shogunal councils.

Among those Abe consulted was Shimazu Nariakira (1809–1858), daimyo of Satsuma in South Kyūshū. Nariakira, whose great-grandfather Shigehide (1745–1833) had been a leading patron of "Dutch learning," was interested in Western science and through his vassal, the king of the Ryūkyū Islands, had a special familiarity with foreign affairs. Thus he contributed to shogunate policy a more broad-minded and realistic point of view than that of the lord of Mito.

The Scholars of "Dutch Learning." Although the primary response to Western pressures was determination to maintain the seclusion policy, certain Japanese began to see the futility of this stand. This was particularly true of the scholars of "Dutch learning," who, knowing the strength of the West, realized that blind resistance was dangerous.

The increasing menace of the West was a stimulus to the study of Western military technology and science through the Dutch language. In 1811 the shogunate itself established an office for the translation of useful Occidental books. This institution, under its later name of Institute for the Investigation of Barbarian Books (*Bansho Shirabesho*), developed in 1857 into a school to teach Western science and various European languages. Similar schools were established at about the same time by several of the larger feudal domains, notably by Satsuma, Chōshū, Mito, Tosa on Shikoku, and Hizen (Saga) on Kyūshū, all of which were to play significant roles in the events following the opening of Japan. Hizen and Satsuma also established experimental scientific laboratories.

The students of "Dutch learning" could see that Japan needed military reforms, and some of them went on to espouse even broader reform programs. As early as 1784 Hayashi Shihei (1738–1793) published *A Discussion of the Military Problems of a Maritime Nation (Kaikoku hei dan)*. This work so severely criticized the government for the weakness of its defense against the Russians in the north that its author was subsequently imprisoned.

A generation later, Takano Chōei (1804–1850), a physician by inheritance and probably the leading scholar of "Dutch learning" in his time, went to Edo and in 1838, inspired by a garbled version of the visit of the *Morrison*, published a pamphlet urging the shogunate to open the country. Both he and one of his close associates, Watanabe Kazan (1793–1841), were imprisoned in the resulting furor. The latter, a gifted painter and a leading official in a small "hereditary" domain, was returned under arrest to his *han*, where he dutifully committed suicide in 1841. Takano escaped after a prison fire in 1844, but in 1850 he committed suicide when forced to kill a pursuing police officer.

Other scholars of "Dutch learning" had more influence. Takashima Shūhan (1798–1866) urged the authorities of his native city of Nagasaki to undertake military reforms. He trained troops in Western military techniques and in 1841, through the influence of friendly shogunate officials, was allowed to demonstrate Western gunnery and drill in Edo with a company of his soldiers, using Dutch commands.

Another man impressed by the military skills of the Occident was Sakuma Shōzan (1811–1864), a samurai of a "hereditary" domain in central Honshū. He started with the study of Western gunnery in 1842 and gradually extended his interest to other aspects of Western science. Echoing a famous passage from the *Analects* of Confucius, he described his expanding vision of the world around him, which at twenty was limited to his *han*, at thirty had extended to the nation, and at forty embraced the world. In time, Western scientific studies and contact with Occidentals brought the same kind of intellectual growth to many other Japanese. Sakuma, attempting to justify the technological changes that he realized were necessary, coined the slogan, "Eastern ethics and Western science." This concept, like its counterpart developed in China, was to prove a comforting idea to the whole generation of modernizers.

The ideas of these students of Western science were useful, but the men themselves had little political impact. Takashima brought down on his head the ire of conservative officials and was imprisoned in 1842. Released after Perry's visit in 1853, he was put in charge of making ordnance and spoke out in favor of opening the country, but he remained politically insignificant. Sakuma too spent long years in prison and was eventually assassinated in 1864 because of his liberal views.

THE FIRST TREATIES

Japan continued to maintain its proud isolation for a decade after the first treaties were imposed on China, but the pressures were mounting. The United States government, undeterred by earlier rebuffs, decided to make a major effort to force open Japan's closed doors.

Perry's First Visit to Japan. The man chosen for this task in 1852 was Commodore Matthew Calbraith Perry. An outstanding naval officer, he was well qualified for the assignment by many of the same character-istics that a century later were to aid another American military hero, General Douglas MacArthur, in an even greater role in Japanese history. Perry was a meticulous planner, a strict disciplinarian, and a forceful leader. His natural dignity — even pomposity — and his sense of personal destiny, combined with a flair for the dramatic, made him an effective negotiator with the Japanese, who attached importance to pomp and ceremony.

Perry approached Japan by the traditional European route around Africa and along the China coast. In China he took aboard seventeen Japanese castaways as a pretext for entering Japanese waters, though the purpose of the mission was to arrange for better treatment of American sailors, to obtain ports of refuge and provisioning for American ships, and to open trade relations. He was joined in China by S. Wells Wil-liams, the American missionary, who had visited Japan on the *Morrison* and had learned some Japanese from castaways aboard that ship. Williams was to be the official interpreter, but the negotiations, as it turned out, were carried on largely in Dutch. He kept a detailed journal, and a long official *Narrative* of the expedition was also compiled.

In the spring of 1853, before proceeding to Japan, Perry stopped at Naha, the chief town on Okinawa and the capital of the Ryūkyū Islands. The Ryūkyūs are inhabited by a people who in culture and language are a variant of the Japanese. Their kings had been tributary to China for many centuries, but since 1609 they had also been vassals of the daimyo of Satsuma. Therefore the attitude of the Ryūkyūans toward Westerners was determined from Japan, but Perry forced the local authorities to treat him with respect and insisted that the regent entertain him officially in the royal palace. Perry also made a side trip to the Bonin Islands, which stretch out in the Pacific some 600 miles south of Japan. Here he raised the American flag, but the United States did not actually occupy these islands until almost a century later.

Finally in July 1853 Perry entered Edo Bay and anchored off Uraga, the regular control point for coastal shipping bound for the shogunal capital. His squadron consisted of two steam frigates, the *Mississippi* and the *Susquehanna*, and two sloops. By a show of firmness and strength, he prevented the Japanese from surrounding his ships in their usual fashion and carried out surveying operations in the bay. Calling himself an "admiral," he refused to deal with any but the highest officials. But the Japanese, playing the same game of prestige, sent relatively minor officers posing as "great lords." After a few days of diplomatic sparring, Perry obliged the Japanese to accept a letter from the President of the United States to the Emperor of Japan. He never discovered what had been well known in the Occident two centuries earlier — that the "emperor" he was attempting to deal with was actually the shogun, and that

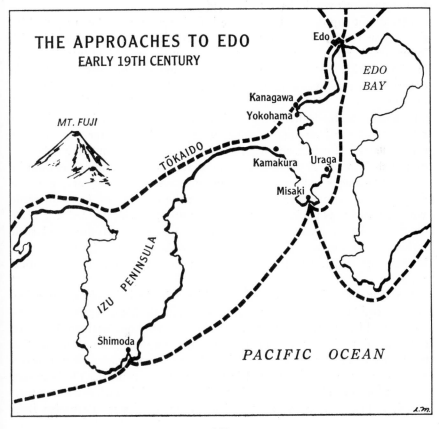

THE APPROACHES TO EDO
EARLY 19TH CENTURY

Edo

EDO BAY

MT. FUJI

TŌKAIDO

Kanagawa

Yokohama

Kamakura   Uraga

Misaki

IZU PENINSULA

Shimoda

PACIFIC OCEAN

the real emperor was in Kyōto. The letter was handed over in an impressive ceremony on shore, after which Perry departed, promising to return for the answer the next spring with greater force.

The Japanese Reaction. Despite the efforts of the shogunate, under Abe's leadership, to consolidate the nation and strengthen coastal defenses, the Japanese were unprepared to withstand Perry's show of force in 1853. Their smaller ships and their antiquated cannon and firearms were no match for the American vessels, and they knew it. Edo, the shogunal capital at the head of the bay, lay exposed to Perry's guns. The food supply of this city of over a million was even more vulnerable, since the bulk of it came by boat through the narrow entrance of the bay, which Perry could easily have blocked. Western aggression in China in the recent Opium War was known in detail to the Japanese. In 1844 and 1847 the Dutch had pointedly advised the shogunate against attempting to maintain its exclusion policy, and warnings about the American expedition had come from the same source. Perry's high-handed conduct in the Ryūkyūs and his adamant demands at Edo made it clear that certain concessions would have to be made.

One might suppose that, since the isolation policy had been created by the Tokugawa shoguns in the seventeenth century, they could with impunity abandon it in the nineteenth. But Japan had changed greatly in the interim. The shogunate was no longer a military dictatorship controlling overwhelming military power. It had become a flabby bureaucratic regime, divided by policy differences among its members. Lacking an unchallengeable leader, it depended on the "public opinion" of its own retainers, of the "hereditary" lords who staffed its higher posts and of the "collateral" lords, who with their retainers were the military bulwarks of the shogunate. It could not be expected that this conglomeration of lords and samurai would present a united front to the rest of the nation on any issue so intensely controversial as the opening of Japan to trade with the West. On this matter, the inner group, being divided, exercised no preponderant power. Thus the views of "outer" daimyo and their retainers had to be considered, and even those of the imperial court, because of its rapid rise in prestige as the source of ultimate political authority.

It is not surprising, therefore, that Abe, who had already taken a few "outer" and "collateral" lords into his councils, decided to refer the problem caused by Perry's demands to all the daimyo. This seemed necessary for general understanding of the intensely unpopular but unavoidable policy of opening the country to more foreign contacts. But it was a momentous step, unprecedented in two and a half centuries of shogunate rule, and it opened the door to discussion and criticism of all government policies. The shogun, whose title had originally meant "Barbarian Subduing Generalissimo" (*Sei-i tai shōgun*), was revealed to be incapable of handling this function. This realization was inevitably followed by others, until by 1868 the whole Tokugawa system had been swept away. Thus Abe's understandable effort to win national support was the beginning of the end of Tokugawa rule. The period between 1853 and 1868 is rightly known as the *Bakumatsu*, that is, the "end (*matsu*) of the shogunate (*Bakufu*)."

The shogun died only a few days after Perry's withdrawal from Edo Bay in the summer of 1853, involving the government in time-consuming ceremonies. Abe nevertheless hastened to strengthen all coastal defenses and removed long-standing restrictions on the size of ships and of *han* defense forces. He also sent translations of the message from the American president to all the daimyo and to certain shogunate officials and Confucian scholars, requesting their frank opinions on the policy to be followed.

The replies were overwhelmingly antiforeign but often vague and ambiguous. This was not surprising in view of the inexperience of the *han* in advising the shogunate and the discrepancy between popular sentiments and actual military conditions. But some of the largest *han* showed considerable awareness of the realities of the situation. About a third of the leading daimyo, including the chief "hereditary" lord, Ii Naosuke of Hikone, were ready to concede some trade, the profits to be used to strengthen Japan's defenses. Other leading daimyo, including Shimazu Nariakira of Satsuma, opposed trade but urged that enough concessions be made to avoid war and to give Japan time for further military preparations. The remainder, including Tokugawa Nariaki of Mito and such powerful "outer" lords as those of Tosa, Chōshū, and Hizen, felt that the Americans should be driven off without making any concessions. Most of the Confucian scholars, isolated from reality, took the same line, and the imperial court, safe from foreign contacts in its inland city of Kyōto, was also known to be strongly isolationist. Abe's bid for national solidarity thus only revealed the depth of the divisions and gave him no clear mandate.

The Signing of the Treaties. When Perry returned to Japan in February 1854, earlier than he had promised, he had with him eight ships, three of them steam frigates — a quarter of the American navy. In the cold light of military reality, American determination appeared to be irresistible, despite Japan's supposedly immovable policy of isolation. All the shogunate could hope to do was to outbluff Perry, or at least keep concessions to a minimum.

The Japanese attempted to negotiate with the Americans again at Uraga, but Perry insisted that the meetings be held further up the bay at Kanagawa, now part of the great port city of Yokohama. Here, with due ceremony on both sides, Perry received the "emperor's" negative reply to the president's letter. Several days of careful diplomatic bargaining followed, in which Perry made vague threats and the Japanese officials, headed by Hayashi, the hereditary Confucian scholar of the shogunate, cautiously accepted what they felt would be the minimum American demands. They were better able to estimate Perry's real intentions than he realized, because they made secret use of a returned Japanese castaway who knew English.

The Treaty of Kanagawa, which was finally signed on March 31, did not differ much from a draft treaty proposed to the Japanese in 1852 by the Dutch. Shimoda, a beautiful but small port isolated from the rest of Japan at the end of the mountainous Izu Peninsula, and Hakodate on the northern island of Hokkaidō, were to be opened to American ships for provisioning and a little trade; shipwrecked Americans were to be well treated in Japan; and an American consular agent was to be allowed to reside in Shimoda. One element of the Chinese treaty system was included, the most-favored-nation clause, stipulating that additional privileges granted to other nations should automatically come to the United States as well.

Before the signing of the treaty there had been a ceremonial exchange of presents and entertainments. Among the gifts from America were a quarter-size locomotive set up on a circular track, a telegraph set, agricultural implements, and a hundred gallons of whiskey. The Japanese put on a demonstration of *sumō* wrestling. The Americans countered with a shipboard minstrel show — which must have completely mystified the Japanese spectators. Then, after sailing past Edo, Perry departed, content to have pried the doors of Japan open a crack.

The reason why Perry had returned to Japan earlier in 1854 than he had promised was his fear that the Russian vice-admiral Putiatin might get ahead of him. Putiatin, aware of Perry's intentions, had gone to Nagasaki a few weeks after Perry first entered Edo Bay in 1853. He failed, however, to negotiate a trade treaty and to settle the boundary in the islands north of Hokkaidō, and was no more successful when he returned again the next January. But following the signing of the Treaty of Kanagawa, the shogunate concluded similar treaties with the British on October 14, with Putiatin at Shimoda on February 7, 1855, and subsequently with the Dutch. The Russian treaty added Nagasaki as an open port and reciprocal extraterritoriality.

The Commercial Treaties and Their Consequences

The agreements signed in 1854 were far from being the full commercial treaties desired by the Western powers, which naturally continued their pressures for increased trade relations. The outbreak of the Anglo-French

War in China in 1856 and the announcement by the British that they intended to negotiate a commercial treaty with Japan made Edo realize that the Perry treaty had given only a brief reprieve. To forestall greater demands, the shogunate signed agreements with the Dutch and Russians in October 1857 for carefully regulated trade at Nagasaki and Hakodate. But it was left to the American consul, Townsend Harris, to force Japan fully open to trade. The story of this accomplishment is told in the fascinating diary of his stay in Japan.

The Harris Treaty. Harris was a man of great perseverance, tact, and patience. When he first arrived in the small town of Shimoda in the summer of 1856, the Japanese attempted to persuade him to leave by isolating him and putting every possible obstacle in his way. But he stayed on in his consulate in a local Buddhist temple, and eventually won the good will and confidence of the Japanese authorities by his sincerity and sympathy. By June of 1857 he had obtained several more concessions, and in December he was even granted an audience with the shogun in Edo. Unlike Perry, he had no military support to strengthen his diplomatic hand, but he skillfully used the imperialist threat of the British, as currently demonstrated in China, arguing that the Japanese would do well to conclude a full commercial treaty with the peaceful and friendly Americans before they were forced to accept a less favorable treaty by the rapacious and unscrupulous Europeans.

The Japanese took Harris' advice, and he lived up to his trust by drawing up a treaty, signed on July 29, 1858, which, though it contained most of the inequalities of the Chinese treaty system, was reasonably fair in view of the international realities of the time. Both ministers and consuls were to be exchanged between the two nations; in addition to Shimoda and Hakodate, Kanagawa on Edo Bay and Nagasaki were to be opened immediately to trade; by stages between 1860 and 1863, Niigata on the west coast and Hyōgo (the modern Kōbe) were to be opened to trade and Edo and Ōsaka to foreign residence; import and export customs duties were to be fixed at moderate rates; Americans were to have extraterritorial privileges in Japan; and the United States was to make available to Japan ships, armaments, and experts.

Within the next several weeks, the Dutch, Russians, British, and French concluded similar commercial treaties, which together with the American treaty are known collectively in Japan as the "Treaties with the Five Nations." These later treaties heightened the inequities of the system by fixing Japanese import duties at low levels and without limit of time. On the other hand, there were no cessions of territory, like that of Hong Kong or the Maritime Province.

Even before the Harris treaty went into effect in the summer of 1859, foreign traders began to settle in large numbers at the harbor of Yokohama, close to Kanagawa, and this unimportant fishing village soon grew into the chief port for foreign trade. Although most of Japan was still off-limits to Occidentals and the old ban on Christianity had not been relaxed, Japan had been opened to an unimpeded flow of foreign trade. Western firms from the treaty ports of China were soon active in Japan.

Controversies within the Shogunate. The relative ease with which Harris obtained his treaty had been the result of political shifts within the shogunate. These had brought to power men who favored a conciliatory policy toward Western demands, while attempting to maintain the shogunate's domestic control.

Abe had placed the shogunate in an anomalous position when he concluded the treaty with Perry. After consulting the imperial court and the *han* for the first time in history, the shogunate had been forced to act contrary to the majority of the opinions expressed. To bolster his position, therefore, Abe took a second novel step by obtaining imperial sanction for the treaty. He also continued his policy of national solidarity by bringing "collateral" and "outer" lords still more fully into the shogunal councils. He put the lord of Mito in charge of coastal defenses and established close relations with another great "collateral" lord, Matsudaira Keiei of Echizen, and with the still greater "outer" lord, Shimazu Nariakira of Satsuma, whose foster daughter was married to the new shogun in 1856. Of these three outsiders, Nariaki, the lord of Mito, became the most influential in government circles and in 1855 even forced the resignation of two of the Elders who were hostile to him.

Opposition slowly built up within the shogunate to Abe and his policies. Many "hereditary" lords resented the infringement of their prerogatives and the compromising of the shogunate's traditional political leadership. Some, because of their close association with the administration of the shogunate, had a clearer appreciation of its military weaknesses than men like the lord of Mito and were more conciliatory toward the Western nations. Thus they represented a group more agreeable to changes in foreign affairs than were Abe's supporters, but less inclined to alter the domestic political system. The lead in this opposition group was taken by Ii Naosuke of Hikone, the greatest of the "hereditary" lords.

Showing the traditional Japanese tendency toward compromise and group responsibility, Abe late in 1855 began to pass his position of leadership among the Elders to a less controversial figure, Hotta Masayoshi, a prominent "hereditary" daimyo. Hotta sharply reduced the political influence of the lord of Mito. He also gravitated toward Ii's faction and became progressively more in favor of granting concessions on foreign trade. The result was the signing of the trade agreements with the Dutch and Russians in October 1857, the permission for Harris' audience with the shogun later that year, and the start of negotiations with him for a full commercial treaty.

Japan's Response to the West

MAJOR EVENTS IN JAPAN 1853–1869

A. *Period of shogunal politics 1853–1861*

1853	July	Perry at Uraga
1854	Mar. 31	Perry's Kanagawa Treaty
1854	Oct. 14	British treaty
1855	Feb. 7	Russian treaty
1855	fall	Abe succeeded by Hotta as shogunate leader
1857	Oct.	Dutch, Russian treaties
1858	May 30	Ii takes power in shogunate
1858	July 29	Harris commercial treaty
1860	Mar. 24	Ii assassinated
1860		Embassy to U.S. to exchange ratifications

B. *Period of han mediation between shogunate and court 1861–1863*

1861		Chōshū emerges to mediate between shogunate and court
1862		Shogunal embassy to Europe
1862	May	Satsuma replaces Chōshū as mediator between shogunate and court
1862	summer	Chōshū adopts extremist position and replaces Satsuma as court favorite
1862	Aug.	Tokugawa Keiki made guardian of shogun; Matsudaira Keiei made shogunal prime minister
1863	June 25	Chōshū fires on foreign ships on date set by shogun for "expelling the barbarians"
1863	July	American and French warships bombard Chōshū
1863	Aug. 15	British ships bombard Kagoshima (the castle town of Satsuma)
1863	Sept. 30	Chōshū forces are driven from Kyōto by a Satsuma-Aizu *coup d'état*

C. *Period of struggles among han military forces — in the name of the court or shogunate 1864–1868*

1864	Aug. 20	Chōshū forces attempt to regain Kyōto, but are defeated
1864	Sept.	Western naval forces demolish Chōshū forts
1864	late	First shogunal expedition against Chōshū
1865	Mar.	Pro-emperor forces triumph in Chōshū civil war
1865	late	Western diplomats move to Ōsaka
1866	Mar. 7	Secret Satsuma-Chōshū entente established
1866	June	British get tariff lowered
1866	Aug. 15	Second shogunal expedition launched against Chōshū
1867	early	Emperor Kōmei dies, succeeded by Mutsuhito
1867	Jan.	Keiki succeeds as shogun
1867	Nov. 8	Keiki attempts an "imperial restoration"
1868	Jan. 3	Satsuma-Chōshū forces seize palace, announce "imperial restoration"

D. *Initial consolidation of the imperial government 1868–1869*

1868	Jan. 27	Shogunal forces defeated at Fushimi, Toba
1868	April 6	"Five Articles Oath"
1868	May	Katsu surrenders Edo
1869	May	Enomoto surrenders Hokkaidō, end of Tokugawa resistance

Before signing the Harris treaty, Hotta followed Abe's lead in asking the advice of the daimyo. The responses again had a strongly antiforeign tone but were, on the whole, more realistic than in 1853. Even the lord of Mito recognized the need to accept some foreign trade. Some daimyo, however, were still strongly isolationist, and few were ready to go as far as the Harris treaty.

Since no clear mandate emerged, Hotta took the unprecedented step of going to Kyōto to obtain the emperor's approval for the treaty in advance. But the imperial court was showing signs of awakening from its long political slumber. In 1845 it had obtained permission from the shogunate to start a school for its nobles. This was the Gakushūin, which later grew into the Peer's School and the present Gakushūin University. Young courtiers were beginning to take an active interest in national politics and felt a new sense of power, as the shogunate began to turn to the court for approval and powerful *han* sent representatives to Kyōto to win the court to their views. Imperial approval of shogunate actions could no longer be counted on as a matter of course. Strengthened by the opposition of many of the largest *han* to Hotta's policies, the court in 1858 gave an ambiguous reply which amounted to a refusal.

The controversy at the court over the Harris treaty was complicated by the efforts of the lord of Mito and his sympathizers to have his son Keiki named heir to the childless and weakly shogun, in preference to the latter's cousin and nearest relative, the child daimyo of the great "collateral" domain of Wakayama. Keiki's claim moreover was legitimate, because he had been adopted into the Hitotsubashi branch of the family, which with the Mito and Wakayama branches and two other collateral lines had been designated to provide a shogun if the main line died out. But the methods of Keiki's supporters were anything but traditional. By appealing to the court for backing, they involved Kyōto for the first time in what was a purely Tokugawa family matter.

Ii's Attempt to Reassert Shogunal Dominance. The lines were hardening between the traditional shogunal officials of "hereditary"-lord status, who were increasingly committed to the opening of Japan, and the national coalition of "collateral" and "outer" lords, who inclined to isolationist views and were turning more and more to the imperial court as a symbol of resistance to the old shogunal monopoly of political power. The first group, once again in firm control of the shogunate, realized that the time had come to make a strong stand if the traditional Tokugawa system was to be maintained.

On May 30, 1858, a month after the court's unsatisfactory answer, Ii Naosuke assumed direct control over the government as Great Elder (*Tairō*), a sort of shogunal premiership that was filled only in times of crisis, usually by a member of the Ii family. Ii signed the commercial

PLATE 19. Plan of Dutch factory on Deshima ("Projecting Island") in Nagasaki harbor. Bridge and guard house control Dutch-Japanese contact. Note, near bridge, a vegetable plot; on right, a Dutch flag. The Dutch dwell above their warehouses; can promenade under a few trees.

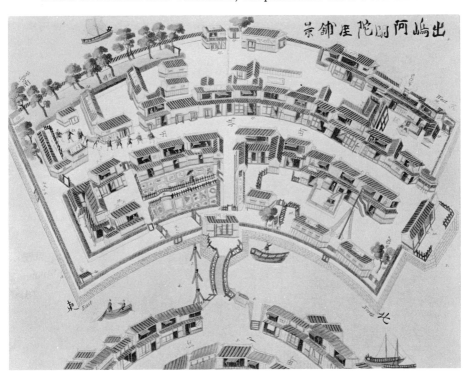

PLATE 20. Dutch Learning: "The seeing mechanism of the eye, the hearing mechanism of the ear" and a hearing trumpet which, while "helpful to the hard of hearing, is no more useful to the deaf than glasses to the blind."

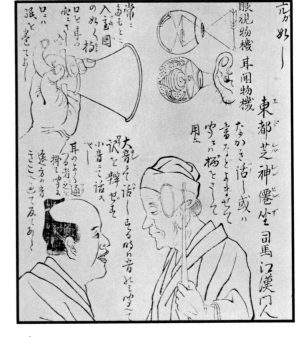

ATE 21. Yoshida Shōin, Chōshū samurai, itary specialist, student of Dutch learning, cuted in 1859 for his anti-Tokugawa plots.

PLATE 22. Satsuma soldiers fresh from victory in the wars against the Tokugawa bakufu. Their average age is 30. All wear Western-style uniform, coats open at the bottom to accommodate samurai swords. Their rifles are not shown. Two have non-samurai haircuts, and one wears shoes.

THE TRANSITION TO THE MEIJI ERA

PLATE 23. From right to left: the old-style "unenlightened man" with samurai swords, the "half-enlightened man" with cap and umbrella, and the "enlightened man of culture" with top hat and cane. Early 1870's.

PLATE 24. Japanese impression of life in America: an 1867 print with the caption, "These are called balloons and they fly through the air as a steamer moves on water."

PLATE 25. This 1877 drawing by Hiroshige IV shows a Japanese balloonist about to attempt a flight in front of the Tsukiji Naval Ministry. Note Western-style architecture, dress, and uniforms, and trackless steam engine.

THE WESTERN FACE OF EARLY MEIJI JAPAN

PLATE 26. "Ladies Sewing," a woodblock print of 1887. From the early 1880's sewing machines were used in fashionable shops on the Ginza. Dresses with long trains reflect the government-supported craze for Westernization. Kageyama Hideko at this time advocated equal rights for women and opened a vocational school to make women economically independent.

PLATE 27. An 1877 print of the Ginza. Brick building, center, is a newspaper office. Shops on left sell colored prints, newspapers, and magazines.

treaties without the sanction of the court or the approval of the daimyo. He had the lord of Wakayama appointed shogunal heir, in preference to Keiki, and the boy succeeded to the position before the year was out. Ii also asserted his defiance of the court by refusing to go to Kyōto when summoned. Instead he sent one of the Elders, who arrested some court nobles for opposing the shogunate and eventually won the court's consent to the commercial treaties.

Ii's strong leadership was no more arbitrary than shogunal rule had always been, but times had changed. There was violent criticism of his measures and an upsurge of subversive, pro-emperor agitation on the part of samurai hotheads. Ii answered with stern repressive measures in 1859. He ordered the lord of Mito, his son Keiki, and their supporters, the "collateral" lord of Echizen and the "outer" lord of Tosa, into domiciliary confinement. He also punished several court nobles and shogunal officials. When he heard of plots to assassinate him, he had many of his samurai critics arrested and some executed. Known from the "year period" as the Ansei purge, this blow fell with particular severity on the pro-emperor intellectuals of Mito.

Ii's strong reassertion of leadership was perhaps the only way the shogunate could have maintained itself. For a while he seemed to succeed, and the political situation momentarily stabilized along the old lines. But on March 24, 1860, a group of extremist samurai from Mito assassinated Ii as he was proceeding through a snowstorm to the shogun's castle.

Had Ii lived, the shogunate might have survived under his strong leadership to play a major role in Japan's subsequent modernization, but this seems improbable, because the shogunate, heavily burdened by tradition, was less capable of revolutionary change than were certain other groups. And Ii's reassertion of Tokugawa absolutism was more apparent than real. Actually, Edo's prestige and authority had both been greatly reduced. Every *han* now felt entitled to express opinions on any matter of national policy. Despite long-standing prohibitions, daimyo and their agents, and even samurai acting on their own initiative, now felt free to approach the court in Kyōto to win it over to their views. It had become clear that now imperial sanction was needed for any major policy decision. Even Ii, by taking care to obtain the emperor's approval of the commercial treaties, tacitly recognized the inability of the shogunate to continue to rule without court backing. Ii's strong measures, moreover, only exacerbated the factional divisions that had produced them. His purge drove the opposition underground, where it built up greater violence. Most thinking Japanese, resentful of foreign pressures and frustrated by their inability to resist them, were bitterly antiforeign. This resentment increasingly was directed against the shogunate which had signed the commercial treaties against popular wishes and the emperor's expressed desires.

The court seemed the logical focal point for opposition to the unpopular foreign policies of the shogunate, and the rising respect for the imperial institution was turned into an important political movement. The slogans "honor the emperor" (*sonnō*) and "expel the barbarian" (*jōi*) became the rallying cries of the opposition. Both had overtones of "down with the shogunate" and were enthusiastically taken up by groups who had long nurtured hidden resentment of Tokugawa rule. This was particularly true of the samurai of Chōshū and Satsuma in Southwest Japan and the "anti-shogunate" Tokugawa retainers of Mito. So strong was the appeal of these slogans that even Ii could not ignore it, and to persuade the court to give its sanction to the treaties, his representative had to make vague promises to "expel the barbarians" as soon as Japan was strong enough.

A definite breakdown in feudal discipline had also occurred under the impact of the foreign crisis and the resulting domestic turmoil. Many *han* asserted their intellectual independence of the shogunate; the more restless of the samurai began to show a determination to participate in national politics. In increasing numbers they requested permission from their daimyo to become *rōnin*, or masterless samurai, to be free to agitate at Kyōto or elsewhere on behalf of the policies they supported. Men of this type killed Ii and left a wide trail of political assassinations throughout the country. Their swords proved potent political weapons. At Edo and Kyōto and in certain *han*, leading advocates of foreign trade or of moderate policies were killed, and many more were cowed into silence.

The Impact of the Treaties. The treaties themselves contributed to the troubles. Foreign traders who started to settle in Yokohama in 1859 found great profit in the gold-silver exchange rate, which was at times as low as 6 to 1 in Japan in contrast to the 15 to 1 ratio elsewhere in the world. Permitted by the treaties to export specie, the traders dumped silver in Japan and exported gold, producing wild fluctuation in prices and serious economic dislocations. Their heavy demands for certain export commodities such as silk and tea also upset the local price structure. The goods they brought to Japan were to prove even more injurious to the national economy. Cotton fabrics and other cheap manufactured goods from abroad began to ruin the corresponding domestic industries, causing severe economic hardship in certain areas. The shogunate did its best to limit foreign trade by every possible tactic of obstruction but was frustrated by the determination of the Westerners and the eagerness of commercial groups in Japan for quick profits.

But the most serious consequence of the treaties was the presence in Japan of considerable numbers of Occidentals, whom most Japanese regarded with great distrust and hostility. Inevitably troubles resulted between fervid samurai activists and Western diplomats and traders. A

Russian naval officer, a sailor, and a Dutch merchant captain were killed in 1859. Then, in January 1861, Harris' Dutch interpreter, Heusken, was cut down at night in the streets of Edo, and the shogunate had to pay an indemnity of $50,000 to the victim's mother. This was followed in July by an attack by Mito *rōnin* on the British legation, in which two Englishmen were wounded. Western diplomats, with the exception of Harris, temporarily withdrew from Edo to Yokohama. But the attacks continued. Early in 1863, for example, *rōnin* burned the British legation in Edo.

The foreign situation also brought new strains on shogunal finances, already in a sorry state of decline. Large sums were needed for defense preparations, and the opening of the ports entailed new and unprecedented expenditures. Worst of all were the heavy indemnities for the incessant attacks made on foreign residents and ships by samurai and *han* now beyond Edo's control.

Thus Ii's firm stand could not conceal the shogunate's hopeless dilemma. Edo could not withstand foreign pressures for trade, yet was forced by public opinion to make promises to "expel the barbarians." Its authority over the *han* and control of the individual samurai was fast ebbing. The shogunate had been forced to recognize the ultimate political authority of the imperial court. Both the political order and the economic system on which it stood were giving way under the Western impact. Ii had sought to shore up the tottering structure, and his death removed its last firm support.

The Emergence of Satsuma and Chōshū

No new Great Elder was appointed, and the council of Elders attempted to win back support for the shogunate by a conciliatory policy. But moderation proved even less successful in maintaining Edo's authority than had Ii's firmness. Even the marriage of the shogun to the emperor's sister in January 1862, after interminable negotiations and further promises to Kyōto to "expel the barbarians," did not improve the situation. The shogunate, while retaining responsibility for national policies, began to lose the initiative to the imperial court and to the "collateral" and "outer" lords, who now looked to Kyōto.

Sources of Strength in Satsuma and Chōshū. Two "outer" *han* — Satsuma in South Kyūshū and Chōshū at the western end of Honshū — came rapidly to the fore. The domination of Japanese history for the next several decades by men from these two of the 265 *han* is surprising but not inexplicable.

Both Satsuma and Chōshū had a combination of advantages. They were among the biggest, and obviously only the larger domains had much hope of influencing national politics. Satsuma was officially ranked second among the *han* in tax yield, and Chōshū ninth, though its actual tax income probably should have placed it fourth or fifth. In both *han* the ratio of fighting men to tax income was much higher than the national average, giving them greater military manpower than their economic strength would suggest. Satsuma had about 27,000 samurai, a large proportion of them "village" or "rural samurai" (*gōshi*), part-time farmers, and Chōshū about 11,000. This high concentration of samurai was the result of a drastic reduction in size, but not in number of retainers, of the Satsuma domain in the late sixteenth century and a similar geographic reduction of Chōshū after 1600.

Another factor in the strength of Satsuma and Chōshū was their internal solidarity. Located far from the major urban centers, both — but particularly Satsuma — were backward economically and socially compared with some of the strongholds of Tokugawa power. Hence the morale of their feudal warrior aristocracy was less eroded, and they were able to take more effective action than *han* located in economically more advanced areas. Their very backwardness contributed to their strength.

In contrast, the "hereditary" *han*, most of which were quite small, were too closely tied to the shogunate to take an independent stand. Some "collateral" *han* were anti-shogunate, as in the case of Mito, but were constrained by their Tokugawa origins from taking the lead in a revolutionary situation. Even Mito, after the death in 1860 of its fiery lord, Tokugawa Nariaki, fell into the hands of a conservative clique and soon became quiescent. Several of the larger "outer" *han* were similarly influenced by history. For example, the greatest of the daimyo, the Maeda of Kanazawa, had a tradition of friendship with the Tokugawa which made openly revolutionary activities distasteful to them.

A few *han* were powerful and had an anti-Tokugawa tradition but lacked the daring and unified leadership needed for a decisive stand or else were financially too insecure to take bold action. The wealth of Satsuma and Chōshū in the middle of the nineteenth century was probably a prerequisite for their success, for without adequate financial resources they would have had neither the strong *han* morale nor the Western arms which made possible their triumph. Feudal morale and financial solvency went hand in hand, each helping to sustain the other. The old warrior virtues of frugality and loyalty which persisted in peripheral areas more than in the commercialized heart of the country had helped Satsuma and Chōshū put their finances in order when the shogunate and other *han* were failing in similar efforts.

Satsuma was lucky to have strong daimyo in Shimazu Shigehide and, later, his great-grandson Nariakira. The latter was succeeded in 1858 by his nephew, whose father, Hisamitsu, soon emerged as another strong leader. Satsuma also had the advantage of trade and contact with the outside world through its vassal domain of Ryūkyū and had become a leading area in the study of Western science and technology. Like most other *han*, it was burdened by a crushing debt, but it started vigorous reforms in 1830, at the very beginning of the so-called "Tempō reforms," which resulted from the crop failures and economic depression of the 1830's. The Satsuma effort consisted primarily in the cancellation of the *han* debt and the strengthening of *han* commercial monopolies. The latter proved particularly successful with sugar, because Satsuma controlled the only parts of Japan where sugar cane grows well. Paradoxically, both these measures were feasible because of Satsuma's backwardness and would probably not have succeeded so well in economically more advanced parts of the country.

Chōshū's "Tempō reform," begun in 1838, included a slashing of *han* expenditures and a reduction of samurai debts. Earlier cuts in samurai stipends were partly restored, and there was a reduction of the *han* monopolies (which was more typical of the "Tempō reforms" in Japan as a whole than was Satsuma's expansion of the monopolies). These measures helped for a while to hold down the ever-mounting *han* debt and heightened samurai morale.

An unusual institution, the "nurturing office," seems to have been the main reason for Chōshū's financial solvency during the period of crisis. Founded in 1762, the "nurturing office" was an emergency fund to help the *han* and its samurai in times of need, but it had become an investment office, particularly successful as a merchandiser of the surplus rice of the domain, and as a storer of goods and provider of funds to other *han* engaged in transport activities on the Inland Sea. By regularly investing part of the *han* revenues through this office, instead of devoting all its financial energies to its debt, Chōshū stumbled into a system of deficit financing. Thus, during this period of creeping inflation, it profited from the gradual diminution of the value of its debt and the enhancement of the value of its investments. Despite the large *han* debt, the "nurturing office" created the surplus needed to modernize the *han's* military establishment in the 1860's.

The Movement for a Coalition of Court and Shogunate. Thus both Chōshū and Satsuma were in a good position to take a strong stand in the turmoil following the full opening of Japan to foreign trade. The main political development of the next decade proved to be a series of alternate, competing bids for national leadership by Chōshū and Satsuma, each more extreme than the last, until finally these two *han* joined to overthrow the shogunate.

The dominant conservative party in Chōshū, which was strongly opposed to any intervention in national politics as too hazardous, was replaced in power in 1857 by the moderate reform party, which was more daring. When the imperial court late that year sent a secret and very cryptic message to Chōshū and thirteen other "outer" and "collateral" *han*, seeking support in its opposition to Ii's signing of the commercial treaties, the reformist party decided that Chōshū should begin to take a part in national politics. This decision was motivated primarily by long-smoldering resentment against Tokugawa rule and by memories of Chōshū's greatness before 1600.

There was also in Chōshū the beginning of an openly pro-imperialist movement by a few of the junior samurai. This was largely the product of Yoshida Shōin (1830–1859), the adopted heir of a hereditary teacher of military tactics. Early in his career, Yoshida had become interested in "Dutch learning," having studied both at Nagasaki and under Sakuma Shōzan in Edo. He had also fallen under the influence of the imperialist and exclusionist Mito school. A dedicated fanatic, Yoshida forfeited his samurai status by setting off on study travels without official permission from the Chōshū government. In 1854, he even attempted to smuggle himself out of Japan on one of Perry's ships, occasioning the imprisonment of his former teacher, Sakuma, in reprisal. Returned to Chōshū for punishment, he was instead permitted to open a school. His original interest in the West and in the Mito line of thought developed into a fanatical determination to overthrow the shogunate and to develop Japan, under the emperor's leadership, into a great imperialist power. To further this cause, he planned in 1859 to assassinate Ii's representative in Kyōto. This ill-considered plot was discovered, and he was handed over to the shogunal authorities, who executed him. Yet Yoshida had already implanted his ideas in the minds of a group of young disciples who contributed an openly anti-shogunate, "honor the emperor" tinge to Chōshū thinking.

It was not until 1861, more than a year after Ii's assassination, that the Chōshū reformers were emboldened to make their first, modest bid for national leadership. They proposed that Chōshū mediate in bringing Edo and Kyōto together — a policy that came to be known as "the union of court and shogunate" (*kōbu gattai*). Specifically they suggested that the emperor order the shogun to embark on a policy of "expansion across the seas." Kyōto accepted this proposal, because it was the first open admission of its political primacy since Ii's repressive measures, and Edo was delighted to have full court support for the foreign policy the shogunate had been forced to accept.

In the end, however, nothing came of the Chōshū efforts at mediation. The policy was undercut within Chōshū itself both by opposition from the extreme pro-imperial disciples of Yoshida Shōin and by the doubts of influential reformers. More important, it was soon eclipsed by a more daring bid for national leadership as Satsuma, in May 1862, proposed itself as mediator between Kyōto and Edo to secure more shogunal respect for the court, the release from domiciliary confinement of Keiki, the defeated candidate for shogun, and his appointment as the Great Elder and guardian of the new shogun. Satsuma won imperial support for this proposal and, with court sanction, it proceeded to suppress the extreme pro-imperial samurai from Satsuma and other *han*, who were causing confusion in Kyōto because of their incessant plots to assassinate moderates. Then the Satsuma leader, Shimazu Hisamitsu, with a representative of the court, took a somewhat modified list of demands to Edo. Yielding to pressure, the shogunate in August made Keiki the guardian of the shogun, with Matsudaira Keiei, the "collateral" lord of Echizen, as a sort of acting prime minister. Thus under Satsuma sponsorship the policy of national solidarity was carried a step beyond what Abe and the lord of Mito had envisioned a few years earlier.

Matsudaira Keiei was advised by a famous Confucian scholar, Yokoi Shōnan, lent him by the conservative "outer" domain of Kumamoto in Kyūshū. Yokoi had a practical bent that had made him much interested in the West and an advocate of foreign trade, for which liberal views he eventually fell by the swords of assassins in 1869. He also had strong imperial leanings and was a firm believer in national solidarity. Under his influence, the whole Tokugawa hostage system was abandoned, and the attendance of the daimyo at Edo in alternate years (*sankin kōtai*) was reduced to a meaningless 100 days every three years. This startling innovation made obvious a change that had already occurred: the shogunate no longer exercised effective control over the *han*.

Chōshū's Bid to Lead a Pro-Imperial Movement. Chōshū was not content to see national leadership slip into the hands of its Satsuma rival. Outbid by Satsuma in the movement for a "union of court and shogunate," it adopted a new approach, which took an openly pro-imperial stand and espoused the sentiment of "expel the barbarians" that was obviously favored by the court. This shift in policy united the extremist disciples of Yoshida Shōin with the dominant reformist faction. The extremists, because of the changing climate of opinion, were now rising in influence, and one of them, Kido Kōin (1833–1877), who was of sufficiently high birth to qualify, even became an important figure in the *han* government.

While the Satsuma leader, Shimazu Hisamitsu, was negotiating in Edo, Chōshū representatives through a few extremist court nobles won control over the court. Chōshū was further strengthened at this point by the official support of Tosa, a major "outer" *han* on the island of Shikoku. The Yamanouchi daimyo of Tosa, who had been given their domain as a reward by Ieyasu, the first Tokugawa shogun, had a tradition of loyalty to the Tokugawa, but among their lesser retainers were many rural samurai (*gōshi*) who had been retainers of the lord whom the Yamanouchi had displaced. These men together with the descendants of rich peasants and merchants who had been allowed to purchase samurai status and the equally prosperous village headmen (*shōya*) formed a rural opposition to the urbanized administration at the *han* capital, Kōchi. Partly because of this division within the *han*, an extremist faction had been able to come to the fore. This party brought Tosa to Chōshū's side, though not for long. Early in 1863, more moderate elements regained control of the *han* and proceeded to suppress the pro-imperialist Tosa samurai who swarmed around the court.

Thus Chōshū again stood alone among the *han*, but it was supported by a wave of pro-imperialist popular sentiment in the Kyōto area. There was a rash of assassinations of moderate leaders, perpetrated by pro-imperialist *rōnin*, and even a peasant uprising. Aroused by the revolutionary fervor, some 2000 peasants, led by samurai extremists, attacked the shogunal authorities in the Nara area south of the capital in September 1863. Though speedily suppressed, this revolt of the so-called "Heavenly Chastising Force" (*Tenchūgumi*) showed that even peasant groups were becoming involved in the confused political situation.

Meanwhile Chōshū continued to develop its pro-imperialist program in Kyōto. Sanjō Sanetomi (1837–1891), a young extremist court noble, was sent to Edo in December 1862, where he got the shogunate to agree again to the expulsion of the "barbarians." Sympathetic court nobles were appointed to three councils, constituting the beginning of an imperial government, and small bodies of "imperial troops" were formed. The Chōshū-dominated court even induced the shogun to come to Kyōto, a policy originally advocated by Yokoi Shōnan. Arriving in Kyōto on April 21, the shogun was soon forced to set June 25, 1863, as the date when the "barbarians" would be expelled.

The shogunal officers knew that expulsion of the foreigners was impossible. They had dispatched an embassy to the United States in 1860 to exchange ratifications of the Harris treaty, and the members of this mission had returned convinced of the hopelessness of resisting the Western nations. A second embassy sent to Europe two years later reached the same conclusion, though it did manage in June 1862 to persuade the British to agree, in view of the obvious turmoil in Japan, to the postponement until 1868 of the opening of trade in Hyōgo and Niigata and the start of foreign residence in Edo and Ōsaka. The other foreign powers subsequently concurred in this postponement.

By this time it was clear that the Chōshū tactics had placed the shogunate in an impossible position. Caught between the intransigence of the forces abetting the court in Kyōto and the superior military power of the West, the shogunate became paralyzed and ineffective. Unable to make policy, it merely waited.

It soon turned out that Chōshū's antiforeignism had gone too far. Chōshū had committed itself and the court to an unrealistic foreign policy, alarming the moderates and realists in other *han* as well as its rivals for power. The folly of the policy was soon revealed. Chōshū alone attempted to carry out the expulsion order. On the appointed day, June 25, its forts along the Strait of Shimonoseki at the western end of the Inland Sea fired on an American merchantman and subsequently on French and Dutch ships. In response, an American warship shelled the forts on July 16 and sank two Chōshū gunboats recently bought at Nagasaki. Four days later a French warship sent ashore landing parties which destroyed the forts and their ammunition.

Alarmed, the shogunate ordered Chōshū to stop its attacks, but Chōshū extremists seized the ship on which the shogunal official had come and eventually killed the unlucky man. Meanwhile Satsuma had taken more effective action in Kyōto, aided by the "collateral" domain of Aizu in North Honshū, whose lord had been appointed military governor of Kyōto. In a *coup d'état* on September 30, troops from these two *han* seized the gates of the imperial palace, restored the more moderate nobles to control of the court, dissolved the court councils created under Chōshū leadership, and disbanded the "imperial troops." The outnumbered forces of Chōshū, which were forced to withdraw from Kyōto to their own *han*, defiantly took with them Sanjō and six other extremist court nobles.

Early in 1864 Shimazu Hisamitsu of Satsuma and the lords of Aizu, Tosa, and one other "outer" domain, together with Keiki and Matsudaira Keiei, representing the shogunate, were appointed as a group of "participating daimyo" to aid the court. This move suggested the creation of a "union of court and daimyo," rather than a "union of court and shogunate," since even Keiki and Keiei, as "collateral" lords, were outsiders in the traditional shogunate government. Lacking real unity and reliable administrative organs, the council of "participating daimyo" broke up in futility in April 1864, and political initiative momentarily returned to the hands of Keiki and the "hereditary" daimyo who staffed the shogunate.

THE FALL OF THE SHOGUNATE

It was too late, however, to reassert Tokugawa supremacy. The situation had entered a new and more critical stage. The anti-shogunate groups had by no means been eliminated, and the use of force by Satsuma and Aizu in 1863 had broken the long peace of the Tokugawa. Thenceforth military power, rather than traditional authority, public opinion, or political skill, was to be the deciding factor in Japanese politics.

Chōshū, despite its expulsion from Kyōto and denunciation by the now Satsuma-dominated court, continued its defiant attitude and rapidly built up its military strength. The reformist faction, after its return to power in 1857, had started to form new rifle units in the *han* forces and in 1860 had begun to purchase, with the money in the "nurturing office," Western ships and guns. Following the disastrous attacks by the American and French warships on Shimonoseki in 1863, the *han* government assigned Takasugi Shinsaku (1839–1867), a member of the extremist faction who was versed in Western military science, to carry out further military reforms. Takasugi formed a peasant militia and established full-time rifle units composed of samurai and commoners. The most famous of these units was the Kiheitai ("irregular troop unit"), but there were many others.

The use of volunteers from the common citizenry was a revolutionary departure from rigid Tokugawa custom, necessitated in part by the reluctance of many samurai to submit to Western-style military discipline and to use guns, which had always been associated with soldiers of the lowest rank. Moreover, the mixed units of samurai and peasants frequently were commanded by the young extremist disciples of Yoshida Shōin, giving these men for the first time a real base of power in Chōshū politics. These units often acted independently, and as early as October 1863 the Kiheitai intervened forcibly in *han* politics to keep the reformist faction in power. Thus, in these mixed units, the forces that were to win the national revolution first came together: the imperialist ideology that justified the revolution, the "expel the barbarian" spirit that gave it popular appeal, the Western military techniques that gave it power, and the ambition of young samurai of relatively humble birth that gave it daring and drive.

The Foreign Attacks on Chōshū and Satsuma. The shogunate and the "participating daimyo" at Kyōto felt that Chōshū should be punished for its defiance of the authority of Edo and Kyōto, but they could not agree on any specific policy, and it was the Chōshū government, goaded by the demands of the leaders of the new mixed units, that finally tried to break the stalemate. Chōshū forces marched on Kyōto in the summer of 1864, hoping to win an easy victory like the Satsuma-Aizu coup of the year before. But they were defeated on August 20 in an encounter at one of the gates of the imperial palace by troops from the same two *han*, and withdrew again in disgrace to their own domain.

This disaster for Chōshū was soon followed by another. It had continued its attacks on foreign vessels in the Straits of Shimonoseki, effectively closing this important waterway to foreign commerce. In retaliation a combined fleet of seventeen English, French, Dutch, and American vessels demolished the Chōshū forts along the straits in September. Chōshū was forced to agree to leave the straits unfortified, and the shogunate had to promise to pay an impossibly large indemnity of $3,000,000. The Western powers subsequently offered to postpone payments in return for further trade concessions. In fact, this financial argument together with the movement of the Western diplomats late in 1865 to Ōsaka, where they could exert more pressure on Kyōto and could threaten to go to the court, induced the shogunate to make a new agreement with the Western powers in June 1866. This removed various restrictions on trade and reduced tariff rates, which had for the most part been at 20 per cent and now were lowered to 5 per cent.

While public sentiment in Chōshū remained bitterly antiforeign, the severe defeat administered by the foreign fleet in 1864 forced the *han* government to recognize that its policy of "expel the barbarians" was impractical. It was also induced to put greater reliance on the new Westernized military units and on individuals who knew the West. For example, two young samurai, who after participating in an unsuccessful attack on the British legation in Edo in 1861 had then gone to England in 1863 to study, found themselves to be men of some importance upon their return to Chōshū. These were Inoue Kaoru (1835–1915) and Itō Hirobumi (1841–1909). The latter was a man of peasant birth who had been adopted as heir of a family of the lowest samurai status and had been a disciple of Yoshida Shōin. Both Itō and Inoue were in time to become prominent statesmen. Though they were unable in 1864 to persuade their *han* leaders to capitulate before the foreign attack occurred, they were subsequently appointed interpreters to deal with the foreign powers and then rose to greater prominence as commanders of two of the new mixed units. Under the influence of men of this type, Chōshū, though not renouncing "expel the barbarians" as a useful slogan, began to adopt a more realistic position on foreign affairs.

In Satsuma there was also much sentiment for expelling the "barbarians," even though the *han* government had taken a realistic attitude toward Western military power. On September 14, 1862, four Britishers riding in the country near Yokohama encountered the procession of Shimazu Hisamitsu of Satsuma at the village of Namamugi, and one of them, Richardson, was killed by irate samurai who felt that the foreigners had not shown the proper respect for their great lord. The British, by threats of naval power, the next year forced the shogunate to pay an indemnity of £100,000. They also demanded an indemnity from Satsuma and the punishment of the culprits. But on August 15, 1863, the Satsuma forts at Kagoshima, the *han* capital, fired on the seven British ships assembled to enforce the demand, whereupon the latter proceeded to level much of the city of Kagoshima and to sink the Japanese ships that were in port.

In the subsequent settlement, Satsuma paid an indemnity of £25,000, mostly borrowed from the shogunate. The incident naturally confirmed the *han* leaders' respect for Western military power and also produced a deep interest on their part in the British navy. British aid was immediately procured to obtain Western naval ships for Satsuma, and the foundations were thus laid for a naval force which became the training ground for many of the first officers of the modern Japanese navy.

The First Chōshū Expedition and Civil War. Chōshū's attempted coup in the summer of 1864 at last induced its opponents to take determined action, and an imperial command for the chastisement of Chōshū was obtained. After much bickering and indecision over who would take the onus of leadership, finally the daimyo of the great "collateral" domain of Nagoya led against Chōshū a force of 150,000 samurai drawn from a large number of *han*. The series of disasters that befell Chōshū in 1864 discredited the reformist clique, and its conservative opponents, who had consistently opposed the policy of involving the *han* in national politics, came back into power in November of that year. Faced with overwhelming might, the conservatives readily capitulated to the mild terms offered by the army sent against them.

This leniency and the good will shown throughout the negotiations were in part due to the influence of Saigō Takamori (1827–1877) of Satsuma, a large man of dominating personality though of lowly samurai birth, who was serving as a staff officer with the shogunal forces. Saigō's attitude probably reflected Satsuma's unwillingness to see the shogunate restored to power by the complete elimination of Chōshū. The shogunate was also weakened by the reluctance of the participating *han* to bear the costs of a long campaign. Thus it exacted only an apology from the Chōshū daimyo, the death of the three "family elders" held to be officially responsible for the attempted coup at Kyōto, and two promises from the *han* government: the return of Sanjō and the other extremist nobles to Kyōto, and the disbanding of the new mixed units which had carried out the attack on Kyōto. On January 24, 1865 the Chōshū government accepted these terms, and the great army marshaled against it started to disband.

Although the Chōshū daimyo and his official *han* government had capitulated to the shogunate, the mixed rifle units, each acting as an independent power group, refused to disband and defied not only the authority of the shogunate and imperial court but also that of their own *han* government. As early as January 13, in the midst of the negotiations with the shogunal forces, Takasugi and Itō led their units in raids on the *han* offices at Shimonoseki and seized an armed sloop. On January 22 the conservative regime dispatched a large, newly formed unit of conservative samurai to suppress Takasugi, who had again raided Shimonoseki, but this force was defeated on the way by other mixed rifle units. The mixed units then took the offensive, winning skirmish after skirmish, and finally seized the *han* capital on March 12. The new *han* government that resulted was a coalition between elements of the old reformist clique and the extremists, with the latter dominant because of their control over the mixed units. Kido soon emerged as the strongest man in *han* politics, and Takasugi also became powerful.

The triumph of the revolutionary mixed units in the Chōshū civil war was a turning point in Japanese history. Their rise — and the subsequent overthrow of the shogunate — has sometimes been pictured as a class movement of commoners and lower samurai, but actually it was little colored by class feelings. A few exceptional peasants showed an active interest in politics. But the overwhelming majority of the peasants and a large part of the samurai remained neutral, if not apathetic. All samurai levels were represented in the divergent parties. Commoners entered the rifle units and low-born samurai rose to their command, for these revolutionary institutions offered the only opportunity for rapid advancement to able and ambitious men of humble birth. But individual ambitions probably contributed a great deal more to the victory of the mixed units than did class interests.

The mixed units also enjoyed certain other advantages which had nothing to do with class interests. They had a slight edge over the conservatives in military discipline and weapons. And they had a tremendous advantage in spirit, because they championed the appealing slogan of "honor the emperor — expel the barbarians" and the equally popular concept of Chōshū leadership in national affairs, while their opponents could only urge compromise and meek submission to outside authority.

The Second Chōshū Expedition. The victory of the mixed units in the civil war in Chōshū nullified the results of the shogunal expedition just concluded. The shogunate, however, was at first unaware of this and, heartened by the apparent success of the expedition, made one more effort to reassert its supremacy over the nation. It reinstituted the attendance of the daimyo at Edo in alternate years, ordered the lord of Chōshū and his heir to come to Edo for punishment, and attempted to reimpose its control over the imperial court. The court, however, under strong Satsuma influence, refused to accept the leadership of the "hereditary" daimyo in Edo's councils. Kyōto countermanded the two other orders as well, and the various daimyo simply ignored the shogunate's demand that they return to Edo.

In June 1865 the shogun himself proceeded with substantial forces to Ōsaka in the hope of reasserting Edo's authority in the old capital area. There followed a year of frantic maneuvering to bring the court and the daimyo into line, and to work out a unified policy against Chōshū, which after the change of *han* government had clearly defied the shogunate's authority by refusing to live up to the terms of surrender. Eventually the shogunate and its half-hearted allies agreed on a mild punishment for Chōshū: the daimyo and his heir were to abdicate in favor of the former's grandson, and the *han* was to be somewhat reduced in size. The new Chōshū government refused to accept these terms. The shogunate in the meantime had marshaled another army, which marched to the borders of Chōshū and finally on August 15, 1866, launched an attack.

In this second punitive expedition against Chōshū, the shogunate did not have the overwhelming superiority it had enjoyed two years earlier. At that time the Chōshū samurai had been sharply divided over policy. But since then the renewed threat of shogunal attack had consolidated opinion, and Kido had proved to be an effective leader of the *han* government. Another sweeping reform of the military had standardized weapons and obtained new ones; the mixed units had been brought under strict *han* control, their members now being executed if they continued to disobey orders; and the rest of the samurai had been organized into new, modernized military units. The shogunal army was less well organized and armed. Its lack of clear purpose and will to fight contrasted sharply with the determination of the Chōshū forces to defend their *han*. Also the shogunate and its allies found the expedition a severe economic drain, to be financed only by borrowing from merchant bankers. The resultant economic strains seem to have contributed to an outbreak of rice riots in the major cities.

In these circumstances, the Chōshū forces, though outnumbered, were clearly superior. The shogunate attackers were immediately thrown on the defensive. Chōshū captured the castle towns of a few nearby participants, and some more distant *han* withdrew their samurai. By October the shogunate was forced to sue for peace and started to withdraw its army in complete defeat.

The Satsuma-Chōshū Coalition. One of the main reasons for the failure of the second expedition against Chōshū was the abstention of Satsuma and some other powerful *han*. The whole Tokugawa system relied on mutual antagonism among the *han*. Satsuma and Chōshū by tradition were as unfriendly toward each other as toward the shogunate, an attitude sharpened by their rivalry for leadership after 1861 and by the diametrically opposed policies they championed. But these differences gradually disappeared as conditions changed.

The attacks by foreign ships on Shimonoseki had forced Chōshū to abandon in reality, even if not in name, its "expel the barbarians" policy, thus bringing it closer to Satsuma's more realistic stand on foreign affairs. Similarly, the ineffectiveness and divided councils of the shogunate had made the Satsuma leaders lose confidence in their original policy of building a strong coalition between the shogunate and the leading *han* through a so-called "union of court and shogunate."

Satsuma also had reason to doubt Edo's real motives. Oguri Tadamasa (1827–1868), an influential shogunate official who had accompanied the embassy to the United States in 1860, was advocating a policy of reform and military modernization to be followed by the complete crushing of Chōshū and the subsequent suppression of other challengers of shogunate power, such as Satsuma. He was strongly backed in this policy by the French Minister, Léon Roches, who since his arrival in 1864 had worked energetically for a restoration of shogunal power under French influence. As a result of his efforts, a French school was opened at Yokohama, a naval dockyard built at Yokosuka nearby, and large quantities of weapons were imported. Not to be outdone, the British Minister, Sir Harry Parkes, who had played a large role in the opening of China, supported Satsuma with information and arms.

Thus through disillusionment as to the shogunate's effectiveness and fear of its possible return to power, the Satsuma leaders began to regard a coalition of strong *han* under the nominal leadership of the court as more feasible and attractive than the "union of court and shogunate." In other words, in Satsuma as well as in Chōshū an "honor the emperor" policy began to seem the best way to assert *han* leadership and create a strong national government.

The first sign of the *rapprochement* between Satsuma and Chōshū may have been Saigō's lenient attitude toward the rebel Chōshu government during the first expedition against Chōshū. Soon he and Ōkubo Toshimichi (1830–1878), who with him and a third samurai controlled the Satsuma government, decided that Chōshū was a preferable ally to the shogunate.

Two pro-imperialist *rōnin* from Tosa, who had taken refuge in Satsuma and Chōshū from the moderates in their own *han*, acted as intermediaries in bringing the traditionally hostile and mutually suspicious leaders of Chōshū and Satsuma together. These men were Sakamoto Ryōma, a "village samurai" descendant of a prosperous merchant family, and Nakaoka Shintarō, of village headman descent. Sakamoto, as a Satsuma agent, also helped Chōshū obtain a warship and rifles from the English firm of Glover and Company, when the shogunate, through its control of the ports of foreign trade, made the direct purchase of foreign arms difficult for Chōshū. The eventual fate of Sakamoto and Nakaoka was typical of that of many of the pro-imperialist *rōnin*. They were felled in a surprise attack in a Kyōto inn by pro-shogunate activists late in 1867, just before the final fruition of their years of plotting.

The gradual *rapprochement* between Satsuma and Chōshū resulted in a secret alliance drawn up in Kyōto on March 7, 1866, by Saigō and Ōkubo with Kido. Satsuma promised to work for Chōshū's reinstatement to favor in Kyōto and, under certain circumstances, to cooperate in the future for the glory of the imperial country. Chōshū's easy victory, however, obviated the necessity for any overt aid from Satsuma at this time and also made clear that the old Tokugawa system had come to an end. The demoralized shogunate had been defeated by a single *han*. Obviously some new balance of power was needed.

The End of the Shogunate. The shogun had died during the second Chōshū expedition, and Keiki, who had been the unsuccessful candidate for shogun a decade earlier, finally achieved this office in January 1867. Though he assumed the post with reluctance, he proved a strong leader, and with advice and aid from Léon Roches started to reorganize the shogunal administration. He placed his major emphasis on modernizing the military establishment but also transformed the Council of Elders into cabinet ministers personally responsible for various branches of the administration, eliminated unnecessary offices, and even took tentative steps toward abandoning the basic feudal principle that birth should determine eligibility for political position.

Late in 1866 Keiki had attempted to organize a council of leading daimyo, through which the shogunate would retain its primacy while surrendering its monopoly of power. This effort, however, was a complete failure. The court insisted on calling the council in its own name, and even then only five of the twenty-four invited daimyo came. The rest stayed at home out of fear or indecision. A small conference, consisting of Keiki and the daimyo of Satsuma, Tosa, Echizen, and Uwajima, was convened in the summer of 1867, but achieved no positive results.

Tosa, which was by tradition friendly to the shogunate but naturally wished to participate in any new division of power, then proposed a compromise solution by which the shogun was to return his political authority to the emperor and head a council of daimyo under the latter. This settlement would have relieved the shogun of the burden of full responsibility for national affairs and foreign relations, while leaving him his source of power — his personal domain, which was at least seven times as large as the largest *han*. It would also have checked the domination of Chōshū and Satsuma, which was feared by Tosa and other *han*. Keiki formally accepted this proposal on November 8, 1867, and was once more entrusted by the court with the government of the nation. But his invitation to all the larger daimyo to join a council in Kyōto went unheeded, and this "imperial restoration" accomplished no real change in the situation.

Meanwhile Satsuma, whose ties with Chōshū had been growing closer since their secret alliance in 1866, decided to join Chōshū in military action to overthrow the shogunate. Both *han* began to move troops into the Kyōto area, and a secret and entirely irregular "rescript" for the destruction of the shogunate was obtained from friendly elements in the court. Control of the court had been alternating between pro-shogunate nobles and moderates who favored the "union of court and shogunate," depending on which outside force was currently paramount at Kyōto. This unofficial "rescript" was obtained through Iwakura Tomomi (1825–1883), a noble who had developed a close association with Ōkubo of Satsuma. Tosa was informed of the plot and agreed, though reluctantly, to cooperate in a new government. Then on January 3, 1868 (the ninth day of the twelfth month of 1867 according to the Japanese calendar), the Satsuma and Chōshū forces, aided by those of the "collateral" *han* of Echizen and Nagoya and of the "outer" domains of Tosa and of Hiroshima in West Honshū, seized the palace and announced another "imperial restoration."

Keiki was inclined to accept the results of this *coup d'état* and retreated with his troops from Kyōto to Ōsaka to avoid clashes with the "imperial" forces. But some of his "collateral" and "hereditary" vassals and many of the officials in the shogunate were not prepared to acquiesce meekly in this power grab by their old rivals. When bands of *rōnin*, recruited at the Satsuma residence in Edo, committed acts of lawlessness, shogunate forces descended on the Satsuma residence and destroyed it. Then, under the leadership of Aizu and another "collateral" *han*, the shogunal troops marched from Ōsaka on Kyōto. The "imperial" forces, though outnumbered, were better armed and better organized, and once again victory went to the side with technological superiority. The shogunal samurai were routed on January 27 at Fushimi and Toba, south of Kyōto, and the whole of the old capital district fell into the hands of the rebels.

The victors then marched on Edo. Despite the pleas of subordinates and the urging of Roches, who continued to hope for a revived shogunate under French influence, Keiki, who himself came originally from pro-imperialist Mito, decided to capitulate. The surrender was arranged by one of his chief officials, Katsu Awa (1823–1899), a Tokugawa "bannerman" who had taken the lead in creating a modernized navy for the shogunate. Katsu, who had briefly visited the United States in 1860 and had helped patch up a settlement with Chōshū in 1866, was leader of a moderate faction in Edo. He also was on such friendly terms with the pro-imperialists of Southwest Japan that he was able to survive the demise of the shogunate to become a leading statesman subsequently. In May 1868 he peacefully surrendered Edo to the imperialist forces and agreed that Keiki should retire into domiciliary confinement in Mito and that his successor as head of the Tokugawa family should have his great shogunal domain cut to about one-tenth its original size.

Some supporters of the shogunate, however, refused to accept this decision. There was fighting in Edo, principally on July 4 at what is now Ueno Park. Die-hard shogunal leaders were executed. The "collateral" domain of Aizu in North Honshū, which since 1863 had taken a determined pro-shogunate stand, put up particularly bitter resistance, but by November had been crushed. Enomoto Takeaki (1836–1908), who had studied for several years in Holland, slipped out of Edo Bay with eight ships of the shogunate navy and seized Hakodate, taking control of the whole of Hokkaidō. But even this last center of resistance, after surviving two heavy attacks, surrendered in May 1869, and the whole of Japan came under the control of the revolutionaries.

THE CREATION OF THE NEW GOVERNMENT

With the shogunate immobilized by the conflicting pressures of foreign demands and "expel the barbarian" sentiment, confused in its councils, and deserted by many of the "collateral" *han* that were supposed to be its chief bulwarks, the overthrow of the Tokugawa had been relatively easy. Most of Japan, divided into units that were either too small or too indecisive to take effective action, simply stood by and watched, while a small group of dynamic young samurai, many of humble birth, seized control of the *han* governments of Satsuma and Chōshū, then with the connivance of a few friendly nobles won control of the court, and finally, through daring use of the military power of Satsuma and Chōshū, won mastery over the whole nation.

Despite the ease with which power had been seized, the creation of a new system of rule and the solving of the problems that had been the undoing of the shogunate were no simple matter. What organs of centralized government Japan possessed had been largely destroyed by the revolution; the new regime, like the old, was virtually powerless before Western military might; and the 5 per cent customs rates imposed by treaty left the country without economic defenses against the cheap manufactured goods of the West.

But the new government had two decided advantages over its predecessor. It was freer of the yoke of tradition and thus more capable of rapid change. More important, the turbulent fifteen years since the coming of Perry had helped clarify what course Japan would have to take to retain its independence. It was obviously impossible to "expel the barbarians." Instead Japan would have to try to match Occidental military power and industrial skills. Only then could it hope to be secure against the West, regain control over its own tariffs, and eliminate the other unequal features of the treaties. It was also becoming clear that, before Japan could match Occidental military and economic power, it would first have to create a much more centralized and modern government and would have to carry out major economic and social reforms.

The New Leadership. In theory, an "imperial restoration" had taken place on January 3, 1868, and various new offices and councils were created at once in Kyōto, but there was as yet no clear plan for a government or any accepted policy for it to carry out, other than the "imperial restoration" itself. And even this cardinal point was more a matter of symbolism than of practical politics. The emperor was to be the source of all legitimate authority, but this did not mean that he was actually to rule. The Japanese were much too accustomed to figurehead emperors, shoguns, and daimyo to return easily to personal imperial rule. The role of the emperor for over a thousand years — from even before the institution of feudalism — had been largely ceremonial and symbolic. Few really expected him to take personal charge of the government.

The Emperor Kōmei, who had been a foe of the extreme imperialists, had died early in 1867, to be succeeded by his son Mutsuhito, then only fourteen. Mutsuhito, who reigned until 1912, was in time to grow into an impressive and possibly influential figure. In 1868 the "year period" was changed to Meiji ("Enlightened Rule"), and the Japanese adopted the system the Chinese had been following since the beginning of the Ming Dynasty in 1368 of having only one "year period" per reign. Mutsuhito thus became known as the Meiji Emperor, and on his death he was given Meiji as his posthumous title, becoming then the Emperor Meiji. He was the personal symbol of the whole modernization of Japan. But in 1868 he was obviously too young to rule, and he seems never to have been more than one among many determiners of policy.

If the emperor was not to rule, then it might be supposed that the court nobles, the descendants of the Fujiwara aristocracy which had ruled Japan in the name of the emperor for many centuries before the establishment of feudalism, should take over the government. This was obviously what they themselves thought, as they busily reinstituted titles and organs of the ancient court. A few of them, controlling the imperial source of all legitimate authority, did become powerful in the new government — especially Iwakura, who had obtained for Satsuma and Chōshū the irregular "rescript" ordering the overthrow of the shogunate. Another noble who figured as a political force was Sanjō, who had returned to Kyōto with the Chōshū forces after his long exile from the court. But few of the other court nobles or imperial princes were fitted by temperament or training for real leadership. They played only symbolic roles as high government dignitaries, manipulated by their subordinates of humbler birth.

Since the extremists of Southwest Japan had acted in the name of their respective daimyo, it was natural for these daimyo to figure in the new government, but again their role was largely symbolic, as it had usually been in their own *han.* Such strong men as Shimazu Hisamitsu of Satsuma and the "collateral" lord Matsudaira Keiei figured in high posts in the early years, but soon even they dropped out.

The real leadership remained largely in the hands of the samurai who had engineered the revolution, though it had to be exercised tactfully through overlying layers of daimyo, court nobles, and the emperor. This cumbersome structure of authority contributed to anonymity and sometimes vagueness of leadership. These features of modern Japanese government were also the product of long-established habits of rule by committee rather than by individuals — habits traceable at least as far back as the thirteenth century.

One outstanding characteristic of the new leaders was their youth. The three most important men of samurai origin, Kido of Chōshū and Ōkubo and Saigō of Satsuma, were also the oldest, but they were between 35 and 41 in 1868 and had already been leading their respective *han* for several years. Inoue and Itō of Chōshū were 33 and 27. The eldest of the group, the court noble Iwakura, was only 43, and Sanjō was a mere 31.

Another feature of the new leadership was its relatively humble origin. Without the changes that started after 1853, Iwakura and Sanjō could never have been more than minor courtiers at an impoverished court, with no political power. A few well-born samurai like Kido might have climbed to positions of authority in their respective *han*, or, in the case of Katsu, in the shogunate, but men of lower samurai birth such as Saigō and Itō could never have been more than soldiers or local intellectual leaders.

The humble origin of these men clarifies two other points about them. Obviously they were men of most exceptional talents, or they would never have risen to power at all, and they had few emotional commitments to the *ancien régime*. Their rise to power had been in defiance of the feudal class system, and most of them, fully conscious of this, had from the start advocated a freer system that would leave careers open to talent.

The New Policies.   Even before the shogunate had been overthrown, the revolutionaries began to chart a new course for their government. On April 6, 1868, they had the young emperor issue a "Five Articles Oath," often called in English the "Charter Oath,"[1] which had been drafted by two samurai from Echizen and Tosa and revised by Kido. The second of the articles was simply a pious wish for national unity, but the others had more significant content. The first, about "deliberative assemblies," was probably not a promise to establish a democracy, of which these men had little knowledge, but was an assurance that elements not then represented in the group in Kyōto would not be frozen out of the government. The framers of the document probably had the ambitious samurai of other *han* in mind. In fact, four successive deliberative assemblies that included *han* representatives were convened between 1868 and 1870, but, for lack of experience with such representative bodies, they proved to be failures and were allowed to lapse.

The third article constituted a revolutionary credo, entirely consistent with the personal ambitions and experience of the young men in control of the government. It promised that persons of all classes should be

---

[1] *The Five Articles Oath of 1868*

1. Deliberative assemblies shall be widely established and all matters decided by public discussion.
2. All classes, high and low, shall unite in vigorously carrying out the administration of affairs of state.
3. The common people, no less than the civil and military officials, shall each be allowed to pursue his own calling so that there may be no discontent.
4. Evil customs of the past shall be broken off and everything based upon the just laws of Nature.
5. Knowledge shall be sought throughout the world so as to strengthen the foundations of imperial rule.

(From *Sources of the Japanese Tradition*, by Tsunoda, de Bary, and Keene, p. 644)

enabled to realize their aspirations without frustration — in effect, the end of the feudal class restrictions that their own careers had already cracked. They followed this with an even more general promise of drastic though undefined changes in the fourth article.

The last article of the oath was the most important of all: "Knowledge shall be sought throughout the world so as to strengthen the foundations of imperial rule." This statement was to be the basic philosophy of the whole movement. Japan was to be modernized and strengthened through the use of Western knowledge. It was a surprisingly frank disavowal of the sentiment to "expel the barbarians" that had been so strong at the imperial court and had contributed so much to the rise of the extremists in Chōshū and Satsuma and to their overthrow of the shogunate. Naturally the new leaders had not forgotten their earlier antiforeign bias. They merely proposed to take a wiser and more feasible approach to the foreign menace. It was obvious that Japan's only defense against the West lay in the creation in modern form of "a rich country and strong military" (*fukoku kyōhei*), which was to be achieved through Western technology.

This about-face on foreign policy had been clearly foreshadowed in March 1868, when the new leaders had arranged for the young emperor to receive representatives of the foreign powers in Kyōto. They also made clear that they would no longer tolerate irresponsible attacks on foreigners. The leaders in two clashes between pro-imperialist forces and French marines and sailors in the Ōsaka area early in 1868 were forced to commit suicide, and indemnities were promptly paid. When two *shishi* attacked the British Minister on his way to an imperial audience, Gotō Shōjirō (1838–1897), a high Tosa samurai who had helped engineer the original Satsuma-Chōshū alliance, decapitated one of the assailants on the spot, and the other was executed like a common criminal.

Centralization of power, though not expressed clearly in the Charter Oath, was another basic policy of the new government. The imperial government was expected not just to replace the shogunate but to exercise more uniform control over the country than had its predecessor. To symbolize their intentions the new leaders on September 3, 1868, renamed Edo as Tōkyō, meaning "Eastern Capital," and the next May moved the emperor to the old shogunal castle in this great city, which had been the true political capital of Japan for two and a half centuries.

The Organs of Government. It was easier to establish general policies than to carry them out. The new government had fallen heir to the position of the shogunate, which was faced with insoluble foreign problems, was financially bankrupt, had never exercised direct rule over most of Japan, and had lost much of the control it had once possessed. None of the new leaders had had any experience in operating a national regime, and they had at their disposal no organs of government suitable for this purpose. But by trial and error, they evolved a system of government that worked, however makeshift its elements.

The first experiment in government, known as the "three offices" (*sanshoku*), was set up on January 3, 1868, the very day of the "restoration." The "three offices" were (1) a General Director, a post occupied by an imperial prince, (2) a group of Conferees, consisting of court nobles and some leading daimyo, and (3) a group of Councilors (*san'yo*, renamed *sangi* in 1869), which included many of the young samurai leaders. This latter body proved to be the most durable of the early political institutions, lasting in one form or another for the next two decades. It was also in many ways the most important, since it usually included the majority of the real leaders.

Shortly after the establishment of the "three offices," a deliberative assembly and a series of administrative departments were added below them, but on June 11, 1868, the governmental structure was completely revised. A constitution was issued, embodying the "Five Articles Oath," and a Council of State (*Dajōkan*), named for an ancient political institution, was made the supreme organ of government. In apparent imitation of the division of powers in the American government, this Council was divided into a legislative body, known as the Department of Deliberation (which was subdivided into two chambers), an executive section called the Department of Administration, and six other administrative departments.

It is not strange that this only half-understood division of powers did not work. The legislative body was reorganized in the spring of 1869, and a complete revision of the government was announced on August 15. The Council of State remained the name for the chief organ, and six administrative departments, now called ministries, were placed under it. A legislative assembly was also attached to the Council of State, but was never reconvened after its second session in 1870. In imitation of the ancient governmental structure and in recognition of the special relationship between Shintō and the imperial family, an Office of Shintō Worship (*Jingikan*, literally the "Office of Deities") was made to outrank even the Council of State. The ancient system of court ranks for government officials was also revived.

Finally on September 13, 1871, a further revision was made. The Council of State was divided into three chambers: a Left Chamber (*Sa-in*), which in theory determined on legislation, a Right Chamber (*U-in*), which was to supervise the various ministries, and a Central Chamber (*Sei-in*), which retained all the actual authority both for legislation and for supervision of the ministries, including the Office of Shintō Worship, which was now reduced to the level of an ordinary ministry.

These rapidly changing organs of government were much less important than the men who staffed them. The emperor had been surrounded for more than a thousand years by three or four ministers of state, and Sanjō and Iwakura were appointed to these high offices in 1868, remaining in them until their deaths. Otherwise the occupants of the chief posts in the government were mainly exalted figureheads, drawn from among the court nobles and leading daimyo. The actual work of government was largely in the hands of young samurai leaders, who served at first as advisers in the main organs of government or as assistants to the heads of departments and ministries. Only slowly did the samurai leaders themselves move up to positions of titular responsibility. This first happened in 1871 when Ōkubo became minister of finance, but not until 1873 did it become the rule for the heads of ministries to be the young samurai who actually ran them.

The Centralization of Government. Central organs of government did not themselves create centralized rule. To do this, the new government had to establish its authority over the 265 separate *han*, which in theory were autonomous and some of which, during the declining years of the shogunate, had become all but independent. This was no easy task, because the new government, despite the theory that the emperor was the source of all legitimate authority, possessed almost no military power except that lent to it by some of the leading domains. The whole "imperial restoration" had been engineered by a few strong *han*, most of whose leaders had hoped to make their own *han* pre-eminent. It had scarcely been their purpose to preside over the dissolution of the *han*, at least not of their own.

In these circumstances, it is surprising how easily the new government led the *han* to their own extinction. This would have been quite impossible if certain of the new leaders, who saw most clearly that a fully centralized government was necessary, had not themselves been influential men in the very *han* that had sponsored the "imperial restoration" and were providing the new government with its chief military support. Moreover, the obscurity of the future helped the new leaders in Tōkyō. It was generally realized that great political changes must take place, and most *han* did not wish to be left behind in these changes for fear of being excluded from national leadership. But few of the *han* leaders realized that the changes actually taking place were leading Japan toward a fully centralized regime in which there would be no place for *han* autonomy.

In the constitution of June 1868, the new government had asserted the supreme authority of the Council of State, placed limits on the retinues of the daimyo when they traveled about the country, and assumed for the central government the right to tax both daimyo and samurai, though no actual system of national taxation was as yet feasible. The former shogunal domain was divided into prefectures for administrative purposes, and certain officers in the *han* were put under the authority of the central government. Then step by step over the next two years the administration of the various *han* was made to approximate that of the prefectures. The economic autonomy of the *han* was ended in 1869 when all highway barriers and custom duties between them were eliminated.

Meanwhile Kido and Ōkubo had persuaded their respective daimyo in Chōshū and Satsuma and the daimyo of two other major "outer" *han* in West Japan — Tosa in Shikoku and Hizen in Kyūshū — to return their domains to the emperor. This was accomplished on March 5, 1869, in a humbly worded document Kido had drafted. Many other daimyo followed suit, not wishing to be discriminated against by the new government, and in July the central government was emboldened to order the remainder to surrender their domains also.

The "return of the *han* registers," as this dramatic act is usually called, was largely symbolic, because the daimyo, as expected, were reappointed as *han* governors. This theoretical change in their status, however, set the stage for the elimination of the *han* two years later. Early in 1871 leading members of the new government went on missions to Satsuma, Chōshū, and Tosa to assure themselves of the support of these powerful domains. Then on August 29 the new government suddenly announced the complete abolition of the *han*. Most of the daimyo and samurai were thunderstruck but complied meekly. A few disgruntled individuals protested through the now-familiar method of political assassination, but there was no organized resistance. All Japan was divided into three urban prefectures (*fu*) and 72 other prefectures (*ken*) under governors appointed by the central government. These divisions have ever since remained the basis for local government, though the number was reduced in 1889 to three urban and 42 other prefectures (exclusive of Hokkaidō and the Ryūkyū Islands).

Consolidating the New Regime

Several factors explain the relative ease with which the *han*, some of which had existed as effective political units for four or more centuries, were pushed into oblivion. Divided by mutual suspicion, they had no basis for cooperation against the new government, while the government could command support from all parts of Japan by championing such popular concepts as the "imperial restoration" and national unity in the face of the foreign menace. Moreover, many of the *han*, crushed by old debts and disrupted by rapid change, had become incapable of functioning as autonomous units. By small steps Tōkyō had already permeated the *han* governments with its own authority. And finally, it offered the *han* and particularly the daimyo a very generous financial settlement.

In 1869, the daimyo, as *han* governors, had been assigned one-tenth of the former *han* taxes as their private income, and this they retained in

1871. Since the central government took over complete responsibility for the costs of local government, the paying of samurai stipends, and the repayment of *han* debts, the daimyo were much better off financially than they had been before.

The treatment of the samurai was less generous. The government reduced their stipends by 50 per cent or more. However, since most *han* had not been paying full stipends for a century or longer, the reductions were not as great as they at first appear, and the higher-grade samurai, whose stipends were cut the most, were also relieved of financial responsibility for their feudal dependents. Nevertheless, the years of transition between 1869 and 1871 did bring a decided lowering of economic status to a large part of the samurai class. The total value of their stipends after 1871 has been estimated at only about two-thirds what it had been three years earlier.

It can be argued that the new government needlessly complicated its financial problems by paying off the daimyo and samurai as generously as it did and that it should simply have dispossessed the feudal classes without recompense. The feasibility of this action, like other historical might-have-beens, can never be proved. It should be remembered, however, that the samurai class numbered about 1,900,000, thus constituting 5 to 6 per cent of Japan's population, or about ten times the percentage of the privileged classes in France at the time of the French Revolution. It would have been no easy task to dispossess so large a number of people who had monopolized the martial arts and political leadership. Moreover, loyalty to the daimyo remained strong despite the rising fervor of loyalty to the emperor, and the new leaders were themselves mostly men of samurai origin with close ties to their own daimyo and *han*.

A less generous settlement with the daimyo and samurai might not have been possible under the psychological, social, and political conditions existing in Japan in the early 1870's. As we shall see, the new government, as it grew stronger, did reduce the terms of its settlement to the point where serious revolts resulted. Actually, the government seems to have steered a successful course between the twin perils of financial bankruptcy on one side and the danger on the other side of pushing the daimyo and samurai to unified opposition, rebellion, or even (as in France) a permanent resistance by believers in the *ancien régime*.

Financing the New Government. Perhaps the settlement with the old order could not safely have been less generous, but it did present the new government with a seemingly hopeless financial problem. Tōkyō possessed no sources of revenue beyond those which had proved inadequate for the shogunate and *han*. Yet to succeed it had to pay the daimyo their large incomes and the samurai their stipends, to service *han* and shogunate debts, to operate local and national governments, and at the same time to shoulder the manifold and extraordinary new costs of modernizing the country. When it assumed authority in 1868, it had to embark on a series of costly military campaigns before it could even gain control over the shogunate domain and tax income. The extension of its authority over the *han* in 1871 increased its financial responsibilities far more than its income.

Little help could be expected from tariffs on foreign trade, since these had been limited by the treaty of 1866 to a mere 5 per cent. This agreement had saddled the Japanese with the expensive obligation of building lighthouses and setting out buoys and lightships at the ports opened to trade. Also the new government had inherited the indemnities and debts for foreign purchases owed by the shogunate and daimyo to various Western nations.

In the mid-twentieth century a technologically backward new regime can usually count on financial aid in the form of loans on easy terms or outright gifts from more advanced nations or from some international agency, but in the mid-nineteenth century this was unthinkable. The Japanese, in their fear of Western encroachments, were reluctant to place themselves under the financial wing of any foreign nation. In any case, the Western nations and bankers looked upon financial aid to the new Japanese government as a dubious investment which would require attractive interest rates and careful guarantees. Late in 1869 a loan of £930,000 at 9 per cent was floated in London to finance the construction of a railway between Tōkyō and Yokohama, and a second loan of £2,400,000 at 7 per cent in 1872 to help cover the increased financial obligations of the government following the liquidation of the *han*. Otherwise foreign capital played little part in meeting the new government's financial needs.

Actually the government's receipts from all sources in 1868 were hardly more than a third of its expenditures, and more than half these receipts were in the form of loans. Some 3,838,000 yen out of total receipts of less than 9,000,000 yen were obtained by the old Tokugawa expedient of exacting forced loans (*goyōkin*) from the great merchant houses. These loans have given rise to the theory that the great merchants had a large role as instigators and guiders of the "imperial restoration," but this was not so. The merchants, wishing to win the favor of the new government, acquiesced in making the loans and in some cases added additional gifts of money, but it never occurred to them to attempt to dictate basic government policy.

The financial situation was little improved in 1869, when income was still less than half of expenditures. Thus the new government had to live to a large extent on credit. For example, to cover its excess expenses in 1868 and 1869, it issued about 48,000,000 yen worth of paper notes, in part through the House of Mitsui and some of the other old merchant-banking firms. The new government notes had little backing and had to compete in a chaotic financial situation with more than 1500 varieties of paper money and credit issued by the *han*. The government notes naturally fell in value — for a while to less than half their face value.

In the early 1870's, however, the government's financial situation improved and with it the value of its paper currency. There were several reasons for this surprising recovery. For one thing, income began to approach expenditure, though in 1872 it had risen to only about 60 per cent of expenditures. More important were rising confidence in the future of the new government and rapid expansion of the Japanese economy, stimulated by foreign trade and freed from the restrictions of feudal political divisions. As a result, the government found that it could float adequate bond issues at home. By 1871 it had repaid all the short-term debts of its first two years, and by 1876, despite a great increase in general economic activity and in government revenue, its issue of paper currency stood at only twice the figure it had reached in 1869. Thus within a decade the new government had overcome its most pressing financial problems.

In the meantime Tōkyō had also carried out monetary, banking, and tax reforms, which had helped stabilize its finances and had contributed to the increasing solvency of the regime. These reforms were carried out largely on the initiative of Itō and Ōkuma Shigenobu (1838–1922). The latter was a Hizen samurai of iconoclastic temperament who had become interested in Western studies at an early age and had risen rapidly in the new government because of his skill in dealing with foreigners and his understanding of financial matters. Ōkuma had been made vice-minister of finance in 1869, and Itō, who had been sent to the United States to study foreign currency systems, served as his assistant. In 1871 Ōkuma and Itō standardized the currency, adopting the decimal system and making the yen the standard coin. It was made equivalent in value to the Mexican dollar used in the international trade of East Asia at that time, worth about half an American dollar. Ōkuma and Itō also set up a modern mint in Ōsaka. In 1872, on Itō's advice, the American system of national banking was instituted, though it worked poorly at first and was never entirely satisfactory.

The Land Settlement. In July 1873, a few months before Ōkuma became minister of finance, a thorough revision of the agricultural tax system was begun. The land tax was heavy in the early Meiji period, since it continued to be the chief source of government income, as it had been under the preceding feudal regime. As late as 1880 it constituted four-fifths of all tax revenue, for Japan was still largely agricultural. Moreover the new regime was unwilling to impose heavy taxes on trade and industry, which had to grow rapidly to meet the foreign economic menace.

Before the tax reform of 1873, agricultural taxes had been figured as percentages of agricultural yields, commonly 40 or even 50 per cent, as they had been in feudal times. Since the amount paid varied with the harvest, government budgeting had been difficult. Hence in 1873 these percentages were changed to fixed taxes in money based on land values. The latter were computed at 16⅔ times the average value of the crop, thus giving theoretically a 6 per cent return for investments in land. Since close to half the crop had always been paid in taxes, the new monetary tax was set at 3 per cent of the assessed value of the land — that is, half its theoretical productivity. This figure proved to be unrealistically high and was reduced to 2½ per cent in 1876.

On the basis of a fixed monetary tax, Ōkuma was able to start a modern budget system in 1873. The tax reform had certain other incidental but important long-range effects. To carry out the new system, the ownership of all land had to be clearly established. This was done in 1872, when all feudal restrictions on the free sale of agricultural land were removed. Hitherto the actual cultivators had usually had rights of a sort to the land, but so also had the feudal lords and their more important enfeoffed retainers, while between cultivators and lords had grown up a stratum of non-cultivating but non-feudal landowners who received rent from tenant farmers and passed part of this on as taxes to the lords. Under the new law it was established that the man paying the tax, either the independent cultivator or the landlord whose fields were worked by tenants, was the owner. Thus in modern Japan, unlike most of post-feudal Europe, there were no feudal estates of any sort but considerable tenancy from the very start.

The conversion of taxes contributed to the further growth of tenancy, because poorer peasants, facing a rigid monetary tax even in bad years, easily fell into debt and often lost their lands by foreclosure. Their plight was further aggravated when some of their subsidiary handicraft industries were ruined by cheap foreign goods. Most of the lands lost by the poor were acquired by their richer peasant neighbors or by urban moneylenders. As a result, tenancy grew steadily. About a quarter of the land was farmed by tenants even before the change in the tax system in 1873, and this figure shot up to 40 per cent in the next two decades and to almost 50 per cent by the 1920's.

The Creation of the New Army. The generous financial settlement with the daimyo in 1871 and the increased financial stability of the central government were major reasons for the ease with which the *han* were eliminated. Another important factor in this and in the social reforms that were to follow was Tōkyō's growing military strength. As early as 1868 and 1869 the new government had enough military support to beat down the die-hard adherents of the shogunate. It hastened to build further military strength both for domestic control and for defense against foreign political and economic domination.

At the time of its victory over the shogunate, the new government had only a few small volunteer units under its direct control and had been forced to rely on the support of *han* armies, principally those of Chōshū and Satsuma. A Chōshū samurai, Ōmura Masujirō (1824–1869), a former student of Dutch medicine and military tactics, emerged as the leading military expert in the new government. He founded arsenals and military academies but was prevented by conservatives from creating a real central army through conscription on the French model.

Ōmura was assassinated by conservative Chōshū samurai in December 1869, but another able Chōshū soldier soon took his place. This was Yamagata Aritomo (1838–1922). Born into a family of the lowest samurai rank, he had studied under Yoshida Shōin, had commanded the Kiheitai in the Chōshū civil war, and had returned to Japan in 1870 after a year and a half of study in Europe. Early in 1871 an Imperial Force (*Goshimpei*), using the French military system, was formed. It was composed of something under 10,000 men provided from the *han* armies of Satsuma, Chōshū, and Tosa. When the *han* were abolished later that year, the central government assumed control of the former *han* armies and divided the country into four garrison districts. Early in 1872 regulations were issued to increase control and discipline over the disparate military elements under Tōkyō. The Imperial Force was renamed the Imperial Guards (*Konoe*), with Yamagata as commander. The next year he assumed full responsibility as army minister.

Another reform early in 1872 was the division of the ministry of military affairs into army and navy ministries. The new government had gained control of the shogunate fleet in 1869 and, with the abolition of the *han* in 1871, had taken over the naval vessels of the various domains. Whereas the army used the French system, the navy from the start was modeled on the British Navy. In 1874 Enomoto, who had been pardoned for leading the last shogunate resistance in Hokkaidō, was made a vice-admiral in the new Imperial Navy, but a large proportion of the higher officers were drawn from the Satsuma naval force, and Satsuma men dominated the navy for several decades.

The most important military innovation came with the issuance on January 10, 1873, of a conscription law, carefully prepared by Yamagata. All men, regardless of social background, were made liable to three years of active military service followed by four in the reserves. Although this reform had been prefigured by the use of commoner volunteers in the mixed units in Chōshū a decade earlier, universal conscription was probably the most revolutionary step in the modernization of Japan. For almost three centuries commoners had been denied the right even to possess swords. The whole division of classes had depended on this clear functional division between them and the samurai. Now the weaponless peasant masses suddenly became the foundation of a greatly expanded and entirely centralized and modernized military system. Naturally it took several years to put universal conscription fully into effect, but as it gradually became a reality the new government established firm control over the whole country.

THE END OF FEUDAL SOCIETY

Universal military service was the death knell for the remnants of feudalism. The feudal political units had gone in 1871; now the chief functional distinction between samurai and commoner was removed. In fact, the whole basis for a feudal class society was disappearing, even though feudal prejudices and attitudes were to survive for another generation or two.

The Abolition of Feudal Privileges. The young samurai leaders, who had risen to power in defiance of feudal restrictions, had promised in the "Five Articles Oath" of 1868 to remove feudal social limitations, and they lived up to this promise with remarkable speed. Class restrictions on professional employment were abolished in 1869, and the next year commoners were permitted to assume family names, which only the wealthier and better educated had hitherto used. In 1871 even the *eta* and other outcast groups, who at the time constituted approximately one per cent of the population, were given full legal equality, though social discrimination against them is strong even today.

But not all class distinctions were removed. The old court aristocracy and the former daimyo were classified as nobles, the former samurai as *shizoku* (gentry), and most of the rest as commoners. The *shizoku*, however, enjoyed no legal privileges denied to commoners. In 1872 the lower echelons of the former samurai class were reclassified as commoners, and in time the distinction between *shizoku* and commoners became merely historical and was abolished.

The samurai were also deprived of their badge of social prestige — the paired long and short swords which only they had been entitled to wear. In 1871 they were permitted to discard them, and in 1876 those who still wore swords were ordered to stop doing so.

The loss of economic privileges was a still more bitter blow to the samurai. Even before 1868 most of them had eked out only an impoverished existence on their small stipends, but these had been reduced by about one-third since then. In 1873 the government offered the poorer samurai the option of a final lump-sum payment of either four or six times their annual income, half in cash and half in government bonds. In 1876 all stipends were commuted into government bonds on a sliding scale. Hereditary pensions were paid off at from five times their annual value for very large pensions to fourteen times for the smallest ones. Pensions limited to the lifetime of the holder were paid off at half these rates.

The total value of the interest payments on the bonds given the samurai was only about half the value of their stipends after these were reduced in 1871. The average lump-sum payment actually amounted to a mere 264 yen. Most samurai, deprived of their hereditary positions as *han* soldiers and officials and unable because of prejudice or inability to adjust to new conditions, soon lost even these pittances. A survey in 1884 showed the samurai in twelve prefectures had lost three-quarters of the bonds issued them only eight years earlier. Another survey made in 1883 of the 6196 former samurai families of the large *han* of Hiroshima revealed that two-thirds were extremely poor and 2701 had used up or otherwise lost all their government bonds and other property, while only 101 had enough in government bonds or other resources to live off income from capital.

The financial settlement with the daimyo was much more generous. They were compelled in 1876 to commute their incomes into lump-sum payments in government bonds, but these were computed so generously that the daimyo became relatively wealthy capitalists, living handsomely off the interest from their bonds. For example, in 1880 more than 40 per cent of the capital of all the national banks had been provided by former daimyo, largely out of these lump-sum payments.

Social Problems. The swift abolition of feudal privileges naturally produced great social turmoil. In all classes the more capable and enterprising took advantage of the new freedom to forge ahead in business or the professions, but the majority found the transition difficult. For example, a large proportion of the big urban merchant firms, accustomed to a close and profitable association with the feudal authorities as bankers and purveyors for the shogunate and *han*, failed to adjust and went into bankruptcy.

The unrest among the peasants was much greater. They were more outraged by the legal rights granted to the *eta* than pleased by their own rise to legal equality with the samurai. Most were bitterly opposed to the fixed monetary tax and to conscription, taking quite literally the unfortunate description of the latter as a "blood tax." (It was rumored that the blood of the conscripts was to be taken and sold to foreigners.) The peasants, in fact, recoiled from almost all changes in their traditional ways. Strange new foreign customs seemed to them abhorrent, and many of the innovations did entail at least transitional hardships. Peasant uprisings, which had more than doubled in frequency during the troubled last eight years of the shogunate, became even more frequent after 1868, rising to a crescendo in 1873 following the conscription act. Then, as the new government gradually established its incontestable military power and authority, they decreased, and became inconsequential soon after the reduction of the land tax in 1876.

Sporadic and uncoordinated peasant uprisings were no more a threat to the new government than to the shogunate, but widespread discontent among the former samurai was another matter. The disaffection within this once dominant group was a real menace to the regime. The leaders in Tōkyō, drawn for the most part from among them, looked upon the plight of their fellow samurai with particular concern. Special relief measures were started in 1869, and efforts were made to settle samurai on newly opened lands and to absorb as many as possible into the new military establishment, the government, and the new industries as foremen or common laborers.

The Debate over Korea. To the more traditional-minded of the new leaders, the re-employment of the samurai through foreign wars also seemed a possible solution of the problem. This approach was additionally attractive because it promised to restore feudal military virtues and other aspects of the *ancien régime* that traditionalists were loath to see lost. For these reasons, despite the precarious domestic position of the new government in the early 1870's, a proposed military expedition against Korea became a major issue.

Three missions had been sent to Korea by the new regime to revise and modernize trade and diplomatic relations, but the Korean government had refused to recognize the political change in Japan or to consider modifying the treaty of 1609 by which a quasi-tributary trade was carried on at Pusan on the south coast of Korea by the Sō, the daimyo of Tsushima. Agitation for a punitive expedition against Korea came to a head in the summer of 1873, partly because Korean officials made insulting references to Japan's Westernization, and partly because of increasing unrest among the samurai after the conscription act had robbed them of their proud monopoly of the military arts.

The situation was complicated by the absence from Japan of many of the stronger government leaders. In November 1871, Iwakura had led abroad a mission of forty-eight members, accompanied by fifty-four students, bent on studying the West and on persuading the foreign powers to modify the unequal treaties which the new government had inherited from the shogunate. With Iwakura had gone Kido and Ōkubo, the two other leading figures in the administration, and a number of rising stars such as Itō. The Iwakura Mission went first to the United States and then to various countries in Europe, returning home in September 1873. While the mission proved of great educational benefit to its members, it failed completely to persuade the Western powers to modify the treaties, even though the Harris agreement of 1858 had stipulated the possibility of revision in 1872.

While Iwakura and his colleagues were abroad, the government was largely in the hands of Ōkuma, Saigō, and Itagaki Taisuke (1837–1919), under Sanjō's general supervision. Ōkuma was among the most ardent of the reformers, but Saigō and Itagaki were typical soldier-samurai and had less sympathy with much of what was happening. Itagaki, a Tosa samurai, had won prominence in the campaign against the shogunate, but was dissatisfied to see the new government dominated by men from Chōshū and Satsuma. Saigō of Satsuma had been the chief military leader in 1868 but was unhappy to see the samurai class go down in ruin. He felt so strongly about the need for a campaign against Korea that he demanded to be sent as an envoy to Korea to invite execution and thus fully justify a war.

Iwakura and his colleagues, somewhat distrustful of the triumvirate they were leaving behind, exacted a promise that no major innovations be made without consultation by letter with the absent members of the government. During these years of rapid flux, however, this restriction was unrealistic. A number of major changes were made by the group left in Tōkyō, including the adoption of conscription. Worried by the plight of the samurai, the authorities remaining in Tōkyō took matters in their own hands in the summer of 1873 and decided on a military expedition against Korea.

The returning members of the Iwakura Mission, now convinced of Japan's backwardness and weakness, were appalled by this decision and managed in October to have it overruled. Saigō, Itagaki, and others resigned from the government in protest at this reversal of their cherished policy, which had already won imperial sanction, and retired in indignation to their former *han*. The result was a dangerous split in leadership.

One less serious effect of the furor over a Korean expedition was a much less hazardous overseas adventure, in part to mollify the defeated party. The kings of Ryūkyū had been the vassals of the daimyo of Satsuma since 1609, and in 1872 the new government extended its control over the islands. The year before, fifty-four shipwrecked Ryūkyūans had been massacred by aborigines on the east coast of Taiwan, and the Japanese government sent a punitive force of about 3600 soldiers against Taiwan in May 1874. Under the leadership of Saigō's younger brother, Tsugumichi, who had accompanied Yamagata to study in Europe in 1870, the Japanese won an easy victory.

Since China claimed suzerainty over both Taiwan and the Ryūkyūs, the expedition produced a diplomatic crisis with Peking. The Chinese, unaware of the niceties of Western international law, settled the dispute by paying Japan an indemnity for the costs of the expedition and for the murdered Ryūkyūans, thus recognizing in Western eyes Japan's claims to the Ryūkyūs. The islands were made Okinawa Prefecture in 1879, and eventually Peking gave up its claim to them.

Relations with Korea were settled soon after. Using Perry's tactics, the Japanese made a show of naval force along the coast of the peninsula in 1875 and again the next year. On their second visit there was a brief military encounter, and the Koreans were frightened into signing the desired agreement. In the Treaty of Kanghwa, February 27, 1876, two ports were opened to Japanese trade in addition to Pusan, where Japanese already resided, and Korea's independence was asserted though China continued to claim suzerainty.

The Suppression of Feudal Opposition. The successful Formosan expedition, however gratifying to the pride of the samurai, did little to help their financial plight. A series of outbreaks followed, some led by disgruntled former leaders of the government, participated in by desperate samurai who hoped to regain some of their lost privileges.

Most of these revolts occurred in the very same large *han* of Southwest Japan that had provided most of the leaders and military power for the new government. This apparent anomaly may have a simple explanation. Samurai of other areas were equally disturbed by the revolutionary changes made by the new government, but, forced into submission in 1868 and 1869, they remained too cowed to dare armed resistance. On the other hand, the disaffected samurai in the leading *han* of the Southwest were less overawed by their former colleagues who had risen to power in Tōkyō, whom they remembered as mere nobodies.

As early as January 1870, there had been a serious mutiny among the Chōshū mixed units, occasioned by local military reforms and resentment over the government's proforeign policies. Saigō's resignation from the government in 1873 induced large Satsuma elements in the Imperial Guards, which he then commanded, to return with him to Satsuma, leaving the army even more strongly dominated by Chōshū men. The next February some two thousand former samurai of Hizen in Kyūshū rose in revolt and captured the former *han* capital of Saga. Their leader, Etō Shimpei, had been influential in the new regime, but had resigned in disgust over the Korean policy.

The Saga revolt was suppressed by firm military action before it could spread, but the commutation of samurai stipends and the prohibition of swords in 1876 sparked new outbreaks that autumn. The first, in the large former domain of Kumamoto in Kyūshū, was followed by smaller risings in a minor domain nearby and in Chōshū. The last of these was led by Maebara Issei, who like Etō of Hizen had formerly been an important official in the new government.

Meanwhile more serious trouble was brewing in Satsuma, where Saigō, the idol of the conservative samurai, had founded schools for training in the military arts and conservative ideals, apparently to prepare for the day when the misguided government would fall of its own folly. His supporters were already in virtual control of the Satsuma area. Tōkyō, alarmed, decided to move government ammunition from Kagoshima, the old Satsuma capital, and some of Saigō's hotheads retaliated by seizing the army and navy installations at Kagoshima in January 1877. Saigō thus found himself the reluctant leader of an armed rebellion against the government he had done so much to found.

Saigō's samurai army, which at its height numbered about 40,000, marched on Kumamoto to the north but was held off by the local garrison until Tōkyō could marshal its forces. These consisted of Yamagata's new conscript army, supported by the navy and the national police force, which was built up mainly of former samurai as a major bulwark of the central government. In bloody fighting the superior government forces slowly pushed the Satsuma army back on Kagoshima, where in September Saigō and his chief lieutenants finally met their end.

The Satsuma Rebellion was by far the strongest challenge to the new regime, and it was also the last. For a while the outcome had been in doubt, but the peasant conscript army, with superior transport and better weapons, won the day. No one could now doubt that the new government, backed by technological superiority and in control of the great reservoir of peasant manpower, could impose its will on any dissident group. Public opinion, far from condemning Saigō, looked upon him as a romantic figure — a great if misguided idealist. In fact he eventually emerged in the popular mind as the hero of the "imperial restoration." But his defeat spelled the end of the old order. The new government had met its last great domestic challenge. Henceforth it could push ahead to modernize Japan and build its power of resistance to the outside world, free of any fear that conservative forces would overthrow it at home.

4

The Development of Meiji Japan

Early Industrialization

The new regime, within a decade of its coming to power, had established a firm grip on the whole nation. But a great deal more had to be done if Japan were to win security from external aggression and equality with the West. These would depend ultimately on the economic strength of the nation and the knowledge and technological progress of its people.

The young leaders saw clearly the broader aspects of the problems they faced. Their breadth of understanding and openness of mind show what remarkable men had been propelled to national leadership by the turmoil of the preceding two decades. The elimination of the *han*, the balancing of the budget, and the suppression of samurai resistance presented them with crises demanding immediate action. Yet they did not overlook the long-range problems of modernization.

The success of the Meiji leaders was probably greater and more rapid than even they had expected. In a mere half century, they built a powerful modern nation out of a feudally fragmented and technologically backward country, thereby winning the national security and equality they longed for. In terms of their own objectives, their achievements constitute the national Cinderella-story of modern times, even though, as in

GENERAL NOZU MICHITSURA, a hero of the Sino-Japanese War, as played by the kabuki actor Kikugorō in a popular patriotic drama. 1894 woodblock print.

Bismarckian Germany, their emphasis on national strength and military power bequeathed serious problems to later generations.

The development of Meiji Japan has particular relevance today, as a nineteenth-century counterpart to the twentieth-century theme of the modernization of underdeveloped countries. But the circumstances were in many ways different. The Japanese could expect no foreign economic aid, though they were surprisingly free from prejudice against foreign expert advice. They were threatened by rampant nineteenth-century imperialism but were not subjected to some of the pressures that are common today. For example, they were not seriously affected by foreign ideological conflicts or menaced by ideological subversion at home. Since no non-Western nation had as yet completely modernized, there was little expectation in Japan and less elsewhere that a great transformation would take place overnight. In contrast with the sometimes unrealistic expectations of the twentieth century, no one assumed that the Japanese should or could suddenly convert their feudal society into a full-fledged democracy or their backward economy into a fully industrial one. Thus they could move step by step toward their objectives, instead of attempting them in one great leap.

The background of the Japanese people was also quite different from that in most of the present underdeveloped nations. We have noted the many unusual features of their economy, society, and intellectual attitudes in the early nineteenth century that facilitated the subsequent transformation. It was the people as a whole, not merely the political leaders, who made possible Japan's rapid modernization.

The question of the respective roles of government and people in the development of Meiji Japan is of special interest today, when the proper balance between the two is an issue in many underdeveloped countries. Undoubtedly the government gave clear and strong leadership. It was the chief modernizing force in many fields. In others it created the necessary conditions of law and order. But strong leadership would have meant little if the people had not been prepared to follow and to exploit the new opportunities provided by the government.

Industrialization, which was so important an aspect of Japan's modernization, is a case in point. The story is complex; but in essence, the government provided political stability and sound monetary institutions, which were prerequisites for industrialization. The government also did the pioneering work in many industrial fields and sponsored the development of others, but it was private initiative that produced most of Japan's industrial development.

Strategic Industries and Communications. The government leaders sought particularly to develop the strategic industries on which modern military power depends. This need had been evident to the shogunate and some of the stronger *han,* which had made progress in this direction even before 1868.

For example, the Hizen domain, which had responsibility in alternate years for the defense of Nagasaki, succeeded with the aid of a Dutch book in building a reverberatory furnace for smelting iron in 1850 and three years later in casting cannon, from the iron it produced, to take the place of outmoded bronze ordnance. Within five years, the shogunate, Mito, and Satsuma followed Hizen in building reverberatory furnaces. Satsuma became the center of a thriving iron industry. The shogunate expanded its activities in this field by employing Dutch experts to set up an imported iron foundry at Nagasaki in 1857 and by establishing other foundries with French aid at Yokohama and Yokosuka in 1865.

Shipbuilding was an equally strategic industry. The shogunate built a Western-style barkentine in 1855 and a steamer at Nagasaki in 1857, apparently without Western technical aid, and constructed a shipyard at Yokosuka in 1865 with French aid. Some fourteen *han* also set up facilities for the construction or repair of Western-style ships. Satsuma had built model steamers as early as 1852, and subsequently constructed full-scale steamers, as did Mito and Hizen. By the time of the Restoration, the shogunate and *han* together owned 138 Western-style ships which they had either constructed themselves or bought from abroad. The Japanese had also acquired considerable knowledge of Western navigational techniques, and as early as 1860 the shogunate sent an entirely Japanese-manned steamer, the *Kanrin-maru,* across the Pacific to accompany the embassy to the United States.

The participants in the struggle for power during the closing years of the Tokugawa found it more practical to buy foreign ships and guns than to make them. But once the crisis was past, the new government set about building up these strategic military industries so as not to be dependent on foreign sources of supply. It set up a shipyard at Hyōgo (the modern Kōbe) to add to the two it had inherited from the shogunate at Nagasaki and Yokosuka. The Yokosuka yard built two naval vessels of more than 1000 tons during the 1870's, and by 1883 the Nagasaki yard had produced 10 steamers for the new regime and the Hyōgo yard 23. In addition, the government operated large works in Tōkyō and Ōsaka for making cannon, rifles, and ammunition and also three small gunpowder factories. The Ōsaka plant alone employed some 1100 workers. Though foreign models were used, foreigners themselves were not employed in these five arsenals for reasons of security.

The government took the lead in developing modern communications, both because of the public nature of this undertaking and because of the great capital sums required for it. A major reason for the economic backwardness of Japan, as compared with the West, was the high cost of internal transportation. There were few navigable rivers, and most goods moved on the backs of horses and men. It was said to cost as much to transport a ton of goods 50 miles within the country as all the way from Europe to Japan. Consequently, railways, once built, proved immensely profitable ventures. The 19-mile line from Tōkyō to Yokohama, completed in 1872, carried almost 40,000 tons of freight in 1877 at one-seventieth the cost of earlier transportation, and 2,000,000 passengers traveled on it in 1880. A second line had been built between Kōbe and Ōsaka by 1874 and was extended to Kyōto in 1877. But railway construction was difficult and costly in mountainous Japan, and by 1881 there were still only 76 miles of track. Telegraph lines, cheaper to construct and important for administrative control of the nation, spread more rapidly. By 1880 most of the major cities had been linked by government lines.

Other Government Industries. Industrialization could not be limited to strategic industries and communications. The production of consumer goods, especially textiles, had to be mechanized if Japan were to compete successfully with the West and eliminate the dangerous imbalance that had developed in its foreign trade.

Although there had been a serious outflow of gold (in exchange for silver) ever since trade had started in 1859, the initial lack of demand by the Japanese public for foreign goods and the strong demand for Japanese silk and silkworm eggs, occasioned by a silk blight in Europe, had created a small favorable balance of trade during the first decade. But the recovery of the European silk industry, the rising local demand for Western goods, and the fixing of import duties at lower rates in 1866 produced large trade deficits after 1869. This unfavorable situation was heightened by charges for shipping, insurance, and other services, which because of Japanese inexperience were almost entirely in foreign hands until well into the 1880's.

Meanwhile the import of cheap foreign manufactured goods was injuring domestic textile production and other handicraft industries on which the peasants depended for much of their livelihood. The draining of specie led to a rapid depreciation of the value of paper money and credits, which, while easing the burden on the heavily indebted government, contributed to the financial collapse of the samurai, especially after their stipends had been commuted into bond payments. New industries were desperately needed to give employment to peasants in certain areas and to samurai everywhere.

The government established a Ministry of Industry in December 1870. The next year Itō took charge of it as vice-minister, and in 1873 he became minister of industry, remaining in this key post until 1878. Under Itō and his successors, the government sought to develop the nonstrategic industries, both directly by starting government enterprises and indirectly by encouraging private industrial development through technical assistance, easy credit, and subsidies.

Even with government aid, however, private industrial ventures met with little initial success. Among their various difficulties were the relative scarcity of private capital and the resulting high interest rates, which were usually above 10 per cent. Hampered by Japanese inexperience with machinery, the need for high-priced foreign experts, and exorbitant transportation costs within Japan, industrial ventures could hardly bring such high returns in their early years. Several promising starts at private industry went bankrupt because of insufficient initial profits. As a result, government subsidies to private industries were felt by some to have been largely wasted.

The government devoted special efforts to mining, as an industry that would reduce the unfavorable balance of trade. By 1873 the Bureau of Mines already employed thirty-four foreigners. The Hizen domain, with English technical and financial aid, had put a modern coal mine into operation in 1869. This was taken over in 1874 by the new government, which bought out the English interests. By 1880 the government had developed eight other modern coal mines. It made a large investment in a modern iron mine in 1881 and in that year was producing 90 per cent of the gold and silver mined in Japan.

The government also built a machine tool factory in 1871, a cement factory in 1875, a glass factory in 1876, and a white brick factory in 1878, all in Tōkyō. The last three were to provide materials for Western-style buildings, since it was official policy to construct government buildings as much as possible in Occidental style, chiefly to impress the West with Japan's modernization.

The most important industrial field was textiles, because these made up more than half of Japan's imports between 1868 and 1882, and the best way to balance trade was to stem this inflow of foreign goods by the development of cheap, machine-made domestic textiles. The role of the government was somewhat different in each major sector of the textile industry. Woolens had become important for the first time in Japan because many men had adopted Western dress and soldiers and government functionaries wore woolen uniforms. Since woolen textiles constituted an entirely new industry, private capital made no effort to develop it, and a government mill, built in 1877–78 by German technicians, remained the chief producer until after 1900.

Cotton yarn and goods were a more important field. Foreign cotton fibers were cheaper and better than those grown in Japan and during the 1890's eliminated Japanese cotton almost completely. Thus the local industry at first depended on relatively costly local fibers and later had to purchase its raw cotton abroad. It had to operate on a very large scale to compete with cheap foreign imports, and naturally found itself handicapped by local inexperience with machinery. Because of these difficulties, it took much capital and a long time before Japanese cotton yarn and goods could match Western products in quality and price, and considerable government aid was necessary in the early stages.

The first modern textile plant was set up by the Satsuma domain in 1868, with 100 looms and 2640 spindles imported from England. Satsuma built a second mill in the Ōsaka area in 1870, but this was taken over two years later by the central government, which added two other government mills in 1881 and 1882. The government raised a 10,000,000-yen loan in 1878 in order to provide imported spinning machinery on easy terms to private companies.

In contrast with the cotton industry, silk reeling was mechanized with relative ease, and the government's role was limited to providing technical advice and operating a few pilot plants. This was because turning the silk reel by steam or water power, which produced much finer silk than reeling by hand, was a simple process requiring only modest capital, while all the other steps in silk filature remained hand processes at which the Japanese were already expert. After the European silk industry recovered in 1869 and the world market again became competitive, the Japanese began to shift to machine reeling. The first mechanical silk-reeling plant was established in 1870 by a "collateral" daimyo in the silk-producing area of central Honshū, and the government established three pilot plants between 1872 and 1877. The first used French technicians until 1875. The last specialized in a new technique — utilization of waste scraps from other mills.

Private Enterprise. Government plants accounted for only a tiny fraction of mechanical silk reeling in Japan. The rest was developed by private entrepreneurs. The house of Ono, which had developed as silk importers in the late seventeenth century and had then branched into banking, built a silk-reeling plant in Tōkyō late in 1870 and seven more in 1872–73. Others, particularly the local businessmen in the silk-producing areas of central Honshū, continued to develop the industry. By 1880 some 30 per cent of Japanese silk exports were machine-reeled products which outclassed the hand-reeled silk of the rest of Asia and competed well with European silk. At this time silk accounted for some 43 per cent of Japanese exports, about double the figure for the next item, tea. Chiefly because of the brisk demand abroad for Japanese silk, foreign trade began to show a favorable balance in the mid-eighties. Thus the industry that contributed most to the balancing of Japan's foreign trade was developed largely by private capital and enterprise.

Private capital moved into the cotton industry more hesitantly. An Edo merchant had ordered spinning machinery from America as early as 1864, but because of slowness of delivery, lack of capital, and technical inexperience, it was not put into operation until 1872, and in 1878 was still bringing in only a 5 per cent return on the original investment.

Two plants built by the Satsuma domain were sold to a private firm in 1878. Mainly because of the government financial aid that became available in 1878, fifteen more private plants were established in the next seven years. Thereafter the growth of private spinning firms was more rapid. Thus cotton spinning, which was to be Meiji Japan's largest industry, was also developed, except in its early stages, almost entirely by private enterprise.

There were other industries besides textiles in which private enterprise was important from the start. Relatively simple processes, such as match and paper making, were well developed by private capital as early as the 1870's. Most mining also was in private hands, though much of it was done in small mines by nonmechanized processes. In 1881, 99 per cent of the coal, 94 per cent of the iron, and 77 per cent of the copper production of Japan came from privately owned mines.

THE DEVELOPMENT OF THE BUSINESS COMMUNITY

The introduction of Western industrial technology was the most spectacular economic innovation after the coming of Perry, but it was on a small scale at first. Meanwhile the growth of other sectors of the economy, such as agriculture, trade, and those traditional handicraft industries that were not destroyed by Western imports, was actually much greater. For example, agricultural acreage increased 7 per cent and average yields per acre about 21 per cent in the 1880's, and total agricultural production doubled in the next 25 years. Although private capital was at first reluctant to enter the unfamiliar and financially hazardous field of machine industry, there was no dearth of capital or enterprise in the more traditional fields of economic activity. New commercial opportunities were enthusiastically exploited, and there was a rush of eager businessmen to the treaty ports when these were opened.

The result was a steady and rapid growth of the whole Japanese economy, and not merely the development of modern industry fostered by the Meiji government. In fact, the success of the government and private interests in industrialization can be explained only by this growth of the rest of the economy, which developed a sound foundation for the industry that the government was trying to construct from the top. This was probably one of the chief differences between Japan's rapid industrialization and the less successful efforts in China and other Asian countries, where modern industry initiated from the top often sank into the quagmire of a stagnant local economy.

The Government and Private Business. Government policies, as well as the opening of Japan, helped to account for this almost explosive growth of the Japanese economy. It could never have happened without the stimulus of foreign trade, the creation of political stability by the government, the economic unification of the country, the reform of the currency system, and the removal of feudal restrictions. The government's development of railways, ports, roads and, in time, such urban services as water systems and street railways also contributed greatly to economic growth.

The government, having originally led the way in many fields of industry, later withdrew from most of its economic activities, but individual government leaders continued to act as the prime movers in developing certain new industries or enterprises. In their eagerness to see Japan grow economically, they cajoled reluctant businessmen into new and still risky fields of activity; they helped them assemble the necessary capital, sometimes by putting pressure on other businessmen, sometimes by providing government subsidies of a type that would now be considered examples of corruption; they helped enterprising younger men to advance at the expense of their more conservative elders; and they forced weak companies to merge into stronger units. Inoue of Chōshū, who became a sort of arbiter in the affairs of the great Mitsui interests, was the most prominent of the government leaders in such economic activities, but others played similar roles. They were probably aided by the well-established Tokugawa tradition that businessmen depended not only on the tolerance of government leaders but on their business patronage as well.

Thus government leaders individually, as well as the government itself, played a large role in industrialization. Yet the fact remains that the great bulk of the economic development of Meiji Japan was the work of private individuals acting largely on their own initiative. It was they who built up agriculture and the small and more traditional lines of enterprise. They also played the major role even in industry.

The immediate political response by large numbers of Japanese has already been noted as an unusual feature of Japan's reaction to the Western menace. The response of an equally large number of private entrepreneurs was even more unusual in modern Asian history. Some of these men broke with the stable, orthodox, Tokugawa patterns to seize new opportunties in the period between 1853 and 1868. Others emerged only afterward in response to the radically new climate created by the early Meiji government. Even though most people clung with bewildered desperation to the old ways of life, a few exceptional persons had the daring to introduce large-scale enterprises based on Western models.

Patriotism often was as much of a motive for these entrepreneurs who industrialized Japan as for the political leaders who reorganized its government. They realized that they too were strengthening the country and establishing its security. In return, Japanese society gave them respect and prestige. As with the political leaders, their dreams of a strong and economically modernized Japan merged indistinguishably with personal ambitions, inducing them to plunge into risky industrial ventures when much higher and more certain profits were to be had in moneylending or in traditional lines of commerce.

The Role of the Merchant Class. The urban merchants, who had dominated much of the culture of Tokugawa Japan as well as its economy, naturally contributed to economic growth in the Meiji period, but in comparison with their former economic role their share was surprisingly small. Their past experience, instead of aiding them, seems to have inhibited their developing new entrepreneurial skills. Their outlook was conservative, conditioned by their long dependence on and subservience to the shogunate and *han*. The house laws of most of the large merchant firms explicitly enjoined their members from entering new lines of business. Thus for the most part they stuck to traditional banking and merchandising activities, waiting until others had pioneered in the new industries and proved their profitability before investing their own considerable capital.

Some of the larger firms that attempted in the early years to branch out into new fields failed during the financially chaotic 1870's. For example, the houses of Shimada and Ono, which with the Mitsui served at first as the bankers for the new government, went bankrupt within a decade after the Restoration. The Kōnoike firm, which had been important in *sake* brewing in the Ōsaka area in the early seventeenth century and had switched to banking toward the end of that century, did manage to survive but gradually lost ground as a leading financial institution.

The house of Mitsui was an outstanding exception among the large old merchant firms. Under the aggressive leadership of Minomura Rizaemon (1821–1877), it made the transition to modern banking methods and subsequently branched out into a variety of new enterprises, becoming in time the largest of the great financial and industrial giants later known as the zaibatsu, a term meaning "the financial clique."

Minomura was an unusual merchant leader, having started as a poor orphan of obscure origin, and his appointment as general manager was unprecedented in Mitsui history. Having shown his ability by successfully conducting the firm's relations with the authorities during the last years of the shogunate, he was equally skillful in dealing with the new government, establishing a particularly close relationship with Inoue. Minomura moved the headquarters of the firm from Kyōto to Tōkyō, sent five members of the Mitsui family and two employees to study in the United States in 1872, and separated the rest of the firm from its merchandising branch. The latter, forced to stand on its own feet, modernized its procedures and eventually developed into Mitsukoshi, the first of those great modern department stores so important in Japanese urban life.

The third largest of the later zaibatsu also grew out of an old merchant company, the Sumitomo firm, which dated back to the early seventeenth century. After the Restoration, an able employee modernized its copper-mining activities and then launched it in banking, foreign trade, and other enterprises. Another great zaibatsu firm was founded by Ōkura Kihachirō (1837–1928), who came from a prosperous merchant house in Niigata on the west coast of Honshū. Abandoning his hereditary business, he traded in rifles during the disturbed period preceding the Restoration and then came to Tōkyō, where he succeeded in foreign trade and branched out into industry.

Samurai Businessmen. In general, entrepreneurial ability emerged from the samurai class more than from the townsmen. This may seem strange in view of the traditional samurai contempt for economic activity and the profit motive, but it is explained by samurai traditions of leadership, their high standards of education, the tremendous interest in economic problems among samurai intellectuals during the second half of the Tokugawa period, the managerial skills some samurai had developed as *han* or shogunate officials, and the severe financial difficulties in which most samurai found themselves in the 1870's.

In the large samurai class as a whole, however, it was only a few rather untypical figures who distinguished themselves as entrepreneurs. The great majority found themselves unprepared, by their inexperience in business and their traditional contempt for the profit motive, to succeed in business life. Samurai did provide almost a third of the capital for the 148 national banks founded in the first two years after the reform of the banking law in 1876. Their capital came from the bonds paid them in 1876 in lieu of their former annual stipends (as was also the case with the 44 per cent of the capital provided by former daimyo). The organization of these banks, however, was supervised by the government and did not represent a very significant entrepreneurial activity on the part of samurai or daimyo. Moreover, almost all of the hundreds of business companies formed by samurai groups during the decade after 1876 failed completely. It was thus only a very small percentage of the men of samurai origin who succeeded in business and still fewer who became important entrepreneurs in industry.

The most outstanding of the new business magnates of samurai origin was Iwasaki Yatarō (1834–1885). He came from the Tosa domain, where he had been a "rural samurai" but had become the supervisor of the *han*'s mercantile operations in Nagasaki before the Restoration. After the dissolution of the *han*, he transformed the *han*'s commercial and shipping interests into his own private concern, which he subsequently named the Mitsubishi Company.

Iwasaki was greatly helped by the government, which saw him as a promising person to develop a Japanese shipping line that would eliminate dependence on foreign ships and reduce payments for haulage in foreign bottoms. The government bought thirteen foreign ships for the Formosan expedition in 1874. It entrusted these to Iwasaki to operate and subsequently gave them to him. He again was put in charge of marine transportation during the Satsuma Rebellion in 1877, being provided by the government with nine more ships and a large subsidy. With this sort of aid and continuing subsidies, he was able to develop a large fleet, which began to operate abroad in 1879. From these beginnings the Mitsubishi Company moved out into other fields, eventually becoming the second largest zaibatsu concern and the major rival of the Mitsui interests.

Peasant Entrepreneurs. Men of peasant origin had an even more remarkable role than the samurai businessmen. Since Japanese agriculture was already quite commercialized by the early nineteenth century, the wealthy peasant class had developed entrepreneurial skills in the processing and sale of local agricultural products. It was not strange, therefore, that these men were able to invest in technological improvements in agriculture and develop their other economic interests. In this they were aided by the prosperity that came to rural Japan in the late 1870's. Though partially a result of the general development of the economy, this also came from the lowering of the land tax in 1876 and the inflation that hit Japan in these years, further reducing the real value of taxes. During the next few years, agriculture bore, by traditional standards, only a modest tax burden, so that the richer and more enterprising peasants were able to invest heavily in agricultural improvements and in commercial and industrial undertakings. The mechanization of silk reeling was mainly the work of wealthy peasants, and many other traditional local enterprises were expanded and modernized by them in much the same way.

The most spectacular of the peasant-born entrepreneurs was Shibusawa Eiichi (1840–1931). Born near Edo into a rich peasant family in the indigo-dyeing business, Shibusawa was given a good education and developed great ambitions. He left home in 1863, determined to achieve samurai status and make a name for himself. He plotted an armed uprising to expel the foreigners, became enrolled as a samurai under Keiki, the future shogun, and accompanied Keiki's younger brother to Europe on an official mission in 1867.

After Keiki's abdication, Shibusawa started a banking and trading company for his former lord but was soon drafted to serve in the new central government. Under the patronage of Ōkuma and Inoue he rose rapidly, becoming one of the major figures in the Treasury and leading the way in establishing the government's first silk-reeling plant. However, he resigned from the government in 1873, after a budgetary disagreement, and then became president of the First National Bank, which he had helped found by forcing Mitsui and Ono banking interests into a merger. In

1880 he organized the Ōsaka Spinning Mill, which soon became Japan's first major industrial success. From this beginning he went on to become one of the nation's greatest entrepreneurs, having a hand in the founding and management of more than a hundred companies spread throughout the major fields of industry and finance.

Another man of rural origin who founded an important zaibatsu firm was Asano Sōichirō (1848–1930), son of a village physician. He ran away from home, came to Tōkyō in 1871, got into the making of cement, acquired control and then ownership of the cement factory that the government had built, turned this hitherto financially disastrous undertaking into a great success, and then launched out into other industries.

The fourth largest of the later zaibatsu firms was founded by still another man of humble origin. This was Yasuda Zenjirō (1838–1921), who in his youth ran away from his home on the west coast of Honshū to Edo where he became a money-changer. After the Restoration he founded a modern banking empire that bore his name and then branched out into railways and other business.

These six men are merely a few outstanding examples among the thousands of individuals of all classes who helped to develop the modern Japanese economy. Many of the most important figures were uprooted men who had fearlessly turned their backs on the past, determined to industrialize Japan, with unbounded faith in the magic of economic modernization. They could have done little without the favorable conditions for economic growth created by the government; for some, direct government aid was crucial to success. But if thousands of private entrepreneurs had not spontaneously appeared, the government's economic efforts might have failed completely or at best would have progressed slowly.

THE GROWTH OF THE ECONOMY

The Development of Hokkaidō. While improved technology permitted some expansion of agricultural acreage throughout Japan, the only large unexploited area was the northern island of Hokkaidō. Since development of this cold, inhospitable region required long-range investment and had important strategic implications, the government took the lead.

The Japanese had exercised some control over Hokkaidō since about the eleventh century, but in the early nineteenth century the Japanese population was still limited chiefly to the coast and the extreme south, while the rest of the island and the smaller ones to the north were inhabited for the most part by the hairy Ainu aborigines. The Matsumae domain in southern Hokkaidō had established fishing settlements as far north as Sakhalin by the late seventeenth century, and the southern Kuril Islands had been developed into rich fishing grounds. Japanese cartographers surveyed and mapped the coasts of this whole northern area in the early nineteenth century. The explorer Mamiya Rinzō (1780–1845) in 1808 proved that Sakhalin was an island and the next year ventured up the Amur River.

Because of the opening of Hakodate to foreign ships through the Treaty of Kanagawa in 1854, the shogunate took over direct control of Hokkaidō from the Matsumae daimyo, as it had on certain previous occasions. This time a serious attempt was made to colonize the island, but with little success. When the shogunate signed its first treaty with the Russians at Shimoda in February 1855, it also agreed to Russian demands for a rough delimitation of the northern boundary. Kunashiri and Etorofu, the two large southern islands in the Kurils, were assigned to Japan and the rest to Russia, while the two countries agreed to continue their joint occupation of Sakhalin.

This settlement of the boundary question did not please the Russians, who kept pressing Japan to modify it. For this purpose, Muraviev, the governor-general of Siberia, went to Kanagawa in 1859 with seven ships but obtained nothing from his show of naval power. In 1861 a Russian naval expedition occupied the island of Tsushima in the straits between Japan and Korea, but soon withdrew from this ill-considered effort to annex Japanese territory. A clear settlement of the Russo-Japanese border was finally reached at St. Petersburg on May 7, 1875, with Admiral Enomoto, the former shogunal naval commander, acting for Japan. The Japanese ceded their interests in Sakhalin to Russia in return for Russia's giving up her claims to the central and northern Kuril Islands.

The Tōkyō government was much more interested in Hokkaidō than in the islands to the north, because of its greater economic potentialities and its strategic value as a bulwark against Russia. As early as 1868 the government had been laying plans for the development of the island. In 1869 the name of the island was changed from Ezo to Hokkaidō, meaning "Northern Sea Circuit," and its development was put in the hands of a Colonization Office (*Kaitakushi*). In 1870 Kuroda Kiyotaka (1840–1900), a Satsuma samurai who had commanded the government forces against Enomoto, assumed charge of this office, serving until a month before it was dissolved in 1882.

Kuroda went to the United States, where, on President Grant's advice, he hired the United States Commissioner of Agriculture, Horace Capron, at the princely salary of $10,000 plus expenses, and a staff of American experts to advise on the development of Hokkaidō. Capron and his group remained in Japan until 1875. The next year William S. Clark, president of the Massachusetts Agricultural College, arrived to take charge of the newly founded Sapporo Agricultural College. Clark left a lasting influence on this institution, which grew eventually into Hokkaidō University. Through the work of such men, the agriculture and rural landscape of the island were given a somewhat American cast. Silos, for example, are a common feature of Hokkaidō farms.

Under government sponsorship, subsidized farmer immigrants came into Hokkaidō, reaching a high point of 13,784 in 1872. Some 2139 colonist militia were settled on the soil in 1875–76. Thus between 1869 and 1881 the total population of the island more than quadrupled, reaching 240,391. Agricultural acreage increased more than tenfold, the fishing industry more than doubled, and many other new industries got started. In these ways, foundations were laid for still greater economic exploitation of this frontier region in the following decades and a further tenfold increase in population by 1918. More important, Hokkaidō was made fully Japanese and secure from Russian penetration. In 1883 it was given a normal prefectural system of local government, though it continued to be called a "circuit" (*dō*) rather than a prefecture (*ken*).

Economic Retrenchment under Matsukata. The development of Hokkaidō, though valuable in the long run, added to the financial drain on the central government during the 1870's. Meanwhile the government's many industrial enterprises for the most part were losing money; even when they were successful, they rarely brought in profits on investment equal to the current rates of interest. This situation was not unexpected, since the government had concentrated on strategic industries and the fields in which the risks were so great and the returns so slow in materializing that private capital was reluctant to enter them. In any case, the ambitious program of economic development in the 1870's helped produce a serious financial crisis in the last years of the decade.

The costs of liquidating the old regime — payments to the daimyo and samurai, repayment of shogunal and *han* debts, and costly military campaigns — were a heavy financial burden, which was augmented by the broad program of modernization. As a result, the government was living beyond its means. It had been able to do all these things through deficit financing, but the rapid increase of its liabilities because of the conversion of daimyo and samurai payments in 1876 and the Satsuma Rebellion the next year overstrained its credit. Its specie coverage for outstanding notes and paper currency fell to less than 5 per cent; by 1880 paper currency depreciated to hardly more than half its face value; a serious inflation set in, with the price of rice more than doubling between 1877 and 1880; and inflation cut the real value of the land tax on which the government largely depended.

In the face of this financial crisis, Ōkuma proposed floating a huge loan in London, but more conservative opinion prevailed, and a policy of economic retrenchment and deflation was adopted. The first major step, announced on November 5, 1880, was the sale of government industrial enterprises. A prime advocate and the chief executor of this retrenchment policy was Matsukata Masayoshi (1835–1924), a Satsuma man of humble samurai origin who had risen rapidly in the new regime because of his financial genius. In 1880 he had been appointed home minister and in 1881 was shifted to be minister of finance, remaining in this key position without interruption until 1892.

At first, because of the weakness of private capital and the unprofitability of most of the government industries, the government could find no buyers at the prices it was asking. Not until 1884 were most of the enterprises sold, and then only at very low rates. Among the major plants and mines for which figures are known, the sale prices ranged between 11 and 90 per cent of the original investment. Almost all were sold, sometimes without competitive bids, to insiders, that is, to businessmen or public servants already closely associated with leading officials. In some cases there was obvious collusion. For example, the proposal to sell the government's assets in Hokkaidō to a group of businessmen and former Colonization Office incumbents for about 3 per cent of the original investment became a major scandal and had to be abandoned.

The sale of the government industries put the development of most sectors of the economy — except for war industries, communications, and public services — entirely into the hands of private enterprise and contributed to the eventual concentration of much of Japanese industry in the hands of a small group of giant corporations. Since the government enterprises formed a large proportion of all the modernized industries of Japan, the rather few firms that acquired them at low prices in the 1880's ultimately found themselves in an advantageous position. As Japan's industrialization overcame its initial handicaps and began to pay off handsomely a few years later, some of these firms got such a head start on possible competitors that they were able to develop into the great zaibatsu combines of the twentieth century.

This outcome of the retrenchment policy has given rise to Marxist interpretations that the chief motive in the sale of government industries was the commitment of the government leaders to large-scale capitalism. There is no real evidence for this theory, however, and it assumes an understanding by the Japanese leaders of the long-range effects of their action and a preference for capitalism over government ownership that seem altogether improbable. Another theory, that the sale was an economic concession by the government to the forces of opposition within Japanese society, appears to have even less basis.

The obvious explanation for the sale of the industries, made amply clear by all contemporary documents, was the financial crisis. Curtailment of government expenses seemed a safer course than large foreign loans. The sale of enterprises was merely one aspect of this budgetary cutback. The funds of almost all branches of government, including the military, were also reduced; costly foreign experts were dismissed; and students were recalled from abroad.

The government leaders probably saw nothing reprehensible in selling industries to insiders at bargain rates. They had been trying to modernize the national economy by all available means, encouraging and assisting private enterprise whenever possible as well as founding government industries when this seemed necessary. Selling the industries at reasonable prices to men they felt were competent seemed the best way to ensure their continued development. This was far more important to the national interest than the payment the government received. As it turned out, most of the industries sold did not for a decade or more make profits comparable to the return in other economic fields. The purchasers' faith in the future of industry in Japan is, in fact, more surprising than the low prices they paid.

Matsukata's retrenchment policies were successful, and by 1886 he had the government back on an even financial keel. New taxes were instituted; a centralized, European-style banking system, under the newly founded Bank of Japan, was substituted in 1882 for the earlier American system; paper currency in circulation was reduced about one-quarter; interest rates dropped; specie reserves were increased to 35 per cent of notes outstanding; and by 1886 paper money had been restored virtually to face value. As a result, the real income from the land tax had also been restored.

The Success of Industrialization. Once back on a sound fiscal basis, the Meiji government thereafter remained financially much stronger than during its first two decades. The general economy, too, though temporarily depressed by Matsukata's deflationary policies, soon recovered and surged ahead even more rapidly than before.

Deflation had weeded out the unsound speculative ventures that had flourished under the inflationary conditions of the late 1870's, leaving only the sounder enterprises. These profited from the return to hard money and the drop in interest rates from around 15 per cent to around 10. Private management of the former government industries, being free from cumbrous bureaucratic control, seems also to have been more efficient. Thus Matsukata's financial policies appear to have provided the last of the prerequisites needed before industrialization could really begin to pay. Political stability, with its assurance of continued law and order, had helped to create adequate domestic capital based in large part on government credit. The Japanese were also beginning to overcome initial handicaps, such as the high cost of internal transport and inexperience with machinery. Long-term investment in industry was thus becoming not only more attractive but also more feasible. In short, Japan was ready for an industrial "breakthrough" or "takeoff" — at least in certain fields of industry.

Shibusawa's Ōsaka Spinning Mill spearheaded the new industrial development. It was much larger than earlier mills, thus cutting overhead costs, and Shibusawa had a highly educated young man specially trained in England to run it with the most up-to-date techniques. The mill had already proved a great financial success by 1884, in the midst of the deflationary depression. In the next few years there was a rush of entrepreneurs into the spinning industry, particularly in Ōsaka, the old center of the cotton trade, and a large number of new firms were founded, including such later giants as the Kanegafuchi Company (Kanebō).

The spinning boom was followed by a more general boom in other industries. New firms prospered in such diverse fields as mining, weaving, cement, beer, chinaware, gas, and electricity, but the greatest growth came in cotton spinning and railway transportation. Between 1883 and 1890, government railways expanded from 181 to 551 miles and private railways from 63 to 898 miles. Cotton spindleage almost tripled between 1882 and 1887 and production grew tenfold in the next five years. In the early 1880's Japan was still importing more than 90 per cent of the cotton yarn it consumed, but after 1889 imports dropped off sharply, and within five years the Japanese spinning industry had become so efficient that its products began to venture into the world market on a significant scale. By 1897 Japan had become a net exporter of cotton yarn, and by the end of the century cotton spinning and weaving employed 247,117 persons, or 63 per cent of all factory workers.

The mid-eighties, which saw the transfer of most government enterprises to private hands and the first industrial boom, also saw the emergence of a pattern of cooperation and cartel-like organization among big business concerns, in place of sharp competition. This was to become a world-wide trend in mature industrial economies, but in Japan's industrialization it appeared at an earlier stage and in greater strength than might have been expected from the experience of Western countries. Perhaps this was partly a result of the old Japanese preference for collective leadership and the long tradition among Tokugawa businessmen of establishing monopolistic associations under official sponsorship. There was also pressure from government authorities, particularly Inoue, for joint business enterprises that would create strong companies. Cooperation between big businessmen does not seem to have stunted Japan's industrial growth; on the contrary, it produced a pooling of resources that facilitated the financing of large-scale new enterprises.

The first clear sign of the new tendency was the merger in 1885 of competing steamship lines owned by the two emerging business giants, the Mitsubishi and Mitsui interests. The resulting Japan Mail Line (Nippon Yūsen Kaisha, commonly known as the N.Y.K.), which was under Mitsubishi domination, has remained ever since the largest component in Japan's merchant marine.

Another example was the development under Shibusawa's leadership of a tight cotton-spinning cartel. The cartel allocated the inadequate supply of skilled labor, organized joint noncompetitive efforts for the purchase of foreign raw cotton and the sale of cotton yarn abroad, assigned quotas in times of overproduction, and lobbied for favorable legislation such as the elimination of duties on raw cotton imports and cotton exports. It also made mutually advantageous compacts with the Mitsui foreign trade network and with Mitsubishi's Japan Mail Line, which brought the spinners their raw cotton and exported their products. Thus by the 1890's the pattern had been set for the development of industry-wide cartels and of "combines" of interlocking business interests in finance, commerce, and manufacturing.

Industrial growth in Japan, as in other countries, was not a straight-line development. The boom years of the 1880's were followed by a period of slower expansion of factory capacity, but Japan's victory in the Sino-Japanese War in 1895 set off another sudden upsurge in all the established industrial fields and in certain new ones such as chemical fertilizers. Not only did the war stimulate the demand for a wide variety of goods, but it proved no financial strain, since the Chinese indemnity of 230,000,000 taels (414,000,000 yen) more than paid for all direct war costs. Subsequently the development of new factories again slowed down, but this was a constructive period of amalgamation of existing companies into a few large and strong units.

Then in 1905, after the Russo-Japanese War, came a third and bigger boom. Cotton weaving began to catch up with cotton spinning; the electric industry grew as railways were electrified and cities installed street lighting; shipping tonnage and services abroad expanded rapidly; the production of coal almost tripled in the decade after 1904; the Yawata Iron Works, founded by the government in 1901 at the northeastern tip of Kyūshū, helped Japan to meet a significant proportion of its iron and steel needs; and a few other heavy industries began to join the simpler light industries as important components of the economy. The scale of the boom can be seen from the increase between 1902 and 1912 of capital invested in various industries: fivefold in sugar refining, eightfold in fertilizer plants, ninefold in the production of machinery, elevenfold in gas companies, and fifteenfold in electricity. Thus, during the two and a half decades following Matsukata's financial reforms, one industry after another came of age, and Japan, with its industrial base now diversified and soundly established, entered a period of sustained industrial growth.

THE TRANSFORMATION OF SOCIETY

Industrialization as well as political and military modernization depended on new skills, new attitudes, and broader knowledge among the

Japanese people. The new leaders had realized from the start that social and intellectual modernization was prerequisite to successful innovation in other fields. But in the social and intellectual areas, as in economics, the responsiveness of thousands of individuals from all classes was more important in the long run than the planning of the authorities.

Westernization. Many innovations were not really necessary to modernization but were merely imitations of Western customs. At the time, however, the distinction between fundamental features of modern technology and mere Occidental peculiarities was by no means clear. If it was necessary to use Western weapons, there might also be virtue in wearing Western clothes or shaking hands in the Occidental manner.

Moreover, the Meiji Japanese had good reason to adopt even the more superficial aspects of Western culture. The international world of the nineteenth century was completely dominated by the Occident, and if Japan were to make its way in this society of nations, it must conform socially to some extent. Indeed, one of the chief problems was to persuade the Western powers to revise the unequal treaties and accept Japan as an equal. Military and economic power was not the only answer to this problem. In view of the arrogant Western assumption of cultural superiority, the Japanese were probably right in judging that they would not be regarded even as quasi-equals until they too possessed not only modern technology but also many of the outward signs of Western culture.

Naturally enough, the Meiji Japanese were extremely sensitive when Occidentals laughed at their customs as quaint or disapproved of them as "barbaric." While this sensitivity reflected the extreme self-consciousness of the Japanese personality, it was also a valid response to the times. The Japanese needed for practical reasons to eliminate, or at least to hide, aspects of their culture that Westerners viewed with contempt or mirth. The resulting effort to borrow almost anything and everything Western may now seem amusingly indiscriminate, but it is perfectly understandable considering the social inequality between the West and Asia in the nineteenth century.

Mixed desires for cultural conformity and technological progress evidently inspired many innovations. For example, Western hygienic practices, such as brushing the teeth with powders and pastes, were gradually popularized through official propaganda, and the Japanese in time became the world's most enthusiastic toothbrush users and consumers of patent medicines. In 1873 a government mail service was inaugurated; in 1872 gas lights were introduced on the streets of Yokohama; and in 1887 electricity was made available in Tōkyō. Japan joined the international metric agreement in 1886 and adopted the metric system for general use in 1924, moving a step in advance of the English-speaking nations.

The Meiji government also adopted the Gregorian calendar of the West, together with its seven-day week and Sunday holiday, in place of the traditional lunar calendar of East Asia. The change was made at the beginning of 1873, when the third day of the twelfth month of 1872 became January 1 of the next year. The Japanese, however, continued to count years primarily by "year periods," 1873 being known as Meiji 6, and the lunar calendar remained in popular use in rural Japan for another generation or two.

The ricksha is a curious hybrid of Westernization, combining superior Western-style wheels with cheap Asian muscle-power. Properly called the *jinrikisha,* or "human power cart," it was a newfangled conveyance invented in Japan in 1869. It proved extremely useful under nineteenth-century conditions in Asia and spread rapidly from Japan to other countries, but in the early twentieth century it was gradually pushed into oblivion in Japan by the introduction of motorized conveyances.

Occidental Fashions. Many innovations were nothing more than fads, justifiable only because superficial Westernization might make Occidentals regard Japan more highly. For instance, the emperor was induced to eat beef in 1872 to help overcome the notion, derived from Buddhist prejudices and the scarcity of farm animals, that the eating of four-legged animals was immoral. Curiously, the beef dish of sukiyaki, developed at this time apparently by iconoclastic students, eventually became one of the popular hallmarks of Japanese culture.

The effort to introduce Western art and architecture to give the cities of Japan a superficial Occidental appearance produced far from happy results. The new buildings were ugly imitations of Victorian style. Their Western ornamentation and the décor of the "Western rooms" in the homes of the great were even worse. Meanwhile native arts and architecture languished. Even the great art of wood-block prints, at its height of technical perfection when Perry arrived, soon degenerated into journalistic illustrations of the curious Western innovations and the rapidly changing scene.

Western-style haircuts became a chief symbol of Westernization. During the later years of the Tokugawa, Japanese had sometimes come back from abroad with Western coiffures, in place of the samurai style, which was to shave the top of the head and leave the rest of the hair long and tied in a knot on top of the shaved area. The military in particular were forced to adopt Western haircuts, since the topknot got in the way of Western military hats. After the Restoration the government leaders and other men in the cities also adopted the Western fashion. Even the then-current Occidental style of wearing heavy beards was followed by many prominent men, aided in this endeavor by the relative hairiness of the Japanese as compared with other Mongoloid peoples. Photographs of the Meiji Emperor, Itō, and many other leaders show them adorned with very fine moustaches and beards.

Similarly, Western-style uniforms were adopted by military and government functionaries, while government leaders and other progressive-minded men shifted to Western civilian attire for general public use. Western dress was prescribed in 1872 for all court and official ceremonies. The emperor always appeared in public dressed in the military manner of the crowned heads of Europe. In the latter part of the Meiji period, the cutaway (called *mōningu* for "morning coat") became so firmly entrenched that it is still widely used in Japan for formal occasions, and *haikara*, meaning "high collar" and referring to the Western styles of the early twentieth century, became the common term for "fashionable" or "swanky." Since the Japanese understood that Englishmen were considered the best-dressed civilians of Europe, they sought to follow English styles. One curious result was the adoption of *sebiro*, a corruption of Saville Row, the street of fine tailors in London, as the Japanese word for the modern business suit.

The dress and styles of women were less affected, since they lived more in seclusion. In 1873, however, the empress set an example by giving up the ancient custom for married women of blackening the teeth and shaving the eyebrows. She and the other court ladies adopted Victorian styles of dress, which are still followed by the court in modified form.

The Swing of the Pendulum. The craze for Westernization reached its height in the 1880's. There was even talk in responsible circles of adopting an official policy of intermarriage with Caucasians to "improve" the Japanese race. There were efforts to make social relations between the sexes conform to Western practice. Women of good families were taught foreign languages and ballroom dancing. In 1883 the government erected in Tōkyō at great expense an elaborate social hall, called the Rokumeikan, where dances were held every Sunday night for the political elite and the diplomatic corps. A great fancy-dress ball was held there in 1887, attended by the chief government dignitaries.

The fancy-dress ball, however, proved to be the last straw for more conservative Japanese. This and other excesses led to a general revulsion against unnecessary imitation of the West, accompanied by a re-emphasis of native values and traditions. The resultant slowing down of Westernization proved to be a useful phase in the general process of modernization. Many superficial aspects of Western culture, such as ballroom dancing, were dropped; thus the significant technological innovations lost the onus of being associated with useless and irritating peculiarities.

The same cycle of enthusiastic and somewhat indiscriminate adoption of Western ways, followed by the rejection of certain less essential aspects of these innovations, was to repeat itself more than once in subsequent Japanese history. Such cycles can also be discerned in other Asian countries. They seem to be a fundamental pattern in the whole process of modernization through borrowing.

Legal Reforms. To win acceptance by the West, it was essential that the Japanese reform their legal institutions along Occidental lines. Extraterritoriality was among the most galling features of the unequal-treaty system, but there was no hope of eliminating it until the Western powers had full confidence in Japanese legal processes.

Legal renovation was also fundamental to technological modernization and was necessitated by the abolition of the old class structure and the other great changes taking place. For example, the Western concept of individual rather than family ownership of property had to be adopted, since it fitted the new economic system and the individual initiative so important in Japan's transformation. On the other hand, for purposes of formal registration of the population, the laws continued to recognize the old extended family, or "house," consisting of a patriarch and those of his descendants and collateral relatives and their wives who had not legally established a new "house." The Western practice of publishing all laws was also necessary, and the Occidental emphasis on legal rights, as opposed to the East Asian emphasis on social obligations, came to permeate the new system. Torture as an accepted legal practice was abolished in 1876, while the structure and procedures of the law courts were made to conform with those of the West.

Most of these legal reforms were instituted in the same piecemeal fashion as the reforms in other fields. Some of the early innovations were obviously designed more to placate Western moral prejudices than to meet the recognized needs of Japanese society. For example, abortion and mixed bathing of the sexes were banned in 1869; pornography, tattooing, and exposure of the body by workers in Tōkyō were proscribed in 1872; and the next year all indentured geisha and prostitutes were ordered freed. Since laws of this type were not essential to the technological changes of the time and rested on no popular support or understanding, they naturally proved ineffective and for the most part were later abandoned.

The new legal system did not reach maturity until the 1890's, by which time the Japanese no longer felt the need of catering to every Western notion. A committee to compile a new civil code had been appointed in 1875. Aided by a French jurist, Boissonade, it submitted drafts in 1881 and 1888. The draft of 1888, which showed strong French influence, was subsequently revised, in part on the basis of German legal precedents, and finally went into effect in 1896.

THOUGHT AND RELIGION

One prominent feature of Western civilization which the Japanese government made no move to borrow was Christianity, even though Westerners would have been more favorably impressed had the Japanese adopted their religion rather than their costumes. This failure and the superficiality of much that was borrowed gave rise to the impression that only the externals of Western civilization were accepted and that native traditions were impervious to the ideas and ideals of the West. Sakuma's old slogan of "Eastern ethics and Western science," which many of the Meiji leaders endorsed, strengthened this interpretation.

In practice, however, no clear line could be drawn between the external aspects of Western civilization and its internal value system. The legal forms of the West, for example, inevitably brought with them the concepts and value judgments on which they were based. Moreover, the Japanese of the early Meiji period, though naturally influenced by the feudal and Confucian elements in their past, remained nonetheless open to the ideas and institutions of the West. Although scientific techniques and external fashions were easier to understand and adopt than were Western ideas and values, no distinction could be made between them in practice.

The Outlook of the Leaders. It would be a mistake to view the Japanese of the early Meiji period, particularly the political leaders, as either ideological traditionalists or intellectual and spiritual followers of the West. They were at the same time both and neither. Any of the leaders — including even those who seem today the most conservative — would champion Western ideas if they seemed useful or an inevitable trend. On the other hand, all of them, even the most Westernized, would defend traditional points of view that seemed of continuing value.

Hence the Meiji leaders might best be described as pragmatists and utilitarians, ready to adopt whatever techniques, institutions, or ideas seemed useful. They had the advantage of being in complete agreement on their ultimate objective and of having the support of most thinking Japanese. The country was to be made strong enough to withstand foreign domination and to win equality. The trial-and-error experience of the late Tokugawa period had shown that the best way to create "a rich country and a strong military" was to centralize Japan politically by means of the convenient imperial symbol and to modernize it by borrowing from the West. But no one as yet had a formula for modernizing an underdeveloped nation, and the leaders, faced with a confused and rapidly changing situation, were flexible rather than doctrinaire about the best way to achieve their ends.

This attitude on the part of the Meiji leaders was perhaps a natural product of the growing pragmatism in Tokugawa thought. They were an extreme expression of this trend, since they had risen to power largely because of their unusual flexibility of mind and ability to meet rapidly changing circumstances. And they found in the West strong encouragement for this point of view. The utilitarian doctrines of Jeremy Bentham and John Stuart Mill clearly supported their own outlook, and Herbert Spencer, as the great popularizer of liberal thought, became the idol of many Japanese intellectuals.

The objectives of the Meiji leaders were entirely secular and largely political, for their primary concern was the future of the nation as a whole. These qualities reflected the growing secularism of Tokugawa society and the agnosticism of the Confucian heritage and at the same time did not conflict with the dominant secularism, materialism, and nationalism that most appealed to them in the nineteenth-century West. Thus the guiding philosophy of Meiji Japan was a natural and easy blend of the Confucian concept of the perfectibility of society through the proper ethico-political organization and leadership, and Western confidence in science as leading to unlimited progress.

This pragmatic, utilitarian approach helps explain the extraordinary moderation of the revolutionary changes in Meiji Japan. The virulent "expel the barbarians" doctrine, which most leaders had supported in their younger days, and the use of assassination during those years as a common political weapon had shown how extreme the Japanese could be. Yet none of the Meiji leaders was a doctrinaire idealist. In typical East Asian fashion, they could see that practical optimums usually lay far short of logical extremes.

Their moderation was also due to their typical Japanese skill at teamwork. They were all strong personalities, yet most of them showed a great capacity for effective cooperation. In contrast with political patterns in many countries, not even the most powerful and influential of these men ever sought to monopolize authority by eliminating the others. When one found that his policies had failed or lost support, he usually stepped aside in favor of someone else who better represented the consensus. The result was extraordinary flexibility in policy for a government that had no formal mechanism for deciding differences of opinion. This flexibility in turn made it easy for the government to retreat from unnecessarily extreme positions and maintain a middle course.

The Native Religions. The Meiji leaders, because of their early Confucian training and entirely secular outlook, were not interested in religion, except as a possible handmaiden of the state. Nor were they particularly interested in Confucianism. They had grown up under its influence, and many of its attitudes persisted in their minds. But as the organized orthodoxy of the Tokugawa system they were destroying, it stood discredited in their eyes. Confucianists were the most effective critics of Christianity, and in time Confucian thinkers managed to win acceptance from government leaders for some of their ideas, but many of the fundamental ideas of Confucianism were obviously not suited to the new situation, and it was unable to provide the guiding philosophy for the new Japan.

Since a revived interest in Shintō had figured among the intellectual trends that had raised the prestige of the imperial house during the late eighteenth and early nineteenth centuries, some of the participants in the Restoration movement had expected the establishment of a Shintō-oriented government, modeled on the semi-theocracy of the Japanese state of more than a millennium earlier. Such ideas lay behind the placing of the Office of Shintō Worship above the organs of civil government in 1869. They also help account for the somewhat violent disestablishment of Buddhism in the first years of the new regime.

The Buddhist clergy, through the system known as Dual Shintō, had gained administrative control over a large proportion of the Shintō shrines almost a thousand years earlier. Under the Tokugawa most Japanese had been forced to register for census purposes as members of Buddhist parishes. Now this latter practice was discontinued, the administrative association of Buddhist and Shintō institutions was dissolved, and Shintō properties were restored to their own priests. These measures inspired a general anti-Buddhist outburst, in which church property and many artistic treasures were destroyed.

Despite the official favor shown to Shintō, the attempted revival had very little inner life and soon faded away completely. Neither institutionally nor intellectually did this simple nature worship have much to offer the men of the new age. The Office of Shintō Worship was downgraded in 1871 and the next year replaced by a religiously neutral Board of Religious Instruction, which was abolished four years later. The government continued to control and support most Shintō shrines, but the Shintō cults themselves lapsed into their traditional passive state, forming no more than a quiet ground swell in the emotional life of the people. Only the so-called popular Shintō Sects, such as Tenrikyō, which were recently founded, eclectic religions, popular among the lower classes, continued to show much vigor.

Buddhism was hard hit by the violent reaction against it in the early years after the Restoration. These attacks indeed shook it from its lethargy of recent centuries. Christianity also proved a stimulating challenge. There was a gradual revival of Buddhist scholarship. The large Shinshū, or True (Pure Land) Sect, showed particular vitality. In time it even adopted some of the organizational techniques of the Christian churches, including foreign missions to the nearby continent, Hawaii, and the West Coast of the United States.

The Reintroduction of Christianity. Both Shintō and Buddhism labored under the handicap of being too closely associated with the feudal past, whereas Christianity had the advantage of being part of the Western civilization that seemed to many Japanese the obvious wave of the future. This assumption contributed to what success Christianity had in Japan, but at first it was offset by strong anti-Christian prejudices inherited from the past.

The new government in 1868 actually re-established the old Tokugawa bulletin boards proscribing Christianity. In the same year it aroused a storm of protest from the foreign diplomats by rooting out a clandestine community of some 3000 Christians which had remained in the Nagasaki area from the period of Catholic missions in the sixteenth and seventeenth centuries. Not until the members of the Iwakura Mission had seen how strongly the Western nations felt about their religion did the government in 1873 drop the old ban on Christianity, and even then only indirectly by removing the public bulletin boards on the grounds that their content was already well known.

But Christianity had in the meantime re-entered Japan. As early as 1859, American Protestant missionaries had taken advantage of the Harris treaty to come to the open ports. One of the first was Guido Verbeck of the Dutch Reformed Church, who, coming to Nagasaki, taught English to Ōkuma and other men who later had important roles in the Meiji government. After the Restoration, Verbeck became a teacher in the forerunner of Tōkyō University and a government adviser. Another early figure was Dr. J. C. Hepburn, a medical missionary of the American Presbyterian Church. He compiled a Japanese-English dictionary, published in Shanghai in 1869, which established the standard system for romanizing Japanese that still bears his name. Catholic missionaries also started to regather their remaining flock in the Nagasaki area, while a French priest established a church in Yokohama in 1862.

The most remarkable of the missionaries was the Russian Orthodox monk Nikolai (1836–1912). He came to Hakodate in 1861 as chaplain of the local Russian community and moved in 1872 to Tōkyō, where he became the bishop and later the archbishop of a flourishing missionary church. In 1884 he started construction of a great cathedral which is still a landmark of the city.

By 1873 there were fifty-three Protestant, Catholic, and Orthodox missionaries in Japan. The prejudice against Christianity subsided only slowly, and occasional acts of overt hostility still occurred. But there was relatively little resistance from the native religious communities, which themselves had been thrown into confusion by the changes sweeping the country. Moreover, during the 1880's the government, partly because of religious indifference and partly to please the Western nations, adopted a policy of complete religious toleration, which was formally written into the new constitution in 1889. Christianity was tacitly accepted, along with Buddhism and Shintō, as one of the three recognized religions.

Although Christianity has never had much mass appeal in modern Japan, it did attract certain inquiring intellectuals. One example was Niishima Jō (1843–1890; also known as Joseph Neesima), a samurai from central Honshū. He managed to leave Japan on an American vessel in 1864, was financed through Amherst College by an interested American ship's captain, and served as an interpreter for the Iwakura Mission. Subsequently he became an ordained Congregational minister. Returning to Japan, he founded in Kyōto in 1875 a private Christian school, which grew into Dōshisha University. A group of young samurai, known as the Kumamoto Band, who had been converted by an American teacher of English at Kumamoto (Captain Janes), transferred to this institution in 1876 and later became prominent Christian leaders.

Similarly Dr. Clark, who came in 1876 to the Sapporo Agricultural College in Hokkaidō, converted several able young Japanese of samurai origin. Among these were Nitobe Inazō (1862–1933), who became a leading scholar and educator, and Uchimura Kanzō (1861–1930), who reacted to the sectarian divisions and close national affiliations of the Protestant missionary societies by founding a "No Church" (Mukyōkai) movement. This, though lacking all formal church organization, won the support of many leading Christian intellectuals. Uemura Masahisa (1857–1925), who was born a shogunal retainer, became the leading clergyman of the Church of Christ in Japan (Nihon Kirisuto Kyōkai), the Calvinist branch of the Protestant movement.

By 1888 the Protestants had translated the Bible into acceptable Japanese and were founding schools all over the country. In Tōkyō alone, American missionary societies founded three institutions — Rikkyō in 1874, Aoyama Gakuin in 1883, and Meiji Gakuin in 1886 — all of which later grew into universities. But in spite of its strength among intellectuals, the Christian movement remained numerically very small. Although Christians had constituted close to two per cent of the Japanese population in the early seventeenth century, in 1889 they numbered less than a quarter of one per cent, divided among 40,000 Catholics, 29,000 Protestants, and 18,000 Orthodox.

EDUCATION

New knowledge was essential for everything that the Meiji leaders hoped to achieve. Their clear realization of this point was evident in the statement in the "Five Articles Oath" of 1868 that "knowledge shall be sought throughout the world so as to strengthen the foundations of imperial rule," as well as in the emphasis they placed on developing a modern educational system.

Study Abroad. The first need was to acquire the necessary new knowledge from the Occident. One obvious way was by study abroad. The shogunate and some of the *han* had started this before the Restoration. Among the first students sent by the shogunate to the Netherlands in 1862 had been Enomoto, the later naval commander, along with others who were to play important roles in modernizing Japan. Itō and Inoue were sent by Chōshū to England in 1863, and in 1865 Mori Arinori (1847–1889), who was to be another important government leader, was sent there by Satsuma.

The sending of students abroad was continued and expanded by the new government to the limit of its financial abilities. Young men and even some young women were sent to Europe and the United States. As noted above, no less than 54 students accompanied the Iwakura Mission in 1871.

Students returned from the West played a critical role in the modernization of Japan. Several of them, such as Itō, Inoue, and Yamagata, were among the chief architects of the Japanese state. Others, such as Saigō Tsugumichi, Enomoto, Mori, and Inoue Kowashi (or Ki; 1844–1895), a samurai from Kumamoto, were only slightly less important as statesmen or advisers to the top leaders. Many others had careers as political, intellectual, and economic innovators and leaders.

A large proportion of the important leaders of the Meiji period studied in the West during their early, formative years, and most of the others traveled in the Occident and observed its institutions at least in a superficial manner. It is significant that, of the top dozen figures, only two never went to Europe or America. These were Ōkuma, who was enough of an iconoclast not to need to see the West, and the elder Saigō, who failed to make the full transition to the new age and became instead the last dangerous opponent of Japan's modernization.

Foreign Experts. Importing foreign experts was another way to get knowledge of the West and mastery of its technology. In the closing years of the old regime, foreign experts had been used in various industrial undertakings. The new government greatly expanded the use of such hired talent. We have already noted the role of Americans in the development of Hokkaidō, the employment of 34 foreigners by the Bureau of Mines in 1873, and the use of various European experts in setting up factories. Between 1868 and 1874 an Englishman, R. H. Brunton, supervised the costly task of installing lights and buoys for navigation. By 1879 the Ministry of Industry employed 130 foreigners, whose salaries accounted for nearly three-fifths of the ministry's fixed expenditures.

Since the "Dutch learning" of the late Tokugawa period had proved to be a half century or more out of date, a new start in Western science and scholarship was made through the use of foreign scholars. A series of German doctors, starting in 1871, gave Japanese medicine a strong German cast that still persists. English and American scholars were more important in other sciences. Professor E. S. Morse of Harvard, who arrived in 1877, is remembered as the founder of modern zoological, anthropological, archaeological, and sociological studies, and the Japanese still feel a strong sense of debt to Ernest Fenollosa of Boston, who came as a professor of philosophy in 1878 and by his own enthusiasm helped to revive an interest in the native artistic tradition.

In the present day, underdeveloped nations can usually secure experts and scholars on easy terms from foreign nations or international agencies, but in the nineteenth century the Japanese had to make a much greater effort to get them and had to pay for them entirely out of their own funds. Perhaps because the foreign experts were hired on Japanese terms, they seem to have been more esteemed and put to better use than is sometimes the case today.

The foreign experts and scholars were inordinately expensive, because they required what were by Japanese standards fabulous salaries and a luxurious style of living and so they were replaced as quickly as possible by their Japanese students and assistants or by Japanese returned from study abroad. For example, the number of foreign employees in the Bureau of Mines was reduced by a third between 1873 and 1880. Subsequently, as a result of Matsukata's retrenchment policy, foreign experts in all fields were eliminated at an even more rapid rate. By the turn of the century few hired foreign experts remained, except as language teachers.

There was, however, one category of foreign teachers that constituted no drain on the Japanese economy and actually grew in numbers. These were the missionaries, who though not usually important scholars nevertheless made a tremendous contribution as transmitters of knowledge about the West and as teachers of English.

Writers and Translators. The printed word had been the chief source of knowledge for the "Dutch scholars" of the Tokugawa period. The shogunate, as we have seen, had founded in 1811 a bureau for the translation of Western books, and this work was continued under the new government by its Translation Bureau. Many private individuals, responding to the challenge of the time, also took up the task and became more effective spreaders of Western knowledge through books than the government itself.

The leading popularizer of knowledge about the West was Fukuzawa Yukichi (1835–1901), probably the most influential man in Meiji Japan outside of government service. His autobiography, which has been translated into English, gives a fascinating account of his early life.

Fukuzawa, by origin a samurai of a North Kyūshū *han*, went in 1854 to Nagasaki to study Dutch and gunnery and the next year moved to Ōsaka to take up Western medicine. Brought in 1858 to the *han* residence in Edo as a teacher of Dutch, he discovered to his consternation that most of the foreign merchants settling in Yokohama spoke not Dutch but English. He therefore shifted his attention to English and in 1860 accompanied the shogunal mission to the United States and in 1862 the mission to Europe.

After returning from Europe, Fukuzawa developed his teaching facilities into a private school devoted largely to the teaching of English and useful knowledge about the West. Named in 1868 the Keiō-gijuku, this school eventually grew into Keiō University, one of Japan's two leading private universities and the source of many business leaders.

Fukuzawa's first fame came from his writings. He published in 1869 a book called *Conditions in the West* (*Seiyō jijō*), in which he described in simple and clear terms the political, economic, and cultural institutions of the Occident, making plain his preference for the British parliamentary form of government. This work sold 150,000 copies in its first edition and had a tremendous influence on Japan. Fukuzawa followed it in the next decade with a number of others, including *The Encouragement of Learning* (*Gakumon no susume*), which is said to have sold over 700,000 copies.

Fukuzawa also encouraged the development of a simple style of written language, in which the number of Chinese characters would be limited to two or three thousand. In 1873 he and fifteen other intellectual leaders, including returned students such as Mori, founded a society known as the Meirokusha ("Sixth Year of Meiji Society"), which through lectures and publication of a magazine popularized many Western ideas. The Meirokusha had only a brief existence, succumbing in 1875 when most of its members deserted it for government service.

Many other private scholars joined Fukuzawa in the task of introducing knowledge about the West to the reading public, often by translating serious works on politics and economics. Two early and influential books translated were Samuel Smiles's *Self-Help* and John Stuart Mill's *On Liberty*, in 1870 and 1871 respectively. Translations of novels and other lighter works were probably just as important in spreading an understanding of Western attitudes. *Robinson Crusoe*, translated in 1859, was followed by a flood of Western classics and popular works of the nineteenth century (works not originally in the English language were usually translated from their English versions). The pseudo-scientific tales of Jules Verne were immensely popular. Translation was the great literary activity of the first decades after the Restoration and over-shadowed creative work, which was at a low ebb during these years.

The New Educational Pattern. In building up an organized school system, the government leaders naturally were influenced by Western theory and practice, but they were not merely imitative. In fact, they proved to be in the forefront of some of the modern educational tendencies.

The Japanese government had some advantages over Western regimes in developing an educational system to meet the needs of a modern state. For one thing, Japanese education, starting almost entirely afresh, was free to apply the latest educational concepts. Not having to contend with the entrenched relationship between religion and education that existed in many Western countries, the government leaders found it easier to standardize education and to shape it to the needs of the nation as they saw them. As a consequence, the lower levels of the Japanese educational system by the early twentieth century showed signs of the complete uniformity and the effective utilization of education for official indoctrination that later in the century were to characterize totalitarian regimes of the West.

During the Tokugawa period, Buddhist "temple schools" (*terakoya*) and private teachers had taught many commoners to read, while the samurai had been given a strongly Chinese Confucian education at the schools maintained by the shogunate and *han* or at small private schools conducted by individual scholars. Almost all of these educational institutions withered away after the Restoration, except for the chief shogunal schools. The Confucian "University" in Edo, the shogunal medical school, and the language programs at the Institute for the Study of Foreign Books were combined in 1869 into a new government university, renamed Tōkyō University in 1877.

During the early years of the new regime, scholars of Shintō orientation hoped to make traditional Japanese culture the core of education at the government university and to relegate Chinese Confucian studies and Western science to a subordinate status. However, this attempted Shintō revival was no more successful in education than in religion. The old Confucian orientation of education was also largely discarded under the vigorous attack of men like Fukuzawa, who championed not only a utilitarian concept of education but specifically the liberal Anglo-Saxon ideal of education as a means of developing independent, self-respecting individuals.

In 1871 the government dropped all but the Western aspects of the work at its university and established a Ministry of Education on Occidental models. The next year this ministry adopted the highly centralized French system, with the country divided into eight university districts, and subdivided into middle school and elementary school districts. Sixteen months of schooling were made compulsory for children of both sexes. Compulsory education was extended to three years in 1880 and later to six years.

It was no easy matter to carry out such a plan because of the insufficiency of both funds and teachers. As late as 1886 only 46 per cent of the children of statutory school age were in school. But by 1905 the figure had risen to 95 per cent, and subsequently it crept up still further, until Japanese literacy rates were among the highest in the world.

In the meantime the original centralized French plan had undergone more than one fundamental change. It had hardly been adopted when more liberal American concepts of education began to dominate the Education Ministry as the result of the influence of men like Fukuzawa and Mori, then stationed in Washington. Dr. David Murray of Rutgers College was brought to Japan in 1873 and for the next six years served as an influential adviser in the Ministry of Education. Elementary education was modeled on that of America, control over the newly founded normal schools was handed over to the prefectural governments, and in 1879 a plan for the complete decentralization of control over education was adopted, though never put into effect.

The liberalization of education was also fostered by private schools. Mention has already been made of Fukuzawa's Keiō-gijuku and of Dōshisha and other Christian schools. Ōkuma, who, as we shall see, was forced out of the government in 1881, answered his political rivals partly by founding in 1882 an institution that grew into Waseda University. Waseda, which is ranked with Keiō as one of the two leading private universities of Japan, became an important source not only of business leaders but also of democratic politicians. During these years many other private schools were founded, and some grew into large universities.

Under Christian auspices a start was also made in women's education. Missionary societies founded many of the early secondary schools for girls, and Christian leaders subsequently introduced higher education for women. Tsuda Umeko, one of the first five girls sent as students to the United States in 1871, founded Tsuda College in 1900 as an institution specializing in the English language. Japan Women's University (Nihon Joshi Daigaku) and Tōkyō Women's University (Tōkyō Joshi Daigaku) were founded under Christian auspices in 1901 and 1918. Though most private schools for men were in time overshadowed by the prestige of government institutions, private schools still remain in the forefront of women's education.

The Perfected Educational System. A great shift in educational policy came during the 1880's. By that time the new leaders, having successfully weathered the grave political and economic crises of their first decades of rule, could turn to the consolidation and rationalization of the system they were creating. A highly centralized, strictly controlled educational system probably appealed to them as being more in keeping with the Confucian concept of the close relationship between education, morality, and government, and better adapted to building a strong and prosperous state than the decentralized and freer American system. The shift in educational policy was also part of the general swing during the 1880's away from unnecessarily close imitation of the West and back toward more traditional values.

The first sign of the change was a decision in 1882 to put a greater emphasis in elementary education on courses in morals, through which undesirable Occidental influences could be combatted and proper attitudes inculcated in the masses. The same tendency was manifest in the issuance in 1890 of a brief document, known as the Imperial Rescript on Education, on which the government laid great emphasis.[1] This document makes only passing reference to education but stresses the ideals of social harmony and loyalty to the throne. Its strongly Confucian tone, reminiscent of the Sacred Edict of the K'ang-hsi Emperor in China (page 85), resulted from the influence of Motoda Eifu (1818–1891), the emperor's venerable Confucian tutor. But the concept of mass indoctrination through formal education, which lay behind the issuance of the document, was entirely modern.

Traditionalists were by no means the primary architects of the new educational policy. The most important figures were men like Mori who

---

[1] *The Imperial Rescript on Education*

Know ye, Our subjects:

Our Imperial Ancestors have founded Our Empire on a basis broad and everlasting, and have deeply and firmly implanted virtue; Our subjects ever united in loyalty and filial piety have from generation to generation illustrated the beauty thereof. This is the glory of the fundamental character of Our Empire, and herein also lies the source of Our education. Ye, Our subjects, be filial to your parents, affectionate to your brothers and sisters; as husbands and wives be harmonious, as friends true; bear yourselves in modesty and moderation; extend your benevolence to all; pursue learning and cultivate arts, and thereby develop intellectual faculties and perfect moral powers; furthermore, advance public good and promote common interests; always respect the Constitution and observe the laws; should emergency arise, offer yourselves courageously to the State; and thus guard and maintain the prosperity of Our Imperial Throne coeval with heaven and earth. So shall ye not only be Our good and faithful subjects, but render illustrious the best traditions of your forefathers.

The Way here set forth is indeed the teaching bequeathed by Our Imperial Ancestors, to be observed alike by Their Descendants and the subjects, infallible for all ages and true in all places. It is Our wish to lay it to heart in all reverence, in common with you, Our subjects, that we may all attain to the same virtue.

October 30, 1890

were earnest students of the West. Mori, who became minister of education in 1885, was one of the most iconoclastic and Westernized of all the Meiji leaders. He was, in fact, assassinated by a fanatic in 1889 for allegedly desecrating the Ise Shrines, greatest of Shintō holy places. Yet Mori felt strongly that an educational system should operate "not for the sake of the pupils but for the sake of the country."

Another student of the West who followed the same line of thought was Katō Hiroyuki (1836-1916), who had been an instructor of Dutch in the old Institute for the Study of Foreign Books and served for many years as president of Tōkyō University. Katō had entertained very liberal political views, but a knowledge of German brought him under the influence of the more authoritarian German tradition, and he came increasingly to emphasize the supremacy of the state in all matters, including education. This German influence was further heightened by Professor Emil Hausknecht, who came to Tōkyō University in 1887 to lecture on pedagogy.

Part of the new educational policy was an entirely healthy emphasis on Japanese and Chinese literature, history, and thought, to balance the hitherto almost exclusive concern with Western subjects. Other aspects of the new policy were an increasing emphasis on indoctrination in education, the standardization of the curriculum, and increased government control over private institutions, especially at the lower educational levels. Still another aspect was the expansion of the government school system and the enhancement of its prestige over the private schools. As a result, private elementary and secondary schools shrank to relative insignificance. In 1896 higher schools were added as a new educational level between the middle schools and universities. In 1903 these were divided between technical schools, which gave terminal training, and academic higher schools, which led on to the universities and, in the case of the government higher schools, enjoyed much prestige.

Tōkyō University was reorganized into a genuine multi-faculty university in 1886 and became the principal training center for future government officials. For a while its graduates were accepted directly into government service without examination. An inevitable result of this policy was the domination of the higher ranks of the bureaucracy by graduates of the Law Faculty of Tōkyō University, a tradition which still persists. Other government universities were subsequently added — Kyōto in 1897, Tōhoku (in Sendai) in 1907, Kyūshū (in Fukuoka) in 1910, Hokkaidō (in Sapporo) in 1918, and others later. Starting with Kyōto University in 1897, the government universities were all named Imperial Universities. In prestige, these Imperial Universities (the "Imperial" was dropped from the name after the Second World War) have usually ranked more or less in the sequence of their founding, and most of them far outrank the private universities.

Early in the twentieth century, the new Japanese educational structure was almost complete. At the bottom were compulsory six-year coeducational elementary schools, designed to produce a literate citizenry for efficient service in the army, factories, and fields. On the level above these were three types of institutions: (1) five-year academic middle schools for boys, (2) various lower technical schools, which produced the lower levels of technical skills, and (3) the girls' higher schools, which were supposed to provide all the education needed even by girls from better families. Above this level stood the three-year academic higher schools and the higher technical schools. And at the top of the pyramid were the three-year government universities (four-year in medicine), which produced the elite.

This was a beautifully logical system, and on the whole it worked very well. The unchallenged prestige of the government institutions, which had the lowest tuition rates, gave Japanese education a more egalitarian flavor than the schools of the English-speaking countries. But the whole seventeen-year educational program was so carefully tailored to fit the needs of the state, as these were envisioned by its leaders, that it did not adequately meet all the educational needs of Japanese society. Women's higher education, for example, grew up largely outside the official educational structure, and the continued rapid growth of private universities showed that there was a demand in Japanese society for much more higher education than that deemed adequate by the government.

The Introduction of Representative Institutions

Universal elementary education and the great expansion of higher learning eventually had a profound impact on Japan, creating social and intellectual conditions comparable to those that contributed to the rise of modern democracy in the West. But long before the new education had produced these results, the Japanese were beginning to experiment with representative government and had decided to create a parliament.

The introduction of democratic institutions was perhaps the most surprising innovation of the Meiji period, because the Japanese had in their background no trace of representative government either in theory or in practice. The group in charge of the government had demonstrated its ability to control the nation without sharing its authority through democratic procedures. But the effort at democracy in Japan was part of a world-wide trend. All countries admired the power of Europe. Constitutional government appeared to be one source of this power. Therefore several non-European countries that had not become European colonies attempted in the late nineteenth or early twentieth century to imitate the Occident and set up constitutional governments. Turkey, Egypt, Persia, and others tried this, but most of them failed.

If one assumes that democracy is the modern political norm, then the limited progress the Japanese made toward democracy during the Meiji period might be described as a failure. But such an assumption is anachronistic because it reads back into the nineteenth century aspirations and conditions more typical of the twentieth. In nineteenth-century terms, the progress of Meiji Japan toward democracy was a significant and surprising success, for it was the first demonstration that elements of democracy could be transplanted and live in a society with neither a native democratic heritage nor a strong belief in democratic ideals.

The Intellectual Background. The successes of democracy in Japan in the twentieth century were no doubt due to the modernization of the society as a whole, but the introduction of democratic ideas and institutions in the nineteenth century must be attributed to other factors. One was the existence at the time of the Restoration of a relatively broad stratum of society that was not only well-educated but also politically conscious. The new government was not dealing only with illiterate peasants and unthinking townsmen. A large percentage of the samurai were men of education, and they had strong traditions of political leadership, fostered by the feudal division of the country into 265 autonomous units. Many townsmen and richer peasants were well-educated and capable of independent thinking. Influenced by new ideals from the West and by changed conditions at home, they, too, quickly developed an interest in politics.

Although a small group of men had won firm control over the nation, these other politically conscious Japanese did not all meekly acquiesce in their rule, as the samurai revolts of the 1870's clearly showed. Among the thousands of Japanese who rushed into new fields of economic or intellectual endeavor, many were subsequently drawn into the government; a few remained proudly aloof — like Fukuzawa, who preferred to make his contribution from outside the government, even though its leaders accepted him as their equal. Others who felt they deserved to be in the government but had found no place in it demanded a share in political leadership.

Demands for the sharing of political power, though a major historical source of democracy in the West, did not force democratic institutions on a reluctant government in Meiji Japan. The governing group had gained such complete and rapid mastery over the nation, and the whole concept of democracy was so unfamiliar to most Japanese, that the new regime at first did not have to worry about such outlandish ideas.

Rather, democratic institutions were introduced chiefly because many government leaders felt that Japan had something to gain from them. They were influenced by prevalent Western beliefs in the triumph of democracy as part of the inevitable course of progress. They saw the specter of the French Revolution as the fate of any too-autocratic regime. They also noted that strong and advanced countries like Great Britain, France, and the United States based their national strength on democracy, while democratic ideas had some currency in all of the more modernized nations. Assuming that representative institutions, like machine production, were among the reasons for the power and dominance of the Occident, most of the government leaders felt impelled to introduce at least some aspects of parliamentary government as a means of modernizing and strengthening the nation. The introduction of democratic institutions, they also felt, would help win the esteem of the West and bring nearer the day of Japan's acceptance as an equal.

If the Japanese leadership, both within and outside the government, had not been as pragmatic and moderate as it was, the experiment with democratic institutions might have been rashly attempted and hastily abandoned. Instead, the Japanese felt their way cautiously and slowly. In this they had the advantage of the nineteenth-century setting for their experiment. Few expected that democracy would be achieved in one giant leap, as is the common twentieth-century assumption. Even in Europe at that time, electorates were usually limited and parliaments circumscribed in their powers. Neither the Japanese nor their foreign advisers expected more for Japan. Former President Grant of the United States, when consulted during his trip to Japan in 1879, advised the emperor to adopt parliamentary institutions only gradually and with great caution.

The introduction of representative government, then, was a slow process — so slow that most critics have described it as a series of failures. But its very slowness helped ensure its success. For a half century, democratic institutions steadily expanded their scope and power, until by the 1920's Japan had become much more democratic than most Meiji Japanese would have desired.

Early Agitation for Representative Government. In the last years of the Tokugawa, a few men had shown interest in the representative political institutions of the West, and had made some proposals. A council of *han* representatives, for example, seemed one way to have the shogunate share its former monopoly of national leadership. It also seemed a way to avoid the transfer of the shogunate's full powers to a single *han*, or to some small group of leaders, which many feared would be the result of the Restoration. Because of such fears the new regime promised in the "Five Articles Oath" of 1868 that "deliberative assemblies shall be widely established and all matters decided by public discussion."

However, both "deliberative assemblies" and "public discussion" were quite unfamiliar to the government leaders and to the would-be participants. The four attempts between 1868 and 1870 to create a deliberative assembly made up partly of *han* representatives seemed to add nothing of value, and there was no great outcry when the effort was quietly dropped. Attempts at local assemblies, first within some of the *han* and later in various new units of local government, proved no more successful. The concepts of representation, majority decision, and a loyal opposition were simply too foreign to the whole Japanese political background.

Interest in representative institutions reached a new level in the autumn of 1873, when the split in the government ranks over Korea brought to a head two very different types of samurai opposition. These were led, respectively, by Saigō and Itagaki, two of the triumvirate that had dominated the government during the absence of the Iwakura Mission. As we have seen, Saigō retired in dudgeon to Satsuma, where he became the focal point of the major military effort to overthrow the government. In contrast, Itagaki of Tosa chose the method of peaceful political agitation in favor of democratic institutions.

In the autumn of 1873 Itagaki, with Etō of Hizen and Gotō and other Tosa leaders, founded a political club, which the next January they named the Public Party of Patriots (Aikoku Kōtō). This was a daring departure from political precedent, because political parties or factions of any sort had usually been regarded in East Asia as disruptive of good government, if not openly subversive. The new "party" included several students returned from the West. It presented the government with a memorial, denouncing its arbitrariness and calling for the establishment of "a council-chamber chosen by the people."

Shortly afterward, Itagaki left Tōkyō and returned to Tosa, where he flatly refused to become involved in Etō's revolt in Saga. Instead he founded a new political organization. In this he was joined by Kataoka Kenkichi (1843–1903), a Tosa samurai who had withdrawn with him from the government. Kataoka served as president of the new organization and in time became a parliamentary leader and a prominent Christian layman. The new group was called the Risshisha, or "Society to Establish One's Moral Will," a name based on the Japanese translation of the title of Samuel Smiles's widely read book, *Self-Help*.

One aim of the Risshisha was the economic rehabilitation of the samurai class, a problem that weighed heavily on Itagaki's mind. The organization, however, was more successful as a political movement devoted to the creation of a popular assembly. It spread rapidly throughout Tosa and from the samurai down to the commoners. To make the movement nationwide, Itagaki founded still another organization, called the Society of Patriots (Aikokusha) in Ōsaka in January 1875.

It is hard to say why Itagaki among the early political leaders took this unusual turn toward popular democratic agitation or why the samurai and commoners of Tosa were so very responsive and produced such a large share of the early leaders of the democratic movement. Tosa does not seem to have been more advanced economically or socially than many other parts of Japan and was probably well behind the more urbanized central regions of Honshū. And Itagaki, like Saigō, was more of a military man than some of the more politically minded new leaders, such as Kido and Itō.

One explanation for the prominence of Tosa men in the democratic movement was their strong resentment over the dominance of men from Satsuma and Chōshū in the new government. Although Tosa had played an important role in its founding and Tosa samurai probably ranked next in numbers in the administration to men from these other two *han*, Itagaki and his associates were disgruntled at their minority status and were quick to assume the role of a political opposition. The great responsiveness of the commoners of Tosa to Itagaki's call for a popular movement may be attributed partly to the strong position of the "rural samurai" and village headmen of Tosa and their tradition of rural opposition to the *han* government (see pages 215–216). This unusual political situation may explain why Tosa, under the leadership of Itagaki and Gotō, led the rest of the country between 1868 and 1871 in wiping out class distinctions and why after 1873 Tosa men took the lead in demands for a parliament.

Government Experiments with Representative Institutions. The government leaders were not particularly shocked by Itagaki's proposals for a representative body, since they still regarded him as one of their own group and were themselves in favor of experiments along this line. Kido on his return from abroad in 1873 had argued that despotic government was essentially weak, whereas a government based on a constitution with reasonable guarantees of popular rights would be stronger. He also implied that, although Japan was not yet ready for even a limited parliamentary government, the people should be guided toward this enlightened end. Between 1872 and 1874, the Left Chamber of the government brought up several proposals for a constitution, and various private study groups, made up largely of officials, began to inquire into the problem of creating a constitution and a parliament. In 1875 the government issued a promise in the emperor's name that in due time a national assembly would be formed.

Itagaki was not committed to an extreme stance in opposition to the government. When the scholar Katō attempted to refute his 1874 proposal by arguing that it was still too early for a national assembly and that Prussia's case showed that national strength did not depend on such an institution, Itagaki made clear that he had only a limited suffrage in mind. In February 1875 he came to a reconciliation with his political foes.

Kido had followed Itagaki out of the government in 1874, when Ōkubo overrode his opposition to sending an expedition to Formosa. Inoue and Itō, distressed at the resignation of Kido, who was the leading figure from their own former *han* of Chōshū, helped arrange meetings between him and Ōkubo early in 1875. At these conferences, which took place in Ōsaka, a four-point program of cooperation was worked out between Kido and Ōkubo; Itagaki, agreeing to these same terms, then disbanded the Society of Patriots he had just founded and together with Kido rejoined the government in March.

Two of the points agreed on at Ōsaka were speedily put into effect. These were the abolition of the Left and Right Chambers and their replacement by a Supreme Court (*Daishin-in*), designed to protect the independence of the judiciary, and a Senate, or more literally a Chamber of Elders (*Genrō-in*). The latter was given the task of preparing for a national assembly. In 1876 it set about drafting a constitution with the aid of a book on English parliamentary government. When the fruits of its labors were finally presented in 1880, however, Itō and Iwakura, then the chief powers in the regime, found the draft too closely modeled on English institutions and shelved it.

A third point agreed on at Ōsaka had been the calling of a conference of prefectural governors as a modest start toward a representative assembly. The conference convened in June 1875 under Kido's chairmanship and engaged in vigorous debates. Subsequent conferences were held in 1878 and 1880, but thereafter this attempt at representation through local officials was allowed to lapse.

The fourth point agreed on at Ōsaka — separation of the functions of Councilors from those of the heads of ministries — was not put into effect. The idea was that ministers should serve purely as administrative officers, while the Councilors should constitute a sort of cabinet to advise the emperor. Piqued by the failure to carry out this agreement and jealous of Ōkubo's continuing domination of the administration, Itagaki again resigned from the government in October 1875.

The government continued with its experiments in representative institutions. The second conference of prefectural governors decided in July 1878 on the establishment of elected prefectural assemblies. This had been under discussion for some time and was put into effect the next March. The franchise was restricted to males who paid five yen or more in land taxes, and the powers of the assemblies were limited to discussing tax and budgetary matters. The local governor had the right to initiate all legislation, to veto the assembly's decisions, and to dissolve it. Nevertheless, these prefectural assemblies constituted a significant step toward democracy, for they were the first successful elected political bodies anywhere in the non-Western world. Similar assemblies were established in 1880 in towns and the other smaller units of local government.

THE CLAMOR FOR PARLIAMENTARY GOVERNMENT

Itagaki, after resigning from the administration a second time, returned to organizing a popular opposition. Some members of the Risshisha in Tosa took advantage of the Satsuma Rebellion in 1877 to plot with a few members of the government an armed uprising in behalf of liberal principles. This led to the imprisonment of the Risshisha president, Kataoka, and a few others. Itagaki and the more moderate elements in the Risshisha decided to avoid all violence, but they did submit a memorial to the government, condemning its despotic nature and demanding that it heed "the will of the people," respect their "rights and privileges," and establish a national assembly. This manifesto was not entirely democratic, however, since it also reflected traditional samurai attitudes in its condemnation of the government for disregarding the emperor's will and for equalizing the status of samurai and commoners.

The "People's Rights" Movement. The next year Itagaki and his associates tried again to make their movement nationwide by reviving the Society of Patriots. The response this time was tremendous. The movement spread rapidly, and similar political associations sprang up all over Japan, particularly in the cities and the economically advanced and prosperous farming areas of central Honshū northwest of Tōkyō.

The burgeoning of political organizations led to some violence, because meetings often resulted in clashes with the overly zealous police. The line between opposition through rebellion and through political agitation was by no means clear to the Japanese at this time. Even assassination seemed a legitimate weapon to some would-be champions of democracy. In one "people's rights" newspaper in 1876 there were articles with captions such as: "Freedom must be bought with fresh blood," and "Tyrannical officials must be assassinated." Indeed, Ōkubo, the most powerful figure in the government, was killed in May 1878 by extremists who had the curiously mixed motives of avenging Saigō's death and defending "people's rights."

Itagaki attempted to coordinate the mushrooming political movement through national conventions of the Society of Patriots. The first was held in September 1878. The second one the following March was attended by representatives of 21 societies from 18 prefectures. The fourth convention in April 1880 was attended by representatives of societies claiming 87,000 members, more than half from Tosa. The conventions uniformly demanded the creation of a national assembly. At the fourth meeting, the Society of Patriots adopted a new name — the League for Establishing a National Assembly (Kokkai Kisei Dōmei).

Two factors lay behind the rapid spread of the demand for parliamentary government, which was now beginning to be known as "the movement for freedom and people's rights" (*jiyū minken undō*). One was its development from a protest movement of disgruntled samurai into a much broader political ground swell, in which men from all classes participated. The most numerous and enthusiastic new members were the prosperous peasant landowners, probably because they, rather than the impoverished samurai, constituted the chief taxpaying group. Men of samurai origin usually remained the top leaders and intellectual guides, but rich peasants provided the chief financial support and the bulk of the members of the new political associations.

Another reason for the spread of the parliamentary movement was the growing knowledge of democratic institutions among Japanese intellectuals. Fukuzawa's *Popular Account of People's Rights* (*Tsūzoku minken ron*), as well as some of his other writings, contributed to this. So also did the works of other writers — for example, those of Ueki Emori (1857–1892), a Tosa samurai by origin, who acted as a political adviser to Itagaki, and Nakae Chōmin (1847–1901), another Tosa samurai, who was even more important. He had studied Dutch and French in his youth, served as an interpreter for the French minister, Roches, during the last years of the shogunate, was sent abroad to study in 1871 on Itagaki's recommendation, and served briefly in the government after his return in 1874. His chief work was the popularizing of the ideas of Rousseau, whose *Contrat social* was first translated into Japanese by another scholar in 1877. By championing Rousseau. Nakae became the spiritual father of the radical intellectual wing of the democratic movement, which looked to French rather than British political philosophy.

Nakae's help in founding the *Oriental Free Press* (*Tōyō Jiyū Shimbun*) in 1881 illustrates the role of newspapers in the parliamentary movement. The shogunate in 1862 had started publishing for its own use translations from the *Batavia Nieuws*. English-language newspapers, published by the foreign port communities, also appeared and were followed by less regular publications in Japanese. The first real Japanese daily, the *Yokohama Daily Newspaper* (*Yokohama Mainichi Shimbun*) was started in 1870. By 1875 there were more than a hundred Japanese periodicals.

None of the newspapers or other periodicals had wide circulation. Most were journals of opinion, reflecting the political views of their backers. Some were sponsored by men in the government but most by political outsiders, like Nakae or Fukuzawa, who founded the *News of the Times* (*Jiji Shimpō*) in 1882. Unemployed samurai flocked into journalism and created a strong tradition of protest against the government. This tradition has persisted to the present, despite many decades of efforts by the authorities to bring newspapers into line with official views. As a result, the vigorous, expanding press has tended to be on the side of the government's critics and has thus played a large role in popularizing democratic ideas.

Government Countermeasures. The government leaders, apprehensive of the growing popular demand for a parliament, were determined to keep the movement under control. In 1875 they adopted new press, publication, and libel laws, designed to prevent newspaper attacks on the government. A running fight resulted between journalists and officials, with the government imprisoning and fining editors, and the newspapers setting up dummy editors as a defensive tactic. Alarmed by the national conventions of the Society of Patriots, the government adopted in 1880 a stringent law on public gatherings. This law required police permission for any public meeting, prohibited soldiers, policemen, teachers, and students from participating in political activities, and gave the authorities such general and vague powers that they could suppress almost any form of political agitation.

The government leaders kept warning one another that firm and speedy action was necessary to keep the "people's rights" movement under control. They were not so much opposed to what was being demanded as they were determined to make the decisions themselves and not be coerced by men they considered irresponsible outsiders. Most of the leaders were convinced that adopting a fixed system of government under a written constitution, with provision for some sort of parliament, would be a decided forward step. But they did not agree as to what sort of constitution or parliament should be created or how rapidly. Opinions were divided in two ways: between those who looked toward Prussian political precedents and those who admired British institutions, and between gradualists and those who felt that the step should be taken at once.

To clarify the situation, all the Councilors were asked in 1879 to submit to the emperor in writing their individual views regarding a constitution and a national assembly. By this time the original composition of the government had changed considerably. Ōkubo and Kido, for long the two most powerful men in the regime, had disappeared from the scene, Kido dying of tuberculosis in 1877 and Ōkubo at the hands of assassins the following year. This left the former second line of samurai leadership, men like Itō, Yamagata, and Ōkuma, in control under the general supervision of the court noble Iwakura.

The responses of the Councilors to the request for their views were predominantly cautious. Yamagata, the army builder, replying in December 1879, decried the popular demands for "freedom" and the decline of traditional virtues such as loyalty, but even he felt that some sort of national assembly should be formed. His specific proposal was to select the better men from the prefectural assemblies as a start and, through this body, work slowly by trial and error toward a real national assembly. Most other leaders took similar stands for the creation in due time of an assembly with strictly limited powers. Only Kuroda, the head of the Hokkaidō Colonization Office, felt that all talk about an assembly was premature.

Most of the men in authority, in power for a decade or more, felt they knew better how to strengthen Japan and persuade the West to grant it equality than did undisciplined, inexperienced political agitators outside the administration. Moreover, they had already put into effect the revolutionary ideas of their youth, such as the abolition of feudalism, legal equality for all classes, universal education, and universal conscription. Now entering their forties, they could hardly be expected to embrace with enthusiasm so new and foreign a concept as democracy. Only a new generation with a different background could do this.

The Crisis of 1881. Consequently it is rather surprising that almost all the government leaders were willing to experiment with a limited national assembly and that one of them, Ōkuma, joined Itagaki, the self-ostracized member of the ruling group, in advocating almost complete democracy. Ōkuma's memorial, not submitted until March 1881, showed the influence of one of his advisers, a student of the British parliamentary system. It suggested that elections be held in 1882, parliament be convened the next year, and the British system of a cabinet responsible to parliament be adopted.

Itō was thunderstruck by the extremism of Ōkuma's proposals. Since Ōkubo's death, he and Ōkuma had emerged as the two strongest contenders for leadership, and he seems to have regarded Ōkuma's proposals as an attempt to get ahead of him by jumping on the bandwagon of the "people's rights" movement. This impression was heightened by the subsequent outbreak of clamorous protests in the press against the proposed sale of the assets of the Hokkaidō Colonization Office — a policy which Ōkuma, among others, had opposed in the government. Ōkuma, it was suspected, was conniving with such powerful outsiders as Fukuzawa and Iwasaki, founder of the Mitsubishi interests, against his colleagues in the government.

These suspicions were probably not justified. Ōkuma seems only to have been trying to tip the scales within the government in favor of his own rather liberal ideas by taking an extreme bargaining position. If this was so, he made a colossal political blunder, though one consistent with his impetuous temperament, for he seriously misjudged the reaction of his colleagues to his provocative proposals. Itō, a consummately skillful politician, may have wanted to seize this opportunity to oust his most formidable political rival. In any case, he and the other leaders decided that Ōkuma must go. The day after the emperor returned from a tour of inspection of the north, on October 11, 1881, Ōkuma was dismissed from office. At the same time, the Hokkaidō sale was canceled as a sop to the opposition, and an Imperial Rescript was issued, promising a national assembly in 1890.

This incident, known as "the crisis of 1881," was a turning point in modern Japanese history. Ōkuma joined Itagaki in the opposition, taking with him a number of able young officials, including Inukai Tsuyoshi (or Ki; 1855–1932) and Ozaki Yukio (1859–1954), two men of samurai origin who became important democratic politicians. Thus the popular democratic movement was strengthened while the liberal element within the government was correspondingly weakened.

Ōkuma's withdrawal from the regime removed the only major leader who was not from Satsuma or Chōshū. Since these two *han* had led the Restoration movement, their samurai had been particularly numerous and strong in the Meiji government from the start. The withdrawal of Itagaki, Etō, and other Tosa and Hizen samurai from Tōkyō in 1873 had concentrated power still more in the hands of Satsuma and Chōshū men. Ōkuma's expulsion furthered the process. Many influential men from other *han* remained, but the top figures — such as Itō, Yamagata, and Inoue of Chōshū, and Kuroda, Matsukata, and Saigō Tsugumichi of Satsuma — were all from these two *han*. This strengthened the rising complaints that the government was a two-*han* oligarchy or a "Sat-Chō clique," as it came to be called.

The shrinking of the ruling group through death increased its oligarchic nature. Ever since 1868 most major political decisions had been made by a group of about a dozen men, who shared their counsels and authority with a few score more. Though this oligarchy was never a clearly defined and specific group, during the two decades after "the crisis of 1881" it was probably more static in membership and more sharply defined than at any other time.

"The crisis of 1881" resulted in a definite date being set for creating a parliament. This is often regarded as a victory for Ōkuma and the whole "people's rights" movement. Certainly Ōkuma had helped force the issue, but the victory was rather Itō's, for the chosen date of 1890 represented his gradualist view. He had already induced Iwakura to appoint him the drafter of the future constitution and to issue a series of very conservative principles for it and the national assembly. These principles, largely the work of the returned student, Inoue Kowashi, who was Itō's chief "brain-truster," included a number of things later embodied in the constitution that Itō finally prepared. Among them were the provisions that the constitution was to be a gift from the emperor, the franchise was to be limited, the upper house was to be a House of Peers on the English model, the cabinet was to be entirely independent of the parliament and was to have a number of important powers reserved to it in the name of the emperor, and the preceding year's budget was automatically to be continued in effect if parliament failed to vote a new one. This last concept, borrowed from the Prussian constitution, was considered a trump card that would keep the purse strings from falling into the hands of parliament.

Preparations for the Constitution

Although the general outline of the constitution and the parliament that would operate under it had already been established, Itō and his colleagues spent the next eight years in careful preparation for this new stage in Japan's political development. So also did Itagaki, Ōkuma, and their associates among the opposition forces. In fact, the first response to the imperial promise to create a national assembly in 1890 was an outburst of organizational activity among the political outsiders.

The Founding of Political Parties. In October 1881 Itagaki, with Gotō and his other political henchmen, reorganized the League for Establishing a National Assembly into a new party, boldly called the Liberty Party (Jiyūto) — though the accepted English translation of its name has always been Liberal Party, a title more consonant with its later history. Drawing on radical French doctrines, the party proclaimed that "liberty is the natural state of man" and its preservation his "great duty." It advocated popular sovereignty and a constitution decided upon at a national convention. While the Tosa samurai around Itagaki took the lead in this party, most of its strength came from the landowners and petty entrepreneurs such as *sake* brewers who, aroused by new government taxes, constituted an important part of its early support.

Ōkuma and his followers founded in March 1882 a less radical party, the Constitutional Progressive Party (Rikken Kaishintō), oriented toward English parliamentary concepts. It initially drew its chief support from urban intellectuals and businessmen. Fukuzawa and the products of his Keiō University were among its most important supporters, as was Iwasaki, head of the great Mitsubishi interests.

Both the Progressive and Liberal Parties supported the imperial institution as the symbol of Japan's political unity. There was no dispute on this point at all. But the parties did challenge the right of what they regarded as a Satsuma-Chōshū oligarchy to speak for the emperor. To the party men it seemed that the imperial will could be better expressed by a parliament.

A third party of transient significance, the Constitutional Imperial Rule Party (Rikken Teiseitō), was also founded in March 1882 to support the government position on the constitutional problem. It was started with the encouragement of some of the government leaders, who apparently hoped to fight fire with fire, but it found little popular support and soon dissolved.

The Liberal and Progressive Parties, though repeatedly disbanded, reorganized, or merged, have continued as major political groupings until the present day. The weaknesses of their first years also persisted for many decades. Although they were able at times of political crisis to stir up enthusiastic mass support, their enrolled membership was very small — at most only a few thousand. Most people felt too close to the feudal past to commit themselves publicly by joining political parties. Moreover, despite this smallness of membership, party control over local affiliates was always tenuous.

Party organization showed strong survivals of feudal patterns. Though the parties had political programs, principles were usually subordinated to personal loyalties. Each party was regarded by the other as less interested in parliamentary government than in replacing the Satsuma-Chōshū oligarchy with its own members. The Tosa leadership of the Liberal Party gave it a regional cast that hurt its cause elsewhere. Moreover, each group, dominated by one towering political figure, was in essence a leader-follower band, split up into smaller leader-follower factions. The parties, in other words, had certain similarities to the personally-organized, daimyo-dominated, and clique-ridden regimes of the *han* of Tokugawa times.

The Collapse of the Party Movement. The weak new political parties faced formidable opponents in the government leaders, who were determined to exclude their noisy critics from participation in drafting the promised constitution. In 1882 the laws on public meetings were made still more stringent. Local party branches were prohibited, making it difficult to organize unified movements. The government also managed to get the chief leaders of the Liberal Party temporarily out of the country, when Inoue Kaoru, the foreign minister, persuaded the Mitsui firm secretly to finance a trip by Itagaki and Gotō to observe European governments. The Progressives insinuated that the Liberals had been bribed; the Liberals in reply violently attacked the Progressives for their connections with that "Sea Monster," the Mitsubishi firm with its big shipping line.

During Itagaki's absence abroad in 1882–83, his party got into serious difficulties. Matsukata's deflationary policy had brought a sharp decline in prices, which made payment of the fixed monetary taxes very difficult for many peasants. The result was a wave of armed uprisings, some of them led by local members of the Liberal Party — thus involving it in open rebellion. The worst outbreaks were in the silk-growing areas on the mountainous fringes of the Kantō Plain around Tōkyō, an area economically more advanced than most of rural Japan and particularly sensitive to general market conditions. The first serious rising occurred in Fukushima Prefecture north of Tōkyō in December 1882, when the local governor had overridden the actions of the prefectural assembly. The unrest culminated in a series of uprisings in the autumn of 1884.

The government, with its solid military backing, had no trouble suppressing these disturbances, which, in any case, soon subsided with the improvement in business conditions. But the uprisings discredited the Liberals and the whole parliamentary movement and helped to split the Liberal Party between the ideological radicals, who had encouraged the peasant unrest, and more moderate elements, backed by the essentially conservative landowners who constituted the financial backbone of the party. This situation, together with the government's restrictive legislation, induced the party to dissolve in October 1884. The faction-ridden Progressives also soon fell apart. Ōkuma and some of his chief associates resigned from the party, which then sank into temporary insignificance.

Another effort was made in 1887 to rally the opposition political groups against the government, this time with new strength drawn from an unexpected source. Inoue as foreign minister had been attempting once again to win from the foreign powers a revision of the unequal treaties, but his terms, when prematurely revealed, aroused a storm of nationalistic protest in Japan. He had proposed the relinquishment of extraterritoriality by the foreign powers but had provided for a transition period during which mixed courts of foreign and Japanese judges would try cases involving foreigners. Both this provision and the proposed opening of all Japan to foreign residence were very unpopular. The 1880's also saw the height of the government-inspired craze for ballroom dancing and other Western customs which irked conservative Japanese. The government thus was open to attack from one side for its failure to adopt the democratic institutions of the Occident and from the opposite direction because of its pro-Westernism.

This simultaneous attack on the government from apparently contradictory points of view suggests a fundamental ambiguity in the party movement. But the party men saw nothing inconsistent in their stand. They advocated Western parliamentarianism as a superior political system that would give them a share in power, but they were not any more committed to other Western institutions or any less chauvinistic than the government leaders. Indeed, as men unencumbered by the responsibilities of national leadership, they could afford to be more extreme on both scores than could the men in power.

The lead in rallying the disparate forces of opposition was taken by Itagaki's old associate, Gotō. Large meetings were held in the autumn of 1887, but the government struck back vigorously. Yamagata, as home minister in control of the police, took strong repressive measures against the political agitators, and on December 25 the government issued a Peace Preservation Law, which gave it the right to expel from the Tōkyō area any person felt to be "a threat to public tranquillity." In the next few days some 570 persons were removed from the capital.

The revived party movement was shaken by this sudden blow and soon collapsed completely when some of its members were inveigled back into the government by offers of high posts. Ōkuma became foreign minister in February 1888 and Gotō communications minister in March of the next year. As foreign minister, Ōkuma replaced the Satsuma-Chōshū oligarchs as the object of popular indignation at the failure to get revision of the unequal treaties, and in October 1889 he lost a leg when a fanatic threw a bomb at him.

Strengthening the Base of Authority: Itō and the Cabinet System. The running fight between the parties and the government leaders had not prevented the latter from going ahead with their plans for writing a constitution and inaugurating limited parliamentary government. The basic scheme had already been adopted in 1881. Itō, though annoyed by the attacks of proponents of French and English political concepts, remained determined that the new constitution should be based on sound Western political theory, with European precedents for its major features. He therefore had himself sent in March 1882 at the head of a group to study European constitutions.

Knowing what he wanted, Itō stayed first for nine months in Germany and Austria, studying with two conservative scholars — in Berlin with Albert Mosse, who had been assigned to him by Rudolf von Gneist, and in Vienna with Lorenz von Stein. These men as well as Bismarck confirmed his previous opinions and gave them the support of the latest conservative European theorizing. In contrast with his long stay in Berlin and Vienna, Itō was in London only six weeks and in the other European capitals for still briefer periods.

Since Iwakura, the court noble, died during his absence, Itō found himself on his return in August 1883 even more powerful than before and quite free to proceed with his plans. He busily set about creating strongholds of executive power against possible encroachments by the future parliament. In March 1884 he assumed the post of imperial household minister and the chairmanship of a special commission set up under this ministry to draft the constitution.

In July 1884 a new peerage was created to form the membership of the projected House of Peers. It was made up of more than 500 persons in five ranks — prince, marquis, count, viscount, and baron (designated by the titles used in ancient Chou China). Most of the new peers were the former daimyo, graded according to the size of their former *han* and the latters' service in the "imperial restoration." A large but impoverished segment of the peerage was made up of the old court aristocracy. The oligarchs also assigned themselves modest positions among the new nobles. Itō, for example, started as a count; but he and a few others, through subsequent promotions, eventually achieved the top rank of prince.

Itō's most important innovation was the creation in December 1885 of a cabinet to take the place of the Council of State, in which a few high court nobles had exercised an uncertain degree of control over the Councilors and the individual ministries. The cabinet was a strong executive body, made up of the heads of ministries under a prime minister. It not only brought Japanese administrative organization into line with the most up-to-date European models but also gave the oligarchs a consolidated base of power, free of supervision by the old court aristocracy and unified against the attacks of the popular opposition. At the same time Itō modernized the system of bureaucratic appointments in keeping with the new cabinet organization. Eventually in 1887 the government adopted a civil service examination system, based on the German model.

Itō and his colleagues made sure that the cabinet, as the chief bastion of executive power, would be entirely in their own hands. The first cabinet is a roster of the top oligarchs. Chōshū was represented by Itō as prime minister, Inoue as foreign minister, Yamagata as home minister, and Yamada Akiyoshi (1844–1892) as justice minister. Satsuma had an equal representation: Matsukata as finance minister, Ōyama Iwao (1842–1916) as army minister, Saigō Tsugumichi as navy minister, and Mori as education minister. The only peripheral figures were Tani Kanjō (1837–1911), a conservative general from Tosa, as minister of agriculture and commerce, and Enomoto, the former leader of the shogunal navy, as communications minister.

To emphasize the unique position of the emperor, Itō created certain posts above the cabinet to speak in the emperor's name. In 1885 he revived the ancient title of Naidaijin, or inner minister, often translated "lord keeper of the privy seal," a post the court noble Sanjō occupied until his death in 1891. Itō also placed the Imperial Household Ministry outside the cabinet, though continuing himself to serve as its minister. Most important of the supra-cabinet organs was the Privy Council (*Sūmitsu-in*), created in April 1888 to approve the constitution then being drafted. Characteristically Itō took the presidency of this new body, relinquishing the prime ministry to do so.

Itō chose Kuroda, formerly head of the Hokkaidō Colonization Office, to be the new prime minister. The choice of Kuroda was particularly appropriate, since it seemed politic to have a Satsuma man follow a Chōshū man at the helm. Though selection of the prime minister was always determined by a complex of factors, the alternation in power of Chōshū and Satsuma men was certainly one important consideration — and as it worked out this practice was strictly observed until 1898.

Kuroda resigned in October 1889, following a serious split in the cabinet over the revision of the unequal treaties and the bomb attack on his foreign minister, Ōkuma. The choice of prime minister fell on Yamagata of Chōshū, just returned from a second trip to Europe. And after Yamagata's resignation in 1891, Matsukata of Satsuma alternated with Itō as prime minister for the next seven years (see chart, page 302). During these shifts in the premiership, the other oligarchs for the most part held their original portfolios or exchanged positions with one another. New men brought into the cabinet were mostly from Satsuma or Chōshū, and even the two outsiders, Ōkuma and Gotō, were former members of the governing group.

While Itō and his colleagues were setting their proposed pattern for the development of Japanese politics, their political philosophies also gradually hardened into a mold. It was becoming increasingly clear that, to maintain their leadership in the face of mounting opposition both by chauvinists and by advocates of democracy, they would have to reserve extensive powers and prerogatives in the name of the emperor. While the "imperial restoration" had been an excellent justification for revolutionary changes, imperial prestige would have to be further enhanced in order to give the oligarchs an impregnable position. To do this, greater efforts would be needed to control and guide public opinion.

Thus the 1880's saw a definite crystallization of the official philosophy. Efforts were redoubled to build up the prestige and power of the imperial institution. As we have seen, education was again put under strict centralized controls, and the imitation of Western social custom was dropped after the fiasco of the fancy-dress ball of 1887. In many fields conservative German theories were given precedence over more liberal theories from other Western countries, and the Confucian and feudal emphasis on loyalty and obedience also came back into fashion, finding expression in 1890 in the so-called Imperial Rescript on Education (page 276).

Strengthening the Base of Authority: Yamagata and the Military.
While Itō had been planning a strong executive system in which, at least initially, the cabinet would remain almost entirely free of influence by parliament, Yamagata, who had even greater misgivings about parliamentary government, had been following a parallel but separate course of institutional innovation. Yamagata seems to have had a more literal and old-fashioned concept of imperial rule than Itō, and as the chief architect of the army, he placed more emphasis on the armed services as a bulwark of strong executive power. Despite the crushing of the Satsuma Rebellion in 1877, the army, made up largely of samurai born in various autonomous *han* and peasants new to their role as soldiers, continued to have major problems of discipline. In fact, there was a serious revolt in the Imperial Guards Division in 1878. Yamagata therefore devoted himself to building up the army's morale and technical competence and to developing a degree of autonomy for the armed services within the government.

In December 1878 Yamagata adopted the German general staff system. This not only was an important advance in military technology but also established the principle that the chief of staff in matters of military command, as opposed to financial and administrative affairs, was independent of the army minister and the civil government and acted only under the command of the emperor, with the right of direct access to him. To emphasize the importance and independence of the chief of staff, Yamagata resigned as army minister and assumed this new post.

In the same year Yamagata put out an "Admonition to the Military," emphasizing the old virtues of loyalty, bravery, and obedience, and in 1882 he had the emperor issue an "Imperial Precept for the Military" (sometimes called the "Rescript to Soldiers and Sailors"). The fact that this document was made public in the name of the emperor increased the prestige of the armed services. The text made clear that "the supreme command" of the army and navy was in the hands of the emperor and would never be delegated to others, thus strengthening the independence of the armed services from the other organs of government.

Yamagata, as home minister between 1883 and 1888, also had a chance to build up strong executive power in other fields in anticipation of the future challenge by parliament. The police force under his control crushed the peasant uprisings of the mid-eighties and dealt severely with political agitators. The Peace Preservation Law of 1887, a prime factor in the breakup of the opposition, was largely his handiwork. Meanwhile he reorganized the police into a more centrally controlled and efficient body. With the aid of Mosse, who had been Itō's teacher in Berlin, he undertook a reorganization of local government into an efficient but highly authoritarian and hierarchic system, embodied in laws promulgated in 1888 and 1890.

The Meiji Constitution. The actual work of drafting the constitution and subsidiary legislation to accompany it did not get under way until 1886. The chief participants under Itō's supervision were Inoue Kowashi, who had helped Yamagata with the "Imperial Precept for the Military"; Itō Miyoji (1857–1934), who was a protégé of the other Itō; Kaneko Kentarō (1853–1942), who came from the Fukuoka domain in North Kyūshū and had studied at the Harvard Law School; and a German, Hermann Roessler. In May 1888 the finished documents were submitted to the newly created Privy Council, under Itō's presidency, which after long deliberation approved them with only minor modifications. The constitution, which had been kept jealously secret from the public, was promulgated on schedule on February 11, 1889, the official anniversary of the supposed founding of the Japanese state in 660 B.C.

The constitution and its subsidiary legislation made good the promise to create a national assembly by 1890 — but with the limitations decided upon by the oligarchs in 1881. The constitution included an extensive series of popular rights, such as freedom of religion, freedom of "speech, publication, public meetings, and association," liberty of residence, and rights to property and due processes of law, but all of these were hedged about with such phrases as "except in cases provided for in the law" or "within limits not prejudicial to peace and order."

A bicameral parliament, called in English the Diet, was to be convened in 1890. The House of Peers was to consist of the higher ranks of the nobility, elected representatives of the lower ranks, and a few imperial appointees, who turned out usually to be men of scholarly distinction. The House of Peers was to be a conservative check on the House of Representatives, which was to be chosen by a strictly limited electorate — adult males who paid national taxes of fifteen yen or more. This category numbered 450,000 in 1890, only a little over one per cent of the population. But the Diet, however restricted in selection, was to exercise real powers and its consent was required for all laws.

The oligarchs, however, set up what they felt were adequate safe-guards against parliamentary domination. The emperor could at any time prorogue (i.e., discontinue) the Diet or dissolve the House of Representatives. When the Diet was not in session, he could issue imperial ordinances which took the place of laws until the Diet could take action on them. Moreover, the oligarchs sought to keep control over the purse strings by providing that, if the Diet failed to vote a new budget, that of the preceding year would continue in effect.

The oligarchs also saw to it that the constitution established un-equivocally those imperial prerogatives which they envisaged as the chief defense of executive leadership. It would be unfair to assume that they cynically used the imperial institution to preserve their personal power. They were men who, since their youth, had been stirred by the concept of an "imperial restoration" and they no doubt believed in it strongly — at least in a mystical sense. It would be impossible to draw a line between their selfish or at least self-confident desires to perpetuate their own powers and their sincere veneration for the imperial institution.

The constitution was presented as the gift of the emperor, who re-served the exclusive right to initiate amendments — none in fact were ever made. It declared the person of the emperor to be "sacred and inviolable" and the locus of sovereignty, as the descendant of a dynasty "which has reigned in an unbroken line of descent for ages past." It made clear that the emperor exercised all executive authority and also "the legislative power with the consent of the Imperial Diet." It specif-ically stated that "the emperor has the supreme command of the army and navy," and it made the individual ministers directly responsible to him, rather than collectively responsible as a cabinet. A judiciary branch of government was created but, being controlled by the justice ministry, it was little more than an extension of the emperor's executive powers.

The Meiji constitution was a blend of many conflicting ideas. Ōkuma, once again in the government, and some of the other oligarchs had urged more liberal principles, while Confucianists like Motoda Eifu had hoped

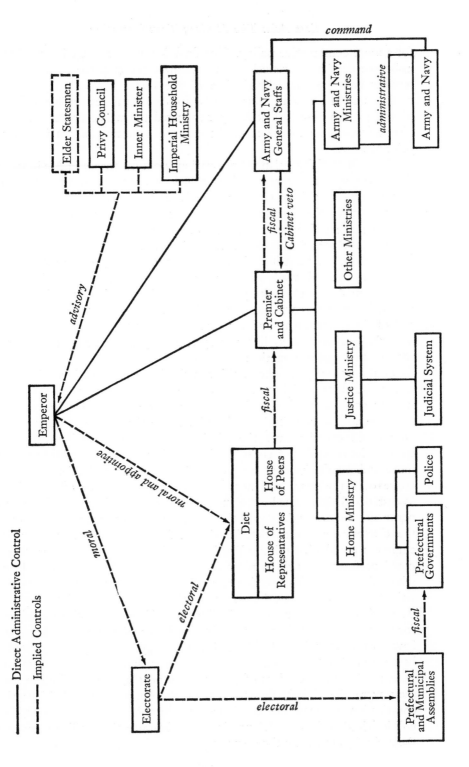

THE POLITICAL SYSTEM UNDER THE MEIJI CONSTITUTION

——— Direct Administrative Control

– – – Implied Controls

297

for a more conservative policy. The final document reflected Yamagata's insistence on the theoretical autonomy under the emperor of the armed services and the parallel principle of the direct responsibility of the ministers to the throne. But clearly Itō had been responsible for the overall pattern. He had skillfully dominated the whole process of constitution-writing, and the result bore the clear stamp of his particular point of view.

Itō so successfully balanced the various political forces in Meiji Japan that there was never any serious attack upon the constitution itself. Enough scope had been given to the advocates of parliamentary government to satisfy their minimal demands. At the same time enough powers had been reserved for the government to satisfy the minimal desires of those of authoritarian outlook. Moreover, the document proved more flexible than had been intended. It gave the parties greater scope than had been expected, while the fact that it was explicitly a gift from the emperor made open attack by conservatives impossible. Considering the period when it was written, the feudal background of the men in control of the government, and the nature of Japanese society and politics, it established perhaps as liberal a system of government as could have worked in Japan at that time.

On the other hand, the Meiji constitution contained inconsistencies and ambiguities which were to plague later generations who had a weaker and less unified leadership than that provided by Itō and his colleagues. The constitution left quite vague the degree of control the Diet could exercise over the administrative processes of government through its functions of voting budgets and approving laws. It left even more ambiguous the degree of control the cabinet and Diet could exercise over the army and navy through control of the purse strings. Worst of all, it assumed clear moral leadership on the part of the emperor, not only over the appointive members of government but also over the electorate and the Diet, but it failed to create a situation where emperors could give this leadership and did not provide organs which could perform this role in place of the emperors. The oligarchs themselves did perform this function of top leadership as long as they remained united and vigorous, but thereafter no other group fully took their place. The Privy Council and other high court offices might claim to speak for the emperor, but the prime minister and his cabinet did not necessarily have to follow their lead. Meanwhile the army and navy general staffs, because of their direct access to the emperor, and the politicians in the Diet, as the representatives of the Japanese people, also could claim that they were the rightful interpreters of the "imperial will." Thus the constitution assumed the continued existence of a strong and unified political leadership that did not in fact exist once the Meiji leaders had themselves passed from the scene.

The Early Years of Constitutional Government

Itō, while reserving the trump cards for the government, had foreseen the possibility that the powers of the Diet might gradually increase until it would even have some share in selecting the cabinet. But development in this direction was more rapid than he had expected. The drafters of the constitution had looked upon the House of Representatives as a safety valve, which would give the advocates of parliamentary government a forum of debate and the prestige of participation in the government. They hoped this would lessen the pressure for further sharing of real power. The opposition, however, proved more obstreperous than had been foreseen.

The oligarchs also discovered that, in stacking the political deck in their own favor, they had made one serious miscalculation. Their chief trump card turned out to be almost valueless. At a time when the national economy and government expenditures were expanding rapidly, the preceding year's budget was never adequate. The national budget actually tripled between 1893 and 1903. Conservative German political theory had proved deficient on this crucial economic point. The oligarchs, dependent upon the Diet to vote their ever expanding budgets, had to make greater concessions to it than even the more liberal of them had anticipated. They fought doggedly to preserve what they felt were the rightful prerogatives of the emperor and his advisers, but bit by bit leadership gravitated from their hands to the Diet.

The First Diet Session. The first elections were held on July 1, 1890, and the Diet was convened in November. The party politicians had acquired considerable experience, both in electioneering and in parliamentary techniques, in the prefectural assemblies that had been in existence since 1878. Some had developed strong constituencies among the local electorate, which, to the consternation of the government, consistently preferred party politicians over announced supporters of the government. Of 300 members of the first House of Representatives, 130 belonged to the newly reconstituted Liberal Party and 41 to the Progressives, while some of the independents were obviously prepared to vote with these opposition parties against the government.

The party men, wanting to establish party control over the cabinet, made immediate use of the one substantial power the constitution had given the Diet. They slashed the budget by about 11 per cent, concentrating on the salaries and perquisites of the bureaucratic followers of the oligarchs.

The government leaders faced the first Diet under the premiership of Yamagata, who was the least inclined to tolerate dictation by the Diet. They had all agreed that the cabinet should remain in a "transcendent" position — that is, unaffected by the support or opposition of the Diet. But the lack of majority support among the members of the lower house was nonetheless embarrassing. The cabinet was reluctant to resort to the extreme measure of dissolving the Diet. In particular, Itō was eager to demonstrate, both to his countrymen and to Westerners, that his constitution was wise and this first experiment in parliamentary institutions a success. Yamagata tried to beat down the opposition by citing a constitutional provision that the Diet could not refuse to vote certain categories of previously fixed expenditures, and there were efforts at bribery and intimidation of the Diet members. Eventually Itagaki and some of his Tosa associates in the Liberal Party agreed to restore about a quarter of the funds cut by the Diet, and the cabinet had to settle for this compromise.

Compromises of this sort were the main pattern of Japanese political development over the next few decades. They were a characteristically Japanese way of solving differences of opinion. Compromise was also a natural product of the somewhat ambiguous situation. The constitution had given neither the cabinet nor the Diet enough power to control the other completely. Nor was either body a fully united group. The Diet was divided between mutually hostile parties and a great many personal factions. The oligarchs also, though a smaller and more cohesive group, included men with sharp differences of attitude.

For the oligarchs, the first Diet session was hardly an auspicious start in constitutional government. It showed they had given away more than they had intended and revealed a growing division of opinion among themselves. Itō was critical of Yamagata's inflexible attitude toward the Diet. Yamagata, who considered himself a soldier rather than a statesman, resigned in May 1891.

Matsukata, who had served so ably as finance minister since 1881, was chosen as the new prime minister. Lacking the strong personal position of Itō or Yamagata and not fully supported by either of them, Matsukata proved so dependent on the group of oligarchs as a whole that his cabinet was dubbed the "puppet cabinet." The leaders who by this time were beginning to be called the Elder Statesmen, or Genrō, consisted essentially of Itō, Yamagata, Inoue Kaoru, and Yamada from Chōshū and Kuroda, Saigō, Ōyama, and Matsukata from Satsuma. Though subsequently depleted by deaths and joined by occasional new recruits, they remained a fairly clear-cut and stable group over the next two decades, serving as the ultimate source of executive authority and making many of the decisions that had been reserved for the emperor. While each did his best to have his own views prevail, they all held to the Japanese ideal of collective rather than individual leadership. Any one of them, when pressed by the others to take the prime ministry, usually accepted with a show of reluctance that was not altogether feigned and, if strongly opposed by the others on any issue, would readily yield rather than bring disagreement to a head.

The Struggle Between the Diet and the Cabinet (1891–1894). Matsukata attempted to carry out the strong repressive policy against the Diet that Yamagata had advocated. When the Diet reconvened in November 1891 and again attempted to slash the budget, he dissolved it. In the following election, on February 15, 1892, the home minister, Shinagawa Yajirō (1843–1900), a Chōshū henchman of Yamagata and former minister to Germany, used all the powers of bribery and force he could muster as head of the police and local government system. It was the bloodiest election in Japanese history. The official figures, probably underestimated, list 25 killed and 388 wounded in melees between the police, hired thugs, and politicians. But this frontal attack failed completely. The opposition forces again won a clear majority, of 163 seats, in the House of Representatives. Shinagawa resigned because of the public clamor, and when the Diet met in May, both houses passed resolutions condemning the government.

Matsukata ignored the vote of nonconfidence and prorogued the Diet for a week as a disciplinary measure. The lower house struck back by cutting the supplementary budget by a third. The House of Peers restored the cuts, raising a constitutional issue, which was referred to the Privy Council, thus setting a constitutional precedent. The Council decided that the two houses would have to compromise their differences on budget matters. Matsukata, however, ran into further trouble with his own colleagues. The army and navy ministers withdrew from his cabinet in August in protest at the punishments of officials who had intervened in the election earlier that year, and Matsukata thereby was forced to resign.

Itō now took his turn at trying to deal with the Diet. Where Yamagata, in his simple devotion to imperial rule, had advocated a straightforward policy of riding roughshod over the party opposition, Itō, with the flexibility of a true politician, took a more ambiguous view of the imperial prerogatives and was more inclined to compromise solutions. He had proposed in January 1892 that the policy of "transcendent" cabinets be abandoned and a government party be formed to capture the Diet, but the other Elder Statesmen had quashed this startling scheme. However, when the Diet, convened again in November 1892, attempted as usual to slash the budget, and sent a memorial to the emperor impeaching the cabinet, Itō showed he had other tricks up his sleeve. He had the emperor admonish the disputants to compose their differences and undermined opposition to the budget by having the emperor surrender some of his own income and order his civil and military officials to follow suit. This invoking of the imperial name and the voluntary reduction of a part of

EARLY PRIME MINISTERS AND DIET ELECTIONS

(c) = Chōshū
(s) = Satsuma

Prime Ministers	Periods in Office	Elections
Itō (c)	Dec. 22, 1885 — Apr. 30, 1888	
Kuroda (s)	Apr. 30, 1888 — Oct. 25, 1889	
Yamagata (c)	Dec. 24, 1889 — May 6, 1891	1st — July 1, 1890
Matsukata (s)	May 6, 1891 — Aug. 8, 1892	2nd — Feb. 15, 1892
Itō (c)	Aug. 8, 1892 — Aug. 31, 1896	3rd — March 1, 1894
		4th — Sept. 1, 1894
Matsukata (s)	Sept. 18, 1896 — Jan. 12, 1898	
Itō (c)	Jan. 12, 1898 — June 30, 1898	5th — March 15, 1898
Ōkuma	June 30, 1898 — Nov. 8, 1898	6th — Aug. 10, 1898
Yamagata (c)	Nov. 8, 1898 — Oct. 19, 1900	
Itō (c)	Oct. 19, 1900 — May 10, 1901	
Katsura (c)	June 2, 1901 — Jan. 7, 1906	7th — Aug. 10, 1902
		8th — March 1, 1903
		9th — March 1, 1904
Saionji	Jan. 7, 1906 — July 1, 1908	10th — May 15, 1908
Katsura (c)	July 14, 1908 — Aug. 30, 1911	
Saionji	Aug. 30, 1911 — Dec. 21, 1912	11th — May 15, 1912
Katsura (c)	Dec. 21, 1912 — Feb. 20, 1913	

the budget in this dramatic way won enough votes to carry the rest of the budget.

Itō was more successful than his predecessors in dividing the opposition. When the Diet met in November 1893, he won some cooperation from the Liberals on matters of foreign policy and so brought them into conflict with the Progressives, who were concentrating their attacks on the failure of the government to obtain revision of the unequal treaties. In the resulting fight in the House of Representatives, the Progressives and their ultranationalist allies impeached Hoshi Tōru (1850–1901), president of the Liberals and speaker of the lower house, on grounds of an improper stock exchange deal, and ousted him from the Diet.

But in the long run, Itō too proved unable to control the Diet even by his more subtle and varied tactics. Its chauvinistic criticism of the treaty-revision negotiations was extremely embarrassing, because they had reached a critical state. Itō twice prorogued the Diet and finally in January 1894 dissolved it. He insisted that the third election, held on March 1, 1894, be strictly fair, and he was justified by the results, which were more favorable to the government. But the new Diet voted to condemn the cabinet for having dissolved the previous Diet, and Itō, faced with war clouds on the continent and Western hesitation at treaty revision, dissolved it again in June, for the second time in six months.

Attempts at Oligarch-Party Coalition (1895–1898). Itō's second dissolution of the Diet was followed not by a renewed storm of protest but by a period of unusual cooperation between Diet and cabinet. A treaty signed with Britain on July 16, 1894, heralded the end in 1899 of extraterritoriality, a major aspect of the unequal-treaty system, thus removing one reason for the Diet's criticism of the government. More important was the outbreak that summer of war with China over Korea. The new Diet, elected on September 1, reacting to a war situation in the same way as most Western parliaments, voted all the war budgets unanimously and almost without discussion.

The Sino-Japanese War (see pages 382 ff.) was a great success from the viewpoint of the Japanese. They were delighted by the quick victory over their giant neighbor and the acquisition of new territories — Taiwan, the adjacent Pescadores Islands, and the Liaotung Peninsula in southern Manchuria. But when joint pressure by Russia, Germany, and France forced the government to give back Liaotung, the public protested bitterly, and the attack on the cabinet was resumed in the Diet.

This time Itō weathered the storm by openly allying himself with the Liberals, thus taking a long step away from the policy of "transcendent" cabinets. Itagaki, again president of the Liberal Party, had been gradually won over to Itō's foreign policy and in November 1895 pledged his support of the cabinet. Prime movers in the formation of this coalition had been Itō's old adviser, Itō Miyoji, and his able foreign minister, Mutsu Munemitsu (1844–1897), who earlier had been a strong advocate of parliamentary government. Originally of the "collateral" *han* of Wakayama, Mutsu had twice studied abroad and in 1877 had been imprisoned with other advocates of parliamentarianism for plotting against the government. To reward Itagaki for his support, Itō gave him the key post of home minister in April 1896, while Hoshi was made minister to the United States, and other party stalwarts were given other political plums.

But the coalition between Itō and the Liberals did not last long. The Progressives responded by joining with other Diet groups in an opposition party, named the Shimpotō, which also is best translated as Progressive Party. The new party, under Ōkuma's leadership, began to cooperate with Matsukata, who, unlike Yamagata, was flexible enough for this kind of political maneuvering. To counter this combination of the forces opposed to him within the Diet and the oligarchy, Itō sought to bring Ōkuma and Matsukata into his cabinet, but Itagaki objected. Itō's tenure as prime minister had already lasted an unprecedented four years, and he resigned in disgust.

Matsukata was selected to try his hand again at dealing with the Diet, and he followed Itō's lead in the new cabinet that he set up in September 1896. He publicly recognized the support of the Progressives by making Ōkuma foreign minister and giving sub-cabinet posts to several of the latter's followers. But the Matsukata-Progressive coalition proved no more durable than that between Itō and the Liberals. The Progressives felt that Matsukata had failed to keep some of his promises, and criticism of the Imperial Household Ministry published by the chief cabinet secretary, a party man, seriously embarrassed the oligarchs in the cabinet. Ōkuma resigned in November 1897, and in December Matsukata, now faced by overwhelming opposition in the Diet, resorted to the old technique of dissolution after a futile effort to win Liberal support. He then resigned the premiership before he would have to face another hostile Diet.

Itō, returning to the helm in January, turned first to the Progressives for their support, but Ōkuma's price of the Home Ministry and three other cabinet posts was too high. Itō also found it impossible to agree with the Liberals. Without party support, he saw his budget attacked and his tax measures voted down by the new Diet elected on March 15, 1898. He had no recourse but to dissolve the Diet again in June and to resign.

As none of the other oligarchs were ready to undertake the premiership, Itō suggested that he be allowed to organize a government party, if necessary resigning his positions in the government, or else that the cabinet be surrendered to the ex-oligarchs, Ōkuma and Itagaki. These two had just merged their followings into the Kenseitō, or Constitutional Party, which was shortly to prove its overwhelming strength by winning 260 of the 300 seats in the lower house in the election of August 10. The Elder Statesmen, who did not like either proposal, finally settled on the second. Thus in a mere eight years they had been forced to abandon completely their original assumption that the cabinet could remain above Diet politics.

The parties, however, were not yet ready for the heavy responsibility of executive leadership. The army and navy ministers, continued from the previous cabinet, held themselves disdainfully aloof from the party men. The bureaucrats, who usually owed personal allegiance to one or another of the oligarchs, were reluctant to cooperate fully with the politicians in charge of the various ministries, thus preventing the party men's control of the administration. The sudden shift from opposition to leadership found the politicians agreed upon vague general principles but without a specific program. Worst of all, the old factional divisions remained strong within the new party. Itagaki as foreign minister had only two of his followers in the cabinet, while Ōkuma as prime minister had four. When one of these, the veteran Progressive, Ozaki Yukio, was forced to resign for having referred in a speech to republicanism in Japan, the cabinet broke up over the naming of his successor. Thus it failed after only a half year in office, without even having faced the Diet.

Yamagata's Efforts to Reassert Oligarchic Control. By 1898 the split between Itō and Yamagata over handling the Diet had become acute. From the start Yamagata had been more insistent than Itō that the Diet should have no control over the cabinet, and he had opposed every compromise step Itō had taken in this direction. He naturally lacked Itō's pride of authorship in the constitution and so felt less committed to its success, at times even suggesting its suspension. He saw Japan's needs primarily in military terms. Stability having been achieved at home, he turned his attention abroad, arguing that the geographic line of national advantage that Japan should defend lay far beyond the line of sovereignty. These imperialistic concepts might be traced to the ardent Chōshū expansionist, Yoshida Shōin, under whom both Yamagata and Itō had studied in their youth. But wholly aside from such early influences, these ideas were natural to any military figure in the late nineteenth century. Since expansion or even a strong defense depended on ever increasing military budgets, it seemed to Yamagata the height of folly to surrender control over the government and its purse strings to the economy-minded representatives of the taxpayers.

There was no concealing the divergence of views between Yamagata, determined to keep what he viewed as the emperor's own military forces and bureaucracy free from control by petty-minded businessmen, and Itō, the agile politician, prepared to make any compromises necessary to win the support of the parliament he had created. But neither Itō, with his strong following in the bureaucracy, nor Yamagata, with his even more powerful following in the military establishment as well as the bureaucracy, attempted to use his base of power against the other. The interests uniting them were greater than those dividing them. Both were devoted to the same dream of creating a strong and rich Japan, and Itō's hopes for a powerful military and firm leadership by the Elder Statesmen differed only in degree from those of Yamagata. They both did their best to continue the cooperation that had started in their revolutionary youth in Chōshū, making what concessions they could to each other. Itō had not objected to the autonomy Yamagata had won for the armed services within the government, and in the wave of nationalistic enthusiasm following the Sino-Japanese War, he obtained Diet approval for a great expansion of the military. The army alone was increased by six divisions and its budget more than fivefold, taking almost a third of the national budget.

Yamagata had been in Europe when Itō established his first coalition with a party by taking Itagaki into his cabinet in 1896. He naturally disapproved of this step and was even more bitterly opposed to the invitation to Itagaki and Ōkuma to form a cabinet. He insisted that the navy and army ministers be appointed separately from the rest of the cabinet. They were Saigō Tsugumichi and Katsura Tarō (1847–1913), a Chōshū general who had returned from study in Germany in time to help Yamagata introduce a general staff system in 1878. Representing his patron's point of view, Katsura worked from within the cabinet to help bring about its downfall in the autumn of 1898. Thereupon Yamagata, taking advantage of Itō's temporary absence in China, took the premiership in November to try out his own concepts of constitutional government.

Yamagata was enough of a realist to know that he had to have some support in the Diet for his policies. As early as 1892 he had encouraged Saigō and the infamous home minister Shinagawa to form a Diet group to support his policies. This was the Kokumin Kyōkai, or Nationalist Association, which was still in existence, though in 1899 it changed its name to Teikokutō, or Imperial Party. This group, however, was not enough.

Fortunately for Yamagata the Constitutional Party, following the collapse of the Ōkuma-Itagaki cabinet, had split into its component elements, the Liberals retaining the name of Constitutional Party and the Progressives calling themselves the Real Constitutional Party (Kenseihontō). With Katsura's aid, Yamagata achieved an alliance, rather than a coalition, with the former. He stubbornly resisted all efforts of the former Liberals to obtain posts in the cabinet, but he worked out a joint legislative program with them. One result was the reduction in 1900 of the tax qualification for voting from 15 yen to 10 yen and the expansion of the House of Representatives to 369 members. Another result was the passage, with the aid of considerable bribery, of Yamagata's budgets and his bills for increased taxation.

Despite these concessions to Diet power, Yamagata's chief efforts were devoted to increasing the autonomy of the armed services and the bureaucracy. Half the members of his cabinet were generals or admirals, and his most important innovations were introduced as imperial ordinances while the Diet was not in session. These included new regulations, issued in 1899, regarding civil service examinations, which were aimed at excluding politicians from the higher ranks. Other measures, adopted in 1900, were the extension of the powers of the Privy Council and a ruling that only officers of the two top ranks on active service could be appointed army or navy ministers. As early as 1873 Yamagata had insisted as an efficiency measure that only professionals, not civilians, should occupy these posts. Now, by specifying their active status, he ensured that the Army and Navy General Staffs would have virtually complete control over the occupants of these two vital cabinet posts.

Itō's Party Government. The cooperation between Yamagata and the Constitutional Party was at best a union of convenience. As Yamagata busily devised ways of freezing the party men out of administrative posts, the latter wearied of supporting him and approached Itō instead. Still determined to have the constitution work according to his own interpretation rather than Yamagata's, Itō finally won approval from the Elder Statesmen and the emperor for his old scheme of organizing a political party. In September 1900 he founded the Rikken Seiyūkai, or Friends of Constitutional Government, made up of the old Liberals, now called the Constitutional Party, and his own supporters in the bureaucracy. Then in October Yamagata, who had for some months been talking of giving up the premiership, finally resigned, and Itō took his place.

Itō's cabinet was ostensibly a party one, since its members, except for the army, navy, and foreign ministers, were party members. However, only some of them, such as Hoshi, the strong man of the Constitutional Party, were real party politicians. Others, like Kaneko, who had helped Itō draft the constitution, were bureaucrats who had just become party members.

Since the Seiyūkai had a majority in the House of Representatives, the Itō cabinet had relatively smooth sailing there, despite determined opposition by the Real Constitutional Party. Overcoming opposition among the Elder Statesmen was more difficult, and Itō found his bill for increased taxes voted down, not by the lower house, but by the House of Peers. He surmounted this difficulty by turning the tables on his conservative opponents. He had the emperor instruct the Peers to pass the bill, which they then did unanimously. But Itō was unable to ride out criticism arising over his inclusion in the cabinet of Hoshi, who had been repeatedly associated with financial scandals. Hoshi was forced to resign in December and was assassinated the next year by a fanatic. Internal dissension soon added to the cabinet's troubles. A bitter dispute over financial measures led Itō, already wearying of his fourth term as prime minister, to resign in May 1901.

The Katsura and Saionji Cabinets (1901–1913). Yamagata was unwilling to resume the arduous duties of prime minister, and after much discussion among the Elder Statesmen, the choice went in June to his protégé, General Katsura. This marked the end of the original oligarchs' titular responsibility for the government. Yamagata served again as chief of the General Staff during the Russo-Japanese War in 1904–5, and he and Itō between them occupied the post of president of the Privy Council from 1903 until Yamagata's death in 1922, but neither they nor any other men of their generation, with the exception of the ex-oligarch Ōkuma, ever assumed the premiership again or held a cabinet post. Instead they let their slightly younger protégés take over, retaining only indirect and gradually fading control as Elder Statesmen.

Katsura established a purely bureaucratic cabinet, in the tradition of his patron Yamagata. At first he had little difficulty with the Diet, because

Itō, as both Elder Statesman and party president, made the Seiyūkai support him. But Katsura ran into trouble when Itō, whose party following represented primarily the rural taxpayers, refused to support his bill for an increased land tax to pay for further naval expansion. The Diet had for the first time lived out its term of four years without dissolution, and a new one had been elected in August 1902, with the Seiyūkai again winning an absolute majority. Katsura dissolved the Diet in December, shortly after it had convened. But the new one, elected on March 1, 1903, was again dominated by the Seiyūkai, and Katsura was forced to compromise, agreeing to pay for the naval expansion by loans rather than by increased taxes.

Yamagata, the other oligarchs, and Katsura naturally were not content to see Itō dominate political decisions through his double role as Elder Statesman and parliamentary politician. In July 1903 Katsura tried to withdraw from the prime ministry in protest. Yamagata then persuaded the emperor to request Itō to resign his party position and resume the presidency of the Privy Council. Itō complied and was joined there by Yamagata and Matsukata, thus making the Privy Council a major organ for policy decisions.

Yamagata's victory, however, was far from complete. Though Itō had withdrawn from party politics, his bureaucratic protégés remained in the Seiyūkai and took his place at its helm. The new president was a figure whose double role was almost as ambiguous as Itō's had been. This was Saionji Kimmochi (1849–1940), a member of the old court nobility who had taken an active part in the "restoration" movement and had then studied for ten years in France, where he became deeply imbued with French and British liberalism. Returning to Japan in 1880, he threw himself into the parliamentary movement, taking the lead in 1881 in publishing with Nakae and others the *Oriental Free Press* (*Tōyō Jiyū Shimbun*). Journalism, however, was considered a shocking profession for a court noble. Iwakura and Sanjō, the two leading members of the group, acting in the name of the emperor, soon forced Saionji to leave the newspaper and brought him into government service, regarded as a more fitting occupation for a man of his high social background.

In the bureaucracy, Saionji became associated with Itō and accompanied him on his trip to Europe in 1882 to study constitutions. In 1894 he joined the cabinet as education minister, and he served as president of the Privy Council between 1900 and 1903. Despite this exalted position, however, he had been one of the prime organizers of the Seiyūkai and was Itō's natural successor as party president. Thus on the one hand he was a hereditary associate of the emperor and a leading member of the bureaucracy, and on the other he was much more deeply committed to parliamentary government than Itō had ever been. This combination of qualities made Saionji's dual role almost as embarrassing to the oligarchs as Itō's.

Katsura managed to hold on as prime minister for four and a half years. He dissolved the Diet in December 1903 but was saved from the usual consequences by the outbreak of the Russo-Japanese War (see page 479). As in the Sino-Japanese War, the new Diet enthusiastically supported the cabinet's war effort and budgets, and the whole nation exulted in the final victory. But once again disappointment over the terms of the treaty revived the attack on the government. In public opinion, control over Korea and South Manchuria and extension of the empire to include the Liaotung Peninsula at last and the southern half of Sakhalin did not compensate for the failure to obtain an indemnity from Russia. The government was accused of having snatched defeat from the jaws of victory. There was widespread rioting. More than a thousand police and citizens were killed or wounded in Tōkyō before order was restored through martial law. Ōkuma's faction — the Real Constitutional Party — which had always had a strong chauvinistic tinge, was particularly violent in its attacks on the government in the Diet. Katsura felt forced to resign in January 1906, and in the face of such strong popular criticism, the Elder Statesmen could only choose Saionji to be his successor.

They insisted that they were selecting Saionji not as president of the Seiyūkai but as a noble and bureaucrat, while he, being by temperament a gradualist, took a very moderate stand on party control of the cabinet. He selected for it only four men of Satsuma or Chōshū origin, as opposed to the eight in Katsura's cabinet, but only two cabinet members besides himself were Seiyūkai members. Like Itō, he had no trouble in keeping support within the Seiyūkai, and it continued to have a majority in the Diet. Moreover, Yamagata's militarist faction in the oligarchy repaid Saionji's earlier cooperation with the Katsura cabinet by giving him support on many issues.

A fairly stable, though ambiguous, solution of the Diet problem had been reached — at least for the time being. The premiership was passed back and forth with relative ease between Saionji and Katsura until 1913, and neither was again forced to dissolve the Diet. The two proved able to cooperate with less open friction than had their respective patrons, Yamagata and Itō. Katsura was more flexible and conciliatory in dealing with the Diet than Yamagata had been, and Saionji, though a more genuine supporter of parliamentary government than Itō, moved only very cautiously toward party control of the cabinet. At the same time, he was as successful as Itō in maintaining the Seiyūkai's support for his own cabinets and the party's cooperation with those of Katsura.

When Saionji's cabinet ran into increasingly hostile pressure from Yamagata, and its Seiyūkai policies were voted down by the House of Peers, Saionji passed the prime ministership back to Katsura in July 1908. Katsura, caught between military demands for another large expansion program and Diet unwillingness to increase taxes, returned the post to Saionji in August 1911. This period of successful cooperation and alternation in power, begun in 1901, continued until the winter of 1912–13, when the military faction forced Saionji to resign by withdrawing the army minister from his cabinet. When Katsura succeeded to the prime ministry for the third time, the enraged Diet almost at once forced his resignation.

The Fulfillment of the Meiji Dream

Even in the period of relative political stability during the alternating Katsura and Saionji cabinets, there had been no clear solution of the constitutional problem. The Japanese government was no longer purely authoritarian nor had it become fully democratic. The Diet had proved unable to control the military and bureaucracy and had shown itself constantly subject to corruption, which undermined the confidence of the public. But the old oligarchy was fading from the scene and even in its heyday had not been able to control the Diet it had created. Saionji and Katsura, representing two irreconcilable views of Japanese politics, had shown the typically Japanese genius for cooperation and compromise. But their *modus vivendi* broke down completely in the winter of 1912–13. That the military faction, using its autonomy within the bureaucracy, had been able to torpedo the Saionji cabinet was indeed an evil augury for the future of democracy in Japan. But the speed with which the Diet in retaliation had forced Katsura to resign showed that the authoritarian traditions of the past could not be easily reconstituted.

Japan's problems were not only political. By 1905 the economy had expanded tremendously, and the country was well on the way toward industrialization, but population growth had also been accelerating. In a mere half century the total had shot up from around 30,000,000 to more than 46,000,000, eating heavily into the economic gains and raising the specter of a deficiency of food and natural resources within the home islands as the population went on increasing. Although Japan had become a strong military power, it had embarked on the unpredictable and stormy seas of world politics. And at home unrest and disunity were growing in the complex society produced by the great innovations of the Meiji period.

In the early years of the twentieth century, however, these were but clouds on the horizon. To the group piloting the Japanese state, the progress made was more obvious than the storms brewing in the distance. They had not set out to create a democracy or an autocracy, but a strong country, and this they had done with spectacular success. However hybrid and anomalous, the political system obviously worked well. Japan had won two major wars — against China and against Russia, the largest of all the Western nations. Political, military, social and educational institutions had been modernized with amazing speed. The economy had been expanded almost unbelievably. Early difficulties in industrialization had been overcome. Though still poor and underdeveloped compared with the advanced nations of the West, Japan was becoming the one really modernized nation in the non-Western world.

The Meiji leaders had clearly succeeded in building the "rich country and strong military" they had dreamed of and in the process had achieved their primary aim of security from and equality with the West. Japan's military security had been unmistakably established in the wars with China and Russia. Equality had also been won. For years the efforts to revise the unequal treaties had been fruitless, despite increasingly explosive demands by the political parties and the public for treaty revision. By 1888 only one nation — Mexico — had surrendered its extraterritorial privileges. But finally Britain, impressed by Japan's legal as well as military progress, relinquished extraterritoriality as of 1899, in a treaty signed in London on July 16, 1894. The United States and the other powers quickly followed. Subsequently Japan regained complete control over its own tariffs through a treaty signed with the United States on February 21, 1911.

Japan also achieved equality in another and more dramatic way. On July 30, 1902, the Anglo-Japanese Alliance was signed — the first military pact on equal terms between a Western and a non-Western nation. The British, seeing their long dominance of the eastern seas threatened by the rise of new naval powers, bolstered their position in East Asia by allying themselves with the only strong naval power in the area. The Japanese, facing war with Russia over Korea, needed the alliance to ensure that Russia would not be joined by another European power. Itō had favored instead an alliance with Russia itself, but Yamagata and Katsura, who wanted the British alliance, were in control of the cabinet at the time and had their way.

In addition to achieving security and equality, Japan had joined the Western powers in the scramble for empire. The intense nationalism that the Japanese had displayed ever since the coming of Perry had often been expressed in expansionist terms. But it would be a mistake to interpret Japanese imperialism in modern times as merely an expression of an inherent trait. The Japanese throughout their history had engaged in rather less foreign aggression than had most other peoples. Except for unorganized marauding by pirates in the medieval period, they had made only one attempt at foreign conquest in historic times — the invasion of Korea by Hideyoshi between 1592 and 1598.

Japan's recent imperialism thus seems to have been more a product of modernization than of native tradition. It was accepted theory and practice in the international Western society which Japan joined in the second half of the nineteenth century for strong nations to build empires at the expense of more backward areas. Yamagata was not being peculiarly

Japanese but merely a military man of his time when he insisted that the line of national advantage which Japan should defend lay far beyond its borders. In keeping with the nineteenth-century zeal for empire-building, the Japanese were as enthusiastically commended by Occidentals for their territorial aggrandizement during the Meiji period as for the more peaceful ways in which they emulated the great Western powers.

The demand for war against Korea in 1873 and the expedition against Taiwan the next year, which confirmed Japan's claims to the Ryūkyū Islands, had been the product of internal difficulties more than of any clear policy of expansionism. But the government's subsequent efforts to dominate Korea showed clearly that it was adopting the imperialistic strategy of the contemporary West. In the resulting Sino-Japanese and Russo-Japanese wars, Japan obtained Taiwan, the Pescadores, southern Sakhalin, and Liaotung, and control over South Manchuria and Korea. The latter it annexed outright in 1910, without protest by any Western nation. Entering World War I as Britain's ally by treaty, Japan picked up the German colonial possessions in East Asia and the North Pacific and sat at Versailles as one of the Five Great Powers — the only non-Western nation to have been accepted as a full equal by the great nations of the West.

Thus even before the original leaders of Meiji Japan had fully passed from the scene, Japan had become a world power. The Meiji leaders had succeeded beyond their fondest dreams. This was clear even before Itō, after serving four years as resident-general in Korea, was assassinated by a Korean while traveling in Manchuria in 1909. It was all the more obvious by the time the last two of the group died as venerable octogenarians — Yamagata in 1922 after a long period as president of the Privy Council and Matsukata in 1924 after several years as inner minister.

China's Response to the West

EARLY WESTERNIZATION IN SELF-DEFENSE

The success story of Meiji Japan from 1868 to 1912 highlighted China's contemporary failure. Both countries had been saddled with unequal treaties that impaired their sovereignty and threatened their economic independence, in an era when expanding Western powers were competing with increasing vigor to make non-European areas into colonies. The dominant Western military and naval power rested on superior industrial technology, commerce, and finance, backed by institutions of education, law, and parliamentary government which constituted, in effect, an entirely different civilization. For Japan to catch up with this modern Western world in all its complexities, across the barriers of language and culture, to compete with it on even terms, and finally to defeat one of the major world powers in a full-scale modern war — all in the space of a single lifetime — was an almost incredible feat. China's inability to do all this is more understandable than Japan's success.

Plainly one reason for Japan's achievement was her capacity, when suddenly thrust into the age of nationalism, to act as a nation with the same degree of patriotic mobilization that nationalism called forth among Western peoples. As in Western countries, this intense nationalism also had its influence on the writing of history and our understanding of what

THE MARBLE BOAT in the Summer Palace lake outside Peking.

happened. The Meiji period has been well documented by Japanese historians with a natural pride in Japan's accomplishments, and their enthusiasm has inevitably influenced foreign students. In China in the same period the collapse of the old order left only a few loyal chroniclers and only a prolonged tragedy for them to record. Undoubtedly the parallel stories of Japan's rise and China's decline, one of the great contrasts of history, have come to us with a certain bias — or at least a fuller record — in favor of those who succeeded. Modern Chinese patriots have probably done less than justice to the Manchu dynasty that failed.

Late Ch'ing history has remained less fully developed since 1912 also because revolutions, though they make history, give little opportunity to write it. China in turmoil offered a less congenial environment to the historian than imperial Japan. In short, Japanese historical writing modernized when Japan did, while in China, historiography, like so much else, remained longer in traditional channels.

Another difference is that Western sources and accounts bulk larger in the historical literature of late nineteenth-century China than of Japan, just as the treaty ports play a more central role in China's history than in Japan's. The greater role of foreigners, their enterprises and their studies, reflects the comparative weakness of nationalism in China, where foreigners participated or even led in modernization over a longer period than the Japanese would permit.

For these and other reasons, we may expect our picture of China's response to the West to change as research progresses. Our own view is that the major determinants of China's response lay within Chinese society, not outside it. First of these was a psychological inertia, as though efforts at Westernization in the 1860's and later were but superficial and temporary responses to immediate dangers, which diminished whenever danger receded. More broadly, we are inclined to think that traditional China never could have achieved modernization as Japan did because Chinese society was so distinctively constituted that it could not follow Western models of organization. In this view a modernized China could not be built up until much of the durable though decaying structure of the old society had been torn down piece by piece. Inevitably, this process was much slower than in Japan, which was far smaller and far more responsive.

This explanation of China's slowness to modernize is sociological and institutional. It differs from the current Marxist-Leninist explanation, that traditional Chinese society was not distinctively different from the West, and that the slowness of modernization was primarily due to the baneful, depressive influence of Western "imperialism." In an extreme form this view, as if echoing the sentiments of nineteenth-century Chinese conservatives, regards all Western contact as having been injurious — almost any foreign contact, in short, was a form of "imperialism." Such an aggrieved attitude, while understandable as patriotic resentment, does not explain why so overwhelming and pervasive an influence as "imperialism" produced such different results in China and Japan. We suggest that in both countries Western influence was at first slight and only gradually increased during the century, that at first it was a stimulant more than a depressant, and that it stimulated Japan to respond successfully. China's initial failure to respond was due to the distinctive features of the Confucian state-and-society. By the time the depressive and exploitative influences of "imperialism" had grown and accumulated, later in the century, it was too late for China to respond successfully.

Even so, some of China's early efforts to modernize were vigorous and at the time impressive, and the contrast with Japan appeared only later. In the 1860's an outsider might well have bet the other way. China had more extensive contact with the West and seemed to have given up after 1860 the kind of die-hard antiforeignism that many Japanese still clung to. Given China's greater size, one might have assumed that in another fifty years a new Middle Kingdom would dominate the islands of the Rising Sun. China seemed ahead of Japan in having come to terms with the West.

"Self-Strengthening" and the Cooperative Policy. As we saw in Chapter 2, the Western encroachment on China had reached a new height in 1860 with the Anglo-French seizure of Peking; the West was appeased only by the final treaty settlement. The great rebellion had come to high tide with the Taipings' campaign of 1860–62; it was defeated with Anglo-French aid reaching inland from the treaty ports of Shanghai and Ningpo. Consequently, in the early 1860's China was most aware of the military superiority of the West, and military Westernization was seen as a solution to both domestic and foreign problems. Tseng Kuo-fan quoted Mencius, "If you can rule your own country, who dares to insult you?" Prince Kung proposed to use suppression of the rebels as a pretext for securing Western arms, which should be carefully kept from the hands of the Chinese people and eventually could be used to overawe the foreigners.

The rationale of this new departure was summed up about 1860 by Feng Kuei-fen, an influential scholar and exponent of "statecraft," who assisted both Tseng and Li Hung-chang. Referring to the Western countries, he asked, "Why are they small and yet strong? Why are we large and yet weak?" He concluded that the reason lay partly in China's ignorance of the hundred countries of the outside world and of their technology, especially military. Western knowledge should be selected and used. China's conventional wisdom invoked by Wei Yüan in the

1840's — use barbarians to control barbarians — was actually useless. "It is utterly impossible for us outsiders to sow dissension among the closely related barbarians. . . . Only one sentence of Wei Yüan is correct — 'Learn the superior technology of the barbarians in order to control them.' "

Thus emerged the movement which we have already identified by the phrase *tzu-ch'iang*, derived from the *Classic of Changes*, meaning "to make oneself strong," or "self-strengthening." As practiced after 1861, "self-strengthening" followed several lines — diplomatic, fiscal, educational, and military.

The diplomatic program was based, as Prince Kung put it, on the ancient saying, "Resort to peace and friendship when temporarily obliged to do so; use war and defense as your actual policy." In January 1861 he proposed a program to establish an office to handle foreign affairs at Peking and two commissioners to do so in the provinces; to expand the new Maritime Customs Service to all the ports; to keep the appropriate officials informed about foreign affairs; to train selected officials in foreign languages; and to secure information and foreign newspapers from the treaty ports. This program now began to supplant the outworn tribute system.

China's new foreign policy was welcomed by the Western powers. The Western ministers were indeed committed to a policy of cooperation both among Britain, France, the United States, and Russia and between them all and China. On the one hand, as Feng Kuei-fen analyzed the situation, "The four countries, Russia, England, France, and America, have too much covert jealousy beneath their outward harmony to let them act together and force China's submission, and no one dares to make the first move." On the other hand, diplomats like Rutherford Alcock (British minister at Peking 1865–1869), who had been a chief architect of the treaty system, tried to keep a balance between foreign treaty rights and China's legitimate interests. To do this, he and the British Foreign Office had constantly to check the aggressive demands of British merchants in the treaty ports, who were constantly pressing for further privileges. Alcock recognized that China's modernization involved "such a revolution as has never been seen since the world began." Progress could not be rapid. "Civilization," he said, "cannot be transferred wholesale from one people to another." The "cooperative policy" of the 1860's was designed to help China modernize gradually.

The Tsungli Yamen. To handle diplomatic relations with the Western ministers who now resided at Peking, there was created in March 1861 a new "office for general management of matters concerning the various countries," generally called by its abbreviated name of Tsungli Yamen ("Office for General Management"). This body was headed by Prince Kung and acted like a foreign office, exchanging official calls and correspondence with the foreign legations. In fact, however, it was not a new ministry but only a subcommittee of the Grand Council, composed usually of about ten high officials who retained their principal posts elsewhere. This informality of organization was probably an advantage, since it permitted a leading group of officials to deal with foreign affairs with a minimum of red tape. The Yamen was proposed as a temporary device, but it soon acquired a staff of some fifty minor officials as secretaries, specially selected to carry on its work in secrecy without relying on clerks.

While the Tsungli Yamen marked a forward step and in fact took the place of a foreign office until one was created in 1901, it also had its inadequacies: all real decisions on foreign policy still had to come from the emperor, usually through the Grand Council, and the Yamen was in charge of the conduct of foreign relations only at Peking. In the coastal provinces there were appointed two commissioners for foreign affairs, respectively for the Southern and Northern ports (in Chinese: *Nan-yang* "Southern Ocean," and *Pei-yang* "Northern Ocean"). These posts eventually came to be held by the governors-general at Nanking and Tientsin, who continued the role that the imperial commissioner for the five early treaty ports had played at Canton between 1842 and 1860, reporting directly to the emperor and Grand Council, not to the Tsungli Yamen. This decentralization, though not admired by the Western diplomats, did in fact accord with the growth of regional power that had occurred during the struggle against the Taipings.

The Maritime Customs Service. The creation of the new order in foreign affairs was much influenced by the demands and the advice of the British negotiators. Among them a prominent part had been played by an aggressive young Englishman, Horatio Nelson Lay (see page 168). Son of one of the first British consuls in China, he had been since 1855 the Chinese-paid "foreign inspector" vigorously administering the assessment of duties at Shanghai. His intimate knowledge of treaty relations and of the Chinese language had helped him play the key role, while on leave from his customs post, in browbeating the Ch'ing treaty negotiators at Tientsin in 1858. Later he had helped draw up the charter of the new customs service, and his appointment as Inspector General of Customs was confirmed by Prince Kung and the Tsungli Yamen in January 1861.

Meanwhile Lay had been joined by another British consular officer, likewise in his twenties, Robert Hart, an Irishman who had come to China in 1854 and become secretary of the Anglo-French commission that governed Canton in 1858–61. At Canton it had also been necessary to appoint a "foreign inspector" to bring order out of anarchy in the customs. Hart took this post in 1859, began to officiate when Lay went to England on leave in 1861, and succeeded him as Inspector General in

1863. By that time the new customs service had been extended from Shanghai to Canton, Swatow, Amoy, Foochow, Ningpo, Chefoo, and Tientsin along the coast and to Chinkiang, Kiukiang, and Hankow up the Yangtze — a total of eleven ports.

These two young men represented two distinct attitudes, one aggressive and the other cooperative, in the British approach to China. This was soon demonstrated in the famous case of the "Lay-Osborn Flotilla." After a decade of sporadic Ch'ing efforts to hire foreign steamers, Prince Kung was persuaded to procure for the Chinese government the ultimate weapon of the day, a fleet of gunboats. Accordingly, Lay in England not only procured a fleet of eight ships with British crews, with the approval of the British government which was just abandoning its neutrality toward the Taipings; he also went further and promised the fleet commander (Captain Sherard Osborn) that all imperial orders to the fleet would be transmitted through, and at the discretion of, himself, H. N. Lay. When this powerful flotilla reached China in 1863, both Prince Kung and Tseng Kuo-fan refused to accept Lay's arrangements. Peking could not let a foreigner control the fleet, and the provincial commanders wanted control themselves. Lay was paid off with a large sum, and the fleet was disposed of by the British. Lay had been the energetic creator of the new Maritime Customs Service, but he had grandly considered himself to be working *for* the Chinese authorities, not *under* them. "The notion," he said, "of a gentleman acting *under* an Asiatic barbarian is preposterous."

Robert Hart built the Customs Service on an entirely different basis. As he told his foreign Commissioners of Customs in a circular of 1864, "those who take the pay, and who are the servants of the Chinese Government . . . are the brother officers" of the native officials and "in a sense, the countrymen" of the Chinese people. The foreign commissioners, who oversaw all aspects of customs procedure, were to be at least nominally subordinate to the Chinese Superintendents of Customs (usually the local taotais) at each port, who received the actual payments of duties. Hart himself remained responsible for the entire foreign staff, which by 1875 included 252 employees from Britain and 156 from sixteen other Western countries. Thus he created with great tact, patience, and foresight an administrative arm of the Ch'ing central government which used foreign employees to handle the foreign merchants and also assisted China's efforts at modernization within the framework of the treaty system.

Western Learning and Armament. The new customs revenue, as well as Hart's discreet advice, supported a new institution at Peking, the T'ung-wen Kuan ("School of Combined Learning" or Interpreters College), which aimed first of all to free China's diplomats from dependence on the old Cantonese linguists as well as from foreign interpreters like H. N. Lay. As the Tsungli Yamen argued, "In any negotiations with foreign nations, the prerequisite is to know their nature and feelings." Or as Li Hung-chang said, "First understand their ambitions, be aware of their desires, and . . . their points of strength and weakness." The Interpreters College, incorporating the old and moribund Russian language school, got started in Peking in 1862; and similar small schools were opened in Shanghai (1863), Canton (1864), and Foochow (1866). Results were at first disappointing. The thirty or so students assigned to the Peking college were mainly middle-aged Manchu bannermen. It had no prestige to attract Chinese scholarly talent. Eventually in 1869, when it had a hundred students, an American missionary-educator, W. A. P. Martin, was made head and developed an eight-year curriculum in Western languages and sciences. In the end the T'ung-wen Kuan produced much of China's diplomatic staff.

Martin had already demonstrated another use of Western learning. With the Yamen's help, he had completed a translation, begun by Hart, of Henry Wheaton's standard work, *Elements of International Law*. Knowledge derived from this translation proved effective in 1864 in obliging the Prussian minister to release three Danish ships he had illegally seized as enemy vessels off Tientsin, within China's territorial waters. Thus foundations were laid for modern China's eventual skill in diplomacy.

A more immediate demand for Western scientific learning was created by the setting up of machine shops, arsenals, and shipyards to make Western arms and vessels. Tseng and Li, after several years of buying foreign arms for use against the rebels and establishing small arsenals at Anking, Soochow, Nanking, and elsewhere, finally combined all their efforts and set up the Kiangnan Arsenal at Shanghai in 1865. By 1868 its Chinese workmen had produced their first steamship, though they used a foreign-built engine. Soon the arsenal was one of the biggest and most impressive in the world, manufacturing not only many kinds of ammunition but also its own tools and machinery. Translation of Western scientific treatises and manuals was an essential part of this development, and during the following decades some 173 works were compiled or translated into Chinese, mainly under the Englishman John Fryer.

At Foochow another arsenal, a navy yard, and a technical school were set up by Tso Tsung-t'ang in 1866 with French assistants. Fifteen vessels were built in the next eight years, and a naval academy began to train a new generation of Fukienese cadets.

Nearly all these steps in Westernization were dealt with at Peking through the new Tsungli Yamen rather than through traditional channels like the Boards of Revenue and War, which did not seek control of such difficult and disesteemed projects. Consequently the Yamen, though in form a temporary committee, became in practice something like a seventh Board in charge of modernization or "foreign matters" (*yang-wu*).

By 1870 many observers felt that China was well started on the building of modern military and naval power. The policy pursued during the 1860's, however, had actually been an indecisive mixture of old and new. The Western aggressors were appeased with trade and contact under the treaties, the secrets of their military strength were learned in order to ward off foreign attack and suppress domestic rebellion, but meanwhile efforts were made to revive the old Confucian type of government. Restoration of the traditional order, with its unity of state and culture, had been the major aim, Westernization in self-defense a minor aim. Western observers impressed by the beginnings of "Westernization" in the 1860's sometimes failed to see that it was a strictly subordinate theme.

THE RESTORATION OF CONFUCIAN GOVERNMENT

As suggested earlier, the Chinese state-and-society had achieved an equilibrium among its political, economic, social, ideological, and other elements, which might decline in vigor and yet remain impervious to outside influence. This stability was the product of three millennia of a distinctive, highly developed civilization, with an unequaled continuity of tradition. The economy and the administration both showed this capacity to continue stably in old ways without responding to new challenges in new ways. Inertia was greatest in the processes of government, where the need for order, the vested interests of the scholar-official and landowning classes, and the conservative ideology of Confucianism all met and reinforced one another. Consequently, China's basic response in the 1860's to the dual menace of foreign aggression and domestic rebellion was to reaffirm, or "restore," the old Confucian system rather than to modernize it.

This reaction expressed a frame of mind. China's great tradition was felt to contain all things. The new was neither expected nor prized, least of all from abroad. As the arch-conservative Mongol scholar Wojen put it in 1867 when opposing the introduction of Western studies at Peking, "The empire is so great, there is no need to worry about a lack of talent. If it is necessary to teach astronomy and mathematics [i.e., Western studies], an extensive search should find someone [in China] who has mastered these techniques. . . . Why must we learn from the barbarian foreigners? . . . They are our enemies."

To this institutional and psychological inertia was added the political weakness of the Ch'ing central power after 1860. The empire was a centralized monarchy. The emperor had to lead the way in any innova-

PLATE 28. The Meiji Emperor dressed in the style of a European monarch.

PLATE 29. Kido Kōin, Chōshū samurai, one of the authors of the Meiji Charter Oath.

LEADERS OF THE MEIJI RESTORATION

PLATE 30. Ōkubo Toshimichi of Satsuma, samurai and official, perhaps the most powerful figure in the Meiji government until his assassination in 1878.

PLATE 31. Saigō Takamori, Satsuma samurai and general in the Restoration wars; withdrew from the government in 1873 and led the Satsuma Rebellion in 1877.

PLATE 32. Prince Kung (personal name, I-hsin; 1833–98), brother of the Hsien-Feng Emperor, signer of the unequal treaties of 1860, head of the Grand Council and Tsungli Yamen.

PLATE 33. The infant Emperor Kuang-hsü (b. 1871) on horseback.

PLATE 34. Sir Robert Hart at work. A drawing from a London periodical, c. 1890, shows the Inspector-General of Customs at his famous standing desk.

PLATE 35. Commissioner of Customs H. F. Merrill (Harvard '74) at Ningpo, about 1894, with his wife, daughter, and household staff: (from left) amah, nurse-girl, number-one boy (in charge), number-two boy, gateman, cook, number-two cook, wash boy, and four chairbearers.

PLATE 36. A Maritime Customs Assistant and his staff, 1892. W. Hancock (Chinese name, Han Wei-li) rose from Third Assistant, Class B, in 1877, to Acting Commissioner in 1904. This photograph was probably taken in Hanoi on his seven-week journey from Hong Kong via the Red River to the Yunnan border. Mr. Lo is accompanied by his two wives and their maids.

PLATES 37 AND 38. American Presbyterian pioneers: The Rev. Calvin W. and Mrs. Julia B. Mateer. In Tengchow, Shantung, Calvin Mateer founded a secondary school, helped translate the Bible, published many textbooks including the widely used *Mandarin Lessons* (1892), and advocated higher education from the West to undergird Christianity in China.

PLATE 39. A Roman Catholic orphanage in transit. A nun (center) inspects babies in process of transportation. Photographed in or near Kiukiang, c. 1891, in the period of anti-Christian riots.

tion. But the T'ung-chih Emperor (reg. 1862–1875) was a weak boy, under a regency dominated by his mother, the Empress Dowager (1835–1908). This remarkable woman, who is usually called Tz'u-hsi from the first two characters of her long title, was clever and strong-willed but narrow-minded. Selected to be a low-ranking concubine in 1851 at the age of sixteen, she had borne the Hsien-feng Emperor his only son in 1856. As empress-mother and therefore co-regent for her son, she soon learned how to use the imperial prerogatives of appointment, promotion, praise, censure, dismissal, and punishment of officials so as to make herself the real ruler of the empire. She became entrenched in power, governing with the aid of palace eunuchs and trusted high officials, but she had no grasp of China's problem of modernization. Prince Kung, the chief official of the early 1860's, could not defy her. Thus progress toward modernization remained slow in the 1860's, and even the restoration of central power was incomplete, contingent upon the continued suppression of rebels, appeasement of foreign powers, and cooperation with the Chinese scholar-generals and their new armies in the provinces. There was still no strong leadership committed to modernization.

China's long-term response to the challenge of Western civilization was consequently halting and uncertain. The revival of Confucian government on Chinese lines was energetic and rather successful, but steps toward modernization which went counter to tradition ran into trouble. Ancient ways could be revived more easily than they could be replaced by Western ways. This trend may be seen first in the success of the Ch'ing "Restoration" after 1864 in suppressing the remaining rebellions, the essential preliminary to reviving Confucian civil government.

Suppression of the Nien Rebellion. The capture of Nanking in 1864 had extinguished the Taiping Kingdom, the only real competitor for dynastic power, but large areas were still in revolt. The most central was that of the Nien rebels on the North China Plain north of the Huai River, where the wheat-millet area of the North merges into the rice-growing region of the Yangtze Valley. Based on the fortified earth-walled villages of this "nest" area, the Nien had developed a defensive strategy of "strengthening the walls and clearing the countryside," similar to that used sixty years earlier by the Ch'ing against the rebels of the White Lotus Society (see page 117). This strategy concentrated both the farming population and the crops from the fields within the earth-walled villages, so that invading imperial forces would find neither manpower nor food supplies (nor even water, where wells had been filled in). With this defense, the Nien combined an offense based on cavalry which used as many as 25,000 horses. Though unable to operate well over the rice fields to the south, they made hit-and-run raids into provinces to the north, using guerrilla tactics, attacking suddenly and eluding pursuers. One imperial commander sent against them was the famous Mongol prince, Senggerinchin (Chinese: Seng-ko-lin-ch'in), who had fought the Anglo-French forces in 1860. He succeeded in capturing and executing the original Nien leader (Chang Lo-hsing) in 1863, but two years later he was induced to pursue the Nien cavalry for a month until, overextended and exhausted, he was ambushed and killed.

This disaster and the addition of Taiping remnants to the Nien forces prompted the appointment in 1865 of Tseng Kuo-fan, the victor over the Taipings, to suppress the Nien. Occupation of the nest area and leveling of its earthen walls had twice been achieved, but to no avail; for the populace and chiefs of village militia corps had continued to support the Nien, and the earthen walls had been rebuilt. Tseng now tried a more fundamental (and traditional) strategy, to separate leaders and followers. He proscribed the Nien leaders, listing them for execution, but promised to pardon and protect their followers and the village chiefs who surrendered. Isolating the nest area with four strong points and blockade lines (see map, page 160), Tseng's forces invaded it and carefully screened one earth-walled village after another, registering the populace in five-family groups for mutual guaranty and formally appointing village chiefs. Meanwhile they revived cultivation in devastated areas, by degrees recovered control of the people and the food supply, and so cut off the Nien raiding forces from their source of manpower and provisions. "Strengthening the walls and clearing the countryside" was thus applied in reverse, against the rebels.

Late in 1866 Li Hung-chang took over the task of suppressing the Nien, since the principal force involved was the Anhwei Army which he had built up. Tseng Kuo-fan had formally disbanded his Hunan Army after the defeat of the Taipings, partly to avoid any suspicion of personal ambition and also to get rid of urgent problems of finance, leadership, and discipline among the troops. As a result Li's Anhwei Army had taken its place as the chief modern force in China. Recruiting many of his soldiers from the unemployed in the former nest area of the Nien, Li put them under commanders of his own choice and supplied them with Western arms from his new arsenal at Shanghai and with tribute rice from the rich Yangtze delta. The Anhwei Army was built up with manpower from that province but with revenues from all the Lower Yangtze region. Soon Li had 30,000 or more muzzle-loading rifles for some 70,000 troops, together with cannon on barges, a water-borne supply service, and 7000 cavalry.

After 1866 the Nien rebels were cut off from their base north of the Huai River and were split into two mobile bands in the eastern and western sectors of the North China Plain. This was done by establishing blockade lines a thousand miles long, manned by 100,000 troops, along the Grand Canal and Yellow River on the west and northwest borders of Shantung province. Gradually the Nien were further hemmed in. The eastern band was destroyed in January and the western in August 1868.

Suppression of the Moslem Rebellions. In Southwest China, where Tu Wen-hsiu had set up his own Moslem state in 1856 (see page 166), there was an even longer struggle to reassert the central Ch'ing authority. Chieftains of local tribal minorities, Moslem commanders loyal to the Ch'ing, and imperial administrators from Peking all played a part in complex and protracted campaigns and negotiations. Eventually the tide was turned by a variety of factors. Tu Wen-hsiu as a religious partisan apparently offered little to the non-Moslem Chinese. In general, the Ch'ing cause seems in the end to have offered a greater degree of orderly administration and nonpartisan justice to all elements of the mixed population. Some Ch'ing generals (like Ts'en Yü-ying, who became governor of Yunnan) came from the local gentry and began their careers as commanders of militia corps. Even Moslem Chinese (like the general Ma Ju-lung after 1861) found it advantageous to take the Ch'ing side. Through death and migration the population meanwhile had been reduced by more than one-half, a fact which may in itself account for the subsidence of rebellion. Walled cities like Yunnanfu (modern Kunming), the capital of Yunnan, underwent long sieges. Tu Wen-hsiu's power at one time was based on 53 walled cities, which the imperial forces captured one after another, often with bloody massacres of the inhabitants. Tali was finally captured in 1873, with a great massacre, and Tu Wen-hsiu killed himself. In the same year the Miao tribesmen in Kweichow were also suppressed.

In Northwest China, in the arid "panhandle" strip of Kansu province that forms the corridor for communication with Turkestan, risings of Chinese Moslems had occurred in the 1780's, inspired partly by the fanaticism of the sect known as the New Teaching. The virtual collapse of Ch'ing power in the mid-nineteenth century set the stage for a new rebellion in the Northwest, which seems to have arisen not against the Ch'ing so much as against discrimination by corrupt local officials. A revolt broke out in Shensi province near Sian in 1862 and spread westward through Kansu. The principal leader of the militant New Teaching, Ma Hua-lung, built up his base near Ning-hsia. The rebellion was marked by wholesale slaughter, especially after the capture of walled cities by either side.

This northwestern region, between Mongolia and Tibet and extending toward Russia, was of greater strategic importance than Southwest China, but its recovery had to wait upon the subjugation first of the Taipings in 1864 and then of the Nien in 1868. The task was given to one of the victorious gentry-generals of Hunan, Tso Tsung-t'ang, who now became a principal figure of the era.

Tso began as a scholar, well connected, but failed three times in the metropolitan examinations. He then devoted himself to studies especially of geography and to practical agriculture in Hunan until the Taiping Rebellion called forth his talents as a commander and administrator. By its end he was governor-general of Fukien and Chekiang with a great record of accomplishment.

Tso Tsung-t'ang's recovery of Shensi and Kansu took five years (1868–1873), precisely as he foresaw. His management of subordinates, maintenance of extended lines of supply, and revival of local civil administration all seemed to prove the efficacy of traditional methods. Systematic and indomitable, he advanced slowly, reducing rebel strongholds and killing as many rebels as possible. By 1871, as he wrote a friend, his wife had died, his hair was white, he had lost most of his teeth, he suffered from dysentery and malaria, and was being criticized for his slowness. However, Ma Hua-lung was finally defeated and, with all his family, executed by slicing. By 1873, though the population had been greatly reduced, peace reigned over the Northwest, and indeed over all the Ch'ing empire except Chinese Turkestan.

The central government's suppression of rebellion, like the rise of the rebels in the first place, had begun in central areas of population and then had spread outward to the Southwest and Northwest. The cycle of rebellion and suppression was marked in each area by a decline and collapse of civil administration, and then by its revival, which the officials of the imperial government alone seemed capable of achieving. The Restoration of the 1860's was thus a triumph both of warfare and of civil government, a genuine pacification in the traditional manner. The great provincial leaders like Tseng, Li, and Tso were not only scholar-generals but also and pre-eminently scholar-administrators. Their success was due not only to hard fighting but also to their application of Confucian moral and political principles, encouragement of economic recovery, effective taxation and, in addition, some use of Western technology.

At the same time, the success of the Restoration did not bring China back to the *status quo ante* but rather to a new equilibrium in which the leading officials at the top of their provincial administrations, though loyal to the dynasty, had strong regional power. The dynastic central power owed its survival to, and henceforth had to contend with, this growth of regionalism.

The Economic Aftermath of Civil War. Like the United States in the same period, China in the late 1860's confronted an enormous task of reconstruction. The forces engaged and casualties sustained in the civil wars in China had been far greater in number, and fighting had occurred over a longer period and in a larger area than in the United States. Modern armament had probably not resulted in as much physical destruction in the Confederate states as had been produced by the old-fashioned methods of pillage and burning in China. Meanwhile the Middle Kingdom lacked a modern industrial capacity to bind up the nation's wounds. Some areas did not recover for decades. Serious losses of capital investment had occurred — for example, in the destruction of irrigation works in the Northwest and in the cutting down of mulberry trees, essential for silkworm culture, in Central China. Great numbers of displaced and homeless persons, like those that had crowded into the Shanghai foreign settlement, had to be fed and put to work. These problems were added to the normal incidence of such natural calamities as flood, drought, famine, and pestilence, which were not at all diminished by warfare.

The traditional methods used to meet these problems consisted principally of fortitude and hard work by the common people all over the country. Leadership was exercised in each locality mainly by the gentry, with official encouragement. Transport and distribution of relief grain, establishment of soup kitchens, orphanages, refugee centers, and other forms of social welfare, as well as public works — "using work in place of charity" — were managed by the upper class of local gentry and officials together. The two basic institutions that mobilized these efforts were China's ancient extended family system and the *pao-chia* system of collective neighborhood responsibility. Government action was mainly in the form of moral exhortation and direction, widespread remission of land-tax payments in devastated areas, some reduction of tax rates, and occasionally large-scale rehabilitation, such as the resettlement of farmers on the land with seeds and tools. On the whole, these measures aided landlords more than tenants; the former might pay less land tax, but the latter seldom secured reductions of rent.

Reconstruction required financing, but the traditional sources of revenue had long since proved inadequate. When rebellion struck after 1850, Peking's savings were quickly exhausted, land taxes due from several rich provinces were cut off, and even the gabelle received from the salt monopoly was disrupted — for instance, the salt produced on the seacoast in North Kiangsu could no longer be shipped for sale in Hupei. Peking increased the sale of rank and office, thus inflating the gentry class, and issued new iron cash, paper, and other cheap forms of money, thus inflating the currency. But these were desperate measures of no long-term value.

This revenue crisis could not be met by increasing the land tax, which had long been set in established quotas for each area ever since the emperor in a time of affluence in 1712 had optimistically decreed that the labor-service tax quotas (which became combined with the land tax quotas) should "never thereafter be increased." This tradition made the land tax difficult to increase at any time, and Ch'ing finance had thus been cursed by inelasticity. The agrarian sector of the economy could not be tapped for new revenues during the rebellion because the peasants might rebel and because they were already too poor, after the mid-Ch'ing growth of population, to bear an increased burden.

To meet the fiscal crisis a censor stationed in Kiangsu (named Lei I-hsien) instituted in 1853 a small tax on merchants and traders, which became known as likin (*li-chin*, "a tax of one-thousandth"). This new tax had three important features: it was too small to be worth a great effort to avoid and hence was easy to collect; it was collected from trade, on articles of consumption, levied either as a transit tax on goods as they passed a likin barrier or as a sales tax on the shops where the goods were sold; and finally the likin revenues were mainly retained and used within the provinces, where the local gentry participated in administering the likin system. By 1860 it had spread to almost every part of China.

The growth of this new tax had kept pace with and aided local efforts to suppress rebellion. Gentry and officials who were mobilizing troops collected likin to support them. Together with a portion of the new Maritime Customs revenues from foreign trade at Shanghai, likin helped finance Li Hung-chang's new Anhwei Army. By the time peace was restored, it could not be dispensed with.

The central government also had become dependent on trade taxes. Its revenue quotas before 1850 had been collected mainly from the agricultural sector of the economy (see table, page 327) and only in small part from the old-style customs houses at seaports and major inland cities. In the 1860's these collections were generally resumed and maintained, but by the end of the century the total central government revenue had more than doubled. The increase was made up by the new taxes on commerce, among which the portions of likin made available to Peking were at first the most important. Meanwhile the new Maritime Customs revenue rose in the 1860's to about 7 million taels a year and subsequently much higher. It included the tax on the foreign opium still being imported in increasing amounts from India.

The fact was that the government of China could no longer be financed by the ancient methods of a superficially centralized agrarian-bureaucratic state. Rebellion had inspired both the growth of regional armies and the spread of the likin system. Both began a trend toward decentralization or regionalism which could not be reversed, although it was held in check in a new equilibrium with the central power by the reaffirmation of the Confucian ideology. Thus change in material matters was somewhat balanced by the intellectual conservatism of the Restoration movement.

ESTIMATES OF CENTRAL GOVERNMENT REVENUES
(receipts nominally expected at Peking, in millions of taels)

	Pre-1850	Early 1890's	Early 1900's
Land tax and grain tribute	30	32	33
Salt gabelle	5 or 6	13 (a)	13 (a)
Old-style customs	4	1	4
New Maritime customs	0	22	35
Likin	0	15 (b)	14 (b)
Sale of rank or office, misc.	1	5	4
Rough total	40	89	103

(a) including salt likin
(b) including native opium likin

The Philosophy and Leadership of the Restoration. Western ideas played a remarkably small part in the revival of the 1860's. On the contrary, the Restoration leaders reaffirmed China's ancient morality and stressed its application to practical affairs through "statecraft" (*ching-shih;* see pages 123 ff.). This emphasis on morality in action followed the teaching of scholars of the T'ung-ch'eng school (named from a city in Anhwei), who found their inspiration in the Neo-Confucianism of the Sung Learning more than in the drier, textual studies of the Han Learning. Tseng Kuo-fan, an eminently practical statesman, derived his own rather eclectic philosophy from this school and his example was widely followed.

The main ideas of this Neo-Confucian morality may be compressed into a series of propositions: that the natural harmony of the universe ought to be reflected in human society; that the harmony of Chinese society depended on hierarchic organization and performance of proper roles from top to bottom, as accepted by superior and inferior alike; that each individual in his own particular status should follow the social norms of conduct, the ancient Confucian *li* ("propriety" or "principles of social usage"); that the proper conduct of each person in his social station should be inspired by the virtuous example of the superior man, which gave him moral authority; and that legal punishments and the use of force were only supplementary to government by virtuous moral example. This doctrine implied that rebels must be chastised, to be sure, and either reformed or eliminated, but that the use of force must be accompanied and followed up by an incorrupt, just, and benevolent government which would ensure the people's livelihood and admonish them as to their proper conduct. Domestic harmony thus restored, peace and prosperity would ensue.

Distinctly "premodern," this philosophy was strongly elitist and hierarchic, as opposed to the egalitarian trend of modern times. It looked backward for its model to the golden age of antiquity and had nothing like the modern concept of progress. Thus the main emphasis of economic policy was not on increased production and revenue but on frugality, the proper use of fixed taxes and resources, including taxation of a presumably constant volume of trade with no attempt to expand it. The Restoration's ideal society was one of static harmony, not of dynamic growth. Its vision was limited to the ancient Confucian model of the agrarian-bureaucratic state.

Within this limit, however, there was a great variety of precedents to draw upon, including a doctrine of cyclical change or "change within tradition" expressed in a famous passage of the *Classic of Changes* (*I ching*): "When a series of changes has run all its course, another change ensues. When it obtains free course, it will continue long." This and similarly cryptic classical quotations were invoked to sanction reform. But reform remained essentially conservative, restricted by two beliefs: that agriculture, providing the "people's livelihood" (*min-sheng*), was the basis of the state, and that a carefully selected elite of "men of talent" (*jen-ts'ai*) was the basis of good government.[1]

As they faced the critical problems of the 1860's, the interests and ideas of Manchu and Chinese leaders became nearly identical, for both were bent on making the traditional system work again, and the Son of Heaven, whether Chinese or non-Chinese, was its keystone. The proportion of Manchus in high positions greatly declined: up to 1850 they had supplied roughly half the officials at Peking and two-thirds of the governors-general and one-third of the governors in the provinces. But in the subsequent suppression of rebellion the new talent that emerged was almost entirely Chinese. They had always staffed the lower levels of bureaucracy. Now Manchus became even scarcer in the provinces, although they continued to hold the top power at Peking through men like Prince Kung and his able colleague Wen-hsiang (1818–1876).

Meanwhile the regulations designed to preserve the Manchus' distinctive position in Chinese society had gradually fallen into abeyance. By the 1860's Manchuria was no longer tightly closed to Chinese migration, the Manchu banners were no longer a potent military force, the Manchu language was hardly used, and the ban on Manchu-Chinese intermarriage was no longer effective. In the common effort to save the Chinese state from invasion and rebellion, the Manchu leadership had almost merged into the Chinese upper class.

[1] See Mary Clabaugh Wright, *The Last Stand of Chinese Conservatism: The T'ungchih Restoration, 1862–1874* (Stanford University Press, 1957).

Thus until the new Chinese nationalism in the 1890's brought the dynasty under attack as racially alien, it functioned as a traditional Chinese institution. The Manchu rulers had the same philosophy of conservative reform as the Chinese leaders in the provinces. Both sought to preserve the great tradition. Modern critics who say that Chinese leaders, by remaining loyal to the Ch'ing in this era, "sold out" to alien rulers are applying a nationalist standard of loyalty anachronistically.

The Examination System and the Gentry Class. The first step in finding the "men of talent" needed for the Restoration was to resume the regular examinations in all regions where order had been restored. This was the most obvious of several measures aimed at stimulating and controlling the flow of talent into government service.

The necessary preliminary was to reopen local academies (*shu-yüan*) and found new ones. This was usually done under the patronage of leading officials who used funds of public origin to provide semi-official support. Libraries also had to be rebuilt and standard works reprinted. In the 1860's provincial officials set up printing offices in major centers, though they often denounced novels and other frivolous or heterodox works. Their sole aim was to spread the classical teaching.

A second effort was to relate the examination questions to real problems of the day — for example, how could troops best be trained, distributed, and maintained? This element of practicality, however, came less from Western example than from the Chinese school of "statecraft," stressing the more skillful use of traditional methods.

A third necessary measure was to restrain the sale of degrees and so maintain the supremacy of entrance into official life by examination over entrance by purchase. The latter practice, used in moderation, had a double value: it provided quick revenue in times of emergency, and it assured the loyalty of the wealthy but presumably nonscholarly man, who was allowed to buy his way into the scholar class without destroying the scholar's supremacy. "Irregular" degrees obtained by purchase were clearly distinguishable from "regular" examination degrees. While the actual sale of *office* was a drastic and dangerous step, taken only in extremity, the sale of *rank* or degree status was a traditional way to reward "contributions" solicited and paid in for famine relief, public works, or military needs (see page 87).

In the first half of the nineteenth century the Ch'ing through the sale of degrees had regularly taken in more than a million, and often two million, taels a year and in return had conferred the lowest degree (*chien-sheng*, which sold for a little over 100 taels) upon roughly 10,000 men annually. These "irregular" gentry by purchase, at the very lowest level of rank, had formed roughly three-tenths of the whole gentry class, which up to 1850 totaled in any given year about 1,100,000 men throughout the empire. To raise money against rebels after 1850, sales of rank had greatly increased.

The Restoration tried with some success to prevent the sale of office and to limit the sale of rank. But here again, it was not possible to go back to the *status quo ante*. The "regular" gentry class had grown by an increase in the quotas of first-level degrees to be awarded by examination in the various provinces, where all administrative areas — districts, departments, and prefectures — had regular quotas of the number of degrees they could award in each examination. As rewards for contributions to military funds, these local examination quotas were gradually raised during the Rebellion by about 18 per cent. Thus richer areas, by securing higher quotas, could get more of their young men into and through the examinations and so into the gentry class. During most of the Ch'ing period the rich and cultured urban centers of the Lower Yangtze had furnished a surprisingly high proportion of the winners in the Peking examinations. About two-fifths of the top men had come from Kiangsu province alone. This continued to be the case.

Meanwhile sale of rank continued and the "irregular" gentry increased even faster than the "regular." By the late nineteenth century the gentry totaled about 1,450,000, more than a third of them qualified only by purchase. Thus despite the revival of the examination system, its position as the font of Confucian government eventually grew weaker. Just as the restored Confucian state was becoming less purely agrarian in its economic base, so its bureaucracy was becoming less firmly rooted in the Classics.

Finally, the restoration of Confucian government was least effective on the lowest level, that of the numerous yamen clerks, runners, and other petty functionaries who normally lived on customary fees or "squeeze." Here the upsetting effects of rebellion and foreign contact were greatest and the traditional morality weakest. One could not select and train "men of talent" at this level. The old system made no adequate provision for the technical specialization that more modern systems require.

CHRISTIAN MISSIONS AND THEIR REPERCUSSIONS IN THE 1860's

To the two themes that characterized China's response to Western contact in the 1860's — Westernization in self-defense, and restoration of Confucian government — a third major theme must be added, similarly defensive in aim and spirit. This was the anti-Christian movement aroused by increased missionary activity, a response to a very concrete religious, social, and political challenge.

The Growth of Missionary Activity. Roman Catholic and Protestant missions differed so much in their circumstances and approaches as to seem like two different movements. The Catholics, with some 150,000 communicants still scattered through the provinces in 1800, had had a firm foundation for the growth which came with the establishment of the first treaties. By 1870 their community approached 400,000 souls, ministered to by some 250 European Jesuits, Franciscans, Lazarists, Dominicans and others, and many Chinese priests and catechists. The French government was the special and active protector of these Catholic missions. The Sino-French convention of 1860 not only promised the missionaries complete toleration and restitution of former properties, such as the Pei-t'ang or northern cathedral in Peking; but in the *Chinese* text, through a French ruse, they were also permitted to lease or buy land and erect buildings anywhere. Thus the Church became a landlord, sometimes renting out its properties, in addition to acting as manager of primary schools, seminaries, and orphanages.

Aided by its long history in China and its political and economic position, Catholicism had become firmly rooted in Chinese society. Impressive rituals and ceremonies, including many prostrations, marked the stages through which a convert became first an adorer, then a catechumen, and finally was baptized. Religious festivals and pilgrimages, family worship, the teaching of moral conduct, the Church's support of its own, all bound the faithful into the Catholic community. The whole effort, tempered by the persecutions of the past, was carefully adjusted to Chinese ways, and intent on saving the maximum number of souls. In fact, by the time toleration was restored in the nineteenth century, Catholicism in China had become less concerned than Matteo Ricci had been to convert the top stratum of society. In the intervening 250 years its vested interests had developed at the lower level among the common people.

The Protestant missionaries, in contrast, were still on the periphery of China, making a beginning. In 1850 they totaled only about 80 persons, representing a score of mission societies, and they were confined almost entirely, as required by treaty, to the five treaty ports, Macao, and Hong Kong. Lacking the long background and tested methods of the Catholic fathers, the Protestant missionaries and their wives, many of whom were also missionaries, did not fit with equal ease into the Chinese scene. They remained clearly a part of the Sino-Western treaty-port society which was growing up on the coast of China, and they had as yet made few converts. Although by 1870 there were 350 or more Protestant missionaries, their converts probably totaled fewer than 6000 persons, not many of whom were in the interior.

There was no single agency, comparable to the Propaganda at Rome, to coordinate Protestant efforts, which were almost as fragmented and pluralistic as those of the Western merchants. Pioneer agencies like the London Missionary Society and the American Board of Commissioners for Foreign Missions (Congregationalist) had been joined by others in great profusion — Dutch Reformed, Gospel Baptist, the Basel Society, Wesleyan Methodist, and many more. Adding to the multiplicity of sects and societies, the American Presbyterians, Baptists, and Methodists were divided over the slavery issue into Northern and Southern bodies.

Despite this confusing variety of affiliations, however, Protestant missionaries from the English-speaking and northern European countries were generally cooperative in their common calling. By difference in language, homeland, and belief they were sharply marked off from the Catholic missionaries, who came mainly from Latin countries and regarded the results of the Reformation as dangerous heresy and evil sectarianism. Protestants repaid this attitude in kind. To them, Rome was anti-Christ, the Catholic faith a rival religion. Cooperation and even contact between the two branches of Christianity were minimal.

Until 1866 Protestantism hardly competed with Catholicism in the populous inland provinces. But in that year a remarkable English evangelist and organizer, Hudson Taylor (1832–1905), began a new approach in the China Inland Mission, which eventually grew into the largest of all mission agencies. This was a mission wholly devoted to the spreading of the gospel throughout China. Taylor had a straightforward belief in salvation through faith in Christ as the only alternative to eternal hellfire and brimstone. China had seemed to him a big problem. *"A million a month* were dying in that land," he said later, "dying without God. This was burned into my very soul. . . . I scarcely slept . . . [thinking about] these souls, and what eternity must mean for every one of them, and what the Gospel might do, would do, for all who believed, if we would take it to them."

For this consuming purpose, Taylor recruited missionaries of any Protestant denomination, from any country, guaranteed them no fixed salaries, asserting that "the Lord will provide," and sent them to inland centers to live simply among the people, dress in Chinese style, and lead Chinese souls to salvation. Making it widely known that he would not solicit support except by prayer, Taylor found contributions and recruits steadily forthcoming. Under his stimulus Protestant mission stations gradually began to appear in the interior provinces where the Catholic Church had long been established. Between them, the two movements eventually brought the foreign religion into the local scene in every part of the country, although in the 1860's the Catholics continued to be the more active.

Causes of Gentry Hostility. The missionaries soon posed a more concrete threat to the local gentry than Western contact had ever done before. Since the days of Yang Kuang-hsien in the seventeenth century (see page 61), Confucians had criticized Christian doctrine as superstitious and heterodox: why, they asked, had an all-powerful and merciful God permitted original sin? Similar questions were raised about the virgin birth and the incarnation of Heaven (*T'ien*) in the Christ. Catholicism had in fact been proscribed as a heterodox teaching in the Yung-cheng Emperor's amplification in 1724 of K'ang-hsi's *Sacred Edict*, and it remained so down to 1846. All this did not commend Christianity to the Chinese scholar class on intellectual grounds.

To this intellectual opposition were added urgent political considerations: the most dire domestic enemies of the established order, the Taiping rebels, claimed to be Christians and used a great deal of Biblical terminology, while the most powerful barbarian invaders of all time, those from the West who had twice defeated the Ch'ing forces in warfare, also professed and promoted the Christian religion. If this were not enough to create suspicion and hostility, the Chinese gentry, as the responsible local elite throughout the country, now found the missionaries beginning to confront them as would-be rivals in the performance of their social functions.

First of all, the missionaries came as teachers, offered religious instruction, and set up schools, thus laying claim to membership in a scholar class which, however, was not Confucian even though Catholics in particular wore the Confucian scholar's gown. Protestants tended to condemn with righteous and sometimes indiscriminate zeal not only the evident evils of poverty, filth, disease, and ignorance in Chinese life but also at times the entire Confucian system. To convey the Christian message of brotherly love and spiritual salvation, missionaries found it necessary, at least by implication, to question the social order of which the gentry were the local protagonists. Frustrated and rebuffed by unappreciative "heathen," some missionaries concluded that the Chinese scholars were "proud and supercilious," "irreconcilable enemies," full of "cunning, ignorance, rudeness, coupled with superstition, vainglory, and inveterate hatred of everything foreign." Missionaries also came into competition with the gentry in practical affairs such as shelter of orphans, relief for the destitute, and welfare aid in time of famine or disaster, thus tending to supplant the gentry in certain of their customary functions.

One important cause of friction was the privileged status claimed by missionaries, or thrust upon them, under extraterritoriality. Just as the gentry were set off from the Chinese populace by their immunity from corporal punishment and their privileged access to and influence with officials, so the missionaries were untouchably privileged, immune to official coercion, able to intercede with and even claim the support of Chinese officialdom and, failing that, to call upon their own governments — and even, at times, upon gunboats. Catholic bishops in particular followed the early Jesuit tradition and assumed a quasi-official status with much pomp and ceremony.

Furthermore, having a privileged position, missionaries, like leading gentry, were often obliged to defend the interests of Chinese, primarily their converts, who became attached to them and regarded them as patrons and protectors. As friction developed between communities of Chinese Christians and non-Christians, missionaries were called upon to intervene with local officials, demanding punishment of culprits and payment of reparations, which usually had to be paid by the gentry and the officials themselves. Thus in three cases in Szechwan in the 1860's, the Catholic Church collected 260,000 taels in recompense for the death of two Catholic missionaries and the destruction of three churches and the homes of many converts.

Hostility was not lessened by the fact that converts were sometimes opportunistic "rice Christians," or from among the underprivileged, least committed to Confucian scholarship as a path of advancement. Christianity seemed likely to mobilize the lower classes and the discontented.

Judging by modern standards of nationalism, it would be hard to imagine a more solid basis for gentry hostility to the incoming priest or evangelist, with his strange speech, uncouth ways, and apparently subversive aims. In retrospect it seems plain that the missionary's purpose, however he expressed it in terms of succor and salvation of his fellow men, was inevitably subversive of the traditional Chinese order. The hostility of the Chinese scholar class is not surprising (nor is the vituperation with which their modern successors, the Chinese Communists, have invoked China's new national pride and berated Christian missions for their "cultural imperialism"). Rather, what calls for explanation is the mildness of the Chinese opposition. It was sufficiently violent to provoke thousands of small incidents and some 240 overt riots or attacks on missionaries between 1860 and 1899, including 55 during the 1860's. Yet it was not adequate to check the missionary movement or to figure largely in the missionary literature that flooded back to the West. Indeed the anti-Christian movement in China has only recently begun to be studied.

The Anti-Christian Movement. Because the Ch'ing government felt committed to maintain the treaty system as a means of limiting foreign aggression, overt official leadership of an anti-Christian movement was lacking, although few officials, we may imagine, could humanly avoid some degree of sympathy for it. The lead was taken sporadically by antiforeign gentry here and there, who used traditional means to arouse popular hostility as opportunity allowed.

Their first device was the printed word, which carried a certain authority in a land where literacy was still an upper-class hallmark. The denunciations of Yang Kuang-hsien and the Yung-cheng Emperor and others were reprinted, together with many traditional accusations — that Christianity was only an offshoot of Buddhism and Islam, that Christian communicants engaged in immoral and perverse practices, that priests administering extreme unction used the opportunity to extract a dying person's eyeballs for alchemic uses, and the like. Private printing and circulation of such writings, in the usual fashion before the days of a modern book trade, were facilitated by the insertion of outright pornography. In the 1860's scatological compilations were passed about which vividly described the sexual perversions and promiscuity attributed to Christian priests and believers, for example, in mixed congregations. This motif attracted readers and discredited Christianity at the same time.

With this literature to prepare the ground, anti-Christian zealots next had recourse to the ancient practice of posting anonymous handbills and placards in public to vent specific complaints and arouse action. Generally this was done in administrative cities at examination time, when hundreds and often thousands of degree candidates, under all the tension that attends such occasions, were concentrated for periods of a week or more.

Local issues might arise from missionary attempts to lease property, build structures which adversely affected the local *feng-shui* or geomantic "spirits of wind and water," or otherwise expand their activities. Disputes, altercations, lawsuits, and other sources of friction were seldom lacking, as well as rumors that exaggerated or fabricated the facts. Among these the most inflammatory were touched off by the willingness of Catholic Sisters of Charity to accept waifs and orphans and sometimes even to pay a small fee to encourage delivery of such unfortunates to their care. This charity, misinterpreted in an atmosphere of popular suspicion, could be linked with the ancient folklore concerning kidnapers who mesmerize small children and lead them off. In a few cases orphanages may actually have been exploited by Chinese kidnapers for the small fees involved. This, of course, was social dynamite.

In such situations overt action could be touched off by placards mobilizing all defenders of propriety and justice to demonstrate in a body at a given time and place. The local riffraff could be counted upon to create a mob. Riot, destruction, burning, beating, and even death might result. Chinese converts, because they were more numerous and more vulnerable, usually suffered more than the missionaries themselves.

This pattern of events was repeated in one incident after another in many parts of China over many decades. It must be seen as a largely unorganized movement of social and political protest, a rather blind and obscurantist defense of the old order, led by the less respectable members of that upper class which felt itself most threatened by the modern processes of change associated with Western contact.

The Failure of Treaty Revision. In the late 1860's missionary incidents in the provinces were troublesome exceptions to the general effort at Sino-Western cooperation being carried on at Peking. There the suppression of the Nien rebels in 1868 and the first steps in pacifying the Southwest and Northwest seemed to go hand in hand with cautious efforts at modernization. These were being promoted by the provincial leaders and by the Tsungli Yamen with the advice of Hart and the encouragement of Alcock and T. F. Wade in the British legation, of Anson Burlingame, the American minister, and others.

The hope of both the Western and the Ch'ing officials who were thus active in the "cooperative policy" was that China could gradually adjust to the outside world without further disaster. Each side had its opponents to contend with. The treaty-port merchants demanded increased privileges — opening the interior to foreign steamers, railways, and mining enterprises, abolition of likin and transit taxes, permission for foreign residence anywhere, and so on. At the opposite extreme, the antiforeign die-hards, both among Ch'ing princes at the capital and among the gentry in the provinces, were buoyed up by the government's success in suppressing rebellion; some were ready to try to expel the barbarian missionaries by force, relying on the sovereign strength of popular sentiment. Between these two camps — the one insatiable and the other irreconcilable — the Western diplomats and the high Ch'ing officials tried to construct peace and security.

Proposals for reforms to strengthen China were submitted in 1865–68 particularly by Hart and by Wade of the British legation, Britain being *primus inter pares* among the Western powers. They put forward arguments which Chinese reformers were to use more fully in later decades. If the dynastic cycle were allowed to run its normal course, China when weak would be overwhelmed by the West before she could grow strong again. Western contact had created an unprecedented foreign problem which required an unprecedented solution by domestic modernization. "If policies are altered," wrote Hart, "China can become the leader of all nations; if policies are not altered, she will become the servant of all nations."

Increased contact with the West, then as so often later, seemed to many one of the best ways to help China remake her civilization. For this purpose diplomatic missions abroad were strongly urged, and in 1868 the retiring American minister, Anson Burlingame, who had been a pillar of the "cooperative policy" since 1861, was sent as China's first envoy to the Western world. As an imperial appointee of the first civil rank, he and his retinue toured the Western capitals. In Washington he concluded a treaty on rather egalitarian terms. But Burlingame was also an orator. His proclamation that a new day of Westernization and Christianity had dawned in the ancient Middle Kingdom was premature and misleading. His mission ended with his sudden death in Russia in 1870.

Meanwhile, since the treaties could be revised after ten years, Alcock with Hart's help had conducted lengthy negotiations in 1868–69, trying to reach agreement on concessions which would partly meet the demands of the British merchants and yet not be utterly rejected by Chinese conservatives. Signed in October 1869, subject to later ratification, the Alcock Convention was negotiated by mutual concession. Its statesmanlike provisions would have put the British expansion and the whole treaty system in China on a more equitable basis for the future. But because Alcock was trying to restrict and so to stabilize the foreign impact on China, his draft treaty was violently attacked by the China trade interests in Britain. Merchants felt they had more to gain from expanding their privileges than from the stability of the Chinese empire. Consequently the British government felt obliged to refuse ratification.

On the Chinese side Prince Kung and Wen-hsiang had consulted the court and Grand Council and high provincial officials like Tseng, Li, and Tso. The Alcock Convention was generally considered a diplomatic victory for China and the imperial approval was considered final. Britain's unexpected rejection of it was therefore a damaging blow to the moderate "cooperative policy" of the 1860's. This setback coincided with a more spectacular disaster.

The Tientsin Massacre, 1870. The incident at Tientsin on June 21, 1870, undid the work of a decade. By revealing the opposed and irreconcilable nature of Western and Chinese aims and attitudes, it marked the end of the "cooperative policy" and also, though less obviously, of the Restoration movement in general.

The British aim had been to put the responsibility for enforcing the treaty system on the Ch'ing central government, while at the same time helping it to inaugurate modernization, particularly in its administration. Yet peaceful suasion could not entirely supersede the threat of force, especially to protect the treaty rights of missionaries. For example, when Hudson Taylor, who had opened a station of the China Inland Mission at Yangchow on the Grand Canal just north of the Yangtze, was mobbed in August 1868, Minister Alcock had eventually sent four gunboats to Nanking to press Tseng Kuo-fan into cashiering the negligent Yangchow authorities and making adequate restitution. There were other cases of this sort. Anglo-Chinese relations, though more enlightened than ever before, were not lacking in acrimony. Alcock tried to restrain his own countrymen and hold Peking responsible for incidents in the provinces. But he also remained ready to take direct action when it seemed necessary.

Sino-French relations were much worse. Having no commercial interests to protect, French officials in China tended to use the protection of Christian missions as a means of expanding French political influence and prestige. In asserting this protectorate, which had become a vested interest, the bellicose chargé d'affaires (Count Julian de Rochechouart) in early 1870 sailed up the Yangtze as far as Hankow with four gunboats, negotiating missionary cases directly with the provincial authorities. His gunboats got results.

Direct foreign action of this sort naturally intensified Chinese xenophobia. Incidents did not cease. The various influences making for an explosion converged at Tientsin. There the French Sisters of Charity had offered fees for orphans delivered to their care; the Chinese local populace believed this stimulated kidnaping and soon accepted rumors that the children's eyes and hearts were being extracted behind the secretive walls of the orphanage. Gentry-patriots agitated for direct action. Tension rose. On June 21 a mob gathered. The truculent French consul, demanding that it disperse, fired on the magistrate, missed him, and was himself torn to pieces. The mob then killed twenty other foreigners, mainly French, including ten nuns, and destroyed the Catholic establishments.

The outraged and fearful foreign powers mobilized gunboats off Tientsin. Meanwhile Chinese die-hard conservatives were joined by many modernizers in the comforting thought that the populace had at last risen in their might and no foreign intruders could withstand their righteous indignation. This was not a Western concept of "popular sovereignty" but the ancient Confucian idea that all government depends on popular support or at least acquiescence. With it, the Ch'ing had suppressed the Taipings and, some hoped, might now even expel the barbarians.

The crisis was laid in the lap of Tseng Kuo-fan, now old and ill, who nevertheless demonstrated once again his character and courage. He investigated and announced to his countrymen the unwelcome facts as he found them: that there was no real evidence of kidnaping by Chinese, or of scooping out eyes and hearts by missionaries. Simultaneously Tseng had to resist severe French demands and threats of war. He temporized and was finally helped by events in Europe, where France's sudden and unforeseen defeat in the Franco-Prussian War left her powerless to coerce China. Later in 1870 Li Hung-chang took over at Tientsin as governor-general of Chihli, backed by his Anhwei Army, while preparations continued to resist the French by force.

The Tientsin massacre ended the honeymoon period of the treaty system and left Sino-Western relations embittered by resentment and fear. The diplomats of both sides, under pressure from the Chinese gentry and the treaty-port communities, could not revive a cooperative policy. At the same time the effort to save China from foreign aggression by a restoration of Confucian government also seemed less promising. Tseng Kuo-fan's death in 1872 marked the end of an era.

ECONOMIC DEVELOPMENTS UNDER THE TREATY SYSTEM

Compared with missionary evangelism in the interior, foreign trade in the treaty ports was a less obvious threat to traditional ways and established interests. China's involvement in the world economy had been increasing for more than a century, and eventually it would affect Chinese life more profoundly than Christianity would. But the Western economic invasion was conducted so largely by Chinese merchants that it did not

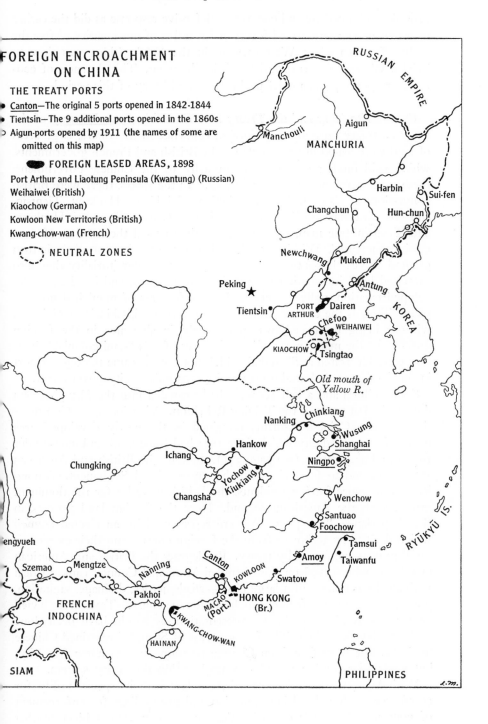

FOREIGN ENCROACHMENT ON CHINA

THE TREATY PORTS

● Canton—The original 5 ports opened in 1842-1844
● Tientsin—The 9 additional ports opened in the 1860s
◌ Aigun-ports opened by 1911 (the names of some are omitted on this map)

🖢 FOREIGN LEASED AREAS, 1898

Port Arthur and Liaotung Peninsula (Kwantung) (Russian)
Weihaiwei (British)
Kiaochow (German)
Kowloon New Territories (British)
Kwang-chow-wan (French)

⬭ NEUTRAL ZONES

RUSSIAN EMPIRE

Manchouli
Aigun
MANCHURIA

Harbin
Sui-fen
Changchun
Hun-chun

Newchwang
Mukden

Peking
Antung

Tientsin
PORT ARTHUR
Dairen
KOREA

Chefoo
WEIHAIWEI

KIAOCHOW
Tsingtao

Old mouth of Yellow R.

Chinkiang
Nanking
Wusung
Hankow
Shanghai
Ichang
Ningpo
Chungking
Yochow
Kiukiang
Changsha
Wenchow
Santuao
Foochow
engyueh
Tamsui
RYŪKYŪ IS.
Szemao
Mengtze
Nanning
Amoy
Taiwanfu
Pakhoi
Canton
KOWLOON
Swatow
FRENCH INDOCHINA
MACAO (Port.)
HONG KONG (Br.)
KWANG-CHOW-WAN
HAINAN
SIAM
PHILIPPINES

provoke so immediate and concrete a defensive response as did the earlier invasions of Western armed forces or the influx of missionaries. After the early efforts to adopt Western arms in the 1860's, China was slow to imitate Western forms of industrial development. This slowness of economic response poses a chief problem in the history of this period.

Extraterritoriality and the Treaty Port Establishment. In many of the fourteen treaty ports open to foreign residence in the 1860's, large areas of land were leased in perpetuity by the British and French governments, which paid modest ground-rents annually to the Chinese government; these areas were known as "concessions." In the 1860's, there were British concessions at Canton, Amoy, Chinkiang, Kiukiang, Hankow, Tientsin, and Newchwang; and French concessions at Canton, Shanghai, Hankow, and Tientsin (see map, page 339). As time passed the number of concessions increased. Within these leased areas the foreign consulates in turn granted 99-year leases to land-renters. Under extraterritoriality they also exercised legal jurisdiction over their own nationals, and by degrees developed taxation, police forces, and other features of municipal government. Thus as the extraterritorial system developed, China's sovereignty, without being destroyed, was put largely in abeyance in the foreign quarters of the major ports. Many features of this "semi-colonial" situation were illustrated at Shanghai, which not only became the biggest port in the foreign trade but also created its own unique city government.

Some million and a half refugees had crowded into the Shanghai area during the last years of the Taiping Rebellion. After its suppression more than 100,000 Chinese residents remained in the newly developed area north of the walled city which since 1854 had come more and more under foreign administration (see page 341). In 1863 the British and American areas coalesced to form the Shanghai International Settlement. Among its 2000 or more foreign residents, the British were by far the dominant group, with the Americans second. Here the foreign land-renters (in British parlance, "rate-payers") were represented by an elected council which derived its authority from the foreign consuls and their extraterritorial powers conferred by treaty. By degrees the British and American merchants who served on this Shanghai Municipal Council came to deal with all the problems of a large city — roads, jetties, drainage, sanitation, police, and recreation facilities such as the race course. Taxes were levied on Chinese residents without representation, as would have been done under a Chinese regime. The foreign areas of Shanghai remained Chinese territory, but were free from Chinese taxation. It was not a free city, but was under foreign consular control within the treaty system.

With Western control came Western law with its special utility for commerce, such as legal incorporation and proceedings for enforcement of contract. Nationals of each Western country were subject to that country's consular court and could be sued by Chinese plaintiffs only in

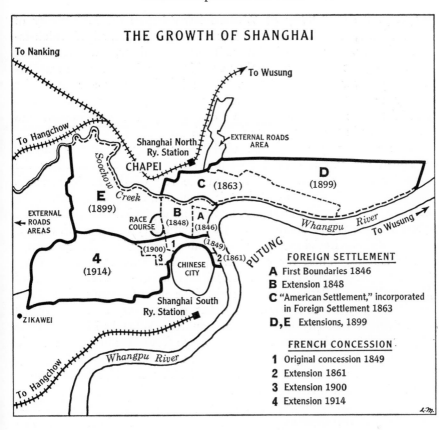

THE GROWTH OF SHANGHAI

To Nanking

To Wusung

To Hangchow

Shanghai North Ry. Station

EXTERNAL ROADS AREA

CHAPEI

Soochow *Creek*

C (1863)

D (1899)

E (1899)

EXTERNAL ROADS AREAS

RACE COURSE

B (1848)

A (1846)

Whangpu *River*

To Wusung

(1900)

4 (1914)

CHINESE CITY

(1849)

2 (1861)

PUTUNG

FOREIGN SETTLEMENT
A First Boundaries 1846
B Extension 1848
C "American Settlement," incorporated in Foreign Settlement 1863
D,E Extensions, 1899

Shanghai South Ry. Station

ZIKAWEI

Whangpu *River*

To Hangchow

FRENCH CONCESSION
1 Original concession 1849
2 Extension 1861
3 Extension 1900
4 Extension 1914

that court. Britain set an example by transferring her Supreme Court for China and Japan from Hong Kong to Shanghai to hear appeals from all her consular courts. But appeals from the French consular court had to go to Saigon in Indo-China, and those from the Spanish, Dutch, or Russian consulates to Manila, Batavia, or Vladivostok, respectively. This made it difficult for Chinese plaintiffs to appeal against consular judgments.

A new invention in 1864 was the Shanghai Mixed Court, which was presided over by a Chinese magistrate but with a foreign consular "assessor" sitting with him as a co-judge and sharing the judicial function. This Mixed Court, using Western procedure, handled cases between Chinese and cases in which Chinese were the defendants. Thus both foreign and Chinese defendants had rights of trial before judges of their own nationality, by the laws of their own countries.

Shanghai existed mainly for business, which developed on the basis of extraterritoriality. The foreign land-renters, as Chinese crowded in and real estate values rose, got high profits by sub-renting the land they had leased. Most of all, foreigners benefited from security of person and property, the availability of Western law (despite the multiplicity of jurisdictions), and freedom from Chinese local taxation, all of which facilitated trade. As Shanghai, Canton, Tientsin, Hankow, and other centers grew into great modern cities, the vested interests dependent on extraterritoriality grew correspondingly. What had begun as a legal device mainly to protect Western individuals against the Chinese custom of judicial torture became even more a device to protect foreign firms and corporations in the treaty ports from Chinese taxation.

Once under way and commended by its many advantages for the foreigner, the extraterritorial system became firmly established as the basis for contact between China and the rest of the modern world. During the 1860's treaties with Prussia, Denmark, the Netherlands, Spain, Belgium, Italy, Austria-Hungary, and others expanded the scope of the system. Nationals of countries which lacked treaty relations with China secured extraterritorial privileges by becoming protégés of foreign treaty-power consuls. Thus, for example, the French consuls, instead of the Chinese government, exercised jurisdiction in China over citizens of Memel, Monaco, Persia, and Rumania. The most-favored-nation clause continued to work as a one-way ratchet, giving every treaty power all the privileges that any one of them acquired. What had begun in the 1840's as a convenient system to control 350 foreigners in 5 ports would eventually, in the twentieth century, come to include some 90 treaty ports or open ports, some 25 ports of call (for steamships), and about a third of a million foreign residents.

The privileged communities of Westerners in the new treaty-port cities brought with them not only the municipal institutions of the urban West — newspapers (like the *North China Herald* at Shanghai), schools, libraries, hospitals, sewage and water systems, paved streets and illumination. They also brought their higher standard of living with its meat diet, leather shoes, spring beds, and modern plumbing. This higher material standard, as well as extraterritoriality and Western learning, automatically made foreigners a kind of upper class in China, as privileged and powerful in their way as the Chinese upper class itself. Those who stayed long enough to be called "Old China Hands" became, like Europeans in their nineteenth-century colonies, well adjusted to their superior status, sure of its moral correctness, and ready to develop it further.

By applying Western technology they also found more efficient uses for Chinese manpower. Instead of the ancient Chinese palanquin or chair carried on bamboo poles by two or more men, the smooth streets of the treaty ports made possible the introduction from Japan of the ricksha (see page 263), which combined bicycle-type, ball-bearing wheels and springs with a coolie to run between the shafts like an intelligent horse.

The Role of the Maritime Customs Service. Development both of the treaty ports and of foreign trade was helped immeasurably by the growth of China's first modern civil service, the Maritime Customs under Robert Hart. It performed a many-sided role under the treaties and also aided Chinese efforts at modernization, forming in fact a chief link between conservative Peking officialdom and the aggressive foreign merchants.

First of all, the Customs ensured to Peking a growing, reliable, and uncommitted source of new revenue at a time when older sources were inelastic and already committed to meet established needs. The Customs revenue paid off the 1860 indemnities of 8 million taels each to Britain and France. In designated treaty ports it became the security for many of the 25 domestic loans floated by various Chinese government authorities between 1861 and 1893.

Meanwhile the Customs preserved the imperial tariff against smuggling and corruption. To check the large-scale Chinese smuggling of opium, salt, and other commodities from the free port of Hong Kong into nearby Chinese territory, two measures were necessary: first, the old Portuguese port of Macao was formally ceded to Portugal in 1887, making it foreign territory; and second, the Maritime Customs at the same time set up offices in both Kowloon (the small continental addition to the island of Hong Kong) and Lappa (close to Macao) to take the place of the corrupt and ineffective old-style offices maintained until then by the Canton customs collector, the "Hoppo" of pre-treaty times. The new offices soon checked smuggling in Chinese junks.

The Customs also completed the charting of the China coast, which the British navy had begun earlier in the century. It installed lighthouses, beacons, markers, and other modern aids to navigation on both coast and rivers, and handled all the management of port facilities including pilotage, berthing, and quarantine. The Customs published trade statistics of value for all merchants and a variety of commercial and scientific reports. In addition, its foreign commissioners in the ports, like Hart at Peking, mediating between foreign treaty rights and Chinese interests, often performed quasi-diplomatic and even political functions, while its Chinese staff provided a modern training ground for civil servants. From 400 Western and 1400 Chinese employees in 1875, the staff grew to 600 and 2000, respectively, in 1885, and to 700 and 3500 in 1895, more than half the Westerners being British.

In brief, Hart and the Customs were at the core of the treaty system, and their work was one of its most constructive aspects, however the system may be judged. Hart and his commissioners in every port set the best example of joint Sino-Western administration in the handling of China's problems of foreign contact and modernization. After 1860, missionaries and foreign merchants built up large organizations radiating from the ports; and many foreign advisers and technicians were employed in Chinese projects. Amongst all this building of new institutions within the old Chinese empire, the Maritime Customs exerted a central leadership and influence.

Growth and Change in China's Foreign Trade. With the growth of the treaty ports into modern cities came the advances in technology that brought China constantly closer to the outside world. The clipper ship era lasted through the 1860's, but first the iron and then in the 1880's the steel steamship offered more and more efficient competition, until the high-pressure, triple-expansion steam engine finally ended the age of sail and increased the speed of sea transport. In 1869 the Suez Canal halved the distance to Europe. In 1870–71 cables were laid connecting Vladivostok, Nagasaki, Shanghai, Hong Kong, and Singapore, whence telegraphic communication went on around the world via London to San Francisco. China was thus drawn further into the world economy and became more subject to the vicissitudes of international prices, business crises, and foreign competition.

Among other deficiencies, China lacked a stable modern currency. During the Rebellion the scarcity of the silver dollars customarily used in foreign trade had led to the adoption in 1857 of an agreed unit of account, the Shanghai silver tael. During the rest of the nineteenth century the China trade was affected by the world-wide fall in the value of silver, as silver output rose and many countries went on the gold standard, demonetizing their silver. This led to a long decline in the gold value of China's silver currency, attended by constant fluctuations which made merchants' calculations uncertain and difficult.

A principal aim of the unequal treaties had been to facilitate foreign commerce, which Consul Alcock for one had regarded as "the true herald of civilization . . . the human agency appointed under a Divine dispensation to work out man's emancipation from the thralldom and evils of a savage isolation." Accordingly the treaty tariff was set at fixed monetary rates which in many cases represented 5 per cent ad valorem in 1858 but generally became lower as prices rose in subsequent decades. Meanwhile foreign imports and Chinese goods for export, as they passed in either direction between treaty ports and the interior, were to pay an additional 2½ per cent (half the tariff duty) as transit dues, and be subsequently free from all the likin and other taxes which goods in China's purely domestic commerce might have to pay. Similarly an additional 2½ per cent could be paid as "coast trade" duty to avoid all further taxes on Chinese goods carried in foreign ships from one Chinese port to another. These arrangements prevented China from imposing a protective tariff, which was a considerable impairment of sovereignty, and furthermore gave the foreign merchant a privileged advantage over his Chinese competitor. Thus aided, foreign merchants after 1860 looked forward to a rich opportunity.

They were correspondingly frustrated and querulous when this Eldorado, on the whole, failed to materialize. During the 1870's and 1880's China failed to provide the expected market for Western products. In an era of world-wide commercial expansion, imports into China tended to stagnate. By 1890 the total value of the China trade, both in and out, was only £50 million, less than that of many small countries. The chief reasons for this stagnation were no doubt China's poverty, self-sufficiency, and conservatism. But British merchants, still the dominant foreign element, ascribed it to a mandarin conspiracy whereby transit taxes still prevented the "opening" of the China market. When the British minister (Wade) negotiated the "Chefoo Convention" in 1876 with Li Hung-chang, over a Burma-Yunnan border incident (see page 372), he secured the opening of five more ports and other concessions. Yet the China trade failed to leap forward.

In the content of the trade, however, the late nineteenth century saw the beginning of a revolution. The great staples of mid-century, opium imports and tea exports, both reached their highest volume and then declined. In the 1830's the importing of 30,000 chests of Indian opium a year had been enough to lead to war. Unmentioned in the first treaties, opium imports had continued to increase. Legalized and taxed under the treaty settlement of 1858–60, they reached a peak of some 87,000 chests in 1879, but thereafter declined because production of opium within China (several times the quantity imported) increasingly supplied the still growing Chinese market. Meanwhile treaty-port firms like Jardine, Matheson and Company largely withdrew from the import trade because of the competition of Indian firms that had organized control over the supply in India.

Similarly tea exports to Britain rose, from a volume of 30 million pounds in the 1830's, to a peak of 150 million pounds in the 1880's but thereafter declined because tea from India and Ceylon, transplanted there from China in mid-century, began to take over the British market. Japanese teas at the same time were beginning to capture the American market. Only the Russian demand for China's brick tea continued to grow. Tea had formed three-fifths of China's exports but after 1900 dropped to a tenth. The reasons lay partly in China's failure to modernize her tea industry. Indian tea, for example, was produced by large-scale methods on big plantations created by capital investment. It was carefully standardized and exported free of duty. Chinese tea was collected from individual farmers on a small-scale basis, its quality was not protected against adulteration by get-rich-quick dealers, and it was taxed both in transit and on export.

China's silk, her most famous product, began to suffer a similar decline after 1900. Both in Europe and in Japan scientific prevention of silkworm disease, mechanization of silk reeling, and modern market organization produced a high-quality standardized product. Unorganized and unaided, the Chinese farming households could not match this quality.

One cause of these setbacks in China's foreign trade was the inability of the Ch'ing government to perform functions of commercial leadership and regulation which governments were performing elsewhere. Domestic opium production, wasteful and corrupt, was allowed to increase; tea and silk exports were handicapped by taxation instead of being fostered; and standards of product were not set and supervised as they were in Japan.

China's production of cotton, mainly in the Yangtze Valley, had supplied a large handicraft industry which wove cotton cloth — for example, the "nankeens" exported in the East India Company trade (see page 97). After the second treaty settlement had opened more ports, imports of cotton goods increased, but in the following decades up to 1890 they failed to achieve the great increase that Lancashire hoped for. The principal growth was not in cotton textiles, which failed in this period to supplant the Chinese handicraft product, but in cotton yarn, imports of which, mainly from India, increased 20-fold from 1872 to 1890. This was because machine-spinning of yarn was some 80 times as productive as hand-spinning, while machine-weaving of cloth was only about 4 times as fast as hand-weaving. Thus the cheaper cotton yarn from abroad crippled the native Chinese spinning industry, while weaving still continued for many years on hand looms in peasant households as before.

Opinions differ as to the net effect of foreign trade on nineteenth-century China. The unfairness of the special privileges set up in the treaties seems obvious. Many have argued from these privileges to economic conclusions, not all of which have yet been validated by research. The classic Marxist concept, of machine-industry products flooding into and disrupting the handicraft industries of a backward country's farm economy, seems to apply to China's experience with only varying degrees of accuracy, for China's involvement in the world economy was less than that of fully colonial areas in Southeast Asia. For example, production of tea, silk, and cotton cloth continued to provide employment for rural man- and woman-power. As tea and silk exports declined, China began to export "sundries," those diverse products which the China trade used to call "chow-chow" cargo or "muck and truck." These included vegetable oils (from peanuts, cotton seed, etc.) and tung oil (from the tung tree, valued as a drying ingredient in varnish), pig bristles (for brushes), hides and skins (largely from Mongolia), and soybeans (particularly from Manchuria). These were mainly by-products of cheap labor on farms rather than in factories.

Compradors and Chinese Capital. Unlike the foreign missionaries and the Chinese gentry, foreign and Chinese merchants needed one another. The China trade was the result of their cooperation, as it had been at Canton before the treaties. The comprador, handling the Chinese side of a foreign firm's business (see page 155), bridged the cultural, linguistic, and institutional gap between East and West. While the term "comprador class" is now sometimes applied with opprobrium to those who aided the foreign commercial invasion, many of them can equally well be extolled as China's pioneers of industry. One of the most famous and successful was Tong King-sing (also called T'ang T'ing-shu, 1832–1892), who came from the Canton delta region and got an English-language missionary education. He served as a Hong Kong government interpreter and then as a Maritime Customs clerk at Shanghai and in 1863 became Jardine, Matheson and Company's comprador there. Another success story is that of Dent and Company's Shanghai comprador, Hsü Jun (known as "Ahyun"), also from the Canton delta, who after seventeen years' service set up his own firm when Dent went out of business in 1867. Typically, both these men purchased official status and titles and so, in addition to their widespread business interests, acquired membership in the official class.

Compradors, however, were only one element in the Chinese trading community. After 1860 Chinese dealers began to compete with foreign firms in the distribution of foreign imports. In this competition they were aided by their guild organization and superior knowledge of local conditions. Soon the foreign firms, which had originally set up branches in every port, began to close them and concentrate their business in major shipping centers like Hong Kong and Shanghai. There they served as commission agents for constituents abroad, procuring foreign goods that were purchased by independent Chinese who now handled the distribution of the import trade.

One channel for this distribution was the interport trade, that is, from one treaty port to another in China's domestic commerce. Admission of foreign vessels and traders to this sphere of trade, one of the unequal-treaty privileges, was now partially nullified by native competition. Chinese merchants became the principal users of the foreign shipping, which was more secure and reliable than native shipping, both for moving Chinese products and for distributing Western imports.

Chinese capitalists, in short, could benefit from the security and facilities of the treaty system once they learned how to do it. The compradors who left foreign employment and became treaty-port entrepreneurs were only the most prominent representatives of this trend. China's treaty ports, where merchants could accumulate and invest capital beyond the reach of a parasitic officialdom, began to play a role in the rise of capitalism not unlike that played in medieval Europe by the growth of chartered cities beyond the reach of feudal exactions.

Shanghai's rise as the capital market of China was marked by the formation in 1865, mainly by British firms, of the Hongkong and Shanghai Banking Corporation, which was set up to serve local needs as well as foreign trade. It and other foreign banks financed Chinese merchants and Chinese banks. They transferred funds between ports, handled remittances from Chinese overseas, and even issued their own local banknote currency.

Chinese capital was attracted to Shanghai, Hong Kong, and other ports by the security of investment in real estate, as well as by traditional opportunities like pawnshops or usury through small Chinese money-shops. But entrepreneurial activity in the port cities was also called forth by the need for many local industries — to process goods for export (tea, silk, cotton textiles) and goods imported for consumption in the ports or shipment to other ports (flour-milling, sugar-refining, brewing); to provide public utilities (water, gas, transport) and urban housing (cement, bricks); and to support the shipping industry (wharves, dockyards, engineering). This cooperative Sino-foreign growth attracted Chinese capital and talent. Funds were invested and skills were learned that created potential resources for China's later industrialization.

One interesting example of this cooperative process occurred in 1862 when the Shanghai partner of Russell and Company, Edward Cunningham, organized a steamship line by securing capital in roughly equal portions from his partners in the United States, from foreign merchants in China, and from Chinese merchants and compradors, who actually put up more capital for this venture than did the Americans in Russell and Company. Among them "Ahyun, Chongfat, Koofunsing" had all served earlier as compradors for the firm. By securing shallow-draft American side-wheeler steamboats and setting up a regular twice-weekly service between Shanghai and Hankow, this American-led, Chinese-backed enterprise inaugurated the great era of steamboating on the Yangtze. It was many years before British firms won their domination of the steamship carrying trade in Chinese waters.

During the quarter century after 1870, economic growth in the treaty ports was creating resources of investment capital and entrepreneurial skill which, in favorable circumstances and in due time, might have been used to bring China through that critical phase of industrialization, the breakthrough into self-sustaining growth. But the treaty ports were only one sector of the Chinese economy. Contemporary experience in Japan showed that success in industrial modernization would have required more central direction and support and more comprehensive scope. It would have needed a whole set of circumstances that were lacking in China outside the treaty ports — a more stable framework of law and monetary practice, a more independent style of entrepreneurship, more clearly defined national political goals, and stronger leadership from the government. A century later, it is not difficult for economists to name the requirements for successful industrialization and to see that China lacked many of them. For the historian, however, it is important to look at what was actually attempted.

EARLY INDUSTRIALIZATION

During the quarter century after 1870 the rate of China's economic modernization, though considerable, fell behind that of Japan and the West. Steamboating on the Yangtze imitated that on the Mississippi, but a subsequent era of railroading, as in the American West, did not ensue. China's slowness to industrialize may be attributed to a complex of factors — intellectual, psychological, social, economic, political, and administrative.

Inadequacy of Government Leadership. To begin with, the idea that the unequal treaties prevented China's industrialization, if we can judge by the Japanese example, is over-simple and inadequate to explain what happened. Decision lay first with the Chinese government; only the government's default gave the treaty port its later dominant role. The restrictive effect of the treaty system was cumulative, and evils visible in its later years were by no means inevitable from the start. In short, the incapacity of government to take the lead was the first great fact in China's slowness to industrialize.

This incapacity of Peking was of course many-sided and inherited from a long past. It was most spectacularly evident in two sectors, finance and policy. Peking's antiquated fiscal system during the last decades of the nineteenth century was still based on tax-farming — that is, provincial officials were expected to make certain tax quotas available to Peking while maintaining themselves and their administrations on the remainder of what they collected. Budgeting, accounting, central planning, and central control were impossible. On the record, about 1890, Peking listed annual revenues totaling roughly 89 million taels (see table, page 327). Of these reported collections, only a part ever reached Peking, the greater part being allotted for manifold provincial uses. However, the unreported collections (except for the Maritime Customs) were probably three to five times as great as those listed for the Peking record. Mobilization and use of fiscal resources was thus beyond the power of the central government and was left by default to provincial officials.

In the provinces ingenious mandarins, by skillful arrangements, could accumulate and invest official funds in new enterprises, but only by taking personal initiative and responsibility. Their leadership in industrialization was usually hindered on the policy level by the purblind conservatism and opposition of most of the official class, in which the inertia of traditional thinking was very evident. Almost all scholars continued to ignore Western learning in favor of the Classics still required for their all-important examinations. Again, as after the Opium War, they avoided the lesson of history. Change in the treaty ports was far more rapid than in the ideas and attitudes of a governing elite who disesteemed merchants.

This intellectual conservatism was evident, for instance, in the economic views of Tseng Kuo-fan. In 1867 he noted with distaste that Western nations for centuries had been annexing one another's territories and squabbling greedily over material gains; their merchants in the treaty ports sought profit at the expense of China; modern steamers, railways, and telegraphs, if managed by foreigners or by Chinese attached to foreigners, would threaten the livelihood of the common people (*min-sheng*); Confucian government must protect the people's livelihood, lest the wrath of the multitude be provoked. Tseng, though a leader in "self-strengthening," had no concept of modern economic development. When he and others did press for "self-strengthening" through Western technology, their efforts had to be limited and circumspect, justified on grounds of immediate defense or direct profit, and supported by the rationalization that Western techniques like mathematics and firearms had originally come from China and been merely developed further in the West. "China invented the method, Westerners adopted it," said Prince Kung.

The advocates of so-called "foreign matters" (*yang-wu*, i.e., Westernization) in the late nineteenth century are now blamed by some in retrospect for their failure to industrialize and strengthen China. At the time, however, they were attacked for attempting too many changes too rapidly. Their attackers, ignorant of the outside world, saw much innovation at home but could not see the larger paradox, that in spite of her considerable rate of change, China was steadily falling behind other nations. This paradox was doubly difficult for the Chinese upper class to understand because both the concept of progress (implying continual change of the established order and rejection of stability) and the concept of nationalism (implying international competition on an equal basis) were new to them.

Warning voices were raised. As early as 1863 Li Hung-chang was pointing to the example of Japan. "The Japanese of today are the 'dwarf pirates' (*wo-k'ou*) of the Ming dynasty," he noted; yet by sending students abroad and even importing machines to make machines, Japan had learned to make and use steamships and cannon, and could already defy the British. If China should become strong, "they will attach themselves to us." If not, "then the Japanese will imitate the Westerners and will share the Westerners' sources of profits." A decade later Japanese expansionists had come close to invading Korea; and when their punitive expedition against Formosan aborigines almost developed into war with China in 1874, the aged Manchu statesman Wen-hsiang warned the throne bluntly that without more vigorous leadership and less complacency, "the country will fall apart, the people's confidence will be shaken, and the disaster will be unspeakable." Yet the great bureaucratic empire continued to drift along during the crucial next two decades up to the reckoning of 1894, when the superiority of Japan's modernization became startlingly plain in warfare. For thirty years the words of a Sung dynasty scholar, quoted by Li Hung-chang in 1863, had remained appropriate: "If you speak in a time of peace . . . no one will believe you; if you speak in a time of trouble . . . it will already be too late."

The Power Structure. Behind the inertia of the Ch'ing leaders lay their vested interests in maintaining the power structure of the day and in using modernization for personal and political aims within that structure. This tendency was illustrated both by the Empress Dowager at Peking and by Li Hung-chang at Tientsin.

During most of the period up to 1894 the court remained firmly under the control of Tz'u-hsi, who steadily built up her bureaucratic machine. She kept a devoted Manchu bannerman, Jung-lu, in command of the military police at the capital and of the new modern-armed Peking Field Force. She dominated the young emperor, and according to legend even encouraged him in a life of excess that brought on his death in January 1875 at the age of nineteen, two years after he had nominally taken control of the government.

To maintain herself in power the Empress Dowager now broke the sacred dynastic law of succession, which required that a new emperor always be chosen from the succeeding generation in order to maintain the ritual observances demanded by filial piety. Instead, she shocked propriety by having her own nephew, a four-year-old boy of the same generation as his predecessor, selected emperor with the reign title of Kuang-hsü ("Glorious Succession," 1875–1908).[1] Until he took on the imperial functions in 1889, she continued to rule. She removed Prince Kung from power in 1884 and entrenched herself by divide-and-rule tactics. Officeholders all over the empire quietly contributed to her personal fortune.

The Empress Dowager's forceful personality was devoted to a conservative end, the maintenance of the dynasty by keeping an equilibrium between the traditional central power and the new regional interests. The latter had grown up in the process of suppressing rebellion — Chinese scholar-generals had created personally led administrative machines in the provinces they governed. Warfare had opened a new avenue to talent and produced civil officials with military experience and local roots. As a result, between 1861 and 1890 almost half the governors-general and

[1] The Empress Dowager manipulated the succession by selecting her younger sister's son, who was also a first cousin of the deceased T'ung-chih Emperor, and adopting him as the heir of herself and the deceased Hsien-feng Emperor. By this device she became the adoptive mother of her own nephew, now the Kuang-hsü Emperor, and could rule as regent for him. But her son, the deceased T'ung-chih Emperor, had had no male offspring and now was left with no heir to perform the important rituals of filial reverence for the dead.

more than half the governors were Chinese who had risen through military command. Almost one-fourth of them lacked the higher (provincial or metropolitan) degrees. They used local revenues like the likin tax to maintain new regionally recruited armies.

Regionalism was buttressed in the post-rebellion era by the modernization projects of leading officials. Thus modernization became a creature of politics. Peking was strengthened by the new Maritime Customs revenues and by projects they supported. But regional interests were also strengthened by new arsenals and industries in provincial centers. Consequently Ch'ing rule depended upon the loyalty of leading officials who had regional bases of personal influence within the imperial administrative structure (see table, page 353). The Empress Dowager could maintain her own position and that of the Manchu dynasty only by cooperating with and manipulating these regional leaders, all of whom with proper Confucian reverence still looked up to the Ch'ing throne for official appointment and for final answers, with no thought as yet of exercising the independent power of warlords.

Li Hung-chang's career illustrates the delicate balance between regional power and dynastic loyalty. During the quarter century after 1870 he remained continuously in power at Tientsin, as governor-general of Chihli and commissioner for the northern ports, quite contrary to the tradition that even the highest official should be shifted every three, or at most six, years. Li's position was based on three elements: first, on the military strength of his Anhwei Army, between 25 and 40 thousand strong, stationed in Chihli and Shantung and for many years also in Kiangsu, and supplied by arsenals at Tientsin, Nanking, and Shanghai; second, on the bureaucratic machine of younger commanders and officials, many of them from Li's native place (Ho-fei) in Anhwei, who worked under him as their patron; and third, on local provincial revenues plus those collected for defense of the metropolitan province of Chihli, mainly from Lower Yangtze sources. Li's trusted German adviser, Gustav Detring, remained commissioner of customs at Tientsin for two decades (from about 1876), despite Hart's usual practice of rotation in the Customs Service.

Li Hung-chang's leadership in foreign diplomacy and in industrial development remained entirely compatible with his loyalty to the throne and to the Empress Dowager in particular. Indeed, the court in bringing Li to North China had evidently decided to join forces with, rather than oppose, his growing power. The two came to depend upon one another in matters both of policy and of profit. As the Empress Dowager through her chief eunuchs (like the notorious Li Lien-ying, d. 1911) built up a traditional system of squeeze, Li Hung-chang was in a position to give her support out of his own resources accumulated in administration and industrialization. This corruption is of course poorly documented, but

SELECTED GOVERNORS-GENERAL IN THE LATE CH'ING PERIOD
with official dates of incumbency

Nanking	Tientsin	Canton	Wuhan	Foochow	Lanchow	Chengtu
Tseng Kuo-fan 1860–1865	Tseng Kuo-fan 1868–1870	Liu K'un-i 1875–1879	Li Han-chang 1867–1868 1870–1875 1876–1882	Tso Tsung-t'ang 1863–1866	Tso Tsung-t'ang 1867–1880	Li Han-chang 1876
Li Hung-chang 1865–1866	Li Hung-chang 1870–1882 1883–1895 1900–1901	Tseng Kuo-ch'üan 1882–1883	Li Hung-chang 1869–1870		Tseng Kuo-ch'üan 1881	
Tseng Kuo-fan 1866–1868 1870–1872	Yüan Shih-k'ai 1901–1907	Chang Chih-tung 1884–1889	Chang Chih-tung 1889–1894 1895–1902 1904–1907			
Liu K'un-i 1875 1880–1881		Li Han-chang 1889–1895				
Tso Tsung-t'ang 1881–1884		Li Hung-chang 1899–1900				
Tseng Kuo-ch'üan 1884–1890						
Liu K'un-i 1891–1894						
Chang Chih-tung 1894–1895						
Liu K'un-i 1896–1899 1900–1902						
Chang Chih-tung 1902						

NOTE: Tseng Kuo-fan (1811–1872) of Hunan sponsored his brother Kuo-ch'üan (1824–1890), Li Hung-chang (1823–1901) of Anhwei, Li's elder brother Han-chang (1821–1899), Liu K'un-i (1830–1902) of Hunan, and Tso Tsung-t'ang (1812–1885) of Hunan. Li Hung-chang sponsored Yüan Shih-k'ai (1859–1916) of Chihli. Chang Chih-tung (1837–1909) of Chihli was sometimes Li's rival. Many other incumbents, usually less important, are of course omitted in this table. It suggests how far one group dominated the two principal regions under the Nanking and Tientsin posts.

353

it seems plain that Li Hung-chang's bureaucratic machine, like that of an American city boss, utilized the flow of public funds through private hands. Thus his long leadership in "foreign matters" had mixed motives, patriotic and personal, ideological and pecuniary.

Among Li's rivals, the other leading survivor from the mid-century era of rebellion was Tso Tsung-t'ang (1812–1885). He, however, was preoccupied with pacification of the Northwest until 1873 and thereafter with the recovery of Chinese Turkestan (see pages 324, 369–370).

"Government Supervision and Merchant Operation." In organizing economic modernization projects, Li Hung-chang and others used the formula "government supervision and merchant operation" (*kuan-tu shang-pan*), meaning that these were profit-oriented enterprises operated by merchants but controlled and directed by government officials. Because officialdom must dominate all large-scale economic activity, enterprises required official initiative; and Li Hung-chang was a natural initiator because of his power within the bureaucracy and his first-hand knowledge of foreign ways.

Li's first venture was naturally in steamships, which had exemplified Western mechanical superiority ever since the Opium War and were now outdoing Chinese junks on coastal and river routes alike. Moreover, Peking's food supply still depended on the Lower Yangtze tribute rice shipments which came by barge up the decaying Grand Canal and by seagoing junk around Shantung. Accordingly, the China Merchants' Steam Navigation Company which Li set up in 1872 was financed partly by an annual government subsidy for haulage of tribute rice. With typical conservatism, however, the now inefficient Grand Canal grain transport, with all its vested interests and perquisites from repair and maintenance (see page 111), was kept going until 1901.

In organizing the China Merchants' steamship line on the principle of "government supervision and merchant operation," Li was following the long tradition of the salt monopoly (see page 113), a fiscal device for milking official taxes and private squeeze from a monopolized staple for which there was an inelastic demand. This static, tax-farming tradition was antithetic to that of the dynamic, risk-taking entrepreneur who founds modern industries. It made for distribution of profits rather than their reinvestment, for profiteering rather than industrialization.

The phrase "merchant operation" also implied the raising of capital from merchant sources. Indeed, the steamship company's name in Chinese is literally "bureau for attracting merchants (to operate) steamships" (*lun-ch'üan chao-shang chü*). Li first appointed as managers men experienced, quite inappropriately, in the junk transport of tribute rice; but he soon turned to Jardine's English-speaking comprador Tong King-sing, who had been directing the operation of their steamships as well as some owned by himself and other Chinese. Tong and others, like Dent's comprador Hsü Jun who came into the management, subscribed shares of capital, but the "attracting" of merchant capital was only partly successful, and Li Hung-chang had to lend funds from his own provincial government. The merchant shareholders generally became managers, with official posts and titles. They secured perquisites and patronage, appointing relatives and friends to the staff. The enterprise was neither government-run nor private in modern terms, but a typical hybrid along traditional lines in which officials and merchants cooperated to get rich. The government meanwhile had no policy of economic development.

Aided by such means as the tribute rice subsidy, the China Merchants' line competed successfully with the foreign lines in Chinese waters. The line managed by the American firm of Russell and Company, which had dominated the Yangtze for a decade, also faced competition after 1872 from British lines set up by Jardine, Matheson and by the new firm of Butterfield and Swire. In 1877, the China Merchants' Company, with seventeen vessels, bought the even larger fleet of Russell and Company. The Americans retired. The Chinese line thus became the biggest, and thereafter maintained monopolistic rate agreements with the British. In the end, however, the latter reinvested their profits more prudently, while the China Merchants' managers took out the profits and let the fleet deteriorate. The Chinese line eventually stagnated, and British ships recovered their dominance in China's carrying trade.

In the history of this company, which served as a prototype for other enterprises, may be seen some of the institutional difficulties that inhibited such developments in China. The system of "government supervision and merchant operation" demonstrated in one enterprise after another that it was a traditional, not a modern, institution. First of all, it was thoroughly tied into the bureaucratic structure and suffered from the evils of nepotistic and cliquish favoritism, squeeze, and lack of risk-taking initiative. Secondly, being under government control, enterprises of this type were subjected to official levies and exactions. Those in charge had to contribute from their available resources to meet urgent government needs elsewhere; consequently, managers were motivated to share profits immediately, lest they be taken by government, rather than to save them for reinvestment in their enterprises. Finally, "government supervision" usually brought with it certain monopoly rights or concessions, originally granted to assist competition with the foreigner, but soon used as props to compensate for inefficiency. Yet despite its economic inefficiency, the merchant-bureaucrat combination became the principal device for initiating industrial enterprises.

Li Hung-chang's Industrial Empire. Impelled by the logic of one industry demanding another, Li with Tong King-sing as his manager began in 1876 to develop a modern coal mine in the Kaiping area about halfway between Tientsin and the Great Wall at Shanhaikuan. This project, also under "government supervision and merchant operation," aimed not only to supply fuel for China Merchants' ships but also to find a southbound cargo for them after they had brought tribute rice north. The use of modern pumps, fans, and hoists soon yielded profits from coal seams that old-style Chinese pit-miners had abandoned. With a dozen Western engineers and modern equipment, the new Kaiping Mining Company (or "Bureau" in Chinese) by 1883 had set up machine shops, produced its own engines, railway cars, and tugboats, and installed local telephones, telegraphs, and a railroad line seven miles long. It was soon producing 250,000 tons of coal a year, most of it consumed in the local North China market. However, Tong King-sing died in 1892 and his successor was a Chinese bannerman close to the Manchu court. Evidently expert in the art of squeeze, the new manager milked the Kaiping Mining Company of its resources, and it became increasingly dependent on foreign loans. In 1900 it was taken over by a British company, represented by an American engineer, (later President) Herbert C. Hoover. After 1912 Kaiping was absorbed into the Sino-British Kailan Mining Administration.

Thus in North China, the steamship brought the coal mine, which required in turn a railroad. They came in succession, but neither quickly nor easily. Early railway projects had been vetoed by officials interested in forestalling foreign exploitation. In 1863 foreign proposals to usher in China's railway age by building a Shanghai-Soochow line had been refused by Governor Li Hung-chang with the oft-repeated dictum that any railways in China should be handled by Chinese. A small, unauthorized Shanghai-Wusung line, opened by foreigners in 1876 (see Plate 42), was purchased the next year by the Nanking governor-general (Shen Pao-chen, 1820–1879, a son-in-law of Commissioner Lin of the Opium War and a foe of corruption), who promptly had it torn up. Against this background the railway begun for Kaiping coal could be extended only slowly — south to Tientsin in 1888, northeast to Shanhaikuan in 1894, and to the outskirts of Peking in 1896, about 240 miles in all. Except for a short line in Formosa, this was the sum of China's response to the railroad age after thirty years of agitation.

The reasons for this retardation are instructive. First, the water transport network, using both cheap manpower and steamships, was well developed and offered severe competition for railways except in North China. Steamships had penetrated China on waterways that went far into the interior, but railroads had to invade Chinese life much more directly, crossing canals and rice fields, disturbing grave mounds, and adversely affecting the spirits of "wind and water" (*feng-shui*) that played a cosmic role in the growth of crops and the prosperity of people.

Popular superstitions, alarm, and xenophobic opposition could be easily aroused. Thus the density of population, the intensive use of land, and the high land values, when combined with popular sentiment, made any right of way a costly and difficult investment. Moreover, capital was not easily mobilized; government finances were weak, while bond issues and other devices for the creation of credit were underdeveloped. Finally, Peking's defensive strategy was to oppose both foreign-run railroads and big foreign loans for Chinese lines.

Enough has been said to indicate that the Chinese who managed industrial enterprises in the late Ch'ing period, contemporaries of those far-distant entrepreneurs who were building up American industries, had to have an unusual combination of social, political, and economic capacities. The mandarin-industrialist who rose to the top of Li Hung-chang's industrial empire was Sheng Hsüan-huai (1844–1916), who had passed the district level examinations but had failed three times at the provincial level. He became Li's principal deputy for industrial matters. After being assistant manager of the China Merchants' line, Sheng organized another "government-supervised, merchant-operated" enterprise, the Imperial Telegraph Administration. Despite its official-sounding name (in Chinese it was called the "central telegraph bureau"), this company built up its capital of some two million dollars by selling shares to "merchants," and particularly to Sheng and others in the management. The government made loans and policed the telegraph lines, to protect them against irate farmers fearful of the tall poles and their effect on geomantic forces of "wind and water"; but the profits went into annual returns of as much as 20 per cent to the shareholders. Beginning with the Tientsin-Shanghai line in 1881, the company installed in the next two decades some 14,000 miles of wires connecting principal cities and reaching strategic places on the frontiers. Meanwhile some 20,000 miles of telegraph lines were installed by provincial governments. Until after 1900, when the company's lines were gradually nationalized, Li Hung-chang through his deputy, Sheng, controlled the telegraph administration all over the country, representing its interests to the throne, appointing its personnel and protecting them against charges of corruption.

In the industrialization of many countries, machine production of cotton goods had been the leading industry. Cotton mills got started in Japan in the 1880's. As early as 1878 Li began to sponsor a Chinese textile mill to compete with foreign imports. Yet the Shanghai Cotton Cloth Mill, on the usual "government-supervised, merchant-operated" basis, did not get into production for many years. The throne granted it tax exemption and a ten-year monopoly to produce cotton cloth and yarn; foreign machinery and engineers arrived. But merchant shares were subscribed in inadequate amounts and the first manager, the famous scholar-comprador Cheng Kuan-ying, invested the funds unwisely, some said for his own profit. After Sheng Hsüan-huai took over the project in 1887, he financed the mill with loans from the China Merchants' steamship company, which he also headed, and from Li Hung-chang's provincial government in Chihli. Beginning in 1890, some 4000 factory workers were soon turning out excellent cloth and yarn, and 25 per cent was paid on shares in 1893, when the mill unfortunately burned down. Undaunted, Li and Sheng planned to set up eleven more mills, monopolize a newly created Chinese textile industry, and eliminate foreign imports. They had five mills in operation when the Sino-Japanese War of 1894–95 cut short their hopes.

There were of course many other, less well known enterprises in China in this period, yet all together they were not enough to keep China from falling behind the other major countries.

THE SLOW PROGRESS OF MODERNIZATION IN THE 1870's AND 1880's

The material growth of the treaty ports with their commerce and industry was of course accompanied by intellectual and cultural innovation. Yet the new ideas and attitudes got from Western contact remained minor elements in the broad stream of Chinese tradition. The wearing of the queue, the long gown of the scholar, the bound feet of women, marriage and funeral processions and the palanquins of officials passing through the crowded streets — the whole appearance of Chinese life remained unaffected by any vogue for things Western such as was sweeping contemporary Japan. Ideas of change were spreading, but very slowly. If we look at such new developments as the modern post office, the press, and the training of students abroad, we see a common pattern: in each case China's modernization was inspired by Western examples and yet had to be superimposed upon old indigenous institutions, which persisted so strongly as to slow down the need or demand for innovation.

The Modern Post Office. Robert Hart early began to work toward setting up a nationwide postal service to facilitate the flow of correspondence, just as the Maritime Customs facilitated the flow of foreign trade. But it took him thirty years because he found China's needs already met, though at a premodern level of efficiency, by several established institutions which formed vested interests against change.

First, there were the 1600 or so official horse-post stations (*i-chan*) on the five main routes radiating from Peking over the empire (see page 105). At an annual cost to Peking of about three million taels, this ancient system moved official persons, correspondence, goods, and money at various rates of speed by all manner of conveyances. An official traveling these routes might use eight chair-bearers, two or three carts, and half a dozen horses on the North China Plain, and up to 100 bearers, porters, and guards in mountainous terrain in the south. This system of official as opposed to public conveyance was a burdensome expense to localities along the way but unavoidable in the absence of a modern road and railway network.

For the postal needs of the common people, secondly, there was a great abundance of commercial "letter hongs" (*min-hsin chü*, lit. "people's letter offices"), which forwarded private mail for small fees according to the distance and profitability of the route. These private enterprises had grown up in the wake of banking and business firms — like the 49 Shansi banks which at one time had 414 branches in 83 places. With commercial correspondence passing regularly, it became profitable to offer privately managed mail services to the general public — without attempting, however, to reach all parts of China. By the end of the century there were 300 letter hongs registered in the 24 treaty ports and many more in the country as a whole.

Finally, Western governments set up their own postal services between major cities in foreign trade and opened this facility to foreign residents. Covered by extraterritorial treaty rights, there were eventually dozens of these foreign post offices operating in China.

Hart succeeded in developing a modern national post, in the midst of all these vested interests, by using the resources of the Maritime Customs with cautious perseverance. Given the task of transmitting legation mails overland to Peking in wintertime, the Customs gradually built up a postal department. Eventually it got foreign steamers in Chinese waters to carry only the mail of the imperial post office, which was formally set up as part of the Customs in 1896. In this way the new Customs post was able to intervene and become the agency for all steamer shipment of the mails of the private letter hongs. By degrees over the decades its broad national service began to put its old-style competitors out of business.

Beginnings of Chinese Journalism. The rise of professional journalism was another index of China's modernization which began under Western stimulus in the treaty ports. Yet the growth of the modern Chinese press was influenced by certain venerable antecedents and limitations.

The famous *Peking Gazette* of the Ming and Ch'ing periods dated back at least to the T'ang when the official network of post stations was already well developed as a means of conveying persons and documents, and so also of spreading news, from the capital to the major provincial centers. Although the *Peking Gazette* reproduced official documents made public at the court, it was not an official publication nor did it appear in one single form: a number of private firms in Peking produced and distributed the so-called gazettes on a commercial basis. Thus they disseminated court news, memorials, and imperial documents among the scholar-gentry class all over the empire, parallel to the flow of secret official correspondence. Similar gazettes were produced commercially in provincial capitals.

In the cities news was also spread by commercial handbills or newsprints (*hsin-wen chih*), produced as a side line by printing shops and hawked in the streets when news seemed salable. This embryonic news press was commonly printed from blocks of clay or wax, on which characters could be incised more quickly but would be correspondingly less legible than on woodblocks. Price lists distributed by guilds and book publishing, done usually under official or scholar-gentry auspices, completed the traditional mechanisms for spreading printed information.

Protestant missionaries injected a revolutionary element into these ancient channels. Barred from the interior until the 1860's, they early resorted to print to spread the gospel in Chinese translation; and they also recognized that Western "knowledge and science are the handmaids of religion." The London Missionary Society set up a press at Malacca in 1815 and published a monthly magazine in Chinese. Other missionaries followed this example, in Batavia, Singapore, Macao, and Canton, and later, after the opening of the treaty ports, in Hong Kong and Shanghai. Besides the missionary periodicals in Chinese, there were English-language newspapers like the *China Mail* (Hong Kong, 1845–) and the *North China Herald* (Shanghai, 1850–) which served the trading community and became the immediate models for modern-style Chinese newspapers.

Chinese journalism finally rose above the purely factual level of imperial gazettes and market reports when men of literary talent began to publish editorial opinion on the news of the day — an activity strictly discountenanced by the dynasty and therefore possible only under treaty-port protection. The pioneer in this field, Wang T'ao (1828–1897?), began life as a classical scholar but then spent the 1850's in Shanghai as Chinese editor of the London Missionary Society press. Having had suspicious contact with the Taiping rebels, he fled to Hong Kong in 1862 under British protection. During the next decade he helped James Legge, who had already translated the *Four Books*, complete his monumental translations of the *Five Classics* (see Vol. I, p. 68). Two years of this period Wang spent with Legge in Scotland. After this long apprenticeship in publishing and contact with the Western world, Wang T'ao became in the 1870's an independent journalist, founding and editing his own daily newspaper in Hong Kong. While he continued to feature court documents from Peking, he also purveyed commercial, local, and foreign news and published his own comments, enriched by his travels in Europe and Japan. After 1884, in Shanghai, he wrote for the leading Chinese daily, *Shun Pao* (founded by an Englishman in 1872).

A hybrid product of Chinese and Western culture, a true denizen of Hong Kong and Shanghai, Wang T'ao was a forerunner — at heart a Chinese patriot, intellectually a critic of the Chinese scene. "When you look at the foreigners," he had written quite early, "with their high noses and deep-set eyes, you can sense how crafty they are. They treat all Chinese very shabbily." Working for them was humiliating. Yet as he saw more of the West, Wang's animus turned also against the apparent causes of China's backwardness — the outworn examinations, the untrained soldiers, the complacent ignorance of technology. Comparing the governments of China and Britain, he saw that borrowing from the West could not stop with mere technical devices but must lead on to institutional change. Western contact generated ideas both of patriotism and of reform.

Sending Students Abroad. The pioneer "returned student" was a poor boy from Macao, Yung Wing (1828–1912), who learned English from the age of seven in missionary schools (partly at the Morrison Education Society, along with the future comprador Tong King-sing) and was sent by missionaries to the United States. He became a Christian and an American citizen and graduated from Yale in 1854. His Yale education revealed to him "responsibilities which the sealed eye of ignorance can never see." He conceived that "through Western education China might be regenerated, become enlightened and powerful." But once he was back in the Sino-foreign society of the treaty ports, Yung Wing, though unusually bilingual, was sometimes hard put to make a living and yet maintain his honor as both a Chinese and a Yale man. He drifted into the tea business. In 1864 he was sent to the United States by Tseng Kuo-fan to buy machinery for the Kiangnan Arsenal.

Not until 1872 were Tseng and Li Hung-chang finally able to realize Yung Wing's long-cherished dream of sending an educational mission to the United States. Under this scheme 120 long-gowned Chinese boys, mainly from poor Cantonese families, went in four classes of 30 each to Hartford, Connecticut, to embark on a proposed fifteen years of Western education as preparation for government service. Under the supervision of Yung Wing and the minor Hanlin scholars who were his colleagues in charge of the mission, the boys were boarded out with families up and down the Connecticut Valley but came periodically to the mission headquarters for Chinese classical studies. Soon, however, they underwent "a gradual but marked transformation" in speech and dress, hiding their queues and developing athletic, exuberant, undecorous ways — becoming Americanized. Yung Wing, who had by now married an American girl and was more Congregational than Confucian in outlook, encouraged this acculturation. His conservative colleagues, however, were appalled, and their outraged criticisms reverberated in Peking. The mission was expensive. Government training schools were developing in China and would cost less. Meanwhile the anti-Chinese movement had been growing up in California, where Oriental exclusion was already a political issue, and a Sino-American treaty of 1880 let the United States unilaterally "suspend" Chinese immigration. West Point and Annapolis were unable to admit Yung Wing's students for training, contrary to the optimistic

Burlingame treaty of 1868. In 1881 the educational mission, for a variety of reasons, was given up.

The incompletely trained students from Hartford who arrived back in Shanghai like displaced persons to kotow before the taotai were greeted with general suspicion. Their advancement would spread heterodoxy and threaten the vested interest of all scholars in the unreformed classical examination system.[1] Consequently Yung Wing's boys contributed to China's modernization mainly through channels that required Western technology or management. Thus 17 went into the navy, 15 and 14 respectively into the telegraph and railroad administrations, 13 into the diplomatic service, 6 to the Kaiping mines, and only 12 became regular officials. However, a number rose to prominence.

In the same era, Li Hung-chang and some other high officials, including those at the Foochow shipyard, sent students to Europe — thirty to England and France in 1877 and others in 1882, 1886, and 1897 — but never on such a large scale as Yung Wing's mission to America. In subsequent Chinese government projects for overseas education, resumed in volume after 1901, care was taken to send abroad students who were above, not below, the critical age of sixteen and therefore less likely to become deracinated.

Christian Missions. The same record of vigorous pioneering and modest results, of great effort and much frustration, typified the missionary movement. After 1870 the growth rate of Christian missions exceeded that of foreign trade or almost any other aspect of Chinese society. Foreign Catholic priests numbered about 250 in 1870, about 750 in 1896. Numbers of Protestants arriving in China roughly doubled every decade. Protestant mission stations increased accordingly — from 35 in 14 places in 1860, to 132 in 79 places by 1880, and to 498 in 356 places in 1900. Yet by 1890, when the 1300 Protestant missionaries outnumbered the Catholics two to one, they had only 37,000 Protestant communicants, compared with the half million Catholics.

The Catholics, by continuing their traditional religious work among the populace in the interior, continued to bear the brunt of the anti-Christian agitation, including scurrilous pamphlets circulated by xenophobic gentry. Riots, attacks, and occasional deaths by violence occurred in various parts of the empire from year to year, culminating in 1891 in several riots in the Yangtze Valley. These were evidently inspired by the receipt of children in Catholic orphanages as well as by the expansion of foreign-style mission properties.

[1] Li Hung-chang and others had been unable to get "foreign matters" (*yang-wu*) into the examinations. The later and oft-cited addition of mathematics as a special subject in 1887 was no real reform: every three years it would permit only 3 out of 283 provincial graduates to know some mathematics!

The Protestants, on the other hand, became more overtly involved in the work of modernization. Their missionary force was composed of Americans and Britishers, men and women, in roughly equal numbers, drawn mainly from the middle class or from rural areas, and including many in the early years without much higher education. They remained thoroughly committed to evangelism in the cause of spiritual salvation, but an increasing minority began to see that good works and social services were more welcome and might be more fruitful than evangelism alone. Reform came naturally to them. Their efforts to change individual conduct set them vigorously against many social customs and institutions — against polygamy, child marriage, foot-binding, gambling, superstitions like fortune-telling, the idolatry of other religions, and even Confucian reverence for ancestors, as well as infanticide and all aspects of the opium evil. On the positive side they continued to spread the holy word by translating, writing tracts, and publishing books and periodicals. Literacy and therefore schooling were necessary to the reception of the gospel, and an educated native pastorate to its propagation. By 1877, when the first General Conference of Protestant Missionaries surveyed the scene, there were 20 theological schools with 231 students who might create a native ministry.

Missionaries generally thought education should serve Christianity and some at first refused to teach English, since it might only help boys seek careers in the treaty ports. Chinese students, to be sure, sometimes accepted Christianity to get an education, and by 1890 the Protestants had almost half as many students in their schools (17,000) as they had communicants in their churches. But the Protestant stress on the individual's comprehension of the Scriptures inevitably led toward Western learning in general.

Protestant primary schools gradually grew to secondary level, came to be called "colleges" (like St. John's College at Shanghai after 1879), and in time became counterparts, if not offshoots, of the denominational colleges which had been created by the New England diaspora in the Middle West earlier in the century. Christian colleges in the United States served as seedbeds of the missionary movement in China. The missionary band from Oberlin College, in 1881, were forerunners of the Student Volunteer Movement for Foreign Missions that began to recruit American youths for mission work, much as the China Inland Mission was doing in Britain, Scandinavia, and Germany, as well as the United States.

Secular education gained ground in the missionary curriculum along with the growth of medical missions, dispensaries, hospitals, and medical schools for Chinese doctors. By 1890, when the second General Conference of Protestant Missionaries met, they had a "Medical Missionary Association of China" in action parallel to their "Educational Association of China." Care was extended to opium addicts, the blind, and the deaf. Soon efforts were being made to meet the immediate crisis of famine. There was no limit to the Christian opportunity for good works in China.

One Baptist who fought the terrible famine of 1877–79 in Shansi was Timothy Richard (1845–1919), a Welshman of broad imagination who believed that Christianity, as the dynamic of Western civilization, could win China more effectively in proportion as China accepted the fruits of Western civilization in general. Hudson Taylor and his China Inland Mission concentrated narrowly on saving souls from hellfire through faith and prayerful conversion with the help of the Bible; Timothy Richard, no less devout, believed that the Kingdom of God was "to be established not only in the hearts of men, but also in all institutions on earth," that "those who did the best to improve this world were best fitted for eternal bliss hereafter." He believed in human progress, Western-style, as part of God's plan, and in good works, especially education, as necessary to progress. From 1891, as secretary of the SDK (Society for the Diffusion of Christian and General Knowledge among the Chinese), he sought to spread Western learning and ideas of reform, particularly among the scholar and official classes.

In this broad enterprise Richard had an ally in Young J. Allen (1836–1907), whose mission support from Georgia had ceased with the Civil War and who had become a translator and editor, publishing from 1868 a weekly "mission news" (*Chiao-hui hsin-pao*) for circulation among the Chinese Christian community. Allen expanded this into *The Globe Magazine* (*Wan-kuo kung-pao*, lit. "international gazette," later translated *Review of the Times*), which spread world news and "knowledge relating to Geography, History, Civilization . . . and general progress of Western countries." Weekly from 1875 to 1883 and monthly from 1889 to 1907 this journal, ably edited by Chinese scholars, presented in literary Chinese a wide selection of Western ideas and information, including Timothy Richard's proposals for remaking China. It became in fact one source of the Reform Movement of the late 1890's.

Yet, like Wang T'ao's editorials and Yung Wing's educational mission, missionary espousals of reform were peripheral to Chinese life, products of the new Sino-Western community in the port cities, remote from the peasant masses or even the bulk of the scholar gentry. Some leading officials might be informed, stimulated, and even guided by this treaty-port or missionary activity. But until Japan's smashing victory of 1895, China remained relatively inert, still firmly in the grip of tradition.

To some Westerners, the Chinese people seemed perversely unchanging. The most widely-read missionary publicist of the day, Arthur H. Smith (1845–1932), used these chapter titles in his classic description of Chinese ways and Western frustration, *Chinese Characteristics* (1890): Face, Economy, Industry, Politeness, The Disregard of Accuracy, The Talent for Misunderstanding, The Talent for Indirection, Flexible Inflexibility, Intellectual Turbidity, The Absence of Nerves, Contempt for Foreigners, The Absence of Public Spirit, Conservatism. Dr. Smith went on to catalogue virtues as well as shortcomings, but the prevailing tone was exasperation.

FOREIGN ENCROACHMENT AND CHINESE RESISTANCE

If knowledge from abroad stimulated change only gradually, foreign aggression induced it more directly. The treaty system had been set up by force and was maintained by the clear threat that the treaty powers would again use force if necessary. So maintained, the treaties provided legal bases for foreign participation in the life of the Chinese people. Sooner or later this increasing foreign activity within the local scene, bringing with it a broader view of the world and the foreign example of patriotic concern for national interests, would rouse a nationalistic Chinese response. More immediately, however, the growth of nationalism was stimulated by the encroachments of foreign powers in the tributary states on the frontiers of the Ch'ing empire.

Imperialist rivalry, nibbling at the periphery of the Chinese world, intensified after 1870 for a number of reasons. In Europe the unification of Italy and Germany in the 1860's brought on an intensified economic nationalism. The oldest established democracies, Britain and France, were soon moved to lead the way in colonial expansion. Britain in particular, convinced that her world-wide trade depended on holding colonies, greatly expanded her empire. The literate citizenry of every European power, newly in contact with world events through the growth of the urban press, developed varying degrees of enthusiasm for national exploits and overseas expansion. These were quickly rationalized by the doctrine of Social Darwinism — that races and nations necessarily struggle for survival, and only the fittest survive. The religious enthusiasm of missionaries was echoed in the idealism, sense of duty, and patriotism of administrators conscious of the "white man's burden."

This general movement of European expansion through great-power rivalry affected China more directly after the Suez Canal in 1869 and telegraph cables in 1870–71 brought the Western public closer to the Far East. Until then, the initiative in Sino-foreign relations had lain with the man-on-the-spot. A Harry Parkes or a Nikolai Muraviev had had to act first and report later. Instructions from home had never quite caught up with the situation on the far frontier. Now, whole nations or at least their newspaper-reading publics became, psychologically, men-on-the-spot, alarmed or elated by the day's events and likely to clamor for action.

Moreover, as the competition for colonies developed, it became apparent that the Chinese empire had uncertain or unstable frontiers. Maps were usually unreliable, historical claims often conflicted, and the limits of Ch'ing authority came increasingly into dispute. To the uncertainties of terrain were added the vagueness and timidity of Peking's claims to suzerainty over tributary states. The tribute system (see page 72) was a defensive more than an imperialistic institution, based less on clear-cut treaty law than on Confucian ethics, less on tangible military domination than on cultural supremacy. When called upon either to take responsibility for disorders in tributary areas and to recompense aggrieved foreigners, or else to renounce suzerain jurisdiction, the Tsungli Yamen's first impulse was to avoid responsibility so as to avoid payment of indemnities. Thus the Ryūkyū (Liu-ch'iu) Islands, Formosa, Korea, Vietnam, and areas of Central Asia gradually became fair game for foreign colonial expansion.

In seizing the opportunities thus presented, the imperialist powers were inspired by mutual fear and emulation. Japan, Britain, Russia, and even the United States and France jockeyed in Korea for positions of influence. Britain and Russia eyed each other suspiciously in Central Asia and Tibet. Britain and France raced to penetrate Southwest China while in the process of absorbing Burma and Indo-China.

Certain patterns characterized this rivalry. Britain, established in China with the lion's share of foreign trade, was on the defensive; yet her defense sometimes took a vigorously aggressive form. The United States in the latter half of the nineteenth century rather passively accepted the fruits, while decrying the methods, of Britain's commercial imperialism. Russia and France, less involved in trade, sought to expand their power territorially from their respective bases in the Maritime Province and in Cochin China, which they had occupied in the 1850's and 1860's. In 1893 they became allies. Japan meanwhile eyed nearby territories with strategic concern for her own defense while building up her military capacity. In this society of warring states, the senescent Ch'ing regime was increasingly threatened.

In this section we look first at the dangers that China faced in a succession of crises in her foreign relations with Russia, France, and Japan. These dangers inspired efforts at military modernization and also ideas about institutional reform. When the military efforts were proved to have been ineffective, by Japan's victory in 1895, reform became the order of the day. We are here concerned, then, with the foreign relations which preceded and formed the background of the Reform Movement in China. The next chapter deals with the broader questions of imperialism and colonialism in East Asia as a whole.

Central Asia and Russia. The territorial integrity of the Ch'ing empire was endangered in the 1870's on its farthest northwestern frontier, in Chinese Turkestan. Of the three principal areas of concern to Ch'ing strategists, the first was the region around Hami (now known by another designation as Komul), which was the key point of ingress to Central Asia across the desert road from China's northwest province of Kansu.

The Hami region, as well as Turfan, Urumchi (Tihwa), and other centers nearby to the west, had been the Manchus' logistic base for military expeditions farther west and also a source of Turkish- or "Turkic"-speaking allies and administrators who could assist in the Ch'ing conquest and rule of Central Asia.

The second strategic area centered on the grazing lands of the Ili River valley, between the Altai Mountains on the north and the "Mountains of Heaven" (T'ien Shan) on the south. This included the corridor through which the Mongol conquerors had debouched westward in the thirteenth century. In the late seventeenth and early eighteenth centuries it had been the homeland of the Dzungar tribe of the Western Mongols. These fierce warriors had sent their expeditions into Eastern Mongolia, the Tarim basin, and even Tibet in bold defiance of the Ch'ing dynasty until it finally succeeded in annihilating them in the 1750's (see Vol. I, pp. 359–60). Thereafter the Ili region had been populated by penal colonies and military garrisons, ruled by a military governor at the chief city, Kuldja. In this and other Ch'ing outposts, Chinese tea, silk, and cotton textiles were traded for horses from the Kazakh tribal lands to the northwest.

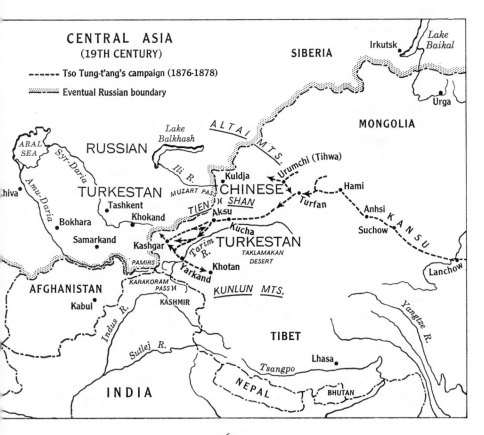

The third region, least firmly under Ch'ing control, consisted of the oasis cities in the Tarim River basin south of the T'ien Shan and east of the Pamir massif, a region sometimes called Kashgaria after the principal oasis and focus of the trade routes. In these centers the population was predominantly Turkic-speaking and Moslem, much the same as in the trading states west of the Pamirs. The two regions were closely connected by language, religion, culture, trade, and politics, for Central Asia both east and west of the Pamirs had been ruled in succession by the Mongol Khanate of Chaghadai, the empire of Tamerlane (in the thirteenth and fourteenth centuries, see Vol. I, pp. 269, 325), and then from the fourteenth to the seventeenth centuries by the Moghuls, warriors who claimed Mongol descent though Turkic in language and Moslem in religion. Latest in this sequence of rulers were the members of a religious clan, the Khoja (also Hodja or Khodja) family, descended from the Prophet, who had risen to power in many of the oasis cities in the late seventeenth century. Khoja rulers in Kashgaria thus had close ties west of the Pamirs and could find support there. Although Khoja rulers were driven out of the oases of Yarkand and Kashgar in 1759–60 by the Ch'ing, some of their descendants took refuge in Khokand (ancient Ferghana) across the mountains to the west. The Khokand khanate became a center of commercial expansion, developing a tributary trade with the Ch'ing. It was also a base for anti-Ch'ing rebels. Khokand aided one of the Khojas (Jehangir) when he launched a holy war against the Ch'ing and invaded Kashgaria in 1826–27 (see Plate 8). This pattern was repeated by others. Ch'ing supremacy was maintained only by constant effort.

In the nineteenth century the Moslems of Central Asia quite lacked a modern sense of nationalism; the name Uighur Turks, for example, was not yet used as a designation. The Ch'ing governors (*amban*) in Kashgaria had conferred the title of *beg*, together with lands and serfs, on some 270 local chiefs who thus formed a local ruling class nominally beholden to Peking. Nevertheless, being on the farthest fringe of the Chinese world, they could not easily be kept under control.

By 1860, after only a century of Ch'ing rule, Chinese or Eastern Turkestan was of increasing interest to the expanding empires of Russia and Britain. The Russians in particular, encroaching steadily southward and southeast across the Kirghiz and Kazakh steppe, were about to take over Western or Russian Turkestan with its cotton production and its strategic access to the northern fringes of British India. Meanwhile Peking kept a tenuous hold on Kashgaria and Ili, at a distance of 3500 miles and six weeks by horse-post. This was dictated by a strong tradition of strategic, rather than economic, concern for the control of the western borders of Mongolia.

In 1862 the Moslem rebellion in Northwest China led to a rising in Chinese Turkestan which got Khoja support from Khokand. A Khokandian adventurer, Yakub Beg, soon seized power and ruled much of the Tarim basin as an independent Moslem state from 1865 to 1877, in militant defiance of the Ch'ing. Yakub Beg found himself at once in the midst of Anglo-Russian rivalry. He had already been among those fighting against the gradual Russian absorption of the khanates west of the Pamirs, where the Russians during the late 1860's and early 1870's took over Tashkent, Samarkand, Bokhara, Khiva, and Khokand. In 1871, to forestall Yakub and British influence, the Russians moved troops into the strategic Ili River valley and occupied the commercial center of Kuldja, where they had had a consul and a regulated trade since 1851 (see page 172). The Russians promised Peking to withdraw from Ili whenever Ch'ing control should be re-established. They then signed a trade treaty with Yakub in 1872. The latter meanwhile got recognition and arms from British India, and a commercial treaty in 1874, as well as arms and the title "Commander of the Faithful" from the Sultan of Turkey, whom Britain was supporting as would-be leader of the Islamic world in a common front against Russian expansion.

Peking by the mid-1870's thus faced a crisis. Its far northwestern territories were out of control. The region north of the T'ien Shan (*T'ien-shan pei-lu*) was occupied by the Russians in Ili and by Chinese-speaking Moslems (called Dungans) who had rebelled in the east. The larger region south of the T'ien Shan (*T'ien-shan nan-lu*) was held by the rebel Moslem regime of Yakub which had been recognized by Russia and Britain and had Anglo-Turkish support. Moreover, the Russians seemed eager to invade the Tarim basin, where the population was predominantly Uighur Turkish with only a small Chinese minority. Although Tso Tsung-t'ang's forces had suppressed the Northwest Moslems in 1873, they were in Kansu province, roughly as far from Yakub's capital at Kashgar as Kansas City is from Los Angeles, on a route that crossed many hundred miles of desert and required ninety days' travel by caravan. At the same time China was embroiled with Japan over the Formosa issue (see page 241).

This crisis evoked two schools of strategy. Li Hung-chang and others concerned with "self-strengthening" and coastal defense against seaborne aggression, opposed the financing of a costly effort by Tso Tsung-t'ang to reconquer unproductive territory in far-off Central Asia. After a great debate in memorials presented to the throne, Tso won out and went ahead. Central Asia had bulked large in the dynasty's traditional strategy of defense against the Mongols; its recovery was also deemed necessary to show reverence for the imperial ancestors. Funds were allocated from eleven provinces. At the same time, Tso through his agent (Hu Kuang-yung), one of the early Chinese financiers in the treaty ports, was raising foreign and Chinese loans in Shanghai to buy his Western cannon and operate an arsenal and a woolen mill at Lanchow. Meanwhile he fed and clothed his troops partly by making them farmers to grow grain and cotton. He built up a base area around Suchow in Kansu, with advanced bases farther west. There he accumulated large grain supplies while reducing his army to a selected 60,000 men, about half from his native Hunan.

In 1876 Tso's troops, led by able commanders, dashed across the desert route and seized Urumchi and other strategic centers giving access to the regions both north and south of the T'ien Shan. Tso mercilessly slaughtered the Chinese-speaking Moslem rebels of the northern region, treating them as domestic traitors. He then invaded the Tarim basin south of the mountains, treating the Uighur Turkish population more leniently as frontier rebels. Yakub died in 1877. By 1878 Tso had recovered all Chinese Turkestan except the Ili region. He had demonstrated China's military capacity and also the efficacy of traditional methods, aided by modern guns, for the control of Central Asia.

This spectacular achievement led Peking to demand that Russia evacuate Ili. For this purpose the Manchu grandee Ch'ung-hou (who had gone to France in 1870 to apologize for the Tientsin massacre) negotiated in 1879 the Treaty of Livadia. But he fatuously conceded so much to Russia — the western part of Ili, the strategic Muzart pass into the Tarim basin, wide-ranging trade concessions, and an indemnity — that he was denounced, tried at Peking, and condemned to be beheaded. A great diplomatic furor and war scare ensued. Foreign diplomats were all against the decapitation of a diplomat. Tso Tsung-t'ang massed troops; and the Russians mobilized troops in Central Asia and ships in the Far East. But the crisis passed. Queen Victoria urged that the Empress Dowager spare Ch'ung-hou, and this was done. Then in 1881 the son of Tseng Kuo-fan, Tseng Chi-tse (known in the West as "Marquis Tseng"), negotiated the Treaty of St. Petersburg by which China paid a larger indemnity but regained most of the Ili area including the strategic passes. In 1884 Chinese Turkestan was made a province under the name Sinkiang (*Hsin-chiang*, "The New Dominion"), given it originally by the Ch'ien-lung Emperor.

This outcome fostered a resurgence of self-confidence in China's military and diplomatic capacity. It also confirmed the conservatives in their easy talk of fighting off foreign aggression while complacently opposing Westernization. During the 1880's the Ch'ing empire continued to avoid the problem of modernizing.

Establishment of Diplomatic Missions Abroad. The Ch'ing had used diplomacy to check foreign invaders. Why then was Peking so slow to send abroad envoys who could observe the enemy's home circumstances and defend China's interests? Western ministers resided in Peking from 1861. But the Burlingame mission of 1868–70, inspired by Robert Hart, achieved no permanent result; later when Ch'ung-hou was sent to France, it was only to apologize for the Tientsin Massacre of 1870. No diplomatic mission functioned abroad until 1877.

This pattern of inertia had its roots in culture, psychology, and politics. Traditionally, envoys had gone abroad in times of strength to spread the imperial prestige, but in times of weakness to beg peace from barbarian tribes. Once the imperial prestige had been shattered by the unequal treaties and the stationing at Peking of Western ministers who need not kotow, foreign relations had become humiliating. Stationing envoys abroad, in this backward-looking view, could only compound the humiliation. No self-respecting official wanted such a post.

Beneath this level of wounded pride and horror of things barbarian lay a practical aspect of Ch'ing politics. The power of Westernizers like Li Hung-chang grew with Western contact but could best be checked and balanced by tolerating the shrill accusations of conservative censors and others who condemned all association with foreigners as simple treason. The Empress Dowager accordingly gave ear to both sides and profited from the stalemate.

The impasse was broken in the 1870's by an object lesson administered by Japan: she had signed a reciprocal commercial treaty, negotiating with Li in 1871, but China failed to exchange envoys and consuls as provided. When Japan's special ambassador in 1873 preceded the other powers' ministers in the audience granted by the T'ung-chih Emperor, he also asked compensation for the Ryūkyū (Liu-ch'iu) islanders killed in Formosa (see page 241). Foolishly, the Tsungli Yamen did not contest Japan's suzerainty over the Ryūkyū Islands, which had long been formally tributary to China although controlled by the Satsuma *han* of Japan. Worse still, to avoid paying Japan compensation, the Yamen disclaimed responsibility for the Formosan aborigines, and so the restive Japanese samurai sent their punitive expedition to Formosa in 1874. With the British minister to China (Sir Thomas Wade) as mediator, war was averted, China paid an indemnity, and the Japanese withdrew from Formosa. But China's weakness had been disclosed. As the British minister to Japan (Sir Harry Parkes) said, she seemed "willing to pay for being invaded."

Li and other Westernizers made the point that a Chinese envoy in Japan might have averted this costly incident. Prolonged debate ensued. But by the time the court decided to establish missions abroad, another incident had already necessitated another mission of apology.

As a British exploratory expedition made its way from Burma into Yunnan in 1875, hoping to open a new overland trade route to tap the fabled wealth of Southwest China, a British interpreter (A. R. Margary) was murdered by armed Chinese. Wade seized the chance to demand indemnity, apology, refinement of rules for Sino-foreign intercourse, and trade concessions, all of which were embodied in the final capstone of the treaty system, the Chefoo Agreement, which he negotiated with Li Hung-chang at the treaty port of Chefoo, Shantung, in 1876.

China's first resident minister abroad, Kuo Sung-tao (1818–1891), came to London in 1877 in this context of humiliation by foreign powers. Kuo was from Hunan, a Hanlin scholar and a friend of Tseng Kuo-fan, loyal and incorruptible. He had studied the barbarians, old and new, and concluded that the Westerners were an unprecedented problem, against whom force would be futile. He was neither tactful nor an opportunist and when appointed to England became the butt of widespread vituperation in China: "Unable to serve men, why is he able to serve devils?", as one critic's scroll put it. In his reports from London, Kuo praised railways, telegraphs, and mines, attacked China's superstitious tolerance of *feng-shui* and supine indulgence in opium, and admired the 200 Japanese whom he found learning British technology: "The Japanese minister . . . said that the natural resources of the universe can be developed by Westerners. They do the hard part — we do the easy part . . . but until now not a single thing had been developed in China. . . . I was so embarrased that I could make no reply."

Kuo's outspoken advocacy of Westernization aggravated the die-hards' defamation of him. As he said, "They impose their ignorant ideas on the court under the guise of public opinion. The court encourages them to do this." When his diary was published by the Tsungli Yamen, the court was prevailed upon to order the printing blocks destroyed. When Kuo returned in 1879 he went straight into retirement in Hunan.

With such acrimony, reluctance, and sense of defeat did the Middle Kingdom enter the modern world. Missions were established in the United States, Germany, France, Japan, and Russia by 1879, only to meet further crises.

Some early diplomats, however, contributed to change at home. For example, the poet Huang Tsun-hsien (1848–1905), onetime counselor of legation in Tōkyō, published in 1890 a laudatory account of Japan's achievements and later became an active reformer. For Chinese officialdom, legations abroad became windows on the Western world.

The Sino-French War. The principal tributary of China on the south, called by its own people Vietnam, was known in China and in the nineteenth-century West as Annam. Between 1858 and 1885 France by degrees made the empire of Annam into a French colony, no longer tributary to China. This colonial venture was a part of French imperialism in East Asia in general, which will be discussed in the next chapter (see pages 453 ff.). Here we are concerned with the war into which France and China drifted in 1883–85 in Tongking (North Vietnam) as a result of French encroachment there.

The concurrent Sino-French hostilities and negotiations during this two-year period confused observers at the time and have confused historians since. One complicating factor was the multiplicity of authorities. In France four cabinets came and went between the first (1880–1881) and the second (1883–1885) ministries of the arch-imperialist Jules Ferry. The French navy was a jealous rival of the foreign office. Negotiations were carried on in Paris, Peking, Shanghai, and Tientsin by three French ministers, a chargé, and a naval officer, and on the Chinese side by Li Hung-chang and Robert Hart among others, in addition to the Tsungli Yamen and its minister in Paris, Marquis Tseng. The negotiators of both sides were harassed by compatriots whose clamor for war increased every time their side was defeated.

A war party had emerged in the councils of the Ch'ing government during the Ili crisis with Russia. The suppression of rebels in the 1860's and 1870's had left the Ch'ing bureaucracy sprinkled with old soldiers in the garb of civil officials, and these took heart at Tso Tsung-t'ang's success in Central Asia. But by 1880 the most bellicose intransigeance in foreign affairs was advocated at Peking by half a dozen younger scholars who had become Hanlin academicians in the 1860's. They were known as the "purification clique" (*ch'ing-liu tang*). Brilliant memorialists and sycophants of the power-holder, these men had defended the Empress Dowager when she outraged genuine Confucians by breaking the imperial succession and having her nephew succeed her son on the throne. Invoking the Classics and the great tradition, they attacked the older advocates of "self-strengthening" as appeasers and supported a militant posture against Russia and France. In 1884 when French victories led to the dismissal of Prince Kung and the Grand Council, the "purification clique" came briefly into positions of power, only to suffer defeat and eclipse in turn through France's further victories. The most able member of this clique, and the only one to survive in power, was Chang Chih-tung (1837–1909), who had clamored for the head of Ch'ung-hou in 1879. He became governor-general of Kwangtung and Kwangsi in 1884 and proved his practical capacity in support of the war effort.

Sino-French negotiations began almost as early as the hostilities. In late 1882 Li Hung-chang worked out a fruitless agreement with the French minister. In May 1884 he drew up with a French naval officer another settlement, known as the Li-Fournier convention, which provided that China should withdraw her troops and admit French trade through Tongking while France should keep Annam and her treaty rights there and claim no indemnity from China. For this deal the war party excoriated Li in forty-seven memorials, the court refused to accept the loss of suzerainty, and hostilities continued, sporadically but more violently, along with abortive negotiations. Robert Hart, being in the counsels of Peking but not its politics, began secret talks. In 1885 he sent his London agent of the Maritime Customs (J. D. Campbell) to Paris and with the court's authority settled peace terms with Jules Ferry on the basis of the Li-Fournier convention. Li signed the peace in June 1885.

The extra year of hostilities was costly for China. One French fleet attacked northern Formosa in August 1884; another anchored in Foochow harbor alongside the eleven small Foochow-built wooden steam warships and gunboats which formed the Fukien fleet of the new Chinese navy. The eight French armor-clad vessels were bigger and had heavier guns. When, after five weeks' indecision, Peking let a French ultimatum expire on August 23, the French destroyed nine Chinese vessels in a few minutes and also the shipyard that Tso Tsung-t'ang had founded in 1866 with the aid of French engineers.

On the land French superiority was less marked. Overconfident French troops were occasionally ambushed by Chinese with Remingtons in the Tongking jungle. The French took the delta around Hanoi and, advancing on the main route north to the Kwangsi border, eventually took Langson just south of Chen-nan-kuan (lit., "the pass that guards the south"). The unexpected Chinese recovery of this strategic spot in March 1885 caused the fall of the Ferry cabinet and somewhat salved Chinese pride.

The war against France was China's first defensive action against a modern enemy since the beginning of the "self-strengthening" movement in the 1860's. It disclosed one major fact, that modern arms are ineffective without modern organization and leadership. The best European guns were useless in Chinese hands without adequate training, tactics, supply, communication, strategy, and command. Pagoda Anchorage at Foochow, for example, was some twenty miles from the sea through a narrow passage past forts armed with new Krupp and Armstrong cannon. Yet the command was so ill-informed, disorganized, and indecisive that neither the modern armament nor even traditional tactics of blockage and harassment were used with any vigor against the French. Again, China in 1884 had more than fifty modern warships, a majority built in Chinese yards, but they were of many sorts and under four separate commands. The Nanyang and Peiyang fleets, respectively under the Southern and Northern Commissioners at Nanking and Tientsin, were larger than the Kwangtung and Fukien fleets, but stayed defensively in their home waters. Caution and bureaucratic rivalry, each official saving his own, prevented a national war effort.

One result of the French war, however, was to call forth vigorous manifestations of nationalism, particularly in Kwangtung, which became the chief base area for the forces in Tongking. The long-standing anti-foreignism of the Cantonese was heightened by several things — fear of a French attack, China's declaration of war after the Foochow debacle and Chang Chih-tung's old-style offer of cash rewards for dead French-men. Even without an invasion of the area, widespread riots and pillaging occurred, especially of Catholic and Protestant missions. The modern Chinese-language press in Hong Kong, which was now purveying in-flammatory news to a social stratum of readers much broader than the scholar-literati class, seems to have helped this growth of an urban-centered mass nationalism.

Korea and Japan. During all the alarms of the Ili crisis and the Tongking fighting, Li Hung-chang had kept his eyes on the danger closest to North China, the growth of Japanese power, particularly in Korea. Beginning in the 1870's, Japan's influence there began to rival that of China, cutting away the foundation stone of the tribute system. The "opening" of Korea that occurred in this period created a whole series of crises for Ch'ing diplomacy, just as it brought revolutionary changes upon the Korean state and populace (see pages 461 ff.).

The "Hermit Kingdom" not only stood first among Peking's tribu-taries but also was the last of the ancient kingdoms of East Asia to be laid open to Western contact. Japanese trade had continued at Pusan on a restricted basis somewhat like the Dutch trade at Nagasaki. Other-wise, Korea's seclusion up to the mid-nineteenth century was more complete than Japan's, for Korea relied on the Middle Kingdom like a younger upon an elder brother, to deal with any and all foreign rela-tions, even while keeping the Sino-Korean border itself tightly sealed. The annual tribute ritual, conducted at Peking with the Board of Rites, continued down to the 1860's to be Korea's only legitimate foreign con-tact except for occasional diplomatic missions to the shogun at Edo.

In the nineteenth century, Western vessels, surveying or in stress of weather, more frequently touched the coast. Korea regularly succored the shipwrecked, expelling them to China, but resisted violently all efforts to open trade or even negotiate. In 1866, for example, to obtain redress for the decapitation of French priests, a French fleet tried to negotiate at the river entrance below Seoul and, when frustrated, took reprisals. Western arms proved superior until the French in a picnic spirit attacked a garrison of North Korean tiger-hunters and met an unexpected reverse before withdrawing.

This and other adventurous incidents excited a degree of rivalry to see who could emulate Commodore Perry and "open" Korea. In 1871 the American minister to China, F. F. Low, was sent with five warships to the river mouth below the capital. His surveyors proceeded upriver. Two Americans were wounded. Low demanded an apology, in vain. In retaliation the American fleet destroyed five forts and killed perhaps 250 Koreans, yet in the end it too could only sail away. In each case

Korea adamantly refused to negotiate and felt confirmed, by her apparent victories, in the old policy of seclusion.

Expanding powers in adjacent territory now began to pose more serious threats than Westerners who came by sea. By the mid-1870's some 4000 Koreans, refugees from hard times and harsh government, had defied the seclusion policy by settling in the newly formed Russian Maritime Province to the north. Meanwhile the provoking of a war with Korea had become a fixed aim of frustrated Japanese samurai. In 1873 their plans for invasion were forestalled by cooler heads in Japan (see page 240), but Tōkyō continued to try to open Korea and draw it away from China.

These pressures put Peking squarely between the irresistible foreigners and the immovable Koreans. The two sides had irreconcilable conceptions of China's proper role in the tributary relationship. As early as 1845 the Ch'ing court had explained to Britain quite accurately, if illogically, that Korea could not be opened to trade by China because it was not part of China, and could not open itself to trade because it was not an independent state. As pressures rose, the Tsungli Yamen tended to seek a neutral posture, restraining both sides but neither taking responsibility for Korea's actions, as the powers demanded, nor undertaking to control the powers, as Korea expected. This was a losing policy.

The "Opening" of Korea. In 1875 a party of Japanese, landing from warships surveying the Korean coast, was fired upon. The Tōkyō government was still strongly opposed to an invasion of Korea, but it now determined, with this incident as a pretext, to emulate Commodore Perry by "opening" Korea peacefully through moderate demands for intercourse backed by a show of superior force. The Tsungli Yamen and Li Hung-chang, when approached by Japan's envoy, stuck to the old Sinocentric concept of China's moral but inactive suzerainty over a tributary state — "though Korea is a dependent country of China, it is not a territorial possession; hence in its domestic and foreign affairs it is self-governing." They finally advised Korea to negotiate with Japan. The Japanese warships and transports that anchored off Inchon below Seoul thus secured in February 1876 an unequal treaty modeled on the Western treaties with China and Japan. It opened three ports for Japanese trade — Pusan (in Japanese, Fusan), Inchon (then known as Chemulpo), and Wŏnsan — and declared Korea to be an "independent state." This revolution in the traditionally limited special relationship between Korea and Japan raised the concrete question, when and how would Korea be "opened" to the West? (See map, page 465.)

From 1880 China's relations with Korea were removed from the control of the Board of Rites, which had traditionally handled tribute relations, and put under Li Hung-chang, who with Chinese and British advice had been developing a comprehensive and active policy. First, he hoped to protect Korea against Japanese or Russian absorption by getting her into treaty relations with all the trading powers, whose commerce would create vested interests in Korea's independence. This was the ancient strategy of "using barbarians to control barbarians." Second, Li hoped through Chinese intervention in Korea's domestic affairs to foster a program of reform and "self-strengthening" concurrent with China's own development of naval and military power. This policy recognized that Korea's seclusion was finished and that modernization must be pursued, but it hoped to see Korea modernized under China's tutelage to ward off foreign (non-Chinese) domination.

The new policy was followed when a United States naval diplomat (Commodore R. W. Shufeldt), again following the Perry tradition, tried first through Japan to negotiate a treaty, without avail, and then succeeded in doing so through Li Hung-chang at Tientsin in 1882. Li negotiated for Korea but failed to get into the treaty a clause describing Korea as "a dependent state of the Chinese Empire." Instead, the American treaty recognized Korea's independence. So did the treaties that followed in 1883–86 with the other Western powers, although only the United States and Japan opened legations in Seoul not under their legations in China. In effect, Western international law, including treaties between sovereign states, could not be combined with China's traditional type of suzerainty under the tribute system. China's only alternatives were to intervene actively or to let Korea follow its own course and perhaps in the end be taken over by Japan or Russia.

During the early 1880's the main threat to China's interests and to Korea seemed to come from Russia, which was also the power most feared by Britain. But as time went on, the basic rivalry for domination of Korea developed between China and Japan. At first China with British encouragement seemed to be ahead in this competition. But as modernization got under way within Korea, the more radical reformers gravitated to the Japanese camp because Japan was modernizing more vigorously than China. Korea's domestic struggles between reformers and conservatives, which we will note in the next chapter, thus were affected by the progress of modernization within her two big neighbors.

China's intervention in Korea's domestic affairs was precipitated by a conservative antiforeign rising at Seoul in the summer of 1882, during which a mob attacked the Japanese legation. Both Japan and China sent troops to Korea, but China sent larger numbers. Japan was mollified with a Korean indemnity, and Li now sought to develop preferential Sino-Korean trade relations, appoint advisers, and dominate Korean politics and policy. Yet foreign contact, such as the Korean mission to the United States in 1883, inevitably encouraged reform and hence the pro-Japanese reformers. In 1884, in a planned coup Kim Ok-kyun, Pak Yŏng-hyo, and others killed leading pro-Chinese conservatives and seized the king. But the vigorous young Chinese commander, Yüan Shih-k'ai (1859–1916), defeated the Japanese legation guards and rescued the king. Kim and Pak fled to shelter in Japan.

This crisis was settled in 1885 when Li and Itō Hirobumi negotiated at Tientsin the Li-Itō Convention. This was a mutual abstention agreement by which the two countries agreed to withdraw their troops and military advisers from Korea and in case of trouble notify the other party before sending them back. Behind this stalemate lay a Japanese decision, following a great debate in Tōkyō, to build up further national strength before becoming involved in hostilities abroad. Itō believed that time was on Japan's side, that to fight for Korea prematurely would only benefit Russia. Li, on his part, felt that historical tradition and geographical proximity favored China. But he also noted prophetically, "In about ten years, the wealth and strength of Japan will be admirable. This is China's future, not present, source of trouble."

Li went ahead with an active program of modernization, urging upon Korea many of the reforms that Britain had urged upon China twenty years before: a Korean Customs Service headed by Westerners lent from the Chinese Maritime Customs; an American adviser on foreign affairs; telegraph lines; military training. Li's lieutenant in Seoul as "Resident" from 1885 to 1894, the young and overbearing Yüan Shih-k'ai, sought to preserve the forms of Chinese suzerainty, while American diplomats and missionaries, among others, benevolently fostered Korean independence. Meantime the decade after 1885 saw a steady increase of Japanese influence among young Korean patriots. China's paramount position at Seoul came to depend less on her ancient cultural and political suzerainty than on her claim to be a strong military-naval power, capable of leading Korea toward modernization.

THE FAILURE OF "SELF-STRENGTHENING" AGAINST JAPAN

After 1885 imperial China had a decade of comparative tranquillity in foreign relations. The recent encroachments of Russia, France, and Japan on peripheral areas stimulated a spirit of nationalism and continued efforts at "self-strengthening." The early "self-strengthening" idea of the 1860's — to use Western devices to defend Chinese civilization — was now giving way to a somewhat different concept: to develop Western-style institutions in order to defend the Chinese nation against the Western powers and Japan. The more drastic reform movement of the period after 1894 was foreshadowed in this preceding decade by the broadened scope of the "self-strengthening" movement. With Peking's formal approval the lead continued to be taken largely by provincial officials, who recruited Chinese experts in "foreign matters," hired foreign technicians, raised loans from foreign firms in the treaty ports, imported foreign machinery, and set up training schools and industries in several parts of the country, though on a rather small scale.

These efforts depended on many factors, such as the continuity of a reforming official in one post, with continued support from the court or a powerful patron. Another factor might be the comparative weakness of local vested interests. This seems to have aided developments in Taiwan, where one of Li's lieutenants, Liu Ming-ch'uan (1836–1896), became in 1885 the first governor. Liu pursued a broad program of modernization — an arsenal at the capital, Taipei; a naval force based on the Pescadores Islands; land tax reform based on a land survey and population registration; development of revenues from the government monopolies of camphor, salt, etc.; a modern post office; more telegraph lines and cables; a short railway; a steamship line; and technical schools. He even built up Taipei in Western style, with paved and lighted streets. Liu was not, unfortunately, a genuine Confucian scholar but had risen from the peasant-bandit level as an able commander against the Taipings and Nien. Conservative critics effected his removal in 1891. His successors in Taiwan let most of his program lapse; it had, however, anticipated later developments under Japan.

Chang Chih-tung's Program. Having been converted to modernization by bitter experience in fighting the French, Chang Chih-tung emerged after 1885 as Li Hung-chang's chief rival in "foreign matters," as well as in regional influence and bureaucratic politics. Although governor-general at Canton in 1885–1889 and at Nanking in 1894–1896, Chang found his main regional base at the Wuhan cities (the joint name for Wuchang, Hanyang, and Hankow at the confluence of the Han and Yangtze rivers), where he served as governor-general of Hunan and Hupei for some fifteen years, 1889–1894 and 1896–1907. This long tenure of one post enabled him to build up the appurtenances of regional power — his own staff of subordinates, local sources of revenue, military forces, industries, and political patronage.

Because of his scholastic brilliance and his record of antiforeignism and loyalty to the throne, Chang was less vulnerable than others to conservative attack when he embarked on modernization. Moreover, he gave to "self-strengthening" a philosophical rationale that helped to obviate criticism. As an aristocrat of the intellect, Chang was sometimes not afraid to follow, with due caution, where reason might lead. Even before 1885 he had sought advice from the Welsh missionary Timothy Richard, and he continued to consult and make use of foreign publications and personnel. Becoming a regional leader twenty years later than Li Hung-chang, he brought to the task a less wide-ranging ability but a greater fiscal probity and a burning desire to establish a philosophical sanction for modernization and to fit it theoretically into China's classical tradition. He ended, however, by adjusting the classical tradition to fit modernization.

As Chang set up one modern institution after another — an arsenal and a mint at Canton, an iron foundry at Hanyang, military academies, and technical schools for telegraphy, mining, railways, and industrial arts generally — he confronted the fact that "self-strengthening" steadily eroded the underpinnings of the Confucian order. Defense, for example, required literate officers trained in academies — military men who also qualified as scholars. This broke down the ancient supremacy of *wen* over *wu*, civil over military. Chang Chih-tung in the fashion of the day found classical sanctions for this. To show that the sages had held civil and military in a more even balance, he could quote the *Spring and Autumn Annals*: "Although there are civil affairs, there must be military preparedness." Again, the fact that military command required a mastery of practical military technology blurred the old distinction between superior (scholar-officials who "labor with their minds") and inferior (artisans and other small men who "labor with their strength"). To meet this problem Chang selected his officer candidates from among the degree-holding gentry or sons of gentry, and kept some classical studies in their curriculum. In the result, his Self-Strengthening Army had fine German-trained troops but an officer corps lacking in initiative.

Chang Chih-tung's defense effort took in more and more of Western technology and yet constantly tried to preserve China's traditional learning. At Canton he set up an old-style academy, the Kuang-ya Shu-yüan, where scholarly editors were assembled and a new press published their large collection of some 176 works by Ch'ing authors. In planning a school of Western studies in 1889, Chang selected the obviously utilitarian subjects of mining, chemistry, electricity, and botany, but also included international law. The Self-Strengthening School that he opened at Wuchang in 1893 stressed Western languages and commercial affairs partly to assist the Chinese tea trade, but soon had to concentrate on languages only, as the essential preliminary to all Western studies. All students, however, were to qualify in the Classics too.

While Chang Chih-tung as a regional leader at Wuhan was thus advancing simultaneously into the past and the future, he met a rival not only in Li Hung-chang at Tientsin but also at the court in Peking. When the Empress Dowager retired in 1889, the Kuang-hsü Emperor (1871–1908) assumed nominal control of the government. His character had been formed from the age of five by his closest adviser, the imperial tutor Weng T'ung-ho (1830–1904), a conservative Hanlin scholar who also held key posts such as the presidency of the Board of Revenue (1886–1898). Weng opposed many of Chang Chih-tung's ambitious schemes, just as he opposed some of Li Hung-chang's policies, in a triangular rivalry for power. But about 1889 Weng T'ung-ho also moved toward reform. He began to read with the emperor the essays on "self-strengthening" which Feng Kuei-fen had circulated in the 1860's but which were published only in 1884. "Self-strengthening" and therefore reform were now becoming the doctrines of the young Son of Heaven.

Building the Peiyang Fleet. Meanwhile Li Hung-chang at Tientsin was confronting the hard problem of China's survival in modern warfare. His had become the main effort. His Tientsin arsenal in the 1870's was able to produce about a ton of gunpowder a day and a million bullets a year. In 1880 he set up a naval school, drawing on Foochow personnel and experience and at the same time competing with the southern lead in naval development.

After the French destroyed the Fukien fleet, a Board of Admiralty or "Naval Yamen" (Hai-chün ya-men) was created in 1885 under the nominal headship of Prince Ch'un (1840–1891), who had succeeded Prince Kung in 1884 as the leading Manchu official at Peking. Father of the reigning Kuang-hsü Emperor, he was a corrupt and compliant tool of the Empress Dowager. This new agency, which Robert Hart had been urging ever since the abortive Lay-Osborn flotilla of 1861, was to centralize naval finance and purchasing and build up China's naval power. Soon, however, the new Board of Admiralty not only became as moribund and ineffective as the Tsungli Yamen had been since the cashiering of Prince Kung in 1884; it also became enmeshed in a system of organized corruption.

Its creation had been a gesture acknowledging that a navy must function as a centralized unit, but in fact the centrifugal forces of regionalism perpetuated four fleets in four regions of the China coast. Naval academies were set up below Canton at Whampoa (1880) and at Nanking (1890), in addition to those at Foochow and at Tientsin.

Li Hung-chang as Northern (Peiyang) Commissioner created the principal fighting force, known as the Peiyang fleet. He contracted with foreign firms to build forts and bases in North China, including a naval base at Port Arthur and a fortified depot at Weihaiwei in Shantung. Instead of building his own vessels as Foochow continued to do, Li bought from the big British and German arms firms, deciding on specifications in this rapidly developing technology as best he could amid advice and inducements from many sides. A British naval officer (Captain W. M. Lang) served as his chief adviser until 1890. By 1888 Li's Peiyang fleet of some 25 vessels had nine warships, two of which were 7500-ton German-built battleships with 12-inch Krupp guns and 14-inch armor. Joint maneuvers were occasionaly held with the Southern (Nanyang) fleet based at Shanghai. Li's fleet received more funds than the other three — over a million taels a year during the 1880's. Yet this was less than half his annual expenditure on his Anhwei Army, and after 1891 even these funds diminished.

This late Ch'ing naval effort, as rumored at the time and since confirmed, was starved by the court, which decided instead to build up the new Summer Palace (I Ho Yüan) northwest of Peking as a retreat for the Empress Dowager on her retirement in 1889. The famous marble barge in the big lake there (see page 313) epitomizes this story. It is reminiscent of the palatial extravagance of the Wan-li Emperor that undid the Ming dynasty just four centuries earlier. In traditional style the chief eunuch (Li Lien-ying) and other courtiers encouraged these expenditures in order to line their own pockets. But in modern style the Imperial Household Department with Li Hung-chang's necessary cooperation tried to conceal this misuse of large levies from the provinces under the heading of "naval funds." It also borrowed from treaty-port sources like Jardine, Matheson and Company. The result was that millions of taels went into the Summer Palace project and no additions were made to the Peiyang fleet in the early 1890's, during a period of intensive naval development in Europe and while nine fast ships were being added to the Japanese navy. The Peiyang fleet's smaller units even took to carrying passengers between Port Arthur and Chefoo. This corruption was not new in kind, merely an exacerbation of customary practice. Li could not check the system, whatever may have been his attitude toward it. By 1894 he realized that the Peiyang fleet was inefficient and he did his best to avoid a showdown with Japan.

The First Sino-Japanese War. The outbreak of domestic rebellion in Korea provided the occasion in 1894 for Japanese intervention, which led to Sino-Japanese hostilities. (For background, see pages 463–467.) In the sequence of events Japanese opinion was inflamed by the spectacular murder of Kim Ok-kyun, the pro-Japanese Korean leader in the coup of 1884, who was lured to Shanghai early in 1894 and killed by a pro-Chinese Korean. His body was shipped on a Chinese warship to Seoul and was there quartered and then displayed in different parts of the kingdom. When the Korean king requested Chinese aid against the rebels, China responded with a small force. Japan, refusing to recognize China's claim of suzerainty, thereupon invoked the Li-Itō Convention of 1885 and sent troops to Korea in larger numbers. Chinese feeling in turn was aroused by the Japanese sinking of the British steamer *Kowshing* carrying Chinese reinforcements. When Japan demanded sweeping reforms in Korea under Sino-Japanese auspices, which would lead to Japanese domination, China refused. The Japanese pressed the conservative Korean court, without avail, and finally seized control over it and had the Korean regent declare war on China. Yüan Shih-k'ai, the Chinese resident, fled. China and Japan declared war on August 1, 1894. Britain, having failed to secure great-power intervention to prevent war, arranged to keep Shanghai and the Yangtze area neutral under British naval protection.

The ensuing hostilities were the first real test of the efforts at military Westernization which China and Japan had been making for a whole generation. Many contemporary observers, lacking our perspective on the two countries, assumed that the Chinese empire would win through sheer size. The world was accordingly startled by the outcome.

With three columns converging on P'yŏngyang, Japan won a succession of land battles and invaded Manchuria. But victory was largely determined by sea power, which in the absence of railways controlled even China's access to Korea. On paper the Ch'ing empire, with some 65 warships listed in its four fleets, seemed more powerful than Japan with its fleet of 32 principal ships. The crucial disparity, however, was in quality. In the major engagement off the Yalu on September 17, one of the first modern naval battles, each side had a dozen ships. But the Japanese fleet, though about the same tonnage, had learned much more from its British instructors. It was also faster and more up-to-date in quick-firing armament and in battle tactics. In two columns it circled the Peiyang warships, which came out like cavalry, line abreast; and in four hours' action four Chinese vessels were sunk, four others fled, and four survived on the scene. The Japanese withdrew intact and thereafter dominated North China waters. Port Arthur, with all its modern seaward-pointing armament, was captured from the landward side in November. The rest of the Peiyang fleet, still a strong force, remained bottled up at Weihaiwei. The Japanese invested the harbor by land and turned the forts against the fleet. It was destroyed or surrendered in February 1895. China has had no naval power since.

Li Hung-chang, now 72, his career in grave peril, was still the leading figure in Ch'ing foreign relations, and it was his responsibility to retrieve the situation. After much maneuvering he was obliged to negotiate with Itō Hirobumi at Shimonoseki. Itō said to him, "Ten years ago at Tientsin I talked with you about reform. Why is it that up to now not a single thing has been changed or reformed?" Li replied, "Affairs in my country have been so confined by tradition."

When a Japanese fanatic shot him, the bullet lodging just below his left eye, Li was able to get more favorable terms. But the Treaty of Shimonoseki (April 17, 1895) nevertheless obliged China to cede Formosa, the Pescadores, and the Liaotung (South Manchuria) Peninsula[1] to Japan; recognize Korea's independence; pay two hundred million taels indemnity; open more ports; and negotiate a commercial treaty. The latter, signed in 1896, gave Japan all the privileges that the Western powers had in China and added the further privilege of carrying on "industries and

[1] Also called Kwantung, "east of the pass," i.e. of Shanhaikwan. Liaotung is "east of the Liao River."

manufactures" using the cheap labor, paid in depreciated silver, in the treaty ports.

Japan's overwhelming victory upset the power balance both within China and on the international scene. British opinion, which had been generally pro-Chinese, underwent a sudden shift, disillusioned by China's appalling incompetence, inspired by admiration for Japanese dash and efficiency, and mindful also of the additional privileges that Japan had secured in China for all the powers under the most-favored-nation clauses in their treaties. Russia, on the other hand, was alarmed for her own ambitions in Korea and South Manchuria; the result (encouraged by Li Hung-chang) was a Russian-German-French diplomatic intervention on April 23, 1895, "advising" Japan to give up the Liaotung Peninsula, which she did in return for thirty million taels additional indemnity. Russia and her associates, having now befriended China in place of the perfidious British, soon demanded compensation. International rivalry was thus intensified in all its many and complex forms. The next few years saw a scramble for concessions which not only threatened the breakup of China but also brought the age of imperialism to a climax in East Asia as a whole (see Chapter 6).

In power politics within China, Li Hung-chang lost his high posts at Tientsin. His protégé Yüan Shih-k'ai took over the training of modern armies in North China. Li's chief mandarin-entrepreneur, Sheng Hsüan-huai, transferred some of his industrial and commercial enterprises to the protection of Li's rival, Chang Chih-tung. Along with Liu K'un-i (1830–1902), the Hunan scholar-soldier who had fought the Taipings and subsequently been governor-general at Nanking for many years, Chang was now a principal figure in "foreign matters." But although Li Hung-chang's empire was divided up, he was too well entrenched, too wealthy, to be cashiered. Instead he was sent on a world tour (see Plate 44).

THE REFORM MOVEMENT

No one was more surprised by China's defeat than the conservatives who had opposed modernization. Remote from the scene of battle, shaken by its unexpected outcome, they were equally violent in accusing Li Hung-chang of treachery and in opposing the peace settlement. Instead, they clamored for the war to continue. Within a twenty-day period the throne received 130 memorials signed by some 2500 persons, many of them scholars too low in rank to memorialize alone. This unprecedented outpouring of patriotic concern stressed that the indemnity, three times Peking's annual revenue, would put the empire in debt to foreigners while the other terms would weaken its prestige and power almost to the point of extinction.

MUSCLE-POWER ECONOMY

PLATE 40. Predecessor of the ricksha. This North China photo of 1873 shows the efficiency of the Chinese barrow: centered wheel bears the weight; the man behind, with shoulder strap, has mainly to balance his two passengers. Passenger on left uses a foot sling.

PLATE 41. Boat-tracking on the Yangtze; photographed in the 1940's. The second junk is held inshore by four lines and hauled upstream by one line attached to 19 or more trackers, who pull with right arm and left shoulder-band.

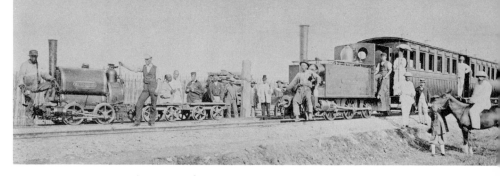

PLATE 42. China's first railway, Shanghai-Wusung, a 30-inch narrow-gauge track built in 1876 by Jardine, Matheson and Company and others. At left: the first engine, the British-made "Pioneer"; note Chinese attendant wearing queue. Center: the 9-ton engine "Celestial Empire," with six 27-inch wheels. Line was purchased and destroyed by Chinese authorities in 1877.

PLATE 43. Li Hung-chang in 1879.

PLATE 44. Li Hung-chang on his world tour, 1896. Li at the age of 72 visited Russia, Germany, France, England, and the United States. Here he stands between the British prime minister, Lord Salisbury (left), and the later Viceroy of India, Lord Curzon.

PLATES 45 AND 46. Yamagata Aritomo, in his early years of power (right), and as a *genrō*, aged 78, during World War I (below).

PLATE 47. Train passing under bridge in Tōkyō, a favorite scene of early Meiji artists. The last two cars carry freight; overland transport by rail was 70 times cheaper than by any other method.

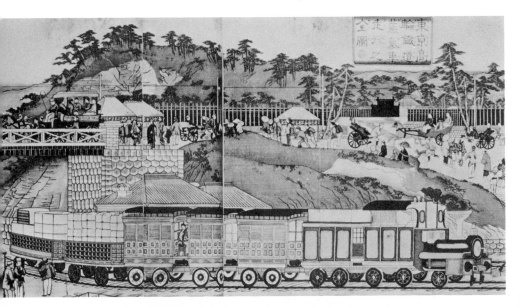

ITŌ HIROBUMI:
THREE AGES OF AN OLIGARCH

PLATES 48–50. Itō as a young official in the
Finance Ministry shortly after the Restoration;
as maker of the Meiji constitution and prime
minister, with his family; and as resident-general
in Korea, with Yi Un, last prince of the dynasty
that began in 1392.

In this atmosphere of alarm and general consternation, a radical reformer, K'ang Yu-wei (1858–1927), led a group of more than 1200 provincial graduates (*chü-jen*), who were at Peking for the triennial examinations, in presenting on May 2, 1895, what became known as the "Ten Thousand Word Memorial" or "Memorial of the Examination Candidates." It advocated rejecting the peace treaty, moving the capital inland for prolonged warfare, and instituting a multitude of reforms. This memorial inaugurated the Reform Movement which absorbed the attention of the scholar-official class during the next four years from 1895 through 1898.

This was the very period when the imperialists' pressure for concessions and spheres of influence was growing constantly more vigorous and menacing. With China's defeat the dam had broken. From without, the foreign powers moved toward dismembering the empire, "cutting up the Chinese melon." Within, the ruling class strove to save the traditional state-and-culture by something more than "self-strengthening" — namely, the "reform of institutions."

The Reform Movement in itself was an institutional innovation, for it led to a great deal of political discussion by scholar-gentry who were not in office. This was quite contrary to the Ch'ing dynasty's established regulations. As early as 1652, mindful how factionalism had weakened the Ming, it had forbidden degree-holders to put forward views on policy, or "to associate with large numbers of others, or to form alliances or join societies." The Yung-cheng and Ch'ien-lung Emperors had denounced all associations of officials as self-seeking "factions" (*tang*), incapable of any disinterested concern for policy, and had demanded that each official be utterly loyal in the sense of taking the emperor's "likes and dislikes as his own will." Although the nineteenth century had seen this authoritarianism modified in practice, the memorial of the examination candidates advocating myriad reforms was almost unprecedented.

Even more revolutionary was the rise of scholar-gentry political associations or "study societies" (*hsüeh-hui*), the most famous of which was the "Society for the Study of Self-Strengthening" (*Ch'iang-hsüeh hui*) founded at Peking in August–September 1895. Branches and similar societies were soon set up in Shanghai and other major centers, with financial support from reform-minded high officials like Chang Chih-tung and Yüan Shih-k'ai.

Scholars once in politics quickly became journalists. The study societies began to publish journals and newspapers to spread their ideas of reform. When K'ang's junior colleague, Liang Ch'i-ch'ao (1873–1929), began in August 1895 to edit a daily for the Self-Strengthening Society, he at first borrowed the title of Young J. Allen's monthly *Wan-kuo kung-pao* and reprinted many articles from it; indeed the young Liang for a time actually assisted Timothy Richard. Journals of scholarly opinion advocating reform sprouted up all over the country. Moreover, the Reform Movement, though it commenced among the scholar class, began to use methods of group organization, with discussion meetings and an active press, strongly reminiscent of missionary methods of seeking China's salvation. With the spread of literacy, these methods could bring a great deal more than the scholar class into participation in political life.

The Ideology of Reform. For scholars indoctrinated by their own studies in the all-embracing social theory of Confucianism, change must be sanctioned by ideas. The theory of reform had developed slowly over two generations, ever since men like Wei Yüan, believers in the traditional type of administrative reform advocated by the school of "statecraft" (*ching-shih*), had first urged the use of Western arms during the Opium War. To justify Western studies, the ancient dictum of the *Sun-tzu*, "Know yourself, know your opponent; in a hundred battles, win a hundred victories," was quoted repeatedly from the 1830's down to the 1890's. But as the pressure to adopt Western ways in self-defense increased, so did the need to justify the process. How could one defend Chinese ways by adopting Western ways?

One answer was to make a distinction between what was defended and what was adopted, as between ends and means. Japanese reformers had used the phrase, "Eastern ethics and Western science." For China, Feng Kuei-fen (see pages 315, 381) had suggested, "Let the moral principles and ethical teachings of China serve as the original foundation . . . supplemented by the methods used by the various (Western) countries for the attainment of wealth and power. . . ." This idea had remained the sanction for "self-strengthening." It was finally summed up in the slogan popularized by Chang Chih-tung in the 1890's: "Chinese learning for the essential principles, Western learning for the practical applications" (*Chung-hsüeh wei t'i, Hsi-hsüeh wei yung*).

To a critical mind, however, this slogan was specious and misleading. It invoked a Sung philosophical distinction between *t'i* "substance" (lit. "body") and *yung* "function" (lit. "use"). This pair of terms designated the interdependence between the inner substance of anything and its outward functioning. It had been applied, for example, to the superior man's inner self-cultivation and outward governing of others, to the ruler's being a sage in spirit and a king in action. Tseng Kuo-fan used "substance" and "function" in this traditional way, as correlative aspects of a given entity.

But Chang Chih-tung's formula now misapplied "substance" and "function" as equivalent to Chinese "ends" and Western "means," or Chinese "values" and Western "technology," or, in a form that has persisted, Eastern "spirit" and Western "matter." Chang was stretching the old ideology of Neo-Confucianism to cover the new practice of Westernization. This was decried by critics like Yen Fu (1853–1921), who in the 1890's was translating J. S. Mill, T. H. Huxley, Herbert Spencer, and other Western writers on evolution and utilitarianism and so knew something of both civilizations. Yen later pointed out that "Chinese learning has its substance and function; Western learning also has its substance and function." The *t'i-yung* formula was a snare, for techniques will affect values, and means that are adopted will determine ends. More than a misuse of the ancient idea of *t'i* and *yung* was needed to sanction the substitution of Western for Chinese ways. The same difficulty confronted those who spoke of protecting the immutable Chinese "way" (*tao*) by the use of Western "instruments" (*ch'i*). Where were they to draw the line in Westernization?

Another approach was to find the sanction for Westernization within China's own tradition. This procedure was a variant of the customary practice of "finding in antiquity the sanction for present-day changes" (*t'o-ku kai-chih*). Thus the prodigious scholar Juan Yüan, who was also governor-general at Canton about 1820 (see page 125), had argued in his biographies of mathematicians that the Western mathematics displayed by the Jesuits had originated in ancient China. Similarly, in the 1860's, Prince Kung justified Western studies in the Interpreters College at Peking by alleging that "Western sciences borrowed their roots from ancient Chinese mathematics." Soon the effort was made to smuggle all the natural sciences into the Chinese curriculum under cover of "mathematics." In the 1880's a vulgar apologetics for Westernization developed along this line — for example, tracing the origin of chemistry to the ancient theory of the "five elements" (Vol. I, p. 77) so as to make chemistry part of China's cultural heritage.

A further step was to find a doctrine of change in China's past. Hsüeh Fu-ch'eng (1838–1894), for instance, had worked under Tseng and Li in foreign affairs and finally served as envoy to European countries in the early 1890's; in essays widely circulated among officialdom in the 1880's, Hsüeh argued that periodic or cyclical change was the way of Heaven. From the age of the sage-kings Yao and Shun until the great change of the Ch'in unification in 221 B.C., two thousand years had elapsed. Now, after another two thousand years, another great change was naturally in order — the sage-kings themselves, if here today, would meet the situation with a "change of method" (*pien-fa*) so as to defend their unchanging way. The same argument was put forward by Wang T'ao in his editorials.

Meanwhile the ancient idea of "change of method" (*pien-fa*) was gradually stretched by expanding the meaning of the term *fa*, which meant literally "method" but also, more broadly, "law" or "institution." The innocuous phrase "change of method" now began to cover "institutional change" of the most basic kind. For example, writers in the early 1890's advocated the inauguration of a parliament, which they justified by quoting classical aphorisms about "ruler and people being one body, superior and inferior being of one mind." But still there was no equivalent in Chinese tradition for the dynamic idea of progress, so dominant in contemporary Western works like Robert Mackenzie's *The Nineteenth Century — A History* (1880), which Timothy Richard translated and circulated widely in 1894.

K'ang Yu-wei's Reinterpretation of Confucianism. K'ang Yu-wei finally supplied the reinterpretation by which the Classics could sanction Westernization, and Confucianism could include progress. He was born into a distinguished scholar-official family of Canton and became a precocious student of the Classics. But soon he found them "all empty and lacking in substance." K'ang said later that his teacher "often cautioned me about my undue feelings of superiority," but nevertheless, at the age of twenty-one, while meditating upon the world, "in a great release of enlightenment I beheld myself a sage. . . ." He proceeded to act like one, and remake the classical tradition.

First of all, he carried further the "new text" movement which had questioned the authenticity of the orthodox "ancient text" versions of certain Confucian Classics (see Vol. I, p. 121, and above, page 122).[1] To reformers committed to working within the classical tradition, the "new text" school of interpretation was very appealing because it broke the monopoly of the Neo-Confucian orthodoxy. K'ang synthesized the studies of Wei Yüan and a number of predecessors in the "new text" school, and in 1891 published his *Hsin-hsüeh wei-ching k'ao* or *Study of the Classics Forged during the Hsin Period* (i.e., the reign of Wang Mang, A.D. 9–23). In this he attacked the authenticity of the *Tso chuan, Chou li,* and *I li* and the major commentary on the *Shih ching* (see Vol. I, p. 68), and concluded that the "Han Learning" was wrongly based, while "the Classics honored and expounded by the Sung scholars are for the most part forged and not those of Confucius." This devastating attack is not now generally accepted by scholars, but it was erudite, persuasive, and therefore most unsettling to the scholarly world of the 1890's. High officials had the printing blocks burned in 1894, but they could not pre-

---

[1] After the Ch'in unifier's "Burning of the Books" in 213 B.C. (see Vol. I, p. 88), certain Classics were written down mainly from memory in new, standardized "modern characters" (*chin-wen*) and these texts became dominant in the Earlier Han. As interpreted by Tung Chung-shu and others, they included many superstitious, extravagant, and irrational concepts of the "five elements," *yin* and *yang,* and the like. Subsequently scholars recovered texts written in the "old characters" (*ku-wen*) of pre-Han times. They made these the dominant versions in the Later Han and on them based more rational, less supernatural interpretations. These became the standard texts of the Classics even though occasional critics arose to question their authenticity. For us today this complex subject is confused by the fact that *chin-wen* is usually translated "new text" though referring to the earlier versions, while *ku-wen* is translated "ancient text" though referring to versions recovered later.

vent K'ang's becoming a metropolitan graduate and Hanlin academician in 1895. He was now at the top of the establishment.

Having brushed aside the orthodox view, K'ang pushed further certain "new text" interpretations and published in 1897 his *K'ung-tzu kai-chih k'ao* (literally *Study of Confucius' Reform of Institutions*, but usually translated *Confucius as a Reformer*). In this work he claimed that Confucius had himself created, rather than merely edited, the principal Classics as a means of invoking antiquity in order to make institutional reforms. This view, if accepted, would allow a near-revolution in the name of the Sage himself. Evidently inspired by Christianity and the Western missionaries, K'ang also proposed to exalt Confucius as the focus of a Chinese national religion.

This was not all. Following the "new text" school and the suggestions of Wang T'ao, K'ang Yu-wei applied to China's problem certain cryptic passages in the *Kung-yang Commentary* on the *Spring and Autumn Annals* and in the *Evolutions of Rites* (*Li yün*) chapter of the *Record of Rituals* (*Li chi*). These set forth a theory of Three Ages. Combining these two classical sources, K'ang derived an evolutionary sequence, consisting of the Ages of (1) Disorder (*shuai-luan*), (2) Approaching Peace (*sheng-p'ing*) and Small Tranquillity (*hsiao-k'ang*), and (3) Great Peace (*t'ai-p'ing*) and Great Unity (*ta-t'ung*). In this analysis, the world had been struggling in the Age of Disorder and with K'ang's reforms evidently would now enter the Age of Approaching Peace and Small Tranquillity. Thus China's classical learning was made to encompass a theory of evolution and progress. As Liang Ch'i-ch'ao later remarked, K'ang could find in a very obscure passage of the *Evolutions of Rites*, as reinterpreted by himself, the "ideas of democracy . . . the League of Nations . . . public upbringing of children . . . sickness and old-age insurance . . . Communism . . . and the sanctity of labor." In his hands, the great tradition could become a modern revolution.

K'ang Yu-wei, in short, was a master of the Classics and yet his loyalty to them was ambiguous. He was not bound by them. From the early 1880's he had developed a secret utopian vision of his own that was not fully published until after his death — *Ta-t'ung shu* (literally *The Book of the Great Unity;* equally well translated as *The Great Commonwealth, Universal Harmony,* or even *One World*). This revolutionary work sought universal peace and equality by eliminating the sufferings created by the nine spheres or barriers that are represented by classes, races, the sexes, the family, private property, and so on. As the means to attain this utopia, K'ang showed a naïve and rather "modern" faith in technological progress of all sorts. He would have everything managed by government under law although paradoxically all states would be abolished. However, for all his daring self-confidence he was sufficiently discreet to hold back during the 1890's many of his more radical ideas, such as the abolition of family bonds and the continuation of marriages only from year to year. For all its Confucian garb, his thinking was broadly eclectic, combining strains of Buddhist and modern Western thought in his own creative mixture. Small wonder that sincere Confucians suspected that K'ang Yu-wei's ultimate commitment was to his own ideas more than to Confucianism.

The Radical Reformers' Rise to Power. Although K'ang Yu-wei had supplied the philosophic groundwork, the Reform Movement did not quickly gain the ascendant. The panic that followed defeat in 1895 soon died down; the Self-Strengthening Society (*Ch'iang-hsüeh hui*) was suppressed in both Peking and Shanghai. K'ang returned to Canton, Liang Ch'i-ch'ao edited a reform journal (*Shih-wu pao*) in Shanghai. Reform activity, though it continued at the capital, fared better in some provincial centers.

Hunan province, though it was the last area still refusing to admit Protestant missionaries, curiously enough became a leading center of the Reform Movement. This productive rice-bowl region with its strong landlord-gentry class had provided leadership against both the Taipings and the missionaries, and now did so for reform. With the blessing of Chang Chih-tung as governor-general, the governor (Ch'en Pao-chen) and other provincial officials (including Huang Tsun-hsien) promoted modernization at Changsha. They soon had results — some paved and lighted streets, steam launches on the river, telegraph lines to the outer world, a modern police system, colleges with modern curricula, a study society with lectures and discussions, a reform paper edited from late 1897 by Liang Ch'i-ch'ao. These achievements of gentry-official cooperation in this one provincial center were symptomatic of a growing movement in many parts of China.

The imperialist powers soon revived the atmosphere of crisis. In November 1897 Germany occupied Kiaochow (Chiao-chou) Bay and the port of Tsingtao in Shantung. This territorial seizure seemed to presage the empire's actual dismemberment, for Russia, France, and Britain likewise moved in early 1898 to secure far-reaching concessions which gave them spheres of influence and many of the attributes of sovereign power in large areas of China. (See pages 468–473.) The resulting crisis at Peking brought K'ang Yu-wei his chance.

True to the great tradition that reform can operate only through the imperial power, K'ang had presented his fifth memorial to the emperor (not all of them got through) after the German seizure of Kiachow. His earlier opposition to Li Hung-chang's peace settlement with Japan had commended him to Li's rival, the former imperial tutor Weng T'ung-ho, who was still close to the young Kuang-hsü Emperor. As a moderate committed to orthodox "self-strengthening," Weng could use a younger expert on reform. He and others recommended K'ang to the emperor. By the time they fully realized K'ang's radicalism, expressed for example in his iconoclastic *Confucius as a Reformer* published late in 1897, it was too late to block his rise.

At forty, K'ang Yu-wei was a senior figure among the radical young scholar-reformers outside the bureaucracy. These men had intense pride of culture and were bubbling over with plans to save China. K'ang's statement for the Self-Strengthening Society in 1895 had proclaimed that "China, on the great earth, has had a ceaseless succession of sacred emperors, and the country has been very famous. Her principles, institutions, and culture are the most elevated in the world. . . . Among all countries on earth none is her equal." With this nationalism, however, was combined a strong sense of Social Darwinism, the struggle for survival of the fittest among nations. Russia under Peter the Great and Japan under Meiji served as models. (K'ang wrote books on both.) The Ottoman Empire and India were warnings. China was now in "imminent peril," with the imperialist powers "sharpening their teeth and watering at the mouth." China must progress or perish. Progress meant change of institutions.

K'ang's program called for the restructuring of internal administration on the grounds that China's traditional checks and double-checks, diffusion of power and surveillance of power-holders, had been developed to preserve the ruling dynasty against enemies arising from within. Now, against enemies from without, this cumbersome machinery was worse than useless. He therefore proposed a cabinet type of domestic administration, with a dozen ministries employing modern-trained experts, to supplant the clumsy Six Boards and Grand Council. Like the Japanese, K'ang was impressed with the usefulness of parliaments not only to raise taxes, check corruption, and promote popular welfare as in Western countries, but also to strengthen the Confucian bond between ruler and people. He called for a national assembly, a constitution, and even local "bureaus of people's affairs" to carry out reforms with scholar-gentry participation. Among his followers all manner of wild ideas were current — democracy, simplification of the written language, even equality of the sexes and Western dress.

The radical reformers' program thus went far beyond the "self-strengtheners'" concept of using Western devices (*yung*) to maintain China's principles (*t'i*). When K'ang Yu-wei first met the officials of the Tsungli Yamen in January 1898, the Empress Dowager's most faithful Manchu supporter, Jung-lu, declared, "The institutions of the ancestors cannot be changed." K'ang replied, "We cannot preserve the realm of the ancestors; what is the use of their institutions?" Li Hung-chang asked, "Shall we abolish all the Six Boards and throw away all the existing institutions and rules?" And K'ang replied, "The laws and governmental system . . . have made China weak and will ruin her. Undoubtedly they should be done away with." Small wonder that Weng T'ung-ho finally judged K'ang to be a heretical "wild fox" with treacherously "unfathomable" intentions. But in the early months of 1898, with the imperialist powers about to tear China apart, action seemed essential, K'ang was full of proposals, and the ardent young emperor, then twenty-seven, finally gave him his confidence.

When K'ang had his first audience, on June 16, it lasted five hours. "China will soon perish," he said. "All that is caused by the conservatives," replied the emperor. "If Your Majesty wishes to rely on them for reform," said K'ang, "it will be like climbing a tree to seek for fish." K'ang then inveighed against the eight-legged essay examinations which prevented officials from understanding foreign countries. The emperor said, "It is so. Westerners are all pursuing useful studies, while we Chinese pursue useless studies."

The Hundred Days of 1898. During the hundred days between June 11 and September 21, 1898, Kuang-hsü, with K'ang Yu-wei, Liang Ch'i-ch'ao, and others as advisers behind the scenes, issued forty or more reform edicts dealing with almost every conceivable subject: setting up modern schools and remaking the examination system; revising the laws as a preliminary to getting rid of extraterritoriality; promoting agriculture, medicine, mining, commerce, inventions, and study abroad; and modernizing the army, navy, police, and postal systems. Few of these orders were carried out, except in Hunan. Officials waited to see how the Empress Dowager, in retirement since 1889, would respond to this radical program.

Conservative opposition was of course vociferous. All the reformers except the emperor were Chinese; the emperor's abolition of sinecure posts threatened many Manchu incumbents; and some feared he would dismiss all Manchus. The proposal to transform monasteries into schools terrified the monks, who had friends among the palace eunuchs. Military reform threatened the ancient Manchu banners and the Chinese constabulary of the Green Standard. The attack on the old examinations as qualification for office threatened all degree-holders who aspired to become officials. The attack on corruption affected nearly everyone in office. In short, as his program unfolded, the emperor found himself at war with the whole establishment, not least with his adoptive "mother," the Empress Dowager, who was still vigorous at sixty-three.

The issue in 1898 was not between reform or no reform, but between K'ang Yu-wei's radicalism and a continuation of the moderate "self-strengthening" which was now in its fourth decade of creeping Westernization. The aims of the latter were summed up in Chang Chih-tung's book, *Exhortation to Study (Ch'üan-hsüeh p'ien)*, which he published during the Hundred Days to state the antiradical position.

This influential work, distributed by imperial order, aimed first of all to preserve the Manchu dynasty by a revival of the Confucian social order. It therefore upheld the "three bonds" (three of the *Mencius'* famous five relationships, namely, those between emperor and official, father and son, husband and wife) and vigorously opposed egalitarianism, democracy, constitutional monarchy, the doctrine of the "people's rights" (*min-ch'üan*), parliaments, the freedom of the individual, and civil liberties of the Western sort.

Second, Chang aimed to save China by education. He proposed to reform the examination system; to set up a hierarchy of schools and colleges at district, prefectural, and provincial levels and an imperial university at Peking; and in the curriculum to stress both the Confucian Classics and Western technology. This program was modeled on Japan's. It would include the sending of students abroad and military education through universal military service.

Third, Chang hoped to save China by industrialization. For this his military "self-strengthening" effort at Wuhan was setting a practical example. One of its aims was to make China less dependent on imported steel. Having begun an iron foundry and arsenal at Hanyang (1890) and an iron mine at Ta-yeh in Hupei (1894), Chang advocated construction of a Peking-Hankow-Canton railway through China's heartland, by a central railway administration under Sheng Hsüan-huai as director-general.

Chang Chih-tung explicitly condemned the "self-strengtheners" of the 1860's, such as Tseng Kuo-fan and Wen-hsiang, for not overcoming the obscurantist opposition of that era. He bewailed China's chronic lack of leadership, funds, policies, and skilled personnel for modernization. But as the imperial edicts of the Hundred Days roused more and more opposition, he joined the majority of officialdom in denouncing the radical reformers.

The Empress Dowager, though not opposed to "self-strengthening," found her entire world threatened by K'ang Yu-wei's attack on those twin pillars of her regime, classical learning and organized corruption. She bided her time while opposition grew. Finally on September 21, 1898, with the help of the top Manchu military commander, Jung-lu, she seized the Kuang-hsü Emperor in a *coup d'état* and began her third regency. K'ang and Liang escaped to Japan; but six of the reformers, including the brilliant young eclectic philosopher from Hunan, T'an Ssu-t'ung (1865–1898), were executed. The emperor remained in forced seclusion, and when the Empress Dowager finally died in 1908, he somehow predeceased her by one day.

The abrupt end of the Hundred Days restored most of the *status quo ante*, yet some moderate reform measures continued, such as the abolition of certain sinecures and the establishment of modern schools. The chief significance of 1898, however, was that the radicals' attempt at a revolution from above, in the pattern of the revolution effected in Japan by the

Meiji Restoration, had failed. The Empress Dowager's counter-coup, though it was followed by another decade of moderate reform, meant that henceforth a really revolutionary change could come only from below, presumably by violence.

Thus gradualism, by being too gradual, made violent revolution more certain. Yet it was still in the future. The Meiji Restoration had not lacked for violence, and while the Chinese program of 1898 sought its revolutionary changes within the nominal framework of Confucian ideas and Ch'ing dynastic power, it would certainly have led to violent clashes of interest and unforeseen results of large proportions. But the ease of the Empress Dowager's *coup d'état* suggests that China as a whole was far from ready for revolution in 1898. After sixty years of attack and stimulus from the Western world, the traditional Chinese order was still strong and capable of violent protest against Westernization.

The Boxer Rising

The radical reforms of 1898 had been a daring effort by Chinese scholars at the very top of the ruling class to respond to the foreign menace by modernizing the whole Ch'ing government. After its failure, the initiative shifted to an opposite wing of the ruling class — die-hard Manchu princes who naïvely believed that they could save their dynasty by throwing the foreigners out of China. Educated in the palace, often kept out of actual government, ignorant of the outside world, these men accepted in 1899 the same purblind slogan that had roused the samurai of Japan forty years earlier — "Expel the barbarians!" They eventually found a vehicle in a traditional type of secret society.

The Origin of the Boxer Movement. This secret society, called *I-ho ch'üan*, had originated as an offshoot of the rebellious Eight Trigrams Society (*Pa-kua chiao*) of the late eighteenth century, which was vaguely affiliated to the antidynastic White Lotus Society in North China. Imperial decrees had identified it and ordered its suppression in the early nineteenth century, but it had survived underground in Shantung and Chihli. The name *I-ho ch'üan*, crudely translated by Westerners as "Righteous and Harmonious Fists," or more simply as "Boxers," indicates that this society under the name of Righteousness and Harmony (*I-ho*) practiced its own form of so-called Chinese "boxing" (*ch'üan*). This was related to the ancient calisthenic "military art" (*wu-shu*), which through a sequence of postures and exercises aimed to harmonize mind and muscle in preparation for combat. The Boxers developed a magic art using Taoist sorcery and a prescribed ritual — members thrice recited an incantation, breathed through clenched teeth, foamed at the mouth, and became possessed by spirits. This gave them supernatural powers, through the support of Buddhist-Taoist divinities, and so made them happily impervious to foreign bullets. Like other traditional secret societies, the Boxers thus invoked the idea of supernatural intervention in human affairs. They found their heroes in the same Chinese folklore that underlay the drama and novels. Their deities were semi-fictional, semi-historic, operatic characters who figured in novels like *Shui-hu-chuan, All Men Are Brothers,* or the so-called "god of war" Kuan Yü or Chu-ko Liang (from the *Romance of the Three Kingdoms*).

Thus the Boxer movement stemmed from the ancient tradition of popular rebellion against the regime in power. To this antidynastic aim it added antiforeignism, and its original slogan early in 1899 was "Overthrow the Ch'ing; destroy the foreigner." In the fall of 1899, however, the aim shifted from antidynastic to prodynastic, "Support the Ch'ing; destroy the foreigner." The target became not the Ch'ing dynasty but the foreign order newly established in China, beginning with the Western missionaries and particularly their Chinese Christian converts. This was the resultant of forces at work in the Chinese political scene.

Anti-Christian hostility was the most obvious of the several factors that combined to inspire the Boxer movement, for the steady growth of missionary activity in the 1890's exacerbated all the problems that had accumulated during the previous decades. Some Christian converts flouted the sacred family relationships, refused to support the local festivals and deities, and got the missionaries to intervene and help them in their disputes. With French support, Catholic prelates could coerce local officials. Scurrilous anti-Christian diatribes continued to circulate, as well as the rumors of lewd, occult, and orgiastic practices, especially in Catholic institutions.

This anti-Christian background was manifest in Boxer proclamations spread among North China villages. Some were on traditional themes like the Ten Coming Disasters ("There will be clothes but no one to wear them, there will be rice but no one to eat it"). But the main attack was on the Chinese Christian community, which had become an organized element and so was drawn into local feuds and set upon by the militant secret society bands. Placards read: "Catholics and Protestants have vilified our gods and sages, have deceived our emperors and ministers above and oppressed the Chinese people below. . . . This forces us to practice the I-ho magic boxing so as to protect our country, expel the foreign bandits and kill Christian converts, in order to save our people from miserable sufferings. . . . The Catholics' Chinese converts have conspired with the foreigners, destroyed Buddhist images, seized our peoples' graveyards. This has angered Heaven."

The sudden rise of the Boxer movement was fostered by current economic and political conditions. Yellow River floods had led to widespread famine in Shantung in 1898. North China suffered generally from drought. Destitute country people were moving about as vagrants. To some degree the importation of foreign cotton goods and oil depressed local industries, while plans for new railways seemed to threaten the livelihood of carters and canal bargemen. The rising foreign menace had been made concrete by the Germans' seizure in 1897 of a position in Shantung. Their surveying for railways and prospecting for mines seemed inimical to the "spirits of wind and water" and endangered the graves of the ancestors.

Throughout the empire, the succession of foreign encroachments on Chinese territory had spread a lively fear of the "breakup of China," currently so much discussed in foreign circles. The late 1890's, in fact, saw disorder, riots, banditry, or local risings in every one of the eighteen provinces. Inspired partly by secret organizations like the Society of Brothers and Elders (*Ko-lao hui*) and the Big Sword Society (*Ta-tao hui*), this widespread unrest was reminiscent of the late 1840's just before the Taiping upheaval. Much of it stemmed from poverty and starvation. But much of it was directed not only against the local government but specifically against Christian converts and foreigners.

In sum, the Boxer movement emerged as a direct-action response to a deepening crisis in the lives of the whole Chinese people. The Boxers themselves were from the peasantry, but their local leaders presumably came from that in-between group of the dispossessed and frustrated, including monks, peddlers, soothsayers and itinerants of many sorts, who had customarily led rebel causes. The rank-and-file members were mostly adolescents.

Finally the movement received its prodynastic impetus from the patronage of Manchu and Chinese officials, both locally and up to the very top of the dynasty. This patronage developed as a by-product of the broad effort led by the Empress Dowager to deal vigorously with the twin menaces of foreign aggression and local disorder, each of which might provoke the other and precipitate a disaster. On resuming the regency in September 1898, determined to resist further foreign humiliation, she had decreed that there should be no more concessions to foreign powers. When the Italians sent a fleet and demanded a leased area in Chekiang in March 1899, they were refused and the southern provinces prepared for war. The court later gave provincial authorities standing orders to resist foreign aggression by force if necessary.

To deal with the domestic missionary problem, inasmuch as the Catholic church organization could not be expelled, Peking moved in March 1899 toward assimilating it, as earlier dynasties had done with Buddhism and even Islam, by giving the Catholic hierarchy official status. As they had long desired, bishops were now entitled to trappings of rank, insignia, retinues and honors, equivalent to those of provincial governors. They and even the lowliest priests could demand audiences and communicate directly with local Chinese authorities, though they were not to intervene in lawsuits.

Meanwhile, to meet the imminent threat of local disorder, Peking adopted another ancient device. The reformers of 1898 had decided to use Chinese-type militia as a substitute for Western-style conscription and universal military training. Now in November 1898 the organization of local militia (*t'uan-lien*) was decreed for North China.

These imperial orders to organize local militia were the court's response to the emergence of armed secret society activity, which had begun in Shantung as early as 1896. In May 1898 came the first official report identifying the Boxer movement there. Soon the hard core of antiforeign and antireformist conservatives in the Ch'ing court began to look to these Boxers as a source of popular support against the foreigners. In this they were invoking the ancient tradition, China's equivalent of Western "popular sovereignty," that the righteous indignation of the common people was the final arbiter of politics and that resistance to tyranny, whether foreign or domestic, could succeed only if based upon popular sentiment. "Heaven sees as the people see, Heaven hears as the people hear," was the classical statement. This was a basic theme in Confucian government, which rested upon the tacit consent of the populace rather than their active participation in politics. Tseng Kuo-fan, in the crisis following the Tientsin Massacre of 1870, had been most concerned for this type of "public opinion." It could never be far from the mind of a Ch'ing magistrate. To claim that the Boxers' antiforeignism now represented the voice of the people carried weight in dynastic councils, for the warning was clear — if the dynasty could not protect the people against foreign aggression, the Boxers might destroy it as well as the foreigners.

Ch'ing Support of the Boxers. The alliance between antiforeign officials and prodynastic Boxers began to take shape in the autumn of 1899, after government troops had defeated and seized some of the antidynastic Boxer rebels in Shantung. The governor, a Manchu named Yü-hsien appointed in March 1899, condoned and thus encouraged Boxer attacks on Christians and actually enrolled Boxer bands as local militia. Boxer leaders gradually abandoned their antidynastic tradition. Their basic village units more and more used the term "militia" (*t'uan*) and so the *I-ho ch'üan* was soon known also as *I-ho t'uan* ("righteous and harmonious militia"), which made it sound semi-official.

All this led some observers then and later to believe that the Boxer organization was an essentially legal militia body brought into being by the government. This view, however, is too simple. Instead, antiforeign officials joined forces with the secret society as it came into the open and made common cause with it against the foreigner. They encouraged the slogan, "Uphold the Ch'ing, exterminate the foreigner," which was pleasantly different from the anti-Ch'ing battle cry of other secret societies. Ch'ing officialdom, in short, by 1899 was split into an ardent pro-Boxer faction, which eventually became dominant, and a much larger but frustrated anti-Boxer element, who despised the superstitious incantations and feared the consequences of Boxer fanaticism, and yet, like patriots tolerant of a Hitler or a McCarthy, sympathized with the extremists' aims while deploring their means, and in any case saw no way to stop them.

The moderates were not strengthened by the anxious demands and threats of foreign diplomats, whose every effort to make the government check the Boxers could be interpreted as further aggressive pressure. Nevertheless, foreign pressure did effect the removal of Yü-hsien as governor of Shantung in December 1899. His replacement, Yüan Shih-k'ai, proceeded to take action against the Boxers by traditional means. Yüan had seen the somewhat similar Tonghak rising in Korea. He proscribed the Boxer movement and established a chain of responsibility running from Chinese local officials down through village headmen to neighbors, fathers, and elder brothers, all of whom must report and oppose Boxer activities within their spheres or suffer severe penalties. He promised to reward informers, punish supporters, kill the leaders, and let the followers redeem themselves. Governor Yüan issued an ode on Confucian lines to be chanted in the schools: "The court loves the people, the people should obey the court. Superior and inferior will thus become attached to each other. Earthly conduct should be allied with heavenly principles." Meanwhile, he ordered foreign missionaries to keep indoors and offer no provocation. With these methods he combined a vigorous use of government troops, who shot Boxers on sight. Yüan the model administrator effectively checked the movement in Shantung, and thus demonstrated that its flourishing depended in large degree upon official tolerance, if not patronage.

In the metropolitan province of Chihli during the first five months of 1900, Boxer bands of hundreds and even thousands spread over the countryside, burning missionary establishments and slaughtering Chinese Christians, with the evident tacit consent of the court. Beginning in April 1899, the leading Manchu princes seem to have gradually persuaded the Empress Dowager that the Boxers' magic invulnerability was real and that they could indeed cast out the foreign scourge from the Middle Kingdom. Repeated identic notes came from the diplomatic corps, demanding suppression. The edicts issued in response, in January and again in April 1900, were highly equivocal — the societies active in missionary cases were "of different kinds," some formed militia bands for worthy ends of "keeping mutual watch and giving mutual help," officials suppressing them must "discriminate" between the good and bad elements. The diplomatic corps, so confident of Western superiority, was slow to recognize that the Empress Dowager, after decades of enforcing foreign privileges under the unequal treaties, was finally prepared to let this popular movement challenge the West by force. In March 1900 Yü-hsien was appointed governor of Shansi. By late May, Boxer bands were terrorizing the countryside around Peking. The principal officials in the provinces and Jung-lu at court urged that imperial troops vigorously suppress them. Troops were duly sent but were still ordered to distinguish between the "good" and "evil" elements among the Boxers.

With the court thus determined to appease rather than suppress the Boxer terror, foreign provocation was hardly necessary to trigger the final explosion; the foreigners had been provocative for sixty years already. The final outbreak was precipitated from both sides. Alarmed by the panic of missionaries who had seen their converts killed, the diplomats agreed that the Boxers must be met by force. They had 17 naval vessels concentrate off Tientsin and brought 426 guards up to the Peking legations by June 3. The Boxers attacked imperial troops along the railway, and the court reproved the imperial general for firing on them. On June 8 the Boxers' leading patron at court, Kang-i, newly appointed as imperial commissioner, accepted the demands of the Boxers and withdrew the imperial forces sent against them. Another pro-Boxer, Prince Tuan, was made head of the Tsungli Yamen on June 10. On the same day an international relief expedition of 2100 troops under the British admiral, Seymour, started from Tientsin for the protection of the Peking legations, acting on the nineteenth-century assumption that "any force of Europeans however small can beat any force of Chinamen however

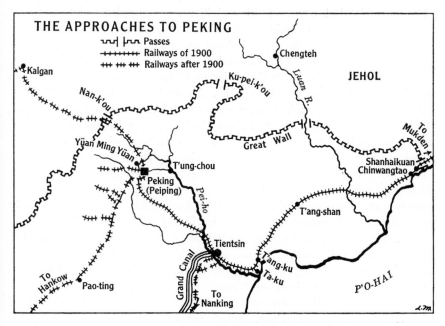

THE APPROACHES TO PEKING

ᴜᴜ| ᴶᴜᴜ Passes
++++++ Railways of 1900
+++ +++ +++ Railways after 1900

Kalgan

Nan-k'ou

Ku-pei-k'ou

Chengteh

Luan R.

JEHOL

Yüan Ming Yüan

Great Wall

To Mukden

Shanhaikuan
Chinwangtao

T'ung-chou

Peking
(Peiping)

Pei-ho

T'ang-shan

Tientsin

T'ang-ku

Ta-ku

P'O-HAI

To
Hankow

Pao-ting

Grand Canal

To
Nanking

large." On June 13, Boxer forces entered Peking, massacred Chinese Christians, and burned foreign establishments outside the legations. An imperial decree ordered the Boxers to resist the invading foreign column, now stuck on the railroad halfway to the capital. On June 14 Boxers burst into Tientsin and besieged the foreign settlements. The Empress Dowager's rationalization was: "China is weak; the only thing we can depend upon is the hearts of the people. If we lose them, how can we maintain our country?"

At this critical point, on June 17, the Empress Dowager was told by the pro-Boxer Manchus at court that the foreign powers had demanded her retirement in favor of the emperor. This fabrication evidently won her over completely to the extremist camp. At about the same time on June 17 the foreign admirals attacked and seized the Taku forts on the coast in order to restore access from the sea up to Tientsin, a distance of 35 miles by road or rail. The next day Seymour's relief column, impeded by Boxer bands and the demolition of the railway, was attacked for the first time by modern-armed imperial troops. The column eventually fought its way back to Tientsin. In Peking the German minister, von Ketteler, started for the Tsungli Yamen on June 20 and was shot dead in the street. On June 21 the Ch'ing dynasty declared war against the foreign powers. In this confusion of events, causation was interactive as both sides moved toward resort to force.

The Siege of the Peking Legations. The eleven foreign legations, in an area about three quarters of a mile square, were besieged from June 20. They contained about 475 foreign civilians, 450 guards of eight nations, perhaps three thousand Chinese Christians who, as it turned out, provided an indispensable labor force, and about 150 racing ponies that ended up providing fresh meat. This embattled community was organized into several fighting units by nationalities and into overall functional committees staffed mainly by missionaries. Meanwhile the Catholic Pei-t'ang or North Cathedral underwent a separate and even more severe ordeal. In this ecclesiastical fortress, Bishop Favier and 43 French and Italian sailors defended 3400 people including 850 Chinese schoolgirls through weeks of increasing starvation. Outside the capital in late June and July some 250 foreigners were killed, most of them missionaries and mainly in Shansi, where Governor Yü-hsien personally presided over the execution of 46. Chinese Christians died in far greater numbers, although several scattered communities succeeded in defending themselves.

This midsummer madness astounded the world. After a month of no news from the diplomats, the missionary leaders, Sir Robert Hart, and the others besieged, they were credibly reported all massacred. Obituaries were published in the London *Times*.

The decentralized nature of the Ch'ing government meanwhile had proved of some practical use. While the benighted Manchus at court

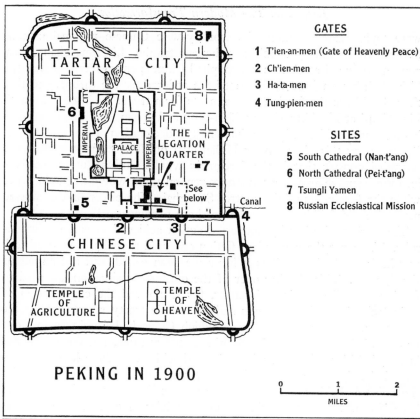

GATES

1 T'ien-an-men (Gate of Heavenly Peace)
2 Ch'ien-men
3 Ha-ta-men
4 Tung-pien-men

SITES

5 South Cathedral (Nan-t'ang)
6 North Cathedral (Pei-t'ang)
7 Tsungli Yamen
8 Russian Ecclesiastical Mission

PEKING IN 1900

0   1   2
MILES

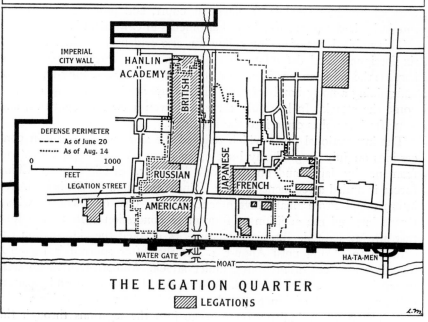

IMPERIAL CITY WALL
HANLIN ACADEMY
BRITISH

DEFENSE PERIMETER
--- As of June 20
···· As of Aug. 14

0   1000
FEET
LEGATION STREET

RUSSIAN
JAPANESE
FRENCH
AMERICAN

WATER GATE
MOAT
HA-TA-MEN

THE LEGATION QUARTER
▨ LEGATIONS

were trying extermination, the worldly-wise Chinese regional officials resorted to diplomacy to mitigate the catastrophe. Li Hung-chang, now governor-general at Canton, telegraphed Chinese envoys abroad that the Taku fighting on June 17 had not been ordered by the throne, and that they should ask the foreign governments for a truce. Li in concert with Liu K'un-i at Nanking, Chang Chih-tung at Wuhan, and Yüan Shih-k'ai in Shantung decided to ignore the dynasty's declaration of war on June 21. Representing this view, Sheng Hsüan-huai on June 26 proposed to the Shanghai consuls that if the foreigners would send no more warships into the Yangtze area, the governors-general there would maintain order while the foreigners might control Shanghai. The effect of this was to neutralize all of China except the northern provinces.

The regional leaders by concerted action achieved several further results. They got the convenient fiction accepted that the Boxer outbreak was in fact a "rebellion," as it has since been called, and not an act of the dynasty. This glossing over of the outrageous situation appealed to foreign as well as Chinese interests, for it allowed the continuation of China's foreign debt payments and the whole treaty system. Thus the Boxer war, the fourth and largest which China had fought against one or more Western powers in the nineteenth century, remained localized in North China while the provincial authorities elsewhere loyally represented the dynasty's interest in peace, corresponding by telegram with the court at Peking and letting the Empress Dowager eat her cake and have it too. She pursued simultaneous policies of extermination, as demanded by the Manchus dominant at court, and peace, as vigorously sought by her envoys abroad and her officials in Central and South China.

This ambivalence of Ch'ing policy was also evident in Peking. Seventy-six foreigners died defending the legations. But the rest survived only because the commander of one part of the imperial forces, Jung-lu, though maintaining a noisy bombardment, did not use available artillery or press home the attack. In late July there was even a twelve-day truce, and some fresh supplies came into the legations.

The international force which relieved the siege of the Tientsin concessions on July 14 gradually built up to some 20,000 troops, about half from nearby Japan and on their best behavior. Britain's North China forces included a regiment of 1200 Chinese recruited at Weihaiwei. An international Provisional Government ran the city of Tientsin, where Russia inspired the addition of four more concession areas to the four that already existed. International rivalries delayed the eight-nation expedition to Peking until August 4, but thereafter spurred it forward. The Boxer forces disintegrated under attack. Modern-trained imperial troops fought but were defeated. Russian, British, American, and Japanese columns vied with one another to be first inside the walls of Peking. The British won when Indian troops broke into the legations through the Water Gate under the city wall on August 14.

Aftermath of the Boxer Incident. As the Western invaders with the usual local assistance began to loot the city, which the Boxers had already despoiled, the Empress Dowager and the Emperor left Peking on August 15 in disguise, traveling by cart across the countryside to the northwest. At the age of 65, this was the Empress Dowager's closest contact with her people's problems of securing shelter, food, and protection against bandits and lawless troops. Traveling south through Shansi, the court eventually reached Sian in late October, still accompanied by the xenophobic Manchu extremists. Meantime, Li Hung-chang at the age of 77 was looked to as usual to save the situation. Still in telegraphic communication with the court on its "western tour," he got Jung-lu appointed to the Grand Council to offset the extremists and temporized skillfully with the foreigners, who accepted his fiction that the hostilities had not been a war at all but a joint effort to suppress rebellion. Although von Ketteler, the German minister, had been the only German killed, the Kaiser demanded the right to name a commander-in-chief (von Waldersee) for the allied forces. The latter reached Peking only on October 17 and devoted himself largely to punitive expeditions to dozens of North China cities, which continued for six months afterward. By late 1900, around 45,000 foreign troops were in North China, and Russia had already occupied Manchuria. The court accepted in December the main points of a settlement, but international jealousies and negotiations consumed another nine months.

The Boxer Protocol was finally signed September 7, 1901, by Prince Ch'ing, Li Hung-chang (who died two months later), and the plenipotentiaries of eleven powers. It required the execution of 10 high officials, including Governor Yü-hsien, and the punishment of 100 others; formal apologies; suspension of examinations in 45 cities, half of them in Shansi, to penalize the gentry class; expansion of the Legation Quarter, to be fortified and permanently garrisoned; destruction of some 25 Chinese forts and occupation of a dozen railway posts to ensure foreign access to Peking from the sea; raising of import duties to an actual 5 per cent; and a staggering indemnity of 450 million taels (about $333 million) to be paid from various customs and salt revenues in gold over forty years at interest rates which would more than double the amount.

The Empress Dowager with her court returned to Peking in January 1902. She received the foreign envoys cordially in audience and later their ladies (see Plate 52). The Tientsin Provisional Government handed over its administration to Li Hung-chang's successor in power, Yüan Shih-k'ai, in August 1902. The British (Mackay) commercial treaty of 1902 tried with only modest success to improve various conditions of trade and evangelism. Abolition of likin taxes, which impeded trade, a national coinage, legal reforms that would pave the way for abolishing extraterritoriality, and many other steps toward modernization which Japan had taken in the 1870's, all proved impossible to achieve. The Boxer rising and the Protocol marked the nadir of the Ch'ing dynasty's foreign relations and left little hope for its long continuance. Yet no alternative had emerged.

CHINA'S RESPONSE IN HISTORICAL PERSPECTIVE

One frequent interpretation of the events of 1900 is that the imperialist powers in their own interest kept the reactionary Ch'ing dynasty in power — that they had in fact already combined with the established order, throughout the six decades of the unequal treaties — the better to exploit the Chinese people. Much evidence can be marshaled to show the inveterate stubbornness, if not rapacity, of foreign groups in defense of their interests in China — witness the failure of the Alcock Convention of 1869 (see page 337) or of the Mackay treaty of 1902 to reform the treaty system for China's benefit. Great changes seldom seemed to the foreigners to be in their interest.

Yet this thesis that China was victimized by the foreign powers, despite its natural attractiveness for modern Chinese patriots, leaves unanswered the basic and prior question — why did China not respond to foreign encroachment earlier and more vigorously? Where were those Chinese revolutionaries who could have responded to Western aggression by modernizing the traditional Chinese state and expelling the imperialists? In the twentieth century such leaders appear. But where were they in the nineteenth century?

The mid-century rebels, being anti-Manchu, were potentially nationalistic but lacked modern ideas. The strongest of them, the Taipings, after ten years' development proved themselves old-fashioned rivals for power and showed little capacity for remaking the traditional order. The "self-strengthening" movement thereafter was more defensive than creative, a conservative compromise avoiding genuine modernization. The radical reformers of 1898, though their plans were potentially revolutionary, viewed themselves as loyal ministers of the dynasty, entirely dependent on the ruling power of the Son of Heaven. The empire's bankruptcy of leadership was finally demonstrated by those Manchu grandees who took up the inane atavism of the hopeless Boxer cause. Talent on a large scale was simply not devoted before 1900 to purposes of real revolution. No one appeared on the historical scene under the old order who had any solid prospect of making drastic changes in it.

This weakness of the forces of change within China was less an achievement of Western imperialism than a tribute to the strength of the Chinese social order, state, and culture. It was the overall cohesion and structural stability of Chinese civilization that basically inhibited its rapid response to the Western menace.

In maintaining this Chinese momentum in established ways, no single factor was all-important. China's remarkable imperviousness to foreign stimuli resulted from a complex of factors, just as did Japan's equally remarkable and opposite capacity for change and modernization. At the highest level of generality, we have suggested that Japan already had the essential ingredients of modern nationalism, in a people ready to strive together for national ends, while China did not. Beneath this level of abstraction, each observer can select his own balance among many interacting factors.

On the material plane, for example, China had vast resources but they were being exploited in traditional ways. Modern ways could not easily be substituted. Japan, as it turned out, was far poorer in raw materials, like iron, necessary for modernization, but her people met the challenge with vigor and adaptability.

The great size of the Chinese empire, which made it potentially a world power, retarded its response in many ways. Economically it was almost self-sufficient. Strategically it was well-nigh invulnerable to conquest, if not to defeat; sea power, to which Japan was so exposed, could dominate many Chinese cities but not the vast interior. Socially, the dense populations of interior areas like Hunan and Szechwan remained beyond foreign contact, reservoirs of traditional attitudes and of talent trained in the old ways; instead of reading newspapers, the elite in these areas still studied the Classics and grew up intellectually almost untouched by the treaty ports. If we consider the logistics of communication alone, Japan being one-tenth China's size might be expected to react to an equal stimulus ten times as fast.

Institutions, however, made an even greater difference than material circumstances. Japan's feudal order, as noted in Chapter 3, had already produced the loyal *han* administrators, the merchant capitalists, the scholars of Dutch learning, the patriotic individual samurai, who could create a nation-state to compete with other nation-states. China was in a different mold, above such competition. Her ancient institutions were finely balanced and well tempered to preserve an equilibrium among three strata — the monarch and his officials, the landlord-scholar-gentry class, the illiterate but cultured farming populace. In this predominantly agrarian empire neither merchant-capitalists nor artisans, neither traders abroad nor inventors and investors at home, could create centers of disequilibrating growth.

The Chinese people, in short, were in the grip of their past. Their national religion was in fact the worship of the past. The prime virtue of filial piety led on into reverence of the ancestors. The world of thought revered the Confucian Classics. Rulers could not counter the injunctions of their dynastic founder. Precedent dominated administration. Social and economic life was ruled by old custom. Even rebels invoked the past, incapable of real revolution. China was under the spell of her own great tradition, incarnate in a written language that kept alive the ancient learning, which was based mainly on history.

This backward-looking self-sufficiency of intellectual life gave China's leaders two major characteristics. First, trained to concentrate on the affairs of the Middle Kingdom, they were wilfully ignorant and correspondingly contemptuous of things abroad. Pride of culture, absorption in the Chinese universe, made them unresponsive to "barbarian" ideas.

Secondly, as supporters of a universal state China's leaders were immune to nationalism. The great empire of continental East Asia, though centered on the dense population of China, had long since had to take in the peripheral peoples of Inner Asia, particularly the nomads and semi-nomads of the steppe whose warrior horsemen had played an ever greater role in China's domestic power politics. As suggested in Volume One, the Mongol and Manchu conquests were fundamental, not superficial, phenomena of the great empire's political life — despite the insouciance regarding them affected by some Chinese chroniclers. As the most sophisticated example of Sino-barbarian administration under an alien dynasty of conquest, the Ch'ing regime vigorously suppressed racist-nationalist sentiment. Through the examination system it recruited talented bureaucrats who had indoctrinated themselves in upward-looking loyalty; it avoided any formal doctrine that officials should represent bottom-level constituencies. Until the rise of treaty-port newspapers and missionary education, presenting a comparative view of other nations, the whole process of government remained highly elitist and lacking in the symbolism, vocabulary, and practices of modern nationalism. Among other things, the elite, trained in loyalty to the ruler and to the past, lacked a common sense of national purpose in making changes, and this inhibited the strong central leadership necessary for modernization. The Manchus, on their part, could not afford to mobilize the Chinese people for participation in political life lest the dynasty become more obviously alien and dispensable and be rejected.

In this specific and seldom understood political situation, China's response to the West was affected positively by one unusual and non-nationalistic factor, the tendency to admit "barbarians" to a peripheral participation in Chinese civilization and even to cooperate in joint enterprises with powerful invaders on the frontier. This produced the long-continued role of the treaty ports, which is otherwise inexplicable. The ports were truly semi-colonial phenomena in the sense that foreign governments dominated them locally while the dynasty continued to rule the broad interior of the empire as a whole. Sea power and land power, foreign ways and interests and Chinese ways and interests, met in the treaty ports in a peculiar, stalemated harmony that modern nationalism would never have tolerated. From the two sides the Chinese and foreign officials divided their authority while the merchants shared their profits. In time the Chinese state, without changing its own nature, met its problems of Western contact by employing foreign administrators and advisers in the Maritime Customs and elsewhere. In the absence of the nationalistic spirit, this employment of foreigners was not used as an opportunity to learn from them quickly and get rid of them, as in Japan; it was more like those inveterate arrangements on the Inner Asian frontier where powerful "barbarians" who could not be defeated were given recognized status in the empire and so used, if possible, to control their fellows beyond the frontier. In their nineteenth-century foreign relations, as elsewhere, the Chinese were drawing on their past.

In the result, Japan's smaller size and greater accessibility, her insular responsiveness to foreign stimuli, the features of intellectual diversity, militarism, and individualism inherited from the feudal order, as well as the intense domestic political struggle which feudalism fostered, all made possible strong leadership that a nationalistic people were ready to accept and follow. China in contrast, was vast in size, self-sufficient, and inaccessible, with traditions of intellectual orthodoxy, civil government, and familism (rather than individualism) devoted to preserving the ongoing Confucian social order. The antinationalistic and superficial Ch'ing regime, approaching the end of its dynastic cycle, was thoroughly on the defensive — strong enough to cling to tradition and suppress rebellion, too weak to provide leadership for change.

The late Ch'ing record in diplomacy, dealing with the imperialist powers with considerable success from a position of weakness, is therefore all the more remarkable; it suggests the richness of China's great tradition. The dynasty did indeed accommodate foreign interests so as to preserve itself. Western "imperialism" should not get all the credit for its longevity.

All this, which tries to account for the contrasting responses of China and Japan to Western contact, is not intended to deny the evil effects of imperialist expansion, of which Western peoples, not having been on the receiving end, have been too often unaware.

6

East and Southeast Asia

in the Age of Imperialism

THE EXPANSION OF EUROPE IN THE LATE NINETEENTH CENTURY

Imperialism in East Asia can be understood only in a broader framework which includes European colonialism on the approaches to the area, principally in Southeast Asia. These two parts of Asia, East and Southeast, went through roughly similar phases of modernization under the stimulus of increasing Western contact. First, the Western powers secured special trading privileges, usually under a semi-colonial, unequal-treaty system. Second, this Western foothold developed in many cases into full colonialism; but in every case it inspired the rise of a native nationalism, which in the colonial areas eventually produced independent nation-states.

The remarkable thing about these later phases of colonialism and nationalism is their speed of development during the past eighty years. The rapid acceleration of European expansion in the 1880's created an "age of imperialism" in the basic sense of one people's domination, by whatever means, over another. Most of the peoples of East and Southeast Asia experienced this European domination in heightened form rather suddenly in the late nineteenth and early twentieth centuries.

The archipelagoes of Indonesia and the Philippines had been partly

ENGLISH WAR-STEAMER, from a Chinese drawing, 1844. The artist included laundry as well as sailors in the rigging, and a band playing on the foredeck.

under European rule for three centuries already. But in the early 1880's most of continental Southeast Asia was still ruled by indigenous, traditional regimes. Superior Western power had gained special treaty privileges throughout East and Southeast Asia, including first of all a legal system of extraterritoriality, similar to that which had earlier been set up in West Asia in relations with the Ottoman Empire and Persia. This semi-colonial system of unequal treaties governed Western relations with Upper Burma, Siam, Vietnam, China, Korea, and Japan. Though the Malay states under Britain and Cambodia under France were already protectorates, there were full British colonies only in Lower Burma, the Malayan Straits Settlements, and Hong Kong and a French colony only in Cochin China (see map, page 410).

After the early 1880's, however, the process of encroachment accelerated. Britain completed her annexation of Burma, and France of Indo-China. Siam, in between, remained independent only under British commercial domination. In the 1890's Japan took Taiwan from China, and the United States took the Philippines from Spain. The Dutch began to expand their rule in Indonesia. Germany, seizing a position in Shantung, precipitated the scramble for concessions in other Chinese provinces. At the turn of the century Russia began to absorb Manchuria, until checked by Japan in warfare. Japan in turn absorbed Korea. Thus semi-colonial treaty relations developed within a generation into outright colonialism, albeit in various forms, in Burma, Malaya, Indo-China, Taiwan, and Korea.

Yet after another generation, the 1940's and 1950's would see colonialism in East and Southeast Asia, including the archipelagoes, almost entirely supplanted by national governments.

The startling rapidity of this rise and fall of colonialism suggests certain observations. First, colonial rule fostered the growth of nationalism and so contributed, for good or ill, to modernization. Second, Japan's achievement in becoming a colonial power in 1895 at the same time that she arranged to get rid of her unequal-treaty status, was a most remarkable performance. Yet it merely followed the European pattern, where national unification and industrial growth, once under way, made possible the equally rapid rise, for example, of imperial Germany. The same type of preponderant power, built on nationalism and industrialism, which had set European colonialism on the march over the world in the 1880's, would enable the Japanese empire to expand in East Asia in the twentieth century. Imperialistic expansion could be one fruit of modernization anywhere. It was no monopoly of the West.

Factors in Europe's Dominance. The acceleration of Western expansion after 1880 was part of a new growth of Western power and influence, manifest on many levels, but most spectacularly on that of material tech-

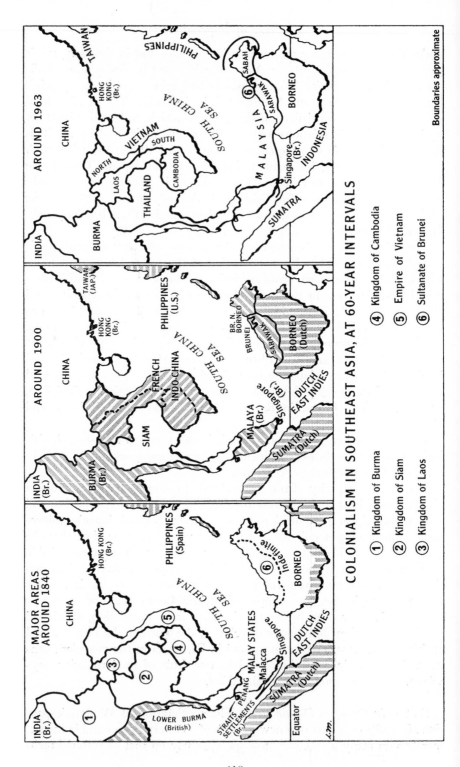

COLONIALISM IN SOUTHEAST ASIA, AT 60-YEAR INTERVALS

(1) Kingdom of Burma   (4) Kingdom of Cambodia

(2) Kingdom of Siam   (5) Empire of Vietnam

(3) Kingdom of Laos   (6) Sultanate of Brunei

Boundaries approximate

nology. Britain, though industrially pre-eminent during the late eighteenth and early nineteenth centuries, was now rivaled by the industrial productivity of the Continent and the United States. Coal, for example, had once been a leading British export, but by the end of the century Germany was mining as much as Britain, and America even more. World production of coal, in this new age of steam, tripled in the last quarter of the century. Railway mileage did the same — from 40,000 miles in 1857, to 150,000 in 1874 and 466,000 in 1898. To iron and steel, railways and steamships, metallurgy, chemistry, and all the other common technology of the industrializing nations, there were added in the 1880's and 1890's electric power and traction, the steam turbine to turn dynamos and propellers, hydroelectric installations and long-distance power lines, internal combustion engines and finally the automobile and (in 1903) the airplane. In the same period the mechanization of agriculture in new lands outside Europe — the United States, Canada, Argentina, Australia, Russia — almost doubled the world production of wheat. Refrigeration brought meat into international trade. New industries developed, like the dairy industry, and markets grew larger, like the European market for Japanese and Chinese silk. Population growth began to accelerate, roughly doubling in Europe and Latin America in the second half of the century and increasing three times in North America. Fifteen million people, the biggest migration in history, went out from Europe between 1878 and 1904.

The new technology revolutionized communication and transport, first of all by sea. Steamship lines, beginning with the Peninsular and Oriental Company, reached Singapore and China in the 1840's. By the late 1860's local steam navigation companies, principally British, were exploiting the existing water routes to and into every country and major island, from Burma all the way around to Japan. They operated in close cooperation with bigger lines that reached Europe, through the Suez Canal after its epoch-making completion in 1869. The China tea clippers that had once sailed to London from Foochow in three months were supplanted by steamships that in the 1870's could make the voyage in two months and subsequently in one month. Meanwhile, shipping enterprisers like Alfred Holt gradually converted their fierce early competition into conference agreements which maintained mutually profitable rates in most of East and Southeast Asia. The advantages of large-scale operation, along with the accumulation of capital, experience, efficiency, and influence, produced ever larger shipping combines, which brought more and more places into world trade.

The revolution in land transport followed close behind that by sea. In the 1860's, for example, when China, Japan, and Siam began to modernize, an American stagecoach still took three weeks and the pony express ten days to cross from the Mississippi to the Pacific, at much the same speed as the official post of the Ch'ing dynasty. But by 1869 American railways (built at the western end by Chinese labor) spanned the American continent, and thus the long voyage around South America or transshipment across Panama was ended in the same year that the Suez Canal eliminated the need to round Africa or transship across Suez.

At the same time, telegraphs and cables, linking up the world, greatly facilitated the flow of trade. The Western, particularly the British, banking services east of Singapore gained greatly in efficiency when telegraphic transfers on London could be substituted after 1871 for the remitting of bills of exchange by sea mail. The telegraph and cable eliminated the old concern as to how exchange rates between currencies might shift while commercial mail was in transit.

The peoples of East and Southeast Asia were thus confronted with an aggressive Western world that was not only different in culture and superior in power but already in the grip of the dynamic technological revolution that was to lead mankind eventually into the nuclear and space age. For Asian countries, the new technology was hard to acquire and still harder to keep up with. An illustration is provided by the history of that original symbol of Western superiority, the steam gunboat. In the 1860's both the Chinese and the Japanese had embarked on their naval programs just at the time when the use of explosive shells was making it necessary to develop ironclad vessels. If the technology had remained static, China as well as Japan could have mastered it. But soon bigger guns necessitated thicker iron plate, and eventually steel plate. Then the maneuverability of torpedo boats had to be met by quick-firing guns — the effectiveness of which was shown by the Japanese against the Chinese battleships off the Yalu in 1894. In buying and building their fleets China and Japan encountered all the complexities of a naval technology that could be mastered only in proportion as their entire societies were modernizing. After Japan defeated China in 1894–95, further developments like wireless, oil fuel, the submarine, the all-big-gun dreadnought, and fire-control systems made it increasingly difficult for China, lacking modernization generally, to attempt a naval comeback. More and more, any modern technology had to have a modern society behind it. Only countries of sufficient technical competence, such as Germany and Japan proved to be, could hope to catch up with leaders like Britain.

Another aspect of Europe's dominance was evident in the capital resources accumulated through the London, Paris, and other money markets and invested, often with an eye on the national interest, in ventures overseas. By the early twentieth century about one-sixth of Britain's national income every year was saved, and of this about one-half was invested abroad. By means of this long-continued process, operating through the complex mechanism of private banks, underwriters, brokers, and other middlemen handling securities on the Stock Exchange, London mainly financed the world-wide economic development of the period. More than a quarter of Britain's national wealth by 1914 consisted of foreign investments, which produced about 10 per cent of the national income. These investments had been distributed roughly one-half to the British Empire and one-fifth each to Latin America and the United States, with somewhat less to Europe and East Asia. Two-fifths of the total had financed the building of railways. The French people meanwhile had also invested heavily in banks which invested abroad. By 1914 the French foreign ownings were almost one-sixth of the total national wealth, producing some 6 per cent of the national income, but these investments were largely confined to Europe and indeed one-quarter to Russia alone. Germany also was beginning to use loans and investments as tools of foreign policy. Thus Europe's capital resources, like her production and technology, facilitated her colonial expansion and grew along with it.

Another feature of nineteenth-century imperialism, too easily forgotten now, was the large role played by individualism, then in its heyday. Colonial expansion was formally achieved in the end by national governments, but the way was prepared by the activities of individuals of every conceivable kind and in large part outside of government control. The late nineteenth century saw a remarkable partnership between individual initiative, private corporate enterprise, and government, on many levels of organization. Western individuals still showed all the diversity of adventurous, acquisitive, religious, and patriotic motives evident in the earlier centuries, as described in Chapter 1.

Theories and Attitudes Concerning Imperialism. As European power expanded, Europeans theorized about the process, and so the age of imperialism produced theories of imperialism suited to the occasion. Victorian Britain took the lead, being in the mid-nineteenth century still the world's workshop, with a near monopoly in industrial exports, particularly textiles. As the competition of the Continent increased, under state protection, the Manchester free-trade doctrine came into question; and when France and Germany began in the 1880's to seize colonies in Africa and Asia and surround them with protective tariffs, Britain quickly acquired more colonies too. Having the largest empire already, she was able to increase it by a third in the period 1885–1900, until it covered a fifth of the globe. Believing in the idea of progress, the world's oldest democracy viewed her acquisition of the world's biggest empire as obviously the reward of virtue.[1]

[1] "What enterprise that an enlightened community may attempt is more noble and more profitable than the reclamation from barbarism of fertile regions and large populations? . . . What more beautiful ideal or more valuable reward can inspire human effort? The act is virtuous, the exercise invigorating, the result often extremely profitable." Winston Churchill, *The River War* (London: 1900).

Many impulses could be discerned in this new British expansion (see pages 365 ff.). The economic urge, to secure trade and investment opportunities, was accompanied by the national competitive spirit, catered to by the popular press and by glorifiers of the "white man's burden" like Rudyard Kipling. Expansion was sanctioned by transferring Darwin's principles of organic evolution from biology to the social scene and speaking of the "struggle for survival of the fittest" among races and nations. This Social Darwinism was believed to ensure progress, because "the strongest tend to be the best." Some went further and glorified the military virtues and war, while others exulted in the benefits brought to "backward" peoples by the Pax Britannica and Anglo-Saxon government.

In all the activities and ideas of European expansion, in France, Germany, and Russia, as well as in England, it is hard to see a sole cause at work. The monocausal interpretation of imperalism as produced by finance capitalism — in its effort to exploit new markets, raw materials, and cheap labor — has been widely accepted in the past and does offer certain emotional satisfactions to those demanding simple explanations of complex situations. This theory was in fact first expounded not by Karl Marx but by liberal-bourgeois writers like J. A. Hobson, and was then developed by neo-Marxian socialists in Germany during the period when Germany was Britain's rival in practicing imperialism as well as in theorizing about it.

Historical experience over the past century and the rapid development of learning, particularly the growth of modern economics and behavioral sciences like sociology and psychology, make it impossible now to accept Marx's historical materialism as the sole guide to history. From a multi-disciplinary point of view that draws upon every branch of knowledge, the spread of imperialism and colonialism and the resurgence of nationalism stand out as phases of broad cultural contact and conflict in the world-wide process of modernization. Psychological, political, and many other factors are now seen to have been at work. The economic, and specifically the capitalistic, aspects of this process seem to have been very important, but by no means all-important. The historical record is in fact biased because the all-importance of economic factors was often assumed in the imperialists' minds and stated in their writings, just as it was in Marx's, though it was not always proved by the outcome of events. The imperialists' hopes at the time regarding the profitability of colonies were in fact often disappointed — some colonies did not become as important outlets for population, or as profitable markets, or as great sources of raw materials as did other countries that were not colonies.

The persisting appeal of the Marxist-Leninist theory that imperialism is caused specifically by capitalism is, however, an important political fact which itself calls for explanation. The continued material imbalance in living standards today between the industrialized and the nonindustrialized nations, which generally correspond respectively to the former imperialist powers and the former colonies, easily sustains in the latter a feeling of frustration and nationalistic grievance. So much present poverty, it is felt, must be the result of previous economic exploitation, especially where the colonial powers proclaimed their intention to exploit their colonies and used their military and political power for the purpose.

Thus the actual facts of imperialism, already complicated, are confused still further by the theories and feelings attached to the subject. Imperialist investment and exploitation can be studied on the factual level of economics, as phenomena helping or hindering the past growth and development of colonies. On the quite different level of attitude and feeling are the nationalistic and exploitative ambitions recorded by the colonial administrations, as well as the resentments and aspirations of the new national regimes. The people of an emerging nation may resent a past colonialism even more bitterly than their less nationalistic grandfathers did at the time.

In trying to understand the East Asian view of imperialism, we Americans are handicapped by our ignorance both of poverty and of the kind of colonial domination experienced in Asia. We should begin by noting that this was colonialism of the Old World type, rather than of the New World. In the New World the indigenous Amerindian peoples were few, and they were culturally less developed than the peoples of Renaissance Europe. In North and South America (and also in Australia and New Zealand) indigenous peoples were soon subjugated, and either eliminated or assimilated; modern civilization in these new areas has been built up largely by the efforts of the European colonists, whose chief struggle was to conquer nature. In the Old World, on the other hand, the struggle of the Europeans for access, trade, privilege, and eventual domination was with civilizations in many ways the equal of premodern Europe, in countries even older and more densely populated. Europeans generally came to the Western hemisphere as colonists in a wilderness, but they went to Asia as the potential rulers of the other peoples. Consequently the colonial era in North and South America led rather soon, in 1775 and 1821, to national rebellions by colonists, mainly of European extraction, against their politico-economic relationship with Europe; whereas colonialism in Asia led, more than a century later, to national rebellions by peoples of purely Asian origin against European domination in all its forms, social and cultural as well as political and economic.

Asian colonialism has thus occurred later in time and been vastly more intensive and comprehensive in scope than the earlier and simpler colonialism of the Americas. In Asia, colonialism has led to a basic confrontation of civilizations, to conflict over cultural values as well as over political and economic issues, and to xenophobic risings in defense of ancient traditions. All this has been much more bitter and soul-searing than, say, the invocation in 1776 of common Anglo-Saxon principles to detach the thirteen American colonies politically from the British Empire. We Americans cannot understand the Asian experience of recent decades from our own national experience of the eighteenth century.

In this chapter we survey two interacting processes — great-power expansion, and the local response to it. However, to understand the response of the Southeast Asian peoples in the smaller regions peripheral to China, where Western colonialism could not be warded off, we must first survey the relations among their traditional societies. Like China, Japan, and Korea, they have suffered invasion, collapse, and metamorphosis in modern times. One hard part of the colonial experience has been the unavoidable necessity to accept at least for a time the superiority of the West, and hence to doubt and disesteem the ancient traditions.

SOUTHEAST ASIA BEFORE THE COLONIAL ERA

"Southeast Asia" is a modern name for a land-and-sea area of about the same size as the United States. On the continental peninsula, geography makes for political and cultural diversity. The headwaters of four great rivers, the Yangtze, Mekong, Salween, and Irrawaddy, flow parallel not many miles apart in the almost impassable Sino-Burmese border region, but their streams enter the ocean through rice-growing deltas on far separate coasts, near Shanghai, Saigon, and Rangoon. The north-south rivers of the Southeast Asian peninsula are paralleled by north-south mountain chains dividing India from Burma, Burma from Thailand, and Thailand from Vietnam. The terrain fosters Balkanization rather than unity. Similarly, the thousands of islands in the four-thousand-mile arc of the Indonesian and Philippine archipelagoes do not lend themselves easily to centralized bureaucratic rule.

Terrain and climate in continental Southeast Asia have made possible two main types of livelihood and social organization. The more primitive or simple has been that of tribal peoples living near the subsistence level by hunting, fishing, or an impermanent, shifting, clear-burn-and-plant type of agriculture, in a tropical frost-free climate that creates minimal demands for clothing and tight shelter but also has its limitations. Thus the monsoon brings torrential summer rains that leach nutrient materials out of the soil, leaving it infertile, while winter is a dry season, especially in upland areas. For such peoples nature is not bounteous despite the warmth and verdure of the tropics.

The second and principal type of livelihood is by rice-cultivation on the flood plains of the rivers, especially the Irrawaddy, the Menam Chao Phraya,[1] the Mekong, and the Red River — or around the Great Lake

---

[1] "Menam" means "river," but Menam is well established in Western literature as the name for the Chao Phraya river.

(Tonle Sap) in Cambodia which acts as a catchment basin for the annual flooding of the Mekong. These flood plains, their soils annually rejuvenated by alluvial deposits, have been steadily developed into rich rice-baskets through the draining, diking, terracing, and irrigating of the fields as well as through the long hours of continuous hard work required from many hands during planting and harvesting. Producing the economic surplus necessary to sustain a higher culture, these areas have become densely populated by tightly knit, complex societies. Large territories in between them, on the other hand, especially in the hilly jungle bordering South China, have remained sparsely settled frontier areas, just as Java with its rich volcanic soil supports one of the densest populations on earth, though many outlying islands are still undeveloped. Except for the irrigated flood plains and their capital cities, continental Southeast Asia is less densely populated and seems on the whole a younger region, less used and worn, than its great neighbors, China and India. Only about one-twelfth of its land surface is cultivated.

The early history of Southeast Asia is relatively unknown but appears to have been quite complicated. Nevertheless, we can see a general pattern, without distorting reality more than is usually required by historical generalization, if we look at Southeast Asian history in four phases: first, a prehistoric period of migration, and the growth of an original culture; second, an inlay of cultural influences, incorporated primarily from India, and the rise of historic kingdoms; third, a further migration of Mongoloid peoples from the north into continental Southeast Asia, with many repercussions; and fourth, additional inlays of external cultural influences coming variously from India, China, Islam, and finally Europe. In short, the long-continued migrations into Southeast Asia have consisted both of peoples and of cultural influences. The latter have commonly been additions to the original culture rather than substitutions for it. The result is an anthropologist's paradise and a historian's nightmare.

The Original Culture. Racial and linguistic evidences in Southeast Asia (summarized in Vol. I, pp. 14–18) indicate that Mongoloid peoples, presumably migrating from the north, became the main inhabitants in prehistoric times, even though many non-Mongoloid racial strains still survive in the area. For the neolithic and early bronze-iron ages, we may posit a basic Southeast Asian racial stock with Mongoloid characteristics which some scholars, to signify its common bonds with the archipelago, call "Indonesian" (though other terms like "Proto-Malay" are also used).

The culture of this prehistoric period (often termed "Austro-Asiatic") was distinctly different from that of either India or China. In technology it included irrigated rice-culture, use of the domesticated ox and water buffalo, metal-working, and skill in seafaring and navigation. In its social organization this Austro-Asiatic culture stressed the importance of women. Its religious expression included ancestor worship and other features which persisted in the mythology and folklore of later times. A bewildering variety of cultural, linguistic, and political differences have been superimposed upon this original culture in the course of history, with China and India providing the major outside influences. But the distinctiveness of the indigenous culture should not be underestimated merely because the archaeological record is as yet undeveloped.

China, as a more ancient, record-keeping state, provides much of our earliest historical knowledge of the area; and the Chinese conquest of North Vietnam in the second century B.C. had two important results. The Red River delta became the first region in Southeast Asia to support a densely populated, centralized society based on rice-culture. And the Chinese empire actually incorporated North Vietnam for a full millennium (111 B.C.–A.D. 907), as we shall note below (page 431). However, this expansion of Chinese society was a matter of military conquest by land, rather than of trade by sea. It did not reach the rest of Southeast Asia, where the major early influence, in the second of the four phases we have listed, came from India.

From prehistoric times men had undoubtedly made their way from one river valley settlement to another along the coasts of South Asia, just as they did from one oasis to another across Central Asia, leaving only a fragmentary record. Thus the "Scythian," "Sino-Siberian," or "animal" style of metal work, found all across the Eurasian steppe from the lower Volga to the Amur (see Vol. I, pp. 109, 248), seems to have been reflected along with Chinese influence in the early Dong-Son culture, named for a site in North Vietnam. Similarly, Indian contact with Southeast Asia must have begun very early, partly by land through Upper Burma but mainly by sea, in ships aided by the monsoon across the Bay of Bengal. From Lower Burma and Malaya routes led eastward through the Straits of Malacca or across the narrow isthmus of Kra on the Malay Peninsula. Trade from India to the east developed early to supply rare tropical goods for the ancient trade between India and the Mediterranean, in which Roman gold flowed continually to Asia. At the site of the ancient port of Oc Eo (see map) archaeologists have found medallions of the Roman emperor Marcus Aurelius (reg. A.D. 161–180).

The idea that Indian influence came with "waves" of actual Indian migration is now no longer accepted. But Indian contact well before the second century A.D. began to shape the higher culture of a whole series of small kingdoms, both on the continent and among the islands.

The Early Indianized States on the Continent. Elements of Indian culture (which was by no means a single entity itself) evidently spread

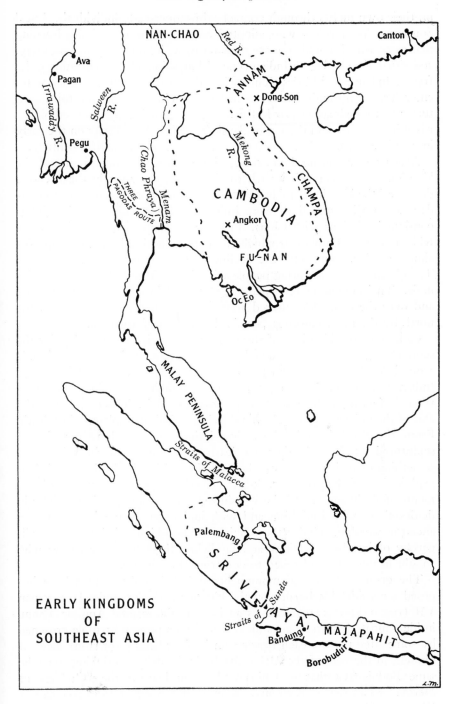

EARLY KINGDOMS
OF
SOUTHEAST ASIA

on their own merits through contact with upper-caste individuals. Local Southeast Asian rulers who adopted Sanskrit writing and the learning that came with it could enhance their status with Hindu myth, genealogy, and ritual, developing an Indian type of kingship and yet remaining quite free of Indian political ties. Thus when the earliest Southeast Asian states enter history through references in Chinese chronicles of the third century A.D., they already show Indian influence in their religious mythology, royal institutions, and the use of Sanskrit, which also appears on the early inscriptions recovered in Southeast Asia, usually from the fifth century.

Archaeology will no doubt fill out our present shadowy picture of the kingdom of Fu-nan (*circa* fifth to sixth centuries A.D.) in the Mekong delta, and the kingdom of Champa to the east of it on the coast of present-day South Vietnam. Both were Indianized states which also had long-continued relations with China. Fu-nan was eclipsed by the rise of the Khmer state of Cambodia, which thereupon coexisted with Champa for almost a millennium, until the decline of both in the fifteenth century. The Chams were a seafaring people with linguistic and other ties to Indonesia. Their kingdom remained decentralized in small coastal enclaves, and over the centuries suffered attack and gradual absorption from the north by the more vigorous, Sinicized kingdom of Vietnam.

Cambodia, the kingdom of the Khmer people, is famous today for the score of great temples recovered by French archaeologists from the jungle around Angkor. Here each god-king, as an incarnation of deity in the Indian fashion, built his own pyramidal temple-mountain, a structure typical of all the Indianized states of Southeast Asia. This temple was the axis of the universe during the king's reign and his mausoleum after death. From the Sanskrit and Khmer inscriptions and the long galleries of sculptured reliefs at Angkor, we learn the sequence of the rulers, and something of their many wars, their religio-political institutions, and their exploitation of the populace. Their eclectic religious life combined elements of Brahmanism and the worship of Siva, Vishnu, and other Hindu deities along with Buddhism and with indigenous cults of animism and ancestor worship. Under the omnipotent god-king ruled a narrow oligarchy of interbred families, and far below these were the masses who fought in the wars and toiled to construct the temples.

The great architectural monuments and their upkeep must have imposed a considerable burden on the kingdom. For example, Jayavarman VII (reg. 1181–c. 1219) built as an impregnable capital Angkor Thom, inside a moat eight miles around, centered on a pyramid-temple crowned by some fifty towers, each bearing on its four sides giant stone faces of himself, in the role of the Mahayana Buddhist deity Avalokitesvara (the same Bodhisattva that in China and Japan became the "Goddess of Mercy," Kuan-yin or Kannon). Soon after this effort the great age of Khmer architecture came to an end. The spread of the simple and austere

Theravada[1] form of Buddhism from Ceylon among the Khmer people seems to have undermined the prestige and power of the god-king as an incarnate Siva or Buddha.

On the west of Cambodia, the Mon people of the lower Menam and lower Irrawaddy basins, who are often grouped with the Khmer as a single linguistic stock called Mon-Khmer, entered history similarly under a pervasive Indian cultural influence. But the western Mon state with its capital at Pegu in Lower Burma was rather soon, in the ninth century, subjected to one of the recurrent phenomena in Southeast Asian history, invasion from the north. (This feature, characteristic of the third of our four phases, will be discussed more fully below.) The invaders were the Burmese, who are sometimes called Burmans to distinguish them from other ethnic groups in Burma, and who came south from the border area roughly between China and Tibet. The first unified kingdom that they established, in the central dry zone with its capital at Pagan (1044–1287), ruled most of the area of modern Burma. It absorbed the more advanced culture of the Mon people, including Theravada Buddhism (emanating from Ceylon), which was superimposed on the native animism and has remained the national religion of Burma. A score of impressive temples and hundreds of stupas still stand beside the Irrawaddy on the site of ancient Pagan. Unlike the monuments to royal despotism at Angkor, some of the temples at Pagan are still being used today by a devout priesthood and populace.

The Early Sea Kingdoms in Sumatra and Java. The first recorded sea power to accept Indian influence and to profit from control of the Straits of Malacca and of Sunda was the kingdom of Srivijaya with its capital probably at modern Palembang on Sumatra, halfway between the two strategic waterways. Chinese Buddhist pilgrims stopping there en route to and from India in the seventh century found Srivijaya a great center of Mahayana Buddhist learning. By the tenth century its growing commercial importance was evidenced in repeated tributary embassies to China and in relations with southeast India, as well as in the writings of Arab geographers. With the aid of vassal states on the Malay Peninsula, Srivijaya controlled the Straits of Malacca and levied a toll, by piracy if not by taxation, on ships passing through. Its hold on the trade route was lost only in the late thirteenth century, when rival powers arose in the islands and on the mainland. This had happened by the time Marco Polo visited Sumatra on his way back to Venice in 1292.

In Central Java the early rule of the dynasty of the Sailendras ("Kings of the Mountain") was marked by great architectural monuments. The

---

[1] The name Theravada, meaning "the doctrine of the elders" or "the teachers," is now preferred instead of Hinayana, meaning "the Lesser Vehicle," although the latter has been the term used in Western literature.

most spectacular, dating probably from the eighth century, is the Boro-budur, a vast stone stupa 150 feet high decorated with innumerable smaller stupas and statues of the Buddha. The miles of galleries on its terraces are adorned with reliefs illustrating Mahayana Buddhist stories with many realistic touches of Javanese life. Though the power of the Sailendras in Central Java declined in the ninth century, they became the rulers of Srivijaya.

Other great monuments in Central and East Java of the tenth century and later, together with Sanskrit inscriptions and the early poetry, laws, and other works of Old Javanese literature, attest the rise of a civiliza-tion which was distinctively Javanese. Its religious life, for example, made eclectic use of Indian forms, especially the Hindu cults of Siva and Vishnu and Mahayana Buddhism, to cloak what was essentially the native ancestor cult. In the politics of this period the kingdom of Majapahit (1293–c.1520) rose to dominance in the region of East Java, Madura, and Bali. In the fourteenth century under a great prime minister named Gadjah Mada (d.1364), this state laid claim, at least in its con-temporary poetry, to a far-reaching sea empire including most of Indonesia and much of Malaya. While historians now find inadequate evidence to support so broad a claim, it has bequeathed to modern times a vision of pan-Indonesian unity, evident for instance in the name of Gadjah Mada University at Jogjakarta.

From even so brief a sketch it seems plain that during the second of our four phases (roughly the first millennium of historic times up to about the fifteenth century) the peninsulas and islands of Southeast Asia, though fragmented and never unified, shared certain elements of expe-rience. Lying on the trade routes between the more ancient civilizations of India and China, they received continual stimuli — commercial, reli-gious and cultural — from contact with their great neighbors, pre-eminently from India. As research continues, the distinctive features of the early indigenous Southeast Asian (Austro-Asiatic or Indonesian) culture may become more apparent, in spite of the great diversity of places and peoples concerned. After all, the sea was a common thorough-fare. Java figures in the early history of Fu-nan, Champa, and Cambodia. The Mon-Khmer people of the Mekong and Irrawaddy flood plains had some degree of racial as well as commercial and political connection with the people of the archipelago. All shared the Indian influence, and Sanskrit inscriptions provided the earliest local records in all these areas.

Continued Invasions from the North. This shadow of early cultural unity, however, was diminished, in the third of the four phases we have listed, by renewed migrations of Mongoloid peoples down the river valleys from the north. Among these, the early Burman influx in the ninth century has already been mentioned. Small states had also been established in the north of present-day Thailand. Further migrations followed in the thirteenth century. These new invaders, like the Burmans before them, spoke languages very different from the Mon-Khmer tongues.[1]

The southward movement of these peoples was presumably given some impetus by the nomadic invasions of China which culminated in the Mongol conquest. The Mongols brought Southwest China into the Chinese empire for the first time. After they had completed their conquest of China in 1279, they sent several sea and land expeditions into Southeast Asia in the late thirteenth century. Among other things, they invaded Champa in 1283 and Vietnam in 1285 and 1287, without success, but on the west they conquered Pagan in 1287 and ruled parts of North and Central Burma until 1303. They also invaded Java unsuccessfully in 1292.

The Mongol threat was followed a century later by the Chinese resurgence under the Ming dynasty and the seven great maritime expeditions under Cheng Ho through the "Southern Ocean" in the period 1403–1433 (see Vol. I, pp. 272–273, 321–325). These marked the fact that the flow of Chinese sea trade and migration into the ports of Southeast Asia had already assumed important dimensions, thus adding still another element to the cultural mixture.

Meanwhile the Mongol conquest of the kingdom of Nan-chao in Southwest China had speeded up the southward migration of the Thai peoples, whose various offshoots had already begun to play a militant role in Southeast Asia. One branch of the Thai, the Shan people ("Shan" being the Burmese term for the Thai people) dominated Upper Burma intermittently after the Mongol conquest of Pagan in 1287; Shan chieftains were frequently at war with the Burman court which was fitfully maintained at Ava. The main branch of the Thai meantime by degrees took control of the upper Menam and upper Mekong valleys. In the latter they took over present-day Laos. In the former they established a succession of capitals, at Chiangmai, Sukhothai, and Ayutthaya, each one farther south.

Rama Kamheng ("Rama the Brave," reg. c. 1283–c. 1317) as king of Sukhothai fostered the Thai assimilation of Mon and Khmer cultural elements from the higher civilizations of both Burma and Cambodia, in-

---

[1] The linguistic history of Southeast Asia is very complex, with many questions still unresolved. Three main families of languages are (1) the Sinitic or Sino-Tibetan family, which includes the Chinese languages as one subgroup and the Tibeto-Burman languages (in Tibet, Burma, Southwest China, etc.) as another subgroup; (2) the Mon-Khmer family of languages (in Lower Burma, Cambodia, and adjoining areas); and (3) the Malayo-Polynesian or Austronesian family (in the Philippines, Malaya, Indonesia, etc.). The Thai group of languages (in Thailand, Laos, the Shan states of Burma, etc.), though plainly much influenced by the Sinitic through contact in Southwest China, are now classified by some as belonging to the Malayo-Polynesian family. Certainly there has been much interaction. Thus Vietnamese, for example, has a system of tones much like Thai but a vocabulary in large part Mon-Khmer as well as Chinese.

cluding political and legal institutions, art, and of course Theravada Buddhism. He adopted a new Thai script, under the influence of the script used in Cambodia, to write the Thai language, the oldest specimen of which is his inscription of 1292. While thus inheriting much from its older Indianized neighbors, this new state showed traces of Mongol influence and also developed close relations with China. In 1350 it established a new capital at Ayutthaya on an island in the Menam. This is taken as the actual founding of Siam. The new kingdom absorbed Sukhothai, and though frequently at war with Chiangmai in the north, built up an administration, promulgated the first recorded system of Thai law, and expanded to dominate much of the Malay Peninsula and Cambodia.

In the fifteenth century King Trailok of Siam (full name: Boromotrailokanat, reg. 1448–1488) developed a central administration with five major civil departments besides the military, each with its bureaucratic functions clearly assigned. The palace law codified in 1450 was reminiscent of Angkor. The traditional Thai status system by which persons were allotted land according to their grade (much as in T'ang China) was regularized with definite rules. By this system an official received a prescribed amount of land instead of a salary and was expected to live on its revenue. A man's status affected his treatment before the law. King Trailok also inaugurated the institution of vice-king and likely heir apparent. Usually a king appointed his eldest son to this post. By the early sixteenth century, the kings of Siam had further instituted a system of compulsory military service, enrolling all men eighteen and over for conscription if needed.

Another Thai state, Laos, was founded in 1353 on the upper Mekong with its capital at Luang Prabang. Lying between Vietnam and Siam, Laos traded with both while receiving cultural influences, including Theravada Buddhism, from Cambodia. Gradually the Thai rulers of Laos expanded their political control southward over the Khmer populace. Siamese pressure on Cambodia had led to the abandonment of Angkor in 1432, and Burmese expansion forced the removal of the capital of Laos south to Vientiane (Vieng Chan) about 1560.

This southward movement of the Thai peoples into present-day Burma, Thailand, and Laos, adding another layer of cultural complexity, was matched on the east by the southward expansion of the Vietnamese. Having thrown off Chinese rule after 907 (see below, page 431), they moved south at the expense of Champa and by 1471 had taken over all but the southernmost part of that ancient state.

These invasions of continental Southeast Asia from the north imposed new rulers and necessitated new cultural syntheses without displacing the indigenous peoples or wiping out their old traditions, for the invaders filtered in as a ruling stratum on top of the ancient societies. The one common theme in all these immensely complex political relations was warfare, carried on continually reign after reign between Burmans and Thai, Thai and Khmer, Khmer and Cham, Cham and Vietnamese, with occasional Javanese or Mongol raids adding variety. Yet out of all this incessant conflict no overall Southeast Asian political unity ever emerged, partly no doubt because of the divisive topography of the region, but partly because of the constant influx of outside influences. The Indian example had been one of political diversity in the first place. History compounded it.

The southward movement of peoples in the thirteenth century not only marked the end of the great millennium of preponderant Indian influence. It also established the states of continental Southeast Asia — Burma, Siam, Cambodia, Laos, Vietnam — in roughly their present positions. Except in Vietnam, their cultural debt to India — in religion and philosophy, monarchic government, law, social organization, science, art, and literature — was much greater than to China; they had remained outside the Chinese culture area.

The Influx of New Influences by Sea. The fourth phase we have listed, that of additional inlays of external cultural influences, had already begun during the Thai migrations on the continent. This new phase was marked by the spread of Islam among the islands and on the Malay Peninsula, along with the rise of Malacca after about 1400 (see page 19). Arab and Persian traders had of course been prominent on the route from the Near East and India to China since the eighth century. But Islam began to take hold in Malaya, Sumatra, Java, Borneo, and the Sulu archipelago only at this late date, after it had become established in northern India and during the same period as the growth of the spice trade to Europe. In this trade the Moslem merchants of Northwest India brought their religion to Malacca along with their textiles, and Islam spread further under the impetus of the trade and sea power which radiated from the new emporium on the Straits. Moslem states in Java encompassed the fall of Majapahit in the early sixteenth century. Just as Malay speech became the lingua franca, so Islam became the major religion of Indonesia, creating a tie with Islamic India and even with Mecca over the long trade route across the Indian Ocean. European trade subsequently overlay this East-West Asian commercial contact.

When a new era dawned with the Portuguese seizure of Malacca in 1511, the Europeans found awaiting their exploitation an area not only potentially rich in tropical products but fragmented by geography and history, divided between Islamic sultanates among the islands and warring Buddhist kingdoms on the mainland, with no political tradition anywhere established that had a claim to unify the whole area. The traditional values and sanctions of social conduct would now be found in Vietnam in the Confucian Classics; in Cambodia, Laos, Siam, and Burma, in the scriptures of Theravada Buddhism; and at some Malayan and Indonesian courts, in the Koran. Coming with their own national values and rivalries, the Europeans in time formed larger and equally diverse units of government, since there was no power like China or Japan to offer resistance.

As noted in Chapter 1, the Portuguese empire of trade, piracy, and evangelism was soon eclipsed by more powerful European nations — particularly, in Southeast Asia, by the Dutch, whose energies in turn became absorbed in the "East Indies." While the Dutch and British empires were developing in Indonesia and India, Europeans were also drawn to the "Far East," to the rich markets and mature civilizations of China and, to a more limited extent, Japan. But the countries of continental Southeast Asia, in between, received less attention. European trade and contact played only minor roles in their history until the nineteenth century.

BURMA AND SIAM IN EARLY MODERN TIMES

If we liken the southward migration of the Burmese, Thai, and Vietnamese peoples to that of the Germanic tribes a thousand years earlier in Europe, then we can compare the centuries-long conflict between Burma and Siam to European struggles like that between the emerging nations of France and England in the Hundred Years' War. As in Europe, institutional growth went on below the surface of this protracted Burmese-Siamese struggle. The Siamese rather easily maintained a unified state after 1350. But Burma suffered periodic disunion, partly because of the ethnic and cultural differences among Mons in the south, Shans in the northeast, and Burmans in between. In two different periods, the latter parts of the sixteenth and eighteenth centuries, the Burman military success in unifying Burma carried over into invasions of Siam. Though the mountains separating Burma and Siam in their respective river valleys make them distinct areas, any unifier of Burma could be tempted by several attractive invasion routes to the east — in the north through Chiangmai and in the south by the Three Pagodas route or the Malay Peninsula.

The Burmese Kingdom. In the sixteenth century Burma was reunified after two centuries of conflict too confusing to trace here. These wars involved the remaining Mon kingdom at Pegu, the Burmanized Shan princes at Ava, and the Shan states in the northeast. The Ming Chinese also intervened in the middle decades of the fifteenth century. Since the Shan warriors had sacked Ava in 1527, the eventual Burman unifier of most of Burma, Tabinshwehti (reg. 1531–1550), developed his capital at Toungoo. He conquered the rich and cultured Mon capital of Pegu in 1539 and subsequently its principal ports at Martaban and Moulmein, at the mouth of the Salween, where Europeans were already trading and could soon be hired to fight as mercenaries. His energetic successor, the conqueror Bayinnaung (reg. 1551–1581), recovered Upper Burma and subjugated the Shan states, then went on to invade Siam and capture Ayutthaya in 1564 and again in 1569. He also invaded Laos twice. Siam remained under Burmese control for fifteen years.

During the course of this sixteenth-century reunification, Burmese vernacular literature developed. The kings, though they boasted of slaughtering thousands, strove to be model Chakravartin rulers, that is, monarchs who achieve universal empire through support of the true Buddhist teaching. They patronized Theravada Buddhism, building pagodas and distributing its Pali scriptures. The ancient Shwe Dagon pagoda (still a religious center in Rangoon) was raised to 300 feet. Ecclesiastical missions went to Ceylon as part of a movement to reform and purify the Buddhist faith.

Despite these developments in war, literature, and religion, however, there seems to have been little innovation in government. The Burman king ruled in the Indian tradition, according to the ancient laws and with the advice of Brahmin priests. His fortified palace was the center of the universe and the abode of the gods; his person was divine. He alone, for example, could use regalia like the white umbrella, or permit the riding of elephants. Finally, the king was the promoter of the Buddhist faith which gave unity and meaning to Burmese life. His supramundane magical and religious status was combined with an absolute despotism in law and politics: the royal family rested parasitically on top of the whole society; all subjects prostrated themselves before the king's "golden feet" and owed him personal service; in law they all belonged to him. The king governed through an executive council (the Hlutdaw) of ancient origin, which met daily in public and handled all aspects of government, subject to his approval. This council, normally composed of four high officials, was not departmentalized and it reviewed the work of each member. Revenue was claimed by the king personally in the form of a household tax of some 10 to 15 per cent of the annual crops, in lieu of direct personal service. He might also assign the revenues of fiefs to princes and high officials. But in neither case was there a territorial bureaucracy capable of maintaining tax collections for the state, as distinct from the king. Government, in short, remained extremely personal, related to the magical potency of the monarch. The death of a king disrupted official appointments, including those of provincial officials, as well as tax payments and even foreign treaties, necessitating new arrangements by his successor. Since, moreover, the succession could easily be disputed, there was little continuity in the control of state

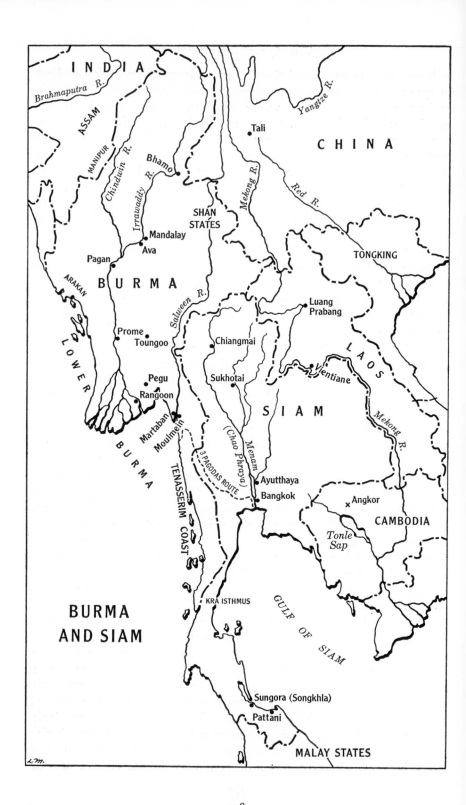

BURMA
AND SIAM

power at the center. Local affairs were supervised by the hereditary chief or headman within each township. This individual customarily handled matters of law and order, taxation, conscription, and social and religious life in a group of villages and generally represented local interests vis-à-vis the royal regime. The institutional weakness of the monarchy was not unrelated to the fact that the Burman kings were continually at odds with the Mons in the south and the Shans in the north. They were unable to build up their central authority and an effective administration.

By the mid-eighteenth century a Mon conquest of Ava had inspired support for another unification of Burma — the third, if we count medieval Pagan as the first. Alaungpaya (reg. 1752–1760) conquered Lower Burma again, invaded Siam unsuccessfully, and founded the Konbaung dynasty (1752–1885). His successors finally captured and burned the Siamese capital at Ayutthaya in 1767 — for the last time, for it was never rebuilt. In the north the Burmese fought the Ch'ing dynasty's punitive expeditions to a standstill in 1766–70 (see Vol. I, p. 390). On the west they conquered Arakan in 1784. Yet these warlike exploits were still not followed by much growth of civil government.

The Rise of Siam. Although Burma gained little permanent benefit from her invasions of Siam, the Siamese state seems to have grown strong from a resurgent patriotism in the face of invasion. Siam developed a stronger monarchy. By 1600, the kings at Ayutthaya had thrown off Burmese rule; thereupon they reasserted their suzerainty over much of the Tenasserim coast of the Malay Peninsula, and also over Cambodia.

The Siamese also differed from the Burmese in their greater receptivity to Western trade. The Burmese rulers had generally avoided such contact during the seventeenth century, and Dutch and English hopes of opening an overland trade through Burma with Southwest China were disappointed. The Siamese rulers, on the contrary, having long accepted Chinese merchants, also welcomed Japanese, Portuguese, Dutch, and English trade at several open ports. In 1609, moreover, they sent a first Siamese mission all the way to Holland.

As European contact developed, the Dutch, who took Malacca from the Portuguese in 1641, outstripped both their Japanese and their European rivals. In fact, they secured such a dominant economic position at Ayutthaya that King Narai (reg. 1657–1688) eventually welcomed as a counterweight the French missionaries sent by Louis XIV. King Narai used a Greek adventurer, Constantine Phaulkon, to superintend the foreign trade and in 1685 received an imposing French embassy from Louis XIV. The next year, seeking French help against the Dutch, King Narai sent an embassy to Versailles. It turned out, however, that the chief French aim, apart from trade, was to convert the king and his subjects to the Roman Catholic faith. Louis sent six warships with 600 troops, who fortified themselves at Bangkok. All these intrigues were suddenly ended by a Siamese palace revolution of 1688 in the course of which King Narai died, Phaulkon was executed, and the French were expelled. European contact was reduced while Chinese contact increased. Thenceforth Siam remained wary of Western entanglements.

The destructive Burmese invasions of the eighteenth century again roused a vigorous Siamese response. After the disaster to Ayutthaya in 1767, a half-Chinese general (called Phraya Tak or Taksin) led the Siamese resistance and largely reunited the country. When he became insane, another general, Chakkri, who may also have been half Chinese, seized power as King Rama I (1782–1809), founding the Chakkri dynasty which still continues, as well as its capital, Bangkok. Beating off the efforts of another vainglorious Burmese king to conquer Siam, Rama I concentrated on consolidating his central power.

The Siamese monarchy, having developed in the shadow of Angkor, was based on the religio-political Indian concept of a god-king who possessed the land and people, — the same concept that had reached Burma from India more directly. As in Burma, the Siamese king though surrounded by Brahmanic ritual was also a Theravada Buddhist. Yet this rough institutional similarity of the Siamese and Burmese monarchies was outweighed by great differences of circumstance — Siam was politically more unified and better governed, the kings were less warlike and more in touch with the outside world. In particular, they had become personally interested in the foreign trade that was carried on principally by Chinese merchants.

Unlike the early expansion of Chinese rule into Vietnam by land, the long-continued Chinese influence in Siam has reached there only by sea and has been commercial rather than political. The gradually increasing Chinese emigration to Southeast Asia was carried in trading junks to ports like Pattani and Sungora (Songkhla, see page 73) on the Malay Peninsula, but most of all to Bangkok, where rice cargoes could be procured to meet the South China demand. The Chinese community in Bangkok included Fukienese and Cantonese, speaking the "Hokkien" (Fukien) and Cantonese languages, but it was dominated by the emigrants from Ch'ao-chou, Kwangtung, who spoke "Teochiu," still another Chinese language. This reflected the fact that, while Canton was already the chief port for Western trade with China, Amoy in Fukien and other ports south of it remained the major center of the junk trade and so of emigration. In the vigorous Overseas Chinese community in Bangkok, the kings found not only merchants to handle the royal rice trade and able men to serve as officials but also Chinese girls for the palace. As a result, all the Chakkri rulers were part Chinese, four of them being at least half Chinese, and the Chinese in Siam before the rise of modern nationalism were not considered foreigners.

By the beginning of the nineteenth century, after long periods of chronic instability in relations with states on all four sides — Burma, Chiangmai, Laos, Cambodia, and Malaya — to say nothing of contacts with Vietnamese, Chinese, and Europeans, the kings of Siam had become strong and wise enough to develop the arts of peace. They avoided wars with Europeans and stabilized their easily disputed eastern borders. The landlocked state of Laos had been split in two in 1707, with capitals at Luang Prabang and Vientiane. These Laotian states had suffered periodic interventions by Burma, Vietnam, and Siam but in the late eighteenth century were finally brought into the Siamese orbit. After a revolt, Vientiane was incorporated into Siam in 1828, while Luang Prabang remained a vassal kingdom. Meanwhile Siamese efforts to seize control of Cambodia were stalemated by equally vigorous Vietnamese efforts, until both invaders accepted in 1847 a joint suzerainty. Thus by the time Britain began to take over Burma, and France to intervene in Vietnam, Siam had achieved a degree of stability.

THE DEVELOPMENT OF VIETNAM

Only one part of Southeast Asia, in close touch with China by land and sea, bears the imprint of Chinese culture so strongly as to be indubitably part of the ancient Chinese culture area. Vietnam is the ancient name, now preferred by the modern inhabitants, for the region previously known to the West by its traditional Chinese name of Annam (in Chinese, *An-nan*, "Pacify the South").

Vietnam invites comparison with Korea as an area contiguous to China, populated by non-Chinese but ruled by China in early times and subsequently a tributary state. For example, the Chinese Han dynasty invaded North Korea in 108 B.C. and set up the commandery of Lo-lang (at modern P'yŏngyang), which remained a Chinese outpost until A.D. 313. Similarly the Han took over North Vietnam in 111 B.C.; but that region remained an administrative part of the Chinese empire until the fall of the T'ang dynasty in A.D. 907. We might therefore expect the Chinese influence to be even greater in Vietnamese history than in Korean, even though Vietnam was also exposed to the Indian influence which permeated Southeast Asia. In any case, the two millennia of Vietnamese history, rather well recorded in Chinese-type chronicles written in Chinese, offer a rich opportunity for institutional and comparative studies.

Vietnam's Achievement of Independence from China. The Vietnamese people (formerly called Annamites in Western writings) are traced back to the bronze-age Dong-Son culture (see page 418). This places them in the general category of the Mongoloid peoples who at an early date migrated from South China into Southeast Asia. The Vietnamese spoken language with its use of tones has affinities to the monosyllabic, tonal Thai group of languages but has many elements of Mon-Khmer mixed in. Thus, like the Burmese and the Siamese, the Vietnamese originated in the north and expanded southward; but of the three peoples, they received the most from China and the least from India. As China quite early pushed south to absorb them, so they eventually pushed farther south to absorb the state of Champa.

North Vietnam, around the rich rice-bowl of the Red River delta at Hanoi, is separated from South China by low mountains and jungle, which form a not impassable but well-defined barrier. Chinese control was first extended to this region in the period of China's earliest unification, near the end of the third century B.C. The Chinese then called it Nam-viet, or, in Mandarin Chinese, Nan-yüeh, "South Yüeh" (though not the same as the character *yüeh* designating modern Kwangtung and Kwangsi). A Chinese type of rice-culture and bureaucratic administration could be set up more easily around Canton and Hanoi, on the watered plains of river deltas, than in the mountain regions of South China that had at first been bypassed in the southward extension of Chinese power. During most of the second century down to 111 B.C., North Vietnam was under a secessionist Chinese state, called Nan-yüeh, centered at Canton. The Han annexation of this state in 111 B.C. firmly established over the North Vietnam region a Chinese government under three commanderies, replete with the Chinese writing system, Confucian classical studies, and a Chinese officialdom, all of which overlay the indigenous culture of the villages.

Thus a Chinese type of administration and indeed most of the higher culture of ancient China spread over the North Vietnam area, much as it spread over South China — building up the agrarian-based civilization of the irrigated plains but leaving the non-Chinese tribal peoples of the mountain fringes relatively untouched. For fully a thousand years these two delta regions, north and south of the low mountain barrier marked by passes such as Chen-nan-kuan, remained outlying parts of the Chinese empire. Under the T'ang, North Vietnam (known as An-nan) was profoundly influenced by the Mahayana form of Buddhism then flourishing in the rest of China, Korea, and Japan. This was still another factor differentiating this southernmost extension of East Asian civilization from the rest of Southeast Asia, including Cambodia and Laos, where the Theravada (Hinayana) form of Buddhism predominated. On this cultural frontier, distinctive styles of art and architecture appeared, a synthesis of influences from Central Asia by way of China and from India and Indonesia by way of the sea route and Champa. Contact was maintained over the sea trade route with the Buddhist center at Srivijaya in Sumatra.

After the fall of the T'ang dynasty in 907, the Vietnamese broke away from Chinese rule and maintained their independence, though as tributaries, in present-day North Vietnam. The principal hero to emerge in this period was Dinh Bo Linh, who unified the country and took the title of emperor in 968. Of the fifteen dynasties usually distinguished during the whole of Vietnamese history, the fourth, known as the Later Li dynasty (1009–1225), for two centuries maintained a unified Chinese-type regime based on the Red River delta, where centrally managed irrigation and diking were needed equally against winter drought and summer floods.

The equally long Tran dynasty which followed (1225–1400) had to defend itself against Mongol invasions from China. The Mongols took Hanoi three times (in 1257, 1285, and 1287) but each time were obliged to withdraw. Under the Ming dynasty the Chinese intervened, occupying Hanoi in 1407. They tried to re-Sinicize Vietnam and make it a Chinese province again, but a guerrilla resistance movement forced them out in 1428, and tributary relations were re-established as the most feasible basis for Sino-Vietnamese contact.

The leader of the resistance, Le Loi, set up the Later Le dynasty (1418–1789). "We have our own mountains and rivers," he said, "our own customs and traditions." His dynasty proved to be almost as long-lived as the Yi dynasty of Korea (1392–1910) and in time showed some signs of a comparable political decay. But Vietnam, though it regularly sent tribute to Peking, was much farther away than Korea and hence able to maintain a greater degree of autonomy: it called itself "great" (Dai Viet) like a Chinese dynasty and its ruler an "emperor" like the emperor of China. (When sending tribute to China, however, the Vietnamese ruler called himself "king.") Throughout its history, moreover, Vietnam was constantly expanding to the south, as Korea could not, and so remained subject to constant non-Chinese influences. A detailed comparison with Korea would probably reveal more differences than similarities.

Growth of the Vietnamese State. The strongest emperor of the Later Le dynasty, Le Thanh-ton (1460–1497), with his capital at Hanoi, built his central administration on the T'ang-Ming model in great detail. He divided the empire into 13 provinces or "circuits," subdivided into 52 prefectures (*phú*), 178 districts (*huyên*), and 50 departments (*châu*).[1] He held triennial examinations and had nine ranks of civil and military officials, each rank subdivided. Triennially they registered the population and revised the tax quotas. The emperor planted military colonies on the expanding southern frontier. He promulgated a code of penal and civil administrative laws, and also a moral code in twenty-four articles or

[1] These are Vietnamese romanizations for characters romanized *fu, hsien,* and *chou* in Mandarin Chinese. We have generally omitted the many diacritical marks used in Vietnamese romanization to indicate tones and the like.

precepts to be read periodically and explained in every village. From the patronage of letters and virtue at the capital to the maintenance of welfare and public works in the provinces, the whole government was modeled on that of China, with dynastic chronicles and other compilations written as usual in Chinese. Indeed, the high degree of similarity between the recorded Vietnamese and Chinese systems of state-and-culture underlines the interesting but as-yet-unanswered question how far the two societies differed in substance, behind the official façade of Chinese structures and terminology.

Vietnam's continual southward expansion against Champa was stimulated by the piratical raids of the Chams, a seafaring people who had suffered repeated invasions from both Vietnam and Cambodia and had repeatedly struck back. Some fourteen dynasties had ruled Champa from the second century A.D. to 1471. They had usually enrolled as tributaries of China and often sought Chinese help against their neighbors. Meantime the Vietnamese, expanding their rule southward along the narrow strip of arable coastal land, had also suffered many vicissitudes in periodic wars with Champa. But by the fourteenth century they had acquired Hué and in 1471 they finally conquered Champa, except for a vestigial remnant which survived in the far south till 1720.

Unfortunately, the peculiarly elongated, narrow waist of the new, greater Vietnam, where the mountains closely parallel the coast, made unity difficult to maintain and dissidence easy to defend. Though the Later Le dynasty reigned from 1418 to 1789, under it the actual ruling power became fragmented. The Mac family ruled as a dynasty in North Vietnam (or Tongking) from 1527 to 1592 and were recognized by China. In the end, however, under the powerless Later Le dynasty, which China also continued to recognize south of Tongking, power was divided between two great ruling families: there was a long civil war from 1620 to 1674 between the Trinh family (reg. 1539–1787) in the north based at Hanoi and the Nguyen family (reg. 1558–1777) in the south-central region based at Hué. The latter blocked the narrow coastal corridor with two great walls north of Hué on about the seventeenth parallel. Stalemated in civil war by 1674, the two family regimes continued to rule separate governments for another century, setting a long precedent for the political division of Vietnam after 1954. The Nguyen family regime also pressed south in conflict with Cambodia, taking over border regions which Vietnamese settlers had infiltrated. They added two provinces in the Saigon area by 1700 and two more in the southern tip of the peninsula by 1750, opening up the whole Mekong delta region.

Both the northern (Trinh) and the southern (Nguyen) family regimes were headed by "princes" (Viet. *vuong*; Chin. *wang*) who professed continued loyalty to the "emperor" (Viet. *hoang-de*; Chin. *huang-ti*) of the Later Le dynasty. Both governments built up their administrations

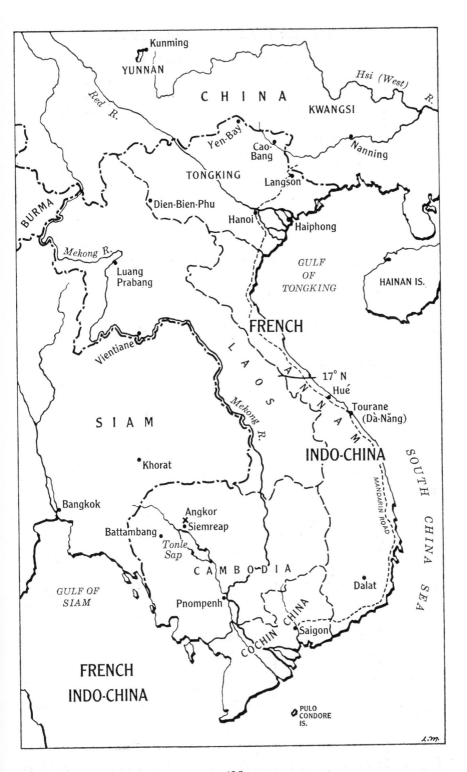

Kunming
YUNNAN

CHINA

Hsi (West) R.

KWANGSI

Red R.

Yen-Bay
Cao-Bang
Nanning

TONGKING

Langson

Dien-Bien-Phu

Hanoi
Haiphong

Mekong R.

GULF
OF
TONGKING

HAINAN IS.

Luang
Prabang

BURMA

FRENCH

Vientiane

L
A
O
S

A
N
N
A
M

17° N
Hué
Tourane
(Dà-Năng)

SIAM

Mekong R.

INDO-CHINA

SOUTH
CHINA
SEA

Khorat

MANDARIN ROAD

Bangkok

Angkor
Siemreap

Battambang

*Tonle
Sap*

CAMBODIA

Dalat

GULF OF
SIAM

Pnompenh

COCHIN CHINA

Saigon

FRENCH

INDO-CHINA

PULO
CONDORE
IS.

L.M.

435

PRINCIPAL REGIMES IN VIETNAM

Later Li Dynasty	1009–1225
Tran Dynasty	1225–1400
Later Le Dynasty	1418–1789
Mac Dynasty (in Tongking; 1592–1677, capital Cao-Bang)	1527–1592
Trinh Family of Tongking (capital Hanoi from 1592)	1539–1787
Nguyen Family of Hué succeeded by the	1558–1777
Nguyen Dynasty (capital Hué)	1802–1945
(Tay-son Rulers	1788–1802)

NOTE: The first four dynasties above had their capitals at Hanoi.

in the Chinese style, classifying landholdings for tax purposes according to productivity, registering the populace, conscripting a territorial army, encouraging cultivation, setting tax quotas, regulating the salt trade and mining, printing the Confucian Classics, and selecting officials by an examination system. Provincial administrations were under a governor, treasurer, and judge. The northern regime, more firmly in the Chinese tradition, led the way in producing its own histories in Chinese (banning the import of books from China) and also in producing poetry in the rather cumbersome native writing system known as *nom* or *chu nom*. This was a system of transcribing spoken Vietnamese with Chinese-like characters created for the purpose, usually by combining two Chinese characters that had phonetic and signific values so as to make one Vietnamese character — much as many Inner Asian neighbors of China had attempted to do, with indifferent success, in the past (see Vol. I, table of scripts on p. 257).

There were many basic differences between the Vietnamese and Chinese cultures, in spoken language, ethnic origins, folklore, and customs; but the Chinese-style family system and elitist government were vigorously and profitably maintained by the Vietnamese ruling class. Vietnam's social problems were also reminiscent of China's: over-taxed and over-conscripted peasants might desert their villages in desperation, local leaders might build up regional power against the central government. While the state cult of Confucius tended to become stereotyped, there was a revival of Buddhism in the seventeenth and eighteenth centuries, nourished from China but expressed in new Vietnamese sects. Religious development, however, tended toward syncretism even more than in China.

Early Contact with the West. Vietnam's relations with the West had begun when Portuguese traders from Macao began to buy raw silk at

Vietnamese ports frequented by Japanese and Chinese merchants. They were followed by Jesuits who, barred from Japan, arrived in 1615. Though proscribed by the Trinh in the north, the missionaries maintained precarious relations with the Nguyen, who were then more interested in Western trade and arms. The vicissitudes of Christianity in its contact with the Confucian-trained ruling class and the common people in Vietnam may be compared with its various ups and downs in China, Japan, and Korea. Christian converts were occasionally massacred and missionaries persecuted. The Christian community remained small, but the missionaries at times played influential roles, both at court through their medical and scientific abilities, and among the populace as supporters of rebellion.

Like their confreres in China, the Jesuits in Vietnam began to write down in the Latin alphabet the sounds of the spoken language. This romanized system of writing, called *quoc-ngu* (corresponding to the Chinese characters *kuo-yü*, "the national language"), became the modern form of written Vietnamese. It soon won out over the earlier and cumbersome *chu nom* system. However, while the romanized *quoc-ngu* began to produce a vernacular literature, Chinese writing in characters continued in use for official and scholarly purposes.

The ambitious French support of Catholic missions through the Société des Missions Étrangères after 1658 (see page 54) was inspired by the celebrated French Jesuit pioneer, Alexandre de Rhodes, who had inaugurated a mission to North Vietnam in 1627 and later printed Christian works in *quoc-ngu*. The French Society was harassed by local persecutions and the jealousy of other Christian powers and societies, but it persevered in the Nguyen territories and created a tradition of French interest in Vietnam. The French East India Company also tried to develop trade there, although both Dutch and British efforts during the seventeenth century had ended in failure. Against this background of continual effort and small success, French missionaries met a great opportunity in the late eighteenth century.

In 1771 there began a widespread peasant rising led by three brothers, who had the surname Nguyen, like so many other Vietnamese, but generally were called Tay-son from the name of a place on the plateau south of Hué. They took the Saigon area by 1778 and Hué and Hanoi in 1786, thus ending the rule of the Nguyen and Trinh families. The Tay-son brothers divided the country into three parts, south, center and north; the northern brother was recognized by Peking even though he had repulsed a Ch'ing invasion and fostered piratical raids on South China. But he died in 1792, when only forty. His regime had offered little new and could not maintain its grip on the country.

Just at this point a priest of the French Society, Pigneau de Behaine (1741–1799), joined forces with the young Nguyen Anh, the surviving heir of the Nguyen family, which had been violently thrown out of power in 1777. Though with different ambitions, the priest and the young pretender were refugees together. In 1787 Pigneau, with Nguyen Anh's small son, got to Versailles and proposed to Louis XVI that France should put Nguyen Anh back in power. In the latter's name he hopefully concluded a treaty of alliance between France and Cochin China (the French name for South Vietnam) and succeeded without much official help in raising enough support to send ships with a few hundred volunteer troops and supplies from Pondichéry in 1789. This French assistance proved of strategic value in consolidating Nguyen Anh's power at Saigon, which he had just recaptured. The French volunteers trained his army and navy and built forts on the best French (Vauban) design, while Pigneau handled his foreign relations. With hard fighting year by year, Nguyen Anh eventually took both Hué and Hanoi, and in 1802 proclaimed himself Emperor Gia-Long of a unified Vietnam, thereby founding the Nguyen dynasty which lasted until 1945. This was the first time that the Mekong delta region of the south (Cochin China) had been brought under a regime ruling the center and north also. In the early-modern centuries of civil war and division, regional administrations had developed in each half of the country, but the symbolic fiction of unity under the Later Le dynasty had never been abandoned. Now that the whole area of modern Vietnam was unified, its government could be reconstructed and strengthened.

Gia-Long at first showed some interest in Westernization, with the help of French comrades-in-arms who had supported his reunification of the country. In fact, several Frenchmen became high mandarins in Vietnam. But France under Napoleon was too preoccupied in Europe to exploit this opportunity for closer relations.

Persistence of the Chinese Pattern in Vietnam. The new dynasty, on the threshold of greater contact with the West, sought to defend itself by conservatism and seclusion. In the manner of a classic Chinese "restoration," it sedulously modeled its government upon the Ch'ing. Both Gia-Long (1802–1820) and Minh-Mang (1820–1841) were vigorous imitators of Ch'ing institutions and copied much of the formal structure and official terminology of the contemporary government at Peking. Though protected by an imposing citadel with twenty-four bastions designed in the European fashion, the capital, Hué, was a small replica of Peking. There were a Grand Secretariat, Six Ministries, a Hanlin Academy, and a Censorate which had the same statutory functions and even the same names in Chinese characters as their Chinese counterparts.[1] The thirty-one provinces in the three major regions of North, Central,

---

[1] In *quoc-ngu* romanization: *Nôi-Các* is equivalent to *Nei-ko* for Grand Secretariat, *Đô-Sát-Viên* to *Tu-ch'a-yüan*, for Censorate, *T'ông-Dôc* to *Tsung-tu* for governor-general, etc.

and South Vietnam were subdivided territorially into a hierarchy of sub-units much as in China. Vietnam continued to be enrolled as a Ch'ing tributary and between 1803 and 1853 sent some fourteen regular missions to Peking. Many features of Chinese administration were carefully copied — tax collections twice a year, five-year census registrations, corvée labor, public granaries, nine grades of officials (each subdivided), allowances added to salaries to "keep integrity," even the demoralizing sale of offices. Gia-Long's law code of 1812 was copied from that of the Ch'ing. Emperor Minh-Mang further strengthened his central government in 1839 by making his officials dependent solely upon stipends, instead of on personal income from villages formerly allotted them. He also built up the old Mandarin Road from the Chinese border to Saigon. Over it the imperial post carried examination candidates, officials, and communications from stage to stage for some 750 miles.

Minh-Mang also sponsored a vigorous Confucian revival, which was naturally xenophobic. He instituted examinations for the *Tan-Si* degree (Chinese, *Chin-shih*, metropolitan graduate) in 1822, and renamed the lower degrees *Tu-Tai* and *Cu-Nhan* to correspond with the Chinese *Hsiu-ts'ai* and *Chü-jen*. Chinese classical studies were encouraged and large geographies and histories compiled. A vernacular poetry also flourished, but this and the native Vietnamese art motifs and other Indian-influenced cultural elements all coexisted with a court architecture, bureaucratic structure, and ritual copied in detail from China. Minh-Mang emulated K'ang-hsi in putting out his own ten-point version of a Sacred Edict (see page 85) exhorting his subjects to respect the Confucian relationships and virtues and to be thrifty and law-abiding.

Meanwhile he refused a number of Western, particularly French, overtures for trade and diplomatic contact. When Christians were involved in a rebellion of 1833, his fears of the corrupting influence of this foreign religion were confirmed, not least by the fact that the French missionaries of the time, equally aware of the tradition of Pigneau, did not keep aloof from politics. Minh-Mang forbade foreign trade and intercourse and persecuted Christianity in a xenophobic effort to avoid influences from abroad. He did try the alternative in 1840 of sending missions to Paris and London, but the animosity of Christian missionaries made them fruitless. An antiforeign policy was continued by his successors Thieu-Tri (reg. 1841–1847) and Tu-Duc (reg. 1848–1883).

With this reassertion of a traditional orthodoxy in form went a serious deterioration of government in fact. The poverty of the farming peasantry was not alleviated nor was trade encouraged. While Vietnamese institutions such as the communal village — the primary unit of peasant society — cannot be understood purely in Chinese terms, it is plain that the difficulties of peasant life were increasing in much the same fashion as in China. The population grew faster than the means to support it.

Concurrently, intellectual life was imprisoned in the specifically Chinese fetters of the classical Confucian orthodoxy and the examination system, which produced a scholarly official class able to monopolize public life but incapable of responding creatively to the Western challenge.

In the midst of these difficulties imperial suspicion and favoritism made many officials disaffected. A succession of revolts put the Nguyen dynasty on the defensive. Some of its leaders were ready in the end to temporize with Western invaders the better to crush domestic rebellion.

The British Empire in Southeast Asia

The kingdoms of continental Southeast Asia entered the nineteenth century with some tradition of contact with Western traders and missionaries, as well as an awareness of Spanish and Dutch rule in the Philippine and Indonesian islands and British rule in India. But they had no idea of the explosive changes that European expansion was about to bring upon them. Worse still, their governments, whether they went back to a Brahmanic Indian model as in Burma and Siam or to a Confucian Chinese model as in Vietnam, were institutionally unsuited and intellectually unprepared to deal with the West.

On the other hand, their rich economic potentialities, as in rice production, tropical forests, and mining, were relatively undeveloped, while their populations in the early nineteenth century were much thinner than those of India or China. There were only some three or four million people in Burma and hardly more in Siam and in Vietnam (not including Cambodia and Laos). Although Vietnam was the smallest of the three major states in area and had the oldest and most densely populated region of rice cultivation, in the Red River delta adjoining South China, still its sparsely populated southern region in the Mekong delta invited modern exploitation in the same way as Lower Burma and Siam.

In the nineteenth century British trade and diplomacy became dominant in much of Southeast Asia. British merchants and empire-builders had been laying the foundations for this expansion during most of the preceding two hundred years. The oft-stated assumption that Britain's nineteenth-century expansion overseas was "caused" by her industrial revolution at home is a half-truth, for the two had gone along together. Just as the early China trade had been built on tea, silk, and opium, not Lancashire textiles, so the British position in Southeast Asia had grown from Asian as well as Western sources. For example, British steamship services, law and order, free trade, and economic development facilitated from the 1840's the immigration of millions of Chinese, who soon provided in much of Southeast Asia a vital labor force and a retail trading class — essential ingredients of economic growth.

One of the chief aims of the British East India Company in the seventeenth and eighteenth centuries had been strategic: to get ahead of the

French and dominate the Bay of Bengal by securing a naval dockyard on its eastern side, since there were no adequate Indian harbors closer than Bombay. A port of call en route to Canton and a trading post to compete with the Dutch at Malacca were also desired. These converging aims inspired many abortive ventures and a long search for a site on the coasts of India, Burma, Siam, Malaya, Borneo, and Java. Finally in 1786, acting on the Company's behalf, a former captain in the "country" trade, Francis Light, purchased the island of Penang from the sultan of Kedah. From 1805 to 1830 Penang was rated with high hopes as a fourth "presidency," along with Bombay, Madras, and Calcutta. But it proved expensive and unsatisfactory for either naval purposes or trade, since it lacked a good dock site and timber and failed to give access to the broad market beyond the Straits. The British still needed a naval-commercial base between India and China.

Raffles and Singapore. When the French took over Holland in 1795, Britain occupied Malacca and other Dutch trading posts to keep them out of French hands, and in 1811 she launched from Malacca a large expedition (12,000 men in 100 ships) which took Java from Franco-Dutch control. These prizes of empire were returned to the Netherlands in 1816 for reasons of state, to strengthen the Netherlands against any revival of French power in Europe. But in the meantime Java was governed for five years (1811–1816) by a young man of genius, Thomas Stamford Raffles (1781–1826).

Poor and self-educated, Raffles had risen in the Company's service at Penang and Malacca, studying the Malay language and people, dreaming of empire in the eastern seas. His task in Java was to get the cooperation of native rulers in ousting the Dutch and then to reform the government along the lines of law, order, and taxation that the British had been developing in Bengal. During his brief administration Raffles tried to apply the principles of free trade and humanitarianism that were currently ascendant in Britain. Although unable to wipe out slavery, forced labor, and forced cultivation, he began to formulate the concept of trusteeship: that the primary aim of colonial government should be the welfare of the subject people. In temperament, however, Raffles was vigorously autocratic, like so many reformers, and he did not actually favor indirect rule through native institutions as much as some empire-builders later assumed. He was inclined to respect "the usages and prejudices of the natives" only when "an anxious solicitude for their gradual improvement and a Christian charity for their weaknesses" made it necessary. He studied Java comprehensively, promoted scientific research (he also founded the original Zoological Society or zoo in London), and left a legacy of philanthropic idealism to later Dutch and British administrators. (On the subsequent history of the Dutch in Java, see Chapter 9.)

When Java and Malacca were given back to the Dutch after the Napoleonic wars, Raffles won the support of his superiors in India for the acquisition of a port "beyond Malacca" which could command the Straits. In 1819, by dealing with one claimant to the sultanate of Johore while the Dutch supported his reigning brother, Raffles secured by treaty the island of Singapore. Chinese merchants flocked to the new settlement; it grew rapidly as a free port and soon paid its way. By a treaty of 1824 the Dutch and British permanently withdrew from each other's commercial spheres, the British giving up posts in Sumatra, the Dutch their posts in India and Malaya including Malacca.

Secure in its footholds at Singapore and Penang and no longer confronted by Dutch competition, the British East India Company in Malaya was now ready to devote itself to trade, without further political involvement or territorial expansion. Yet the Company's officials on the spot, trying to facilitate trade, had constantly to push for that primal requisite of economic development, law and order. While keeping Siam from expanding farther south on the Malay Peninsula, they undertook to suppress the growing menace of piracy which had been stimulated by the growth of trade. Pirate vessels (proas or praus, i.e. war boats), equipped with sails, oars, and even cannon, and sometimes displacing 100 tons and carrying 50 men or more, could raid commerce and elude capture in shallow estuaries and island waters all the way from the Celebes and the Philippines to Sumatra, but especially on the long northwest coast of Borneo.

The White Man's Burden in Borneo. Except for some gold mined by Chinese immigrant communities, Borneo's inhospitable, roadless terrain of swampy jungles and inland mountains offered little opportunity for trade. But Borneo adjoined the ancient Chinese junk routes, now used by the China trade, which passed it both east and west. The disunity of the local Malay chieftains, who ruled as Moslem sultans, together with the monopolistic Dutch repression of local trade and the influx of modern arms, had encouraged piracy among the hardy, head-hunting Sea Dyaks and other tribes of Sarawak and of Brunei (from which the name of Borneo was derived). Hope of trade and the weakness of local administration had repeatedly attracted the attention of the British East India Company, but without permanent result. Raffles, when in Java, had prepared, fruitlessly, to take over Borneo. Most of it lay north of the equator and out of the Dutch sphere delimited by the 1824 treaty.

Law and order were brought to Sarawak, and piracy and eventually head-hunting suppressed, by James Brooke (1803–1868), a magnetic Englishman who was an ardent admirer of Raffles. He had grown up in India and inherited a small fortune; in 1839 he arrived at Kuching in his own schooner, entered into the local life and politics, and made friends with the Malay ruler. The latter was heir to and regent of the Brunei sultanate, to which Sarawak was tributary, but was having a hard time keeping control of Sarawak in the face of piracy, corruption, and rebellion. After James Brooke with benevolent enthusiasm helped him fight rebels and pirates, he formally installed Brooke as raja and governor of Sarawak in 1841.

Raja Brooke became indispensable as a giver of impartial justice and a suppressor of piracy. Steamers of the British navy helped him attack pirates, a service they were also performing on the China coast. Brooke and his family successors, ruling Sarawak as benevolent despots for more than a century, gave the Dyaks and other local Malay peoples a distinctly personal, humane, and conscientious government. Not least, they discouraged the influx of Western enterprise and exploitation.

Sarawak under the Rajas Brooke gradually grew northward, absorbing parts of the effete Brunei sultanate. Both became British protectorates in 1888, as did also the concession area of North Borneo, which had been leased from the sultans of Brunei and Sulu by the British North Borneo Company. This organization, whose backers included a partner of the China firm of Dent and Company, had secured a royal charter in 1881. It was the last of the British chartered companies empowered to administer foreign territory. Thus under different forms the northwest coast of Borneo came under British rule.

The Malay States. British East India Company rule in the Straits Settlements (formed in 1826 out of Singapore, Malacca, and the island of Penang with its hinterland called Province Wellesley) aimed at promoting trade but not intervening in the kaleidoscopic politics of the Malay states. The northern states — Kedah, Perlis, Kelantan, and Trengganu — were tributary to Siam. All were plagued by succession disputes and occasional disorders, quite contrary to the economic interest of the Singapore Chamber of Commerce. After the Straits Settlements were transferred from the India Office to a more independent status as a crown colony under the Colonial Office in 1867, British administrators by degrees had more opportunity to intervene and undergird the Malayan economy with a modern administration.

Pressure for British intervention grew out of the increasing incompetence of the Malay sultans' traditional administration in the face of new developments — not least, the influx of immigrants from South China who set up their own ethnocentric communities each under a headman or "Capitan China." Small-scale Chinese capitalists were soon developing the Malayan tin mines, where the Chinese miners were organized in rival branches of the ubiquitous Triad Society and fought fratricidal wars. Singapore had long been half Chinese, and the secret societies there dominated an underworld of opium dens, rackets, and brothels (men out-

BURMA

FRENCH
INDO-CHINA

KRA ISTHMUS

MALAYA
IN THE
BRITISH PERIOD

S
I
A
M
(THAILAND)

Federated Malay States

Unfederated Malay States

Straits Settlements

Sungora

Pattani

BAY
OF
BENGAL

PERLIS

KEDAH

PROVINCE
WELLESLEY

LIGOR

SOUTH CHINA SEA

PENANG

KELANTAN

TRENGGANU

M
A
L
A
Y
A

PERAK

PAHANG

SELANGOR

Kuala Lumpur

NEGRI
SEMBILAN

Malacca

JOHORE

STRAITS OF MALACCA

SINGAPORE

S
U
M
A
T
R
A

L.m.

numbered women something like 10 to 1 in these early Overseas Chinese communities). With pirates on the coasts, Chinese riots and gang fights in major centers, and British traders demanding law and order, the Malay sultans in the late nineteenth century generally found it expedient to seek British aid in government.

The main innovation was to install a British resident at the native ruler's request, nominally to be his adviser but actually to run his government for him in all matters except "Malay religion and custom." This was done first in Perak in 1874 and then in Selangor — as the sultan put it, "I should be very glad if my friend [i.e., the British adviser, Frank Swettenham] would set my country to right and collect all its taxes." This system of indirect rule through residents next spread to Negri Sembilan and Pahang. The sultans retained their political status, pomp and ceremony, and a guaranteed income. Arbitrary taxes, impediments to trade, slavery, and debt-slavery were abolished. Roads to the tin mines, regular taxes, a government treasury, a police force, and public health and educational services were instituted. These innovations were accomplished, for the most part, through cooperation. Each resident tried, as one wrote, to get "the Malay ruling class to work with him so that they shared in all administrative acts, and took pride in schemes for which they rightly considered themselves in part responsible." The sultan presided over a state council which included the British resident, Malay chiefs, and leading Chinese. It passed all legislation and reviewed the administration, including that of justice.

This developing system required coordination, which was supplied after 1896 when Perak, Selangor, Negri Sembilan, and Pahang were brought together as the Federated Malay States, with a common civil service and central government at Kuala Lumpur. Sir Frank Swettenham became the first resident-general, and a Federal Council including the sultans and residents was set up in 1909. In the same year Siam gave up suzerain claims to Kedah, Perlis, Kelantan, and Trengganu and these states, along with Johore, retained a considerable degree of internal autonomy as the Unfederated Malay States, under British suzerainty. Meanwhile the Malayan economy was producing about half the world's tin and soon would be producing half its rubber.

This British success in bringing modern administration to Malaya was due to many things: the fragmentation of authority among a dozen autocratic rulers, each a local despot but none a national leader; the rapid rise of unassimilable but industrious and productive Chinese communities, which gave the British and Malayan authorities a common problem; the surprising wealth in tin and rubber exports, which would have helped any regime to succeed. Thus armed conquest had been unnecessary, economic and political development began early, and Malayan nationalism arose only slowly — in fact, only half of the population was Malay, for the invasion of British capital and administration had come hand in hand with immigration of a foreign labor force, first of Chinese for the tin mines and later of Indians for the rubber plantations. British, Chinese, and Indian capital dominated the prosperous new economy. In Malaya as in Borneo, both the political organization and the traditional culture had been fragmented and impotent to create the reign of peace and law and the rapid growth of communication, trade, investment, and production which the British administration could offer. As a result, the Malays found their homeland transformed by modernization but themselves no longer masters of it.

The Absorption of Burma. Burma too acquired a political structure of law and order adequate to facilitate economic growth, but again the price was loss of sovereignty. During the nineteenth century the traditional power of the Burmese kings withered and finally collapsed, partly from British pressure, partly from internal weakness. The Burmans had conquered Burma only at the cost of subjugating minority peoples who remained politically unassimilated. These included the cultured Mon people (today called Talaings) and the rural Karen folk in Lower Burma, Arakanese on the western coast, rather primitive Chin tribes in the northwest, warlike Kachins in the far north, and finally the Shan people whose princes had once ruled Upper Burma for several centuries.

The principal force for cultural unity was the Buddhist church, whose sacred order of monks (the Sangha), custodians of the moral order of society, made the same religious values available to every racial and cultural group. Boys got their elementary education in the monastery schools. A three months' sojourn or even a longer career as a Buddhist monk was open to almost all males.

Unfortunately, the Burman kings of the Konbaung dynasty, after its founding by Alaungpaya in 1752, seem to have used their despotic powers chiefly to wage wars of conquest and impoverish the country by exacting forced labor and building palaces and pagodas. In his first four years as king, Bodawpaya (reg. 1782–1819) slaughtered all his rivals in the royal family, built a new capital outside Ava, conquered Arakan, and attacked Siam by four routes but without success.

Burman suppression of rebels in Arakan after the conquest created periodic border problems with British India. Friction increased in the 1820's when an ambitious Burman general took over Assam and Manipur and prepared to invade Bengal. The British countered with a surprise seizure of Rangoon in 1824. Though delayed by the rains, lack of transport, and heavy losses from disease, the British Indian forces finally advanced from Prome up the Irrawaddy (which is navigable for a thousand miles). In 1826 they secured at Yandabo, not far from Ava, a treaty ceding Arakan, Manipur, Assam, and the Tenasserim coast, a big indemnity of a million pounds sterling, and promises to exchange envoys and negotiate a commercial treaty.

The First Anglo-Burmese War thus installed British East India Company rule in Tenasserim, closing off its use as a main corridor for Burmese-Siamese invasions. A system of law courts and regular taxes was instituted, but the administration at Moulmein was kept subordinate to Calcutta. Not only was British Indian law imported but also Indian contract labor, while Chinese immigrated from Penang. The old social order in this part of Burma began to collapse, though population and rice production rapidly increased. Arakan meanwhile was ruled from Bengal on more purely Indian lines.

Meantime, back at the capital, the Burman kings seem to have remained tyrannical and arrogant. Bagyidaw (reg. 1819–1838) and Tharrawaddy (1838–1846) both became insane. The latter and Pagan Min (1846–1853) slaughtered their relatives and rivals. Government grew more extortionate and was dominated by anti-British extremists with little knowledge of the outside world. Diplomatic contact broke down even as British trade increased. In the Second Anglo-Burmese War of 1852–53, which was precipitated by a minor incident, the British occupied Rangoon and Pegu province, which Britain annexed by unilateral proclamation in 1852. In 1862 Tenasserim, Arakan, and Pegu were combined in British Burma (Lower Burma) as a province of India. Its capital at Rangoon, laid out to be a modern port, became the outlet for valuable shipments of teak wood and steadily-growing rice exports from the rich Irrawaddy delta, a swamp-and-jungle area that awaited modern exploitation. Heavy immigration from the central dry zone of Upper Burma, combined with local and international steamship haulage to the Indian market and via Suez to Europe, helped produce a sixfold increase in rice cultivation in the second half of the nineteenth century.

By degrees the British administration of Lower Burma, with the co-operation of the Talaing and Karen minorities, suppressed the resistance and disorder created by dacoit bands (dacoity is an Indian term for gang robbery), which were often led by the hereditary Burman township headmen. The British raj installed new types of local administrators — village headmen, police constables, revenue collectors, and semi-permanent township magistrates. But this new structure installed by the foreigner, being essentially artificial, did not check the continued disintegration of the old society.

The next Burman king, Mindon Min, who reigned from 1853 to 1878, was very different from his predecessors — a sincere Buddhist, humanely opposed to war and bloodshed, and aware of the underlying problems of Western contact. Though not a powerful ruler in his traditionally turbulent but now weak and landlocked kingdom, he nevertheless succeeded in maintaining peaceful relations with the British while acting as a great patron of Buddhism. He began in 1857 to build up a new capital at Mandalay, near Ava, as a religious and cultural center, with ornate monasteries, pagodas, and palaces, as well as a royal city inside five miles of moats and walls. There in 1871 Mindon Min convoked the Fifth Buddhist Council, a great assembly of monks at which the whole Burmese version of the Tripitaka, the sacred texts of Buddhism, was recited. He also began to modernize his administration by establishing fixed salaries for officials and regular income taxes on households. But modernization was severely inhibited by lack of Western contact. Christian missionaries had been active in Lower Burma, especially among the Karens, ever since the arrival of the pioneer American Baptist, Adoniram Judson, in 1813. But Upper Burma remained largely inaccessible.

As foreign trade in Lower Burma began to prosper, British merchants inevitably pressed for trade privileges within the kingdom in Upper Burma. Commercial treaties of 1862 and 1867, though reciprocal in many respects, set up a system of British privileges rather similar in effect to the unequal-treaty system in China: rights of trade everywhere, a 5 per cent customs tariff, a British resident at the Mandalay court, navigation of the Irrawaddy up to Bhamo, a consulate there, and a degree of British extraterritorial jurisdiction over British subjects. British companies developed vested interests and even greater expectations in handling teak and rice exports and steamer traffic on the great river. In the 1860's, moreover, the Rangoon Chamber of Commerce joined those who envisioned Southwest China as a mineral Eldorado and hence sought to open up the old China-Burma trade route to forestall the French. Intrepid Englishmen explored this route in 1863 and 1868, while equally intrepid Frenchmen went up the Mekong and into Yunnan in the same period. China's eventual suppression of the Moslem (in Burmese, Panthay) rebellion in Southwest China in 1873 and French activity at Hanoi and on the new Red River route to Yunnan (see page 452) heightened this Anglo-French rivalry.

King Mindon Min in desperation tried to play off European rivalries. He sent a mission to Europe in the mid-1850's and another in 1872, trying to assert his independence of the British, who now controlled his chief access to the world, including access to Western arms. He sought support from France in particular, and French Catholic missionaries at Mandalay were soon joined by various French and Italian military adventurers.

Unfortunately Mindon Min died in 1878. His successor, Thibaw (1878–1885), a weakling manipulated by an unscrupulous palace clique, could only preside over the collapse of the kingdom. He slaughtered his relatives in the traditional way, let bribery and corruption spread widely from the palace down, and soon faced sizable Shan and Kachin rebellions. At the same time he became deeply involved in schemes for French arms and loans, including French aid for a railway and a state bank. Anglo-French rivalry over empire was then near the flash point in any case, and Thibaw's levy of an exorbitant fine on a British teak company in 1885 merely provided a convenient *casus belli*. In a quick steamer campaign the British seized Mandalay and deposed the king. Upper Burma was annexed in 1886, and the whole of Burma thenceforth was directly administered as part of British India.

The British proceeded to apply to Burma the methods of direct rule developed in India. Having easily disposed of Thibaw, they made little effort to preserve the monarchy under a protectorate and soon abolished even the traditional king's council (Hlutdaw). Without the monarchy, however, there was in Upper Burma no authority adequate to carry on a central government, and the British found themselves involved in a costly guerrilla war of Burman national resistance which required some five years and 40,000 troops to suppress. This contrasted with their success in the same period in establishing suzerainty over the Shan states in the northeast on a basis of indirect rule.

The disappearance of the monarchy also deprived the Buddhist church, which had been the state religion, of its central authority. It came under secular law and lost its prestige and morale. Undisciplined and ignorant Buddhist monks became an element of disorder. As a result Burma's phenomenal economic growth was now paralleled by an increasing breakdown of social and political order, which the impersonal and "universalistic" British-Indian type of legal system and government services could not check. The selection of Burmans and others by civil service examinations gradually produced a new lower-level bureaucratic class, but British administrators from India could not re-create the social and cultural leadership which the royal court and its official class had formerly supplied.

By the late nineteenth century, Britain had developed a position of colonial rule in Malaya, Borneo, and Burma which depended only in part on superior arms and force held in reserve. It also depended on two capacities demonstrated by British administrators and private enterprisers — first, to provide government services establishing political order, equitable taxation, legal process, public health measures, and some educational facilities; and second, through this creation of a congenial environment, to stimulate economic development. Production, population, trade, and investment flourished; but in this climate of material growth the native social order, political leadership, and culture were overshadowed and sometimes almost eclipsed by new foreign elements — British, Chinese, and Indian. Just as Chinese immigrants formed a separate economic community in the tin mines and trade of Malaya, so in Burma as rice culture expanded, there was an influx of Indian laborers and South Indian moneylenders (Chettyars), with a consequent rise in tenantry. The resultant colonial societies were bifurcated or pluralistic, both ethnically and culturally. The indigenous social order became less integrated and self-contained than it had been.

THE FRENCH ESTABLISHMENT OF INDO-CHINA

British expansion in Southeast Asia stemmed naturally from the great and primary fact of British rule in India. Trade, personnel, naval and military power, and administrative practice flowed steadily eastward from the Indian subcontinent. French influence in East Asia in the nineteenth century had no such local and natural center from which to be diffused. Most fundamentally, French expansion had no basis in trade. Having lost her empire to Britain in the eighteenth century, France lacked even an outpost in the Far East.

The Growth of French Imperialism. As a result, patriotic Frenchmen, feeling themselves imperial have-nots, were under pressure to emulate and catch up with Britain. "In the China seas," as one put it, they had to avoid falling "into a state of contemptible inferiority." Their quest frequently met frustration. After the British acquired Hong Kong, for example, the French tried to get a Far Eastern island base but failed even in the out-of-the-way region of the Sulu archipelago. Yet French diplomats and naval officers, searching restlessly for glory and empire, displayed no lack of individual initiative. Consul Montigny at Shanghai, since he had no French trade to protect, could not usefully echo the faith expressed by the British consul (Alcock) that trade is "the true herald of civilization." Nevertheless Montigny secured the separate French Concession area (see map, page 341) for the use of the one French merchant at Shanghai and found an alternative basis for France's *mission civilisatrice* in the protection of Roman Catholic missions.

With the religious revival in France, the revived Jesuit order was once again penetrating East Asia. From 1844 to 1860, fourteen new Catholic vicariates were established in eleven provinces of China. Unlike Protestant missionaries who generally stayed with their families within treaty limits in the ports, French priests in native garb infiltrated the still-forbidden interiors of China, Korea, and Vietnam, and some even penetrated Mongolia and Tibet, showing the utmost energy, daring, and devotion. Consequently, while British consuls intervened with the Chinese authorities under the early treaties mainly on behalf of trade, French consuls did so almost solely on behalf of religion. This growing Catholic missionary activity met increased persecution in both China and Vietnam, thus giving the ambitious Napoleon III an active Far Eastern policy: namely, to champion Catholic missions, and meanwhile to keep up with British expansion by cooperating with it.

The opening of China and Japan inspired repeated Western efforts to open relations with Southeast Asian countries. In addition to the British activity we have already noted, American envoys tried their hand. Edmund Roberts was rebuffed in South Vietnam, though he made an ineffectual commercial treaty with Siam in 1833. Another American got no results in either Siam or Vietnam in 1850, and Washington showed no interest in acquiring bases, as some proposed, in the Bonin or Ryūkyū Islands or Taiwan. But American activity, together with that of Russians in Northeast Asia, spurred the French to further efforts. The British in 1855 made a fruitless approach to Vietnam but secured the opening of Siam (see page 457). Townsend Harris for the United States and Montigny for France secured similar treaties at Bangkok in 1856. Montigny then tried to get treaties with both Cambodia and Vietnam, but his exorbitant demands were backed by inadequate force, and the French had to withdraw in frustration from the principal port for foreign contact, Tourane (in Vietnamese, Da-Nang).

By this time the vested interests of Catholic missions in both China and Vietnam were considerable — of little material value compared with the China trade of Britain and the United States but certainly substantial in human and spiritual terms. The communities of Catholic converts vastly outnumbered those of Protestants. When Emperor Tu-Duc of Vietnam (reg. 1848–1883), a sincere Confucian, faced serious domestic rebellion, he moved harshly to break up the Christian communities in order to eliminate foreign religious influence. This involved him in destroying villages and killing thousands of Vietnamese Christians as well as some French missionaries. In 1857 he executed the Spanish bishop of Tongking. These events, together with the execution by the Chinese of Fr. Chapdelaine in Kwangsi in 1856, provided the French with a plain *casus belli* in the Far East.

Early Encroachment on Vietnam and Cambodia. Just as the British had been concluding in the 1850's that they must either advance in China or lose ground, so the French now felt that they must either support the Christian position in Vietnam by force or see it suppressed. Therefore, while joining with Britain against China in 1857–60 (see page 169), France also used her forces against Vietnam. In September 1858 some two thousand French troops and a thousand Spanish from Manila occupied Tourane. But they soon fell prey to heat, dysentery, scurvy, cholera, monsoon rains, and eventually typhus, while native Christian and rebel support, promised by the missionaries, failed to materialize.

Unable to advance on the capital at Hué, the French went south and seized Saigon in February 1859, but by early 1860 they had to make an ignominious retreat from Tourane for the second time.

Following the Anglo-French subjugation of Peking in 1860, however, the French forces enlarged their foothold at Saigon. Emperor Tu-Duc, hard pressed by rebellion in Tongking, signed the treaty of Saigon with France and Spain in June 1862. Spain got part of an indemnity. France was ceded the three eastern provinces of Cochin China and got promises of trade, religious freedom, and a vague protectorate over Vietnam's foreign relations.

To the Vietnamese rebellion against Tu-Duc in the north were now added Vietnamese risings against the French in the south. The local mandarins fled; hence the French, instead of being able to rule through them, had to undertake direct rule themselves. In consolidating their position in Cochin China, and eying the possibility of trade with China up the Mekong, they established a protectorate over nearby Cambodia in 1863–64: first they offered help to King Norodom (reg. 1860–1904), who was also beset by rebels; and then with a show of force at his capital, Pnompenh, they obliged him to give up his dependence on Siam. In 1867 a Franco-Siamese treaty confirmed this arrangement. In the same year the French occupied the three western provinces of Cochin China.

This French lodgement in South Vietnam was mainly the work of the navy, with missionaries playing only a secondary role and merchants almost unrepresented. The home government of Napoleon III was meanwhile preoccupied by difficulties elsewhere — with Italy, Mexico, and finally Prussia. French admirals therefore ruled Cochin China largely on their own. The geographical exploration of the Mekong in 1866–68, which stirred the French public's appetite for an Indo-Chinese empire, was carried through by a talented young naval officer, François Garnier. The expedition explored the ruins of Angkor; it went through Vientiane and Luang Prabang to Tali in Yunnan, and thence down the Yangtze through Hankow. It proved that the Mekong could never rival even the Irrawaddy as a trade route leading to Southwest China, and French interest now shifted to the Red River (Song Koi) route through Tongking. Here a French arms-salesman (J. Dupuis) began to ship arms to Yunnan.

On this frontier, French expansionists like Garnier saw themselves building in Indo-China the empire that Dupleix had been unable to create in India; after the Prussian defeat of 1870, they felt they were reasserting France's vitality, competing with Anglo-American dominance, guiding and helping lesser peoples and thus, for example, liberating Cambodians and Annamites (the French term for the Vietnamese) from the "brutal" encroachment of Siam and, above all, from the evils of backwardness. "The true, the legitimate conqueror today," wrote Garnier, "is science." France, he believed, was predestined to spread its civilizing benefits.

Imperialist sentiment in France during the 1870's was stirred not only by this idealistic rationale of colonialism, together with some hopes of economic gain, but also by the daring exploits of Frenchmen risking death overseas. Garnier provided such an example in 1873, when the admiral governing at Saigon sent him to Hanoi with 200 men, ostensibly to remove the arms merchant Dupuis at Emperor Tu-Duc's request, but actually to seize control of Tongking. Before Garnier was killed, his small force captured the citadel at Hanoi and other strongholds. Although France had to retreat and disavow this military exploit, it ushered in a decade of increasing disorder in Tongking, friction between France and China, and growing imperialist sentiment in France.

Absorption of Tongking and Laos. By the 1880's sovereignty over "Annam" was claimed both by France, on the basis of a Franco-Vietnamese treaty of 1874, and by China, on the basis of some fifty tribute missions sent to Peking by rulers of Vietnam since 1664, most recently in 1877 and 1881. France, however, had control over her colony of Cochin China in the south and a preponderant influence at the Vietnamese capital, Hué. Franco-Chinese hostilities developed on the Chinese border in the north, where Tongking had been in disorder for a decade. Not only was there disaffection here against the ruling Nguyen dynasty of Vietnam, but also an infiltration of Chinese "Black Flag" irregulars, remnants of the Taiping and Panthay rebels, under an able commander (Liu Yung-fu). The resulting turmoil prevented the French from using their new treaty rights such as that of trade on the Red River. The Vietnamese ruler encouraged the Black Flags against the French and invited in the Chinese army against both. Finally, in 1882, the French seized Hanoi, set up by treaty a protectorate over "Annam," and at once had to send for reinforcements. China gave support to the Black Flags and by late 1883 had also sent regular troops from Yunnan and Kwangsi across the border into Tongking, where they met the French in pitched battles.

The Sino-French war of 1883–85 (see pages 372 ff.) eliminated China's traditional claim to suzerainty over Vietnam and established French rule over four regions: Cochin China, governed directly as a colony, and Cambodia, Annam (i.e., central Vietnam), and Tongking, ruled more indirectly as protectorates. These regions were combined in the Indo-Chinese Union in 1887.

French residents had been governing Cambodia on behalf of King Norodom since the 1860's, but the Nguyen throne of Vietnam now posed greater difficulties. After Tu-Duc's death in 1883, two of his successors met untimely ends and the third, the boy-emperor Ham-Nghi, fled in 1885 to lead a resistance in the hills until captured three years later. The French finally installed a compliant emperor of their own choice so as to rule through the Nguyen dynasty, and suppressed rebellion with networks of posts and punitive flying columns. Nevertheless a sporadic resistance continued until about 1895, led by loyalist mandarins (like the chief censor, Phan-Dinh-Phung) or guerrilla fighters (like De-Tham in Tongking, d. 1913).

Meanwhile the French in Indo-China inherited with enthusiasm the old Vietnamese claims to areas lying between the expanding states of Vietnam and Siam. Cambodia, formerly under joint suzerainty, had already been taken over, in the 1860's, and energetic French empire-builders, even before the conquest of Tongking, had pursued intensive explorations of Laos and adjoining areas on the upper Mekong. It will be recalled that Laos had been split in 1707 into two hostile parts with capitals at Luang Prabang and Vientiane, and that the latter had been absorbed by Siam in 1828 while the former remained a tributary kingdom. With disorder in Tongking, Chinese bandits entered Luang Prabang, Siamese forces came in to suppress them, and the French began to intervene against this Siamese "expansion."

In the 1890's French imperialism, already confronting Britain in Africa and elsewhere, became aroused to "recover" for Vietnam all areas east of the Mekong. Frontier incidents threatened to bring on a Franco-Siamese war. In 1893 the French sent gunboats and an ultimatum to Bangkok, whereupon the British urged moderation on France and compliance on Siam. Thus pressed, Siam ceded to France Laos and the whole east bank of the Mekong and evacuated the old Cambodian areas around Angkor (Siemreap and Battambang, eventually ceded to France in 1907).

French expansion, stimulated by this absorption of Laos in 1893, was not stabilized until the Anglo-French agreement of 1896, which averted war and guaranteed the independence of Siam in the area of the Menam Valley. This was the real heart of the country and also the main area for British trade. The French expansionists had in effect been bought off with large territories which, however, had little economic value.

The French administrators in Indo-China believed that French culture was of universal value and superiority. In Cochin China they followed a general policy of "assimilation," training Vietnamese in French ways and incorporating them in the lower levels of a single bureaucracy. Superficially in the other, protectorate areas they tried also a policy of "association," bringing cooperative Vietnamese, Cambodian, and Laotian officials at higher levels into a parallel though powerless structure of native agencies of government, so that French rule would be indirect in appearance. For this purpose an imposing façade of rulers was maintained — the emperor of Vietnam and kings of Cambodia and Laos (at Luang Prabang) together with courts, councils, and consultative assemblies — and it served to make French rule more palatable. Yet in fact the aim could only be assimilation, for to the French the imposition of their culture seemed the only genuine means of modernization available.

Paul Doumer, governor-general from 1897 to 1902, instead of trying to build a modern government indirectly through the protectorate system, laid the fiscal and administrative foundations of a self-supporting centralized regime. From his capital at Hanoi the governor-general ruled Cochin China through its governor, and the four protectorates of Cambodia, Annam, Tongking, and Laos through French *résidents supérieurs*, under whom French residents in turn ruled the provinces through the native officialdom. This use of Vietnamese mandarins, though indirect in form like the Dutch use of Javanese princes, left no doubt as to who held power. In the Napoleonic fashion, major central ministries were now built up to direct a unified tax-collection, including government monopolies of salt, opium, and alcohol, as well as public services and programs of public works — port facilities, canals, roads, and railways. This created a framework for a national government and for economic expansion. French investment opened coal mines and plantations.

But the general effect of French rule was to weaken if not liquidate traditional institutions of law, ethics, family, and village community, without as yet creating a new social order to take their place. While breaking down the village commune, French rule built up landlordism with its attendant evils of sharecropping, usury, and inefficient production on fragmented holdings, so that the rice-farming economy, especially of the northern delta, soon became overpopulated and undercapitalized. Both the social order and the standard of living suffered.

MODERNIZATION IN SIAM

Siam escaped colonialism through a combination of circumstances, beginning with a fortunate geographic location. Shielded from India by Burma and from China by Vietnam, it lay squarely between those two great civilizations which became the main foci of European expansion, yet was situated some 700 miles off the sea route connecting them. In the late nineteenth century Siam also lay between the countervailing expansions of the British in Burma and the French in Indo-China, a buffer state. Moreover, it had its own protective fringe of tributary territories, which it gradually surrendered to Britain (on the Malay Peninsula) and to France (in Cambodia and Laos) while in the process of preserving Siamese independence.

Commercial Development and Western Contact. The modernization of the Siamese kingdom began with the growth of foreign trade. This was traditionally monopolized by the king and was increasingly stimulated in the early nineteenth century by immigration from China and by exports in the large junk trade to Amoy and Canton. Tribute missions — which in the Ch'ing were a sign of official trading activity — went from Siam to China only eleven times between 1662 and 1776, averaging every tenth year, but thirty-eight times between 1777 and 1853, averaging every other year (the tribute regulations specified once every three years). Significantly, such missions ceased after the inauguration of trade under the treaty system in 1855. Siam's biggest export before 1851 was sugar to China, since rice exports were still nominally forbidden. In addition to handling this foreign trade, the growing Chinese community in Siam was moving into domestic retail trade. Thus while Upper Burma and Vietnam at mid-century still played no part in world commerce, Siam had already begun to receive the impact of a money economy and foreign contact.

The Siamese monarchy rode the tide of this commercial development. As of 1850 the government of King Rama III (1824–1851), though it required some taxes and labor service, remained still superficial to the life of the villages and dealt in premodern fashion mainly with ceremonies, domestic peace and order, and foreign relations. But the king had already built his own fleet of a dozen square-rigged, Western-style ships for foreign trade and was getting important revenues from it. These had increased when, in place of his royal monopolies on many export products, he substituted Chinese-style tax-farming by private collectors, mostly Chinese, who bid for the privilege. Thus the monarchy, with its absolute and comprehensive powers, had become interested in trade, not opposed to it. There was no anti-merchant dogma like that of Confucianism to hold it back.

Diplomatic relations with the West had also developed auspiciously. The early heyday of Western contact and intrigue had led to Siam's comparative seclusion after 1688 (see page 430). A British mission (under Raffles' co-worker, John Crawfurd) failed to open treaty relations in 1822. But Britain's humbling of the all-conquering Burmese, in the first Anglo-Burmese war of 1824–26, facilitated negotiations at Bangkok by another British envoy, Henry Burney. In 1826 he secured a treaty, on equal and reciprocal terms, which stabilized Anglo-Siamese relations in Malaya and regularized trade. Perhaps from their varied experience with so many neighboring states — Burma, Vietnam, Cambodia, and Laos — the Siamese seem early to have mastered the principle of balancing one foreign power against another. In 1833 the American envoy (Edmund Roberts) was given his treaty, on the model of Burney's, in record time. Altogether six Western diplomats were granted audiences between 1826 and 1839.

During the last years of Rama III, however, Western aggression in China and foreign objections to the king's tax-farming and trade practices led to strained relations. Even the persuasive Sir James Brooke of Sarawak, who came as a British envoy in 1850, failed to open Siam in the way Japan was about to be opened. In view of the Anglo-French expansion in East Asia that was soon to follow, it is plain that by the 1850's Siam was facing great dangers from abroad.

Mongkut and the Opening of Siam. In this era of crisis the kingdom was saved by still another fortunate circumstance — her rulers' extraordinary capacity to carry through a long-term program of modernization.

King Rama III's younger brother, Prince Mongkut, though eligible for the throne, had been passed over in 1824. Forsaking the palace, he became a Buddhist monk and made pilgrimages throughout the country. In addition, he became a scholar of the Pali scriptures, an examiner of the priesthood, an abbot, and leader of a reform movement that was concerned not only with monastic discipline and ritual but also with rediscovery of the pure Buddhist canon. As a reforming monk, Prince Mongkut pressed for a rational faith stripped of superstition and devoted less to monasticism than to popular enlightenment. Catholic and Protestant missions had become established in Siam in 1830 and 1833; Mongkut's Buddhist priests now began to compete with them in preaching to the people. The prince studied Latin, mathematics, and astronomy with the Western missionaries. English became his second language. He set up the first Siamese printing press. Working outside the confines of the court, traveling among his people, reading widely and meeting foreigners, Prince Mongkut had a long and unparalleled preparation for the kingship, which he was invited to assume as Rama IV (1851–1868). For vice-king he chose a brother well versed in the English language and culture.

As king, Mongkut had a combination of despotic power and personal wisdom which enabled him to meet the Western threat by voluntarily opening his country. For Britain, having just seized Lower Burma and helped open Japan, sent two righteous champions in 1855 to open Siam. These two men, respectively concerned for free trade (Sir John Bowring) and British prestige (young Harry Parkes), were the same who in the following year would start the second war with China. The Siamese king and his advisers realized that they had dynamite on their hands, and Mongkut utilized a personal diplomacy that left Bowring, at least, much impressed by royal intimacies and Oriental splendor.[1]

The Anglo-Siamese treaty of 1855 set up an unequal-treaty system of the Chinese type, with a most-favored-nation clause and provisions for no duty on opium imports, a very low fixed treaty tariff, and a British consul exercising extraterritorial jurisdiction over all British subjects. Treaties were signed with France and the United States (Town-

---

[1] Mongkut to Bowring in his own hand: "My respected gracious Friend, — I am now indeed very glad for your Excellency's arrival, as mostly it is the fulfilling of my longly expecting mind and earnest desire" etc., signed "S.P.P.M. Mongkut, Rex Siamensium." Bowring's journal: "How can I describe the barbaric grandeur, the parade, the show, the glitter, the real magnificence . . . of today's Royal audience! We went, as usual, in the State barges: mine had scarlet and gold curtains, the others had none. Parkes sent them back, and they all returned with the needful appendages: he understands the art of managing Orientals marvellously well."

send Harris) in 1856 and subsequently with other countries in an effort to give them a countervailing interest in Siam's independence of Britain. At the same time a Siamese embassy went to London in 1857.

Great changes followed the opening of the country by treaty. There was a spurt in foreign trade (particularly teak and rice exports), and some investment, predominantly British, came in from abroad. King Mongkut promoted public works, especially canals and roads, and the study of foreign languages and science. He also developed an extensive correspondence with Western dignitaries and heads of state.[1]

Reform and Survival under Chulalongkorn. Thus begun, the modernization of Siam was pursued by Mongkut's son Chulalongkorn, whose reign as Rama V (1868–1910) was almost coterminous and in some ways comparable with that of the Meiji Emperor in Japan. In comparison, however, Siam was a much younger, smaller, and weaker country, less mature and dynamic, with a simpler division of labor and a greater need of many basic changes. It was concerned less with building national power than with fending off a foreign take-over. Siam under Chulalongkorn had farther to go, and went less rapidly, than Japan under Meiji.

Since Chulalongkorn was only sixteen years old at his accession, he prepared himself during a five-year regency by travel to Java and India. After 1873 he began a long process of reform from the top down. The absolute power of the king, which made these basic changes easier, was itself symptomatic of Siam's political and social underdevelopment. Chulalongkorn's first act on his coronation was to abolish the custom that required all his subjects to remain flat on their faces in his presence.

Siam was still a simple agrarian society of rulers and ruled. The government's demands on the peasantry for taxes and corvée labor were not onerous. Rice was the country's main crop, produced especially on the plain of Lower Siam where the Menam Chao Phraya deposits fertile alluvium during its annual summer flooding. The expanding Chinese community handled much of the rice-milling. Siam, like Lower Burma and southern Vietnam, still had an abundance of undeveloped land for rice-farming, and restive Thai peasants could develop new lands on the frontier of cultivation. The royal aristocracy was not a caste, because a king's collateral descendants in five generations became commoners, and

---

[1] He once offered to provide young elephants to populate the American forest (President Lincoln politely declined), and signed himself to Queen Victoria "by race of royalty your affectionate brother" (she replied as "your affectionate sister"). King Mongkut had altogether 82 children during his seventeen-year reign. His children's tutor for five years, Mrs. Anna Leonowens, misrepresented him in her book *The English Governess at the Siamese Court* (1870), and the progressive distortions of this work in a popular novel, a musical comedy, and a Hollywood film have recently depicted this remarkable man as little more than a Gilbert and Sullivan type of noble savage.

while the king made appointments to a bureaucracy with five levels of nobility, this bureaucratic nobility was not hereditary. But perhaps a third of the population were in a status of slavery, into which one might fall through capture in warfare, or more generally by selling oneself to meet a debt. Chulalongkorn prohibited this practice, but gambling, a chief cause of debt-slavery, was not suppressed.

Political modernization came only slowly. The customary, premodern type of corruption among self-seeking officials and commoners could be checked only by reforms of taxation and administration, and for these tasks the king hired European advisers, often from smaller or less aggressive nations like Belgium, Denmark, or Italy, as well as many Britishers experienced in nearby areas. Even so, the first budget was not published until 1901. Abolition of tax-farming and forced-labor taxes took several decades as part of a centralized reform of local administration on the model of British Burma. This was carried through by Prince Damrong, a representative of the new aristocracy who had been given a European education in palace schools and then sent abroad. He also set up a state educational system, building upon the Buddhist monastery schools which had traditionally given boys their primary education. In all these gradual reforms, British models were the most influential.

Meanwhile, as in Malaya, Chinese immigration contributed greatly to Siam's growth. Taksin, the half-Chinese king who reigned for fourteen years after 1767 (see page 430), had been the son of a Chinese migrant (surnamed Cheng) from Ch'ao-chou and consequently spoke "Teochiu" Chinese. He fostered Chinese immigration and patronized his half-countrymen in Siam. "Teochiu"-speakers became the dominant Chinese element there. The population of Bangkok was thus half or more Chinese from the start.

With modernization, Chinese immigration accelerated. By the 1870's steamships, including some in the Siamese merchant marine, were supplanting both the traditional trading junks and the modern square-rigged sailing ships as the main carriers of Chinese overseas. Emigration from China was now funneled through Hong Kong from treaty ports like Swatow, Amoy, and Hoihow on Hainan Island, opened in 1876. From a net increase (surplus of arrivals over departures) of a few thousand a year in the early 1800's, this flow of Chinese to Bangkok and other Siamese ports on the Malay Peninsula rose to about 7000 in the 1880's and 15,000 in the following decades down to World War I. As a result, Siam's total population in 1917 (estimated at 9,232,000) was about one-tenth Chinese (roughly 900,000).

The disproportionate importance of the Chinese in Thai economic life was due to several factors: their greater concern for getting ahead by hard work, money-making, and thrift, inherited from the more crowded and competitive social scene of China; and their related concern for kin-group solidarity and continuity, in such contrast with the weak kinship system of the Thai, who lacked an ancestor cult and even surnames. Self-selected emigrants from Fukien and Kwangtung, the most commercial-minded areas of China, were likely to be unusually enterprising individuals; and in Siamese cities and towns they were allowed a freedom for modern enterprise that was largely denied the rice-farming Thai freeman or debt-slave until the end of the century. As a result, Western merchants in Siam relied on Chinese compradors as they did in China. British and Chinese commercial interests grew up in an interplay of partnership and competition, but the Chinese kept the inside track. The astute kings of Siam, for example, took leading Chinese into the ranks of the government and the bureaucratic nobility.

The success of the Siamese aristocracy under Chulalongkorn in developing a more modern government also aided economic growth, making it possible for British interests under the unequal-treaty system to prosper in conditions of law and order and eventually to handle nine-tenths of Siam's foreign trade. This in turn obviated any demand for British colonial expansion in the interests of commerce and civilization. The semi-colonial treaty system proved adequate for commercial domination, and outright colonialism was unnecessary. This favored situation, as well as her position in Burma, led Britain to support Siam diplomatically against French encroachment from the east. As imperialist rivalry increased in the 1890's, Siam passed through another era of crisis in its foreign relations, but the danger of war with France was finally averted by the Anglo-French agreement of 1896.

KOREA'S RESPONSE TO THE OUTSIDE WORLD

The tragedy of Korea's experience in modern times may be highlighted by contrast with the success story of Siam, and by comparison with the parallel tragedies of Burma and Vietnam. All four were small kingdoms, by Asian though not by European standards, in the shadow of the Chinese empire. Korea with 86,000 square miles of area was roughly one-third the size of Burma (260,000 sq. mi.), two-fifths the size of Siam (200,000 sq. mi.), and two-thirds the size of Vietnam (127,000 sq. mi.). But in population Korea in the early nineteenth century was perhaps the largest of the four — about 7 or 8 million.

Geography helped decide the fate of these four kingdoms. None could escape foreign encroachment, but Siam was the most favorably situated, for it lay safely off the main sea routes, on the far periphery of British and French expansion, and offered no corridor of land contact with the assumed riches of China. Burma had the misfortune to offer such a corridor, at least in the hopes of Europeans, while also adjoining the heart of British expansion in India. Vietnam similarly presented a river route to China, not up the Mekong as first supposed, but up the Red River. But Korea was in the worst position, lying in the path of Russia's continental expansion and serving as an invasion corridor between Japan and the continent. In the age of imperialist expansion Korea became inevitably a vortex of great-power rivalry: a bone of contention between China and Japan; then a focus of Russian interest in an ice-free port; and, for Japan, "a dagger pointed at the heart" and, later, a bridge to the continent. Whereas the Southeast Asian states fell temporary victim to maritime powers expanding far overseas, Korea was inextricably lodged in a nutcracker between an island-empire and two land-empires. Her geographical position had long since destined the country for trouble.

Political institutions also influenced the fate of these four states. While the Burmese monarchy was institutionally weak and over-warlike, the Siamese kings turned their despotic powers to good account. Unencumbered by xenophobic doctrines derived from Confucian political philosophy, Siam had had direct experience of European relations earlier and more fully than the three other states and in the nineteenth century was the first to accept the necessity of modernization. In contrast, both Vietnam and Korea, geographically and historically closer to China, were more genuine tributaries, culturally and intellectually as well as diplomatically. One may speculate that their intellectual dependence on the Confucian system of thought and government, with its font of origin outside their own boundaries or control, made the scholar-official classes in both Vietnam and Korea respond to the Western challenge even less creatively than did the scholar-officials of China.

At all events, the blighting influence of imperial Confucianism in general and its tributary system in particular was even more marked in Korea, China's principal tributary, than in Vietnam. For centuries the foreign relations of Korea had been limited to the sending of regular tribute missions to China and some other missions to Japan. The Korean kings, though weak as domestic rulers, were consistently hostile to all Western contact. They maintained a rigid policy of seclusion until it was almost too late to learn the art of diplomacy. The reluctance and confusion of aim in Korea's response to the imperialist menace were major reasons for the disastrous outcome. For here, as elsewhere, imperialist expansion, though irresistible in its later phases, had seemed at first to be little more than an intellectual challenge on the outer horizon.

Korea's Unpreparedness for Western Contact. While the development of Korean society and culture up to modern times has been summarized in Volume I (Chapter 10), and the diplomatic opening of the country during the late nineteenth century has been sketched in the preceding chapter (pages 375–378), we have not yet tried to look at Korea's modern history from the inside. Though still little studied, the last centuries of the inordinately long Yi dynasty (1392–1910) seem to present a picture of social and cultural stagnation. Perhaps this was due in part to the fact that so much had been borrowed from China. In actuality, Korea remained distinctly different from China in historical experiences, social structure, and worldly situation. But, like the Manchus when they ruled the Middle Kingdom, the Korean ruling class felt themselves to be conservators of a great tradition, not innovators.

Accordingly the hereditary, aristocratic, and nonproductive *yangban* class used Chinese forms to support a monopoly of public life much more narrow than that of the gentry class in China. To do this, they clung to the very letter of Confucianism, tolerated no deviation from orthodoxy, and maintained the private academies (*sŏwŏn;* Chinese, *shu-yüan*) and the examination system without opening them to non-*yangban* talent. They controlled and restricted trade, mining, and technological innovation, and even at times banned the circulation of money in certain areas.

The fifteenth century, an age of brilliant cultural activity, witnessed an outpouring of histories, encyclopedias, classical commentaries, and the like (printed with movable type fifty years before Gutenberg) and the innovation of a highly scientific phonetic writing system (*han'gŭl*). But thereafter the dynasty fell prey to bureaucratic schism. The sixteenth century saw a series of great purges when dominant individuals and groups, whether motivated by Confucian idealism or unscrupulous ambition, harassed or destroyed their rivals through manipulation of the censoring organs of the state. Out of these purges there developed a virulent factionalism that eventually became entrenched on a family and regional basis and hardened into hereditary groupings in permanent rivalry, undermining orderly government and diverting attention from pressing problems of state.

In similar fashion, foreign trade and contact had been growing in the early years of the Yi dynasty, in the era of the great Ming voyages to South Asia; and Korea had then received tribute missions from the Ryūkyū Islands, Siam, and Luzon, as well as from minor Jürched and Japanese rulers. But this early, expansive contact with the outer world had given way to seclusion, especially after friction with the Japanese had been followed by massive Japanese invasions. Hideyoshi's 160,000 warriors from Japan overran most of Korea in 1592, and were followed by another wave of some 140,000 invaders in 1597. Whatever the Japanese did not destroy was at the mercy of Korea's allies, the armies sent by Ming China. In 1636, finally, a Manchu invasion force of perhaps 100,000 came across the Yalu; but although the Manchus soon set up the new Ch'ing dynasty in Peking, they kept the Yi dynasty in power under tight restrictions as their number-one vassal.

The devastated Korean kingdom was thus denied even the benefit of a dynastic new deal. Rural poverty, exploitation by landlords, removal of land from taxation, nepotism, corruption among officials, weak government, famine, pestilence, and banditry — these became the Korean way of life. Though the eighteenth century saw certain specific achievements in literature, art, and administration, the country was in no way prepared for Western contact. Whereas Japan had fought off all invaders, dealt firmly with earlier Europeans, grown economically despite its self-imposed isolation, and now was ready to burst open again with self-generated energy, Korea was politically moribund and economically stagnant. This, at least, is the picture thus far available.

The Failure of Rebellion and Reform. The Korean state in the 1860's met a challenge on two fronts, foreign and domestic, just as China and Vietnam had done a few years earlier. On the domestic front a large-scale peasant-based rebellion, led by a religious cult, broke out in southeastern Korea in 1862–63, the most serious revolt for several hundred years past. Though primarily in protest against poverty and *yangban* misgovernment, this rising was also inspired by the upsetting news of the Taiping rebellion and foreign invasion in China. In Korea, however, domestic rebellion and foreign religion became differently related to one another than in China.

Catholic Christianity had reached Korea first in the form of Chinese writings from the Jesuits at Peking and became known as the "Western Learning" (*Sŏhak;* in Chinese, *Hsi-hsüeh*). The first Chinese Catholic missionary penetrated Korea only in the late eighteenth century. Gaining adherents, Christianity was soon persecuted, in 1801 and later, as a heterodox sect and also a foreign menace. It became perforce a secret society, ministered to by Chinese priests and, after 1836, by French priests who were smuggled into the country.

In violent opposition to this "Western Learning," but also partly inspired by its example, there arose in the 1860's a syncretic religious cult known as the *Tonghak* (in Chinese, *Tung-hsüeh*) or "Eastern Learning." The founder, Ch'oe Che-u (1824–1864), was the guilt-ridden son of a poor village scholar of North Kyŏngsang province. He suffered repeated frustrations in the official examinations, much like his Chinese contemporary, Hung Hsiu-ch'üan. After years of study and meditation, Ch'oe felt impelled, partly by the news of the Taiping movement and the Anglo-French attack in China, to seek the mandate of the Lord of Heaven (*Ch'ŏnju;* in Chinese *T'ien-chu*, the same as the Catholic term for God). This he claimed to have received on May 25, 1860, in the form of divine instructions to found a religion which could make the East as strong as the West. His teachings used concepts from Taoist, Buddhist, Neo-Confucian, and even Catholic cosmology, but with a strong admixture of native Korean shamanism and an apocalyptic emphasis, somewhat like that of Christianity, on the spiritual union of the believer with the

Creator. In the "new era," a "world of new creation," the *Tonghak* "way" would overcome the Westerners by its magic and supersede Confucianism and Buddhism to begin a new cycle, enriching the poor and exalting the lowly. The new sect naturally appealed to the poverty-stricken peasantry, spread rapidly, and contributed to risings in southeast and south Korea. Though Ch'oe, when arrested and tried in 1864, maintained that the *Tonghak* aimed to defeat Catholicism, he was decapitated as a subversive. Presumably his teaching seemed to be too similar to Taiping Christianity. Under his successors the *Tonghak* faith spread quietly into every province.

The rulers of Korea in the 1860's met domestic rebellion and the Western challenge much as Vietnam had earlier in the century, by an anti-Christian policy of seclusion and a revival and reform of traditional institutions. A vigorous conservative reform program was pursued by the Korean regent of the decade 1864–73, who was known by his title as the Taewŏngun or Grand Prince (literally "Lord of the Great Court"). This man's personal name was Yi Ha-ŭng (1821–1898) and he was father of the boy-king Kojong (reg. 1864–1907); he was also a newcomer, quite prepared to challenge the whole establishment. He met the crisis in the domestic fortunes of the Yi dynasty by seeking reforms which would effect a "restoration" (*yusin*) of the golden age of the dynastic founder (Yi Sŏng-gye), a bit like the contemporary T'ung-chih Restoration in China. These reforms aimed to restore the proper functioning of the traditional Korean "three systems" of land tax, relief grain, and military service, all of which had become thoroughly corrupted. The Taewŏngun used many devices to strengthen the central administration, the monarchy, and the royal family. (These included rebuilding the fifteenth-century Kyŏngbok palace; see Vol. I, Plate 42.) He tried to wipe out factionalism by closing almost all the private academies (*sŏwŏn*) which nurtured factional adherents, by depriving the censoring organs of their power in the government, and by directly taxing the *yangban* class. He recruited talent much more widely, reorganized the central administration, and revised the law codes. He also tried to create military strength by giving more prestige to the military class, building fortresses, and training some 12,000 riflemen with modern arms.

With all this effort to revitalize tradition and even use modern means to defend it, the Taewŏngun was vigorously exclusionist. When his execution of French priests brought on the French attack of 1866 (see page 375), his commander lectured the invaders with Confucian righteousness: "How can you tell us to abandon the teachings of our fore-fathers and accept those of others?" After the French had left in defeat, as the Koreans assumed, the Taewŏngun redoubled the persecution of Christians, but in keeping with established custom he left Korea's foreign relations for Peking to handle.

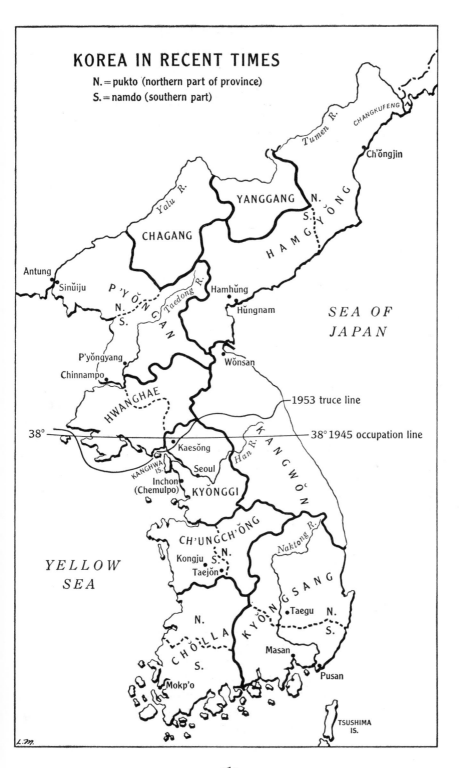

KOREA IN RECENT TIMES

N. = pukto (northern part of province)
S. = namdo (southern part)

CHANGKUFENG

Tumen R.

Ch'ŏngjin

YANGGANG

N.

S.

Yalu R.

CHAGANG

HAMGYŎNG

Antung

Sinŭiju

P'YŎ *Taedong R.*

N.

S.

Hamhŭng

Hŭngnam

SEA OF
JAPAN

P'yŏngyang

Chinnampo

Wŏnsan

HWANGHAE

1953 truce line

38°

38° 1945 occupation line

KANGWŎN

Kaesŏng

Han R.

KANGHWA IS.

Seoul

Inchon
(Chemulpo)

KYŎNGGI

CH'UNGCH'ŎNG

Naktong R.

YELLOW
SEA

Kongju

N.

S.

Taejŏn

KYŎNGSANG

N.

S.

Taegu

N.

CHŎLLA

S.

Masan

Pusan

Mokp'o

TSUSHIMA
IS.

L.M.

The subsequent opening of Korea produced violent repercussions at Seoul. The Taewŏngun, still intransigent though out of power after 1873, opposed the Japanese treaty of 1876. He played a key role in the anti-Japanese outbreak of 1882, and he was thereupon kidnaped by the Chinese as a troublemaker and held for three years in China. This left in power his enemies, the entrenched Min family, who were represented at court by King Kojong's queen (often referred to as "Queen Min"). The queen and her Min family faction now cooperated with China, undid some of the Taewŏngun's reforms, and similarly opposed the modernization efforts of those who wanted to follow the Japanese example. The lack of national unity, manifested in the curse of factionalism, continued to upset Korean efforts to achieve independence and modernization.

Foreign influences flooded into Korean politics. After cultural missions went in 1881 to both China and Japan, a Korean mission visited the United States in 1883, and another set up a legation in Washington in 1888. American influence, strong in Japan in the 1880's, also reached Korea through missionary-educators and sympathetic diplomats, who espoused Korean independence even though, as later with the "integrity of China," the use of force to support the idea was never contemplated in Washington.

Paradoxically, during the era of Chinese ascendancy at Seoul from 1882 to 1894, it was mainly contact with Japan that inspired a growing number of patriots with Western ideas of nationalism and reform. Japanese liberals, like Fukuzawa Yukichi who advised the young reformers Kim Ok-kyun and Pak Yŏng-hyo in the early 1880's (see page 377), saw Japan inaugurating a new day in Korea much as the United States had done in Japan. But these Korean reformers, who wanted to Westernize on the Japanese model, found their hopes blocked by the ruling Min faction and the dominant Chinese influence, and so attempted their *coup d'état* of December 4, 1884. With the knowledge of the Japanese legation, they assassinated conservative ministers and seized the king, only to be thwarted by the Chinese commander (Yüan Shih-k'ai) and forced to flee. Rising foreign pressure had not eliminated factional disunity.

During the 1880's the misery of the populace was not alleviated, and the *Tonghak* movement, venerating its martyred founder, continued to appeal to the oppressed. As in the ancient tradition of shamanism, *Tonghak* members worshiped at altars in the hills with chanting and ritual dancing in order to ward off illness. Occasionally they organized demonstrations with bells and drums at the royal palace, seeking a posthumous pardon in traditional fashion so as "to claim redress of grievances for the cult founder." In 1893 the sect became more explicitly antiforeign and, soon, more violent against the government. Its uprising in the southern provinces in 1894, though quickly suppressed, provided the occasion for the Japanese invasion.[1]

By 1894, Japanese of all camps were involved in Korean politics. Militant expansionists like Uchida Ryōhei of the *Genyōsha* (Black Ocean Society) came to help the *Tonghaks,* just as liberals like Fukuzawa publicly mourned the assassination of his disciple Kim Ok-kyun (see page 382). It was one thing, however, to expel Chinese influences and declare Korea independent, and quite another to set the Korean government on the path of Japanese-type modernization.

Three successive Japanese ministers to Korea failed in this task. The first (Ōtori), after Japanese troops took over Seoul in July 1894, installed in power the Taewŏngun, of all people, to head a sweeping reform program; but the Japanese soon found the old man interested "only in grasping power and purging his opponents." The second minister (Inoue Kaoru) then brought the exiled reformer of 1884, Pak Yŏng-hyo, and other pro-Japanese modernizers into power in a government of all parties, but Pak was forced to flee again in Inoue's absence. The third minister (General Miura) finally conspired with the Taewŏngun in October 1895 to effect at last the brutal murder of the old man's daughter-in-law, "Queen Min," whose body was burned in her palace grounds. After this, Japanese influence was eclipsed for a couple of years by that of Russia — especially after the king fled for safety to the Russian legation (February 1896), where he stayed for more than a year.

Dynastic weakness and foreign aggression inspired at Seoul in 1896–98 a Korean counterpart of the Reform Movement then blossoming at Peking. The main protagonist, Sŏ Chae-p'il, had been a leader of the attempted coup of 1884 but then had got safely away. He came to the United States and as "Philip Jaisohn" acquired an American wife, citizenship, and a medical degree from George Washington University. Returning in 1896 as a government adviser, he founded two reformist institutions: a newspaper, *The Independent* (*Tongnip Shinmun*), which used only the vernacular *han'gŭl* without Chinese characters, and an embryonic political party, the Independence Club (*Tongnip Hyŏphoe*), which began to debate political issues and soon organized large demonstrations to promote national independence through governmental reforms. Like their Chinese contemporaries, the Korean reformers had no contact with peasant-based movements like the *Tonghak,* and they endangered the vested interests of dominant court conservatives, who suppressed the reform movement at the end of 1898.

But the weak Korean king, though he took the title of emperor in 1897, was incapable of holding power. Since Japan's victory had ended the influence of China, which had been backed by Britain, Korea's fate

[1] After 1905 the *Tonghak* sect, now pacified, took the name *Ch'ŏndogyo,* "Society of the Heavenly Way."

was left poised between Japan and Russia. Their agreements over Korea in 1896 and 1898 did little to check their rivalry, and only Japan's victory of 1905 finally established her domination of the peninsula as a protectorate (see pages 482 ff.).

Korea's response to foreign contact had thus been doubly handicapped. Within the protecting cocoon of the Chinese tribute system the country's leaders had been less well prepared for outside relations than those of Siam, Burma, or Vietnam. But by the time Korea was opened, the pressures emanating from great-power rivalries had become much greater. Not one power but five pushed their way into Seoul — Chinese and Japanese troops, Russian, British, and American diplomats, together with Catholic and Protestant missionaries, all exerted their several influences in this hermit kingdom that lacked any tradition or experience of multi-state foreign relations. The Koreans were caught off balance from the beginning. So multifarious were the foreign pressures upon them that we have already had to deal with the opening of Korea within the broad context of foreign encroachment on the Ch'ing empire in Chapter 5. Even more, the fate of Korea after 1898 can be understood only within the framework of power politics in the heyday of imperialism.

POWER POLITICS OVER CHINA, 1894–1901

One way to bring order into the kaleidoscopic picture of imperialism in Asia in the 1890's is to view it against a background of Anglo-Russian rivalry all across the continent, from the Afghan border on the northwest approach to India, through Central Asia, Tibet, and Mongolia, and around to Manchuria and Korea. As of 1890, Britain was entrenched on the south as ruler of India, Malaya, and Burma and as dominant trading power in Siam, China, and adjacent areas. Britain's particular rival in Siam and Burma had been France, but Anglo-French rivalry, which had been especially bitter in Africa, was compounded after 1893 by the Franco-Russian alliance. And so one element precipitating the intensi-fied European imperialism in the Far East in the 1890's was Russia's accelerated expansion as a land power across the north of Asia.

Russia's Re-emergence in the Far East. After Count Muraviev's suc-cessful mid-century invasion of the Amur and the acquisition of the Maritime Province in 1860 (see pages 171–173), Russian expansion ran into serious difficulties of food supply and transportation. The cossacks in the sixty villages that formed a communication route along the Amur could not grow enough crops to feed themselves in the unfavorable climate; in summer they could navigate upstream only with difficulty, and in winter they lacked draft animals for transport on the ice. With the sale of Alaska to the United States in 1867 and the decline of the sea-otter fur trade in the Pacific, even the Russian garrisons and naval forces in Northeast Asia were reduced. Finally, the Suez Canal after 1869 wrecked the hopes of developing trade via the Amur between China and European Russia. Even China's brick-tea exports to Russia began to go by sea. By 1880 the population of the Russian Far East was still less than 100,000; the combined immigration of Chinese, Tungus from Manchuria, and Koreans exceeded that of Russians; trade was mainly in non-Russian hands. The area's connections with European Russia were maintained more by sea than by land.

This weak Russian position had been accompanied by a passive policy. After the Sino-Russian settlement of the Ili crisis in 1881 (see pages 366–370), the Russians felt rather on the defensive in the Far East, where they faced such developments as the Ch'ing empire's active colonization program in Manchuria in the 1880's, as well as Li Hung-chang's build-up of his Peiyang fleet and Port Arthur naval base and the contemporary growth of the Japanese fleet.

However, Russia's passivity in the Far East had diminished neither the expansive proclivities of her rulers nor the distrust of Russian designs which had become traditional in Japan, China, Britain, and the United States. In 1885–87 the British navy occupied Port Hamilton, an anchorage in a group of small islands on the south coast of Korea, in order to forestall Russia's pushing south for an ice-free port in Korea. In 1886 Tsar Alexander III concluded that all the weaknesses in the Russian position — in population, food supply, land transport, and naval power — could be overcome by building a trans-Siberian railway which would strengthen Russian land power in the Far East. Diplomatic isolation and frustration in Russian policy elsewhere made it easier to turn eastward again, and French capital was available. In 1891 work was started on the Trans-Siberian Railway from both ends, with completion scheduled for 1903.

Once under way, Russia's turning to the east was justified by ideologists of the time as a sacred "historical mission" to spread Western culture to the Orient and "liberate" its "oppressed" peoples. The influential Prince E. E. Ukhtomskii stressed a pan-Asian cultural kinship of Russians and Asians: "All these people of various races feel themselves drawn to us, and are ours, by blood, by tradition, and by ideas." Meanwhile on the plane of action the powerful Sergei Witte, a self-made man who was minister of finance from 1892 to 1903 and chief architect of Russia's industrialization, got the personal support of the new tsar, Nicholas II, for the Trans-Siberian Railway. It became a key element in the Russian state program of heavy industry.

As Russia's interest and power thus increased, her Far Eastern policy became more vigorous. After long initial hesitation, she led France and Germany in the triple intervention of April 1895 which forced victorious Japan to restore the Liaotung Peninsula to China. Pressing this advantage, Witte in July 1895 got French and Russian banks to loan China 400 million gold francs (£15,820,000, or about $76,890,000) at the relatively low rate of 4 per cent interest, to help pay China's indemnity of 230,000,000 taels (about £30,000,000 or $146,000,000) due to Japan. By December he had got the French banks to join in setting up the Russo-Chinese Bank, an agency capable of using French capital to promote commercial, industrial, and railway projects in China.

By April of 1896 Russia was asking Chinese permission to build a railway 950 miles across Manchuria to Vladivostok, in order to avoid by this short-cut the costly tunnels and bridges which the Trans-Siberian line would require on the 350-mile-longer Amur route. Peking at first refused; but after Li Hung-chang arrived in St. Petersburg for Nicholas II's coronation, accompanied by Prince Ukhtomskii, he negotiated and got Peking's agreement to his signing in June 1896 a secret Russo-Chinese treaty of alliance. By it, China and Russia were to fight together against any Japanese expansion on the continent, and the Russo-Chinese Bank was to build the Chinese Eastern Railway across Manchuria. (A protocol promised Li a bribe of three million rubles, only one million of which was eventually paid him, in May 1897.) After much maneuvering and confusion of counsels, Russia followed up this treaty by sending a naval squadron into Port Arthur in December 1897 and getting from China in March 1898 a 25-year lease of the southern tip of the Kwantung Peninsula,[1] including the port of Dairen (in Chinese, Ta-lien; in Russian, Dalny) and the Port Arthur naval base. Russia also got the right to connect these ports with the Chinese Eastern Railway by a north-south line 650 miles long, the South Manchurian Railway.

The "Scramble for Concessions." This Russian success in acquiring the long-sought ice-free port, to be connected with Europe by rail, illustrated the novel methods of a new phase of imperialist penetration in China. The new approach used loans, railways, leased areas, reduced land tariffs, and rights of local jurisdiction, of police power, and of mining exploitation to create in effect "spheres of influence." Great-power rivalry chiefly motivated the rapid maneuvers by which Britain, France, Germany, Russia, Japan, and to some extent the United States variously challenged, assisted, forestalled, and cooperated with one another to take advantage of the expected breakup of China. While the details of these maneuvers are almost as confusing to historians today as they were to diplomats at the time, certain patterns can be picked out.

First of all, no power followed a straight and single course of action, because each was influenced by all the others. The Russian moves sum-

---

[1] Kwantung ("east of the pass," i.e. at Shanhaikwan, also spelled Shanhaikuan) is not to be confused with Kwangtung, the province around Canton. Kwantung, the term used by Japan, actually designated a larger area than Liaotung ("east of the Liao River") but the two names were used interchangeably.

marized above, for example, were only one thread in the tapestry and were partly responses to the moves of others. Thus both Germany and Britain in 1895–96 had actively encouraged Russia to press forward in the Far East in order to lessen her pressure elsewhere; and Russia occupied Port Arthur in December 1897 only after Kaiser William II had offered encouragement and set an example by sending a German squadron into Kiaochow, Shantung, in November. Russia's counsels were often divided, many of her efforts failed, events were often unforeseen, and bold action alternated with worried hesitation. So it was with the other powers.

Secondly, there was a certain degree of alignment among the European nations, as we can see by putting a selection of main events in a chart (page 472). The Franco-Russian allies, having little sea trade, encroached on China from their land-based positions on the south and north, in Indo-China and the Russian Far East. France actually was the first to act, in June 1895, extorting a concession to open mines in Southwest China and to extend her railways there from Tongking. This success, after decades of Anglo-French competition in planning the railway penetration of Yunnan, was eventually followed up by French construction of the narrow-gauge line from Hanoi up the Red River to Yunnan-fu (Kunming), completed in 1910. On their land frontiers, moreover, France and Russia secured reductions in the Chinese customs tariff. Working through a Belgian syndicate, they also secured the concession for a Peking-Hankow railway through the Chinese interior, in May 1897.

Britain and Germany, on the other hand, as trading and naval powers without important land frontiers with China, sought their spheres in the Yangtze Valley and Shantung, respectively. They also had greater capital resources, and their bankers lent two-thirds of the funds that China required to pay the Japanese indemnity.

Of these two maritime powers, however, the British were defending a long-established commercial position which gave them four-fifths of the foreign trade of China, while the Germans were newcomers, already Britain's chief trade competitors, aggressively seeking markets and naval bases. The Kaiser kept on friendly terms with his cousin the Tsar and, after much prospecting for a naval base elsewhere, won the latter's tacit consent for the German occupation of Kiaochow in November 1897, which in fact precipitated the general scramble.

In the ensuing melée, the British government, under vigorous pressure from the China Association and other spokesmen for the China trade and imperial expansion, pragmatically followed a policy of "compensation." While still espousing the traditional principle of the integrity of China, the Open Door, and equal opportunity for the trade of all comers, Britain nevertheless carved out her own "sphere," applying in effect the same two-power standard as in the naval race to keep abreast of any combination of two competitors. Thus, as it turned out, France acquired a "sphere" in Kwangtung-Kwangsi-Yunnan with a naval base at Kwang-

EUROPEAN RIVALRY IN CHINA, 1895–98

Russia	*France*	*England*	*Germany*
	S.W. China treaty June 1895: reduced land tariff, exclusive land treaty ports		
First (Franco-Russian) *loan* July 1895: 400 million francs, 36 years, secured on Chinese Maritime Customs			
	Anglo-French S.W. China agreement Jan. 1896: share privileges in S.W.		
			Second (Anglo-German) *loan* Mar. 1896: 16 million pounds, 36 years, Customs administration to "continue as at present"
Russo-Chinese secret alliance June 1896: Russo-Chinese Bank, Chinese Eastern Railway rights, reduced land tariff			
		S.W. China treaty Feb. 1897: railroad and trade concessions	
	Peking-Hankow railway agreement July 1897; final contract June 1898: Belgian syndicate to lend funds and operate for 30 years.		
			Kiaochow (Tsingtao) occupied Nov. 1897, leased Mar. 1898 for 99 years with railway rights, etc.
Port Arthur occupied Dec. 1897, leased Mar. 1898 for 25 years, railway rights, etc.			
		Third (Anglo-German) *loan* Mar. 1898: 16 million pounds, 45 years, British I.G. of Customs as long as British trade greatest (nonalienation of Yangtze Valley to another power)	
	Kwang-chow Bay leased April 1898 for 99 years	*Weihaiwei* leased April-July 1898 "for so long as Port Arthur shall remain" Russian	
		Kowloon (New Territories) leased June 1898 for 99 years	

(American Open Door Notes, Sept.-Nov. 1899; Hay circular, July 1900)

NOTE: The items listed are arbitrarily selected as illustrative. For an authoritative discussion, see W. L. Langer, *The Diplomacy of Imperialism 1890–1902* (2 vols.; New York: 1935, 1950).

chow Bay (April 1898), while Russia got a "sphere" in Manchuria, and Germany one in Shantung, each with a leased territory enclosed by a neutral zone and with railways projected from the main port. But meanwhile Britain had kept pace with France by opening Southwest China to trade up the West River from Canton and by a projected Burma railroad (February 1897). Moreover, through a nonalienation agreement (that China would not cede the territory to any other power) Britain had got a claim to the entire Yangtze Valley — the whole hinterland of Shanghai, half the China market. Britain also got concessions to build some 2800 miles of railways, roughly equal to the combined length of the French (420 miles), Russian (1530), and Belgian (650) concessions. In addition Britain leased Weihaiwei in Shantung, opposite Port Arthur, as a naval base and increased eightfold the territory leased on the mainland next to Hong Kong. She also tried to ensure the survival of the treaty system, which had been so largely a British creation, by securing the opening of more treaty ports in the southwest and northeast and a promise that the office of Inspector General of Chinese Maritime Customs would remain British-held as long as Britain's share of the China trade remained the largest. Yet this outcome tended to weaken Britain's position in China, since her taking "compensation" only confirmed the special positions of the other powers in Yunnan, Shantung, and Manchuria, contrary to her interests there.

The results of the scramble of 1898 were most evident in the political scene. It threatened the Ch'ing empire with extinction and directly inspired both the Reform Movement and the Boxer rising. It also inaugurated a new and more ominous phase of the treaty system, because "spheres of influence" were plainly part-way steps toward making China into a congeries of outright European colonies. Up to this time the trading powers led by Britain had dominated China's foreign trade, ports of access, and internal waterways. Now, Germany and Russia were moving in to dominate entire provinces with new railways, mines, industries, and seaports. The leased territories and railway zones, to be governed and policed by foreigners in Manchuria and Shantung, would become quasi-colonial areas, much more extensive and more menacing to China's integrity than the old treaty-port concessions.

Foreign Financial Exploitation. The new imperialist domination, moreover, was not confined to "spheres of influence" but extended to Peking's entire financial structure. Up to 1893, some 25 loans had been made to Chinese government agencies by foreign sources in China. Thus, for example, the Chinese superintendent of customs at Shanghai in 1886 had secured 700,000 silver taels from a loan authorized by an imperial edict and floated by the Hongkong and Shanghai Banking Corporation in the form of some 3000 bonds bearing 7 per cent interest and redeemable over

30 years. The total indebtedness still outstanding from such loans, which were all secured on the Maritime Customs revenue, was inconsiderable in 1894. The Sino-Japanese war, however, brought financial crisis. Loans of about £6,500,000 were raised during the war. The Japanese indemnity (200 million taels plus 30 million more for the retrocession of Liaotung) came to about £30,000,000, and the big loans used to meet it in 1895, 1896, and 1898 were secured from the foreign banks on onerous terms: China received less than the face value to begin with (say 94 per cent), had to pay rather high interest for as long as 45 years, and also had to pay in gold, at the mercy of the gold/silver exchange rate. Thus the three big loans, with a nominal value of £47,820,000, actually brought China only £43,210,000 and yet would require an eventual repayment of interest and principal totaling £102,360,000.

To cap this, in 1901 it was arranged that the Boxer indemnity of 450 million taels (about £67,000,000 or $333,000,000) was to be paid in bonds which bore interest at 4 per cent in gold, so that by the conclusion of payments in 1940, interest and principal repaid would total 982 million taels (or $739,000,000). Russia was to receive roughly 29 per cent, Germany 20, France 16, Britain 11, Japan 7.7, the United States 7.3, and Italy 6 per cent. As scheduled by the international commission of bankers, China's remittances on all her foreign debts would run at 42 or 43 million taels a year, a figure larger than Peking's annual revenue had been in the early nineteenth century.

The Japanese and Boxer indemnities, unlike productive loans, were complete losses to China. Their payment drained off the Ch'ing government's revenue collected from foreign trade by the Maritime Customs, which had theretofore provided funds for armament and modernization. (Even this limited revenue had been further limited as the rise of prices gradually reduced the ad valorem percentage value of tariff duties fixed in money terms in 1858.) Henceforth even large portions of the provincial revenues and of the likin and salt revenues on domestic trade would have to be added to the Maritime Customs revenue, just to pay the foreign bondholders. The historian H. B. Morse in his *International Relations of the Chinese Empire*, having labeled 1834–1860 a period of "conflict," and 1861–1893 a period of "submission," quite rightly called 1894–1911 a period of "subjection."

To be sure, imperialism's bark was sometimes worse than its bite. The Boxer indemnity is a case in point: in the end, with the eclipse of Tsarist Russia and Imperial Germany during World War I, and with the remission of American, British, and other portions of the indemnity, and other changes, less than a third of the original assessment was actually paid (total payments made or scheduled as of 1935 were about 320 million taels). Similarly, Japan's claim to a sphere in Fukien, obtained through a non-alienation agreement in April 1898, was never followed up. Italy's demand for a sphere in Chekiang in March 1899 was successfully refused. A number of the railway concessions made in the late 1890's were never actively pursued. That the "breakup of China" did not occur was partly owing to Chinese dexterity, as yet little studied, in balancing one imperialist power against another. Yet this era of financial imperialism, with its insatiable great-power rivalries and exploitative demands, has tended to overshadow the preceding decades of quieter commercial penetration and economic growth and has given patriotic Chinese ever since an indelible hatred for the whole treaty system as a "foreign imperialist yoke."

American Expansion and the Open Door. Many Americans in the 1890's were righteously proud that the United States, unlike European powers, had never fought wars and seized colonies in Asia. To be sure, British wars to open Burma and China had paved the way for the less violent opening of Japan, Siam, and Korea, and in all these countries American missionaries and traders had enjoyed the special privileges secured and maintained in large part by the British navy. Yet the fact remained that American activity, at least in the American view, had avoided "imperialism" in the Far East just as it avoided "entangling alliances" in Europe. By invoking Britain's own doctrine of most-favored-nation treatment and equal opportunity, the United States had got the benefits of Britain's free-trade empire without its odium or responsibilities.

However, as the European race for colonies developed, new expansionist tendencies together with certain accidents of history brought the United States also onto the Far Eastern scene as a great power. The American people were more susceptible to the imperialist virus than they liked to think.

The expansion of the United States, like that of the European powers, was due to a mixture of causes — in our case, the rise of industries manufacturing cheap export products, the disappearance of the frontier at home, and a missionary tradition abroad. As the navy's great proponent of seapower, Captain A. T. Mahan, put it, America was "looking outward" in an era when doctrines of Social Darwinism and Nordic racial superiority provided a sanction for keeping up with other nations in the search for markets, colonies, and naval bases. Mahan's advocacy of bases overseas coincided with the decision of the Congress in 1890 to build a first-class battle fleet and with public agitation for a canal across Nicaragua so that the fleet could operate in both oceans.

Meanwhile there had been a long-continued interest in Hawaii, where the white sugar planters in 1893 deposed Queen Liliuokalani and sought annexation to the United States, only to be frustrated when the Cleveland administration left the question unsettled. Similarly in Samoa, American interest in the harbor of Pago Pago, in a spirit of competition mainly with Germany, had led in 1889 to a three-power Anglo-American-

German joint protectorate over the Samoan Islands. These developments, reminiscent of the first era of "manifest destiny" in the 1840's and '50's, had prepared the way by 1898 for an American counterpart of the European "scramble" in China.

The American expansion of 1898 in the Far East was triggered by the accidental coincidence of the war with Spain over Cuba, declared on April 24. In anticipation of war, Theodore Roosevelt, assistant secretary of the navy, had prepared Commodore Dewey and his American Asiatic Squadron at Hong Kong to attack the Spanish fleet which happened to be at Manila. Dewey did so at dawn on May 1; by lunchtime the Spanish fleet was sunk or burning, only eight Americans had been injured, and Dewey was a national hero. Seeing no alternative, the United States occupied Manila with a force of 11,000 in the summer of 1898. After a great debate over imperialism, the United States received the Philippines from Spain by a peace treaty in December, and at once become involved in suppressing a full-fledged Filipino struggle for independence (see pages 727–728). Meantime Hawaii had been annexed by Congressional action in July, and the western Pacific island of Guam had been taken from Spain. By the end of 1899 a three-power agreement gave the United States part of Samoa.

These American acquisitions in 1898–99, outstripping those of any imperialist power in China, gave the United States potential naval bases at Pearl Harbor, Guam, Pago Pago, and Manila, as well as the Hawaiian Islands and the entire Philippine archipelago.

It was right in the middle of this period, in September 1899, that Secretary of State John Hay issued his first Open Door notes. Hay had recently been minister to London, where the British early in 1898 had consulted him on how to preserve the tradition of equal opportunity, an open door for trade, in the face of imperialist "spheres of influence" developing in China. The British, though they then considered using the "collective influence of the trading nations," reverted after March 1898 to their more concrete program of keeping up with imperialism by getting a Yangtze "sphere" of their own.

Secretary Hay, however, went ahead with the equal-opportunity idea. His chief adviser, W. W. Rockhill, had long favored the idea of supporting the integrity of China. Rockhill now got the first-hand advice of an old friend, an Englishman named A. E. Hippisley, one of Robert Hart's chief commissioners in the Chinese Maritime Customs. As a result, the American Open Door notes reflected the specific interest of Hart and the Maritime Customs in maintaining that original principle of the treaty system — the equal taxation of foreign trade in all treaty ports, inside as well as outside the new "spheres of influence." American business interests and missionary societies, seeking protection for their established rights of trade and access, were, to be sure, demanding that Washington act.

But the action taken in Hay's notes of 1899 was limited to requesting concretely, first, that each power not interfere with "any treaty port or any vested interest" within its "sphere"; second, that only the Chinese government should collect duties on trade at such ports, and only according to the treaty tariff; and third, that no preferential harbor dues or railroad charges should benefit the subjects of a power having a "sphere." In short, these first Open Door notes sought to preserve equality of trade in China, not the Chinese state.

Britain, Germany, France, Italy, and Japan all agreed to accept these provisions if everyone else did so. The Russian reply was negative inasmuch as it said nothing about preferential rates on the railroads Russia was building in Manchuria. However, Russia had already declared Dairen a free port. Hay's success was limited, but he made the best of it by blandly notifying all concerned that their unanimous acceptance of his notes had been "final and definitive."

As the Boxer rising brought foreign armies into North China in the summer of 1900, China's chances of survival as a state seemed more dubious than ever. Hay's second note, a circular of July 1900, therefore stated the American desire for a "solution" that would bring "permanent safety and peace to China, preserve Chinese territorial and administrative entity, protect all rights guaranteed to friendly powers by treaty and international law, and safeguard for the world the principle of equal and impartial trade with all parts of the Chinese Empire." Everyone agreed, and the Open Door became publicly established as the traditional American policy toward China. In time its essential concept became the preservation, not merely of foreign commercial opportunity, but of China's integrity as a nation. But in origin it was an effort by a maritime power at a distance to maintain the treaty system against the spread of colonialism in China. It was a statement of principle in words, put forward as a good thing in itself, without thought of forceful action to back it up. The United States was simultaneously acquiring a colony in the Philippines. It is safe to say that the Open Door policy was taken more seriously in the United States than elsewhere.

THE RUSSO-JAPANESE RIVALRY IN NORTHEAST ASIA

In 1900 the United States had joined the other powers and the leading officials of Central and South China in the convenient fiction that the Boxer war was actually a "rebellion," not an act of the dynasty; the dynasty, therefore, could be preserved, along with the treaty system (see pages 400–403). Preserving the dynasty had seemed the only practical alternative to the breakup of China into a number of European colonies. But the Boxer settlement of 1901 did not end the period of intense suspicion, rivalry, and jockeying for position among the powers. The pre-

1894 picture of stability — in which a slowly modernizing Chinese empire had remained open for trade, mainly British, under the British-managed treaty system — had been shattered beyond repair. In its place, the newly expansive powers — Japan, Russia, France, Germany, even the United States — now crowded the scene. Amid the resulting turmoil and confusion, the Russian attempt to absorb Manchuria gradually emerged as the principal threat to the territorial interests of both China and Japan and to the commercial interests of Britain and the United States. Great-power relations in the Far East continued in a state of flux and ferment until the Anglo-Japanese alliance of 1902 and the subsequent showdown between Russia and Japan, after which a degree of international stability was once more established.

The Anglo-Japanese Alliance. The maneuvers of the powers cannot be followed here in detail, and are not even fully known, but certain patterns of ambivalence emerged as each power confronted its range of alternatives. For example, Russian railroad building in Manchuria proved costly and difficult, and Russian counsels became seriously split between the soft line of peaceful economic penetration of Manchuria through friendship with China, advocated by Witte as finance minister, and the hard line of military occupation regardless of expense and ill will, advocated by the ambitious Russian military. The German effort, again, was to encourage Russian expansion in the Far East while hoping that Britain's difficulties, partly caused thereby, would lead to an Anglo-German alliance. Japanese counsels were divided between those like Itō who sought agreement with Russia, so that Japan could dominate Korea while Russia took Manchuria, and those like Yamagata and Katsura who were convinced that Russia could be stopped only by force and so were building up the Japanese army and navy for that purpose. The British, meanwhile, with 250,000 men fighting in the Boer War (October 1899–May 1902), were on the defensive in China and had found no way to stop the Russian encroachment in Manchuria. An Anglo-Russian agreement of April 1899 and an Anglo-German agreement of October 1900 both recognized Britain's pre-eminence in the Yangtze Valley, but neither interposed any bar to Russia's taking Manchuria. Nevertheless the British felt that, in the long run, stable relations could be achieved with Russia, by agreeing to her territorial ambitions, more easily than with Germany, which was a more direct rival of Britain in the race for trade and naval power.

During the Boxer war of 1900 the Chinese forces in Manchuria, artillery and all, had conducted hostilities against the Russians and compelled them to evacuate major centers. By October, however, with 175,000 troops deployed in the Far East, the Russians had got back to Mukden. While reoccupying their positions on the new railway routes, they were at the same time dealing with Li Hung-chang to get a separate agreement, apart from the international Boxer protocol, which would consolidate their control of Manchuria. Late in 1900 they forced the Ch'ing governor-general (Tseng) to sign a sweeping draft agreement (the so-called Alexeiev-Tseng agreement) which seemed to imply Russian absorption of Manchuria. As Li had hoped, the terms when known inspired such British, Japanese, and American protests that China was able to avoid ratifying the agreement and Russia finally withdrew it. After the signing of the Anglo-Japanese alliance in January 1902, Russia felt obliged to agree in April to evacuate Manchuria, in three stages, within eighteen months. The effort of the Russian military to use the Boxer crisis to absorb Manchuria thus ended in diplomatic frustration, although the Russian forces in 1902 were still in control of the area.

A similar competition between alternative policies occurred among the Japanese leaders, who were negotiating late in 1901 with both Russia and Britain. With Russia, Itō Hirobumi worked out a draft settlement by which Russia and Japan would have recognized each other's special positions in Manchuria and Korea. But instead of this settlement, the Japanese leaders chose to sign the Anglo-Japanese alliance in January 1902. Their aim was to isolate Russia in case of a military showdown, for each ally promised to fight any third power alone and expect the other ally's support only against a fourth power. In effect this meant Japan against Russia would fight alone; Britain would help Japan only if France helped Russia; and thus the Anglo-Japanese alliance would "hold the ring," keeping France and also Germany out of any Russian war against Japan.

For Britain the alliance marked the end of "splendid isolation." It also ended the current effort to come to terms with Russia, as well as the idea of an alliance with Germany, with whom relations were now strained in any case. Britain in 1902 forestalled any Russo-Japanese agreement to partition Northeast Asia and instead secured Japan's support in maintaining the treaty system in China. In return, Japan received a free hand in Korea, being, as the alliance stated, interested in that country "in a peculiar degree politically as well as commercially and industrially."

The Russo-Japanese War and Its Aftermath. Viewed in the context of 1902, the Anglo-Japanese alliance made for international stability rather than war. Amicable settlements with Russia were still sought by Japan and Britain, and indeed were to be achieved five years later, in 1907. But unfortunately, Russia's frustration in Manchuria had become not only diplomatic but also economic. The Russian railroads, with their large purchases from abroad, their Chinese labor force, their new city-building and subsidiary installations, had proved an enormous drain on the state treasury, uncompensated by any growth of Russian trade. Despite Witte's tariff arrangements favoring the rail route, Russian trade with the Far East continued to go more cheaply by sea. Rail traffic from

Europe first came through to Dairen in March 1903, but the 6000-mile haul took nearly a month, while non-Russian trade in Manchuria had quickly profited from the new opportunities created by the railways there. By early 1903 Russia's economic hold on Manchuria was plainly precarious but her military evacuation was still scheduled.

Confronting this dilemma, the Russians dragged their feet. The evacuation of troops, though promised, was delayed. In August 1903, Tsar Nicholas II created a Viceroyalty of the Far East and dismissed the gradualist Witte from power. When China again refused to accept Russian demands portending control of Manchuria, the Russians felt compelled to negotiate with Japan.

Japanese power had been growing rapidly. The big indemnity of 1895 from China had allowed Japan to go on the gold standard in 1897 and greatly expand her economy, foreign trade, and use of Western credits. Her military and naval expenditures had increased several times over, and she was already the dominant foreign power in Korea.

In the protracted Russo-Japanese negotiations of August 1903-February 1904 Japan got a fairly free hand in Korea. But instead of giving Russia the same in Manchuria, Japan offered to recognize only the Russian rights along the railways, and otherwise insisted on preserving China's integrity. The tsar and his advisers, still uncertain as to their long-term aims, played for time to transport more troops, 7000 a month, over the Trans-Siberian. The Japanese, suspicious, resolute, and in a hurry, broke off relations on February 6, 1904; with a night torpedo-boat attack they surprised the Russian fleet at Port Arthur, bottling it up there, on the 8th; and they declared war on the 10th. In May, Japanese forces transported to Korea crossed the Yalu River into Manchuria; others invested Port Arthur and occupied Dairen. Port Arthur finally surrendered in January 1905, after a long and costly siege. Meantime in a series of great land battles, the aggressive Japanese forced the defense-minded Russians to withdraw north along their vital supply line, the railway, by constantly outflanking them. By March 1905, when a 17-day battle for Mukden ended again in Russian withdrawal, both sides were exhausted and the Russians were further embarrassed by widespread revolutionary disorders at home.

The Russians' last hope was their Baltic fleet. Denied by Britain the use of the Suez Canal and Britain's world-wide system of ports, the Russians had dispatched around Africa in October 1904 a collection of 45 ill-assorted vessels, deficient in wireless communication, joint maneuverability, equipment, training, and morale. Nevertheless, with dogged determination Admiral Rodjestvensky surmounted illness and mutiny while delayed at Madagascar and then, in 28 days during March-April 1905, steamed 5000 miles direct to another French haven in Indo-China. Thence he made a dash for Vladivostok, but on May 27 ran head on into the thoroughly prepared Japanese battle fleet in the Straits of Tsushima. Admiral Tōgō "crossed the enemy's T" (turning his column across the

PLATE 51. The Empress Dowager transported by palace eunuchs in court dress, as photographed in 1903 by a young Manchu official. In a mat-roofed Summer Palace courtyard under a dragon-embroidered umbrella, the Empress wears small shoes raised on gilt platforms. At right front is the chief eunuch, Li Lien-ying.

DYNASTIC DECLINE AT PEKING

PLATE 52. The Empress Dowager receiving wives of Western envoys, 1903. After the Boxer Incident, the Empress Dowager had to conciliate the foreigners. Here she is photographed with ladies of the diplomatic corps, who stand close about and over her, Western fashion. The Empress holds hands with the American minister's wife, Sarah Pike Conger, who had survived the siege of the Peking legations and was now deeply impressed by the Ch'ing ruler's "womanly tenderness" and "intuitive ability."

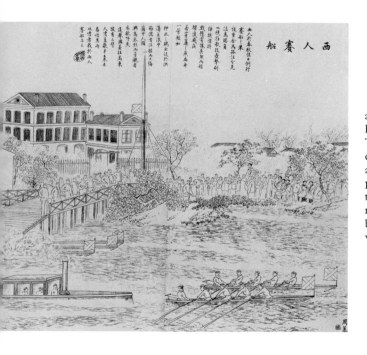

西人賽船

西人於春秋佳日例行
賽船以來

"In the fair weather of spr
and autumn, Westerners regula
hold boat races for high sta┃
The little oars fly by like swall┃
crossing a screen; the shallow b┃
are like leaves, light as seag┃
playing on water. Amid the wa┃
the high-spirited participants d┃
mind getting wet. Spectators┃
both banks cheer them on. Th┃
whole country is mad about i┃

WESTERNERS THROUGH CHINESE EYES

PLATES 53–56. Four sketches from a Shanghai picture magazine (*Tien-shih-chai hua-pao*) founded in 1884. Illustrated are Western sports (boat-racing, Plate 53, and a paper chase, Plate 54), a cautionary tale of a French opium addict (Plate 55), and an instance of foreign medical skill (Plate 56). The Chinese explanations are summarized.

"In the fine weather of spring and autumn, on two occasions in each season and each time on three days only, Westerners compete in racing on horseback with high wagers. This autumn at Shanghai they have added paper-chasing: up to 50 or 60 riders gather in one place, one goes ahead scattering multi-colored paper strips, and the others follow, racing madly. Whoever first gets over the paper course is the winner."

法人吸烟

"Opium coming to China has become an evil beyond control. If it is not Heaven's will to stop it, there is no other way to save the situation. Heretofore it has been said that only we Chinese are opium smokers. Not so. A French addict in the prime of life, traveling with his wife, an English friend, and a French servant, lay down to smoke in a Singapore hotel but next morning became ill and died — the doctor said from smoking too much. How can one not be afraid!"

"A foreign woman doctor, specialized in women's ailments and also in surgery, examined at the T'ung-jen Hospital in Hongkew a woman patient with a huge growth. Saying, 'This can be cured,' she took out a sharp knife, cut it off (it weighed one-fourth as much as the patient) and applied medicine, and after a month it was cured. The patient was fortunate to find this doctor, and the doctor fortunate to find this patient on whom to demonstrate such miraculous skill, which leaves Chinese doctors speechless and ashamed."

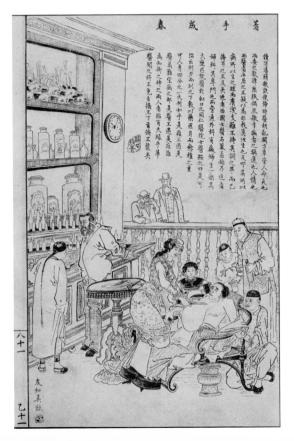

著手成春

大清光緒三十一年崇佑庭七十有四小照

尚書銜軍功花翎
福州將軍閩海關監督船政大臣
兼署閩浙總督兼福建鹽政大臣世襲奉恩將軍

NON-CHINESE OFFICIALS IN CHINA

PLATE 57. A Manchu official: Ch'ung-shan, courtesy name Yu-t'ing, of the Bordered Red Banner, Foochow Tartar General 1903–07, and sometime Acting Governor-General. *Inscription on right:* "Tartar General of hereditary rank by receipt of Imperial Grace, with brevet rank of Board President and Peacock Feather bestowed for military merit," etc. *On left:* "Portrait of Ch'ung Yu-t'ing at 74 *sui*, 1905" (with his seals "Yu-t'ing" and "Ch'ung-shan of the imperial family").

PLATE 58. Sino-foreign officials, Foochow, c. 1905. Front row, from left: Customs Commissioner E. B. Drew (American); Salt Intendant Lu; Japanese Consul; Tartar General Ch'ung-shan; American Consul (Dr. S. L. Gracey); Grain Intendant Ch'i-yueh; French Consul. In the back row are interpreters for English, French, and Japanese and officials concerned with Customs, Foreign Affairs, Defense, and Navy.

Russian line of advance to bring all his broadsides to bear), followed up with torpedo boats, and destroyed 32 out of 35 Russian vessels, to end the war.

Through President Theodore Roosevelt's diplomatic initiative, the peace conference met at Portsmouth, New Hampshire (to escape the heat of Washington). The Treaty of Portsmouth, September 5, 1905, recognized Japan's "paramount interests" in Korea, restored China's sovereignty and administration in Manchuria, and gave Japan the Russian lease on the Liaotung Peninsula in South Manchuria and the Russian-built railway as far north as Chang-chun. Japan got the southern half of Sakhalin Island but, after some altercation, no indemnity. Already, on August 12, the Anglo-Japanese alliance had been renewed for another five years, this time providing that the allies would fight together against any third power and including India within its scope.

Japan's spectacular victory stabilized great-power relations in East Asia and ended the high period of imperialist rivalry there, at the same time that the powers again became absorbed in their relations in Europe. Britain and France had already formed their *entente cordial* in April 1904. In June 1907 France and Japan agreed by treaty, first, to respect the independence and integrity of China (nearly all treaties after 1900 made a pious bow to the Open Door), and second, to support each other's "situation and territorial rights" on the continent, meaning, in effect, their "spheres of influence" within the Ch'ing empire. All this paved the way for the Russo-Japanese conventions of July 1907, by which the late adversaries publicly agreed to support China's "independence and territorial integrity" and secretly agreed to divide Manchuria into a northern sphere for Russian exploitation and a southern sphere for Japan. This was capped by the Anglo-Russian entente of August 1907, which harmonized the two powers' interests in Persia, Afghanistan, and Tibet. Thus the Anglo-Japanese and Franco-Russian alliances became interconnected in East Asia, leaving Germany and the United States isolated. The resulting stability of great-power relations left the treaty system intact, formally supported by repeated Open Door declarations in favor of China's integrity, but still threatened by the simultaneous growth of "spheres of influence."

The immediate result of the Russo-Japanese War was to make Japan a full-fledged imperialist power, not only ruling Taiwan (Formosa) but also dominating Korea and expanding in Manchuria. Western expansion, growing into imperialist rivalry, had set the stage in Japan for a national effort overseas which was no less dynamic than those of Western nations. Even the most race-minded Westerners, though still convinced of Nordic supremacy, had to admit that Japan was an exception.

Among Asian peoples, on the other hand, the long-term effect of Japan's victory was to stimulate the rise of nationalism. Not only in China but also in the Philippines, Vietnam, Indonesia, and elsewhere, the

Japanese example inspired modern patriots to stand up against Western domination. In one colony after another, 1905 marked the beginning of organized independence movements (see Chapter 9).

The decade of high imperialism in East Asia thus had a multiple significance: as the climax of Western colonial expansion and great-power rivalry; as the seedtime of indigenous Asian nationalism; and as the beginning of the Japanese drive toward empire. Indeed, Japan within a generation was to become the instrument to destroy Western colonialism and the semi-colonial treaty system. Japan's expansion would both oppress and arouse the new nationalisms of East and Southeast Asia while bringing Western dominance there to an end sooner than anyone in 1905 could have foreseen.

Japan's Annexation of Korea. In this context of the Asian peoples' awakening to modern nationhood, it was particularly tragic that the Korean people, having come last into contact with the modern world, should be so soon subjugated by Asia's first leader in modernization, Japan. However, Japan's aim in Korea was originally not so extreme as it later became. Itō Hirobumi took on the task of working out the relationship between the two countries. Backed by Japanese troops, he secured in November 1905 a convention making Korea a Japanese protectorate and ending its diplomatic contact with other powers. He set up a Residency General to administer the Japanese protectorate, exercising wide powers immediately under the Meiji Emperor but leaving the Korean emperor still reigning. Itō aimed at a modernizing, benevolent administration capable of winning Korean collaboration and good will while making Japan's dominance secure.

This moderate approach met difficulties. When the Korean emperor sent a secret mission to the Second Hague Peace Conference of 1907 to protest Japan's domination, he was forced to abdicate in favor of his feeble-minded son. Itō assumed wider powers, arranged that Japanese could serve as Korean officials, and disbanded the Korean army. Widespread "riots" ensued, amounting in fact to a nationwide rebellion, which the Japanese vigorously suppressed by burning villages and killing some 12,000 "rioters" in the course of twelve months. In this war the Japanese reported 1450 engagements in 1908, 900 in 1909, and 147 in 1910. Itō attempted to work with a Korean ministry, including would-be reformers of the 1890's, and held out against immediate annexation, which was advocated by Yamagata and Katsura, as well as by ultranationalist pressure groups like the Black Dragon (i.e., Amur River) Society organized by Uchida Ryōhei in 1901.

But Itō was assassinated in Manchuria by a Korean patriot in October 1909, after his resignation as resident-general; and the annexation of Korea which followed in August 1910 was generally approved by Japanese opinion, liberal and otherwise. Now called Chōsen, Korea was governed for Japan's strategic and economic purposes by Japanese officials at the middle and higher levels, as a colony outside the Japanese constitutional process. Korean nationhood was thus suppressed at the very time when conservative *yangban* (the Japanese had abolished their class status), reformist students, disbanded soldiers, and impoverished peasants, rebelling alike against foreign rule, were developing a common sentiment of nationalism.

Colonialism in Retrospect

In this chapter we have briefly traced the steps by which Malaya, British Borneo, Burma, Vietnam, Cambodia, and Laos during the nineteenth century became European colonies in Southeast Asia, where Spanish and Dutch colonies already existed in the Philippines and Indonesia. We have also outlined with equal brevity the great-power rivalry of the late 1890's over China, which made that giant country, more populous than all these others put together, into a semi-colony, divided into "spheres of influence" and financially in bondage to the foreign powers. Finally, we have noted the fate that overtook Korea, absorbed into the new empire of Japan. What can now be said of this broad process as a whole?

First of all, Western expansion in the late nineteenth century had accelerated and intensified. East and Southeast Asia had had prolonged contact with Portuguese and Spanish adventurers, Catholic missionaries, and Dutch, British, and French East India companies, during more than three centuries. But by 1850 the expansion of Western private traders, Protestant and Catholic missionaries, and official empire-builders had taken on a new vigor, which soon became overwhelming.

In the second place, so much of this vigor came from Britain that British imperialism became the model in the minds of most Western powers, including Britain. But if, as is customary, one ascribes Western (primarily British) nineteenth-century expansion in general to the "industrial revolution," the latter term must be interpreted very broadly to embrace ideas as well as inventions, forms of business organization and political philosophy as well as machine production.

In the realm of economic institutions, for example, the growth of Eastern commerce in Western hands had accompanied the rise of the British doctrine of free trade, with its impassioned linking of capitalist enterprise and individual freedom. This had led to a whole series of legislative and diplomatic steps — the abolition of the East India Company monopolies of British trade with India (1813) and then with China (1834), the founding of free ports at Singapore (1819) and then at Hong Kong (1841), and the establishment of the unequal-treaty system to protect the free enterprise of Western merchants and missionaries in China (1842), Japan (1854, 1858), Siam (1855), Upper Burma (1867), and other areas.

Next, Western commerce had taken local root and stimulated Asian economic activity. The new methods and ideas of the free-trade era facilitated a reciprocal growth of local Asian production and export, usually with Asian merchants participating under Western auspices. The various roles of Indian opium, Chinese tea, and Japanese silk exports, mainly in Western hands, have been stressed already. After mid-century, Burmese and Siamese rice and teak and Malayan (mainly Chinese) tin exports were soon facilitating the inflow of British textiles and other manufactures.

Finally, law and order were as essential to economic progress in Asia as in Europe. A rational administration of taxes and of justice with some humanitarian concern for health and education, it was believed, would assist the inevitable progress of (Western) civilization. This was the sanction for British colonialism in its gradual expansion: free trade would bring material development; both required modern government. Freedom of the individual person or corporation to trade required first the imposition, by force or the threat of force, of the modern (Western) system of law and order. This helped explain the paradox that the Western powers most democratic at home got the biggest empires abroad — democracy and empire both testified to their advanced status in the world.

The foregoing picture of colonialism as the natural result of economic expansion seemed a century ago to be verified by the British experience. It has colored most thinking on the subject ever since. Unfortunately it grossly oversimplifies the manifold causes of imperialism, as the French and Russian examples make evident.

The proud French nation had experienced much glory, frustration, and defeat in the century from 1763 to 1871. Its expansion into Indo-China, in comparison with that of the British elsewhere, had to be pursued more suddenly and aggressively, without a comparable basis in commerce and therefore with a more strident assertion of certain Western values — the spiritual claims of Catholic Christianity and the superiority of French culture. Economic interests were at first only a small part of the French national craving for empire. Similarly Tsarist Russia turned eastward late in the nineteenth century more for strategic and political than for commercial reasons. It was Russian imperialism trying to create trade, rather than trade creating imperialism. Finally, although Germany and Japan show a more even balance of economic-strategic motives, neither expanded in the British pattern.

The idea of colonialism as a product purely or at least primarily of economic forces is belied also by the missionary movement, which was expansionist in the realm of spirit, intellect, and culture, and which gave opportunity to many ardent and energetic Western individuals. Christian missions required law and order quite as much as did Western trade. The idea that Christianity and education would bring spiritual development, and that both required a climate of modern government, was also a sanction for colonial expansion.

If we now try to look at the Western invasion as seen by the ruling class in each invaded Asian country, we may well imagine that it presented a very broad range of evils, among which the economic menace was at first by no means the most obvious. The subversive influence of Christianity and the danger of Western military power both seemed more fearsome than trade.

Perhaps the most positive Asian response was to the Western religious, ideological, and cultural challenge. This was met very generally by an effort to reaffirm the native religious and cultural tradition while shunning all things foreign. In each country there were movements through which the rulers tried to revivify the traditional faith. Confucianism had a revival under Minh-Mang in Vietnam after 1820. Buddhism was vigorously revived under Mongkut in Siam before 1850 and more tardily and ineffectually under Mindon Min in Burma after that date. At the same time both Burma and Vietnam attempted a xenophobic exclusion of the West. The Koreans even more vigorously sought to keep out foreigners while invoking Confucianism or "Eastern Learning" and reviving traditional institutions. On the whole, the Confucian states, Vietnam and Korea, were more violent and less flexible in meeting the challenge of foreign faiths and ideas than the Buddhist kingdoms of Burma and Siam, to say nothing of the weak Islamic sultanates of Malaya and Borneo.

When finally forced into greater contact with the West, the rulers of all these smaller, threatened states were able generally to respond on the political plane more readily than on the economic. For instance, they had little concept of protecting their native industries, but knew instinctively how to ward off Western military conquest by playing one foreign power against another. Thus Tu-Duc in Vietnam called in the Chinese against the French, and Thibaw in Burma sought to rely upon France against Britain, though both without avail. When Chulalongkorn got British help to save Siam from France in 1896, the Siamese economy had long been a British preserve; he was able to maintain the political independence of his state because he had already given up much of the control over its economy. In Korea, finally, the factionally divided rulers were so accustomed, as tributaries of China, to relying on an outside power that they devoted themselves from the first to factionalism linked with foreign alliances. Between the suzerainty of China and that of Japan there was only a brief Russian interlude, and Korea never achieved an independent, factionally undivided foreign policy.

China was able to survive principally, no doubt, because of her great size. At the same time, China's political sophistication and use of "barbarians" against one another were demonstrated in classic fashion at Peking during the ultraimperialist decade after 1894. Since the diplomatic history of this period has been studied chiefly through the records of the great powers, the skill of the Ch'ing diplomats has probably been underrated. Part of their skill lay in using China's obvious weakness to motivate the foreigners to stultify one another's ambitions. The Ch'ing negotiators spread rumors and leaked secrets. They appeared panic-stricken and at their wits' end. They accepted bribes while making alliances and granting concessions. But China survived, and their diplomacy deserves re-examination as having been more effective than foreigners realized at the time.

In the smaller countries, however, the ruling regimes were offered no alternatives: they usually faced a single aggressor, in a smaller terrain; they could accept imperialist dominance in one form or another, or cease to rule. In the event, the Burman and Korean monarchies perished and were superseded; the Vietnamese, Cambodian, and Laotian monarchies were embalmed as protectorates, and became outdated and vestigial; while the Siamese monarchy survived only because the extraordinary statesmanship of King Mongkut had made it an advocate of modernization. This disappearance or discrediting of the old rulers in British Burma, French Indo-China, and Japanese Korea deprived those societies of their traditional leadership, not merely in politics but also in letters, art, philosophy, and culture generally. The old social order was decapitated. Even where this was not the case, as in Malaya and Siam, a new order of leadership had still to be created.

For the common people of the new colonial areas, the changes of the nineteenth century were many-sided. Both standards of living and standards of administration seem very generally to have suffered a decline during the early nineteenth century. In Korea and Vietnam, at least, peasant unrest preceded Western invasion, and it may be inferred that population increase, as in China, underlay the Korean and Vietnamese movements of domestic rebellion. Once Western contact began, great revolutionary changes ensued in all the colonial countries in much the same fashion as in contemporary China and Japan — the establishment of special privileges for the foreigner, the growth of foreign trade and drawing of the domestic economy into the world economy, the rise of modern port cities, the growth of farming populations and usually of landlordism and tenantry, and the modernization of governments with their central services and public works.

All these concrete, material changes had their intellectual, social, and psychological counterparts. Old ways were discredited, ancient institutions undermined, proud ruling classes humiliated — and in the fully colonial areas, unlike China, Japan, and Siam, the indigenous leadership was largely destroyed or suppressed. Small-scale but persistent rebellions against the new colonial authority continued for many years in Vietnam and Burma after 1885 and 1886 and in Korea for several years after 1907. But all were eventually suppressed, and with them the irreconcilable elements among the old ruling classes.

As a result, the colonial populations suffered a grievous hiatus in leadership, in the period between the discrediting of the old regimes and the slow and niggardly training up of modern leaders. In this respect the fully colonial areas suffered as Japan, China and Siam did not. But in all these countries the refashioning of intellectual traditions, social values, ethical creeds, and institutional practices was quite as necessary as the development of the economy and government structure.

Thus the "evils" of colonialism were not merely economic but also political, social, and cultural. Indeed it may be seriously questioned whether the conventional view of colonialism as consisting essentially of economic exploitation is not in need of being stood upon its head. Economic exploitation, to be sure, was very much in the imperialists' minds. But what actually happened? As we shall see in Chapter 9, the attempt at economic exploitation in most cases meant a considerable degree of economic growth in the aggregate, though not necessarily in production per capita. Judging by the performance of the indigenous rulers before colonialism overwhelmed them, it may be doubted that this economic growth would have come any sooner under indigenous auspices, or would have been any the less inequitable for the masses had the traditional native leadership remained in power. But the psychological evils of colonialism — the depth of humiliation, the loss of self-confidence, the confused sense of identity — might have been avoided, and with them some of the obstacles to healthy modernization. If they had escaped colonialism, the small countries of East and Southeast Asia might have emerged little or no better off economically, but perhaps much better off in their political, social, and cultural life.

7

THE CENTRAL REVIEW

Imperial Japan:

From Triumph to Tragedy

THE SECOND PHASE OF MODERNIZATION

Japan's rise from semi-colonial status under the unequal treaties to the level of a great power and ally of Britain, while most of Asia continued to fall further under Western domination, was a spectacular and unparalleled success story. Japan's modernization in Western style had even included the acquisition of an East Asian empire in Taiwan and Korea.

For this new Japan the early decades of the twentieth century were a golden age. The gripping fears and self-doubts that had persisted through the nineteenth century had now been largely dispelled. Who could doubt that the nation would continue to modernize its institutions and society and build up economic strength, political prestige, and military power? Having successfully met the great challenge presented by the Western powers in the nineteenth century — in fact having been the only non-Western nation to do so — why should Japan not overcome the seemingly simpler problems ahead?

Indeed, Japan in the first quarter of the twentieth century gave every promise of living up to this optimistic prospect. The nation moved ahead rapidly in all fields, continuing with amazing speed to close the technological gap between itself and the West that had so terrified the Japa-

COVER of May 1936 issue of *The Central Review*, a Japanese intellectual magazine, announcing the special feature, "The Full Picture of the International Crisis and the Hirota Cabinet."

nese only a generation or two earlier. By 1925 Japan was a far more modernized country and much more of a world power than at the close of the Russo-Japanese War.

The next two decades saw a continuation of the same rapid technological progress, growth of power, and modernization of institutions, but meanwhile a profound change had come over the country. The easy successes of earlier years had somehow turned into staggering new problems. Confidence had been replaced by new fears, the old unity of purpose by great inner conflict. Japan continued to rush forward, but the Japanese themselves began to wonder apprehensively where they were going. And their worries proved to be justified. Japan became embroiled in wars of increasing magnitude, until in 1945 her newly won empire and ancient homeland both fell in complete ruins in perhaps the largest single catastrophe to overwhelm any nation in modern times. Japan's unparalleled success had turned to ashes.

This second great phase in Japan's modernization, culminating in the rapid transition from success to failure, is doubtless pregnant with meaning — especially since Japan is still the only non-Western nation to have passed completely through the first phase. But no one is as yet sure just what this reversal of fortune fully signifies. We have some idea of the dynamics of Japan's modernization in the nineteenth century, and the disaster that struck in the 1930's and 1940's may be clear enough, but how and why did the one so quickly turn into the other? The few who have attempted to answer the question have usually treated the disaster as if it were a direct outgrowth of the imperfections of the Meiji system — in fact, as if the same actors were receiving their punishment for their earlier oversights — but we must remember that two generations separated the original Meiji leaders from the men who led Japan to her great defeat. One whole generation of glorious success lies between the Meiji oligarchs and the later crisis.

Unfortunately, the early decades of the twentieth century are the least studied and least understood period in modern Japanese history, both in Japan and elsewhere. It is clear, however, that during this "golden age" there appeared problems that were soon to overwhelm Japan. True, these problems usually grew from seeds planted in the Meiji system itself, but it was the first quarter of the twentieth century that nourished the growth which in later years was to overshadow some of the more desirable products of the Meiji transformation.

The New Problems. In transforming their society to meet the problems they faced in the nineteenth century, the Japanese inevitably created new ones to be faced in the twentieth. A great spurt in population naturally accompanied the modernization of the economy and the introduction of modern medical science and hygiene. Hence Japan, long virtually self-sufficient and even an exporter of food in the nineteenth century, now became increasingly dependent on imports of rice for her people and raw materials for her industrial enterprises. Thus the quest for economic security from the West led to dependence on foreign markets to pay for imports.

Similarly the quest for military security from the West had resulted in a rapid build-up of military might, which, in the nineteenth-century setting, led almost inevitably to expansion abroad. While no longer fearful of foreign domination at home, the Japanese now found themselves embroiled in imperialistic rivalries and the rising difficulties that beset all colonial powers in the twentieth century.

But even more serious were the less obvious and less understood social and intellectual problems of a country undergoing rapid modernization. The new economy, universal education, and many other factors were producing a vastly more complex society than before, with decidedly more complicated problems. Modernization had moved at varying paces in different parts of Japan and in different social strata. Urban Japan had changed much more rapidly than the socially more stagnant countryside, and the gap in thought and attitudes was widening between the masses, who received a few years of elementary schooling with a high content of indoctrination, and those who underwent the new higher education, which tended to be strongly oriented toward the West. Even among the more educated, divergencies of attitude were becoming greater than those that had existed among the Meiji leaders, with their common feudal background. Professional military men, civil administrators, educators, men of letters, businessmen, and politicians were living very different kinds of lives and thinking very different thoughts.

In this new, more diverse society, there were fresh stirrings of discontent among the lower classes. Tenancy, as we have seen, had grown steadily in the countryside as a result of a modernized landholding and tax system, and the new urban proletariat of factory workers, as it gradually became divorced from its peasant origins, became more vulnerable to fluctuations in the industrial economy. Neither group was as underprivileged as its poor-peasant ancestors had been. Living standards for the Japanese as a whole, including even food consumption, had moved steadily upward. But in a country liberated from its feudal bonds and provided with universal education, economic expectancies apparently rose faster than realities — at least for the lowest strata of society. The unhappy conditions of life among tenant farmers and factory workers posed a major problem, both for these less fortunate Japanese themselves and for the more educated groups.

The Failure of Leadership. Problems of this sort are not unusual in societies that are modernizing and certainly do not seem very grave when compared with those which the Meiji leaders had faced. But the new generation of leaders proved much less able to cope with the problems of their time, perhaps because they no longer had a clear unity of purpose. The Meiji leaders had been a close-knit group, sharing a common educational experience and similar feudal backgrounds, and they had been united on their goal: to achieve security and equality for Japan by using Western technology. There had been differences of opinion as to procedure but no disagreement over the objective. But after this end had been achieved it was no longer clear what should come next, and just at this time the original leadership began to fade from the scene, leaving Japan in the hands of a larger and more diverse leadership group. Thus professional military men who were much more narrowly specialized than their predecessors might argue that Japan's future lay in increased military strength in order to seize a larger empire, whereas business leaders or the politicians they helped elect might feel that such a course was both expensive and dangerous and that Japan would do better to invest in industrial expansion.

Such divisions of opinion are not infrequent in modern societies, but their resolution requires either strong leadership or an effective mechanism for settling disagreements — both of which Japan lacked. The Meiji oligarchs created a government which they could direct from above. They saw it realistically for what it was: man-made, based on a German constitutional model, and embodying a compromise between different forces in Japanese society. They assumed the continuation of a strong and unified leadership group like themselves. The second and third generation of leaders, however, were the heirs and not the architects of the system. They were in it, not above it. Its framework they accepted almost as a part of nature — ordained by the emperor and sanctioned by the successes of Japan in the decade or two after 1890. As a consequence, they were more limited and less flexible in dealing with problems.

The Meiji constitution, moreover, provided no clear mechanism for resolving differences of opinion or policy. On the contrary, it guaranteed that each of the governmental elites would have at least the powers needed to maintain its elite position. The Diet, the civil bureaucracy, and the armed services were knit together by implicit mutual controls, but no one of them was clearly subordinate to any other (see chart, page 297). In normal times compromises were worked out and considerable advances were achieved despite this system. But in major crises — lacking a true ruling emperor or an all-powerful group of leaders who could speak in his name — Japan had no sure way to resolve disagreements between these different elites of the government.

Behind the political ambiguities was an even more serious ideological ambiguity — or perhaps one might better call it a growing diversity of values. The guiding spirit of the Meiji transformation was an emperor-oriented nationalism with deep roots in the loyalty ethic of the Tokugawa period. This had been expressed in a driving ambition to strengthen Japan, to preserve her political independence, and to make her into a powerful state. This had been enough as long as the factors which had created the nationalistic upsurge in Japan remained still active and the initial revolutionary leadership was at the helm. But once Japan achieved security and equality, her goals became diverse, even though the core elements of nationalism remained the strongest and most widely accepted spiritual values. One man's image of the nation came to differ radically from another's. Social liberation, universal education, a working parliamentary system, and other factors stimulated the growth of a democratic ideology, but this was circumscribed by the Meiji constitution, which made any too-open espousal of democracy seem like *lèse majesté* and anti-nationalism. To find meaning or purpose in the midst of this confusion of ideals, some iconoclasts turned to socialism or other radical Western ideologies. Other seekers turned to religion: to Christianity, to new Shintō religious groups, or to reawakened Buddhist sects. Still others attempted to fuse tradition with elements from the modern West to prepare new supports for an illiberal nationalism. In comparison with the Meiji period, the Japanese as a whole began to drift along with no clear, unifying ideology to define political goals.

Japan's political life in the late nineteenth and early twentieth centuries was partly free and partly unfree. Political parties, if not too radical, might agitate, and were eventually given a voice in the government. Various streams of Western thought entered Japan, and intellectual freedom was considerable. Yet at the same time police supervision was close, slander laws were ridiculously severe, and the right to assemble was restricted. As Japan's society became more modern, this half-way position was increasingly difficult to preserve. A demand for greater freedom was created by the leveling of feudal barriers, a heightened social mobility, more and better education, and a greater participation by a growing percentage of the people in the political control of the society. This reflected the major trend in Japanese politics through the 1920's: the step-by-step increase in the power of the Diet and in the strength of the political parties in relation to the other governmental elites. Yet during the same period the potential for greater authoritarian controls also increased through such factors as the growing centralization and strength of police and military powers, more indoctrination in primary schools, the development of mass media of communication, and the slow breakdown of the traditional society which began to produce greater social fluidity in the third and fourth decades of the century. When crises arose in the early 1930's that Japan's leaders could not solve, a shift occurred in the balance of elites and Japan became a militarist state. In part this was because Japanese society was not sufficiently democratic to withstand these crises. Few spoke up in defense of constitutional government or individual rights.

But the shift to military control demonstrated also that the evils as well as the benefits of modernization could appear in non-Western as in Western nations.

THE MATURING OF THE ECONOMY

The base for Japan's modern industrial development was formed during the last thirty years of the nineteenth century. In part this was the result of vigorous government action that created the framework within which individual enterprise could flourish. With a rapidity perhaps unparalleled in history, the Japanese had fashioned for themselves a strong centralized political order, a modern educational system, a stable monetary system, banks, transportation networks, and other new institutions.

The response to these measures during the nineteenth century came in two overlapping waves. The first was in the traditional sector of the economy. Freed from Tokugawa restrictions and given impetus by the institutional innovations and reforms, Japan's traditional small industries underwent a notable expansion. This was accompanied by a proportional increase in commerce and in the size of the internal market. The second wave of advance came in the burgeoning modern sector of the economy during the late 1880's and the 1890's. This was in part a response to the high level of demand formed by the earlier growth, in part the successful expansion of industries that had begun as government enterprises.

But we must keep this nineteenth-century economic growth in proper perspective. In spite of its qualitative brilliance, it was small. In a quantitative sense Japan's "takeoff" period of sustained industrial growth really began only after the Russo-Japanese War. At the end of the nineteenth century the country was still technologically backward, exporting for the most part raw or semi-processed materials such as silk. Japan had indeed started to export a considerable quantity of cotton yarn, a very simple manufactured product, but contemporary observers felt that Japanese factories would never really compete with those of the West.

It is important to keep this economic situation in mind when considering political history. When we ask to what extent Japanese society in the 1930's was "modern," we must note that even though the impact of Westernizing institutional reforms and intellectual currents had been felt for two or three generations, the transformation of society under the impact of modern industry had begun only a single generation before. We therefore should not be surprised to find that the life and thought of the Japanese were not modernized overnight; in many ways they remained tenaciously traditional in outlook.

However, the rate of economic growth after 1900 was spectacular; the upsurge of the late nineteenth century continued almost without interruption for the next four decades, until the debacle of the 1940's. Between 1900 and the late 1930's the production of raw materials seems to have more than tripled, and the output of manufactured goods increased well over twelve-fold — at least four times the world average for this period. By the late 1930's the Japanese economy was relatively mature even in its heavy industries. Close to 60 per cent of the export trade, which had grown about twenty-fold in the meantime, was made up of fully manufactured goods, and certain industries within the great manufacturing nations of the West had become almost hysterically afraid of Japanese competition. Plotting Japan's growth against Western models shows that at the beginning of this period Japan's economy was at least as backward as that of Russia, the most backward of the industrializing countries in the West. However, its growth, as measured by percentage increase in its total product, was greater than that of any European nation. That such high rates of capital formation could be achieved in a country with low per capita incomes underlines the contribution to Japan's economic advance of the traditional values of frugality, saving, and endurance — the cultural setting that Thorstein Veblen once referred to as "Japan's opportunity."

Many scholars have attributed this great economic growth largely to Japan's exploitation of her new colonial empire, but there seems to be little basis for this theory. The Japanese certainly wrested from their colonies what they could, and control over the agricultural products and mineral resources of Korea and Taiwan in particular proved to be of great strategic advantage. But in purely economic terms, the empire was probably more a drain than an asset. More went into investment in these areas than was derived from them, even if we disregard the greatly increased military expenses required for their seizure and defense.

Some scholars have stressed the role of foreign markets (of which colonial markets were but a very small part) to explain Japan's economic growth. They have argued that the inequities of landlordism and zaibatsu concentration of wealth limited domestic consumption and forced Japan to turn outward for markets. This hypothesis also is not borne out by the facts. As a source of raw materials and producers' durable goods, foreign trade was necessary. But it accounted for a smaller percentage of Japan's total national product than was true of most European countries during the same period. Japan's economy was dominant, not satellitic. Its growth, as during the nineteenth century, continued to be largely self-generated.

Some of the growth was used up by an increase in the population, which came close to doubling — from 43,847,000 in 1900 to 73,100,000 in 1940. Much went into investment in the new empire and into the greatly increased military expenditure required because of Japan's new role as a world power. And, as we have seen, a high percentage was plowed back as capital investment, perhaps 15 per cent or more of net income in boom years. Yet despite all these claims on Japan's total product, enough remained to effect a substantial rise in per capita consumption during the first four decades of the twentieth century. At all levels of society, living standards advanced somewhat, although relative disparities between different groups in the population also increased.

As the Japanese economy developed, it became closely integrated with the world economy. Japan lacked the extensive mineral resources possessed by most other major industrial powers. As industrial output rose, it became necessary to import ever increasing amounts of raw materials, which of course could be paid for only by a corresponding expansion in exports. Most of the time these were easily obtained. But the psychological awareness of dependence became more and more intense, particularly after 1929. Moreover, while foreign trade was not the motor of Japan's economic growth, it bulked large enough to make the difference between an economy running in high or in low gear. This is reflected in the character of Japanese business cycles. During the late nineteenth century, as during the Tokugawa period, the ups and downs of the economy had been to a large extent determined by political or financial decisions at home. After the Russo-Japanese War, however, the Japanese economy became more sensitively attuned to world conditions. The pattern of government investment remained important, but Japanese business cycles largely corresponded to international patterns of boom and retrenchment. More recently it has been said that when New York coughs, Tōkyō comes down with a cold. The beginnings of this situation are clearly visible in the 1920's and 1930's.

Expansion and Boom. The economic history of modern Japan falls into sharply differentiated periods. The first began after 1905 with a boom that developed into a period of sustained overall growth continuing until 1913. The three types of demand that were central to this advance are worth treating in detail because they typify the forces that sustained Japanese economic growth into the 1930's. The first, as we have seen, was continuing growth in the traditional sector of the economy. As wages rose, consumer taste, remaining relatively constant, demanded more of the traditional goods, rather than the products of new industry. Satisfying these demands utilized surplus labor, required very little capital, and, by contributing to aggregate demand, helped to keep the economy at a high level. The second type of demand, domestic and foreign, was for cottons, bicycles, and other products of Japan's light industries. The third type of demand was that created by government expenditures, which increased sixfold in the two decades before 1913. Most of this increase was military. Throughout the period 1887–1940 government investment in the economy, as a proportion of total investment, averaged well over 40 per cent. This is a higher proportion than that of any European country (excluding the Soviet Union), and one reached by the United States only during the peak years of the Great Depression. It has been suggested that the high level of this government-created demand and its relative steadiness — as contrasted with Tsarist Russia, where government expenditures played a comparable role in economic development — were crucial factors in Japan's prewar pattern of industrialization.[1] Such government investment took many forms: bridges, harbors, roads, rolling stock, public utilities, iron and steel works, as well as military expenses for ships and ordnance. All of these created a steady market for the products of Japan's heavy industries at a time when these were not yet competitive with those of the West.

Heavier government expenses were met by increased taxes, which the expanding economy could safely bear, and by new government monopolies, such as that begun on tobacco in 1898 and on salt in 1904. Foreign capital was also used extensively for the first time, though its role in the total picture was small. Some foreign companies such as General Electric and Dunlop (rubber) contributed directly to the development of new industries. In such cases the import of capital was synonymous with the import of advanced technology. Most foreign investment in Japan, however, took the form of purchases of government bonds. The sale of these helped to establish the government-operated Yawata Iron and Steel Works, to pay for the Russo-Japanese War, and to pay for the state railway system that was nationalized after 1906. At a time when the economy was strained by war, by rising domestic consumption, and by an expanding foreign trade, the availability of foreign capital was important. This large-scale use of foreign capital was made possible by two factors. The Japanese, confident of their own strength, were no longer fearful of foreign economic domination, and financiers and businessmen abroad now looked upon Japan as an attractive place for investment. Another new element was Japan's control over her own tariffs, partial after 1899 and complete after 1911. She could now use these to protect strategic or infant industries, even though, on the whole, Japanese tariffs remained moderate and were only a secondary factor in shaping economic development.

Japan's rate of government expenditure and industrial investment in the years after 1905 proved too high for her to maintain, and by 1911 she was facing a serious financial crisis. When the first World War broke out in August 1914, the initial effect was a serious dislocation of Japan's foreign trade, but by early 1915 the war had produced a strong new impetus for economic expansion. This was undoubtedly the "best" war

[1] Henry Rosovsky, *Capital Formation in Japan*, p. 104.

in Japan's history: her military participation was minimal, orders for munitions poured in from her allies, and there was a vast increase in demand for Japanese manufactured goods in Asian and other markets now cut off from their usual European sources of supply.

Between 1915 and 1920 the Japanese economy grew by leaps and bounds. The destruction of European shipping played into the hands of the Japanese merchant marine, which almost doubled in size and, with the aid of soaring freight rates, increased its net income about ten times. The number of factory workers almost doubled, as did the export of cotton goods. Profits were huge and, despite a sharp rise in prices, permitted a rate of capital investment in industry that was unusually high even for Japan. In addition, Japan became for the first time a creditor nation, with gold reserves at home and abroad of more than two billion yen, a sixfold increase in six years.

Readjustment and New Growth. A spiraling inflation kept Japan's war boom going for more than a year after the armistice, but prices collapsed in March 1920, and deflation set in. The next twelve years were economically among the least impressive of Japan's modern history. One reason was that Japanese agriculture and the domestic production of raw materials reached a plateau. Between 1920 and 1930 there was no increase in the amount of land cultivated, no increase in the farming population, and very little increase in agricultural product. This mirrored the generally advanced character of the Japanese economy. On the one hand, it had become more profitable to invest in industry than in agriculture, cheaper to import grains from the colonies or elsewhere than to apply more capital to Japan's overworked soil. On the other hand, the limits of agricultural exploitation at the scientific levels of the 1920's had just about been reached. This leveling off in the production of raw materials and agricultural crops not only accentuated the growing gap between rural and urban income levels; it also put the burden of absorbing the expanding population and of maintaining overall growth on the industrial sector of the economy, which had problems of its own.

A second reason for the uneven performance of this period was a relative decline in government expenditures. During the earlier periods such expenditures had provided a minimal constant level of demand that buffered fluctuations in the economy. But during the 1920's, a time of peace, of internationalism, and of democratic tendencies, military expenses were cut sharply without a compensatory increase in other public expenditures. This was one of the few times in the prewar period when the role of the government in capital formation was smaller than that of the private sector. The result was to leave the Japanese much more exposed to the ups and downs of the internal and foreign markets.

A third type of economic problem came from the character of the world economy during this period. The price structure of most countries had been more thoroughly deflated after World War I than had that of Japan. This led to an unfavorable balance of trade during the early 1920's and to the loss of the foreign credits obtained during the war. Conditions at home did not permit an easy resolution of this problem during the middle twenties. Japan's exports were buoyed up by the prosperity of the United States during the later twenties, but were dealt a disastrous blow by the economic consequences of the Great Depression that followed the American stock market crash in 1929.

Other domestic factors also contributed to the checkered pattern of Japan's economic life. The postwar depression had begun to lift in 1922, but on September 1, 1923, a great earthquake occurred in the Tōkyō area in which more than 130,000 persons died and billions of dollars' worth of property was destroyed. This set off a construction boom that was financed in part by a second wave of foreign borrowing. After 1924 Japan temporarily went off the gold standard, letting the value of the yen depreciate and thus further stimulating foreign trade. An inflationary expansion of the economy ensued; but this was checked by a bank crisis in the spring of 1927, when a number of important banks failed, and deflation once more set in. Then, after springing back briefly, the economy experienced an even greater shock in 1930. In January, Inoue Junnosuke, the orthodox-minded finance minister, unwisely put Japan back on the gold standard, just two months after the American crash and at a time when world prices had already started a precipitous descent. The resultant rise in the value of the yen heightened the deflationary impact of world economic conditions, and Japan sank into a serious depression in which she was forced to make her final readjustment from the overinflated values of the war years to the price structure of the postwar world.

Despite all these difficulties, the Japanese economy was not stagnant between 1920 and 1930: advances were made in technology, industry was diversified more widely, manufacturing came close to doubling in output, and the gains of World War I and of the period of inflationary expansion from 1922 to 1927 were consolidated by the elimination of unsound enterprises. But the price paid for this progress, in human suffering and social unrest, was high; one facet can be seen in the wild fluctuations of prices during this period. The price of rice, Japan's staple food, which had risen 174 per cent in the preceding six years, fell by more than half within a year after the 1920 deflation, recovered almost to the old high by 1925, and then sank almost to the 1914 level by 1931. Silk, the chief export and the most important secondary product of Japan's agriculture, was subject to similar movements: its price fell by more than two-thirds between 1925 and 1929.

Recovery and the Rise of a War Economy. Though the depression lasted for many years in the United States, Japan was already recovering by 1932, and in the next few years her economy forged ahead faster than that of any other nation. The first major factor contributing to this recovery was an expansion of foreign trade. Inoue's successor as finance minister, Takahashi Korekiyo (1854–1936), again took Japan off the gold standard in December 1931, and the yen, which had been worth 50 cents, eventually stabilized at around 30 cents. Such a severe devaluation produced a boom in exports. The market for silk was not regained, because of the displacement of silk by synthetic fibers, but increased exports of cotton cloth and other manufactured goods more than made up for its loss. Particularly, in the period of world depression, cheaper Japanese goods were able to capture many of those markets in Asia and Africa that were not sealed up within European empires. The second factor responsible for Japan's rapid recovery was the return to military adventure in the Manchurian Incident of 1931, which re-created the high level of military expenditures that had been lacking during the previous decade. Because there was considerable slack in the economy, these two factors were complementary: trade helped build industrial strength which could serve the military, and military demand contributed generally to the recovery from depression. As a result, by 1936 industry was more diversified, great technological advances had occurred in the metallurgical, machine, and chemical industries, the volume of exports abroad and to the colonies had doubled in six years, and the net national product had increased by half.

The reaction in the West to the expansion of Japanese exports was wholly negative: tariffs were raised, quantitative restrictions were sought, and voices were lifted against "dumping" and cheap Oriental labor. In a few specific cases these responses were not unjustified. Yet when one considers that Japanese exports were only 4 per cent of world exports, and that Japanese imports from the United States and Europe were far greater than exports to those areas, such Western fears in retrospect seem hypochondriac — reflecting grave doubts in the West itself regarding the viability of the international economic order.

In any case, the reaction of the West provided fuel for the arguments of those groups in Japan favoring a policy of imperial expansion. Sentiment for this was not primarily an economic matter. Yet the economic arguments for it, while they varied from time to time and from group to group, were not without a certain logic. Other industrial powers had either extensive colonies or vast internal resources. Japan, the Britain of Asia, was deficient in both respects. It appeared that the only way to fulfill the national destiny in the face of Western restrictions was to create an economically self-sufficient empire. Those who argued this way stressed the primacy for Japan of the Asian market, the availability of iron ore and coal in China and of tin, oil, and rubber in Southeast Asia, and the fact that Japan, by the mid-thirties, had almost reached the point where she was no longer dependent on the West for heavy industrial equipment.

But events as they unfolded after 1936 show that even in purely economic terms these arguments were fallacious. The first point to note is that, despite raised tariffs abroad, Japan had successfully recovered from the depression. This recovery was based on a multilateral pattern of trade: Japan sold more than she bought in Asia and Africa, and bought from the United States and Europe more than she sold to them. This geographical imbalance was possible because currencies could be converted. After 1936, however, more and more of Japan's exports went to her colonies from which no convertible currencies were obtained. This led to diminishing foreign credits at a time when military demands were rising, thus forcing Japan to impose controls on dollar imports.[1] Second, by 1936 the Japanese economy was taut. The rapid economic expansion of the early 1930's had created conditions of virtual full employment and few resources were idle. Hence there was little possibility of another round of growth when Japan went to war, first with China in 1937 and then with the United States and the Western Allies in 1941. Already on what was called a "quasi-wartime" footing, Japan could increase her strategic economic potential only by imposing an elaborate system of strict controls to reduce consumption and shift productive capacities to war industries. A heavy dependence on foreign sources of raw materials, which war soon cut off, further limited her economic potential, heightening the industrial discrepancy between Japan and her chief opponent, the United States, which possessed vast sources of raw materials and, at the beginning of the war, was far from enjoying full employment.

Textile Industries.   A more detailed look at some of the major aspects of the Japanese economy will help us see what was happening to the economy and, through it, to the society as a whole. Japan's industrialization, like that of Britain, moved from traditional industries, mainly handicrafts, to light industries, and then to heavy industries. At first glance this sequence of development appears natural, even inevitable. But in fact, when we compare Japan with other late-developers — Germany, France, and Russia — we find the pattern to be anomalous. In the European countries the early industrial breakthrough came in iron and steel. Modern labor — men able to accept the discipline of industrial production — was scarce and therefore expensive, and capital was relatively cheap. This dictated an early development of capital-intensive

[1] William Lockwood, *The Economic Development of Japan*, pp. 394, 531.

industries which used fairly small amounts of labor. Since these developments began with the most advanced technology of that era, these countries very quickly became competitive with England.

That the Japanese pattern of development differed can be explained by three factors. The first was that capital in Japan, in comparison with Europe, was relatively expensive. The second was that industrial labor was relatively cheap, mainly because of the built-in labor surplus which appears to have existed in the Japanese pattern of intensive agriculture. This surplus, moreover, possessed characteristics enabling it to adapt rapidly to the conditions of modern industry. Even in farming, the practice of contractual wage labor had begun. Perhaps technological skills comparable to those of the European modernizers were lacking, but workers at least did not quit their jobs after earning enough to live on for a few weeks — as frequently happened in other pre-industrial societies. One is tempted to generalize, on the basis of developments in Japan and in the treaty ports of China where there was a Japanese-like framework of political stability, that wherever there is a combination of intensive agriculture and East Asian cultural values, the creation of a disciplined labor force will not be a problem for industrialization.

The third factor in Japan's development was that the unequal treaties, by excluding the possibility of tariff protection for infant industries, had prevented Japan from directing her maximum efforts toward heavy industrialization during the late nineteenth century. Enforced free trade opened Japan to the manufactures of Europe. In order to preserve her balance of payments, Japan was forced to develop competitive consumer industries. Rich in labor and poor in capital, she naturally developed along the lines of greatest economic advantage: the labor-intensive textile industries. Like the European late-developers, the Japanese textile industries imported the most modern equipment and soon became competitive with the mills of England.

During the early and middle years of Japan's industrialization (the 1880's to 1920's), textiles were central among her light industries, and the mainstay of her development. In 1912 they constituted 50 per cent of industrial production; in 1919, 45 per cent; and in 1926, 40 per cent. Their importance among Japan's exports was even greater: in 1929 they constituted 70 per cent of all exports, and as late as 1937, 60 per cent. In the mid-thirties, over 40 per cent of Japan's industrial labor force was still employed in textiles. This was the area in which private entrepreneurs obtained their first successes; it was the textile sector of industry that led in Japan's "takeoff," creating a demand that pulled other industries along with it.

Silk accounted at the turn of the century for about 29 per cent of the exports. Except for the reeling process, a very simple mechanical step, this was entirely a product of agricultural and hand labor. Between 1900 and 1929, production increased almost eight times over, most of it for export to America. On the eve of the Great Depression it constituted about 37 per cent of Japanese exports. A sharp drop in world prices, however, started in 1925, and the American crash of 1929 reduced the value of the export market, though production remained almost level. By 1936, raw silk exports were down about a tenth in bulk and exactly half in value, constituting a mere 12 per cent of the total.

The cotton-spinning industry, again a relatively simple one, had found the only sizable foreign market for Japanese manufactures before the end of the nineteenth century. This market more than doubled between 1900 and 1913, by which time Japan provided a quarter of world exports, but it had started to fall off by the end of the war as other technologically backward countries began to master this simple industrial process and supply their own needs. By the late 1930's exports of cotton yarn were a mere quarter of what they had once been, though productive capacity had increased about threefold to meet domestic needs.

Cotton textiles, which require somewhat more complex industrial skills, had meanwhile more than taken the place of yarn in the export field, also finding their market largely in the underdeveloped countries of Asia. Starting from almost nothing at the turn of the century, cotton textile exports had passed the slumping yarn trade before the end of the war, had come close to doubling again by the mid-1920's, and, after falling during the depression, scored further gains in the 1930's. By 1936 Japan had even passed Great Britain to become the leading exporter of cotton piece goods. By 1937 she had also become the greatest producer of rayon in the world.

The woolen textile industry, though never as large as cotton textiles, showed even more remarkable growth. In 1900, despite a protective tariff instituted the year before, Japan was still importing close to three-quarters of the woolen fabrics she used. By 1936 domestic production had grown more than 80-fold, imports had been virtually eliminated, and a sizable export trade had been established. The shift in relative importance from silk to cotton and wool, however, further highlighted Japan's dependence on foreign raw materials. To meet domestic and export needs, imports of raw cotton had increased more than fivefold since 1900 and of wool almost 40-fold.

Transport, Heavy Industries, and Raw Materials. In discussing Japan's textile industries there is a danger of overemphasizing the role of private enterprise and neglecting the indirect role of government in creating a constant environment in which planning and other manifestations of economic rationality could flourish. But in transport and heavy industries, government action in the form of subsidies and direct investment looms so large that it is easy to forget that most of the developments took place in private hands.

The Meiji leaders, as we have seen, placed strong emphasis from the start on railways and shipping. Railway mileage was more than tripled in the decade preceding World War I and had doubled again by the mid-1930's. Between 1906 and 1909 the main trunk lines were all purchased by the government and nationalized, but private enterprise continued to build many feeder lines and commuting networks around the great cities. Discriminatory legislation in 1906 also helped speed a shift from imported to domestically produced rolling stock. By the 1930's Japan had one of the finest and most efficient railroad networks in the world.

Laws passed in 1896, granting general subsidies to shipping lines and shipbuilders, together with the adoption in 1899 of differential subsidies in favor of Japanese-made ships, helped stimulate ship construction and the merchant marine. Shipbuilding increased more than fivefold in the fourteen years before the outbreak of World War I, by which time Japanese lines were carrying about half of Japan's trade. We have already seen what a stimulus the war was to Japanese shipping, and ship launchings increased more than sevenfold. But in the face of renewed Western competition after the war, the merchant marine leveled off in size, while shipbuilding fell drastically, recovering in the 1930's to only half the figure achieved in 1919.

The collapse of the shipbuilding boom at the end of the war showed that it was still difficult for Japan to compete with the Occident in heavy industries, but by the 1930's she had made impressive advances even in these more difficult technological fields. The early starts in heavy industry, which, as we have seen, date back to the late Tokugawa period, had been justified on strategic, not economic, grounds. During the Meiji period economic considerations reinforced strategy, but even then things went very slowly. In iron and steel production, for example, it was difficult for private entrepreneurs to get sufficient capital, the technical difficulties were severe, domestic supplies of ore and coking coal were inadequate, and after 1881 the government was reluctant to re-enter the field of state enterprise. This reluctance was overcome in 1901 with the founding of the Yawata Iron and Steel Works in northern Kyūshū, which by 1913 was meeting almost half of Japan's iron needs and close to a third of her steel needs. Steel output increased fourfold between 1913 and 1929, and had more than doubled again by 1936, though it still fell short of meeting domestic demand.

The production of machinery had also made a small start before World

War I. For example, the Shibaura Engineering Works, one of the predecessors of the present Tōshiba, was founded in 1887, and Hitachi, another present giant, in 1910. But even as late as the mid-1920's Japan was largely dependent on foreign imports of machinery. In the next decade, however, a great change occurred. By 1936 Japan was able to provide for much of her machinery needs and was beginning to export simple machine tools and, of course, products manufactured by machines, such as electrical goods, bicycles, and a wide variety of cheap consumer goods.

Other fields showed this same coming-of-age of the industrial economy. The production of chemicals, which had risen steeply since prewar years, almost doubled between 1929 and 1937. Electric power more than doubled between 1913 and 1920, came close to expanding fourfold in the next decade, and almost doubled again by 1937. Much of this increase resulted from extensive exploitation of Japan's rich hydroelectric resources. By the late 1930's nearly two-fifths of the industrial workers were occupied in metals, machinery, and chemicals, and the share of metals, metal products, and machinery in the export trade rose from 4 to 14 per cent between 1929 and 1936.

Thus Japan by the mid-1930's had laid the foundations for an advanced, diversified, and booming industrial economy, supplying virtually all her own needs for manufactured goods and able to compete in many fields with the most advanced industrial nations of the West. Primarily an exporter of raw and semi-processed materials in the late nineteenth century, she had become predominantly an exporter of finished goods by the 1930's. Parallel to this change, however, Japan became increasingly dependent on foreign sources of raw materials. Despite a sharply rising consumption of ores, mining in Japan reached a point of diminishing growth. Copper historically had been the one important mineral export, and even as late as 1914 Japan was the world's second largest exporter, but production grew only slowly thereafter, and in the 1920's Japan became a net importer of copper. Coal production, the largest mining industry, increased about fourfold in the first two decades of the twentieth century, but thereafter, although significant gains in productivity per worker were scored, there was only a small increase in total production. The coal seams were too narrow and broken to permit easy exploitation, and Japan had become a net importer of coal before the end of the 1920's. Her deficiencies in many other important minerals were even greater. For example, by 1930, even before the big industrial upsurge of the next few years, Japan was already dependent on overseas sources for 100 per cent of her aluminum, 93 per cent of her lead, 85 per cent of her iron and steel materials, 79 per cent of her petroleum, and 74 per cent of her tin. Moreover, Japan also had to import a significant proportion of the food for her people, and virtually all of the fibers for their clothing. The wars on which Japan embarked after 1937 first imperiled and then cut off most of her essential markets and sources of raw materials. Thus the ill-fated attempt to create an empire of East Asia dealt the economy an almost fatal blow, which the destruction of the Japanese cities and industrial machine only intensified.

The Zaibatsu System. One of the distinctive features of the Japanese economy by the 1920's was the extraordinary concentration of wealth and economic power in the hands of a few giant concerns and the families that owned them. The scarcity of capital in early Meiji Japan, the government's willingness to give financial aid and extraordinary privileges to entrepreneurs who gave promise of building up the economy, and Matsukata's sale in the 1880's of government industries to the few who were able to buy them—all these factors, as we have seen, combined to enable a relatively small group of business leaders to gain control over a large proportion of Japan's new industrial economy, just before industrialization started to pay off. New entrepreneurs continued to appear in the rising big industries, and many prospered, while a growing host of small businessmen competed desperately in the small industries. But the business giants that had established themselves in the late nineteenth century grew faster than the economy as a whole and by the 1920's controlled a major part of the nation's wealth and a much larger share of its economic power.

In the industrial upsurge of World War I, those industrialists who already had a head start expanded enormously, and during the decade of economic uncertainties that followed the war they fastened their hold on the economy even more firmly. At least half of Japan's banks were eliminated during this period, leaving the financial power needed for large-scale industrial expansion concentrated in the hands of a few giant institutions. The leading financial and industrial groups had from the start cooperated closely and submissively with the government and had benefited greatly from its patronage, but now a greater equalization of roles began to take place. Businessmen continued to work within a framework of government fiscal policy, to depend on the government for foreign exchange, to require the cooperation of the various ministries, and to profit from government purchases. But they were no longer dependent on the government for their capital requirements—on the contrary, the government came to depend on them for aid in floating bond issues. And while continuing as instruments of government policy, big business, by its ties within the bureaucracy and by its financial influence on the political parties, came to have a growing voice in the formation of policy as well. To many Japanese it appeared that the tail was beginning to wag the dog. The term zaibatsu, or "financial clique," which came into common use at this time for these business giants, had a strongly pejorative flavor.

There has never been any clear agreement on how many or exactly which companies constituted the zaibatsu group, but the top four are always listed, in order of their size, as Mitsui, Mitsubishi, Sumitomo, and Yasuda. The origins of these four and of two other members of the zaibatsu group, Shibusawa and Asano, have been described in Chapter 4. In addition, no one would dispute the inclusion of other giants such as the Furukawa, Kuhara, and Kawasaki interests, as well as Aikawa's Nissan interests and other "new zaibatsu" which rose in the 1930's in the armaments industries and through aiding the army to exploit Manchuria.

The zaibatsu firms concentrated almost completely on the newer and more rapidly growing sectors of the economy, but few of them ever established the degree of partial monopoly that was becoming characteristic of the newer industries in the United States and some other Western lands at the turn of the century. Instead they commonly established conditions of oligopoly, that is, the control of the market in some product by a relatively small group of sellers. Two zaibatsu firms or as many as five or six might control half or more of some product or service, thus jointly dominating that particular economic field. Often such producers joined in voluntary associations to regulate the quality of their common product. Such associations not infrequently also acted to curb undue competition within the domestic market. This sort of semi-competitive oligopoly, rather than monopoly, afforded an interesting parallel in Japanese economic life to the pattern of oligarchic rule, rather than dictatorship, that dominated politics.

The greatest difference between a typical zaibatsu firm and a typical Western corporation was that the former, instead of concentrating in one type of venture, usually spread over a variety of fields, constituting thus a "combine" of business enterprises rather than a single great company. Such a combine might spread horizontally through a variety of manufacturing or mining industries and also vertically through the different stages of activity concerned with a single product. Thus one of the Mitsubishi mining companies might extract the minerals which one of the Mitsubishi manufacturing companies then fashioned into a product which a Mitsubishi trading firm in turn marketed abroad, transporting it in ships of another Mitsubishi affiliate, and the whole process would be financed through the Mitsubishi banking interests.

Such combines grew to enormous size during the 1920's and 1930's, and the top two, Mitsui and Mitsubishi, were at that time probably the two largest private economic empires in the world. By 1941, the sprawling Mitsui interests consisted basically of a main holding company, with 70 direct corporate affiliates. The two largest, Mitsui Trading and Mitsui

ORGANIZATION OF THE MITSUI COMBINE
(based on specific examples among major units in the combine)

Arrows indicate percentage of stock ownership. Numbers in parentheses are paid-up
capital in millions of yen (roughly 3 to the
dollar).

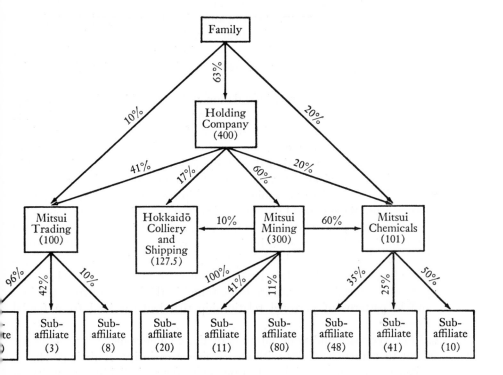

Mining, controlled respectively 126 and 31 other affiliates, while 108 other companies were under the control of the other 68 direct affiliates. It is estimated that the Mitsui interests at their peak employed about a million people in Japan proper and another million in the empire and abroad.

The structure of control within the combines in some ways paralleled and in others contrasted sharply with Western corporations. Mitsui was owned basically by the original Mitsui family, by then divided into eleven branches, which held some 90 per cent of their wealth jointly and were strictly controlled in their actions and expenditures by family laws, dating back two or more centuries but brought up to date in 1900. The family as such held shares directly in many of the Mitsui companies and owned a majority interest in the central holding company. This distinction between family and holding company did not exist in the more recently risen zaibatsu firms. Another difference between Mitsui and most of the others was that, while in the former actual business control of the combine had long since passed into the hands of managers, in the newer zaibatsu firms the original entrepreneur or his immediate descendants might still be in operating control.

The zaibatsu holding companies held stocks in their direct affiliates and these in turn in their own affiliates, and sometimes these various sub-units held one another's stocks. Interlocking directorates also helped tie the ramified interests of a combine together. Thus directors of the holding company might also serve in key posts in its affiliates, or a single man might serve as a director or the treasurer of a whole series of companies in the combine.

This pattern of corporate infeudation and interlocking directorates may be understandable enough from Western practices, but a sharp difference with the Occident was that the majority of the stocks in an affiliate might not be owned by the combine, and yet the latter's control over the affiliate remained unquestioned. Family and holding company interests in some direct Mitsui affiliates, for example, amounted to only 20 per cent, and in indirect affiliates combine ownership sometimes was no more than 10 per cent. Such control without majority ownership naturally expanded the economic power of those running the central holding company far beyond the point warranted by its actual wealth. It was possible in part because of the extreme laxity of Japanese corporation law, which permitted outside stockholders little control over management. More important reasons, however, were to be found in the nature of the combines and in patterns of personal relationship that had survived from feudal times.

The very size and wide interests of the combines made it possible for them to control affiliates without owning a majority of their stock. A zaibatsu combine was simply too powerful for an individual company to challenge. The combine controlled the financial resources the company normally drew on; it also controlled the trading companies which marketed the company's products and the shipping lines that transported them. An individual company could scarcely afford to build up, in competition with the combine, its own marketing outlets, especially in foreign trade. A combine, with its vast and widespread resources, could easily crush through a price war any revolt by one of its affiliates. For the latter, obedient cooperation was obviously more advantageous than defiance. In fact, entirely independent business enterprises, and particularly those seeking foreign markets, found it desirable to play the role of humble satellites and thus gain some of the advantages of participants in the system. Consequently, far from failing to control their own partially-owned affiliates, the great combines exercised strong influence over large

numbers of smaller businesses in which they had no direct financial investment at all.

Moreover, even apart from economic sanctions, it would have been
unthinkable for an affiliate to transfer its allegiance from one combine to
another. The survival from feudal times of a sense of personal relationship between employer and employee in industry was paralleled by a
strong sense of personal or corporate loyalty within management itself.
The college graduate who joined a combine usually did so for life. He
started in a subordinate position in a minor affiliate but hoped that, through
displaying absolute loyalty as well as talent, he would rise eventually to a
position of power in a major affiliate or in the holding company itself.
He was, as it were, a samurai for life in that particular zaibatsu *han*, and
his loyalty assured the loyalty of the affiliate for which he worked.

There has been a hot debate over the economic efficiency of the zaibatsu
system as it had developed by the 1920's. Today, most economists tend
to feel that the system was very efficient, and in its era almost inevitable.
When any backward country industrializes, there is a shortage of capital,
skilled labor, and technological know-how. To obtain rapid growth, these
must be brought together in as concentrated a form as possible. In the
twentieth century, with its ideological emphasis on economic equality
(witness the use of "socialism" as a slogan by agrarian-based modernizers),
this concentration most frequently takes place under the aegis of the state.
But during the second half of the nineteenth century — the heyday of
Manchester liberalism, when free enterprise was strong and there existed
no historical model of socialist development — it was only natural for
this to occur in private hands.

One often-voiced criticism of the zaibatsu system was that it tended
toward monopoly, which normally produces economic stagnation. While
the combines were usually engaged in keen competition with one another,
the smallness of their number and the weakness of the laws permitted
collusive arrangements which at times probably raised prices and increased
profits beyond levels that would have prevailed in a more fully competitive system. Such tendencies, however, never went very far. The large
place of foreign raw materials and markets in the zaibatsu enterprises
helped keep their prices highly competitive; not until the 1930's and under
pressure from the government, rather than from the zaibatsu themselves,
did the Japanese economy begin to suffer from the restrictions of excessive cartelization.

On the other hand, the very size and breadth of interests of the zaibatsu
combines permitted them to venture into new and costly fields or develop
large-scale enterprises, which might otherwise have gone undeveloped or
been left to less efficient government management. In short, the profits
from established enterprises could be effectively used by the combines

as risk capital to pioneer new fields. Moreover, their great size and ramified interests permitted an unusually high degree of economic integration, which in other countries has normally been achieved only through government regulation.

The concentration of a large proportion of Japan's wealth in the hands of the zaibatsu families was also probably a net economic gain. If ownership of the zaibatsu firms had been spread among a wide segment of the population, their profits might have been largely absorbed in modest rises in living standards for a large number of families. As it was, the zaibatsu families, being few in number, could not possibly consume all their vast income, and in fact, with their typically Japanese love of simplicity and dislike of ostentation, they consumed very little of it. As a result, the bulk of the profits from the combines was reinvested in their expansion, a fact which helps to explain Japan's phenomenal economic growth during this period. The whole economic history of Japan down to World War II proves that the zaibatsu system must have worked with considerable economic efficiency.

It is more difficult, however, to evaluate the social and political effects of the system. Obviously the zaibatsu were in many ways undemocratic. They were marked by hierarchy, authority, and unquestioning personal loyalties. Yet they were not more undemocratic than the surrounding society. On the contrary, within their bureaucratic framework, ability, efficiency, and education counted for a great deal. They gave no support to individualism, yet, after the Japanese managerial revolution of the 1890's, the zaibatsu probably offered a career more open to talent than any other part of Japanese society except the military services.

Some have criticized the heavy concentration of wealth in the hands of the zaibatsu families as an obstacle to the development of a strong middle class. No doubt a wider distribution of corporate stock ownership would have contributed to this. On the other hand, the middle management of the zaibatsu concerns (along with the professions, small businessmen, landlords, and upper levels of the bureaucracy) did constitute a recognizable middle class even during the 1920's, with homes, savings, a high concern for their children's education, and so on. It can easily be argued that rapid economic growth, which the zaibatsu system promoted, did more to strengthen this group than economic concentration did to weaken it. As we shall note later, what this group lacked, in comparison with similar groups in the West, appears to have been more the result of its culture and values than of its lack of economic perquisites.

In the political sphere the effects of zaibatsu concentration of wealth were certainly bad. Whether the actual influence of big business on government was much greater than in the Western democracies is doubtful. Yet in Japan the fact that the financial power of the zaibatsu completely outweighed that of rural landlords and small business interests was highly visible. The political activities of the zaibatsu early became a target for popular criticism and helped to tarnish the whole concept of democracy in many Japanese minds.

Yet, though nondemocratic, the zaibatsu did not fit in very well with militarism, the other political trend then developing in Japan. Their ties to the conservative political parties led them to favor representative government as it existed during the 1920's. The education and experience in foreign countries of their managers, together with an awareness of the importance of foreign trade, tended to give the zaibatsu an international outlook. After World War II the zaibatsu were singled out as the greatest object of attack by democratic reformers during the American occupation. Before the war, however, it was the supporters of militarism, rather than the believers in democracy, who, borrowing the arguments of the left, were the most violent critics of the zaibatsu system. The officer bureaucrats of the Japanese Kwantung Army in Manchuria, for example, viewing the zaibatsu as Western, urban, liberal, and corrupt, shut them out of the early phase of Manchurian development after 1931. As Japan slipped deeper into war after 1937, the zaibatsu industries inevitably became the core of the war economy. Even then they proved difficult to control. The government could easily dominate smaller economic units, but the zaibatsu represented such aggregates of economic power and expertise that it seemed more expedient to seek their cooperation than to force their submission. Administratively, the zaibatsu combines proved to be the only major residuum of private power able to maintain some autonomy during the rising militarism of the late 1930's and World War II.

The Double Structure of the Japanese Economy. Another distinctive feature of the Japanese economy was the tremendous number of small concerns with less than five workers. In 1930, for example, more than half (2,772,183) of Japan's manufacturing labor force (4,759,921) was employed in such small businesses. It is difficult to estimate their productive capacity since their reports for tax purposes grossly underestimated their actual role in the economy. It is clear, however, that they were far less efficient than the big modern factories, and that the value of their output was considerably less than their numerical strength would indicate. They cannot, however, be simply dismissed as the declining sector of traditional small industries. Relative to medium and large industry, their percentage of total production was slowly declining, yet in Tōkyō alone their number increased phenomenally from about 3000 in 1923 after the Tōkyō earthquake to almost 26,000 in 1932.

Bimodality thus marked the Japanese economy: a handful of giant combines, thousands of tiny workshops, and, in between, relatively few medium-sized industries. Japanese economic historians refer to this pattern as the "double structure" of the economy. In part it was a result of a split technology: zaibatsu engineers versed in Western science as contrasted with the small shops rooted in the Tokugawa artisan tradition. The availability of capital was also bimodal. Zaibatsu banks catered to industries within the same combine, but small businesses could be started with private savings or a loan from a patron. The two extremes also reflect clear differences in social organization: the zaibatsu, although deeply paternalistic, were recognizably modern or "Western"; the workshops, even when newly formed, assimilated to traditional Japanese small-group organization. By the late 1930's some of these distinctions had begun to blur. Universal education and ties to larger industries led to a rising level of technology in the small businesses. And changes were also taking place in social organization. In general, however, the relative differences continued into the postwar period, along with a double standard of wages.

Among the small concerns with fewer than five workers were traditional handicrafts, woven textiles, shops producing daily necessities, and repair shops, all areas of expanding demand as standards of living rose. Yet we must stress not simply their functions in relation to the consumer, but also the integration of small business with the most advanced sector of the economy. Estimates vary widely, but probably over half of Japan's small concerns subsisted entirely on sub-contracts from zaibatsu-type industries. Modern assembly line production depended to a varying extent on elements produced outside of the modern industrial sector itself. A simple machined part or the time-consuming assembly of an electrical device, for example, might take place in a farm village shop serviced by a trunk railway line one hundred miles from the factory.

What this double structure meant is still highly controversial. Was the low efficiency of small business a drag on the economy, an obstacle to modernization, or should such small concerns be viewed as an area of supplementary strength that enabled the modern sector to direct all its energies to technological advance and industrial production? If the former position is taken, one can go on to see the relation between the zaibatsu and small business as exploitative: putting out simple tasks to the workers in these shops kept cheap labor cheap and maintained social patterns that permitted continued exploitation. Had the total productive process been brought into the factory, a greater equalization of wages, more favorable conditions for labor organization, and new social patterns would have developed.

In any human terms, this system was exploitative: working conditions in the small shops were poor, only a step removed from those of tenant farm labor. The use of such shops, however, was the cheapest way to produce, and it was this economic consideration, rather than any zaibatsu social policy, that led to the putting out of work. Moreover, we can say that to a considerable extent the double structure developed not because of zaibatsu planning, but in spite of zaibatsu growth. That it was not destroyed by rapid industrial growth was owing to the high rate of population growth which kept up the supply of cheap labor. In the postwar period, the same type of growth in the modern sector — in combination with a sharply decreased rate of population growth — has pulled labor out of small industries and out of the farm villages more rapidly than it could be replaced. This has forced wages up within the small concerns and is breaking through the prewar bimodality; but the "double structure" still remains a characteristic, even if declining, aspect of Japan's economy.

SOCIAL STRUCTURE AND SOCIAL CHANGE

Like the economy, social organization represents not an independent dimension of history but one that is interdependent — one that while abstractable as an independent structure must also be intellectually recombined. In the writing of Western history this dimension is often taken for granted. Everybody knows, or thinks he knows, what the family is, and to discourse on it may seem a statement of the obvious. The same assumption, however, does not work in East Asian history; there is much that needs to be made explicit if the nature of historical change is to be understood.

The Japanese Family. The family was of political as well as social importance before World War II in Japan. It was seen as the building block of the unique Japanese "national polity." Its ideal virtues of harmony, solidarity, and loyalty were projected onto the Japanese state. It was the last stronghold of Confucian social practices. The family changed greatly, as we shall see, but the pace of change was usually slower than that of the surrounding society. Even the city dweller, whose life was modern in most respects, was through the family in touch to some degree with a still vital area of Japan's premodern tradition.

In the family as it existed in the late nineteenth century, lineage, not marriage, was sacred. The emphasis was placed on the relation between self and parents and ancestors, not self and wife. This view of the family mirrored the stress within the traditional family system on the ancestral house as an entity continuing in time. The duties of the individual were to the "house." Marriage was for the purpose of obtaining heirs for the house. The position of the daughter-in-law was partly defined by the proverb, "The womb is borrowed." If a marriage was childless the "bride" might be returned, or an heir might be adopted, or in a well-to-do family a concubine might be set up. Both daughter-in-law and eldest son, as well as other, unmarried children, lived with his parents. Both were subordinated to his father, the family head. The ideal family was three generations under a single roof. Unlike the extended family that was the traditional Chinese ideal, there was no provision for lateral spread in Japan. Younger brothers left the "house" when they married, forming separate "branch families." These were ceremonially subordinate to the main family; but in fact, where property or close residence or some other compelling tie did not exist to hold them together (as in a rural situation, or in a family business like the Mitsui), ties rapidly weakened and branch houses tended within a generation or two to become autonomous main houses in their own right.

Most aspects of this traditional model of the family, and in particular the powers of the family head, were given the force of law in the revised Civil Code of 1898 (which continued in force until after World War II). Family property was held by the family head as an individual, not by the family as a collective entity; the establishment of the right of the individual to own property was perhaps a necessary concession to Japan's capitalist economic order. But most of it went to one son, usually the eldest or the most able, who succeeded as the family head. The family head had the power to expunge from the family register (kept at the local government office) the name of any offender against family honor or his own authority. He could also dissolve a marriage of a son under thirty or a daughter under twenty-five. Yet for all his legal powers, the family head, more than in China, represented the consensus existing among the other family members, rather than a dictatorial figure standing above it. If the use of this legal power was judged by the family, including relatives, to be excessively arbitrary and against the good of the family as a whole, the head could be forced to retire by a council of family elders.

Change in an institution as basic as the family proceeds very slowly. Even after World War II the pattern described above is still recognizable in most areas of rural Japan. Yet in urban Japan important changes were already under way during the late nineteenth century. The expanding population that accompanied Japan's early industrialization produced a greater than usual number of second and third sons who moved to cities and formed (in fact if not in ideal) conjugal-type families, centered on the husband-wife relationship rather than the line of "house." As the rationalization of the economy continued, impersonal factors became more important, more time was spent away from the family, and for the increasing numbers of wage employees the economic unity of the family as the unit of production began to disappear. Changes in the social base created potentials for new institutions. These were realized, little by little, under the influence of new ideal patterns introduced from the West. The women's rights movement, the doctrine of political rights, romantic literary currents, Protestant Christianity, socialism, and other influences contributed to the shift in emphasis from lineage to the conjugal tie. All tended to point up the ideal equality of the woman in marriage. The debate on the family continues on many fronts even today. Thus when the bill banning prostitution was before the Diet in 1957, one conservative party representative argued that prostitution was necessary so that decent women could remain decent, whereupon a somewhat intellectual woman's magazine replied that the wife must become a prostitute (i.e., a sexual companion) to her husband. The transition to the conjugal-type family is still not complete. Even in urban areas most marriages are still arranged by parents and go-betweens, though the future partners are usually consulted and at least exercise veto powers. And love, although extremely popular as a concept, is not considered necessary in marriage. The overall change, however, is in the direction taken by the modern West.

The change in the family can be seen quantitatively in divorce statistics. In the West, as industrialization and social modernization proceeded, the percentage of divorces increased. In the United States, an extreme case, the increase was from .3 per 1000 of population in 1867 to 2.2 in 1957. The conjugal family of the nineteenth century was anchored by other crisscrossing ties — kinship, local, economic, religious, social. As these ties weakened, the husband-wife nexus became more important than ever, yet less secure. But in Japan the trend of the divorce rate is reversed: 3.39 per 1000 in 1883, 1.43 in 1900, and .79 in 1957. The actual drop in the divorce rate was much more precipitous than these figures suggest since in the past many rural marriages went unregistered until demonstrated "successful." It is ironic that the "Japanese family system" so eulogized by traditionalists should have had one of the highest divorce rates in history. The Japanese statistics reveal an increasing stability resulting from a change in family type from lineal to conjugal. Durkheim expressed this, saying, "As the family [lineage] loses ground, marriage on the contrary is strengthened." In Japan it was only during the 1950's that one could begin to see in the statistics of the largest cities the modern phenomenon of a rising rate of divorce among nuclear families. Until the last decade or so this had been lost statistically in the much greater movement in the other direction.

Rural Society. Japanese rural society by the turn of the century was in no simple sense a peasant society that could be defined as tradition-directed. Primary education was on the point of becoming universal. Children of the rural well-to-do often went on to intermediate and higher education. Newspapers were read. Many rural Japanese had traveled as soldiers in the army. Most had relatives in the proliferating cities. New agricultural methods had been accepted and proven successful. As railway lines were built, agricultural markets became nationwide. Government influence, though often indirect, was pervasive, and rural hearts thrilled to Japanese military victories. Change was apparent, and a degree of "openness" had developed that made the village qualitatively different from the Tokugawa village. Yet it was not a modern society. In many important ways the "cake of custom" remained unbroken. Religiously, socially, politically, there continued the practice of community solidarity that was directly derived from the "traditional society" of Tokugawa Japan.

The unit of the local "organic" society was the *buraku* or hamlet — a grouping of households, from ten to seventy or so in number, such as dot the Japanese countryside. The social cohesion within such groupings had several sources. In part it was the expression of the ethic of harmony, of the necessary etiquette found in most face-to-face groups in Japan. This was reinforced by the rituals of hamlet shrines or temples which stressed community solidarity. Irrigation in most areas required community decisions regarding the allocation of limited water resources. And from the Tokugawa era most hamlets possessed communal pastures or wooded hills; decisions concerning these were made by a hamlet council to which each household sent one representative. This council also handled collections, aid to families in time of crises, and even plans for community recreation.

The combined force of these various and necessary community functions was too great to be resisted. If a member of the hamlet rebelled against the discipline of the group or too seriously affronted the honor of the community, his family might be subject to ostracism, although this was rarely necessary. Instances are recorded, however, even after World War II. In one, a high school girl brought shame on her community when her essay exposing corrupt local politics was picked up by the newspapers and gained nationwide attention; both the girl's family and her school-teacher were ostracized and forced to move to another area. It is often said that government by law stopped at the village, the lowest level in the administrative hierarchy. In the several hamlets of which a village was composed, all decisions affecting the community as a whole were carried out by group consensus. Even after 1937, when semi-official recognition was given to the hamlet to aid in wartime mobilization and requisitioning, directives from above were given effect by the consensus of the hamlet council, not by the legal authority of the hamlet head.

Within the solidarity of the geographically defined local hamlet there were several overlapping types of internal organization. One factor, especially clear in the more traditional rural society of northeastern Japan, but also surviving less markedly elsewhere, was kinship. In one well-studied hamlet (one of eight in a village) there were 51 families. These were divided into eleven lineages, each with main and branch families. Some of the branch families were not strictly related to their "main houses" by blood ties, but either had been hereditary servants in the past or had joined an existing lineage on entering the hamlet as a "new family" in order to participate in hamlet affairs. One lineage was superior to the others: its head was the "parent" to the heads of the other ten. In a community such as this the lineage often acted as a bloc within the hamlet council.

Another and more important factor influencing hamlet organization was the pattern of land ownership. At the time of the Meiji Restoration about 25 to 30 per cent of the land was worked by tenants. The proportion slowly rose to 45 per cent in 1908 and was maintained at this level until after World War II (46 per cent in 1941). Japanese landlords, however, were not a local aristocracy as in Iran or Poland, nor were they wealthy absentees as in some areas of South China in pre-Communist days. Most were small landowners, with a few more acres than they could work themselves. Those with larger holdings almost invariably lived on their land. And there were infinite gradations in the size and patterns of holdings. Only 20 per cent of farm families were pure tenants; 35 per cent were part owners, part tenants; and 45 per cent owned all the land they worked.

In areas where landlordism was extensive, patterns of paternalism and subordination were related to this, and community solidarity was hierarchical. (In a fishing village, boat ownership was the equivalent of land ownership in an agricultural village.) There were always more people willing to work the land than land available to be worked. This gave the landlord the upper hand. Tenants were protected by custom — the same custom that supported their inferior status — but written contracts were rare. In times of distress the tenantry actually depended for their life on the practice of paternalism. The power of the landlords was also bulwarked by ideologies such as "Agriculturism," a Confucian-tinged concept stressing the virtues of obedience, loyalty, harmony, and frugality.

Landlordism gave rise to serious inequities within rural society. Taxes that took about 35 per cent of the value of the crop during the early Meiji period dropped by 1902 to about 20 per cent as a result of tax cuts and creeping inflation. This decline was not unrelated to the great influence of the rural landlords on the political parties. But rents collected from tenants remained at almost Tokugawa levels, about 50 per cent of the crop. This imbalance, which made landlordism very profitable, was compounded by the general decline of agriculture as farm productivity leveled off during the 1920's. Cities grew and prospered, but the farmers, who even in the late 1930's constituted 44 per cent of the total population, received a shrinking proportion of the national wealth. The prosperity of urban life made the hardship of the countryside, where expectations also rose with education, less tolerable than before. One index of this decline was that government subsidies, earlier given almost wholly to industry, were after 1920 increasingly given to agriculture; by 1931, 40 per cent went to rural areas.

As the relative position of agriculture in the economy declined, tenant unions (called Farmers Unions) began to form, first in prefectures about Tōkyō and then spreading to the northeast and other areas. These paralleled the rising labor unions in the cities, and for the most part began

under the influence of city intellectuals. As in city-based unions, a major
role was played during the early years by Christian socialists, but by the
mid-twenties Marxists were dominant. A national organization of these
unions was formed in 1922. Parts of this were active in supporting prole-
tariat-peasant parties. In villages where landlords practiced the paternalism
which they preached, trouble was often avoided, and compromises were
reached. But in some areas where unions were organized, bloody riots
occurred, the landlords obtaining police support. It is possible to exaggerate the importance of these unions. Even in the peak year of 1927
they had only 365,000 members, while almost four million families were
wholly or partially tenants. Yet it is symptomatic of the new openness
of rural society that ideas so at odds with tradition could have entered
and been accepted at all.

After the Manchurian Incident of 1931 the tenant movement fell apart.
Leftist leaders of the movement were arrested in the police crackdowns
of 1928 and the early 1930's. The All-Japan Peasants' Union, which before
the Incident had criticized "Japanese imperialism" in Leninist terms,
swung around to a national socialist position supporting Japan's expansion abroad. At the same time the villages of Japan experienced bitter
suffering. Agricultural prices dropped: particularly hard hit were the
40 per cent of rural families whose incomes depended in part on silk-
stocking prosperity in the United States. Under these conditions, and
within Japan's particular social structure, solidarity became more necessary
and class struggle gradually disappeared. Yet the village harmony that was
re-created at this time was somewhat less hierarchical than before. Partly
because of new government rural policies, the position of the owner-
farmers was improved, and that of the landlords made less all-powerful

The Growth of the Tenant Movement

Year	Tenant-Landlord Disputes	Tenant Unions	Union Membership (in thousands)
1917	85	—	—
1919	326	—	—
1921	1,680	681	—
1923	1,917	1,530	164
1925	2,206	3,496	307
1927	2,053	4,582	365
1929	2,434	4,156	316
1931	3,419	4,414	306
1933	4,000	4,810	303
1935	6,824	4,011	242
1937	6,170	3,879	227
1939	3,578	3,509	210
1941	3,308	293	24

in village councils. Conditions, however, remained poor. The frustrations and aggressions that earlier had been directed against the landlords were now turned outward against the urban rich and Japan's "enemies" abroad. When land reform was announced after World War II, it was discovered that the tenants had little "rights consciousness" toward the land they worked. As one writer has put it, "What they were now promised seemed almost too good to be true, and they were prepared to take what gifts the gods gave them and not complain if they were not all they might have been."[1]

Politics in Rural Japan. A final aspect of rural Japan that must be considered is its relation to national political organization. After 1890 there were two interlocking national political hierarchies, one of the bureaucracy, the other of the political parties or of party politicians. Both were in part grounded in the semi-traditional rural society.

Local bureaucracy began in the Home Ministry and extended downward through prefectures to counties (abolished in 1921) and then to cities, towns, and villages. All executive positions were filled by appointment from above, and the chain of authority was marked by a high degree of submissiveness and responsibility toward higher echelons of government. An adjunct of the official hierarchy, under the Home Ministry, was the police. Social censure was so powerful and family attachments so strong that crime was rare in prewar rural Japan. As a consequence, the police were primarily roving guardians of public morality, working with local leaders as a uniformed expression of official approval for the local order. The political role of the Home Ministry changed with time. It was early used by the government against the parties. Then, as the party men gained power in the government and as the bureaucracy became infiltrated with party appointees, it was used by one or another party, usually the party in power, for the advancement of their candidates. At all times, but especially during the 1930's, it was the watchdog on guard against "dangerous thought."

The village was the lowest administrative level in the bureaucratic hierarchy. Here modern bureaucracy with its records, directives, individual responsibility, and impersonality met the personally-oriented, family-based solidarity of the hamlet. Village organization itself can be seen as a compromise between the two. Mayors were appointed by the prefectural governor. Yet the men appointed were usually men of influence in their communities, men of good family, men with education, personality, and experience with farming and with agricultural finance. Under the mayor was an elected village council. This decided on matters of local importance, and gave an expression of local sentiment intended to guide the mayor in the execution of government directives. It also provided

[1] Ronald Dore, *Land Reform in Japan*, p. 168.

a channel by which information could pass from the government to the hamlet.

A second political hierarchy was that of the political parties, or more accurately, of party politicians. This began with Diet members and reached back through prefectural assemblymen to county and village men of influence. Such men of influence on the local scene have often been called bosses. In truth, their political influence was great within their "roped off areas," and they could throw blocs of votes to the candidate of their choice. Yet we must dig deeper to see their real character. First, they were not bosses in the pejorative sense that the term has when applied to ward bosses in some American cities. Rather, they usually possessed the Japanese equivalent of the solid social position that a Protestant banker might have in a midwestern American town. Second, if their control was not democratic, neither was it authoritarian. Voting in rural, prewar Japan was largely an expression of local solidarity. It was socially approved; a higher percentage of eligible voters always exercised their franchise in the country than in cities. There was a strong feeling against wasting votes; a vote counted if it joined other votes in a bloc for a candidate who would obtain benefits (roads, bridges, schools, tax reliefs, and so on) for the area. Bosses maintained their influence by tending to their personal ties with village and hamlet leaders, and by securing benefits for their areas. In contrast to this pattern, both democracy and authoritarianism as they exist in the West are based on support from, or control over, a more highly individualized, differentiated social base.

Japan was predominantly a rural country until recent times. As late as 1918 more than two-thirds of the Japanese lived in places of less than 10,000 population. Thus, a national politician to win an election had to obtain the support of prefectural assemblymen and of the men of influence associated with them who controlled votes at the "grass roots." This required a dual approach. On the one hand, it was necessary to obtain concrete benefits for the district and prefecture. The local politician, with such evidences of the esteem in which he was held by the nation's leaders, could more easily hold his following in line. On the other hand, personal ties also had to be carefully cultivated. Entertainment, gifts, and money were continuously employed to lubricate the personal machine of the candidate. Most of the funds for this came not from the party, but directly from some wealthy person or combine, whose influence continued after the election. The lack of party control over such funds was, and is today, one of the contributing causes of factionalism within the Diet. If either the material or the personal needs of the political machine were neglected, support might shift to other, more able politicians.

The strongest political organization that has been studied thus far was the "iron constituency" in Okayama Prefecture which sent a member of the Inukai family to the Diet in every election from 1890. From this area 76 per cent of the votes went to Inukai (or to the candidates whom he designated) in the decades after 1890, 47 per cent of the votes after 1932 when the son inherited the "fief" from the father, and 35 per cent (still enough to win a Diet seat) in the years immediately after World War II. This constant support was exceptional. In most areas, even though bloc-voting occurred, local bosses tended to swing their influence from one party to the other — usually to get the patronage of the party in power.

Yet the progressive weakening of control within the Inukai machine does reflect a nationwide movement away from the tightly-integrated, hierarchical, community-conscious character of Meiji society. This movement was slow. It represents in part a rise in individual political awareness, and in part the rising position of owner-farmers vis-à-vis landlords, a trend which continued even during the 1930's and early 1940's and provided the groundwork for the greater "rural democracy" that followed the Occupation's land reform.

Urban Society. The city in Japan was traditionally freer than the countryside. Different types of restrictive organizations did exist — ward associations, shrine groups, guilds, fire-fighting groups, and so on; and in commoners' districts where houses adjoined, privacy was slight and immediate neighbors were close and familiar. But personal ties could not be formed between all residents in a city district. Movement in and out of communities was frequent. And in the absence of the cooperative forms demanded by agriculture and communal property, and of the physical demarcation of the hamlet, the sense of community solidarity was weaker.

The modern city in Japan is in some respects an outgrowth of the traditional city, while qualitatively new in other ways. Observed objectively, the rise of the modern city was an epiphenomenon of Japan's modern economic growth. In 1895 only 12 per cent of the 42 million Japanese lived in cities or towns of more than 10,000 persons. This shows a slight increase over estimates of the city population in late Tokugawa Japan, mainly reflecting growth in the traditional sector of the economy. By the mid-1930's, however, over 45 per cent of the 69 million Japanese lived in such urban areas, and over a quarter of the population lived in cities of more than 100,000 persons. The growth of the big cities in particular was phenomenal. By 1940 Tōkyō was rivaling London and New York with a population of 6,779,000, while Ōsaka, Kyōto, Nagoya, and the new port cities of Yokohama and Kōbe together accounted for an equal number.

Cities were from the start the center of Japan's modern cultural transformation. During the 1870's and 1880's material signs of the new times appeared, first in Tōkyō: horse-drawn streetcars, gas lamps, meatshops selling beef, Western-style buildings, barbershops offering a non-samurai cut, Western dress, and the new schools and colleges. Change was uneven. As late as 1901 an ordinance was issued in Tōkyō against going barefoot. Yet by this time primary school education was almost universal, and those moving in from the rural areas as well as those growing up in the cities were for the most part literate. When one considers that Japan's school-age population increased from 4.2 million in 1873, to 7.2 million in 1893, to 11.3 million in 1935, the magnitude of this accomplishment becomes apparent. The cities also became the centers for higher education that created and spread the new culture of modern Japan.

THE GROWTH OF HIGHER EDUCATION IN JAPAN

Year	University Students	Students in Technical Colleges	Students in Teachers Colleges
1900	3,240	19,670	16,442
1910	7,239	32,969	26,900
1920	21,915	49,007	28,610
1930	69,605	90,043	46,624
1940	81,999	141,478	44,454

By the end of World War I further changes had emerged. Standards of living had risen; workers drank beer and soft drinks; weekly magazines, movie houses, bars, restaurants, and other manifestations of popular culture had appeared. The *narikin*, the *nouveau riche* who had risen during the war, were much in evidence. This was the age of the *mobo* and *moga* (*modan boi* and *modan garu*) who strolled on the Ginza or the main thoroughfares of Ōsaka, boys who wore Harold Lloyd glasses and girls who drank, smoked, and read literature. These were the years of the permanent wave, the bathing suit, the bare-legged chorus line, the dance hall and cabaret. It was a time when students not concerned with the leftist political movement became engrossed in the "three S's" — sports, screen, and sex. During the early 1930's Japan Victor and other gramo-phone companies suddenly expanded, selling hundreds of thousands of sad songs suggesting the transiency of life, the indistinguishability of tears and *sake*, the pleasures of jazz, liquor, and dancing, the passing of time and the languid beauty of willows along the Ginza. Sales of records jumped from 10,483,000 in 1929 to 16,895,000 in 1931.

Though this efflorescence of popular culture was tame by any European standard, it seemed outrageously extreme to many in Japan. Some essay-ists called the period culminating in 1931 and 1932 the era of *"ero, guro, and nansensu"* (the erotic, the grotesque, and the nonsensical). To some the empty ostentation of city culture appeared to parallel the seeming impasse reached by Japan's contemporary writers, for whom the only moral choices remaining were suicide, Marxism, or the extreme, sensual, experimental writing of the non-left. That Japan's modern, urban culture had reached this point made the dichotomy between city and village seem almost unbridgeable. In normal times even the flamboyance and pleasure-seeking of the city might have been tolerated. But in 1931 and 1932 Japan was at the pit of its depression, and rural conditions were particularly

RCENTAGE OF SCHOOL AGE CHILDREN ATTENDING PRIMARY SCHOOLS

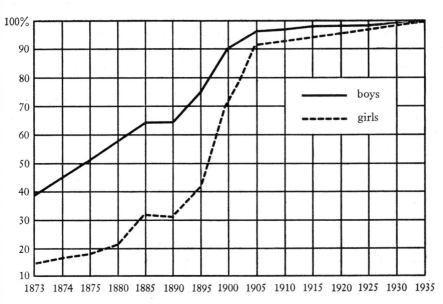

bad. As a result, the cities and their mode of life were castigated by rightist spokesmen as the antipode of what was truly Japanese.

Another effect of the changing urban scene was generational change. In the 1930's there were many families in which three generations lived together: grandparents in their eighties, parents in their fifties, and children in their twenties. The grandparents had been born in Tokugawa Japan. The second generation had come of age just after the turn of the century when Japan's modern culture was beginning to appear. Many had come to the cities from rural areas bringing with them the social reflexes of the countryside. The third generation became adults amid the democracy, jazz, depression, and crisis of the late 1920's and early 1930's. Often in such a family there existed close, warm ties between its members. We earlier suggested that the strengthening of marriage in Japan in modern times was the result of the development of women's rights and of the conjugal family. One might also suggest that the rapidity of changes in other spheres tended to create a greater dependence on the family. Yet in spite of the real sense of solidarity emerging from this, three such generations were in many ways three different kinds of people, far more so than in Europe or the United States where the tempo of change had been slower.

The two aspects of the modern Japanese city treated above, its social and cultural divergence from the countryside and the generational differences within it, were important and obvious. Equally important, though less obvious, was the variety of social patterns within the prewar Japanese city. Some were traditional, based on kinship, or on the boss-follower relationship which stressed loyalty and service in exchange for paternal care. Druggists, dyers, cloth merchants, restaurateurs, and performers of traditional arts were often organized in main and branch families. The sons of branch families, after completing their formal education, would train in the store (or workshop or school) of the main house. The main family would aid the branches in time of need. The relationships between them were mostly informal and diffuse.

A variation of this pattern was found among those employed in urban or rural small businesses, the less fortunate segment of Japan's prewar economic "double structure." The average concern consisted of a boss and a few workers. If not related to the boss, the workers were at least introduced and vouched for by persons of responsibility to whom they were related or obligated. The hours of work were long. Contact with the boss was close and informal: unmarried workers often lived in the home-office-shop of their employer. They were called on to help with work about his house. They aided the boss in time of trouble and were cared for in time of need. As skills increased, as educational standards rose, as business grew, as the new generation came along, there occurred a general shift in the direction of contractual relationships. Yet, until after World War II, the millions who worked in such businesses were in many ways closer to rural than urban Japan, even though they lived in cities.

The most difficult sector of urban society to discuss is the most modern: that of large factories, universities, government offices, banks, and political parties. People who worked in such organizations led lives similar to those of their Western counterparts — rising by the alarm clock, snatching a quick breakfast, commuting to work by bus or train, spending a workday among acquaintances doing the same type of work entirely separate from home or community, returning home in the evening, and playing with the children, if at all, on weekends. The organizations within which these people worked were also profoundly influenced by Western models, created as they were to fill the needs of a modern society. They emphasized performance. Top-level personnel were recruited from the universities; the most favorable conditions were offered to graduates of the best schools. Among those of the same age group and same educational background, ability was a primary criterion for advancement. Jobs were specific, pay schedules fixed, authority limited to the requirements of the position, and relations less personal than in the older types of businesses. And all these bureaucratic aspects were gaining ground. Yet at the same time the people who worked in such organizations were not modern enough in their training, values, and ideas for the Western structure to function without adjustment. As a consequence, there early developed in the interstices a good many particular Japanese features. Once established, these not only reflected the importance of personal ties in Japanese tradition, but also tended to preserve them.

One feature of virtually all modern organizations in Japan was an emphasis on loyalty. Another was paternalism. The employee joined a company for life. Once accepted, he had the assurance that he would be kept, even in hard times, and advanced, within the limits of his education and ability, according to seniority. A high official could graduate, as it were, from a government ministry to a company presidency or to important political posts. But lateral moves from company to company (or university to university, or ministry to ministry) were rare and disapproved. They were seen as a sign of shallow character, and they involved a loss of seniority. Even today, inter-company mobility is only beginning to appear among engineers and scientists, the technicians of industry. Executive skills, however, are not viewed as interchangeable; the feeling is strong that they can only be used effectively by one who is accepted as a member of the company "family."

Loyalty to the company was buttressed by personal loyalties within it. There are many proverbs in Japan, such as "Move into the shade of a big tree," which suggest the helplessness of the individual without a patron. In most organizations personal ties were formed between important senior men and juniors loyal to them. When a senior was moved from one post to another he might take with him members of his clique. Belonging to such a group was considered important for promotion. One reason why lateral movement between companies did not work was that a new man brought in found it difficult to enter such a group. Even men entering the bureaucracy directly from the university might feel themselves to be "outsiders" for many years if they were not graduates of, say, the Law Faculty of Tōkyō Imperial University.

The solidarity in modern bureaucratic organizations in Japan is in one sense akin to the much greater organic solidarity of the hamlet; both, at different levels, embody the same values of harmony, loyalty, and paternalism that we shall see in the orthodox family-state philosophy. Or, to put the matter negatively, they reflect the same weakness of individualism that is a part of the Japanese tradition.

Industrial Labor. In Japan the shift from an agricultural to an industrial economy, as in so many other countries, was accompanied by a number of social ills, from which urban labor suffered more than any other group except tenants. The government was dominated from the start by men who thought in terms of national strength rather than the individual well-being of the citizens. Even in the political parties the interests of property owners and the business community were much more strongly represented than those of the underprivileged. As a result, Japan was extremely slow to adopt social legislation designed to protect urban workers. There were at first no limits on the conditions or hours of factory work or the ages of workers. Children sometimes worked fourteen hours a day. And vast, noisome slums grew up in the cities, as they had in the West during the early years of industrialization.

Apart from government aims and policies, one reason why labor was so slow to share the gains from industry was that it was abundant and consequently cheap. Industrial output rose fantastically; but much of its gains reflected technological advances that reduced the need for labor per unit of production. Labor requirements therefore grew more slowly than industry. Burgeoning peasant families provided a stream of industrial recruits that easily met the increased demands, thus keeping urban wages geared to the depressed rural economy. Some gains were made; the real incomes of industrial workers increased by more than half between 1914 and 1929. But unskilled labor had very little bargaining power.

Population was not the only factor tying labor to the farm. Many went to work in industry only briefly and then returned to their rural homes. This was especially true in textiles, Japan's largest industry. Here, as in other countries, the early workers were largely girls. In cotton spinning, for example, women constituted 80 per cent of the working force at the turn of the century, and they still made up 44 per cent of all factory workers in the 1930's. Most women in the textile industries were farm girls recruited on contract, often by false representations, housed and fed in dormitories, where their lives were strictly regimented, and paid a mere pittance, which they assiduously saved toward their dowries. Ideally, the assumption of moral as well as economic responsibility, by which the company became the surrogate for the parents in the period between school-leaving and marriage, was for the welfare of the girls and was sanctioned by their families. In practice it often became a modern form of peonage. Such workers naturally intended from the start to return to the farm, and many others also melted back into the rural population, especially in time of depression. Industrial unemployment was thus largely met by an increase in the number of mouths to be fed at the farmer's dinner table. This made social legislation less pressing. But it also inhibited the modernization of labor: even in the 1930's urban labor still stood with one foot planted in the stagnant economy of the paddy fields.

Under conditions such as these the labor union movement remained fairly small. Such developments as did occur were integrally associated with the Christian social movement and socialism. The first phase came between the late 1890's and 1911. By 1897 there were 400,000 workers in factories employing more than five; and by 1907, 600,000. Among these workers a number of unions with about 10,000 members were formed before the turn of the century. The Police Regulation Law of 1900, though drafted to check the spread of socialism, sharply curtailed union activities; consequently, what began as an attempt at legal trade unionism evolved into a political movement, and ended as an anarchist plot to assassinate the emperor. After 1911 a second phase began under the extremely moderate leadership of a Christian, Suzuki Bunji. By the end of World War I there were 1,700,000 factory laborers in Japan. The industrial expansion and greater emphasis on democracy at this time combined with the moderate tactics of Suzuki to produce steady gains for the union movement.

THE RISE OF LABOR UNIONS, 1914–1920

Year	Newly Founded Unions
1914	6
1915	4
1916	13
1917	14
1918	11
1919	71
1920	86

In 1918 the spiraling price of rice led to a wave of large-scale riots which swept most of the cities and larger towns. The riots were often directed against rice merchants and landlords. Police were called out, but in some cases the violence then turned against the police, so that in 42 locales it became necessary to call in army troops to suppress the uprising. The effect on labor of the World War I boom that continued until 1920 can be seen in the accompanying table of prices and wages.

PRICES AND WAGES, 1912–1919

Year	Wage Index	Price Index
1912	100	100
1913	102	101
1914	102	99
1915	101	94
1916	104	109
1917	102	145
1918	157	200
1919	224	238

The sudden drop in real income as prices outpaced wages after 1916 led to a burst of union activity and labor unrest.

LABOR DISPUTES, 1912–1920

Year	Number of Disputes	Number of Men Involved
1912	49	6,000
1914	50	8,000
1916	108	8,000
1917	398	57,309
1918	417	66,000
1919	2,388	335,225
1920	1,069	127,000

In 1920, as the wartime boom collapsed, a third phase of unionism began. Once again the movement turned from economic to political ends, coming first under the influence of anarcho-syndicalist leaders and then after 1922 of Marxist socialists. The tendency to adopt a European rather than an American type of unionism was related to the position of labor in the economy, which more nearly resembled that of certain European countries. To combat this militant unionism the government used police pressure on the one hand, while making certain limited concessions on the other. Unions were legalized in 1923, universal manhood suffrage was established in 1925, and some trifling controls over the exploitation of labor that had gone into effect in 1916 were extended in the 1920's by a variety of laws which gave industrial workers some rudimentary protection. For example, the workday was reduced to ten hours for women and children, and children under fourteen were banned from factory work, except for twelve- and thirteen-year-olds who had completed their elementary education.

The reaction of the unions to these reforms was in a parliamentary direction. By 1925 the moderate socialists had driven the Communists and revolutionary socialists out of the *Sōdōmei*, the largest federation of unions in Japan, containing about 70 per cent of all organized labor. This federation, while subject to many changes, continued as the central force in the union movement into the 1930's, becoming one of the main supports for the parliamentary socialist movement. Other smaller union federations were formed parallel to less moderate and revolutionary socialist groups. Total union strength increased as follows:

UNION MEMBERSHIP, 1922–1942

Year	Number of Unions	Members
1922	389	137,381
1924	469	228,278
1926	488	284,739
1928	501	308,900
1930	712	354,312
1932	932	377,625
1934	965	387,964
1936	973	420,589
1938	731	375,191
1940	49	9,455
1942	3	111

Even in the peak year of 1936, however, unionized labor represented a very small percentage of Japan's total industrial labor force of 6,090,116. Moreover, the unions were generally weak. The average union had only

500 or so members and was usually confined to a single company. The rank-and-file members, caught up in the solidarity of the company, were entirely removed from the activist leaders of the central federations. These weaknesses, combining with external pressures, led to the switch from socialism to nationalist socialism that took place in the major federation in 1937. That the same change had occurred in tenant unions almost six years earlier is a measure of the gap between the city and the countryside.

CURRENTS OF THOUGHT

Intellectuals in Japan today are the heirs not of the early Meiji thinkers but of the generation that came to maturity just after the turn of the century. Where the early Meiji thinkers were morally, socially, and even politically akin to the Restoration leaders, intellectuals after the turn of the century became increasingly alienated both from society and from the late Meiji political order. It is ironic that this alienation should have appeared and spread during a period marked generally by optimism and progress.

To Western eyes, the advanced intellectuals of this era seem almost to have bridged the cultural chasm and to be contemporary with their Western peers. Romanticism gave way to realism and then to naturalism; and socialism and anarchism were issues of the day. The 1909 diary of the poet Ishikawa Takuboku reveals a life that is strikingly modern: detached introspection, reading Turgenev in bed, commuting to work on the streetcar, listening to the sounds of the Kyōto University tennis team from the room next door. Even his poetic images are drawn from the modern world: "If I could . . . throw away this garment of obligation my body would become as light as hydrogen," "Your eyes must have the mechanism of a fountain pen — you are always shedding tears." Partly because he was so modern, his feeling of isolation and estrangement in the Japan of his day was profound:

> Do not be loved by others, do not accept their charity, do not promise anything. Do nothing which entails asking forgiveness. Never talk to anyone about yourself. Always wear a mask. Always be ready for a fight — be able to hit the next man on the head at any time. Don't forget that when you make friends with someone you are sooner or later certain to break with him.[1]

The social and cultural reasons for the appearance of this sense of alienation are several. During the early and middle years of the Meiji era,

---

[1] Translated by Donald Keene. From *Modern Japanese Literature:* An Anthology Compiled and Edited by Donald Keene; copyright © 1956 by Grove Press, published by Grove Press, Inc. (British publisher, Thames & Hudson).

Western-educated intellectuals were few and government positions relatively easy to obtain. But by the turn of the century there were more university graduates than jobs. Government jobs were almost wholly monopolized by the graduates of the national universities, especially of Tōkyō Imperial University. Then, too, the Western-oriented generation appeared just as the government was more and more assuming a neo-traditionalist position, and this heightened its sense of not belonging. But even more basic was a growing concern over the problem of cultural identity, an increasing awareness of the problems posed by modern Western culture in Japan. In the West the transition from the premodern to the modern world was difficult in that the modern had to be created, it could not be borrowed. Yet the transition was made easier by occurring within a single continuous cultural tradition over a long period of time. Tremendous changes were involved, but each step was organically linked to previous developments. In Japan, however, the modern was abruptly borrowed. It was culturally discontinuous. And when it was assimilated to a degree, it led to deep intellectual and moral dislocations.

During the early Meiji period few realized how difficult a lasting solution to this problem would be. The early Meiji intellectuals, whatever their Western training, had in common a Confucian education. Most of them rejected Confucianism as an explicit philosophy, yet they retained a body of assumptions that are recognizably Confucian. Considering the period in which they wrote, and their relatively short contact with the West, it was perhaps inevitable that Western ideas would be grafted onto branches of Japanese thought without too nice a concern for the assumptions underlying them in the West. Perhaps only a few Japanese Christians attempted to grapple with this problem at a fundamental level.

By 1900 there appeared the first generation educated within the new school system. It was a generation still profoundly influenced by Japanese tradition, although it no longer possessed a common background of Confucian learning. Yet at the same time this generation's understanding of the West went far deeper than that of the early Meiji intellectuals. It therefore felt dissatisfied with the synthesis of Japanese and Western thought effected by earlier thinkers; it was dissatisfied with the official philosophy that continued to emphasize the instrumental use of Western ideas in order to build a strong state. It was aware that the acceptance, for example, of Western individualism implied the rejection of much of Japanese tradition, and that the rapid rejection of the latter would create tremendous tensions. Natsume Sōseki, Japan's greatest modern novelist, wrote that Japan had only superficially mastered the teachings of the West; he asked what would be the consequences if Japan could advance and achieve a modern enlightenment within fifty years:

If, then, by our physical and mental exertions, and by ignoring the difficulties and suffering involved in our precipitous advance, we end by passing through, in merely one-half the time it took the more prosperous
Westerners to reach their stage of specialization, to our stage of internally
developed enlightenment, the consequences will be serious indeed. We will
be able to boast of a fantastic acquisition of knowledge, but at the same
time, the inevitable result will be a nervous collapse from which we will
not be able to recover.

Before examining some of the positions taken by major Japanese
thinkers during the early twentieth century, we must first ask what was
the Japanese tradition at this time. What were the ideas with which, in
one way or another, modern thinkers took issue? At the turn of the
century the old ideas appeared in many guises: in hereditary schools of
painting, tea ceremony, drama, and flower arrangement; in traditional
forms of literature; and in the multiple permutations of Japan's historical
religions. Yet, for an understanding of Japan's modern history, the most
important locus of tradition was the several interpretations of state
philosophy that together constituted orthodoxy in Japan between 1890
and 1945.

The Orthodox Philosophies of the Japanese State. It would be wrong
to say that Japan's leaders consciously set to work after 1890 to create
an orthodox philosophy. On the contrary, the aim from the time of the
Meiji Restoration had been to create a strong state structure. Other
world powers had constitutions; those out of power in Japan demanded
a constitution; this confluence of forces led to the establishment of the
Meiji constitutional order. But, having written a constitution, Japanese
leaders and thinkers had to say what it meant in relation to Japanese tradition and to define how it would function legally. The results of their
efforts produced a number of interrelated philosophies of state. These
marked the limits of orthodox, officially sanctioned political thought until
the end of World War II.

One feature common to all these philosophies was the affirmation of a
unique Japanese "national polity" (*kokutai*). This made Japan different
from, and in some ways superior to, all other nations. One of the unique
characteristics of this polity was the Imperial House, portrayed in the
Meiji constitution as "a single lineage for 10,000 generations." The end-
product of this lineage, the emperor, was described as "sacred and inviolable." The meaning of these terms varied, but in every case the emperor
was seen as the ultimate power in the state. As such, the emperor and the
various dimensions of traditional significance with which he was invested
were used as a bulwark for the Meiji constitutional order. The rights
granted by the constitution were new, real, and a part of the modern

world. Yet they were proclaimed in the constitution as "the immutable law of the land," they were seen as grounded in Japanese tradition.

A second characteristic of the Japanese "national polity" was that it was moral. Japan had certain virtues that other nations lacked: loyalty that bound the people to the emperor; filial piety that undergirded the family units of which the nation was composed. Integrated by such moral principles, Japanese society was viewed as a harmonious whole. (During World War II a Tōkyō University economist lecturing on "Japanese capitalism" was reproved by a member of his audience who said that Japan could not be called capitalist since, harmonious and tranquil, it had never experienced the class conflict present in other industrial societies.) Values such as these were still quite vigorous in Japan at the turn of the century; it is only natural that they should have been used in combination with newer Western principles. Yet the way they were joined to the philosophy of the imperial state fixed them in modern Japanese thought at a time when Japanese society was changing rapidly. Because of the philosophical significance of the emperor, these traditional values were given a religious dimension that made them difficult to attack.

The way in which "national polity" thought furnished the guidelines for political action between 1900 and 1945 can be understood only by grasping separately some of the different strands of interpretation which it contained.

One of the earliest and most important interpretations of the character of the Japanese state was, even if conservative, still rational. Itō Hirobumi saw the Japanese polity in terms of the German organic view of the state. Itō compared the emperor, as "the head of state" in the constitution, to the brain which "in the human body is the source of all mental activity manifested through the four limbs and the different parts of the body." He did not see the Japanese state as a mystical entity. Rather it was the product of a long historical development which, while moral in content, was naturalistic in process. Loyalty, filial piety, social harmony, and the imperial lineage were the unique heritage of the Japanese *volk;* yet they were nonetheless the products of an evolutionary process.

Moreover, though Itō undoubtedly revered the imperial institution, his affirmation of these elements from the Japanese tradition was not simply a token of his own belief. He was well aware of his own creative role as an innovator. His attribution of absolute authority to the emperor was in part the conscious act of a social engineer. Reporting to the Privy Council on the constitution, he wrote in 1888: "In Europe the beginnings of constitutional rule go back for over 1000 years; and not only are the people well versed in this system, but there is religion as a common principle. It penetrates deeply into the hearts of the people and unites them." Itō then pointed out that constitutional government is "entirely new" in

Japan and that a basis must be found on which it can be built. But did such a basis exist?

> In our country religion is weak. There is not one that could serve as a principle of state. Buddhism today has fallen into decline. Shintō is based on the precepts of our forefathers and transmits them, yet as a religion it has little power to move men's hearts. In our country, as a common principle [literally, "the rotor of an engine"], there is only the Imperial House.

Itō was always willing to use fragments of the Confucian cosmology or bits of Shintō myths when he felt that they would serve his ends. It is unlikely that he believed in them in any literal or religious sense.

The most rational elements in Itō's view of the state were further developed by Minobe Tatsukichi, a professor of administrative law at Tōkyō University between 1900 and 1932. Minobe accepted the core elements of *kokutai* theory. He wrote, "I am second to none in my deeply rooted conviction that our unique national polity is our people's greatest glory and that therein partly lies the strength of the nation." But Minobe superimposed upon this a newer German theory that described the state as a legal person possessing both sovereignty and the authority to rule. The emperor was merely the highest organ of the state with the ultimate right to carry out the executive functions of the state.

The differences beween this view and Itō's may appear subtle, and are indeed slight. Yet the consequences were important. In Minobe's eyes the emperor is clearly less than the state and subordinate to the law of the state. The effect was to reduce in theory the absolute character of the emperor's authority, and to balance against it the authority of other legally constituted organs of the state. This interpretation weakened the sanction for autocratic rule by the bureaucracy (in the name of the emperor), it attacked the role of nonconstitutional bodies around the emperor, and it opened the way for increased Diet power. It would be no exaggeration to say that Minobe's theory furnished the theoretical scaffolding for the movement to establish party cabinets during the 1910's and 1920's. Minobe himself frequently wrote that only government by a Diet embodying the will of the people can be called constitutional.

Minobe's interpretation never obtained a monopoly even in academic circles. It was, however, the dominant legal interpretation of the constitution from World War I until 1935 when Minobe was attacked in the Diet and his works proscribed. It not only influenced scholars and intellectuals, but also became the prescribed subject matter in constitutional law for the higher civil service examinations, the door to the Japanese bureaucracy. The considerable measure of rationality that can be found in the functioning of the government during those two decades was not unrelated to the rationality of this theory. In particular, one should note that the narrow political definition of the emperor's position created an almost secular view of the state. Unfortunately for Japan, the conservatism of the bureaucrats was such that they were unwilling to have taught to others what they believed themselves. Within the state system of education other less rational views predominated.

These views were more deeply rooted in Japan's cultural tradition, and have overtones that are clearly religious. The earliest form was recognizably Tokugawa Confucian in inspiration. Confucianism as a coherent system of ideas was already fast fading away during the early and middle Meiji period. By the last decade of the century it was clearly out of step with the times. Yet men such as Motoda Eifu, the emperor's Confucian tutor, could still be found, and "Confucian" assumptions were still widely held. In this view Japan's national polity was seen as an eternal, immanent, moral order. The unique Imperial House, as described in the Imperial Rescript on Education, was seen as "coeval with Heaven and Earth." That is to say, the emperor was viewed as the personification of the Confucian cosmological order. He was not an absolute monarch in the Hobbesian sense: he was unfree, bound by the moral order and by the tradition that surrounds it. Yet he was greater than the absolute monarch of Hobbes in that he embodied this order and as such was often seen as the ultimate source of value. On this point General Araki Sadao, for example, wrote of the emperor as "the eternal culmination of the True, the Good, and the Beautiful throughout all ages and in all places." This type of logic permeated the thought of those who argued during the 1930's that action by the government and army was taken under the direction of the emperor and was therefore moral in character.

A second development in the religious view of the national polity was the conceptualization of Japan as a "family-state." The elements from which this concept was formed had existed in Japan for centuries. They were first joined in the course of the 1892–98 debate over a proposed Civil Code strongly influenced by the individualistic Napoleonic Code. The proponents of the code, such as Ume Kenjirō, a Tōkyō University professor, argued that "the power of the family head is a survival of feudalism" and must be abolished. Implicit in this view was the acceptance of a considerable amount of eighteenth-century European thought about natural rights.

Chief among the opponents of the code was Hozumi Yatsuka, another Tōkyō professor. His argument in brief was that the family joined the past with the present. The past of a particular family in the form of its ancestors constitutes a spiritual conglomerate that is united with the presently existing generations through ancestor worship. "The family is a continual religious service for the ancestors. The family head . . . represents them in this world." Japan, however, is not simply a congeries of separate families. On the contrary, all Japanese are ultimately descended from a "common folk ancestor" identified with the imperial ancestor. All Japan is thus a single racial and spiritual family. The authority of the family head and that of the emperor are identical in character. Loyalty to the state and filial piety are but a single virtue.

These arguments by Hozumi carried the day. Property law in the revised Civil Code remained individualistic, but family law was revised to strengthen the powers of the family head. Just as important as this legal enactment was the adoption of many of Hozumi's regressive ideas by certain segments of Japanese officialdom. Particularly, the concept of the family-state was incorporated into the school texts on moral education during a period of revision between 1908 and 1911. These were texts used in all primary schools in Japan. It is ironic that such views began to infect the content of mass education just as Minobe's more enlightened views were spreading in the universities.

It is worth comparing texts in order to grasp the qualitative change from the straightforward nationalism of the Meiji period to the family-statism that appeared in the early Taishō era. In a 1904 text under the title "Be loyal to the emperor and love the country" was the following:

> Those who are peasants, merchants, and artisans increase the wealth of the nation by diligently performing their jobs; those who are concerned with scholarship and the arts strive to advance the nation's civilization by perfecting their work. In comparing the conditions of our country with America and other powers, there are still many areas in which we do not measure up. Keeping this in mind, we must plan to fulfill the nation's strength.

Representative of the revised texts is the following excerpt from a 1911 article on "Loyalty and filial piety":

> The feeling of respect and love of the child for his parents comes from nature. The great virtue of loyalty-filial piety emerges from the highest form of such feelings. . . . Our country takes as its base the family system: the nation is but a single great family, the Imperial family is our main-house. We the people worship the unbroken Imperial line with the same feeling of respect and love that a child feels towards his parents. Thus loyalty and filial piety are one and indivisible. . . . The union of loyalty and filial piety is truly the special character of our national polity.[1]

One is struck by the increase in official self-satisfaction in the second quotation. This was not unrelated to Japan's victory in the Russo-Japanese War, and was a characteristic that continued to develop through the 1920's. But more important was the accompanying vision of a conservative society, a vision that did not change basically thereafter, even

[1] Ishida Takeshi, *Meiji seiji shisōshi kenkyū*, pp. 7–8.

though subsequent revisions of the texts during World War I introduced complementary material that was more liberal and more international in character.

A third development in the religious view of the *kokutai* was the union of history and Shintō myth. This amalgam entered the school texts toward the end of the first decade of this century; one Japanese historian has called it "Japan's myth of the twentieth century." This can be viewed as the second phase of a revival of Shintō legend that had begun during the Tokugawa period, declined after the earliest years of the Meiji period, but was still ardently supported by some conservative thinkers. Even in the progressive, enlightened middle years of the Meiji period a number of strands prefigured this development. Hozumi's explanation of the family-state suggests a living Shintō past. The extension into the past of Itō's historical view brings Japanese history ultimately to either myth or archaeology; and, by defining, in his *Commentaries on the Constitution*, the sacredness of the emperor with a quotation from Shintō legend, even Itō's writings lean at times to the conservative safety of myth.

Once history is linked to myth, a quite different interpretation of the "national polity" emerges. The emperor is sacred not simply as the embodiment of a moral order, but also as a lineal descendent of the Shintō gods. And, in legend, Japan itself is also divine in origin. To this theory Uesugi Shinkichi, another Tōkyō University professor, appended a revised form of the theory of absolute monarchy in which the emperor was mystically identified with the body of the state. This was the theory that opposed Minobe's during the second, third, and fourth decades of the twentieth century. Its adherents in academic circles and at the higher levels of the bureaucracy were generally less successful than their opponents. Yet they came into their own during the late 1930's as the ideologists of a military Japan.

We may generalize to say that the range of orthodox belief before the turn of the century was narrow: in both the Meiji constitution and the Imperial Rescript on Education the rational, conservative historicism of Itō was blended with more conservative, Confucian ideas, such as those of Motoda Eifu. This mixture contained contradictions, but it was workable. The more extreme, Shintōistic views of Hozumi were not representative at this time. But by about 1914 there had developed within the "state orthodoxy" bitterly antagonistic theoretical positions — the liberal, constitutional monarchism of Minobe and the absolute monarchical, "Shintō" statism of Uesugi. It would be wrong to see the latter trend as a ground swell that gathered force in the 1920's and came to a crest during the 1930's. On the contrary, in spite of the support it received from patriotic societies, military groups, rural groups, and others, it was losing ground during the early 1920's to more liberal, international opinion. Yet two points may be validly made. First, the generation that came to maturity in the 1930's had begun its education in the very years when this "Shintō" view of Japanese tradition began to enter the school texts. Second, in the conservative nationalism of the 1930's and 1940's there can be found little (except a critique of liberalism borrowed from European fascist thought) that had not already been fully developed thirty years earlier.

If the distribution and influence of ideas could be reduced to statistics, we might estimate that well over 90 per cent of political action in Japan between 1900 and 1945 was rationalized in terms of one or another of the above-described strains of orthodox thought. Unless one sees the important differences between these diverse strains of emperor-thought, the meaning of the struggles within modern Japanese politics cannot be comprehended. At the same time, however, it is also important to stress what all these positions had in common. It has been suggested that in the traditional religious symbolizations of East Asia (including Tokugawa Japan) man, society, and nature tend to fuse: society is seen as a part of eternal being, and the individual is subordinated to society by a number of particular values which constitute obligations rather than rights.[1] In this symbolization there is no transcendent moral position from which society can be judged, nor cultural support for the individualism characteristic of the modern West.

It is clear that the Meiji and late Meiji versions of the earlier symbolization did not imply a vision of a changeless society. The class theory, the economic ideas, and the political hierarchy that had provided the Tokugawa image of the "natural society" had all been dropped. By the turn of the century only a few points remained fixed — loyalty, filial piety, harmony, and the emperor — in the moral order of the *kokutai*. This "stripped down" *kokutai* was a necessary precondition for the revolution of the early years of the Meiji era, and the successive changes that followed. Yet, although the content of the Tokugawa symbolization had been discarded, many of the underlying assumptions persisted. In many ways nature, society, and self continued as symbolically undifferentiated areas.

We have seen this, first, in the Confucian strain of interpretation where the moral *kokutai*, which informs Japanese society, is coeval with Heaven and Earth, the Confucian cosmological order. Society and the natural order are not distinct. Secondly, in the Shintō interpretation, Heaven and Earth are replaced by (or merged with) an irrational god-world in which myth is history, and history the more recent portion of a spiritual continuum. The transition from deities that are half human to humans that partake of divinity is imperceptible. Hozumi wrote of filial piety: "Even when

[1] Robert Bellah, "The Religious Situation in the Far East," *Harvard Divinity Bulletin*, Vol. 26, No. 4 (July 1962).

parents lose their bodily forms, their spirits still live to protect their off-spring." Also, it was this sense of a spiritual continuum between the human and the divine that permitted the attribution of divinity to the emperor before 1945. He was never seen as a transcendental deity; such a notion would have been ridiculous. He was merely the highest figure in a world-view in which the political, social, and religious spheres were not clearly distinguished. He possessed the same sort of "sacred authority" as a parent, although in greater degree. Thirdly, even in the most secular view of the "national polity" — the historical and organic view that prevailed among the more highly educated — there was still some ambiguity regarding the relation between nature and society. History is natural. It was a short step from the affirmation of the moral content of Japan's historical development to a view of the development itself as moral.

Moreover, just as society and nature were not clearly separate, so the distinction between the individual and society was also weak. Whether the group was the family, the work-group, or the nation, its claims virtually always had priority over those of the component member as an individual. In orthodox thought there were no grounds upon which the individual could withhold loyalty to the social order. On the contrary, the realization of self came through fulfilling one's duties to society. Apart from society, the only other channels for self-fulfillment were an asocial absorption in nature or a personal expressiveness of a sort that did not conflict with one's obligations to society.

Modern Japanese intellectuals have shown deep concern with the problem of self. This has at times taken the form of a search for philosophic principles that will enable the individual to stand up against society. What this search has meant can be understood only by measuring it against the lack of individualism in traditional thought. Some answers have been found in Western culture, others by transforming elements of Japanese tradition to this end. Yet, at a time when the ultimate value of the individual was being increasingly questioned in the West itself, the search was difficult. Against the background of Japanese orthodox thought it was far easier to stress equality within the social group than independence from it.

Modern Japanese Literature. One of the least used but most interesting perspectives on modern Japanese intellectual history is afforded by literature. During the last decades of the nineteenth century the development of the novel in Japan was, with a few notable exceptions, political — giving a romantic expression of the envisioned heroic destiny of Japan. It was in step with the times. But with the emergence of the illiberal, unheroic reality of the Japanese state after 1890, with new currents of literary thought, and with the sense of alienation mentioned earlier, the Japanese novel turned away from public concerns (just a decade or so before the modern political novel appeared in China). Instead, it became intensely concerned with the private lives of individuals, with personal relations in and out of the family. Since the emperor, the army, politics, the financial world, and the like were ignored, this literature would seem to have little to do with "orthodox" thought. However, the orthodoxy was social as well as political. Most of modern Japanese literature has been consciously antitraditional: it has attacked the old family system and has been preoccupied with the problem of the individual. That the dominant form of the novel has been autobiographical reflects this focus on the individual. Yet in spite of this focus it is doubtful if a satisfactory individualism, or any satisfactory alternative to the old society under attack, was ever successfully portrayed. That it could not be is important, for what an author can express in literature represents the limits to which an idea is meaningful. The result was, by and large, a literature of despair and melancholy in which the lonely mood of the author is softened only by a refined identification with nature — a traditional avenue of escape from the demands of society. In this sense, what began as a conscious attack on orthodox society often ended in a new statement of a traditional, episodic lyricism.

The school of naturalism which began after the turn of the century exemplifies certain aspects of this trend. Naturalist writers in Japan identified the true self with the forces of nature. Self-realization involved not the control but the release of these forces; man learns what he is by liberating his natural desires, especially sex, from the constraints of an artificial society. The naturalist writers were critical of the suffering caused by Japan's traditional society, so iconoclastically critical that fear of their influence may have been a factor leading the government to begin ethical education in the public schools. But their dissatisfaction with tradition did not lead them to a dynamic view of men working to change society — such as was implied in Western naturalism, which stressed scientific control of nature. Instead, both man and society were submissive to the internal and external demands of time, age, death, sickness, hunger, and sex.

In *Life*, a novel by the naturalist writer Tayama Katai, a younger generation of sons and their wives endures the tyranny of a mother. Eventually the mother dies and a quieter, more tranquil, more humane time arrives. The change from the old to a newer, more bearable society is the work of nature; while the mother is there she is accepted, almost as nature's will. In another novel by the same author the forces of nature impelling the hero are sexual; their release leads to his destruction when he disregards the conventions of the existing society. In these novels a sort of self-awareness was at times achieved. But since purposive action was largely precluded, great stress was put on the moods evoked by changing circumstance and on a sensitive description of the feelings of those caught up by these natural forces. The delicate, introspective, moody character of the works of the naturalists is reflected even in their titles: *Mediocrity, Dust, Mildew, Life, Loneliness, Indulgence.*[1]

The greatest novelist of this period, and of modern Japan, was Natsume Sōseki. A professor of English literature at Tōkyō Imperial University, Sōseki held that the tremendous progress of modern Japan was the result of an "external enlightenment" the achievement of which had led Japan to sever its ties with tradition, to lose its "ancestral energies," and to become engrossed in "mere appearances." Sōseki criticized those who continually took their cues from abroad and based their opinions on Western writers. He stressed in his essays that a true understanding of Western culture would lead, instead, to an independent spirit based on individually-held internal values. As an example he praised the "egalitarian" poetry of Whitman as revealing a truly free man who, "bound only by his own conscience, could calmly live and act amidst the evil of the world." This, contended Sōseki, "is the spirit of a republican people." From this standpoint Sōseki was not unwilling to touch on politics, and was one of the few writers to do so. He held that individual morality was higher than state morality and ridiculed those who justified their every action in terms of patriotism:

> When the bean curd man peddles his wares he is not doing it for the state. His basic purpose is to gain the means by which to live . . . though indirectly this may benefit the state. . . . But, wouldn't it be awful if he always had to keep that in mind and eat his meals for the state, wash his face for the state, and go to the toilet for the state.

This positive individualistic side of Sōseki's thought was further developed by certain of his disciples to become one of the few philosophies contributing a measure of liberalism to modern Japanese thought. One strain was the "ethical individualism" of the thinker Abe Jirō. Abe's basic position was a neo-Kantian philosophy of culture which furnished universal principles of conscience and universal standards for action. In Abe's writings the sense of inner self deriving from these principles was combined with Sōseki's individualism in an ethical position that was popular among students and, in the Japan of his day, modern. From this position, Abe criticized the sensual individualism of the naturalists, he attacked the family-state ideal of the government, and he supported the movement for women's rights.

A second group, also influenced by Sōseki, that contributed to the intellectual ferment of the second and third decades was the White Birch school of novelists. Well born, educated at the aristocratic Gakushūin University, the writers of this group were romantically individualistic. They held that mankind best advanced by developing the abilities

[1] Howard Hibbett, "The Portrait of the Artist in Japanese Fiction," *Far Eastern Quarterly,* Vol. 14 (1955), p. 350.

of each person to the fullest, and they extolled genius. Mushakōji Saneatsu, for example, born of the Kyōto nobility, held that nature was kind, its bounty unlimited, and that love was natural. He was deeply influenced by the religious humanism of Tolstoi's later years; he wrote, "Had I not known Tolstoi I might have become a politician, living from day to day without faith or a reason for existence." In his novels he contrasted an altruistic humanism based on the genuine feelings of man with the artificial morality of the old society. Some critics derided the optimism of Mushakōji as "silly," and others argued that writers who had never known hardship could not escape superficiality. Certainly the Tolstoian emphasis on love that was meaningful in a deeper sense in Western tradition was only shallowly rooted in Japan. Yet this was the only literary school in prewar Japan that went a step beyond a criticism of the old and attempted to define a new morality on which human and family relations could be based.[1]

However, both in Sōseki and in modern Japanese literature generally, liberal and positive strains were scarce. Predominant was a darker, pessimistic, even fatalistic note, as in the naturalists. In the novels of the mature Sōseki, the complete development of the individual led, not to freedom, but to a bleak world of fear, despair, and absolute loneliness. In *The Gate* the hero, having stolen the wife of a friend, spends the rest of his life in secluded misery with her, each sharing the loneliness and pain of the other. At the end he attempts to find an answer in Zen Buddhism, but without success. The "gate" does not open. In *Passers-by* the protagonist is beset with even greater fears and anxieties until at the end only religion, madness, or death remains. But for Sōseki, neither religion nor madness was a live option. In *Kokoro* (Mind) the end is suicide, in *Grass by the Road* it is resignation to an answerless fate. Sōseki differs from the naturalists primarily in that suffering, in his view of life, affirms the ethical character of man — even though man's lot is hopeless.

Even among the optimistic White Birch writers the same vein of despair occasionally comes to the surface. Shiga Naoya describes the state of mind of a man convalescing at a hot spring resort after having narrowly escaped death in a train accident:

> I had been saved this time, something had failed to kill me, there were things I must do. — I remembered reading in middle school how Lord Clive was stirred to new efforts by thoughts like these. I wanted to react so to the crisis I had been through. I even did. But my heart was strangely quiet. Something had made it friendly to death.

While at the resort he sees a dead bee and the death of a rat; and he himself, by accident, kills a lizard.

[1] Tatsuo Arima, "The Failure of Freedom," Harvard University Ph.D. thesis, 1962.

Quite by accident I had lived. Quite by accident the lizard had died. . . .
I knew I should be grateful. But the proper feeling of happiness refused
to come. To be alive and to be dead were not two opposite extremes.
There did not seem to be much difference between them. It was now fairly
dark. My sense of sight took in only the distant lights, and the feel of
my feet against the ground, cut off from my sight, seemed uncertain in the
extreme. Only my head worked on as it would. It led me deeper and
deeper into these fancies.[1]

The despair here is not complete. Rather than cruel, nature is amorphous
and union with it has a positive side. One Japanese critic finds in the
passages cited above a traditional sense of "the sublime tranquillity of a
man who lives in a world apart, beyond life and death." Yet even this
appreciation can be questioned. When Buddhism was a live, intellectual
force, the sense of a self merging into oneness with all other being was
meaningful. But in modern Japan few found more than a gloomy
aesthetic satisfaction in the vague impalpability of such a state. A more
modern reaction to the same lack of clear-cut values was that of Sōseki's
character Ichirō in the novel *Passers-by* (*Kōjin*):

He suffers because nothing he does appears to him as either an end or a
means. He is perpetually uneasy and cannot relax. He cannot sleep so he
gets out of bed. But when he is awake, he cannot stay still, so he begins to
walk. As he walks, he finds that he has to begin running. Once he has
begun running he cannot stop. To have to keep on running is bad enough,
but he feels compelled to increase his speed with every step he takes.
When he imagines what the end of all this will be, he is so frightened that
he breaks out in a cold sweat. And the fear becomes unbearable.

Ichirō's friend, relating the rest of the conversation, replied to the above:

"This uneasiness of yours is no more than the uneasiness that all men
experience. All you have to do is to realize that there is no need for you
alone to worry so much about it. What I mean to say is that it is our fate
to wander blindly through life."
Not only were my words vague in meaning but they lacked sincerity.
Your brother [Ichirō] gave me one shrewd, contemptuous glance; that
was all my remarks deserved. He then said:
"You know, our uneasiness comes from this thing called scientific
progress. Science does not know where to stop and does not permit us
to stop either. From walking to rickshaws, from rickshaws to horsedrawn
cabs, from cabs to trains, from trains to automobiles, from automobiles . . .
to airplanes — when will we ever be allowed to stop and rest? Where
will it finally take us? It is really frightening."
"Yes, it is frightening," I said.
Your brother smiled.

[1] From "At Kinosaki," translated by Edward Seidensticker, in *Modern Japanese
Literature*: An Anthology Compiled and Edited by Donald Keene; copyright © 1956
by Grove Press, published by Grove Press, Inc. (British publisher, Thames & Hudson).

"You say so, but you don't really mean it. You aren't really frightened. This fear that you say you feel, it is only of the theoretical kind. My fear is different from yours. I feel it in my heart. It is an alive, pulsating kind of fear."[1]

Ichirō's friend typifies the less self-conscious Japanese majority, who were pleased with trains, airplanes, science, their rising standard of living, and the rest of their modern plight. He is representative of the student who proceeds successfully and happily from higher school to university law school to a job in government or industry. Ichirō, however, speaks for the alienated intellectual, unable to integrate, or find meaning in, the elements of his life.

Another great writer of modern Japan, hailed as the genius of his age during the 1920's, was Akutagawa Ryūnosuke (the author of *Rashōmon*). Also a disciple of Sōseki, Akutagawa continued his concern with the problem of the meaning of Western culture in Japan. Yet where Sōseki felt that "internal modernization" would come in time, Akutagawa was doubtful. In *The Faint Smiles of the Gods* Akutagawa writes from the point of view of a Portuguese priest in Japan during the last half of the sixteenth century, struggling to sustain his faith in the power of an absolute God while on every side he feels beset by strange animistic forces that hinder his mission. At one time the priest is spoken to by an old man, a god of Japan in human form:

> Perhaps even God will become a native of this country. China and India changed. The West must also change. We exist in the midst of trees, in the flow of shallow water, in the wind that passes through the roses, in the evening light lingering on the wall of a temple. Everywhere and at all times. Watch out for us!

Obviously Japan as a part of East Asian culture had far more to its tradition than animism. Yet after the explicit rejection of Buddhism and Confucianism during the early Meiji period, it is not strange that Akutagawa should use this as a symbol of the particularity of Japanese culture in contrast with the universal values of the West. Elsewhere Akutagawa likened Japan to an Olympics run by the insane. Projecting his own uncertainties onto Japan, he suggested that even Dante's hell would be better: at least it had law, fixed rules. Akutagawa's suicide in 1927 was hailed by Japanese leftists as the end of bourgeois literature, symbolic of the impasse reached by "middle-class culture."

It would be exaggerating to say that religion, or its lack, was central as a literary concern in twentieth-century Japan. The dominant genre was the autobiographical novel — confessional or contemplative — in which the author appears as his own, often dissolute, hero. (The literary history

[1] From Edwin McClellan, "An Introduction to Sōseki," *Harvard Journal of Asiatic Studies*, Vol. 22 (December 1959).

of this period yields at least one comic incident, in which the wife of an author obtained a divorce after discovering her spouse's infidelity in his writings.) With this self-focus was combined a *haiku*-like description of the texture of sensual experience, often of great beauty. Yet, though religion was not a central concern of literature, one can say that literature reflected certain cultural anxieties that were widespread among intellectuals in Japan. These were not unrelated to the fact that Japan had jettisoned most of its own philosophic tradition without finding anything more substantial to replace it than emperor-centered nationalism.

Philosophy. In a newspaper opinion poll taken after World War II, readers were asked which books they would like to see republished. The three writers whose works drew the greatest response were prewar philosophers, the first two were Nishida Kitarō and Abe Jirō. The "boom" which this poll reflected was of short duration; but there has been in postwar Japan a continuing interest in the writings of those who attempted to reconcile philosophically the traditions of Japan and the West.

The philosophical history of Japan in modern times is incredibly complex. Virtually every school of thought in Europe or America, not to mention schools of Buddhist philosophy and the like, has been represented in one form or another. Yet in general, the strongest current of Western philosophical thought in Japan, beginning in the late nineteenth century and gaining ground in the twentieth, was German. A song sung by higher school students in the late Meiji period began

> Dekanshō [Descartes, Kant, and Schopenhauer]
> Dekanshō
> Half the year we live with them,
> The other half we sleep.

By the 1920's the most popular Western philosophy was German idealism; the most popular philosopher, perhaps, Hegel. That this type of thought should have found acceptance in Japan is in part related to the earlier Japanese interest in German state philosophy. In part, too, there was an affinity between intellectual life in twentieth-century Japan and the anguish of German metaphysics. As student types in Japan, the "literary youth" and the Werther-like "philosophic youth" replaced the "political youth" of the late nineteenth century. Within this broad current of thought, the most original and most influential synthesis with Japanese tradition was undoubtedly that of Nishida Kitarō.

Nishida was born in 1870, only three years after Natsume Sōseki. His graduation from the philosophy department of Tōkyō Imperial University in 1894 was followed by a period of hardship. He taught in high schools and junior colleges, receiving little recognition. During these years he began the practice of Zen Buddhism. But as late as 1901 he could write in his diary: "Several years have passed since I began Zen; I have not advanced, but have gone back a step and gained nothing." Two years later he still wrote: "Though I meditate I find it difficult to concentrate. I think of this or that, of how nice it would be to travel abroad or to become a university professor, or my body aches and my mind remains clouded." Not until 1905 does the entry appear: "Zen is music, Zen is art, Zen is action; beyond this there is nothing that need be sought to give peace of mind." From this time Nishida's philosophic task was "to provide a philosophic foundation" for "the vision of the shapeless shape, the voice of the voiceless reality" which he felt was the "basis of oriental culture."[1]

To accomplish this task Nishida drew on a wide range of Western philosophers — whose writings had constituted the core of his university education. Particularly important were Hegel, James, and Bergson, all of whom were concerned with the philosophic expression of religious experience. Nishida's first concern was to find universal categories for the "moment of true existence" he had found in Zen. In his first work, *A Study of the Good*, published in 1911 after he had become an assistant professor at Kyōto Imperial University, he termed this "pure experience," experience before the differentiation of knower and known. In his later works he called it "active intuition." Nishida's second concern was to relate this insight to the universe of existence. Here his arguments, while too complex to reproduce, were Hegelian (for example, a typical sentence reads: "All that exists has the character of the absolutely contradictory self-identity of this manyness and oneness."[2]). Nishida's third concern was to apply the "logic of nothingness (*mu*)" to define the position of Japan and Japanese culture in relation to the world and world culture. Not surprisingly, the essence of Japanese culture he found in Zen and Pure Land Buddhism rather than in Confucianism.

The meaning of Nishida's philosophy for prewar Japan was ambiguous. Like the constitutional thought of Itō or Minobe it was a mixture of Japanese and Western strains; it attempted to enclose elements of Japanese experience in Western conceptual forms without affecting their essence. On the one hand, this appears to be a philosophy with no social implications, since once the self is unified in "pure experience," all conflicts are resolved and further action is unnecessary. Some Japanese critics have even labeled this and other "idealistic" philosophies as "bureaucratic" because of their asocial character and because of their popularity in academic and government circles during the 1920's and 1930's. It is certainly true that Nishida stressed the importance of harmony, community, and other values found in orthodox thought, and that some of

[1] Ueyama Shumpei, "Nishida Kitarō," in *Nihon no shisōka II*.
[2] For the context from which this was taken, see p. 866 of Tsunoda, deBary, and Keene (ed.), *Sources of the Japanese Tradition*.

his followers, emphasizing these, became scholarly propagandists for the Greater East Asia Co-Prosperity Sphere during World War II. They argued that the contradictions inherent in modern culture could be transcended only by a return to the unique spirituality of Japan. On the other hand, the social implications of Nishida's philosophy were not wholly negative. Nishida himself spoke up in 1938 and 1939 to criticize those who attacked science and free inquiry in the name of patriotism. He continually stressed in his philosophy of culture that Japanese culture, though unique, was meaningful only as a part of a universal, world culture composed of unique particulars. Likewise, his emphasis on the Japanese state was in a similar context of a world society of nations. Cast in the concepts of Western philosophy, his experience of religious individuality took on implications that were lacking in Japanese Zen.

Christianity in Modern Japan. Christianity entered Japan in the Meiji period as a part of Western culture. Many of those who accepted it were concerned with the Meiji task of strengthening Japan and gaining equality with the West. Many who were converted to Christianity in the early years were former samurai, the intellectual class of feudal Japan. Partly because of this social base and partly because it could participate in the general vogue of Westernization, Christianity became widely distributed in both urban and rural areas. During the 1890's, however, as the new nationalism arose and as the intellectual center of gravity moved to the cities, Christianity declined rapidly in rural areas and became concentrated among the urban middle class or among intellectuals. The percentage of Christians in Japan remained small and even today constitutes less than one half of one per cent of the population.

The lack of success of Christianity in Japan — during a century in which Japan has undergone successive waves of Westernization — argues a basic incompatibility between it and the dominant intellectual tendencies. One obvious area of difficulty was the Christian myth. Science had been encouraged since the Meiji Restoration: one can say it acted as a sieve straining out the thought of the premodern West. Those in Japan who attacked Christianity, even those who were defenders of some version of the Japanese orthodoxy, often appealed to science for their arguments.

Beyond the problem of myth there were other fundamental obstacles. One was the idea of a loyalty transcending other loyalties to family or country. When an early samurai convert, Ebina Danjō, "took God as his feudal lord," he described the change within himself — from world-immanent loyalties to a transcendental loyalty — as "Copernican." The same radical secularization of the family-state ideal is reflected in the statement of Niishima Jō, the founder of Dōshisha University: "God, not my parents, created me." Shorn of their religious sanctions, the personal, particularistic ties of the Japanese orthodoxy, which previously had been sacred and therefore unquestionable, were opened to scrutiny and in many cases found lacking. Uchimura Kanzō, for example, broke with the orthodoxy of his day when he refused to bow to the Imperial Rescript on Education at a school ceremony and when he opposed Japan's actions in the Russo-Japanese War on the grounds of Christian pacificism. Uchimura was not unnationalistic: He always spoke of the "two J's," Jesus and Japan, and he felt that the moral discipline of *bushidō* (the way of the samurai) was better suited to Christianity than the mores of the modern West. He also opposed the missionary churches of his day, founding what he called the "No Church" movement. This was radically Protestant and stressed the direct confrontation of the individual and God. It centered on Bible study groups and for a time was influential at Tōkyō University. Yet his attachment to Japan was moral, not religious, and was always subordinated to his Christianity.

Thus a corollary of the observation that Christianity was incompatible with the orthodoxy of modern Japan is that, when it was accepted, it could effect at times a radical change. In fact, although the number of Christians in Japan has been small, they have produced a considerable ferment in Japanese society. A high percentage of those who studied abroad were either Christian or under Christian auspices. Christian education in Japan, especially women's education, has been influential. Many intellectuals, particularly literary men, went through a Christian phase in the course of their development. A great number of social welfare projects, in areas in which the Meiji government had little interest, were also begun by Christians: orphanages, work with outcast (*eta*) communities, welfare work with prostitutes, and the women's rights movement. Moreover, Christianity was also the major vehicle by which socialism first was carried to Japan. Of the six founders of Japan's first socialist party in 1901, five were Christians. The labor union movement during and after World War I was begun by Suzuki Bunji and aided by Kagawa Toyohiko, who was also active in welfare work in the slums of Kōbe. By the mid-1920's the socialist movement in Japan had drawn away from the positions taken by its earlier Christian leaders. Yet among the leaders of the moderate socialist parties even in the 1930's, many Christian socialists were still to be found, and postwar Japan's only socialist prime minister (Katayama Tetsu) was a Christian.

Equally notable in prewar Japan was the occasional association between Christianity and parliamentary government. Christian thinkers, when politically minded, usually reacted to the excesses and shortcomings of Diet politics not with totalistic plans to jettison the entire system but with programs to reform it from within. The most prominent example was Yoshino Sakuzō.

Yoshino, born in 1879, became a Christian while in higher school. While studying at the Law Faculty of Tōkyō Imperial University he attended the church of Ebina Danjō; he helped to edit a Christian journal, and associated with Christian socialists like Abe Isoo. During 1906–09 he went to China as the tutor of the eldest son of Yüan Shih-k'ai. In 1909 he became an assistant professor at Tōkyō Imperial University; he studied abroad from 1910 to 1913, and became a full professor on his return. From 1916, when he wrote "The Essence of Constitutional Government" for the *Central Review* (*Chūō Kōron*), into the early 1920's he was one of the most prolific and penetrating advocates of parliamentary government in Japan.

Yoshino's ideas may be seen, basically, as a more advanced program of reform within the fundamental position elaborated by Minobe. Like Minobe, Yoshino recognized the sovereignty of the emperor, since not to recognize it would have brought his entire program under fire. Therefore he rejected the concept of democracy in which "national sovereignty resides legally in the people" for one in which "the basic goals of state action lie politically in the people": that is, government by the people and for the people, but in the name of the emperor. Yet his formal recognition of the emperor's sovereignty did not prevent him from criticizing those "in the political world who, placing their major emphasis on idols [the emperor]," demand "the blind obedience of the people." The majority of Yoshino's political writings dealt not with sovereignty but with what should be done. He was concerned first with changes needed to make the Japanese government into a true parliamentary democracy. His articles treated universal suffrage, suggestions for the reform of the House of Peers, the need for the complete subordination of the army to the cabinet, and so on. Yoshino's second concern was with social democracy. He argued for gradual evolution toward socialism within a parliamentary framework.

Yoshino's writings are distinguished by the quality of his analysis and the steadfastness of his commitment to parliamentary government. To the Western observer, the program he advocated seems to contain just what was needed in the Japan of the 1920's. Had this gained intellectual support it would undoubtedly have been a bulwark for the political parties and a force working against the militaristic tendencies that appeared during the 1930's. However, except within the political parties and among journalists, this program won only momentary acclaim. For most of the politically minded young intellectuals, it was only a way-station on the road to Marxism. One Japanese historian wrote in 1956 that while "Europeans and Americans find it difficult to understand" the degree to which Marxism has entered the consciousness of the Japanese intellectual, "Japanese intellectuals have not understood the extent of the attraction held by the word 'liberal' in the historical life of Europe and America."[1] Why

---

[1] Tsurumi Shunsuke, in *Gendai Nihon no shisō*, p. 55.

did Yoshino arrive at, and consistently maintain, a liberal position that for most other thinkers was at best transitional? The answer would seem to be that he not only supported social equality, like the Marxists, but was also committed to the value of the individual, a position that seems a consequence of his modern Christianity. For Yoshino, democracy was not simply a question of the formal organization of government; it was based on faith in the individual and a belief in the possibility of limitless individual development. "To thoroughly realize democracy, humanism must function as a living concept." The basic source of humanism Yoshino found in the Christian belief that "sees all men as the children of God, and recognizes in all men a spark of divinity." Or more briefly: "Christian belief, as it asserts itself in every aspect of society, is democracy."[1]

Marxism in Japan. The years between the middle 1920's and the early 1930's saw the sudden rise of Marxism among the intellectuals, labor leaders, and writers of Japan. One writer refers to it as a "typhoon" that struck suddenly, and powerfully affected Japan's intellectual life. Considered strictly as an intellectual phenomenon, Marxism was probably stronger in Japan than in China at this time. However, since Japan was an industrialized nation, the role of its intellectuals was different from that of the intellectuals in China. Further, the Japanese police power, far more centralized than in the United States, was incomparably more efficient than that of China. Finally, it was impossible to create a Hunan-like territorial base within centralized Japan, and the organizational offshoots of Marxist theory, apart from the universities, were without staying power.

Marxism was not new to Japan in the 1920's. Socialism, as a theory, entered during the last decade of the nineteenth century, with Christianity, as we have seen, playing a major role in its introduction. A second, secular stream of socialist thought was introduced by men associated with the left wing of the "people's rights" movement of the late 1880's. The two forces converged in 1901 when Christians and political activists joined to organize a political party on the basis of Unitarian social thought, the ideas of Henry George, and French socialist doctrines. The result was the Social Democratic Party, banned the day it was formed. Secular socialists began to move away from the leadership of Christians as early as 1903 when Sakai Toshihiko, one of the later founders of the Japanese Communist Party, and Kōtoku Shūsui started a weekly paper, "The People's News." Yet the two groups could still join in opposing the Russo-Japanese War and unite in 1906 to form the Japanese Socialist Party. The thought of the left wing at this time was a mixture of pre-Marxist socialism, Marxist socialism, anarchism, and syndicalism. The final split oc-

---

[1] Takeda Kiyoko, "Yoshino Sakuzō," in *Nihon no shisōka II.*

curred in 1907 when Kōtoku, fired by revolutionary syndicalism, which he got from the Industrial Workers of the World on a trip to San Francisco, began to emphasize the primacy of direct action. This came to its logical conclusion in a plot to assassinate the emperor in 1911. Four men appear to have actually planned such an incident. Yet hundreds were arrested, more than twenty were brought to trial, and Kōtoku, who was not in the plot, and eleven others were executed. This trial brought socialism to an abrupt halt. Many of those remaining turned to scholarship, and the socialist movement, if such it can be called, went into hibernation for a decade.

The second wave of socialist thought came in the years after World War I: the age of liberalism and internationalism. The economy had leaped ahead during the war, and society, with the emergence of a modern city culture and a union movement, had become more diverse. The influences of the Russian Revolution, of the Comintern, and of European social democracy also entered Japan at this time. As a result of these favorable conditions, Marxism spread in unions and in intellectual circles; and new socialist political parties were formed.

It was the universities, rather than the workingmen's associations, that were both organizationally and intellectually central to the rise of Marxism, providing the sustenance that enabled it to spread despite police action. The "New Men's Association" (*Shinjinkai*) was founded by Yoshino Sakuzō, another professor, and two students of the Debating Club of the Law School of Tōkyō Imperial University in 1918. Its platform was "the liberation of mankind and the rationalistic reform of present-day Japan." The intellectual diversity it represented — in a sense picking up where the earlier socialism had left off — was reflected in the early issues of its magazines, which carried pictures of Lincoln, Rousseau, the anarchist Kropotkin, Marx, Lenin, and the Communist Rosa Luxemburg. By 1924 Lincoln, Rousseau, and anarchism had been dropped; the Association was overwhelmingly Marxist, and it had become the central force behind the student movement in the area around Tōkyō. Parallel to this organization were the "social science study groups" at various universities throughout Japan. These were Marxist from their inception, and in 1924 they joined to form the Students' Social Science Federation with 600 members at 53 schools. Its program was, first, "to implant a proletarian consciousness among students," and second, "to organize awakened students to contribute, within the limits open to students, to the proletarian movement." By 1928 the Federation had 1700 members and had come under the influence of the Japanese Communist Party. After 1929 these groups were dissolved and the student movement became more directly subordinate to the Communist Party or its Youth League. Partly to counter increased police activity, study groups were organized even within the universities as cell groups. From this time, matters of party policy, such as the debates on Comintern theses, became academic concerns, and multi-volume works, like the 1931–33 *Symposium on the Development of Japanese Capitalism*, were produced to justify one or another position. In the development of theory and in the volume of scholarly Marxism produced at this time, Japan was probably ahead of all countries except Russia and Germany. Even after 1933, when the student movement declined and the Japanese Communist Party became almost extinct, these writings continued to be read and studied in Japan's universities, and informal study groups continued to be formed. Numerically the latter were gradually overwhelmed by ultranationalist groups espousing various extreme versions of the emperor ideology. Yet the rapid rise of Marxism after World War II was largely due to the generation of academicians trained during these prewar years.

Among unions and in the newly formed socialist parties, as in the universities, Marxism spread rapidly. Syndicalism and anarchism declined after 1922, and by 1924 the more disciplined analysis of Marx and Lenin had become the orthodoxy of the left. The party organizations of the leftist movement are conventionally divided into three categories: revolutionary parties, centrist parties, and the anticommunist, parliamentary left. Parties of all three groups splintered, broke into factions, combined and recombined so frequently that it is almost impossible to treat them by name. The revolutionary left, including the Japanese Communist Party founded in 1922, was the smallest in size, the most plagued by internal dissensions, and the object of the most vigorous police suppression. As organizations, the revolutionary parties flickered in and out of existence; often there were more leading Communists in jail than out. Yet the revolutionary leftists were extremely influential within other organizations, whether from Leninist organizational techniques, or from their intellectual vitality, is hard to say without further studies. By the early 1930's the revolutionary parties were almost totally crushed.

The centrist parties were also revolutionary-Marxist in ideology but more moderate in practice. After 1925 they attempted to function as parliamentary groups, and during the early 1930's some joined with the socialist right to form the Social Mass Party. The parliamentary socialists were in many ways early advocates of the welfare state in Japan. Numerically they were the dominant element in the socialist movement and drew wide support from intellectuals and white-collar workers as well as from labor. They were led by Christian socialists with Fabian ideals. Yet even here the influence of a lukewarm Marxism, if not Marx-Leninism, was pervasive at all but the highest levels of the party organization.

One of the clearest signs of the intellectual vitality of Marxism in Japan was its strength in literature. Arishma Takeo of the White Birch school, a year before his death in a double suicide in 1923, gave his family estates to his tenants and acknowledged the justness of the proletarian cause.

From the mid-twenties there appeared an increasing number of novels, poems, and critical essays which attempted to replace the earlier natural-scientific literary ideal with a "social-scientific" outlook, and aimed at fulfilling the dictum that the purpose of literature is social enlightenment. Many portrayed the aimless, frivolous, empty character of bourgeois existence. Others described the heroism born in the midst of the hardships suffered by the working classes. Still others, as in the following poem by Nakano Shigeharu, attacked the effete character of traditional Japanese aestheticism:

> Don't sing
> Don't sing of scarlet blossoms or the wings of dragonflies
> Don't sing of murmuring breezes or the scent of a woman's hair.
> All of the weak, delicate things
> All the false, lying things
> All the languid things, omit.
> Reject every elegance
> And sing what is wholly true,
> Filling the stomach,
> Flooding the breast at the moment of desperation,
> Songs which rebound when beaten
> Songs which scoop up courage from the pit of shame.
> These songs
> Sing in a powerful rhythm with swelling throats!
> These songs
> Hammer into the hearts of all who pass you by![1]

Like the political leftists, the proletarian writers early took diverse ideological positions. These were tolerated for a time; but in 1926 a milestone was reached when anarchists and other non-Marxists were excluded from the Proletarian Literary Federation. The multifarious literary societies and magazines that emerged thereafter generally operated as organs of the various revolutionary political groups and mirrored the twistings and turnings of leftist thought. The proletarian school of writers was the dominant force in Japanese letters between 1927 and 1932, after which it rapidly declined. During its heyday the only real opposition came from the neo-impressionists, who from time to time protested against what they called the tyranny of the left in literature.

Why was Marxism so attractive in Japan? Why did it spread so rapidly? One reason is that there was a certain resonance between Marxism and orthodox Japanese thought. In both the individual is slighted, subordinated to his social group. In Marxist groups in Japan the demand to sacrifice individual goals for the "good of the people" was almost as com-

[1] Translated by Donald Keene. From *Modern Japanese Literature:* An Anthology Compiled and Edited by Donald Keene; copyright © 1956 by Grove Press, published by Grove Press, Inc. (British publisher, Thames & Hudson).

pelling as the demand in other contexts to sacrifice "for the state." The weakness of individualism in modern Japan, together with the similarity between the traditional collectivity, with its unspoken identification of the individual and group, and the ideal communism of Marx, has even led some Japanese scholars to suggest that Japan will move from premodern society to "postmodern" (socialist) society without ever passing through the stage of modern (individualistic) society. Others have pointed out the affinities between the extreme right and left during the 1930's: both criticized the decadence of "bourgeois city culture" and argued that "modernism should be overcome." To the extent that this premodern emphasis on group solidarity was important to its spread, Marxism in Japan may perhaps be compared with Marxism in other Asian countries.

Yet, even while noting similarities between Marxist values and those of the Japanese cultural tradition and suggesting comparisons with other Asian countries, we should also keep in mind that Marxist ideas found a very different application in Japan. In China and other Asian areas where Communism became identified with nationalism, it was the anti-imperialist dogma that was crucial. But in Japan, which was more sinner than sinned against, Lenin's theory of imperialism had only a secondary appeal. Rather, the responsibility for the ills of Japanese society was laid primarily at the door of its landlord and capitalist classes. In this connection, Marx's analysis of the politics of a capitalist society — his view of the parliament as a "committee of the bourgeoisie" — was central. And that there was much in Japan that fitted this view, cannot be denied.

A second factor contributing to the rapid rise of Marxism among intellectuals was the character of Japan's modern academic tradition. The historical-evolutionary view of the state was already deeply rooted and was even a central component in orthodox thought. Various forms of naturalism were prevalent; science was highly esteemed by all, and German philosophy was widespread. By the end of World War I some economists, including Kawakami Hajime of Kyōto Imperial University, were moving from classical to Marxist theories. And they were joined by other scholars who saw in Marxism a unified social science which could break through departmental barriers.

Yet the spiritual significance of Marxism in modern Japan was not in the main either traditional or academic. Rather, the attraction that it exercised came from the clarity of its break with orthodox thought. It held that the world was material, and therefore not only comprehensible, but also changeable by historical human forces. It attacked the central institutions of Japanese orthodoxy: the family, the state, and the emperor. Stripped of their religious coloration, these were exposed as the exploitative forms of a particular historical stage. It demanded action for the good of all men rather than fulfillment of particular obligations. Its further requirement that those who accepted it become actors in history led to the flow of energy from the universities to leftist politics. In fact, however, those who held Marxist views were so isolated from the mainstream of society that their theory became almost an end in itself and was taken as a substitute for reality. Marxism ended in the prewar years not in a remaking of society, but in manipulation of theory and in factional strife. Yet its impact was such that some have compared it to the Christianity of the Meiji period, suggesting that, although diametrically opposed as intellectual positions, the two had a common spiritual function in Japanese intellectual life: to radically reject the imperial cosmology.[1]

POLITICS FROM 1900 TO 1918

One of the salient features of the period between 1900 and 1918 was the change in the political role of the emperor. The Restoration had proclaimed direct imperial rule. This was largely a façade behind which those who had carried out the Restoration ruled, yet the Meiji Emperor was vigorous and to a limited extent participated in decision-making. His successor, the Taishō Emperor (1912–1926), however, was sickly as a child and later mentally deranged. No one could even pretend that he wrote his own edicts. The spiritualization of the emperor institution that we noted earlier is not unrelated to the personal deficiencies of Taishō. After 1912 the emperor was more and more removed from decision-making and was relegated to an almost purely symbolic role in government.

Parallel to the change in the position of the emperor was the decline of the oligarchy, largely as the result of assassination, death, illness, or simply old age. By 1912, the oligarchs were few in number, often feeble, and removed from the centers of power. We should not underestimate them — Yamagata in particular; they continued to participate in the process of naming a new prime minister, and their personal ties to government leaders gave them a potential power which they wisely conserved through sparing use. But their day was passing. The feeling was strong that younger men should be given a chance.

Political Elites. Nakae Chōmin, criticizing oligarchic control, called the early Meiji government "a strange creature with one body and many heads." By the end of the Meiji period, however, one might more accurately depict it as an even stranger creature with one head and several bodies. The original oligarchs (the many heads) were rapidly fading away. In their place, coordinating the various branches of the government, appeared a cabinet (a single collective head). Yet, below the cabinet

[1] Maruyama Masao, *Nihon no shisō*, p. 15.

there had come into being a number of differentiated elites — the political parties, the military services, the civil bureaucracy, and others — which struggled for power. Perhaps the most striking single change in Japanese government organization after the turn of the century was the maturation of these plural elites. As the political history of Japan between the late Meiji period and World War II is largely the history of the relations between these elites, they are worth considering in detail.

Central to the government was the civil bureaucracy: a vast group of men ranging from local officials and uniformed station attendants of the government railway system to the top officials in the ministries of the central government. When treating the bureaucracy as a governmental elite, one is concerned chiefly with the few thousand career bureaucrats who actually exercised the executive power of the central government. These men were recruited by a system of civil service examinations. Those in the top positions were overwhelmingly graduates of the Law Faculty of Tōkyō Imperial University. They were relatively young, they advanced rapidly and retired early — going on to other careers in politics, government companies, economic associations, and the like. They were able, proud, and autocratic. They saw themselves as an educational and social elite, and until the 1920's, when company executives pulled ahead, they were also the economic elite of Japan. They were actually called "the officials of the emperor." The unit of Japanese officialdom was the ministry, although factions existed within each ministry as well. Each minister was legally responsible to the emperor rather than to the cabinet and prime minister, whose powers, in comparison with the far greater powers of European premiers, were relatively weak. Serious disagreement between ministers could force the dissolution of a cabinet.

Another pair of elites were the army and navy. In many ways these were similar to the civil bureaucracy. Both had relatively high prestige within Japan. Both claimed a special relation to the emperor. The army and navy ministers, like the heads of other ministries, were directly responsible to the emperor. Yet, in addition to the two service ministers, the two chiefs of staff as well as the army inspector-general of education were also directly responsible to the emperor. That the chiefs of staff were directly responsible to the emperor meant that their "right of command" over the services was autonomous. The chiefs of staff were not under the cabinet; and not even clearly subject to interference from the service ministers — since within the services a clear distinction was made between the duties of the General Staff and the service ministers. In the mid-Meiji period when responsibility to the emperor meant subordination to the oligarchs, this raised few problems. But when the oligarchs passed from the scene and no one took their place, it meant that the army and navy had a dimension of autonomy which the other ministries lacked. The services were never regularized under the control of civil government as in the West. Even in the palmiest days of party government during the 1920's, the potential for independent policy-making existed within the services.

The political parties constituted yet another elite. They were originally formed, before the existence of a Diet, as political pressure groups acting on the government from without. Then, in the first phase of constitutional politics (1890–1900), the parties entered the newly formed Diet. Their powers, though limited, were greater than had been intended, and they quickly learned techniques to harass the government. But in this first period of constitutional government their role was still primarily that of an opposition group. During the second period of constitutional government (1900–1918), the parties joined with bureaucratic leaders and were taken, one step further, into the government. The Seiyūkai formed in 1900 and the Dōshikai of 1913 were the two most important mergers of politicians and bureaucrats which opened the way for a party role in government beyond that of opposition. From this time on, one party would be allied with the government and the other would be the opposition, and for the first time the function of political parties in Japan began to resemble that of parties in modern Western governments. Yet until the election reforms of 1918 and 1925 the parties represented only a very small percentage of the adult male population of Japan, a privileged group of landlords, businessmen, officials, and other taxpayers. And even then, the parties functioned within a framework that required them at times to be more responsive to the demands of the other elites than to those of their constituencies.

Another elite or group of elites consisted of various legal and nonlegal bodies close to the emperor. Some — such as the inner minister, imperial household minister, and Senior Statesmen (Jūshin) — advised the emperor. Another, the House of Peers, was appointed by him, or by others in his place, to exercise a moderating influence in the Diet. With the exception of the Senior Statesmen, these groups were originally under the tight control of the oligarchs. As the oligarchy became the Elder Statesmen (Genrō) and then gradually disappeared, these groups about the emperor weakened, although their negative or obstructive powers were still substantial. They inherited the mantle of the former oligarchy, but could not inherit its powers. In part their decline stemmed from the stand of Prince Saionji, who was determined to be the last Elder Statesman, and who was unwilling to have such offices — over which he possessed great influence — interfere with party government. Thus, by the twenties the Peers had been partly infiltrated by political party appointees and was calling for reforms to make itself a more representative body. The Privy Council, once the stronghold of the oligarchs, became more and more a place of retirement for former prime ministers and important ex-ministers, though some party men were appointed as well. Its only real strength was its constitutional authority to ratify treaties. After 1932 the Privy Council was again strengthened by Saionji, who hoped to use it to curb the military. The Senior Statesmen, a new group that appeared during the 1930's, consisted of the inner minister, the president of the Privy Council, and former prime ministers. In 1932 they informally gave their opinions to Saionji regarding the appointment of the new prime minister. From 1937 this decision was made by the inner minister. In 1940 a Senior Statesmen Conference was formally convened to make this decision. Continuing until 1945, this was the group that forced the retirement of Prime Minister Tōjō in 1944.

Finally, there were the zaibatsu, comprising an elite obviously different from the others. This elite did not derive its power from a position, legal or traditional, within the government. It was not chiefly concerned with power, or with a voice in political decision-making. While socially its top executives were of a status such that they could intermarry with the other elites, politically speaking it would be more accurate to see this as the most powerful outside pressure group in prewar Japan. The close ties that the zaibatsu maintained with party politicians enabled them to exert influence at a number of levels, when such influence was deemed necessary to their fortunes.

When we ask how government actually functioned in Japan before World War II, we find that it was not a case of self-contained, united elites, each working against the others and jockeying for position and power within the government. Rather, there existed hostile groupings, rival cliques, within each elite: Itō and Saionji versus Yamagata among the oligarchs; Mitsui versus Mitsubishi and others among the zaibatsu; party pitted against party; army against navy, or Chōshū and Satsuma cliques within the services against other cliques; coteries competing within the Peers and bureaucratic factions within the ministries. Government in prewar Japan was carried on by a horizontal coalition of groupings that cut through the structure of plural elites. Such coalitions were in effect demanded by the powers given to each elite. Any one of the elites could block the work of government; all had to join for government to function. As a result, compromise between elites was built into the system.

The ties joining a faction of one elite with a party or faction of another were, in Japanese fashion, usually personal. Often personal ties antedating the formation of the Diet furnished the connections which later brought together such factions into an inter-elite coalition. Hoshi Tōru, one of the leading politicians in what became in 1900 the Seiyūkai, was an old friend of Mutsu Munemitsu — who as foreign minister had carried out the revision of the unequal treaties. Mutsu was a protégé of Itō, and these ties were one factor which led to Itō's leadership of Hoshi's party after 1900. The Mitsui house was indebted both for aid at a time of crisis and for organizational reforms to Inoue Kaoru who was close to Itō. This led to the role of the Mitsui as the financial helpmate of the Seiyūkai during the early decades of the century. Similar personal ties can be found joining Ōkuma, Katsura, the Mitsubishi concern, Katō Kōmei (prime minister 1924–26), and Shidehara to the other major political party. In general such coalitions were put together under oligarchic supervision until 1912. As long as coalitions were manipulated from above, competition between elites was severely restricted. But after 1912, as the elites gained greater independence, the coordination from above disappeared. Personal ties were still important in the construction of coalitions, but they did not prevent rivalries and struggles between the elites for greater powers.

Politics was thus, even macroscopically viewed, terribly complex. On the one hand, the elites were divided into factions which formed inter-elite coalitions. On the other, it is still meaningful to speak of competition between elites as wholes, since all members of an elite, however factionalized, had the same kind of power within the structure of government. This gave them common attitudes and interests. Even a shift from one coalition to the other did not greatly affect the position of one elite relative to another. This struggle continued whichever coalition was in power. A gain by a faction of one elite within its coalition automatically enhanced the bargaining power of the other faction of the elite in the opposite coalition.

Until the late 1920's the political parties were the most successful among the elites in such struggles. The pattern of their advance was erratic, but that it was an advance seems undeniable. Often, of course, a party went back on its principles in order to return to power. Yet once again in power, or once again out, party politicians, whatever their beliefs or personalities, were led to demand lower taxes, the extension of suffrage, or more party ministers. When they were successful they advanced in their party, their party gained popularity at the expense of its opposition, and both parties gained in relation to the other elites. The mechanism for change in the relative position of the elites was compromise within a coalition. However much the party out of power might decry compromise, it was the means by which the political parties gained ground. But, as the situation changed, it was also the means by which they lost power thereafter.

When an issue arose on which no compromise could be worked out, several things might happen. A coalition might be shuffled, one faction of one elite replacing another. Since each party was composed of a number of personal factions, one or several of these might splinter off to join the opposite party or to form a third party. Or power might switch to a rival coalition. In extreme cases the coalitions themselves might be radically reorganized. And on a few dramatic occasions the opposing factions within an elite united to reject compromise arrangements with other elites, and the government came to a standstill until a new coalition could be worked out. One such moment came in the winter of 1912–13, the "Taishō Political Crisis." It is worth treating in some detail since it exemplifies some of the complexities described above, while at the same time marking one of the earliest incidents of widespread popular participation in party politics, the "Movement for the Protection of the Constitution." Instead of an oligarchic prime minister dissolving a recalcitrant Diet, we see the power of the majority party in the Diet combine with public opinion to destroy a sometime protégé of Yamagata.

The "Taishō Political Crisis" of 1912–13. Saionji became prime minister for the second time in the summer of 1911. In line with the demands of his party, the Seiyūkai, and in response to Japan's economic needs, he was determined to enforce a policy of retrenchment. Both the army and navy, however, pressed for increased allocations. The two were bitterly competitive; each was determined not to be outdone by the other. In the end, after months of negotiations, both were turned down. The army minister, therefore, after conferring with Yamagata, sent his resignation to the emperor without previously informing Saionji. With this, Saionji's cabinet fell.

The remaining oligarchs, faced with finding a new man, first asked Saionji to form another cabinet. He refused. Yamagata wanted General Terauchi, but the others refused, feeling that the appointment of an army man would not be accepted by the parties. As an authority on financial matters Matsukata was chosen, but he refused too, as did Hirata Tōsuke, another Yamagata favorite. Admiral Yamamoto Gombei (Satsuma) also turned down the post, saying in effect that the Chōshū army clique should clean up its own mess. Finally, as a last resort, Katsura Tarō was asked. He accepted.

It is necessary to distinguish between Katsura the man and Katsura the symbol. Katsura had risen within the army at a time when it was led by men with great breadth of vision. He can best be seen as a transitional figure between statesmen-soldiers such as Yamagata and later narrow military specialists. At the turn of the century he shared the view of his mentor Yamagata that cabinets should be "transcendent," above party control. Yet in the years (1901–1912) in which he alternated as prime minister with Saionji he had become accustomed to working in cooperation with the parties, and was ready to form one himself. He saw himself not as a representative of the army but as a statesman, and he accepted the premiership with the intention of continuing the retrenchment policy of his predecessor and of extending civil control over the military. Nor was he simply a pawn of Yamagata. In 1911 he had recommended Saionji as his successor in direct opposition to Yamagata; and he had been reported to the old man as having said, "When I come back [from a trip to Europe] I will push into retirement such people as Yamagata."

Yet Katsura was anathema to the parties and the public. He was blamed for the loss of the peace after the Russo-Japanese War. He had been responsible for a heavy-handed campaign to root out "subversive" thought after the 1911 assassination plot against the emperor. He had risen as an army general, and worst of all, he was from Chōshū. In 1912 he had been pushed out of active politics into semi-retirement as the inner minister. This post apparently was forced on him as punishment for his earlier independence, but the public saw it as an attempt by Katsura to obtain direct control over the emperor. And since none of those who chose Katsura as prime minister took overt responsibility for the imperial rescript appointing him prime minister, it appeared to the public that he had with diabolical cunning contrived the army's overthrow of the Saionji cabinet and then used his ascendancy over the emperor to secure his own appointment.

The first problem that faced Katsura as prime minister was the navy's demand for new battleships. Following the example of the army, it threatened to withhold a minister if its claims were not met. Countering this, Katsura issued an imperial rescript directing the navy to furnish a minister. The newspapers and parties, ready for a fight, seized upon this use of imperial authority as further evidence of Katsura's undemocratic character. That he had used it against the military did not matter to the party leaders; their enemies were the authoritarian oligarchs of Chōshū and Satsuma who had ruled Japan for forty years, not the services which were showing their first signs of independence.

The League for the Protection of the Constitution was begun in December 1912, when the army toppled Saionji's cabinet. Formed of some businessmen, some intellectuals, and a few professional men, and organized by the parties, which at this time formed a common front, it called at its first meeting for a "Taishō Restoration." The early years of the Meiji Emperor had witnessed sweeping reforms toward a modern Japan; the reign of the Taishō Emperor must open with similar changes toward a democratic Japan. When Katsura became prime minister this movement for constitutional government took the form of a popular front against Katsura. Massive rallies were held. Most newspapers supported the movement. Local party officials pledged their support (Katsura never dissolved the Diet to call for an election since he knew he would lose). Orators at meetings in the main cities of Japan shouted "Destroy the *han* leaders and off with Katsura's head." For a time the top ex-bureaucrat leaders of the Seiyūkai, Saionji, Hara Kei, and Matsuda, stood aside and watched. The Seiyūkai was led from the ranks by Ozaki Yukio, and the other main party, the Kokumintō, by Inukai. When it became apparent that the movement was a great success, they halfheartedly joined. By late January it was decided to call for a no-confidence vote against Katsura in the Diet.

Katsura's first counter-move was to form his own political party. To gain time he prorogued the Diet for fifteen days, using another imperial rescript. As Itō had based the Seiyūkai on the old Liberal Party of Itagaki, Katsura wanted to base his on the Kokumintō, the successor to the Progressive Party of Ōkuma. As his foreign minister, Katsura drafted Katō Kōmei, later party president and prime minister in 1924. Katō had begun his career with the backing of Mitsubishi (he was married to a daughter of its founder, Iwasaki) and had also been Ōkuma's secretary in 1888. Katsura's plan was to use Mitsubishi funds, the personal influence of Katō and Ōkuma, and the attractions of power to win followers away from the opposing common front. In the long run the party founded by Katsura became one of the two major parties in prewar Japan. But over the short term it was a failure, obtaining less than one-fourth of the number of Diet members in the opposition Seiyūkai.

When the Diet met again after the fifteen-day recess, Katsura was questioned regarding the source of the rescript used to prorogue it. He replied that the matter was too sacred to discuss. This led to Ozaki's famous speech:

> They always mouth "loyalty" and "patriotism" but what they are actually doing is to hide themselves behind the Throne, and shoot at their political enemies from their secure ambush. The Throne is their rampart. Rescripts are their missiles.

Eventually Katsura became desperate and turning to Saionji asked whether it was not inconsistent to have agreed to his appointment as prime minister yet permit the party to destroy his cabinet. Saionji finally agreed to transmit a rescript to his party ordering it to retract its decision for a no-confidence vote. What followed was complex, but in the end the managing board of the Seiyūkai rejected the imperial order. Katsura then prorogued the Diet for a third time in order to save face by resigning before the formal vote was taken. As a consequence, the crowds that had gathered to cheer for the victory of the Seiyūkai turned into an angry mob that vented its displeasure by destroying the offices of pro-government newspapers and burning police boxes. Katsura died later in the year, a broken man.

Domestic Politics during the First World War. The meaning of the "Taishō Political Crisis" for the years that followed between 1913 and 1918 was not self-evident. Unstudied, these years are among the most opaque in modern Japanese history. Certainly the parties did not attempt to live up to the pretensions voiced in their speeches during the winter of 1912–13. The increases demanded by the services, which occasioned the "Crisis," were all granted in the next few years, although in part this was a consequence of an emergent factor, Japan's participation in the war. And even a step-by-step constitutional decline can be seen in the character of the three prime ministers who followed Katsura. The first was a

Satsuma admiral, Yamamoto Gombei (February 1913 to April 1914); the second, Ōkuma (April 1914 to October 1916), though a leader in the party movement so disliked by Yamagata and the others, was almost an oligarch himself; the third was Terauchi (October 1916 to September 1918), like Katsura a Chōshū general. The circumstances surrounding the appointment of Yamamoto mirrored the balance of forces in 1913. Katsura was too discredited to be reappointed. Hara, the new president of the Seiyūkai, could not be appointed because of Yamagata's opposition. Yamagata's man, Terauchi, could not be named because of Seiyūkai opposition. Therefore, Yamamoto, a worldly military bureaucrat—a type viewed with contempt by the "pure" younger officers of the 1930's—was chosen as a compromise candidate.

Yet, the "Crisis" did have appreciable consequences. One major area of advance was the entry of the second political party lineage (the Kaishintō-Kokumintō) into the ranks of the elites. Until 1912–13 only the Seiyūkai had at its top levels the bureaucratic leadership necessary for participation in government. This supplied the support for the cabinets of both the Itō (Saionji) and Yamagata (Katsura) oligarchical cliques. After 1913 two-party politics became possible with the development of the Dōshikai (Kenseikai) under Katō Kōmei. The effects were slow to emerge, but the shift was crucial for the 1920's.

A second consequence of the "Crisis" was an immediate increase in party power. Virtually all of the ministers in Yamamoto's cabinet were party men, bureaucrats who at Hara's insistence joined the party in order to enter the cabinet. The legislation carried out under Yamamoto was also highly favorable to the parties. Patronage was increased; high posts in the Home Ministry and in the prefectural police departments, posts that could be used to influence voters at election times, were removed from civil service jurisdiction and opened to party politicians. The budget was cut by more than 13 per cent and the bureaucracy was reduced by more than 10,000 persons. Most important of all, the posts of army and navy minister, heretofore limited to active-service generals and admirals under service control, were opened to retired general-rank and flag-rank officers. None were ever appointed, but the fact that they could be, increased the potential leverage of the cabinet over the services.

The new face of politics was also visible in the election of March 1915. Ōkuma the prime minister was tremendously popular in Japan. Known as "the sage of Waseda," he was viewed almost as the god of constitutional politics. Allied with the Dōshikai (Katsura's party and the lineal descendant of the Progressive Party Ōkuma had founded in 1881) he had run into Seiyūkai opposition during the first Diet session of his premiership. He therefore dissolved the Diet and called a new election. On the one hand, this election was one of the most corrupt in Japanese constitutional history. Bribery was used to split the opposition Seiyūkai. Ōura, the home minister, used local officials and police to help candidates of Ōkuma's party and hinder those of the opposition. Such tactics were so blatant that Ōkuma was denounced by Ozaki, and three of Ōkuma's ministers, including Katō, president of his party, indignantly quit the cabinet. But, on the other hand, this election also saw the beginning of the modern party political campaign in Japan. Ministers of the government as well as Ōkuma himself traveled about speaking on behalf of their candidates — earlier this had been considered beneath the dignity of a cabinet minister. For the first time in Japanese political history a speech by the prime minister, "The Power of Public Opinion in Constitutional Politics," was recorded and played from victrolas on platforms all over Japan. And on election morning telegrams requesting votes were sent in Ōkuma's name to the homes of voters in areas that were deemed crucial. Ōkuma's party won an absolute majority in the Diet.

The war years ended with the cabinet of General Terauchi. The appointment of a Chōshū general as prime minister, which had been an impossibility in 1913, was merely an anachronism in 1916. The Seiyūkai, having been out of power since 1914 and badly off in the Diet since the election of 1915, took a step backward, gave up the principles for which it had fought at the time of the "Taishō Crisis," and supported the all-bureaucratic cabinet of Terauchi. For this it was richly rewarded: once again orders went out to prefectural governors to help out in the election, which proved to be a hands-down victory for the Seiyūkai. But this alliance was tenuous at best; the party opposed the government when it pleased, and when Terauchi's cabinet fell in the aftermath of the rice riots of 1918, the Seiyūkai was waiting with demands for more democracy and increased party power.

Japan's Early Imperialism. The first phase of Japan's modern imperialism, from the Taiwan Expedition of 1874 to World War I, was fairly consistent in character. Action was carried out by a unified government establishment for the sake of commonly held objectives. This contrasts strongly with a later phase of imperialism which began with autonomous action by a single elite.

After the Meiji Restoration Japan's objectives were autonomy and security within her own waters. These were gained early, complete political independence followed the revision of the unequal treaties during the mid-1890's, and Japan began to redefine her security needs in terms of her relations with other powers in East Asia. During the 1880's this concern centered on Korea and the balance there between Japan and China. Yet well before the Sino-Japanese War of 1894–95 Japan had shifted attention to the European powers. During the peace negotiations of 1895 Yamagata wrote to a friend that the situation in the Far East would grow worse and that Japan "must be prepared for

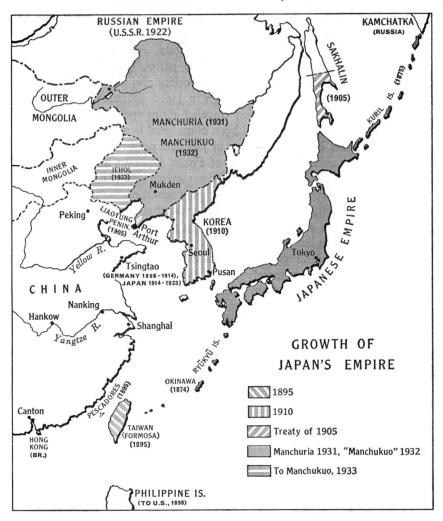

GROWTH OF
JAPAN'S EMPIRE

1895

1910

Treaty of 1905

Manchuria 1931, "Manchukuo" 1932

To Manchukuo, 1933

another war in ten years." The war with Russia came as predicted. From it Japan gained the southern half of the island of Sakhalin, the recognition of Japan's paramount interests in Korea, the lease of the Liaotung Peninsula, and railway rights in southern Manchuria. From this time Japan saw her strategic line of defense as curving through southern Manchuria. The importance of this line was heightened by Japan's annexation of Korea in 1910.

Another aspect of this early phase of imperialism was Japan's desire to get great-power credentials. The great powers of the world had either empires or vast internal territories under their control. Japan's early concern for security quickly blossomed into a desire for empire as well. Yet, aware of her weaknesses, Japan moved slowly from one limited objective to the next. Her leaders quashed the 1873 proposal for an invasion of Korea, they stepped gingerly during the 1880's, they gave in to the three powers and retroceded Liaotung in 1895, and they supported the Open Door in 1899, since they felt that the nation was still too weak to expand its spheres of influence in China against the positions held by the European powers. The Anglo-Japanese Alliance of 1902 marked Japan's recognition as a great Far Eastern power. Her victory, however shaky, in the Russo-Japanese War confirmed this. And by the time of Versailles, Japan was a world power. By then her empire had become less a needed symbol of political prestige, and more an accepted part of the Japanese body politic, integrated economically with the homeland.

The economic dimension of this early phase of imperialism is hard to pin down. During the 1870's and 1880's economic factors were minimal. By the turn of the century they were more important, though difficult to evaluate. Marxist historians in Japan have had trouble explaining why early Japanese capitalism, still blighted with feudal survivals, should have manifested the expansionist tendencies that "ought" only to appear in the most advanced capitalist nations. One explanation that has been suggested is that in Japan the shortage of capital, rather than its surplus, led to imperialism; that the Japanese, unable to compete with the West under conditions of free competition, attempted to establish protected zones on the continent to which Japanese exports might be sent. Judging from the speeches of the military, this view seems plausible. Yet a reading of business journals would point to an opposite conclusion: that businessmen did not want expansion before 1904, that they were not interested in Manchuria, and that they saw empire itself as unprofitable. Arguments based on the structure of the Japanese economy are equally inconclusive. Japan did need raw materials. Particularly during World War I the zaibatsu encouraged the government in its demands for iron, coal, and other raw materials from China. Yet, until later, raw materials were available on the open market. Japan's economic development also benefited from the usual high level of military demand. But, here, too, other alternatives are conceivable; that they were not chosen seems more politically than economically determined.

In the area of ideology a considerable number of elements joined together in support of imperialism. One over-arching element was the sanction of Japan's "political religion." Before the formation of the constitutional orthodoxy, very diverse positions were taken regarding the emperor, and even after the turn of the century, the content of emperor-thought was rather broad. Yet, since the emperor, rather than law or an abstract ethic, was the ultimate ground both of morality and of political legitimacy, the imperial mission of the emperor's army could hardly be found morally wrong. Expansion did not need to be justified as long as it was successful.

A second element coloring Japanese perceptions of international relations was the lack of a tradition of international law. Unlike European nations, Japan was not traditionally part of a multi-state international community. Japan lacked the idea of a universal law to which all nations might agree. Fukuzawa Yukichi, therefore, felt that while law was useful in dealing with the West, it was of little value in Japan's relations with the rest of the world. And even in relation to the West, in spite of his general commitment to law, Fukuzawa early observed:

> One hundred volumes of International Law are not the equal of a few cannon; a handful of Treaties of Friendship are not worth a basket of gunpowder. Cannon and gunpowder are not aids for the enforcement of given moral principles; they are the implements for the creation of morality where none exists.

This view was reinforced toward the end of the nineteenth century by the impact of Social Darwinism. Spencer was for a time the darling of the intellectuals. His ideas on individualism aroused little interest, but the ideas that the fittest societies not only survived but conquered was readily accepted and joined to ideas regarding Japan's moral superiority.

A third ideological factor at this early stage was the support given to expansionism by the proponents of constitutional government. For one thing, some in the political parties spoke of "Japan's Monroe Doctrine." They argued that it was Japan's mission to help China and keep out European influences as had the United States in Latin America. For another, party politicians had argued from the start that constitutional government was strong government. Constitutional government and colonial expansion were not seen as incompatible: England had both. Thus Fukuzawa supported the Sino-Japanese War as a means of advancing "modern civilization" on the continent, and Ōkuma violently criticized the government for not getting more out of the Russo-Japanese War. Certainly Yamagata's fulminations against the parties, that they wanted successful wars without military expenses, were not without justice. This complex mixture of extreme chauvinism and halfhearted liberalism can also be seen in the Japanese government during World War I. Ōkuma, the democrat, presented the notorious Twenty-One Demands to China and became the arch-imperialist, while also supporting his old friend, Sun Yat-sen, as a liberal out of power. Yamagata, the imperial conservative, opposed the Demands since he supported Yüan Shih-k'ai, the anti-republican conservative in power. As in Japanese liberal meddling in Korean politics in the 1880's, liberals in Japan hoped to strengthen themselves at home by allying themselves with liberals abroad. The latter in every case were betrayed by the realities of Japanese imperialism.

Ties between party politicians and the Japanese patriotic societies also grew out of this mixture. The early doctrines of ultranationalist societies joined liberalism and expansionism; therefore their members could go from the party movement to continental adventures with little sense of contradiction.[1] Yet by 1920 this combination was beginning to come apart. The parties were slowly moving toward an anti-imperialist position; and the patriotic societies were losing interest in liberalism, the "left" of the early years, and beginning to receive the influence of the new left of socialism.

By World War I imperialism was less popular than it had been earlier. Where only a handful of Christian and socialist intellectuals had opposed the Russo-Japanese conflict, criticism was now more widespread and respectable. One of Japan's influential magazines, the *Eastern Economic News* (*Tōyō keizai shimpō*), editorialized,

> Japan's greatest responsibility is to prevent the unhappy war [of Europe] from extending to the Far East. For the Japanese army to attack the German soldiers in Shantung just because they are few in number is an aggressive action that passes beyond our limits of obligation under the Anglo-Japanese Alliance.

Contributing to this attitude was the awareness that the security of Japan was not at stake; moreover her economy was doing very well apart from the war, and many felt that the vaunted moral superiority of the West was being tarnished by the ferocity with which European killed European. On the other hand, most newspapers supported Japan's limited participation in the war. East Asia had for years been in an uneasy balance between the power of Britain in central China, Russia in the north, Japan in Korea and Manchuria, France in the south, and Germany in Shantung. Now all except Japan were busy in Europe, leaving a power vacuum in East Asia. Some Japanese were aware that the era of imperialism was passing. Yet most felt that, since Japan had begun late, the powers, her allies, should not begrudge her a few more years of activity.

The last fling of this early phase of imperialism stemming from decisions by a unified government, as well as the first presage of something new, was the Siberian Expedition of 1918–22. Desirous of getting Russia back into the war against Germany, the Allied powers sent troops to Siberia. In Japan, Saionji and Hara were willing to send troops only if the United States did so as well. Yamagata and Terauchi favored intervention to get control of the Trans-Siberian Railway and thereby strengthen Japan's position in Manchuria. General Tanaka and other army officers had even more grandiose dreams of a Siberian empire as far west as Lake Baikal, under Japanese influence. These opposing factions were balanced for a time. But then American troops were sent, the Allies invited Japan to participate, and in Japan the decision went to those who favored intervention.[2] The decision having been made, the expedition became a military and not a civil matter. The General Staff, there-

[1] Marius Jansen, *The Japanese and Sun Yat-sen.*
[2] James Morley, *The Japanese Thrust into Siberia, 1918.*

fore, took advantage of its "autonomy of command" and sent in many times the number of troops originally agreed upon. Battles were fought and young officers connived with White Russian officers. When the war ended, other nations withdrew their troops. The United States hinted that Japan should do the same. Prime Minister Hara succeeded in getting Yamagata's support for a withdrawal of the Japanese forces. The army, however, was no longer in the hands of officers who felt loyalty to Yamagata. It held, moreover, that its honor was involved, and therefore refused. In Japan the campaign became grossly unpopular. It cost two-thirds as much as the Russo-Japanese War, and in the end nothing was gained. One music hall comedian amused his audience by punning that the Siberia *shuppei* (sending of troops) had become the Siberia *shippai* (failure); and a general going to take up his command wore civilian clothes so as to travel unnoticed. This was the first clear case in modern Japanese foreign policy of autonomous action by the military as a refractory elite.

THE YEARS OF PARTY GOVERNMENT: 1918–1931

The years between 1918 and 1931 witnessed developments in the direction of constitutional government at least as important as those marked by earlier milestones: the first election under the Meiji constitution in 1890, the formation of the Seiyūkai in 1900, or the "Taishō Political Crisis" of 1913. These advances were greatly influenced by a sweeping change that took place during the years of World War I and immediately thereafter. Social, intellectual, and political energies joined with foreign influences in favor of an internationalist, peaceful foreign policy and constitutional government at home. It would not exaggerate if, searching for comparable bursts of new ideas leading to sudden shifts in the climate of opinion, we were to liken this period to the pro-emperor movement after 1858, or to the abrupt shift to Western ideas in the early Meiji era.

The New Liberalism. When Itō went to Europe in search of a constitution in the 1880's, he found German principles most to his liking. In 1918, however, the democracies were strong and victorious. As one Japanese historian has put it, the popular image of the war in Japan was that of the *Punch* stereotypes: the bearded Kaiser of German militarism fighting the beautiful goddess of liberty, who represented the Allied cause. The influence of this democratic current was felt as early as 1916–17 when school texts were revised to include (alongside the religious view of the emperor) an emphasis on internationalism. Needless to say, this was oriented toward Europe; virtually no one in Japan at this time was intellectually concerned with the changes in neighboring China, not to speak of changes in the rest of the non-Western world.

Liberal intellectual currents within Japan, always sensitive to European opinion, were strengthened at this time. This was the age when Minobe's theory of the emperor as an organ of the government triumphed over the monarchism of Uesugi. This was the time when Yoshino Sakuzō presented in various magazine articles his plans for the reorganization of government structure so as to subordinate the various elites to a party cabinet. The spirit of the age was reflected in the romantic individualism of Mushakōji Saneatsu, who wrote that "only a country without authorities is livable," and hoped that at last Goethes and Emersons would be born in Japan.

A Japanese writer has described a universal suffrage rally he attended as a youth in 1919. It was held under the auspices of the Yūaikai, the Gompers-like labor union which had risen after 1912 under the moderate leadership of the Christian Suzuki Bunji. The three hundred who went to meet the speaker, Ozaki Yukio, sang a song written by the pioneer social worker Kagawa Toyohiko, as they marched through the streets of Kyōto: "Realizing that labor is a sacred vocation, let our spirits bravely advance, aiming at a distant ideal. . . ." The lecture hall was packed, and the crowds that were turned away broke windows and doors in order to hear Ozaki's oration. The manifesto passed that day amidst tumultuous applause pointed out "the misery of the proletariat and their oppression by the propertied classes," and, while "pledging loyalty to the sacred Emperor," demanded universal suffrage as a means of "extirpating the injustices of the [present] socio-economic system."[1]

In the above one can see in microcosm the temporary union of labor, the leftist political movement, the Christian social movement, liberal party politicians, and intellectuals, which was the outstanding characteristic of the early 1920's. The same ideological variety could also be found in a number of "reconstructionist" organizations born at this time in Tōkyō: all were vitally concerned with new doctrines, and their efforts, for their brief moment, converged in support of parliamentary government. The potentials of this combination should not, however, be overrated. One writer described its intellectual content as a melange of different ingredients "swallowed whole without sufficient chewing," and his own position in his student years as a "leftist, emperor-oriented faith in democracy." Certainly any one element, when examined closely, shows basic weaknesses. Yet new democratic symbols did emerge. Egalitarian thought began to spread. Workers' and tenants' organizations mushroomed overnight. The first signs of a consumer society appeared. Intellectuals became actively involved in the social movement. In part the movement at this time was strong because it was sufficiently diffuse to draw support or sympathy from virtually every group that opposed some aspect of the state orthodoxy. It is not too much to say that this combination of elements did for the early 1920's what the right wing did in the

[1] Kuwabara Takeo, "Taishō gojūnen," *Bungei shunjū*, Feb. 1962, p. 72.

1930's in changing the spirit of the times. And it influenced the overall direction of change among the plural elites of Japan's state structure.

By the mid-1920's, however, the combination had dissolved. Politically-minded younger intellectuals moved on to Marxism and to a basic distrust of the parliamentary state. Certainly there was much in the conduct of the Japanese Diet that contributed to this move. Yet it is ironic that the distrust should have arisen just as the Japanese working classes for the first time gained the right to vote. Christian socialists and moderate socialists (the truest heirs of this early liberal social movement) continued to work for parliamentary government and democracy, but they were deeply affected by the considerable loss of intellectual support, and became themselves more and more influenced by Marxist theory. The major parties, having absorbed some of the non-radical programs — such as universal suffrage — of this early liberal movement, were in some ways doing better than ever in the mid-twenties. But they were also moving into a period in which they increasingly were attacked by both the left and the right.

Internationalism. Related to the new liberalism of the years 1917–25 was a sharp shift in Japan's foreign policy. One contributing factor was the failure of militarism during the war. Prime Minister Terauchi's attempt to use 145 million yen of Finance Ministry and army special-account funds to fish in the muddy waters of Chinese warlord politics had ended in empty-handed failure. Japan's military participation in the war brought no territorial gains apart from the former German colonies in the Pacific. At the Washington Conference of 1921–22 (see pages 674–676) Japan finally agreed to withdraw from Siberia. The various concessions extracted from China during the war could not be put into effect. Moreover, Japan's attempt to dominate China by threat of force had stirred up violent anti-Japanese feeling in China. Thus, apart from her 1905 gains in Manchuria, Japan had by 1922 retreated to the common position of the other powers, that guaranteed by the unequal treaties.

Also involved in Japan's changing foreign policy was her growing diplomatic isolation. The last phase of her earlier imperialism had been underwritten by England; this support was lost in 1921 when the Anglo-Japanese Alliance was replaced by the Four-Power Treaty. The Nine-Power Treaty which pledged the territorial integrity of China also lined up world opinion against further aggression in China. Japan's special position in Korea and Manchuria had also been protected earlier by a series of four pacts with Tsarist Russia signed between 1907 and 1916. These were subsequently repudiated by the Soviet Union, which put forward a new criticism of Japan's position in Eastern Asia based on Lenin's analysis of imperialism, and closer Soviet ties with China strengthened the latter's position against Japan. The United States too had given some recognition to Japan: Taft and Katsura in 1905 gave mutual assurances regarding the Philippines and Korea, and the Lansing-Ishii Agreement of 1917, negotiated during the war, recognized that "territorial propinquity" gave Japan special interests in China. But after the war these assurances also vanished in Wilson's "New Diplomacy" that emphasized self-determination and the sovereign rights of each people. They vanished in the multi-national conferences and agreements which reflected — to a degree — the shift that had occurred in the doctrines of international relations. This change can easily be exaggerated. It did not lead to the abandonment of entrenched imperialist positions or privileges. Even United States policy was far from congruent with the Wilsonian principles. Yet it did lead to a criticism of new imperialist aggression. From this standpoint the United States looked coolly, even hostilely, at Japan's continental aspirations.

The result was a change-over to internationalism as a means in Japanese foreign policy. This new policy is sometimes called "Shidehara diplomacy" after Shidehara Kijūrō, Japan's foreign minister in 1924–27 and 1929–31. Yet in a broader sense it characterized all of Japan's relations with foreign powers during the 1920's. Recent research has demonstrated that even the "positive" policy of Prime Minister Tanaka (1927–29), while more belligerent in tone, was in its execution basically similar to that of his predecessor. This political internationalism was not unrelated to economic internationalism. Japan's gains during the war were achieved through peaceful, multilateral trade; her postwar economic leadership, more powerful than ever, was mainly interested in lower taxes and continued opportunities for trade.

Hara and the Rise of Party Government, 1918–24. In the "Taishō Crisis" of 1912–13 the parties were experimenting with the limits of their power within Japan's constitutional system. Even at that time they were ideologically committed to parliamentary government; but their actual expectations were far less than one would gather from their speeches. When the hue and cry was over, they compromised and settled for a small advance. By 1918 their expectations were higher. General feeling throughout the country was that the non-party government of General Terauchi had been a failure, and world trends suggested that democracy was best. This led in 1918 to the appointment of Hara Kei, president of the Seiyūkai, as prime minister. His cabinet was the first in which both the prime minister and the majority of ministers were from a single party. It was hailed by many in the party movement as the beginning of a new era of party government in Japan.

Hara was called the "Great Commoner." He was the first person not an oligarch or titled bureaucrat to become prime minister. Enormously talented and of higher samurai rank by birth than any of the Meiji oligarchs, he had not been born in one of the *han* that carried out the Restoration. This fact together with a generational difference — he was born in 1856, almost a generation later than the oligarchs — dictated a new career pattern: rapid promotion within a ministry and then a succession of postbureaucratic jobs leading to the premiership. At twenty-three Hara became a newspaper reporter, then a profession close to politics. He entered the Foreign Office at twenty-six and advanced steadily until fifteen years later he became ambassador to Korea. He then went on to become the editor of one of Japan's great daily papers, he helped Itō to found the Seiyūkai, and was in turn a bank official, the president of a company, and a member of the Diet. He held ministerial positions in a number of cabinets and became the president of the Seiyūkai after Saionji's retirement in 1913. All accounts agree that he was the most able politician in the Japan of his day. He was at best a halfhearted liberal; nationalistic and paternalistic within his party, he regarded politics as a very complicated game. One writer has described the administrative harmony of the Hara cabinet as due to its success in conciliating the plural elites:

> Hara's policy toward the Genrō was deferential; toward the militarists, ambivalent; toward the Privy Council and Peers, conciliatory; toward the Seiyūkai rank and file, arbitrary; and toward the opposition parties and the general public (except certain industrial and landed interests), unconcerned.[1]

The ends for which he played the game of politics can be seen in the four main emphases of his program: "the perfection of national defense, the expansion of education, the encouragement of industry, and the expansion of communications." This might be summed up as production-oriented; even his antagonism to labor unions was not simply a result of his zaibatsu ties, but also expressed his belief that they interfered with the development of the nation's economy.

But Hara was more than a detached political engineer who could make the system work. Whatever his personality and political ideals (and in these he was not so different from conservative Anglo-American politicians of his day), he was a product of party politics and the election system. He worked sedulously to promote the power of his party in government. He reduced the taxpayer's qualification for the vote from ten to three yen — the effects of this being greatest among the small landowners of rural Japan where Hara's Seiyūkai had its most important strength. He was successful in opening the bureaucracy, the Peers, and even the colonial bureaucracy to party adherents, appointing party politicians among the twenty-seven new prefectural governors that he named. He held that the civil administration of Japan's empire should not be subordinate to the military, and he opposed the presence of the Japanese army in Siberia. Within narrow limits he was able actually to exert stronger civil control over the navy: when Katō Tomosaburō, the navy

---

[1] Robert Scalapino, *Democracy and the Party Movement in Prewar Japan*, p. 212.

PARTIES AND PRIME MINISTERS, 1918–1932

Seiyūkai		*Kenseikai-Minseitō*
1918–21 Hara		
1921–22 Takahashi		
	[1922–24 The "transcendental" cabinets of Katō Tomosaburō, Yamamoto, and Kiyoura]	
		1924–26 Katō Kōmei
		1926–27 Wakatsuki
1927–29 Tanaka		
		1929–30 Hamaguchi
		1931 Wakatsuki
1931–32 Inukai		

minister, went to Washington in 1921, Hara though a civilian took over his post until his return. The army was forced to accept this, placated by a promise that even in the future no civilian control would be imposed on it. Here were the beginnings of tendencies that became clear only after 1924. Hara was assassinated by a rightist youth in 1921, and the years that followed showed that the principle of party government was still not firmly established. Takahashi, who became party president and then prime minister after Hara, was unpopular and unsuccessful in manipulating the other elites. After his resignation in June 1922, the Seiyūkai agreed to support Katō Tomosaburō, a non-party admiral, as a candidate for the premiership, rather than see power pass to Katō Kōmei, the president of the opposition party. The steps taken by the new prime minister included naval disarmament, the partial liquidation at the Washington Conference of 1922 of Japan's gains in World War I, a cut in the army, and administrative and financial retrenchment. All this was largely the program of the Seiyūkai.

Katō's successors, however, were increasingly bureaucratic and less responsive to the demands of the parties, and this was the basic reason for their lack of success. The "earthquake cabinet" of Yamamoto was formed the day after the great Tōkyō quake of September 1, 1923, in which 132,807 persons died and 576,262 homes were destroyed. Against a background of material destruction, martial law, mob and police violence against Koreans and leftists (common objects of public prejudice), the cabinet bent all its efforts to restore order and services in the capital area. Yet only four months after the Yamamoto cabinet was formed it assumed "responsibility" for an attempted attack on the prince regent (who became emperor in 1926) and resigned. The Kiyoura cabinet which followed (January-June 1924) was viewed with particular hostility by the parties (except for one segment of the Seiyūkai, which split in two at this time). In fact, the two major parties united to form the Second Movement for the Protection of the Constitution. As in 1913 the newspapers supported the constitutional movement, and this time its popular base was broader, since labor unions and other elements of the democratic coalition discussed earlier gave it some support. The Diet was dissolved and an election called in which the government used all its resources to defeat the parties in the movement, but the opposition parties won a huge majority anyway, forcing Kiyoura to resign.

Katō and Party Government, 1924–26. Kiyoura was followed as prime minister by Katō Kōmei at the head of a victorious three-party coalition cabinet. With this administration the principle of government by party politicians at last seemed firmly established. It was not party government in the British sense of the term, since the majority party in the Diet did not automatically have the right to form the cabinet. At times the premiership was given to the head of the minority party, who then went out and got his majority in an election. But government was by party leaders, and majority support in the Diet was recognized as necessary for rule.

Since the administration of Katō was the high-water mark of parliamentary government in prewar Japan, it is well to define clearly both its achievements and its limitations. We will examine first the party, then the man, and finally the program carried out between 1924 and 1926.

Katō's party, the Kenseikai, was in 1924 professedly more democratic than its opposition. It had been out of power since 1916, and the attachment of Japanese parties to parliamentary ideals was always greater when out of power and separated from the necessity (and rewards) of compromise. The Kenseikai, moreover, had been out of power during the burst of democratic sentiment after World War I and had absorbed a considerable amount of it, as symbolized by its leadership of the movement for universal suffrage after 1920. In some small measure the greater democracy of the Kenseikai, compared with the Seiyūkai, may have been compositional: it had a few more intellectuals and ex-officials from the relatively "liberal" Finance and Foreign Ministries; it was also slightly more oriented to urban centers, so that its policies tended to stress the general interests of groups in the more open sectors of Japanese society. Yet after its return to power, the need to compromise with other elites led the Kenseikai to ally itself with one of the most backward factions in the House of Peers, and the need for a Diet majority led it to take into its ranks, when in June 1927 it changed its name to Minseitō, that segment of the Seiyūkai which had supported the reactionary government of Kiyoura. Thus it lost much of its reformist zeal.

Katō Kōmei has been aptly described by one student as the very model of a modern Meiji bureaucrat. Born in 1860, he got his start (like his successors in the Minseitō, Wakatsuki and Hamaguchi) as a graduate of Tōkyō University. He entered Mitsubishi at twenty-one, married the daughter of Iwasaki, spent some time in England, entered the Foreign Ministry (unlike Wakatsuki and Hamaguchi, who rose in the Ministry of Finance), and at the age of forty became foreign minister. Like Hara he was a man of parts, becoming in rapid succession a Diet member, the president of a large newspaper, several times foreign minister, ambassador to England, and from the time of its formation the president of the Kenseikai. His last cabinet office prior to 1924 was as foreign minister in Ōkuma's cabinet at the time of the Twenty-One Demands on China. As a man Katō was blunt, pure, cold, haughty, and respected if not popular. He has been called an "enlightened conservative," a term that might be applied to his government as well. An Anglophile, he both understood and staunchly supported constitutional government.

The accomplishments of the Katō cabinet were considerable, yet each seems to have had a darker as well as a brighter side. One major achievement was the passage of a universal manhood suffrage bill in 1925. With this the electorate increased from three to more than twelve million. When one considers that the national electoral system had begun only in 1890, this was an amazingly rapid advance. Yet earlier in the same year Katō agreed to pass a strengthened antisubversive measure, the so-called Peace Preservation Law, which prohibited the formation of groups that advocated a change in the Japanese "national polity" (*kokutai*) or the abolition of private property. Penalties up to ten years in prison were provided for membership in such a group; these terms were made even more harsh in 1928 for use against the Japanese Communist Party. The conjunction of this law with the suffrage act indicated a willingness to recognize the political potential of everyman, but a conservative desire to limit the range of political alternatives to which he would be exposed. Also involved in the bargaining for this bill was the restoration of diplomatic relations with the Soviet Union, which Shidehara pushed through (eight years before a similar action by the United States) in spite of Privy Council opposition.

A second accomplishment of the Katō ministry was a program of social legislation favorable to labor. Article 17 of the Public Peace Police Law, which had been used against unions, was abolished. A Factory Law, a National Health Insurance Law, and a Labor Disputes Mediation Law were enacted. These, together with the suffrage bill, in effect legalized union support for the nonrevolutionary socialist movement that was rising at this time. Against the revolutionary left, against those who advocated the overthrow of the emperor, the Katō cabinet was draconian; but toward those who were willing to work within a parliamentary framework, Katō was permissive, since the threat they represented was small.

A third reform dealt with the Peers. This body, heavy with the post-

The Criteria of Eligibility	Election Year	Size of Electorate	Total Population
1889: male subjects 25 and over, paying 15 yen or more in taxes	1890	453,474	40,072,000
1900: male subjects 25 and over, paying 10 yen or more in taxes	1902	983,193	45,227,000
1919: male subjects 25 or over, paying 3 yen or more in taxes	1920	3,069,787	55,963,000
1925: all male subjects 25 and over	1928	12,409,078	63,863,000
1947: all citizens 20 and over	1949	42,105,300	78,100,000

1885 nobility, was a thorn in the side of party government, often blocking bills passed by the lower house. Katō originally had wanted to change the constitution so as to curtail the functions of the Peers. This proved impossible, but he was able to change the Peers' composition, limiting the number of members from the nobility and increasing the number of imperial appointees, who were usually men of legal, academic, or other achievement.

The best illustration of the balance existing between the parties and the other elites at this time is the case of the army. In this era of "Shidehara diplomacy," of international trade and world prosperity, of party ascendancy, the services were unquestionably losing ground. Army prestige was so low that off-duty officers took to wearing civilian clothes. In this atmosphere, as a part of a broader retrenchment program that cut the civil bureaucracy by 20,000 men, Army Minister Ugaki agreed to cut four divisions out of the army. Bitter army protest was of no avail. And total military expenses, which had comprised 42 per cent of the national budget in 1922, were pared to 29 per cent in 1925 and 28 per cent in 1927. Yet the army was not out of the picture. Some of the money saved by reducing its size went into a sorely needed program to mechanize and modernize it. At the same time, military training was injected into the middle and higher schools, and local military training units were set up for youths who did not continue their education. Many officers of the four eliminated divisions became instructors under this program. Even at the height of party power in December 1925, General Ugaki could write in his diary:

More than 200,000 troops in active service, more than 3,000,000 in the veterans organization, 500,000 or 600,000 middle and higher school students, and more than 800,000 trainees in local units: all of these will be controlled by the army, and their power will work as the central force aiding the Emperor in war and peace alike. The right of autonomous command over the Emperor's army is, in a time of emergency, not limited to the command of troops, but contains the authority to control the people.

The Twilight Years of Party Government, 1927–31. The powers of the parties from 1927 to the Manchurian Incident of 1931 remained basically unchanged. Yet the parties were increasingly buffeted and on the defensive. The Seiyūkai returned to power in 1927, its fortunes revived by the popular Tanaka, who had become its president in 1925. Tanaka was born in Chōshū in 1863. Entering the army, he rose to become army minister in the Hara cabinet in 1918. His association with party politicians was so close that some generals viewed him with distrust, feeling that his ambition might work against the best interests of the army. Like Terauchi, or even Katsura, Tanaka was a transitional figure: less powerful than the oligarchs and more inclined to favor party government, but broader in outlook and more astute than the more narrowly professional generals of the 1930's. As prime minister, Tanaka spoke of a "positive foreign policy," of strengthening Japan's position in Manchuria, and of taking a tougher attitude toward the Chinese. In fact, however, Japan's relations with China remained by and large in the same hands as under Shidehara; but Tanaka's bellicose tones provoked an anti-Japanese reaction in China. This boomeranged on the Tanaka cabinet when in 1928 officers of the Japanese Kwantung Army in Manchuria assassinated Chang Tso-lin, Japan's client warlord in the area, in the hope that his son would be less nationalistic and more compliant with Japanese suggestions. Tanaka, with imperial approval, moved to punish those responsible. The army leaders, however, refused on the grounds that such action would damage the prestige of the entire army. Unable to force the army to comply, Tanaka's cabinet fell.

The return of the Minseitō to power in 1929 (the cabinets of Hamaguchi and Wakatsuki with Shidehara as foreign minister in both) was a return to a more committed constitutional government. At the time of the London Naval Conference of 1930, Premier Hamaguchi went beyond either Hara or Katō in his determination to enforce his will upon the services. Basing his policy on friendship with Britain and the United States, he compelled the navy to accept a limitation on cruisers that even American naval experts (in private) agreed was unfavorable to Japan. This led subsequently to the weakening of the moderate admirals who had cooperated with him. Yet Hamaguchi, until shot by a rightist "patriot" in November 1930, was able to withstand the criticism both of the Navy General Staff, which declared that he had infringed on its right of supreme command, and of the Privy Council, the Peers, and the Seiyūkai, which joined to attack the concessions he had made to Japan's naval rivals at the London Naval Conference.

In addition to the furor over the cruiser ratio, the political mudslinging at times, as in the elections of 1928 and 1930, was such that it almost seemed as if the two major parties themselves were intent on hastening the downfall of party government. The Minseitō called the government of the Seiyūkai between 1927 and 1929 a "Mitsui cabinet," since the bank crisis of 1927 had been settled on terms highly favorable to the Mitsui. In reply, in 1930 the Seiyūkai called the government of Hamaguchi a "Mitsubishi cabinet." Whether the Japanese politicians of this period were in fact more venal than those in the West can be questioned. But the sources of their campaign funds were more obvious, and infractions of the election laws were legion. Furthermore, there was probably a higher level of ethical expectation regarding government morality (deriving from the same Confucian assumptions that lay behind Yamagata's belief that government should be above parties and other private interest groups). Corruption, magnified by suffering due to the depression and by the Marxist critique that held it to be inevitable in a capitalist society, thus attracted much attention, and faith in party government weakened. For all of the strength earlier displayed by party leaders, when the Manchurian Incident occurred in 1931 they proved helpless.

Reviewing the political history of 1918–31, we see first that it occurred within the post-1890 structure of constitutional, multiple elites. The power balance within this structure altered in favor of the parties, the economy diversified, mass media appeared, and society became somewhat more open; yet the total impact of these changes did not produce a breakthrough to a new political structure. At the local level, even the enactment of universal manhood suffrage did not disrupt the balance of power within the rural community. The newly enfranchised were accommodated within the existing political scheme. The intermediate institutions — prefectural political organizations, veterans' associations, temple and shrine organizations, business groups, the police, the bureaucracy, and the system of education — that served as the transmission belt between village and nation also remained firm. And within the central government there occurred no redefinition of the legal powers of the different elites.

It is possible to place the responsibility for this lack of progress on the parties themselves and on the party leaders who came to the parties only after serving long apprenticeships in the other, more conservative elites. But it is also possible to say that the parties were about as liberal as they could have been at the time if they were to cooperate effectively with the other elites. The two major parties were both conservative, and they were alike in most respects; the choice between them was rarely such as to inspire a voter with democratic fervor. But it seems likely that the essential similarity of the parties was the precondition for the small gains that were made; the slight differences between them at any one time — such as the Kenseikai stress on universal manhood suffrage before 1924 — represented the area open for parliamentary advance. Had one party been significantly more advanced than the other, significantly more democratic in character, then the government might have feared the consequences of the alternation of power by party leaders, and a stable alliance might have emerged between the more conservative of the parties and the other government elites. Had this occurred, as it did in Germany in the period before World War I, then the shifts back and forth between parties would have been precluded, and progress made more difficult.

Comparative history is still in its infancy, but a contrast between Japan during these years and pre-Weimar Germany with its comparable government of plural elites seems to offer, at the least, a relief from the perspective that comes from interpreting Japanese government in terms of the Anglo-American democracies. Both Japan and Germany were late developers and both had semi-feudal survivals, such as the power of the family head. Both had imperial constitutions, Prussian in origin, that limited the powers of the legislature. Both were run by academic, elitest bureaucracies, and the services in both were directly under the monarchy. One significant difference between them was that Japan's society was much more homogeneous: there were no politically significant religious splits, no Junker class with its own party, and no powerful socialist party with widespread political support. Rather, the pace of evolutionary change was so even that both major parties represented, by and large, the same social groups — rural landlords, "men of influence" in the rural political structure, and urban industrial interests. A comparison with the underdeveloped parliamentary state of Germany before World War I also suggests a higher evaluation of Japan's gains under the Meiji constitution — especially when one considers that Japan not only had to build its parliamentary organization, but also to implant the very vocabulary necessary for its articulation. Yet considerable as these gains were, they were not sufficient to cope with the challenges of the 1930's.

THE RISE OF MILITARISM IN THE 1930'S

Within Japan's multi-elite structure of government, as we have seen, the political parties steadily gained in power from 1890 to the late 1920's. The early gains were made in a government in which oligarchs coordinated the functions of the different elites. After the "Taishō Crisis" of 1913, gains were made more and more in direct competition with other elites, without coordination from above. Particularly during the 1920's, so great were party gains that Japan almost appeared to be moving toward full party government, and Katō Kōmei could maintain that party cabinets were an unwritten principle of the constitution. In the 1930's this trend ended. There was no reversion to the pre-1913 pattern of oligarchic control; nor was there a revolutionary destruction of the post-1890 structure of government. Rather, what occurred was a small shift in the balance between the elites, the advantage passing from the parties to the services and the higher ranks of the bureaucracy. This small shift produced an enormous change in political climate and policy, setting Japan upon the course that led to disaster in World War II. By the late 1930's a new type of leader had emerged, and the powers that the parties had wielded ten years earlier appeared in retrospect almost apparitional.

The causes behind this shift away from party cabinets were many. First, new forces from outside were impinging on Japan: the world depression that exacerbated tensions within Japanese society, the rise of militant Chinese nationalism that threatened Japan's colonial interests in Manchuria, and the rise of undemocratic states in Europe as examples for a Japan always sensitive to European trends. Second, there were the internal responses to these external factors: independent action by the army in 1931 that reduced Manchuria to a military colony and exposed the impotence of civil government to control the services, the application of terror to the "establishment" by the revolutionary right between 1932 and 1936, and the war in China after 1937.

Third, in explaining the tendencies of the 1930's, it must be kept in mind that both Japan's responses to external forces and the reverberations of these responses on its political life were mediated by the society and culture which we examined earlier. Modern society has both democratic and totalitarian potentials. Industrialization, universal education, the nationalism that enables a government to tap the political energies of the masses, modern communications and transport, can all be used either to create new freedoms or to suppress all human rights. Both Nazi Germany and the Soviet Union of Stalin exemplify the totalitarian side of modern, or modernizing, societies. Japan by the 1930's was modern in many respects, and its shift away from parliamentary government had many points of similarity with, say, what occurred in Germany. Yet, fundamentally, what happened was different, for though the first buds of the mass society that would bloom in the 1960's were visible, Japan was not yet sufficiently free of traditional values to follow the European pattern of fascism. What developed in Japan was not a purely modern totalitarianism but rather a militarism that in its early phase was spurred on by would-be fascist-type groups, and in its later phase mobilized Japan for war by applying modern controls where they would work and using "organic" social groupings where they would not.

CABINETS 1929-1945

Party Cabinets	Hamaguchi	July 1929–April 1931	(Minseitō)
	Wakatsuki	April–Dec. 1931	(Minseitō)
	Inukai	Dec. 1931–May 1932	(Seiyūkai)
Moderate	Saitō	May 1932–July 1934	
Admirals	Okada	July 1934–Mar. 1936	
Growing	Hirota	March 1936–Feb. 1937	
Militarism	Hayashi	Feb.–June 1937	
China War	Konoe	June 1937–Jan. 1939	
	Hiranuma	Jan.–Aug. 1939	
Diplomatic	Abe	Aug. 1939–Jan. 1940	
Pause	Yonai	Jan.–July 1940	
Axis Pact	Konoe	July 1940–July 1941	
	Konoe	July 1941–Oct. 1941	
World War II	Tōjō	Oct. 1941–July 1944	
Ending the War	Koiso	July 1944–April 1945	
	Suzuki	April–Aug. 1945	

Party Cabinets and the Depression. The decline of the political parties began in 1927. In that year ex-General Tanaka, who was less of a constitutionalist than his predecessors, became prime minister. The domestic depression of 1926 led to the bank crisis of 1927 in which a great number of weak and overextended banks were wiped out. Further tensions were aroused by the assassination of Chang Tso-lin in 1928 and the storm of protest that followed Japan's concessions at the London Naval Disarmament Conference in 1930. And minor crises were finally followed by a major catastrophe when the world depression hit Japan early in 1930.

That the depression had the effect it did was in part bad luck. Japan's economic growth had lagged during the 1920's. After the inflationary policies of Tanaka, taken to counter the economic crisis of 1927, Prime Minister Hamaguchi of the Minseitō was determined to effect a stern cure for Japan's economic doldrums by a policy of government retrenchment, a return to the gold standard that had been abandoned in 1917, and the promotion of mechanization and rationalization in industry. Certainly the latter measures were needed if Japan were to compete with other industrial nations, and even the fiscal aspects of the Hamaguchi program, though harsh, might have been effective at another time. As it was, the deflationary effects of these measures were joined with the deflationary impact of the world depression, worsening its initial social impact.

The value of Japanese exports dropped 50 per cent from 1929 to 1931. Workers' real incomes dropped, from an index of 100 in 1926, to 81 in 1930, to 69 in 1931. Unemployment rose to about 3 million, with much of the burden falling on farm families. Rural Japan bore the brunt of the depression suffering: between September 1929 and September 1930 the price of silk cocoons fell 65 per cent. In 1930 the "bumper crop famine" occurred. On October 2 a crop 12 per cent greater than that of the previous years was predicted; by the following day the price per unit (5 bushels) of rice had fallen to 16 yen, although the cost of production was 17 yen per unit. By October 10 the price had fallen to about 10 yen. In 1931 the evil of too much was followed by the greater evil of too little: an unprecedented crop failure occurred in northeastern Japan and Hokkaidō. Images of the depression in Japan were formed by this event: children begging for food outside the dining cars of trains, starving peasants stripping off the tender inner bark of pine trees or digging for the roots of wild plants, the agents for city brothels bargaining with farmers who had nothing left to sell but their daughters. Between 1926 and 1931, rural cash incomes fell from an index of 100 to 33, and by 1934 were back only to 44. Because of lower prices, the peasants' real incomes, never high, were now down about one-third. The conditions of tenants and poorer farmers, at near-subsistence levels even in good times, were far worse than statistical averages would suggest.

The blame for the depression fell on the political parties. This was not merely because the party leaders were in power when the depression took place. Rather, in the public mind, the parties were intimately associated with the zaibatsu, the bureaucracy, the landlords, and the urban white-collar class. All the groups of this "parliamentary coalition," with the possible exception of the landlords, had a common vision of economic advance and growth by participation in the international, multilateral economic order that paralleled the comity of democratic nations represented by various international conferences and the League of Nations. This was the 1920 outgrowth of the Meiji vision of limited democracy and paternalistic capitalism at home working in cooperation with the great powers abroad. The depression called into question the validity of the international economic order; this in turn cast doubts on the worth of the comity of democratic nations and Japan's constitutional order at home.

The economic question was whether Japan could afford to depend on the world economy in view of rising tariff barriers, protests against the flood of cheap Japanese exports, and the problem of finding adequate raw materials and markets. The political question was posed by the emergence of Fascism in Italy, the rise of Naziism in Germany, and their attack on democracy as weak and ineffective. These developments revived the unsolved question of the Meiji constitution: Who would rule in Japan — who best represented the will of the emperor and the interests of the people? Was it the party politicians, influenced by the zaibatsu and working with the complacent bureaucracy, under whose government the farmers had suffered so much? Or was the emperor's army, which had preserved untarnished the earlier emphasis on loyalty and duty, best fitted to rule? Those who advocated a greater role for the army at home also argued that military expansion abroad could create an autonomous economic empire within which Japan could be insulated from the vagaries of the world economy — a controlled imperial economy within which the livelihood of farmer and worker would be guaranteed.

Party government acted effectively, if late, to counter the depression. Inukai of the Seiyūkai, who became prime minister in December 1931, reversed the decision of his Minseitō predecessors and took Japan off the gold standard. This produced the boom in exports and production that made Japan the first of the world's industrial nations to recover. (It also brought millions of yen of profits to speculators, especially to the Mitsui, who had bought American dollars in the expectation of such a move. This led to fresh cries of corruption from the opposition.) By 1936 domestic consumption was up 20 per cent. Some of this was taken up by a 7 per cent rise in population to 70 million, but a rise greater than 10 per cent in real incomes occurred for the nation as a whole. This was not evenly distributed. The salaried classes benefited the most. But unemployment dropped, and the real wages of workers rose from an index figure of 155 for 1925–29 to 174 for 1930–34 (and then declined to 166 for 1935–39 as a moderate inflation set in). Rural incomes recovered somewhat, but because the debts incurred since 1929 made even heavier the earlier burden of taxes and rents, few gains were made. The main political consequences of the rising incomes in the mid-thirties was a weakening of sympathies for the radical right. Yet, though the radical right declined, the recovery came too late to benefit the parties. Other trends had begun in the meantime that proved irreversible.

The Army in Politics: The Manchurian Incident. Even more injurious to constitutional government than the depression was the Manchurian Incident of September 1931. Independent action by the army in defiance of the government gave rise to what is often called dual diplomacy: the usurpation of foreign policy formation by the army in the name of its right of autonomous command. In almost every case such independent actions were recognized by the government after the fact, since not to do so was to admit both at home and abroad that the civil government was unable to control the military.

From the point of view of the army, 1931 was not a break with the past but rather a response, to a new challenge, in terms of a potential that the army had maintained all along. Ever since the decline of the oligarchy, the army had had the capacity for independent action. This was guaranteed by the position of the General Staff directly under the emperor and the position of the army minister under the emperor as well as the prime minister. The use of this autonomy was not new in 1931. In the budget struggle of 1912, Army Minister Uehara had toppled the cabinet of Saionji, thus precipitating the "Taishō Political Crisis." The army had also used its powers to prolong the Siberian Expedition in the early 1920's, and to fight for military appropriations at other times. And at a different level, examples also can be found of independent actions by field-grade officers that, when successful, tended to commit the army as a whole to some policy that it might not otherwise have chosen. In this category fall an abortive "Mongolian-Manchurian Independence Movement" planned by officers of the Japanese Kwantung Army in Manchuria with General Staff support in 1915–16 and plots hatched between Japanese colonels and White Russian officers during the Siberian Expedition. On the whole, however, a decline in the army relative to the other elites, combined with moderate leadership by a transitional generation of generals willing to cooperate with the parties, kept the army somewhat free from politics until the late twenties. Then, a new generation of narrower, more professional generals began to appear just as the political parties began to move away from Japan's earlier, expansionist, military policies. This set the stage for a clash over policy that was triggered by other forces in 1931.

The attachment of the army and of Japan as a whole to Manchuria was of long standing. In popular sentiment Manchuria was viewed as a recompense for the 100,000 Japanese lives lost in the Russo-Japanese War. Militarily, the army had seen Manchuria since 1905 as a buffer against Russian power in the north. Military considerations were strengthened after 1918 by a policy of ideological containment of Communism. Of foreign investment in Manchuria, 75 per cent was Japanese; particularly important was the South Manchurian Railway Company. There were a million Japanese subjects in Manchuria, mostly Korean, and 40 per cent of Japan's China trade was with this area. Arguments in favor of the expansion of this economic position had been powerfully bolstered by the depression.

In spite of these various interests Japan was not originally determined to reduce Manchuria to a colony. It was content to maintain a façade of Chinese sovereignty under a semi-puppet warlord, a balance possible only because of Chinese disunity. By the late 1920's this balance had been upset by the Kuomintang's unification of China and the rise of Chinese nationalism that changed the character of politics in Manchuria itself. Faced with this new situation, no important group in Japan considered withdrawing. Japan's liberal leaders, Wakatsuki and Shidehara, argued for peaceful diplomacy and international trade but also for the *status quo*. A do-nothing policy was also favored by Saionji, who was undoubtedly behind the emperor's communication to General Minami on Septem-

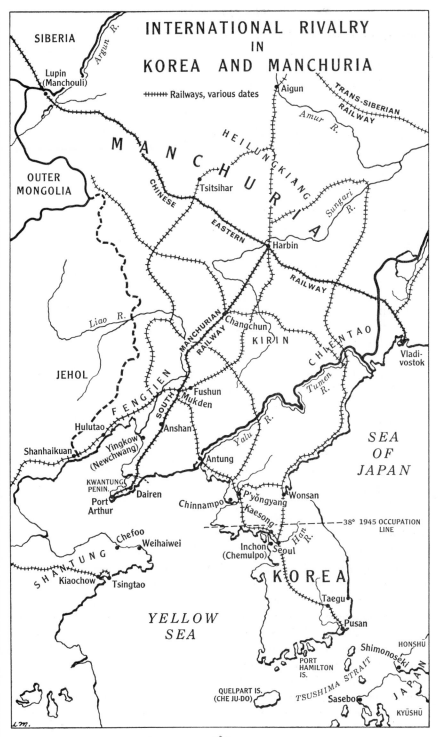

INTERNATIONAL RIVALRY
IN
KOREA AND MANCHURIA

++++++ Railways, various dates

SIBERIA

Lupin
(Manchouli)

Argun R.

Aigun

TRANS-SIBERIAN
RAILWAY

Amur R.

HEILUNGKIANG

M A N C H U R I A

OUTER
MONGOLIA

CHINESE

Tsitsihar

EASTERN

Harbin

Sungari R.

RAILWAY

Liao R.

Changchun

K I R I N

C H I E N T A O

Vladi-
vostok

JEHOL

MANCHURIAN RAILWAY

SOUTH

FENGTIEN

Fushun
Mukden

Tumen R.

Anshan

Yalu R.

SEA
OF
JAPAN

Hulutao

Shanhaikuan

Yingkow
(Newchwang)

Antung

KWANTUNG
PENIN.

Dairen

Port
Arthur

Chinnampo

P'yŏngyang

Wonsan

Kaesong

— 38° 1945 OCCUPATION
LINE

Chefoo

Weihaiwei

Inchon
(Chemulpo)

Han R.

Seoul

S H A N T U N G

Kiaochow

Tsingtao

K O R E A

Taegu

YELLOW
SEA

Pusan

HONSHŪ

Shimonoseki

PORT
HAMILTON
IS.

TSUSHIMA STRAIT

J A P A N

QUELPART IS.
(CHE JU-DO)

Sasebo

KYŪSHŪ

L.m.

ber 11, 1931, asking the army to be careful in Manchuria. Yet the *status quo* was crumbling; action was necessary if Japan's political position in Manchuria were to be maintained. Even many in the parties recognized this, and all groups in the army favored some kind of action. In August 1931, Minami, the most powerful of the moderate generals, drew up a plan. While predicated on cooperation with the Foreign Office, it aimed at the formation of a "fundamental policy for Manchuria" to obtain practical results by the spring of 1932. A second group, the army's China experts, under General Tatekawa, favored direct action by the army, as did many other groups of field-grade officers both in Tōkyō and within the Kwantung Army.

Internationally, the situation in East Asia was defined in terms of a number of multilateral international agreements (Washington Conference treaties, Kellogg-Briand Pact, London Disarmament treaty) which promised peace but contained no apparatus for the enforcement of collective security. Replacing the bilateral pacts defining spheres of imperialist interests, these provided during the 1920's the international atmosphere that contributed to the rise of "Shidehara diplomacy." In the 1930's the fact that these agreements were merely expressions of sentiment enabled Japan to act aggressively without the expectation of international sanctions.

The actual incident which led to the Japanese take-over of Manchuria has often been described as a coup carried out by junior officers without the knowledge of their superiors. This is not strictly true. The architects of the plot were field-grade officers, Colonel Itagaki and Lieutenant-Colonel Ishiwara of the Kwantung Army. Late in August 1931, Ishiwara told General Tatekawa of the General Staff and others of his plan to provoke an incident that would lead to Japanese military control of Manchuria. No one objected. He also told General Honjō, the commanding general of the Kwantung Army, who is said to have replied that he would take "immediate action" in case of a crisis. When the chief of staff of the Kwantung Army heard of the plot he asked the army in Tōkyō to send someone to inform the Kwantung Army of Tōkyō's policy. Tatekawa was sent, but before leaving dispatched a cable to the plotters, who stepped up their plans. Tatekawa arrived in Manchuria on the evening of September 18 and went straight to a geisha house; his message, whatever it may have been, went undelivered. On the same night a bomb exploded on the tracks of the Japanese railway north of Mukden. Colonel Itagaki ordered a full-scale attack against the Chinese troops in Mukden, bombs were thrown in other areas as well, and General Honjō, hearing of the crisis, took responsibility for calling out the Kwantung Army. Once action had begun, no one in the army was willing to consider a return to the earlier situation.

The effects on the Japanese government of the army's aggression in Manchuria were disastrous. On the day after the fighting began the Wakatsuki cabinet decided on a policy of "nonexpansion of hostilities." But on September 21 the Japanese army began to advance into areas beyond the South Manchurian Railway zone. On September 24 the Japanese government announced that "the action of the Japanese army was taken in self-defense and hence unavoidable"; but that "the army was already returning to the railway zone." Actually the army continued to advance, attacking the capital city of Chang Hsüeh-liang on October 8. The Japanese government was unable to stop the aggression. After each army advance it was forced to eat its words, and little by little it became an apologist for the deeds of the military. By early 1932 the conquest was completed. Japan recognized Manchuria (called "Manchukuo") as an independent state under the last Ch'ing ruler, Pu-yi, in September 1932. The Lytton Commission of the League of Nations visited Manchuria in the spring months of 1932, and its report issued in the fall condemned Japan as an aggressor. The report was adopted by the League of Nations, from which Japan accordingly withdrew in March of the following year. By this time the Japanese armies had already moved south from Manchuria to occupy about 5000 square miles of the province of Jehol.

One reason why the Wakatsuki cabinet was unable to take effective action was that the cabinet itself was split. Several ministers supported the action of the Kwantung Army, most disapproved silently, only two were openly critical. Divided, the cabinet vacillated for several months and resigned in December. The next cabinet was formed by Inukai Tsuyoshi, the president of the Seiyūkai and the last party prime minister in prewar Japan. Like its opposition, the Seiyūkai was not united on policy. One faction favored military expansion — reflecting the "positive foreign policy" that had for years been a slogan of the party. The majority however, including the prime minister, opposed the action of the army. Long a fighter for party rule, Inukai was particularly opposed to the army's usurpation of the decision-making functions of the cabinet. He therefore attempted to negotiate directly with the Chinese, sending a personal representative to Nanking to talk with Chiang Kai-shek and other Chinese leaders. It appears, on the evidence of his son, that Inukai also sought, unsuccessfully, to obtain an imperial rescript to restrain the army in Manchuria. But such moves were without effect. Inukai and others of his government were assassinated by ultranationalists on May 15, 1932.

At this point the parties became the victims of the methods which they had used so successfully for four decades. They had risen to power by manipulating other elites and by compromise. Faced with the military coup of 1932, compromise could lead only to regress. They needed strong leaders who could dig in their heels and fight. But none was forthcoming. Had Saionji been a stronger person, had he spoken resolutely against the army in the name of the emperor, it is barely possible that the "parliamentary coalition" might have rallied to some degree. The whole rationale of the army's defiance of the cabinet was based on the fiction that the army acted on the direct orders of the emperor. But Saionji saw as his first duty the protection of the emperor from involvement in political controversy; this took precedence over his far weaker concern for parliamentary government.

The year 1932 was the pit of the depression, the peak of agitation by the revolutionary right. Stirred by the conquest of Manchuria, by the fighting between Japanese and Chinese forces that had broken out in Shanghai in January and February, and by the "patriotic assassinations" of liberal and conservative figures, many in Japan hoped that an army general would be chosen prime minister. In this situation the most that Saionji could do was to appoint as prime minister Saitō Makoto (1862–1952), a moderate admiral, in the hope of reconciling the opposing forces of the parties and services. Had the president of the Seiyūkai been named to the premiership, the services might have refused to furnish ministers and thus blocked the formation of the cabinet. As military men, both Saitō (prime minister May 1932-July 1934), and his successor Admiral Okada (prime minister July 1934-March 1936), were not unacceptable to the army in spite of their moderate character. Saitō's cabinet "of national unity" was made up both of ex-bureaucrats and of politicians appointed from both parties. Split into factions and jealous of each other, the parties were willing to accept their reduction to a ministerial role in government. The parties continued a vigorous criticism of the military from the floor of the Diet, but, in general, the four years of the Saitō and Okada cabinets saw a steady drift away from the policies of the 1920's.

The Rise and Fall of the Revolutionary Right, 1932–36. The most significant movement during the four years of government by the two moderate admirals was the emergence of patriotic societies which espoused a wide range of ultranationalist doctrines. Some of these groups were formed by civilians, some by military men. They represented only a tiny fraction of Japan's total population. Yet, judging by the consequences of their actions, they were undoubtedly the most effective pressure groups of the 1930's. They drove the conservative center of the government away from the ideas of Minobe into a more jingoistic, nationalistic, emperor-centered position. Indirectly they brought about an increase in the persecution of leftist and liberal groups. By the time they themselves were suppressed in 1936, the relative intellectual openness that had characterized the late 1920's had disappeared.

The first component in the ultranationalist movement were the civilian patriotic societies. Usually these were composed, in a traditional fashion, of a leader and his followers. On occasion a somewhat larger association was formed, and several times such larger groups tried to organize political parties. Such associations, however, were highly schismatic. They usually dissolved into their component factions very rapidly, and the parties they formed were never successful at the polls. Though these organizations had first formed in the years after the Satsuma Rebellion, they were few until the mid-1920's. They then began to proliferate and became extremely numerous during the 1930's and 1940's. Charts drawn by Japanese scholars to show the lineages and interrelationships of these groups look like the wiring diagrams for electronic computers.

Ideologically, all had in common a concern for the "national polity," and within it, the emperor, the subject's duties to the state, social harmony, and other unique Japanese virtues. All had a keen sense of Japan's mission or destiny. Virtually all favored pan-Asianism and the exclusion of the West from continental Asia, and opposed internationalism. Most members of these groups saw themselves as in the *shishi* tradition of the political activists who helped bring about the Meiji Restoration. Like the *shishi*, they directed their attacks against the "traitors at the side of the emperor." They called for a "Shōwa Restoration" (after the reign name of the emperor who succeeded Taishō in 1926). At the trials after the political murders of the 1930's, the assassins defended their actions as having been "purely motivated." That such actions were purely destructive was of no account; they believed that others — from the army — would emerge to govern when the evil politicians were swept away. Combined with these basic ideas were a variety of others. Kita Ikki, one of the few thinkers in Japan that can with any accuracy be labeled "fascist," formulated a radical national socialism combining Marx with elements of traditional nationalism. Other thinkers combined with the purity of direct action either Taoist Know-Nothingism or Buddhist ideas regarding the unique spirituality of the East, or the Confucian emphasis on the farmer as the base of the country. Just as the small, independent farmer is politically important in the United States as the possessor of virtues akin to those of the founders of the American tradition, so in Japan the rural community was seen as the repository of traditional Japanese virtues. The greatest weakness or contradiction in the doctrines of these rightist groups was that the emperor-centered nationalism which they proclaimed was accepted in one vague form or another by almost everyone in Japan. They therefore had little new to offer except a radical attack on the government, which was inescapably the imperial government ordained by the imperial Meiji constitution.

This movement was not scholarly. It lacked systematic thinkers. Its combination of traditional values and populist radicalism was expressed in thought as amorphous as that of the conservative orthodoxy discussed earlier. Its recourse to "direct action" was parallel to samurai assassinations of foreigners in the last years of the Tokugawa era. In fact the patriots of the earliest ultranationalistic societies were ex-samurai from Fukuoka, men who had lost out in the Meiji Restoration. The samurai as a class disappeared, but even in the 1920's these organizations continued to represent social strata that were traditional but unsuccessful. From these strata they drew upon active and able young men who had been denied, or were unable to adapt to, the normal academic channels for advancement. Like European rightists they reacted against those in power: they felt that they had suffered at the expense of the academically successful, Western-oriented elites which had garnered the honors and fruits of Japan's modernization. They were opposed to the zaibatsu, the bureaucracy, and the political parties, which epitomized in their eyes all that was selfish and vile. A few even included in their attack the higher echelons of the army which they rightly saw as a part of the establishment. Like populist patriots in Europe they were in reaction against the modern world: the Japanese right saw the culture of Tōkyō's Ginza as Hitler saw that of Berlin — as antipathetic to the honest, good, true character of the nation. Like their European counterparts they disliked freedom. But they differ in one important respect. The revolutionary right in Europe has been described as seeking an "escape from freedom," as having been forced to become individuals without having been given the values and upbringing that make social individuation tolerable. But in Japan it was not so directly threatened. Freedom was an external enemy, visible in the cities or in foreign culture. Usually the rightists came from strata that were fairly well integrated but depressed, from among small businessmen, farmers, contractors, or lower officers in the army. They acted out of frustration, seeking redress for their social group.

The second component in the revolutionary rightist movement of the 1930's was the army. Professionally modern, the army was, in its spiritual culture, a stronghold of orthodox values. The officer corps, educated in army schools after graduation from middle school, constituted a society within a society. Close to the rural scene from which the army obtained most of its recruits and sympathetic to the suffering of the farmer, many in the army were early susceptible to the radical ideas of civilian thinkers. These ideas reinforced tensions within the army which antedated the depression and the rise of Chinese nationalism.

One area of tension within the army since Meiji times had been its domination by officers from Yamaguchi prefecture, the former Chōshū *han*. By 1912 the Chōshū monopoly of the highest ranks had been broken, and by 1922 some top General Staff and Army Ministry posts went to men from other areas. Yet the lineage of Chōshū generals that can be traced from Ōmura to Yamagata, Katsura, Terauchi, and Tanaka continued to dominate the "heights" of the army until 1924. At this point it became necessary to appoint Ugaki Kazushige, a general born in Okayama, as army minister. This signaled the end of the Chōshū faction as a geographically based group. Yet the lineage in some sense maintained its identity as the group of officers exercising top leadership of the army under Ugaki. Associated in this faction during the 1920's and 1930's with General Ugaki was Nagata Tetsuzan. Like Ugaki, Nagata had studied in Germany after graduation from the Army War College; like Ugaki, Nagata favored a policy of greater mechanization for the army. The early monopoly of power by a single geographically determined clique called into existence an anti-Chōshū clique of generals centering on Uehara, Araki, Mazaki, Yanagawa, and others, who resented their exclusion from the army's centers of power. Even after the Chōshū clique had turned into the Ugaki clique, this faction remained united as an opposition, barred from the top positions. Once in 1924 and again in 1930 it tried to break the monopoly, but in each case was outmaneuvered. As in politics, struggles for power took on an ideological coloration. In contrast to mechanization, the anti-Ugaki group stressed mass tactics, spiritual training, and the "imperial way." Unable to obtain power legally by promotion and appointment, and unwilling to do so by ties to party politicians, this element began to flirt with factions of younger officers who advocated nonparty military government and direct action.

A second cleavage within the army was between those who had, after middle school or after the special army "military preparatory school," gone only to an officers' training school, and those who after several years in the field had been selected to go on to the Army War College. Those who had merely graduated from the officers' training schools were non-elite and of relatively low prestige in the army. Their education was tactical, mathematical, and ethical. They rarely attained top army commands, but usually ended as field-grade officers in rural posts. When young they were often radical. They formed the patriotic societies within the military which furnished a goodly number of the political assassins of the 1930's. In contrast, the graduates of the War College were the elite of the army. They were relatively well educated. Those with the best records were sent abroad a few years after graduation for foreign-language training. They held virtually all of the important posts in the General Staff and Army Ministry, and the best usually got at least a divisional command. They wore a special lapel insignia and were deeply resented by the others. It is misleading to overstate the depth of these cleavages, since in the face of outside criticism the army, more often than not, closed its ranks and acted as a unit. Yet the interaction of conservative generals, who tried to use factions of extremist-minded younger officers in their quest for power, and younger officers, who tried to play off one group of generals against another, is central to the story of terrorism during the thirties.[1]

The beginnings of direct political action by military and civilian extremists can be traced to the plots of March and October 1931. These were worked out by field-grade officers of the Cherry Blossom (a symbol of Japan) Society in conjunction with the civilian, ultranationalist thinker, Ōkawa Shūmei. The March plot called for popular demonstrations, the ordering out of troops to "protect" the Diet, and then the resignations of party politicians and the establishment of a "national defense state" under a new cabinet headed by General Ugaki. Ugaki, however, quashed the plot as soon as he heard of it. Members of the same group then turned to General Araki, of the anti-Ugaki faction, and rescheduled their plot for October; but again word leaked out and the plot was halted. Both incidents were hushed up to protect the good name of the army. Two of the leaders were punished by light confinement to quarters.

Other incidents occurred in the first months of 1932 as part of this same early, revolutionary elan. First, members of a civilian society, the League of Blood, assassinated a prominent party politician, and then a Mitsui executive. Second, on May 15 a group of junior officers of the navy and army, acting in coordination with members of a rural patriotic society, murdered Prime Minister Inukai and other political figures, and attacked the Seiyūkai party headquarters, the Bank of Japan, various official residences, and the Tōkyō Police Headquarters.

In the meantime Araki of the anti-Ugaki faction had been appointed army minister in the cabinet of Inukai formed in December 1931. This appointment was possible, first, because Ugaki was away in Korea and unable to block it, and second, because many in the army felt that only Araki, the champion of the ultranationalists, would be able to control the young firebrands of the army. In fact, in his two years as army minister Araki alienated almost every important group in the army. His first action was to carry out a purge of the Ugaki faction generals: some were sent to field commands, others were given unimportant posts; Tatekawa, the general most directly implicated in the Manchurian Incident, was sent as the Japanese representative to the Geneva Disarmament Conference. Araki's treatment of the younger officers was ambiguous. On his first day as army minister he made a speech in which he compared the younger officers to the patriots of the Restoration who were concerned with the nation's troubles, and the higher ranks of the army to the Elders of the *han* who thought only of narrow, local interests. This speech and Araki's subsequent "fraternization" with the younger officers

---

[1] James Crowley, "Japan's China Policy, 1931–1938: A Study of the Role of the Military in the Determination of Foreign Policy," University of Michigan dissertation, 1959.

PLATE 59. An 1877 print depicting elementary education. First-grade vocabulary chart at left is one of a set of eight produced by the Ministry of Education in 1875.

PLATES 60 AND 61. Two scenes from schools in 1905, by which time all children in Japan were receiving an elementary education. Right: boys in kimonos, with hair cropped short, read from their national language textbooks. Below: girls exercise in their schoolyard.

PLATE 62. Saionji Kimmochi   PLATE 63. Katsura Tarō

POLITICAL LEADERS OF IMPERIAL JAPAN

Unlike the earlier Meiji leaders (PLATES 28–31), the political leaders of twentieth-century Japan were men of compromise as well as of power amid competing elites, factions, and coalitions.

PLATE 64. Hara Kei   PLATE 65. Tanaka Giichi

Thinkers of Modern Japan

PLATES 66–68. Above (left): Minobe Tatsukichi, professor of law at Tōkyō Imperial University, who saw the Emperor as an "organ" of the government. Above (right): Yoshino Sakuzō, political liberal and professor at Tōkyō Imperial University. Below: Natsume Sōseki, novelist and critic, seated in the book-filled room of the Japanese scholar.

PLATE 69. Ceremonial send-off given by schoolmates for student entering army.

PLATE 70. Children dressed up as navy officer, samurai, and army officers. "Banzai," they shout, waving the fan and the flag.

PLATE 71. A hamlet discussion during the depression year of 1934 in Aomori Prefecture. Topic is how to survive without selling daughters.

disappointed those who had expected stronger leadership. Yet when the younger officers pressed Araki for action they were told to "leave it to Araki," and they soon began to feel that "Araki is only talk" and switched their hopes to General Mazaki, another of the anti-Ugaki clique.

A final and important group was that of Nagata (under whom were Tōjō, Mutō, Imamura, and most of the other generals who were to lead Japan's army during World War II), which felt, first, that Araki had not advanced the army's program of mechanization, and second, that clique struggles were bad for the army. These several forces combined; in January 1934 Araki was dropped, and later in the year Mazaki was relieved of his post for complicity in a plot to carry out another round of assassinations.

With the ouster of the Araki-Mazaki leadership, those younger officers who hoped to see the creation of a military state became even more desperate. One of these, Lieutenant-Colonel Aizawa, blaming General Nagata for the dismissal of Mazaki, walked into his office and cut him down with his sword. His trial turned into an emotional circus at which the defense was permitted to grill various zaibatsu executives, and Aizawa stated that his only regret was that he had been unable to kill Nagata with a single stroke.

The last attempted coup by the revolutionary right, the final act of the plots that had failed in 1931, was the Tōkyō rebellion of February 26, 1936. Young officers of the First Division stationed in Tōkyō led 1400 troops into the streets; they attacked government offices and assassinated a number of cabinet ministers and members of the Imperial Household Ministry. For three days the center of Tōkyō was in a state of siege, with soldiers of the rebellion occupying the Diet, the Army Ministry, the General Staff Headquarters, and other government centers. Against the background of snow-covered streets, troops with machine guns at the ready bore banners inscribed with the slogan of the Restoration: "Down with the traitors about the throne." At first, some among the army's generals were inclined to make concessions to the demands for "national reconstruction." For once, however, Saionji had the emperor stand firm, and virtually all other important segments of opinion in Japan, including the navy, joined in opposing the First Division troops. Therefore, on the 28th the insurgents were officially branded as rebels and put down by soldiers brought in from outside commands.

The rebellion was followed by purges, increased activity of the military police, and the re-establishment of army discipline. Central in carrying this out were members of the group formerly under General Nagata, the so-called control faction, which came into power at this time. The leaders of the rebellion, and also the civilian ideologists Kita Ikki and Nishida Zei, were quietly tried and quickly executed. The leading generals of both the anti-Ugaki and Ugaki cliques were either put on inactive duty or barred from critical posts within the army. The powers of the army police were augmented. In army police manuals dealing with Communism and "dangerous thought" were included the names and doctrines of those who advocated direct action, with the instruction that these were as dangerous as the leftists and must be rooted out of the army. General Tōjō, in particular, was instrumental in the clean-up, in which many army extremists sympathizing with the rebellion were arrested in Manchuria and Japan. Deprived of their ties to the military, civilian superpatriots slipped back into the noisy but ineffective position they had occupied before 1931. The restoration of discipline did not mean that the army had become an automaton manipulated by outside political forces. On the contrary, its independence as an elite continued and its voice in Japanese politics was, if anything, made greater by the deeds of those who were now suppressed. The threat of renewed turbulence, if the army were not given its way, became one of its most convincing arguments in political councils.

A second overall consequence of the period of terror was a stepped-up campaign against unorthodox thought. Under attack by extremists, the government, including some party politicians, intensified its persecution of leftists and liberals in order to demonstrate that it too was 100 per cent Japanese, and no less patriotic than its detractors. The effects of the weaknesses of Japanese constitutional thought and the lack of any tradition or belief in the civil rights of minority groups now became only too apparent. Underlying the persecutions of the thirties was the socioreligious current of emperor-thought examined earlier. The earliest attacks were directed against the revolutionary left, which was openly heretical in its denial of the emperor. Instead of the sporadic arrests of the middle twenties, there now were mass arrests. In 1932, 1500 socialists, union organizers, and Communists were arrested, and as many again in 1933. Many were sentenced to prison, and a few Communist leaders as well as the leading writer of proletarian literature, Kobayashi Takiji, were tortured to death in prison.

In 1933, attacks against liberals began with the dismissal of a Kyōto University professor who overstressed the constitutional character of constitutional monarchy and criticized the "Japanese family system." The president and law faculty of the university protested and some resigned, but to no avail. The education minister, Hatoyama Ichirō (prime minister 1954–56), declared: "Let all of the professors resign if that is how they feel." In 1935 in a movement "to clarify the national polity" Minobe was attacked in the Diet for having suggested that the emperor was an "organ" of the state. Eventually he was forced to recant and his works were banned. Although his works had been central in Japanese constitutional thought for over two decades, few spoke up in his behalf. After this time, what had been orthodox liberalism became heresy. All problems touching on the character of the emperor came under a taboo, and the religious interpretation of the state became official.

Cross-Currents, February 1936–July 1937. The period after the February Rebellion of 1936 and before the beginning of the China war in the summer of the following year is one of considerable ambiguity. In it two cross-currents appeared: a stronger voice for the army in a government preparing for war, and a resurgence of the political parties in opposition to the army-dominated government.

The Okada cabinet resigned after the rebellion. The new cabinet was formed by Hirota Kōki, the former foreign minister, a career diplomat and an advocate of a stronger foreign policy. The army interfered from the start, vetoing as cabinet ministers Yoshida Shigeru (prime minister 1946–47, 1948–54) and several others on the grounds that they were too liberal. In the end, only four party men were able to enter the cabinet. The policies carried out by this cabinet, and that of Hayashi which followed it, form a logical bridge between the conservatism of the years 1932–36 and the intensified militarism after the onset of the China war.

One of the acts of the Hirota cabinet was the passage of more stringent laws for the control of dangerous thought and seditious materials. Another, under the rubric of "National Defense in the Broad Sense of the Term," was the passage of a greatly augmented budget for military expenditures. This marked a sharp break with the policies of the twenties and provided the funds for the modernization of the army that the military had long been advocating. In foreign policy the cabinet brought its policies in line with those of the army. It called for the neutralization of five northern Chinese provinces. It also stressed, for the first time, Japan's concern with the regions to the south of China. And in December 1936 Japan signed the Anti-Comintern Pact with Germany. Ostensibly this pact merely provided for the exchange of information regarding the activities of international Communism. In fact, there was also a secret agreement to the effect that should either Japan or Germany be attacked by the Soviet Union, the other would take no action that might relieve the position of the Soviet Union.

Still another action taken by the Hirota cabinet was to re-establish the law that only generals and admirals on active duty might be appointed as army or navy minister. One purpose of this was to prevent the generals ousted after the 1936 rebellion from re-entering politics by this side door. Its result, however, was to make cabinets dependent on the goodwill of the army as they had been before the First Movement for the Protection of the Constitution in 1913. The effect of this change became clear early in 1937 when General Ugaki was asked to form the next cabinet. Because of his close ties with the political parties, his association with cliquism in the army, and his responsibility for the 1924 reduction in armaments, the army opposed his nomination and refused to furnish an army minister. As a retired general Ugaki was unable to become his own army minister and was forced to withdraw. In his place, General Hayashi Senjūrō, who faithfully followed the line of the control faction of the army, became prime minister. The reactionary character of the four short months of this ineffective cabinet is summed up in the slogans it used: "Respect the gods and honor the emperor," and "The union of government and religion."

The second cross-current during this period was the revival of party strength and its opposition to the army. In the election of February 1936 (one week before the rebellion) the Seiyūkai, with its more nationalistic "positive" foreign policy, entered with 301 incumbent Diet seats to the Minseitō's 146. Yet the Minseitō, using slogans such as "What shall it be, parliamentary government or fascism?" won a notable victory at the polls, coming out of the election with 205 seats to the Seiyūkai's 174. Such support of democracy was not simply habitual voting by a lethargic populace. Rather, it was sensitively attuned to the problems of the day.

Increasingly ignored by the bureaucratic-military cabinets, the parties gradually formed a united opposition. In January 1937 a Seiyūkai Diet member made an impassioned speech attacking the army's interference in government. The army minister replied, an angry debate followed, the Diet member recommended that the army minister commit *hara-kiri*, the army minister wanted to dissolve the Diet. The navy minister and others refused, and therefore the Okada cabinet resigned. The Hayashi cabinet, which lasted only four months, was also brought down by the parties. Like Yamagata at the turn of the century, Hayashi felt that cabinets should be above the factional strife which the parties represented. He demanded that those who entered his cabinet renounce their party ties. To attain the unity he desired he dissolved the Diet shortly after getting the budget passed and threw the support of the government behind the Shōwa-kai, a pro-militarist party. Apparently his idea was to realize in Japan the "one country, one party" formula of the Nazis. Yet in the ensuing election of April 1937 he was totally defeated and forced to resign. It had again been made plain, as in the late Meiji period, that rule without party support was impossible.

The election of 1937 reveals the extent to which, in spite of the drift to the right in the balance of governmental elites, the Japanese people had maintained a moderate, antimilitary position. Devotion to the emperor and Japan did not automatically lead them to favor the more extreme forms of nationalism in politics. The bulk of the people, as in the elections of 1930, 1932, and 1936, stayed with the two major parties, which although severely factionalized, made a common front against militarism. These parties received over 7 million votes and 354 seats in the Diet. Only slightly more than 400,000 voted for the government-supported party, which won only 19 seats. By and large, the voting pattern of the 1930's represents, not a break with that of the 1920's, but a continuation. This also can be seen in the gradual growth of moderate socialism, which won 8 Diet seats in 1928, 5 seats in 1930 and 1932, 18 in 1936, and 37 in 1937 (receiving over 900,000 votes). Since the Social Mass Party (formed in 1932) was plagued by a nationalist-socialist fringe on one side and by antiparliamentary Marxism on the other, it cannot simply be described as a democratic force. Yet it was led by moderates such as the Christians Abe Isoo and Katayama Tetsu (prime minister 1947–48), and its slogan, "Anticommunism, antifascism, anticapitalism" undoubtedly had a genuinely democratic appeal in the Japan of its day. Votes for this party were concentrated in the cities and represented the current of socialist support that would emerge so much stronger in postwar Japan.

To resolve the conflict between the parties and the government, Konoe Fumimaro was asked to form the next cabinet after the fall of Hayashi. Konoe had ties with the army, the political parties, and the Japanese financial world. A civilian, a member of the old aristocracy, a protégé of the liberal Saionji, a skillful and popular writer, a man who in his youth had gone to Kyōto University expressly to study with the philosopher Nishida and the Marxist economist Kawakami Hajime, Konoe had some appeal for every group. His appointment was greeted enthusiastically in all quarters. Certainly the parties expected from him a greater liberality than had existed under Hayashi. Yet, whatever potential he might have had in peacetime, in the course of the war that broke out a month after the formation of his cabinet, he proved to be a compromiser, too weak to resist the demands of the military and the belligerent civilians whose hold on the government became stronger and stronger.

Japan at War

In 1937 all Japanese army planning was predicated on the assumption that the Soviet Union was Japan's only serious enemy in the Far East. By 1935 Russia had more troops in its Far Eastern provinces (about 240,000) than Japan had in Manchuria (160,000), as well as more planes and greater mechanized strength. At the Seventh Comintern Congress of 1935 it was proclaimed that the fascist states of Germany and Japan were the enemies of the Soviet Union. In March 1936 the Soviet Union concluded a mutual defense pact with Outer Mongolia, and Russia obviously benefited from the united front policy which led to a truce between the Kuomintang and the Chinese Communists after the Sian Incident of 1936. To match the military strength of the Soviet Union in the Far East, the Japanese army in the summer of 1937 drew up a "Five-Year Plan for the Production of War Material." To fulfill this required time and peace; the last thing Japan needed was a full-scale war with China.

Indeed, apart from Manchuria, Japan's strategic concern in China was limited to the formation of buffer zones in North China to protect the Japanese rear in Manchuria from surprise attack during a possible war with Russia. By the end of the summer of 1935 these limited objectives, by and large, had been obtained. Agreements were reached in June 1935 for the withdrawal of Chinese Nationalist troops from Hopei and Chahar, and in December 1935 an "Autonomous Political Council" was established under a Chinese general — neither a Nationalist official nor a Japanese puppet — to govern these areas. The Japanese army wanted more: an "independent" North China, or government by a pro-Japanese Kuomintang. Throughout 1936 and the early months of 1937 Japan actively negotiated with Nanking to obtain recognition of its position in these areas. But such desires were to be achieved solely by economic or political pressures. To prevent the use of force, three steps were taken to reduce the influence of the bellicose Kwantung Army: the commander of Japan's army in North China was given a rank equal to that of the commander of the Kwantung Army; General Tashiro, who accepted the discipline that followed the army purges of 1936, was given command of the North China Army; the influence of the Special Intelligence Bureau at Mukden under General Doihara was excluded from North China by the establishment of a separate bureau in Peking subordinate to the North China Army. Advocates of a more aggressive China policy did exist among the army's China experts and in the Kwantung Army. These argued that the Nanking Government should be crushed before it had time to enter into an alliance with Russia and so pose a menace to Manchuria from the south. But such a differing tactical emphasis represented a minority opinion within the overall strategy directed against the Soviet Union.

In spite of these precautions, when on July 7, 1937, a local, unplanned clash took place between Chinese and Japanese troops in the Peiping area, it spread and developed into a general war, with disastrous results for Japan and the Far East.[1]

One reason for this was that the moral assumptions of Japan and China were vastly different. Japan saw its position in China as based on national destiny, economic need, and history. It judged events, as have other colonial powers in more recent times, in terms of the *status quo*. In Japanese eyes, the disturbing element in a situation that had existed since 1905 was Chinese nationalism. Most Japanese had come to feel that the steps taken since 1931 were not aggressive, but necessary to protect legitimate imperial interests. China, on the contrary, saw its own modern history as one of continued aggression by foreigners. Japan's encroachments were the most recent and the most outrageous. That these occurred just as Chinese nationalism rose to new heights was intolerable. The outbreak

---

[1] For developments in China in the "Nanking decade" to 1937, see pages 691 ff.

of fighting in 1937 was seen as a Japanese attempt to manufacture a new Manchurian Incident for the take-over of North China.

A second reason for the spread of the fighting was that there was little flexibility on either side. The Hopei-Chahar political council represented a delicate balance of interests. With the outbreak of hostilities each side felt threatened. The National Government felt that it could not afford to lose another inch of territory. Some have suggested that Chiang alone, depending on the terms, might have been willing to consider joining Japan in an anticommunist front. His position within the Chinese government, however, required him to respond vigorously to the Japanese threat. The National Government was militarily more capable than it had been, owing to its truce with the Chinese Communists and its new German-trained divisions. Therefore, when it learned of plans for the sending of Japanese troops to North China (subsequently canceled), it sent four divisions to South Hopei, breaking the truce agreement of 1935. Japan was alarmed at the rising tide of anti-Japanese sentiment in China and felt that its post-1935 position was in danger. Particularly in the face of Chinese troop movements it felt that its small force of less than 5000 in North China must be strengthened.

This crisis of mobilization was further complicated on the Japanese side by a hydra-like profusion of policy-making organs. It was hard enough for the General Staff and Army Ministry to reach agreement, split as they were by jealousies regarding who should plan what. The navy and other cabinet ministers also had to give their approval. Yet at times it was difficult for the cabinet even to know what the army planned to do. At one cabinet meeting, about three weeks after the fighting began, the minister for colonial affairs asked the army minister, "At about what line would military action be stopped?" The army minister, intent on preserving the army's independence of command, sat silent without replying. Thinking this reprehensible, the navy minister answered in his place. Thereupon the army minister turned pale with anger and attacked the navy minister: "Is it all right to divulge such information in a place like this?" Eventually a compromise was reached by which only the prime minister and the foreign minister would be apprised of the army's plans. Konoe was often infuriated by the army's interference in policy-making and resorted to incredible measures to keep the army in its place — such as appointing the purged General Araki as his minister of education in 1938 to counterbalance the control faction of the army. Yet one must stress that there was no simple dichotomy at this time between a civilian peace party and an aggressive army. More often than not the struggle within the Japanese government was over policy control, not over policy. The drift to the right continued. More and more extremists such as Hiranuma Kiichirō, Yanagawa Heisuke, or Suetsugu Nobumasa appeared in top government posts. In December 1937 the army, navy, and

Foreign Ministry had reached an agreement on terms for peace with the Chinese, but Suetsugu was able to have them rejected by asking whether they would be acceptable to the Japanese people. Several times armistices were reached by the armies in the field only to be overturned by army or cabinet decisions made in Tōkyō.

Fighting broke out in Shanghai in August 1937: the navy was unable to sit still and let the army get the glory. Soon the "North China Incident" developed into the "China Incident." (Even the United States treated this as an incident. To have called it a war would have made it even more difficult to settle. It would also have forced the United States, under the provisions of the 1937 Neutrality Act, to cut off war supplies to both Japan and China — which would have hurt China more than Japan.) The Japanese army minister promised the emperor that the incident "would be cleared up in two months." As the fighting increased, so did sentiment for a knockout blow against the Chinese. The General Staff argued that if Nanking fell, the Chinese government would give in to Japanese demands. The Chinese capital was captured in December. The willingness of army commanders to see this former center of anti-Japanese agitation punished led to the days of wanton slaughter known as the "rape of Nanking." Chiang Kai-shek, however, held out, and Chinese troops, though no match for those of Japan, fought fiercely, making the war costly and long. In January 1938 it was decided, over the opposition of the General Staff, to launch an all-out offensive in China and to establish a new central government favorable to Japan. By October 1938 Hankow and Canton had been captured and on November 3 Konoe could say that the Kuomintang regime had been reduced to a local government (in Szechwan), and announce the establishment of Japan's New Order in East Asia.

Apart from the portions of western and southwestern China ruled from Chungking and the Chinese Communist region in the northwest, the most heavily populated areas of China came under Japanese military control. Yet the reality of Japan's New Order was one of divided rule. The Kwantung Army controlled Manchuria and the puppet state of Inner Mongolia. The North China Army created a regime in Peking. The Central China Army set up a government based on Nanking. In part these were kept separate by army rivalries, in part by the hope of many in Japan that the Kuomintang would realize the helplessness of its plight and re-emerge as the government of a united China under Japanese tutelege. Japan probably could have driven the National Government from Szechwan, but Chiang might merely have moved further west. The threat of Russia in the north led Japan to limit its commitment in China to the control of the railroads and major cities. When hopes regarding the collapse of Chinese resistance proved futile, Japan turned to Wang Ching-wei who, reviving the pro-Japanese writings of Sun Yat-sen, came to the Japanese in 1939, and became the head of a new puppet government at Nanking in March 1940. There was perhaps a sufficient affinity between the idealistic slogans of the New Order and the illiberal modernism of the Kuomintang for such a government to have worked in a fashion had World War II not occurred. As it was, the behavior of Japanese troops in the field, the continual guerrilla warfare in the countryside, the tactics of the Japanese military police, and wartime demands combined to destroy illusion.

The Structure of Militarist Japan. The rationalization for war came after the outbreak of the "China Incident." The burden which the limited war in China placed on the domestic economy was not overwhelming. Yet it became a pretext for the passage of various laws that little by little transformed Japan into a militarist state; war became the national cause in the face of which resistance became impossible. The opposition of the major parties to the government, which had typified the stormy period of the Hirota and Hayashi cabinets, vanished almost overnight. War budgets were passed without protest. The Social Mass Party at its November 1937 Congress decided to "positively support the holy war for the fulfillment of the historical mission of the Japanese people." When one Minseitō Diet member protested a national mobilization law as unconstitutional, a lieutenant-colonel told him to shut up. Two years later, when the same man made a speech criticizing the New Order in East Asia, he was expelled from the Diet for having sullied the "holy war." Only five members of the Diet opposed his expulsion, and eight members of the Social Mass Party were expelled from their party for being absent from the Diet when the vote was taken. Long before the parties were formally dissolved in 1940, the Diet had lost its power and become a body which docilely rubber-stamped the decisions of the government.

Power in the government was now in the hands of the cabinet and the services. The Imperial Headquarters was formed in November 1937 to coordinate planning and operations between the two services. The political power of the services was institutionalized in the same month with the inauguration of the Liaison Council which brought together for policy-planning the prime minister, the service ministers, the foreign minister, the army and navy chiefs of staff, and, at times, the home and finance ministers. Council meetings were held during the latter part of 1937 and the early months of 1938. There then occurred a falling-out between the cabinet and the services which lasted until mid-1940. During these two years no meetings were held. They were revived, however, at the time of the second Konoe cabinet in the summer of 1940. After this the Liaison Council became the most important decision-making body in the government. Its most crucial decisions were confirmed at Imperial Conferences.

Economically, the most vital organ of government was the Planning Board established in October 1937 for total national policy formation.

Directly under the prime minister, this board planned Japan's wartime economic expansion and administered the controls that were gradually imposed after 1937. Central to its functions were the powers contained in the National Mobilization Law of April 1938, which provided for the control of resources, labor, materials, trade, prices, wages, and services, for censorship of the press and other mass media, and for compulsory registration and savings. This was an enabling act which the Konoe cabinet promised not to use as long as the war remained limited to China. Yet beginning in July 1938, little by little, ordinances were issued putting these controls into effect. Many able men served on the Planning Board. Some had previous experience in the semi-planned economy of Manchuria, some were national-socialists who brought to their work an enthusiasm for planning which overrode their immediate objectives, and some were bright young bureaucrats who had chafed under the seniority system within the other ministries. In 1941 a conflict arose between the Planning Board and the business world. The zaibatsu, while not unwilling to fulfill defense requirements, wished to maintain overall control of their own enterprises within cartelistic associations. They attacked the Planning Board slogan of "public profit first" as Communistic and were able to effect the purge of seventeen leftists from that body. (Some of those arrested at that time, e.g. Wada Hiroo, became prominent in the postwar Socialist Party; some who remained became prominent in the postwar conservative party or in business.) After this incident Lieutenant-General Suzuki became the head of the board, making it more responsive than ever to army influence. And later in 1941 new laws were passed giving it sweeping powers over private enterprise. By the first years of the Pacific war the economy was laced and overlaced with regulations and controls, and was moving largely in response to government direction. In 1943 the Planning Board was absorbed into the new Military Procurement Ministry.

A final aspect of Japan's wartime structure was the national spiritual mobilization movement, also inaugurated after the start of the China war. Directing this movement was the Central Alliance for the Mobilization of the National Spirit, a wrapper-organization which, by the end of 1938, contained 94 lesser organizations — such as the Imperial Veterans Association, the National Mayors Organization, the Japan Labor Unions Council, and so on. The original purpose of the Central Alliance was to coordinate propaganda and promote nationalist and Shintōist activities. As time passed, the alliance took over community defense functions, the sale of war bonds, the collection and distribution of materials, and so on. In October 1940 at the time of the second Konoe cabinet a further advance was made and the Central Alliance was absorbed into the Imperial Rule Assistance Association. This association was patterned after the Nazi "one country, one party" model, and all of Japan's major political parties were dissolved and brought within it. Apparently Konoe hoped at the time of its formation to use it as a counterweight to the army. However, apart from the negative fact that many other organizations were dissolved in order to form it, it came to very little and totally lacked the dynamism of a political party. Power lay in the government structure, not in the association, which was no more than a façade plastered over great heterogeneity. The political parties, for example, maintained their factional contentions within its confines. Leadership in the association came into the hands of government leaders: prefectural governors became the heads of the prefectural branches. At the lowest level this devolved into neighborhood associations, units of about ten families each, which were also under the effective control of local government offices. These were, at best, an attempt to use the remaining sense of local solidarity to marshal all possible energies for modern total war.

The Nature of Japanese Militarism. Japanese historians have been almost unanimous in terming the changes described above as the growth of fascism in Japan. In part this reflects the continuation of prewar Marxist historiography in postwar Japan, for in Marxist theory a state that is both capitalist and dictatorial can only be fascist. There are, indeed, many critical points of similarity. Both Japan and Germany, for example, moved away from parliamentary government. In both countries a narrow-minded nationalism and the use of terror by a revolutionary right contributed to the rise of authoritarianism. Both abolished the freedoms of speech, press, and assembly; and in both, liberals and leftists who attempted to speak out against aggression or oppressive legislation were persecuted. Both were expansionist, aggressive states. Thus, at a very high level of abstraction it is not impossible to combine these features of Japan and Germany with their common historical character as late modernizers (see page 579) and construct a "fascist model" of political change. Yet, on the whole, the differences between Japan and Germany seem as important as the similarities.

First, their governmental structures were different. Germany had undergone the Weimar change; its government was completely parliamentary and power was in the hands of the dominant coalition of parties in the Reichstag. To gain power the Nazis had to obtain a plurality of the votes in a national election. Japanese government in the 1930's was still at the "pre-Weimar" stage. As in Germany before World War I, the Diet was only one of several elites. A shift could occur in the character of the government without a shift in the balance of party power in the Diet. Victory at the polls was not a prerequisite for the rise of authoritarian government.

Second, not only was Japanese government in the 1930's more like that in Germany before World War I, but its society was also considerably less "modern" than that of Hitler's Germany. In Germany there was an almost point-to-point correlation between economic change and political polarization. After the runaway inflation of 1922–23 both the Nazis and the Communists rose from very small beginnings to become major parties in the elections of 1924 — at the expense of the centrist parties. The economic stabilization achieved by 1928 caused both parties to decline sharply at the polls. Then, under the influence of the world depression both spurted ahead in the early thirties and the numerically superior Nazis maneuvered themselves into power. In this pattern the direct relation between the individual's awareness of his predicament and his reaction to politics at the national level was pathological, not normal. It reflected the breakdown of intermediate institutions — business, welfare, judicial, police (the rise of private armies) — that ordinarily buffered the relation between the individual and the state. The Weimar framework was used to carry out what amounted to direct plebiscites between two extreme, antiparliamentary programs.

In contrast, the traditional (post-1890) social structure was relatively firm in Japan. The two major parties were both centrist, and they were never seriously challenged by an extremist mass party. They continued to get the bulk of the votes, and often the votes went to the more parliamentary of the two. The revolutionary extremist groups that came to prominence in 1931–36 had little influence on the support given to the Seiyūkai and the Minseitō at the polls. And these two parties totally defeated the government-supported, rightist-conservative Shōwa-kai in the 1936 and 1937 elections. The only other tendency visible in the elections of the 1930's was the slow secular trend in favor of semi-liberal socialist parties. Behind the stability in Japanese voting was the fact that intermediate institutions — as in the 1920's — were in good condition. They "contained" the misery of the poorer peasants and workers in the worst years of the depression. The tenant movement was not spurred on but overwhelmed by the coming of the depression, and the rural "community" was re-established — in a somewhat more egalitarian form. The Japanese middle class, such as it was, was also in better shape than its German equivalent. War and inflation wiped out the savings of the middle class in Germany; when the depression came there was nothing for it to fall back on. The Japanese middle class did very well during the war and the 1920's without encountering any serious inflation. The depression hurt small and medium-sized businesses, but bank savings and salaries were worth more than ever. Many remember the early thirties as the "best" period in prewar Japan.

Third, because the government structures and societies were different, the process by which the "antiparliamentary forces" rose was also very different. The Nazis rose as a mass party with a revolutionary program. Taking over the government, the Nazi party remade it in its own image, step by step establishing authoritarian controls. Having created a totalitarian regime, it then made war. Without exaggerating its efficiency, there is no denying its dynamism. But in Japan the antiparliamentary forces were not a dynamic, purposive, united group. It is hard even to describe those who in the 1930's gradually replaced the party leaders in the cabinets, except to say that they were ex-bureaucrats and ex-military men, former members of the Peers and former members of the Privy Council. These men did not plot to seize power. Rather, since the times were not propitious for the parties, nonparty prime ministers were appointed and then more and more nonparty ministers. Behind this "drift" within the establishment were the disputes, maneuvers, and compromises among the multiple elites of government. Communications were often poor and actions uncoordinated. One Japanese scholar has described Japan's path to war as a gradual nervous breakdown within the system. The most dynamic group was the army, which tended to confuse military strategy with national policy. Armies tend to be politically strong in early modernizing states and weak in fully modern states. Japan was not fully modern, and yet its army clearly was not an enlightened counter-elite as in some of the more backward Latin American countries. Rather, within a relatively modern state structure, the power of the Japanese army stemmed from the fact that legally it had never been subordinated to civil control. Its power was exercised within the government organization. By the summer of 1937 Japan was less parliamentary than in 1931, but was not yet totalitarian.

The turning point came when Japan blundered into war with China. The war led to wartime controls. Aiming at the total mobilization of national resources for war, these were sufficiently rigorous by 1941 to be called totalitarian. The official controls were reinforced by community and family pressures of a sort not existing in the West. These demanded not only "right actions" but also "right thoughts," and led to the ethical climate in which university students could be recruited as suicide pilots during the last desperate years of the war. But Japan in this period is better labeled militarist than fascist. The basic state apparatus was not new or revolutionary, but merely the "establishment" overlaid by controls and permeated by an unchecked spiritual nationalism. When the war ended, opinion shifted and the controls were removed, and until the reforms of the Occupation took hold, the basic state structure was much the same as it had been earlier.

Finally, the spiritual difference between Nazi Germany and militarist Japan was immense. In Germany Teutonic myths were used as a vehicle for a value-configuration that would sanction the aggression of the Nazis. Their values were demonic as were their ideas on race, but the myths were never presented as literally true. The problem of reconciling them with natural science did not arise. Rather, the break with the past was a break with the moral position of Christianity, liberalism, and socialism.

The enormity of this break necessitated concentration camps and brought about the sense of guilt in the postwar period. In Japan it was not necessary to disinter archaic myths; they were still very much alive and compelled a considerable degree of literal belief. These could be used, almost without change, to justify Japanese expansion. Under the impact of various economic arguments, most people could make the transition from the liberal orthodoxy of the 1920's to the conservative orthodoxy of the 1930's with little sense of a moral break. Many persons were sent to prison, but concentration camps were unnecessary. And after the war, although antimilitarism (the total rejection of the policies of the former leadership) was strong, there was little sense of individual guilt — except in intellectuals' attitudes toward the countries overrun in Asia.

The Background of the Pacific War. It is not surprising that militarist Japan eventually became allied with Nazi Germany and Fascist Italy. These were the only two states in the West that were not critical of Japan's aggression in China. And in Japan there was a great deal of admiration for the accomplishments of the Nazis. In fact, Japan's "New Order in East Asia" sounds like a translation from the German. Moreover, the 1936 Anti-Comintern Pact, while it provided for little, expressed a common animus that prefigured later, more compelling ties. Finally, Japan, Germany, and Italy, among the great powers, were have-not nations, covetous of the riches in the empires held by the European democracies. Yet diplomacy often produces strange bedfellows. Certainly there was no straight line linking the Japanese situation in 1937 and 1938 to the 1941 attack on Pearl Harbor.

Japan's concerns were Asian, not European. Europe counted only as it affected the balance of power in the Far East. From the end of 1938, Japan's main problem in Asia was how to settle the mess in China. Each new cabinet proclaimed its intention to extricate Japan from China. Obviously this was to occur on terms favorable to Japan. Much of Japan's diplomatic and military strategy during the late 1930's was directed to bringing about a situation in which the Chinese government would give in to Japan. A second, continuing problem was the Soviet Union. The Russian military potential in the Far East was affected by the degree to which Russia was involved in Europe. This fact was the most important concern in the pattern of Japan's relations with Europe, and in particular with Germany. A third problem was the United States navy in the Pacific. Japan's navy viewed this in the same way that the army viewed the Soviet army, as its greatest threat; hence the navy was generally predisposed to stress good relations with the United States. A fourth area of Japanese concern was Southeast Asia, rich in the raw materials Japan needed for an autonomous economy. Here Japan was faced by France, Holland, and Britain.

Throughout the early part of 1939 Japan sought to strengthen its position against the Soviet Union and to bring pressure to bear on the Chinese government by establishing an alliance either with Germany and Italy or with Britain. Most of the army and many politicians, including Hiranuma (prime minister January–August 1939), favored Germany. Germany, however, was not willing to ally with Japan against Russia alone and insisted that Japan commit itself against Britain and the United States as well. The leaders of both the Japanese navy and the Foreign Ministry resisted an alliance on these terms.

Pro-German groups in Japan were gaining ground when in August 1939 Germany signed a nonaggression pact with the Soviet Union and turned to war on the West. The reaction of the Japanese was unequivocal; they felt that they had been made fools of by Germany. Hiranuma said on resigning the premiership: "Japan's foreign policy is in a state of having been practically betrayed." Japan had wanted an alliance as protection against Russia. Concern with this had increased during 1938 as Russia extended aid to China and as Japanese and Russian troops fought for two weeks along the Russian-Korean border near Changkufeng. But far more serious, during the summer months from May to September 1939, even as Germany was concluding the pact, Japanese troops were battling several Russian divisions in a large-scale war near Nomonhan on the Mongolian-Manchurian border. An armistice was signed in September, but victory went to the more mechanized Soviet forces. Now Germany had freed the Soviet Union to take an even stronger stance in the Far East, and had gone to war with Britain.

This brought about a sudden reorientation of Japanese policy. Hiranuma was succeeded as prime minister first by General Abe Nobuyuki and then by Admiral Yonai Mitsumasa, noted for his pro-British and American leanings. During this period (August 1939–July 1940) new German diplomatic advances were repelled by the Japanese, and many leaders attempted to improve relations with the United States and Britain. China remained the stumbling block. Britain and France were willing to approach Japan and apparently thought of compromising on China in order to preserve the West's position in the treaty ports and at the same time block a future Japanese-German entente. But the United States secretary of state, Cordell Hull, was not willing to countenance aggression through the abandonment of China; hence negotiations in this direction came to nothing. Some have argued in retrospect that this was a critical moment in diplomatic history; that had the United States been more flexible, it might have reached agreement with Japan that would have precluded the later Japanese pact with Germany and Italy. Yet it should be borne in mind that these were also the years in which the Liaison Council was not functioning, in which the cabinet and the army were not in close cooperation. Even if the Japanese Foreign Ministry had concluded an agreement with Britain, France, and the United States, the agreement subsequently might have been repudiated by the army.

By late spring of 1940 the situation was changing again. All in Japan were amazed at the German victories in Europe. The fall of Britain appeared at hand. Once again voices were raised in favor of an alliance with Germany. In July the army withdrew its minister, thus overthrowing the Yonai cabinet. The second Konoe cabinet that replaced it was clearly the most militant yet formed. General Tōjō came in as the representative of the army. Hoshino Naoki, a former economic planner in Manchuria, entered as minister without portfolio and head of the Planning Board. And blunt, erratic, contradictory, unstable, and wildly pro-German Matsuoka Yōsuke, whom Hull described as "crooked as a basket of fishhooks," became foreign minister.[1]

The most important act of this government was the signing of the Tripartite Pact with Germany and Italy in September 1940. This provided that the signatories would go to war against any nation attacking one of their number — excepting those already at war at the time the Pact was signed. Japan hoped to get four things from this Pact: (1) Japan wanted better relations with the Soviet Union. Germany, ostensibly on good terms with Russia, offered to act as a go-between. The negotiations took time, but in April 1941 Japan got a neutrality pact with the U.S.S.R. (2) Germany was defeating the colonial powers; Japan wanted assurances that their ex-colonies in Asia would enter its New Order. (3) Japan wanted to end the war in China. It felt that China would collapse if material and moral support from outside were cut off. It hoped that a Eurasia divided into spheres among Germany, Russia, and Japan would bring about this end. (4) Japan felt that in the face of this pact the United States would be more isolated than ever, and therefore less likely to interfere in China or elsewhere. In fact, the most immediate consequence of the pact was the worsening image of Japan in the United States.

United States policy in the Far East in the years between 1931 and Pearl Harbor espoused the principles of the Open Door, China's integrity, and nonaggression, but avoided any idea of trying to support these principles by military action. The result was a mixture of inaction, high moral statements, and free-trade theory. In part the United States was incapable of action: its army was small and its navy was divided between two oceans. In the face of Japanese aggression, the United States disapproved. Public indignation at Japanese actions in China slowly rose. The decline of equal commercial opportunity in those areas of China under Japanese control was an affront to the traditional American Open Door policy. The bombing of Chinese cities — with bombs made from American scrap, and planes using fuel bought from American companies — was

---

[1] Saionji, when his secretary suggested that Matsuoka must be insane, said, "It would improve him to become insane."

viewed with horror. But, on the whole, the American people were firmly behind the government policy of noninvolvement. The election campaign of 1940 saw each candidate out-peacing the other. And when Japan began to move southward in the face of American warnings, the most the United States could do was to invoke mild economic sanctions. Japanese army observers were sent to Tongking in northern Indo-China in June 1940, and in September army units followed. In reply, after a great deal of soul-searching, the United States placed an embargo on aviation gasoline in July (not effective since other grades could be cracked) and on steel and scrap iron in September (this hurt, though it posed no insuperable problems). Until this time the United States was chiefly oriented toward Europe. It had only a secondary concern for East Asia and wished to avoid any entanglement there that would weaken its power in the Atlantic. But, when the Tripartite Pact was signed in September 1940, the European crisis merged with the Far Eastern crisis. This had the effect of joining to the slowly rising public opinion against Japan the great antagonism already existing against Germany. Consequently, far from further isolating the United States as Japan had intended, the Tripartite Pact made the United States more anti-Japanese than before.

The months between the signing of the pact in September 1940 and mid-1941 were in Japan a time of cautious preparation for a further move to the south. Japan wanted, first, to cut off the Chinese government from southern supply routes and, second, to obtain strategic resources. It was felt in Japan that a total embargo might be put into effect by the United States at any moment, and that a self-sufficient empire, including the oil-rich Dutch East Indies, was a military necessity. Some in Japan favored a move south even at the risk of war. Many, however, were hesitant about moving against Dutch and British colonies while Britain still stood. They did not want war with the United States, which through Lend-Lease and joint military planning, was increasingly involved on the British side.

In June 1941 Japan again found itself betrayed by Germany. Instead of finishing off Britain, and thus opening the way for a Japanese move to the south, Germany attacked Russia, giving Japan, its ally, little advance notice. Foreign Minister Matsuoka, until the fighting actually began, did not believe that Germany would invade Russia. The German attack put Japan in the ridiculous position of having concluded its neutrality pact with Russia through the good offices of Germany, even while Germany was preparing its troops for the attack. Germany then compounded the insult by asking Japan to attack the Soviet Union in the East. This occasioned a fierce debate in the army between those who favored war with Russia and those who wanted to move to the south. At an Imperial Conference on July 2, 1941, it was decided to fight Russia if the German armies proved victorious in the West. By September the German armies had been stopped short of Moscow. Japan therefore decided to honor its neutrality pact with Russia and ignore the German request. Instead, with its northern flank in Manchuria now safe from a Soviet attack, Japan decided to proceed south even at the risk of war with Britain and the United States. But at the same time it was also decided to begin new negotiations in order to lessen the danger of war. These two policies proved mutually contradictory.

Japanese troops entered southern Indo-China in July 1941. The United States, together with Britain and the Dutch East Indies, reacted by placing a total embargo on all exports to Japan. This effectively cut Japanese oil imports to 10 per cent of their previous volume and produced in Japan the "crisis of the dwindling stockpile." Navy staff officers and junior planners, not averse to war, said that Japan's oil reserves would last only two years. If no action were taken by October, action would become impossible and Japan would be forced to retreat step by step until all her gains were lost. Senior naval admirals were unable to oppose their juniors. Therefore "an outline plan for carrying out the national policy of the empire" was drafted and submitted to the meeting of the Liaison Council on September 3, 1941. Faced with the either-or logic of this plan, Japan's leaders agreed to go to war with the United States if an agreement regarding oil was not reached by early October. Two days later at a briefing for an Imperial Conference the emperor said, "This would seem to give precedence to war." Konoe replied that such was not the case. War would come only if diplomacy failed. The naval chief of staff, when asked what a war would mean, compared Japan to a patient critically ill. An operation, though extremely dangerous, might save his life. At the Imperial Conference next day that approved this fateful decision, the emperor read a poem by the Meiji Emperor:

> Since all are brothers in the world,
> Why is there such constant turmoil?

What Japan had in mind when considering the possibility of war was quite different from what actually happened. During World War II some rather fantastic reports of Japanese aims were circulated in the United States: for example, that Japan expected to dictate the terms of peace from the White House, or to reduce the United States to the original Thirteen Colonies. This was nonsense. No person in a position of responsibility in Japan held such views. The plan of strategy was to carve out an area within which economic self-sufficiency was possible and to defend it until the United States tired of war. This was to be achieved by sinking America's Pacific fleet — a stroke in which Japan succeeded, missing only the aircraft carriers. The Japanese plan assumed the victory of Germany in Europe, the defeat of England, and the collapse of the Chinese government, all of which seemed probable in mid-1941. It further assumed that, with these conditions fulfilled, Japan could fight the United

States on a one-to-one basis in East Asia. It bet the land-based airpower and shorter supply lines of Japan against the greater productivity of America. Beyond war were vague schemes for the division of the world into spheres (Japanese, German, Russian, and American) and the transformation of international relations into intersphere relations.

Yet, though the decision had been taken to go to war if oil were not obtained, most Japanese leaders still felt that diplomacy would win out. Japanese efforts to this end began seriously in July 1941 and continued frantically even after the September decision and the formation of the Tōjō cabinet in October. (Of course, the negotiations for peace were accompanied by the move into Indo-China mentioned earlier and by preparations for the Pacific war — Pearl Harbor was rehearsed for months in advance at Kagoshima Bay in southern Kyūshū.)

In July 1941 the second Konoe cabinet was dissolved and the third Konoe cabinet formed in order to get rid of the pro-German foreign minister, Matsuoka. Personnel changes were made in the Foreign Ministry as well. Concessions were also planned. Within the framework of emperor-centered nationalism, the reasoning of Japan's leaders was that of *realpolitik*. The United States had little effective power in the Far East. It was not directly involved in China or Southeast Asia. If Japan pledged to maintain the *status quo*, or to make minor withdrawals, then the United States ought to be willing to rescind its embargo on oil. This would avoid war, and leave the long-term political outcome in the Far East to depend on the result of the war in Europe. To reach such an agreement Konoe pressed for a meeting with Roosevelt. Konoe was apparently willing to stipulate that Japan would not go to war with the United States under the Axis Pact even if American actions in the Atlantic involved it in a war with Germany. More than this the "peace party" in Japan could not offer. Had negotiations been successful, it is conjectural whether the Japanese army would have accepted this much. The army was clearly not willing to give up its conquests in China, or even to return to the *status quo ante* of 1937. Perhaps Japanese military planning had progressed so far that all of these negotiations were little more than window dressing — however seriously they were intended.

In contrast to Konoe, the reasoning of Secretary of State Cordell Hull, the dominant voice in shaping American Far Eastern policy, was moral. Japan was an aggressor. Any compromise would sanction aggression. The United States should not negotiate unless Japan underwent a change of heart. Roosevelt was willing to meet with Konoe. He brought to diplomatic problems the same mixture of pragmatism and morality found in the New Deal. Hull, however, distrusting the Japanese overtures, vetoed the meeting.

The last chance to postpone the war came in November when Japan offered as a temporary *modus vivendi* to turn the clock back to June

1941: withdrawal of Japanese troops from southern Indo-China in return for oil and a United States "hands off" policy towards China. Roosevelt was interested, but again Hull blocked acceptance. He feared that any sudden change in American policy would endanger the network of relations that had been established between the United States and Britain, Holland, Australia, and China. Therefore, he in turn submitted to the Japanese a ten-point program requiring them to withdraw all their armed forces from Indo-China and China (including Manchuria). Behind this uncompromising stand was a calmness and a sense of the ampleness of time that ultimately rested on the belief that Japan would not dare to attack the United States.

The Japanese took Hull's program as the rejection of further negotiations. Possessed by the vision of an East Asia dominated by Japan, and trapped in a timetable of their own making, they attacked Pearl Harbor on December 7, 1941.

8

The Rise of the Chinese Republic

THE LATE CH'ING REFORM MOVEMENT

Japan's drive for imperial hegemony over East and Southeast Asia was generated from within the Japanese nation by the stimulus of foreign contact. Long before this militarist expansion there had been the sustained Meiji effort to defend the country by modernization. Thus throughout the eighty-eight years from Perry to Pearl Harbor, Japan's leaders had responded to outside influences; and so a different configuration of forces in the outside world would no doubt have led Japan's expansion in the 1930's and 1940's into different channels. Pearl Harbor was not inevitable. Yet after Japan became a great power in 1905, the expansion of her influence in some fashion on the Chinese continent was certainly unavoidable. Since the form of this Japanese expansion would depend partly on conditions and responses in China, the fate of imperial Japan in the twentieth century became interlocked with that of the Chinese Republic.

Behind the mutual tragedy that resulted lay not only Japan's success in developing national power but also China's painful slowness in achieving institutional change, national unity, and regeneration. Because of this time-lag, China in the early twentieth century was still absorbed in a

POLITICAL DEMONSTRATION at a Peking city gate by students carrying banner reading "National Tsing Hua University." Redrawn from photographs.

process of incipient revolution such as Japan had gone through in the 1860's. The old order under the Ch'ing dynasty had begun to crack after Japan's attack in 1894–95, but its political structure remained standing for another fifteen years.

The final decade of the Ch'ing dynasty from 1901 to 1911 was not a period of collapse so much as of metamorphosis. Institutional and social change began early and political disaster came only at the end. Up to 1911, in fact, instead of falling apart, the traditional Chinese state began a gradual reconstruction along lines of institutional change which had been advocated unavailingly in the 1890's. The Empress Dowager and her conservative supporters, having thrown the Kuang-hsü Emperor and K'ang Yu-wei out of power in 1898 (see page 393), proceeded to give effect after 1901 to most of their radical reform program. In truth, they had no alternative. The Boxer war had shown the bankruptcy of mere antiforeignism, while the threat of anti-Ch'ing rebellion goaded the regime into constructive action to save itself. Conservative reform was thus the principal movement of the early 1900's in the Chinese public scene, while the republican revolutionary movement grew up on the periphery. Its principal leader, Sun Yat-sen (1866–1925), was already identified with anti-Ch'ing rebellion after his attempted rising at Canton in 1895, but the rebel cause remained fragmented and inconsequential until about 1905. Its early history until then (to be noted in the next section) was a minor eddy in the stream of change.

Reformers, not revolutionists, mainly prepared the ground for revolution. Great changes were at last under way in Chinese life, and the alien Ch'ing dynasty, trying to guide these changes, could not avoid nurturing anti-Ch'ing and centrifugal forces that would eventually destroy it. Students the government trained abroad, new armies it trained at home, merchants it encouraged in domestic enterprise, political assemblies it convoked in the provinces, all sooner or later turned against the dynasty. In political quicksand, the more the dynasty struggled to save itself, the deeper it sank. For modernization now meant Chinese nationalism, which might mean the end of Manchu rule, and the fact that modernization was strongest in the coastal and Yangtze provinces boded ill for the central power at Peking.

Along this one-way street leading to its political demise, however, the dynasty's reform efforts were a great deal more than merely opportunist responses to the pressure of the revolutionary movement, which was rather tardy, weak, and ineffective, and never a serious military threat. The late Ch'ing reforms deserve study in their own right, as attempted solutions to China's peculiar problems of modernization.

In January 1901, while still at Sian, the Empress Dowager repentantly announced a policy of adopting the "strong points of foreign countries in order to make up China's shortcomings." By this she meant serious institutional reform. Foreign languages and machines were only "the skin and hair of Western technology . . . not the fundamental source of Western government." This policy, supported at court by Jung-lu, marked the ascendancy in the government reform program of Chang Chih-tung and Liu K'un-i, the Yangtze "viceroys" (governors-general respectively of Hunan-Hupei and of Kiangsi-Anhwei-Kiangsu) who in 1900 had dexterously remained both at peace with the foreigners and loyal to the dynasty.

In three joint memorials of July 1901, Chang and Liu outlined a broad program reminiscent of the Hundred Days of 1898, but under the cover of all the usual sanctions for "self-strengthening" — that Western countries now used ancient Chinese methods, that borrowing from them would follow the ancestors' practice and "recover our forgotten ceremonies from abroad," while "never neglecting" the Classics, etc. By turns sanctimonious and shrewd, Chang Chih-tung as the principal author also stated a few blunt truths: ". . . popular feelings are not the same as thirty years ago. The people admire the wealth of foreign countries and despise the poverty of the Middle Kingdom." Similarly they admire foreign troops, the "fair play" of the Maritime Customs Service, the strict orderliness of foreign concessions. "Rebels are slowly emerging" and spreading subversive doctrines. Hence the urgency of establishing new school systems, sending students abroad, adopting Western military methods, developing agriculture and industry, instituting better laws and taxes, abolishing sinecures and corruption, and all the rest. The catalogue of needed reforms was longer than ever, but education, to nourish "human talent" for government, was still first on the list.

Education: New Schools, New Scholars. The general aim of the educational program was to train and select officials more effectively. The original aim was not public education of the Chinese people (which became an ideal only later) nor was it liberal education of the Chinese individual. The means was to be a hierarchy of schools at all the territorial levels of government — district, prefecture, province, and imperial capital — parallel to and feeding into the traditional examinations. In time, say after ten years, the new schools, supported by contributions from the public, would supplant the old examination system, which could then be discarded. But meantime, it was hoped, the two systems could be used side by side. Candidates prepared in the new schools and candidates prepared privately in the traditional way would alike take the regular examinations, which would be somewhat modernized in content. As first steps, in August 1901 the "eight-legged essay," against which scholars had protested for centuries, was abolished and in September the old-style academies (*shu-yüan*) were ordered converted into government schools.

To get the new school system accepted as the main channel for advancement, an attempt was made to appease the contemporary generation of scholar-officials in office and classically-trained aspirants for office, all of whom had a vested interest in the classical examination system. It was to conciliate these conservatives that the new schools were expected to prepare their students at each level to take the regular examinations, which from 1902 were now to include modern as well as classical subjects. But it soon appeared that of these parallel routes to office, the traditional route of private, individual preparation for the examinations would continue to be cheaper, easier, and more attractive than the new route, which led through years of costly schooling in a prescribed curriculum of already formidable proportions. The majority of old-style aspirants for office would shun the new government schools. On the other hand, the minority of restive, modern-minded youth, potential leaders, must be recruited into the government schools lest they become outright enemies of the established order. Already, the foreign missionary schools in China, the new flow of students to Japan, and the public demand for modern education of all kinds had shattered the monopoly of the examination system.

The new government schools faced competition, first of all, from the example of Christian missionary education in strategic urban centers. By 1905, Protestant missions had some 2200 kindergartens and primary schools with 42,000 pupils, and reported 389 "intermediate and high schools and colleges" with 15,000 students.[1] St. John's College at Shanghai was one example of the gradual rise of the Christian colleges. Stemming from a Protestant Episcopal boys' school founded in 1847, the St. John's campus had been built up after 1879 by a vigorous bishop (S. I. J. Schereschewsky). The mixed Sino-foreign faculty included five of Yung Wing's boys from the Chinese Educational Mission at Hartford, Connecticut. By 1904, the three schools of arts and sciences, medicine, and theology had 187 students. Only 57 were Christians. Most were the sons of merchants and officials.

Missionary institutions were fostering Christianity, individualism, education of women, and Western ways generally, all under the protection of extraterritoriality, and were setting a revolutionary example. They refused to have their students pay homage to Confucius or the emperor, as required in government schools. Peking countered by barring mission school graduates from official careers.

Private Chinese modern education was also beginning. In 1904 an able young graduate of the Peiyang naval academy, Chang Po-ling, opened at Tientsin a middle school with 73 students. In 1907 he acquired a campus, thus founding Nankai Middle School and later (in 1919) Nankai University.

---

[1] The "Centenary Conference" celebrating the growth of Protestant missions from 1807 to 1907 recorded 3500 missionaries working under some 70 societies and residing at 632 stations to minister to 250,000 Chinese Christians.

Thus the combination of the new government schools and the old examination system, put together in 1901, seemed unlikely to attract either the old-fashioned, who clung to the examinations, or the modern-minded, who flocked to missionary and private schools. A committee headed by Chang Chih-tung after much debate concluded in 1903 that the new school system could secure neither students nor popular financial support until the examination system ceased to exist as an alternative. They promised that the schools would include "everything that has been taught and practiced in the examination system," only do it better, with examiners still sent from the capital and jobs still available for all degree-winners. Accordingly in January 1904 the court ordered a gradual reduction of the quotas, i.e., the numbers who might receive degrees, in each old-style examination. Yet this could only dismay many young men who had hoped to rise through the traditional channel.

Soon, under the continued pressure of events in 1905 — such as the Japanese victory over Russia and the further organization of the anti-Ch'ing Chinese revolutionaries in Tōkyō — the leading provincial officials, beginning with Chang Chih-tung and Yüan Shih-k'ai, felt compelled to move more quickly. In August 1905 they urged the immediate abolition of the examination system, and the court ordered this to take effect in 1906. The government's educational hopes now lay entirely with the new schools. A Ministry of Education (Hsüeh Pu) was created in 1906 to supervise them.

The Ch'ing government school system was modeled on the Japanese. It called for specialization after middle school so as to produce specialists for government service. The system was slow in getting started, undercut until 1905 by the continued existence of the old examination system. The massive and detailed regulations issued in 1904 followed Japan's example in leading students through higher elementary school (4 years), middle school (5 years), and higher school (3 years, achieving the degree of *chü-jen*) to the Imperial University (3 years, achieving the degree of *chin-shih*). The entire curriculum was minutely prescribed.

Thus the late Ch'ing reformers of education were not trying merely to abolish the ancient examinations, but wanted, more positively, to create a modern school system. This effort, like so many others, had begun at the top, with the Imperial University set up during the Hundred Days of reform in 1898. W. A. P. Martin, the American who had been head of the Interpreters College (T'ung-wen Kuan) from 1869 to 1895, served at first as dean of Western studies. In 1902 the university absorbed the Interpreters College. Eventually it became National Peking University (generally abbreviated as Peita, from Pei-ching ta-hsüeh). But below this top institution the new school system lacked modern-trained faculties, buildings, equipment, funds, and leadership.

Progress in building the school system was achieved, as in industrialization, mainly at the provincial level. For example, that exemplary leader in educational reform, Chang Chih-tung, had a great variety of small pilot-model schools operating in Hupei — a normal school to train teachers, five higher primary schools, civil and military middle and high schools, and special schools for foreign languages, agriculture, industry, and the training of officials already in service. Other provinces followed this example. But it was easier to found colleges than middle schools, easier to set up middle schools than primary schools. The system remained weak at the base.

Provincial educators now found their chief inspiration and resource in Japan. Chang Chih-tung sent two missions to study the Japanese school system and buy textbooks. He began to see the need for general public education, to find talent anywhere among the people. Soon he imported Japanese professors, who could communicate with their Chinese colleagues and students at least in writing. He began to look to Japan as the best training ground for the new generation of Chinese schoolteachers — cheaper than the West because Japan was near at hand, easier because Japan's "language, literature, and customs" were close to China's, and because many Western books had already been translated into Japanese. In addition, Chinese students could be supervised more easily in Japan by Chinese government inspectors.

The flow of Chinese youth seeking modern education in Tōkyō had begun by 1896. In 1898 there were still only 18 or so recorded, but after the suppression of the reform movement in that year the Chinese student population in Japan rose to about 200 in 1899. This increase continued after 1901, reaching about 1000 in 1903, 1300 in 1904, and roughly 8000 by the end of 1905, after the abolition of the examination system. Even more Chinese students seem to have been in Japan in 1906, estimated at 13,000 or more, but the number who went exceeded by far the number who enrolled in serious academic studies, which in turn far exceeded the number who eventually graduated. Indeed, the Chinese graduates from reputable Japanese institutions never exceeded 700 in any year (623 in 1908, 536 in 1909, 682 in 1910, and a peak of 691 in 1911). Even so, this was an impressive number at that time.

Among these many thousands of Chinese youths who went to Japan in the last decade of the Ch'ing period, something like one-half were on Chinese government funds, mainly of provincial governments. Students were often prepared in new provincial schools and usually were sent in annual delegations to Tōkyō. There they followed the ancient Chinese practice of organizing associations or guilds (*hui*) among fellow provincials, reminiscent of the regional guilds (*t'ung-hsiang hui*) organized by officials, gentry, and merchants in Peking and other major cities over the centuries. Thus the new educational system brought young men and even some young women together more intimately, over a longer period and in circumstances more stimulating to group cohesion, than the old examination system had ever done. Just as the new student life in China nurtured provincial consciousness (often based on dialect) and provincial loyalties, so life in Tōkyō nourished nationalism.

In this way Chinese education was quietly revolutionized in the five years between 1901 and 1906. Classical studies gave way to a mixed Sino-Western curriculum. Private preparation for triennial examinations on traditional themes gave way to school life day by day, a broader range of ideas, more social and intellectual contact. Instead of indoctrinated scholar-gentry loyal to Confucius and the Son of Heaven, the new system produced revolutionists. Chang Chih-tung could carefully prescribe light-blue gowns, hats with red tassels, and a multitude of rules to foster decorum among his students, and an edifying song — "The Holy Son of Heaven plans for self-strengthening. . . . Hygiene makes the people strong and healthy. . . . Honor Parents, respect rulers. . . ." But once the examination system had been washed away, there was no checking the tides of change.

The intellectual content of the new education, in China as in Japan, now contained much from the West. Despite so many decades of increasing Western contact, it was only after 1900 that the Chinese scholar class really began to absorb Western ideas. The famous popularizer of Western fiction, Lin Shu (1852–1924), had already been turning out by hearsay (i.e., by listening to oral translations) his Chinese versions of Dickens, Dumas, Scott, Balzac, and others — 156 works in all. To this continuing literary fare were now added the translations and interpretations of the classics of Western liberalism by Yen Fu (1853–1921). Having joined the navy, Yen saw the world, especially England, in the 1870's and concluded that the secret of Western power was Western thought. He became a convert to Herbert Spencer's Social Darwinism: the individual's energetic self-realization must help the nation to compete and survive. Liberal principles, however, Yen Fu felt were needed to augment China's national wealth and power rather than to foster individual freedom. Democratic self-government would be premature. The translator tried especially to convey those ideas of Victorian Britain that seemed most meaningful for late-Ch'ing China. T. H. Huxley's *Evolution and Ethics* appeared in classical Chinese with Yen's commentaries in 1898, Adam Smith's *Wealth of Nations* in 1900, J. S. Mill's *On Liberty* in 1903, part of his *System of Logic* in 1905, Montesquieu's *Spirit of the Laws* in 1909. These and other works, by exalting Western logic, law, science, and evolution, severely indicted China's sages as the cause of her backwardness, yet did it as an inside job, in classical Chinese for the literati.

New Armies: The Rise of Yüan Shih-k'ai. By 1901 China had inherited from her far and recent past three main types of military organization. The oldest, largest (at least on paper), and most useless of the military were the effete Manchu banner forces, still subsisting on their inadequate stipends, and the decentralized Chinese constabulary ("Army of the

Green Standard"). A few thousand bannermen had been given modern guns and formed into the Peking Field Force in 1862. Later, selected units of the constabulary, especially around Peking, had received some modern arms and training and so had become known as the Disciplined Forces (Lien-chün). But in general the officers were still chosen by the ancient military examination system, which was an elaborate, three-tiered imitation of the civil system in form, but in content stressed mainly physical prowess in mounted and dismounted archery, sword-brandishing, pulling a powerful bow, and lifting a heavy stone. This antic ritual being no preparation for modern war, the old-style military examinations were finally abolished in August 1901, and new military academies ordered established.

The second type of military organization was that of the regional armies inherited from the Taiping period. Their genealogy went back to the Hunan Army (see page 164) which Tseng Kuo-fan recruited after 1852 from the peasantry and organized in battalions of 500 soldiers plus some 180 carriers for logistic support — nominally, one coolie for every three soldiers. Despite Tseng's formal disbandment of the Hunan Army (see page 322), it had continued to exist, along with the Anhwei Army created by Li Hung-chang in 1862 and similar forces organized by Tso Tsung-t'ang and others against the mid-century rebels. These personally-led, regionally-recruited armies were not composed of militia (*t'uan-lien*) in the sense of part-time farmer-soldiers but rather of professional fighting men (*yung*, "braves"). As ongoing military institutions with their own leaders and sources of support, they became vested interests. They in effect supplanted the traditional bannermen and constabulary in the provinces and came to be known generically as the Defense Army (Fang chün). The Anhwei Army (under Li at Tientsin) and the Hunan Army (led by Liu K'un-i at Nanking) remained the dominant rivals among these forces. Though usually equipped with modern rifles and artillery, instead of matchlocks, gingals, and smoothbore cannon, they lacked standardized armament as well as modern-trained officers and staff specialists, to say nothing of engineer, signal, quartermaster, modern transport, or medical services. In short, they were still only semi-modern.

The third and most recent type of military organization had been developed in response to Japanese aggression. Both Li Hung-chang and Chang Chih-tung had set up military academies in the 1880's and hired German instructors to train a new officer corps, but little was achieved until after Japan's startling victories in 1894. Out of the ensuing welter of proposals and efforts a number of new units emerged, among which two set a new standard.

One was Chang Chih-tung's Self-Strengthening Army, which he organized while temporarily governor-general at Nanking in 1895. Chang employed 35 German officers to command and train 13 battalions (about

3000 men), which included on the German model eight battalions of infantry, two of artillery, one of engineers, and two squadrons of cavalry, all with European equipment. The troops were carefully selected country boys and were well paid. Unfortunately, when Liu K'un-i again became governor-general at Nanking in 1896, he watered down this program, subordinating it to his own Hunan Army, while Chang, returning to his usual post in Hunan-Hupei, continued his military efforts on a modest scale.

The other and more significant unit developed under Yüan Shih-k'ai, who had risen as Li's proconsul in Korea and as a military more than a civil official (see page 378). He was appointed in 1895 to train a new imperial army on the German model and with German instructors, to be financed by the Board of Revenue. Near Tientsin he soon had 7000 men in training, recruited from several provinces and well paid, with precautions against the usual corruption. It was here in his personal leadership of this new force, later to be known as the Peiyang Army, that Yüan laid the foundation of the "Peiyang clique" of a later day and became the "father of the warlords," for among his early Peiyang officers were ten men who later, after the revolution, were to become military governors of provinces, and five (in addition to Yüan himself) who became presidents or premiers of the Peking government under the republic.

Yüan's emergence as an efficient military modernizer, with an earlier interest in the Self-Strengthening Society of 1895, had led K'ang Yu-wei and the other radical reformers of 1898 to seek his help to ward off the Empress Dowager's conservative coup in that year. Yüan did not respond, and the exiled reformers thereafter accused him of betraying them and the Kuang-hsü Emperor (see pages 385, 393), while the Empress Dowager and her commander-in-chief, Jung-lu, continued to rely on him. During the crisis of 1900 he had been admired by foreigners as vigorously anti-Boxer, but he was also loyal to the dynasty, so much so that in July 1901 the throne transferred to Yüan's command the Self-Strengthening Army from Kiangsu.

The subsequent deaths of Li Hung-chang (1901), Liu K'un-i (1902), and Jung-lu (1903) left Yüan Shih-k'ai, in his mid-forties, the chief army-builder in the empire. Inheriting Li Hung-chang's position as governor-general of Chihli and Peiyang Commissioner from 1901 to 1907, he worked closely with the top Manchu, the notoriously corrupt Prince Ch'ing (I-k'uang, 1836–1916), who had held the highest positions in foreign affairs at Peking ever since the dismissal of Prince Kung in 1884. Thus Prince Ch'ing headed the central government's commission set up in 1903 to reorganize the armed forces, but Yüan as associate director appointed his own officers to run it, as well as the Board of War at Peking.

Yüan Shih-k'ai's build-up of six divisions of his Peiyang Army, with its half-dozen diversified military schools, miniature general staff, well-drilled troops, and impressive maneuvers, had been imitated, incompletely and less effectively, in most of the provinces, first of all under Chang Chih-tung in Hupei. For the Ch'ing empire, however, still fragmented by regional-provincial interests, genuine military centralization was politically impossible. The reorganization program of 1904 therefore proposed to have China's armies still developed and controlled essentially at the provincial level, thus leaving intact the balance of domestic power relations betwen Peking and the major provinces. Though the New Army (Lu-chün) blueprint called for 36 divisions, each of 12,500 men, and followed the Japanese model in many details, it lacked the essential ingredients of centralized direction, adequate financing, and industrial support. The ancient banners and much of the constabulary still remained on the rolls.

This general military growth, under the stimulus of the Russian ambitions in Manchuria and then the Russo-Japanese War of 1904–1905, developed several new features. First, the new military schools, like that at Paoting near Peking, had begun to produce a whole new class of scholar-officers, military activists imbued with patriotism, who combined modern military knowledge with some of the scholar's sense of responsibility for putting the empire in order. Secondly, Japanese instructors, cheaper than Germans, were now hired in increasing numbers, and Chinese officer candidates were sent to military academies in Japan, where their patriotism was further aroused by the example of a foreign land. Chiang Kai-shek, of Chekiang, aged eighteen, attended Paoting in 1906 and the Japanese Military Cadets Academy in 1907.

Administrative Reform and the Central Power. The Ch'ing administration of 1901 had been inherited from the early Ming of 500 years before. Refined gradually during more than four centuries, this decentralized but rather sophisticated and highly articulated bureaucratic structure, with its established procedures and built-in balances and safeguards, had served the agrarian-based Chinese empire well enough until about 1800. But now, just as the mounted archer had been supplanted, rather suddenly, by the railroad and rifle, and the sailing junk by the steamship, so the imperial government faced a technological revolution, first of all toward centralization.

For modern purposes, China needed dynamic central organs to perform new functions with unwonted initiative and speed, to apply new laws and fiscal procedures, and to be more fully acknowledged by the provinces as their superior and coordinator. But such a unitary national government would upset the ancient balance between Peking and the provinces. The provincial administrations still reported directly to the emperor and were merely supervised and serviced, rather than directed and controlled, by the Six Boards at the capital. Moreover, the late nineteenth-century growth of regionalism, helped by the growth of treaty-port industries and local trade revenues, regional armies and personal bureaucratic machines, had now strengthened the position of the major provincial governments in the power structure, in spite of the increasing national need for stronger government at the center. Reform at Peking consequently faced both the bureaucratic inertia of old vested interests and the restive jealousy of new provincial interests.

Reforms of the administrative structure at Peking were generally begun by new agencies set up alongside, within, or under the ancient organs of government; whereupon the new organs grew stronger while the ancient ones withered. So in 1901, as required by the Boxer Protocol, the Tsungli Yamen, which had long functioned alongside the Six Boards (Liu Pu), became a full-scale Ministry of Foreign Affairs (Wai-wu Pu). (*Pu* is customarily translated "board" in the Ch'ing period, but in both earlier and later periods as "ministry.") In 1905 a Ministry of Police was inaugurated, forerunner of a Ministry of Internal Affairs. In the reorganization of 1906, the new Ministry of Education took over the examining function of the Board of Ceremonies, while the old Board of War (Ping Pu), customarily headed by civil officers, was expanded into the Lu-chün Pu (literally, Army Ministry). It absorbed the new Japanese-type military administration, and was headed by ambitious Manchu generals, who tried vigorously but in the end unsuccessfully to cut down the influence of Yüan Shih-k'ai and his Peiyang clique.

It was typical of this period that innovations started by "bureaus" (*chü*) in the coastal provinces now began to be pursued by committees or new ministries at Peking. Thus after bureaus of commercial affairs had first promoted chambers of commerce, commercial newspapers, and business and industrial schools in leading provinces, a Ministry of Commerce (Shang-wu Pu) was set up at Peking in 1903. It eventually absorbed the old Board of Works (Kung Pu) and became a Ministry of Agriculture, Industry, and Commerce (Nung-kung-shang Pu), trying to promote railroad-building, industrial exhibits, standard weights and measures, registration of firms, mining regulations, company law, farmers' associations, and other measures of modern economic growth or administration. Typically, it offered official rank to reward economic achievement.

New structures at Peking were easier to inaugurate than new processes over the empire. Legal reform, for example, was held by the foreign powers to be prerequisite, as in Japan, to any abolition of extraterritoriality. In 1904 a law-compilation bureau began work under Shen Chia-pen, a 65-year-old scholar-veteran of the Board of Punishments. He began by trying to give modern expression to traditional social values but ended up proposing revolutionary changes.

Thus in 1907 Shen put forward a draft criminal code based on Japanese and German models which would have distinguished law from morality —

that is, it would have made the Confucian rules of propriety, like filial piety, legally unenforceable as such. By also making all persons outside the imperial family equal before the law, Shen would have dealt a blow to the five relationships and the whole hierarchic social order based on distinctions of status, age, and sex. His draft was rejected.

Shen also presented, however, a less drastic revision of the Ch'ing code or *Ta-Ch'ing lü-li*, which was finally promulgated in 1910 and remained in force until after 1928. Though entitled a "current criminal code" (*Ta-Ch'ing hsien-hsing hsing-lü*), this revision still included civil as well as criminal matters, and both law and procedure. It contributed to modernization by reducing corporal punishment and torture; abolishing branding, slicing, slavery, and public exposure of heads and corpses; substituting individual for collective responsibility; distinguishing between civil and criminal law; and enunciating certain general principles to guide the application of the numerous specific regulations or "supplementary laws" (*li*). These had accumulated during the dynasty to a total of about 1900 items, a corpus of rather concrete but often mutually contradictory rules which magistrates could not apply with any degree of consistency or predictability. This ambiguity and uncertainty as to the law applicable to a case, added to the fact that law had been neither primary nor pervasive in Chinese society, had left the judicial function of magistrates stunted and undeveloped, to say nothing of the whole world of legal philosophy and phraseology and the legal profession itself. Though he reduced the number of *li*, Shen Chia-pen could not remake this situation. He presented other draft codes which remained unaccepted by the Ch'ing but pointed the way toward subsequent modernization.

Financial reform was even more difficult, not only because it threatened so many "rice bowls" (individual incomes) but also because the inherited fiscal system was so superficial and weak to begin with. In the first place, the actual tax collections over the empire remained largely unknown, unbudgeted, and unaccounted for. Local tax collectors, as well as the provincial regimes above them, had to live on what they collected. What they should report to Peking was fixed by traditional quotas. At a guess, it was perhaps a third, possibly only a fifth, of the actual collection.

Second, the taxes officially received, more or less according to quota, were not centralized in a "common purse." Instead, they were listed as a congeries of fixed sums due from a multitude of specific sources and allotted to a multitude of specific uses. Sums listed at Peking were seldom received or disbursed there, for revenues from a province were allotted in bits and pieces to meet needs in it or elsewhere. Of the 18 provinces, 13 regularly forwarded fixed allotments for specific purposes to other provinces. For example, the 7 million taels allotted to maintain the bannermen in Peking came from 52 different sources over the empire. This *ad hoc* procedure tied the imperial revenues to an infinite number of vested interests, mainly the support of officials and soldiers.

Finally, even at Peking there was no single fiscal authority. The imperial revenues about 1905 totaled on the books roughly 102 million taels (say 70 million dollars or 14½ million pounds sterling), a small sum for so large a country (see table, page 327). To make up this total the Board of Revenue listed its receipts from the land tax and tribute grain still at the traditional figure of about 33 million taels, to which the salt tax added 13 million and other taxes about 7 million. The Board listed the provincial likin collections at the nominal figure reported to it of 14 million taels. Meanwhile the new and growing Maritime Customs revenue, 35 million taels in 1905, was handled separately, under the Tsungli Yamen, and in any case was earmarked for foreign indemnity payments. Thus the new trade taxes — customs and likin — were hardly under Peking's control, while the traditional land tax quotas remained inelastic. With authority thus divided, actual revenues unknown, and many expenditures entrenched as vested interests, fiscal reform could come only through an unprecedented assertion of central power, changing the balance on which the Manchu dynasty had so long maintained itself.

The ancient Board of Revenue, though reorganized in 1906 as a Ministry of Finance, still could not centralize fiscal control. Other ministries continued to receive and expend their traditional revenues and even set up their own banks, like the Bank of Communications (1907).

A novel effort to make a national budget began with nationwide revenue surveys in 1908 and the compilation of budget estimates in 1910, in which central-and-provincial government revenues and expenditures were differentiated from local. This produced estimates of total revenues (297 million taels) and expenditures (national-including-provincial, 338 million taels; local, 37 million taels) which presaged a sizable deficit (78 million taels). Unfortunately, planning and budgeting, collecting statistics and setting tax rates, went on in both the central ministries and the provinces, uncoordinated, with the provinces not subordinate to the ministries and yet expected to supply the revenues.

These many inadequacies of the old regime, in administration, law, and finance, were deeply rooted in Chinese custom, political values, and social structure. It became apparent that the Ch'ing government, which had been superficial, passive, and indeed parasitic for so long, could become modern only by expanding its functions and asserting its central leadership. For an alien dynasty in an era of rising nationalism, this was a formidable task.

Constitutionalism and Provincial Support. When Japan's constitutional monarchy defeated Russia's tsarist autocracy in 1905, constitutionalism seemed to have proved its efficacy as a basis for unity between rulers and ruled in a national effort. Even Russia now moved in 1905 toward parliamentary government. Constitutionalism in China, it was hoped, if combined with government reorganization to strengthen the central administrative power, might give the rising provincial interests a meaningful share in the government and so keep them loyal to it. Between 1906 and 1911 Peking actively pursued this dual program, combining administrative modernization and constitutionalism. Such changes, however, precipitated a struggle for power, both within the central government and between it and the provinces.

In the power struggle at the capital, the Manchu princes succeeded in maintaining, or even enlarging, their grip on key posts while preventing really fundamental reforms. This pro-Manchu and therefore anti-Chinese coloration at the capital handicapped Peking's efforts to create a new and more centralized relationship with the provinces.

Anti-Ch'ing sentiment came not only from the revolutionary students in Tōkyō but also from a rising spirit of nationalism within China. This was manifest in 1905 in China's first modern boycott, against the United States' discriminatory treatment of Chinese, particularly the total exclusion of laborers. In this boycott, the old tradition of cessation of business by local merchant guilds was expanded nationwide to most of the treaty ports, especially Shanghai and Canton, where students joined merchants in mass meetings and modern press agitation. American trade was damaged for some months, and Peking hesitated to repress this popular anti-foreign movement lest it become antidynastic also.

Under the pressure of rising nationalist sentiment, the court sent two official missions in the first half of 1906 to study constitutionalism abroad. One visited mainly the United States and Germany; the other, Japan, England, and France. Prince Itō lectured the visitors on the necessity of the emperor's retaining supreme power, not letting it fall into the hands of the people. On their return they recommended following this Japanese view, that a constitution and civil liberties including "public discussion," all granted by the emperor, could actually strengthen his position because he would remain above them all. In September 1906 the Empress Dowager promised "a constitutional polity" after due preparation. Further missions visited Japan and Germany in 1907–08.

In order to build up a modern central government, the Six Boards in November 1906 were expanded to make eleven ministries (Foreign Affairs, Civil Appointments, Internal Affairs, Finance, Rites, Education, War, Justice, Agriculture-Industry-and-Commerce, Posts-and-Communications, and Dependencies). Parallel with this executive echelon of government it was proposed to establish a Military Staff Office and four *yüan* (lit., "a courtyard," a common term for organs of government, usually left untranslated): namely, a Censorate (Tu-ch'a Yüan), National Consultative Yüan (i.e., a "popular assembly"), Audit Yüan, and Administrative Justice Yüan. This proposal would seem to combine the Western separation of three powers — executive, legislative, and judicial — with the Chinese tradition of three echelons of administration — military, civil, and censorial. While the three last-named *yüan* (Consultative, Audit, and Justice) were only talked about in 1906, they paralleled Sun Yat-sen's scheme for a "five-power" or five-*yüan* constitution, eventually adopted in the 1920's.

In August 1908 the Empress Dowager proclaimed a set of constitutional principles to guide a nine-year program to prepare for constitutional self-government. Accordingly, consultative provincial assemblies were to be convened in 1909 and a consultative national assembly in 1910. This idea of a nine years' tutelage imitated Japan, where in 1881 a Diet had been promised for 1890. Sun Yat-sen, as we shall note below, had also proposed a nine-year preparation for constitutional government, in three stages. Ardent constitutionalists, however, objected to so long a period.

The Ch'ing regime was further weakened by the death of the Empress Dowager on November 15, 1908. For half a century the "Old Buddha" (*Lao Fo-yeh*), as she was respectfully called in common parlance, had been at the center of power, exerting an influence upon the course of China's history that is still almost unstudied and certainly incalculable. She was a great patron, for example, of the colorful, northern-style "Peking opera" but lacked the ability of a K'ang-hsi or Ch'ien-lung, in far different times, to be a leading connoisseur of art and patron of literature. On her death, the demise of the hapless but usually healthy Kuang-hsü Emperor was announced as having occurred on the preceding day, November 14. The Empress Dowager had named as his successor her three-year-old grand-nephew P'u-i (also Pu-yi), who reigned as the Hsüan-t'ung Emperor (1909–1912), with his father, the second Prince Ch'un, as regent. Kuang-hsü's mysterious death at 37 destroyed the best chance of China's transition to a constitutional monarchy and left the throne in the hands of a group of ignorant and vainglorious Manchu princes, striving to maintain their power in the midst of reform. Sir Robert Hart returned to England on leave in 1908, Yüan Shih-k'ai was dismissed in January 1909, and Chang Chih-tung died in October.

The late Ch'ing reform movement, too grudging and too slow, now faced more problems than it could solve. For example, the new central administration under eleven ministries at Peking needed coordination through a cabinet. But such an agency, it was feared, might become too powerful, if packed and dominated by the premier, who might eclipse the throne. The Ch'ing regency hesitated to give up its power.

In order to survive, the Manchu dynasty needed to retain the support of the non-official Chinese elite, the stratum of local leadership throughout the provinces, which traditionally had been the class of degree-holders or "gentry." Since the opening of the treaty ports, this elite had undergone a considerable change. Out of the old landlord-*scholar*-official gentry class, already fragmented and after 1905 no longer produced by examinations, a new landlord-*merchant*-official class had begun to emerge, more ready to invest in commercial and industrial enterprises. This shift of values, from Confucian scholar to modern businessman, was a subtle process. Landowning and officeholding continued to be supports of the ruling class, but on the third leg of the tripod of power, the modern-minded merchant now began to supplant the classical degree-holder. The public functions formerly carried out by landlord-scholar-gentry in their semi-private capacities — maintaining local public works (irrigation ditches, bridges, temples), educational institutions (academies, libraries), relief agencies, and the like — were being neglected even as the local need for them increased. But the new landlord-merchant "gentry," though increasingly atomized, urbanized, and diversified by modern developments, were still the potential leaders in local and provincial government, to whom Peking must look for cooperation.

One exemplary leader of this type, prominent in the constitutional movement, was Chang Chien (1853–1926) of Kiangsu. A prefectural degree-holder (*hsiu-ts'ai*) at fifteen in 1868, he took the triennial provincial examination six times, becoming a *chü-jen* only in 1885, and then the metropolitan examination five times, finally becoming a *chin-shih* in 1894 and being selected in the palace examination as the top scholar of the empire (*chuang-yüan*) at the age of forty-one. This success coincided, however, with Japan's defeat of China. To save his country, Chang now became a pioneer industrialist. He decided to utilize the skilled labor and long-staple cotton produced in his home district of Nantung, Kiangsu, so as to spin cotton yarn that could compete with the rapidly growing Indian and Japanese imports. Through his prestige as a scholar and his high-level connections with officials like Chang Chih-tung, Liu K'un-i, and Sheng Hsüan-huai, he received encouragement, status, tax benefits, and some of the capital and machinery necessary to launch his Dah-Sun (Ta-sheng) cotton-spinning mill in 1899. In comparison, his half-dozen merchant-partners were of little help.

Chang Chien used Western technical advice and production methods but handled his labor force like a Confucian Robert Owen, paternally concerned with their "joys and sorrows alike" as well as their living quarters and education. Prospering, he built three more mills and branched out into cotton-growing, steamship transport, and consumer industries — flour, oil, and salt production — and also became a philanthropist, eventually making Nantung a model district with schools and technical colleges, roads, parks, homes for the orphaned and aged, even a new jail. Having thus made the transition from scholar-gentry to entrepreneur, Chang Chien became head of the Kiangsu Education Association, a promoter of railways, and in 1909 president of the Kiangsu Provincial Assembly, where he pushed for constitutional government.

In February 1910, representatives of all sixteen provincial assemblies met at Peking. Representing a vociferous, nationwide movement, they petitioned the throne to set up a national parliament. This was rejected, but the petitioning continued. The demand for government by a genuine parliament and cabinet became intensified after the consultative national assembly, consisting of 100 appointees of the throne and 100 of the provincial assemblies, convened in October 1910. Thus pressed, the regent promised a parliament for 1913 and meanwhile, in April 1911, at long last established a cabinet; but with incredible ineptitude he appointed eight Manchus, one Mongol bannerman, and only four Chinese!

The Railway Controversy. Provincial conflict with the central power came to a head over railway-building. China's late nineteenth-century policy of avoiding foreign-financed and foreign-run railways had been smashed in the scramble of 1898. Foreign-controlled lines — Russian and Japanese in Manchuria, German in Shantung, and French in Yunnan — had now become tools of economic imperialism, preliminary to opening mines, extracting resources, and exploiting markets. Other lines, though nominally owned by the Ch'ing government, had been financed under contract by foreign banking syndicates, which commonly floated bond issues to raise funds as foreign loans to the Chinese government. They then built the lines and managed them as trustees for the foreign bond-holders, holding a first mortgage on the railway as security for the original loan and so remaining mortgagees in possession. China was thus entering the railway age with foreign financiers awaiting the profits.

Consequently a patriotic "rights recovery" movement became active in most provinces, where local groups demanded redemption of the foreign lines and formed companies to build Chinese provincial lines. With the moral support of provincial gentry in Hupei, Hunan, and Kwangtung, Chang Chih-tung got a British loan in 1905 and redeemed the American China Development Company's contract of 1898 to build the Hankow-Canton railway. But provincial resources proved inadequate to finance construction. Though doubly inspired by patriotism and hope of profit, these merchant-gentry railway companies found it difficult to raise the capital needed to purchase a right of way, pay the land tax on it, and buy foreign rolling stock. Speculation and corruption also handicapped their efforts, which in any case ran counter to the technological need for central planning and direction of any railroad network.

The chief proponent of railway centralization was Sheng Hsüan-huai, who had risen under the patronage of Li Hung-chang and Chang Chih-tung in turn (see pages 357–358 and 384) and by 1908 had got control over both the China Merchants' steamship line and Chang Chih-tung's industrial base around Hankow. In that year Sheng combined the Han-yang arsenal, the Ta-yeh iron mines (80 miles away in Hupei), and the coal mines at P'ing-hsiang (250 miles south in Kiangsi) to form the Han-Yeh-P'ing Coal and Iron Company. To finance it he had already become dependent on Japanese loans, just as Japan's steel works at Yawata, begun in 1896, had become dependent on iron ore from Ta-yeh. Already illicitly rich from his "official supervision" of textile mills, telegraphs, and other enterprises, Sheng now worked with the Manchu minister of finance at Peking to float foreign loans, in particular to build railways from Hankow to Canton and from Hankow into Szechwan. These were the so-called "Hukuang railways" (the line from Hankow to Peking had been completed in 1905). Thus railway building had become a major political issue. Peking's technically necessary leadership in railway development, and the foreign loans needed for it, had got thoroughly embrangled with Sheng Hsüan-huai's well-known corruption, the provincial opposition to central power, and anti-Manchu feeling in general.

Since railroad loans had become a chief tool of imperialist encroachment, the United States now became quixotically involved under the Taft administration in defending the Open Door through the contradictory method of "dollar diplomacy." Secretary of State Philander C. Knox made a vague proposal in November 1909 for "neutralization" of the railways in Manchuria. This, however, ran counter to the British policy after 1907 of acquiescing in the Russo-Japanese expansion in Manchuria. Knox's ill-conceived proposal only stimulated Japan and Russia to reaffirm secretly in 1910 their division of spheres in the Northeast. Meanwhile, in July 1909 President Taft had intervened in the Hukuang railway loan negotiations with a personal telegram to the regent at Peking, demanding "equal participation by American capital" so that it could promote "the welfare of China and . . . her territorial integrity." This got the Morgan group of banks included in a four-power (French, British, German, American) banking consortium set up in 1910.

The final contract of the consortium, signed with Sheng in May 1911, coincided with an imperial decree, which Sheng had advocated, to nationalize, buy out, and put under Peking's control all provincial railway projects. This rebuff to provincial interests threw the fat in the fire. To patriots in the provinces it seemed that the Manchus and their corrupt henchmen were selling China to foreign bankers for their own profit. A "railway protection" movement sprang up, particularly in Szechwan, with mass meetings and anguished petitions to Peking, all in vain. The Szechwan movement intensified. Shops and schools were closed. Tax payments were stopped. Peasant support was mobilized. In September the government moved troops, shot down demonstrators, and seized the gentry leaders. Typically, these men were degree-holders of means, with landlord-merchant backgrounds, who had studied in Japan, were now prominent in the provincial assembly, and had invested heavily in railway projects. Their antiforeign slogan "Szechwan for the Szechwanese" represented the interest of the provincial ruling class, which had now become violently antidynastic.

Thus the decade of late Ch'ing reforms had seen the beginning of a social and institutional metamorphosis. Some of the landlord gentry, less and less oriented toward official examinations and imperial preferment, had developed commercial and industrial interests centered in their own provinces. Basically conservative, this provincial elite had supported the constitutional movement in hopes that a parliament at Peking could link them with the ruling power, and that a cabinet responsible to parliament, holding the bureaucracy responsible in turn, could modernize China's finances, administration, and public services. After 1909 the provincial assemblies had become new political institutions, centers of policy discussion and political organization.

Meanwhile the modern press in the treaty ports increasingly served as the bloodstream of this new life of politics. Up to 1895, Chinese periodicals had been started mainly by British and American missionaries, but most of the 60 or so publications begun during the next 15 years down to 1911 were purely Chinese ventures that combined commercial journalism with reformist ideas. New dailies sprang up in Shanghai to join the *Shun Pao* (see page 360), which had reached a circulation of 15,000 by 1895. And the Commercial Press, a pioneer in modern publishing, founded in 1897, was spreading new textbooks among the schools.

By 1911 the provincial assemblies and the press provided a forum for both the "gentry" interests and the new class of young students and military officers, "Young China." Constitutional monarchy was still the slogan of the day, but the dynastic order had been fatally undermined by revolutionary ideas.

THE REPUBLICAN REVOLUTION OF 1911

New regimes in China have often started their conquest from an external base — witness the Khitan, Jürched, Mongol, and Manchu conquerors between the tenth and the seventeenth centuries. In the early twentieth century the treaty ports, the Overseas Chinese communities in Southeast Asia and elsewhere, and the Japanese empire all gave shelter to Chinese rebels. In fact, the Revolution of 1911 was largely made in Japan.

The Japanese Influence. This idea of the formative role of Japan has been unpalatable and rather disregarded, both among Western peoples, whose forebears stimulated China's Westernization, and among Chinese patriots, who have suffered from later Japanese aggression. Nevertheless, the period from 1898 to 1914 saw a major Japanese influence on the course of Chinese history. Japan was alike the model of Ch'ing government reformers and (until about 1907) the home base for anti-Ch'ing revolutionaries. Republican China went to school in Tōkyō. The Japanese stimulus to modern education, militarism, and constitutionalism in China, already noted, was part of a broader contribution to the rise of Chinese nationalism in general.

Japan's influence in this brief period was more direct, profound, and far-reaching than that of Britain in the nineteenth century or of the United States from 1915 to 1949, or even, one may suspect, of the Soviet Union after 1949. One reason for this was Japan's much closer cultural as well as geographical propinquity. Another reason was the historical circumstance that, in this dawn of their modern age, China was most eager to learn and Japan most eager to teach, as yet without serious conflicts of national interest.

Japan's coming of age as a great power between 1895 and 1905 made her the model for Asia in the eyes of patriots not only in other Asian lands but also in Japan. It fortified the dream of Japan's pan-Asian leadership toward modernization and against Western imperialism. A Japanese movement developed for the study of contemporary China, aimed at helping her maintain her national integrity and achieve political reform and economic modernization. This was expressed in organizations such as the *Tōa Dōbun Kai* (East Asian Common Culture — in Chinese, *t'ung-wen* — Society) founded by political, cultural, and expansionist leaders in 1898. In addition to programs of historical studies of China at Tōkyō and Kyōto, centers of contemporary research were established in Taiwan, at Mukden by the South Manchurian Railway Company, and at Shanghai in the productive training academy, *Tōa Dōbun Shoin.* Scholarly and idealistic interest in China's problems merged, at the other end of a broad spectrum, with plots of activist *shishi,* "men of high purpose," associated especially with the ultrapatriotic Amur River Society (lit., "Black Dragon Society," from the Chinese name for the Amur, Hei-lung-chiang), which was founded in 1901 by Tōyama Mitsuru (1855–1944) and headed by Uchida Ryōhei (1874–1937). The primary aim of this society was to promote Japan's continental expansion beyond Korea and against Russia. It encouraged Japanese adventurers who penetrated East Asia as students, travelers, and businessmen; and these in turn fostered nationalist revolution and prepared the ground, sometimes unconsciously, for Japan's imperialist expansion at a later time. In addition to the expansionism of the chauvinists, the opposition leaders of the Liberal and Progressive parties regularly demanded from the government, as a domestic political tactic, a more vigorous foreign policy. Some of them also became actively interested in reform and revolution in China.

In 1898 Japanese protection and shelter were accordingly given K'ang Yu-wei and Liang Ch'i-ch'ao as leaders of the ill-fated radical reform movement of that year at Peking. K'ang stayed for a time in the house of the Progressive Party founder, Ōkuma, who had been prime minister briefly in 1898 and who gave Japan's growing commercial and ideological interest in China a classic formulation in his so-called "Ōkuma doctrine":

that Japan, having modernized first, should repay her ancient cultural debt to China by now guaranteeing her freedom and aiding her modernization. Fifteen years later Ōkuma still saw Japan as "the point of contact between the civilizations of the East and of the West," destined to raise "the civilization of the Orient to the high level of . . . the Occident so that the two might coexist in harmony." (Even Yamagata, founder of Japan's military power, in 1914 decried "the application of force alone" and wanted "to instill in China a sense of abiding trust in us.")

Ōkuma's follower, Inukai (destined to be assassinated as prime minister in 1932), cultivated the various groups of Chinese political exiles. In 1898 he got Liang and Sun Yat-sen together to discuss cooperation between the radical reformers led by K'ang Yu-wei and the anti-Ch'ing revolutionaries represented by Sun. K'ang, however, not only refused to meet Sun unless he became a disciple; he also remained a monarchist, stubbornly loyal to his Kuang-hsü Emperor. In 1899 he began to visit Overseas Chinese communities around the world to set up units of his "Protect-the-Emperor Society" (*Pao-huang hui*), collect funds, and stimulate a reformist press. In his teacher's absence, Liang for a time contemplated joining forces with Sun, but K'ang prevented it. The Japanese effort at unity failed; and after 1900 the two Chinese exile groups, reformers and revolutionaries, though both patriotic and both proscribed by Peking, became bitter rivals.

Two Protagonists: Liang Ch'i-ch'ao and Sun Yat-sen. Liang visited Honolulu and Southeast Asia in 1900–1901, and the United States in 1903, but spent most of the decade in Japan. Already a master of classical learning, he absorbed modern ideas voraciously and wrote upon all manner of subjects in an eloquent, clear, and forceful style that soon made him the most influential writer of the period — the Chinese students' window on the world. The titles of his successive journals indicate the trend of his thinking — "Public Opinion" (*Ch'ing-i pao*, 1898 . . .), "The Renovation of the People" (*Hsin-min ts'ung-pao*, 1902 . . .), "The National Spirit" (*Kuo-feng pao*, 1910 . . .). Still only thirty in 1903, Liang Ch'i-ch'ao soon left his teacher behind. K'ang Yu-wei was then forty-five, past changing, and Liang had already put him in his place by praising him as "the Martin Luther of Confucianism" and a great thinker of the period "before Darwinism came to China." Thus as he absorbed modern learning in Japan, Liang began to put China's problems in a context of Western or world history, not merely Chinese history. To justify reform and progress in China, he no longer cited K'ang's radical reinterpretation of Confucius' teaching but instead took up the then world-wide doctrine of Social Darwinism, that history consists essentially of races and nations competing for survival in the process of evolution. Having made this transition, he could compare China's long development with that of other nations, compare Columbus and Vasco da Gama with Cheng Ho, Immanuel Kant with Wang Yang-ming, and look back on the "new text" movement, in which he had been so ardent in the nineties, as comparable to the revival of Greek learning in the Renaissance. In short, he had got outside of China's classical learning and was beginning the modern re-appraisal of Chinese history which is still going on.

Liang's hope for China lay in popular education for nationalism, a moral "renovation of the people" (*hsin-min*). Echoing Fukuzawa and other Westernizers in Japan, he espoused an Anglo-Saxon ideal of self-respect, individualism, enterprise, and public-spirited citizenship. De-nouncing China's political decadence, he urged the transfer of loyalty from ruler to nation, from Confucian personal relationships to principles of law, and the establishment of new institutions — "a constitution, a par-liament, and a responsible government." He also sponsored literary maga-zines, the writing of short stories and other fiction, and translations of world literature, mainly from Japanese versions, into Chinese.

In politics, however, Liang refrained from blaming China's ills on the Manchu dynasty. Like any member of the gentry elite as well as most foreign observers, he believed his people unprepared for representative democracy. He remained therefore a gradualist and a constitutional monarchist, antirepublican and not actively revolutionary. The Political Culture Association (*Cheng-wen she*) which he organized in 1907 advo-cated orderly political processes and had great influence in the constitu-tional movement, though it fell into the usual liberal position — both the Ch'ing government and the anti-Ch'ing revolutionaries attacked it, from opposite sides.

While Liang was an upper-class aristocrat of the intellect and a leader of thought more than of action, his fellow-Cantonese Sun Yat-sen (formal name: Sun Wen; 1866–1925) was one of the early professional revolution-aries of modern times. The two men approached China's problems from opposite social contexts, with antithetic preconceptions, and through dif-ferent media. While Liang was expounding the ideology of Chinese na-tionalism, Sun built up the structure of the early revolutionary movement.

Sun had, or acquired, a remarkable list of qualifications for revolution-ary leadership. He came from Hsiang-shan, the district next to Macao, longest in touch with Westerners, farthest from Peking's control, home of the original "returned student" Yung Wing, of the comprador Tong King-sing, and of countless emigrants to the Overseas Chinese communi-ties abroad. Socially as well as geographically, Sun's origin was op-portune. Son of a peasant, he was schooled by an uncle who had fought for the lost cause of the Taipings (modern China's romantic equivalent of the American Confederacy), and Hung Hsiu-ch'üan was his boyhood hero.

Sun's early career was equally unoriented toward the emperor at Peking, for at thirteen he sailed in a British steamship to join his elder brother in Honolulu, where he stayed three years and studied an English curriculum in a Church of England boarding school. He sang in the choir and accepted Christianity. Returning to his native village an iconoclast, he broke local idols and was sent away. He studied in Hong Kong, supported by his brother overseas, and after another visit to Honolulu, spent five years (1886–1892) in Canton and Hong Kong studying such subjects as chemistry, physiology, surgery, and clinical medicine for his medical degree from a British mission hospital. In 1892 he began to practice in Macao but was forced out for lack of a diploma from Portugal. Having been concerned over the fate of China ever since her defeat by France in 1885, Sun submitted a reformist petition to the chief Westernizer of the day, Li Hung-chang, but got no reply. Thwarted as a doctor, disregarded by those in power, he now turned to a new calling — neither merchant, peasant, scholar, nor medical practitioner, but revolutionist, a man of no class, ready to work with all classes.

Sun had already made contact with that traditional rebel body, the Triad Society (see pages 119–120). By 1894 he had a secret society of his own, the *Hsing-Chung hui* (lit., "Revive China Society"), with branches in Hawaii as well as in the Macao-Hong Kong-Canton area. In 1895 its first plot, to seize the Canton provincial government offices, was discovered, and several of Sun's fellow conspirators were executed. But he himself escaped to Japan, cut his queue, grew a mustache, and in Western-style clothes soon passed for a Japanese under the name of Nakayama (lit., "central mountain," which in its Chinese form, Chung-shan, would later be applied to public parks and thoroughfares, educational institutions, and even a style of clothing in Nationalist China). Now "wanted" by Peking, Sun went by way of the United States to London. There in 1896 he was recognized at the Chinese legation, "kidnaped," and held for twelve days preparatory to being shipped back to China for execution; but his old teacher of medicine, Sir James Cantlie, who had also taught him cricket in Hong Kong, mobilized British opinion and got him released. Thus at the age of thirty, already world-famous as the leading anti-Ch'ing revolutionary, Sun felt himself a man of destiny.

By the time he returned to Japan in 1897, and took the aid and advice of expansionists there, Sun had put together several ingredients of rebellion, some new, some old. New elements included financial support from Overseas Chinese communities which had grown up outside the traditional mainland society with nonconformist, commercial values, nationalistic but frustrated in their political loyalties; and leadership from a small group of semi-Westernized, sometimes Christian, patriotic youth who came like Sun from the Canton area, particularly his native district of Hsiang-shan, on the modernizing fringe of Chinese life. Old-style ingredients included the bands of armed rebels that could be assembled by the mainland secret societies; and the simple antidynastic aim of seizing local power somewhere by force, hoping thereby to set off a chain reaction that would topple the imperial government.

In October 1900 a two-week rising was engineered with Triad Society aid at Waichow (Hui-chou) north of Hong Kong, though it had to be broken off when Japanese arms and men from Taiwan failed to materialize. Trying to combine traditional and modern means, Sun joined the *Chih-kung t'ang* lodge of the Triad Society in Hawaii in 1903 and worked through it all over the United States.

By this time, however, he faced a new problem — how to compete with other revolutionists by appealing to the new generation of Chinese students abroad, especially in Japan. For this purpose he needed to develop a rationale of revolution. K'ang Yu-wei still had most of the support of the rather conservative Overseas Chinese merchants in Southeast Asia, and Liang Ch'i-ch'ao's writings were forming the ideas of the new student class. Meanwhile risings had been attempted by others, like T'ang Ts'ai-ch'ang, a Hunan reformer and follower of K'ang and Liang, who arranged for his own student group (the *Tzu-li hui* or "Independence Society") to join with the central Yangtze branches of the ancient *Ko-lao hui* (Brothers and Elders Society) for a rising at Hankow in 1900 — only to be discovered, seized, and executed.

Revolutionary societies, schools, and journals were springing up among students in the treaty ports as well as in Japan. A Kiangsu-Chekiang group in Shanghai was led by classical scholars like Chang Ping-lin (Chang T'ai-yen) and Ts'ai Yüan-p'ei, who attacked K'ang and Liang. In 1903 their inflammatory anti-Manchu paper in Shanghai, the *Su-pao*, was suppressed, and Chang was imprisoned for three years. In 1904 Ts'ai Yüan-p'ei headed the *Kuang-fu hui* ("Restoration Society"; lit., "return-of-light society") composed of students from Chekiang and the Lower Yangtze provinces. In Hunan, Huang Hsing founded the *Hua-hsing hui* ("China Revival Society") in 1903 and tried to unite army officers, students, and secret society members for a rising at Changsha in 1904, but as so often happened, the plot was discovered and broken up. One widely circulated and influential call to action was *The Revolutionary Army* published by an eighteen-year-old youth, Tsou Jung, in 1903. Revolutionary activity was thus growing, but it lacked coordination, specific ideology, and a long-term program.

Facing this competition, and opportunity, Sun Yat-sen now developed his own ideological appeal. In 1903 he wrote his first newspaper articles in Tōkyō and Honolulu. By mid-1905, after organizing Chinese student groups in Brussels, Berlin, and Paris, he was back in Tōkyō again. Dedicated in aim but flexible, if not indeed opportunist, as to means, Sun now put together from his multi-cultural background in China, Japan, the United States, and Europe a set of ideas to justify and guide a republican revolution. This was the Three Principles of the People (*San-min chu-i*): *min-tsu chu-i* (a term connoting both people and race), national-ism; *min-ch'üan chu-i* ("people's rights"), democracy; and *min-sheng chu-i* ("people's livelihood"), socialism.

These three protean concepts summed up much of the ferment of the age and yet could undergo much change in specific content. "National-ism" was at this time both anti-Manchu, hence pro-republican, and anti-imperialist, though this latter aspect was not stressed by those seeking foreign aid for the revolution. "Democracy" implied an anti-Confucian egalitarianism, to be guaranteed by a constitution (which stole Liang's thunder) with five powers — executive, legislative, and judicial as in the United States, plus examination and censorial or "control" powers drawn from the Chinese tradition. This "five-power constitution" was apparently Sun's own invention. Finally, his "socialism," to meet the new problems of industrial growth, involved no Marxist class struggle but instead fol-lowed Henry George's then popular idea of a single tax to appropriate future unearned increase of land value and thus check the enrichment of speculators and monopolists. Thus the ancient term *min-sheng* (later translated as "people's livelihood") in 1905 meant principally this urban "equalization of land rights" in the specific Western single-tax sense, not an agrarian land-redistribution. The latter would as yet kindle little enthusiasm among the sons of merchants and landlords, eager though they might be for a political revolution.

The T'ung-meng Hui and Its Vicissitudes. All these ingredients — Overseas Chinese funds, secret society contacts, new student leadership, and revolutionary ideology — were finally combined in 1905 under Japa-nese encouragement. Bringing rival groups together, Sun's oldest friend in Japan, Miyazaki Torazō, introduced him to Huang Hsing and others of the Hunan group. At a big Tōkyō meeting in August the *T'ung-meng hui* ("United League," a typical secret society name) was founded with Sun as chief executive (*tsung-li*), Huang Hsing second in command, and Chang Ping-lin and others named to key posts. Overseas offices in Singa-pore, Brussels, San Francisco, and Honolulu were to be coordinated with branches in seventeen provinces (every one but Kansu). Among roughly a thousand early members, the largest group was from the provinces of Hunan and Hupei (so long governed by that modernizer of education, Chang Chih-tung), while the Cantonese were second, and the Szech-wanese and Lower Yangtze contingents third and fourth in size. Huang's society (*Hua-hsing hui*) contributed far more members than Sun's *Hsing-Chung hui*.

Felt by many to be a magnetic personality, Sun at thirty-nine was not only the eldest but also the most famous, the most widely traveled, and the most experienced among this revolutionary band, with the greatest number of contacts in Japan and overseas, though not in the Yangtze provinces. On the other hand, as a "foreignized" Chinese and not one of the scholar elite, a man known for conspiracy and desperate action rather than for literary production, and indeed intellectually rather superficial, he could not stand forth in the role of modern sage to guide the thinking of his generation. And yet, given the multi-cultural confusion produced by the collapse of China's great tradition and the variety of foreign models to choose among, probably no systematic thinker could have had even as much success as Sun Yat-sen.

The new ideology of republicanism was expounded by Sun's literary lieutenants in the *T'ung-meng hui* journal *Min-pao* ("The People"). In 1905–1907, in a vigorous attack on Liang Ch'i-ch'ao's ideas of gradualist reform and constitutional monarchy, *Min-pao* writers like Wang Ching-wei (1883–1944), Hu Han-min (1879–1936), and Chang Ping-lin (1868–1936) largely succeeded in winning Chinese student support for the attractive thesis that China could catch up with and indeed surpass the West by a speedy revolution — Sun used the ancient phrase, "make one all-out effort and be forever after at ease" — instead of gradual evolution. These polemicists argued that China's past experience held many bases for domestic development; that "men of determination," providing strong leadership (as in Japan), could intervene to speed up the process of modernization. Further to meet Liang's argument that the Chinese people would need an enlightened despotism and much popular education to prepare them for modern political life, the *T'ung-meng hui* put forward Sun's three-stage program: (1) three years of military government, with local self-government beginning district by district; (2) six years under a provisional constitution (*yüeh-fa*), which later came to be known as a period of "tutelage" (*hsun-cheng*); and (3) eventual constitutional government with an elected president and parliament. These optimistic assumptions and over-simple promises soon proved more popular than the cooler rationality of Liang Ch'i-ch'ao, whose espousal of benevolent monarchy was in any case torpedoed by the death of the Kuang-hsü Emperor in 1908.

Despite its new unity, the revolutionary movement suffered repeated frustrations. In the most rebellious province, Hunan, an independent revolt of the Brothers and Elders Society in October 1906, caused partly by famine, was joined by coal miners at P'ing-hsiang in Kiangsi but was suppressed in a month by government troops from four provinces. In 1907, Ch'ing protests led Japan to expel Sun Yat-sen. He and Huang Hsing moved to Hanoi in French Indo-China and between May 1907 and May 1908 staged six outbreaks in Kwangtung, Kwangsi, and Yunnan. But the friendly French soon found that the Chinese example stimulated Vietnamese unrest. They in turn expelled the *T'ung-meng hui* conspirators. By 1909, Ch'ing arrests and executions, combined with the revolutionists' failure of coordination and lack of success, had discouraged Overseas Chinese financial support and led to dissension within the movement. It practically came to a standstill, and Sun went to the West again seeking funds. Others took up anarchism, advocated especially by a group of students from Paris, and, like Russian anarchists, resorted to assassination to dramatize their cause. In 1910 the handsome Wang Ching-wei tried to bomb the prince regent in Peking but was caught and imprisoned. Anti-Manchu feeling was rising, but the revolutionary movement seemed thoroughly frustrated.

Huang Hsing pursued the most hopeful course of subverting imperial troops. An army revolt engineered at Canton in February 1910 was suppressed, but another overseas fund drive collected 187,000 Hong Kong dollars, mainly from Southeast Asia and Canada, and financed the smuggling of arms and "dare-to-die" attack forces into Canton in April 1911. Like most earlier plots, the "Canton Revolution" of April 27 (the 29th of the third month of the lunar calendar) was doomed, despite individual heroism, by a sequence of difficulties — inadequate secrecy, government precautions, last-minute changes of plan, lack of coordination, general confusion, and practical futility. Huang Hsing's men in several groups tried as usual to seize the chief government offices; but one group mistook another's identity, and they dispersed each other with gunfire, thus helping to produce the famous "72 martyrs" of Canton. Sun Yat-sen listed this as the tenth failure of his forces since 1895. Huang Hsing concluded that "in instigating revolution, dictatorship is imperative. Once a dissenting voice is permitted, the revolution is bound to fail."

All these risings, of the *T'ung-meng hui* and other groups, had been more political than military in their ulterior purpose, to destroy the dynasty's prestige and claim to power. Outbreaks and assassinations, funds and arms from abroad, had been used for their destructive effect on that tacit popular acquiescence which constituted Heaven's mandate. It was also endangered by worsening economic conditions, manifested in peasant rice riots (as in Hunan in 1910). The frustration of gentry interests which supported provincial "railway protection" movements (as in Szechwan in 1911) also contributed to the gradual and widespread decline of the central authority of the Ch'ing dynasty, and therefore of the monarchy as an institution.

The End of the Ch'ing Dynasty. The denouement when it came was partly accidental, locally improvised, and out of *T'ung-meng hui* control. Students and soldiers had organized a succession of revolutionary study societies in Hupei, founding new ones as the old were suppressed. One group (the *Kung-chin hui*, "Common Advancement Society"), loosely affiliated to the *T'ung-meng hui*, set up a Shanghai headquarters and cells in Hankow. A larger local group, posing as a literary society, was composed mainly of soldiers. The two groups finally agreed to cooperate in

September 1911, their plot was as usual discovered (on October 9), and some of the soldiers in Wuchang revolted in order to save themselves on October 10 (since celebrated as the "Double Ten," i.e., tenth day of the tenth solar month). Although fewer than three thousand out of a much larger body of troops rebelled, the Manchu governor-general fled the city, as did his military commander. Wuchang fell to the rebels. The foreign consuls declared neutrality. Since no revolutionary leader was on the scene, a brigade commander (Li Yüan-hung) was pressed into leadership.

This anti-Manchu rebellion received spontaneous popular support locally. Within a few weeks it inspired anti-Manchu declarations in some two dozen other centers, usually backed by the *T'ung-meng hui*, the New Army, and provincial assemblies. By early December all the southern and central and even the northwestern provinces had declared their independence, usually under Ch'ing army officers who became military governors and held power jointly with provincial assembly leaders of the constitutional movement. Fighting occurred in only half a dozen places. The Ch'ing court now recalled Yüan Shih-k'ai to power, since the best troops were loyal to him, but he came on his own terms, as premier of a new cabinet government as well as commander of the armed forces. Meanwhile the rebellious provinces and the *T'ung-meng hui* revolutionists joined forces in setting up a provisional government at Nanking.

Sun Yat-sen, who had read of the Wuchang revolt in a Denver newspaper, had gone on to England seeking a loan and British help to prevent Japan's giving financial or military aid to the dynasty. He reached Shanghai just in time to be elected, as a senior figurehead, to the provisional presidency of the Chinese Republic. He was inaugurated at Nanking on January 1, 1912, but at the same time offered to resign in favor of Premier Yüan Shih-k'ai whenever the latter would support the new republic.

Though some sharp fighting occurred, particularly at the Wuhan cities, the 1911 revolution was singularly unviolent. It was also inconclusive because its main aim was purely negative, to get rid of Manchu rule. However, there was a widespread consensus on a few positive points — that the provinces must be represented in a parliament; that Chinese unity was needed to forestall foreign, probably Japanese, intervention; and that Yüan Shih-k'ai was the one man with sufficient experience, ability, and backing to head a new government. Sun Yat-sen, Huang Hsing, and other revolutionists had generally agreed by late December 1911 that Yüan represented the chief hope of avoiding civil war, chaos, and foreign intervention. On his part, Yüan, backed by his military commanders, negotiated both publicly and secretly on various levels, from a central position, with the Ch'ing court on the one hand and with the revolutionists and their Nanking provisional government on the other, and gradually engineered a general settlement: on February 12, 1912, the Hsüan-t'ung Emperor (later known as Henry Pu-yi) bowed to "the Mandate of Heaven . . . manifested through the wish of the people" and abdicated, ending the Ch'ing dynasty, as well as the ancient Chinese monarchy and empire. Sun Yat-sen then resigned as provisional president and Yüan was elected his successor at Nanking. A violent army mutiny at Peking, however, necessitated Yüan's presence, and so he avoided moving the capital south. He was inaugurated on March 10 in his own bailiwick at Peking, to govern under a provisional constitution until a parliament should be elected and full constitutional government established. While gradualist, this program was not considered to be "tutelage," which must wait until a central authority could be re-established over the present federation of autonomous provinces.

The Son of Heaven could disappear from the scene so easily, with scarcely a bang or a whimper, because modernization — in new ideas, reform of institutions, and nationalistic aspirations — had progressed so rapidly during the preceding decade. As one symbol of this, China now adopted the international (solar) calendar instead of the ancient lunar one. The custom of dating years from the accession of the ruler was retained, except that 1912 was called the first year not of an emperor but of "the Republic," *Min-kuo*.

Yüan as president, however, was later to "betray" the revolutionists who had elected him, just as he had "betrayed" the Ch'ing court that had made him premier. To get power and keep it from 1912 to 1916, he or his entourage made use of bribery, military riots, and assassinations, coerced the parliament, revised the constitution at will, and finally tried to revive the monarchy. All these manipulations left Yüan few friends in modern China and branded him an enemy of the people and their republic. He has had a poor press and been little studied. Perhaps his greatest fault was simple incomprehension of democratic processes.

In the context of his times, Yüan Shih-k'ai may eventually appear to have performed, in addition to his evil deeds, certain useful functions. In 1912 he had no rival of equal stature capable of holding power at that unprecedented moment when the Chinese leviathan had been decapitated and no Son of Heaven was left to perform the crucial imperial functions at the apex of state and society. In this great political crisis the Manchus might have tried to fight rather than be pensioned off, the northern armies might have been used against the Nanking regime, and the Japanese, who were soon to become aggressive, might have seized this earlier opportunity. As it happened, however, Yüan had the skill and chicanery to oust the Manchus, court foreign recognition, beguile the revolutionists, and maintain an administration through a time of great uncertainty. The Japanese, with divided counsels, were unable to agree in 1911–12 on an active policy. Britain pressed for Chinese unity. Sun and his republican colleagues, having neither armed forces nor vested interests and constituencies in the provinces, knew that China needed strong and unified rule, and that they could not provide it. With nationalist sentiment of every type calling for unity under a strong man, Yüan emerged as the sole candidate.

Thus when China's immemorial monarchy was abolished, the emergence of a power-holder cushioned the shock. But Chinese political life without the Son of Heaven inevitably deteriorated, because the chief of state now lacked the traditional ideological and ceremonial sanctions for the exercise of supreme power. While not exactly theocratic in Western terms, the Chinese ruler had been indubitably placed above mankind, as Yüan was not. Lacking the traditional sanctions and not yet having developed modern ones, the Son of Heaven's successors — both Yüan and the warlords — had to rely increasingly on military force. When new sanctions were eventually established, years later, they were not those of the Anglo-Saxon model of government which the revolutionists had vaguely had in mind. In this way 1911, though it marked the end of an era, was also significant as the beginning of a prolonged crisis of central power in the world's most ancient government.

The Republic's Decline into Warlordism

The great modern transformations of economy, politics, society, thought, and culture, which have swept about the world like tidal waves, by 1912 had already begun to smash China's traditional civilization to bits and pieces. Chinese who have lived through the unprecedented era since that time have thus experienced chaos on every level, private and public, practical and theoretical. Nowhere has the search for a new order, a revival of national power, a remaking of the national life, been more prolonged or more frustrating. But the Chinese revolution, the greatest in history, has steadily accelerated and is still unfolding.

Unfortunately for historians, the recent past of the last few decades lies back beyond the range of sharp personal memory and present-day journalism but is still largely opaque to the analytic eye of historical research. Statistics are meager, and monographs few. Many developments remain only vaguely perceived. China is many times the size of Japan; less is known of its modern history. We can say more of personalities and politics than of underlying economic and social changes.

Domestic Politics: Yüan vs. the Kuomintang. The new provisional president, Yüan Shih-k'ai, having taken over the principal administrative functions of the extinct monarchy, soon became involved in the successive phases of a power struggle with the revolutionary leaders. The first phase saw disagreement but no open break. In March 1912 Yüan inaugurated the republican system of government by appointing his protégé T'ang Shao-i (who had been educated at Hartford, Connecticut, under Yung Wing) to be premier and form a ten-man cabinet. It contained four *T'ung-meng hui* members, among them Sung Chiao-jen of Hunan, a close colleague of Huang Hsing and a leading drafter of the new provisional constitution. This document had divided authority between president and parliament, and disagreement soon arose over which should control the cabinet and its administration. Premier T'ang could not establish his new role and gain authority. He had no party organization, no patronage, no budget, and no control over his cabinet ministers. When he found that Yüan Shih-k'ai would not let him run the administration, he and the four *T'ung-meng hui* members resigned (June 1912), and the cabinet thereafter became in effect responsible only to the president, not the parliament. President Yüan, however, avoiding a rupture, invited Sun Yat-sen and Huang Hsing to Peking, where each spent almost a month in the period August–October 1912. Yüan saw them frequently, expressing full and cordial agreement with their views, and appointed Sun director of railways to mastermind a great national railway system, all on paper.

The older *T'ung-meng hui* leaders, generally unskilled in government affairs, were unable to achieve, or even demand, party government. Their ideas about it were vague, their aims uncertain, their counsels divided; and the institution itself was undeveloped and untested in the Chinese scene. Political parties in fact were just taking shape, emerging out of two traditions.

One tradition was that of the clique or faction (*tang*) of scholar-officials, stemming from K'ang Yu-wei's Self-Strengthening Society (*Ch'iang-hsüeh hui*) and the other political study groups formed after 1895. This element had contributed to the nationwide constitutional movement of the last few years and now in May 1912 was expressed in a Republican Party (*Kung-ho tang*) which generally supported Yüan's administration. After Liang Ch'i-ch'ao returned from Japan to a hero's welcome, in October, he formed a Democratic Party (*Min-chu tang*) and in May 1913 amalgamated these Republicans, Democrats, and other small groups into the Progressive Party (*Chin-pu tang*), still generally in support of the government in power.

The other source of party tradition was the conspiratorial societies of revolutionists, like the *Hsing-Chung hui* and the *Hua-hsing hui*, which had coalesced in the *T'ung-meng hui*. Many political groups partook of both traditions. Many politicians belonged to several parties. No party was more than a congeries of upper-class individuals who were drawn together by personal ties or common background, but who lacked reliable electoral constituencies, political status, and experience. In short, the adaptation of Western methods of political association and agitation, such as had begun in Japan in the 1870's, was barely starting in China. Genuine issues of party policy could not be seriously debated because the institutional role of parties was itself still an issue.

Instead of a separation of powers under the supremacy of law as the central myth of the state, the Chinese monarch had traditionally integrated in his person all the powers of government. Yüan had got control over the cabinet and civil administration and was expanding it over the provincial military governors. He was asserting China's claims to Mongolia and Tibet as parts of the Ch'ing empire. Bearing all these burdens of personal responsibility, he was unprepared by experience or tradition to countenance a "loyal opposition" that might attack his policies and thwart his power while professing a higher loyalty to the Chinese Republic. Nevertheless this was precisely what the Western model of parliamentary government seemed to call for; the way seemed open for an opposition party to try to dominate the parliament, and the attempt was made.

In this next phase the power struggle was led by Sung Chiao-jen, who now ranked just after Sun and Huang among the revolutionists. He persuaded four small political groups in August 1912 to join with the *T'ung-meng hui* in forming an open party, the *Kuo-min tang* or "National People's Party." National elections, held on the basis of a very restricted and indirect franchise in each province, gave the Kuomintang a majority in the bicameral parliament by February 1913. Sung Chiao-jen thereupon campaigned widely in Central China, criticizing the administration and demanding that the Kuomintang should now control the cabinet, though Yüan should remain president.

This was a high point of parliamentary democracy in modern China, but Sung Chiao-jen's creation of the Kuomintang and inauguration of electioneering had a denouement that spectacularly blighted this promising development. Through his premier (Chao Ping-chün) and the cabinet secretary, Yüan Shih-k'ai hired assassins, as the Shanghai Mixed Court later documented in detail, and on March 20, 1913, at the Shanghai station Sung Chiao-jen was shot down. He was not yet thirty-one. Yüan temporarily confused the public with fabricated charges against Huang Hsing. Assassination had heretofore been a weapon of the anti-Ch'ing revolutionists out of power, but President Yüan had now developed its use in power, having already had various pro-revolutionist generals assassinated or executed. The strategic murder of Sung asserted a principle (that the power-holder is above the law) and demonstrated a tactic (that an opposition movement can best be checked by eliminating its leader) which have been used to strangle democracy in China ever since. In 1913 the Kuomintang activists were left leaderless, while the moderates still fondly hoped to control the president by legal means through the parliament.

In this same period the revulsion of the revolutionary party against Yüan was heightened by his getting money and recognition from the imperialist powers on onerous terms: while blasting party government at home, he seemed to be mortgaging China's revenues to the foreigners. All this stemmed from his urgent financial needs. Although Yüan now had personal control over the military governors who commanded most of the armies in the provinces, having been their old commander, he was no more able than his Ch'ing predecessors to augment the land tax and other meager revenues flowing to Peking. The Ch'ing had staved off bankruptcy by borrowing 10 million pounds sterling in April 1911 for "currency reform and Manchurian industrial development" from the four-power consortium of British, French, German, and American banks. To this group Russian and Japanese banks were added in June 1912 to make a six-power consortium.

Yüan had early begun to seek massive foreign funds, but the consortium, while maintaining its virtual monopoly over loans to China, demanded that China's salt taxes be the security and that they be collected, like the maritime customs, by a joint Sino-foreign administration. Patriotic Chinese of all persuasions protested against these terms. President Wilson in March 1913, reversing President Taft's position of 1909, refused to support American participation on the grounds that the conditions of the loan threatened China's administrative independence. But after fourteen months of negotiation the consortium contract for the great Reorganization Loan of 25 million pounds sterling was nevertheless signed (April 26, 1913). This was done with the remaining five-power group of banks, without the parliament's approval and on the same day that the evidence was published concerning Sung's assassination. (Since the bonds were floated at only 90 per cent with 6 per cent commission to the banks, China actually received only 84 per cent, or £21,000,000, and yet would have to repay principal and 5 per cent interest until 1960, a total of £67,893,597.)

Yüan's success in smashing the idea of an opposition party and in borrowing foreign money to pay his armies was largely due to the widespread belief that only he could keep China united and at peace. In mid-1913 he was still backed by the Progressive Party, tolerated by much of the Kuomintang, and supported by the northern military governors, who were his own men of the Peiyang clique. He therefore spurned various concessions offered by the Kuomintang, dismissed the military governors who supported it in Central and South China, and moved troops against them. Reacting to Yüan's aggressiveness, during July and August 1913 seven provincial governments, though ill-armed, again declared their independence of Peking in the short-lived "second revolution." This movement, the last in which Huang Hsing figured, lacked popular or foreign support and was suppressed within two months with little fighting. Sun Yat-sen, Huang, and other leaders, fleeing to Japan, found themselves back where they had started, while Yüan's generals of the Peiyang clique expanded their control as military governors over most of the remaining provinces.

The final phase of parliamentarism began when the Progressive Party, with moderate Kuomintang help, formed a cabinet at Peking in September 1913 which included some of Yüan's henchmen (Hsiung Hsi-ling as premier, Tuan Ch'i-jui as minister of war) and also Liang Ch'i-ch'ao (minister of justice) and Chang Chien (minister of agriculture and commerce). Yüan's aim, now becoming more clear, was to get himself at last formally elected president by the parliament, in the agreed-upon procedure, and then dispense with it. Bribery and strong-arm intimidation bent the parliament to his will. On October 6 it finally elected him president. On the 7th he succeeded through diplomatic bargaining in getting the major powers to recognize the Chinese Republic. On October 10 he was formally inaugurated as its first president. Soon he destroyed it. In November he ordered the Kuomintang dissolved and excluded 438 members or former members from the parliament. In January 1914 he suspended the parliament and then the provincial assemblies. In February the cabinet resigned. Yüan, at fifty-four, was now dictator.

Though execrated by patriots of a later day, Yüan's piecemeal dismantling of the thin façade of parliamentarism seems to have been of great concern only to a minor part of the public, especially to the sprinkling of would-be parliamentarians who had just begun to emerge in the treaty ports and the provincial and national capitals. Neither the rival foreign powers nor the inarticulate common people nor the city merchant class offered much objection, while the administrative bureaucracy, the army, and most of the provincial military governors simply favored stability under the one essential man at the top. Unlike the diffusion of responsibility in Japanese politics, the Chinese polity was accustomed to a single head who could balance the many conflicting interests and give final decisions. Yüan now did so, ruling through appointed organs and under a new document, the Constitutional Compact promulgated on May 1, 1914, which gave him comprehensive dictatorial powers. He muzzled the press, encouraged local "self-government" by gentry and elders, and revived the censorate and the state cult of Confucius. Alighting from his armored car, he conducted the ancient imperial rites at the Temple of Heaven. By the end of 1915 he was president for life, emperor in all but name.

Foreign Relations: The Republic vs. the Foreign Powers. Yüan Shih-k'ai's rise as a dictator was due not only to the immaturity of any institutional alternative to a Son-of-Heaven autocracy, but also to the continued Chinese desire for a strong government to ward off foreign encroachment. Nevertheless, the new Chinese Republic lost control over the outlying regions of the Ch'ing empire. This was particularly ironic because the Ch'ing dynasty in its last years had been pursuing a vigorous forward policy in Mongolia and Tibet (see pages 800–801) as well as in Manchuria.

To offset railroad penetration by Russia in northern Manchuria and by Japan in the south, the Ch'ing had abolished the traditional military government in 1907 and made Manchuria (as foreigners have called it) into the "Three Eastern Provinces" or "Northeast" as the area is known in Chinese (Fengtien, Kirin, and Heilungkiang). Under the stimulus of railroads, industrial development, and more modern administration, Chinese migrated in large numbers from North China and sovereignty remained Chinese.

Inner Mongolia, meanwhile, had seen a vigorous government-led Chinese expansion of agriculture and trade. This "secondary imperialism" was facilitated after 1909 by the Peking-Kalgan railway, the first Chinese-built line (engineered by a Hartford and Yale graduate, Chan T'ien-yu, or "Jeme Tien Yow"). Outer Mongolia, on the other hand, declared its independence in December 1911 and gradually moved into the Russian sphere. Similarly, the Ch'ing government had asserted its control and decreed reforms in Tibet in 1908, with such vigor that the Dalai Lama had fled to India in 1910. But the revolution in China led to the surrender and withdrawal of troops from Lhasa in 1912.

Thus Tibet and Outer Mongolia, which had long acknowledged the Manchu emperor, broke away from the Chinese Republic and became oriented to Britain and Russia, respectively, more than to Peking. (For details, see Chapter 9.) Having cast out the Manchus in the name of national-racial self-determination, the Chinese revolution had little claim to Inner Asia. But Yüan Shih-k'ai, inheriting power at Peking, maintained the traditional claim nevertheless. Russia, Outer Mongolia, and China soon agreed on the formula: Chinese suzerainty and Outer Mongolian autonomy (which permitted actual Russian domination); while Britain and China agreed on a similar formula: Chinese suzerainty and Tibetan autonomy (allowing a British permanent interest). Thereupon both Russia and Britain finally recognized Yüan's government on November 7, 1913. Russian influence in Outer Mongolia was already far greater than that of Britain in Tibet.

This expansion of great-power influence in China's borderlands was paralleled by a further growth of foreign control over China's revenues from foreign trade. Soon after the revolution began, Hart's successor as Inspector-General of Customs (Sir Francis Aglen) got the imperial government's agreement in November 1911 to a fundamental change in the handling of the Maritime Customs revenue, which was now fully pledged to meet China's foreign loan and indemnity payments. Previously the foreign commissioners had reported to Peking their accounts of revenues collected, but the Chinese superintendents of customs at each port had actually received and handled the funds. Now, as most of the provinces declared their independence, the unity of the Maritime Customs Service and China's foreign credit and debt payments were all preserved by arranging that the foreign commissioners should for the first time actually receive the revenue funds. After deducting the fixed allowances for local maintenance of the service and certain first charges on the revenue, they transmitted the remaining revenue funds through the inspector-general to an International Commission of Bankers at Shanghai representing China's foreign creditors.

The foreign position at Shanghai as the hub of foreign trade and investment in China was further strengthened, in the face of revolution and collapse of the Ch'ing government, when the consular body in late 1911 took control over the Mixed Court (see pages 341 and 689). This made Shanghai more than ever a foreign-run city.

This expansion of foreign control over Shanghai and over the customs revenues, together with the modernization and foreign direction of the new Salt Revenue Administration under Sir Richard Dane as Chief Inspector, had the same ambiguous value as many earlier aspects of the unequal-treaty system — infringing further upon China's sovereignty and yet in the short run giving the government certain benefits. In this case, for example, China's credit was sustained, thus facilitating foreign loans, and the salt revenues were greatly increased at a time of desperate financial need.

One other ambivalent merit of the treaty system had been that the rapacity of any one treaty power was somewhat checked by the jealousy of all the others. This had been true once again during the years 1911–13. World War I, however, nullified this restraining capacity of the treaty system and let Japan embark on a course of aggression which in the next thirty years would galvanize the whole Chinese people into a new national consciousness.

In August 1914 China declared her neutrality, but the Ōkuma government in Japan declared war on Germany, landed troops in north Shantung, flouting China's neutrality, and with token British assistance captured the German-held port of Tsingtao by early November. Japan then took over the whole German position in Shantung, and in addition put Japanese military police in the railway zones running through that province.

Japan followed this on January 18, 1915, by presenting to Yüan Shih-k'ai, secretly, Twenty-One Demands in five groups. The fifth group would have given Japan general control over the Chinese government through a system of advisers and specific control over the police, arms-purchases, arsenals, and the development of Fukien province. By the usual device of leaking these outrageous terms to the foreign press, Yüan obliged Japan to leave group five for some "future discussion," but under a Japanese ultimatum of May 7 he was forced to accept most of the first four groups of demands. No Western power came to his aid, though the British minister (Sir John Jordan) opined that "Japan's action toward China is worse than that of Germany in the case of Belgium." Embodying these demands, the Sino-Japanese treaties and notes of May 25, 1915, in effect confirmed Japan's dominant position in Shantung, inherited from Germany, and in South Manchuria and Eastern Inner Mongolia, long recognized as Japan's sphere, where her leases were now extended to 99 years. In addition Japan was acknowledged to have a special interest in the Han-Yeh-P'ing industrial base in Central China, which had long been used as security to get Japanese loans, even by Sun Yat-sen in 1912. Though never ratified by a Chinese parliament, these treaties served Japan as a charter for continental expansion.

The aim of the Twenty-One Demands, presented by the Ōkuma cabinet which represented Japan's new industrial interests, was basically economic (see page 566). But the effect in China was mainly political, for they roused a new spirit of nationalism, expressed in mass rallies, strikes, boycotts of Japanese goods, and vigorous protests by Liang Ch'i-ch'ao and other writers in the press. Japan emerged as China's principal foreign menace just as domestic politics were about to enter their period of greatest frustration in the warlord era. The high though vague hopes of the republican revolution for parliamentary democracy had met disaster, but a new national-racial enemy now took the place of the Manchu dynasty as the common foreign target of all patriots.

The Nature of Warlordism. Yüan Shih-k'ai was the "father of the warlords" not merely because he gave them their early training and promotions but also because he set them an influential example of how to govern the Chinese people after the collapse of the traditional system. His formula began with his duty to give the people peace and order, for which purpose he kept power through terrorism and bribery — knowing only that human beings "fear weapons and love gold," as Liang Ch'i-ch'ao phrased it. Yüan's considerable administrative achievements have been little studied; on the other hand, his manipulation of ancient and modern forms of popular consent, though skillful, was soon seen to be thoroughly cynical and consequently was rather ineffective. Moreover, Yüan's Confucianism was vestigial at best (he had never passed the examinations), and his enforced retirement from 1909 to 1911 had disillusioned him as to the virtue of loyalty. He was in an ideological vacuum: the ancient Confucian ethical sanctions and the ceremonial forms of imperial rule had lost their potency, while modern beliefs and institutions of popular government, either parties in competition or party dictatorships, had not yet become established. In the absence of a clear ethical consensus or political creed in the society of their day, Yüan and the warlords governed in a somewhat "Legalist" rather than "Confucian" tradition, by force and manipulation, with little faith even in themselves, using whatever means came to hand.

This poverty of political belief was illustrated in Yüan's decline and fall as a would-be emperor. In 1915 his stout anti-Japanism, for which he had been famous since his start in Korea, won him nationwide support, and this, as well as his eldest son's enthusiasm at the prospect, evidently fed his monarchical ambition. Yüan may also have been impelled by the very weakness of his government at Peking: he received few provincial revenues and needed further means to check the growing local power of his various military followers — men like Tuan Ch'i-jui in the north and Feng Kuo-chang at Nanking. Having already shown the uninhibited ruthlessness of a traditional aspirant for the throne, Yüan in August 1915 launched from behind the scenes a monarchical movement complete with a Yüan-for-emperor association to "plan for peace" (*Ch'ou-an hui*), nationwide "people's petitions," a unanimous vote by "elected" representatives, old-style memorials, and similar contrivances, all demanding his enthronement. Moreover, Yüan's American adviser on constitutions, Dr. F. J. Goodnow, told him that China's government, with its tradition of autocracy rather than of popular participation, would be less endangered by disorder and dictatorship if its continuity were ensured by a monarchy. This recommendation has often been cited, without, however, Goodnow's strict qualifications that there must first be no opposition to the monarchy and that it must develop constitutional forms. In any event, this "expert" opinion from a foreigner was exploited in Yüan's campaign, as were the names of conservative Westernizers like Yen Fu who had long been dubious of the Chinese people's readiness for democratic processes. After all, constitutional monarchy was associated with the success and power of Britain and Japan and had been the main program in China up to 1911.

In response to the demand he had manufactured, Yüan after appropriate hesitation consented in December 1915 to accept the throne. He announced as his reign title "Grand Constitutional Era" (*Hung-hsien*), to begin with 1916.

All this came to nothing. Within six months Yüan Shih-k'ai was undone and discountenanced; on June 6, 1916, he died of uremia due to nervous prostration. The super-realist had somehow misjudged the political realities.

One factor in his failure was the disaffection of his generals, who bore him no love. Another was the opposition of the Japanese government, which mobilized an almost unanimous treaty-power opinion and "advised" against the monarchy. But the precipitating factor was military opposition within China, sparked by Liang Ch'i-ch'ao, the anti-revolutionist who yet saw history as irreversible and now advocated the continuity of the Chinese Republic just as he had earlier advocated the continuity of the Ch'ing dynasty. He plotted with his old Hunanese student, Ts'ai Ao, who had been military governor of Yunnan in 1912. The latter, feigning dissipation, escaped from Yüan's surveillance at Peking and returned to Yunnan, the province farthest from Yüan's control and most sympathetic to his enemies of all parties. On December 25, 1915, the governor (T'ang Chi-yao) declared Yunnan's independence. There followed six months of limited fighting, mainly in Szechwan, and intensive negotiation. By degrees eight southern and Western provinces turned against Yüan, while he first postponed his enthronement, then renounced the throne, and finally died a broken man.

In the background other forces, both ideological and geopolitical, worked against Yüan. In seeking imperial legitimacy as a prop to central power, he seems not to have realized that the sanction of power in China no longer was thought to come from an impersonal heaven, whose will might be expressed in popular acquiescence or other portents. On the contrary, the idea had now taken hold that the people, the body politic of the nation, were the active makers of history. The Son of Heaven as an institution had been gradually discredited in the long years leading up to 1911. For Heaven's Mandate had been substituted the modern idea of the people's will, the consent of the governed. The apotheosis of "the people" (*min*) permeated the new nationalist thinking — the "people's army" (*min-chün*), the "national people's party" (*Kuomintang*), the "three people's principles." Yüan the strong man had been too scornful of the modern idea of representation, even though it was demanded only by the upper classes, not the common mass. At the same time, in traditional terms he had been too disloyal to his followers to command their loyalty in return.

Geopolitical factors working against Yüan included the centrifugal tendency of the provinces, which were distinct geographic and cultural as well as administrative regions. They had grown steadily more independent of Peking, in a process under way since the 1850's. There were also the ineradicable climatic, economic, and historical differences that produced a divergence of interest and outlook between South China and North China, such as had plagued every dynasty.

After Yüan's death still other, foreign influences inhibited China's unity and continued to checkmate his successors in the struggle for power: first, the political sanctuary and strategic resources available to local power-holders in the treaty ports, beyond central control; second, the interests and capacities of the imperialist powers in their respective spheres of influence, which enabled them almost to dominate whole provinces; third, the power of the foreign banks, both in and outside the consortium, to make and unmake Chinese governments by giving or withholding loans; and finally, the constant inflow from abroad of new ideas and techniques, ranging from the anarchism of Kropotkin and the individualism of Ibsen to armored trains and bicycles, all of which contributed to China's ongoing cultural revolution and the disintegration of the old order.

In short, Yüan and the military governors who competed as "warlords" from 1916 to 1928 and later, were men in between. They were not in the traditional circumstances of a dynastic interregnum, where "change within tradition" could be expected to bring forth a new dynasty. Yet they were not modernizers with a new order in mind. Their armies, newly swollen and Western-armed, using the new transport facilities of railways and river steamers, could now more easily dominate the terrain, yet they could not create a new political order. In 1911 the revolutionists, with a party but no army, had failed to gain power. Now the warlords, with armies but no parties, were equally incapable of organizing a national government. Their repeated use and misuse of parliaments and political slogans only highlighted their lack of adequate political principles and institutions. Since 1913 the armies had proliferated but the parties had splintered. No one could integrate the new military power with a new political organization. Under the warlords China's government deteriorated, the people suffered, and Chinese society after a century of decline reached a nadir of demoralization.

Behind the surface parade of hundreds of bemedaled commanders leading their shambling legions across the historical scene in these years, certain typical characteristics emerge. First of all, a warlord had to have a strong personality, subordinate officers, and troops. His problem was to feed and supply them all. For this he needed support from the revenues of a great city, a province, a trade route or railway, or from other militarists or a foreign power. The geography of a region might give him a strategic advantage, but its land and people could provide only food and manpower to be requisitioned, not a true territorial base in the modern guerrilla sense, with support among the peasantry. The typical warlord army had no roots among the local people but was a scourge upon them, exacting taxes, living off the villages, feared and despised. An army moving to a new province might therefore better itself, at least temporarily. It was both parasitic and peripatetic.

In the second place, because military force created political power only when legitimized and mediated through institutions, the warlords sought formal appointments, seals of office, and documents properly signed by others, and also justified their every move by pronouncements in favor of the public welfare and patriotic principles. In short, they needed the help of civilian politicians and civil government. Warlordism did not substitute military force for the other elements of government; it merely balanced them differently.

This different balance between military and civil came partly from the disintegration of the sanctions and values of China's traditional civil government which we have already noted. Partly it came from the warlords' new technical military capacities, greater mobility and fire-power, which were not balanced by an equilibrating growth of new political institutions. This has become, of course, a major motif in modern world history — material technology, especially military, outrunning the growth of popular participation in government. In this respect warlord-ism was less an old Chinese custom, as foreigners have generally assumed, than a result of unbalanced modernization, armaments growing faster than political agencies capable of controlling them.

Finally, as to the nature of warlord politics, everyone at the time and since has found them remarkably confusing, partly because the war-lords were so venal and treacherous, so given to sudden shifts of allegiance and wily stratagems reminiscent of Ts'ao Ts'ao and Chu-ko Liang in the *Romance of the Three Kingdoms*. However, despite all the con-fusion and the absence of clearly formulated ideological cleavages, regional interests gave some shape to the fluctuating political alignments. Region-alism of course is only a more general term for provincialism, which is based on common backgrounds, early personal associations, and mutual interests, the stuff of which bureaucratic cliques were made in times of strong central government. Thus while the traditional power structure was decapitated, its lower, regional levels continued to function, and tried to create nationwide organs at higher levels. The ultimate aims of the warlords were political, and they sought all manner of institutional means to bolster and expand their power, working with parliaments and as-semblies, even convoking conferences of military governors (now called *tu-chün,* "directors of armies"). Being deficient in their capacity for modern political organization, the competing warlord groups could not rise above the regional level. Nevertheless they always assumed and acknowledged the existence of the Chinese state. Throughout this period the Peking government continued to function abroad diplomatically and maintained many of its services, like that of the post office, at home. No warlord ventured to proclaim a new dynasty in the pattern which as-pirants for power had followed for so many centuries. Times had changed.

Patterns in the Power Struggle. The struggle among the warlords, among the politicians in the parliament, and between the warlords and the politicians went through a sequence of phases with a general trend toward the weakening of the parliament and fragmentation of the country.

In the first phase, after Yüan's death in June 1916, order was sought by reviving the provisional constitution of March 1912 and reconvening the parliament of 1913, with a sincere constitutionalist, Vice-President Li Yüan-hung, succeeding to the presidency and the chief Peiyang mili-tarist, Tuan Ch'i-jui, as premier. In the parliament Liang Ch'i-ch'ao and others of the former Progressive Party now formed the "Research clique" (*Yen-chiu hsi*), which generally tried to work with the Tuan government and was opposed by the Kuomintang remnants from the south. Meanwhile, the Peiyang *tu-chün*, who dominated a dozen northern and central provinces, formed an "interprovincial association," under an old Manchu supporter (General Chang Hsün) as chairman, ostensibly to maintain national peace and unity and actually to control the government and parliament.

In May 1917 the Peiyang warlords, favoring war with Germany, used a mob to pressure the parliament into a declaration, but without success. In retaliation the parliament and President Li obliged Premier Tuan Ch'i-jui to resign; Li under warlord pressure sought the mediation of General Chang Hsün; Chang secured the dissolution of parliament in June and occupied Peking, his troops still wearing the queue as required under the Ch'ing. With the support of K'ang Yu-wei he then announced the restoration of the last Ch'ing emperor, Henry Pu-yi. This restoration lasted two weeks. The other warlords joined in suppressing it and making Tuan premier again, supported by Liang and the Research clique in a reorganized parliament, with General Feng Kuo-chang as acting president (d. 1918).

The net result of this first phase was to bring the parliament more completely under warlord domination, thus estranging the southern provinces. The next phase saw a wider north-south split, further fragmentation of power, and greater frustration of civilian politicians.

In this second phase, the defection of the southerners from the Peking parliament in 1917 marked a turning point, for it gave another opportunity to Sun Yat-sen. In Japan he had reverted to his earlier secret-society approach to revolution and in July 1914 had founded the "Chinese Revolutionary Party" (*Chung-hua ko-ming tang*) as a disciplined underground elite who were to be fingerprinted and sworn to personal loyalty to Sun. His aim was to overcome "that lack of party discipline . . . the cause of our failure." Huang Hsing and many others, however, refused to take the oath; this revived conspiratorial effort was plainly not democratic, nor did it appeal to the rising patriotism of the time, for Sun Yat-sen omitted from his new party platform of 1914 the principle of nationalism. Originally anti-Manchu, this principle (incredible as it may seem) apparently held no more significance for him; his thinking was now pan-Asian, directed toward cooperation with Japan, not against imperialism. Out of tune with the times, Sun contributed little to the frustrating of Yüan Shih-k'ai in 1916.

In 1917, however, Sun Yat-sen re-emerged and jumped into the warlord-parliamentary fray. In July he went to Canton along with other former Kuomintang colleagues and most of the Chinese navy. He convened some 250 southern members of parliament and formed a military government with himself as generalissimo (*ta yüan-shuai*), but the local warlords were the real power-holders. Sun at Canton, trying to team up with the local men in power, was like Liang Ch'i-ch'ao at Peking, trying to provide a civilian component of government for Premier Tuan Ch'i-jui. Both were soon frustrated.

The deterioration of political standards continued. From the north, Premier Tuan tried to take over Hunan and Szechwan for the Peiyang clique, but failed. (He resigned in November 1917, and became premier again from March to October 1918.) In the year after he declared war on Germany (August 14, 1917), Tuan financed his domestic warfare by borrowing enormous sums from Japan, the "Nishihara loans," partly on the excuse of preparing to fight Germany. He now made a military alliance with Japan, imported Japanese military instructors, and worked closely with a pro-Japanese group of politicians and with his own Anhwei group of militarists known as the An-fu (Anhwei-Fukien) clique (*an* and *fu* also, ironically, happened to mean "peace" and "happiness"). They were opposed by Feng Kuo-chang leading a Chihli clique, thus splitting the Peiyang militarists into two factions. Many patriots began to protest that the power-holder (Tuan) was again selling China to the foreigners in order to build his own military power. Liang Ch'i-ch'ao finally withdrew from politics in frustration. Tuan assembled a packed "tuchuns' parliament" and had Hsü Shih-ch'ang (who had been the last governor-general of Manchuria and very close to Yüan Shih-k'ai) made president in October 1918.

In the south Sun Yat-sen's Canton parliament was also split. One element (the Political Study clique, *Cheng-hsüeh hsi*) cooperated with the warlords, who nevertheless began to assassinate Sun's men and forced him to retire to Shanghai in May 1918. A Kwangsi clique of militarists now dominated the south, much as the An-fu clique controlled the north.

The end of World War I put north and south under pressure to patch things up, and in 1919 the two factions negotiated at Shanghai in a fruitless peace conference. During 1920, however, China's fragmentation entered a third phase: minority elements both north and south, seeking allies wherever possible, ousted the groups in power but still could not stabilize their own control.

In the north the Chihli clique of warlords (now led by Ts'ao K'un and Wu P'ei-fu) joined in July 1920 with a "Fengtien," i.e., South Manchurian, clique (under Chang Tso-lin) and forced the An-fu clique of Premier Tuan Ch'i-jui out of power. This, however, soon led to war between the Chihli and Fengtien cliques. In the south, Kwangtung militarists in August 1920 ousted the Kwangsi clique and dissolved the military government at Canton. By this time almost every province was held by a semi-independent militarist, who was usually allied loosely with a warlord clique.

This situation gave impetus to the idea of federal government as a political order for China. The idea of federalism had been current since the beginning of the century, and particularly in 1911. It expressed the widespread desire of burgeoning provincial interests to control their own systems of local taxation, administration, and even defense. In the early 1920's this constitutional concept of federalism was taken up by a number of warlords in the south and southwest as a convenient means to buttress their local positions. Scholars also urged that a federal division of powers between the central and provincial governments could stabilize the power struggle. This approach was supported by a nationwide federalist movement in 1922 and was actually worked out in the provincial constitution of Hunan in 1922–25. But federalism seemed to most patriots a cloak for provincial autonomy and so a barrier to real unity. It clashed both with Chinese tradition and with modern patriotism and did not become an ongoing movement.

After 1922 the disintegration of China's civil government entered still another phase and began to produce divergent results north and south, which must be separately discussed.

In the north the warlord melee cast up new leading personalities, less directly indebted to Yüan Shih-k'ai for their early careers.[1] Three men eventually stood out; in the course of their triangular relations, each allied himself in turn with each of the other two against the third, and thus each was double-crossed by the others. These three were:

(1) Chang Tso-lin (d. 1928), "Warlord of Manchuria," an ex-bandit who had risen as Japan's ally against Russia and been military governor at Mukden since 1911, buttressed by the resources of the Three Eastern Provinces and their strategic defensibility vis-à-vis North China.

(2) Wu P'ei-fu (1872–1939), a division commander under Ts'ao K'un, who had been trained in the Confucian Classics and then by Japanese officers at the Paoting military academy, and who became the repository of many Chinese and British hopes for peace and order in Central China.

(3) Feng Yü-hsiang (1882–1948), a big, burly man of peasant origin, a soldier from the age of eleven and a graduate of Paoting, who was baptized by John R. Mott of the Y.M.C.A. in 1913 and was known to his foreign missionary friends as the "Christian General" because he urged his well-disciplined troops to pursue Protestantism, austerity, practical education, and social reform. Seizing Peking in 1924, Feng broke the power of the Peiyang warlords and destroyed their false façade of parliamentary government.

The intricate relations among these warlord figures defy detailed description. Even a bare listing of events, such as the following, perhaps confuses as much as it clarifies:

[1] Among the leading figures of this period who had been officers under Yüan Shih-k'ai in the late 1890's were Chang Hsün, Feng Kuo-chang, Hsü Shih-ch'ang, Ts'ao K'un, and Tuan Ch'i-jui.

1921. July-Oct. Hunan-Szechwan militarists invade Hupei to expel Chihli clique, and are suppressed by Wu P'ei-fu.

1922. Jan.-May. "First Fengtien-Chihli War" around Peking; Chang Tso-lin defeated by Wu P'ei-fu and forced back to Manchuria. Li Yüan-hung made president again by the Chihli clique (Ts'ao K'un and Wu P'ei-fu).

1923. Li Yüan-hung forced out of presidency (June); Ts'ao K'un elected president by bribing parliament (October).

1924. Peiyang militarist cliques fight the "Kiangsu-Chekiang War" in the Shanghai-Nanking area, Chihli clique wins (Sept.-Oct.); meanwhile in the "Second Fengtien-Chihli War," Feng Yü-hsiang turns against his superior Wu P'ei-fu, cooperates with Chang Tso-lin, and seizes Peking (Oct.) and Tientsin (Nov.); Ts'ao K'un ousted from presidency, replaced by Tuan Ch'i-jui as "chief executive" of a provisional government (Nov.), which major treaty powers recognize (Dec.). Rivalry between Fengtien clique of Chang Tso-lin (based on Manchuria and along Tientsin-Pukow Railway) and Feng Yü-hsiang's "Nationalist Army" (*Kuo-min chün,* named to denote a putative affinity with the Kuomintang) based on Honan and Northwest.

1925. "Second Kiangsu-Chekiang War" (winter 1924–25): Fengtien forces take Shanghai area. Fighting in Honan (Feb.-April) strengthens Feng Yü-hsiang's "Nationalist Army." "Fengtien-Chekiang War" (Oct.-Nov.): Fengtien clique forced out of Lower Yangtze area by Sun Ch'uan-fang of Chihli clique.

1926. War between Fengtien clique and Feng Yü-hsiang's clique (Nov. 1925–April 1926): Kuo Sung-ling revolts against Fengtien clique (Nov.), Feng Yü-hsiang occupies Chihli; Wu P'ei-fu (of Chihli clique, based at Hankow) allies with Chang Tso-lin of Fengtien (Jan. 1926). Fengtien and Chihli cliques expel Feng Yü-hsiang from Peking (April): Chang Tso-lin and Wu P'ei-fu in power, but fail to create a civil government.

The result of all the marching and countermarching was to leave North and Central China divided under warlord cliques roughly as follows: Manchuria, the Peking-Tientsin area, and Shantung under Chang Tso-lin and his Fengtien clique; the Lower Yangtze provinces, Chekiang, and Fukien under Sun Ch'uan-fang of the Chihli clique; Hupei, Honan, and the Peking-Hankow Railway under Wu P'ei-fu of the Chihli clique. Three minor elements were (1) the "Model Governor" Yen Hsi-shan, who had controlled strategically defensible Shansi province since 1911; (2) remnants of Feng Yü-hsiang's "Nationalist Army" in the Northwest, from Chahar and Suiyan around to Shensi; and (3) Governor T'ang Sheng-chih in Hunan. Such was the situation in the north in mid-1926.

By this time in South China the new forces of the Nationalist Revolution had finally been organized (see pages 682–683). In 1926–28 they swept north, got the cooperation of the three minor elements mentioned above, and unified China under a new order in which a party army accepted the control of a party dictatorship. With military force and civil government now reunited, the warlord era was at least nominally at an end.

Besides the incalculable sufferings of a populace oppressed by systematic pillaging and over-taxation, the material results of warlordism included inflation of the currency, disruption of trade, and deterioration in railways and in public works for flood control and irrigation. Another typical result was the recrudescence of the opium evil. The Ch'ing government in 1906 had begun a concerted attack on opium production and smoking, with such widespread patriotic support that the British Indian importation, already down to 50,000 chests a year, was gradually reduced and stopped at the end of 1917. The much larger Chinese production, well on the way to extinction, was now revived by the simple warlord device of levying such high taxes on land suitable for poppy-growing that nothing but opium could meet the payments. Another device, as under "Model Governor" Yen in Shansi, was to prohibit opium production within the province but unofficially levy a monopoly tax on the opium imported from adjoining areas.

The impact of warlordism with all its evils was greatest on the minds of patriotic youth. "In China today only cunning, crooked, vile, and ruthless people can flourish," wrote Liang Ch'i-ch'ao. Out of the desperation and humiliation of the period came a new revolution which began among the intellectual class.

THE REVOLUTION IN THOUGHT AND CULTURE

The warlord era, roughly from 1916 to 1928, was both chaotic and creative. This was no paradox, for in China's tradition-bound society, so long accustomed to central authority and orthodoxy, new ways could be tried out and adopted only after traditional patterns had broken down. With the end of monarchy and the decline of central power, all sorts of ideas and practices, fads and experiments, bubbled forth unrestrained by authority. The pluralism of this era was illustrated by the divergence between political decline on the one hand and intellectual, economic, and social developments on the other. Along with political disorder came a great intellectual ferment. Underlying it were processes of economic growth in the cities and of social change generally.

The Economic and Social Background. Just as the decline of central political power permitted the rise of warlordism and disorder in the countryside, so the decline of Western imports into China during and after World War I facilitated the rise of native industry in the cities. With the pressure of Western competition removed by war in Europe, both Japanese and Chinese entrepreneurs in China seized the chance to expand. This industrial growth was compatible with the political disorder of the time because it occurred mainly in the foreign-administered treaty ports, protected by the treaty system from the warlordism which flourished outside in the provinces.

A new merchant class, less trammeled by official control and existing outside the ancient guild system, had long been growing, indeed had been fostered by government policies after 1901. By 1914 there were over a thousand local chambers of commerce and they had more than 200,000 members. Large-scale enterprise, however, had been dominated by foreign firms, mostly British, but also American (particularly in Shanghai) and German (in Shantung until 1915). Among consumption goods, for example, China's relative lack of known petroleum resources had given a clear field to foreign imports of kerosene (to supplant vegetable oils for illumination) and fuel oil (to compete with coal). These imports were dominated by Standard Oil subsidiaries and by the Asiatic Petroleum Company (A.P.C.), an affiliate of the Anglo-Dutch combine, Royal Dutch-Shell, formed in 1907. On the other hand, the long-continued import of cotton yarn and then of textiles had stimulated Chinese cotton-growing to supply British, Chinese, and now Japanese textile mills in Shanghai, Tientsin, and other centers. Similarly, the market for cigarettes was first developed by an American-organized, London-based combine, the British-American Tobacco Company (B.A.T.), formed in 1902, which soon began through its compradors to lend seed and credit to North China cultivators. It set up a network of collecting points and curing factories to supply Chinese tobacco to half-a-dozen big B.A.T. cigarette factories. But Chinese firms, like the Nanyang Brothers formed in 1905, were soon competing.

By 1914 a modern Chinese administrative and entrepreneurial class had begun to emerge. Often loosely called the "comprador class," it grew up under the wing of foreign educators, civil servants, and businessmen. It acquired experience in mission and other schools with mixed Sino-Western curricula; in the Maritime Customs; in the Post Office, which was separated from the Customs in 1911 and by 1918 employed a hundred foreigners and 27,000 Chinese; in the steamship lines, mills, shops, and general commerce of old treaty-port firms like Jardine, Matheson or Butterfield and Swire; or in new specialized concerns like the A.P.C. and B.A.T. Thus this nascent middle class consisted mainly of Chinese who had learned modern economic ways in the treaty ports or from association with foreigners. They had accumulated the attitudes, interests, and skills necessary for economic development, and World War I gave them their opportunity.

Of the other ingredients necessary for industrialization, Chinese capital had been accumulated both in the overseas communities and in Hong Kong and the treaty ports. It was now handled through modern Chinese banks, some of which grew up under government auspices (like the Bank of Communications, founded in 1907, and the Bank of China, 1913) and some as private concerns (like the Shanghai Commercial and Savings Bank, 1915, and the Kincheng Banking Corporation, 1917). Modern banks, increasing from 17 in 1914 to 102 in 1926, now put the old-style Shansi banks out of business. Yet many domestic factors still retarded the growth of financial resources. As an alternative to productive investment, old-fashioned moneylending, for instance, could still bring 12 per cent or more a year, as compared with much lower rates in the West. Efforts at currency reform and unification had still not succeeded in abolishing the ancient but variable unit of account, the silver tael, although silver dollars from government mints had come into general use under Yüan Shih-k'ai, most of them bearing his image.

A labor force meanwhile had been drawn to urban centers. Urbanization was evident in the growth of cities at railroad junctions like Tsinan, Hsuchow, and Chengchow. More and more, cheap labor was needed to tend cotton spindles or sort tobacco, or to work in factories producing matches, flour, canned food, cement, and other mass-produced commodities in Shanghai, Tientsin, and Hankow. These opportunities for employment, newly accessible by railway and steamship, opened up alternatives to the closed routine of peasant life. Warlord taxation and conscription, population increase (presumably), and natural calamities stimulated migration from the countryside to the cities. City life and factory work tended to break the bonds of the old family system. As wage-earning sons and womenfolk became financially independent, the family ceased to be a self-contained economic and social unit controlling the individual. Instead, the impersonal, universalistic criteria of function, not those of status or specific kinship and personal ties, were applied in the urban labor market. In crowded slums and sweatshops, new values began to take over, and true proletarian factory workers began slowly to accumulate. By 1919 they numbered over a million, perhaps a million and a half persons.

Social change was evident not only in the rise of new capitalist and labor classes but also in a new status for youth and for women. Young men, principally returned students, had led the *T'ung-meng hui* in the Revolution of 1911, and students now claimed the old privileged status of the scholar class. By 1915 the Ministry of Education listed 120,000 government schools of all sorts with about four million students — an increase over the old days, though only a few thousand at most reached the college level. Mission schools both Catholic and Protestant in 1919 had perhaps half a million students, with Protestant colleges leading the way in higher education. Missionaries had also pioneered in teaching girls. In 1915 the first women's institution of higher education, Ginling College, was opened at Nanking. Girls were a sizable proportion of the 13,000 students in Protestant middle schools.

The emergence of these new social classes — merchant-entrepreneurs, factory laborers, and modern-style students — fostered the metamorphosis of China's traditional society. The old landlord-scholar-official trinity, the gentry class in its broad sense, began to disappear from the countryside. Classical degree-holders (gentry in the narrow sense) gave way to younger men, students trained in the cities or even abroad. Landlords tended to become absentee city-dwellers, no longer available to preside over the rural society. Modern-trained officials recruited from the student class were more specialized, less omnicompetent, no longer the personal representatives of a Son of Heaven who ruled all mankind. In short, the rise of modern city life, with its various classes responsive to mass movements, was accompanied by a corresponding decline of rural life, where the leadership of the big households disappeared at the top and the peasant masses met grievous problems in the villages. With improvements in transportation and public health, China's rural population was probably increasing in numbers, but its standard of living was probably falling. Tenantry seems to have grown, as well as the landless peasantry — illiterate, rootless, jobless, and so available for banditry, warlord armies, or dirt-cheap coolie labor.

This trend toward collapse of the old society pressed the new student class to stand forth as leaders and saviors. They had inherited the tradition that scholars should advise the ruler and serve the state-and-culture. In the present crisis they felt uniquely qualified by their studies to modernize and "save" the nation.

The motives and ideas of the new student leadership sprang increasingly from their foreign contacts. Japan still took the largest number of students abroad (about two-fifths), but one-third now went to the United States. The remission to China in 1908 of $12 million (about two-thirds) of the American share of the Boxer indemnity had led to the establishment of Tsing Hua College at Peking, whence a steady flow of scholarship students to the United States began in 1911. (In 1924 the remainder of the indemnity was remitted, and the China Foundation for the Promotion of Education and Culture was established to use the remitted payments as they fell due.) Meantime, to provide a labor force during the war in Europe, some 140,000 Chinese contract workers were recruited in 1916–18 and sent to France, where Chinese student workers like James Yen (Yen Yang-ch'u) of the Y.M.C.A. began to develop methods of mass education. In France a work-and-study movement had already been initiated by Ts'ai Yüan-p'ei and others among Chinese students. This movement and the wartime experience in organizing and educating Chinese workers in France exemplified a trend toward dissolving the ancient barrier between scholarship and labor. France more than America became a source of political movements and doctrines among the returned students in China.

Socialism had appealed to students in Japan after 1900, and state socialism, particularly as discerned in the rise of Germany and Japan, had been espoused by some *T'ung-meng hui* members before 1911. In that year a small Chinese Socialist Party had been organized, though soon suppressed. But the industrial capitalism and factory labor class which gave socialism its *raison d'être* in Europe were still on a comparatively small scale in China.

European theories of anarchism, on the other hand, especially the anarcho-communism of Peter Kropotkin, found a wide response among Chinese intellectuals bent upon destroying the traditional order. Kropotkin's *Mutual Aid: A Factor of Evolution* (1902) argued that mutual aid was as much a law of nature as mutual struggle, though restraints upon freedom must of course be destroyed before cooperation could flourish. Chinese students in Tōkyō and especially in Paris, led by classically trained scions of the official class (like Wu Chih-hui, 1865–1953, and Li Shih-tseng, 1882–   ), applied the anarchist teachings to China by opposing all elitist organizations and all government (hence nationalism itself), while advocating egalitarianism, mass movements, and direct action including assassination. This anarchist line of thought, combining puritanism, self-sacrifice, and the destruction of the established order with a utopian faith in the public will and voluntary association, was taken up by many students in China. Despite the early death of the leading figure (Liu Ssu-fu, known as Shih-fu, 1884–1915), anarchist groups by 1919 were active in major centers.

The New Thought at Peita. The intellectual revolution centered at Peking National University (Peita) partly because of its prestige at the top of the educational system — only two other government universities as yet existed — and partly because of the faculty collected there in 1917 by the new chancellor, Ts'ai Yüan-p'ei (1867–1940). As a classical scholar, Ts'ai had risen to the Hanlin Academy at twenty-five, but later he had joined the *T'ung-meng hui*, studied Kant and many other Western philosophers during four years in Germany, and served as minister of education for six months in the first republican cabinet under Sun and Yüan in 1912. Returning from further study in Germany and France, he now set about converting Peita from a bureaucrat-ridden school that prepared officials to hold sinecures into a center of learning where all the world's ideas might compete.

Ts'ai Yüan-p'ei's clarion call in 1912 for freedom of thought, for "education above politics . . . beyond political control," had been silenced by Yüan Shih-k'ai's authoritarian effort to revive Confucianism, and it would be muffled again by the rise of party dictatorship; in the long run, Chinese efforts at reconstruction would seek a new orthodoxy to buttress a new political order. But in the years after 1917 the very weakness of the political order (not its strength, as under a pluralistic rule of law) permitted freedom of thought to flourish for a time in a genuinely liberal fashion. Ts'ai encouraged the most divergent views at Peita and even the activity of professors and students, as individuals, in politics. The result was a sudden intellectual flowering which now formed, on the plane of ideas, a counterpart to the political revolution of 1911.

This revolution in thought was carried on by men of a rare transitional generation, born generally around the 1880's, who had acquired a grounding in Chinese classical studies and then immersed themselves in Western culture abroad. Thus they stood astride two worlds, as few have done before or since, and rejected the traditional orthodoxy out of knowledge, not ignorance.

Ts'ai brought to Peita to be Dean of Letters a leading revolutionary journalist, Ch'en Tu-hsiu (1879–1942). Coming from a well-to-do official family, Ch'en had passed the classical examinations (1896–97), studied in Japan (1902, 1906) and in France (1907–10), and participated in the 1911 revolution and the revolt of 1913 against Yüan. He had taught in several schools, founded vernacular magazines, and become a zealous advocate of the principles of individual freedom in the style of the French Revolution — "Liberty, equality, fraternity." He attributed China's decay to Confucianism: its social and family obligations enervated the individual, its disdain of commerce and wealth impoverished the economy. In the monthly he founded in 1915, *New Youth* (*Hsin ch'ing-nien*, "La Jeunesse"), Ch'en therefore called upon Chinese youth to "be independent, not servile . . . progressive, not conservative . . . dynamic, not passive . . . cosmopolitan, not isolationist . . . utilitarian, not emptily formalistic . . . scientific, not (merely) imaginative." Launching a radical attack on the ethics and values, the whole civilization, represented by Confucianism, Ch'en Tu-hsiu in this period uncritically and almost romantically extolled the individualism, dynamism, and utilitarianism of the modern West — the very un-Confucian idea of each man's material self-interest as the basis of society. At Peita, Ch'en continued to edit *New Youth,* which soon became a wide-open forum for discussion, printing letters to the editor, distributing as many as 16,000 copies, stirring up the student class all over the country.

Ch'en Tu-hsiu's principal ally at Peita was a younger man, Hu Shih (1891–1962), who, like Ch'en, came from a scholar-official family in Anhwei with an early training in the Classics. In the United States on a government scholarship between 1910 and 1917, Hu Shih studied philosophy at Cornell (B.A. 1915), and at Columbia (Ph.D. 1917) under John Dewey. Quite early he had picked up the idea, advocated by many revolutionists since 1898, of using vernacular speech (*pai-hua*) as the basis for literary writing instead of the classical written style (*wen-yen*). The vernacular novels of the Ming and Ch'ing (see Vol. I, pp. 287, 386) and the Western missionary writings from 1815 on had paved the way for writing *pai-hua*. Hu Shih in 1915, reflecting the "New Tide" in American poetry, pioneered in writing Chinese poetry in everyday words. He and a brilliant specialist in linguistics (Y. R. Chao) stated the case for written *pai-hua* in 1916; the movement was launched in China in 1917 with Ch'en Tu-hsiu's support in the pages of *New Youth,* which soon was written entirely in the vernacular.

The literary revolution, or "literary renaissance," had several aims — first of all, to create a new written style to go with modern thought. "A dead language," declared Hu Shih, "cannot produce a living literature." His Columbia thesis on "The Development of Logical Method in Ancient China," his advocacy of Dewey's pragmatism, his stress on the scientific method, all led him to seek precision and clarity of statement, a new written language as a tool of critical thinking for the scholar.

A second aim of the literary revolution was to reach the common people, both by making literacy more accessible to them and by creating a popular literature more directly related to their lives. Ch'en Tu-hsiu wanted not only to abandon "stereotyped and over-ornamental" classicism in favor of "fresh and sincere" realism, but also to overthrow the "pedantic, unintelligible and obscurantist literature . . . of the aristocratic few" and create a "plain, simple, and expressive literature of the people." A great step in this direction was the Education Ministry's decree of 1920 substituting *pai-hua* for the classical language in elementary schools.

A further aim of the movement was to emancipate the individual, partly by destroying the written language which had been "the repository of Confucian morality and Taoist superstition." A new literature of protest was called for, and soon emerged. Ch'en, Hu, and the others editing *New Youth* published in May 1918 a satirical short story, the first written in the vernacular, entitled "The Diary of a Madman." In it the madman, convinced that people want to kill and eat him, examines a history book: "This history recorded no dates, but over every page were scrawled the words 'benevolence, righteousness, truth, virtue.' " Looking closer, however, he "discovered all over it a succession of two words between the lines: 'Eat men!' " This indictment of China's traditional society was typical of the author, Lu Hsün (pen name of Chou Shu-jen, 1881–1936). He had come from an impoverished official family in Chekiang, studied on a government scholarship in Japan (1902–1909), learning Japanese and some German, and after teaching in Chekiang had become a minor official at Peking (1912–1925). In the years after 1918 Lu Hsün's writings, both short stories and short essays, soon made him the great pioneer figure in China's modern popular literature.

Thus by 1919 the university at Peking had become a meeting ground of manifold influences from abroad — from Japan and from the West, especially France and the United States — as well as from China's classical tradition. *New Youth* had been joined by other journals of discussion, such as *Weekly Critic (Mei-chou p'ing-lun)* which Ch'en Tu-hsiu founded with the university librarian, Li Ta-chao (1888–1927), and *New*

Tide (*Hsin ch'ao*) founded by a group of students many of whom later became academic leaders.[1]

In the ferment of their discussions and writings, all the social and philosophical theories then current in the Western world and Japan were given expression, whether or not fully grasped — realism, utilitarianism, pragmatism, liberalism, individualism, socialism, anarchism, Darwinism, materialism, etc. Utilizing this armory of ideas, the wholesale criticism of the old society supported two principal protagonists, called by Ch'en Tu-hsiu "Mr. Democracy" and "Mr. Science." "Only these two gentlemen," he wrote in January 1919, "can cure the dark maladies in Chinese politics, morality, learning, and thought." The ground was thus prepared, in ideas and means of communication, for a great explosion of intellectual energy, in politics as well as in learning.

The May Fourth Incident. The phrase "May Fourth," which derived from the 1919 student demonstration of that date in Peking, has been taken in the Chinese numerary fashion to designate the whole intellectual movement roughly from 1917 to 1921 or even later, of which we have noted the beginning. The immediate significance of the incident of May 4 was that nationalism then emerged as the dominant force in politics.

This patriotic concern had been mounting ever since Japan's seizure of Shantung in 1914 and her Twenty-One Demands of 1915. China's entrance into World War I in August 1917 had been urged by some as a means of ensuring China's presence at the peace settlement in order to counter Japan's wartime expansion, especially in Shantung. Forehandedly, however, Japan by secret notes in 1917 had got British, French, and Italian agreement to her retaining the ex-German rights in Shantung (as well as Germany's North Pacific islands). She followed these secret moves with the Lansing-Ishii agreement of November 1917 in which the United States publicly though vaguely acknowledged that Japan's "territorial propinquity" gave her "special interests" in China. Consequently, although November 1918 brought jubilation at the victory of democracy over militarism in Europe, the Chinese delegation representing both Peking and Canton at the Paris Peace Conference in January 1919 soon found, like President Wilson, that his doctrines of self-determination and open diplomacy did not apply to the Far East. It developed that in 1918 Peking also had signed secret agreements confirming Japan's Shantung position. The arguments of able young diplomats (like V. K. Wellington Koo and C. T. Wang) were unavailing. Meanwhile Chinese

---

[1] For example: *Fu Ssu-nien,* later head of the Academia Sinica Institute of History and Philology, of Peita after World War II, and of National Taiwan University; *Lo Chia-lun,* later head of Tsing Hua and National Central Universities and of the Kuomintang historical commission; *Ku Chieh-kang,* historian; *Fung Yu-lan,* philosopher; *Chu Tzu-ch'ing,* writer.

public concern had become unprecedentedly aroused, with hundreds of associations of Overseas Chinese, students, merchants, educators, labor unions, and political groups telegraphing their protests to Paris.

As student indignation mounted, both at the Paris decision and at the Peking government's secret sell-out to Japan, a demonstration to commemorate the Twenty-One Demands on May 7, "National Humiliation Day," was advanced to May 4. On that afternoon over 3000 college students from 13 institutions in Peking assembled at the Gate of Heavenly Peace (*T'ien-an men*) and endorsed a manifesto which concluded: "China's territory may be conquered, but it cannot be given away. The Chinese people may be massacred, but they will not surrender. Our country is about to be annihilated. Up, brethren!" The subsequent demonstration began in good order but erupted into violence when students beat one pro-Japanese official as a "traitor" and burned the house of a cabinet minister.

The May Fourth incident reflected a long build-up of patriotic indignation, but its historical impact really came from the students' subsequent program of continuing political organization and agitation. The warlord government's ill-advised and drastic punishments and reprisals gave the students wide public support as defenders of China's national interest against pro-Japanese politicians. The Peking students organized a union, including girls as well as boys. They quickly secured nationwide support from the press and the merchants, from Sun Yat-sen and the Canton government, from warlord rivals of the An-fu clique and indeed from all its many enemies. Students in other cities, similarly organized, staged demonstrations, began boycotts of Japanese goods, and mobilized general public support with speeches in the streets, working often in small "Groups of Ten for National Salvation." They stimulated a similar organization of the modern scholar class — professors, teachers, writers, journalists — for political action. In late May and early June students staged general strikes closing the schools in more than two hundred cities all over the country. They proved themselves a new force in politics, under the banner of anti-Japanese patriotism.

The warlord Peking government, true to its belief in force, tried early in June to suppress the movement by imprisoning some 1150 student agitators, turning part of Peita into a jail. In response, girl students now began to join the boys in the streets. Even more important, Shanghai merchants sympathetically closed their shops in a week-long patriotic strike, and workers struck for patriotic reasons in some forty Shanghai factories. This truly national movement, involving major classes and reaching a new level of popular political activity, won the day. The Peking students marched victoriously out of jail. The three pro-Japanese "traitor" officials were dismissed. The cabinet resigned. And China refused to sign the Versailles peace treaty with Germany.

The New Culture Movement. Out of the political activity of the May Fourth incident came China's new nationalism of the 1920's, which was to be marked by the rise of party dictatorship, the growth of socialist thinking, and the struggle against imperialism (see pages 673–688). Meanwhile the process of intellectual ferment, out of which political activity had been precipitated, went steadily on — media of communication increased, Western ideas were eagerly sought after, old evils were more vigorously attacked and new values debated. All this activity, in the year or two following May 4, 1919, generally stopped short of social and political action and was given the name "New Culture Movement."

First of all, several hundred new periodicals in the written vernacular made their appearance, though some only briefly. Touching every kind of subject, nearly all aimed to contribute to the remaking of Chinese society. Newspapers, too, catered to the new thought and its re-examination of all values. Publication of books, including translations of Western works, rose sharply. By these means the intellectual revolution, begun by young professors in their thirties and students in their twenties, spread from Peita all over the country. Associations for innumerable purposes sprang up everywhere.

Leading foreign scholars were invited to lecture. John Dewey spent two years in China (May 1919–July 1921), traveling in eleven provinces. He lectured frequently, often with Hu Shih interpreting, and roused wide interest in his views on education and on pragmatism generally. Bertrand Russell was in China for almost a year (October 1920–July 1921). He lectured with Y. R. Chao interpreting, and as an advocate of state socialism was even more widely read than Dewey. Others came later, like the Indian poet Rabindranath Tagore in 1924, whose more abstract message of peace and spiritual brotherhood by that time received a poor response.

The attack on old evils continued with the campaign to "overthrow Confucius and Sons," as Hu Shih called it. It denied the validity of the ancient "Three Bonds" (which were also the most important of the "Five Relationships"), namely, the subordination of subject to ruler, of son to father, and of wife to husband. The three corresponding virtues — loyalty to superiors, filial piety, and female chastity — were now seen as props of despotism in both state and family. The anti-Confucianists attacked the tyranny of parents, their arrangement of marriages, and the subordination of youth under the family system. The idea of the emancipation of women spread rapidly. Like the contemporary movement for women's suffrage and equal rights in the West, it encountered a demoralized and passive, rather than active and doctrinal, resistance from males. Meanwhile the many conservatives who wanted to defend the Confucian ethical order by making Confucianism a state religion, which K'ang Yu-wei still advocated as he had in 1898, provoked increasing opposition. The Confucian proprieties or principles of social usage (*li;* literally, "ceremony," "ritual," "decorum") were denounced as fetters on the individual. The old social harmony based on a hierarchic inequality of roles was anathematized in the name of egalitarianism. "Chinese culture," wrote Lu Hsün, "is a culture of serving one's masters, who are triumphant at the cost of the misery of the multitude."

The attack on Confucianism stimulated the critical re-evaluation of Chinese antiquity. Scholars at Peita ("antiquity-doubters" like Ch'ien Hsüan-t'ung and Ku Chieh-kang) re-appraised the authenticity of the Classics and rejected the tradition that Confucius had been their author or even editor. More positively, Liang Ch'i-ch'ao, now retired from politics, and Hu Shih among others led a wide-ranging "reorganization of the national heritage," winnowing the grain from the chaff within the great tradition. Thus they restudied the ancient philosopher Mo-tzu, the political thought of the era before 221 B.C., and the history of many major developments — Buddhism in China, Taoism, the vernacular novels, the thought of the Ch'ing period.

Concern for China's national heritage was heightened by disillusionment with European "materialism" after World War I. Liang Ch'i-ch'ao returned from the Paris Peace Conference convinced of the spiritual bankruptcy of Western civilization. With its development of scientific technology and acceptance of Social Darwinism, the West had become materialistic, withered, dry, and sick from a "spiritual famine." This theme was carried further in an influential book by a Peita philosopher, Liang Sou-ming, on *Civilization and Philosophy of the Orient and Occident* (1922), which compared the West, China, and India as embodying three distinct ways of life, respectively characterized, for example, by struggle, adjustment, and self-denial, or by rationalism, intuition, and religion.

Thus a whole series of controversies and polemics argued the merits of one issue after another. Among intellectuals, religion was debated, defended, and widely decried. When the World Student Christian Federation met in Peking in 1922, a nationwide anti-religious and anti-Christian movement was organized among student youth. In a polemic on "science vs. philosophy of life" in 1923, the omnipotence of science was questioned by a Tsing Hua professor (Chang Chün-mai, "Carsun Chang") while metaphysics was attacked by a Peita geologist (V. K. Ting), with many others participating.

In proportion as the intellectual and cultural revolution triumphed over the traditional order, it lost its unity of emphasis. A split occurred, partly because of background and personal temperament, between those inclined toward academic studies, reform, and gradual evolution, and those inclined toward political action, rebellion, and violent revolution. People sorted themselves out.

The rational, pragmatic approach to re-creating China's civilization was led by Hu Shih, who as early as July 1919 inveighed against "isms," by which he meant the various forms of socialism and other all-embracing creeds. Instead, he urged a concentration on "problems," which must be analyzed as to their causes by the "genetic method" and with "a critical attitude": "There is no liberation *in toto*, or reconstruction *in toto*. Liberation means liberation from this or that institution, from this or that belief, for this or that individual; it is liberation bit by bit, drop by drop. Reconstruction . . . is bit by bit, drop by drop." To many, this very logical, dispassionate application of pragmatism seemed inadequate to meet China's problems, as well as emotionally unsatisfying. Hu's long-term program of education had no short-term political method. It could only produce liberal manifestoes, in which intellectuals asked warlord governments to guarantee civil liberties, all in vain.

The academic wing of the New Culture movement was led by returned students from the West, who used their training to develop higher education, libraries, humanistic studies, and scientific research. But building new institutions of learning was slow work, constantly impeded by the lack of a modern government.

In general, during the period 1917–21 the focus of concern had been how to emancipate the individual. But after 1921 it shifted back to the more customary theme, how to strengthen the nation. To put it another way, the supporters of individualism stressed emancipation from family domination and other outworn restraints but they seldom asserted a positive doctrine of individual rights and freedoms like that of Western liberalism. The latter had been derived from the Western doctrines of natural rights and of the supremacy of law, but these had no counterparts in China capable of supporting a genuine Chinese liberalism. Instead, the would-be liberal in warlord China, before he could "selfishly" demand his own civil liberties from the state, had to help create a modern nation-state, as his new loyalty to country also demanded. Consequently the ancient aim of Chinese and Japanese statesmen, to "enrich the kingdom and increase its military power" (Chin. *fu-kuo ch'iang-ping*: Jap. *fukoku kyōhei*), could now reappear in China in modern dress as "national salvation," much as it had in Meiji Japan. Nationalism took precedence over individualism and liberalism. Political movements soon arose which would again try to dominate the individual and his cultural activity.

The Introduction of Marxism-Leninism. The May Fourth incident had shown what student youth could accomplish when organized for political action. This potentiality was plain to Sun Yat-sen, then in Shanghai, and he set about recruiting students as part of his general reorganization of the Kuomintang, which began in October 1919. Political action also appealed to the romantic temperament of Ch'en Tu-hsiu, who as a leader of the May Fourth movement had been imprisoned at Peking from June to September 1919 and thereafter went to Shanghai. Just at this point the example and the doctrines of Soviet Russia came to hand in practical form. One whole wing of the New Culture movement, like some of the major Kuomintang leaders, soon felt they had found the action program they had been seeking.

The intellectual appeal of Marxism lay partly in its claim to being "scientific," in an age when science seemed to be the secret of Western material superiority. Marx's concept of "historical materialism" — that society progresses through a sequence of stages (primitive, slave-owning, feudal, capitalist, and socialist) by virtue of "class struggle" between ruling and exploited classes for control of the "means of production" — appealed to students in need of a system to explain "progress" and simplify the confusing events of history. The optimistic belief that class struggle and exploitation could be obviated by abolishing private ownership of the means of production was particularly attractive in an underdeveloped country where industrialization and all its problems were just beginning. Moreover, Marxism had been capped by Lenin's concept of the revolutionary vanguard, the disciplined intellectual elite of the Communist Party, and by his explanation of colonial imperialism as due to the growth of international monopoly capitalism.

While European Marxism, originally prescribed for advanced industrial societies, had thus far been a very minor motif in China's intellectual history, Marxism-Leninism was something new. In the China of 1919 its messianic vision was made more credible by the startling Soviet success in seizing power. It seemed to offer an all-embracing solution to China's problems on several levels. On the intellectual plane, it provided a self-consistent, universalistic, and "scientific" view of the world's history which enabled one to reject the imperialistic West in the name of Western "scientific thought" and explain China's humiliating backwardness as due to her bondage to "capitalist imperialism" (e.g., Japan and the Western treaty powers) which had allied itself with "warlord feudalism" (e.g., the An-fu clique). On the political level, Leninism offered a new and tighter method of party organization and a technique for seizing power and using it to mobilize the populace and re-create society — actually, the latest step in borrowing political technology from the Western world. For the individual, finally, Leninism claimed to offer a way to discipline and self-sacrifice for patriotic ends.

While many of these appeals would grow stronger with time, they made their appearance at a propitious moment, when the nationalistic fervor of 1919 had been aroused and was seeking organized expression. China's "betrayal" at Versailles offered dramatic proof to many that the national enemy really was "imperialism." Henceforth nationalism and anti-imperialism seemed interlinked, just as Lenin said. Some of the participants in the New Culture movement proceeded to take political action.

In the *New Youth* of November 1918, Li Ta-chao, a professor of broad philosophical bent much concerned for the Chinese peasant's liberation, celebrated the anniversary of the October 1917 Revolution and hailed "The Victory of Bolshevism." In May 1919 he edited that journal's issue on Marxism. Study groups in Peking and Shanghai took up various kinds of socialist theory. (A Hunan student, Mao Tse-tung, who had assisted Li in the Peita library in the fall of 1918, returned to Changsha in March 1919 and led another such group.) In August 1920 a Socialist Youth Corps was founded in Shanghai. By mid-1920 Ch'en Tu-hsiu and Li Ta-chao had wholeheartedly accepted Marxism-Leninism. Ch'en met with others in September to plan the founding of a Chinese Communist Party. By the time Mao and eleven others attended the Shanghai meeting of July 1921, now regarded as the founding First Congress of the Chinese Communist Party, small party branches existed also in Peking, Changsha, Wuhan, Canton, and Tsinan.

The Soviet contribution to this rather sudden development had begun with an offer in July 1918 to give up the tsarist position in Manchuria. This was later developed in a manifesto put out by Leo Karakhan of the foreign ministry in July 1919, offering to give up all privileges under the old tsarist unequal treaties. The offer merely capitalized upon Soviet impotence, but when it became generally known in China, in March 1920, it aroused widespread pro-Soviet enthusiasm. Karakhan repeated it in September 1920, with some qualifications, as a basis for negotiation.

Meantime, an agent of the Third or Communist International (Comintern, organized in March 1919), Gregory Voitinsky, reached Peking and then Shanghai in early 1920. He helped set up the first Communist organization in Shanghai, with its news agency and publications, and with various branches elsewhere. His successor, Maring, assisted at the First Congress of the Chinese Communist Party. At this stage Comintern know-how was an essential ingredient.

Another early source of Chinese Communist organization was the group of activists among the worker-students in postwar France, many of them from Hunan, who in 1921 set up their own Young China Communist Party in Paris. Chou En-lai (1898–   ), a graduate of Nankai University, is only the most famous of the considerable group of Communist leaders who later returned from France.

After 1921, as we shall see, the growth of centralized and disciplined party organizations, both Communist and Kuomintang, confronted intellectuals with a painful choice, to pursue scholarship eschewing politics, or to subordinate learning to political action. When Hu Shih and Ch'en Tu-hsiu parted company early in 1921, after four years' collaboration, they symbolized the alternatives.

Writers in the new vernacular style soon faced a similar choice. For most of them the overwhelming preoccupation became the social revolution — the evils of the old order and the struggle to remake it. Most writers believed that theirs was a didactic social function, to instruct their fellow countrymen and save China from its decay and corruption. Those who individualistically pursued "art for art's sake," often on Anglo-American models, were soon overshadowed by writers with a social purpose, like Lu Hsün, desirous of serving their country as spiritual physicians. The latter were particularly inspired by the great Russian novelists of the nineteenth century whose circumstances and concerns seemed so close to their own and who were already so influential in Japan. Writers, more than scholars, increasingly felt themselves to be in the forefront of revolutionary change, as servants of revolution rather than of literary art.

The most influential early group, the Literary Association (*Wen-hsüeh yen-chiu hui*, lit. "society for literary studies") formed late in 1920, took over the editing of *Short Story* magazine (*Hsiao-shuo yüeh-pao*) published by the Commercial Press. The first editor was Mao Tun (pen name of Shen Yen-ping, 1896–   ), who later became a leading novelist (see page 701). The group advocated a varied and realistic "humane literature," stressed the translation of Western fiction, and encouraged new talent, including several women writers. In the 1920's *Short Story* magazine gave opportunity to several major writers whose best work emerged a decade later.

A rival group was the Creation Society (*Ch'uang-tsao she*) formed by Kuo Mo-jo (1892–   ) and others in Japan in 1921. It was dedicated at first to an all-out, rebellious romanticism. Yü Ta-fu (1896–1945), for example, wrote candid semi-autobiographical confessions in which sexual desire and patriotic sentiment alike met frustration and left the hero usually remorseful and guilt-ridden, presumably still under the influence of the Confucian ethic of his childhood.

In the mid-1920's, however, the Creation Society turned with equal energy to Marxism. As Kuo Mo-jo wrote on his conversion in 1924, "I am now able to impose order on all the ideas which I could not reconcile; I have found the key to all the problems which appeared to me self-contradictory and insoluble" — a statement which epitomized the simplistic intellectual appeal of Marxism-Leninism and augured ill for the liberal-individualist approach to literature as art. Kuo Mo-jo (who twenty-five years later under the Communist regime became head of the Academy of Sciences at Peking) went on to say, "The literature of today can only justify its existence by its ability to hasten the realization of socialist revolution. . . . This is the age of propaganda and literature is the trenchant weapon for propaganda." While this view did not become officially dominant for another quarter century, it gained ground steadily among writers in the 1920's. Lacking a modern literary tradition and established artistic canons in a new medium, they perhaps more readily accepted a primarily social function in the revolutionary process.

The Rise of the Chinese Republic

BACKGROUND OF THE NATIONALIST REVOLUTION

The 1920's saw the height of warlord disorder in Chinese politics and the rise of a revolutionary movement to re-establish central power. The first aim of the revolution was national reunification. Beyond this were other goals, foreign and domestic. In foreign relations the revolution aimed to abolish foreign privileges and domination of China under the unequal treaties. Every patriot was anti-imperialist. In the domestic scene, however, interests diverged. Social revolution, through mass organization of factory labor and even of peasants in the countryside, emerged as a political possibility. But the main leadership of the revolutionary movement, for a variety of reasons, eventually turned against the social revolution, suppressed the mass movements, and consolidated its power on a platform of national unity and anti-imperialism.

As a political process the revolution first accumulated its various elements during a preparatory period from 1921 to mid-1925, came to high tide for two years thereafter, and then receded.

As a step in China's political modernization, the rise to power of the Kuomintang meant that a new form of government, party dictatorship, had finally been devised to supplant the dynastic system. The treaty system also took on its final form, modified to permit more exercise of Chinese sovereignty. Yet both these developments stopped part way. The Kuomintang dictatorship did not get firm control over all the provinces of China, and the revolution which brought it to power, mainly in the cities, also stopped short of the countryside. Similarly China's recovery of sovereignty failed to abolish extraterritoriality. Thus the Nationalist Revolution, like the Revolution of 1911, got limited results.

Unfortunately, the potentialities of domestic revolution continued to be unlimited, because the disintegration of China's ancient rural society was still proceeding apace. Beneath all the events of the period lay the fact of poverty and demoralization in the villages. China's population was believed to be increasing, and estimates during the 1920's put the total well over 400 million, even approaching 500 million. The farm handicraft economy, however, was now receiving the full impact of factory products and imported goods. Machine-made textiles, paper, matches, pottery, and the like put the old farm industries, such as the weaving of cotton cloth, out of business, just as kerosene by the tin had supplanted the making of vegetable oil for illumination. Farming was drawn further into the money economy but remained undercapitalized. The cultivator was too poor to store his crops, improve his seeds and tools, or avoid borrowing from the moneylender. Tenantry seemed to be increasing, especially in South China. Rents and prices were rising. Meanwhile calamities multiplied, like the great Northwest famine of 1920–21. The mercenary armies of the warlords lived off opium production and distribution. A market was growing for morphine, heroin, and other narcotic concentrates. Destitution, malnutrition, and banditry were becoming widespread. The human and material conditions for revolutionary movements, in short, continued to accumulate.

While this perspective suggests that the revolutionary achievements of the 1920's were on the plane of politics more than of economic life and social structure, this should not surprise us. The remaking of China had been attempted from many angles and on many levels during the preceding seventy-five years, always with disappointing results. This high incidence of frustration, which has plagued every wielder of power in modern China, engendered much recrimination during the 1920's — against the imperialist powers, the warlords, the Comintern, the Kuomintang, or others. No group could ever claim more than partial or temporary success.

Among all the elements exercising some degree of power in China, the influence of foreigners was now meeting its inevitable limitations. For China's domestic crisis they could offer no solution. Neither Western entrepreneurs developing trade and industry in the treaty ports nor missionaries promoting education and Christian values in the interior could deal with the problem of China's political unity and order. No treaty-power government could offer China a model for the political reorganization of an underdeveloped country, or show how to harness her new nationalism for purposes of industrialization. The foreigner had helped destroy the old order, but could he now help to build a new one? This question underlay the post-World War I diplomatic settlement of 1921–22.

The Washington Conference and Treaty Revision. The treaty-power diplomats generally looked forward to China's developing a stable central government like any other nation. The treaty system had always retained the possibility of its own liquidation, since the treaties were all made between two sovereign powers, one of which (China) accepted limitations on its sovereignty. Foreign diplomats and Chinese nationalists disagreed less on the aim of China's recovering her sovereignty than on the speed and procedures with which to accomplish it. In contrast with this long-run idealism of the diplomats, however, foreign nationals protecting vested interests in China were generally short-run conservatives, supporters of the established treaty-port order, enemies of violent change. In the 1920's, unwilling to assist the Nationalist Revolution, they became its chief targets.

The treaty powers' principal diplomatic effort to deal with the China problem was made at the Washington Conference (November 12, 1921–

February 2, 1922), which was called mainly on American initiative and constituted the chief postwar settlement in the Far East. To the two principles of the Open Door doctrine — equal opportunity for foreign trade and preservation of the integrity of the Chinese nation-state — Woodrow Wilson had added the further concept of national self-determination. But the Western powers had been unable during World War I either to compete with Japan's economic expansion in China or to check her political aggression exemplified in the Twenty-One Demands of 1915; they had felt obliged to acknowledge, in their secret treaties, Japan's claim to retain Shantung. Partly because the Paris Peace Conference of 1919 had acquiesced in Japan's gains, the United States had not ratified the Versailles treaty. One American aim in the Washington Conference was to counter Japan's wartime expansion.

The treaties signed at the Washington Conference provided a possible basis for international stability in the Far East and for China's development as a nation. This was achieved partly because Japan cooperated in the settlement and was willing to give up her wartime territorial gains. Even so, the settlement lacked any means of enforcement, either in sanctions and operative clauses or in binding commitments of power politics, to maintain the arrangements it proclaimed.

In the first place, the Anglo-Japanese alliance, which had not particularly restrained Japan and might embroil Britain and the Commonwealth in any further Japanese-American conflict, was now abolished, with no equally firm alliance to take its place. Second, limitation of naval armament, one primary purpose of the Conference, was accepted on a five-five-three ratio for Britain, the United States, and Japan, with the proviso that no Anglo-American naval bases would be developed east of Singapore or west of Hawaii. Third, Japan agreed to withdraw from Shantung and also withdraw her forces from the Northeast Asian mainland, where intervention against the Bolshevik revolution in mid-1918 had brought Allied forces, especially Japanese, into the Maritime Province, northern Manchuria, and eastern Siberia. Thus, in return for an assurance of her naval domination of the western Pacific, Japan withdrew to her territorial position of 1905, except for Korea. Finally, the Nine-Power Treaty signed at Washington in 1922 formally proclaimed everyone's support of the Open Door and the territorial integrity and administrative independence of China and moved toward gradual liquidation of the treaty system by calling for conferences on the Chinese customs tariff and on extraterritoriality.

As a consequence of these agreements, Japan withdrew from Shantung, and China recovered the port of Tsingtao which Germany and Japan had developed. Britain eventually restored Weihaiwei. But the tariff conference was not held until 1925–26, and even then, because of divergent foreign aims and the lack of any genuine Chinese central government, it failed to agree except on the important point that China might exercise tariff autonomy by 1929. Similarly the extraterritoriality commission, meeting in Peking only in 1926, achieved no result. An effort of the United States, in 1920 and later, to revive the international consortium with British, French, American, and Japanese bankers as a means of financing China's economic growth, failed to achieve the extension of financial aid for reconstruction or troop disbandment. This was partly because the bankers could not agree on whether to redeem earlier unsecured debts, particularly Japan's Nishihara loans amounting to some 188 million Chinese dollars.

Inhibiting this international effort to facilitate China's development as a nation-state was the lack of an effective central government. Banditry and warlord excesses endangered foreign lives and property. The inability of the Chinese authorities to perform their international obligations undercut their claims to exercise rights of sovereignty. Thus China's internal disorder checked the proposed revision of the unequal-treaty system.

In addition, there was no firm basis for British-American-Japanese cooperation. The United States Exclusion Act of 1924 poisoned American-Japanese relations, while Britain's attention was monopolized by European problems. The principal contribution of France was to demand repayment of her loans in gold francs and thus hold up ratification of the Washington treaties until 1925.

The Soviet Approach to the Chinese Revolution. The Soviet impact on China in the 1920's was still another phase of Western influence. But in contrast with the treaty powers' halfhearted and halting efforts at a gradual reform of China's foreign relations, Moscow offered China a working model of domestic revolution. The Soviets' ideology and techniques of revolution together seemed to some Chinese patriots to offer an immediately feasible means of creating a new political order. This was something the Western treaty powers had never quite been able to do; indeed, their ideology and political methods had come to seem inapplicable to China's situation.

As early as 1912, Lenin had suggested that the Communist-led proletarian revolution of industrialized Europe should support Asian nationalist revolutions that might be led, according to the Communist definition, by "bourgeois-democratic" movements against colonialism and imperialism. At the second Comintern congress in the summer of 1920 Lenin's "theses on the national and colonial question" argued that, just as Western capitalism had prolonged its life by exploiting the cheap labor and raw materials of its Asian colonies, so the Western proletariat could now, by a "flank attack," ally with the Asian bourgeoisie against their common enemy; for "capitalist imperialism" was the economic exploiter of the colonial peoples and the political ally of the reactionary "feudal" ruling class in Asia.

Lenin's theory of imperialism thus unified the world scene. It gave historical significance, within a single cosmology, to all the elements in Chinese politics. One's military rivals could be stigmatized as "warlords" representing the "feudal reaction" of a dying order. Merchants and middle-class individuals in the cities could be classified as part of the "national bourgeoisie," representing the capitalist stage of history, which it would now be possible to "leap over" by applying Lenin's adaptation of Marxism. With the use of Soviet aid and of the Chinese peasantry, a "united front" could be developed, led by the "proletariat" in the Communist Party. By this tactic the "bourgeois nationalist" movement could be supported to defeat foreign "imperialism" while at the same time (and this was essential) the "proletarian party" could be organized to seize power from within. Lenin foresaw a wide range of opportunities — Communist parties in Asia could make "temporary agreements and even alliances" with "bourgeois nationalist" movements in a united front, or alternatively, they could develop their own communist "soviets of workers and peasants" as centers of independent power.

This range of theoretical alternatives was inherited by Lenin's successors. Trotsky advocated independent development of soviets in China, while Stalin advocated a united front in cooperation with the Nationalist Party, the Kuomintang. In Marxist thinking a true party must represent a class, and so Stalin had to argue, in cooperating with the Kuomintang, that it was not actually a party but rather a coalition or "bloc of four classes": proletarian workers, peasants, petty bourgeoisie, and capitalists, later called national bourgeoisie. These alternatives gave the Soviet approach to China a built-in dualism — it could stress either a united front of all revolutionary classes against foreign imperialism and its "lackeys," or a class struggle within China, with soviets of proletarians and peasants fighting the Chinese bourgeoisie plus the feudal reactionaries, landlords, militarists, and their imperialist supporters. Between these two tactics lay a middle ground of coalition with some classes against others, for example, with the "petty bourgeoisie" but against the "national bourgeoisie."

In addition to this flexibility of doctrine vis-à-vis the revolution, the Soviet government also pursued a dual approach to China on the two levels of open diplomacy and revolutionary subversion. Diplomacy conducted by the Soviet foreign ministry had begun with the Karakhan manifestoes of 1919 and 1920, already noted, which offered to give up the former tsarist privileges. This diplomacy was pursued by several missions to Peking and led to hard bargaining and an actual reassertion of former tsarist aims in Northeast Asia. The eventual Soviet treaty with the Peking government (May 31, 1924) provided for joint administration of the Chinese Eastern Railway and the preservation of a dominant Russian influence in Outer Mongolia. Karakhan became an ambassador, out-ranking the old treaty-power ministers and so diminishing the influence of the diplomatic body at Peking.

Meanwhile, under the Soviet program of revolutionary subversion, Comintern agents like Voitinsky and Maring were sent to China. They assisted in developing the Chinese Communist Party apparatus and a Communist-led labor movement, and simultaneously made contact with leading warlords in the north, Wu P'ei-fu and Feng Yü-hsiang, and with Sun Yat-sen in the south.

By this time civil war in Russia and the Soviet economic revolution, together with the allied blockade and intervention, had produced an economic collapse necessitating Lenin's introduction in 1921 of the New Economic Policy of retrenchment, a "temporary retreat" from Communism. This was the less extreme and less fearsome Soviet image presented to Sun and his followers in the early 1920's. The struggle between Stalin and Trotsky that later contorted Soviet policy toward China was precipitated only after Lenin's death on January 21, 1924.

The Kuomintang Reorganization and Alliance with the Comintern. Sun Yat-sen's charismatic sincerity and hopeful opportunism had led him, during a long revolutionary career, to join with a series of allies — secret societies in South China, Japanese expansionists, Chinese merchants overseas, students in Tōkyō, and military-political leaders of provincial autonomy movements in the Revolution of 1911. Increasingly Sun had groped for some kind of party organization which could make the transition from a military seizure of power to a form of civil government exercising a "political tutelage" over the unsophisticated Chinese masses. The early idea of "tutelage" (*yüeh-fa*) had been forgotten in the domestic power struggle of 1912–13. After the failure of the early Kuomintang to become a Western-type parliamentary party, Sun had moved toward the idea of party dictatorship, trying in 1914 to organize his "Chinese Revolutionary Party" as a carefully selected and disciplined elite, secretly bound to himself. When in 1917 he entered into the frustrating warlord politics of South China, Sun was still seeking the organizational key to power. Now the rise of the Soviet party dictatorship seemed to be part of a broader postwar European movement toward authoritarian party organization. The rise of Fascism in Italy after 1919 and Mussolini's successful march on Rome in 1922 offered an example of party dictatorship not based on a doctrine of class war. Finally the student activity in the May Fourth incident inspired Sun Yat-sen in October 1919 to begin a reorganization of his political forces. He re-established the Kuomintang as an open party and during the next four years built up its structure.

Using his prestige as the senior revolutionist of the day, as well as his wide knowledge of personnel, Sun now re-emerged as a leader trying to mobilize the increasingly ardent revolutionary talent of the era. He created a party headquarters, began the drafting of the Kuomintang's general regulations, which underwent several revisions, and appointed committees to write a statement of party principles and a party manifesto. All three documents were issued January 1, 1923. The reorganization was formally completed at the First Congress of the Kuomintang in January 1924. By this time, and as part of the process, Sun had made his working alliance with the Comintern.

The Kuomintang-Comintern alliance developed gradually over the years 1921–24, favored by several circumstances — first of all, the apparent indifference of the Washington Conference treaty powers. They dealt only with the Peking government, though not as a fully sovereign power, and their good intentions, stated in the Nine-Power Treaty, were long delayed in execution. Although Japan's expansion was checked, little was done to liquidate the treaty system of foreign privilege. Sun Yat-sen's repeated but grandiose proposals for Western aid in China's reconstruction got no response. Indeed, his demand in September 1923 that the diplomatic body let his Canton government use the local Maritime Customs surplus was sharply refused; the treaty powers in December concentrated fifteen naval vessels at Canton to prevent his seizing the Customs.

Meanwhile Sun's domestic vicissitudes were equally disappointing. The Kuomintang rump parliament at Canton was as prone to splintering as the warlord parliament at Peking. Sun's uneasy cooperation with the Kwangtung warlord, Ch'en Chiung-ming, collapsed in 1922, frustrating his attempt to mount a northern expedition for the unification of China and forcing him to flee to Shanghai in August. Ch'en Chiung-ming himself had certain democratic ideas and an interest in the New Culture movement, but his regional military power was so independent that the Kuomintang could not regard it as a reliable base for its national revolution.

When the Comintern agent Maring (who under the name of Sneevliet had had some success in forming a united front in Indonesia; see pages 735–736) visited Sun in the autumn of 1921 at Kweilin, his report of Lenin's New Economic Policy impressed Sun as similar to his own rather vague ideas about economic reconstruction. In January 1922, Kuomintang delegates went to a Moscow congress organized to counter the Washington Conference (see pages 763–764). The Second Congress of the Chinese Communist Party (CCP) in mid-1922, which stated its adherence to the Comintern and subordination to its discipline, favored an alliance with the Kuomintang (KMT) on a parallel or equal basis. However, this was soon modified so that, instead of an alliance between parties, the members of the Communist Party would join the Kuomintang as individuals, thus forming a "bloc within" instead of a "bloc without." This change, forced through by Maring, was required also by Sun Yat-sen, who believed in one-party government. He permitted Li Ta-chao to retain his Communist Party membership when he joined the Kuomintang. Ch'en Tu-hsiu then joined the Kuomintang on similar terms and was given high positions in it. Others followed.

This was the background of a statement issued in Shanghai on January 26, 1923, by Dr. Sun and a representative of the Soviet foreign ministry, Adolph Joffe, who had just been negotiating unsuccessfully in Peking. They agreed "the Soviet system cannot actually be introduced into China," conditions being inappropriate. Joffe, however, promised Russian support of China's national unification and reaffirmed that Russia would renegotiate the tsarist treaties, while Sun accepted Russia's claims that the Chinese Eastern Railway should be reorganized by mutual agreement and that Russian aims in Outer Mongolia were not imperialistic. Sun then sent his assistant Liao Chung-k'ai with Joffe to Japan to learn more of the Soviet system. With Soviet advice Sun also began the establishment of a party army and in August 1923 sent his devoted military assistant, Chiang Kai-shek (1888–   ), to the Soviet Union to study its methods. The KMT began to be represented at Comintern meetings.

After he succeeded in returning to Canton early in 1923, Sun Yat-sen began using Chinese Communist Party members in important posts and taking the intimate technical guidance of an able Soviet adviser, Michael Borodin, who was sent to Canton in September by Karakhan as an official representative of the Russian government. After living in the United States from 1905 to 1917, Borodin had been a Comintern agent in Mexico, Spain, and finally Turkey, whither Lenin sent him in 1921 to operate the Soviet alliance with Kemal on the basis of their common anti-British aims. (Kemal subsequently, while maintaining friendly relations with the Comintern, had turned upon the Turkish Communists.) At Canton Borodin drafted the KMT's new constitution and soon had a political institute teaching propagandists how to organize mass support. On the Soviet model the KMT now set up local cells (*tang-pu*) which in turn elected delegates to congresses at higher levels (*hsien* and province), each of which elected an executive committee, up to the national party congress, which chose a central executive committee, whose standing committee could now by "democratic centralism" dominate a centralized Leninist-type party.

On the Communist side of this marriage of convenience, the Fourth Congress of the Comintern in late 1922 had ordered the Chinese Communists to join the Kuomintang as individuals but to keep their separate organization, as we have noted. In June 1923 the Third CCP Congress by a bare majority acquiesced in this "bloc within" type of alliance and agreed that the KMT should be the "central force of the national revolution." Mao Tse-tung, for example, as head of the CCP organizational department, cooperated for a time with the Kuomintang stalwart Hu Han-min in "coordinating" the two party organizations. But the small CCP, with fewer than a thousand members, opposed close coordination as giving the KMT too much control over its membership. Mao resigned from his post and the Communists pushed their independent organization of labor unions. Their dual strategy was now to capture the Kuomintang organization from within while developing their own mass organizations outside it.

Sun Yat-sen's attitude in welcoming individual Communists into his party was both self-confident and practical. He saw how effectively students in the Socialist Youth Corps could develop local organizations of workers and peasants. The few hundred members of the CCP were a mere handful compared with the scores of thousands of Kuomintang members and supporters. While Lenin is said to have referred to Sun Yat-sen's "inimitable, one might say, virginal naïveté," Sun felt certain that his party could remain the principal Chinese partner of the Russians, who he felt would "not be fooled by these youngsters" of the CCP. If the latter did not obey the KMT they would be ousted; if the Russians tried to favor them, Sun would turn against Russia.

Development of Kuomintang Ideology and the Party Army. To go with the new party organization, Sun Yat-sen needed as always a revolutionary ideology. In his own rather empirical, superficial, and sometimes contradictory thinking, while on the sidelines in Shanghai in 1918 and later, he had developed a theory of "psychological reconstruction." This included the idea that "knowing is more difficult than doing" (*hsing-i, chih-nan*), an acknowledgment that the revolution thus far had lacked in ideas. He also wrote a plan for material reconstruction, published in English as *The International Development of China*, which envisioned extensive foreign investment and indeed foreign financial control over China's economic growth, with an enormous railroad net and other unrealistic aspects. In his own mind Sun did not accept the Leninist thesis that capitalism inevitably produces imperialism. The latter he regarded as merely political oppression. He favored the struggle of oppressed nations against oppressing nations, but he did not link this with a class struggle inside each nation. Instead, in response to Borodin's request that the Kuomintang be given a more formal ideology, he put forward his own revised statement of the *Three Principles of the People* (see page 636).

In these rather discursive lectures given in the winter of 1923–24, the principle of nationalism (*min-tsu chu-i*, a term with some connotations of racialism), which in 1905 had been anti-Manchu and in 1914 had been disregarded in Sun's platform, now stressed anti-imperialism. It also included self-determination both for the Chinese people and for minorities within China. The principle of people's rights (*min-ch'üan*), often translated as democracy, distinguished between popular sovereignty (*ch'üan*) and the administrative capacity of the government (*neng*). Sun piously hoped to "make the government the machinery, and the people the engineer," but this was to be done only through the devices of election, initiative, referendum, and recall (copied from the American Progressive movement of a bygone era) which had never become operative in China. The principle of people's livelihood (*min-sheng*) remained the vaguest of all, since Sun specifically denied the Marxist thesis of class struggle and reiterated his earlier concepts of the limitation of capital and the equalization of landholdings on the single-tax basis advocated by Henry George — all of which was a good deal more tepid than socialism, to say nothing of Marxism-Leninism.

Of the three principles, nationalism was the dominant core and the one point upon which unanimity could be achieved. For all his offhand remarks that his principle of people's livelihood was the same as communism or socialism, Sun Yat-sen remained unconverted to historical materialism, the idea of the withering away of the state, the collapse of capitalism, or class war. At the Kuomintang First Congress in January 1924, he accepted the three tactical principles of alliance with the Soviet Union, collaboration with the Chinese Communists, and development of the workers' and peasants' mass movement. These policies were later to be exalted by the Chinese Communists as Sun Yat-sen's "Three Great Policies."

Just as important as the party apparatus and its ideology was the indoctrinated party army. The revolutionary government at Canton was most united upon the need to reunify China by defeating the warlord forces to the north. After Chiang Kai-shek's return from the Soviet Union in December, the Kuomintang decided in January 1924 to develop a military academy, which was opened in June at Whampoa below Canton with 490 cadets selected from 3000 applicants. Chiang was the superintendent. Liao Chung-k'ai, as the chief administrator, mediated between Chiang and a corps of Soviet advisers. (By 1925 there were some thousand Russian military representatives in China; this early aid program was a forerunner of the much larger efforts of the U.S.A. in the 1940's and the U.S.S.R. in the 1950's.) The Whampoa Military Academy's six-months course was taught by a Chinese faculty who had either been trained in Japan or, more generally, in the Chinese academies at Paoting and Yunnan, both founded by Japanese-trained officers. The leading CCP representative, Chou En-lai, was deputy head of the political education department, which Communists steadily infiltrated but without ultimate success. A first shipment of 8000 Russian rifles arrived in October 1924. Soon two regiments of cadets constituted a KMT "party army," trained to fight for Sun Yat-sen's ideology above all. In May 1925 Chiang became its commander, dedicated to the army's role as the agent of national revolution. He recognized in the KMT army the new key to power in China that Sun Yat-sen had sought all his life.

The figure of Sun Yat-sen, after his untimely death on March 12, 1925, now became the object of a revolutionary cult reminiscent of the ancestor reverence accorded a dynastic founder. His writings became a creed of "Sun Yat-senism." To carry on his cause, the National Government (*Kuo-min cheng-fu*)[1] was formed at Canton on July 1 as a military-party dictatorship with Wang Ching-wei, one of Sun's principal political heirs, as its chairman, just as the revolution developed into a great mass movement.

THE KUOMINTANG'S RISE TO POWER

Labor Organization and the May Thirtieth Movement. By the summer of 1925 the two revolutionary parties, the dominant KMT and the small CCP, faced an explosive opportunity: an upsurge of patriotic anti-imperialism combined with a militant anti-capitalist labor movement. Each of these movements had its own rationale. Six years after May Fourth, patriots could see that the treaty powers, despite the Washington Conference settlement and declarations, still continued to exercise nearly all their accumulated privileges. For example, the Japanese Kwantung leased territory and South Manchurian Railway dominated southern Manchuria. The South Manchurian Railway and the British-owned Kailan Mining Administration policed China's biggest coal mines. At Tientsin, concession areas were still governed by the British, French, Japanese, and Italians. Legation guards still paraded through Peking. Most of Shanghai was governed by the foreign (mainly British) ratepayers through the Shanghai Municipal Council. The trade of South China was largely dominated by Hong Kong. Foreigners still held the top posts in the Chinese Maritime Customs, Salt Revenue, and Post Office administrations, revenues from which went chiefly to pay China's foreign creditors. Foreign steamship lines and gunboats plied China's inland waters all the way into Hunan and Szechwan. Many modern industrial enterprises were foreign-owned.

Any middle school student could have added details to this humiliating picture of semi-colonialism, which the competing warlords of North and Central China and Manchuria could not alter, some of them indeed being part of it. The stimuli for anti-imperialism were most visible in the great port cities — Shanghai, Canton, Hong Kong, Wuhan, Tientsin —

---

[1] Sun Yat-sen in 1920 decreed that *Kuo-min* should be translated "Nationalist," making the Kuomintang the "Nationalist Party." However, "National Government" became preferred by the government itself, while "Nationalist" has gained currency abroad since 1949.

where the new factory labor class was also heavily concentrated. In these centers an anti-capitalist labor movement could fuse explosively with patriotic anti-imperialism.

The evils of factory work in China had become as great as the unlimited supply of manpower: a twelve-hour day, more or less; a seven-day week with a very few festival holidays; unskilled peasants paid by piece-work, with a high rate of turnover; child labor exploited along with that of mothers, their nursing babies often parked under the basins of boiling water in the silk filatures; uncontrolled hazards to body and health; friction with Chinese labor-contractors and foreign managers and foremen; and pay so low that all family adults must work — such conditions, reminiscent of Europe a century earlier, gave the Chinese labor movement its own impetus.

A modern labor movement required, of course, new forms of labor organization. In China's traditional handicraft guilds, shop masters still dominated the artisans and apprentices, and craft solidarity was stressed, not working-class solidarity. Moreover, local or provincial origin was usually a criterion of membership, as in the regional guilds or provincial associations (*t'ung-hsiang hui*). Nor were the old secret societies suited to leading a labor movement. In Shanghai, for example, the powerful "green gang" and "red gang" (*ch'ing-pang, hung-pang*) could not rise above the underworld level of opium-smuggling, prostitution, crime, and protection rackets.

With the growth of modern industries, workingmen's benefit associations or clubs had been formed, mostly among miners or railway workers, although the most efficient early union was built up after 1914 among Chinese seamen in international shipping. From 1895 to 1918 some 150 strikes had been recorded, usually spontaneous measures of economic protest, poorly organized, generally futile. With the May Fourth movement came a wave of strikes, and such activity continued with somewhat better organization and success in 1919–21. Thereafter the organizing efforts of anarchist, Kuomintang, and other political groups were gradually overshadowed by those of the Chinese Communist Party. Protestant missionaries, Y M.C.A. workers, and representatives of the International Labor Office were trying in the early 1920's to expose and reform the evils oppressing China's factory labor class, but the CCP now began to take the lead in organizing and using labor for militant political action.

The CCP initiated the first all-China congress of labor organizations at Canton in May 1922, but it could not get the anarchist, KMT, and other independent regional and craft groups represented there to join in a nationwide, all-industry, politically oriented labor organization. More success attended the efforts of young CCP organizers, like Mao's schoolmate from Hunan, Liu Shao-ch'i (1898–   ), who set up unions and fomented strikes in Hunan, Hupei, and along the North China railways later in 1922. But this was checked when General Wu P'ei-fu in February 1923 bloodily suppressed a general strike on the Peking-Hankow line. Integration and coordination of the new labor movement in the revolution as a whole came only with the united front of 1924.

By this time the foreign treaty-port establishment, particularly the big firms, and the provincial military governors seemed to much of the articulate Chinese public to constitute an evil partnership of "imperialism" and "warlordism." KMT and CCP alike saw these twin evils as the enemies of "nationalism." Chinese industrialists were the more ready to oppose them because of the recrudescence of foreign competition in the treaty ports since World War I. In Shanghai early in 1925 union organization and strikes increased, and at the same time merchants in the Chinese General Chamber of Commerce protested against regulation and "taxation without representation" under the Shanghai Municipal Council.

When British-officered police of the Municipal Council killed 13 demonstrators in Nanking Road on May 30, there ensued a nationwide multiclass movement of protests, demonstrations, strikes, boycotts, and militant anti-imperialism. This "May Thirtieth movement" dwarfed all previous antiforeign demonstrations. In similar fashion, on June 23, a demonstration on the so-called Shaki bund, the roadway facing the consular island of Shameen at Canton, led to shooting between Whampoa cadets and Anglo-French troops and to the death of 52 Chinese. There then ensued a great 15-month strike and boycott against Hong Kong, crippling British trade in South China.

These tumultuous events, with many smaller incidents and issues, afforded a great opportunity for student agitation and for the mobilization of all classes in a great national cause. The CCP exploited this opportunity. Its young enthusiasts moved into the center of affairs. Its membership, including the Youth Corps, rapidly increased to about 20,000 by late 1925. It bade fair to capture the leadership of the mass movement in the cities.

The Northern Expedition and the KMT-CCP Split. The nationwide response to the May Thirtieth movement of 1925 marked the onset of high tide for the Nationalist Revolution. It also raised the question of the revolution's ultimate aims and began to strain the unity of the disparate groups that were working together as the heirs of Sun Yat-sen at Canton. In the parlance of the day, a "left wing" of the Kuomintang emerged as the central group holding an uneasy balance between the Communists on one side and an anti-Communist "right wing" of the Kuomintang on the other.

Faced with the growth of the Chinese Communist Party, which was abetted and used by the ambitious leaders of the left-wing Kuomintang who now dominated the Canton government, the right wing of the

Kuomintang chose that alternative position which opened before politicians in so many countries in this period. Sun's long-time follower Tai Chi-t'ao (1890–1949), for example, had early become interested in Marxism and then in Marxism-Leninism, but his major interest was anti-imperialism on a united, national basis rather than through class warfare. In mid-1925 he stated the case for an ideology of national unity which would be multi-class and both anti-imperialist and anticommunist. This view could be compared in many respects with contemporary ideas of anticommunism in Europe. Alarmed by the Communists' divisive, ulterior designs, it tried to counter them. In August 1925, Liao Chung-k'ai, a leader of the left-wing KMT, was mysteriously assassinated. In November some right-wing leaders left Canton and became identified as the "Western hills" group, meeting outside Peking, in front of Sun Yat-sen's coffin, to concert their anticommunist efforts.

For the CCP and the Comintern which controlled its party line, the choice was difficult — either to break with the Kuomintang entirely, facing the danger of being overpowered by it, or to keep working with the still dominant left KMT against the right, hoping to split the two to Communist advantage. As things were, the Communists were developing independent power in the labor movement; they had also, since 1921, been leading peasant movements like that in the Hai-lu-feng districts of Kwangtung. Mao Tse-tung now began to organize peasant associations in his native Hunan. On balance, the trend of events seemed still to justify the KMT-CCP united front, and Stalin chose to continue it.

The Second Kuomintang Congress of January 1926, at which the left KMT held the balance of power, also continued the alliance. It kept leading Communists in the KMT secretariat and organization bureau, and seven (constituting 20 per cent) on the central executive committee. This arrangement was approved by both Wang Ching-wei, the leader of the left wing, and Chiang Kai-shek, the principal military commander. Chiang's Whampoa cadets had already defeated local forces in the Canton area. But the militant organization for the Hong Kong strike and boycott had been taken over by the CCP and was creating at Canton an armed, Communist-led government-within-a-government. Communist influence was expanding within the KMT apparatus and mass organizations. Communists took over the navy. Evidently in self-defense, Chiang on March 20 staged a *coup d'état* at Canton, ousting part of the Communist leadership and some Soviet advisers while simultaneously reaffirming his loyalty to the Canton-Moscow alliance. Later he kept both the right KMT and the Communists from increasing their power, while prevailing upon Borodin to continue giving arms only to the KMT army rather than building up separate CCP forces.

Thus in the spring of 1926 Chiang Kai-shek emerged as the principal proponent of China's military unification, and the Communists again faced the choice of continuing to work with the KMT or turning against it. Once again Moscow favored collaboration: Stalin needed his alliance with Chiang as a means of arguing against Trotsky, just as Chiang still needed a united revolutionary effort with CCP and Soviet support for the forthcoming Northern Expedition.

This great military campaign, long planned by Sun to smash the warlords to the north and unify China, was also aimed at rising above local conflicts at Canton and expanding the revenue area of the government. It was launched in July 1926 under Chiang as commander-in-chief. Of its six main armies, mostly reorganized warlord forces, only one, commanded by Ho Ying-ch'in, was the product of the Whampoa Academy. Preceded by its newly trained propagandists, the expedition advanced rapidly against opposition much weaker than the Taipings had met 74 years earlier. The Nationalist troops showed respect for the people and were welcomed by them. They absorbed some 34 warlord armies or contingents by the time they reached the Yangtze. Only one regiment eventually proved to be under Communist control; CCP cells had not been widely established in the military forces.

At the end of 1926 the National Government moved from Canton to Wuhan where it was dominated by the left KMT, now more fearful of Chiang Kai-shek's growing military power. Three Communists still held top posts in it. In December the Comintern, meeting in Moscow, followed Stalin's lead and ordered the CCP to stay with the left KMT in the Wuhan government, which it now defined as a "bloc of three classes" (workers, peasants, and petty bourgeoisie), thus trying to exclude the "national bourgeoisie," meaning the right KMT, from the revolutionary movement. The CCP therefore continued as a "bloc within," subordinate to Wuhan and largely prevented from exploiting peasant unrest or building independent military power.

As the Northern Expedition in the spring of 1927 continued its successful take-over of Central China, the Nationalist Revolution entered a phase in which the military forces played a larger role, over a broader terrain, and purely political manipulation of the movement was less feasible. The preponderant anticommunist view of the military soon fostered a split — first Chiang and the KMT military joined the right KMT in turning against the left KMT and the CCP; then the left KMT also turned against the CCP, eventually rejoining the right. Thus the Nationalist drive for unity and a new political order rejected the divisive Communist program for class struggle and social revolution.

The confused and still-disputed events of early 1927 highlighted the rise of Chiang Kai-shek. He established his headquarters at Nanchang in Kiangsi and moved to take over the rice basket and industrial base of the Lower Yangtze region and Shanghai. Just at this point, on April 6, the Peking authorities raided the Soviet Embassy and seized incriminating evidence of subversion; Li Ta-chao and other Communist leaders were later executed. Meanwhile at Shanghai, on April 12, Chiang's forces with foreign concurrence supported local anticommunist elements who destroyed the armed Chinese Communist organization and labor movement by a sudden coup and reign of terror. On April 18 Chiang set up his own government at Nanking with the support of most of the KMT central executive committee and in defiance of Wuhan. He continued to proclaim his friendship for the Soviet Union while destroying the Communist-led labor movement in the Nationalist areas he controlled.

In this crisis the Comintern representatives and CCP leaders at Wuhan were still instructed from Moscow to follow Stalin's line of cooperation with the left KMT. But the latter, finally disillusioned and alarmed, broke in July with its Communist colleagues and expelled them. Borodin, Sun Yat-sen's young widow (Soong Ch'ing-ling, 1890–   ), and others left for the Soviet Union. On August 1 an uprising of Communist troops at Nanchang began an open civil war between the two parties. The Comintern blamed Ch'en Tu-hsiu, as secretary-general of the CCP, for the "opportunism" which had led to failure, "in complete contradiction to the instructions of the Comintern." (He was expelled as a scapegoat in 1929.) Mao Tse-tung, who in his February 1927 report on the peasant movement in Hunan had advocated a peasant rising contrary to the Moscow directive of that period, now led a so-called "Autumn Harvest" insurrection in Hunan. It was soon suppressed. Communist putsches at Swatow in September and Canton in December 1927 both failed. The youthful Communist leadership was executed, driven underground in the cities, or forced into the countryside of South China, where Mao and Chu Teh (1886–   ) joined forces at Ching-kang-shan in the mountains on the Hunan-Kiangsi border in May 1928.

The way was now open for Chiang Kai-shek and the right-wing Kuomintang leaders, with the support of the Chinese bankers and businessmen of Shanghai, to make peace with the left KMT and build up the Nanking regime as the central government of China. Warlordism was not yet wiped out, but China was more nearly united than for a decade. Even more important, at long last it had a central government intent on building a modern nation-state and reasserting the national dignity.

The Revolution and the Foreign Powers. The response of the treaty powers to China's dramatic awakening to nationalism and striving for reunification had been slow and cautious. Already committed to China's gradual development as a nation, the powers were chiefly concerned to defend foreign lives and property without taking sides in the domestic power struggle. In response to the "anti-imperialist" movement, they gave ground and acknowledged many of the claims of nationalism. At the height of antiforeign agitation in 1925–27, most of the Protestant missionaries withdrew from the interior, while an international force of 40,000 troops gathered to defend Shanghai. After the May Thirtieth movement, Chinese representatives were added to the Shanghai Municipal Council; municipal parks were eventually opened to Chinese residents of the city; and the Shanghai Mixed Court, which the foreign powers had controlled since 1911, was supplanted in 1927 by a purely Chinese district court to deal with Chinese nationals. The powers in 1926 permitted Canton to collect the customs surtaxes they had refused to Sun Yat-sen in 1923. After Chinese mobs took over the British concessions in Hankow and Kiukiang early in 1927, Britain negotiated and gave them up. When Nationalist troops, taking Nanking on March 24, killed six foreigners, British and American gunboats laid down a protective barrage but later a settlement was worked out. Considering the passions and fears of the day, rather little Sino-foreign violence erupted.

The British, with the largest foreign stake in China, maintained a defensive posture but expressed their readiness to liquidate the unequal treaties whenever a sufficiently strong government existed. The American State Department followed suit, maintaining neutrality toward the civil war, refusing to be obsessed by the Bolshevik menace, and waiting to deal with a unified China despite the conviction of the Shanghai foreign community that Chinese antiforeignism was a Moscow plot. The Western powers in fact did little either to prevent the rise or precipitate the fall of Soviet influence on the revolution.

Another Nationalist northern expedition, mounted in the spring of 1928, occupied Peking (*Pei-ching*, "Northern Capital") in June and renamed it Peiping ("Northern Peace"), inasmuch as the capital was now Nanking (*Nan-ching*, "Southern Capital"). The United States signed a new tariff treaty, recognizing Nanking, in July. By the end of 1928 the National Government had received general international recognition. The "Young Marshal" of Manchuria, Chang Hsüeh-liang, son of Marshal Chang Tso-lin, brought the Three Eastern Provinces into political union with the rest of China by the end of the year. China's unity was nominally complete, even though Japan and Russia still held special positions in Manchuria.

Led by a new generation of "returned students" who had studied mainly in the West, the government strove to consolidate the new national unity and abolish the unequal treaties. The chief aim of the foreign minister (C. T. Wang, a Yale graduate and former Y.M.C.A. secretary), was "rights recovery." Extraterritoriality for the major powers continued, but by 1930 Nanking had issued new civil and criminal law codes and secured new treaties which placed many minor foreign nationalities under Chinese jurisdiction. Negotiations to abolish all extraterritoriality reached an advanced stage. Tariff autonomy was fully recovered by 1933, as well as control over the Maritime Customs, the

Salt Revenue Administration, and the Post Office. The foreign concession areas were reduced from 33 to 13. This vigorous Nationalist foreign policy, with its whittling away of treaty privileges, slowed down after 1931 mainly because the new aggression of Japan gave China and the Western powers a common defensive interest in preserving the foreign treaty rights and privileges, especially in major centers like Shanghai.

The treaty powers' natural preference for order over violence led them in 1927–28, as in 1861, 1901, and 1913, to accept and work with the regime that gave the greatest promise of stability. Evidence is lacking to show that they played an effective role in the victory of the right KMT over the left and the CCP. On the other hand, foreign interest was still so pervasive, particularly in Shanghai, that it formed a natural ally ready and waiting to cooperate with the Chinese bankers, administrators, politicians, and militarists who organized the new Nanking Government. The foreign influence on the revolution derived less from diplomatic policy than from the continuing fact of foreign participation on a large scale in so many aspects of Chinese life under the modified treaty system. Thus foreign statesmen could remain correctly neutral and non-interventionist in their official policies toward China's revolution while their preservation of foreign rights at Shanghai, which was China's strategic financial center, made cooperation with the foreigner preferable to continued anti-imperialism. As Nanking turned against Marxist-Leninist class struggle and confronted Japanese aggression, it toned down its attack on foreign privilege. This reflected the Nationalists' temporary community of interest with the foreigners, particularly the British, Americans, French, and Canadians, who continued to participate in Chinese life as privileged persons, maintaining colleges and hospitals, banks, trading firms, and their investments.

Anachronistic thinking, reading the conditions of the 1940's back into the 1920's, no doubt still colors historical interpretation of this period. For example, scholarly researches on the KMT-CCP rivalry, made use of above, outnumber those on all the other aspects of the era, including the warlords, the rise of the Kuomintang, and its subsequent achievements.

In any case, the Comintern strategy of the 1920's seems in retrospect to have had little chance of success. Political organization of urban labor, in order to seize power as in Europe, was still a forlorn hope in China because labor unions could develop strength only in the few port cities where the new Nationalist leadership and foreign interests were also most heavily concentrated. The Nationalist movement embraced political-military-commercial-industrial elements sufficient to form a new composite ruling stratum. It could command the talent of returned students, the funds flowing in from Overseas Chinese and from landlords in the provinces, and the arms of KMT troops. Lacking a party army, the CCP could not seize the cities. Nor could it seize the Kuomintang from within, since the Comintern had given the KMT a centralized Soviet-style party structure, difficult to subvert. The peasantry meanwhile remained largely passive and unexploited for political purposes in the 1920's. With the CCP so small and inexperienced and Moscow's directives coming from such an obfuscating distance, a Communist victory was hardly to be expected, least of all on the classic lines of city insurrection.

From their victory the Kuomintang and Chiang Kai-shek seem to have drawn the fatal conclusion, typical of the time, that national political power depended fundamentally on armies supported by industries. Once victorious, they remained blind to the potentialities of peasant organization as another source of political power, also capable of lending support to armies. Their ideology of Sun Yat-senism had less attraction than Marxism-Leninism for student youth, the potential organizers of peasants. The Nationalist faith was in unification and rights recovery; it was against imperialism from without and against class war within. This was the view of an entire generation, older than the Communists, with more ties to the cities and the landlord class than to the peasantry, whose ambitions did not include a social revolution led by youthful activists in the countryside. Chinese society, in short, or at least its leadership, was unprepared in the 1920's for the kind of totalitarian mobilization of revolutionary forces that was to become more feasible a quarter of a century later.

THE DECADE OF THE NANKING GOVERNMENT

Although Kuomintang China is only the day before yesterday, and the record much less complete than on contemporary Japan, certain historical trends seem to stand out clearly. The Nanking period, from the nominal reunification of China in 1928 to the full-fledged Japanese attack of 1937, forms a distinct epoch during which China faced toward the Western world while the latter, unfortunately, was absorbed in its own problems. This decade saw the onset of Stalinism in the Soviet Union, the Great Depression in the United States, and Nazism in Germany. Japan's aggression against China was therefore unchecked from outside the East Asian scene. Nanking thus balanced precariously among three major influences — the pervasive though somewhat superficial Western contact and influence in all aspects of modern Chinese life; the gradually mounting aggression of Japan, near at hand; and the unresolved problems of the Chinese countryside where the Chinese Communists kept alive a movement utilizing peasant unrest.

Throughout its existence the Nationalist party dictatorship under Chiang Kai-shek showed a disconcerting ambivalence, almost a dual personality, due no doubt to the mixture of discordant elements from which it was put together. Neither democratic nor totalitarian, neither socialist nor capitalist, the regime looked both to the modern West and to the Chinese past as though stuck in between. Indeed this bifocal character of the Nanking Government, with all its hopes and frustrations, may be typical of many new nations modernizing late on the ruins of ancient empires. The old domestic traditions are bankrupt, Western models do not fit the local scene — patriotic leaders look to both, but in vain.

Another feature of Nationalist China was the comparatively small size and underdeveloped condition of the modern government and economy. Even at the end of the Nanking decade, the 400 or possibly 500 millions of Chinese were served by about the same mileage of modern highways as the 25 million people of Spain, less railroad mileage than Italy or the state of Illinois, less than a third the telegraph lines of France, less industrial production than the 8 million people of Belgium. Other aspects of technological modernity were equally meager. Modernization, in short, was still very superficial.

This condition of national underdevelopment tied the Nanking Government, as a modernizing agency, to its Western orientation. It had little choice, if it was to build a modern state; for Japan was an enemy and the Soviet model of industrialization, not yet developed for export, could not yet claim to be a feasible alternative. The whole capacity of the Chinese state as of 1928, in all its elements from popular literacy to specialized technology, was inadequate to mount a national effort even for totalitarian development. Too many prerequisites had still to be achieved.

This dependence upon Western models, which created the community of interest between Nanking and the West, goes far to explain the superficial character of the regime. Its program of modernization verged upon Westernization, for Western-trained officials naturally tried to apply what they had learned abroad, and their efforts reflected the administrative institutions, technology, and values of life in the industrialized nations, where agricultural backwardness and peasant discontent were not dominant problems. Consequently Nanking often understood modern finance, foreign trade and exchange, transport and telecommunications better than it understood its own hinterland. Its modern-minded officials seldom felt at home in the villages. The regime was based on the treaty-port cities and foreign trade, not on the countryside and the grain tax. Its central administration therefore remained almost as superficial as that of the Ch'ing and earlier dynasties. In some ways Nanking had more contact with the outside world than with the Chinese peasant population, for it left much of the countryside in the hands of those landlord-warlord remnants of the old order who had not yet been displaced in the outlying provinces.

These considerations make it less useful to dwell on the shortcomings of the National Government, which were plain enough, than to appraise the magnitude of its problems and its efforts to solve them.

Chiang Kai-shek and the Kuomintang in Power. A bare fifteen years after the demise of the monarchy, Chinese politics still required a single power-holder at the top to give final answers, which neither a presidium nor a balance of constitutional powers could supply. Unification (against warlords) and resistance (against Japan) were the dominant needs of the day; the power-holder must be a military leader. Chiang Kai-shek by degrees became indispensable.

Chiang was a man of patriotic dedication and strong-willed determination, politically astute but with certain intellectual limitations. To his early landlord background in Chekiang and an abiding respect for the virtues of Tseng Kuo-fan had been added some of the samurai ideals of the Japanese Military Cadets Academy and finally the experience of warlord politics in a period when armies counted heavily. From Soviet Russia Chiang had evidently learned more about armies than about mass movements. He did not believe in the efficacy of popular mobilization vis-à-vis military force. In any case, he faced the continuing problem of all holders of power: how to keep on holding it. Dealing with all possible rivals required the constant and jealous manipulation of personnel and resources. Chiang's dual task was to stay on top and simultaneously build the military strength of a modern state. To this urgent end he subordinated the question of industrialization and economic growth and, even more, the question of rural reconstruction and peasant mobilization.

After his marriage in 1927 to Soong Mei-ling, a Wellesley graduate and sister of Sun Yat-sen's widow, Chiang became a confirmed Methodist and maintained contact with the West through his wife, her brother T. V. Soong (a Harvard graduate), and her brother-in-law H. H. Kung (Oberlin). He used these relatives with American background in top financial posts, and long-time colleagues of Japanese background in military posts.

Given the continued increase of his military power, Chiang's major problem in party politics, as an outsider not of the old guard, was how to cooperate with and divide the KMT leaders descended from the early days of the party, especially Wang Ching-wei of the left wing and Hu Han-min of the right. During 1927 Chiang cooperated at different times with each against the other. Then for three years, 1928–31, he worked with Hu, leaving Wang out of power. When the two of them briefly joined up against him in 1931, Chiang proved more than ever indispensable as military commander against the Japanese. He then joined with Wang for four years, 1932–35. Hu died in 1936, and Chiang became Party Leader in 1938. Wang, who had considered himself Sun Yat-sen's heir, survived an assassination attempt in 1935, and in 1939 went over to the Japanese, evidently out of sheer frustration.

In time the supremacy of the "Generalissimo" (the title used for Chiang Kai-shek by the foreign press) came to rest on a tripod of army, party, and government, in each of which he balanced his personal bureaucratic machine against regional or rival groups. The army was dominated by the "Whampoa clique" of officers who had been his students in the academy at Canton (only half had survived the fighting of the revolution). They controlled the great military bureaucracy and the secret military police and generally held the balance against the Kwangsi militarists and various other regional forces.

In the party, Chiang relied on the "Organization clique" headed by the brothers Ch'en Kuo-fu and Ch'en Li-fu (hence commonly called the "CC clique"), who built up the Central Political Institute for training civil servants and the KMT central secretariat and Organization Ministry, with all their personnel files, financial resources, and secret party police. Their major rivals were the "Political Study clique," a looser-knit group of politicians and administrators with business and financial connections, partially descended from Liang Ch'i-ch'ao's "Research clique," once a competitor of the KMT. Although the "Whampoa clique" and the "CC clique" shared a vigorously nationalistic, anticommunist, but vaguely state-socialist orientation, they remained rival segments of the bureaucracy, respectively military and civil, joined only at the top by their personal loyalty to Chiang.

The Kuomintang, though still Leninist in structure, never achieved a tight totalitarian discipline over its members, whose effective number remained somewhere between two and four million, not counting the automatic membership of some millions of the armed forces. In the power structure stretching down from the party congresses[1] there was a gradual expansion of membership which was offset by a continual concentration of power. The First Party Congress of 1924 had had 150 delegates; the Sixth in 1945 had 600, a catch-all of prominent personalities. The Central Executive Committee had begun in 1924 with 24 regular members and 17 reserves, but by 1945 totaled 222 regular members with 90 in reserve. Similar growth occurred in the Central Supervisory Committee. Since the Central Executive Committee had only two or three meetings a year, power gravitated to its Standing Committee, which began as 8 persons but increased to 50, meeting more or less weekly. After Chiang became Party Leader (*Tsung-ts'ai*, "General Director") in 1938, he held a veto over the Central Executive Committee and presided over the Standing Committee. There being no institution of a loyal opposition, the tendency was to bring everyone of importance under the KMT aegis and into a personal relationship with the leader.

Since the party, not the people, controlled the National (or Nationalist) Government during the "period of tutelage" (1928–1948), the Political Council which usually headed the government was a subcommittee of the

[1] KMT National Congresses were held as follows: First Congress, Jan. 20–30, 1924 (Canton); Second, Jan. 4–19, 1926 (Canton); Third, Mar. 18–27, 1929 (Nanking); Fourth, Nov. 12–23, 1931 (Nanking); Fifth, Nov. 12–22, 1935 (Nanking); Extraordinary, Mar. 29-Apr. 1, 1938 (Wuchang); Sixth, May 5–21, 1945 (Chungking).

Central Executive Committee of the party. A number of party ministries — Organization, Information, Social Affairs, Overseas Affairs — functioned as part of the central administration. Party and government thus interpenetrated and became practically indistinguishable. Considered historically, China's first experiment in party government echoed many aspects of dynastic government — the separate military and civil bureaucracies were united only at the top, under a ruler chosen from a continuing body (the party) which retained the statutory power, and he was aided by open and secret supervisory personnel at all levels.

In comparison with these realities of power, the government structure remained relatively unimportant. Sun Yat-sen's "five-*yüan*" or "five-power" system was dutifully installed at Nanking under five Yüan — Executive, Legislative, Judicial, Control (i.e., censorial and auditing), and Examination (i.e., civil service). But the Executive Yüan with its dozen big ministries (*pu*) of Foreign Affairs, Finance, Economic Affairs, Education, Justice, Communications, War, Navy, and the like, at once overshadowed the other Yüan. Conversely, the Legislative Yüan drafted laws with care but had much less power than a parliament — for example, very little financial control. Under the presidency of Sun Fo (Sun Yat-sen's son by his first wife) from 1932 to 1948, this Yüan's 80 or so members, all appointed by the party leadership and many in sinecure posts, passed laws at their weekly meetings but did not function as a legislature responsible to an electorate. Even less creative vigor and independence were displayed by the Judicial Yüan, sitting atop the three-tiered court system, or the Control Yüan, trying to find modern equivalents of the ancient censorial functions, or the Examination Yüan, which produced less than 8000 successful candidates in 16 years, only a tiny part of the bureaucracy. Perhaps these agencies could have developed key roles in peacetime. As it was, the civil government under all five Yüan was paralleled by the innumerable agencies of the military establishment, which took most of the national revenues.

The Growth of Nationalist Militarism. Much can be said for the thesis that Japan's aggression changed China's history by necessitating military defense, distracting attention from domestic problems. When Japanese militarism was finally destroyed after an unbridled career of fourteen years (1931–1945), the Chinese government, or what was left of it, had little but militarism with which to reconstruct the country. The Japanese militarists had forced China to go in the same direction, negating the Western influence of the 1920's and '30's, exacerbating the already pressing problems of the Chinese people, and destroying all chance of gradualism, reform, and evolution in meeting them.

While maintaining this view, one can also see domestic reasons for Chiang Kai-shek's rise as a military politician. After the 1927 split, Nanking was committed to unification and national development without class war. Kuomintang labor unions ("yellow" unions in Communist parlance) were promoted to compete with leftist unions, but peasant associations were generally suppressed. Forgoing mass mobilization at the village level as a source of power, the National Government had to compete with the remaining warlords and provincial power groups pretty much on their own level, not fomenting popular uprisings against them.

This was evident in the continuation, already mentioned, of the Northern Expedition to take over North China. From April to June 1928, Chiang Kai-shek was supreme commander over four armies led respectively by himself, the top Kwangsi general (Li Tsung-jen), the "Model Governor" of Shansi (Yen Hsi-shan), and the "Christian General," Feng Yü-hsiang, now more interested in the Soviet system (see Plate 78). Both Yen and Feng had their own forces, while Li represented a provincial power group with its own armies and program of provincial regeneration. A post-unification conference in 1929 to disband the swollen armies and usher in a new era of peaceful reconstruction reached no agreement. A great war involving a million men subsequently erupted in North China from March to September 1930, in which Yen and Feng, joined by Wang Ching-wei, tried to destroy the power of Chiang Kai-shek. The latter's victory, aided by the support of the "Young Marshal" from Manchuria, made the National Government at Nanking supreme, but on a shaky foundation. Warlordism died only slowly, and military unification was never achieved. An anti-Chiang wing of the Kuomintang centered at Canton. In Yunnan, Szechwan, Shansi, Sinkiang, and other provinces local militarists maintained control, giving only lip service to Nanking. The Communists in Kiangsi until 1934 and in Shensi thereafter constituted a regionally based rebel power. The Japanese in Manchuria from 1931 and in Jehol and part of Hopei from 1933 became a foreign-based regional power in China. Year after year central government forces had to take the field to fight or negotiate in some part of the country in the name of national unity.[1]

Plainly, in this post-warlord era of the 1930's, militarism based on regional resources and interests continued to be a principal mode of political organization and expression. Nanking, controlling the key

[1] Principal campaigns of the Nanking decade:

1928 Northern Expedition continued to Peking.
1929 Kwangsi armies' insurrection suppressed. Hunan revolt (pro-Wang Ching-wei) suppressed.
1930 Suppression of Feng, Yen, and Wang Ching-wei's rival KMT regime at Peking.
1931 First Communist-extermination campaign in Kiangsi.
1932 Shanghai "undeclared war" launched by Japan (see p. 707). Second and third anticommunist campaigns.
1933 Fourth anticommunist campaign. Southerners' revolt in Fukien suppressed.
1934 Fifth anticommunist campaign.
1935 Pursuit of Communists on Long March (see p. 851).
1936 Southwest (Kwangtung-Kwangsi) insurrection averted. Northeastern (Manchurian) forces "kidnap" Chiang at Sian (see p. 711).
1937 China's military leaders finally united under Chiang against Japan.

economic area of the Middle and Lower Yangtze Valley, the major ports (except Dairen), and the foreign trade revenues, held preponderant power but had to contend with regional forces on the south, southwest, north-west, north, and northeast. Nanking's comparative success in this task was Chiang Kai-shek's success. Under him the Nationalist military establishment became less a Soviet-type party army controlled by the Kuomintang than a semi-government under its own leader who had created it.

The Nationalist military structure steadily grew and developed. When Chiang was president of the government in 1928–31, he put the military under a separate general headquarters of the commander-in-chief. When he was forced out of the presidency by party rivals late in 1931, he became chairman of the Military Affairs Commission (1932–1946), under which the separate growth continued. Having dispensed with the Soviet military mission in 1927, Chiang shifted to German advisers and the German military structure, similar to that of Japan. Thus the Nationalist forces remained independent of civil government and free from legislative interference. The general staff was autonomous and separate from the minister of war under the Executive Yüan (a post filled by General Ho Ying-ch'in continuously from 1930 to 1944). "Chairman" Chiang (as he was usually called in Chinese) and his generals thus had complete control of the military sphere, in which the Military Affairs Commission created more and more ministries for economic and political as well as strictly military purposes and eventually had fifteen special service training schools in addition to the Central Military Academy. All this was under an enormous bureaucracy in which sessile Whampoa graduates held top posts without further training and expended the larger part of the Na-tionalist revenues on an unbudgeted basis. From 1932, furthermore, Chiang's military "headquarters for bandit-suppression" took over the administration of provincial regions recovered from the Communists, superseding both party and government in an increasing area.

German military aid from 1933 was planned out by the former com-mander of the Reichswehr (General von Seeckt), who stressed the build-ing of a high-quality officer corps with a unified command and clear lines of organization. General von Falkenhausen, who headed the German military mission of some 70 officers, also urged the building of a military industrial base, incidentally using German equipment. A central army of 80,000 men was developed, the best troops in China, who soon grew to a crack force of 300,000. The Yangtze delta between Shanghai and Nan-king was fortified. Arsenals were established to produce German-type weapons. The German specialists got results although their programs were, as usual in such cases, based upon World War I assumptions, e.g. of trench warfare and positional fighting. Their military doctrine did not envisage cooperation with the peasantry or a war of maneuver and "scorched earth" such as eventually came.

The continued existence of regional Chinese militarists and the continual aggression of Japan thus fostered the growth of central government militarism throughout the 1930's: it grew as a law unto itself for conventional military purposes of self-maintenance and domination by force; it could do little to meet the long-term social and economic needs of Chinese society.

Nanking and the Economy. During the Nanking decade the chief models of economic growth were provided by nations that were in varying degrees totalitarian — Nazi Germany, the Soviet Union, and Japan. But the government of Nationalist China, in an underdeveloped country, could not aspire to a comparable mobilization of the national resources. Trying to inaugurate effective budgeting and auditing but with the military out of hand, it was never sufficiently in control of its finances, let alone the national economy, to pursue a plan of development. The League of Nations gave it technical aid in public health work, and under this stimulus in 1933 Nanking created the National Economic Council which tried fruitlessly to initiate and coordinate development. Economic growth could have been stimulated by aid from abroad, but America was isolationist, absorbed in the depression and the New Deal, and as yet had no concept of government-to-government programs of foreign aid.

Finance was the government's most pressing need and hence the chief focus of its economic effort. More than thirty foreign banks still operated in the treaty ports, financing foreign trade, monopolizing foreign exchange transactions, in some cases issuing their own bank notes, and generally serving as repositories also of the private funds of Chinese politicians, militarists, speculators, and businessmen. Sometimes they held as much as half the silver stock in Shanghai, where silver was the basic medium of exchange. The biggest was the Hongkong and Shanghai Banking Corporation. Its original capital of 2,500,000 Hong Kong dollars in 1864 had grown by the 1930's to twenty million with a reserve of one hundred million and assets of a billion (the Hong Kong dollar equaled two shillings, say half an American dollar). Meanwhile the hundred or so modern Chinese banks — government, provincial, or private — had issued great quantities of depreciating bank notes and chiefly financed short-term commercial transactions or made loans and advances to government agencies. But customs and salt revenues were mostly pledged for foreign debts.

To finance the revolution the Kuomintang had established the Central Bank of China at Canton in 1924 with T. V. Soong as manager. In 1928 it was reorganized in Shanghai to act as a central bank of issue and a government treasury. At the same time the Bank of China (descended from the Board of Revenue Bank of 1905) was reorganized to dominate the foreign exchange business, much as Japan had set up the Yokohama

Specie Bank in the 1880's to compete with foreign banks. The Bank of Communications (dating from 1907) was also reorganized to foster transportation and industry. In 1933 the Farmers Bank of China was set up to provide farm credit. Despite their intended differences of function, these four government banks all issued bank notes and tended to duplicate one another's activities, forming a quadripartite equivalent of a European-type central government bank. Their deposits increased almost five times, and by 1935 they dominated the scene with two-fifths of the capital and reserves, and over half the deposits, of all the modern Chinese banks.

As finance minister until 1933, T. V. Soong carried through a fiscal revolution — recovery of tariff autonomy and increase of customs revenue, readjustment of foreign debts and domestic loans, reforms of taxation, suppression of likin taxes, and abolition of the multiform unit of account, the tael. These reforms brought the modern sector of the economy and its capital resources increasingly under the government's financial influence. In this way it was possible to move toward government control of credit. From 1933 the American silver-buying program siphoned the silver currency out of China most disastrously. In self-defense China's monetary reform of November 1935 nationalized all the old silver currency in the country, thus taking it out of circulation, and substituted a managed paper currency. With British and American support, this reform enabled the government to unify and administer the financial reserves it held against note issue. It could now change these reserves gradually from the form of silver currency into the form of foreign exchange. The effort was to nationalize control of foreign exchange, stabilize the international value of China's money, and build a banking system independent of foreign powers. Accordingly the notes of the four government banks were substituted for silver and other notes. In 1936–37 there was still no inflation.

These fiscal developments were accompanied by other aspects of modernization, such as branch banking and interbank cooperation, some long-term financing of industry, and the organization of bankers' associations, all in the cities. But it proved well-nigh impossible, even through credit cooperatives or the Agricultural Credit Administration set up in 1937, to make credit readily available to the farming population. Rural bank credit was still used for seasonal short-term needs, not for long-term productive investment, and merely competed with the usury of old-style moneylenders. Many fine rural programs were blueprinted, and some begun, for everything from land reclamation, reforestation, irrigation, and water conservancy to pest control, improved seeds and tools, and crop and animal breeding. Farm extension work, American-style, was introduced. But no sustained effort could be mounted at the critical level of the village to increase the farmer's productivity nationwide.

Public finance showed the same concentration of activity in the modern, treaty-port sector of the economy. Partly this was necessitated by the important fact that the Nanking Government had given up any claim to the land tax and left it for provincial administrations to exploit, thus making a virtue out of its initial inability to control large regions of the interior. This renunciation of the tax which had been the main resource of most dynasties was symptomatic of Nanking's tendency to avoid disturbing the rural scene, with all its vested interests and explosive problems. Instead, the National Government got about 50 per cent of its revenue from the Maritime Customs (as compared with about one per cent in the United States). In addition, it taxed the consuming public through consolidated excise taxes on staples like tobacco, kerosene, and flour, as well as through the salt monopoly. Since there was no income tax, this regressive taxation fell on the average consumer as heavily as on the wealthy and so tended to reduce mass purchasing power. Central government revenues doubled between 1929 and 1936, yet the customs duties, on exports as well as imports, handicapped as much as they helped trade and industry. In effect, the regime lived off the modern sector of the economy which, ideally, it should have tried by all means to develop.

Constant deficits were met by borrowing from the four government banks about 25 per cent of the amounts the government expended. The four banks in turn sold bonds on the domestic market, debt payments on which soon exceeded the large payments still due to foreign creditors. Servicing all these debts took about a third of all expenditures. The domestic bondholders included many Nanking bureaucrats, and they often got high interest rates (up to 20 to 40 per cent if one allows for discounts they received on the purchase price). Such ill-gotten gains, paid to Chinese within the Chinese scene, were no doubt a good deal less odious than, for example, the enormous indemnity payments that had been extorted by foreign powers after 1901. But Nanking's policy was not designed to encourage production at home or capital loans from abroad, and it achieved little saving and investment for long-term industrial growth. The nation's capital resources were not mobilized, while the available resources went mainly to support the military or to benefit what the Marxists called "bureaucratic capitalists." The latter might be identified historically as the latest form of the traditional money manipulators, who used official connections, monopolies, development schemes, usury, foreign exchange and real estate speculation, as in Shanghai, to profit parasitically rather than investing in production.

More progress was perhaps made in transportation than in industry. Railroad building, largely in abeyance since World War I, was resumed by getting foreign firms to finance the foreign-built equipment, paid for partly by British-returned Boxer indemnity funds, while Chinese sources financed the local construction. This obviated both foreign control of the lines and foreign concern about security of investment. Total mileage grew from 7700 in 1926 to 9800 by 1935, although one-third of this total was by then under Japanese control in Manchuria. The National Government completed the Canton-Hankow line and an east-west Chekiang-Kiangsi line connecting with it from Shanghai (see map, page 853). The building of 60,000 miles of motor roads also facilitated cross-country bus lines. But sailing junks and river steamers still were the main contact with Szechwan, and two-fifths of China's steamer tonnage still sailed under the British flag.

After deflation and depression in the early 1930's, the Chinese economy by 1937 seemed more prosperous and dynamic. But Nanking's comparative economic weakness was symbolized by the fact that the principal industrialization of the thirties, using Chinese labor, had occurred in Manchuria under Japanese control.

Cultural Life and American Influence. Living in the shadow of rebellion-suppression and imminent invasion, those Chinese in the 1930's who felt themselves the intellectual inheritors of the May Fourth period still were divided into two main wings — reformist and revolutionist. Representative of the former were academically inclined scholars who fostered science, technology, and learning divorced from politics. Typical of the latter were activist-minded writers who tried to produce a literature of social revolution and were increasingly drawn into the leftist camp.

In literary circles Lu Hsün after 1927 became a public senior figure, encouraging younger writers, denouncing the Nationalist censorship and persecution of left-wing literature, and at the same time deploring the lowered, propagandist standards of the leftists. "Good literary works," he asserted, "have never been composed in accordance with other people's orders." Yet as a rebel against social injustice he became emotionally converted to the Communist cause, though never a party member, and was accordingly persuaded in 1930 to join with the novelist Mao Tun and some fifty others in forming the League of Left-Wing Writers. The Creation Society had been banned in 1929, and this new and broader organization with its many subsidized publications and polemical tactics marked the beginning of Communist ascendancy in the Chinese literary world, under the recently unfurled Soviet banner of "socialist realism." Although Lu Hsün was a prominent polemicist of the League, its policy leader in 1931–33 was Ch'ü Ch'iu-pai (CCP secretary general in 1927), who advocated the use of folk speech, the most common vernacular, in a literature for the masses.

Mao Tun was the chief novelist to emerge from the leftist ranks. In his first great success, *The Eclipse*, written in 1928, his young heroines reflect the revolutionary enthusiasms and disillusionments of the Northern Expedition. Through their eyes Mao Tun looks at the many anomalies of a time of upheaval — the discrepancies between aspiration and reality, the conflicts between love and duty, conscience and ambition, and the way despotism arises in the name of freedom.

Another popular novelist of the 1930's was a convinced anarchist, Pa Chin (1904–   ); his pen name is in fact the first transliterated syllable of Bakunin (Pa) and the last of Kropotkin (Chin). Influenced by Turgenev and other Russians, his novels such as the long trilogy *Family* (1933), *Spring* (1938), and *Autumn* (1940) depicted the experience of Chinese youth — its struggles against the decadent family system, with marriages arranged and true love frustrated, and its sacrifices for revolution.

Still another major figure, Lao She (1898–   ), was an urbane Pekingite who spent 1926–31 in England. Influenced by Dickens, he developed a great capacity for comic satire of the corrupt old society and the weaknesses to be found alike among cowardly compromisers and romantic revolutionaries.[1] Unfortunately the translator of Lao She's tragedy *Rickshaw Boy* gave it a spurious boy-gets-girl ending to help it sell in America.

American reformist influence in the 1930's was greatest among the nonrevolutionary wing of the intelligentsia, those who were foreign-trained and worked in academic and scientific institutions. The Christian colleges represented the cooperation of 21 Protestant mission boards and a dozen American institutions.[2] They now got more than half their income from Chinese sources including tuition fees, and were controlled locally by Chinese boards of directors. Their faculties in 1936 were two-thirds Chinese (466 out of 652 teachers). Although they had only 6500 students, as compared with 41,000 in the hundred or so government institutions of higher education, the Christian colleges still were pace-setters in instruction as well as in standards of living and social life. However, the big national universities like Peita and Tsing Hua also had staffs largely trained abroad, mostly in the United States. American influence was similarly evident in the Geological Survey of China, the National Library of Peiping, and the dozen research institutes of the central government's Academia Sinica, the National Agricultural Research

---

[1] "There are two great forces in the new society: soldiers and students. Though they won't fight foreigners, soldiers give everybody three lashes. Though they won't fight soldiers, students beat everybody with their canes. Consequently, these two great forces march on in unison, giving people some idea of the 'new militarism.' If the soldiers who daren't fight foreigners did not oppress and maltreat the people, they would forfeit their title to soldiers. If the students who daren't fight soldiers did not beat the presidents, deans and teachers, they would forfeit their rights to be called righteous youths." (Lao She in *Chao Tzu-yüeh*, 1928.)

[2] The principal Protestant universities were Cheeloo (at Tsinan), Yenching (Peiping), St. John's (Shanghai), colleges at Shanghai, Soochow, and Hangchow, West China Union (Chengtu), Nanking, Ginling College for Women (Nanking), two institutions at Foochow, and a group forming Hua Chung (Central China, at Hankow). Principal Catholic universities were Aurora (Shanghai) and Fu-jen (Peiping).

Returned Students from Britain, France, and the United States

Sikh Policeman directing Shanghai Traffic

Both drawings by the Mexican artist, Covarrubias, in China *by Marc Chadourne (Covici Friede, 1932)*

Institute at Nanking, and the big Rockefeller-supported Peking Union Medical College at Peiping, as well as the national health service which benefited from its pioneer work.

This institutional growth was the fruit of training Chinese students in the West. Some 2400 had entered American universities between 1901 and 1920; 5500 did so between 1921 and 1940, studying altogether in 370 institutions, primarily in branches of engineering or business economics — practical subjects. Returning to work in Shanghai firms or Nanking agencies or in institutions such as those just listed, these modern-trained graduates were a new cultural elite. They had close ties with the West and lived, if not at a Western level, at least on a material and intellectual plane far above the poverty and illiteracy of the Chinese village.

In the 1920's and '30's also, a modern generation of Chinese scholars, stimulated by study abroad, began to take the lead in reappraising China's history and culture. They achieved creative beginnings in many lines — for example, discovering Peking Man and the Shang dynasty capital at An-yang (see Vol. I, pp. 13 and 39), finding previously unknown architectural monuments, publishing and using Ch'ing archives, and in general assimilating into Chinese the vocabularies and concepts of modern science.

Missionaries and Rural Reconstruction. The missionary response to China's problems, while still evangelical, had also taken on many practical forms. Christian missions in China had expanded under the stimulus of late nineteenth-century evangelism, which had enlisted thousands of American youth, for example, in the Student Volunteers for Foreign Missions. After 1909 the laymen's movement had sponsored annual National Missionary Campaigns, holding as many as 75 conventions and collecting millions of dollars, with China a principal focus of concern. By World War I, revivalists like Sherwood Eddy and John R. Mott were touring Chinese cities. From 1900 to 1920, Protestant converts increased four times, and by 1936 six times, to a total of more than half a million. The thousand or so American missionaries of 1900, representing 28 societies, had increased by 1930 to more than 3000 representing 60 societies.

Meantime the Protestant message, with an enthusiasm represented by Mott's book *The Evangelization of the World in This Generation*, had become less narrowly denominational, more concerned with the "social gospel," with seeking "the kingdom of God in the social order." Where pioneer missionaries had found their chief response in the smaller market towns, the new concern for social service was expressed principally in the cities. By the 1930's all but about 100 *hsien* had been invaded by the gospel, but two-thirds of the Protestant missionaries were working in cities of 50,000 or more. With the rise of nationalism, the effort now was to make the Christian church in China indigenous, led by a Chinese pastorate and partially self-supporting, with the foreign missionary only advising and assisting.

These new interests had been expressed in the growth of the Y.M.C.A. (founded in China in 1885) and Y.W.C.A. Their city branches now developed programs for literacy and social work among factory laborers. With its lessened stress on the gospel and its direct concern for social service, the Y.M.C.A. attracted an able young Chinese leadership and gave an impetus to a whole generation of Chinese humanitarians.

Christian compassion found other outlets in practical good works. The North China famine of 1920–21 led to the creation of the China International Famine Relief Commission. By 1936 it had used $50 million in foreign contributions for pioneer programs of rural improvement in cooperation with local authorities in famine areas — building wells, roads, and river dikes. Responding to rural needs, it had also formed farm credit cooperatives in North China with some 200,000 members. Many missionaries participated in its work.

As Christianity in China became increasingly concerned with social welfare, an interdenominational Protestant conference of 1922 organized the National Christian Council, partly to apply the social gospel, partly to promote the "indigenous" Chinese Christian church. In addition to its urban program, this body began to develop a rural program and to strengthen rural churches. It also encouraged agricultural research and extension activities, as under Dr. J. L. Buck at the University of Nanking. Christian missions were thus by the 1930's approaching the problems of "rural reconstruction" at the village level.

A pioneer in this movement, Dr. James Y. C. Yen, a graduate of Yale and the Y.M.C.A., began work at Ting-hsien near Peking in 1926 with subsequent support from the Rockefeller Foundation. Here his Mass Education Movement began with foreign assistance to attack the problems of the Chinese peasantry, pioneering in the application of agricultural science and the spread of elementary education. It soon confronted questions of farm credit, marketing, cooperatives, and farmers' associations. This last type of organization, when combined with literacy, could give voice to peasant grievances and eventually raise questions of land tenure and local politics. At this point, the gradualist approach of the social worker and educator ran into the vested interests of local power-holders, those remnants of the erstwhile "gentry" who now often functioned with the military support of militarists or secret societies.

Thus "rural reconstruction," which was much more than a merely agronomic movement, affected the interests of government and became in fact an opportunity for it. Chiang Kai-shek through Madame Chiang, who was in close touch with church and Y.M.C.A. leaders, invited American missionaries to set up a model *hsien* administration among the peasantry in a part of Kiangsi recovered from the Communists. While little enough could be achieved in religious or community work in the midst of so much poverty, this and other projects of the 1930's developed methods to deal with basic rural problems. A broader North China rural reconstruction program, coordinated with Rockefeller Foundation support, was just beginning when Japan struck.

As power-holder, committed to being sage as well as hero, Chiang Kai-shek mounted his own program for China's regeneration in the New Life movement, stressing the ancient virtues of moral conduct — propriety, righteousness, integrity, and the sense of shame — while using some Y.M.C.A. methods. A network of 1300 branches during 1934–37 exhorted the public to concrete practices of hygiene, physical fitness, cleanliness, and orderliness — "Do not eat noisily," "Correct your posture," "Kill rats and flies," "Be prompt," and so on — a direct attack on the problem of remaking social conduct, in just the way that the commandant of a military academy might attempt it.

These many activities of the Nanking decade, when China was most oriented toward the West, still await serious study. Conditions among the populace in the villages were seldom recorded in statistics. Most movements, like the attempts at "rural reconstruction" or the official effort to revive Confucianism, remained piecemeal and superficial. The gulf persisted between those holding military-political power and the scattered intellectual leadership of the new nation. A further gulf separated the intellectuals from the Americans and other foreigners in China, who were still protected by extraterritorial privileges and could assist but not themselves take the lead in social changes for which there were few Western models available. Thus the noncommunist prescriptions and programs for China's cultural and social remaking in the 1930's, largely Western-inspired, were diverse and scattered. The ferment of these new developments was in any case cut short by military invasion and devastating warfare.

JAPAN'S AGGRESSION ON CHINA

Japan in Manchuria and China's Response. China's "Northeast" of 300,000 square miles was a big, new frontier area, about a quarter the size of China proper south of the Great Wall, yet containing much less than a tenth as many people. Population had tripled from perhaps 11 million in 1900 to 34 million in 1930, partly through migration from North China, and was 95 per cent Chinese. But the Japanese military felt that the blood shed in defeating Russia in 1905 and all the developments since then had given them a special position and claim to hegemony. The South Manchurian Railway Company (SMR) had developed near Mukden the enormous open-cut Fushun coal mine and the Anshan steel works. The Kwantung Civil Government administered the leased territory in which the port of Dairen handled a trade second only to that of Shanghai. Manchuria accounted for a fifth of China's total trade, and her exports of coal, iron, soy beans, and other products tied her increasingly into the Japanese economy. The Kwantung Army officers, responsible to the Japanese Army, not the civil government, were filled with a sense of imperial mission. Their concern over Manchuria as Japan's "lifeline" mounted during the 1920's as part of that general movement which eventually brought the military to power in Japan (see pages 579–588).

The rise of the National Government and its patriotic claims to Manchuria as racially, historically, and legally part of China thus clashed head on with the explosive militarism of the Kwantung Army. Friction developed over Chinese railway-building parallel to and competing with the SMR system, and over a whole series of incidents. Moreover, in 1929 the Chinese Nationalist seizure of the Sino-Soviet-administered Chinese Eastern Railway led to a rupture of Sino-Soviet relations and sharp Sino-Soviet hostilities in North Manchuria; when the *status quo ante* was restored at the end of the year, it suggested that Soviet interest in Manchuria might still rival Japan's.

Young Kwantung Army officers began to take things into their own hands, pressuring their superiors to acquiesce in their schemes for expansion. When Japan sent troops into Shantung in 1928, for example, young officers incited hostilities with the Nationalist Northern Expedition at Tsinan in May; in June they assassinated Marshal Chang Tso-lin (see pages 581, 656). Failing by such isolated acts to shut out Nanking's political influence and keep Manchuria independent under Japan's tutelage, some officers conspired to set up a puppet regime of their own by force. When they arranged the "Mukden incident," and proceeded without authorization from the civil government in Japan to take over Manchuria, the Chinese patriotic reaction and boycott led to an "undeclared war" at Shanghai (January 28–March 3, 1932). With difficulty 70,000 Japanese troops battled the surprisingly vigorous Chinese resistance. Rather than expand the fighting, both sides accepted an armistice. But meanwhile the successful coup in Manchuria had shattered the collective security system of the League of Nations. Neither the League nor Secretary Stimson's policy of American "nonrecognition" could now stop Japan's expansion. The Washington Conference treaties were in the discard.

Mindful of the tradition of barbarian conquest of China with Chinese help in ages past, the Japanese set up a puppet government in Manchuria with Japanese advisers exerting an indirect control. The state of "Manchukuo" ("Manchu-land") was proclaimed at Mukden on March 1, 1932, with the last Ch'ing boy-emperor, Henry Pu-yi (1906–), as regent. In 1934 he was enthroned as Emperor K'ang-te. Local Chinese were brought into "self-government committees" proclaiming "national independence," while the mystique of the "Kingly Way" (Chinese *Wang-tao*, Japanese *Ōdō*) was exemplified in Pu-yi's policy of "morality, benevolence, and love." Japanese control was centralized under an ambassador who was at the same time governor of the Kwantung leased territory and commander-in-chief of the Kwantung Army. The convenient fiction of an independent state justified the exclusion of foreign interests as long as the powers did not recognize the new government. The army program for "Manchukuo" aimed to keep out both capitalists and politicians and to foster the spiritual and patriotic harmony of the populace. Branches of the "Concordia Association" were organized under committees of local residents, together with a youth corps, public meetings, and "patriotic" campaigns, all managed by the army behind the scenes, deceiving no one. Mongol, Manchu, and other minorities received special treatment. Japanese migration was encouraged. But the recruitment of volunteers, the establishment of training institutes for them in Japan, and the settlement of colonists on new land proved expensive. By 1941 over 100,000 Japanese colonists had settled 89 places; by 1944 the record showed 220,000 Japanese in rural centers in Manchuria, heavily subsidized — in short, a failure.

Industrialization, on the other hand, progressed rapidly. A five-year plan was begun in 1936. New companies were chartered with special privileges and inducements to mobilize private capital. While the older zaibatsu were kept out, newer financial interests under Aikawa Yoshisuke were given a special opportunity. A badly needed unification and reform of the currency was achieved under a central bank; and communications, transport, and hydroelectric power were rapidly developed. Strategic railroads were pushed toward the Russian frontiers of Manchuria, and the formerly competing Chinese lines parallel to the SMR were incorporated into a single system. In 1935 "Manchukuo" bought out the Soviet interest in the Chinese Eastern Railway. In addition to the drainage of produce through Dairen, new ports on the northeast coast of Korea were developed to provide another direct route to Japan.

All this created in Manchuria an industrial base in competition with the homeland and required a heavy capital investment. Growth was aided by inflation. In four years after 1931 Japan's investment doubled, far exceeding that in Korea and Formosa. The China market was lost through the boycott while Japan's balance of trade with Manchuria was reversed. Thus Japan's economic gains were minimal, but the new strategic base on the continent provided the satisfactions of imperial glory and also a vested interest in further expansion.

Moving inexorably on North China, the Japanese in 1933 rounded out "Manchukuo" north of the Wall by taking over Jehol province, which the Nationalists had separated from the "Three Eastern Provinces." Japan further secured the creation of a demilitarized zone, just south of the Wall but north of Peiping and Tientsin, from which a Chinese puppet regime fostered infiltration of smuggled goods and narcotics into North China. In 1935 North China was made a neutral zone by agreement; then Japanese officers tried to incite a separatist movement to make its five provinces (Shantung, Hopei, Shansi, Chahar, and Suiyuan) into a puppet "North China-land" (*Hua-pei kuo*). This effort collapsed in December in the face of Peiping student demonstrations which dramatized Nanking's dilemma — when and where to resist by force.

China's non-military resistance in the form of a boycott after the "Mukden incident" had been very effective, spreading over the whole country and overseas, inhibiting Japanese sales and even contact with Japanese banks or business concerns. The boycott was coordinated by the Kuomintang with much initiative from students and merchants. It operated underground in the treaty ports, using terrorism when necessary, and enforced its program elsewhere by public meetings, propaganda, inspection, fines, and actual punishment of malefactors. Japanese exports to China proper were cut in half, back to the level of 1908. Japan's aggression was provoking a more thoroughgoing national response at a new level of public participation in patriotic action.

Nanking, however, discounted the capabilities of non-military and para-military (guerrilla) resistance. The Nationalist experts in firepower knew that unarmed civilians could not stop Japan's tanks and planes. The indubitable correctness of this view was confirmed by common sense as well as by military opinion in most of the world. Yet it overlooked what was later demonstrated in the Spanish civil war and in World War II: the effectiveness of popular resistance when mobilized in support of, and coordinated with, conventional firepower.

Chiang Kai-shek expressed the conventional wisdom of the day in his strategy of building up his German-trained army before committing it to battle. For almost six years after September 1931, with considerable skill and tenacity, he temporized, negotiated, withdrew, and avoided a showdown with Japan while creating his new army. This was plainly a harsh necessity. Yet alongside his new army Chiang had little success in using mass organizations for a total mobilization of the nation. On the contrary, opposed to the class war by which the Communists were rallying peasants against landlords (see pages 850–851), Chiang used his new army to follow a strategy of "unification before resistance" and so mounted his five anticommunist "extermination campaigns" in 1931–34. This effort to wipe out practitioners of class war was represented by the Communists as class warfare itself, against the peasantry of whom they claimed to be the champions.

Nanking's policy of fighting Chinese rebels but not Japanese invaders further aroused patriotic concern. A "National Salvation Association," ably organized in 1936 by noncommunist politicians and intellectuals critical of Nationalist policy, expressed this view. Other groups, both Communist and non-Communist, organized student strikes and demonstrations, calling for immediate resistance and a united front. Since this was the current Communist line, the broadening public support of it put Nanking under heavy pressure. By this time Nationalist China was not, as Japan claimed, a mere "geographical expression," but neither was it a fully mobilized nation, ready to rise as one man. In the 1940's the Communists were to achieve a great success in mobilizing the peasantry; but the Kuomintang did not attempt to add this tactic to its military resources in the thirties.

The Japanese Invasion and Its Repercussions. Japan's full-scale aggression in 1937, first near Peiping on July 7, then at Shanghai in August, really opened World War II, which in China lasted a full eight years, longer than the war in Europe. During the first four years, moreover, down to December 8, 1941, Free China fought alone while isolationist America continued with a growing sense of guilt to sell essential oil and iron to Japan's war machine, until mid-1941. By that time the National Government and its leader had shown both inspiring fortitude and the same limitations that had characterized their rule at Nanking. Their regime, oriented toward Western trade and contact, was progressively cut off from the West and confined to the hinterland whose problems it had only begun to deal with.

Chiang foresaw correctly that Japan's fanatical aggressiveness would sooner or later bring other powers to China's aid. The war became a test of stamina. At Shanghai the new Nationalist armies fought the Japanese to a standstill but suffered severe losses. Once outflanked in late 1937, they withdrew westward, "trading space for time" and using "scorched earth" tactics to destroy many of the industrial installations that could not be transported inland. After a pause at Hankow in 1938 the National Government moved up above the Yangtze gorges to Chungking in the mists of Szechwan. Whole arsenals and factories, and faculties and student bodies of universities, migrated beyond the reach of Japan's tanks, though not of her planes. With their superior firepower, the invaders took over China's plains areas and rail net except in Hunan, which became a battleground during the rice harvests.

Occupied China was soon divided between two puppet regimes, each with its own currency. In North China the Japanese army, pre-empting the rail lines as invasion routes and seizing the cities, rather quickly overcame resistance except in the densely populated plains inside the rail network where popular guerrilla movements began to take shape. After the fall of Nanking in December 1937, Japan's North China army kept ahead of its Central China rivals by setting up a puppet "Provisional Government of China" at Peiping, using as figureheads old men who had once been students in Japan and officials of the Japan-oriented Peking government. Soon a New People's Association (*Hsin-min hui*, reminiscent of Liang Ch'i-ch'ao's slogan, *hsin-min*, "the renovation of the people") began to urge a return to the classical virtues and pan-Asian cooperation, in press and school propaganda which was both anti-Western and anti-communist.

In Central China, after German mediation had failed to produce any mutually acceptable terms, Japan also installed a puppet "Reform Government" at Nanking in March 1938. After the fall of Canton and Hankow in October, Japan announced the creation of the "New Order in East Asia," which would substitute Japan's overlordship in China for the Western treaty system. This induced the frustrated patriot and one-time student in Japan, Wang Ching-wei, to seek peace by defecting from Chungking and Chiang Kai-shek; and on March 30, 1940, after much negotiation, Wang became head of a "Reorganized" National Government at Nanking, a shadowy replica of the former Nanking Government, under the nominal control of the "Orthodox Kuomintang," a rump group of anti-Chiang KMT members who had defected along with Wang.

These puppet façades at Peiping and Nanking, like "Manchukuo," fooled no one and rested on force. Yet, as in Europe a bit later, the invaders' superior arms made urban resistance suicidal and collaboration almost unavoidable. Collaboration, moreover, permitted Chinese to mitigate the conqueror's harshness even while working under him, and so was not wholly unpatriotic. The relative ease with which Japan recruited collaborators and governed a large part of China in the 1930's suggests that not all the Chinese people were ready for mobilized popular resistance. By the time this capacity became evident later, in the 1940's, it had grown with bitter experience under the invader.

Beyond the southwestern periphery of Japan's superior military power, Nationalist China and its armies survived in the less developed hinterland. This brought it into competition with the Communists, who had survived their Long March of 1934-35 from Kiangsi and now had a territorial base in the Northwest as well as a special capacity for peasant mobilization in the patriotic war of resistance (see page 854). Both the CCP and the Comintern had proposed a second united front in August 1935, this time for China's national defense against Japan. This tactical shift was aimed to take Japanese pressure off the Soviet Union and Nationalist pressure off the CCP. In late 1936 the formation of the Rome-Berlin Axis and the German-Italian-Japanese Anti-Comintern Pact heightened the danger of aggression. When Chiang was forcibly held or "kidnaped" in December at Sian by Chinese troops from Manchuria, who were more eager to resist Japan than to exterminate Chinese Communist rebels, the latter mediated to release him; whereupon the united front gradually took shape. It gave the CCP again a legal status and opportunity to expand its influence, using its tactics of village organization and control in the war of resistance.

The second united front thus began another period of KMT-CCP collaboration and scarcely veiled competition. In 1938 it became apparent which party might gain the more from the social transformations of wartime, including mass mobilization and the arming of peasants. The KMT soon turned against such developments in the area under its control, and Nationalist troops, eventually 200,000 or more, blockaded the CCP in its base in the Northwest. The united front continued only as a façade of national unity, to paper over the fact that two armed party dictatorships were still rivals for ultimate power.

The National Government, within the limitation which made it avoid social change in the countryside, took several measures to buttress its political power. A People's Political Council, chosen of broadly representative public figures, was created in 1938 to meet the demand for representative government, though it was given advisory powers only. Its questions did not have to be answered. From 1939 to 1947 the *San-min chu-i* Youth Corps under Chiang as chief built up a pyramidal structure parallel to that of the party. However, as the youthful membership grew older, it became a rival of the party, with no new or different ideas, and finally had to be absorbed back into it. A Central Training Corps, set up at Chungking as an indoctrination mill, brought together group after group of assorted magistrates, officers, professors, administrators, and the like from all over the country. Each group, in two or three weeks of tightly scheduled lectures, calisthenics, and other exercises became informed on the Kuomintang's principles and heard and saw the Party Leader in person. Meantime on the level of local government a "new *hsien* system" was introduced in 1939. It aimed to invigorate economic and welfare activities at the district level, which proved difficult, and also to revive the ancient *pao-chia* mutual-responsibility and surveillance system, which proved of some effect in maintaining local order. This revival had new features of "self-government" through election of *pao* representatives to participate in village administration, but there is little record of the election process taking hold in the back country.

All these measures, like Chungking's indomitable wartime performance as a whole, betrayed a conservative poverty of ideas. The original leaders of the National Government still clung to power. The Military Affairs Commission expanded and took over more and more of the civil government's functions. As many as five million troops were under arms at one time, with half a million officers and an enormous bureaucracy in charge of industrial, political, and cultural as well as military activities, in a war effort which was also a vested interest. Yet the ideological leadership of this massive effort was confined to the meager set of ideas put forth in *China's Destiny*, a treatise Chiang Kai-shek published in 1943 and made required reading in the study of "party principles."

The first theme of this book is nationalistic anti-imperialism — the humiliations of foreign aggression, the manifold evils brought upon modern China by the unequal treaties. The patriotic sense of grievance is plain and understandable, whether or not one agrees that the many evils and all the other maladjustments of modernization have in fact been due to Western victimization of China. The second theme concerns what to do about it all, and Chiang's proposal, as in the New Life movement of a decade before, was to revive the ancient virtues of the Confucian social order and subordinate the individual properly to the state. At the same time he would industrialize on a grand scale for national defense and collectivize the peasants to make them farmer-soldiers. In its patriotic anti-imperialism and authoritarian tendencies, *China's Destiny* had certain points in common with the ideology developed by Mao Tse-tung (see page 861), but its traditionalism invoked ideas even more out-of-date. It was a poor competitor among student youth.

The sufferings of the government civil servants, the people from "down-river," who had migrated to the crowded housing and consumer-goods shortages of wartime Szechwan, were capped by the continuing inflation, which destroyed their government stipends and living standards by a process of slow strangulation. Although it was in a self-sufficient agricultural region with a considerable food supply, the government failed to develop its tax revenues and relied heavily on note-issue to finance its needs. This left the rural subsistence economy relatively unaffected, but put the government's urban stipendiaries, the whole modern sector of Free China, through an inflationary wringer. White-collar salaries never kept up. Books, clothing, furnishings went for food. Malnutrition produced skin disease, stomach ailments, tuberculosis. Poverty led many to the ultimate humiliation of trying to survive by corruption. The privileged few in business enterprises tended to hoard commodities or gold rather than invest their untaxed profits. But most of the modern stratum of Free China was enervated and demoralized, and eventually blamed the regime in power.

This tragic process coincided in the universities with the Kuomintang's effort to both expand and control the system of higher education for political purposes. This government effort, facilitated by its control of the rice supply, was natural enough in wartime, but its lack of new ideas and use of police intimidation made it more repressive than creative. Even the academic wing of the intelligentsia began to question what the KMT leadership had to offer.

American Aid to China in World War II. In the first two and one-half years of China's struggle the National Government received far more help from the Soviet Union than from America, Britain, and France. Soviet credits of $250 million in 1937–39 almost equaled the Western credits of $263.5 million received in the four years from 1937 up to

Pearl Harbor. Soviet arms came by sea as well as over the 1700-mile Central Asian camel and truck route, and an entire Soviet "volunteer" air force fought Japan in China. But Soviet aid died away after the onset of World War II in September 1939.

In this early period of the war, Free China's cause won American public acclaim but little help. Access through Hong Kong was blocked by Japan's seizure of Canton in October 1938, while access via the Indo-China rail route from Haiphong to Kunming was finally cut after the fall of France in 1940. Meanwhile the Burma Road, a 715-mile truck route over high mountains and deep river gorges from the railhead at Lashio to Kunming, had come into use early in 1939. But Free China, thus besieged, was practically cut off.

Since Japan's attack on China coincided with the era of American isolationism, United States Government assistance was long delayed. Washington's domestic silver-buying policy, after China gave up her traditional silver currency in 1935, contributed $252 million to her finances by late 1941. But American support of China's strategic necessities, such as her currency or her air force, was slow and cautious before 1941.

When Pearl Harbor made active allies of Washington and Chungking, the United States Government through its military aid began for the first time to play a major role, albeit involuntarily, in China's domestic affairs. The wartime alliance, from 1941 to 1945 and immediately afterward, brought to its highest point the American participation in Chinese life that had been growing for a century past. Revision of the British and American treaties with China in January 1943 formally ended the unequal-treaty system; yet, ironically, the war effort created an American presence — manifest in air forces and bases, training schools, supply and transport services, and other wartime agencies with their radio networks and airlines — greater than had ever been seen before. Most spectacular was the success of the Fourteenth U.S. Air Force under General C. L. Chennault in stopping the Japanese bombing of Free China's cities.

But American aid suffered a series of handicaps. First, Japan's quick seizure of Burma in early 1942 cut the Burma Road supply route. The only substitute was an airlift from India over the mountainous "Hump" of northern Burma to Kunming — a costly route of limited capacity (see map, opposite) which only in 1944 equaled the Burma Road's tonnage of 1941. Second, the Allied strategy, to defeat Germany before Japan, gave the distant China-Burma-India theater a low priority. After Lend-lease aid to China once began in the spring of 1941, it amounted by early 1946 to $1.5 billion, but this was only about 3 per cent of the $50 billion Lend-lease aid given to all countries in World War II. China was neither easy to help nor strategically of first importance. General Joseph Stilwell, designated Chiang Kai-shek's "chief of staff," tenaciously

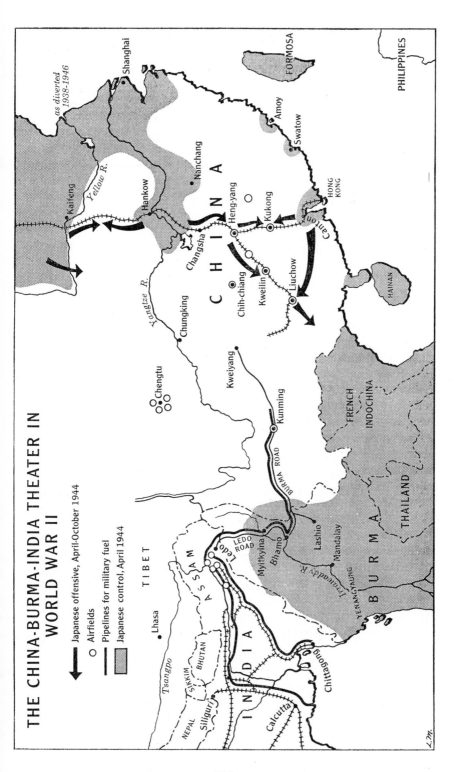

THE CHINA-BURMA-INDIA THEATER IN
WORLD WAR II

➤ Japanese offensive, April-October 1944
○ Airfields
▬ Pipelines for military fuel
▨ Japanese control, April 1944

set about the difficult reconquest of North Burma to reopen a land route to China as the putative base for attacking Japan. By early 1945 a road and a pipeline accomplished this, but the naval campaign in the Pacific had long since carried the war directly to Japan. American bombers had hardly begun in 1944 to use airfields built with great effort around Chengtu before they were shifted to the Mariana Islands, supplied by sea and nearer Tōkyō.

Thus warfare outpaced diplomacy. The initial American political aim, to help China become a "great power" capable of stabilizing East Asia once Japan had been defeated, had been joined with a parallel military aim, to help the National Government build up its military capacity. If the Allied attack on Japan had indeed gone through China, conditions there after the war might have been more viable and less inviting to Communist rebellion. In fact, however, China was bypassed and became a sideshow. This exacerbated the inevitable frictions of any alliance and produced much bitterness and recrimination, between the Americans and the British, between Stilwell and Chennault, between Chiang Kai-shek and his allies, eventually between America and China.

The American war effort, so concentrated on defeating Japan, expressed the outlook of a people accustomed to peace in a stable society, who had never themselves suffered invasion or revolution at home and who viewed the war overseas as a brief interlude, not as a phase of a continuing process. In China, on the other hand, the principal war effort had already been expended, to survive Japan's aggression in 1937 and the four years of disruption and scarcity since then. The Kuomintang ideal of unifying China militarily, the Communist hope of seizing power by armed revolution, underlay Chinese politics. Americans eager to win the war pressed for a more efficient, unified KMT-CCP war effort, only to meet frustration. Partly over this issue, General Stilwell was recalled in November 1944.

Once Japan was defeated in August 1945, the United States quickly demobilized its powerful forces with no thought of further military action in East Asia. But the arms it had provided made the National Government commanders apparently overconfident of their capacity to suppress the Communist rebellion. Their government emerged from World War II economically debilitated and politically insecure but with superior firepower. This combination of circumstances led it into a civil war that proved its undoing (see pages 858–860).

The decline and fall of the Kuomintang, after its early promise, is a recent tragedy still hotly disputed among observers and still awaiting thorough research. Certain points may be made. First, the KMT-CCP rivalry was continuous from the very moment in 1923 when the KMT was reorganized as a Leninist-style party dictatorship. The potentialities for revolutionary change, such as the mobilization of the peasantry to take part in war and politics, steadily increased, yet the Kuomintang did not succeed in grasping and using them. Second, Japan's aggression after 1931 was an ever present fact in China's national life, even more immediately pressing than the potentialities of revolution. It undoubtedly diverted the National Government from many constructive tasks and altered its history. Third, American aid to the National Government after 1941, though it climaxed a century of American help toward meeting China's problems, came too late. If in the early 1930's substantial United States Government aid had gone to Nanking, as it has gone to so many regimes since 1941, Chinese history might well have been changed. But American aid in wartime, coming late to a hard-pressed government, served more as a crutch to lean on than as a means to cure its ailments. American financial and military aid may have made the Chungking regime less dependent on other, more purely political and domestic, sources of support than might otherwise have been the case. If this is so, it may, ironically, have accentuated the Nationalist reliance on military power, which Japan's aggression had already necessitated, in preference to programs of social revolution, which the CCP had increasingly pre-empted.

Finally, Nationalist China's deterioration during eight years of wartime attrition reflected both the impact of overwhelming circumstance and an inadequacy of leadership, in proportions still being debated. For the Nanking Government, based on the coastal cities, removal inland was all but fatal. The Chinese Communists' comparatively successful wartime expansion was accomplished without the oppressive burden of frontal resistance and national responsibilities that exhausted Chungking's energies. National Government forces tied down most of Japan's troops in China, roughly half her armies overseas, and suffered the great part of China's three million or more battle casualties. Meanwhile the CCP regime built up its power on a more primitive level. (On the Chinese Communist war of resistance, see pages 852–857.)

Chinese tradition sees history in more personal terms than modern social science. Chiang Kai-shek, who took responsibility as the holder of power, has been by many assigned responsibility for losing it. Study may show, however, that he was seldom master of Free China's circumstances; his cause was damaged less by inadequacies of virtue than by an excess of virtues that were out of date, less by initial corruption among his followers than by disregard of economics. His inflexible rectitude mirrored the inertia of a whole political tradition, still in the shadow of the Confucian monarchy.

In short, just as Western aid was unable to prevent Free China's deterioration, so Western models were of little use to the Chinese republic in wartime. After several generations of increasing American contact, the Chinese people emerged from World War II more susceptible to totalitarianism than the American people could imagine possible. Their ways soon parted.

9

Colonialism and Nationalism

in the Peripheral Areas

THE PERIPHERAL AREAS IN MODERN EAST ASIAN HISTORY

Around the edge of East Asia are a dozen or more areas, stretching from the Russian territories in the Maritime Province and Siberia on the north around through Mongolia, Central Asia, and Tibet to Burma, Thailand, Vietnam, and the rest of Southeast Asia.[1] This great arc forms the geographical context of the modern expansion of China and Japan. It has been the matrix within which, in modern times, three vigorous regimes in succession — the Ch'ing empire, militarist Japan, and Communist China — have tried to develop an East Asian political order separate from the international order of the outside world created by the Western powers. China and Japan have competed in Taiwan, Korea, Manchuria, and Mongolia. Overseas Chinese emigrants have played strategic roles in the growth of the Philippines, Indonesia, Malaya, Burma, Thailand, Cambodia, and Vietnam; and Japanese militarists in the 1940's overran all these countries. Recently China has reasserted its claims to Sinkiang and Tibet. Today Communist China adjoins the Soviet Union on the northern and western continental segment of this periphery, and nations aided by the United States on the eastern and southern maritime segment.

[1] On the peripheral areas of East Asian civilization, see Vol. I, pp. 395ff.

JAPANESE SOLDIER of World War II.

Since the peripheral areas, with all their diversity of peoples and cultures, figure in the modern history of East Asia, they cannot be disregarded; and yet they cannot be adequately included here. This is the status of "peripheral" areas in any history — by definition not the main actors, they still play significant roles that must be briefly characterized. In this chapter we must deal with the modern history of the peripheral areas too briefly to do them full justice, and with a disproportionate concern for their relations with China and Japan.

We have already noted in Chapter 1 how Siberia and Southeast Asia provided Europe's first routes of access to East Asia, and in Chapter 6 how these areas fell under European domination. The imperialist rivalries in China at the turn of the century could not be understood without reference to the expansion of Russia in Central Asia and Manchuria, Britain in Burma, France in Vietnam, and the United States in the Philippines. Areas along the borders of the Ch'ing empire — Ili, Tongking, Taiwan, Korea, and Manchuria — became in succession the focal points of Sino-foreign conflict, just as Tibet has been more recently. Meanwhile the Republican Revolution of 1911 was greatly aided by the Overseas Chinese in Southeast Asia.

In a larger view we have suggested that the "Chinese culture area" of early East Asian history included not only China, Korea, and Japan but also Vietnam, and that the successive processes of Western intrusion and national modernization in this whole area should be studied comparatively, not only as between Japan and China but also as between, for example, Korea and Vietnam. Each of the separate histories of the peripheral areas has great interest in itself, for the modernization of each traditional society and culture is a unique story. At the same time they offer fascinating though perilous opportunities for comparative study.

There is of course a tremendous contrast between the vast thinly-populated reaches of the pastoral Inner Asian lands — Outer Mongolia, Sinkiang, and Tibet, with hardly ten million people — and the tropical, rice-growing lands of Southeast Asia with a total population now over 220 million. Yet the peoples of both regions have been subjected in modern times to the pressures and stimuli of conquest and colonial domination, whether by European empire-builders or by the expansion of Japan or China more recently. The forms of this colonial domination, pressing upon the peripheral states from outside and also from inside East Asia, have been many and various, but in recent times they have invariably stimulated a growth of nationalism.

Coming after the expansion of European imperialism and colonialism in the late nineteenth century, already described in Chapter 6, this rapid growth of nationalism in Inner Asia and Southeast Asia was marked by certain milestones. First was Japan's defeat of Russia in 1905, which shattered the contemporary myth of white racial superiority. Second, in

1912 the Chinese Republic eclipsed the Son of Heaven, the most ancient and central authority in East Asia. This was soon followed by the incredible spectacle, in World War I, of mutual slaughter among the leading peoples of Western civilization — a serious blow to their prestige in Asia. Then out of the war came the explosive ideas of the Russian Revolution, and also the principle of the self-determination of small nations, applied in Europe, though not overseas. New political principles spread from the West even as old monarchies crumbled. The collapse of the Ch'ing empire facilitated both the rise of Japan as a world power and the eastward expansion of Communism from Soviet Russia as an international revolutionary movement. Communism and nationalism, in the 1920's, began to undermine the established order of European colonialism in Southeast Asia. It was further strained by the world-wide depression of the early 1930's.

Finally in World War II Japan's military expansion southward over "Greater East Asia" within a few months supplanted the colonial regimes which Western powers had built up through many decades or even centuries. And in each country national sentiment was stimulated by the humbling of the Western regimes and the subsequent Japanese occupation. Though the Western powers, after Japan's defeat in 1945, returned for shorter or longer periods, colonialism was dead; and purblind efforts to revive it, as under the Dutch in Indonesia and the French in Vietnam, ended only in disaster.

Since World War II a dozen regimes have begun to function as independent nation-states — even when dependent to some degree, as satellite or client, upon an outside power. These new states are still involved in the history of East Asia — as neighbors, for example, of the new China, or trading partners of the new Japan, or allies of the Soviet Union or of the United States. In any picture of East Asia today we must therefore sketch the main outlines of the history of Inner Asia and Southeast Asia, as we try to do in this chapter, looking first at the growth of the colonial administrations and their economies and then at the rise of nationalist movements. In every case the changes have come with extraordinary and accelerating swiftness.

VARIETIES OF EXPERIENCE UNDER COLONIALISM: INDONESIA AND THE PHILIPPINES

The essential fact of the colonial era was that the expansion of the Western powers brought peoples of East and West into contact and sometimes conflict; and as the colonial powers became dominant in their various areas, the peoples they ruled began to learn some of their ways. In other words, colonial rule fostered certain aspects of Westernization and eventually modernization, for better or worse, including in the long run the final rejection of colonialism in the name of nationalism. It was a fact of the colonial relationship, as a muted form of power politics, that in certain ways the conquerors came to be imitated by the conquered in self-defense. The dominant capacity of the Western peoples, though derived from many sources, was expressed most obviously in their spirit of nationalism, which usually ran high in the process of colonial aggrandizement. This Western example eventually helped inspire in the subject Asian peoples a similar devotion to a nationalism of their own.

Among these peoples, as in Japan and China, Western superiority was first demonstrated on the material, military, and commercial plane, while Western ideas and institutions were accepted more slowly. Modernization, as a process of incorporating some inherited traditions and some modern Western ways in a new and unique mixture, was not less hard in Southeast Asia than in the more ancient and developed societies of Japan and China, and turned out to be a rather different experience for each colonial people. Each had its own background and circumstances and, in addition, a different Western nation and culture to contend with. The resultant diversity can be illustrated by the contrast between Indonesia and the Philippines. These areas had lacked the political unity and strong governments that confronted the Westerners in Japan and China, but as archipelagoes had remained readily accessible by sea.

Indonesia under the Dutch. When the Dutch East India Company was taken over by the state in 1800 (see pages 66–68), the French Revolution was remaking Europe; but its ideas could not easily be applied to Asia. As the Dutch authorities at Batavia put it in 1796, "we can hardly imagine in what way a revolution based upon the system of liberty and rights of the people could be introduced into this country without destroying its value for the home country . . . the whole existence of this state is founded upon the moral and political conditions actually existing among these princes and peoples. . . ." This statement was prophetic. European ideals and Asian conditions continued in conflict throughout the succeeding century and a half of colonial rule. Colonial administrators were caught in between.

The nineteenth century in Indonesia began with two vigorous administrations. The first, from 1808 to 1811, was that of the Dutchman, Marshal H. W. Daendels, who tried on Napoleon's behalf to centralize and rationalize the administration of Java while building up its defense against Britain. The second, from 1811 to 1816, was that of the Englishman, Stamford Raffles, who helped oust the Franco-Dutch regime and governed Java on behalf of the British East India Company until Dutch rule was resumed in 1816 (see pages 440–442). These two administrations, though conducted by enemies, had some common aims — to reduce corruption, increase revenues, reform the judicial system, and better the lot of the common people. Both fell short of their hopes. Under Daendels, military dictatorship antagonized the local Javanese rulers, whom Raffles therefore wooed the more easily. But Raffles in turn was unable by rational administrative reforms on paper to make liberalism supplant "feudalism," or to get rid of the established practices of compulsory cultivation and forced deliveries, by which the valuable Javanese coffee crop, for example, was collected for export from cultivators who were presumed to be naturally "lazy."

The Dutch, when put back in control in 1816, were similarly committed to promote the "general welfare" of the Indonesians. In practice they retained or developed many of the Daendels-Raffles reforms — rule through a territorial administration under a hierarchy, in descending order, of Dutch residents, Javanese regents, and district chiefs down to the village (*desa*) level; a dual system of justice with separate courts for foreigners (Europeans, Chinese, and others) and for Javanese, the latter applying the local customary law (*adat*). On the other hand, the rationalized system of land tenure by individual cultivators, who were to grow what crops they pleased and pay land rent to the government as the owner of the soil, proved almost impossible to establish. Moreover, it produced little domestic revenue, while the profits of overseas trade were increasingly taken by British merchants trading with Indonesia rather than by Dutch merchants. The government deficit mounted further during a Javanese rebellion (led by a devout Moslem, Prince Diponegoro of Jogjakarta) which cost the lives of some 8000 European troops and perhaps 200,000 Javanese in the five years from 1825 to 1830. Just at this point Belgium rebelled against the Netherlands at home. Financial disaster was thus the immediate sanction for the so-called Culture System introduced into the Dutch East Indies in 1830.

Under the Culture (or, more correctly, Cultivation) System of government-controlled agricultural production, each village was to be asked either to pay its land rent (normally two-fifths of the rice crop) or to devote one-fifth of its cultivated land to export products for Europe — mainly cane sugar, coffee, and indigo, but also tea (transplanted first from China and then from Assam), tobacco, cotton, cinchona trees (for quinine), and various spices. In theory, villagers were to labor on export crops no more than they would have done in producing rice on the same area. In theory, they were free agents, and would be paid for transporting crops or working in processing factories. In fact, however, government contracts had to be made with village headmen and created a new tax to be paid in labor. The tradition of compulsory cultivation was thus continued, except that now, instead of receiving tribute from Javanese rulers, the government was directly involved, as never before, in organizing and superintending production. Java became a big and profitable plantation. Exports shipped by the Royal Netherlands Trading Company soon made the Dutch merchant fleet the third largest in the world. During the era of the Cultivation System, from 1831 to 1877, the Netherlands treasury received some 832 million guilders as "surplus" from the East Indies, constituting usually between a quarter and a half of its annual budget.

It is easy to join the Dutch liberals of the time in denouncing the evils of exploitation which grew up under the Cultivation System. The original limitations often gave way to extortion by Javanese regents, Dutch controllers, and Chinese tax-farmers and sugar-millers, who now began to form a composite ruling class over the uneducated peasantry. The exploiters profited. On the other hand, Java's population roughly doubled during the half century of the Cultivation System. Thereafter, in a continued multiplication of poverty and ignorance, aided by admirable public health measures, roads, irrigation, and new export crops, it became one of the densest populations in the world (estimated at 5 million in 1815, 48 million by 1942). Here again the disruption caused by colonial development was not purely economic but also social and political. Javanese regents and even village headmen, since they could rely upon the Dutch, became more authoritarian toward their own people, who were thus alienated from their rulers. Government monopolies and taxes on market trade, sales of opium and liquor, bridge traffic, pawnshops and the like, were farmed out to Chinese, who thus consolidated their position in the colonial society as the local entrepreneurial class. The Javanese peasant, imbedded in his traditional village society, remained an uneducated laborer, generally unable to compete in trade or other enterprise. A plural economy and society grew up, sharply divided on three levels among the Dutch-Javanese rulers profiting from export trade, the Chinese tax-farming and retail trading class, and the impecunious Javanese villagers working and multiplying in their own subsistence economy on the land.

The revolutionary year of 1848 in Europe brought an increase of liberalism in the Dutch home government, yet the Cultivation System was so profitable and so entrenched that, despite continual reforms of obvious abuses, it was not supplanted by free enterprise until the 1870's. Even then, the liberal reforms mainly provided opportunity for Dutch capitalists, who were now allowed to lease (but not own) plantation land and take over the export trade. The Dutch prohibition of landowning by non-Indonesians was to prove a great boon to the Indonesian peasantry, in comparison with the widespread tenancy in colonial Burma or in Korea under Japan. But the peasants were still burdened by state monopolies and compulsory labor. This labor, arranged through the village headmen, was required either through contracts with private Dutch planters or by law (for perhaps one month a year or less) on road-building and other public works. The colonial government gave up its general export monopoly in 1877 but retained that on coffee, still based on compulsory labor, down to 1917. In general it tended to preserve the traditional Javanese village life, which subordinated the individual to his village community and thus reinforced its authoritarian features.

The economic development of the Dutch East Indies in the late nineteenth century was marked by the growth of steamship services, tin-mining on the islands of Bangka and Billiton, oil production on Borneo by the Anglo-Dutch company Royal Dutch-Shell, and a general doubling of the value of the export trade. As in British Malaya, a "forward movement" or expansion of the colonial regime's central power began in the 1870's. The aim was to suppress illegal trade and freebooting and promote order in the generally neglected area of the Outer Provinces (i.e., outside Java and Madura), and also to forestall encroachment there by other powers in the age of imperialism. Efforts to suppress the piracy carried on by Moslem rulers of Acheh in north Sumatra involved the Dutch in an intermittent war of conquest for thirty-five years. By the early twentieth century, however, Dutch rule had penetrated to every island of the great archipelago. Peace and order, steamships, railways, telegraphs, cables, and an efficient colonial administration, all facilitated the new economic dominance of the big private corporations. But education had remained stunted, and local self-government was undeveloped.

The contrast between Dutch dynamism and prosperity and the apparent inertia and backwardness of the Indonesian populace lay behind the "new course" announced by the Netherlands in 1901, an "ethical policy" of Dutch moral responsibility for native welfare. It called for widespread reforms — administrative decentralization, more use of Indonesian civil servants, promotion of village schools and welfare, and the like — but all within a continuing framework of Dutch paternalism. Preparation of Indonesia for independence was not contemplated, and the islands entered the twentieth century as an efficiently-run, economically-productive colony, politically backward.

The Philippines under Spain. The peoples of the Philippine archipelago, unlike those of the Indonesian islands, had had relatively little contact with the Asian mainland before they came into contact with the West. This left them in a condition of "backwardness" which paradoxically facilitated "Westernization" or at least obviated the clash between Western and indigenous ideas and institutions. For example, the Filipinos had not become converts to Buddhism or, in any number, to Islam and so were more readily converted, without bloodshed, to Catholic Christianity. The chief exceptions, the Magindanao confederacy in the far south and the sultanate of Sulu in the far southwest, both Moslem, remained the most warlike and least assimilable areas. Pre-colonial political institutions were similarly less developed than in Indonesia. The power of the local rulers (called *datu* or *raja*) among the various Malayan ethnic groups (Visayan, Tagalog, Ilocano, and others) was not so great as to make them necessary tools of indirect rule under a colonial power. The Philippines had not yet developed the kind of complex society or "civilization" that in Java had already incorporated local rulers in a traditional hierarchy under sultans whom the Dutch could utilize.

At the same time the colonizing power, Spain, was committed to a civilizing (Christianizing) mission, unlike her purely commercial rivals, Holland and England. Moreover she was soon overshadowed by them without, however, losing the Philippines. Thus Spanish colonialism remained economically less dynamic and hence less exploitative. While the Dutch and British East India Companies were building governments based on an expanding European trade in Java and India, the Spaniards at Manila developed their colony more slowly and, lacking much naval power or a large merchant fleet, quietly continued for 250 years to send their annual Manila-Acapulco galleons across the Pacific to Mexico—not even directly to Spain, since the Philippines remained an outpost under New Spain.

Spain's Christianizing mission had important social results. The Roman Catholic friars — Augustinians, Dominicans, Franciscans, Jesuits, and Recollects—though they engrossed much land for themselves, also provided religious education for Christian Filipinos. The establishment of early seminaries led in 1611 to the founding at Manila of the college of Santo Tomas which still continues today, older than any university in the United States. While the comparatively few Dutch missionaries in Moslem Java eventually gained only a scattering of converts, the Catholic fathers succeeded much earlier in making the Filipinos a Christian people. This contributed to the growth of a mixed Spanish-Filipino elite. At the same time the Spanish administration opposed, in the Philippines as in Spain, the growth of a non-Catholic commercial minority and so was more disposed to repress the Chinese merchants as a class than to make them a special group for tax-farming as the Dutch did on Java. Though set apart in their own community with a distinct legal status, the Chinese were able to marry into the elite, which accepted Catholic offspring of mixed marriages, and so by the late eighteenth century an ethnically mixed but culturally homogeneous Spanish-Filipino-Chinese upper class had begun to emerge, in a society that was far less stratified than the Javanese.

Thus a great many circumstances contributed to make the Philippines' colonial development very different from Indonesia's. Luzon, for example, was four-fifths the size of Java but had nothing like its heavy population. Java by 1900 held 28.4 million people; but all the Philippines, more than twice the area of Java, had only 7.6 million in 1903. The Philippine economy was correspondingly smaller, plantation agriculture was less developed, and the export trade less of a vested interest. The indigenous societies of Luzon and Java had been very different in the first place — perhaps even more different than the contrasting aims and policies of Spain and Holland. Under these two powers, religious and commercial goals had been pursued in different proportions.

By the early nineteenth century Manila was being drawn into international contact. After the brief British conquest of Manila in 1762–64, Spain promoted direct trade, eventually under a royal company, in competition with the entrenched galleon trade. The latter ceased in 1815, and Mexico's independence of Spain in 1821 put the Philippines directly under Madrid, more accessible to European influences including the new spirit of free trade. Finally in the early 1830's (just as the British East India Company monopoly was being ended at Canton), Manila was made an open port. American firms (like Russell, Sturgis and Company of Boston) for some decades played a major role in foreign trade at Manila; but by the 1870's they were eclipsed by British firms aided by British banks (like the Chartered Bank of India, Australia, and China and the Hongkong and Shanghai Banking Corporation). Filipino banks, both private and governmental, also facilitated the growth of export trade in tropical products — indigo, sugar, coffee, coconuts, and, especially, fine tobacco for Manila cigars and hemp for the world's fleets. Meanwhile the development of communications — roads, a local press, postal service, steamship lines, telegraph, and in 1891 a railroad — had accompanied the rise of urban middle classes, Filipino-Spanish and Chinese in racial origin. The dominant class was Hispano-Christian in culture, already nationalistic in politics.

The early rise of nationalism in the Philippines, in such contrast with its retardation in Indonesia, was stimulated by the liberal, though short-lived, revolution of 1868 in Spain which promoted ideas of reform in Manila, including freedom of political discussion and Filipinization of the parish priesthood. The subsequent Spanish monarchist reaction culminated in the Philippines in the harsh suppression of a mutiny of Filipino forces at the Cavite naval base near Manila in 1872, and the ensuing trumped-up trial and martyrdom of three nationalist Filipino priests. Thereafter the colonial government, in refusing to grant minimum liberal reforms to Filipinos, fanned the sparks of nationalism.

Leadership in a nationalist movement was provided by *ilustrados*, scions of the property-based Filipino elite seeking education in Spain and inspired both by the ideals taught in Madrid and the evils practiced in Manila. From 1872 stemmed the "Propaganda Movement," an agitation demanding reforms such as Filipino-Spanish legal equality and representation in the Spanish Cortes. A group of talented young men founded the *Asociación Hispano-Filipina* in Madrid in 1889; in their periodical, *La Solidaridad*, and in novels, pamphlets, and essays, they began to create in Spanish a national literature of the Philippines. But this liberal reform movement, though tolerated in Spain, was savagely suppressed in the islands. One of Southeast Asia's earliest martyrs to the idea of nationalism was the Philippines' José Rizal (1861–1896), a man of universal genius, a gifted linguist, artist, and writer. He had studied medicine and published political novels in Europe, but when he returned to Manila in 1892 and founded a patriotic reform society, the *Liga Filipina,* he was arrested and later executed.

At about the same time a revolutionary movement began with the founding of a secret society, the *Katipunan.* It had rites modeled on the Masonic order, teachings printed in Tagalog, and a widespread organization. When the Spanish authorities discovered it in August 1896, a rebellion erupted which received further impetus from the execution of Rizal.[1] Spanish troops and payments to the rebels eventually effected a truce in December 1897, and the Filipino commander, General Emilio Aguinaldo, went into exile at Hong Kong. After the United States squadron under Admiral Dewey destroyed the Spanish fleet at Manila on May 1, 1898 (see pages 475–477), Aguinaldo returned. Believing (incorrectly, as it turned out) that he had American government assurances of Philippine independence, he raised an army and besieged the Spaniards in Manila before the arrival of the American expeditionary force which led to the final Spanish surrender.

The Philippines' Preparation for National Independence. Without decrying the worthy altruism of American policy toward the Philippines, we may nevertheless note certain historical circumstances which facilitated it — first, the long-continued Spanish contribution to Philippine life, and the vigor of the Philippine national independence movement which had already grown up under Spanish rule; and second, the fact that American commercial and other vested interests had not become dominant in the islands before the unforeseen American take-over of 1898. Thus it was possible for American political motives, ideologically anticolonial, to take precedence from the first over commercial interests. The Spanish-American treaty of 1898 preserved the old Spanish tariff and the Philippine-Spanish trade for ten years. By the time full Philippine-American free trade began in 1913, creating a colonial type of Philippine economic dependence on the American market, the program of preparation for political independence was well under way.

Philippine nationalism was vigorously asserted from 1898 to 1901 by the revolutionary republic created by an eloquent group of patriots under the youthful Aguinaldo. Their declaration of independence of June 1898 was the first of the several Asian documents to be modeled on the American declaration of 1776. A revolutionary congress at Malolos, north of Manila, in September framed a constitution on mixed Spanish and Ameri-

[1] From Rizal's novel *El Filibusterismo (The Subversive,* 1891): "You ask parity of rights, the Spanish way of life, and you do not realize that what you are asking is the destruction of your national identity. . . . Take advantage of the prejudices of our rulers. So they refuse to integrate you into the Spanish nation. So much the better! Take the lead in forming your own individuality, try to lay the foundations of a Filipino nation . . . develop an independent, not a colonial, mentality."

can lines; diplomatic representatives went abroad; and arms, though they never reached the Philippines, were secured from Japanese pan-Asian expansionists, supporters of Sun Yat-sen. The American decision of December 1898 to retain the islands precipitated another Philippine war for independence. Although Aguinaldo was captured in March 1901, a Filipino guerrilla resistance continued until 1902, not unlike the resistance met by the respective colonial powers in Vietnam after 1885, Burma after 1886, and Korea after 1907. Suppressing it took many thousand American troops, of whom 4200 died. The cause of independence, though lost for the time being, was dramatized unforgettably.

Meanwhile, however, the American military government had brought Filipinos into its administration, begun to hold local elections, and encouraged the growth of an active political organization: the Federal (later Progressive) Party. Civil government was inaugurated under William H. Taft on July 4, 1901, on terms developed by an American civilian commission which had held public hearings in 33 provinces. Taft declared, "We are the trustees and guardians of the *whole Filipino people.*" The political aim expressed by President McKinley, to train the Filipinos "in the science of self-government," was pursued step by step under the authority of an organic act passed by the United States Congress in 1902. The first election, in 1907, with six parties competing, gave the Nacionalista Party 32 out of 80 seats in the lower house or Assembly, while the Philippine Commission, an appointive body, acted as the upper house. In 1913 the Commission's American-Filipino ratio of 5 to 4 was reversed, so that henceforth Filipinos controlled both legislative houses, under the American governor-general as chief executive.

This accelerated Filipinization reflected also a fact of American domestic politics: that since the Philippines had been acquired under the Republicans, the Democrats championed their independence. Under the Democratic administrations between 1913 and 1921, the Americans in the civil service decreased from 2600 to 600 while the Filipinos increased from 6300 to 13,200. The Jones Law of 1916 revised the organic act of 1902 and promised independence "as soon as a stable government can be established." It substituted an elected Senate for the Commission and a House of Representatives for the old Assembly.

Meanwhile the Nacionalista Party had continued to dominate the elections and the political process. Its head, Sergio Osmeña, by an unwritten constitutional development was regularly elected speaker of the Assembly (or House), and became the top Filipino political figure, closely consulted by the American governor-general. The president of the new Senate after 1916 was the number-two Nacionalista Party leader, Manuel Quezon, who as resident commissioner in Washington had lobbied so successfully for the Jones Law. The system of party government by the Nacionalistas, based on their country-wide organization of landowning local leaders (*caciques*) and their election campaigns on the sacred national issue of independence, now became firmly established: Nacionalista members of both houses in a joint caucus followed Osmeña as party leader. The six department heads in the executive branch became answerable to the majority party in the legislature; in general its leader controlled patronage, legislation, and policy; the Philippines were informally developing a parliamentary type of government.

This trend was checked after 1922, for the new Republican governor-general (Leonard Wood), halting the Filipinization program of his Democratic predecessor in the name of "American efficiency," was less ready to let the Filipino political leaders build up their unwritten constitutional powers. Quezon, moreover, supported the constitutional separation of powers. In a coalition with Osmeña, but reversing their power relationship, he won the elections of 1925. Henceforth the political leader of the Philippines, as official spokesman for the legislative majority, was the president of the Senate (Quezon), but the parliamentary body did not control the executive branch of the government.

This domination of the legislature by one party was a single facet of a complex constitutional development. It illustrated the degree of sophistication attained by the leadership in the Philippine political process, in which independence overshadowed all other issues. Sectional interests, church-state relations, the tariff, capital vs. labor, and other questions received little attention from the political oligarchy. Having split with Osmeña over the terms of independence in 1933, Quezon won the election of 1934, but in 1935 the two men again formed a dominant coalition.

While the political oligarchy was striving for complete independence, economic developments had paradoxically tied the Philippines closer to the American market. By the late 1930's four-fifths of Philippine exports went to the United States, mainly the four staples of sugar, coconuts, tobacco, and hemp, while three-fifths of the islands' imports came from there. Sugar exports indeed overshadowed all others combined, sugar production having been stimulated by American needs during World War I.

The size of this trade during the depression years brought new supporters to the cause of Philippine independence: beet-sugar producers in the United States, dairymen fearful of the competition of coconut oil in margarine, and Cuban cane-sugar interests, even though little direct competition of Philippine against American products could be shown. Since plantation-owning by non-Filipinos had been prevented and American investments in Philippine sugar, unlike those in Hawaii, were not great, no large vested interests opposed independence and the tariff barriers it would bring against Philippine products in the U.S.A. On the other hand, American political sentiment, repeatedly and altruistically on record, favored the claims to freedom eloquently voiced by Filipino representatives in Washington. The main issue thus became how to cut the umbilical cord of Philippine-American trade. The Tydings-McDuffie Act, passed in 1934 after the Philippine legislature had rejected a similar act of 1933, finally gave the islands a ten-year commonwealth status prior to independence. During this decade the United States would handle foreign affairs, defense, and monetary policy, and gradually impose American tariffs.

This dependence on the American market was not the only economic problem that accompanied preparations for political independence. The landlordism inherited as a social institution from the Spanish regime had been protected by the American concern for property rights. Local ruling families, typically of Spanish or Chinese immigrant origins, through landowning, moneylending, and political influence had long provided the leaders or bosses (*caciques*). They had continued to exploit impoverished tenant farmers and landless laborers while supporting independence and the political oligarchy. Agrarian discontent, including demands for the breakup of large estates and Church lands, was exploited after 1930 by the Sakdal movement (*sakdal* meaning in Tagalog "to accuse," "to strike"), which staged brief uprisings around Manila in May 1935.

Thus when the Philippine Commonwealth, as a ten-year preliminary to independence, was joyously inaugurated under a new constitution on November 15, 1935, with Quezon and Osmeña as president and vice-president, it faced domestic problems both economic and social. But there was no question of the vitality of the election-based political process which Manuel Quezon had learned how to dominate. Underlying it was the fact that 1,230,000 children were attending 7800 public schools, while 99,000 others were at some 500 church-supported and other private institutions, and almost half the population had become literate.

The United States, committed to the self-determination of all peoples, had never called the Philippines a "colony" and from the beginning had trained the Filipino populace for nationhood both in the school system and in public life. Nevertheless the Philippines fit into a discussion of "colonialism"; for it turns out in retrospect that all colonialisms have been no more than part-way stages on the road to nationalism — even when the colonial power, as in the case of the Dutch, had long cherished other hopes.

The Rise of Indonesian Nationalism. The comparative retardation of nationalism in Indonesia was due to a complex of factors roughly the obverse of those operating in the Philippines: in the latter, the pre-colonial society had been less highly developed, and the colonial regime of Spain consequently had had little difficulty in Christianizing the populace, while the fresh regime of the United States, more free of vested interests, could try to hasten political Westernization and independence. In Indonesia, on the other hand, the relative size and strength of the old order made it less amenable to quick modernization, while the Dutch until 1901 had been primarily economic administrators, not religious crusaders or political reformers. In political life, the ancient Indonesian tradition had produced hereditary rulers with autocratic prerogatives, who could not be overthrown by their own subjects as easily as they could be subjugated and used as regents by the Dutch. Colonial rule preserved itself by preserving the Javanese ruling class as local allies. "Indirect rule" through 269 native states eventually covered more than half the area outside Java. In economic life, since the aims of the Dutch were commercial rather than proselytizing, their rule had been superimposed on the old society in the villages and had fostered the rise of Chinese middlemen and tax-farmers in place of a new native middle class.

Thus Indonesia under the Dutch presented a more difficult problem of modernization than the Philippines. The balance between the traditional native civilization and the Western colonial influence was very different. The East Indian archipelago covered an enormous area, with roughly six times the land mass and four or five times the population of the Philippines. Conversely, the tiny Netherlands were no bigger than a state of the American union. The Netherlands' responsibilities and vested interests were both correspondingly greater.

In cultural inheritance Indonesia was richer and more diverse than the Philippines, and so less malleable and instructable. In religion, it was 85 per cent at least nominally Moslem, with a minority who maintained active ties to Mecca (52,000 Indonesians made their pilgrimage in 1927, for example). Bali was still Hindu. Christianity found converts mainly in the Outer Islands. Thus on the whole, religion produced a cleavage between rulers and ruled, instead of a common bond. Problems of modernization were correspondingly complex, for the traditional society lived on beneath the colonial one imposed upon it. In 1900, for instance, only 75,000 Javanese out of 30 million had been listed as in school. Though much progress was made, by 1931 only 1,666,000 out of 60 million Indonesians were listed as in primary schools conducted in the vernacular, and 16,000 in such vocational schools, while the schools of all sorts conducted in Dutch contained some 52,000 Europeans, 92,000 Indonesians, and 32,500 "Foreign Orientals," mainly Chinese. This backwardness in education, compared with the situation in the Philippines, in part reflected the basic fact of slower modernization in a disunified plural society.

In the face of this great contrast between the two archipelagoes, any American criticism of Dutch colonial policy as retarding the rise of Indonesian nationalism would be over-simple. The conflict (or stalemate) of cultures was so great, on the plane of social institutions, customs, and values, that Dutch achievement was easier on the material plane, in economic life.

However, the "ethical policy" after 1901 expressed an intense Dutch desire to promote among the Indonesian people a development more general than that which the Cultivation System had produced earlier in the economy. Dedicated Dutch administrators now devised innumerable programs for native welfare. These included legal limitations on the capitalistic exploitation of cheap and unorganized native labor; state-sponsored village banks, pawnshops, and cooperatives to provide rural credit in competition with the Chinese moneylenders; public health measures; education; and village development through instituting village treasuries, banks, budgets, schools, records, and public meetings. This whole welfare movement, coming from the top down, was criticized for its paternalistic methods and ultimately material motives — "Capitalism dressed up like Christianity." For all its altruistic enthusiasm, its hopes of fostering village democracy and an Indonesian middle class were generally disappointed. From 1905 to 1947 the population more than doubled (from about 37 to 76 million), but within this general trend the European (including a sizable Eurasian element integrated with the Dutch) and Chinese communities advanced more rapidly both in rate of growth and in standards of living. The more numerous Indonesian peasantry were, if anything, worse off than before. Those few who got educated found few jobs open to them in the modern sector of society already dominated by the European-Eurasian and Chinese communities. Thus despite Dutch efforts to ameliorate native life, the non-Indonesian rich got richer and the Indonesian peasantry generally poorer, while more education and contact with the foreign communities nurtured an increasingly bitter antiforeign nationalism.

The growth of national consciousness, among diverse islands stretching 3100 miles west to east, was facilitated by the success of the Dutch in finally spreading their administration all over the area. For thus were created most of the material elements of a unified state — facilities for travel and communication, and a central government bureaucracy supervising taxation, police, justice, and public works and services — where none had existed before. While the shadowy tradition of Srivijaya and Majapahit had symbolic value for modern patriots, these ancient empires had not ruled the whole area even in theory. The late nineteenth-century expansion of Dutch rule over this vast region was a unifying influence, both in setting an example of modern nationalism at work and in rousing opposition to it. For example, the rapid spread of Islam over Java seems originally to have been an in-group response to the early intrusion of the foreign power of the Portuguese and then the Dutch. Similarly the Indonesian national language developed out of the early lingua franca of the trade routes, bazaar Malay, partly because some early Dutch administrators promoted its use, instead of Dutch, as a means of keeping the "natives" in their place.

These ingredients of nationalism — an overall government in a recognized area with a common tradition, religion, and language — have accumulated only gradually and are still far from being completely pervasive.

That they were not fused into a modern movement before the twentieth century was partly owing to the lack of leadership. The Dutch system of indirect rule made the traditional Indonesian ruling class a part of the colonial order. Eurasians produced by Dutch-Indonesian miscegenation were accepted as part of the European establishment. Meanwhile the limited opportunity for Indonesian commoners — either to get a modern Dutch education and enter government service, or to rise in business by competing with the Chinese — inhibited the emergence of a new elite from the villages. In the end, of course, this early side-tracking of native leadership, along with colonial economic exploitation, fostered a patriotic sense of grievance, especially after 1901 when humanitarian Dutch reformers, modernizing the villages under the "ethical policy," gave the Indonesian masses more perspective on the world and their place in it. Inevitably, education raised up a new generation of patriots.

Another long-term stimulant to Indonesian nationalism was the example of the growth of Chinese nationalism. By 1900 the Chinese minority of half a million included two groups of roughly equal size — the urban Chinese commercial class, whose ancestors had come mainly from southern Fukien but who were now "native-born" in Indonesia (hence called *Peranakan*), and the recently arrived immigrant labor class, who were principally from Kwangtung and were employed in the Outer Provinces (called *Singkeh* from Chinese *hsin-k'o*, "new guest"; or *Totok*, an Indonesian term meaning culturally pure Chinese).

The earlier *Peranakan* Chinese by the nineteenth century had created a distinctive hybrid culture in Indonesia, speaking the local Indonesian language but retaining Chinese surnames, developing mixed forms of cuisine, drama, and music, and adopting Indonesian types of dress and kinship structure while retaining many Chinese kinship terms. This was in marked contrast with the Chinese experience in Siam (see pages 455–460), where the self-confident and vigorous leaders of Thai society down to the 1880's had given Chinese immigrants opportunity, used their skills in foreign trade and government service, and assimilated them to the point where the Chinese had adopted Thai names, customs, and values and lost their Chinese identity. In Indonesia the Chinese had not been assimilated because the Indonesian leadership had remained fragmented and demoralized under Dutch domination, no longer masters of their own country but defeated and forced to turn inward on the defensive. As Moslems, they avoided intermarriage with non-Moslems, using religious and racial criteria for admission to their in-group, which the Chinese immigrants on their part had no incentive to join. Moreover, the Dutch masters of the Indies took care to keep the *Peranakan* Chinese restricted to their role as traders and middlemen. They were confined to Chinese ghettos in the towns, listed as "Foreign Orientals," and not allowed to mix with the local labor class or village society.

Hedged in by these racial, economic, and legal barriers, the *Peranakan* Chinese minority by 1900 had lost or feared the loss of its traditional functions of tax-farming and moneylending. To promote Indonesian welfare, the Dutch were now substituting a government opium monopoly, government ferries and abattoirs, and rural credit institutions to take the place of Chinese activity in these various lines. Yet the Chinese were still forced to obtain passes in order to travel, even on business; were allowed to dwell only in certain zones within the cities; and were further discriminated against in law by being under police court jurisdiction with fewer rights than Europeans. Generally excluded from the Dutch schools and from government office, the *Peranakan* minority developed its own cohesion.

The arrival of culturally pure *Totok* Chinese immigrants in increasing numbers after 1900 created, alongside the *Peranakans*, a new and distinct Chinese community in Indonesia, in closer touch with the homeland and more directly responsive to pan-Chinese nationalism. Through Singapore as their main window on the outer world, many Indonesian Chinese responded to the stirrings of nationalism present in the Chinese reform movement of the late 1890's. Chinese leaders in Batavia in 1900 established a pan-Chinese society (*Chung-hua hui-kuan*, "Chinese guild" or "association") to promote Confucianism as an alternative to Christianity and also Chinese education using the "national language" (*kuo-yü*), as well as communal unity between the *Peranakan* and the new *Totok* arrivals. Increasingly, the late-Ch'ing reform movement after 1901 and the revolutionary movements of both K'ang Yu-wei and the *T'ung-meng hui* had their repercussions among the two groups of Overseas Chinese, who now possessed the wealth with which to take action.

Soon there were hundreds of Chinese private schools, newspapers, chambers of commerce, and even political associations in major centers throughout the archipelago — modern, Western-type institutions to meet the needs of the growing *Totok* community. The local Dutch-appointed Chinese headmen or "officers" (often called *Kapitein*) of the old *Peranakan* community now lost their traditional role of passive leadership. Through their communal cohesiveness, expressed when necessary in boycotts or cessations of trade, the newly organized Chinese minority obliged the Dutch to provide them with government schools and abolish much of the earlier discrimination — even though the two Chinese communities, the older and the newer, failed to coalesce and left the Overseas Chinese minority divided into two wings, respectively more and less assimilable into modern Indonesian society.

To the Chinese example of nationalism close at hand was added that of the Japanese, who from 1899 got the Dutch to treat them as "Europeans," a bit of realism soon justified by Japan's victory of 1905.

One of the first Indonesian nationalistic organizations in a Western style was an upper-class cultural-uplift society, *Boedi Oetomo* ("The

Noble Endeavor").[1] Formed by Javanese intellectuals in 1908, and non-political at first, it gradually became more nationalist and Indonesian in scope. With 10,000 members, mainly aristocrats, civil servants, and students, it was only the most prominent of many new associations, including regional clubs (e.g., of Sumatrans in Java) and women's societies.

From the beginning of European contact, Islam had been a rallying point for Indonesian resistance to the intruders. The first large-scale expression of early nationalism took the form of an Islamic economic-religious movement called *Sarekat Islam* ("Islamic Association"), founded in 1912 partly to counter Christian missionary work, partly to promote cooperatives and commercial enterprise among middle-class Javanese in competition with the pervasive economic influence of the Chinese community. Professedly nonpolitical, within five years it had a membership of 800,000, both urban and rural, including village religious leaders who gave vent to rural discontent and for a while were welded into a mass movement. At the same time the Modernist Islamic movement in India and Egypt, where reform leaders particularly in Cairo sought to purify and revive the faith while taking account of Western learning and modern social values, stimulated in Java the founding, also in 1912, of a reform society, *Muhammadiyah*. This became a major religious movement. *Sarekat Islam* meanwhile became more politically radical and nationalistic; for example, it gave opportunity to a Dutch social democrat, Hendrik Sneevliet, who in 1914 began to propagate revolutionary Marxism in its local branches. By the time he was expelled in December 1918 (to reappear in China in 1921 as the Comintern agent "Maring," see pages 671, 679), *Sarekat Islam* was demanding independence instead of mere self-government as at first.

Meanwhile the Dutch were weakened by their relative defenselessness during World War I. On top of various earlier organs for local self-government and regional and city councils, they now set up a People's Council (*Volksraad*). It met in May 1918, with Netherlanders in the majority, and had only advisory powers. Rather than symbolizing democracy, it became a symbol of stubborn Dutch determination to retain paternalistic control until the Indonesians should be "ripe for self-government" at some undefined future time. Nationalist leaders were pushed by this attitude into an opposition which the Dutch considered disloyal.

The fourth congress of *Sarekat Islam*, representing almost two and one-half million members, met in 1919 and reasserted its religious principles. Shortly thereafter, in May 1920, Marxist elements broke off to form the Indonesian Communist Party or PKI (*Perserikaten Kommunist di India*) and joined the Comintern. Soon the PKI and *Sarekat Islam* were struggling for control of the new labor movement — not unlike the CCP and

---

[1] The Dutch spelling *oe* for the sound of *u* as in *flute* has been changed since independence to *u*. Thus *Budi Utomo* is also correct.

KMT in China at that time. Though the Communists succeeded in dominating the labor unions, they antagonized many Moslems, neglected and estranged the peasantry, and failed to form a united front with reformist and "bourgeois-democratic" nationalists against the Dutch. One faction finally planned a premature revolutionary rising for 1926, against the advice of the Comintern agent for Southeast Asia (Tan Malaka), who warned against a "left deviation" of putschism without well-organized mass support. Meantime the Dutch banned all meetings, suppressed strikes, systematically arrested PKI leaders, and disrupted the organization. When risings were attempted, November 1926 in Java and early 1927 in Sumatra, the PKI had only about 3000 members plus 30,000 in peasant organizations. The risings were crushed, and some 13,000 people were arrested, of whom 4000 were imprisoned and 1300 interned, mainly in detention camps far in the jungle of Dutch New Guinea.

Communism was thus discredited and driven underground, but Islam, in both its reformist and orthodox wings, was opposed to Westernization and hence could not serve as the main vehicle of Indonesian nationalism. Leadership in a secular nationalist movement was now taken by students, many of them returning from Holland with leftist leanings, who advocated independence through a broad united effort and through tactics of non-cooperation rather than of violence. On such a platform an eloquent young engineer named Sukarno (also Soekarno) and others formed in June 1927 the Indonesian Nationalist Party or PNI (*Partai Nasional Indonesia*) and soon were leading a loose federation of all the major national organizations.

When the Dutch authorities arrested and imprisoned Sukarno and others in 1930, and later outlawed the PNI, the nationalists countered with a new tactic. Two able student leaders who returned from Holland in 1932 (Sutan Sjahrir and Mohammad Hatta) abandoned the effort to build up a mass movement, which could be continually decapitated by arrests. Instead, before their own arrest in 1934, they concentrated on training a small but ever widening circle of self-reliant leaders at lower levels. In the ensuing years before the Japanese invasion, this method kept the independence movement alive while the public scene was filled with more moderate activities.

During the 1920's the Netherlands Indies greatly increased its production of rubber, tin, coal, oil, sugar, tea, and copra, providing as much as 12 or 15 per cent of the Netherlands' national income. In the next decades, disillusionment with the results of reforms under the "ethical policy" and loss of markets during the depression made the regime even more exploitative and repressive. Any discussion of policies looking toward "independence" (*merdeka*) was thenceforth banned in political life. The very name "Indonesia," a modern term, was similarly refused official recognition.

Thus by World War II the Indonesian nationalist movement was under police repression and, with some exceptions, was following a policy of noncooperation, while the Philippine nationalist movement was already governing the domestic affairs of the Philippine Commonwealth and preparing for full independence. Economically, on the other hand, the contrast was not so great: Philippine exports still depended largely on privileged access to the American market, while the larger and more diversified Indonesian economy, with its oil, hydroelectric, and other developments, was less dependent on the small metropolitan economy of the Netherlands and more subject to government stimulation and management. Moreover, the early Dutch restrictions on landlordism had checked the spread of tenantry such as now plagued Luzon.

COLONIAL DEVELOPMENT IN CONTINENTAL SOUTHEAST ASIA

Malaya, Burma, Siam, and Indo-China, with their diverse peoples and cultures, cannot be treated here in satisfactory detail, nor can they be omitted, any more than Indonesia and the Philippines. In this dilemma, our only recourse is to be analytically selective, as historians have to be in any event. After all, if "Japan" and "China" with their great internal diversities of climate, terrain, local customs, and regional interests can usefully be thought of as complex entities, so can continental Southeast Asia. Here we shall sketch, first, socio-economic changes, and then political developments.

Aspects of Economic Growth. In the late nineteenth century, after British domination had been established over Malaya and Burma generally and over Siam commercially, and French control over Indo-China, economic growth in these areas occurred first of all through commerce fostered by transportation. Steamships provided easy access to the many ports on the Malay Peninsula and up the Irrawaddy, Chindwin, and Menam (or Chao Phraya), as well as on the lower reaches and canal systems of the Mekong and Red rivers. The railway from Rangoon reached Prome in 1877, and Mandalay in 1889; railways were begun in Cochin China in 1881 and Tongking in 1890, and pushed north from Bangkok in 1892. Eventually Malaya and Siam were joined by rail. Cochin China and Tongking were similarly connected, though French lines did not go through to Siam or to China except in Yunnan.

Secondly, major exports were developed with the aid of European and Asian capital investment and some migration of Asian labor. In Malaya tin-mining was first developed by Chinese labor and capital, but as production grew, more Western capital came in and modernized the mining and smelting processes. Thus Chinese controlled four-fifths of Malaya's

tin output in 1912 but only about a third in 1936. Meantime the automobile age and British investment created the great Malayan rubber
industry: exports amounted to 200 tons in 1905 and 195,000 in 1920, half
the world's supply. By 1948 total production was nearly 700,000 tons,
much of it from small-scale peasant cultivation or small Asian companies.
At the same time immigration of Chinese and Indian labor had left the
Malays outnumbered in a plural society. (In 1911 there were 1,437,000
Malays, 916,000 Chinese, and 267,000 Indians; in 1941, 2,278,000 Malays,
2,379,000 Chinese, and 744,000 Indians.) Tin and rubber brought Malaya
great changes but a precarious prosperity, since sales were dependent on
the American market and fluctuating world prices.

In Burma the great export product became rice. Lower Burma produced rice on three million acres in 1880, and on nearly ten million in
1930. About two-thirds of the crop was exported, mainly to India. Indian
laborers migrated seasonally by the hundreds of thousands to work the
new rice lands. Indian moneylenders, financing this expansion of cultivation, by 1938 had become owners of half the occupied land in Lower
Burma and made many local peasants into a landless proletariat amid their
former rice-fields. Oil wells in the Yenangyaung region of central Burma,
teakwood forests, lead-silver and other mines also contributed exports,
but the great part of this modern industry and much rice-land remained
foreign-owned.

Siam's exports of rice and teak were similarly developed, at different
levels of activity, by British and Chinese traders and investors. Chinese
migrated to Siam in large numbers and by the 1930's totaled two million
or more, perhaps one-sixth of the population. By that time Siam's trade
and industry were 95 per cent in European or Chinese hands.

In Indo-China rice production in the Mekong delta increased fourfold
in the sixty years after 1880. The colony exported rice and rubber and
had uncultivated land still available in the south, as well as coal and other
minerals in the north. But France lacked the extensive commercial resources of the British Empire and so avoided its competition by a protectionist policy, seeking from Indo-China only raw materials and a
market for French products, excluding investment by third parties. As a
result, by the late 1930's over half the foreign trade and almost all the
investments were French, except for about one-fifth, which were Chinese.
Meanwhile in the northern and southern delta regions, population pressure
and overcrowding, fragmentation of holdings, and tenantry and landlordism on big estates had increased.

This "colonial" pattern of economic growth in continental Southeast
Asia included investment of foreign capital, immigration of foreign labor,
and increase of agricultural and mining production for export. Several
features are noteworthy. For one thing, public health and other measures
led to a rapid increase of population: from about 1800 to the 1940's,

Malaya grew in population from perhaps half a million to 6 million; Burma from perhaps 4 million to 17 million; Siam about the same; and Indo-China from roughly 7 to 27 million (see table, page 740). The rate of increase had accelerated after 1900. While modern cities, civil administrations, and public services had been built up, in most of the crowded delta areas the common people were hardly better off economically than before.

One feature of this growth was thus the paradox that greater economic production went hand in hand with greater poverty at the lowest levels. Consumer purchasing power and domestic consumer-goods industries grew only slowly. This situation became less supportable when the world-wide depression after 1929 lowered the demand for tropical exports. The disastrous dependence of colonial economies on an unpredictable world market seemed to many to justify the Marxist-Leninist analysis of the evils of "capitalist imperialism."

Another feature of Southeast Asia's development was the immigration of Chinese, whose small-scale business in the port cities was under the shadow of European firms but who often dominated trade in the hinterland. Like the Indian element in Malaya and Burma, the Chinese all over Southeast Asia, with their sophistication in the ways of a money economy, had been principal participants and beneficiaries in European colonialism. This increased the native people's sense of frustration at being exploited by foreigners, including Asians from the more ancient neighboring countries of India and China.

Still another feature was the plural society. Europeans and the native aristocracy formed a top class, Chinese (and in British areas, Indians) provided middle-class activities of small-scale capitalism and skilled labor, and the great mass of local cultivators constituted the substratum. The growth of port cities, foreign trade, and industrial investment in Southeast Asia brought about a European and Chinese economic collaboration that was rather similar to their collaboration in the treaty ports of China. In this respect, Singapore was not unlike Shanghai — British interests guided an administration which facilitated Chinese as well as Western enterprise, though in different communities.

A plural economy and society, when developed to such an extreme as in Malaya, served to inhibit the rise of nationalism. The colonial governments in Burma and Indo-China were hardly committed to it. Only the Siamese had a free field for national political growth. Their experience shows the long-term and basic difficulties of the process.

National Development in Siam (Thailand). During the first third of the twentieth century the absolute monarchy of Siam continued to deal skillfully with the foreign powers and carry on a program of gradual modernization. Unequal treaties and extraterritorial rights accorded to

POPULATION GROWTH IN EAST AND SOUTHEAST ASIA

(Seldom based on modern census enumerations, usually representing only an order of magnitude, and compiled from often contradictory sources)

Country	Area (Sq. mi.)	Estimated populations at dates indicated (in millions) →						
Japan	142,000	35.9 (1875–1879)	42.2 (1895–1899)	54 (1915–1919)	61.3 (1925–1929)	71.2 (1935–1939)	92 (1958)	93.4 (1960)
Taiwan	13,000	3 (1905)	3.6 (1920)	4.6 (1930)	5.9 (1940)	7.5 (1950)	9.8 (1956)	13 (1961)
Korea	85,000	13.3 (1910)	16.9 (1920)	21 (1930)	24.3 (1940)	30 (1953)		
So. Korea	37,400					20.2 (1949)		25 (1960)
No. Korea	47,600					{ 12 / 9 (1956)		8.4 (1961)
China	{ 3,900,000 / 2,450,000				472.6 (1938)	582.6 (1953)	646.5 (1958)	
including China Proper	1,400,000							
Manchuria	309,000	14.9 (1910)	25.3 (1926)	44.5 (1940)		53 (1953)		
Sinkiang	{ 600,000 / 660,000			3.7 (1941)	3.9 (1945)	4.9 (1953)		
Tibet	470,000				{ 1.5 / 3 (1948)			

740

POPULATION GROWTH IN EAST AND SOUTHEAST ASIA (*continued*)

Country	Area (*Sq. mi.*)	⸻ *Estimated populations at dates indicated* (*in millions*) ⸻→						
Outer Mongolia	{ 626,000 / 580,000	.647 (1918)	.709 (1928)	.750 (1945)	.850 (1951)			.954 (1961)
Burma	262,000	10.5 (1901)	14.7 (1931)	16.8 (1941)	17 (1947)	19.2 (1954)	19.5 (1960)	22.5 / 21.5 (1961)
Siam (Thailand)	200,000	8.3 (1911)	11.9 (1931)		17.3 (1947)	20.3 (1955)	26.2 / 25.5 (1960)	26.3 (1961)
Malaysia	131,000							10.4 (1962)
Malaya	50,690	{ 2.7 (1911)	} 4.4 (1931)	4.9 (1947)	} 7.5 (1955)	6.3 (1957)	6.9 (1960)	7.3 (1962)
Singapore	224			.941 (1947)		1.4 (1957)	1.66 (1960)	1.75 (1962)
No. Borneo (Sabah)	29,388						.454 (1960)	.473 (1962)
Brunei	2,226	(see note to table, p. 782)			} 1 (1955)		.083 (1960)	.091 (1962)
Sarawak	48,250						.744 (1960)	.776 (1962)
Hong Kong	391	.625 (1927?)	.840 (1931)	1.786 (1941)	2.4 (1956)		3.133 (1960)	

POPULATION GROWTH IN EAST AND SOUTHEAST ASIA (*continued*)

—— Estimated populations at dates indicated (*in millions*) ——>

Country	Area (Sq. mi.)							
Indo-China	285,000	21.5 (1931)	27 (1947)	31.5 (1955)				
South Vietnam	66,000			12 (1955)		13.8 (1959)	14.1 (1960)	14.3 (1961)
North Vietnam	60,000			14 (1952)			15.9 (1960)	15.8 (1961)
Cambodia	67,560			4.1 (1950)	4.1 (1954)	5 (1958)	5.3 (1961)	{ 5.0 / 5.7 (1962)
Laos	91,000			2.1 (1951)	1.4 (1954)	1.7 (1958)	2.2 (1960)	{ 2 / 1.85 (1961)
Philippines	115,600	7.6 (1903)	12.3 (1930)	16 (1939)	19.2 (1948)	22.3 (1956)	{ 24 / 27.5 (1960)	28.6 (1961)
Indonesia including W. New Guinea (W. Irian)	753,000		60.7 (1930)	76.4 (1947)			92.6 (1960)	96.4 / 95.9 (1961)
W. New Guinea (W. Irian)	180,000			.3 (1930)		.7 (1956)		
Borneo (Kalimantan)	208,000						3.6 (1958?)	4 (1961)
Sumatra	183,000						11.5 (1958?)	15.4 (1961)
Java (and Madura)	51,000	4.5 (1816)	13 (1860)	30 (1905)	41 (1930)	52 (1952)	53–54 (1955)	62.7 (1961)

foreigners left Siam in a "semi-colonial" status until the mid-1920's. One principal aim of legal and social reforms was to get rid of extraterritoriality. Meanwhile the traditional absolutism of the monarchy was gradually supplanted by an oligarchic government of aristocratic political and military leaders.

King Chulalongkorn, who died in 1910 after a long reign, did not have a successor of equal vigor and ability. King Maha Vajiravudh,[1] who ruled as Rama VI (1910–1925), promoted Westernization and nationalism but was not a strong personality. He had been prepared by so many years of education in England that he dispensed with the customary use of royal relatives in government and built up his own entourage, which was, however, no less corrupt. He reduced the number of Western advisers in government but continued to send many young aristocrats abroad for education. Vajiravudh made himself a national symbol through costly ceremonies and created, for example, the Wild Tiger Scout Corps as a quasi-military patriotic movement under his personal leadership.

Siamese nationalism, like that of Indonesia, was particularly stimulated by reformist and revolutionary activity within the Overseas Chinese community. Anti-Manchu feeling had been traditional among Chinese emigrants ever since the Ming dynasty and was kept alive by secret societies like the Hung League (Triads). The danger of China's dismemberment and the drama of K'ang Yu-wei's reform efforts in 1898 and later had roused the interest of Chinese in Siam as elsewhere abroad. After the *T'ung-meng hui* had been founded in Tōkyō and had established a branch at Singapore in 1905, it set up a branch in Siam which Sun Yat-sen himself visited in 1908. Soon Chinese newspapers, propaganda cells organized around "book and newspaper societies," Chinese-vernacular schools, and money-raising campaigns were all being utilized by the two competing movements headed by K'ang and Sun.

This newly self-conscious Chinese patriotism, however, inspired anti-Chinese feeling in the Siamese upper class, some of whom were acquiring with their Western education the current Western fear of the "Yellow Peril." When Bangkok was paralyzed for several days in 1910 by a Chinese cessation of business, in protest against taxes, this "foreign" community's economic stranglehold on retail trade was alarmingly dramatized. Most of all it alarmed the new king, Vajiravudh, whose patriotic writings began to depict the Chinese as unassimilable and self-seeking materialists, bent only on gain.

As in Japan and China, the new Siamese nationalism found another principal target in extraterritoriality. Western privileges had been built up into a very complex legal structure, which at its height gave the French and the British jurisdiction over their Asian subjects (Cambodians and

[1] Romanized more correctly Wajirawut. In Thai romanizations, we have followed convention, which is not systematic.

Malays, for example), stipulated that Siam employ European legal advisers in her "international" courts dealing with all foreigners, limited import duties to three per cent ad valorem, and exempted registered foreign nationals from Siamese laws on such matters as declaration of exports, public health, or operation of pawnshops. These impairments of Siamese sovereignty could be exploited by the Chinese merchant minority who controlled most retail trade and rice-milling.

The dismantling of the extraterritorial system had therefore been started under Chulalongkorn, notably in 1909 when Siam gave up claims to four of the Malay states (see pages 443–445) in return for British agreement in principle that all British subjects should be under Siamese jurisdiction. The extraterritorial system was further dismantled after World War I. Siam joined the Allies in July 1917, sent a small expeditionary force to fight in Europe, and become a signer of the Versailles treaty and a member of the League of Nations. For Siam as for China, war and revolution ended the extraterritorial privileges of the Central Powers and Tsarist Russia. In December 1920 the United States also gave up her extraterritorial rights, setting a model for others to follow. The real end of the system, however, as well as the achievement of tariff autonomy, depended on action by the other powers and the promulgation of new law codes by Siam. In 1924–25 a mission headed by an American adviser (F. B. Sayre) negotiated new treaties with France, Britain, and eight other European states. By 1927 tariff autonomy was recovered; and it was agreed that as soon as new law codes were in force, the last forms of extraterritoriality would disappear, though this did not finally happen until after new treaties were concluded in 1937.

The long-continued effort to get rid of extraterritoriality involved the king of Siam, like the leaders of Meiji Japan, in social as well as legal reforms. Vajiravudh forbade polygamy. He popularized Western dress and sports, in particular association ("soccer") football. He also founded Chulalongkorn University (1917) and made elementary education compulsory (1921). Another policy was to promote Buddhism as the state religion — every true patriot should be a Buddhist. Modern methods of proselytism eventually led to conversions from Christianity to Buddhism. Even more than Chulalongkorn, Vajiravudh tried to lead this national development from the top, using the king's absolute power. As the functions of the central government multiplied, his absolutism increased, along with the corruption of his regime.

When his successor, King Prajadhipok (1925–1935), sought to reduce the swollen bureaucracy and its emoluments, he roused opposition not from the common citizenry, who were still largely excluded from politics, nor from the new Siamese merchant and labor classes, which were still small, but from within the ruling class itself. The new king conscientiously tried to revive cabinet government and secure advice from various councils of aristocratic advisers, but his necessary economies during the depression in 1930–32 created discontent in both army and civil service. These mainly Western-trained groups now chafed at the dominant governmental roles of the king's innumerable brothers, uncles, and other royal relations.

A bloodless *coup d'état* or "revolution" occurred on June 24, 1932. It was led by a French-trained law professor, Luang Pradist Manudharm, generally known by his personal name of Pridi Banomyong, and a group of military officers including General Phya Bahol and Luang Phibun Songgram. (Phya and Luang are titles of rank.) In December the revolutionists promulgated a constitution, to which the king at once agreed, having already promoted the idea, participated in the drafting, and preserved certain prerogatives. The new government, with a cabinet responsible to an elected unicameral assembly, continued to be subject to periodic coups. In June 1933 General Phya Bahol led another and until 1938 presided as prime minister over the ruling oligarchy or "People's Party." This was divided into two competing groups — a military faction headed by Phibun, and a more popular civilian faction under Pridi. The role of the monarchy was further diminished when in 1935 Prajadhipok abdicated in favor of his nephew (Ananda Mahidol), a ten-year-old schoolboy who reigned under a regency. Rule by oligarchic factions, instead of autocratic rule by the royal family, was consolidated when Phibun took over as premier from 1938 to 1944.

In the decade following the constitutional revolution of 1932, Siamese nationalism developed an increasingly chauvinistic, rather than a democratic, spirit. The national name was changed to Thailand in 1939 as a translation of the native term *Muang Thai*, "Land of the Thai." Thai language and culture were promoted in an expanding school system which tried to incorporate the children of the large Malay and Chinese minorities. Vigorous measures were taken against Chinese schools, secret societies, and newspapers; Chinese immigration (at a new height in the 1920's) was now checked; and the commercial class, mainly Chinese, was taxed more heavily. All this was part of a broad attack on the powerful Chinese trading community and foreign economic interests. Limitations and restrictions on foreign control of industries and foreign investment were combined with attempts to build up Thai government enterprises in shipping, oil refining, teak lumbering, and the production of sugar, tobacco, alcohol, silk, and other consumer goods. As a result of this effort to free Thailand from foreign economic domination, the military-political leadership under Phibun was less friendly toward the nearby powers, China, Britain, and France, than toward the more distant, rising power of Japan. By the late 1930's Japanese military training, financial advisers, trade, and economic investments were all being utilized by the nationalistic Siamese leadership.

The Rise of Nationalism in Burma. Chinese-British economic domination of Thailand was paralleled in Burma by Indian-British-Chinese predominance. Burma not only came under British rule in 1886 (see pages 446–449), it became an integral part of British India. Consequently both moneylenders and cheap labor, as already noted, began to flood in from the more commercialized and densely populated regions of India. Burma's foreign population rose from 5.5 per cent in 1872 to almost 10 per cent in 1931. More significantly, by the latter date the few large towns were 50 per cent Indian and over 6 per cent Chinese. Modern skills as well as urban life were largely monopolized by Indians who outdid the Burmese on nearly all levels. Cheaper Indian coolie labor predominated in the rice mills. More sophisticated Indian merchants distributed the imported factory-made textiles. Better-trained Indian personnel served in many government offices and generally staffed the new public services — hospitals and public health, the post office, the telegraph and telephone administrations, railways, steamships, and engineering projects.

Meanwhile British administrative efficiency had contributed to the breakdown of the local Burmese village community. Formerly these rather large village groupings or townships had been the scene of various forms of social life — festivals, plays, puppet shows, boat races, and other popular amusements — and had been under the superficial administration of hereditary headmen. The British in Lower Burma had generally maintained these township headmen as agents of indirect rule, yet after 1886 the need for efficient revenue collection and local administration led them to create smaller, artificial village units and appoint new, impermanent headmen on salaries, who served under the British deputy commissioner in each district. After 1900, specialized government agencies dealing with courts, jails, hospitals, land revenues, conservation, public health, education, cooperatives, and so on began to reach down to the village unit. But by this time the rather loose, organic social life had gone out of it, for the traditional rural community had now been fragmented into individual families and persons. Western property law, for example, facilitated the breakup of family holdings. Where British rule at first had brought civil order and some prosperity, it now was disintegrating the traditional society. The individual farmer was becoming typically an insecure tenant dependent on commercialized agriculture, lacking any personal connection with local government, only narrowly educated in the Buddhist monastic school, and alienated from the new English-speaking Anglo-Indian world. Subjected to the competition of cheaper Indian labor, he was at the mercy of foreigners in his own homeland. The growth of crime, such as murder and gang robbery (dacoity), reflected this breakdown of community life. The foreigner's democratic procedures could not easily be transplanted into it.[1]

[1] See J. S. Furnivall, *Colonial Policy and Practice* (1956), passim.

Nationalism in Burma was stimulated by the example of the Indian Congress Party early in the century, but found its initial expression through Buddhist organizations, including the Young Men's Buddhist Association (Y.M.B.A.) founded in 1906. However, since the British regime had not succeeded in modernizing the traditional monastic schools, they remained unable to provide a modern education and gradually deteriorated. Private missionary schools with a combined Anglo-vernacular curriculum were therefore encouraged, and eventually the government University of Rangoon was created in 1920; at that date there were fewer than 400 Burmese college graduates.

The rise of nationalism was complicated by conflicts of interest between the dominant Burman leadership and minority ethnic groups — principally Shan and Karen, but also Chin and Kachin. Christian missionaries had found their converts, and British administrators their best allies, among these minorities rather than among the descendants of the former conquerors and rulers of Burma, whom we have distinguished above as "Burmans." (While ethnographically useful in earlier periods, this term with the passage of time has become descriptively less precise.)

Political agitation developed after Britain's promise of eventual self-government for India, made during World War I, had led with some painful delay to a similar commitment for Burma. The system of dyarchy, decided upon for India in 1919, set up in each province a legislative council, most of it elected, with the more important provincial government functions "reserved" to British governors and their executive councils, and the less important functions "transferred" to newly installed Indian ministers. When Burma was at first excluded from this system, as being less ready for self-rule, delegations were sent to London representing the Western-oriented elite to demand home rule and separation from India. Meanwhile, along with the rise in India of the noncooperation movement led by the Indian National Congress under Gandhi, nationalist agitation grew up in Burma on a broad popular scale among students, the Buddhist monkhood (*sangha*), and even in the villages. Students boycotted the new university. School strikes ensued. The Y.M.B.A. early in 1921 organized a General Council of Burmese Associations, which soon began to mobilize nationalist complaints by organizing at the village level. A Buddhist monk named U Ottama (U is a term of respectful address) called for rebellion to defend the Buddhist faith against foreign rule which would destroy it. A whole class of nationalist-oriented monks (*pongyi*) arose in the villages to inflame popular feeling against the foreigners and their government. Sentiment in Burma as in India thus crystallized against alien rule.

Dyarchy was applied to Burma after January 1, 1923, on liberal terms. The old legislative council was now enlarged, to be mainly elected on a broad franchise, and the new degree of self-government at all levels was supported by expanding education. But the elections were boycotted, and a violent movement arose against paying capitation taxes. Among the Western-oriented urban elite, some cooperated in dyarchy, but many joined in noncooperation, along with the more radical Buddhist-led rural elements. The principal nationalist group in the legislative council elected in 1926, the People's Party, remained in opposition, refusing all ministerial posts. Hatred of dyarchy and apathy toward elections inhibited local participation in the new district councils, which therefore all the more easily became both corrupt and ineffective. Municipal government also deteriorated. Thus antiforeignism nurtured the popular indifference and indeed irresponsibility that hampered the growth of democratic self-government.

When the world depression in 1930 brought economic distress, destitute Burmese laborers turned upon Indian dockworkers and Chinese traders in several bloody riots. On December 22, a small, secretly planned rebellion broke out in Lower Burma (Tharrawaddy District) to restore the ancient Kingdom. Its leader, Saya San, revived the whole panoply of traditional mythology, insignia, and religious sanctions of the Burman monarchy, with charms, amulets, and tattooing to make one "invulnerable." A number of small-scale, poorly armed outbreaks during the first half of 1931 were suppressed by some 10,000 troops; Saya San was captured and executed, but only after becoming a patriotic symbol. He was defended at his trial by an ambitious and nationalistic French-trained lawyer, Dr. Ba Maw.

When Britain late in 1931 held a "round-table" conference in London on Burma's future, similar to those held on India, nationalist sentiment was split between "separationists," anxious to get rid of all forms of Indian domination in Burmese life, and "anti-separationists," fearful of being isolated from the great Indian independence movement. One of the latter, Dr. Ba Maw, won the 1932 election, and proceeded with much tergiversation to bargain with both Britain and India as to Burma's future status. The decision for separation, with temporary safeguards for Indian trade and immigration, was finally reached in London, and an act of 1935 modified the system of dyarchy and gave Burma a separate constitution and government. A British governor would still be responsible for defense, finance, and foreign relations, but there would be an elected bicameral legislature, and a Burmese prime minister and cabinet to handle the general administration of internal affairs. When separation was carried out in 1937, Dr. Ba Maw became the first prime minister, inaugurating a stormy four years of parliamentary self-government.

One segment of Burma's new nationalist leadership in the late 1930's stemmed from the Student Union at the University of Rangoon. The students were an elite, generally of middle-class background, strategically placed to get a hearing and organize a following. Their principal vehicle became the *Dobama Asiayone* (We Burmans Society). They soon had followers in high schools and, under some superficial Marxist influence from England, tried their hand at organizing labor unions. To demonstrate their defiance of British rule they addressed one another by the term for "lord" or "master," *Thakin*, used in Upper Burma for Englishmen (like *Sahib* in India). They also sent delegates to Indian Congress Party meetings. In 1936, when the president of the Student Union (Thakin Nu) was expelled and its secretary (Thakin Aung San) was also disciplined, a school strike erupted and the student leaders succeeded in getting the legislative council to investigate the university, which increasingly came under political influence. While many in the student movement took up the study of Marxism and a few later became Communist leaders, the majority continued, like Aung San, to put the nationalist aim of independence ahead of socialism or Communism. With the outbreak of war in Europe in 1939, several Thakin leaders joined with Dr. Ba Maw, who had been driven from power, to organize a "Freedom Bloc" of ultranationalist groups. When they opposed the war effort in mid-1940, Dr. Ba Maw, Thakin Nu, and others were imprisoned, while Thakin Aung San fled to China and the Japanese camp.

Nationalism and Communism in Vietnam. Just as Burmese patriots were encouraged by the example of nearby India, so the Vietnamese took heart from reformers and revolutionaries in China. True to the pattern of imitating the Ch'ing, Vietnamese scholars who traveled abroad in the 1860's and 1870's had vainly advocated Westernization in self-defense. By the end of the century a new generation of scholars, still versed in Confucianism, was ready to respond to K'ang Yu-wei's reform program of 1898 and the subsequent Chinese movements of reform and revolution. Though these Vietnamese scholars, like their Chinese counterparts, centered in Tōkyō, they used ideas of Rousseau, Montesquieu, Adam Smith, Mill, Spencer, and Huxley, among others, as intellectual substance. Only later would the spread of French education in Vietnam give another, more direct channel of access to the Western national-revolutionary tradition.

Japan's victory in 1905 drew several young Vietnamese to Tōkyō in an "exodus to the East." A leader among them was Phan Boi Chau (d. 1940), who became acquainted with Liang Ch'i-ch'ao, Sun Yat-sen, and those Japanese patrons of pan-Asianism, Ōkuma and Inukai. Inspired by works of K'ang and Liang, Chau[1] wrote a *History of the Eclipse of Vietnam* (*Viet Nam vong quoc su*) and formed a political association to

---

[1] Vietnamese names are written in the Chinese order, surname first, but it is customary to use the personal name which is written last as though it were the surname. Thus Ngo Dinh Diem, though of the surname Ngo, was called "Mr. Diem." This is said to result from a few surnames like Nguyen being so prevalent as to lack particularity.

aim at Vietnamese independence under a constitutional monarchy. Unfortunately Japan's great-power friendship with France caused Chau, like Sun Yat-sen earlier, to be expelled from Tōkyō in 1910. The success of the Chinese revolution of 1911 and contact with the *T'ung-meng hui* leader, Hu Han-min, at Canton inspired him to organize a Society for the Restoration of Vietnam (Viet Nam Quang Phuc Hoi), aiming now at a republic. But Chau's efforts to foment anti-French risings led to his imprisonment for some years after 1913 amid the general suppression of all revolutionary efforts.

Would-be reformers fared no better. Scholars who tried to develop Sino-French-Vietnamese education, and to push for national modernization within a framework of cooperation with France, made no headway. This failure was partly due to the disconcerting oscillations of French policy: conservative administrators might crack down on schools and reform groups which their liberal or socialist predecessors had permitted. It was also true that anti-French feeling remained so strong among the scholar class that any reform venture might get out of hand. When the University of Hanoi opened in 1907, nationalist agitation was so violent that the French closed it the next year, and it remained closed until 1918.

All this reflected the fact that the French had seized power from a ruling class steeped in traditions of government by scholar-officials, loyalty to the emperor, and rebellion against foreign rule. Young Vietnamese scholars regarded themselves as the future ruling class and therefore as natural saviors of their oppressed country. As late as 1916 the young Nguyen Emperor (Duy-Tan) helped organize a rebellion, and fled to the mountains when it was prematurely discovered.

Against this upper-class rebelliousness, French rule was maintained by force and manipulation, principally by keeping Indo-China divided and by utilizing the old mandarinate as a bulwark of authority. The French preserved the façade of the traditional government, instead of destroying it as the British had done in Burma; at the same time, for logical reasons, they delayed the creation of a new system of popular government. This amounted to using the past against the future, letting the strength of tradition stifle new growth. There was less native participation at the lower administrative levels in Cochin China than in Burma. Meanwhile the mandarinates in the other "protectorate" areas were staffed with compliant functionaries who depended on the French. The enforced collaboration of the Nguyen dynasty with French rule robbed it of nationalist influence at the top. The Nguyen Emperor who came to the throne in 1925 at the age of twelve with the reign-title Bao-Dai was left only ritual functions to perform. When a Grand Council of Economic and Financial Interests was created in 1928, it included Vietnamese but remained French-dominated. Even at lower levels, Frenchmen still staffed much of the civil service. As late as 1942 there were 5100 French officials and only 27,000 Indo-Chinese, the highest proportion of Europeans in any Asian colonial government. Indigenous political activity was smothered by French police control over travel, mail communication, and publication, and by the repression of free assembly, labor organization, and political movements. Suspects were summarily shipped to the island of Pulo Condore.

Among many anachronisms, the classical examinations, inculcating an outworn orthodoxy, were preserved until 1915–18. Modern education for a new order developed slowly. Modern research on Indo-China's several cultures and complex history, though brilliantly pursued by l'École Française d'Extrême-Orient at Hanoi from 1899, long remained a French preserve. As the Sino-Vietnamese classical education ceased, some vernacular instruction using *quoc-gnu* developed, but the French regime stressed French education and even offered French citizenship as a goal of one's career. Though French learning eventually brought with it the ideas and vocabulary of European nationalism, its first effect was to estrange the student from his own national tradition. In any case, it reached only a tiny minority. In the 1930's, with four-fifths of the population still illiterate, only half a million students were usually in government primary schools and only a few thousand at higher levels.

These various traditional, divisive, diversionary, and repressive measures served to maintain French control well enough during the early decades of modernization. The old order was clearly bankrupt. French energy was creating, in the attractive new capital-cities like Saigon, a new administration with modern services. A revolutionary Vietnamese leadership had not yet emerged. The 1920's saw a great investment of French capital, an expanded production, and some interest on the part of French socialists in Franco-Vietnamese collaboration. But meanwhile French achievements in public health, another of the two-edged benefits of modernization, helped the population to increase faster even than the food supply. Sharecropping cultivators on the very margin of subsistence could offer no market for consumer goods, and mass living standards in the crowded delta areas evidently declined. The big French rubber-plantation, coal-mining, and other export concerns, together with the Banque de l'Indochine and the Chinese rice-monopolists and money-lenders, increasingly dominated the colonial economy and formed an interest-group wedded to colonialism, while the condition of the populace worsened.

To this economic exploitation, political repression, and cultural stagnation, not reform but revolution seemed to many Vietnamese the only answer. Of the 100,000 Vietnamese soldiers and laborers who were sent to France during World War I, many returned with dangerous thoughts.

The ideas of national self-determination, revolutionary class struggle, and party dictatorship which flourished in China in the early 1920's had immediate repercussions south of the border. Revolution began in Vietnam through similar nationalist and Communist organizations.

The Vietnam Nationalist Party (Viet Nam Quoc Dan Dang, i.e. Vietnam Kuomintang) was indebted to the Kuomintang of China for much of its ideology, method, and support. Denied any chance to function in an established electoral process, it turned in the late twenties to terrorism. Meantime a more highly-trained professional revolutionary movement was being set in motion by Ho Chi Minh (ca. 1892–   ), who like Sun Yat-sen began as a nationalist (using the name Nguyen Ai Quoc, "Nguyen the patriot") but, being a generation younger than Sun, turned to Communism. Getting to France before World War I, he helped found the French Communist Party in 1920, and was sent by it to Moscow in 1923 to study at the University for the Toilers of the East. He participated in the Comintern Fifth Congress of 1924, and arrived in Canton in 1925 to work under Borodin. There he recruited Vietnamese to form the Vietnam Revolutionary Youth League as a first step toward a Communist Party, and published a paper, *Youth* (*Thanh Nien*). Through this indoctrination in Leninism he began to create for the first time a centralized subversive movement, to be based on secret cells in Indo-China, more capable of surviving French police repression. Some members were trained at the Whampoa Military Academy. After the Kuomintang-Communist split in China, Ho Chi Minh as a principal Comintern agent succeeded at Hong Kong in 1930 in uniting regional splinter groups into the Communist Party (Cong-san Dang) of "Vietnam," a title soon broadened to "Indo-China." It soon had some 1500 members and Comintern support.

The first phase of the Vietnamese revolution began in 1930 partly because the world depression then began to hit the Indo-Chinese export economy while simultaneous crop failures and famines intensified the popular suffering. The Vietnam Nationalist Party attempted a military rising, starting in February with a mutiny of troops at Yen Bay on the Chinese border, which the French crushed with such severity that the party was all but destroyed. The newly unified Communist network, however, receiving a great influx of ardent revolutionaries, proceeded in 1931 to stir up many strikes, demonstrations, incidents, and even peasant risings. The French used their Foreign Legion in a small-scale war to get the situation under control, and as a result thousands were killed, tried, executed, or deported. Ho Chi Minh was jailed in Hong Kong (1931–33) and the Communist Party structure and Comintern contact were temporarily broken.

This defeat fostered among some Vietnamese Communists the Trotskyist view that any united front with "bourgeois nationalists" was inherently "reactionary" and unreliable — as witness the 1927 split in China. Later in the 1930's the orthodox Stalinist party, rebuilding its underground apparatus with help from Moscow and via Siam, joined with Trotskyists and others in local Saigon politics during the period of the Popular Front. Political activity was freer in Saigon because Cochin China was a full French colony, not a protectorate. When the united front policy dictated from Moscow ended on the outbreak of World War II, Vietnamese Communists as well as nationalists again staged risings against French rule and were again ruthlessly suppressed. Nevertheless the Communist movement had clearly become a major vehicle of Vietnamese nationalism.

Communists became leaders of the national revolution in Vietnam, more than in any other part of Southeast Asia, for a variety of reasons. One was the influence of China, so near at hand, the traditional model for Vietnamese political innovation. The geographical and cultural propinquity of Vietnam and China, together with the similarity of their political institutions (e.g., ideological authority as the base of government, secret societies as the only opposition), made it natural for the Vietnamese to follow a Chinese example.

But Vietnam as a revolutionary problem was politically and socially somewhat less complex, if militarily more difficult, than China. First, on the level of theory, the imperialism of the treaty powers in the Chinese treaty ports was many-headed and limited; only indirectly could it be blamed for the domestic problems of Chinese poverty, warlordism, and political disunity. In Vietnam imperialism had but one embodiment, the French regime, which bore direct responsibility for domestic affairs; every evil could be denounced in terms of the Marxist-Leninist doctrine of imperialism. National unity in Vietnam was not the major problem; "national reunification before social reconstruction" was not a meaningful slogan. The anti-French aims of nationalists and Communists almost coincided. Second, on the practical level, the centralized French regime, controlling all the communications and the police, financial, and military powers of the state, represented imperialism in full possession of the country, not confined to treaty ports on the periphery — a very different antagonist from the rival imperialist powers in China. This made regional power bases impossible and external aid important, if not essential, for revolutionaries in Vietnam; and in this respect the Comintern apparatus could outdistance all rivals.

A multi-class coalition on united front lines was also an indicated tactic in Vietnam, where so little proletariat as yet existed. Revolt was just beginning in the 1920's when Ho Chi Minh in Moscow and Canton made his Vietnamese translations and applications of Marxism-Leninism. He then envisaged a two-stage revolution — first a "bourgeois-democratic" struggle of all revolutionary classes to achieve independence, then the "proletarian revolution" itself. As he said in 1927, no one in Vietnam "as yet understood the significance of the word Communism." In the end Communism in Vietnam was nourished from both France and China and was no doubt sustained by its own sophisticated techniques, as well as by its ideological ardor against the fascist tendencies of the 1930's; yet even so it hardly more than survived French repression into the period of World War II.

A backward look over the sixty years from about 1880 to 1940 suggests that economic modernization — with its classical phenomena of growth in trade, transport, industry, investment resources, and propertied or managerial and laboring classes — was complicated in continental Southeast Asia by geographic, social, and political factors peculiar to the area. First, the availability of uncultivated lands for rice-growing, mainly in the southern deltas of Burma, Siam, and Cochin China, combined with modern medical and transport facilities to make possible an enormous and rapid increase of population. But this came suddenly, without time for a commensurate rise in education, or living standards, or social cohesion and civic consciousness.

Second, this great multiplication of poverty, among socially deracinated, illiterate, debt-ridden, frequently landless farmers, was facilitated and accompanied by foreign invasion — military, political, economic, and cultural. The two disasters, from within and without, came hand in hand. Foreign domination, rather suddenly imposed in Burma and Indo-China, intensified the inevitable psychic stress of modern changes. Alien colonial rulers, the evident agents of change, became the natural objects of fear and hatred. These sentiments were not diminished when some white Europeans claimed innate racial superiority.

Historical evaluation of the colonial era has not yet even begun to reach a consensus among scholars, to say nothing of political leaders and their publics. Long before economic planning and the welfare state became respectable ideals in the West, the colonial regimes found themselves inevitably monopolizing the channels of modernization and therefore often pioneering in programs of economic development and social welfare. Yet they were quite unable in their day and age to forestall the growth of population or to concentrate on raising standards of living, or, in short, to realize more than a few of the increasingly obvious potentialities of the modernization process. The profitability of colonies, so generally assumed by imperialists at the time and still assumed in retrospect by so many nationalists as well as by Marxist-Leninists, is open to some doubt; the enthusiasm of colonial empire-builders tended to go beyond the economic facts. But for the subject peoples the plain reality of foreign political and social domination, whatever its material or cultural benefits, was in itself sufficient cause for anticolonial nationalism.

The forms of government, though they bulked large in people's minds, seem to have been rather superficial to the material and social conditions of the colonial era. The old monarchy and the aristocratic class continued to rule in Siam, disappeared completely in Burma, and remained as puppets in Vietnam — three very different fates. Yet in the end the basic problems in these three countries were rather similar — upset and decline of the traditional culture and society; economic domination by foreigners, both from distant Europe and from nearby India or China; inadequacy of education, training, and experience to produce a new leadership; and consequently a long-drawn-out struggle for national self-assertion.

One test of a colonial regime's success was therefore the degree to which it was able to inaugurate self-government, as was done, for example, in Manila and Rangoon, as a step toward the liquidation of colonialism. The Dutch and the French hung back for many reasons, perhaps roughly in proportion as they let themselves feel dependent on their colonial position.

A third way, between the old colonial regimes and the new nationalist movements, was offered by international Communism. After the Second Congress of the Comintern in 1920, its Far Eastern bureau at Shanghai had helped found Communist parties in several countries, notably in Indonesia (1920) and China (1921). When the early participation of these parties in the nationalist movements of the 1920's had led by 1927 to frustration, the Sixth Comintern Congress of 1928 called for a "left" strategy of proletariat-based parties and insurrectionary efforts. Yet this only widened the gap between Communism and the nationalist movements. Communist parties founded in Indo-China (1930) and the Philippines (1931–32) made little progress. Coalitions with nationalist movements were resumed only under the united front line of the Seventh Comintern Congress (August 1935), fostered by the growing menace of the Nazi-Fascist Axis and then by Japan's joining the Axis. By the 1940's the vision of world revolution by the brotherhood of all oppressed peoples against capitalist imperialism, which had inspired the international Communist movement in Southeast Asia in the 1920's, was being gradually supplanted by interest in the separate local struggles for national independence in each country.

Even with Communist help, the nationalist movements in Southeast Asia might not have been able for many years to oust the foreign regimes, except in the Philippines where full independence was scheduled for 1946. But suddenly in the course of the single year 1941–42, Western rule was wiped out by an intruding force from East Asia, the expansion of imperial Japan — an expansion originally stimulated, of course, by Western dominance.

JAPANESE COLONIALISM: TAIWAN AND KOREA

In no respect did Meiji Japan catch up with the West more quickly than in colonial development. She began quite early to develop the northern island of Hokkaidō (see pages 256–257). Within a decade of the final British and French conquests of Burma and Indo-China, Japan took over Taiwan. In another decade she had Korea. Given her late start, compared with the Dutch in Indonesia or the French in Indo-China, Japan's achievement of her aims in Taiwan and Korea, both in integrating the colonial economies into that of the homeland and in suppressing nationalist political developments, is all the more noteworthy.

Several factors obviously favored Japan's empire-building — not only geographic proximity and easy communication by sea with an island and a peninsula which sea power could control, but also (and equally important) cultural proximity. For Japan, Taiwan, and Korea were all parts of the Chinese culture area. Chinese characters, used in all three writing systems, still provided a common medium of communication, so that a literate Korean or Taiwanese could understand a Japanese official's orders written in classical Chinese. The devices of indirect rule, which blunted the efficiency of other colonial regimes, were thus less necessary. Moreover, the traditional phraseology and concepts of imperial Confucianism — benevolent rule, family morality, the social order — could be utilized by the new masters, who by the same token were not imbued with alien ideas like individualism, the rights of man, or the White Man's Burden. This common background made it easy for Japan to update and use the *pao-chia* system, for example, in Taiwan. The Chinese cultural tradition even in its Korean variation tended to support established authority. Japan could thus work from the inside; moreover she did so in the East Asian area where ideas and methods of authoritarian rule had gained maturity, balance, and sophistication through a long development. Cultural proximity made it easier for some Taiwan-Chinese and Koreans to become Japanized collaborators and for Japanese police spies to infiltrate the populace. Japan was close enough culturally, in fact, to envision an actual absorption and assimilation of her colonial subjects, more complete than any Western power, even France, had been able to contemplate elsewhere.

Japan's Development of Taiwan. The mountainous island of Taiwan, 250 miles long by 60 to 80 miles wide, offered Japan a golden opportunity for economic development. Controllable from the sea and a short sea haul from the home islands, Taiwan was comparatively underpopulated by some three million industrious Chinese peasants and a small minority of about 120,000 aborigines of Malayo-Polynesian origin. The island was underdeveloped but was capable of producing semi-tropical food crops to meet Japan's needs.

Politically, Taiwan was still almost a Chinese frontier area. It had been settled principally since the late Ming, and was accustomed to being

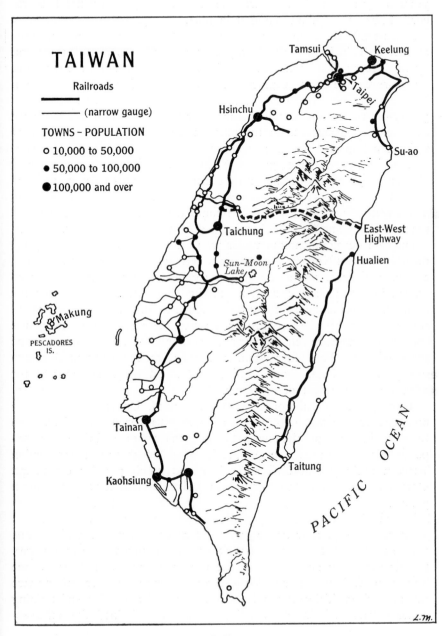

TAIWAN

Railroads

━━━━━ (narrow gauge)

TOWNS – POPULATION

o 10,000 to 50,000

● 50,000 to 100,000

⬤ 100,000 and over

Tamsui

Keelung

Taipei

Hsinchu

Su-ao

Taichung

East-West Highway

Sun–Moon Lake

Hualien

Makung

PESCADORES IS.

Tainan

Taitung

Kaohsiung

PACIFIC OCEAN

L.m.

governed from a distance, having become a separate province only in 1885 (see page 379). There was little tradition of independent rule, and Koxinga and the Dutch of the seventeenth century were only distant memories. Local disorder was endemic — "a small rebellion every three years, a big one every five," was the saying. Many risings had been recorded since the Ch'ing conquest in 1683.

Against this background, the short-lived "Republic of Taiwan," proclaimed at Taipei in May 1895 in protest against the cession of the island by the Treaty of Shimonoseki, had been encouraged from the mainland by die-hards like Chang Chih-tung in a vain hope of stimulating Western intervention. The "Republic" had also expressed a native Taiwan-Chinese gentry-led patriotism, which was manifest in the anti-Japanese resistance and banditry maintained in the hills for years afterward. But in 1895 Chinese nationalism had not yet produced even the Reform Movement of 1898 on the mainland, and the Ch'ing dynasty's helpless surrender of Taiwan to Japan bequeathed no irredentist heritage to future patriots. Japan took over a prenationalistic polity as well as a premodern economy. The hastily contrived Taiwan "Republic" had been more transitory than the first Philippine Republic proclaimed by Aguinaldo in 1898.

Japanese development got under way only in 1898 with the appointment of General Kodama Gentarō as governor-general and Gotō Shimpei, a doctor of medicine, as head of the civil administration. These two leaders in Japan's modernization inherited a chaotic situation, for the traditional subsistence economy was plagued by disorder, and the central administration had largely broken down. They set out to make the colony economically self-supporting, a strategic bulwark of Japan, come peace or war. They first established order, then conducted thorough surveys of the land, people, and customs, and thereupon pressed for scientific development of resources.

To establish peace and order was the first need. Under Gotō's Japanese predecessors, the task of suppressing bandits had been divided between the army in one zone, the civil police in another zone, and the army-and-police jointly in a third zone, an inefficient system that produced friction between military and civil authorities and much popular discontent. Gotō rebuilt the old *pao-chia* system and integrated it with a modern police network, so that local police offices worked closely with the household groupings of mutual responsibility in the villages. Meantime the Japanese military, now under civil government control, were only one of the means used to induce bandit groups to surrender, area by area. Offering amnesty or liquidation, the regime extinguished the resistance by mid-1902. The rank and file of the police force were recruited more and more from Taiwanese, who received special education and training under Japanese administrators. Well paid and disciplined, the police assisted in many kinds of administration — registration of households, collection of taxes, sanitation, water control, and even afforestation.

Next, the Japanese administration reorganized the land tenure system. Cadastral surveys reduced the confusion of land rights. Prior to this time large landowners had rented to smaller landowners who had sub-rented in turn, so that a single piece of soil might owe rents to several parties. Meanwhile the Chinese government land tax had remained stationary and much new land remained untaxed. The facts of land-ownership and productivity being largely unknown, farm land as a whole was under-taxed. The Japanese had new land registers and maps drawn up and in 1904 bought out the noncultivating landowners by giving them public bonds. This move created a society of owner-farmers responsible for taxes on their own private property, and more than tripled the land tax revenue. Weights and measures and the currency were similarly unified and simplified. The Bank of Taiwan by 1909 was able to shift to a note issue backed by gold.

On the social plane, Japanese superiority was asserted and enforced with many forms of discrimination to keep the Chinese populace subordinate. The Japanese language was widely promoted for administrative purposes and technical education. After World War I, to further the policy of assimilation, Japanese was taught in the elementary schools, but higher education for Taiwanese remained very limited.

Material development came rapidly, mainly through government leadership and investment. Gotō inaugurated many public health measures; the elimination of epidemic diseases and malaria contributed significantly to a doubling of the population between 1905 and 1940. By 1903 the railway linked up the north and south of the island, and some 6000 miles of roads eventually reached the countryside. Harbors, telegraph lines, and postal services were also developed.

Production efforts centered on rice, tea, and especially sugar cane. Agricultural experiment stations, importing Hawaiian cane, encouraged production for new Japanese-financed sugar mills, which invested in land improvement, irrigation, fertilizer, and transport. Labor was attracted, and cultivators were persuaded to plant new, free land, on condition that part of it produce cane. Standards and marketing methods were scientifically developed. By monopolizing the sugar mills, Japanese capital controlled this new export industry. Fostered by heavy early investment and a protectionist policy (Taiwan sugar entered Japan duty free), Taiwan's sugar industry by 1914 had increased about fourfold — a triumph of capitalist development — and supplied a great part of Japan's needs.

By 1905 Kodama and Gotō had already made their Taiwan regime fiscally independent, financed by its own government monopolies and land tax, no longer in need of large subsidies from Tōkyō. Eventually the individual tax burden in Taiwan was about four times as great as that in Korea, contributing to a larger per capita budget and resting on a higher per capita living standard. After World War I, the cultivation of rice was increasingly fostered for export to Japan. On the whole, Taiwan's colonial economy had been developed by state rather than private capitalism. Heavy industrialization was not contemplated.

Taiwan-Chinese political resistance in terms of nationalism developed rather slowly. For one thing, Japanese rule did not require the suppression of a local ruling house or the entire discrediting of the traditional civilization. Nor did it break up the rural community. On the contrary, the Japanese regime sponsored farmers' associations to promote agrarian improvements (thereby laying a foundation for the later success of rural reconstruction in the 1950's), and the Taiwan farmer's brick house and use of electricity and scientific technology testified to his comparative welfare in the Asian scene. Thus economic progress, reinforced by police controls, discouraged anti-Japanism. During World War I, however, Taiwanese political associations were formed to seek Taiwan-Chinese equality with the Japanese and specifically to abolish the 1896 ordinance that gave the law-making power to Japan's government-general. After the May Fourth movement of 1919, ideas of personal freedom and political reform spread more rapidly among Taiwan students in the private universities and middle schools in Japan, where there were then some two thousand seeking education. The 1920's brought repeated petitions for representative government, the organization of cultural and youth groups, and some abortive Communist activity. But Japan's aggression in China after 1931 was accompanied by intensified police repression in Taiwan, and comparatively few incidents erupted.

Korean Nationalism under Japan. When Japan swallowed the ancient Korean kingdom in 1910 (see pages 482–483), she confronted a situation in some ways quite opposite to that of Taiwan fifteen years earlier. In economic matters Korea's long-used soils, deforested hills, and north-temperate-zone climate held no promise of agricultural growth like that of lush, semi-tropical Taiwan. Politically, on the other hand, the long tradition of Korean independence and the recent struggle to preserve it nurtured an ineradicable anti-Japanese nationalism. In Taiwan, a rather new Chinese province had been brought under Japanese control before the rise of the Chinese nationalist movement. In Korea, nationalism was already very active among the upper class. The crucial fifteen years between 1895 and 1910 indeed had been the watershed between traditional xenophobia and modern nationalism in most of Asia. Korea thus presented a very different political problem.

As one stimulant of Korean nationalism, Christian missions, especially Presbyterian and Methodist, had made great progress in the decades after the opening of Korea to Western contact in 1882. The pioneer Protestant, Horace N. Allen, M.D., had arrived in 1884, eventually becoming active in the international intrigue of the day as American consul-general and minister. Others, like Horace G. Underwood, founded hospitals and schools, including facilities for educating women (Ewha Girls' School, 1886) and for training up a Korean pastorate.[1] By 1910 there were some 200,000 Korean Christians under about 50 foreign Catholic priests and more than 300 Protestant missionaries, most of whom were American.

Thus Western and especially American missionaries, with their religious, medical, and educational institutions, though repeatedly enjoined by their governments from "intermeddling" in Korean politics, nevertheless constituted a vested interest sympathetic to Korean nationalism. By the same token, Japanese administrators found Christianity subversive. In 1911, they accused more than a hundred leading Korean Christians of conspiring to assassinate the governor-general. They were arrested, hung by the thumbs or otherwise pressured into confessions, and sentenced to prison terms. Christian protests, mainly from the United States, in time got many of them released. Missionaries continued to give the small but elite Christian community a sustaining contact with the outside world.

The nature and limitations of American missionary support of Korean nationalism were illustrated in the long career of Syngman Rhee (Yi Sŭng-man, 1875–   ). Rhee got his start in the English language, in Western studies, and in Christianity at the Pai Jai School, an institution established by the Methodists in Seoul in 1885 and recognized by the government as a source of modern-trained officials. The journalism and debating activities in which he became a student leader were also a training for revolutionary politics. During Korea's mounting domestic crisis in 1896 he joined the Independence Club and helped organize mass demonstrations in the traditional manner. The Korean royal government accordingly, with the usual torture, imprisoned Rhee for seven years (1898–1904). After his release, he came to the United States, an emigré nationalist, studied at George Washington University and Harvard, received his Ph.D. at Princeton from Woodrow Wilson in 1910, and returned to Korea as a Y.M.C.A. worker. When the Japanese staged their anti-Christian conspiracy case in 1911, they omitted Rhee as too well-connected. He then settled for twenty-five years in Hawaii, becoming the leader of a faction of Korean nationalists abroad and remaining unreconciled to the Western missionaries' acquiescence in Japanese rule.

The Japanese attitude of superiority toward the Koreans, so evident

[1] Late nineteenth-century missionaries seem to have anticipated the terms of the "Three-self" movement (later utilized in Communist China), advocating "A Korean ministry for a Korean church . . . no namby-pamby, half-foreignized mercenary ministry for an invertebrate mass of jelly-fish Christians but a self-sacrificing, self-reliant, self-respecting Korean pastorate over a self-supporting, self-governing, self-propagating Korean church." W. D. Reynolds, *The Korean Repository*, May, 1896.

in their military administration after 1910, went back to the tradition of conquest established by Hideyoshi's expeditions of the 1590's (see Volume I, pp. 332, 443, and 589) and revived in the great debate of the 1870's (see above, pages 240–242). The efficiency of Japan's exploitation was unchecked by egalitarian pangs of conscience. Japan's experience in Taiwan suggested that the Koreans should be ruled paternalistically but rigorously, as an inferior, subject people, with no idea of trusteeship, self-government, or training for future independence. Thus the bureaucracy — in the government-general at Seoul, in the provinces, counties, and municipalities, and in education — became three-fifths Japanese (52,000 Japanese to 35,000 Koreans in 1936). All political activity was prohibited and all publication tightly controlled.

Japan installed an exemplary network of railways and roads, as well as postal services and telecommunications, hydroelectric plants, mines, and a few modern industries. Aided by public health measures and peace and order, the Korean population increased by about five-sixths between 1910 and 1940. But Japanese large-scale landlordism increased several times over, while Korean living standards remained very low. By the 1930's half the rice crop was being exported to feed Japan, but the per capita consumption of rice in Korea had reportedly dropped 45 per cent — a clear sign of lowered welfare. Japan's program of economic modernization could not achieve in Korea a success like that in Taiwan.

The spread of poverty went hand in hand with new ideas. Modern education, in schools established by the Japanese regime, by private Koreans, and by foreign missionaries, nourished patriotic discontent. Korean students in Japan became ardent nationalists. Christian and liberal attitudes grew stronger after World War I. They included a Wilsonian belief in the self-determination of peoples and in the moral influence of world opinion. This faith underlay the great March First (*Samil*) movement of 1919, a nationwide unarmed demonstration of Korean nationalist sentiment. (The May Fourth movement was to be launched in Peking a few weeks later in a similar atmosphere though with very different results.)

Hoping to impress the statesmen reshaping the world at Versailles, Korean patriots fixed on their late emperor's commemoration day as the occasion for a protest, secretly organized and dramatically made public. On March 1, thirty-three cultural and religious leaders, including both Christians and heads of the modern syncretic "Society of the Heavenly Way" (*Ch'ŏndogyo*), and their co-conspirators in every township over the country, read an eloquent "Proclamation of Independence."[1] A mil-

[1] "We herewith proclaim the independence of Korea . . . in witness of the equality of all nations, and we pass it on to our posterity as their inherent right. . . . Victims of an older age, when brute force and the spirit of plunder ruled, we have come after these long thousands of years to experience the agony of ten years of foreign oppression, with . . . every restriction of the freedom of thought, every damage done to the dignity of life, every opportunity lost for a share in the intelligent advance of

lion or so demonstrators marched chanting *"Tongnip manse! Manse!"* ("Independence — hurrah! Hurrah!"; cf. Jap. *"Banzai,"* Chin. *"Wan-sui"*). In brutally suppressing them, the frightened Japanese recorded 19,000 persons jailed and 2000 casualties. (Korean sources give 7000 killed in the following twelve months.) In April, meetings in Shanghai and in Seoul set up a provisional government of the Korean Republic. But the world's leaders, including Wilson, trying to organize the postwar world in cooperation with Japan, made no response.

The nationalist movement thus launched suffered severely from factionalism. In traditional Korean politics, factionalism had been nurtured by the intensity of leader-follower relationships within small, almost family-like groups, with the result that primary loyalty was often to the group or faction. In the modern nationalist movement this factional tradition was kept alive by the dispersion of Korean patriots to many foreign lands, especially to Russia, China, Japan, and the United States, where they acquired different ideas, conflicting approaches, and discordant allies. Influences from these larger countries pulled Korean nationalists in different directions. But the failure of the March First movement and the survival of the Soviet revolution now favored the rise of Communism as the chief vehicle for Korea's anti-Japanese patriots in the 1920's.

Since the late nineteenth century an expatriate community of Korean emigrants had grown up across the Tumen River in the Chientao region of southeastern Manchuria near the Korean-Russian border (see map, page 585). Ever since 1910, remnants of the old Korean royal army under one of its commanders, General Yi Tong-hwi, had staged border raids across the Tumen against the Japanese regime. Other Korean emigrants had formed communities in Siberian cities along the Trans-Siberian Railway. Koreans were consequently the first East Asians to participate in the Soviet revolution, both in the armed forces and under the Comintern. As early as 1918–19 General Yi Tong-hwi organized an embryonic "Korean Communist Party" in Khabarovsk and Vladivostok and sought Soviet arms and aid. As Lenin turned to the East, Korean patriots were the most readily available allies — and the most anti-Japanese. More Koreans than Chinese attended the Congress of the Toilers of the East, held in Moscow in January 1922 to counter the Washington Conference (see page 674). Speakers like Zinoviev drove home the point that at Washington the status-quo Allied powers acted "as though Korea did not exist . . . the word 'Korea' was not even mentioned," whereas Moscow offered Korea full equality and brotherhood in the world revolution.

Patriots like An Ch'ang-ho, who tried to organize the "Korean Pro-

---

the age in which we live. . . . The result of annexation, brought about against the will of the Korean people, is that the Japanese are concerned only for their own gain . . . digging a trench of everlasting resentment deeper and deeper the farther they go. . . ."

visional Government" in Shanghai between 1919 and 1921, soon met frustration. The American-oriented Syngman Rhee, though nominal president, stayed in the United States to seek moral support through diplomacy. The Soviet-oriented Yi Tong-hwi as premier sought Soviet aid for military operations in Manchuria. Another leader, Kim Ku, was addicted to terrorism and grew closer to the Chinese Nationalists. Differences of ideology, program, and personality soon produced fractures: not only on the right, between gradualist negotiators like Rhee and activists like Kim Ku, but also on the left, between the long-time patriot General Yi, leading a "Shanghai faction," and a younger, more Russified Communist element based at Irkutsk. Koreans also worked in the Chinese Communist Party.

To unify the Korean Communist groups the Comintern staged get-togethers in Moscow and Vladivostok but never could quite patch things up. Progress within Korea also proved difficult. A Korean Communist Party was finally inaugurated in Seoul in 1925, and a coalition of Communists and Nationalists, the *Shinganhoe* or New Korea Society, was maintained from 1927 to 1931. But dissidence was continually suppressed by the Japanese police, who actually knew more about the Korean Communist movement than any of its members.

Meanwhile, among the exiled patriots seeking aid from noncommunist powers, Syngman Rhee negotiated during the 1930's in Washington, Geneva, and Moscow; but Kim Ku gradually supplanted him as president of the dormant "Provisional Government" in Chungking. By World War II the Korean factions in Chungking and Washington were small and ineffective compared with the troops and cadres secretly prepared over the years in the Soviet Union — though all had been equally frustrated by the Japanese police in Korea.

The postwar wave of liberalism in Japan in the 1920's had produced a movement for conciliation and reform of the Korean administration under Admiral Saitō Minoru as governor-general. This was accompanied by many promises, seldom realized, of nondiscrimination, Japanese-Korean friendship, and civil liberties. Korean journalism and labor and youth organizations, however, had a brief opportunity to develop. Japan made renewed efforts to secure the collaboration of upper-class Koreans. The vestigial aristocracy and embryonic middle class were given representation in powerless advisory councils which were partially elected at various levels.

These liberal beginnings were choked off when militarism swept the Japanese empire in the 1930's. Japan's heightened dominance now produced a sullen and restive though largely helpless people, whose resentment was nourished by the belief that their increasing poverty was due to Japanese exploitation. Police controls, backed by the army, were well developed and ever alert against all expressions of nationalism. Even the Korean language was banned in the late 1930's. Koreans were expected to take Japanese surnames, and the Korean language press was almost eliminated. Korean of course remained the language of the home, while Christianity continued to hold its small share of converts — half a million in 1938 in an increased total population. But under the pressure of Japan's war effort, Korean agriculture continued to deteriorate, while tenantry and landlordism (especially Japanese landlordism) increased. As Japan's power grew in Manchuria and spread into China, Korea became even more abjectly submerged in the Japanese empire.

Thus until 1940 Japan's experience of colonialism had been almost entirely within the Chinese culture area of East Asia, in Taiwan, Korea, and Manchuria, over peoples with a Confucian tradition of government and social order. This common cultural background had eased Japan's task of control and administration. Not unnaturally, the comparative success of Japan's rule over her East Asian empire since 1895 had established certain precedents and confirmed certain attitudes that would be applied to the far different societies and cultures of Southeast Asia, once Japanese expansion engulfed them in World War II. Japan's imperialism, in short, was no less culture-bound than that of non-Asian powers.

SOUTHEAST ASIA IN WORLD WAR II

Japan conquered Southeast Asia with a two-edged sword, which in the view of the local peoples cut down the stature both of the conquered white men and of the Japanese conquerors themselves. European colonialism was shattered, but Japan's New Order was not established in its place. The net result during the five years 1940–45 was a violent stimulus to nationalism and, in less degree, to social revolution.

Japan's "Greater East Asia Co-Prosperity Sphere." Japan's anticommunist "New Order in East Asia," proclaimed in November 1938 to include Manchukuo and China under Japanese hegemony, was given its logical extension, once Japan turned southward, in the "Greater East Asia Co-Prosperity Sphere" (*Dai Tōa Kyōeiken*). This was envisaged in 1940–41 as including, in addition to the above-named areas, the mandated Pacific islands, all of Southeast Asia both continental and insular, and even Australia and New Zealand (possibly India also, though this possibility was never pushed). This vast area was to become economically self-sufficient and free from Western exploitation under Japan's political hegemony, with Britain and the other colonial powers excluded and "independent" regimes in most countries functioning in treaty relations as "protectorates," i.e. satellites, of Japan. The Japanese military's sacred mission was to bring peace and stability to all these peoples by creating a new moral order free of the materialism and social disruption brought by the West. Implicit in this conception were two assumptions — the innate superiority of the Japanese to their fellow Asians, entitling them to domination, and the need to revive the traditional, authoritarian social order, in place of corrupting Western ways.

Even in its original planning, however, this essentially backward-looking program ran into difficulties, for the immediate aim of the Co-Prosperity Sphere would have to be the economic support of Japan's war effort, and so it would be necessary to set up Japanese military governments and oppose "premature independence movements." Thus it was proposed to leave the French in control of Indo-China and some of the Dutch in posts in Indonesia, meanwhile training a limited number of Southeast Asian intellectuals in Japan so as to convert them from "European and American liberalism and Communist ideas" to "Oriental moralism" and a "new spirit" in support of Japan. The explosive potentialities of nationalism in Southeast Asia were evidently not perceived in Tōkyō.

The speed of Japan's well-planned conquest was spectacular,[1] and by mid-1942 Greater East Asia was within Japan's sphere. Similar steps were taken in each area (with variations to be noted below), once the military were in control: a single political organization was set up, using local collaborators, on the model of the Imperial Rule Assistance Association in Japan, the Concordia Society in Manchukuo, and the New People's Society in North China. This body tried to monopolize political expression, staged formal demonstrations of support, spread Japanese culture and propaganda, and mobilized economic cooperation. Neighborhood associations were organized to maintain local order on a basis of mutual responsibility. The educational system was overhauled and instruction revised for Japanese purposes. Japanese was made the second language and its study promoted. The local religious tradition was given special support, just as Confucianism and the "Kingly Way" had been in Manchukuo and North China (see pages 708, 711). In Siam and Burma the Japanese encouraged Buddhism; in Malaya and Indonesia, Islam; in the

---

[1] Chronology of Japanese Conquests:

Late 1940. Dominant position established in French Indo-China and Thailand
Dec. 8, 1941. Attacks on Hawaii, the Philippines, Hong Kong, and Malaya
Dec. 13. Guam falls
Dec. 20. Wake Island falls
Dec. 25. Hong Kong falls
Jan. 2, 1942. Manila falls
Jan. 11. Landings in the Netherlands East Indies
Feb. 15. Singapore falls

March 6. Batavia falls
March 8. Rangoon falls
April 9. Bataan Peninsula (north of Manila Bay) falls
April 30. Lashio (Burma Road) falls
May 2. Mandalay falls
May 6. Corregidor (Manila Bay) falls
June 12. Attu (Aleutian Is.) falls
June 3–6. Battle of Midway; Japan is checked

Philippines, Catholicism. Simultaneously they advocated as part of their pan-Asian ideal a recrudescence of traditional forms of social authority — the superiority of heads of families, the subordination of women, doctrines of blood-kinship and filial piety, of loyalty and group responsibility. Along with these ideals, however, went the supremacy of the Japanese emperor in theory and the brutal and arrogant rule of the military police (*kempeitai*) in daily life.

To forestall Foreign Office interference with military rule, a Greater East Asia Ministry was created in Tōkyō in November 1942, incorporating the Manchurian Affairs Board, the China Affairs Board, and other agencies, and charged with handling relations, promoting development, and spreading cultural propaganda in the conquered areas. It busily sent Japanese language teachers abroad, brought Asian students and goodwill missions to Japan, and summoned a Greater East Asian Conference of Japan's "independent" allies — Manchukuo, China, Thailand, Burma, and the Philippines. But by the time this conference convened, in 1943 in Tōkyō, co-prosperity had been eclipsed by economic disruption and suffering, and Japan was losing the "Greater East Asia War" (*Dai Tōa Sensō*).

By their great effort in Southeast Asia the Japanese had seized a vast empire at the farthest remove from the centers of Allied power in Europe and America. At the same time, however, it was also several thousand miles from Japan; and, as we shall note in Chapter 10, when the Allies gradually brought their superior industrial-military-naval might to bear, Japan's contact with Southeast Asia was increasingly interrupted. Shipping did not get through. In the end the whole vast area of Southeast Asia was cut off and left to wither, as the Japanese homeland came under direct assault. Only in the Pacific islands, the Philippines, and Burma did the white men fight their way back into the local scene.

Thus Japan's empire-building in Southeast Asia was defeated from without, by the course of the total struggle. But meanwhile the several factors that worked against it from within suggest that it might not have had much long-term viability in any case. First, Japan was unable to substitute for the world economy and keep trade going at its customary level. She could neither absorb all the tropical exports of Southeast Asia nor supply all the needed industrial products. The region was consequently thrown back onto a stagnant, subsistence economy subject to maldistribution, shortages, and inflation. Second, the Southeast Asian peoples' cultural contact with the Japanese military was an unmitigated disaster. The Japanese soldier, systematically brutalized in his army training, became overseas a doubly brutal conqueror, his moral instincts blunted in an alien social context. Finally Japan faced the dilemma whether to suppress nationalist movements in Southeast Asia or encourage them for wartime Japanese ends. However attractive, the latter policy would inevitably summon the genie out of the bottle.

The Japanese Impact. Japanese policy toward colonial nationalism was first set in Indo-China, where military necessity dictated the utilization rather than the overthrow of the French. Thus at the very beginning the realization of "Asia for the Asiatics"[1] had to be deferred.

Japan's southward expansion had begun with the fall of France in June 1940, when Japanese demands obliged the French to close the Haiphong-Kunming railroad as a supply route to Free China. Then, strengthened by the German-Italian-Japanese Tripartite Pact of September 27, Japan arranged with the collaborationist French government at Vichy to occupy strategic bases in Tongking for an attack on China. When Thailand under the chauvinist leadership of Luang Phibun launched hostilities against the French to recover territories along the Mekong (October 1940-January 1941), Japan mediated and in the process strengthened her preponderant influence in both Indo-China and Thailand. By late 1941 she was prepared to leap south and west from bases in southern Indo-China.

Japan made no effort to "liberate" the Vietnamese nation. Quite the contrary. She continued to recognize French sovereignty represented by the Vichy governor (Admiral Decoux), who skillfully maintained France's position on a diplomatic tightrope until the Japanese military take-over near the end of the war (March 9, 1945). And so Vietnamese revolutionists of all camps were smothered under the combined weight of French repression and Japanese occupation.

Nationalist China, however, gave the Vietnamese support and a staging area across the border, where in the spring of 1941 the Vietnamese Communists led the way in creating a united front organization, the League for the Independence of Vietnam (Viet Nam Doc Lap Dong Minh Hoi) or Viet Minh ("Viet League"), with Ho Chi Minh secretary-general. Nationalist China tried hard to counteract Communist predominance in the Vietnamese united front, but it nevertheless increased as the Communists built up their organization inside the country, using broad social, patriotic, and liberal appeals like those of Mao Tse-tung's "New Democracy." By 1945 Vo Nguyen Giap (1912–), a young Vietnamese teacher-turned-general, trained by the Chinese Communists at Yenan, was in command of guerrilla forces in Tongking. These included strategically placed non-Vietnamese tribal peoples of the mountains (called by the French "montagnards").

When the Japanese forcibly seized power from the French administration in March 1945, they acknowledged the "long-suppressed" aspiration for national independence but nevertheless created another regime like that the French had maintained. Nominally it was under Emperor Bao-Dai and other dignitaries, but actual control rested with Japan. The

[1] "Asiatic" has since become, in many minds, a pejorative term. "Asian" is now preferred.

Viet Minh therefore cooperated with the Allies while building up an independent base in Tongking. As soon as the Japanese and Bao-Dai were out of power, Ho Chi Minh declared Vietnam's independence at Hanoi on September 2, 1945.

In Thailand as in Indo-China, Japan's military occupation was superimposed upon the established government with considerable benefit to the Japanese war effort. Thailand furnished many supplies, and the Malaya and Burma campaigns were mounted there. The pro-Japanese and irredentist government of Luang Phibun secured by treaties not only Mekong territories from France but also two of the Shan states from Burma and the four northern Malay states. The Thai economy, however, suffered under war conditions, and trade with Japan failed to develop as hoped. Goodwill missions and cultural propaganda availed little in the face of Japan's gradual defeat. The fall of the Tōjō cabinet in Tōkyō (July 21, 1944) was followed in Bangkok by that of Phibun, whose rival Pridi came back into power, secretly conspiring with the "Free Thai" underground preparations for Allied landings. However, the war ended too quickly for Thailand to join the Allies by fighting Japan. The peace settlement took away all the newly acquired territories; but the United States, never having acknowledged Thailand's declaration of war, held out against British proposals to treat the country as an enemy state, and so there was little penalty for Thailand's wartime alliance with Japan. Once again by clever diplomacy the Thai leadership had avoided both the devastation and the defeat of warfare, as well as the social dislocation that usually accompanies them. The persistence of oligarchy was demonstrated in November 1947 when Phibun by a military coup came back into power for another decade.

In the Philippines Japan dealt with the oligarchy of the dominant Nacionalista Party and gave little support to social revolution. When the president of the Commonwealth, Manuel Quezon, and his close colleague, Sergio Osmeña, reluctantly left the Islands in March 1942 (at the same time as the commander of the American and Filipino forces, General Douglas MacArthur), many of their lieutenants stayed in Manila by agreement to collaborate with Japan as an unavoidable duty.

The Japanese military created a single political party, the "Association for Service to the New Philippines" (abbreviated in Tagalog as *Kalibapi*), as an agency to support the "New Order." The government was run by a Philippine Executive Commission, headed by Nacionalista Party figures formerly close to Quezon but now controlled by Japanese advisers. The content of education was recast to build the Co-Prosperity Sphere into a brotherhood of Asian peoples under Japan's leadership. Japanese generals exhorted the Filipinos to get rid of "the degenerate influence of American culture," which was based upon "individualism, liberalism, and democracy," and which stressed materialism, hedonism, and "the corruptive custom of showing excessive esteem toward the weaker sex," breaking down that "time-honored principle of the East — to respect the head of the family."

At the same time the Japanese army's treatment of civilians won it few friends. Face-slappings, public beatings, execution on evidence of informers, punishment of groups for acts of individuals — all these combined with the economic requisitions and hardships of wartime to rouse popular hatred. After the surrender of the American-Filipino forces on the Bataan Peninsula (April 1942), anti-Japanese resistance activities spread in the provinces, supplied increasingly from early 1943 by MacArthur's command in Australia.

Japan's grant of Philippine "independence" was ostentatiously preceded by a new constitution (September 1943) and the election of a new collaborationist president (José Laurel). The final signing of an alliance with Japan (October) conferred independence in name though the Japanese army continued to rule. The collaborating Nacionalista leaders defended their people and the established social order and obstructed Japanese efforts in many ways. They delayed declaring war on the United States and Britain until September 1944, and avoided conscription. The frustrated Japanese finally, in December 1944, gave power to a more radical and pro-Japanese leader (Benigno Ramos, organizer of the anti-government Sakdal movement of 1935), but by this time the Allied reconquest had already begun. Japanese rule ended with the defense of Manila in February 1945, amid great destruction and suffering for its inhabitants.

Since Quezon had died in 1944, MacArthur now transferred civil authority to Osmeña as Commonwealth president; but in the elections of April 1946, Osmeña was defeated by Manuel Roxas, the next most prominent Nacionalista leader, who had worked publicly with the Japanese but secretly against them, and whom MacArthur had exonerated of "collaboration." Roxas thus became the first president of the independent Republic of the Philippines on July 4, 1946.

In Indonesia the Dutch, unlike the French in Indo-China, refused to collaborate and continue running the government, but they were unable to resist Japan and fight their way back as the Americans did in the Philippines. Instead, the Dutch surrendered quickly and were ignominiously interned, some 60,000 altogether. They were partly replaced by Japanese administrators, who eventually totaled more than 23,000. Not only the Dutch but other Europeans, Eurasians, Indonesian Christians, and the influential Chinese minority suffered maltreatment and humiliation, and in their place many Indonesians moved into posts of greater responsibility. The substitution of Japanese for Dutch as the second language only stimulated the continuing spread of bazaar Malay as the new universal Indonesian tongue (*Bahasa Indonesia*), necessary even for the Japanese administration because of the increased number of Indonesian personnel.

Japan's aims, to exploit the islands economically in an all-out war effort without thought of independence, created a regime much harsher than that of the Dutch, with more direct demands upon the villages. As tools for this exploitation, Japan tried to use both Islam, through organizations that reached the villages, and the urban-centered nationalist movement. When the conquerors brought the nationalist leaders back from exile, however, the latter are said to have agreed among themselves that Sukarno and Hatta would collaborate while Sjahrir would help organize the resistance. In March 1943 Sukarno and Hatta became heads of the political organization set up by Japan, the "Center of People's Power" (*Pusat Tenaga Rakjat*, abbreviated as *Putera*). Through this and other agencies the Japanese tried to realize their short-term aim of promoting the war effort, while the nationalists tried to keep alive their long-term goal of independence.

Japan experienced many frustrations in her efforts to utilize the Islamic movement, indoctrinate the masses, mobilize economic resources, recruit labor battalions, and even train a volunteer Indonesian army, which by 1945 totaled 120,000 men. As one result of the nationalist leaders' collaboration, loudspeakers of the expanded radio network filled every marketplace with Sukarno's oratory. Possibly his strictures against Western "imperialism" nurtured anti-Japanism too. But it was already endemic because of *kempeitai* brutality, inflation, exploitation, and the collapse of the export economy in the absence of overseas trade. In March 1944 the Japanese replaced the *Putera* with a more all-inclusive and closely-controlled organization, still headed by Sukarno but under military supervision and buttressed by neighborhood associations among the populace, who were thus brought a bit further into political life. Japan's effort to utilize Islam built up a large Moslem organization (*Masjumi*), but this encouraged nationalism more readily than pro-Japanism — as when Moslems were forced, for a time, to bow toward the emperor in Tōkyō instead of toward Mecca. Finally, a number of youth and student organizations gave opportunity, as did the army, for the emergence of talent from a new generation no longer dependent on the old criteria of aristocratic birth, religious training, or Western education. Among these young people, skilled at least in the arts of organization, were potential leaders for the future.

As Japan's fortunes waned, the widespread Indonesian underground prepared to rebel whenever Allied forces landed, while Japan prepared to give Indonesia independence before this could occur. In the end, Japan's surrender came first (August 14, 1945), and Indonesian independence was proclaimed from Sukarno's residence on August 17. In addition to his administrative cabinet, Sukarno appointed a broadly representative advisory body, the Central Indonesian National Committee (Komité Nasional Indonesia Pusat, or KNIP). Forces of the new Republic of Indonesia attacked some of the Japanese city garrisons, in time to ensure maximum difficulty for the Dutch effort to reassert control.

In Malaya, as well as Sumatra, Japan intended at first to create strategic Japanese territories. English captives were systematically humiliated in public; and the populace were harshly regimented and propagandized, asked to bow toward Tōkyō and learn the Japanese language. However, the Japanese mobilization of anti-British sentiment among Malays and Indians, including an "Indian National Army," was soon undercut by the conquerors' brutal and minatory attitude and the collapse of the export economy along with the currency and the Singapore food supply. Both passive noncooperation and a guerrilla resistance developed among the Chinese population, and Communist influence grew among the guerrillas. The Japanese army, locally undefeated, never got to the point of encouraging a declaration of independence.

In Burma, as in Thailand, the nationalist leaders before the war had already looked toward Japan, responsive to the cry of "Asia for the Asiatics." Japanese propaganda had been spread by inviting nationalist politicians to Tōkyō and financing their newspapers in Rangoon. By 1941 some thirty Thakin leaders, including Aung San and Ne Win, had received Japanese training on Hainan Island preparatory to forming a Burma Independence Army. As the Japanese overran Burma in early 1942, constantly outflanking the poorly prepared British and then the Chinese as they retreated northward, this army rapidly built up a force of patriotic youth and assisted in both military operations and local government. Soon, however, the Japanese disbanded it and created a new, small Burma Defense (later National) Army under Major-General Aung San. A nationalist administration was set up in August 1942 under Dr. Ba Maw, who was assisted by an able group of Thakin leaders, including Thakin Nu. Many were disillusioned by the *kempeitai* treatment of civilians, but they had already been denounced by Britain as traitors.

To counteract the rise of anti-Japanese feeling in Burma, as in the Philippines, Premier Tōjō in early 1943 promised formal independence for both countries. On August 1, Burma became an "independent" ally of Japan and declared war on the Allies. Dr. Ba Maw, proclaiming "One Blood! One Voice! One Command!", headed a dictatorial regime under Japanese control. He catered to the politically active Buddhist monks and asserted national interests which made him increasingly a thorn in the side of the Japanese occupation. The young Thakin nationalist leaders, meantime, got experience in running the administration, and in pursuit of Burma's future independence they gradually organized a comprehensive resistance movement.

By the spring of 1944, when Japan's attempted invasion of India with the "Indian National Army" proved a failure, the resistance had made an agreement with the British, who were about to begin their reconquest of Burma. A united front was created, the Anti-Fascist People's Freedom League (AFPFL). Circulating in secret a postwar program for freedom, democracy, and welfare, the League built up a widespread organization in which Communists were only one element among many. Its strategic opportunity came in late March 1945, when most of the 10,000-man Burma National Army turned upon the hard-pressed Japanese in time to help decisively in their defeat and in the recapture of Rangoon by May 2, just before the monsoon rains began.

The war ended with most of Burma's cities and transportation bombed and ruined, much riceland gone back to jungle, and the country economically prostrate. But wartime had destroyed the position of Indian landowners and moneylenders, as well as of the British, and had created a new national political unity under the AFPFL. This nationalist united front, moreover, had the armed support of Aung San's National Army. The returning British imperial power thus confronted in the ashes of Japan's empire the same kind of problem that was about to face the Dutch in Indonesia and the French in Indo-China.

Despite the diversity of their cultures and current circumstances, the Southeast Asian peoples shared a series of similar experiences during World War II. When Japan suddenly knocked out the colonial powers, the leaders of the nationalist movements in most areas collaborated in the "New Order," hoping to advance the nationalist cause. Soon disillusioned, both by Japanese brutality and exploitation and by the vigor of the Allied counterattack, they accepted the forms of "independence" proffered by the Japanese and at the same time prepared to turn against them in defeat. Between the Japanese arming of local forces, notably in Indonesia and Burma, and the Allied arming of resistance movements, as in the Philippines, Malaya, Burma, and Indo-China, the war ended with nationalist forces of some sort armed, active, and ready to support independence in almost every country. Meanwhile "independent" domestic regimes under Japan had been inaugurated in Burma in August 1943 and in the Philippines in October 1943. Independence had been proclaimed by Sukarno on August 17, 1945, and by Ho Chi Minh on September 2. When the Allies reoccupied all these areas in late 1945, the situation was profoundly altered from 1941.

THE EMERGENCE OF INDEPENDENT NATIONS IN SOUTHEAST ASIA

Allied reoccupation of Southeast Asia was deemed essential both to arrange the surrender and repatriation of the Japanese forces and to succor prisoners and bring in outside aid for postwar relief and rehabilitation. The colonial powers after their long absence returned with out-of-date assumptions as to their own indispensability, which were reinforced by a very practical recognition of the value of colonies in wartime defense of the homeland. Both the colonial administrator's sense of responsibility and the colonial businessman's interests called for restoring the *status quo ante.* Consequently, in the postwar decade nationalism and colonialism clashed head on, while the international Communist movement tried to seize opportunities. In the end nationalism proved to be the strongest of all these forces, and eight nation-states, of varying sizes and types, emerged in Southeast Asia. While their individual histories present complex problems of interpretation and are quite beyond the scope of this volume, we note below the main phases of their emergence and also the roles of the Communist movements and the Chinese minorities in each country, as part of the international context of Communist China's entrance on the world scene.

The postwar settlement with Thailand (known again as Siam from 1945 to 1948) and the establishment of Philippine independence in 1946 obviated a national-colonial clash in these countries, but their ruling oligarchies nevertheless faced serious problems.

In the Philippines the attainment of political freedom on schedule in 1946 could not be matched in economic relations. American aid (which eventually came to two billion dollars) was necessary for postwar rehabilitation, and free trade with the United States could not be ended without disaster. It was therefore arranged to continue free trade until 1954 and restrict it only gradually for 20 years thereafter; Americans were also to be allowed to participate in the exploitation of Philippine natural resources. United States naval and military bases were leased for 99 years. Colonialism had been liquidated in the political sphere more easily than in the economic or strategic.

One result of enemy occupation had been the sanction given for peasant guerrilla organizations, which became active not only against the Japanese invader but also against the Filipino landlord interest that often had collaborated in requisitioning heavy quotas of rice and other products for shipment to Japan. The principal guerrilla force on Luzon, the Anti-Japanese Resistance Army (abbreviated as *Hukbalahap*) or "Huks," though American-supplied, turned out to be Communist-controlled. The Huks divided up landlord estates or reduced rents, set up local administrations over wide areas, and had an army of some 80,000 to oppose the gendarmerie that now tried to reassert landlord rights. Thus the penury of the mass of tenant farmers, which Japanese occupation had intensified and the Nacionalista Party oligarchy back in power did little to alleviate, gave the postwar Communist movement a promising opportunity.

Neither negotiation with the Communist leader (Luis Taruc) nor gendarmerie terrorism met the Huk problem. But in 1950 the minister of defense, Ramon Magsaysay, a gifted leader of humble origin, replaced the gendarmerie with the Philippine regular army, fully supplied and disciplined. This and other reforms reduced the corrupt and exploitative power of the local *caciques* and alleviated the tenant farmers' plight sufficiently to enervate the Communist movement. This success made Magsaysay president in 1953 and injected into Philippine politics a new element of appeal to the underprivileged, which persisted despite Magsaysay's death in a plane crash in March 1957.

In Burma the British civil government, once reinstalled, began by assuming that the need to rebuild the economy required and justified the return of British firms and even of Indian Chettyar moneylenders, with compensation and restored property rights. It refused to recognize that, despite the war's economic devastation, Burma had come of age politically. The returning governor at first denied the nationwide representative capacity of the Anti-Fascist People's Freedom League headed by the popular hero U Aung San and other Thakin leaders like U Nu. In the end, however, the British postwar Labor Government, having agreed to India's independence, accepted the inevitable in Burma also and put the AFPFL leaders in charge of the government. The AFPFL had earlier in 1946 ousted the Communists from their ranks, and now cooperated in the orderly negotiation of Burma's future in spite of continual disorder, strikes, Communist agitation, and friction among minority groups.

In January 1947 Aung San and Prime Minister Attlee agreed in London on steps to take toward independence, leaving Burma free to accept or reject dominion status. In July Aung San (aged 32) and most of his cabinet were assassinated by a political rival; but U Nu took his place, and in October arranged for complete independence, from January 4, 1948, outside the British Commonwealth in spite of the generous terms of the British settlement. The Republic of the Union of Burma, thus formed, survived domestic rebellions by two Communist factions ("White Flag" and "Red Flag"), former guerrilla forces, and Karen and other minority groups. The rebels failed to make common cause or defeat the army under General Ne Win. A decade later in the face of mounting corruption and governmental difficulties, Ne Win seized power (October 1958) for a year of more efficient army administration. In the elections of February 1960, U Nu once more became premier. But in March 1962 Ne Win again seized power, with no announced limit to his nonparliamentary rule.

In Malaya, where the Malays were hard put to dominate the peninsula while its port of Singapore was overwhelmingly Chinese, a unified nationalism could not easily be aroused against British colonialism. However, the British proposed in 1946 to move with the times by subordinating the Malay states and their rulers to a new Malayan union, with union citizenship for all races equally, including the Chinese in Singapore. Since on this basis the Chinese might have dominated the Malays, the plan was vigorously opposed by a newly created and widely representative United Malays National Organization (UMNO). The British accordingly reversed their policy and in February 1948 set up the Federation of Malaya, based on the Malay states, now strengthened as protectors of the Malay community against the Chinese, and excluding Singapore.

Shortly after, in June 1948, there began a Communist uprising, with international Communist prompting — the Cominform ("Communist Information Bureau") had been created in October 1947, as a revised version of the Comintern, and an international meeting had been held in Calcutta in February 1948. The Malayan rebellion was carried on for nine years by a few thousand Chinese guerrillas. Operating from the jungle and provisioned by the villages of some 300,000 Chinese squatters who had originally fled there from the Japanese, this "Malayan National Liberation Army," espousing a "New Democracy" type of program, terrorized the plantations and disrupted production and trade. In the end many tens of thousands of British and Malayan troops, with naval forces controlling both coasts, were needed to bring Chinese squatters into controlled government villages and so starve the terrorists of supplies — a strategy reminiscent of the traditional Chinese "strengthening the walls and clearing the countryside." The rebellion finally declined after the two communal political parties, the UMNO (under Prince Abdul Rahman) and the Malayan Chinese Association, agreed to join forces and press for national independence. Their alliance, joined by the Malayan Indian Congress, won 51 out of 52 legislative seats open to election in July 1955. This unanimity for national independence led to the Federation of Malaya becoming an independent member of the British Commonwealth in September 1957, with Abdul Rahman the first prime minister.

Singapore, though the metropolis of Malaya, is a Chinese city and a strategic British port. In June 1959 it became a self-governing state, with the British Queen's representative as head of state. The solution of its relationship to Malaya was sought in 1963 by the creation of Malaysia as a new state to include Malaya and Singapore along with Sarawak and Sabah (North Borneo).

In Indonesia in the autumn of 1945, Dutch colonial administrators returned with the British take-over forces to find that the Indonesian Republican army was fighting the Japanese for control of Djakarta (the ancient name for Batavia revived under the Japanese) and other main cities. On the assumption that Dutch rule should and could be reimposed, Dutch forces were soon in conflict with Indonesian at many points. Faced with widespread disorder, the British for a time stopped disarming the Japanese and had them recapture cities from the Indonesians. But the strength of nationalist feeling, among other things, convinced Britain that the Dutch must negotiate. After some 280,000 Japanese had been repatriated and the British had gone in late 1946, there ensued a three-year Dutch-Indonesian struggle marked by bitter fighting and disillusioning negotiations.

In the accompanying turmoil of Republican politics, Sjahrir became premier (November 1945–June 1947) to facilitate negotiations with the Dutch, since he had been a noncollaborator under the Japanese occupation. Sukarno as president maintained his position as the charismatic leader most able to move the common people.

In the struggle with the Dutch, the Republic first settled (in the Cheribon or Linggadjati agreement, November 1946) for recognition as the *de facto* authority in Java and Sumatra, over some 85 per cent of the Indonesian population and economy. The Dutch hoped still to maintain an overall

Netherlands-Indonesian Union under the Queen, in which the Indonesian component (the federal "United States of Indonesia") would consist of Borneo and the Great Eastern State (all the eastern islands) as well as the Republic. The Dutch continued their economic blockade of exports from the Republican area, and in July 1947 launched a full-scale military attack ("police action") on it. Their armor, fanning out over transport routes as the Japanese had done in North China a decade earlier, quickly seized cities, ports, and communications on Java and Sumatra while the Republican forces melted into the hills and villages. The United Nations intervened. Negotiations were resumed. But the Dutch unilaterally created new states out of their newly occupied territory, until the Republic retained less than half of Java. Nevertheless it accepted in January 1948 the Dutch truce terms negotiated on board the U.S.S. *Renville*, counting on future American support to ensure that plebiscites would be properly held. As the Dutch maneuvered to avoid this, however, American inactivity seemed to be in fact on their side, and some nationalists began to look more hopefully to the Soviet Union and its protagonist the Indonesian Communist Party (PKI).

This was the situation when the Communists attempted to seize power. Musso, a leader of the Communist rising of 1926, was now suddenly sent back from Moscow, evidently in connection with the 1948 Cominform effort to foment rebellion in Malaya, Burma, India, and elsewhere. Musso quickly vitalized and expanded the Communist organization. The Republican government, however, followed the view of Mohammad Hatta, premier in 1948–49, that "our national revolution is certain to break down midway if we allow elements of social revolution to creep into it." Facing government preventive measures, the Communist rising was begun prematurely in September, by minor elements. Musso denounced the failure of the "national bourgeois class," but Sukarno called for support of "an independent Indonesia which is not subjected to any other country whatsoever." The rising was suppressed in a couple of months.

Next came the second Dutch "police action," breaking the *Renville* truce agreement in an all-out war suddenly launched in December 1948 with bombers, parachutists, and armored columns. The Dutch seized the remaining cities and also captured Sukarno, Hatta, Sjahrir, and other leaders, who were interned on the island of Bangka and told the existence of their government was no longer recognized. Disregarding resolutions by the United Nations, the Dutch created a pro-Dutch federal government by dividing Indonesia into a dozen major states headed by Indonesians and controlled by Dutch arms, the local Republicans having been shot, jailed, or intimidated. This power play, it was hoped, would bring into being a cooperative, Dutch-dominated Indonesia in which the Republic would be outvoted and contained or even suppressed. The effort failed partly because of opposition from the outer world, though the United States at first hesitated to do anything inimical to the Netherlands' economic role in European recovery. But mainly it failed because of the ubiquitous noncooperation and guerrilla resistance put up by the Indonesian populace, even with a minimum of leadership. As this resistance grew, American influence on both parties facilitated another agreement, the

777

reinstallation of the Republican leaders at Jogjakarta in July 1949, and a round-table conference at the Hague (August–November). Thus was finally created, on December 27, 1949, the sovereign and federal United States of Indonesia, headed by Sukarno as president and Hatta as premier, with the Republic as its largest component. West New Guinea (West Irian), which is inhabited by peoples racially distinct from the rest of Indonesia, was left in Dutch hands.

In August 1950 the federal United States of Indonesia changed itself into the unitary Republic of Indonesia, obliterating the Dutch-created federal system. Indonesia's remaining connections with the Netherlands were progressively reduced by the dissolution of the Dutch-Indonesian union in 1954, repudiation in 1956 of the debt assumed by the U.S.I. in 1949, gradual expulsion of more than 50,000 Dutch nationals after 1957, expropriation of Dutch air and shipping lines, and eventually, in 1963, the negotiated take-over of West Irian.

While Indonesia followed a neutralist line in foreign affairs, domestic politics produced an uneasy balance of forces between the army and various political parties, including the nationalist party (PNI), the large Moslem party (*Masjumi*), a number of smaller groups like the fanatically fundamentalist *Darul Islam,* and the Communist party (PKI). After a great increase of Communist strength in the first general election held in 1955, and subsequent revolts by the army, which was anticommunist, Sukarno developed what he called a "guided democracy," under which he eclipsed all other leaders and assumed dictatorial powers in 1960 in the hope of maintaining a government less susceptible to party politics.

In Indo-China the French were in a stronger position than the Dutch in Indonesia, first of all in numbers. Where the Netherlands had one-eighth the population of Indonesia (9.6 million to about 76.4 million in 1947), the French nation was half again as populous as Indo-China (42 million to 27 million). Moreover the French (Vichy) administration had continued to govern the colony until six months before Ho Chi Minh raised the flag of independence in 1945. The French no less than the Dutch were convinced of the duty, expediency, and feasibility of their postwar reoccupation. In men, resources, and firepower they could outdo the Dutch, except in one strategic respect — the Dutch navy had been able to blockade the Indonesian Republic, but Vietnam adjoined China, where the Communists triumphed in 1949. In the end, this made a great difference.

Japan's military take-over of March 1945, displacing and disarming the French, had not extended to the mountainous fringe of Tongking, where the Viet Minh established a "Liberated Zone" on the Chinese border, not unlike the Chinese Communists' "Liberated Areas" farther north. From this territorial base they steadily infiltrated the Red River delta and even the puppet regime of Bao-Dai. On Japan's sudden surrender in August, the Viet Minh and Vo Nguyen Giap's small army found themselves for the moment the only effective power in Vietnam. The Japanese remained neutral, and Emperor Bao-Dai abdicated at Hué on August 26 in favor of the Democratic Republic of Vietnam. Its independence was joyfully proclaimed at Hanoi by Ho Chi Minh on September 2.

As in Indonesia, Japan's surrender created immediate problems of public order, especially in Cochin China where rival, armed religious sects (the syncretic Cao Dai sect with its own church and pope, and the Hoa Hao, a Buddhist secret society) had their own anticommunist forces and challenged the Viet Minh united front, which was broadly inclusive in form though dominated by the orthodox or Stalinist Indochinese Communist Party.

The Allied take-over to disarm and repatriate the Japanese was divided between Chinese forces north of the sixteenth parallel and British forces south of it. With the British in mid-September 1945 came the Free French, concerned for the 20,000 French civilians still in Saigon, and determined like General de Gaulle not to diminish the national glory by giving up the empire. Under local British orders the French, re-armed, forcibly retook control of Saigon (September 23), and by January 1946, when the British left, they had reoccupied principal cities, routes, and plantations in Cochin China, though resistance continued sporadically in the countryside.

In Tongking, on the other hand, the Nationalist Chinese forces arriving in mid-September had let the Viet Minh go on functioning at Hanoi while the French representatives looked on in impotence. Having removed the Japanese and got French agreements in favor of Chinese commercial interests, Nationalist China withdrew her forces during the spring of 1946. By that time the Viet Minh was well entrenched.

Compared with Indonesia, the nationalists in Vietnam were handicapped by having had less experience of actual government; Japan had used French collaborators rather than Vietnamese to run the administration during most of the war. The rather simple unifying aims of xenophobic anticolonialism, to expel the French and achieve independence, were also cut across by the aims of domestic social revolution. The poverty and inequalities of the crowded North Vietnam delta country fostered a combined social and national movement such as Ho Chi Minh advocated. To pursue both these revolutions at once involved a struggle on two fronts, a united national struggle of patriots against foreigners and a divisive class struggle mobilizing the poor and insecure mass against the propertied and well-to-do minority. Against Franco-Japanese repression the Communists, with their tighter organizational methods, had survived better than other groups; and Ho Chi Minh despite his years in Moscow had emerged as a senior figure in the national revolution with something of Sun Yat-sen's capacity for bringing rival groups together. Finally, among many factors, the success of Communism in the form of Mao's "New Democracy" in China in the late 1940's naturally strengthened the sister movement south of the border. In this period the Vietnamese Communists made continual efforts to minimize the Communist core of their united front. They formally dissolved the Indochinese Communist Party in November 1945, held an election for the first time, brought more non-Communists into the Hanoi government, and set up a popular front (the Lien Viet) with a program of "independence and democracy."

Ho Chi Minh was beset by rival groups, such as the anticommunist patriots supported by Nationalist China, and saw no prospect of aid to Vietnamese independence from China or the United States. He made an agreement with the French on March 6, 1946. France recognized the Democratic Republic of Vietnam as "a free state with its own government, parliament, army, and finances, forming part of the Indochinese Federation and the French Union" —

a formula (used later by the Dutch) putting the Republic into a colonial federation which would in turn form a "union" with the metropolitan power. In return, French troops came back to Hanoi unopposed. General promises were made on both sides, subject to further working out of specifics; but continued negotiations including a conference in France (at Fontainebleau in July-August) proved only how irreconcilable were the differences of aim and attitude. The French unilaterally put Cochin China under a puppet regime, detached from the rest of Vietnam. Relations worsened, especially after a French naval and air bombardment of Haiphong on November 23 killed 6000 or more civilians. The Vietnamese made a surprise attack on the French in Hanoi on December 19, and a full-scale war ensued, with the Viet Minh organizing a national resistance throughout the countryside against 115,000 or more French troops.

As this Franco-Vietnamese colonial war continued month after month during 1947 and 1948, it gradually became a focus of the international power politics of the cold war. In brief, as the Chinese Communists began to gain the upper hand in China and the international Soviet-directed movement fostered the Communist risings of 1948 in Burma, Malaya, the Philippines, and Indonesia, anticommunist resistance also stiffened in many countries in a world-wide tendency toward polarization. The Communist core of the Viet Minh became more overt; and *pari passu* the French finally succeeded in June 1949 in setting up a Vietnamese regime at Saigon under the ex-emperor Bao-Dai as chief of state and a rallying point for nationalist anticommunists.

Attracting nationalists to an "independent" Vietnam that would still be French-controlled was not easy. The anticommunist Catholic ex-mandarin, Ngo Dinh Diem, who had been Bao-Dai's chief minister in 1933, now refused to head Bao-Dai's new government, even though the French had at last agreed to make Cochin China part of a united Vietnam "associated" with France. The French colonial regime could not relax its grip, least of all with a war on its hands. By the time the French National Assembly in January 1950 finally confirmed the treaties making Bao-Dai's Vietnam and also Cambodia and Laos into independent but "associated" states, the war in Vietnam was escalating to a new level. Communist China, now on the border of Tongking, and the Soviet Union recognized Ho Chi Minh's government; the United States and Britain recognized Bao-Dai's. American arms were soon flowing to the French in Vietnam, while Chinese economic aid, arms, and training (based on South China) henceforth bolstered the Viet Minh forces.

During the seven-year struggle with France economic shortages and political regimentation overtook North Vietnam. The regime became more thoroughly Communist on the Chinese model. A successor to the Indochinese Communist Party (dissolved in 1945) reappeared early in 1951 in the form of the Vietnam Workers (Viet Nam Lao Dong) Party headed by Truong Chinh. As mobilization of men and materiel proceeded, the French forces totaling some 420,000 men, including a Vietnamese army of 200,000, met a constantly more formidable military challenge from a Viet Minh army almost as large, entrenched in mountain bases and ineradicable among the populace. When a Communist-led "Free Laotian" (Pathet Lao) movement invaded Laos to the west, the French finally decided to block the main route by airborne build-up of the mountain-ringed post of Dien Bien Phu. Thither in April–May 1954 Vo Nguyen Giap un-expectedly transported artillery — which destroyed the French empire. The surrender of this post, on May 7, 1954, pushed an international conference already in session at Geneva to recognize North and South Vietnam, divided a little north of Hué on about the seventeenth parallel: the Communist-controlled Democratic Republic of Vietnam ruled the north from Hanoi; France withdrew in favor of the Bao-Dai government of the Republic of Vietnam with Ngo Dinh Diem now premier at Saigon. He vigorously sup-pressed the armed religious sects and other corrupt elements, and in late 1955 won elections which ousted Bao-Dai and made himself chief of state. The United States gave the Diem government more direct assistance against Communist-led infiltration and rebellion after 1960. Diem was assassinated in 1963 when army generals took power, but there was still little prospect of a unified Vietnamese nation.

On the west of Vietnam, Laos by 1960 was torn by a similar tug-of-war between Communist and anticommunist movements backed by the two great power blocs. Cambodia under its last king (Norodom Sihanouk, who abdicated in 1955 but remained chief of state), tried to preserve a precarious neutrality between these blocs and in relation to its traditional enemies, Vietnam and Thailand.

All these new nations face a common problem in their Chinese minori-ties. The Overseas Chinese communities became one stratum in the plural economies of the Southeast Asian countries precisely because these were colonial economies, oriented toward production for market and com-mercial growth. Once the European rulers were expelled by the nation-alist movements, the Chinese communities that had grown up during the European era were the next targets in line. In Thailand, Indonesia, and the Philippines, the areas least in touch with China, they suffered some-times severe discrimination, including a ban on Chinese schools in order to cut off the linguistic-cultural tradition. Equally important, immigra-tion was stopped and the old system of dual nationality no longer recog-nized. Nationalistic campaigns were mounted, with varying success, to break down the economic position of the Chinese and effect their political and even cultural assimilation.

It was easier, however, to get rid of the Europeans, who were few in number, far from home, and fit only for superior positions, than to absorb the more numerous Chinese, who had established themselves as laborers and merchants in economic competition, rather than by military con-quest, and whose homeland was nearer at hand, sometimes just over the border. The flow of family remittances back to China and, more recently, a flow of students have been encouraged by both the Nationalist and Communist Chinese governments. Thus the degree of assimilation of the Overseas Chinese into the new nations of Southeast Asia may be expected to differ in each case.

OVERSEAS CHINESE IN SOUTHEAST ASIA
(1961 estimates)

	Ethnic Chinese *(in thousands)*	*Per cent of* *total population*
North Vietnam	90	0.6
South Vietnam	830	5.8
Cambodia	280	5.5
Laos	40	2.
Thailand	2,480	9.4
Burma	400	1.8
Federation of Malaya	2,672	36.9
Singapore	1,273	75.2
British Borneo (Sarawak, No. Borneo, and Brunei)	370	28.2
Philippines	400	1.4
Indonesia	2,480	2.6
Southeast Asia total	11,315	5.1

Within Indonesia: Indonesian Borneo 375 (9.2), Sumatra 700 (4.5), Java and Madura 1,240 (2.), East Indonesia 165 (1.2).

Within Malaysia (formed in 1963, as estimated in 1962): Federation of Malaya 2,712 (36.9), Singapore 1,315 (75.1), total for all Malaya 4,027 (44.3); Sarawak 244 (31.4), Brunei 24 (26.4), Sabah (North Borneo) 111 (23.5), total for all Borneo formerly British 379 (28.3); total for all Malaysia 4,406 (42.2). (Brunei is included for reference, not as part of Malaysia. The same is true on page 741 in the population table.)

(For this table we are indebted to Professor G. W. Skinner.)

CHINA'S INNER ASIAN FRONTIERS: MONGOLIA AND SINKIANG

In all the areas peripheral to China on the south and east, colonialism had relied upon access by sea, with maritime trade nourishing the international order, and sea power (such as that of Britain or the Anglo-Japanese alliance) guaranteeing it. Since all the colonial powers — Portuguese, Spanish, Dutch, British, American, and Japanese — had reached their colonies only by ship, not by caravan or railway on a land route, one was able to displace another whenever its naval power became dominant — witness most recently the Japanese expansion in 1941–42 and the Allied, mainly American, riposte in 1943–45. The rapidity with which one navy could displace another in the waters of East and Southeast Asia was matched by the thinness of the colonial occupation there. The maritime powers had not been able to populate their colonies by emigration more than superficially; hence, when nationalism arose, the few foreigners could be driven out rather quickly, even those who (like many Dutchmen in Indonesia) had been born in the colony and called it their native land.

Without succumbing to a mystique of geopolitics, we can still view the continental relations of the Russian and Chinese empires and the intervening peripheral areas — Mongolia, Sinkiang, and Tibet — as in a different category from maritime colonialism. These Inner Asian areas were not only inaccessible from the public highways of the sea, they were also slower to change in modern times, more imbedded in ancient tradition. We have noted in Volume I, Chapter 7, for example, the persistent and increasing role of the Inner Asian "barbarians" in the government of China; one may even regard the Chinese empire since the thirteenth century as a Sino-"barbarian" empire that normally tended to embrace all of continental East Asia, including both China and the areas north and west. This tendency reached its height after the Manchu conquest of the seventeenth century, when the Ch'ing dynasty first defeated the Western Mongols and then in the eighteenth century established its suzerainty over both the Ili region and Chinese Turkestan (jointly now called Sinkiang) as well as Tibet (see Vol. I, Chap. 9).

In modern times this hard-won Ch'ing suzerainty over continental East Asia survived, at least in form, as long as the dynasty itself. However, as the dynastic power declined during the late nineteenth century, Inner Asia was invaded by the imperialist encroachments of the rival British and Russian empires, expanding on the south and north, respectively. We have already noted (pages 43–52) the slow but irreversible nature of Russia's eastward expansion. It was stopped short of Manchuria and Mongolia after the treaties of 1689 and 1727, only to be resumed successfully in the 1850's and with great vigor in the heyday of imperialism in the 1890's, up to Japan's victory over Russia in 1905.

The demise of the Ch'ing dynasty in 1912 found Russians long since installed in the Maritime Province as both populace and rulers, dominant in North Manchuria (their acknowledged sphere of influence), and participating in the foreign trade of both Outer Mongolia and Sinkiang. Because of the Russian colonization of Siberia, with the Trans-Siberian and other railways serving as trade routes, the Russian position on the north and west of China was now becoming far more permanent and powerful than the British influence established over Tibet in 1904 and later. Thus the end of the Ch'ing imperial order in 1912 was followed within a decade by a new expansion of Russian power in continental East Asia, as the energy of the Soviet revolution began to contribute to the ongoing Chinese revolution. These two great movements came into contact not only in Manchuria but also in the Inner Asian areas lying between them — Outer Mongolia and Sinkiang. But the primary fact in the new situation was the powerful growth on the Russian side, in Soviet Asia.

The Expansion of Russia in Asia. The renewed Russian expansion into the Far East in the late nineteenth century had been energized by the

Trans-Siberian Railway; it culminated in the decade of tsarist imperialism from 1895 to 1905. World War I, the Russian revolution of 1917, and the civil war that followed created a pause in this Russian expansion. During the civil war the anticommunist White forces set up a Siberian government at Omsk in June 1918, soon headed by Admiral Kolchak. The Allied intervention of 1918–22 brought principally Japanese forces, though also some American and other troops, into the Maritime Province and along the Trans-Siberian west of Manchuria almost to Lake Baikal. In this region the Soviets joined with local elements in creating a buffer state, the Far Eastern Republic of Siberia with its capital at Chita, to counter the continuing Japanese occupation. In November 1922, after the Japanese had withdrawn, it was incorporated into the Soviet Union. By the mid-1920's the Soviets had got back much of the old tsarist position in the Far East. Their treaty with Peking in 1924 revived the joint Sino-Russian administration of the Chinese Eastern Railway. A Soviet-Japanese treaty of 1925 withdrew Japanese forces from Russian northern Sakhalin and regularized relations.

In Russia's economic growth under the Soviet five-year plans after 1928, many big cities with populations over 100,000 arose east of the Urals, until by 1940 Soviet Asia held almost a third of the population of the U.S.S.R. A great new industrial base was built, for example, in the Kuznetsk Basin (Kuzbas) in Western Siberia, which was rich in mineral resources, especially coal, and was remote from the frontiers of other great powers. The Turkestan-Siberian (Turk-Sib) railroad connected the Trans-Siberian with Russian Turkestan (Soviet Central Asia), where new industries rose in old oasis cities like Tashkent and newly irrigated plains supplied raw cotton for textiles. Soviet industrialization along the Trans-Siberian in Eastern Siberia and the Soviet Far East was accompanied by the development of mining and lumbering in the Arctic. The Trans-Siberian was double-tracked, and a branch extended north of Lake Baikal to the 2600-mile-long Lena River. Communication was developed down the great rivers to the north in the summertime and thence, with the use of ice breakers, through the Arctic Sea to European Russia. Airlines were also built up. This great economic growth, including the railroads, dams, mines, and lumbering, rested partly on the large-scale exploitation of millions of criminal and political prisoners at forced labor camps, especially in Siberia.

The Soviet revolution and the subsequent expansion of its totalitarian state power over Soviet Asia provided the peoples of East Asia with still another set of examples of modernization. Soviet policy toward ethnic minorities, for instance, at first promised them cultural equality and local autonomy, along with literacy, technical training, and the use of native languages. With this went the recruitment and training of native leaders to function in the Communist parties and governments of each of the

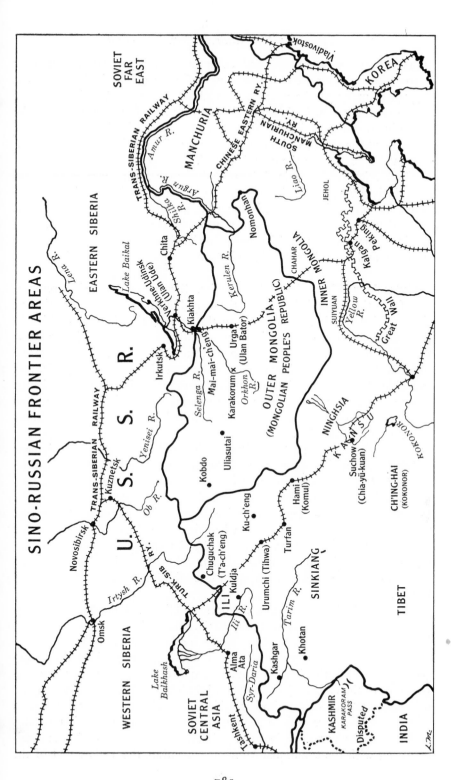

SINO-RUSSIAN FRONTIER AREAS

fourteen "ethnic" republics and other autonomous regions. But after 1929 collectivization destroyed the nomad way of life in Central Asia, as well as many of the nomads themselves; and after Stalin's purges of the 1930's the national minorities lost all prospect of autonomy under the mounting pressure for Russification and uniformity of culture and thought throughout the U.S.S.R. Much of this story, like the forced labor system, remained hidden from the outside world.

The Soviet expansion in Asia, with its many facets both institutional and ideological, is beyond our scope to characterize further, but in general it inaugurated a new era in Inner Asia, even more quickly and ruthlessly than the treaty system of a century before had inaugurated a new era in China and Japan. The new Russian influence began to supplant the older and more distant Chinese influence, especially in Outer Mongolia.

Outer Mongolia in the Ch'ing Empire. Because of Mongolia's remoteness from the sea and the rest of the world, a modern transformation of the traditional order, comparable to the process that began in China in the mid-nineteenth century, did not really get started until the early twentieth century. Even then, the traditional order in Mongolia was so different from that of the maritime, commercial areas of East Asia, and so stable after a millennium of autochthonous development, that change came at first only very slowly. Consequently, the effort to move from medieval to modern times has been telescoped in Outer Mongolia almost into a single generation.

The society of the steppe that we have characterized in Volume I (Chapter 7), in the vast terrain of the grasslands, had remained distinctively pastoral in its sheep-and-horse economy and tribal in its political organization. The grazing of sheep and the nomadic seasonal migration to different pasture were part of a long-established way of life that included Tibetan Lamaism, which had first spread into Mongolia in the thirteenth century. Subsequently, in the sixteenth and seventeenth centuries, two profound changes overtook Mongol society — the further growth of the Lamaist church and the establishment of the Ch'ing state power.

First of all, the second introduction of Tibetan Buddhism into Mongolia (see Vol. I, p. 361) was part of the process by which the reformist Yellow sect of Lamaism became the temporal power in Tibet and created a great monastic order in Mongolia. There it was headed by the Living Buddha at Urga (the Jebtsun-damba-hutukhtu; Mongolian *hutukhtu* corresponds to the Chinese *huo-fo*, "living Buddha," meaning a reincarnation of a *bodhisattva*, a deity who has achieved enlightenment but has elected to remain in this world to help others); the first incarnation of this Living Buddha was born in 1635. Displacing and to some degree amalgamating with the traditional Mongol shamanism, the Yellow sect of the

Lamaist church won converts quickly and became pervasively influential in Mongol life. In this same period the heads of the sect, the Dalai Lamas, gradually became installed at Lhasa as temporal rulers of Tibet, by an institutional development extending from the sixteenth century up to 1751. Similarly the primate of Tibetan Buddhism in Mongolia, the Living Buddha at Urga, gained wealth and influence though he had little centralized power — he was only *primus inter pares* among some eighty reincarnations who presided over various monasteries. As ongoing institutions, the monasteries accumulated something like half the landed property, as well as a near monopoly over learning, since church writings were in Tibetan, not Mongolian. By the nineteenth century the clergy in the monasteries constituted about a fifth of the population. Another fifth of the population customarily served the monasteries as retainers or vassals on their lands.

Meanwhile the Ch'ing state power had also spread over Mongolia. The dynasty of the Manchus, after its establishment at Peking in 1644, had developed its rule over its early Mongol allies in Inner Mongolia and had also extended it northward in defense of the Eastern Mongols (Khalkas; see map, page 47). Both helped the Ch'ing carry on the long struggle to subdue the Western Mongols, in particular the Dzungar tribe, who were not finally crushed until the Ch'ing conquest of Ili and Chinese Turkestan in the 1750's. The establishment of the Ch'ing protectorate over Tibet in this same period was motivated partly by concern for the control of the Lamaist church in Mongolia, as well as of the Mongol chieftains themselves.

Of the three main groups of Mongols, those in Inner Mongolia remained under the dominant influence of China, while the Western Mongols, farthest away, after being subjugated with much slaughter, remained scattered and uncohesive, some on the north Tibetan plateau in the Kokonor (Ch'ing-hai) region, some still in southern Russia on the lower Volga (called by the Russians "Kalmuks," see page 50). Only Outer Mongolia, the ancient homeland of Chinggis Khan, had the obvious ingredients for a modern state — a homogeneous population dominating a recognized area with their own tradition, language, and way of life. Here the Ch'ing perfected their system of control.

Under the Ch'ing secular order in all parts of Mongolia the mass of simple herdsmen-commoners were vassals who might own private property but also usually owed tribute or levies to the various grades of feudal nobility, who constituted about eight per cent of the population. At the top of this "nomadic feudalism," as it has been called, were the princes (in Chinese, *wang*), hereditary chieftains of the large tribal migrating units (*aimak*), each unit's members being descended from a common ancestor or at least having a common tradition, territory, and chieftain.

As a principle of organization the Manchus had applied to the Mongols their own "banner-arrow" system, creating basic groups of ten and, above them, a hierarchy of decimal units, so that within each tribe there were 150-man cavalry squadrons (called "arrows") that were grouped into "banners" and, in turn, into tribes (*aimak*) and leagues. (In the most populous region, Inner Mongolia, the Ch'ing listed 1256 "arrows" under 51 "banners" in 24 tribes in 6 leagues. Among the Western Mongols were 104 or more "arrows" under 66 "banners"; and in Outer Mongolia some 170 "arrows" were listed under 86 "banners.") Thus the Ch'ing did not disrupt the ancient tribes, but fragmented their military organization. The once fluid Mongol nation-in-arms could now be dominated by the Manchu rulers, its organization turned inward as a control mechanism, no longer a war machine for expansion. The once warlike Mongol nobility now received their titles and much-prized seals of office, their allotments of retainers and gifts (in return for tribute), all from the Ch'ing court. They had lost their independence but gained security and a personal relationship with the emperor at Peking.

After the mid-eighteenth century the Mongols were carefully controlled by ten or a dozen Ch'ing military governors or agents installed at strategic points, all connected with Peking by horse-post routes. The principal administrators of the system were the military governors at Uliasutai and Kobdo and the imperial agent or resident (*amban*) at Urga. Through these officials the Ch'ing used all the old devices inherited from the Ming and new ones in addition — assigning the tribes to fixed territories, confirming the succession of chieftains, conferring honors and titles, closely supervising all inter-tribal councils, keeping track of postal communication among leaders, and regulating trade at fixed markets — a comprehensive control system which brought tribute missions regularly to Peking and at the same time froze the inter-tribal political scene so that no new Chinggis Khan could possibly arise to mobilize the Mongol tribes for aggression. This strategy was aided by the fact that the age of firearms had already ended the millennial supremacy of the mounted archer in warfare.

Part of the Ch'ing strategy was to confirm in office and similarly control and sponsor the unwarlike dignitaries of the Lamaist church. As a result, Mongol society by the nineteenth century was divided between church and state. Channels of social and political mobility led into the respective hierarchies of the monasteries and the lay nobility, which now exhibited certain features of bureaucratic government. The Ch'ing protected this established order by forbidding Chinese colonization, controlling trade, and limiting contact. But in the late nineteenth century the whole system began to break down.

Outer Mongolia's National Revolution. By 1900, the pastoral economy, with its complex and sophisticated techniques for managing herds and flocks amid all the variations of pasture and weather, was being invaded from the Great Wall northward and from North Manchuria westward by the very different commercial-agricultural economy of China. Alarmed at Russian expansion in Manchuria, the Ch'ing in 1902 formally opened Mongolia to Chinese settlement, thus permitting a Chinese "secondary imperialism" to encroach upon Mongolia even as the outside world was invading China. Mongol princes soon lost their economic independence. Many found it expedient to let Chinese cultivators colonize their lands. Chinese traders selling tea, utensils, luxuries, and manufactured wares (like *yurt* frames) on credit to the Mongol princes got them into debt at interest and their tribal revenues and resources mortgaged far into the future. Ch'ing exactions added to the mounting burden on the common Mongol herdsmen. Large-scale Chinese immigration was facilitated after 1909 by the completion of the Chinese-built Peking-Kalgan-Suiyuan railway. All this led to the eventual absorption of Inner Mongolia into Chinese provincial administrations.

The chief modernizing influence on Outer Mongolia had come through contact with Russia via the communities along the Trans-Siberian Railway such as Irkutsk and Verkhne Udinsk (now Ulan-Ude) and on the Selenga River connecting with Lake Baikal. In this region ever since 1727 the Sino-Russian caravan trade had centered at the entrepot established by treaty at Mai-mai-ch'eng opposite Kiakhta, whence trade went via Urga to Peking. As Russian expansion was resumed in the nineteenth century, more centers were opened to trade, and the right to install consuls was granted by two Sino-Russian treaties: in 1860, consuls at Urga, Ili (Kuldja), Chuguchak, and Kashgar in the west; in 1881, consuls at Suchow (Chia-yü-kuan) and Turfan and, if trade developed, at Kobdo (installed 1911), Uliasutai (1905), Hami, Urumchi, and Ku-ch'eng. In short, Russia's "opening" of Mongolia and Sinkiang had paralleled, at least on paper, the contemporary "opening" of treaty ports in China.

In addition to this access to Outer Mongolia from the north, the Russification of the Buryat Mongols who had settled in the Lake Baikal region of Siberia created a community of Russian subjects who were still Mongolian-speaking and followers of the Lamaist church even though no longer pastoral nomads of the open steppe. The Buryats, cultural cousins from across the border, some of them Russian-educated, were natural diffusers of modernization. One of them settled in Urga as early as 1895 and began to print the first Mongolian newspaper and publish Western literature in translation. The Russian revolution of 1905 accordingly found echoes in Urga.

Russian-Outer Mongolian trade — for example, in Chinese tea and Mongolian meat for Siberia — was only part of Russia's long-term expansive interest. In 1907 Japan and Russia agreed on a division of spheres that allotted North Manchuria and Outer Mongolia to Russia, South

Manchuria and "eastern Inner Mongolia" to Japan (see page 481) — a division of interests which their ally Britain and their victim China both recognized by 1911.

To the Mongols, the more distant tsarist regime seemed less dangerous than the influx of Chinese settlers and exploitative traders under the Ch'ing overlords. The eighth Living Buddha at Urga (1870–1924), a Tibetan, though reputedly an alcoholic was an intelligent man and was still revered as a holy figure above party; he appealed for Russian aid to resist reforms and payments demanded by Peking in 1910. A Mongol mission went to Russia in July 1911. The Chinese revolution of October quickly precipitated a declaration of Outer Mongolian independence: on December 28, 1911, the Living Buddha was enthroned at Urga as king or *Bogdo-gegen*, a theocratic ruler advised by a council of nobles (*Khuriltai*), and Chinese debts were repudiated.

Instead of recognizing Outer Mongolia's independence, however, Russia worked out a formula: Chinese suzerainty and Outer Mongolian auton-omy under a *de facto* Russian protectorate. This left Russia free to develop her influence in the area without the interference of outside powers, since Outer Mongolia was not a sovereign state in international relations. Thus in January 1912 Russia, having begun to arm and train the Mongol army, disclaimed any territorial designs in Mongolia, and urged China to give up direct rule, stationing of troops, or colonization while still retaining "suzerainty." In November a Russian-Mongolian treaty recognized Mongolia's autonomy and Russia's trading privileges. A year later, in November 1913, a Sino-Russian agreement confirmed the formula of Chinese suzerainty and Mongolian autonomy. Finally, long negotiations produced in June 1915 a triangular Sino-Russian-Mongolian agreement reconfirming both this formula and Russia's economic rights, now made more urgent by her wartime demand for Mongolian livestock. Chinese merchants still outdid the Russians in Mongolia's retail trade, but Russia acquired in effect a protectorate, almost a co-suzerainty with China.

Outer Mongolian nationalism thus arose in an era of social change and wartime disorder. The church and the nobility, no longer protected by a Manchu emperor at Peking, were impotent in the face of Chinese eco-nomic encroachment and could only increase their exactions upon the impoverished Mongol commoners. The latter, however, as herdsmen and huntsmen, had the capacity to flee with their livestock and arms from their overlords' domains, especially toward the west. Banditry, disorder, and risings by secret organizations resulted.

Into this disintegrating political and social scene came foreign armies. During the civil war in Siberia, the Japanese in 1918 encouraged an army of the An-fu clique of North China warlords (under Hsü Shu-tseng, called "Little Hsü" to distinguish him from larger Hsüs) to occupy Urga, where Chinese claims were soon violently reasserted. In 1920, however, White

Russians (under the "Mad Baron," Ungern von Sternberg), also with Japanese support, drove out the Chinese in a reign of terror. Out of the Mongol partisan resistance to these invaders arose a revolutionary leadership allied with the Soviet revolution, which now proved a more powerful influence than either Japan or China.

The first leader, Sukebator (1893–1923), had served from 1912 to 1919 in the new Mongol army trained by Russian officers. His associate and successor, Choibalsang (1895–1952), also a poor boy from eastern Mongolia, had run away from a monastery, joined an interpreters' school, and studied among Russians at Irkutsk. In the winter of 1919–20, these two men, each then head of a resistance group, joined forces. Sukebator's leadership among militant lower-class nationalists and Choibalsang's acquaintance with Soviet doctrines of world revolution were combined in creating with Soviet guidance the Mongolian People's Revolutionary Party. With the help of Soviet troops it expelled the "Mad Baron" and set up a government in 1921.

In November, Sukebator and others visited Moscow: Lenin advised them, instead of calling their party Communist in a land without a middle class or proletariat, to develop toward socialism by promoting cooperatives and generally bypassing capitalism. Thus advised, the Mongol revolutionists moved first against the hated privileges of the nobility, leaving the more popular Lamaist church at first undisturbed. When the eighth Living Buddha died in 1924, they deferred seeking a successor and declared Mongolia a republic. But in this period the nobles and monasteries still possessed about half the wealth and most of the literacy and administrative skills, in a country far too vast and too thinly populated to be controlled from the one center of Urga (re-named Ulan Bator, "Red Hero"), much less by the Soviet Union from outside.

The revolution developed slowly. In 1925–28, later called a period of "Right deviation," the old ruling classes invested in the new cooperatives, foreign trade flourished, and even a "capitalist class," it is said, began to arise, with some pro-Chinese leanings. By 1929–32, however, later known as the period of "Left deviation," the Youth League and others within the People's Revolutionary Party had mobilized enough support in the countryside, where cooperatives now handled about a quarter of the trade, to begin under Choibalsang a more revolutionary program, confiscating the wealth of some 1500 noble families (including 200 clerics), expelling their members from office, and at its height imprisoning or executing several hundred persons. These excesses, generally paralleling contemporary developments in the U.S.S.R., led on to attempts at forced collectivization and the eviction of lamas from monasteries. This provoked a slaughter of livestock — a serious disinvestment — and large risings, so large that Soviet forces had to be called in to help suppress them. Moscow and the Comintern called a halt in mid-1932.

The next phase, known as the "new turn," installed Marshal Choibalsang as head of both party and government, increasingly close to the Soviet Union but espousing a gradualist, less coercive program. From 1933 the new attack on the church used divisive class warfare, trying to recruit the poor majority of lamas and monastic retainers to join cooperatives based on land or livestock expropriated from some of the 760-odd monasteries. Since these contained perhaps 100,000 persons, about a third of the adult males of the nation, the new government with its new security police and Soviet backers struggled to liquidate the church organization, get control of its manpower, and destroy its economic base, social status, and cultural tradition. Police-state terror completed this liquidation of religion in the late 1930's, again with many excesses. Only two chief monasteries now survive as relics.

This bitter social revolution was sanctioned partly by the menace of Japan's expanding militarism, which purposely stimulated Mongol nationalism against China on Outer Mongolia's eastern and southern borders. Inner Mongolian nationalists had long sought autonomy from the Chinese Republic. Nanking's Mongolian and Tibetan Affairs Commission had still served to link the Mongol nobility directly with the central government of China, but in the newly created Chinese border provinces of Chahar and Suiyuan local Chinese militarists had imposed their rule upon the remnants of the old Mongol polity. A leading Inner Mongolian anti-Chinese nationalist (Prince Demchukdonggrub; in Chinese, Te Wang) was accordingly supported by the Japanese, who invaded Chahar and Suiyuan in 1936–37 and backed him as head of a puppet regime which later became, from 1941 to 1945, the "Mongolian Autonomous Nation." Thus Japan competed with Russia for control of the Mongols in between them.

To counter Japan's expansion, a Soviet-Mongol mutual-aid treaty in 1936 brought in Soviet troops. Japanese probing of the Manchurian-Mongolian border near Nomonhan (Nomynkhan) and the Khalkhyn Gol (*gol* means river) — much like their probing of the Korean-Manchurian-U.S.S.R. border in the Changkufeng-Lake Khassan area in July–August 1938 — led to a great battle from May to September 1939, in which the Japanese were worsted. Thereafter they turned south to Greater East Asia.

The Mongolian People's Republic achieved formal independence from China in 1946 as a result of a plebiscite to which China had agreed in a Sino-Soviet treaty of 1945. The Republic entered the United Nations in 1961. It has benefited in its economic development from a favorable balance between thin population and extensive natural resources. Old industries like the manufacture of woolen and leather goods, dairying, and meat-packing have been modernized, and new mines and railways built up, as part of a general technological improvement affecting animal husbandry and agriculture as well. A university was founded in 1947.

The party dictatorship that has presided over these transformations, while thoroughly dependent on its Soviet mentors and allies, has dealt with a people and a way of life so distinctively different from that of both Europe and China as to make comparison very difficult.

Outer Mongolia's orientation toward the Soviet Union, though due to many factors, was doubtless facilitated by the tradition of orientation toward higher authorities abroad. Each of the two great institutions of Mongol society — the church and the nobility — for centuries past had had its apex outside Mongolia, in Lhasa and Peking, respectively. Meanwhile Inner Mongolia's absorption into the Chinese republic echoes the tradition of a strong China dominating her Inner Asian frontier.

China's Government of Sinkiang. Lying between Mongolia and Tibet, in the western arc of China's Inner Asian dependencies, Chinese Turkestan served for two thousand years as the pivotal communications zone between East and West Asia. Rulers of China, whenever they could, sent armies and planted military colonies in this zone as far as the Pamir massif and the Ili Valley.

Chinese Turkestan, however, was only the eastern part of the vast Central Asian region of ancient oasis-cities, trade routes, and grazing lands both east and west of the Pamirs that formed the traditional homeland of the Eastern Turks. These peoples — Uighurs, Kazakhs, Kirghiz, Uzbeks, and others — are distinct linguistic rather than racial sub-groups or "nationalities." They form the Turkic-speaking group within the Altaic family of languages, in which the other main groups are Mongolian and Tungusic (Manchu). The Eastern Turks were generally of Moslem faith, used the Arabic script, and shared a tradition of imperial grandeur going back to Chinggis Khan and Tamerlane. Yet in modern times, politically fragmented and scattered geographically on both sides of the Pamirs, they have been encroached upon and absorbed by the expanding empires of Russia and China. The name Turkestan, though used by geographers, has not designated a modern political unit embracing all these peoples.

In the late nineteenth century, Russian expansion into Central Asia west of the Pamirs came up against the rival British position on the south in Afghanistan and Kashmir. By 1907, when the two powers stabilized their relations all across Asia, they had long since given up any designs on Chinese Turkestan, leaving it for China to govern. Meantime, after Tso Tsung-t'ang's reconquest in the 1870's (see page 370), Peking in 1884 had combined the Ili region north of the T'ien Shan range with the Tarim basin on the south to create the new province of Sinkiang (the "New Dominion") with its capital at Urumchi (Tihwa). In this domain, twice the size of Texas, a complete Chinese administration was installed. Staffed partly from Tso's native province of Hunan, it continued to rule through the *beg* and other leaders of the local ruling class. Uighur Turks formed nine-tenths of the agricultural population in the oases of the Tarim basin and four-fifths of the total population (perhaps three million) of the whole province. The Kazakh and Kirghiz pastoral nomads of the Ili region were eastern offshoots of tribal peoples most of whom had come under Russian domination farther west. Chinese bureaucrats, military colonists, and merchants, the separate community of Chinese Moslems (Dungans), and remnants of various Mongol tribes added to the cultural and linguistic diversity of Sinkiang under Ch'ing rule.

From 1911 to 1949, Sinkiang remained under Chinese control but largely independent of the central government. In the disorder of the republican revolution, the last imperial governor "appointed" as his successor an experienced official from Yunnan, Yang Tseng-hsin (1859–1928), a metropolitan graduate of 1889 who had served twenty years in Kansu and Sinkiang. Yang vigorously suppressed disorder and by the usual Chinese divide-and-rule tactics continued to govern the mixed population of the province almost independently of the Peking government until his assassination sixteen years later in 1928.

The Soviet revolution, forcibly transforming the economy and society of the Kazakhs, Kirghiz, and other peoples of Soviet Central Asia in the 1920's and 1930's, brought new influences to bear upon Sinkiang. Trade between the two regions was encouraged by Sino-Soviet treaties of 1920 and 1924. Consulates were reopened on either side. Completion of the Turk-Sib Railway in 1930, another trade agreement, and reduced customs duties further facilitated the drainage of Sinkiang's commerce to the U.S.S.R. During the fifteen years of Japan's encroachment on Kuomintang China, far-off Sinkiang came more and more into the Soviet economic orbit.

Yet government from a distance through a Chinese minority was so deeply entrenched in this region of mixed population that no pro-Soviet or Uighur nationalist movement came to power. The strong man who ruled from 1933 to 1944 was General Sheng Shih-ts'ai (1895–   ), a Chinese from Manchuria who had studied in Japan and served under Chiang Kai-shek in the Northern Expedition of 1926–27. Faced with anti-Chinese rebellion, he proclaimed broad administrative reforms, promised religious freedom and equality among the linguistic "nationalities," and developed schools, newspapers, and cultural activities for Uighurs, Kazakhs, and other groups. Meanwhile he obtained Soviet loans, advisers, technical aid, arms, and even, when needed, the intervention of Soviet planes and troops, some of whom did not go home. Thus aided, Sheng defeated Chinese Moslem rebels, built up his secret police, and ruled like an autocrat. Sheng Shih-ts'ai's authoritarian reforms, though evidently opportunistic, encouraged the growth of a Uighur nationalist movement and contact with the U.S.S.R., and won the collaboration during the united front period of both Communist and non-Communist Chinese.

Soviet aid to Nationalist China, traversing Sinkiang in the years 1937–39, buttressed the growing Soviet influence. In 1942, however, Sheng turned against Soviet Russia and engineered a rapprochement with Chiang Kai-shek, who forehandedly removed him in 1944 before he could switch back to the Soviets.

In the late 1940's the Chinese National Government brought extensive military forces into Sinkiang but was unable to suppress a Uighur-Kazakh rebellion that had broken out in the Ili region in late 1944. It demanded representation of the non-Chinese in local government and set up a Soviet-oriented "East Turkestan Republic." By 1949, when all of Sinkiang went over to the new Chinese Communist regime, Soviet Russian influence in the province was at a high point.

Britain and China in Tibet

In both Tibet and Mongolia the lack of rainfall has made a sparse population rely on pastoral nomadism rather than agriculture. As outlying regions of the Ch'ing empire, Mongolia early confronted the expansion of Russia, and Tibet confronted that of British India. Yet the parallel is made superficial by the great difference in geography.

The Mongolian deserts and grasslands at altitudes of about 5000 feet provide corridors for trade, and the caravans that had crossed Mongolia between China and Russia for hundreds of years could be supplemented in the early twentieth century by automotive transport across the roadless steppe and eventually by railways, which reached Urga from the Trans-Siberian in 1949 and from China in 1955. In contrast, Tibet is geographically a sequestered plateau, much of it treeless and windswept at 16,000 feet, ringed by mountain ranges at 20,000 feet or more that make it difficult of access. The medieval European and Arab travelers who followed the caravan routes to the Mongol capitals at Karakorum or Peking (see Vol. I, p. 283) usually heard about Tibet but never got there. Wheeled vehicles were largely unknown in Tibet until the building of motor roads in the 1950's; railways are still in the future.

Tibet's relative inaccessibility within its mountain barriers made possible an eclectic synthesis of cultural elements that filtered in from all four sides — India, China, West Asia, and even Mongolia — to produce, for example, a distinctive alphabet, calendar, architecture, religion, and religious art. Under the seventh-century unifier, Song-tsan Gam-po,[1] who founded his capital at Lhasa, the Tibetans began to play a role on the fringes of Chinese, Indian, and Central Asian history. It was a late, rather debased Buddhism from Northern India, developing its Tibetan form by fusion with the local Bon cult, that produced the Lamaist church

---

[1] The scholarly transcription Srong-btsan sGam-po includes letters of the Tibetan alphabet still written but not pronounced.

with its concern for magic and demons. Nevertheless the reformed or Yellow sect founded by Tsong-kha-pa (d. 1419), by spreading over Mongolia, eventually gave Lhasa the importance we have noted in Ch'ing imperial politics.

The Manchu and British empires had a first confrontation in Tibet in the late eighteenth century. The Ch'ing interventions of 1720, 1728, and 1750 had made the Dalai Lama the temporal ruler at Lhasa under the supervision of residents (*ambans*) sent from Peking. Ch'ing influence discouraged the fitful activity pursued by Jesuit and Capuchin missionaries at Lhasa until the 1740's but could not yet seal Tibet off from India. In the late eighteenth century the number-two reincarnation in the church, the Tashi Lama (generally known as the Panchen Lama), at his monastery of Tashi-lhunpo at Shigatse acquired great influence as temporal ruler in western Tibet. This dignitary, the sixth Panchen Lama (d. 1780), whose monastery played a great role in trade with India, received the East India Company's first emissary, George Bogle, sent by Warren Hastings in 1774–75; and another emissary, Samuel Turner, visited his successor in 1783.

The potentialities of British trade with western Tibet were eclipsed when the warlike Gurkhas, having conquered Nepal in the 1760's, invaded Tibet in 1788 and again in 1791, capturing Shigatse and plundering Tashi-lhunpo. The Panchen Lama's appeals to the British at Calcutta were in vain, whereas the Ch'ien-lung Emperor, whose forces had already waged nine victorious campaigns on the frontiers of the empire (see Vol. I, p. 390), now capped them all by sending two armies, by forced marches from the east and north, over the roof of the world to drive the Gurkhas all the way back into the vale of Khatmandu, the Nepalese capital. The Gurkhas made amends and were enrolled as tributaries of the Ch'ing, to send missions to Peking every five years. (From 1792 to 1908, at least ten such missions were recorded.) Meanwhile British neutrality, motivated partly by concern for the Canton trade, had earned only the ill will of both sides. The Ch'ing closed Tibet to Europeans and perfected their control over the Dalai Lama, who was no longer rivaled by the Panchen Lama.

Thus despite the continuous contact with India, history had overcome geography to connect Tibet politically with the Ch'ing empire of East Asia. Tibetan life centered in the southern river valley of the Tsangpo (Brahmaputra) at the comparatively low altitude of 12,000 feet, in a region which was farthest from China and closest to India; but the spectacular triple cordon of the Himalaya ranges, rising from the subtropical heat of India to an arctic climate within 100 miles, had become a historical, cultural, and psychological barrier as much as a physical one. In the late nineteenth century, with Lhasa only 330 miles (for the modern mail, eight days) from Gangtok — the capital of Sikkim, near the Indian railway built to Darjeeling in 1881 — the Dalai Lama still acknowledged the overlordship of the Son of Heaven, more than 2000 miles away in Peking.

The eighteenth-century achievement of the Ch'ing protectorate over Tibet, just in time to close the country and forestall European contact, takes on added luster if we look at the close relations of Tibet with the hill states along the 1500-mile arc of the Himalayas, from Ladakh through Nepal, Sikkim, Bhutan, and Assam to Northern Burma (see map, page 798). Of the caravan routes converging on Lhasa, the long northern road from Lanchow and Sining crosses mountains nearly 20,000 feet high, while the eastern road from Szechwan via Tachienlu, Batang, and Chamdo is equally tortuous, crossing the parallel defiles of the Yangtze, Mekong, and Salween rivers. The easier road from Lhasa west up the Tsangpo Valley, on the other hand, connects with short routes leading south to the hill states and India — from Gyantse down the Chumbi Valley to Gangtok and Darjeeling; from other Western junctions south to Khatmandu and Taklakot; and from Gartok westward down the Indus River to Leh, the capital of Ladakh, 900 miles from Lhasa. This western route connects both with Kashmir farther west and also, via the Karakoram and other passes in the Aksai Chin area, with the trade centers of Khotan, Yarkand, and Kashgar to the north in Sinkiang. Over these routes moved not only the brick tea and other exports from China and the wool exports from Tibet but also the pilgrims visiting Lhasa both from Mongolia and from the Himalayan states. Ladakh in particular was close to Tibet in race, religion, and culture and sent triennial tribute-and-trade missions to Lhasa. In return, Chinese tea was brought to Leh annually by the Dalai Lama's personal trader, and Ladakh also monopolized the supply of Tibetan wool to make Kashmir shawls.

As Britain by degrees established protectorates over the hill states, an ambiguous dual allegiance made them face two ways — traditionally and culturally toward Tibet, but now increasingly in trade and politics toward British India. War with Nepal in 1814–16 established a British resident in Khatmandu, a protectorate over Sikkim (1817) on the east, and control over territories up to the Tibetan frontier on the west. China did not retaliate against the British trade at Canton, as had been feared, but Ch'ing officials at Gartok and other posts continued to turn back all commercial prospectors from Simla and elsewhere who sought access to Tibet.

International relations among the Himalayan states became very complex. A conqueror from the Sikh kingdom, expanding on the upper Indus, took over Ladakh in 1834, and in 1841 invaded western Tibet beyond Gartok almost to Nepal. Tibetan forces retaliated vigorously, invading Ladakh and besieging Leh. A Ladakh-Tibet treaty signed there in October 1842 restored the *status quo ante*. This continued when the British acquired in 1846 their protectorate over Ladakh and Kashmir. In 1861 a British military expedition "opened" Sikkim. In 1865 a war stabil-

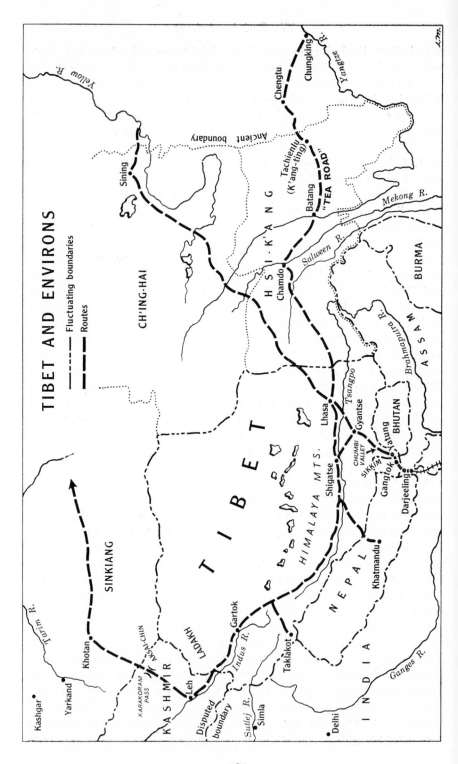

TIBET AND ENVIRONS

- –·– Fluctuating boundaries
- ▬ ▬ Routes

ized British relations with Bhutan. Meanwhile the tribute missions from Nepal via Lhasa to Peking strained relations between the Tibetans and the Gurkhas, who in 1856 had bellicosely forced Tibet by treaty to accept a Nepalese resident in Lhasa and actually pay an annual tribute to them in Khatmandu. But for Europeans Tibet continued to be the "Forbidden Land."

Peking's suzerainty over the Dalai Lama, who in turn had a politico-commercial-religious influence among the hill states, was eventually called into question in much the same way as Peking's suzerainty over Liu-ch'iu (Ryūkyū), Korea, or Vietnam. An overlordship that premodern distances had made traditionally passive now was required to be actively asserted or else relinquished — Peking had to take responsibility for the tangled foreign relations of Tibet. The original Ch'ing strategic interest in Lhasa as the key to the Lamaist church in Mongolia had been reinforced by the Chinese commercial interest in the valuable brick tea trade from Szechwan to Lhasa. Peking's concern to preserve the *status quo* generally coincided with the interests of the Tibetan hierarchy. Their dominance at Lhasa and in monasteries throughout Tibet rested on twin monopolies of religious and commercial life, which could be undermined by an inflow of tea imports, irreligious persons, or even ideas.

From the late 1860's to the end of the century the Ch'ing seclusion policy in Tibet challenged a whole generation of Westerners — French Catholic missionaries in eastern Tibet, British consular travelers on the trade routes, innumerable chambers of commerce with hopeful schemes for expanding trade, and a notable series of explorers from many lands, who emulated their fellows in the Congo or the Arctic. Many tried to reach the sacred city of Lhasa. The intrepid French Lazarists, Huc and Gabet, had reached it from Mongolia in 1846. Their would-be successors included the great Russian explorer Prjevalski, who completed four expeditions between 1870 and 1885; the American diplomat W. W. Rockhill, whose second trip in 1892 covered 8000 miles in eleven months, crossing 69 passes at over 14,500 feet; Prince Henry of Orleans; and many others. All were turned back from Lhasa.

The Ch'ing seclusion policy was acceptable to Britain as long as it was enforced to keep others, especially Russia, out of Tibet and so away from the hill states on India's border. Britain had formally acknowledged Ch'ing control over the foreign relations of Tibet by a Sino-British "Burma-Tibet convention" of 1886, in return for China's recognition of British rule over Upper Burma. By another Sino-British convention on Sikkim and Tibet, Peking in 1890 gave up the Sino-Tibetan claims to suzerainty over Sikkim; and Sino-British regulations for India-Tibet trade via the Chumbi Valley were signed in 1893. But trade from the new trading post of Yatung, supervised by the Chinese Maritime Customs at the foot of the valley, was obstructed at the top by Tibetan officials who followed the old instead of the new regulations, to which they had not been a party. Britain's effort to stabilize her Tibetan relations by a settlement with Peking also ran into the fact that after 1893 Peking's old-style suzerainty over Lhasa grew weaker there and less popular than ever; yet Britain had no means of direct contact with Lhasa either to negotiate frontier grievances or to deal with the new nationalistic spirit of independence from China which attended the coming-of-age of the Thirteenth Dalai Lama. (His predecessors since 1804 had all died in various unfortunate ways before maturity, leaving the regents to continue in power.)

The British finally undertook a forward move in Tibet out of fear of Russia. Trade was an excuse more than a motive. The traditional fear of Russian expansion reached a new height soon after the energetic Lord Curzon became viceroy of India in 1899, for the young Dalai Lama not only established an arsenal at Lhasa but seems to have moved to offset Chinese weakness, French proselytism, and British expansiveness by contact with Russia. Among his tutors was a Russian subject, a learned Buryat Mongol named Dorjiev, who had studied in Lhasa since the 1880's at the great Drepung monastery. He was now used by the young Dalai to develop direct contact with Tsar Nicholas II.

Dorjiev's journeys from Lhasa unobserved through India to Russia to see the tsar, in 1900 and 1901, roused a host of rumors about Russian ambitions. Seeing Russia's current expansion in Manchuria and elsewhere and Britain's difficulties world-wide, Curzon feared that Russian influence, once lodged in Tibet, could penetrate the hill states. "Tibet itself," he wrote, "and not Nepal must be the buffer state that we endeavor to create." Yet his repeated efforts just to communicate with the Dalai Lama all failed. Sino-British trade and boundary negotiations in 1902–03 could not meet the basic need to keep Russia out of Lhasa. Yet rumors persisted, in Khatmandu, Darjeeling, Peking, and elsewhere, of secret treaties giving Russia a protectorate over Tibet. Curzon's response was the Younghusband mission, backed by 8000 troops, which alternately fought and negotiated its way to Gyantse and Lhasa in 1904 and there signed an Anglo-Tibetan convention that would have established in effect a British protectorate.

By late 1904, however, the Russian menace had already been diminished by the Russo-Japanese War, while Curzon's superiors in London were anxious to curb him and get a rapprochement with St. Petersburg. Colonel Francis Younghusband's convention was therefore modified, its indemnity reduced, and British access to Lhasa given up. Yet, ironically, the authority of the Dalai Lama, who had fled to Mongolia, and his capacity for independence had been impaired. In 1906 Ch'ing suzerainty was reasserted and acknowledged in an Anglo-Chinese agreement. Finally, the overall Anglo-Russian agreement of 1907 provided for mutual abstention from Tibet.

Britain's uncertainty whether to deal with China as suzerain power or with Tibet as an independent country was thereafter resolved by events.

As part of the late Ch'ing "secondary imperialism" already noted in the case of Mongolia, Peking announced a broad reform program, suppressed risings in eastern Tibet, and sent an army to Lhasa in 1910. The Dalai Lama and his faithful Dorjiev fled this time to India.

Contrapuntally, the Chinese revolution of 1911 led to a collapse of this newly asserted control. Yüan Shih-k'ai's government laid claim to Tibet and Mongolia but lacked strength to reconquer them. Chinese forces and officials having been expelled, the Dalai Lama in January 1913 declared the independence of his country and made a treaty with the Living Buddha at Urga in which the two prelates recognized the independence of their respective states. After Anglo-Chinese-Tibetan negotiations at Simla, Britain in 1914 recognized Tibetan independence while China refused to do so. Eastern (or "Inner") Tibet, retained under Chinese administration, was made after 1928 into the provinces of Hsi-k'ang and Ch'ing-hai. "Outer" Tibet, the central and western areas, developed its independent relations with British India, accepting British missions and eventually a trade agent at Lhasa and some aid in education and modernization. British or Indian suzerainty was never asserted. China, both Nationalist and Communist, retained her claims.

PROBLEMS OF MODERNIZATION AMONG CHINA'S NEIGHBORS

In the 1960's we may look back on colonialism and semi-colonialism (the unequal-treaty system) as a transitory phase in the process of modernization, based on the hard contemporary facts of the superior power and skill of the colonial and treaty powers. It is further evident that the colonial and treaty systems, by which the powers dominated East and Southeast Asia in this era, were undermined and overthrown by the continued diffusion of the very factors of modernization that had created them. The precise designation of these factors may vary with the observer, without invalidating this proposition. Commerce, evangelism, nationalism, individualism, and technology, it was suggested in Chapter 1, all contributed to the original expansion of Europeans to the East. Both Japan and China responded by assimilating elements of Western material technology, learning, political institutions, and social values, transmuting these into the twin drives toward nationalism and industrialism. A similar diffusion in the peripheral areas has culminated in the rise of nationalist movements and independent states.

The political ideas and values of the Western peoples included doctrines of national sovereignty, individual rights, and self-government under law that always conflicted with colonialism. Once adopted by native elites, such ideas enabled them to lead their peoples toward national independence. At the same time missionaries who built up a local Christian community and Western educators or other specialists who trained their Asian counterparts, insofar as they succeeded, made themselves both unnecessary and unwanted. The end of colonialism has altered the circumstances of this diffusion without necessarily checking it. The difference now is that national independence offers more freedom to select and synthesize modern ways with the underlying tradition of the local society and culture. Modernization is now world-wide; it is not Westernization.

Yet within this broad (and optimistic) framework, the less numerous peoples around the edge of China labor under severe handicaps. Independence once acquired must be defended, but the smaller size of the peripheral states, compared with China, leaves them vulnerable to a new Chinese power that has inherited a tradition of Chinese supremacy over surrounding peoples. The vitality of the Sinocentric tradition in East Asian politics is indicated by the fact that most states or peoples on China's borders are split in two politically — witness Vietnam, Laos, Mongolia, Korea, and the Turkic-speaking peoples of Central Asia.

Meanwhile, the strenuous and costly internal process of modernizing an ancient society and culture taxes the material and human resources of each new state. Tremendous effort and skill are required, for example, to build up and staff mass media in one's own language. Yet how long can a modernizing nation survive without its own press, radio, and television networks? Such considerations suggest that new states, formed in an age when national sovereignty is shadowed by the rise of super-powers with super-technology, cannot meet their problems on the characteristic national basis of the nineteenth century. In short, the past experience of nationalism in the West offers no reliable models for the future of nationalism elsewhere. Warfare between neighbors, one chief expression of nationalism in the past, today involves the rest of the world.

It would be stretching a point to discern common cultural traits or other denominators among the many peoples and dozen nations on the periphery of China. The local synthesis resulting from the infusion of Western and modern ways into traditional Asian societies has been different and unique in each case. Without attempting here to forecast the future balance between the influences of "Western" and "Asian" traditions, we would note only one point: in the rise of nationalism in all these countries, the fate of individualism has generally remained obscure.

The Western liberal assertion of the supreme importance of the individual — resting on such concepts as the sanctity of the person (the immortality of the soul), the supremacy of law, and natural rights — grew to maturity in the era of Europe's expansion, and this expansion into the open spaces of the New World eventually fostered the egalitarian frontier societies of America and the British Commonwealth countries. European expansion into the Old World's crowded lands, on the other hand, generally created colonial regimes under ruling classes composed of the European colonial elite and the local Asian aristocracy, old or new, associated with it.

When imperialism in time gave rise to nationalism, and the nationalist leadership emerged from the new social class of the Western-educated native elite, determined to end Western domination, it remained a small elite, leading peoples traditionally accustomed to aristocratic rule. Nationalism as a political ideal grew faster than mass education and the election process as a political way of life. Conscientious colonial administrators in fact often distrusted the nationalist leadership because of its oligarchic tendencies.

National independence has thus left unresolved the fate of individualism in most of these Asian countries. As a matter of necessary strategy, national freedom has taken precedence over individual freedom and legal rights. Indeed the Western ideal of individualism, in these older and more crowded societies, has sometimes seemed antisocial, selfish, and anarchic, just as Confucian scholars, Japanese generals, and Comintern organizers, among others, have at various times so roundly declared. The result, both in the new nations of Southeast Asia and in the half-dozen republics of the Chinese culture area, has frequently been party tutelage and strong-man rule.

This collectivist tendency, toward the political mobilization of newly educated masses under an organizing elite, gains internal strength from the urgent need for dominant leadership in making great changes. Traditions of social harmony under monarchic rule, moreover, make it difficult to distinguish power-holders from their policies and hence to let opponents of policy function as a loyal opposition. In any case, the influence of nearby China, though it rouses some neighbors to seek allies from a distance, is portentous; for here is an overt example of collectivism under party dictatorship as the way of modernization. China's metamorphosis is the biggest fact on her neighbors' horizon.

10

East Asia in the New

International World

THE PACIFIC WAR

The transformation of East Asia in modern times comes to a climax with the military defeat and reconstruction of Japan and the Communist-led revolution in China. The war brought great suffering to all the peoples of East Asia. Although the Japanese, utilizing the skills of an advanced economy, eventually won through to an era of prosperity, they experienced many years of confusion and travail, while the Chinese and the Koreans (like the Vietnamese) have suffered disunity, civil war, exhaustion, and constant anxiety. Americans have undergone no comparable disasters or difficulties. This divergent experience of the American and the Asian peoples tends to widen the gap between them. Since the past affects the East Asian present more pervasively than is usually realized, the Japanese, Korean, and Chinese peoples' views of their recent history, like our own grasp of the world process, will influence future relations across the Pacific.

MASS EDUCATION. This woodcut of a "winter school," showing warmly clad pupils studying on a brick bed (*k'ang*) heated by a coal fire, illustrates the Chinese Communist use of an old pictorial form that can be cheaply reproduced for mass distribution and propaganda.

Pearl Harbor and Japan's Blitzkrieg in East Asia. The surprise attack by carrier-based planes of a Japanese striking force, sinking most of the battleships of the United States Pacific Fleet at its Pearl Harbor base in Hawaii on the morning of December 7, 1941, was both a brilliant tactical victory and a disastrous psychological error. Seven battleships, many lesser vessels, and over half the American aircraft on the island were destroyed or gravely damaged in a few minutes. But opinion within the United States, so long divided by isolationism, was unified within a few hours. Continued Japanese expansion in Southeast Asia might have left the American people still divided and uncertain. Pearl Harbor shocked them into an all-out war effort.

The shock became all the greater when it was realized that America's unprecedented defeat at Pearl Harbor was due to unpreparedness of mind more than of materiel. Ambassador Grew had warned from Tōkyō that Japan might attack with dramatic suddenness, as in previous wars. Decoding Japanese secret messages, Washington had for weeks been expecting an attack somewhere. At Pearl Harbor, enemy submarines had been sighted and depth charges dropped, and the approaching planes had actually been detected by radar, well before the attack. Yet the American forces on that Sunday morning were not mentally alert to the danger.

The Pearl Harbor disaster was lessened by the fact that three aircraft carriers of the Pacific Fleet were at sea, unharmed, and the sunken battleships had been close to obsolescence. But a second disaster, in some ways even greater though less publicized, followed in the Philippines. Despite the imminence of war, United States bases under General Douglas MacArthur were undermanned, poorly armed, and inadequately linked by communications. Their bombers and fighters took to the air but landed for lunch and refueling. Eight or nine hours after Pearl Harbor, Japanese air attacks caught them on the ground, lined up wing to wing. Stripped of air cover and without naval strength, the Philippines became indefensible. Invaded on December 10, they were completely in Japanese hands by May 6, 1942, after bitter fighting on the mountainous Bataan Peninsula and the island fortress of Corregidor in Manila Bay. The crippling of the United States Pacific Fleet and the destruction of American air power in the Philippines pulled the cork from the Southeast Asian bottle. Within hours the way lay open for Japanese amphibious drives through the Philippines, Borneo, and Celebes, and through Malaya and Sumatra, to Java. (See chronology, page 766.)

Meanwhile a Japanese offensive was mounted from Indo-China through Thailand to Burma. By the end of May 1942, Japanese troops had pushed far into northern Burma, closing the Burma Road and cutting off supplies to China except for the small quantities that could be flown in over the "Hump" from India. Trying to counter Japan's seaborne offensive against Malaya, the British battleship *Prince of Wales* and the battle-cruiser *Repulse* lost their air cover and were sunk by carrier-based planes on December 10. Japanese troops then advanced through "impenetrable" jungles to take Singapore from the rear. The great naval base, its defenses facing the sea, fell on February 15. Invading the Netherlands East Indies on January 11, 1942, the Japanese found the Dutch forces small and the Indonesians uninterested in a defense for the sake of the Dutch; by March the islands were in Japanese hands.

Elated by success, the Japanese army favored concentrating on the Asian continent to subdue China and deal with Russia, while the navy proposed to take Hawaii and cut American-Australian communications in the South and Southwest Pacific. Wake Island had been taken on December 13 and Guam on the 20th; and in the early months of 1942 the Japanese moved into the Solomon, Ellice, and Gilbert island chains, and into northern New Guinea. In the summer the western Aleutian islands of Kiska and Attu were occupied. By this time Japan possessed a vast oceanic and continental empire stretching from Sakhalin 4000 miles south almost to Australia, and from Burma 6000 miles east to the Gilberts.

Japan's military leaders, however, missed the lesson of their victory: they failed to give immediate top priority to building air power. Their military technology also failed to keep up with the American develop-ment of weapons systems that used radar, homing torpedoes, proximity fuses, and other novel devices. Meanwhile Tōkyō and Berlin, unlike the Allies, failed to coordinate their efforts or even exchange adequate intelli-gence. Worse still, competing interests within Japan's high command prevented an efficient unity of effort: the army, for example, preferred invading India to defending the Pacific islands.

In the second phase of the war, from mid-1942 to mid-1944, the Japanese tried to consolidate their empire and exploit it economically, while the Allies assailed its periphery. The American counterattack was slowed by two factors: the "Germany first" decision of the Anglo-American Combined Chiefs of Staff, and the time-lag between the beginning of the war and the full conversion of the American economy to war production. But Anglo-American plans were coordinated by the combined staffs in Washington and at top-level conferences at Casablanca in January 1943, at Quebec in August, and at Cairo in December.

The first major engagement that was not a disaster for the Allies was the naval Battle of the Coral Sea fought to the northeast of Australia on May 7–8, 1942. Losses were about equal. But since United States produc-tion was greater, this meant an Allied gain. A greater victory came with the Battle of Midway a month later. A major Japanese armada came to take Midway Island, the westernmost of the Hawaiian chain, and to annihilate the remainder of the United States Pacific Fleet. But Japanese codes had been broken, and American planes were thereby enabled to destroy the four carriers that were the heart of the superior Japanese fleet. Losing its striking force, Japan's far-flung empire was henceforth on the defensive.

Two other Allied actions during these years occurred at the southern rim of the Japanese sphere. In New Guinea, amid jungles and mountains inhabited only by a people of the stone age, a small force first checked the Japanese advance from the north, and then, in fighting that lasted from October 1942 to August 1944, won the island. In the Solomons, an Allied counteroffensive was begun in Guadalcanal at the southern end of the island chain in August 1942. By February 1943, after desperate fighting, the island was completely in Allied hands.

The Allied Drive on Japan. In the final phase of the war two great island-hopping, amphibious offensives brought Allied troops to the doorstep of Japan. One of these returned MacArthur to the Philippines (Leyte, October 1944), where one of the most destructive campaigns of the war was fought. By June 1945 the Philippines were in Allied hands. The other offensive swung up from the South Pacific. It began in the Gilbert Islands (Tarawa, November 1943), then moved to the Marshalls and the Carolines; it next took a 1000-mile jump to the Marianas (Saipan, June 1944) and then to Iwo Jima. Saipan brought Japan within bomber range; Iwo Jima was taken to provide a haven for disabled bombers. In April 1945 the two offensives converged on Okinawa, which fell in June. These offensives required the development of new amphibious techniques that combined air superiority, naval barrages, landing craft, and men. Defensive techniques were also perfected. Considering the minuteness of the territories that were fought over, the losses were enormous. On the Japanese side more than 85 per cent of the defenders at Okinawa were killed; on the Allied side there were 49,100 casualties, about a fifth of which were at sea where massed attacks by suicide planes called *kamikaze*[1] sank 34 ships and damaged 368 others.

In the overall strategy of the war two factors were perhaps crucial. One was the Allied success in isolating Japan from her empire. This was accomplished by the destruction of her merchant marine, navy, and naval air power. At the start of the war Japan had a merchant marine of six million tons. Conquest and new construction brought this to a total of over ten million. But by the end of the war all but 1.8 million tons, mostly small wooden ships plying in coastal waters, had been sunk. Attacks by surface ships accounted for 10 per cent of the Japanese losses; aircraft for 30 per cent; and submarines, a major offensive weapon, for 60 per cent. As Japan became increasingly less able to transport men, equipment, food supplies, or raw materials, her economy began to weaken

---

[1] "Divine winds," referring to the typhoons which destroyed invading Mongol fleets in the thirteenth century; see Vol. I, page 542.

and her empire to wither on the vine. Once cut off, Burma, Malaya, Thailand, Indo-China, the Dutch East Indies, China, and Japanese military bases on Pacific islands became almost irrelevant to the course of the war. Nevertheless, fighting continued on many fronts. Anglo-American-Chinese forces launched offensives in Burma (March 1944 to July 1945), Russia invaded Manchuria in the last days of the war, and Chinese forces, both Nationalist and Communist, attacked Japanese positions in China along a front of several thousand miles. These actions affected the situation in postwar Asia, but they contributed only indirectly to the defeat of Japan.

A second crucial strategic factor was the destruction by firebomb raids of Japan's industrial facilities and civilian housing. Begun during the last half of 1944, the raids mounted in intensity and culminated in saturation bombing by thousand-plane flights in the months preceding surrender. Fearful destruction was wrought in Japan's densely populated cities built of wood, paper, reeds, and tile. On March 10, 1945, for example, one hundred and thirty B-29's dropped incendiary bombs in parallel swathes through Tōkyō, killing over 100,000 persons. In all, 668,000 civilians died and 2.3 million homes were destroyed. By the last days of the war, railroads were breaking down, coal production was falling short of industrial needs, oil was almost gone, aircraft production was dropping, nonmilitary production was nil, and the average civilian was consuming less than 1500 calories a day. Japan was beaten, yet would not acknowledge defeat.

The Politics of War and Defeat. At the outset of the war, Tōjō Hideki had been in a strong position. A general on active duty, he was both prime minister and his own army minister. Wearing two hats, he could oversee both civil and military affairs. He donned a third in February 1944, becoming chief of the General Staff to coordinate administrative and command functions within the army. In a general election in April 1942, the Imperial Rule Assistance Association (see page 602) secured the election of a pro-Tōjō Diet which assured him of support in that quarter as well. Controlling the top posts and with this broad base, he continued in power until July 1944.

Yet Tōjō was not a dictator like Hitler, Mussolini, or Franco. He was the first among many generals and admirals who led the military, the most powerful elite of wartime Japan. Above Tōjō was the emperor, and about the emperor were the senior statesmen (*jūshin*) — the inner minister, the president of the Privy Council, and various former prime ministers such as Konoe, Yonai, and Hiranuma — who maintained extensive contacts with officials of the numerous wartime ministries.

At the start, Japan's strategy was to negotiate a peace when the United States grew tired of fighting. But from 1943, as the tide of battle turned

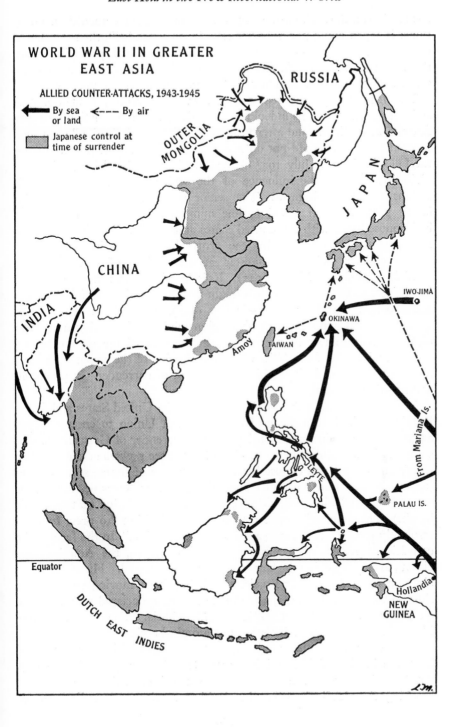

WORLD WAR II IN GREATER
EAST ASIA

ALLIED COUNTER-ATTACKS, 1943-1945

By sea or land   By air

Japanese control at time of surrender

RUSSIA

OUTER MONGOLIA

CHINA

INDIA

JAPAN

IWO-JIMA

OKINAWA

Amoy

TAIWAN

LEYTE

From Mariana Is.

PALAU IS.

Equator

Hollandia

NEW GUINEA

DUTCH EAST INDIES

against Japan, those about the emperor began to favor immediate negotiations: if Japan could not fight her enemies to a standstill, then she should make peace before all was lost. In the minds of several, pessimism about the war was mingled with fear that radicals in the army would impose a system of "imperial communism" if conditions in Japan grew worse.

The meetings of the senior statesmen were secret, their thoughts ambiguous, their actions indecisive. The danger of assassination by army fanatics was still real, and after years of "spiritual mobilization" even such veteran politicians could not openly speak out in favor of peace. Finally the fall of Saipan in July 1944 created a crisis. Ministerial opposition to Tōjō joined with the influence of the senior statesmen to force his resignation and retirement. The senior statesmen wanted to appoint in his place Admiral Yonai (prime minister January-July 1940), who had opposed war with the United States and Britain. But Yonai was too moderate to be accepted by the army; he became, instead, deputy prime minister and naval minister in the cabinet of General Koiso Kuniaki (July 1944–March 1945). Koiso's cabinet was in turn toppled by the fall of Okinawa, which brought to power retired Admiral Suzuki Kantarō (prime minister April–August 1945), former head of the Privy Council. Suzuki appointed as his foreign minister Tōgō Shigenori, who clearly favored an early peace. Yet, in the face of the unconditional-surrender demand of the Allies which left the fate of the emperor unclear, not even Tōgō could bring himself to speak of surrender. In public all reaffirmed Japan's intention to fight to the end.

At the Yalta Conference in February 1945 the United States and Great Britain had obtained a pledge from the Soviet Union to enter the war against Japan within three months after the surrender of Germany, which came in May. In July the declaration of the three powers at the Potsdam Conference bid Japan choose between an "order of peace, security, and justice" if she would surrender unconditionally, or "utter destruction" if she refused. (Behind this ultimatum was the knowledge of the atomic bomb.) The official Japanese response was a decision "to press forward resolutely to carry the war to a successful conclusion." In the face of the casualties expected in an autumn invasion of Japan, the American decision to use the bomb was virtually uncontested. Hiroshima was obliterated on August 6. Russia, which had been moving troops from Europe to East Asia since the German surrender, declared war on Japan on August 8, and began to invade Manchuria. The following day Nagasaki was destroyed by a second atomic bomb.

Even after these shocks the military remained adamant, unmoved by those in the cabinet and Supreme Council who favored surrender. An Imperial Conference was therefore called at which the emperor, breaking the deadlock, gave the decision to those counseling surrender. One condition, however, was agreed on by all: the prerogatives of the emperor as "sovereign ruler" must not be prejudiced. This was rejected by the Allies. On the morning of August 14 a second Imperial Conference was called; opinion split three to three, the two chiefs of staff and the army minister opposing Naval Minister Yonai, Prime Minister Suzuki, and Foreign Minister Tōgō. Again the emperor, saying that "the unendurable must be endured," gave his support to the latter group favoring unconditional surrender. It was a final commentary on the orthodoxy that had emerged in Japan after 1890: although Japan was smashed and beaten, only the emperor could put the imperial system in jeopardy. On August 17 a new cabinet was formed by Prince Higashikuni to represent Japan in the surrender ceremonies. By the end of the month General Douglas MacArthur and his forces had moved into the Tōkyō area, and the signing of the Instrument of Surrender took place on September 2 on the U.S.S. *Missouri* in Tōkyō Bay.

THE OCCUPATION OF JAPAN

Japan's history was significantly changed by America's postwar occupation of the country. Though lasting only seven years, it was decisive for Japan's subsequent development. The Occupation was a success because it built on earlier trends, yet in crucial respects it produced changes which would not have occurred had Japan not fallen into American hands. In some ways the changes were revolutionary, even though imposed from outside.

Japan in August 1945 was in chaos, her people physically spent and psychically benumbed. Cities had been gutted by bombs, factories destroyed or damaged by fire. Railroads were dilapidated. People were hungry and ill-clothed. There was, moreover, no precedent in Japanese history for defeat. In war the Japanese soldier usually fought until killed, or often killed himself when the situation became hopeless. Surrender was socially unacceptable — and social pressures were far stronger than in the West. Even the civilian populace was psychologically prepared to fight to the end and was girding for the final "battle of Japan" (training, in some cases, with bamboo spears) when the emperor's surrender speech was broadcast. This shivered the sense of national mission. Most Japanese seem to have felt sad, relieved that the war was over, but apprehensive at what might follow.

Expecting a cruel and harsh Occupation, the Japanese found it benevolent. Fearing a vindictive rule, they found it constructive. Under these conditions the sense of duty that had enabled them to bear the sacrifices of war was turned to cooperation with the new authorities. The rejection of wartime policies and the shift toward democracy were reinforced by the discovery that, contrary to what the Japanese people had believed during the war, their nation was reviled in all the countries that had been a part of its Co-Prosperity Sphere.

That the Occupation was American was of great significance. In 1945 Japan had both democratic and totalitarian potentials. On the one hand was the post-1890 parliamentary tradition; on the other, the prewar factors that had stifled this tradition, and the wartime structure of economic controls and national mobilization. Had Japan been occupied by the Soviet Union, Japanese capabilities for national planning and collective endeavor could undoubtedly have made her a model Communist state. Occupied by the United States, however, she built on the parliamentary institutions of her modern tradition to move in the direction of a more open society.

The Structure of the Occupation. In theory, at least, the Occupation was international, directed by a thirteen-nation Far Eastern Commission in Washington and advised by a four-power Allied Council in Tōkyō. Accordingly, General Douglas MacArthur was given the title of Supreme Commander for the Allied Powers (SCAP). In fact, the Occupation was almost purely American. Apart from twelve printed pages of Initial Post-Surrender Policies sent to SCAP by the Joint Chiefs of Staff, it was carried out almost entirely by MacArthur, his staff, and the American and some British troops under his command. MacArthur was in many ways the ideal man for the post. He viewed himself as a man of destiny acting on the stage of history. Self-confident and speaking in broad historical themes, he inspired the Japanese during the hard early years, giving them hope for a better future. He was also the ideal commander from the point of view of American politics: as a confirmed Republican under a Democratic administration, he could carry out the most radical reforms without arousing criticism at home.

Unlike Germany, Japan was not governed directly by foreign troops. The army of occupation ruled through the Japanese administrative structure. In Tōkyō under MacArthur was Headquarters SCAP, which contained various staff sections roughly parallel to the ministries of the Japanese government. In the prefectures were "military government" teams, which acted as an inspectorate to ascertain that reforms enacted into law were carried out. Liaison between the SCAP sections in which policy was formulated and the Japanese government was undertaken by the Central Liaison Office, staffed chiefly by Foreign Ministry personnel. (After 1948 the liaison arrangement was eliminated in favor of direct contact with government ministries.) Some criticized this pattern of rule, saying that the same bureaucracy which had formerly followed the dictates of the Japanese military now followed the American military, and pointing out that this was poor preparation for democracy. In truth, in the early years there was uneasy tension between the supposed power of a democratized Diet and the actual power of SCAP. Yet in practice, after the initial reforms, the military gradually withdrew its hand, and so the problem never became acute.

The assumptions of the Occupation were based on a devil-theory of history: that Japan's leaders since the early 1930's had been engaged in a giant conspiracy to wage aggressive war. This view was clearly brought out in the indictment of the Tōkyō war crimes trials. The leaders had attained their ends because Japanese society was "feudal," its values militaristic, its huge financial combines "merchants of death," and its political system reactionary. So faulted was Japan's character that only the most radical action could reform it. This theory of conspiracy was partly false and partly a gross exaggeration, but it was responsible for the thoroughness of the early wave of reforms. Conservatives became radical, and reforms were successfully enacted that would not have been possible without this climate of opinion. From the highest staff offices down to the lower ranks, the army of occupation threw itself into the job of democratizing Japan. And if its enthusiasm at times outran its grasp of the situation and its knowledge of Japan, still it was dedicated and sometimes even imaginative, and the results were on the whole successful.

Demilitarization and Reform. Liquidation of the apparatus of Japanese militarism and enactment of a series of democratic reforms characterized the first phase of the Occupation (1945–48). The empire was dismembered, and all Japanese abroad, military and civilians, were returned to Japan. The military services were demobilized; ultranationalist and paramilitary organizations were dissolved. Shintō shrines were disestablished. Armaments industries were dismantled or shut down. The Home Ministry that had controlled police and local government was abolished. The police were decentralized, their powers curtailed, and their authority to regulate speech and "thought" revoked. Political prisoners were released from jail.

The Occupation also acted to remove the old leadership from positions of responsibility. War crimes trials were held to punish those guilty of atrocities and to discover those responsible for the war. Twenty-five of the latter were brought to trial, an immense effort at documentation took place, and seven of the wartime leaders, including Tōjō, were hanged in December 1948. Most of the others were sentenced to long prison terms, later commuted. At the time the Japanese people took little interest in the trials. The war was lost, the wartime policies repudiated, the men themselves bypassed by the current of events.

A second step in this process of demilitarization was a purge of the former officers of Japan's military services and of the top officialdom of wartime governmental and business organizations. About 200,000 persons were affected. This was a purge by category, not one that attempted to weigh individual responsibility for wartime actions. Had the purge been attempted as a judicial and not an administrative action, it would have been impossible to carry out. In the words of an Occupation general, the purpose was "to cleanse the government of elements which by their acts or associations participated in Japanese expansion." As a denial of the civil rights of individuals, this involved a confusion of ends and means. But it was effective. It led to a change in the top leadership of Japan, a younger generation coming to the fore. Many of the new leaders were little different from those purged except in being junior. Occurring, however, just as democratic reforms were being carried out, it brought into power men able to adjust themselves more easily to the new ways than their predecessors could have done.

The most significant reform of the Occupation was the establishment of the 1947 constitution. The Meiji constitution had begun:

> Having, by virtue of the glories of Our Ancestors, ascended the Throne of a lineal succession unbroken for ages eternal; desiring to promote the welfare of, and to give development to the moral and intellectual faculties of Our beloved subjects, the very same that have been favored with the benevolent care and affectionate vigilance of Our Ancestors . . . We hereby promulgate . . . a fundamental law of the State, to exhibit the principles, by which We are to be guided in Our conduct, and to point out to what Our descendants and Our subjects and their descendants are forever to conform.

In contrast, the new constitution began:

> We, the Japanese people, acting through our duly elected representatives in the National Diet, determined that we shall secure for ourselves and our posterity the fruits of peaceful cooperation with all nations and the blessings of liberty throughout this land, and resolved that never again shall we be visited with the horrors of war through the action of government, do proclaim that sovereign power resides with the people and do firmly establish this Constitution.

The 1947 constitution transformed Japan's political life, making Japan into a truly parliamentary state. Some of the major changes were:

1. The prewar multiple elites were either abolished (the services, Privy Council, and special officials close to the emperor) or strictly subordinated to the cabinet (the bureaucracy).

2. Between cabinet and Diet there was established a relation on the British model. The cabinet became a "committee" of the majority party or coalition in the Diet.

3. Both houses of the Diet became fully elective, and the franchise was extended to all men and women aged 20 or over. The 467 members of the more powerful House of Representatives are chosen from 118 electoral districts.

The 250 members of the House of Councillors are chosen partly from prefectures and partly from the nation at large.

4. The judiciary was made independent, and the Supreme Court was given the power to pass on the constitutionality of Diet legislation.

5. Top local government offices became elective and were given increased powers.

6. Human rights were guaranteed. Among these were the classic rights of eighteenth-century thought — life, liberty, equality, and the pursuit of happiness; but also included were newer rights such as "the right to maintain the minimum standards of wholesome and cultural living," "academic freedom," and the right of workers to bargain collectively.

The position of the emperor was also changed. Formerly sacred as well as sovereign, he was stripped of all "powers related to government" to become "the symbol of the state and of the unity of the people, deriving his position from the will of the people with whom resides sovereign power." What "symbol" means in this context is uncertain. That the emperor was not thrown out altogether eased to some degree the transition to the postwar world. Yet the effect of his changed position, going far beyond the political restructuring demanded by Yoshino Sakuzō in the 1920's, was to weaken myth and secularize the state. This was a decisive break with Japan's long Shintō tradition and the form it had taken in the Meiji constitution. It had implications for ethical action at every level of society. The minority of conservatives who lament the change usually care less for the imperial institution itself than for the traditional moral order associated with it. They sense in the emperor a talismanic power by which the Humpty Dumpty of tradition might be put back together again. Those who have fought to preserve the present constitution see their struggle as directed against the total prewar syndrome of emperor, state, Japanese family-system, and the obligations associated with each.

The constitutional change in the emperor's position has been effective because it has been matched by a shift in public opinion, education, and popular culture. By the 1940's Japan's Shintō past was becoming less and less meaningful even to the majority of the less well-educated citizens. During the early years of the Occupation the emperor traveled about to create the image of a human emperor. Since 1959 attention to the royal family has focused more on the crown prince, whose marriage to the commoner daughter of a wealthy businessman was a spectacle of enormous popularity. Most marked is the generational difference in attitudes: among the old a diminishing number still view the emperor with awe; the generation that came to maturity immediately before or during the war are either mildly favorable to his present symbolic position or are violently against him; the young are either wholly indifferent or, what is much the same, view him as a celebrity.

That Japan was ready for the new constitution is evident in the almost twenty years of parliamentary government that have ensued. Yet the steps required to effect this reform illustrate clearly the essential nature of the Occupation as a revolution from outside. In September 1945 the Occupation informed the prime minister of the importance of constitutional change. A cabinet committee was formed. Its draft revision, however, was an ambiguous document in which only words were changed: "armed services," for example, substituted for "army" and "navy." The sovereignty of the emperor was preserved intact. Thereupon the Government Section of SCAP prepared its own draft, which was given to the Japanese for use as a "guide." The Japanese government now understood what was to be done. In time, and in accordance with "the freely expressed will of the Japanese people," a slightly modified version of the SCAP draft was adopted by the Diet as an amendment of the Meiji constitution. (The official history of the Government Section of SCAP cites as a precedent for the legality of this mode of amendment the constitutional revision of the State of Georgia during the 1940's.) When the new constitution was promulgated, one Japanese journalist wrote that some passages "by Japanese literary standards, sound quaintly and exotically American." His comment, like all references to the Occupation's direction of government reforms, was censored and went unpublished.

A second major achievement of the Occupation was land reform. In 1945 about 46 per cent of the cultivated land in Japan was worked by tenants, who paid 75 per cent of their rents in kind. Socially and economically subordinate to landlords, tenants often deferred politically as well, thus giving the landlord effective power over blocs of votes in the village. If any sector of Japanese society could be labeled "feudal," it was this. The Occupation accordingly secured legislation which provided for government purchase of all land held by absentee landlords and all but ten acres as a maximum per family of other holdings. Carried out by Japan's remarkably efficient bureaucracy, the new laws left former landlords with at most three small farms to work themselves and an additional $2\frac{1}{2}$ acres to rent out. Since the land was paid for at pre-inflation prices, this was tantamount to expropriation. Land so purchased was then sold to the former tenants at the same low prices on easy credit terms. At the end of the reform the percentage of land worked by tenants had dropped from 46 to 10, and rents in kind were cut almost to zero. Because of agricultural shortages in postwar Japan, debts were quickly paid off, and there emerged a countryside of small but independent farmers, who became the base for subsequent social and political change in rural Japan.

Economic reforms in the modern sector of the Japanese economy were primarily directed against the zaibatsu. The rationale was that these economic giants had furnished the motive power for Japan's militaristic imperialism. The first wave of reforms dissolved eighty-three zaibatsu holding companies, froze the assets of zaibatsu families, and then con-

PLATE 72. The Japanese Emperor visits General MacArthur. In his 1946 New Year's rescript Emperor Hirohito reaffirmed the Meiji Charter Oath, including the "elimination of misguided practices of the past" and "love of mankind," and referred to "the false conception that the Emperor is divine." MacArthur commented that the Emperor "squarely takes his stand for the future along liberal lines. His action reflects the irresistible influence of a sound idea."

PLATE 73. At Nanking, early 1912 (front, left to right): Ts'ai Yüan-p'ei, Minister of Education; Huang Hsing, Army Minister; Sun Yat-sen, Provisional President.

PLATE 74. Sun Yat-sen and his young wife, Soong Ching-ling, a graduate of Wesleyan College for Women (Macon, Georgia), en route to Peking at the end of 1924.

PLATE 75. Dr. Hu Shih in 1946, at Cornell University, lecturing on the history of Chinese philosophy. He was China's ambassador to the United States in the early war years 1938–42.

PLATE 76. Chiang Kai-shek as super-intendent of the Whampoa Military Academy in 1925, aged 38.

PLATE 77. Mao Tse-tung at Yenan in 1937, aged 39.

PLATE 78. Generalissimo and warlords. Chiang Kai-shek (center) in late 1928, after taking over North China, with two of his army commanders: the "Model Governor" Yen Hsi-shan (right), and the "Christian General" Feng Yü-hsiang (left, in common soldier's uniform). In 1930 Yen and Feng fought Chiang for power but were defeated.

PLATE 79. The problem of distribution in China in the 1940's: the
well-nourished woman sits in front
of a grain shop; the beggar boy
has come into town from a famine
area.

PLATE 80. October 1, 1963, in
Peking. Paraders through the great
square before the reviewing stand
(behind Mao's portrait on the
T'ien-an Men or "Gate of Heavenly Peace" leading to the Palace)
bear portraits of Marx, Engels,
Lenin, and Stalin, with slogans
against "Modern Revisionism", and
for socialist unity.

fiscated the major part of such family fortunes by a capital levy. This broke the former zaibatsu into their component sub-combines, companies, and banks. At the same time, an anti-monopoly law was passed to preclude recombination, and new inheritance and income taxes were established to prevent the formation anew of huge private fortunes. In December 1947 a law was passed under which the further deconcentration of 1200 companies was planned. But at this point the emphasis in Occupation policy swung from reform to recovery, so that in the end only nine companies were affected.

Some critics have argued that these reforms meant little, that the Occupation abandoned them in midstream, and that the Japanese government has since ignored the antitrust laws. It is true that, although zaibatsu families and holding companies have disappeared, former zaibatsu companies have tended to re-establish relations with the bank of their former combine — on which they often continue to depend for financing. This has resulted in loose coalitions of industries centering on one bank or another. It is possible to view these as merely a more modern form of the same old combines. But there are important differences too. The new coalitions are less hierarchical. The degree of control is less, since banks may be changed or several dealt with at once. Some companies have not "rejoined." And many new companies have emerged completely outside the zaibatsu tradition. More and more the organization of Japanese business has come to resemble that of the modern West. Perhaps the main difference is that mergers, industry-wide associations, and cartels are still more prominent in Japan than in the United States.

Parallel to "zaibatsu-busting," the Occupation initiated a program to promote labor organization. A Trade Union Law was passed in 1945, giving workers the right to organize, bargain, and strike. A Labor Relations Adjustment Law was enacted in 1946 and a Labor Standards Law in 1947. Within this changed legal climate the remains of the prewar union forces expanded and grew strong. Unionists increased to 6.5 million in 1949 and then gradually to almost 9 million in 1962. In terms of the total labor force, unionism is slightly more developed than in the United States, but somewhat less so than in England. The vigor of labor's response at first delighted Occupation reformers. Their enthusiasm dimmed, however, as the movement grew into a leftist political force under Marxist, and at times Communist, leaders. As early as February 1947 the Occupation forbade a railway general strike. And when economic recovery came to be emphasized, the Occupation took the position that further wage gains must await increases in production. In 1949, earlier labor laws were revised and a more restrictive Taft-Hartley type of legislation was passed. In 1950, Communist leaders were driven from the unions in the so-called "red purge." Since that time the dominant position in Japanese unionism has been held by Marxist, non-Communist unions — which usually have been deeply suspicious of the United States.

Another vital reform was in education. Prewar education had been marked by special channels leading to vocational training, higher technical schools, or universities. Once underway, a student found it hard to alter his course. This was changed; levels were standardized so that the completion of any school became sufficient preparation to enter the next higher level of any other school. Entrance to high schools and universities came to depend on success in highly competitive examinations. Within the new system compulsory education was extended from six to nine years. The content of education also changed. New textbooks embodying democratic principles were introduced. Classroom projects replaced rote learning. "Social studies" replaced history in the lower grades. In every area an attempt was made to end indoctrination and promote independent thought.

Higher education was also reformed. Though all of Japan is smaller in area than California, educational experts within the Occupation felt that each prefecture should have a prefectural university. This required that higher schools, normal schools, and technical colleges, though lacking both libraries and faculties, be made over into multi-faculty universities in the American pattern. As time went on, the first wave of experts gave way to a second and Japan saw overnight a proliferation of junior colleges. Today Japan has 260 universities (more than half of which are private) and 305 junior colleges. As in American universities, the first two years are given over to general studies, followed by two years of specialization. Recently many objections have been raised to this system. In part the criticism reflects a valid concern about a weakening of specialized training at the better state universities — for which graduate studies have not yet compensated. In part it stems from the nostalgia of scholars and officials for the elitist atmosphere of the prewar higher school, with its "philosophical freedom" to read German metaphysics and think on life. Yet, though college students have increased from 268,000 in 1940 to 834,000 in 1962, the demand for graduates in recent years has generally exceeded the number available. Therefore, even though modifications may occur to improve the quality of the major national universities, the system as a whole will probably not be drastically revised.

The Conservative Phase of the Occupation and the Peace Treaty. By the end of 1947 the work of the Occupation was done. Structural reforms had been carried out. The Japanese response demonstrated a willingness to accept reforms that went far beyond the democracy of the 1920's. The further presence of American troops in Japan's main cities, of censorship, of government direction by SCAP, could only provoke a negative reaction. The United States wanted to sign an early peace treaty with Japan, but the Soviet Union demanded a veto in the negotiations. With a treaty thus blocked, the Occupation continued on for several more years. Increasingly, however, decision-making passed into Japanese hands.

When a peace treaty was finally signed, the transition was almost imperceptible to the average citizen.

The American interest in Japan also changed after the "cold war" began in 1947. By the middle of 1948 it was clear that the Communists would win in the Chinese civil war. As a result, Japan became pivotally important; her industrial and potential military strength made her the balance wheel of American policy in East Asia. At the same time, it was hoped that Japan would flourish as a democratic nation. Thus the foe of 1945 became the friend of 1948. For Japan to become a successful parliamentary state, economic stability was necessary. American policy therefore turned away from radical reform toward reconstruction. This conservative tendency was accelerated when South Korea was invaded by the North in June 1950 (see page 847). As American troops and then United Nations troops fought to repel the invasion, Japan became a staging ground and workshop for the United Nations forces, a privileged sanctuary like that of the Chinese Communists in Manchuria. General MacArthur, commander of the United Nations troops in Korea as well as of the Occupation in Japan, was dismissed in April 1951, after having disagreed with President Truman over the conduct of the war. That so great a general could be so summarily removed from power provided MacArthur's last object lesson in democracy to the Japanese. He was replaced as SCAP by General Matthew Ridgway, who came in to head the final, caretaker phase of the Occupation.

In 1951 the United States and forty-seven other nations signed a peace treaty with Japan, by which Japan regained her independence but renounced her claim to former colonies and some islands formerly under her control. China, India, and the Soviet Union did not sign, but as the Occupation was American, their abstention had no effect. India signed a separate treaty shortly thereafter as did the Nationalist Chinese government on Taiwan. Diplomatic relations with the Soviet Union were restored in 1956 (though without a full peace treaty) and were followed by Japan's admission to the United Nations. Diplomatic relations with Communist China have not been established, although commercial and cultural contacts have become quite extensive. The longings of the political left, the hopes of businessmen, the conservatives' sense of Japan's traditional ties with China, and geographical propinquity combined to make the Japanese feel that relations with China constituted an unsolved problem of extreme importance. France's recognition of China in 1964 added to the great debate within Japan; there are many who would have Japan mediate between China and the West.

On the same day as the peace treaty with the United States, the Japanese government signed a security treaty which provided for the continuation of American bases in Japan and committed the United States to defend Japan in case of need. Such a treaty was necessary, for Japan in 1951 was weak; yet it created tension in two areas. First, it was signed with the expectation that Japan would "increasingly assume responsibility for its own defense." This conflicted with Article 9 of the 1947 constitution in which the Japanese had pledged to "forever renounce war as a sovereign right of the nation," and hence never to maintain "land, sea, or air forces" or "other war potential." By 1949 both the United States and Japan's conservative government viewed this article with some embarrassment. In 1950 a 75,000-man "National Police Reserve" was established. Sea and air arms were added, and by the 1960's this had become a 200,000-man "National Defense Force" with tanks, artillery, destroyers, and over a thousand planes. The formation of this force involved a distinction, of dubious constitutionality, between "war potential" and "defense potential." Anti-war feeling was so strong in Japan that even this very limited rearmament was a volatile issue. As a second source of tension, some felt that the security treaty was the price Japan had to pay for the peace treaty, and that it cast a shadow over Japan's independence since it left military forces in Japan under foreign control. The government supported the treaty, but many in the opposition argued that the United States bases would make Japan a target for attack in time of war, and so jeopardize rather than guarantee the nation's security. This feeling was one cause of the riots in 1960 at the time of the treaty's revision.

Still another thorny problem arising from the peace treaty was the American take-over of the Ryūkyūs and the Russian absorption of the Kurils. In the treaty Japan renounced her claim to these territories, but their ultimate disposal was left undefined. The problem of the Kurils rankled, since these northern islands were traditionally claimed as a part of Japan and were not among her modern conquests. Japanese claims to two large southern islands of this chain still block the signing of a formal peace treaty with the Soviet Union. The problem of the Ryūkyūs — ethnically a part of Japan and traditionally under both China and Satsuma — rankled more, since they were in the hands of a friendly power and had a population of about 900,000, whereas all Japanese had been expelled from the Kurils. After World War II the United States transformed Okinawa into a bastion of American military strength in the Far East, and it has continued to bulk large in American military thinking. American military rule after the war was so inept that the Okinawans once elected a Communist mayor in their capital city of Naha. Since then the internal economic situation has improved. As a result of Japanese protestations, the United States recognized the "residual sovereignity" of Japan over the Ryūkyūs. Though murky as a legal concept, this means that the United States will continue to administer Okinawa and use it as a military base for the time being, but that in the indefinite future it will revert to Japan. Until this occurs, the political situation on the islands may remain unstable.

Relations with an independent Korea, to which Japan renounced all claim, had been left open in the peace treaty; but as Korea was divided into North and South, Japan could not establish relations with one without estranging the other. "Nondiplomatic" South Korean missions functioned in Japan from the Occupation era — originally to attend to the welfare of the nearly 600,000 Koreans in Japan. Japanese businessmen in increasing numbers traveled to Seoul and occasionally to the North as well, and the Red Cross handled the voluntary repatriation of some 80,000 Koreans in Japan to North Korea. Japan was interested in South Korea primarily for reasons of security: an all-Communist Korea would be a worrisome neighbor. Economically, Korea could not be very important to Japan; but Japanese capital and know-how, if South Korea could bring itself to use them, could be of enormous benefit to the Korean economy. The combination of rapid population growth, economic torpor, and political and social turmoil in South Korea was so disquieting that the United States strongly favored its closer relations with Japan. But anti-Japanese feeling and the entanglement of the issue in domestic politics on both sides have made the establishment of diplomatic relations a difficult issue for the two nations.

JAPAN'S YEARS OF PROSPERITY AND CHANGE

The most casual visitor to Japan is assaulted with evidences of well-being: television antennas sprouting from tile roofs, stylish dress, new buildings, the bustle of the cities and the whir of mechanized cultivators in the countryside. Tōkyō in 1961 had 700,000 cars, trucks, and motorcycles in comparison with 59,000 before the war. The life expectancy has risen to 65 for men and 70 for women. The Asian pattern of near-subsistence living, still visible in prewar days, has largely vanished. Some have labeled this growth miraculous. The gross national product rose from a stuporous $1.3 billion in 1946 to $15.1 billion in 1951, exceeding prewar levels, and to an almost incredible $51.9 billion in 1962. Through a cyclic spiral of booms and pauses, growth has averaged about 10 per cent a year. Wages increased as productivity rose; equally important, the pattern of income distribution changed. Where only 38 per cent of prewar national income went to wages, 48 per cent was taken by wages in 1956. In contrast, income from rents and interest dropped from 18 to

RISE IN PER CAPITA REAL INCOME
(indices: 1934–36 = 100)

1934–36	100
1946	51.9
1954	99.5
1962	215.2

4 per cent. Sweeping social changes have been the result. Indeed, without such economic growth, Japan's success in parliamentary government and the gradual democratization of the society might not have occurred.

Reconstruction and Economic Advance. Economic recuperation began slowly. Production in 1947 was only 37 per cent of the prewar level. With her empire lost, her foreign relations severed, her population swollen to 72 million, and her industries half-smashed, dismantled, or unmoving for want of raw materials, Japan's prospects were bleak. The Occupation's purges and deconcentration program inhibited economic planning. While many businessmen and government officials waited uncertainly, inflation, an effective capital levy, wiped out the savings of the prewar middle class.

American aid began with $400 million in 1947, much of it in the form of foodstuffs to prevent starvation in the cities; by 1952 two billion dollars had been given. Foreign trade developed slowly because of the inflation, and in 1949 the Occupation forced Japan to adopt a politically unpopular austerity program to halt it. (Joseph Dodge, Detroit banker and planner of this policy, was awarded in 1962 the First Class Order of the Grand Cordon of the Rising Sun for services to Japan.) The reduction of prices led to a small spurt in exports. The first major advance in manufacturing came in 1950–53 when four billion dollars' worth of military procurement orders were placed in Japan during the Korean War. This coincided with the quiescent phase of the Occupation, the peace treaty, and the launching of government and private plans for industrial development. The Korean War boom was followed by a recession in 1953–54, a new export boom in 1955–57, and then other deflationary pauses and rounds of renewed growth. By the early 1960's Japan had regained her pre-eminent economic position in Asia.

ECONOMIC GROWTH

	1955–60 (average yearly rate)	1960
Japan	10.2%	13.2%
United States	2.3	2.7
England	2.4	4.3
France	5.3	5.3
West Germany	6.1	8.7

Many causes underlay Japan's recovery and phenomenal growth. Her workers were hardworking, technically advanced, and literate. Her populace achieved a high rate of saving. Like Germany, Japan had the combination of managerial, corporate, and banking skills necessary for the administration of an advanced economy. Wartime destruction notwithstanding, these characteristics enabled Japan to rebuild as she had built in the past. Importing new equipment, her industries became among the most efficient in the world.

The relatively light burden of military spending, made possible by the security treaty with the United States, has minimized this sort of nonproductive investment. Where the United States spends about 9.6 per cent of its gross national product on military expenses, and Western European countries about 5 per cent, Japan spends only about 1.2 per cent. Of Japan's 1962 national budget, defense expenses took up only 8.6 per cent — in contrast to the 12.5 per cent spent on education.

Another condition for growth was the resumption of multilateral world trade.

EXPORTS AND IMPORTS
(in millions of dollars)

	Exports	*Imports*
1951	1354	1995
1953	1274	2409
1955	2010	2471
1957	2858	4283
1959	3456	3599
1961	4235	5810

Even before the war Japan was poor in raw materials; today she is more than ever dependent on imports. In all, 60 per cent of Japan's imports are raw materials: 14 per cent raw cotton and wool, 12 per cent oil, 7 per cent steel scrap, and 5 per cent coke. Without these, Japan's industries could not exist. That they are obtainable only through peaceful trade is one of the facts conditioning Japanese attitudes to international relations. Continent by continent, the distribution of Japanese exports in 1961 was as follows:

Asia	37.3%
North America	27.6
Europe	12
Africa	9
Central and South America	8
Oceania	3.6
Communist Countries	2.4

Yet a country-by-country consideration of Japan's most important markets in 1961 reveals the pre-eminent position of the United States, which took 24.8 per cent of exports and supplied 35.8 per cent of Japan's imports, far more than any other country. After the United States, the next two most important markets for Japanese exports were Indonesia and Hong Kong, each of which took 3.6 per cent of her export total. The remaining 68 per cent of Japan's exports was spread out over a great number of other countries. The United States also contributed to the Japanese economy through support for Japan's participation in European economic organizations, by loans for plant modernization, by grants of commodity credits, and through technical licensing agreements between American and Japanese firms. None of these are unilateral relations; as in trade, where Japan is America's second biggest export market, both sides

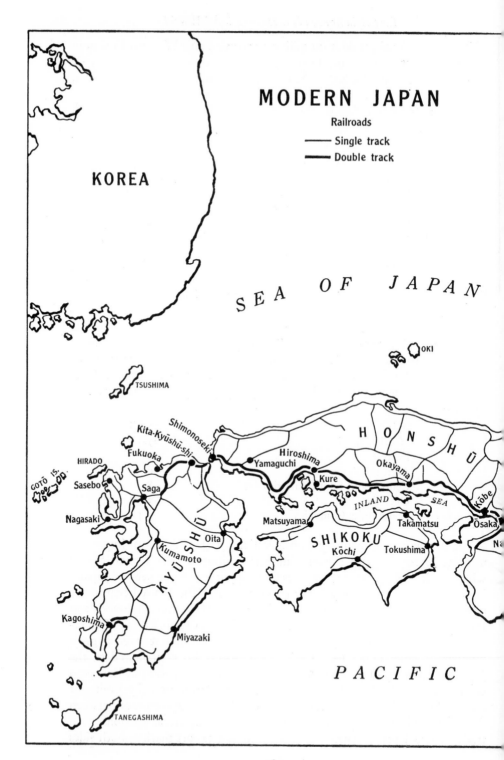

MODERN JAPAN

Railroads

—— Single track
━━ Double track

KOREA

SEA OF JAPAN

OKI

TSUSHIMA

HONSHŪ

Shimonoseki
Kita-Kyūshū-shi
Fukuoka
HIRADO
Hiroshima
Yamaguchi
Okayama
GOTŌ IS.
Sasebo
Saga
Kure
Kōbe
Nagasaki
KYŪSHŪ
Oita
Matsuyama
INLAND
SEA
Ōsaka
Kumamoto
SHIKOKU
Takamatsu
Na
Kōchi
Tokushima

Kagoshima

Miyazaki

PACIFIC

TANEGASHIMA

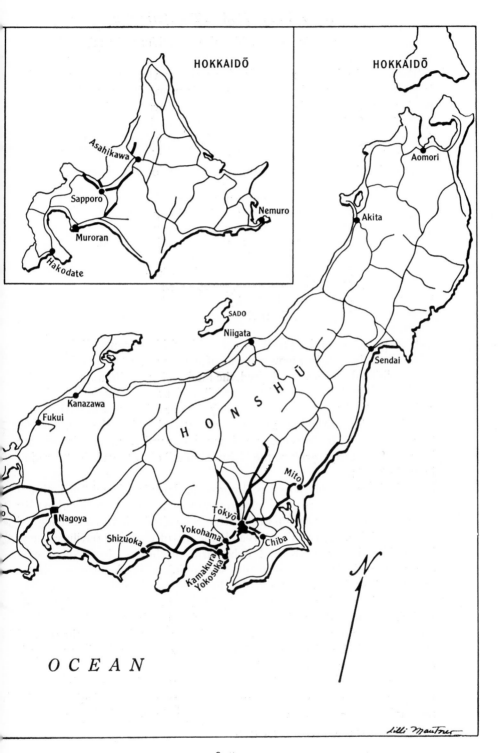

HOKKAIDŌ

HOKKAIDŌ

Asahikawa

Sapporo

Nemuro

Muroran

Hakodate

Aomori

Akita

SADO

Niigata

Sendai

Kanazawa

Fukui

H O N S H Ū

Mito

Tōkyō

Nagoya

Yokohama

Chiba

Shizuoka

Kamakura
Yokosuka

N

O C E A N

Lilli Mautner

profit. This economic partnership also conditions Japan's attitude to world politics.

To stress the importance of foreign trade as a source of raw materials is not to say that the Japanese economy is primarily oriented to foreign markets. Even more than before the war, growth has depended on the expansion of the domestic consumer market. Postwar giants such as Matsushita Electric have risen to produce new goods for the Japanese masses. The company song intoned each morning by Matsushita managers and uniformed workers suggests international horizons:

> For the building of a new Japan,
> Let's put our strength and mind together,
> Doing our best to promote production,
> Sending our goods to the people of the world,
> Endlessly and continuously,
> Like water gushing from a fountain,
> Grow industry, grow, grow, grow!
> Harmony and sincerity,
> Matsushita Electric![1]

Yet 90 per cent of its products are sold within Japan. Higher wages and benefits have led to new patterns of consumption. Where before the war traditional goods were desired, the modern housewife now wants new products. The "three sacred treasures," anciently the mirror, the jewel, and the sword, became in the late 1950's the television set, the refrigerator, and the washing machine, and more recently the hi-fi, the car, and the "room cooler." At the same time Japan has passed from the "investment boom" of the early 1950's to the "leisure boom" of 1960 and the "vacation boom" of 1963.

Agricultural productivity has also grown. Japan's original "agricultural revolution" (1868–1920) was contemporary with its industrialization. By the 1920's the import of foodstuffs from the colonies led to a leveling-off of productivity. Since World War II the use of chemical fertilizers, new insecticides, better seeds, and light farm machinery, has led to new advances, making Japan virtually self-sufficient in foodstuffs. Better foods, such as fruits and vegetables, have increased, while between 1953 and 1962 the number of chickens doubled, cows tripled, and pigs quadrupled. Though the agricultural population continues to decline absolutely, land is now three times more productive than it was at the start of the Meiji period, and three times more productive than land generally is today in India or Southeast Asia.

Finally, Japan's combination of government guidance and free enterprise has contributed to her growth. Three points in particular may be noted: (1) More was spent on investment, particularly during recessions,

---

[1] Quoted in *Time*, February 23, 1962.

than was available, on the assumption that great increases in productivity would provide surpluses to cancel out debts later on. This turned out well. (2) Commercial banks have lent out over 97 per cent of their funds for purchases of fixed capital equipment. This has had the tacit backing of the Bank of Japan. Where two-thirds of the capital requirements of the average American company are met by stock and only one-third by loans, in Japan the percentages are reversed. This type of "dangerously overextended banking practice," channeling both government and private capital into investment, refinanced industry during the 1950's. (3) The Japanese government, working through a cabinet-level Economic Planning Agency, has played a greater role in charting Japan's future growth than has the government of any other non-socialist state. Government economists estimate foreign markets and set internal production targets. The government rewards growth with high depreciation allowances, cheap loans, and light taxes. This policy of maximum incentives and the voluntary cooperation of business and government led to a sudden rise of industries based on new technologies. Shipbuilding and heavy machinery advanced from a prewar base; but electronics, petrochemicals, and optical instruments started from almost nothing, and growing, have changed the character of the Japanese economy.

Appearances can be deceiving. Japan's economy is not one of plenty. The baseline from which postwar growth began was so low that it is easy to exaggerate the results. Houses remain flimsy. Sanitation is often poor and heating is inadequate. Transport is crowded and roads and harbors are bad. The average family, apart from a few calculated luxuries and extravagances, lives on a tight budget. And in Japan, as in the United States, there are about 15 or 20 per cent of the population who do not share in the new prosperity. The standard of living has risen to about that of Italy; it is still considerably below that of England, France, or West Germany.

Social Change. The slowdown in the rate of population growth has been one of the major changes in postwar Japan. One can compare this with a leveling-off in the populations of other advanced industrial nations and view it almost as a natural phenomenon. But it is important to see it as man-made, the result of an increase in rationality and planning.

Expanding from 35 million in 1875, to 44 million in 1900, to 59 million in 1925, to 85 million in 1950, Japan faced the specter of eventually becoming — like China today — so heavily populated that further industrialization could only fractionally improve the lot of her people. To stay this tide the government passed in 1948 a Eugenics Protection Law legalizing abortion for economic as well as medical reasons. Public and private efforts were also made to spread birth-control practices: posters in post offices, for example, contrasted small families of well-fed, happy children with large families of ill-fed, poorly clothed, cheerless children. Some factories also cooperated in establishing family planning groups. Longer years of higher education, modern couples who postpone marriage to avoid living with in-laws, a spreading desire to prolong the pleasures of single life into the early twenties (notably, high-school girl graduates who want to spend a few romantic years as business girls before accepting the cares of marriage) — all have contributed to population decline. By the late 1950's over 40 per cent of Japanese families queried in opinion polls practiced contraception. Most of the remainder resorted to abortions, the number of which for a time exceeded live births. As a consequence, the rate of natural increase has declined to less than one per cent or about 900,000 persons a year. Outside of Western Europe this is one of the lowest rates in the world.

The combination of population stability and rapid growth in the modern sector of the economy has resulted in men being drawn willy-nilly from agriculture and small and medium industry into the new large industries. During the 1950's this leaching process began to erode the "double structure" characteristic of the prewar economy. To compete against the high wages, greater security, and extra fringe benefits offered by large industry, small and medium businesses have had to pay higher wages. This has required that they become more efficient, with marginal producers being forced out of business. On Japan's farms the same tightness in the supply of labor has made it economical to spend more on fertilizers, insecticides, and light machinery in order to increase the productivity of those who stayed behind.

Growth in the modern sector has also expanded the manufacturing cities. One out of every nine Japanese lives in Tōkyō, a megapolis containing, in addition to the Ginza, eight or nine "downtowns," each with department stores, shopping areas, movie houses, coffee shops, restaurants, bars, and night clubs. So crowded was Tōkyō's transportation in the late 1950's that electric train lines hired students as "pushers" to help pack in the passengers. (The situation has recently grown worse. To expedite the departure of trains arriving only two minutes apart, "pullers" are now employed to detach passengers whose attempted entry prevents car doors from closing.) Surrounding the expanding cities are belts of new, middle-class housing. And farther out, often clustering about rail lines, are aggregates of apartment developments, often set down incongruously in the middle of rice fields in areas under cultivation since the beginning of Japanese history.

The new education, the consumer society, new economic patterns, the rise in the status of women, the slow advance of the conjugal family ideal (newspapers occasionally receive letters complaining of brides who are cruel to their mothers-in-law), unionization, the pursuit of happiness, the new religious freedom, all can be seen as quantitative change along lines begun in prewar Japan. Yet the changes are not simply linear. Rather, the total effect is a new social configuration, a new way of life. The older generation recognize this by saying, often, that the *apure* (*après la guerre* generation) are entirely different — more relaxed, frank, less polite, and perhaps egoistic. They regret the change, viewing the appearance of juvenile delinquency and other modern urban phenomena as signs of moral decay, and criticizing the new system of education. Yet the old themselves accept and participate in a way of life that could not have been foreseen twenty years ago.

Changes in the village are less apparent. On the surface, the tiled or thatched roofed houses, the green terraced fields, and the ubiquitous shrines and temples have an air of timelessness. Yet in fact the social transformation of rural Japan, starting as it did from more backward conditions, has been greater than that of the cities. Farming, even more than before the war, has become commercialized with considerable amounts of capital involved. It is carried out for maximum profits, not subsistence: if pigs are in oversupply, they are slaughtered and chickens raised, and the same attitude applies to agricultural crops.

In many farm families at least one member, often the husband, commutes to a nearby city. Farmers in more remote areas commute to smaller towns, to replace others who have migrated to cities. Often the bulk of the farm work is performed by the wife, with the help of grandparents or older children. Thus, in 1960, of the average farmer's income of 1133 dollars, 542 dollars came from non-agricultural pursuits. Moreover, while agricultural income had risen 6 per cent over the previous year, non-agricultural income was up almost 16 per cent.

Even the hamlet dweller now looks outward. Administrative amalgamation has consolidated former villages into cities of "district" level, where decisions governing hamlet life are made. In 80 per cent of rural Japanese homes, television brings in world news and the whole gamut of Japanese and American programs (the latter with Japanese dubbed in). Farm boys are oriented more and more to educational success and city jobs, and farm girls do not want to become farmers' wives. As household heads and other able-bodied men leave the countryside during the working day, as the youth emigrate to the cities, the fabric of traditional society wears thin. Hamlet solidarity erodes. Men with land and an outside source of income have little interest in spending their weekends on communal functions, which in many regions near cities are close to collapse.

Japan is still marked by small-plot farming. Sentiment attached to land was not wholly dissipated by the Occupation reform. Holding land is viewed as insurance, as something to fall back on in time of trouble. Farming also furnishes a second income. Thus there has been no rush to sell land, and change in the pattern of landholding will inevitably be slow. But if present trends continue, the younger generation may eventually sell off marginal holdings, and larger farms worked by mechanized equipment may appear.

This sketch of postwar society should not imply that changes proceed at the same rate in all spheres. On the contrary, the transformation of Japan suggested by the vital, social indices has not been matched by equally rapid changes in manners and mores. Nor do the end-products of change, in every case, resemble the institutions of the modern West. More than in the West, the individual still relies on his group and obtains satisfaction from belonging to it. Social obligations are taken only slightly less seriously than before the war, and favors are carefully returned. Human relations within the man's work group are still too important, and too delicately balanced, to permit the unsettling influence of wives: the spouses of company managers, of officials in a government bureau, or of professors in the same department of a university do not as a rule know one another; their social circles are separate from those of their husbands, usually centering on the local community, the P.T.A., or relatives.

Intellectual Currents. Japan maintained her identity while modernizing by destroying the traditional order in the name of the nation. Her nationalism, however, was not diffuse and democratic, not wholly modern. Rather, at its core were enshrined traditional concepts of emperor, state, and family, so as to preserve symbolically what was being destroyed in fact. Though a kind of hocus-pocus, this self-deception worked. Mesmerized by the emperor-ideology as a "teaching . . . infallible for all ages and true in all places," the Japanese marched ahead into the modern world. In postwar Japan the most important ideological change was negative: the destruction of the socio-political identity that had functioned as the basis of orthodoxy until 1945.

Nationalism in the broad sense of the term (*kokuminshugi*) was not lost. The Japanese sense of "we-ness" versus "they-ness" remained strong. A Japanese victory in sports or the conquest of a Himalayan peak was hailed enthusiastically. The admission of Japan to the United Nations brought a sense of national fulfillment. But the state (or *kokkashugi*) and its works came under a dark cloud. Patriotism was for a time repudiated as narrow and parochial. Nationalistic holidays were abolished. The Japanese flag was rarely flown. *Nippon*, a term with supposedly imperial overtones, went out of fashion and peaceful *Nihon* came in. Actions could no longer be justified "for the sake of the nation." Or, if a sanction was sought, it was "for the sake of a new Japan" international in outlook and democratic in practice. And militarism, or anything pertaining to war, was viewed by intellectuals and by most of the people as anathema.

Some critics in Japan argue that it is naïve to say that the "emperor-system" is dead as long as the emperor remains. But there is a good deal of truth in such naïveté. Not only has the prewar emperor-ideology broken into pieces, but the pieces themselves have been discarded. The emperor has become a mere symbol, like a flag; he has lost his awe. The old family ideal is dying and no one views the state as an aggregate of families, no one speaks of a unique Japanese "national polity." Individualism has become a consciously sought goal among students and younger Japanese. Before the war this was expressed as a concern for "self-consciousness" (*jiga ishiki*), a term with few political overtones. In recent years the demand has been for the development of an "independent self" (*shutaisei*) capable, when necessary, of acting in the face of authority. Opinion even appears to be shifting concerning the proper relationship of man and nature. In a national opinion poll in 1953, 64 per cent of those queried felt that man must use or conquer nature in order to be happy; 27 per cent opined that man should adapt himself to nature. Five years later the percentage who would conquer and use had risen to 66, while the adapters had declined to 20 per cent. On the other hand, it is also true that, in spite of these changes, many of the psychological orientations and behavior patterns of the old orthodoxy continue in various guises; institutions survive after the values that inspired them have passed.

The rejection of the old left many in a state of aimlessness. No ideology of comparable coherence emerged to replace emperor-thought. Internationalism, pacificism, and a vague humanism gained some currency; but these did not tell how or why to live. One literary reaction to this sudden deprivation of values was an early vogue of existentialism and existentialist literature — with philosophical roots in the prewar German tradition. *The Stranger* by Albert Camus became a best-seller. Many intellectuals felt that this novel depicted their predicament and sense of estrangement as accurately as did the writings of Japanese authors. The brilliant writer Dazai Osamu, indulging in women, alcohol, and drugs, continued the nihilism of Akutagawa that had become all the more palatable as a result of a meaningless war and a sodden defeat. The "hero" of Dazai's *Setting Sun* speaks: "It is painful for the plant which is myself to live in the atmosphere and the light of this world. Somewhere an element is lacking which would permit me to continue." Dazai died in a double suicide in 1948.

The terrible bleakness of the immediate postwar years has vanished. In 1961 Japan published more books than any other country but the Soviet Union and England. The Japanese read more newspapers per person than any other people but the English and the Swedes. Literature has been marked by an ample variety. Tanizaki, Kawabata, and other prewar figures continue to write. Popular literature abounds with tales of samurai and contemporary stories with sad-happy endings. Detective stories, called "novels of deduction," are widely read. An anti-war literature arose, describing the brutality of army life or the horror of Hiroshima. Proletarian literature was also revived. Younger writers generally have been sympathetic to the left, yet not so sympathetic as to take contemporary Russian or Chinese novels as models. In form and content they build directly on Japan's prewar syncretism of the European and the traditional. In spite of the variety, most serious novels deal with the prewar themes of death, sex, loneliness, man's inability to communicate, mental aberrations, and the dissolute lives of novelists. And younger writers are often more nihilistic, more openly questing for sensual immediacy, than those who began writing before the war.

Another current in the post-1945 intellectual scene was Marxism, which for a time exerted great influence in universities, unions, and journals of opinion. Many who had partially repudiated it during the late 1930's picked it up again after Japan's defeat. To many students it seemed the antithesis of militarism, offering a historical schema in terms of which the upheavals of modern Japan could be seen in world-wide perspective. Student government associations, established by Occupation fiat to aid in the democratization of Japan, were taken over by Marxists to become the organizational network of the student political movement. Known by the name of their national federation, the Zengakuren, these student organizations figured prominently in the Tōkyō demonstrations of 1960. In fact, however, they were stronger and more united during the early and middle fifties: 1960 was the eve of their disintegration into smaller, squabbling, ideological factions. The Japan Teacher's Union was early dominated by Marxists and often followed closely the line of the Japanese Communist Party. And the majority of unions, even after the expulsion of Communists, maintained a fairly orthodox Marxism, though this seems to be weakening in recent years.

Since 1955, and even more clearly since the anti-security-treaty riots of 1960, Marxism in Japan has been undergoing a thaw. The revelation of Stalin's crimes, followed by the Sino-Soviet split, has created schisms in the leftist movement. One writer, who repudiated his Marxism in 1964, suggests that these revelations have had the effect on Japanese Marxists that the 1936 Russian purge trials had on the European intelligentsia. Japanese economic growth has demonstrated, even to leftist critics, that the present social order is not only viable, but has something to recommend it. All but a small percentage of students have lost interest in demonstrations and strikes; the political awareness of students is still very high, but sports or clubs have replaced politics as the most favored extracurricular activity. Parallel to the shift in student attitudes, journals of opinion and scholarly journals that previously were Marxist and violently anti-American have adopted a more moderate position. Marxism is still more powerful in Japan than, say, anywhere in Western Europe. Even Japanese businessmen will often unconsciously think of politics in categories derived from it. As a total system of thought, however, it is losing ground; the insights it offers are gradually being enveloped in other, newer intellectual currents.

In the face of frenetic social and economic change and the destruction of orthodoxy, some have sought to return to more traditional, "organic" social organizations. The most successful of such groups was the Sōka Gakkai (Value Creating Association) — one of Japan's "new religions" — which rose from a few thousand families in the early 1950's to claim 4.3 million families in March 1964. (The Japanese Communist Party paid it the supreme compliment of studying its organizational techniques.) Probably about one of every fifteen Japanese is a member, and each member pledges to convert three others. It aims at "seven million households in seven years." Like the radical right during the 1930's its appeal has been largely directed toward traditionally-minded groups that have not fully shared in Japan's prosperity. First spreading among shopkeepers, taxi drivers, coal miners, unskilled labor, and other segments of the lower and lower-middle classes, it has more recently begun to penetrate other strata of society. It is notable for its successes among younger Japanese. Its appeal is down-to-earth. Members ask potential converts: "Why are you living? Are you satisfied with your life?" Against the spiritual malaise of modernity it gives a traditional answer: that only Nichiren Buddhism and faith in the Lotus Sutra can bring salvation to the individual, the nation, and the world. It also teaches faith healing and mutual assistance, and, for a Buddhist-based sect, it places an extraordinary emphasis on "profit" in this world as a sign of the efficacy of belief. The Sōka Gakkai is also politically active. It has elected many members to local assemblies; in the House of Councillors election in 1962 its candidates received 4,120,000 votes (11.2 per cent), making it the third most important political group in Japan today. In 1964 it announced that it would run candidates in the next general election for the lower house. Its political program is good government through religion: it is for peace, the present constitution, and clean elections, and is against nuclear weapons.

Marxism, nihilism, and the Sōka Gakkai have been among the most highly visible phenomena of the postwar era, but the era itself was generally characterized by a new receptivity toward all recent Western ideas and by the strong re-emergence of universalistic tendencies of Japan's own modern tradition. Comparing postwar Japan with the years after the arrival of Perry, some Japanese scholars have even called 1945 the second "opening of Japan." After being secluded from new Western intellectual influences since the start of the China War in 1937 (some

Japanese would say that in fact this "seclusion" started with the rise of the emperor-orthodoxy during the 1890's), Japan quickly made up for lost time. Particularly influential among new intellectual currents that entered from the West were those from the United States. A legacy of the Occupation and of the maturation of American scholarship during the mid-twentieth century, this was especially noticeable within the Japanese universities. American texts became widely used in medicine, law, the sciences, and engineering. Schools of education became somewhat more like those in the United States. Economics faculties translated American books on business management. American anthropology, psychology, and sociology entered to mix with Marx, Weber, and English social science. Perhaps only in the arts and letters did the European influence continue dominant, but here too Japan was receptive to England and the United States as well. These multiple influences are not doctrinally coherent. Yet on the whole they foster assumptions that reinforce Japan's growing democracy. Combining with liberal ideas that existed in the penumbra of the prewar orthodoxy, they have shaped the pluralism that marks Japanese intellectual life today.

A final point worth mentioning is that most Japanese intellectuals tend to be critical and idealistic. They do not compare Japan with Java or Burma, or even with China or India, and ask others to admire. Instead, they compare the Japanese *reality* with the English, American, or Soviet *ideal* and point out its tremendous shortcomings. The situation appears to be improving, they will say, but if you probe beneath the surface, things are worse than they seem. This attitude, as a bar to retrogression and an impetus to further progress, is undoubtedly healthy. And, today, Japan *is* more like the advanced nations of Europe than like other Asian countries. Yet such critical comparisons can mislead. An outside observer, reading only the journals and magazines which mold intellectual opinion in Japan, would never guess that Japan has been doing well. The combination of literary nihilism, the Marxist criticism of government and society, and the amorphous pluralism of doctrines (the lack of a consensus based on a unitary belief-system) gives an extremely negative impression of life in Japan. Evidence from a 1964 opinion poll (printed in the leading intellectual journal, the *Central Review*) would suggest, however, that intellectual gloom is not representative. When asked to choose the best period in Japan's modern history, the majority of respondents selected the present. When asked what country they would choose if they could be reborn in the land of their choice, 74 per cent picked Japan. When asked "What color is the present age?" the largest number replied "pink." Next came green and blue; only 2 per cent picked gray and 1.3 per cent black. After decades of deprivation the average Japanese appears to be enjoying his new well-being, not overly concerned with unresolved problems of cultural values.

Some thinkers dismiss the results of such polls as easy optimism. They feel keenly the lack of a doctrinally coherent, democratic consensus rooted in Japan's history. They lament the shallowness of Japanese liberalism in contrast to Western nations which, having experienced a Renaissance, Reformation, and Enlightenment, were able to fashion their own democratic institutions. They argue that the postwar changes are even more of an "external enlightenment" than those so designated by Natsume Sōseki at the turn of the century. They question whether the present parliamentary system could weather a severe crisis. Other Japanese, however, argue that Japan is already more Western than East Asian in the traditional sense. They feel that the values and experiences that shaped the West are implicit in contemporary Japanese culture, and that their social realization is an ongoing process.

The Problem of Political Consensus. Although in part a foreign product, Japan's new constitutional structure has worked remarkably well. Buoyed up by economic development, it has been strengthened by the social and intellectual changes described above. It has been given external support by Japan's ties to the West and by her new internationalism — stronger and more sincere than in the best days of Shidehara diplomacy. Above all, it has built on the prewar political tradition. First, both the conservative and socialist parties are the continuations of prewar parties. Second, the nature of vertical relations between Diet members and their parties, prefectural political circles, and local politicians is very much what it was before the war. The shift from bloc voting to a more open pattern of individual voting has made the electoral process more democratic; but this also is the continuation of a tendency that began in late Meiji times.

The continuity of political life that is now obvious was not so clear in 1945. At that time there was considerable flux, and no one was sure what the outcome would be. Alongside the major parties was a welter of smaller groupings. In the election of 1946 there were 363 "parties." Of those elected in 1946 to the lower house, 81 per cent were new members. Gradually, however, small fringe parties were absorbed into the major parties and the turnover of Diet seats decreased. By 1953 only 10 per cent of those elected had not previously served in the Diet. The system had stabilized.

Another area of uncertainty was whether there would be government by single parties or government by coalitions of parties. When the two major prewar parties emerged from the cocoon of the Imperial Rule Assistance Association in 1945, the Seiyūkai became the Liberal Party and the Minseitō became what at different times was called the Progressive Party and the Democratic Party. Under their new names these parties continued for several years to oppose each other as before the war. In 1947–48 the conservative Democratic Party even joined the socialists in the formation of two cabinets, rather than join with the equally conservative Liberals. Such coalitions, however, were failures: socialists and conservatives could not work together. From 1948 the government was continuously in the hands of the conservatives, while the socialists became a permanent opposition. A *de facto* two-party system gradually emerged out of this balance, becoming formalized in 1955 when right and left socialists rejoined to form a united Socialist Party, and the Liberals and Democrats joined to form a single, conservative Liberal-Democratic Party. These parties have not become monolithic: they are made up of a number of factions, each composed of a leader and his followers. Struggles for advantage within the parties follow the lines of clique cleavages. As in 1959, when the Nishio faction bolted the Socialist Party to organize the Democratic Socialist Party, factionalism can lead to the formation of splinter parties. But in general the parties are stable: to remain in power the Liberal-Democrats must stay together, to come to power in the future the socialists must reunite.

One serious problem affecting Japanese politics is a lack of consensus between the Socialists and the Liberal-Democrats. For parliamentary government to function well over the long term there must be some measure of agreement between the major parties. This is a precondition for the existence of a "loyal opposition." It permits change in administration without total discontinuity in government policies and programs. It provides a base of popular support for the government whoever may be in power. In the years since the war Japan has largely lacked such a consensus. The platforms of the two main parties have had little in common; the speeches of the respective party spokesmen are often not in the same universe of discourse.

The lack of consensus has not been fatal, and has not caused upsetting dislocations, only because the conservatives have been in power continuously and because this has been an era of steadily rising prosperity. Conservative government has provided continuity of policies and policy makers. During the early years, after the purge of many former leaders, the conservative cabinets were headed by members of the prewar "Anglo-American" clique of the Foreign Ministry — men who assumed the premiership with the blessings of Occupation authorities. Among these Yoshida Shigeru, prime minister for seven of the first eight and one-half years, was outstanding. Building a strong personal following among the members of the Liberal Party, he ruled autocratically in a fashion some termed "one-man government." Since Yoshida no prime minister has been able to construct a faction of comparable size. As a result, the tenure of each prime minister, a factional leader in his own right, has depended on his skill in maintaining a coalition with several of the seven or so other party factions. When an opportunity occurs, the other factional leaders are usually ready to withdraw their support and vie for a turn as prime minister. One of the most successful since Yoshida was Ikeda Hayato, a former Finance Ministry bureaucrat, who first ran for the Diet in 1948 and became prime minister in 1960. Adopting a "low posture" (one of compromise) toward the Socialists, he avoided head-on clashes in the Diet. Displaying a conciliatory attitude and distributing party offices to members of other factions, he mollified his opposition within the Liberal-Democratic Party. He also gained considerable popular support as a bluff, honest, outspoken man, as a planner of Japan's prosperity, and as the prime minister who obtained greater recognition for Japan from the United States and Europe.

In power continuously, the ruling conservative party, in conjunction with bureaucrats and big business, forms "the establishment" of present-day Japan. Years of cooperation with the bureaucracy have led to a considerable identification of interests and outlook between higher officials and minister-level politicians. Since there is no longer a Privy Council or an appointive House of Peers, officials who reach the limit of advancement within the civil service now frequently join the conservative party to run for a Diet seat. In 1964 about one-quarter of the Liberal-Democratic Diet members were ex-bureaucrats. Familiarity with administrative detail has given these men an important role in the party. Likewise there has been an intimate and efficient relationship between government and big business. The Economic Planning Agency, the Finance Ministry, the Ministry of International Trade and Industry, and other government bodies cooperate closely with Japan's industrial and banking leaders. Conservatives have directed the work of these ministries and have received their campaign funds from big business.

As leaders of the "establishment" the conservatives project a mixed image. Their ties to the business world make them appear, in the eyes of some, the defenders of particular, moneyed interests. Their dependence on the rural vote is viewed as a reliance on "bossism." The desire of many in the conservative party to pay compensation to landlords who lost their land in the postwar land reform is seen as "backward-looking." The conservatives are clearly the heirs of the prewar parties and ethos, and even, to a limited extent, of prewar militarism. Hatoyama Ichirō, prime minister 1954–56, was the minister of education who purged liberals from the faculty of Kyōto University in the 1930's; Kishi Nobusuke, prime minister 1957–60, was a minister in the Tōjō cabinet that declared war on the United States. Such men may indeed have undergone a "democratic rebirth" in the postwar era, but it seems unlikely that parliamentary government has become the institutional expression of their basic values. The conservatives are patriotic and lament the decline in national feeling among the postwar generation. They are concerned with Japan's reputation in the world. They favor the maintainance of an army both for practical reasons and as a necessary appurtenance of a sovereign nation.

Most would be happy to get rid of Article 9 of the constitution by which Japan renounced the right to maintain war potential. The patriotism of the older conservative members of Japan's gerontocratic Diet (in 1962 the average age was 61) is still colored by a certain traditionalism as well. Most conservatives would prefer that the emperor be the "head of state" rather than its "symbol." This would have no effect on the locus of sovereignty. Some older members of the Liberal-Democratic Party still wish to restore the national holiday celebrating the mythical establishment of the Japanese state in 660 B.C. The conservatives have been ideologically the most affected by the demise of emperor-thought. In its place, for lack of a clear-cut political philosophy, they have tended to rely on what might be termed economism: a stress on material achievements and goals.

On the other hand, the conservatives have also shown themselves to be extremely competent managers, men who with great skill can make the system work. They are the men who have brought Japan from postwar devastation to its present well-being. They accept parliamentary government; if the Socialists won at the polls, they would undoubtedly relinquish power. Moreover, they are clearly not "conservatives" in the sense in which this term is used in the United States. The Liberal-Democratic Party advocates, like everyone else in Japan, a highly centralized government. They believe in free enterprise, but, Keynesian in theory and paternalistic by instinct, they also feel it is the job of the government to direct growth and to keep the economy running in high gear. They are closer to French "planners" than to the *laissez faire* posture of the American Republican Party. Internationally, they are pro-Western and anti-Communist. They would, however, be willing to expand Japan's trade with China and the Soviet Union if this could be done without weakening their ties to the United States. Thus, while emphasizing cooperation with the free nations of the world, Prime Minister Ikeda in 1964 also stressed the importance of "economic diplomacy" in Japan's foreign policy.

The socialist opposition, continuously out of power, depends on labor unions for campaign funds and organized support at the polls. With union backing candidates run well, without it they do poorly. This has led some to call the socialists a "one-pressure-group" party, in the same sense in which the conservatives are labeled the party of business. It has also led the extreme socialist left to demand that it be a class, not mass, party. The largest national labor federation in Japan is Sōhyō, which in 1962 included 45.9 per cent of all unionized labor. Support by Sōhyō enabled the socialist left to gradually rise in strength during the 1950's. During these years many men were recruited from unions into the parties; at the end of the 1963 elections about 37 per cent of socialist Diet members had risen through union channels. On the socialist right is another large federation, Dōmei Kaigi, which supports the Democratic Socialist Party with its 13.4 per cent of organized labor. In between these two federations are smaller groups with local and national ties to socialist politicians and factions of the party. Since socialists tend to rely on unions rather than local political organizations, they do best at the national level where union support is effective, decline somewhat in the prefectural assemblies, and are weakest at the local level where union support is more difficult to mobilize. That the socialists have no political organization in almost two-thirds of Japan's towns and villages points up their weakness at the grass roots. This has led some to compare the Socialist Party to an inverted triangle.

In spite of organizational weaknesses, the socialists have gradually risen in strength at the expense of the conservatives. Their rise is most easily explained as a consequence of the economic and social changes of the postwar era. Occupational groups that have tended to vote conservative are declining, while groups that support the socialists are growing

DISTRIBUTION OF VOTES FOR THE HOUSE OF REPRESENTATIVES

Election Year	Conservatives	Socialists
1946	46.3%	17.1%
1947	58.9	26.2
1949	63.0	15.5
1952	66.1	21.9
1953	65.7	27.6
1955	63.2	30.2
1958	57.8	32.9
1960	57.6	36.3
1963	54.9	36.2

in size. Agricultural and forest workers, about 75 per cent of whom vote conservative, have dropped from 16.1 million in 1953 to 13.7 million in 1963, and the same sort of attrition has also affected other small, traditional businesses. In the meantime employees in manufacturing industries rose from 7.2 million in 1953 to 11.5 million in 1962, and the total number of employed persons rose from 15.7 to 25 million. That about 75 per cent of industrial workers vote socialist in accord with union policy is understandable. What is striking, however, is that perhaps half of the "new middle class" of salaried employees in government offices or large corporations also vote socialist. This is anomalous since this group is an admired part of the established order of present-day Japan: its salary, regular bonuses, fixed working hours, vacations, and job security represent the *summum bonum* to which Japanese in other, less-favored occupations aspire. Apparently, the explanation for the socialist leanings of these middle-class voters is that they are well educated enough to share in some of the Marxist orientations of intellectuals; they are partially unionized; and they are sufficiently low within the hierarchy of Japanese bureaucracy to be filled with a sense of their own unimportance and powerlessness. They vote socialist as a protest against the powers that be.

It is impossible to foresee the day when labor alone will bring the socialists to power. Their hopes for an eventual majority in the Diet depend on the new middle class. Whether support from sections of this group will continue is an open question. The weakening of Marxism in Japan, the decline of the radical student movement, the quantitative increase in the number of older Japanese who tend to vote conservative, and continued economic growth may make the white-collar class more conservative. Their growing awareness of their own critical importance in the political process may also affect their voting behavior. In any case, the emergent importance of this group in the early 1960's has been a powerful argument for those within the Socialist Party who want a mass, not class, movement.

Japanese socialist ideology is easy to describe since, out of power, the socialists spend much time in elaborating it. But it is difficult to evaluate since the socialists usually have not acted in accordance with their Marxist doctrines: in action they are pragmatic, more or less accepting parliamentary procedures. Many still cling to the symbols of revolution, but perhaps the party has already begun to change in the direction taken by the socialist parties of Western Europe. During the postwar period socialist positions have run the gamut from welfare-statism on the right to revolutionary Marxism almost indistinguishable from that of the Japanese Communist Party on the extreme left. Within this spectrum of belief two modal points could be discerned: (1) On the right was a Fabian or Christian Socialist position in many ways resembling that of the British Labour Party, though somewhat more neutralist in international affairs. While opposed to Japan's security treaty with the United States, it viewed the world struggle as one between democracy and totalitarianism. Domestically, it was anticommunist, and a supporter of democracy and the welfare state. During the 1950's the strength of this right wing declined from about 40 to 30 per cent or less of socialist forces in the Diet. (2) Occupying a left-of-center position was a Marxist socialist group of Diet members, supported by Sōhyō. Formally committed to revolution, this left wing viewed the struggle in the world as one between capitalism and socialism and called the Soviet Union "the camp of peace." One of the main debates between the left and the extreme left within the Socialist Party was whether the "immediate enemy" of the Japanese people was "domestic monopoly capitalism" or "American imperialism." The former view won out, but a number of prominent socialist leaders on trips to Peking affirmed their ideological unity with the Chinese Communists against "American imperialism." At home the left favored nationalization of large industry and the collectivization of small and

medium enterprise. And while vociferously supporting the 1947 constitution on tactical grounds, the socialist left spoke from time to time of
the ultimate need to replace it with a socialist constitution.

Since 1960 there has begun an ideological shift toward a somewhat more
moderate position both within unions and within the socialist ranks.
Sōhyō, for example, bringing theory into accord with practice, has
acknowledged that it is meaningful for labor to work for economic goals
even within the framework of a capitalistic society. The former right
wing of the socialist movement — composed largely of older and even
prewar socialists — has not grown stronger: the percentage of votes it
receives in elections continues slowly to decline. But the left has assumed
a less revolutionary stance. In fact, the left of the 1950's has broken into
two groups of factions. The more moderate of these has moved to a
position to the right of center (in terms of the 1950 spectrum) and has
allied itself with a portion of the socialist right wing to form a new,
reformistic, "mainstream" group within the Socialist Party. In 1960 this
dominant coalition of factions announced the doctrine of "structural
reform," which proclaimed that revolution, if necessary at all, could be
relegated to an indefinite, later time, and that by gaining power at the
polls the socialists could step by step reform the present economic and
political structure of Japan. Inspired by Togliatti's Italian Communist
Party, this cannot be called a giant stride toward moderation. Yet, like
the revisionism of Bernstein before World War I in Germany, it opens
the way for a gradual shucking-off of Marxist tenets. Taking off from
this position, Secretary General Eda Saburō could in 1962 unofficially
announce his "vision" for a Japanese future in which Soviet welfare
measures, the American standard of living, British parliamentarianism,
and the Japanese "peace constitution" would be joined.

The Liberal-Democratic Party, seeking to capitalize on its economic
achievements, apprehensive over the socialists' program to woo the new
middle class, and gravely concerned with the decline in its vote, has
given renewed thought to its own party program. Prime Minister Ikeda's
1960 plan to double Japanese income in ten years seemed a first step in
this direction. Then, in 1962, certain groups in the conservative party
put together a platform labeled "new conservatism" and drew up plans
for party "modernization." The drafters of this program were leaders
of certain liberal, "pure politician" factions containing fewer ex-bureaucrats and ex-businessmen. Underlying their program was the explicit
assumption that in Japan as in Europe a new middle class is emerging,
that in Japan this class still has attitudes characteristic of the working class,
though its aspirations are socially upward, and that the Liberal-Democratic
Party must champion this class to obtain its support. Their program to
attain this end, put simply, is to establish a conservative welfare state.
Some backers of the program, going beyond welfare measures, have

framed a "labor charter" for the conservative party; they argue that the party should be neutral between business and labor, reconciling the interests of both for the good of the nation as a whole. Meeting opposition within the party, this idea has not yet been adopted.

The socialists' "structural reform" and the conservatives' "new conservatism" are convergent doctrines. Both aim at the white-collar vote. To get this the socialists have dropped "violent revolution" in favor of a program of graduated reforms (still within a Marxist framework). The conservatives are moving in a direction that is non-traditional, still pro-business, but not anti-labor, toward a welfare state built on a New Deal type of economy. A consensus that would envelop both parties is still distant, but less so than in the 1950's. The right-wing socialists are closer to liberal elements in the conservative party than to the socialist extreme left. If these convergent trends continue, there may then emerge a political consensus which would undergird Japan's parliamentary structure, strengthening it for future trials.

The hopes of liberal Japanese for such a development are not unrealistic. The polar separation of the two parties, reflecting differences in thinking between middle-aged union leaders and late-middle-aged businessmen and conservative politicians has been unnatural all along. Public opinion polls reveal that the Japanese people in the mass have been less divided than party platforms suggest. The majority of Japanese want neither Marxist government nor a changed constitution. Those who vote conservative do so because they are satisfied with the progress of the past decade and a half. And of the votes for the socialists, "only a few are votes for socialism, the majority are votes for democracy," as Eda Saburō, the Secretary General of the Socialist Party, openly admitted in 1961. The balance between the two parties has tended to benefit parliamentary government in postwar Japan: the conservatives have been given the power to carry out government, and the socialists, sufficient seats in the Diet to block the revision of the constitution. The very slow gains of the socialists in successive elections have made the socialists more moderate and the conservatives more liberal. As the conservative legacy of the prewar period and the Marxism of the immediate postwar era grow gradually weaker, both parties show signs of assuming positions more nearly in line with those of the electorate.

Moving from the center, right and left, to the extreme fringes of the Japanese political scene, one finds the Japanese Communist Party and a variety of small ultra-rightist organizations. The Japanese Communist Party, reorganized as a legal body during the early years of the Occupation, got 3.9 per cent of the votes in 1946 and, projecting the image of a "lovable Communist Party," rose to a postwar high of 9.7 per cent in 1949. Cominform criticism of this stance led, however, to new militancy after 1951. Since then at the most it has gained only 4 per cent of the vote. The Japanese Communist Party, badly divided by the Sino-Soviet split, has recently come out in favor of the Chinese, expelling Shiga Yoshio and several other old-time leaders for having supported the nuclear test ban treaty. Except in a segment of the student movement, in a handful of unions on the extreme left, and in a few "front" organizations, the Communist Party does not really count in Japanese politics.

The ultra-right has been even less successful. Of the not inconsiderable number of such organizations that have been formed or reformed since the war, a few favor "direct action" and will occasionally harass a socialist rally. Twice misguided youths, inflamed by older ultranationalists who survived the war, have carried out political murders. But these super-patriotic advocates of "direct action" are universally abhorred. The umbilical sustenance they derived from the emperor-orthodoxy in prewar times no longer flows. They have difficulty in obtaining funds; they can recruit only misfits and the mentally disturbed. In sum, the weakness of the political extremes is another sign of the postwar middle-of-the-road orientation of the Japanese people.

Conclusions about the only non-Western state to have successfully industrialized are not difficult to reach. Economic and educational statistics, census returns, and the results of public opinion polls are sufficiently numerous that even foreigners may know more about certain aspects of Japan than the leaders of other Asian nations know about their own countries. Like other parliamentary states, Japan since the end of World War II has been a goldfish bowl open to scrutiny by all.

Yet the very openness may deceive: faced with an overwhelming amount of data we are forced to ask which aspects are fundamental and which indices pivotal. Unlike other neighboring states in which an apparatus of modern government has been imposed on societies that are still predominantly agricultural, Japanese society is complex. The blurring of class lines, the ideological diversity, the release from the restraints of tradition, the range of choices open to individuals in society, the vigor of her modern culture — these make appreciations possible from differing, or even conflicting, points of view.

Since many of these same characteristics are found in Europe and America, we find Japan more intelligible than the rest of Asia. In contrast, the impact of revolutionary organization and doctrines on tradition-bound, immobile peoples is almost beyond the ken of our understanding. But, at the same time, there remains the influence of Japan's recent non-Western past within her modern life. The meaning of this compels us to ask questions for which there is no exact parallel in the study of the West. As the only non-Western modern nation, Japan stands as an archetype to which other developing nations may fruitfully be compared. The study of this archetype has only just begun.

THE DIVISION OF KOREA

Japan's growth and stability, just across the water, have highlighted the Korean people's tribulations. Once again after World War II, Korea's fateful location between China, Japan, and the Soviet Far East brought disunity and disaster upon the peninsula.

By accidents of geography and history North and South Korea present certain parallels with North and South Vietnam. The northern parts of these unhappily divided nations border on China and possess more resources for industrialization — in North Vietnam, anthracite coal, tin, and other minerals; in North Korea, coal, iron, graphite, tungsten, copper, and other minerals, and hydroelectric power, especially along the Yalu River. In both cases the southern economy is more agricultural and less industrialized. While this parallel should not be overworked, it is plain that in North Korea, as in North Vietnam, influences of history and of power politics have coincided: these two border areas, the principal ones that were anciently under direct Chinese rule, are now the two countries in all East and Southeast Asia that have gone along with mainland China into the Communist world with its program of industrial development through totalitarian regimentation.

The Postwar Occupations. Unlike the European colonies liberated from Japan in Southeast Asia, Korea suffered no reoccupation by former rulers. Instead, she was taken over and bisected by two victorious powers, one of which (the U.S.S.R.) had prepared for this, the other of which (the U.S.A.) had not.

The American idea of self-determination, more an attitude than a concrete program, was reflected in the Cairo Conference statement of December 1, 1943, by Roosevelt, Churchill, and Chiang Kai-shek, that "in due course Korea shall become free and independent." The phrase "in due course" expressed Allied uncertainty as to how Korean self-government might be achieved. International trusteeship by Britain, China, the United States, and the Soviet Union was subsequently agreed to. But in contrast with the distant American overseas interest in the principle of independence of small nations, the continental Soviet interest across a common border (albeit only a dozen miles long) reflected long-term strategic concerns and the very different ideology and procedures of Russian Communism. Soviet troops entered North Korea on August 9, 1945, just before Japan's surrender on August 15 (August 14, American time); but American troops, unprepared for the task, arrived only on September 8. By arranging to take Japanese surrenders north and south of the 38th parallel, the two powers, as it turned out, created two countries. International trusteeship was never achieved. Unification proved impossible.

In the north the Russian aim, to create a Communist satellite state, was comparatively definite and was achieved in successive stages. As the Soviet forces came in, the Japanese generally fled to the south, and Communist-trained Koreans were guided in building up a Soviet-type state north of the closed border on the 38th parallel. First, Communist elements got control of the "people's committees" that were being organized at each level of government — county, municipal, and provincial — while opponents were got rid of in one way or another (something like a million North Koreans migrated to the South). Secondly, a number of manipulated "democratic" parties were set up to mobilize workers, farmers, youth, women (now "emancipated"), adherents of the *Ch'ŏngdogyo* sect, and others in a national front. Finally, Soviet intransigeance having doomed any reunification, elections were held in November 1946, with almost everyone voting, followed by a Convention of People's Committees at the capital, P'yŏngyang, in February 1947, which in turn set up a People's Assembly. This at once elected a People's Committee to run a provisional Korean government. At its head was the original Soviet nominee, Kim Il-sung, a young man now bearing the name of a former guerrilla leader. The whole process of political indoctrination and mobilization was managed by the dominant Labor (i.e., Communist) Party, supported by Korean "people's militia" numbering 150,000 or more and guided by Soviet advisers in the background. Along with this political structure went vigorous programs for rural reorganization in the guise of land reform, beginning with confiscation and redistribution of landlords' estates, together with nationalization of industry and a planned economy in general.

Organized forcibly from the top down, the North Korean Communist dictatorship, though little studied, seems to have displayed most of the strong and weak points typical of such regimes. Being Korean in form, though actually under Soviet control, it was less offensive than Japanese rule; and its reforms had their attractions for various groups, particularly in the early stages of the totalitarian metamorphosis. In any case, Russian domination left no alternative.

In the south the American aim, to foster but not control the growth of an independent, self-governing nation, was immensely more complex, uncertain, and difficult. In addition, unlike the British, Dutch, French, and Russians who moved into other liberated areas noted above, the Americans had made no preparations to take over South Korea even temporarily. Drawn suddenly into a power vacuum, they arrived three weeks after the war's end to find that the Japanese governor-general had prompted formation after August 15 of an interim government headed by a moderate, Lyuh Woon-hyung. This regime had organized local "people's committees" all over the country. It had helped maintain order, convened provincial delegates at Seoul, and on September 6 proclaimed a "People's

Republic" with a broad economic and political reform program. Its potentialities of becoming a noncommunist regime were never tested, for the American military government, taking responsibility, refused to recognize it. Instead the Americans gained odium by dealing initially with the Japanese, all of whom, however, were soon repatriated.

While trying to postpone political decisions, the United States Occupation faced urgent economic problems. The Korean economy had been enervated by the war, yet it was integrally tied into that of Japan and suffered when the tie was cut.

The Americans generally assumed in 1945 that Korea would soon be unified. But their hopes of peaceful reconstruction by international cooperation were increasingly frustrated as the impasse created by the Soviet Union's power interests marked the unhappy trend toward cold war. In December 1945 the Moscow conference of foreign ministers, seeking a way out of this impasse, agreed that a Soviet-American joint commission should superintend creation of a unified Korean government, under a four-power trusteeship for five years. But the Koreans themselves, except those under Communist control, opposed trusteeship. In any case, the Soviet determination to control the country, or at least half of it, made this scheme clearly hopeless by mid-1946.

The American military government in the south therefore proceeded to give steadily increasing responsibility to its Korean personnel and inaugurated in December 1946 a partly elected legislative assembly. Trying to establish a rule of law as a basis for political and economic freedom, the United States' policy was more intent on political than economic ends, much as it had been in the Philippines earlier in the century. The aim was to get a stable, representative government established as soon as possible without attempting basic economic reforms. As a result, land reform to aid the mass of impoverished tenant cultivators by redistribution of Japanese holdings was delayed until 1948. This delay was partly due to the fact that in the meantime the nascent political process, in the shadow of Communism across the border, had become dominated by landlord-minded conservatives.

Syngman Rhee, now 70 after a long career of emigré agitation, succeeded in returning to Korea by October 16, 1945, ahead of Kim Ku and others of the old "Provisional Government." Reappearing to save his people like a latter-day Moses, Rhee espoused ultranationalism — independence without delay and unification at any price — against the current American policy of trusteeship and settlement by negotiation. Touring the provinces in an eloquent bid for support while quietly organizing a strategic following among the police, Rhee used whatever political methods served his cause. He soon built his "Society for the Rapid Realization of Independence" into a political party, complete with mass demonstrations and strong-arm squads. As Communist intransigeance became more obvious on the left, including a resort to terrorism in South Korea, anticommunism gained strength on the right. In this polarized political scene the moderates gradually lost out while the extremists took over. Lyuh Woon-hyung was assassinated in July 1947, Kim Ku in June 1949.

Meantime the United States placed the Korean problem in September 1947 before the United Nations, which set up a Commission on Korea to aid Korean unification and to observe Korean elections for the creation of a national assembly and government. Rhee's party won the elections in South Korea in May 1948; he headed the new assembly, and on August 15 became president of the new Republic of Korea with wide executive powers, thus terminating the American military government.

Having excluded the U.N. election commission, the North Korean regime hastily held its own elections and on September 9, 1948, proclaimed itself a Democratic People's Republic. Within a year Soviet and American forces had been largely withdrawn from the divided peninsula. By June 1950, when North Korea mounted its attack on the South, it was the stronger state, both industrially because of its mineral and hydro-power resources and militarily because of Soviet armament for offensive warfare.

The Korean War and After. The North Korean surprise attack on June 25, 1950, was at once condemned by the United Nations Security Council. (The Soviet Union, having boycotted the Council for six months as a protest against the presence of Nationalist China, was not present to cast a veto.) President Truman, mindful of the historical lesson of the 1930's in China and Europe, that aggression unchecked fosters more general warfare, committed United States forces in support of the U.N. collective security system. They were eventually joined by contingents from Britain, Turkey, and thirteen other member countries, though Korea supplied two-fifths of the ground forces and the United States one-half, as well as most of the naval and air power. All were put under the unified command of General MacArthur. The 142,000 casualties suffered by the United States made the Korean War the fourth largest in American history. (South Korean casualties were estimated at 300,000, North Korean at roughly 520,000, and Chinese at perhaps 900,000.)

The war had four phases. First, under the well-prepared, Soviet-armed North Korean assault, the outnumbered Korean-American forces initially were forced back southeast of the Naktong River to protect a rectangular 50-by-80-mile perimeter around Pusan. They beat off violent North Korean attacks while gathering strength from abroad. In the second phase, MacArthur demonstrated the offensive power of modern military technology with a massive amphibious landing on September 15 at Inchon — a gamble that succeeded brilliantly and was soon followed by recovery of Seoul and destruction of the North Korean invasion. (See map, p. 465.)

The war entered a third phase when U.N. forces crossed the 38th parallel in early October and, in an effort to reunite Korea by force, pushed north toward the Yalu. The two main American thrusts were under separate commands, divided by fifty miles of "impassable" mountains. In mid-October massively organized Chinese Communist "volunteers" began to cross the Yalu into North Korea to defend China's vital interest in the region. Marching long distances through the mountains by night, lying hidden from air reconnaissance by day, they remained undetected until by late November they totaled 300,000 or more. Unexpected Chinese flank attacks then forced the American columns into a costly retreat of 275 miles in the winter cold, all the way south of Seoul. But China's attempt to use her vast resources of manpower to unify Korea by force was now contained by U.N. firepower that eventually produced a stalemate on about the 38th parallel. General MacArthur's increasingly public disagreement with the fixed American policy of limited war led to his dismissal by President Truman on April 11, 1951. In the fourth phase of the war, truce talks began in July 1951 and dragged on at Panmunjom for two years. An armistice was finally signed July 27, 1953; in 1964 it was still in effect, with a closed border across the peninsula.

To the political inexperience and economic problems of South Korea were now added the burdens of a postwar rehabilitation. In the continuing crisis, President Syngman Rhee's autocratic methods reflected his personality; but they also bespoke the precedence of nationalism over liberalism in a newly emerging state threatened by subversion and invasion. Police repression, corruption, and rigging of elections finally touched off spontaneous student demonstrations in Seoul in April 1960. They could not be stopped by gunfire, though scores were shot; and after twelve years in power Rhee was obliged to retire, leaving Korean politics to an uneasy contest between the election process and army rule. In 1961 General Chung-hee Park seized power to form a military government; in 1963 he won election as head of a civil government. But when he sought to "normalize" relations with Japan as a means of helping the Korean economy, student demonstrations again broke out. Meanwhile American aid tapered off. Rural poverty and population pressures could not quickly be relieved, and the unification of all Korea remained a dream.

THE CHINESE COMMUNISTS' RISE TO POWER

The paradoxical reversal of roles in the last twenty years of East Asian-American relations, our ally China becoming our enemy, our enemy Japan becoming a friend, suggests how quickly modern governments, in changed circumstances, may lead their peoples into new alignments. While postwar Japan and South Korea saw new leaders emerge with American aid, North Korea and China experienced drastic revolutions on the Soviet model.

The emergent Chinese leaders had had the longest preparation as a group. The People's Republic of China in the 1960's is still headed by revolutionists who gradually rose to power within China between 1921 and 1949. This long revolutionary experience has given them both cohesion as a group and certain tested assumptions about Chinese politics which, despite possible limitations, have been applied by them to the world scene.

The defeat of the Nationalists by the Communists effected a change of ruling parties somewhat like a dynastic succession. In the take-over during 1949–50, the Communist army and bureaucracy absorbed much of the Nationalist army and bureaucracy, while the CCP party dictatorship supplanted the KMT in control of the military-administrative-supervisory tripod of power.[1] After 1923, innovation had been most evident on the supervisory side, where party members functioned somewhat like censors of old. Meanwhile the top leaders of the party dictatorships, first of the KMT and then of the CCP, had supplanted the dynastic family as the ultimate power-holders. Unlike the Ch'ing ruling family, created in the harem where K'ang-hsi, for example, begot twenty sons, the KMT and CCP central executive committees were ruling groups selected in the competition of intra-party politics. Each party dictatorship had its indispensable leader, the one man at the top to give final answers. But Chiang Kai-shek's early reliance on his wife's relatives (T. V. Soong and H. H. Kung) and later on his son (Chiang Ching-kuo) was a bit in the dynastic style, reflecting the transitional character of the KMT polity. Mao Tse-tung held power without reliance on kinship.

The rival parties make a fascinating comparison: each had an early but ephemeral success (in 1911–12 and 1925–26, respectively) followed by a decade in the wilderness (1913–23 and 1927–37). Each came to power with bright hopes (1928 and 1949) but within another decade met serious trouble. In both parties the original organizers were an educated elite, typically "alienated intellectuals," who found their calling as full-time revolutionaries.

Contrasts are even more striking. Sun Yat-sen's followers were city men, often of merchant background, typically from Canton. Chiang's closest supporters were from Shanghai and the Lower Yangtze provinces. Many had been abroad. More of Mao Tse-tung's followers were, like him, from rural areas, and his closest colleagues came especially from his native Hunan. Only a few had ever been outside China. In time the

---

[1] See Vol. I, page 297 for the Ming system of control and pages 363 ff. for the Ch'ing.

CCP even recruited leaders of true peasant origin. The difference in age between the two groups, due to their respective founding dates of 1905 and 1921, put them on different sides of a great historical watershed.

The rise of the CCP to power, after its initial decade had ended in disaster (see page 688), came partly from an internal development, the ascendancy of Mao and Maoism, and partly from propitious circumstances, the Japanese destruction of Kuomintang power and the anti-Japanese war of resistance.

Ideology and Survival to 1937. The KMT and the CCP differed most in the degree of discipline they imposed on their members. This reflected the relative importance of ideology in the two parties, as well as their respective situations. As revolutionists seeking power, the Communists could survive and make history only by obeying their party line as a unit. The Nationalists, partly from being in power, were more torn by cliquish rivalries and regional interests. Ideological control was also essential for the CCP program of revolutionary change, which has hinged upon the application of Marxist-Leninist assumptions to solve the many "contradictions" in the current Chinese scene.

After the KMT-CCP split of 1927, the small Sixth Congress of the Chinese Communist Party met in defeat in Moscow (June-July 1928). It concluded that the revolution was in a "trough between two waves" and should therefore prepare for a new "rising tide"; although agrarian revolution was the main "content" of the movement, it could be led only by "proletarian hegemony"; hence the CCP must recapture leadership of the urban proletariat through its labor unions while also preparing for armed insurrection.

This was the task of the new Moscow-appointed secretary general, Li Li-san, and his close ally, Chou En-lai (1896–). In 1929–30 they tried to get city workers to engage in political strikes, and they also tried armed insurrection. But no tide rose. CCP forces that seized Changsha in July 1930, for example, were expelled in a few days. The "Li Li-san line" was then condemned by the Comintern as both "opportunism" and "putschism." Li went to Moscow for "study" (to re-emerge in Manchuria in 1946) while Chou confessed his "cowardly rotten opportunism" but remained on the Central Committee. It was now dominated by returned students, Moscow-trained, who still assumed that the urban proletariat must lead the revolution. Yet in 1930, out of an alleged total of 120,000 CCP members, only about 2000 were industrial workers.

This first decade of failure was the background for Mao Tse-tung's rise to leadership. In his strategy, foreshadowed in his unorthodox report on the Hunan peasant movement in February 1927, the "revolutionary vanguard" in China were not city workers but "poor peasantry." By using the CCP to organize peasants, creating rural "soviets" (as Trotsky had urged) even before this was sanctioned by the Comintern, Mao and his military commander Chu Teh built up a military force, the Red Army, in a territorial base on the rugged Kiangsi-Hunan border. Like rebels of old, they collected manpower and food in a defensible area on provincial frontiers. Yet they used the new institution of a Leninist party and new, ideologically orthodox, Marxist-Leninist terminology. Proclaiming a "Chinese Soviet Republic" at Juichin, Kiangsi, in November 1931, they called it a "democratic dictatorship of the proletariat and peasantry," echoing Lenin's formula of 1905 in far different circumstances. The "proletariat," though nonexistent in these mountain hamlets, was given a favored legal status as in Russia. The violent redistribution of land in the ancient fashion of peasant uprisings was now called class warfare against "feudal" landlordism.

Mao's unorthodox methods worked, and he rose to power without any decree from Moscow. Arrests and executions in Shanghai drove the Central Committee out to Kiangsi in 1932, and Chiang Kai-shek's five "extermination" campaigns by October 1934 forced some 100,000 CCP personnel to break through the strangling network of Nationalist block-houses and embark on their Long March.

The extraordinary cohesion of Mao's followers grew out of this amazing hegira. Moving swiftly by night through the mountains of the southwest, CCP forces covered 5000 miles or more on foot across 18 mountain ranges and 24 rivers in about a year. Only at this point, when out of radio contact with Moscow and dependent on Mao's organization, was the Soviet-trained leadership obliged to acknowledge Mao's dominance in the CCP. While many perished on the Long March, the survivors were battle-hardened, tempered by perils and hardships now legendary. Out of this endurance test the CCP emerged in the latter part of 1935 in Shensi province on China's northwest frontier, closer to the U.S.S.R., and with the party nucleus intact, unified under Mao. Making Yenan their capital at the end of 1936, the Communists were ready to seize new opportunities. Including Shensi forces under the local leader Kao Kang, the Red Army had perhaps 50,000 troops, controlled by a centralized Leninist party.

The political environment in China now gave the CCP another chance. Since 1931, Nanking's effort at military unification and Japan's long-continued aggression had already undermined the central government, obliging it to put its resources into military defense more than economic growth or rural reconstruction. After 1937, the Nationalist regime was perforce further militarized, yet its central power was weakened vis-à-vis regional forces, and its civil administration was exhausted by exile in the hinterland and by inflation. Meanwhile warfare pulverized the old Chinese society. Migration of million of refugees and conscription of millions of soldiers broke up families and whole communities. Movement of soldiers and officials over the land further shattered the old regional power structure. While the war effort created common national goals, war weariness brought an overwhelming desire for peace and a new order.

Organizing the War of Resistance. Japan's conquest of the communication routes and cities of North China destroyed the existing fabric of government, yet remained superficial. Unlike the Nationalist area in Central China, there was not much geographical front in North China for positional warfare, but there was an omnipresent social front for popular resistance. The invaders' tanks and trucks, guided by aircraft, could reach every hamlet to kill and burn, loot and humiliate, but seldom could stay. Resistance during eight years of war became the North China peasant's way of life. It made him politically active as never before, and responsive to patriotic organization. The CCP had had to put group survival ahead of doctrinal orthodoxy on the Long March; now in its Yenan period (1936–45) it subordinated class warfare to the national war of resistance.

The united front, agreed upon between the National Government and the CCP in 1937, soon degenerated into an uneasy armed truce. The CCP had promised to support Sun's *Three Principles,* give up armed rebellion and anti-landlordism, democratize its local regime, and put the Red Army under the National Government's command as the Eighth Route Army. But in fact the CCP, riding on the tide of popular resistance to Japan and expanding to fill a vacuum of authority, gradually became the overall government in North China, the only coordinating mechanism among local movements, some of which had been at first autonomous.

CCP forces from Yenan pushed across the Yellow River into Shansi province, thence out onto the North China plain and across to Shantung. In 1937, by agreement with the Nationalists, the Communists began to build up their New Fourth Army in the Lower Yangtze region, using remnants from Kiangsi. In the Northwest in 1938 they joined with local patriots in setting up the Shansi-Hopei-Chahar Border Region Government as a separate administrative entity. Other base areas, usually inside the enemy-held rail net, were in historic bandit terrain, like the Hopei-Honan border-region corridor connecting Shansi and Shantung where the Nien rebels had operated in the 1860's, or the Liang-shan moor in western Shantung, lair of the twelfth-century bandit heroes of *Shui-hu chuan.* By the end of the war, the CCP listed 19 such territorial bases, mostly called "liberated areas," embracing a total population of perhaps 90 million. The regular and guerrilla forces, supposing they totaled only 500,000 instead of 910,000 as Mao claimed, had still increased tenfold, and in addition there were about two million in village militia forces. The National Government, never locally dominant in much of North China and absorbed in its own problems, had been unable to prevent this expansion of Communist rule, even in the Lower Yangtze region of North Kiangsu.

THE RISE OF THE CHINESE COMMUNISTS

───── Routes of the Long March, 1934-1935

"LIBERATED AREAS" AS CLAIMED (BUT ONLY PARTLY CONTROLLED) BY THE CCP IN EARLY 1944

1 Shansi-Hopei-Chahar Border Region
2 Hopei-Honan Border Region
3 Shensi-Kansu-Ninghsia Border Region
4 Shansi-Suiyuan Border Region
5 Shantung
6 North Kiangsu
7 Central Kiangsu
8 South Kiangsu
9 East Chekiang
10 North Huai
11 South Huai

12 Central Anhwei
13 Hupei-Anhwei
14 Canton
15 Hainan

Using resistance to Japan as a sanction, the Chinese Communists directed from Yenan a far-flung process of popular mobilization. They had to compete for peasant support with the KMT and other noncommunist patriots as well as with puppets of the Japanese. They learned how to combine patriotic resistance to a national enemy with social revolution in the villages. The Eighth Route Army, through constant indoctrination by its political department, was trained to help and befriend the common people so that it could rely upon them in turn for supplies, recruits, transport, and intelligence. Where the army became established, magistrates were installed to provide orderly government. Mass organizations for youth, women, and other groups could then be built up to indoctrinate the whole population. The peasant was encouraged to become literate and to participate in village meetings, farmers' associations, and even elections. Instead of dispossessing landlords, the Communist-led regimes generally reduced their revenues by invoking the Nationalist law of 1930, which limited rent to 37½ per cent of the crop. The peasant economy was stimulated by production drives for self-sufficiency in food and cotton and by encouraging cooperation on many levels — labor exchange in mutual-aid teams, cooperatives for transport and for the small-scale industrial production of consumer goods.

All this political, social, and economic innovation made North China the proving ground for the new technology of guerrilla warfare based on a crowded countryside. During the Yenan period, violent class warfare was less expedient than total mobilization against the foreign invader. The Japanese conscript, moreover, was so conveniently uncomprehending of the local scene, so vulnerable in his fortified town or blockhouse! The Japanese superiority in arms, like that of some later American-backed forces in other parts of East Asia, was offset by the political organization, economic efforts, and social cohesion of the resistance movement, now united by a heightened spirit of nationalism.

By 1945 the CCP regime was active over an area of 250,000 square miles where travel was by foot of man or beast and quick communication was limited to radio. Party membership had burgeoned in the war years: Mao claimed 40,000 members in 1937, 1,200,000 in 1945, mainly students and peasants. To inspire, guide, and control the wartime construction of a decentralized state-within-a-state, while keeping the CCP a centrally-disciplined Leninist party, was a formidable task.

To ensure ideological orthodoxy, party schools at Yenan processed thousands of students, and in 1942 Mao inaugurated a reform movement for "correcting unorthodox tendencies" (*cheng-feng*) in thought, in personal relations inside and outside the party, and in speech and writing. Prolonged criticism and self-criticism in "small groups," confessions of guilt and repentance in public meetings, became standard procedures. Behind the jargon of "subjectivism, sectarianism, and formalism" (the three main evils attacked) was a strenuous effort to re-educate and discipline new followers still contaminated by a liberal background, an individualistic temperament, or traditional morality.

Thought reform at Yenan marked the final eclipse of the doctrinaire Soviet-trained returned-student group of CCP leaders. Marxist-Leninist theory must now be applied to rural China's concrete realities: this testing of theory in action became the basis of "Maoism." As the new CCP constitution of 1945 put it, "the ideas of Mao Tse-tung, the combined principles derived from the practical experience of the Chinese revolution," were now added to Marxism-Leninism as the party's guiding star. This growth of "Maoism" represented the Sinification of Communism in China, in a period of wartime nationalism and minimal Soviet influence. Its principal achievement was to build a Leninist party on a peasant base, demonstrating (contrary to its own theory) that the Chinese Communist Party was in fact independent of the proletariat.

The party line for public consumption in the Yenan period was laid down in Mao's essay of 1940, *On the New Democracy*, a persuasive propagandist document which justified the united front of 1937 as a temporary phase and reaffirmed the party's long-term mission. The New Democracy aimed to develop a type of "democratic" state ruled by an alliance of several revolutionary classes under "proletarian hegemony" (unlike either the "dictatorship of the proletariat" in the U.S.S.R., or Western democracy, which was considered a "dictatorship of the bourgeoisie"), before proceeding to a second stage of "socialism." To appeal to his non-Marxist audience, Mao claimed the mantle of Sun Yat-sen and skillfully identified the May Fourth movement as the origin of Chinese Communism. Meanwhile, for the benefit of Marxists, he claimed to be, like Marx, Engels, Lenin, and Stalin, an original contributor to Communist theory, though in fact his "innovations" had been mainly in the realm of practice, not theory.

The Communists' organizational ability, their current egalitarianism, reasonableness, and moderation, their militant and messianic faith, all contributed to spread a new cult of the common people. "Liberation" aimed at the political awakening and activation of the Chinese peasant masses. The CCP cultural movement stressed pictorial art in the form of the woodcut, which could be cheaply reproduced for mass distribution. It also utilized the modern Chinese drama (*hua-chü*, "speaking plays") that had developed principally in Shanghai under the stimulus of foreign examples. Simplified characters and even a romanized script in the Latin alphabet, *latin-xua*, were used to print the didactic short stories of revolutionary literature. All these media spread a new faith, that technology and a new social order could remake, enrich, and modernize the life of every peasant. Meanwhile, in order that the revolution might draw perpetual sustenance from the masses, the party worker (*kan-pu*, "cadre")

Woodcuts from North China in Wartime

"Support Our Common People's Own Army." From top: Peasants bring in flocks for food and pack animals for transport. They welcome soldiers with music and a banner, stand guard, provide hot water to drink, carry the wounded, give new recruits a send-off, and care for the disabled. Matching placards at the service man's door read, "Fine clothing and sufficient food; a well-established household."

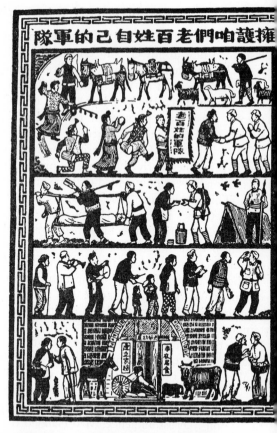

"Marriage Registration." A couple arrange their own marriage in modern style and sign the register on the k'ang-table of a local official. Right: brick cooking stove, folded quilts.

was expected to live in the village, work with the peasant, eat his food, lead his life, think his thoughts.

This concept of individual "liberation" became a dynamic of the Communist movement and also the sanction for the new party dictatorship. The logic of this paradox was as follows: (1) the revolution aimed to give the masses a new life, beginning with their economic betterment; (2) this betterment could be achieved only through the exercise of absolute political power, sufficient to remake the old order; (3) political power could not be achieved by uncoordinated individuals but only through organization in a centralized party; (4) a party could be effective only if its members submitted to absolute party discipline — in party councils all might have a voice, it was claimed, but once the party decision was taken, all must obey it. The party took on the character of an ongoing, living entity with a historic mission, transcendent over individuals, who could find fulfillment by expending themselves in its cause.

Negotiation and Victory in Civil War. After the New Fourth Army incident of January 1941, when Nationalist troops fought an eight-day battle with a CCP force allegedly out of bounds south of the Yangtze, the government blockaded the CCP area in the Northwest more intensively, and a general fear arose that World War II would be followed by civil war. Both Chungking and Yenan responded by promising to seek a political rather than military solution of their differences. Mao now declared that, being still in the stage of "bourgeois-democratic revolution," China needed a "New Democratic government of a coalition nature embracing all parties and nonpartisan representatives." When the CCP in April-June 1945 held its seventh congress, the first since 1928,[1] it perfected its strategy for the postwar period by adopting the flexible line of "coalition government." Depending on expediency, this could mean a coalition *including* the KMT, as was to be proposed in 1946, or a coalition with minor parties and liberals *against* the KMT, as was to be achieved in 1949. Meanwhile this line appealed particularly to the modern-minded but frustrated intellectuals of Free China — professors, students, journalists, the literate and technically trained, who formed a basic resource for postwar reconstruction.

American diplomats also saw the inherent danger in the KMT-CCP rivalry, which might hamstring the war effort against Japan and might eventually let Russia back the Communists against the National Government. The Americans aimed therefore to get a united Chinese war effort under a "war council" representing both parties; to avert civil war by

[1] Congresses of the Chinese Communist Party: First, July 1921 (Shanghai); Second, May 1922 (Hangchow); Third, September 1923 (Canton); Fourth, January 1925 (Canton); Fifth, April 1927 (Hankow); Sixth, July 1928 (Moscow); Seventh, April 1945 (Yenan); Eighth, September 1956 (Peking); Eighth Congress, second session, May 1958 (Peking).

encouraging a political settlement, to which Chiang Kai-shek committed himself as early as September 1943; and meanwhile to strengthen the position of the National Government by building up its armies and securing "reforms" to broaden the base of its authority. Unfortunately, the original American program of 1942, to help Nationalist China become a "great power" (principally by modernizing its armies under General Joseph Stilwell as Chiang's chief of staff), had been undercut by events. The attack on Japan was made by sea across the Pacific instead of being based on China as initially expected. The China-Burma-India theater therefore received a lower priority, and American influence in China was lessened. Though China was kept in the war, Washington did not bargain with Chiang Kai-shek to secure a broader political base for the Nationalist regime in return for American aid. Gravely weakened by Japan's aggression, Chiang strove to buttress his personal power in the traditional fashion.

The Japanese surrender in August 1945 was followed by an American air-and-sea lift of half a million Nationalist troops back to the coastal centers, a Communist race overland to expand by taking Japanese surrenders in North China, and American repatriation of 1,200,000 Japanese troops. Even as the United States began to demobilize its forces, the long-foreseen Chinese civil war began in the KMT-CCP rivalry to reoccupy North China.

General George C. Marshall, the top American officer in World War II, was sent to Chungking in December 1945 to seek a political settlement of the burgeoning civil war. The only apparent alternative to war was to get the Chinese Communists into the political and military framework of a constitutional regime, in a position similar to that of Communist opposition parties in Western Europe. The two contending parties would both be represented in a reorganized coalition government under Chiang; their armies would be merged and reduced, whereupon American economic aid would be forthcoming. In January 1946 a cease-fire was issued by both armies and plans were drawn for a coalition government. In February a military merger was agreed to.

General Marshall during his year in China made a strenuous effort to remain neutral in the domestic political struggle, and simultaneously to uphold the supremacy of the recognized National Government without being used by it. The truce of January 1946 collapsed first in Manchuria, which had remained beyond the effective cease-fire limits. Behind the renewal of civil war in mid-1946 lay the Nationalists' confidence in their superior armament and the Communists' shrewd calculation of the Nationalists' vulnerability. And though Stalin showed little confidence in the prospects of an early victory for the Chinese Communists, his inauguration of a cold war with the West gave them the stimulus and opportunity to bid for power.

The eight-year Japanese invasion was followed by four years of civil war, 1946–49, one of the big wars of modern times. The Nationalist forces totaled at the beginning about three million men, the Communists about one million. The cost of United States aid to China between August 1945 and early 1948 was estimated at over two billion dollars — this in addition to the billion and a half committed during World War II. By sheer weight of arms the Nationalist forces spread out to major cities and provincial capitals, and, when eventually permitted by Russia, into Manchuria. In- numerable factors undid them: the Nationalist forces, going against American advice, became overextended; the military under Chiang were out of civilian economic control and never established a sound economic base; a postwar American-style military reorganization produced con- fusion; the Whampoa clique discriminated against provincial commanders and armies, particularly those of Kwangsi. The strategy of the Nation- alists was to hold strong positions defensively; their instinct was to hoard supplies and wait for others to move first; their field tactics were some- times masterminded by the Generalissimo from a great distance. Corrup- tion, demoralization, and desertion steadily depleted their armies.

The Communists pursued opposite tactics, maneuvering in the country- side, recruiting among the populace, destroying railroads, avoiding unfavorable terms of battle. They grew in numbers and armament, both from the big Japanese Manchurian stocks made available by Russia and from Nationalist defections and surrenders. By June 1948 the CCP roughly equaled the Nationalists in numbers of men, rifles, and cannon. Having cut off the government's Manchurian garrisons, in October 1948 they forced their surrender — a third of a million men.

The Nationalist cause had meanwhile been gutted in its city bases by an economic collapse. During World War II Chungking had steadily in- creased its expenditures, with income lagging far behind outlay. In 1941, when revenues provided only 15 per cent of expenditures, the government took over the land tax in kind and kept its bureaucracy alive on rice stipends. But the situation deteriorated. Prices doubled at first every few months, then by the week. In September 1945 the volume of note issue was 465 times that of July 1937. The end of World War II gave a brief respite as the Nationalist currency spread back over all China, but large government expenditures continued. Hyperinflation was resumed. Prices doubled 67 times between January 1946 and August 1948 and then rose 85,000 times in six months, destroying the last remnant of urban enthusiasm for the Nationalist cause.

Intellectuals meanwhile had been increasingly alienated from the government. When many professors joined in widespread agitation for domestic peace and against civil war, the CCP catered to this feeling, but KMT rightists tried to suppress it by force, even by assassination — such as the shooting in Kunming in mid-1946 of the Tsing Hua professor

Wen I-to, a poet and patriot educated in the United States. More and more students crossed the lines to join the CCP cause, which now seemed to possess the "Mandate of Heaven."

The showdown in the civil war came in a great two-month battle fought in the old Nien area of the Huai River basin. Chiang (against the advice of his staff) committed 50 divisions, out of 200 remaining, to form a strong point on the plains around Hsuchow. The Communists, however, not only controlled the villages but, by reactivating railways as they advanced, were able to deploy large forces and to surround and immobilize the well-armed Nationalists. By mid-November four Nationalist army groups, about 340,000 men, had been cut off and encircled on the plain. By late December the 130,000 surviving Nationalists, out of 66 divisions now committed, were squeezed into six square miles, surrounded by 300,000 of the People's Liberation Army. They surrendered on January 10, 1949. Of 550,000 Nationalists lost, the Communists claimed 327,000 surrendered. Jealous noncooperation among the Whampoa commanders, failure to use the Nationalist monopoly of the air, inability to bring their American weapons to bear on the enemy, every aspect of this great defeat underlines the old adage that armament alone cannot bring victory. Tientsin and Peking, long since cut off, surrendered in January 1949. In April the Communists stormed across the Yangtze, in May they entered Shanghai, in October Canton, in November Chungking. Chiang Kai-shek and most of the National Government leaders established themselves on Taiwan.

THE CHINESE COMMUNISTS' CONSOLIDATION OF POWER

Terminology is the first of many difficulties impeding the study of a contemporary revolution: in the 1950's, for example, "Red China" and "People's China" referred to the same entity from different angles. In the early 1960's, factually intended terms like "Mainland China" or "Communist China" run the danger of becoming outdated. Secondly, factual generalizations, never easy to make about a people as numerous as all the Europeans and Americans combined, have been impeded by lack of data. The revolutionary changes in China after 1949 occurred under a cover of totalitarian control of information and expression. Consequently the new regime was able to project its self-image to the outside world as well as to the Chinese people; but in the process, plans and achievements, hopes and facts, often became confused, sometimes even in the minds of the Communist leaders themselves.

Finally, patriotic Chinese resentment over China's unhappy fate in modern times rose to a new height after 1949 and was focused by the regime on "American imperialism" as the main source of China's troubles.

This animosity from Peking in turn roused American resentment at its unfair extremism.

Our effort to comprehend this political, ideological, economic, and social metamorphosis among 600 or 700 million people, so recent and yet so far away and difficult to observe, must begin with certain assumptions. First, Chinese governments over the centuries, struggling to spread and maintain a unified state and a uniform culture over a vast and diverse sub-continent, have become skilled at imposing centralized military, social, and ideological controls and large-scale bureaucratic administration; and the Chinese Communists have inherited this great tradition of unified government from Peking. Like scholar-officials trained to apply Confucian principles on behalf of the emperor, party members can act effectively for the CCP in far places roughly in proportion as they are trained in Marxism-Leninism and the thought of Mao Tse-tung.

Second, the ingredients of the central power that Mao wielded after 1949 had accumulated over several decades — not only in the 28-year experience of the Chinese Communist Party before its achievement of power but also in the experience of the whole Chinese people. The long era of warlordism and the Nationalist revolution, followed by the eight years of Japanese invasion and the four years of civil war, had produced a nationwide craving for central authority, firm leadership, peace and order. The forms and methods of a new order had also accumulated: the Leninist system of party dictatorship used by both parties; the moral and practical organization of student youth, developed ever since the pioneer days of the Chinese Y.M.C.A. and the Reform Movement of the 1890's; the techniques of material improvement in the village — famine relief, public health measures, fly-swatting, well-digging, tree-planting, crop improvement, the whole program of rural reconstruction, tracing back to nineteenth-century missionary beginnings and the mass education move-ment. Meanwhile, inspiring the use of these new methods was the spirit of devotion to country above all — including, for example, the ideals of citizenship espoused by Liang Ch'i-ch'ao, the welfare of "the people" invoked by Sun Yat-sen, the national honor once embodied in Chiang Kai-shek. Most of these developments could be classified as aspects of "modernization."[1]

Such perspectives may suggest that the new regime in Peking was less monolithic than it liked to think it was and less purely a product of Marxism-Leninism than it claimed to be. Its achievement was less to

[1] We defined "modernization" in Chapter 1 as an over-arching descriptive term that may be used to tie together the analyses of modern East Asian history derivable from the various disciplines of economics, political science, sociology, and the like. It is still slippery as an analytic concept, however, and tends to impute positive value ("modern" is "good") to processes that still require evaluation, by each observer of history.

invent all the parts of the new order than to put them together, under an unprecedented degree of central control made possible by Communist theory and practice. The result, in any case, was something quite new in Chinese experience.

Organization of Political Control. The CCP military take-over occupied a year and a half, from the end of 1948 until the occupation of all the mainland and Hainan Island by May 1950. In the midst of this process the People's Republic of China was proclaimed at Peking on October 1, 1949. The take-over left in office most local administrators. On the surface the Communist cadres gave it a festive air, proclaiming peace and "liberation." The troops generally behaved with restraint. It was a honeymoon period. Modern-trained Chinese came home from abroad to help rebuild their country.

The announced policy of the CCP for the first few years was to get rid of the KMT, supplant it with a "coalition" government, rehabilitate the economy, and reform China's armies and foreign relations. Mao's statement of July 1, 1949, "On the People's democratic dictatorship," propounded the dual thesis that the new government should be a "democratic coalition" under Communist leadership and at the same time a dictatorship directed against the reactionary classes or "enemies of the people." The "people" were composed of four classes: proletariat, peasantry, petty bourgeoisie, and national bourgeoisie. For the peasantry there was a prospect of maintaining, at least temporarily, private property in land, and for the bourgeoisie, a sector of privately owned industry. This carried out the original idea of the New Democracy. Since any individual could be transferred by a stroke of the pen to the category of reactionaries or "enemies of the people," this framework provided a means for sifting out dissident members of the population. The power of class imputation remained with the Communist Party.

The Preparatory Committee of the People's Political Consultative Conference was set up at Peking in June 1949, nominally representing 23 parties or groups. The PPCC itself was convened in September for 10 days, with 662 delegates. It passed the Common Program, a general statement of aims of the new coalition government, and the Organic Law of the Central People's Government, which made the working class the leader of the republic. Since the CCP represented the working class, this meant that the government was to be its administrative arm. Four committees and 30 ministries were created, 15 of them connected with economic affairs. In the top committee, 31 out of 56 seats were occupied by Communists. Chou En-lai became premier.

This powerful autocratic administration left half a dozen minor parties in existence, and gave posts of prominence to noncommunists. It was essential for Communist China to use the training and ability of that majority of the upper class which had never been Communist. Liberal intellectuals were therefore catered to, given some scope for their talents, and placed in high positions. (One is reminded of dynasties of conquest making use of Chinese administrators.) Most Western-returned scholars were in this category. Devoted to their country's future, long since estranged from the Kuomintang, they saw little alternative.

The constitution adopted in 1954 diminished the role of noncommunists. It did not remake the governmental structure but concentrated more authority in Peking under the State Council, which soon had five million persons working under its direction. Central authority was strengthened by abolishing the six regional military-political bureaus into which China had been divided during the take-over. The head of the principal industrial region in the Northeast (Manchuria) was the Shensi leader Kao Kang, now head of the State Planning Commission. In 1954, accused of excessive regional independence, he reportedly killed himself — one of the few cases of purge within the top leadership.

The tripod of power — army, government, and Party, each a separate hierarchy — was held together by the Communist leaders in the Party's Central Committee. The supreme power of its 94 members and 93 alternate members, as of 1962, was exercised by its Political Bureau of 19 members and six alternates (who might participate in discussions but not vote), and ultimately by this bureau's Standing Committee of seven persons. Below the Central Committee the party structure descended through roughly eight levels, the principal ones being six regional bureaus (re-established since 1960); 28 provincial or equivalent committees; 258 special district committees; 2200 *hsien* or similar committees; about 74,000 commune committees; and more than one million branch committees in the villages, factories, schools, and so on. These myriad committees exercised the Party's powers of leadership, supervision, patronage, and control.

The party structure was paralleled by the government structure that its members interpenetrated. Communist government reached far below the old Kuomintang level. On a territorial basis, People's Representative Congresses, like Russian soviets, were set up in a hierarchy from the village on up to the National People's Congress at Peking, which was first convened in 1954. These government congresses had quasi-legislative functions and were used mainly as sounding boards and transmission belts for policy from above. They provided an arena for popular participation in "democratic centralism" but had no real power in a Western legal sense.

Cutting across the territorial structure of the government congresses were the new nationwide mass organizations. The All-China Federation of Trade Unions, founded in 1922, by 1956 claimed a membership of over 13 million. In 1949 several parallel bodies were created: All-China Federations of Democratic Women, of Democratic Youth, of Cooperative Workers, and of Literature and Art. There were also an All-China Students Federation, a Children's Pioneer Corps, and many comparable bodies of more specialized character. Finally in 1953 there was established the All-China Association of Industry and Commerce for the national bourgeoisie, who still existed.

These mass organizations mobilized individuals according to their professional or social functions, in ways that territorial government could not. Controlled from key posts at the top by party members, they reached out to organize the general public through broad programs and an extensive administrative apparatus. The entire Chinese population was thus brought into one or another action group and its program of meetings, study, and agitation. Big training programs, with schools and indoctrination centers, recruited talent and activist personnel. Welfare and cultural programs under the mass organizations included such things as labor insurance, leave and pension systems, literacy classes, maternity hospitals, and midwife training. All this had its ultimate effect through the local units of organization, the neighborhood (street) committees and small groups at places of work.

The mass organizations were institutions of a new type in China, fulfilling primarily political functions as quasi-governmental agencies, bridging the immemorial gap between populace and officialdom. They were one part of the apparatus which applied the concept of the "mass line": that the CCP leadership must be guided by constant contact with the worker-peasant masses, first securing from the party workers full and accurate reports as to the masses' problems and opinions, then issuing policy directives to meet these problems, and finally getting the masses to adopt the policies as their own and carry them out. The mass organizations received government aid and even representation in the People's Congresses. In actuality, their main function was to indoctrinate. Working directly with the populace through meetings and demonstrations as well as propagandizing through mass media, they were able to manipulate the climate of opinion. Local police stations also used the street committees, whose duty it was to promote not only welfare measures but also mutual surveillance and denunciation among neighbors and within families. When coordinated in each locality, this whole apparatus could bring to bear upon every individual a pervasive and overwhelming public pressure.

The mechanism to increase this pressure was the campaign or drive. Campaigns might appear to start spontaneously, but they developed only as the Central Committee of the Party decreed. Campaigns quickly set in motion the enormous new apparatus of party, state, and mass organizations and directed its hammer blows against one target after another among the various classes and their institutions. The campaign method of revolutionary development, encouraging the cadres to attack certain heterodox ideas or undesired activities, could develop a high momentum and easily overshoot the mark, achieving "excesses." Each campaign therefore gave rise to another to check, redirect, or supersede the previous one.

Standing behind this apparatus were well-paid security forces and secret services. Locally the police stations handled cases or passed them on to the hierarchy of "people's courts," also an arm of the central administration. Cases normally came to trial only after the accused had fully confessed and denounced any others concerned in the crime with which he had been charged. Since law expressed the revolutionary policy of the Party, it remained largely uncodified and changeable. This uncertainty of the law for both judges and accused was, to be sure, reminiscent of the traditional Chinese system. Justice was still personal and particular, to be secured by applying universal principles to the circumstances discerned in each case, with a minimum of procedure. Litigation was disesteemed, legislation unimportant.

Economic Reconstruction. Early in 1949 Mao had announced a "shift to the cities" as the focus of a vigorous economic effort, reaffirming the primacy of the urban proletariat in a party which was now about 90 per cent of peasant origin. The first goal was to get production back to its prewar level within about three years. In Manchuria, the industrial progress achieved under the Japanese received a setback in 1945 when the Russians removed more than half the capital equipment. In China proper, railroads had been torn up by civil war, and urban labor had been demoralized by hyperinflation. It took some time to convince the city worker that "liberation" had brought him the "opportunity" to work harder. Wartime blockades between city and country had increased rural self-sufficiency; market crops like cotton had to be revived. Meanwhile inflation was still the major problem. The substitution of a new "people's currency" for Nationalist banknotes, even at favorable rates, left the regime still obliged to expand its note issue steadily to meet a budget deficit of perhaps 75 per cent. Prices in Shanghai rose 70 times in nine months.

The first move toward quelling inflation was to get the budget more or less balanced by increasing revenue, first in the countryside by collecting agricultural taxes in kind, then in the cities through devices like sales taxes on major commodities and business taxes set by the "democratic appraisals" of trade associations. Second, the entire fiscal administration was reorganized and rationalized. The central regime gradually made the tax-collection process more efficient, controlling it for the first time directly down to the village level. The regime also got control of money and credit through the banks and set up six government trading corporations to dominate prices in major consumer commodities. One device for restoring confidence was to express wages, salaries, bank deposits, and some government payments and bond issues in terms of commodity units, linked to quantities of goods in daily use rather than to monetary prices: thus a typical unit might be composed of 6 catties (8 lbs.) of rice, 1½ catties of flour, 16 catties of coal, and 4 feet of white cotton shirting. As prices rose, the commodity-based unit would rise accordingly in money terms, protected against further inflation. Thus by a variety of vigorous measures a balance was struck between the supply of goods and the flow of money income, and by mid-1950 inflation was conquered, an impressive achievement.

Among the accomplishments of the first year was an extensive reopening of railways, and by 1952 railways and highways had expanded to the modest totals of 15,000 and 75,000 miles respectively. Economic recovery was also aided by good harvests in 1950–52. Moreover, a centralized banking system and single uniform currency now covered the country. Budgeting could be attempted realistically for the first time.

Peking's long-term economic goal was to mobilize China's resources and reallocate them for industrialization. The first requirement was extension of government control over all segments of the economy. Private enterprise was permitted to continue in form, but in fact it was brought increasingly under state control. By controlling credit and raw materials and monopolizing key commodities, the state could now dominate production and commerce. The second requirement was control of the surplus product of the land.

The nationwide land reform, begun in mid-1950 and completed by late 1952 or early 1953, was not merely economic in aim but also social and political. Cadres coming to a village first identified out-and-out enemies, and then explained land reform to the poor peasantry in particular. After this a period of "class struggle" was inaugurated. In "struggle meetings" the accumulated grievances of the populace against local landlords or others could be brought forth in "speaking bitterness" or "settling accounts." Hatred could be fanned into mob violence. The entire community, by taking violent measures against local "enemies of the people," committed themselves to the new order.

The next phase temporarily used peasants' associations, which defined the class status of each individual as landlord, rich peasant, middle peasant, poor peasant, or farm laborer. Everyone was thus sorted out and brought under control. The peasants' associations also carried out the classification, confiscation, and redistribution of landholdings. The resulting "equalization of land tenure" was in the old tradition of peasant rebellions. The tiller now generally had title to his land.

But though it had been announced in 1950 that this New Democracy phase of private ownership would last for a "rather long time," in fact the Communist regime moved at once to lay the foundation of the new collectivist agrarian system. The first stage was a program for cooperatives, which moved gradually from North China to the south through a series of phases — first setting up temporary, usually seasonal, small-scale mutual-aid teams; then larger permanent ones; and then "lower-level" agricultural producers' cooperatives. In these, the peasants began to cultivate in common and share a common product in proportion to their pooled contributions of land, equipment, and labor. Up to this point the program was still posited on private ownership of land and voluntary cooperation for mutual benefit. Soon, however, the goal began to shift. The regime argued that only eventual collectivization could produce enough to pay for industrialization.

Social Reorganization. China's traditional ancestor-reverence, family cohesiveness, and filial piety had long been eroding. Communist "liberation" furthered the process. By the new marriage law of 1950, women were given full equality with men in rights of marriage, divorce, and property ownership. In the various campaigns of the 1950's, children were commended for denouncing their parents. Extended family ties were disparaged as feudal, and romantic love as bourgeois. The new state with its ubiquitous branches tried to displace the Chinese patrilineal family system, leaving the nuclear family as the norm.

The totalitarian mobilization of the populace was made easier in late 1950 by the Korean War. Reports of China's early victories and later of alleged "germ warfare" by the United States provided a useful sanction for intensifying anti-American sentiment and destroying the generally favorable Chinese image of America. War was also an opportunity to get rid of irreconcilables. Two major campaigns were mounted, to "Resist America, aid Korea," and to "Suppress counter-revolutionaries." They called for patriotic spying on relatives and neighbors, public denunciation even of parents, and consignment of enemies of the people, reactionaries, and counter-revolutionaries to "reform through labor." Executions were in the hundreds of thousands, some say many millions. The honeymoon was over.

In this context of terror and patriotism, foreign missionaries both Catholic and Protestant were denounced as spies and jailed or expelled. Among the Protestant churches in China, a "three-self" movement was set going, for "self-government, self-support, and self-propagation," free of the missionaries' alleged "cultural imperialism." In 1958, having cut off foreign support and pressured Chinese Christian leaders to join up, the movement unified the worship of all denominations in each locality. A Chinese Catholic church was also created, independent of the Pope, who responded with excommunication. All these efforts tried to reverse China's Western orientation.

The mechanisms for bringing public pressure to bear on designated types of individuals were used more and more plainly for refashioning China's social structure. The "Three-anti" and "Five-anti" movements of 1951–52 proceeded through well-defined phases. The "Three-anti" campaign, directed against officialdom, was anti-corruption, anti-waste, and anti-bureaucratism — an attempt to invigorate the vast new administrative apparatus. It brought the enlarged bureaucracy more thoroughly under central control with spectacular denunciations, public "trials," and great publicity.

The "Five-anti" movement, a similarly well-organized attack on the bourgeoisie, nominally was against bribery, tax evasion, theft of state assets, cheating in labor or materials, and stealing state economic intelligence. Employees were inspired to accuse employers, customers to accuse shopowners, and there was a general screening of all persons in urban trade and industry. As in all campaigns, the public was skillfully mobilized, and an appearance was created of great popular initiative, righteous anger, and enthusiasm for the triumph of virtue. Confessions, apologies, and the reform or elimination of culprits by labor camp, suicide, or execution followed. One immediate aim was financial. Large sums were milked from the business class. From this time the national bourgeoisie existed on sufferance. Eventually they were all expropriated and in January 1956 dutifully celebrated their own demise as a social class.

All these manipulations of the body politic squeezed out great numbers of "enemies of the state." Forced labor camps were the natural result, built both on the Soviet model and on the ancient Chinese tradition of *corvée* or labor service. The modern mobilization of the populace for labor service was no great innovation except for its increased scope: as many as four million persons might work on one project, like the much-publicized Huai River dikes and dams.

Precommunist China had been premodern and particularistic in many ways — in the neglect of punctuality, in the lack of civic consciousness and public neatness, in putting family before community and personal interests before national, in all those attitudes and habits that Chiang Kai-shek's futile New Life movement had condemned in 1935. In the old days everyone haggled over prices, took note of other people's manners, and treated every situation *ad hoc* and every person according to the circumstances if not on his merits. This premodern character of the old Chinese society, its "medieval" traits, had fascinated foreigners and humiliated patriots for a century. The Confucian scholars who sought a panacea in gunboats, then in technology, and finally in the reform of institutions had now been succeeded by radical social revolutionaries. With reforming zeal the CCP applied itself to remaking not only the economy and social order but also the Chinese individual.

Reform of Thought and Culture. Building upon methods used in Yenan to Leninize the Party, Liu Shao-ch'i and other organizers developed empirical procedures to deal with every type of enemy or supporter, including party members. The Communist aim was to change Chinese thinking and behavior in general, but especially to create reliable cadres for the enormous new apparatus and to recondition intellectuals inherited from the old order.

Thought reform usually had certain common features: control of the environment, both of the person physically and of the information available to him; the stimuli of idealism and terror intermixed; and a grim psychological experience, undergone with guidance through successive phases and intensified by manipulation of the individual's sense of guilt and shame. Privation, fatigue, prolonged insecurity, and tension, combined with exhausting repetitive indoctrination, could shatter any individual's sense of inner identity. The only escape for many was submission to authority and at least temporary acceptance of new attitudes and concepts. Perhaps it was not surprising that in China, where the practical art of human relations had been more fully developed than anywhere else, these psychological methods should be most advanced.

For Chinese students, this intellectual-emotional reconditioning was carried out in the big revolutionary colleges set up through the reorganization and expansion of the educational system. Trainees went through indoctrination courses of several months' duration in study groups of six to ten persons. A typical six-month course of thought reform had three stages. The first was group identification, a period of togetherness and considerable freedom and enthusiasm, leading the trainee to expose himself freely and engage wholeheartedly in a "thought mobilization." The second phase was induced emotional conflict. The individual submitted his first summary of his own life and thought. Group pressures were focused by experienced leaders so that each individual became heavily involved emotionally, under assault. He might struggle with himself and be "struggled with" by his group-mates over an excess of subjectivism or objectivism, of opportunism or dogmatism, and so forth. The individual was now psychologically alone, isolated within himself. He soon felt a guilt that turned him against himself and prepared him to achieve through confession a psychological catharsis. The third phase was submission and rebirth. When his final thought summary or confession was accepted he usually felt exhilarated, cleansed, a new person. In some cases this months-long process might constitute an induced conversion of almost religious proportions. Through it, the individual was manipulated to associate his relief from tension with the external authority of the group and the Party, on which he would henceforth, it was hoped, be dependent.

Out of the Chinese inheritance, many traditions can be invoked or prostituted for modern purposes. While Chinese Communist self-criticism is partly in Soviet style, it is also a bit reminiscent of the Confucian doctrine of self-cultivation. Thus Wang Yang-ming (1472–1529) had attacked the dualism of "knowledge and action" and urged self-cultivation as a process by which the true philosopher brought his thought and conduct into consonance, so that knowledge was realized in action and action contributed to knowledge. This idea was echoed by Sun Yat-sen ("Knowledge is difficult, action is easy") and later by Chiang Kai-shek. Although Confucian self-cultivation was not a group affair, it stressed the moral improvability of human nature, the ancient Chinese belief that through proper ethical instruction and exhortation man can be made into a more social being. Thought reform, at Yenan and later, made use of traditional Chinese terminology and invoked Confucian sanctions. The good Communist, according to Liu Shao-ch'i, must discipline himself through self-cultivation, through "watching himself when alone," so as to become flexibly and resourcefully obedient to the Party's leadership. Where Confucianism instilled loyalty to family, father, and emperor, Maoism now focused it on the "people," the Party, and the leader.

Thought reform seemed particularly necessary in the Chinese intellectual and literary world. Mao Tse-tung's dicta of 1942 on literature and art, that they are political tools in the class struggle and wholly subordinate to politics, supplied the major premises. The full force of meetings, denunciations, and special publications was assembled, for example, to attack Hu Shih as the symbol of "decadent American bourgeois pragmatism." The same campaign discredited Western-type literary criticism, particularly that based on individual taste or historical research, as part of the effort to stamp out the "worship America" tendency and the intellectual freedom associated with the West. But the Communist Party's creative writers still tended occasionally to be critics, the same as in the Soviet Union. Some who had gained fame attacking the evils of the old order now criticized imperfections in the new, particularly the Central Committee's claim through its literary commissar, Chou Yang, to be the final arbiter of artistic excellence. A rebellious disciple of Lu Hsun named Hu Feng was pilloried for this in a nationwide campaign. Eventually his denunciators, like the revolutionary woman novelist Ting Ling, were also denounced and purged by Chou Yang.

Just as thought reform and other campaigns winnowed the population, separating out potential enemies and recruits, so the great corpus of China's historical inheritance had to be reappraised in Marxist-Leninist terms and integrated into the new state-and-culture. "Applying the universal principles of Marxism-Leninism to the concrete realities of China" was a never-ending process. Most of China's glorious past, for example, had to be put by definition within the Marxian period of "feudalism." Precisely when "capitalism" had begun in China was disputed; but since 1840, it was argued, foreign "capitalist imperialism," allied with domestic "feudal reaction," had checked and distorted China's "normal" capitalist development. Such formulas, imposed upon academic learning for political purposes, raised some new questions and absorbed scholarly attention.

Military Strength and Soviet Aid. Having early in 1949 proclaimed his policy of "leaning to one side" against "capitalist imperialism," Mao Tse-tung spent nine weeks of hard bargaining in Moscow (December 1949–February 1950). Finally he signed a thirty-year Sino-Soviet alliance treaty against aggression by Japan or any power (meaning the U.S.A.) joined with Japan. Soviet power thenceforth provided a shield behind which the Chinese Communists could pursue their domestic revolution, get rid of the last vestiges of "imperialist" rights and privileges in the former treaty ports and in the economy, religion, and education, and try to reassert China's control over border areas.

It is not certain that Peking expected to join in the Soviet-armed North Korean aggression of June 1950 against South Korea. Instead, the CCP evidently hoped to seize Taiwan from Nationalist hands, but this was prevented when President Truman ordered the American Seventh Fleet to stop invasion either way across the Taiwan Strait. Impelled presumably by strategic concern for the industrial base in Manchuria, Peking entered the Korean War in October after U.N. forces advanced northward across the 38th parallel. Aided by Russian-made tanks, planes, and artillery, battle-hardened Chinese forces were soon boasting of victories over the American "imperialists," and they continued to receive Russian military support even after the prolonged truce talks began in July 1951. The People's Liberation Army also invaded Tibet in October 1950 and reasserted Chinese control in a year-long campaign of "liberation" and subjugation. Despite their cost, these campaigns built up China's military power. Afterward, military modernization was pushed with Russian help; and in 1955 compulsory military service began to draw on the five million young men reaching the age of 20 each year, to create the largest reservoir of military manpower in history. A professional officer class developed on the top level of a regular army of about 2.5 million men. But jet planes and their fuel, for example, still had to be procured from the U.S.S.R.

From the start, Soviet aid came only at a price. In 1950 Sino-Soviet "joint-stock" companies were set up, on the model used in Eastern Europe, for the development of mining in Sinkiang and similar purposes potentially beneficial to the U.S.S.R. However, after the death of Stalin (March 5, 1953) these companies were liquidated (in 1954). Similarly the Soviets gradually gave up their special position in Manchuria, ending joint control of the main railway in early 1953 and withdrawing from the Port Arthur naval base in 1955.

In industrialization the Soviet example and expertise were at first the Chinese Communists' greatest inspiration. Thousands of Chinese trainees went to the U.S.S.R., and thousands of Russian technicians armed with blueprints came to help renovate or build the 211 old and new projects that led the industrial program (125 more projects were added in 1958–59). Starting in 1950, the Soviet Union loaned China $60 million a year in economic aid for five years, to be repaid by Chinese exports of raw materials. China's prewar pattern of foreign trade was reversed, flowing to the Soviet bloc instead of to the West and Japan. A second loan in 1954 provided $26 million a year for five years, though by that time such a sum would hardly cover the repayments due the U.S.S.R. on the first loan. China received essential help in technology, military hardware, and capital equipment but went into debt accordingly.

Though the limitations of the Soviet example were not at first apparent to Peking, Communist China's capacity to follow the Stalinist Russian industrial model was inhibited by certain specific conditions. China had extensive coal and iron ore reserves, and other mineral and oil resources greater than had been realized, but utilizing them would require a costly investment in power and transport. China at her level of industrial development in the early 1950's was actually closer to the Russia of 1900 than to the Soviet Union of 1928 when the five-year plans began the Soviet industrialization. Russia *in 1900* already had a higher per capita production of pig iron, steel, and cotton goods, and more railroad track per square mile, than China *in 1952* — and only one-quarter the rural population density. By 1928 Russia had a much more extensive rail network and her production of coal, iron, steel, power, textile products, and the like in per capita terms was far greater than China's in 1952. The Soviet model of industrialization, which stressed heavy industry at the expense of the peasant, was therefore not suited to China's situation. Yet the CCP was determined to stress heavy industry even more than the Soviets had.

Viewed against the population increase and the balance between population and food resources in the two countries, China's prospects of emulating Russia grew perceptibly dimmer. The superabundance of people (estimated by the census of 1953 at 583 million and increasing about 12 to 14 million yearly), together with the comparative lack of new land for cultivation, meant that China's population must press upon the food supply even more than Russia's had. The standard of living therefore could not be modernized very far, in the sense of raising it from the bamboo-and-rice/millet level, within the foreseeable future. Even though the centralized Chinese state might build up a superstructure of heavy industry and military power, it would remain a colossus weak in the stomach, vulnerable to natural calamity.

Mao and his colleagues were loath to accept any limits on their hopes. Consequently the ineradicable limitations in China's material resources, combined with the CCP's success in consolidating its power and mobilizing the country's human resources, set the stage by 1955 for one of the great national efforts and frustrations of history.

THE CHINESE EFFORT AT "SOCIALIST TRANSFORMATION"

From 1953 the CCP leadership inaugurated a second phase of the effort to modernize China, Communist fashion, through planned development toward "socialism" in both industry and agriculture. The initial results, usually couched in the very un-Confucian terms of "struggle," appeared impressive.

The Struggle for Agricultural Collectivization and Industrialization. The practical completion of land reform by the end of 1952, together with the tightening of controls over the urban and industrial sector of the economy, put Peking by 1953 in a position to plan joint programs for industrialization and for the collectivization of agriculture. Catching up with the West materially would require a harsh regimentation of economic effort over a prolonged period. Industrialization would make it necessary to import Soviet-bloc capital goods, to be paid for by exporting mainly agricultural products. To extract more from the farm economy, a squeezing mechanism would have to be created in the form of true collectives. While these might lower incentives among agricultural workers, they seemed, in CCP thinking, to be the only sure way to enforce saving and check the growth of a "rich peasant" class based on private landowning. Collectives also seemed the most efficient channels for introducing agronomic technical improvements. Moreover, the 1953 grain output failed to increase as hoped, and a state grain trade monopoly was instituted in November. Heavy floods in 1954 and continued stringency led in August 1955 to tax quotas for each grain-producing household. The drive for collectivization was an integral part of this effort to control rural production and consumption.

The initial decision to move toward collectivization, announced in December 1953 after some intra-party debate, got results faster than anticipated. By mid-1955, fifteen per cent of the farm lands and farming families were said to be in agricultural producers' cooperatives, defined as "semi-socialist" collectives. Mao Tse-tung now decided against those colleagues who wanted a more "gradual" and "voluntary" program; he proposed to move rapidly toward the final elimination of the rich peasant, the merchant-speculator, land rent, and all capitalistic tendencies in rural life. In July, accordingly, he called for 250 million peasants to be in agricultural producers' cooperatives of a "semi-socialist" type by early 1958. Within China's million villages, each such cooperative would include about 50 families. This bold plan, pushed by party cadres in the countryside, again went faster than expected. Within less than a year, by May 1956, nine-tenths of the peasantry were reported to have joined the cooperatives, which were soon being asked to move on to the "higher" level of socialized agriculture by turning themselves into full collective farms.

Warned by the disastrous Soviet collectivization of 1929–32, when so much of the livestock and other farming capital was destroyed, the CCP made the process more gradual: it did not lead directly to state ownership of the land, but rather to ownership by the individual cooperatives, which formally bought out the peasant proprietors. The process moved by stages from temporary mutual-aid teams to permanent full-scale cooperatives, from small groups to large ones. Most peasants evidently saw no alternative but to have faith in Chairman Mao and the Party. Still fresh in their memory was the burning of landlords' title deeds, which had given them at least temporary ownership of the land. Moreover, all noncommunist leadership in the villages had been eliminated.

The cooperatives, usually one or two to a village, now became the central actors in the Chinese rural program, owning all fields and equipment. As the new focus of village life, the cooperatives undertook the local public works and welfare activities which under the empire had been the province of gentry leadership. State farms (3300 at the end of 1955, using graduates of 26 agricultural colleges) served mainly as pilot operations to meet technical problems in their localities and set an example. Mechanized agriculture, with machine tractor stations like those of the Soviet Union, remained for the distant future except on the broad plains of Manchuria.

The ambitious twelve-year rural plan for 1956–67 set forth bright promises: cultural amenities would be introduced (radios, libraries, cinemas, etc.); disease, flood, and drought would be eliminated, forests widely planted, labor fully employed. Mainly through full employment, the plan envisioned 400 man-days of work applied annually to every hectare of land, thus doubling production in South China and increasing it nationally by half. Equally ambitious was the long-term plan to control the Yellow River by a "staircase" of big dams on the main stream, with accompanying benefits of hydro-power for multi-purpose projects, and irrigation for much of North China. For the farm boy just learning to read, this confident vision was undoubtedly inspiring. For doubters and dissenters there was "reform through labor." Meantime food rationing was instituted and quotas were set for the compulsory delivery of commercial crops. How to resolve the competing investment demands of agriculture and industry was not indicated.

Preparation for a Soviet-type forced-draft industrial development had gone forward with the nationalization of banking, industry, and trade: the state took control of enterprises, making them joint state-private concerns, and launched campaigns to exhaust the entrepreneur and make him in effect a state employee. The first five-year plan, nominally for 1953–57, was not really drawn up until two and a half years had elapsed in building an administrative structure, training technicians, and creating statistical services. When disclosed in July 1955, it was heralded as inaugurating the "transition to socialism," which had formally super-seded the New Democracy as of 1953.

The conflict between the development of agriculture and of industry, and the consequent subordination of the former, was apparent in the first five-year-plan targets announced in 1955: steel output would be tripled, power and cement doubled, machine tools more than tripled; but cotton piece goods would increase by less than one-half, and food grains by less than one-fifth. In other words, industry could grow only as the farmer kept his consumption down. Collectivization had put him in a box: through price manipulation in favor of industry, his product could be taken from him indirectly as well as by outright collection of crops and taxes. Just as men had been cheaper than armaments in Chinese warfare, so in her agricultural development China would have to stress capital-cheap, labor-intensive projects like flood-control dikes. For China's capital investment was to be concentrated in heavy industry, which would receive seven or eight times the investment in light (consumer goods) industry.

The enthusiasts who now dominated the CCP Central Committee beat down the "rightist conservatism" of their policy opponents by calling in 1956 for a "leap forward" in which the people's productive energies would be psychologically liberated and devices such as emulation cam-paigns among competing workers' groups would achieve "quantity, speed, quality, and economy" of production all at once. This forced-draft industrialization was soon able to channel something like 30 per cent of the Chinese people's gross national product through the government, which used it approximately one-fourth for defense, one-fourth for administration and social services, and one-half for investment. Com-munist China's industrial growth in this period seemed rapid and formid-able — as of 1957, the fastest of any underdeveloped Asian country.

The Struggles with Intellectuals and with Cadres. "Socialist construc-tion" required the mobilization of all the nation's energies, including those of the thin stratum of about 100,000 technical, professional, and academic "higher intellectuals" who were still mainly Western-trained. The party heads seem to have believed, optimistically, that their leadership and doctrines had by this time re-educated, "spiritually transformed," and won allegiance from this group; but they were evidently concerned that the new party apparatus with its host of young cadres had stifled intellectual life and tyrannized over the older intellectuals. Campaigns were therefore

mounted in 1956–57 to manipulate these two strategic elements, intellectuals and cadres.

The Party early in 1956 initiated a "struggle against rightist conservative
ideology" among intellectuals in order to ensure their fullest contribution
to the tasks of socialist transformation. This was to be achieved by
improving the intellectuals' working conditions, giving them more access
to foreign publications, more free time, more scope for initiative, and at
the same time getting them to "remold" themselves ideologically and
qualify in large numbers for party membership. A campaign for freer
criticism of the cadres and bureaucracy was also begun in May 1956 under
the classical slogan "Let a hundred flowers bloom together, let the hundred
schools of thought contend." This was not a clarion call for free speech.
Criticism must not overstep the implicitly assumed limits of complete
devotion to the Party's final authority. (This would be in the imperial
censor's tradition of "loyal remonstrance," not like a "loyal opposition"
in the West.)

It is a neat trick to foster intellectual vitality within a framework of
uncritical loyalty. Mao announced his doctrine of contradictions — some
"antagonistic" as between the regime and its "enemies" abroad or at home,
and some "non-antagonistic," normal and arguable, as between the
bureaucracy and "the people." Within this framework he evidently
hoped that a continuing "struggle" over the execution of policy, using his
method of "unity-criticism-unity," could be healthily pursued and yet
contained. As in the *cheng-feng* movement of the Yenan period, this
dialectical process would call forth criticism and then would meet it,
letting extreme views emerge to be dealt with through open argument, in
order to discover faults and correct them and also to discover fault-
finders and reform them. Any of "the people" who seemed hypercritical
and disloyal could be classed as "enemies" to be coerced.

Repeated invitations eventually released a surprising torrent of publicly
expressed dissatisfaction on the part of intellectuals with the CCP's
totalitarian political system, its ideas, aims, and methods. This widespread
and basic criticism startled the Party in the late spring of 1957 and was
harshly suppressed. The recent critics were soon obliged to publicly
accuse themselves and condemn one another in an "Anti-rightist" campaign.

Meanwhile the Party's Central Committee faced the even more serious
problem of controlling the enormous apparatus of cadres that executed
its policies. By 1957 the twin drives in agriculture and industry had
achieved spectacular results. The face of the country was changed with
new roads, factories, cities, dikes, dams, lakes, afforestation, and new
cultivation, for which the 650 million of China, at least a fifth of mankind,
had been mobilized in nationwide efforts of unparalleled intensity and

magnitude. Yet this vast "surging tide of socialism" had entailed a struggle not only against material conditions but also against recalcitrant personalities and human nature under the guidance and urging of the party cadres.

The rapid growth of this apparatus of activists was indexed by the rise in party membership — from 4.4 million in 1949 to 17 million in 1961.[1] In addition, there were the Young Communist League (about 25 million in 1959) and the Young Pioneers (about 50 million in 1962). This multitude was needed to do the Party's work, yet it was largely unseasoned and inexperienced. Four-fifths of the party members probably lacked a secondary or high school education. Young cadres fresh from their indoctrination, though given the prestige of learning and a code of leadership through self-sacrifice, might easily fall into the evils of "blind optimism," "dogmatism," and "commandism," or of "conservatism," "empiricism," and "blind opportunism," instead of manipulating the peasantry through discussion, logic, and persuasion. Cadres could be stimulated, by Mao's ideological pronouncements and the party line, more easily than they could be restrained and given wisdom, or saved from the corruption and false reporting that had inveterately characterized peasant-official relations in the past. Agricultural collectivization had in fact proceeded unevenly, with considerable friction on the spot and overoptimistic reporting to superiors. The Eighth Party Congress, meeting in September 1956, found that the peasantry had been widely misled by the cadres' false promises. Industrial projects had similarly been overambitious. The masses had actually suffered a lowering of their standard of living.

Roused by the dangers of excessive "commandism" and of being "out of touch with the masses," an evil that also seemed to be exemplified in the Hungarian revolt of October-November 1956, the CCP inaugurated in April 1957 a great ideological campaign for "rectification" of the Party's working style. Parallel at first to the "Hundred Flowers" campaign to induce criticism from the intellectuals, the "Rectification" drive to control party cadres was soon merged with the "Anti-rightist" campaign to control intellectuals. Both groups were brought into a big campaign for "downward transfer," *hsia-fang*, to move teachers, students, and city cadres and functionaries into the countryside so that by manual labor among the villagers they could avoid "separation from the masses" and could also help agricultural production.

But it proved easier to discipline the small number of intellectuals than to curb the overenthusiasm of the millions of cadres — or indeed to

[1] Growth of CCP membership:

1921	57	1949	4,488,000
1927	58,000	1953	6,612,000
1940	800,000	1957	12,720,000
1945	1,211,000	1961	17,000,000

remain uninfected by it. The fanaticism of the revolution reached a new height in 1958. The top leadership fell victim to its own enthusiasm.

The Great Leap Forward and the Communes. The "Great Leap" in industrial production and the formation of large-scale rural "communes" in 1958 aimed to meet China's economic problems by intensive use of labor. But both measures proved inefficient, and too intensive to be sustained.

The Great Leap drive for increased production — to "catch up with Britain" in fifteen years (a mortifying goal for a nation twelve times as populous) — was epitomized by the frenzied effort to increase iron and steel production by unskilled use of small, uneconomic backyard smelters. This was part of a general attempt to energize local party leadership and to decentralize economic management. The task of gathering statistics now devolved onto the "rectified" local cadres; and the result was a spate of raw production statistics that misled Peking into believing that socialist enthusiasm, skill, and self-sacrifice could somehow in one year, for example, double China's food production. The incredible figures that the Central Committee trumpeted abroad in 1958 had to be humiliatingly withdrawn in 1959.[1]

The same period saw a movement to amalgamate cooperative farms into planned, gigantic, self-sufficient communes, averaging some 5000 households (say about 22,500 people) in a military type of organization. These were designed to combine all the local organs of government administration and of agricultural and industrial production. This would bring large-scale efficiency to the village and get all its labor, including its womanpower, into full employment. This grandiose concept was pursued with utopian fervor — for example, by trying to set up a free supply of food and other necessities "according to need." But it proved impossible in practice. China's intensive hand-gardening agriculture could not be organized even on the big scale of the Russian *kolkhoz*, especially in the absence of mechanization. In a few years the unit of production was again at the village level in the cooperative farm of about 20 to 40 households that could function in personal contact, now called a "production team."

After overleaping itself in this way in 1958–59, with "politics in command" and the Party almost merged with the government, Communist China underwent several years of serious economic dislocation. Malnutrition was widespread; the people were exhausted and apathetic. Transportation broke down. Industry stagnated, as in a severe economic

---

[1] Thus the CCP claims and hopes for grain production were announced as follows: production in 1957, 185 million metric tons; production in 1958 (as claimed in December 1958 and April 1959), 357 million tons; forecast (in December 1958) for 1959, 525 million tons; revised claim for 1958 (as of August 1959), 250 million tons.

depression. Many plants closed down, and statistics were no longer published. The regime acknowledged that agriculture, short-changed for a decade, must now receive top priority. Though nature was blamed, it became apparent that Mao and the CCP, using their political power, had made economic errors on a gigantic scale.

The mounting extremism of the Chinese revolution during the 1950's, the feverish tendency to accelerate campaigns and revise targets upward, is reminiscent of other great social upheavals. This tendency was continually encouraged by Mao and the Central Committee in the faith that the masses would respond to a Marxist-Leninist leadership that knew how to unleash the latent "productive forces" of the society and free the "creative capacity" of the Chinese working class that had previously, it was believed, been held in check by domestic and foreign exploiting classes. Seldom has faith been frustrated on so vast a scale. By the 1960's the Chinese people had learned how to coexist with the CCP regime, as they had with autocracies in the past, but the initial enthusiasm of the revolution had been spent.

CHINA IN THE WORLD SCENE

Revolution at home went with a revolutionary attitude toward the outside world, and CCP thinking became fixed upon the universalistic theme of "American imperialism" as the enemy and China's "liberation" as the model for all colonial and semi-colonial peoples. Circumstance imposed upon Peking the traditional aim of strong dynasties: to dominate contiguous areas in defense of the Middle Kingdom. But this practical aim of conventional power politics was seen as part of a great world-wide struggle of the progressive "socialist camp" against the reactionary "imperialist camp." In these terms China's newly heightened nationalism found expression in a more-than-nationalistic universalism, a vision of People's China at the top of a new revolutionary world. In this spirit, Peking during the 1950's utilized both coercion and persuasion in foreign policy, as on the home front, and similarly ran into difficulties after 1957.

Expansion of Chinese Influence. The first phase, 1950 to 1954, began belligerently. In October 1950, Chinese troops intervened in Korea and entered Tibet, as we have noted, and soon thereafter Chinese military support aided the Viet Minh in Indo-China. But after two years of negotiation, the Korean armistice was signed in July 1953; and after the defeat of the French at Dien Bien Phu, France's withdrawal from Indo-China was agreed upon, with China participating as a great power, at Geneva in July 1954. This expansion of Peking's influence, however, roused defensive measures. In September 1954 a joint defense system, the Southeast Asia Treaty Organization (SEATO), was created by the

United States, Britain, France, Australia, New Zealand, the Philippines, Thailand, and Pakistan. Washington also signed defensive alliances with Seoul (October 1953) and Taipei (December 1954). Thus, by the time the Communist-Nationalist confrontation over the offshore island of Quemoy in Amoy harbor led to a crisis in early 1955, Communist China's activity concerning four contiguous areas was matched by an American-led anticommunist effort at "containment."

After the militancy of these early years came a phase of greater reliance on diplomatic persuasion. At the Geneva conference of April-July 1954, Chou En-lai joined the foreign ministers of the other powers in the effort to create stability in Indo-China as France withdrew. In negotiating at this time with India and Burma, Chou enunciated five principles of "peaceful coexistence." These also formed his main theme at the conference held in April 1955 at Bandung in western Java by leaders of 29 Asian and African states. In tune with the "Bandung spirit," the American and Communist Chinese ambassadors at Warsaw began to hold periodic talks.

Yet this "soft" line soon yielded to a "hard" one. In late 1957, after the Soviets' spectacular success in orbiting their first "sputniks," Mao went to Moscow to celebrate the fortieth anniversary of the Bolshevik revolution. Declaring that "the east wind prevails over the west wind," he called for a new belligerency in East-West relations. This was becoming evident on several fronts: first, in the Taiwan Strait. The American build-up of Nationalist military power had been resumed in 1951. Thereafter the Nationalists increasingly harassed the mainland by espionage, reconnaissance and leaflet-dropping flights, and commando raids. They also strengthened the fortification of "the front" on Quemoy, committing thereto a third of the Nationalist forces. Communist bombardment in August-September 1958 created a second Quemoy crisis, which subsided but left Quemoy a bone of contention, still held by the Nationalists as a recognized part of the mainland.

Another area of renewed belligerency was Tibet, whose people after 1956 were pressed toward a socialist revolution that would amount to Sinicization. A rising at Lhasa in March 1959, when the Dalai Lama fled to India, led to harsh repression by the Chinese and to Tibetan charges of genocide. During the following summer Sino-Indian friction increased on both ends of the Himalayan frontier and finally erupted in hostilities in October 1962. China got control of the strategic route between Tibet and Sinkiang through the Aksai-Chin region (see map, p. 798) but shattered the Indian dream of peaceful coexistence. Intensified efforts were now made to absorb the Tibetans into the Chinese state as a minority nationality in an Autonomous Region, like the Inner Mongolian Autonomous Region founded in 1947 and the Sinkiang Uighur Autonomous Region founded in 1955. Accordingly Han (i.e., Chinese) settlers as well as troops and officials were sent into Tibet, while Tibetans were taken into the People's

Liberation Army and their old social groupings broken up. Tibet ceased to be a buffer state.

Similarly the Chinese population expanded into the thinly populated border regions of northern Manchuria, Inner Mongolia, Kansu, Ch'ing-hai, Sinkiang, and even Hainan Island. Settlers, prisoners, and volunteers brought in to cultivate virgin lands or develop mineral resources tended to dominate the local minority peoples. The vast area once ruled by the Ch'ing dynasty as a multi-racial empire was now largely occupied by the Chinese nation.

Peking's dominant influence in North Korea after the war gave a new form to the old tributary relationship. In the same way North Vietnam continued its tradition of local independence of Chinese rule while imitating Chinese institutions. North Vietnam's systematic aggression against the South after 1959, first supporting the development of guerrilla warfare, assassination, sabotage, and terrorism, then intervening more directly with troops, made full use of CCP techniques and support. It also capitalized on the long-established gulf between city and countryside, between the urban upper class and the peasant village, where a new and tighter social and political order could now be created. The fighting in South Vietnam and Laos increased Chinese influence in the whole region.

The Struggle against Soviet "Revisionism." The Sino-Soviet bloc after 1949, as though joined on a geological fault line, was highly vulnerable to ideological earthquake. For under Mao the CCP had long since asserted its organizational and ideological autonomy in applying Marxism-Leninism to China. Peking, like Moscow, was now an autonomous center of doctrinal authority; international Communism was no longer monolithic; and under the pull of national interests, friction if not rupture was inevitable. Under the party lines of the "united front" and "coalition government," the CCP had stressed that the whole Chinese "people," as a combination of all "revolutionary classes," rather than the one class of the "proletariat," were the makers of China's history. After 1949 this nationalistic trend grew stronger as the CCP organized a multi-class regime under its own "hegemony" and the new People's Republic of China began to fulfill nationalist aspirations long latent. Inevitably, this autonomous growth under the CCP diverged from contemporary Soviet developments, which were at a different level of industrialization and political stability. Mao proclaimed that, by a determined use of organized will power, men could transform their consciousness and release energies hitherto untapped; this concept of the primacy of "subjective" forces underlay the Great Leap Forward of 1958 but met with little favor in Moscow.

The mutual denunciations issued by Peking and Moscow in the summer of 1963 indicated that their differences went back at least to 1956, the beginning of Soviet "de-Stalinization," which had surprised and embarrassed the CCP at a time when it was still invoking Stalin's name and building a "cult of personality" around Mao Tse-tung. Animosity increased in 1960, when Soviet technicians and blueprints were suddenly withdrawn from China. From the outset, Soviet aid had been rather limited and had required repayment; it had stopped short of nuclear weapons (evidently promised in 1957) and finally ceased supporting China's own efforts to develop them. Since nonsupply of Soviet equipment hamstrung China's development, the U.S.S.R. became a target for the vexation caused by the failure of the Great Leap of 1958.

The bitterness of this sectarian controversy, attacking error and apostasy among the faithful, was expressed in ideological terms. The Chinese Communist Party saw itself as the real heir of Lenin's and Stalin's revolution and Soviet policy under Khrushchev as an opportunist "revision" of orthodox truths. With the Great Leap Forward and the communes, Mao had claimed to be surpassing Moscow on the road to Communism, but the Communist Party of the Soviet Union ridiculed these efforts as foolhardy pretensions. It decried Peking's fanaticism as a dangerous deviation from the international Soviet-led program for the eventual victory of Communism.

The doctrinal conflict between the two fraternal parties was also an international power struggle between the two nation-states that they ruled. National interests were in opposition at some sensitive points: for example, concerning the Turkic peoples in the trans-Pamir regions of Sinkiang and Russian Turkestan. There were personal differences too. Indeed, the causes of the split, as a major event, may be found on economic, strategic, political, and personal levels, as well as cultural and ideological.

Historically, the recent decade of Soviet paramountcy in China's foreign affairs may be compared with the decades of British influence, for example, in the 1860's, or of Japanese influence after 1900, or of American influence during the period of the Nanking Government. Many outside peoples have had their day in aiding the transformation of the Middle Kingdom, but none permanently; all have been cast off.

As the Sino-Soviet split widened, Peking sought to capture the leadership of the Communist world revolution by all possible means, exporting cultural missions, exhibitions, militant propaganda, and aid to new nations, supporting "national liberation movements," especially in Asia and Africa, even claiming to lead the "colored races" against the "whites." These efforts had varying success. At least until 1964, more states recognized the Republic of China on Taiwan than the People's Republic at Peking, which mainly through American opposition year after year was still refused admission to the United Nations.

The Chinese Republic on Taiwan. After the Ch'ing dynasty took Peking in 1644, it could not rest content until it conquered Taiwan in

1683. Similarly, fifteen years after taking the mainland, the CCP continued to claim supremacy over all parts of the Chinese world as vigorously as any dynasty. It joined the Nationalist Government at Taipei in asserting the unity of all Chinese; and it denounced the idea of "two Chinas" (one on the mainland, one on Taiwan) as a threat sustained only by American "aggression."

In a similar spirit the (Nationalist) Government of the Republic of China in exile, still dominated by the Kuomintang (though since 1948 under a constitution instead of "party tutelage"), considered itself only temporarily superimposed upon Taiwan as one of its provinces and maintained a posture of militant readiness for "counterattack" to recover the mainland.

Political life on Taiwan reflected the psychology of rulers in exile, proudly determined not to give up claims the assertion of which sustained their hopes and sense of historical consistency. As a consequence, the Nationalist Government continued, as on the mainland though in different circumstances, to devote itself in large part to military preparation for counterattack, rather than concentrating its energies, under the protection of the American Seventh Fleet, on more general development. In this garrison atmosphere the tradition of an almost monarchic, one-man leadership died slowly. After all, it was barely fifty years since the abdication of the Son of Heaven.

Relations between the ruling minority from the mainland and the Taiwan-Chinese majority met an initial disaster in March 1947. The flagrant corruption of the Nationalist take-over authorities, before the arrival of most of their compatriots, provoked widespread demonstrations that were countered by the systematic killing of several thousand leading Taiwanese. As time passed, most of the two million or so political leaders, civil servants, teachers, and soldiers who came from the mainland had to depend on modest stipends from the National Government, while the ten million Taiwan-Chinese in agriculture and trade began to participate more directly in the island's economic growth. On the other hand, the Taiwanese participated in political life for the most part only under the provincial government. Under it the election process gradually developed. Taiwanese became the majority among students and faculties in higher education and held most of the offices in local government.

Economic growth was assisted by American aid, both military and economic, as well as by land reform. The Sino-American Joint Commission on Rural Reconstruction, after beginning on the mainland in 1948 by simply fostering agronomic technology, found that rent reduction, improvement of tenant contracts, and eventually land ownership by the cultivator (achieved by 1964) were all needed to settle the age-old landlord-tenant problem. Fostered through farmers' associations (inherited from the Japanese era), the combination of technical education, rural handicrafts, credits, and cooperatives soon set an example of development that was of interest to other countries. The high birth-rate gradually declined. As the administration became more stable and efficient, the repressive police controls of its early years became less evident, and hope emerged that democratic processes would grow as living standards continued to rise.

The peoples of East Asia have a vigorous capacity for nationalism due to their distinctive and ancient cultural traditions and social cohesiveness. But the fact that the Chinese have always been the center of their own world still sets them apart. Indeed, they are hobbled by their great inheritance; their writing system, for example, still lacks the phonetic capacity of Japanese, Korean, or Vietnamese to assimilate foreign words and hence ideas. Writing Chinese in Latin letters, now being attempted, cannot succeed for many years. The world's largest nation, with the longest tradition of ethnocentricity, is therefore the last to participate fully in the new international world.

A distinctive modern Chinese order, to supplant the traditional order, is still being worked out. In it we may foresee certain constant problems due to China's bigness: the problem of feeding and employing so dense a population, the problem of maintaining morale in so large an adminis-tration. If government is still to operate by persuasion and manipulation through a party apparatus, using morality more than legal process to sanction the state's use of violence, then public and especially party morale will continue to be all-important, and ideological orthodoxy essential. The size of the state and its problems, the vigor of its nationalism and its authoritarian tradition, all suggest that individualism under law will be long deferred; and Sino-American relations may remain in jeopardy over this issue, among others.

Conclusions about the world's largest state, or even about Taiwan, which is more populous than two-thirds of the members of the United Nations, are inhibited by our profound ignorance not only of today's rapid changes but even of China's inheritance. We are still under the spell of the dynastic chroniclers, who treated China as a unit, lumping together half a dozen distinct regions each the size of Japan. Historians have barely begun to get behind the official myths of imperial Confucianism and appraise the autocracy and elitism by which state and society con-trolled the individual. China still confronts us with a separate tradition and a radically different modern revolution. Acknowledgment of our ignorance is the necessary beginning of wisdom.

The Pronunciation
of Chinese, Korean, and Japanese

The romanization systems used in this book are those generally considered standard in the English-speaking world: Wade-Giles for Chinese (with the omission of a few unnecessary diacritical marks); McCune-Reischauer for Korean; and Hepburn for Japanese. There is one major exception to this rule, however. Common Chinese geographical names are normally given according to the Chinese Post Office system, which often follows southern Chinese pronunciations and not the Peking pronunciation of standard Northern Chinese (Mandarin or *kuan-hua*). For example, the city that has been the capital of China for most of the past five and a half centuries is generally romanized Peking and pronounced accordingly, but the Wade-Giles romanization of the name would be Pei-ching, pronounced something like Bay-jing.

The three standard systems of romanization have points of similarity and therefore can be considered together. The following guide to pronunciation is a nontechnical presentation which ignores many finer points but will be adequate for the general reader.

Vowels. The basic vowels, *a, e, i, o,* and *u,* in Chinese, Korean, and Japanese transcriptions are pronounced as in Italian, German, and Spanish.

a as in f*a*ther

e as in *e*nd

i as the first *e* in *e*ve

o as in *o*ld (but with less of the *ou* sound of English)

u as in r*u*de

There are, however, some exceptions in CHINESE:

e (except when following *i* or *y*) is pronounced like the *u* in *u*p

ih is pronounced something like the *ir* in st*ir*

o is often pronounced more like the *o* of s*o*ft

u when it follows *ss* or *tz* is sometimes hardly pronounced (and in Japanese too it is often barely audible; e.g., *desu = des'*)

Diphthongs and long vowels:

> In CHINESE two vowels coming together are pronounced always as diphthongs, that is, run together (*ai* as the *i* in *i*ce; *ou* as the *o* in *o*bey; *ao* as the *ow* in c*ow*).

> In JAPANESE only *ai* and *ei* (like the *a* in *a*le) are diphthongs; other vowels coming together are pronounced as separate syllables. Long vowels (*ō* and *ū*) are formed like the corresponding short vowels (*o* and *u*) but are held much longer. This distinction between long and short vowels is very important in Japanese.

> In KOREAN *ae* is like the *a* in *a*dd; *oe* like the *ö* of German; and *ŭi* like the *uee* in q*uee*r.

Other vowels:

> *ŏ* in Korean is like the *u* of b*u*t
>
> *ŭ* in Korean is something like the *oo* in f*oo*t
>
> *ü* in Chinese is like the *ü* of German or *u* of French

Consonants. The consonants and the semi-vowels *w* and *y* in Chinese, Korean, and Japanese transcriptions are generally pronounced as they are in English. The following are the chief exceptions:

> In the paired aspirated consonants (*ch', k', p', t', ts', tz'*) and unaspirated consonants (*ch, k, p, t, ts, tz*) of CHINESE and KOREAN (the last two in each listing do not occur in Korean), the aspirated forms are more like the corresponding English consonants, which are usually aspirated, that is, are accompanied by a marked exhalation of air, and the unaspirated forms are closer to the corresponding consonants in French.[1] To the ears of English-speaking persons, however, the unaspirated consonants of Chinese often sound like the corresponding voiced consonants and are usually so pronounced by all but expert speakers of Chinese. Thus, in Chinese *ch* is pronounced as *j*, *k* as *g*, *p* as *b*, *t* as *d*, *ts* and *tz* as *dz*.

In CHINESE:

> *hs* (which occurs only before *i* and *ü*) is pronounced rather like *sh* (which occurs before *a*, *e*, and *u*)
>
> *j* is pronounced something like *r* (*jen* sounds like *run*)
>
> *ss* (which occurs only before the lightly pronounced *u*) is not to be distinguished from *s*

Correspondence in Pronunciation. Words and names of Chinese origin, as used in Korean and Japanese, are pronounced somewhat differently from Chinese. Actually, the Korean forms are sometimes closer to ancient Chinese than are the modern Chinese. Both Korean and Japanese preserve certain

---

[1] The use of ' in Japanese transcriptions has nothing to do with aspiration. It follows *n* when the *n* is part of the preceding syllable and not the initial consonant for the vowel which follows.

consonantal finals to syllables that have been lost in standard modern Chinese (though they are retained in the southern coastal "dialects"). The general nature of the correspondence in pronunciation for words and names of Chinese origin in the three languages can be seen in the following chart of the cardinal points, which are much used in place names in all three countries and also appear in the names of the Korean political factions. (There are also native Japanese words for the cardinal points, which have no relationship to these Chinese-derived words.) The names are given below in their traditional East Asian order:

	CHINESE	KOREAN	JAPANESE
EAST	*tung*	*tong*	*tō*
WEST	*hsi*	*sŏ*	*sai*
SOUTH	*nan*	*nam*	*nan*
NORTH	*pei*	*puk*	*hoku*

Bibliographical Suggestions

Any brief, introductory selection of books is of course inadequate and also embarrassing for authors to attempt; for many works on which they have relied, sometimes with great indebtedness, must be omitted. Here we have tried to list recent books, through which reference may be found to earlier, and sometimes even more important, writings. Our suggestions of materials in English do not attempt to indicate the large bodies of literature in East Asian and in other European languages, nor do they include the bibliographies, journals, survey books, and other reference works in English useful for the modern history of East Asia that have already been listed in the "Bibliography" in Volume One (pages 679–686).

The best bibliographical starting point is *The American Historical Association's Guide to Historical Literature* (New York: Macmillan, 1963); see pages 278–295 on Modern China, 297–318 on Japan, 241–248 on Korea, 248–257 on Inner Asia. In what follows we should like to assume the reader's acquaintance with this admirable reference tool, and so we list mainly more recent publications.

On Asian geography, Norton Ginsburg, ed., *The Pattern of Asia* (Englewood Cliffs, N.J.: Prentice-Hall, 1958) has valuable maps and data, and George B. Cressey, *Asia's Lands and Peoples* (New York: McGraw-Hill, 3d ed., 1963) gives a vivid and up-to-date description.

China. Among recent bibliographies on China, Charles O. Hucker, *China, A Critical Bibliography* (Tucson: University of Arizona Press, 1962) contains 2285 annotated entries topically arranged with some repetitions on all aspects of Chinese civilization; over 400 entries concern modern history. An even more comprehensive listing, under a useful topical breakdown though not annotated, is in Tung-li Yuan, *China in Western Literature, A Continuation of Cordier's Bibliotheca Sinica* (New Haven: Far Eastern Publications, 1958, 802 pages). Most general works also include extensive bibliographies: Franz H. Michael and George E. Taylor, *The Far East in the Modern World* (New York: Holt, Rinehart, and Winston, rev. ed., 1964) provides a full 26-page list of books and articles on East and Southeast Asia and United States policy. George M. Beckmann, *The Modernization of China and Japan* (New York: Harper and Row, 1962) has 25 pages of comprehensive "Bibliographical Notes." Paul Hibbert Clyde, *The Far East, A History of the Impact of the West on Eastern Asia* (Englewood Cliffs, N.J.: Prentice-Hall, 3d ed., 1958) and Harold M. Vinacke, *A History of the Far East in Modern Times* (New York: Appleton-Century-Crofts, 6th ed., 1961) both have lists at the end of each chapter. J. K.

Fairbank, *The United States and China* (Cambridge: Harvard University Press, rev. ed., 1958) in its paperback form (Compass Books, Viking Press, 1962) contains a 28-page bibliography down to 1961. The most recent survey, also with a bibliography, is by O. Edmund Clubb, *20th Century China* (New York: Columbia University Press, 1964).

Translations of source materials on Modern China include William Theodore de Bary, Wing-tsit Chan, and Burton Watson, comps., *Sources of Chinese Tradition* (New York: Columbia University Press, 1960); and Ssu-yü Teng and John K. Fairbank (with E-tu Zen Sun and Chaoying Fang), *China's Response to the West. A Documentary Survey 1839–1923* (Cambridge: Harvard University Press, 1954).

Among recent studies of China's traditional social and political institutions are T'ung-tsu Ch'ü, *Law and Society in Traditional China* (Paris and La Haye: Mouton, 1961) and *Local Administration in China under the Ch'ing* (Cambridge: Harvard University Press, 1962); Sybille van der Sprenkel, *Legal Institutions in Manchu China, A Sociological Analysis* (London: Athlone Press, 1962); Kung-chuan Hsiao, *Rural China: Imperial Control in the Nineteenth Century* (Seattle: University of Washington Press, 1960); and Ping-ti Ho, *The Ladder of Success in Imperial China, Aspects of Social Mobility, 1368–1911* (New York: Columbia University Press, 1962). Etienne Balazs, *Chinese Civilization and Bureaucracy, Variations on a Theme* (New Haven: Yale University Press, 1964) makes available major writings of a great scholar.

Early European contact with the Far East is most recently surveyed in John H. Parry, *The Age of Reconnaissance* (London: Weidenfeld and Nicolson; Cleveland: World Publishing Co. 1963).

For the Ch'ing period the one indispensable work is still A. W. Hummel, ed., *Eminent Chinese of the Ch'ing Period 1644–1912* (Washington, D.C.: Government Printing Office, 1943–44). The following works provide basic treatments of certain subjects or are starting points in their fields: K. S. Latourette, *A History of the Expansion of Christianity*, Vol. 6, *The Great Century in Northern Africa and Asia A.D.1800–A.D.1914* (New York: Harper, 1944), chap. 5, "The Chinese Empire"; John King Fairbank, *Trade and Diplomacy on the China Coast: The Opening of the Treaty Ports, 1842–1854* (Cambridge: Harvard University Press, 1953); Mary C. Wright, *The Last Stand of Chinese Conservatism, The T'ung-chih Restoration, 1862–1874* (Stanford: Stanford University Press, 1957); Stanley F. Wright, *Hart and the Chinese Customs* (Belfast, Ireland: Mullan, 1950); Knight Biggerstaff, *The Earliest Modern Government Schools in China* (Ithaca: Cornell University Press, 1961); Albert Feuerwerker, *China's Early Industrialization: Sheng Hsuan-huai and Mandarin Enterprise* (Cambridge: Harvard University Press, 1958); Ralph L. Powell, *The Rise of Chinese Military Power 1895–1912* (Princeton: Princeton University Press, 1955); and Marius B. Jansen, *The Japanese and Sun Yat-sen* (Cambridge: Harvard University Press, 1954).

China's modern history and foreign relations are further pursued in Hsin-pao Chang, *Commissioner Lin and the Opium War* (Cambridge: Harvard University Press, 1964); Masataka Banno, *China and the West 1858–1861: The Origins of the Tsungli Yamen* (Harvard University Press, 1964); C. Y. Hsu, *China's Entrance into the Family of Nations: The Diplomatic Phase, 1856–*

1880 (Harvard University Press, 1960); Paul A. Cohen, *China and Christianity: The Missionary Movement and the Growth of Chinese Antiforeignism 1860–1870* (Harvard University Press, 1963); Stanley Spector, *Li Hung-chang and the Huai Army* (Seattle: University of Washington Press, 1964); Victor Purcell, *The Boxer Uprising, A Background Study* (Cambridge, Eng.: Cambridge University Press, 1963); Chun-tu Hsueh, *Huang Hsing and the Chinese Revolution* (Stanford: Stanford University Press, 1961); and Jerome Ch'en, *Yuan Shih-k'ai 1859–1916* (Stanford University Press, 1961).

Modern intellectual history is further opened up in Benjamin I. Schwartz, *In Search of Wealth and Power: Yen Fu and the West* (Cambridge: Harvard University Press, 1964); Joseph R. Levenson, *Confucian China and Its Modern Fate*: Vol. I, *The Problem of Intellectual Continuity*, and Vol. II, *The Problem of Monarchical Decay* (Berkeley: University of California Press, 1958, 1964); Chow Tse-tsung, *The May Fourth Movement: Intellectual Revolution in Modern China* (Cambridge: Harvard University Press, 1960); and the same, *Research Guide to the May Fourth Movement* (Harvard University Press, 1963).

In literature, C. T. Hsia, *A History of Modern Chinese Fiction 1917–1957* (New Haven: Yale University Press, 1961) refers to English translations from Lu Hsun, Lao She, Mao Tun, Pa Chin and others. Useful surveys are Kai-yu Hsu, transl. and ed., *Twentieth Century Chinese Poetry, An Anthology* (New York: Doubleday, 1963); and A. C. Scott, *Literature and the Arts in Twentieth Century China* (Garden City, N. Y.: Doubleday Anchor Books, 1963).

Materials on American relations with China are surveyed in Kwang-Ching Liu, *Americans and Chinese: A Historical Essay and a Bibliography* (Cambridge: Harvard University Press, 1963), with an extensive listing of American source materials. American policy is analyzed by Dorothy Borg, *The United States and the Far Eastern Crisis of 1933–1938* (Cambridge: Harvard University Press, 1964); Herbert Feis, *The China Tangle: The American Effort in China from Pearl Harbor to the Marshall Mission* (Princeton: Princeton University Press, 1953); C. F. Romanus and R. Sunderland, *Stilwell's Mission to China; Stilwell's Command Problems;* and *Time Runs Out in CBI* (*United States Army in World War II, China-Burma-India Theater*, 3 vols., Washington, D. C.: Department of the Army, 1953, 1956, 1958); Arthur N. Young, *China and the Helping Hand 1937–1945* (Cambridge: Harvard University Press, 1963); and Tang Tsou, *America's Failure in China 1941–1950* (Chicago: University of Chicago Press, 1963).

Political and institutional studies of Republican China are still rather meager. *20th Century China* by O. Edmund Clubb, already noted, is the most recent and comprehensive.

The rise and course of Sino-Soviet and KMT-CCP relations, on the other hand, has produced a considerable series of studies, too long to list here. For the latest selections of documents, see Tso-liang Hsiao, *Power Relations within the Chinese Communist Movement, 1930–34* (Seattle: University of Washington Press, 1961); Stuart R. Schram, *The Political Thought of Mao Tse-tung* (New York: Praeger, 1963); and *Communist China, 1955–1959: Policy Documents with Analysis* (Cambridge: Harvard University Press, 1963) with a one-page foreword by R. R. Bowie and J. K. Fairbank. Two books influential in their day are Edgar Snow, *Red Star over China* (New York: Random House, 1938); and Chiang Kai-shek, *China's Destiny* (New York: Macmillan, 1947), trans. Wang Chung-hui. Monographs are numerous; see notes and bibliography in Robert C. North, *Moscow and Chinese Communists* (Stanford: Stanford University Press, 2d ed., 1963).

Communist China is depicted in many works of journalism but rather few of scholarship. An informative survey is Chang-tu Hu and others, *China, its people, its society, its culture* (New Haven: HRAF Press, 1960) with a good topical bibliography. A. Doak Barnett, *Communist China and Asia, Challenge to American Policy* (New York: Harper, 1960) also has a 12-page "Bibliographic Note." Recent studies of the economy include Choh-ming Li, *Economic Development in Communist China: An Appraisal of the First Five Years of Industrialization* (Berkeley: University of California Press, 1959); T. J. Hughes and D. E. T. Luard, *The Economic Development of Communist China, 1949-1958 (-1960)* (London and New York: Oxford University Press, 1959; 2d ed., 1961); and Alexander Eckstein, *Communist China's National Income* (New York: The Free Press of Glencoe, 1961). On thought reform see Mu Fu-sheng, *The Wilting of the Hundred Flowers: The Chinese Intelligentsia under Mao* (New York: Praeger, 1962); Theodore H. E. Chen, *Thought Reform of the Chinese Intellectuals* (Hong Kong: University of Hong Kong Press, 1960); and Robert Jay Lifton, *Thought Reform and the Psychology of Totalism. A Study of "Brainwashing" in China* (New York: Norton, 1961). Two recent studies in political science are by Chalmers A. Johnson, *Peasant Nationalism and Communist Power, The Emergence of Revolutionary China, 1937-1945* (Stanford: Stanford University Press, 1962); and John Wilson Lewis, *Leadership in Communist China* (Ithaca: Cornell University Press, 1963). Among many studies of Chinese-Russian relations see Donald S. Zagoria, *The Sino-Soviet Conflict, 1956-1961* (Princeton: Princeton University Press, 1962).

On Inner Asia, recent studies that list earlier works are H. E. Richardson, *A Short History of Tibet* (New York: Dutton, 1962), and Owen Lattimore, *Nomads and Commissars: Mongolia Revisited* (New York: Oxford University Press, 1962). Owen Lattimore, *Studies in Frontier History, Collected Papers 1928-1958* (London: Oxford University Press, 1962) contains a wealth of reflection and observation on China's Inner Asian relations.

Southeast Asia. This volume has touched upon Southeast Asia only as a peripheral area. Stephen N. Hay and Margaret H. Case, *Southeast Asian History, A Bibliographic Guide* (New York: Praeger, 1962) provides annotated entries on 632 bibliographies, books, articles, and doctoral dissertations, frequently quoting book reviews. The most recent and useful general work is John F. Cady, *Southeast Asia, Its Historical Development* (New York: McGraw-Hill, 1964), a compact yet comprehensive account with copious footnote citations of major books and articles in this broad field. D. G. E. Hall, *A History of South-East Asia* (New York: St. Martin's Press, 1955) gives a detailed summary of the political history of the Southeast Asian countries, excepting the Philippines, with a 27-page bibliography.

Korea. In addition to S. McCune, *Korea's Heritage: A Regional and Social Geography* (Tokyo: Tuttle, 1956) and C. Osgood, *The Koreans and Their Culture* (New York: Ronald Press, 1951), both cited in Volume One, there are now two other general surveys: *Korea: Its Land, People, and Culture of All Ages* (Seoul: Hakwon-Sa, 1960; rev. ed., 1963) and, less comprehensive, Korean National Commission for UNESCO, *UNESCO Korean Survey* (Seoul: Dong-a, 1960).

The extensive literature on late nineteenth-century foreign relations is cited in F. Hilary Conroy, *The Japanese Seizure of Korea, 1868–1910* (Philadelphia: University of Pennsylvania Press, 1960). On the succeeding era of Japanese rule see Chong-sik Lee, *The Politics of Korean Nationalism* (Berkeley: University of California Press, 1963). For the period after World War II see George M. McCune, *Korea Today* (Cambridge: Harvard University Press, 1950) and E. Grant Meade, *American Military Government in Korea* (New York: King's Crown Press, 1951).

The most recent of some 50 titles on the Korean War is David Rees, *Korea: The Limited War* (New York: St. Martin's Press, 1964). The most recent studies on the south and north, respectively, are W. D. Reeve, *The Republic of Korea: A Political and Economic Study* (London: Oxford University Press, 1963), and R. A. Scalapino, ed., *North Korea Today* (New York: Praeger, 1963).

Japan. In the past few years there has been a deluge of excellent books on modern Japan. Based on primary sources and the results of recent Japanese research, these have extended in many directions our knowledge of the world's most modern non-Western nation. Here we will name only a few of the best of these works. For the rest the reader may consult the bibliographies in Edwin O. Reischauer, *Japan Past and Present* (New York: Knopf, 1964); Hugh Borton, *Japan's Modern Century* (New York: Ronald Press, 1955); Richard Storry, *A History of Modern Japan* (Baltimore: Penguin Books, 1960); W. G. Beasley, *The Modern History of Japan* (New York: Praeger, 1963). The best annotated bibliography in this field is John W. Hall, *Japanese History, New Dimensions of Approach and Understanding* (Washington, D. C.: Service Center for Teachers of History, 1961).

For the background of modern Japan and the Meiji Restoration the reader might begin with: W. G. Beasley, *Select Documents on Japanese Foreign Policy 1853–1868* (London and New York: Oxford University Press, 1955); Robert Bellah, *Tokugawa Religion* (Glencoe, Ill.: Free Press, 1957); Albert Craig, *Chōshū in the Meiji Restoration* (Cambridge: Harvard University Press, 1961); Marius Jansen, *Sakamoto Ryōma and the Meiji Restoration* (Princeton: Princeton University Press, 1961); Thomas C. Smith, *The Agrarian Origins of Modern Japan* (Stanford: Stanford University Press, 1959).

For the modern intellectual scene George B. Sansom, *The Western World and Japan* (New York: Knopf, 1951) is a well-written account of early Japanese and Western cultural contacts. Kosaka Masaaki, *Japanese Thought in the Meiji Era* (Tokyo: Pan-Pacific Press, 1958), trans. David Abosch, provides a more encyclopedic coverage of thinkers. The most important volume of source materials for intellectual history is Ryusaku Tsunoda, William Theodore de Bary, and Donald Keene, *Sources of the Japanese Tradition* (New York: Columbia University Press, 1958). The two best monographic studies of single thinkers are Carmen Blacker, *The Japanese Enlightenment: A Study of the Writings of Fukuzawa Yukichi* (Cambridge, Eng.: Cambridge University Press, 1964) and Hyman Kublin, *Asian Revolutionary: The Life of Sen Katayama* (Princeton: Princeton University Press, 1964). A brilliant work of political science as well as intellectual history is Masao Maruyama, *Thought and Behavior in Modern Japanese Politics* (London: Oxford University Press, 1963).

The history of political parties in Japan is covered in Robert A. Scalapino, *Democracy and the Party Movement in Prewar Japan* (Berkeley: University of California Press, 1953) and Nobutaka Ike, *The Beginnings of Political Democracy in Japan* (Baltimore: Johns Hopkins University Press, 1950). A more recent, revisionistic analysis is George Akita, *The Foundations of Constitutional Government in Modern Japan, 1868–1900* (Cambridge: Harvard University Press, 1965). An in-depth study of politics is given in James W. Morley, *The Japanese Thrust into Siberia 1918* (New York: Columbia University Press, 1957).

The best integrated description of life in rural Japan is Richard K. Beardsley, John W. Hall, and Robert E. Ward, *Village Japan* (Chicago: University of Chicago Press, 1959). Both city and country are dealt with in Ronald P. Dore, *City Life in Japan* (Berkeley: University of California Press, 1958) and *Land Reform in Japan* (London and New York: Oxford University Press, 1959). Japanese character — as it used to be — is analyzed in Ruth Benedict, *The Chrysanthemum and the Sword* (Boston: Houghton Mifflin, 1946). Also noteworthy is Irene Taeuber, *The Population of Japan* (Princeton: Princeton University Press, 1958). The new problem of leisure is treated in David Plath, *The After Hours: Modern Japan and the Search for Enjoyment* (Berkeley: University of California Press, 1964). A fascinating analysis of urban family and community life is presented in Ezra Vogel, *Japan's New Middle Class* (Berkeley: University of California Press, 1964).

The two best analyses of Japanese economic development are William Lockwood, *The Economic Development of Japan; Growth and Structural Change 1868–1938* (Princeton: Princeton University Press, 1954) and Henry Rosovsky, *Capital Formation in Japan* (Glencoe, Ill.: Free Press, 1961). For the non-economist, Chapter 3 of the latter is particularly meaningful. Other aspects of Japanese economic life are discussed in: Thomas C. Smith, *Political Change and Industrial Development in Japan: Government Enterprise, 1868–1880* (Stanford: Stanford University Press, 1955); John W. Bennett and Iwao Ishino, *Paternalism in the Japanese Economy* (Minneapolis: University of Minnesota Press, 1963); Johannes Hirschmeier, *The Origins of Entrepreneurship in Meiji Japan* (Cambridge: Harvard University Press, 1964).

For the 1930's, the reader might begin with: Richard Storry, *The Double Patriots* (London: Chatto and Windus, 1957); F. C. Jones, *Japan's New Order in East Asia: Its Rise and Fall, 1937–1945* (London: Oxford University Press, 1954); Herbert Feis, *The Road to Pearl Harbor* (Princeton: Princeton University Press, 1950); *Tojo and the Coming of the War* (Princeton: Princeton University Press, 1961) and *Japan's Decision to Surrender* (Stanford: Stanford University Press, 1954) by Robert J. C. Butow.

Bibliographical Suggestions

The best survey on the American occupation of Japan is Kazuo Kawai, *Japan's American Interlude* (Chicago: University of Chicago Press, 1960). Edwin O. Reischauer, *The United States and Japan* (Cambridge: Harvard University Press, 1957) treats Japanese-American relations in the postwar period in terms of Japanese psychology and history. Also to be recommended on postwar Japan are: Robert A. Scalapino and Junnosuke Masumi, *Parties and Politics in Contemporary Japan* (Berkeley: University of California Press, 1962) and Lawrence Olson, *Dimensions of Japan* (New York: American Universities Field Staff, 1963).

Finally, literature is important in modern Japan. Donald Keene's *Modern Japanese Literature; an Anthology* (New York: Grove Press, 1956) is a good place to start sampling. Some of the best novels are: Natsume Soseki, *Kokoro* (Chicago: Regnery, 1957), trans. Edwin McClellan; Tanizaki, *The Makioka Sisters* (New York: Knopf, 1957), trans. Edward Seidensticker; Osamu Dazai, *The Setting Sun* (New York: New Directions, 1956), trans. Donald Keene; Yasunari Kawabata, *Thousand Cranes* (New York: Knopf, 1959), trans. Edward Seidensticker; *Seven Japanese Tales by Junichiro Tanizaki* (New York: Knopf, 1963), trans. Howard Hibbett.

Illustration Acknowledgments

The maps on the endpapers of this book and the text maps were drawn by Lilli Mautner in collaboration with the authors.

Following are acknowledgments or explanations of illustrations not included elsewhere in the text.

Title page: The Chinese characters *Fu-kuo ch'iang-ping* (Japanese *fukoku kyōhei*), lit., "to enrich the kingdom and increase its military power," the ancient slogan used by so many East Asian modernizers, were written for us by Dr. Chow Tse-tsung, author of *The May Fourth Movement, Intellectual Revolution in Modern China* (Harvard University Press, 1960). This is combined with a stamped tile design probably from about the third century B.C.

Page 3   Detail of text signed by Ricci from Iwasaki Library.

Page 80   Detail from Chinese engraving, "Conquests of The Emperor of China."

Page 179   From *Edo meisho zue*, Volume One.

Page 183   From the Boehringer Collection, "Americans — A View from the East"; Smithsonian Institution.

Page 244   From an 1894 wood-block print entitled "Generals and Admirals of the Sino-Japanese War."

Page 313   Redrawing of the Marble Boat from photographs.

Page 408   "Curious Chinese drawing of an English War-Steamer" from *The Illustrated London News,* December 1844.

Page 488   Facsimile of the cover of May 1936 issue of *The Central Review.*

Page 613   Redrawing from photos of student demonstrations.

Page 703   From *China* by Marc Chadourne. Copyright, 1932, by Marc Chadourne. Reprinted by permission of Crown Publishers, Inc.

Page 718   Redrawing from photo of a Japanese soldier during World War II.

Page 804   By Wang Liu-ch'iu.

Page 856   By Ku Yuan.

CREDITS FOR PLATES

Plates 1–2 Nieuhof: *An Embassy from the East India Company of the United Provinces to the Grand Tartar.* Rare Book Room, New York Public Library.

Plate 3 Houghton Library, Harvard University.

Plate 4 Victoria and Albert Museum.

Plate 5 Musée Guimet.

Plates 6–8 Houghton Library, Harvard University.

Plate 9 From Thomas Allom, esq., *China in a series of views, displaying the scenery, architecture, and Social habits of that Ancient Empire* (London, preface 1843).

Plates 10–11 From *Wan shou sheng tien,* Chinese-Japanese Library of the Harvard-Yenching Institute at Harvard University.

Plate 12 From Thomson, *Illustrations of China and Its People,* Volume IV; London, 1874.

Plate 13 Courtesy Mr. W. J. Keswick, from *George Chinnery 1774–1852 'Artist of the China Coast'* by Henry and Sidney Berry-Hill; F. Lewis, Publishers, Limited, Essex, England.

Plate 14 The Peabody Museum of Salem.

Plate 15 Radio Times Hulton Picture Library.

Plates 16–17 The Peabody Museum of Salem.

Plate 18 Hong Kong Government Information Services.

Plate 19 From *Illustrations of Japan* by M. Titsingh; London, 1822.

Plate 20 From *Shiba Kōkan* by Nakai Shūtarō (Tōkyō, 1942).

Plate 22 Courtesy, Asoka Shobō Book Company. From *Utsusareta bakumatsu,* Volume 3.

Plate 23 Kanagaki Robun; *Seiyō dōchū hizakurige.*

Plate 24 From the Boehringer Collection, "Americans — A View from the East"; Smithsonian Institution.

Plate 25 From *Meiji bunka zenshu, kagaku-hen,* Volume 24.

Plate 26 From *Gendai hanga.*

Plate 27 From *Meiji bunka zenshu, zasshi-hen,* Volume 18.

Plate 28 Radio Times Hulton Picture Library.

Plates 29–31 From *Kensei hiroku.* Courtesy Yamada Shoin Publishing Company.

Plate 32 Radio Times Hulton Picture Library.

Plate 33 From the Collection of the American Bible Society Agent, C. F. Gammon. Courtesy, Essex Institute.

Plate 34 From the Drew Collection at Harvard Chinese-Japanese Library.

Plate 35 Mrs. Helen Merrill Groff-Smith.

Plates 36–39 From the Drew Collection at Harvard Chinese-Japanese Library.

Illustration Acknowledgments

Plate 40 The Peabody Museum of Salem.

Plate 41 Dimitri Kessel — courtesy, LIFE Magazine © 1956 Time Inc.

Plate 42 Courtesy, The Essex Institute Library.

Plate 43 Courtesy, The Essex Institute Library.

Plate 44 Radio Times Hulton Picture Library.

Plate 45 Courtesy, Yamada Shoin Publishing Company.

Plate 46 Courtesy, International Society for Educational Information, Tōkyō.

Plate 48 Courtesy, International Society for Educational Information, Tōkyō.

Plate 49 Reproduced from the Collections of The Library of Congress.

Plate 50 From *Kensei hiroku*. Courtesy, Yamada Shoin Publishing Company.

Plates 51–52 Part of the Oriental Collection of the late Ernst von Harringa.

Plates 53–56 From *Tien-shih-chai hua pao*, Shanghai.

Plates 57–58 From the Drew Collection at Harvard Chinese-Japanese Library.

Plate 59 From *Meiji bunka zenshu, kyōiku-hen*, Volume 10.

Plates 60–61 The Library of Congress.

Plate 62 From *Kensei hiroku*. Courtesy, Yamada Shoin Publishing Company.

Plate 63 Radio Times Hulton Picture Library.

Plates 64–65 From *Kensei hiroku*. Courtesy, Yamada Shoin Publishing Company.

Plate 66 Courtesy Asahi Shimbun.

Plate 67 Courtesy, International Society for Educational Information, Tōkyō.

Plates 68–71 Courtesy, Kodansha Publishers, Limited, *Nihon 100 Nen No Kiroku.*

Plate 72 Courtesy, International Society for Educational Information, Tōkyō.

Plate 73 Eastfoto.

Plate 74 Wide World Photos.

Plate 75 Courtesy, Cornell University.

Plates 76–78 Radio Times Hulton Picture Library.

Plate 79 Photo by Silk. Courtesy, LIFE Magazine © 1946 Time Inc.

Plate 80 Eastfoto.

Index

(Since practice varies widely in the use of hyphens and word divisions in non-Western names and words, hyphens and word divisions have been ignored in the listing of the non-Western names and words in this Index. Page numbers given in italics refer to maps or illustrations in text. "Pl." refers to plates by number.)

Abe Isoo, 548, 597
Abe Jirō, 540, 544
Abe Masahiro, 198, 202, 203, 206, 207, 208, 215
Abe Nobuyuki, 581, 607
Academia Sinica, 702
Academies (*shu-yüan*) in China, 102, 138, 329, 615
Academies in Korea, 462, 464
Acapulco, 25, 34, 725
Acheh (Achin), *17*, 19, 724
Adams, Will, 28
Aden, *16*, 18
Administration, Department of, Japan, 230
Administrative district (*hsien*), China, 100, 104; administrative areas, Ch'ing, *94-95*
Administrative Justice Yüan, 626, 627, 695
"Admonition to the Military" (Yamagata), 295
Afghanistan, *367*, 481, 793
"Agency houses," 70, 129, 130
Aglen, Francis, 647
Agricultural Credit Administration, China, 699
Agricultural producers' cooperatives, 867, 873
Agriculture, in China, 91-92, 673, 699, 705, 867, 873-875, 877; in Japan, 190, 192, 235-236, 250, 254, 256, 257, 497, 501, 517, 589, 826, 829; mechanization of, 411; plantation, in Southeast Asia, 455, 722, 723; Culture System, in Dutch East Indies, 722-723; in Burma, 746; sharecropping, in Vietnam, 751; in Taiwan, 759, 760; in Korea, 764, 765; collectivized, in China, 867, 873-875, 877; *see also* Farmers' associations *and* Tenant farming
Agriculture, Industry, and Commerce, Ministry of (Nung-kung-shang Pu), 623, 626

"Agriculturism," Japan, 517
Aguinaldo, Emilio, 727, 728
"Ahyun." *See* Hsü Jun
Aigun, *47, 339, 585;* Treaty of, 173
Aikawa Yoshisuke, 506, 708
Aikoku Kōtō (Public Party of Patriots), 281
Aikokusha (Society of Patriots), 281 283, 284
Ainu, 787, 788
Aizawa, Lt.-Col., 593
Aizawa Yasushi (or Seishisai), 197
Aizu, *187*, 217, 225
Akita, *187, 825*
Aksai-Chin area, 797, *798*, 880
Aksu, *367*
Akutagawa Ryūnosuke, 543, 831
Alaska, 171, 468
Alaungpaya, 429, 446
Albazin, *47*, 48, 49, 50
Albuquerque, Afonso d', *16-17*, 18
Alcock, Rutherford, 167, 316, 344, 336-337, 450
Alcock Convention, 336-337
Aleutian Islands, 171, 806
Alexander III, Tsar, 469
Alexeiev-Tseng agreement, 479
Alexis, Tsar, 46
Alienation, sense of, in Japan, 529-530, 538, 542-543, 830-835
All-China Association of Industry and Commerce, 864
All-China Federation of Trade Unions, 863-864
All-China Federations of Democratic Women, Democratic Youth, Cooperative Workers, Literature and Art, 864
All-China Students Federation, 864
All-Japan Peasants' Union, 518
All Men Are Brothers (Shui-hu-chuan), 395
Allen, Horace N., 761
Allen, Young J., 364, 385

Allied Council in Tōkyō, 812
Alma Ata, *785*
Altai Mountains, *47, 367*
Altaic family of languages, 793
Amban, 788, 796
Amboina, 19, 29, 67
American Board of Commissioners for Foreign Missions, 152, 331
"American Settlement", Shanghai, 340, *341*
Amherst, Lord, 53, 78
Amoy, *17*, 29, 30, 92, *95, 160, 339, 715, 809,* 880; junk trade at, 71, 72, 73, 430; gazetteer of (*Hsia-men chih*), 127; British in, 143, 340; as treaty port, 144, 152, 154, 459; rebellion at, 163; customs service in, 318
Amsterdam, 27, 67, 69
Amu Daria, *16, 367*
Amur River and region, *17*, 46, 47, 48, 171, 256, *585, 785;* Russian invasions of, 45, 49, 50, 172, 468
Amur River Society, 632
An Ch'ang-ho, 763
An Lu-shan rebellion, 174
Analects of Confucius, 199
Ananda Mahidol, 745
Anarchism, in Japan, 549, 551; in China, 639, 651, 662
Ancester worship, 59, 61, 405, 418, 420, 422, 534
"Ancient text" (*ku-wen*) versions of Classics, 123, 388
An-fu (Anhwei-Fukien) clique, 655, 790
Angkor, *419, 420, 424, 428, 430, 435,* 452
Angkor Thom, 420
Anglo-Burmese wars, 447, 456
Anglo-Chinese College, Malacca, 152
Anglo-Chinese War (Opium War), 81, 136–146, 150, 166
Anglo-French War in China, 168–171, 204–205
Anglo-Japanese Alliance, 311, 478–479, 481, 565, 675
Anglo-Russian agreements, 478, 481, 800
Anglo-Siamese treaty, 457
Anhsi, *367*
Anhwei, 92, *94*, 104, 106, 164, *176, 853*
Anhwei Army, 174, 175, 322, 326, 338, 352, 382, 620
Animism, 420, 421, 543
Anking, *94, 105,* 319
Annam, *419,* 431, 432, *435,* 453, 455; *see also* Vietnam
Ansei purge, 209
Anshan, *585,* 706
Anti-Christian agitation, 147, 269, 330, 332–335, 362, 395, 396, 463, 464, 668
Anti-Comintern Pact, 595, 606, 711

Anticommunism, in China, 686, 687, 709, 880; in Europe, 686; in Southeast Asia, 779, 780; in Siberia, 784; in South Korea, 847
Anti-Fascist People's Freedom League, Burma, 773, 775
Antiforeignism, 485; in China, 143, 146, 150, 168, 174, 334, 336, 337–338, 362, 374–375, 395, 396, 397, 630, 685, 860–861, 866, 870, 879; in Japan, 203, 208, 209, 210–211, 216, 219, 264–265, 294; in Korea, 377–378; in Vietnam, 439; in Indonesia, 732; in Burma, 748; *see also* "Barbarians" *and* Nationalism
Anti-imperialism, Chinese, 365–378, 670, 673, 683, 684, 685, 686, 713
Anti-Japanese feeling, in China, 570, 650, 666; in Korea, 760–765; in the Philippines, 770, 774; in Indonesia, 771; in Burma, 772
Anti-Japanese Resistance Army (*Hukbalahap*), 774
Anti-opium campaign, 136–141, 152
"Anti-rightist" campaign, China, 876, 877
"Anti-separationists," Burma, 748
Antung, *339, 465, 585*
Antwerp, 69
An-yang, 704
Aomori, Pl. 71
Aoyama Gakuin, 270
Approaching Peace (*sheng-p'ing*), Age of, 389
Arab traders, 10, 12, 14, 19, 20, 425
Arabic influence in China, 38
Arakan, *17*, 28, *428*, 429, 446, 447
Araki Sadao, 534, 591, 592–593, 599
Arima, Tatsuo, 541n.
Arima domain, *186*
Arishima Takeo, 551
Army, in China, malpractices of, 142; late Ch'ing, 619–622; Army Ministry (Lu-chün Pu), 623; revolts of, 639, 640, 641
Army, in Japan, 182, 199, 220, 224–225, 236–238, 242–243, 246, 297; modernization of, 576, 595; as political elite, 555–556, 559, 562, 568, 594; power of, 577, 583–588, 595–596, 598, 599, 601–606; and rightist movement, 590–593; "Five-Year Plan" of, 597
Army of the Green Standard (*Lü-ying*), 116, 142, 392, 619–620
"Arrows" (cavalry squadrons), 788
Artillery, 13, 42, 80
Asano domain, *186*
Asano Sōichirō, 255, 506
Asia (*Ya-hsi-ya*), 42
"Asia for the Asiatics," 768, 772
Asiatic Petroleum Company, 659
Asociación Hispano-Filipina, Madrid, 726

Index

Assam, *428*, 446, 447, 7*15*, 797, *798*
"Association" policy, 454–455
"Association for Service to the New Philippines" (*Kalibapi*), 769
Astrolabe, 24
Astronomy in China, 38, 42; Imperial Board of, Pl. 2
Atomic bomb, 810
Attlee, Clement, 775
Attu, 806
Audit Yüan, 626, 627
Augustinians, 36, 43, 54, 55, 725
Aung San, 749, 772, 773, 775
Australia, *17*, 155; in SEATO, 880
Austria, 54, 292
Austria-Hungary, 342
Austro-Asiatic culture, 417–418
"Autonomous Political Council," North China, 598, 599
Autumn (Pa Chin), 702
"Autumn Harvest" insurrection, 688
Ava, *419*, 423, 426, *428*, 429, 446
Avalokitesvara, 420
"Avoidance, law of," in China, 101, 102
Ayutthaya (Ayuthia), *17*, 20, 28, 54, 423, 424, 427, *428*, 429

Ba Maw, 748, 749, 772
Bagyidaw, 447
Bahasa Indonesia, 770
Bahol, Phya, 745
Baikal, Lake, *17*, 45, 47, *367*, *785*, 789
Baikov, Fedor Isakovich, 46, 52, 53
Bakumatsu ("end of the shogunate"), 203
Bali, 422, 731
Balkhash, Lake, *16*, *47*, *367*, *785*
Balloons, Pl. 24
Banda Islands, *17*, 18
Banditry, 157, 758
Bandung, *419;* conference, 880
Bangka, 724, 777
Bangkok, *428*, *435*, 451, 454, 456, 769; Chinese in, 29, 459, 743; French in, 430
Bank of China, 659, 698
Bank of Communications, China, 625, 659, 699
Bank of Taiwan, 759
Banque de l'Indochine, 751
Bannermen, Manchu, 116, 121, 157, 165, 351, 392, 619–620, 788; Tokugawa, 183
Bansho Shirabesho (Institute for the Investigation of Barbarian Books), 199
Bantam, *17*, 18, 19, 29, *41*
Bao-Dai, 750, 768, 769, 778, 780, 781
Baptists in China, 332
"Barbarian Subduing Generalissimo" (*Sei-i tai shōgun*), 202–203
"Barbarians" (foreigners), 35, 178, 183, 197, 216; superior techniques of, 147;

use of rivalry of, by China, 486; of Inner Asia, 783; *see also* Antiforeignism *and* "Expel the barbarians"
Basel Society, 332
Bataan Peninsula, 805
Batang, 797, *798*
Batavia, *17*, 28, 29, 66, 67, 196, 341, 776; Chinese in, 120, 734; missionaries at, 360
Batavia Nieuws, 285
Battambang, *435*, 454
Bayinnaung, 427
Belgium, 342, 722
Bellah, Robert, 537n.
Bengal, *16*, 68, 70, 76, 130, 446; Bay of, 441
Benkulen, *17*, 70
Bentham, Jeremy, 267
Bergson, 545
Bering, Vitus, 171, 195
"Bernardo," 32
Bhamo, *428*, 448, 7*15*
Bhutan, *367*, 7*15*, 797, *798*, 799
Biddle, James, 196
"Big households," 111
Big Sword Society (*Ta-tao hui*), 396
Billiton, 724
Birth control in Japan, 827–828
Bismarck, 292
Black Dragon Society, 482, 632
Black Flags, 453
Black Ocean Society (*Genyōsha*), 467
Board of Revenue Bank, China, 698
Boat racing, Shanghai, Pl. 53; boat tracking, Pl. 41
Boca Tigris. See Bogue
Bodawpaya, 446
Boedi Oetomo (*Budi Utomo*) ("The Noble Endeavor"), 734–735
Boer War, 478
Bogdo-gegen (king), 790
Bogle, George, 796
Bogue, Boca Tigris, *133*, 135; British Supplementary Treaty of the, 144, 145
Boissonade, 265
Bokhara, *16*, 172, *367*, 369
Bombay, *16*, 68, 70, 76, 130, 441
Bon cult, 795
Bonin Islands, *17*, 201
Book of the Great Unity (*Ta-t'ung shu*), 389
Book of History (*Shu-ching*), 123
Borneo, *17*, 29, *410*, 724; Islam in, 425, 485; British in, 442–443, 449; Chinese in, 782
Borobudur, *419*, 422
Borodin, Michael, 680, 686, 688, 752
Boromotrailokanat (Trailok), 424
Boston Tea Party, 75
"Bourgeois nationalist" movements, 676–677, 752

Bowring, John, 145, 457
Boxer movement, 119, 394–404, 473, 474, 477, 478; origin of, 394–397; Ch'ing support of, 396, 397–400; and siege of Peking legations, 400–402; aftermath of, 403–404
Boxer Protocol, 403
Boycott, use of, in China, 626, 666, 707, 708, 709; against Hong Kong, 685
Boym, Michael, 38
Brahmanism, 420
Brahmaputra River (Tsangpo), *17, 367, 428, 715, 796, 797, 798*
Brandenburg, 54
Brazil, 19, 24
Brief Survey of the Maritime Circuit (*Ying-huan chih-lueh*), 150
British-American Tobacco Company, 659
British East India Company, 14, 28, 129; power of, 66, 68–69, 70; and the China trade, 74, 75, 76, 77, 78, 130, 132, 133, 134, 136; in Southeast Asia, 440–441, 442, 443, 447, 721, 725; breaking of monopoly of, 483, 726; in Tibet, 796
British North Borneo Company, 443
Brito, Felipe de, 20
Brokerage houses in opium trade (*yao-k'ou*), 131; brokers (*ya-hang*), 73, 92
Brooke, James, 442–443, 456
Brothers and Elders Society (*Ko-lao hui*), 396, 636, 638
Brunei, *410,* 442, 443, 741, 782
Brunton, R. H., 272
Buck, J. L., 705
Buddhism, Christianity and, 31, 56; in Japan, 31, 32, 59, 181, 268, 269, 270, 492, 533, 542, 833; in China, 42, 56, 61, 120; Pure Land, 269, 545; "temple schools" of, 274; in Cambodia, 420, 421; Mahayana, 420, 422, 432; Theravada, 421, 424, 426, 427, 430, 432; in Burma, 427, 446, 448, 449, 485, 747, 748, 766, 772; in Vietnam, 436; Fifth Buddhist Council, 448; in Siam, 457, 485, 744, 766; Zen, 541, 544–545; Tibetan, 786, 787, 795; Nichiren, 833
Buppō, 31; *see also* Buddhism
Buraku (hamlet), 516–517
Bureaucracy, in China, 84, 99–103; in Japan, 202, 230–232, 236–237, 276–278, 297, 519, 525, 555, 562, 829; in Korea, 762
Burlingame, Anson, 336, 370
Burma, *17,* 421, 423, 424, 425, *428, 435, 444,* 473, *715,* 755; and Portugal, 20; Japan in, 26, 714, 766; and the Dutch, 28, 67; as a Ch'ing tributary, 72; and Moslem rebellion, 166; British in, 366, 409, *410,* 446–449, 468, 486, 487, 746,

747, 748, 754; Lower, 409, *410,* 421, *428,* 429, 440, 446, 447, 448, 738, 748; Upper, 409, 423, 446, 447, 449, 716, 797, *798;* reunification of, 426–429; struggle of Siam and, 426–431; Buddhism in, 427, 446, 448, 449, 485, 747, 748, 766, 772; population of, 440, 739, 741; size of, 460; in and after World War II, 714, 772–773, 775, 805, 808; Chinese in, 718, 782; economy of, 738; nationalism in, 746–749, 772, 773; communism in, 773, 775, 780; independence of, 775
Burma Defense (National) Army, 772, 773
Burma Road, 714, *715,* 805
"Burma-Tibet convention" of 1886, 799
Burmese (Burmans), 421, 426, 446, 447, 747
Burney, Henry, 456
"Burning of the Books," 388n.
Buryats, 789, 800
Bushidō, 547
Butterfield and Swire Company, 355, 659

Cabinet, in China, 391, 629, 640, 643, 646; in Burma, 748; in Siam, 745; *see also* Cabinet, Japanese
Cabinet, Japanese, 297, 298, 554, 555, 562, 577, 580, 581; Itō and, 292–294; "transcendent," 299–300, 559, 573; struggle of Diet and, 301–310; Hara and, 571, 572, 577; "earthquake," 573; coalition, of Katō, 574, 575; "Mitsubishi," 578; "Mitsui," 578; and the depression, 581–583
Caciques, 729, 730, 775
Cairo, *16,* 20, 735
Cairo Conference, 806, 844
Calcutta, *17,* 68, 130, 441, *715;* Cominform in, 776
California, 171, 361
Cano, John Sebastian del, 24
"Cambalu," *40*
Cambodia, *17,* 128, *419,* 420, 422, 425, 426, *428,* 432, *435:* Spanish in, 26; Dutch in, 28; French in, 54, 409, *410,* 451, 452, 453, 454, 455, 486; rice-cultivation in, 417; temples in, 421; and Laos, 424; and Siam, 429, 431; and Vietnam, 431, 434; Chinese in, 718, 782; area and population growth of, 742; after World War II, 780, 781
Campaigns (drives), in Communist China, 864–865, 867, 870, 875–877
Campbell, J. D., 374
Camus, Albert, 831
Cantlie, James, 635
Canton, *17,* 30, 51, 72, 92, *95, 105, 113, 133, 160, 339, 419,* 430, 473, *564, 715,*

853; early contacts with, 21, 22, 44; and junk trade, 73; Christianity in, 121, 152, 158; Juan Yüan in, 125, 126; opium trade in, 137, 138, 139–141; as treaty port, 144, 151, 154; antiforeignism in, 143, 374, 626; missionary magazine in, 360; Cohong at, 155; rise of nationalism in, 157; British capture of, 170; customs service in, 317, 318; interpreters' schools in, 319; foreign concessions at, 340; arsenal and mint at, 380; Kuang-ya Shu-yüan at, 380; Nan-yüeh centered at, 432; Japanese capture of, 600, 711; revolutionary movement in, 637, 639; "72 martyrs of," 639; communism in, 671, 686, 688, 857n., 860; treaty powers' opposition to Sun at, 679; labor movement in, 684; anti-Chiang wing of KMT at, 696; Central Bank of China at, 698; Vietnam Revolutionary Youth League, in, 752

Canton Factories. *See* "Thirteen Factories"

Canton-Hankow railroad, 393, 629, 630, 701

Canton system, 71–78, 79, 96–97, 141; decline and collapse of, 128–136, 168

Cao-Bang, *435,* 436

Cao Dai sect, 779

Capital Formation in Japan (Rosovsky), 496

Capitalism, extension of, 11, 412–413; in Japan, 258, 494, 495, 497, 553, 565; in China, 347–348; in Mongolia, 791

Capron, Horace, 256

Capuchins, 796

Carmelites, 62

Caroline Islands, 807

Cartelization in Japan, 260–261, 506–509

Cartesian philosophers, 58

Casablanca Conference, 806

Castiglione, G., 63; Pl. 5

Cathay, *40, 43;* writings about, 55–56; *see also* China

Catherine the Great, 172

Catholicism, in China, 39, 54, 121–122, 153–154, 330–331, 332, 333, 334, 335, 362, 396, 660, 702n., 868; in Japan, 269, 270; in Southeast Asia, 429, 448, 450–451; in Korea, 463, 468; in the Philippines, 724, 725, 767; *see also* Missionaries, Protestantism, *and* Religion

"CC clique," 694

"Celestial Empire," steam engine, Pl. 42

Censorate (Tu-ch'a Yüan), 626, 646

"Center of People's Power" (*Pusat Tenaga Rakjat* or *Putera*), 771

Central Alliance for the Mobilization of the National Spirit, 602

Central Asia, Western imperialism in, 366–370; collectivization in, 786; *see also* Ili *and* Russian Turkestan

Central Bank of China, 698

Central Chamber (*Sei-in*), 230

Central China Army (of Japan), 600

"Central Country" (*Chung-kuo*), 82

Central Executive Committee, Central Supervisory Committee, KMT, 694, 695

Central Indonesian National Committee (Komité Nasional Indonesia Pusat), 772

Central Liaison Office, Tōkyō, during Occupation, 812

Central Political Institute, China, 694

Central Review (*Chūō Kōron*), 488, 548, 834

Central Training Corps, Chungking, 712

Ceremonies, Board of, China, 623

Certificate (*yin*) system, 115, 124

Ceylon, *16,* 28, 31, 67, 345, 421

Chaghadai, 368

Chahar, 598, 709, *785,* 792

Chakkri dynasty, 430; *see also* Rama I, Rama III, *etc.*

Chakravartin rulers, 427

Chamdo, 797, *798*

Champa, 90, *419,* 420, 422, 423, 424, 432, 434

Chams, 434

Chan T'ien-yu ("Jeme Tien Yow"), 647

Chang (headmen), 89

Chang Chien, 628, 646

Chang Chih-tung, 353, 373, 375, 384, 385, 758; modernization program of, 379–381, 390; educational reforms of, 386, 392, 393, 617, 618, 619; and the Boxer rising, 402; military reforms of, 620, 621, 622; death of, 627; and British loan, 629

Chang Chün-mai ("Carsun Chang"), 668

Chang Hsüeh-liang ("Young Marshal"), 587, 689, 696

Chang Hsün, 654, 656n.

Chang Lo-hsing, 165, 322

Chang Ping-lin (Chang T'ai-yen), 636, 637, 638

Chang Po-ling, 616

Chang Tso-lin, 577, 581, 655, 656, 657, 689, 707

Changchun, *339,* 481, *585,*

"Change of method" (*pien-fa*), 387

"Change within tradition," 327

Changkufeng, *465,* 607

Ch'ang-lu region, 113, 115, 116, 165

Changsha, 95, *105, 113,* 159, *160,* 164, *339, 715, 853;* modernization at, 390; Communist Party in, 671

Chao, Y. R., 664, 667

Chao Phraya (Menam) River, 416, *419*, 421, 423, *428*, 454, 458, 737
Chao Ping-chün, 644
Chao Tzu-yüeh (Lao She), 702n.
Chao-ch'ing (Shiuhing), 36, *95*
Chao-chou, 430
Chapdelaine, Father, 169, 451
Chapei, Shanghai, *341*
Chapu, *94*, 143, 144, *176*
Charter Oath, 228, 229, 230, 238, 271, 280; Pl. 29, Pl. 72
Chartered Bank of India, Australia, and China, 726
Chau, Phan Boi, 749–750
Cheeloo University, 702n.
Chefoo, 318, *339*, *585*
Chefoo Agreement, 145, 345, 372
Chekiang, 26, *95*, 106, 113, 119, 174, *176*, 324, 396, *853*
Chekiang-Kiangsi railroad, 701
Chemicals, production of, in Japan, 504
Chemulpo. *See* Inchon
Ch'en Chiung-ming, 679
Ch'en Kuo-fu, 694
Ch'en Li-fu, 694
Ch'en Pao-chen, 390
Ch'en Tu-hsiu, 663, 664, 665, 669, 671, 680, 688
Cheng Ch'eng-kung ("Koxinga"), 28, 118, 758
Cheng Ho, 63, 126, 423, 633
Cheng Kuan-ying, 357–358
Chengchow, *94*, 660, *853*
Cheng-feng movement, 854, 876; *see also* Thought reform
Cheng-hsüeh hsi (Political Study clique), 655, 694
Chengteh, *94*, *105*, *853*
Chengtu, *94*, 105, 715, *798*, *853*, 702n.
Cheng-wen she (Political Culture Association), 634
Chen-nan-kuan, 374, 432
Chennault, C. L., 714, 716
Cheribon or Linggadjati agreement, 776
Cherry Blossom Society, 592
Chettyars, 450, 775
Chia-ch'ing, 108, 117, 121
Chiang Ching-kuo, 849
Chiang Kai-shek, 587, 599, 600, 795; and Sun, 680; as superintendent of Whampoa Military Academy, 682; as leader of KMT and Nationalist China, 683, 686, 849, 851, 858, 859, 860, 861, 868; early anticommunist campaign of, 687–688; and the Northern Expedition, 687–688, 696; Nanking government of, 691–706; militarism under, 695, 696, 697; "kidnaping" of, 696n., 711; "rural reconstruction" under, 705–706; as com-

mander of army, 709; in World War II, 710, 712, 844; ideology of, 712–713; bound by tradition, 717; anticommunist "extermination" campaigns of, 709, 851; photographs, Pl. 76, Pl. 78
Ch'iang-hsüeh hui ("Self-Strengthening Society"), 385, 390, 391, 621, 643
Chiangmai, 423, 424, 426, *428*
Chiao (religious sect), 119–120
Chiao-chou (Kiaochow) Bay, 390
Chiao-hui hsin-pao ("mission news"), 364
Chia-yü-kuan (Suchow), *17*, 43, *105*, *367*, 370, *785*, 789
Ch'ien Hsüan-t'ung, 668
Ch'ien-lung, 77, 90, 107, 116, 129, 370, 796; persecution of Christians by, 63, 121; Voltaire's description of, 65; and Flint, 75; patronage of learning by, 88; death of, 117; authoritarianism of, 385; Pl. 5–7
Chien-sheng (degree-holder by "contributions"), 86, 87, 329
Chientao region, 763
Chi-hsien, 98
Chih-ho, *160*
Chih-kung t'ang (lodge of Triad Society, Hawaii), 636
Chihli, *94*, 111, 120, 159, 338, 352, 358; Boxers in, 398; Chihli clique, 655, 657
Children's Pioneer Corps, China, 864
Chin tribes, 446, 747
China, 3, 9, *17*, *40–41*, *428*, *435*, *564*; ancient trade of, with the West, 10, 25–26, 73–75; inventions by, 10; under the Yüan, 10; central power in, 14–15; self-image of, 21, 82–84; relations of Russia and, 43–52, 171–172, 570, 707; relations of Europe and, 60–66, 409; on the eve of change, 80–88; premodern change of, 88–99; growth and change in foreign trade of, 128, 157, 344–346; diplomatic missions abroad from, 240, 269, 270, 370–372; civil war in, 321–326; and Vietnam, 418, 431–433, 434, 436, 438–440, 453, 461, 749; and Siam, 455–456, 743, 745; and Korea, 461, 462, 468, 485; power politics over, 468–477, 483; in Manchuria, 469, 478–479, 481; Open Door in, 471, 472, 476–477, 481, 565, 608; independence and integrity of, 481, 570, 675; anti-Japanese feeling in, 570, 650, 666; unification of, 584, 657, 688, 689, 691, 693; Japanese war on, 598–601, 606, 706–717; reform movement in, late Ch'ing, 613–631; republican revolution of 1911 in, 631–642, 790, 801; Republic of, 640–706, 720; rise of warlordism in, 642–658; foreign relations of, under the Republic, 646–649;

in World War I, 648, 655, 665; and military alliance with Japan, 655; intellectual currents in, under the Republic, 658–672; Nationalist revolution in, 673–683; Nationalist government in, 683–706 (*see also* Kuomintang); in World War II, 710, 713–717, 808, *809;* area and population growth of, 740; Inner Asian frontiers of, 782–795, *785;* and Tibet, 795–801, 871, 879, 880–881; and the Korean War, 848, 867, 871; People's Republic of, proclaimed, 862; friction between India and, 880; *see also* Ch'ing dynasty, Communism in China, Ming dynasty, Republican China, Restoration period, Sung period, *and* T'ang dynasty

China Affairs Board, 767

China-Burma-India (CBI) theater, 714, *715*

China Development Company, 629

China Association, 471

China Foundation for the Promotion of Education and Culture, 661

China Illustrata (Kircher), 56

"China Incident," 600–601

China Inland Mission, 332, 337, 363, 364

China International Famine Relief Commission, 705

China Mail, 360

China Merchants' Steam Navigation Company, 354, 355, 358, 629

"China Revival Society" (*Hua-hsing hui*), 636, 637, 643

China's Destiny (Chiang), 712–713

"Chinatowns," 29

Chinchew (Ch'üan-chou), *17, 22, 40, 95, 132*

Chindwin River, *428,* 737

Chinese Characteristics (Smith), 364–365

Chinese Classics. See Classics, Chinese

Chinese Communist Party, Long March of, 163, 696n., 711, 851, *853;* Congresses of, 671, 679, 680, 857n., 877; development of, 671, 678, 683, 755; and labor movement, 678, 684; and Sun, 680; and Kuomintang, 680–681, 682, 685–686, 687, 688, 716; weakness of, 690, 691; united front with, 711–712; rise of, to power, 717, 849–851; Koreans in, 764; Yenan period of, 852–857; political control by, 861, 862–865, 881; structure of, 863; reform of thought and culture in, 869–871; internal struggles of, 875–878; growth of membership in, 877 (table); and Soviet Union, 882

Chinese Eastern Railway, 470, *585,* 680, 707, 708, 784, *785;* joint Soviet-Chinese administration of, 677

Chinese Educational Mission, Hartford, Conn., 361, 362, 616

Chinese emigration, 154–155, 423, 430, 443, 455, 459. See Chinese overseas

Chinese governors-general, 351–352, 353, 615

Chinese Imperial Maritime Customs Service. *See* Maritime Customs Service, Chinese

Chinese overseas, in Philippines, 26, 725; in Siam, 429, 430, 456, 459–460, 733, 738, 743, 745; in Malaya, 443–445, 738, 772; in Burma, 447, 746, 772; in Southeast Asia, 450, 739, 781, 782; in Indonesia, 731, 733–734; in Singapore, 775, 776; table of, in Southeast Asia, 782; *see also* Overseas Chinese

Chinese Repository, 152

Chinese Revolutionary Party (*Chung-hua ko-ming tang*), 654, 678

"Chinese rococo," Pl. 3

"Chinese Soviet Republic," 851

Chinese Turkestan, 172, 366, *367,* 368, 370, 787, 793

Ch'ing, Prince (I-k'uang), 403, 621

Ch'ing (Manchu) dynasty and empire, 29, 35, 157, 462; Christianity and, 36, 42–43; and Russia, 45–52; relations of, with Europe, 52–66; trade in, 71–78, 79; tradition in, 80–88; population and economic structure of, 88–99; administrative areas under, *94–95;* and local government, 99–102; administrative control and process in, 102–108; corruption in, 108–116; declining power of, 116–122; scholarship and thought in, 122–128; collapse of Canton system in, 128–136; and Opium War, 136–146, 166; revolts against, 155–166; Confucian support of, 163–164; propped up by West, 167, 175, 177; restoration of, 173–178 (*see also* Restoration period); and struggle for Central Asia, 366–370, 469; and political discussion, 385; support of Boxers by, 397–400, 402; suppression of nationalism by, 406; and the Burmese, 429; and the "scramble for concessions," 473; diplomacy of, 486; reform movement in, 613–631; rising sentiment against, 625; end of, 639–642, 720, 783; and Outer Mongolia, 786–788, 789; and Sinkiang, 793–794; and Tibet, 796–801

Chinggis Khan, 787, 788, 793

Ch'ing-hai, *785,* 787, *798,* 801, 881

Ch'ing-i pao ("Public Opinion"), 633

Ching-kang-shan, 688

Ch'ing-liu tang ("purification clique"), 373

Ch'ing-p'u, *176*

Ching-shih ("statecraft"), 123–125, 139, 150, 164, 327, 329, 386
Chin-hai, 22
Chinkiang, *94*, 143, 144, *176*, 318, *339*, 340
Chinnery, G., Pl. 13
Chinoiserie, 64, 65–66; Pl. 4
Chin-pu tang (Progressive Party), 643, 645, 646, 654
Chin-shih (metropolitan graduate), 39, 86, 87, 164, 439, 617
Chin-t'ien, 159, *160*
Chinwangtao, *399*
Chin-wen ("new text") movement, 122–123, 124, 388n., 389, 634
Chippendale, Pl. 4
Ch'i-shan, 143, 144
Chita, 784, *785*
Ch'i-ying, 144, 146, 168
Ch'oe Che-u, 463–464
Choibalsang, 791
Ch'öndogyo ("Society of the Heavenly Way"), 467n., 762, 845
Chongfat, 348
Chōsen, 483; *see also* Korea
Chōshū, 184, *186*, 203, 207, 211–217, 224; schools in, 199; samurai in, 210, 226, 242; foreign attacks on, 218–219; expeditions against, 219–222; coalition of Satsuma and, 222–223; and overthrow of the shogunate, 226, 227, 229; surrender of domains of, to emperor, 232; dominance of, in new government, 237, 282, 288, 293, 294, 302, 560, 562, 563; domination of army by, 590–591; portraits, Pl. 21, Pl. 29
Chou (*Viet. châu*) (department), 104, 433
Chou En-lai, 671, 682, 850, 862, 880
Chou Shu-jen (Lu Hsün), 664, 668, 672, 701
Chou Yang, 870
Ch'ou-an hui (association to "plan for peace") 650
Chou-li (*Rituals of Chou*), 161, 388
"Chow-chow" cargo, 346
Christian evangelism, 10, 11, 12, 152, 363
"Christian General." *See* Feng Yü-hsiang
Christian socialism in Japan, 518, 526, 547, 551, 570, 840
Christianity, spread of, 10, 11, 12, 20, 24, 25, 26; in Japan, 11, 30–35, 78, 182, 269–270, 492, 546–549; crusade of, against Islam, 19; hostility to, 33–35, 60, 63, 78, 121, 122, 147, 362, 395, 396, 439, 451, 463, 464; and Confucianism, 37, 55–58, 59, 60, 61; as heterodox sect, 62, 120–122, 463; in Southeast Asia, 429, 437, 439, 450–451; in Burma, 448, 747; in Korea, 463–464, 468, 760–761, 765; Marxism compared to, in Japan, 554; in the Philippines, 724, 725; in Indonesia, 731; in the peripheral areas, 801; *see also* Catholicism, Christianity in China, Missionaries, Protestantism, *and* Religion
Christianity in China, 10, 11, 35–43, 49, 50, 51, 52–60, 172, 177, 362–365, 450, 656; rejection of, 60–62, 63–64, 78, 121, 122, 362, 395, 396, 451, 668; entrance of, through treaty ports, 152–153, 158; mixture of, with Chinese elements, 161, 162; and Taiping movement, 168; in 1860's, 330–332; and Boxers, 395, 396; and education, 616, 660, 702; accepted by Sun, 635; accepted by Chiang, 693; as indigenous movement, 704–705
Chronometer, 14
Ch'ü Ch'iu-pai, 701
Chu Hsi, 56, 181
Chu nom writing system, 436, 437
Chu Teh, 688, 851
Chu Tzu-ch'ing, 665n.
Ch'üan (popular sovereignty), 682
Ch'üan-chou (Chinchew), *17*, 22, *40*, *95*, 132
Chuang Ts'un-yü, 123
Ch'uang-tsao she (Creation Society), 672, 701
Ch'üan-hsüeh p'ien (*Exhortation to Study*) (Chang), 392–393
Chuenpi, *133*; Chuenpi (Ch'uan-pi) Convention, 143; battle, Pl. 15
Chuguchak, *47*, *785*, 789
Chü-jen (provincial graduate), 86, 87, 385, 439, 617
Chu-ko Liang, 395
Chulalongkorn (Rama V), 458–459, 460, 485, 743
Chulalongkorn University, 744
Chumbi Valley, 797, *798*, 799
Ch'un, Prince, 381; second, 627, 629
Chün-chi-ch'u (Grand Council), 107, 317, 373, 391, 403
Ch'un-ch'iu (*Spring and Autumn Annals*), 123, 380
Ch'ung-hou, 370, 371, 373
Chung-hsüeh wei t'i, Hsi hsüeh wei yung ("Chinese learning . . ., Western learning . . ."), 386
Chung-hua hui-kuan ("Chinese guild"), 734
Chung-hua ko-ming tang (Chinese Revolutionary Party), 654, 678
Chungking, *95*, 98, *105*, *339*, 715, *798*, *853*, 858, 859, 860; Chinese capital at, 600, 710, 712; Korean "Provisional Government" in, 764
Chung-kuo ("Central Country"), 82
Ch'ung-ming Island, *176*

Index

Chung-shan. *See* Sun Yat-sen

Ch'ung-shan (Ch'ung Yu-t'ing), Pl. 57

Chūō Kōron (Central Review), 488, 548, 834

Church of Christ in Japan (Nihon Kirisuto Kyōkai), 270

Churchill, Winston, 413n., 844

Chusan Island, *17, 94,* 71, 133, 141, 143

Cigarettes, China, 659

"Circuit", 257 *(dō)*, 104 *(tao)*

Civil Appointments, Ministry of, China, 626

Civil Code, Japan, 265–266, 514, 534, 535; China, 624

Civil service, Chinese, 101 *(see also* Examination system); Japanese, 293, 555

Civilization and Philosophy of the Orient and Occident (Liang), 668

Clark, William S., 256, 270

Class divisions, in Japan, 184, 191–192, 237–238; in China, 82, 659–661, 866, 868, 881

Classic of Changes (I ching), 316, 328

Classic of Documents (Shu ching), 123, 174

Classics, Chinese, 37, 56, 58, 64, 82, 84, 101, 150, 159, 162, 181, 360, 388, 389, 405, 426; reinterpretation of, 123, 125

Clavius, 36

Cleveland, Grover, 475

Clock, 36

Coal production, in Japan, 248, 250, 261, 504; in China, 356, 629, 706; world, 411; in Southeast Asia, 455; in Indonesia, 736; in Indo-China, 738; in Vietnam, 751; in Soviet Union, 784

"Coalition government," 857, 858, 862, 881

Cochin China, 366, *435,* 737, 778–779; French in, 409, 438, 452, 453, 454, 455, 750, 753; puppet regime in, 780

Coconuts, 726, 729

Coen, Jan Pieterszoon, 28, 29, 66

Coffee, 68, 79, 726

Cohong *(kung-hang),* 73–74, 134, 135, 144, 146, 155

Colao, Pl. 1

Cold war, 780, 819, 846, 858

"Collateral" branches of Tokugawa family *(Shimpan),* 183, 184, *186–187,* 193, 211, 212, 220, 303; nationalism in, 197; and shogunate, 198, 202, 206, 208, 217, 225; and Ansei purge, 209; and "imperial restoration," 224

Collected Essays on Statecraft under the Reigning Dynasty (Huang-ch'ao ching-shih wen-pien), 124

Collective security, 586, 707

Collectivization, in Central Asia, 786; in Mongolia, 791; in China, 803, 867, 873–875, 877

Colleges and universities, in Japan, 208, 256, 270, 274, 275, 277, 278, 522, 530, 540, 550, 555, 818; in China, 363, 616, 617, 660, 661, 669, 702–704; in the Philippines and Siam, 725, 744; *see also* Education

Colonial Policy and Practice (Furnivall), 746n.

Colonialism, 408–416; revolts against, 415; idealistic rationale of, 452–453; in retrospect, 483–487; psychological evils of, 487; and Westernization, 720–721; in Indonesia, 721–724, 730–737; in the Philippines, 724–730; in continental Southeast Asia, 737–765; in Taiwan and Korea, 756–765; and nationalism, 774; as phase of modernization, 801; end of, 802; *see also* Imperialism

Colonization Office *(Kaitakushi),* 256, 287

Columbus, 11

Cominform, 776, 777

Comintern, 597, 671, 676, 735, 736, 755, 850; and KMT, 679, 680, 686, 687, 688, 711; and China, 690; and Vietnam, 752, 753; and Korea, 764; and Mongolia, 791; *see also* Anti-Comintern Pact

Commentaries on the Constitution (Itō), 536

Commerce, Ministry of (Shang-wu Pu), 623

Commercial Press, China, 631, 672

"Common Advancement Society" *(Kung-chin hui),* 639

Common Program, China, 862

Commoners, Japan, 184, 192, 237–238; education for, 274; democratic movement among, 281, 282

Communes, China, 863, 878, 882

Communication, in Meiji Japan, 246–247; in China, 344, 357, 365 *(see also* Postal service); revolution in, 411–412; modernization of, 802; in the Philippines, 726; *see also* Transportation

Communications, Bank of, China, 625, 659, 699

Communism, primitive (economic), 161; policy of ideological containment of, 584; international, 595, 720, 774 *(see also* Cominform *and* Comintern); in Germany, 604; in Vietnam, 752–754, 779, 780, 781; in Malaya, 772, 776, 780; in Burma, 773, 775, 780; in the Philippines, 774, 780; in Indonesia, 777, 778, 780; in Indo-China, 779, 780; in Japan, 817; in North Korea, 845; *see also* Communism in China *and* Communist parties

Communism in China, 36, 600, 774; and Taiping movement, compared, 162; and Christianity, 334; and nationalism, 553; pre-World War II, 597, 599; and literature, 701; rise of, to power, 778, 780, 795, 848–860, *853*; and French recognition, 819; and relations with Japan, 819; consolidation of power of, 860–873; and 1954 constitution, 863; and "socialist transformation," 873–879; and the world scene, 879–884

Communist parties, in Japan, 549, 550, 551, 575, 594, 833, 842–843; in Indonesia, 735–736, 755, 777, 778; in France, 752; Indochinese, 752, 755, 779, 780; in Vietnam, 752, 768; Philippine, 755; Korean, 763, 764; in Soviet Union, 882; *see also* Chinese Communist Party

Commutation Act, 76

Compass, 14, 24

"Compensation" policy, of Britain in China, 471, 473

Compradors, 155, 346–347, 348, 354–355, 460, 659

"Concessions" in treaty ports, 340–342

"Concordia Association," Manchukuo, 708, 766

Conditions in the West (Seiyō jijō) (Fukuzawa), 273

Confucian "University," 274

Confucianism, and Christianity, 37, 55–58, 59, 60, 61; as world-view, 88; and "new text" movement, 122–123, 124, 388, 389, 634; attacks on, 162, 663, 664, 667–668; in Japan, 181, 193, 267, 268, 274, 276, 530, 534, 756; in China, 320–330, 388–390, 634, 646, 649, 663, 667–668; revival of, 326, 327–329, 393, 485, 646, 713; K'ang Yu-wei's reinterpretation of, 388–390, 633; in Vietnam, 436, 439, 440, 485; in Korea, 461, 462; in Indonesia, 734; *see also* Classics, Chinese, *and* Neo-Confucianism

Confucius, *Analects* of, 199

Confucius as a Reformer (K'ung-tzu kai-chih k'ao) (K'ang), 389, 391

Confucius Sinarum Philosophus, 56, 57

Conger, Sarah Pike, Pl. 52

Congregationalists, 331

Congresses, Chinese Communist Party, 857n.

Congreve rocket, Pl. 15

Cong-san Dang (Communist Party of Vietnam), 752, 768

Conquests of the Emperor of China, *80*, Pl. *6–7*

Conquistadores, 26

Conscription, military, in Japan, 237–238, 239, 241, 243

Conservative party, Japan, 836–838, 841–842; *see also* Liberal-Democratic Party, Japan

Consortium of bankers, international, 630, 645, 676

Constantinople, 12, *16*, 166

Constitution, constitutional government, in Japan, 270, 278, 282, 283, 286, 288, 295–298, 299–310, 556, 560, 566, 568–579, 574, 577, 814–815; in China, 625–629, 637, 638, 643, 653, 863; in the Philippines, 727–729, 730; in Siam, 745; in Burma, 748; *see also* Meiji Constitution

Constitutional Compact, China, 646

Constitutional Imperial Rule Party (Rikken Teiseitō), 289

Constitutional Party (Kenseitō), 304, 306, 307

Constitutional Progressive Party (Rikken Kaishintō), 289, 290, 291, 299, 302, 303, 304, 562

Consultative Yüan, 626, 627, 629

Contract labor, 154–155, 501, 661

Contrat social (Rousseau), 285

Control faction, Japan, 593, 596, 599

Control system, Chinese government, 102–103, 695

Convention of People's Committees, North Korea, 845

Cook, James, 195

Coolie trade, 154–155

Cooperation, in Japanese government, 267, 300, 303, 309–310; between Western powers and China, 316, 335–336, 337; of Chinese and foreign merchants, 135, 141, 346–348

Cooperatives, in Mongolia, 791, 792; producers', in Communist China, 867, 873, 874

Copenhagen, 69

Copernicus, 36

Copperplate engraving, 80, Pl. 3, Pl. 6–8

Copper production, Japan, 250, 504

Copper-silver exchange rate, China, 137–138

Copra, 736

Coral Sea, Battle of the, 806

Cornell University, Pl. 75

Coromandel, 28

Corporations, 12; giant, in Japan, 258–259, 260–261, 506–509; *see also* Zaibatsu

Corregidor, 805

Corruption, in China, 108–116, 132, 167, 352, 381, 382, 713, 717, 877, 883; in Japan, 310, 578, 583; in Korea, 464; *see also* Squeeze

Cossacks, 44, 45, 50, 468

Index

Cottage industries, 6, 192
Cotton production and industry, in India, 70, 76, 79, 130; in China, 97, 346, 357–358, 659; in Japan, 210, 248–249, 250, 260, 261, 493, 497, 499, 502
Council of State (*Dajōkan*), 230, 231, 293
Councilors (*san'yo* or *sangi*), 230, 283, 286, 293
"Country" trade, 69–71, 76, 97, 129–130
Court of Directors, of British East India Company, 69, 77
Covarrubias, 703
Crawfurd, John, 456
Creation Society (*Ch'uang-tsao she*), 672, 701
Crimean War, 168
"Crimps," 154
Crowley, James, 592n.
Crusades, 12, 21
Cuba, 154, 476
"Cultural imperialism," 334
Cultural life, in Nationalist China, 701–704; in Communist China, 855, 869–871; *see also* Intellectual currents
Culturalism, Chinese, 84
Culture (Cultivation) System, Dutch East Indies, 722–723, 731
Cu-Nhan (*Chü-jen*) degree, 439
Cunningham, Edward, 348
Currency problems and reforms, in China, 137, 344, 660, 699; in Japan, 190, 235, 257–259; in Taiwan, 759; *see also* Money and banking
Curzon, George N., 800; Pl. 44
Cushing, Caleb, 146
Customs duties, in China, 109, 168, 342–343, 359 (*see also* Maritime Customs Service); in Japan, 205, 226

Dacoity, 447, 746
Daendels, H. W., 721, 722
Dah-Sun (Ta-sheng) cotton-spinning mill, 628
Dai Nihon shi (*History of Great Japan*), 193
Dai Tōa Kyōeiken ("Greater East Asia Co-Prosperity Sphere"), 546, 765–767
Dai Tōa Sensō ("Greater East Asia War"), 767
Dai Viet, 433
Daimyo, 31, 32, 34, 179, 202; three categories of, 183–184; domains of, 186–187; "participating," 217, 218; reappointed as *han* governors, 232; financial settlement on, 233, 239, 257; classified as nobles, 238; in new House of Peers, 292; *see also* "Collateral branches," *Han*, "Hereditary" daimyo, *and* "Outer" daimyo

Dairen (Ta-lien; Dalny), 339, 470, 477, 480, 585, 706, 708
Daishin-in (Supreme Court), 283
Dajōkan (Council of State), 230, 231, 293
Dalai Lama, 647, 787, 796, 797, 799, 800, 801, 880
Dalat, 435
Damrong, Prince, 459
Da-Nang (Tourane), 435, 451, 452
Dane, Richard, 648
Danish East India Company, 69, 75
Darjeeling, 797, 798
Darul Islam, 778
Date, 186; daimyo of, 34
Dazai Osamu, 831
Decoux, Admiral, 768
Defense Army (Fang chün), 620
Deflation, in Japan, 257, 259, 290, 497, 498, 581, 822; world, 498
De Gaulle, Charles, 779
Degrees, degree-holders, 84, 86, 87, 88, 111, 164, 439, 617; "irregular" and "regular," 329, 330; *see also* Examination system, in China
Deism, 58, 65
Delhi, 16, 798
Deliberation, Department of, Japan, 230
Demchukdonggrub, Prince, 792
Democracy, and imperialism, 484; "New," in China, 768, 779; "guided," in Indonesia, 778
Democracy (*min-ch'üan chu-i*) in China, 637, 644, 665, 682, 768, 779, 855
Democracy in Japan, during Meiji period, 278–283; and parliamentary government, 283–288; parliamentary and social, 548; and Christianity, 549; and the new liberalism, 568–571, 764; political party support for, 574, 596, 597; during the Occupation, 811, 813, 818, 819, 832; and intellectual currents, 830, 834; and political consensus, 835; *see also* Political parties in Japan
Democracy and the Party Movement in Prewar Japan (Scalapino), 572n.
Democratic Party (*Min-chu tang*), China, 643
Democratic Party, Japan, 835
Democratic Republic of Vietnam, 778–780
Democratic Socialist Party, Japan, 836, 839
Demonstration, student, 613
Denmark, 128, 342
Dent, Thomas, 129, 130
Dent and Company, 135, 347, 443; Pl. 13
Department, government (*chou*), 104, 433

Dependencies, Ministry of, China, 626
Depression, in Japan, 498, 581–583, 604; Pl. 71; world, 498, 580, 604, 730, 748; in Burma, 748; in Indo-China, 752
Description ... de l'Empire de la Chine (du Halde), 56
Deshima, 34, 179; Pl. 19
Despotism of China (Quesnay), 65
"De-Stalinization," 881–882
De-Tham, 454
Detring, Gustav, 352
Dewey, George, 476, 727
Dewey, John, 663, 664, 667
Dias, Bartolomeu, 18
Dictatorship, Yüan, 646, 650; party, in China, 673, 678, 685–706; in Indonesia, 778
Diem, Ngo Dinh, 780, 781
Diemen, Antonie van, 66–67
Dien Bien Phu, *435*, 781, 879
Diet, Japanese, 296, 297, 298, 310, 556, 601, 603; first session of, 299–301; struggle between cabinet and, 301–310; after World War II, 814–815, 837; *see also* House of Peers *and* House of Representatives
Dinh Bo Linh, 433
Diplomacy of Imperialism 1890–1902 (Langer), 472n.
Diponegoro, Prince, 722
Disciplined Forces (Lien-chün), 620
Discussion of the Military Problems of a Maritime Nation (Kaikoku hei dan) (Hayashi Shihei), 199
Disorder (*shuai-luan*), Age of, 389
District (*hsien*), 100, 104, 167, 433
District magistrate, China, 100, 101, 104, 108–109
"Divine spirit" (*Shen*), 154
Divorce, U.S. and Japan, 515
Djakarta, 776; *see also* Batavia
Dominicans, 26; in Japan, 33; in China, 43, 54, 59, 60, 63, 121, 153, 331; in the Philippines, 725
Dō ("circuit"), 257
Dobama Asiayone (We Burmans Society), 749
Dodge, Joseph, 822
Doihara, General, 598
"Dollar diplomacy," 630
Dōmei Kaigi, 839
Dong-Son culture, 418, *419*, 431
Dore, Ronald, 519n.
Dorgon, 42
Dorjiev, 800, 801
Dōshikai (Kenseikai), 556, 562, 574, 579
Dōshisha University, 270, 275
"Double structure" of Japanese economy, 511–513, 524, 827–828
"Double Ten," 640

Doumer, Paul, 455
"Downward transfer" (*hsia-fang*), 877
Drake, Sir Francis, 27
Dress, Westernized, in Meiji Japan, 264
Drew, E. B., Pl. 58
Dual diplomacy in Japan, 568, 583, 586–588
Dual Shintō, 268; *see also* Shintō
Dungans, 794
Dunlop Rubber Company, 496
Dupleix, Joseph Francis, 452
Dupuis, J., 452, 453
Durkheim, Emile, 515
Dust, 540
Dutch, in East Asia, 27–28, 29, 34, 43, 441; and China, 52, 53, 77–78; and Japan, 79, 169, 179, 204, 205, 206, 207, 770; in Indonesia, 409, *410*, 426, 610, 721–724, 730–737, 755, 770, 776, 777, 778, 806, *809*; in Siam, 429; *see also* Netherlands
Dutch East India Company, 14, 28, 34, 66, 67, 68, 69, 75, 721, 725
Dutch East Indies. *See* Indonesia *and* Netherlands East Indies
"Dutch learning" (*Rangaku*), 182, 189, 191, 198–200, 214, 272, 405; Pl. 20–21
Dutch New Guinea, 736
Dutch Reformed Church, in Japan, 269; in China, 332
Duy-Tan, 750
Dyaks, 442, 443
Dyarchy system, Burma, 747–748
Dynastic cycle, traditional Chinese, 80–82; Pl. *51–52*
Dzungars, 46, 47, 48, 49–50, 367, 787

Earlier Han. *See* Han, Earlier
East Asia, modernization of, 3–10; historical viewpoints on, 4–6, 9–10; Westernization of, 6–7; role of tradition in, 8–10; responses of, to European expansion, 14–15; international rivalries in, 24–30; and unequal-treaty system, 144–146; *see also* Imperialism, Modernization, Westernization, *and various countries*
East Asian Common Culture Society (*Tōa Dōbun Kai*), 632
East India Companies, 96, 121, 346; French, 54, 68, 69, 75, 437; Danish, 69, 75; Swedish, 75; *see also* British East India Company *and* Dutch East India Company
"East Indies," 426; *see also* Indonesia *and* Netherlands East Indies
"East Turkestan Republic," 795
Eastern Economic News (Tōyō keizai shimpō), 567
Eastern Han. *See* Han, Later

Index

Eastern King (*Tung-wang*), 159
"Eastern Learning" (*Tonghak* or *Tung-hsüeh*), 398, 463-464, 466-467, 485
Eastern Turkestan. See Chinese Turkestan
Ebina Danjō, 546, 548
Echizen, *186*; daimyo of, 206, 209, 215, 224
Eclipse (Mao Tun), 701
École Française d'Extrême-Orient, Hanoi, 751
Economic conditions and development, 5-6, 7; in premodern China, 91-96; in Tokugawa Japan, 189-191; after Japanese treaties, 210; under new Japanese government, 234; in Meiji Japan, 255-261; in Restoration China, 324-326, 328; under treaty system, 338-348, 658-662; world, in 19th century, 412-413; in modern Japan, 493-513, 524, 816-817, 822-827; in Nationalist China, 692, 698-701; in Indonesia, 724, 736, 737; in the Philippines, 729, 730, 737; in Southeast Asia, 737-739; in Vietnam, 751; in Taiwan, 756, 759-760; in Soviet Union, 784; in Communist China, 865-867; see also Exports and imports, Industrialization, *and* Labor
Economic factors, in rise of rebellion, 157; in colonialism, 483-484, 487
Economic Planning Agency, Japan, 827, 837
Eda Saburō, 841, 842
Eddy, Sherwood, 704
Edo, 79, 182, 184, *187*, 190, 214; as capital of Tokugawa shogunate, 34, 183; alternate years in (*sankin kōtai* system), 182, 215, 221; approaches to, *201*; Perry at, 202; opened to foreign residence, 205; antiforeignism in, 210, 211; surrendered to imperialist forces, 225; renamed Tōkyō, 229; industry in, 249; Confucian "University" in, 274
Edo Bay, 195, 196, 201, 205, 225
Education, Western, impact of, 8, 274, 275; Christianity and, 152, 269, 270, 275, 331, 363, 364, 466, 547, 616, 660, 702, 704, 747, 761; in Burma, 446, 747; in Siam (Thailand), 459, 744, 745; in the Philippines, 725, 730, 769; in Indonesia, 731, 733; in Vietnam, 751; in Taiwan, 759; in Korea, 761, 762; see also "Eastern Learning," Education in China, *and* Education in Japan
Education in China, tradition of, 84; missionary efforts to extend, 152, 331, 363, 364, 616, 660, 702, 704; and study abroad, 361-362, 661, 671, 704; Western studies, in China, 380, 387; proposed reforms in, 393; in late Ch'ing, 615-619;

higher, 616, 617, 660, 661, 669, 702-704; Ministry of (Hsüeh Pu), 617, 623, 626, 660, 664, 695; under the Republic, 660-661; see also Examination system, in China
Education in Japan, in Tokugawa period, 185, 192, 193; and Christianity, 269, 270, 275, 547; higher, 270, 274, 275, 277, 278, 522, 530, 535, 550, 555, 818; in Meiji period, 271-278; and study abroad, 271; compulsory, 275; for women, 275, 278, 547; Imperial Rescript on, 276, 294, 534, 536, 547; shifting policy for, 276-278; centralized, 294; universal, 512, 515, 535; primary, 522, 523; and Shintō, 536-538; reforms in, 818; Pl. 59-61; see also "Dutch learning"
Educational Association of China, 363-364
Egalitarianism, 161, 162, 181, 278, 514, 547, 549, 551, 553, 569
Egypt, *16*, 278
Eight Banners, 116
"Eight-legged essay" (*pa-ku wen*), 122, 392, 615
Eight Trigrams Society (*Pa-kua chiao*), 120, 394
Eighth Route Army, 852, 854
Elder Statesmen (*Genrō*), 297, 300, 304, 307, 309, 491, 554, 556, 557, 559; Pl. 45-46, Pl. 48-50, Pl. 62; see also Oligarchy, Japanese
Elders (*Rōjū*), 198, 206, 209, 211
Elders, Chamber of (*Genrō-in*), 283
Elders, Council of, 224
Electorate, growth of in Japan, 576
Electric power production, Japan, 504
Elements of International Law (Wheaton), 319
E-le-teng-pao, 117
Elgin, Lord, 170, 171
Elites, political, in Japan, 297, 554-559, 562, 568, 572, 579, 594; in China, 87, 627
Elizabeth I of England, 28
Ellice Islands, 806
Elliot, Charles, 139, 140, 141, 143
Emperor, Chinese, role of, 84; disappearance of, 641; discrediting of, 651; Plates 5-11; see also Tz'u-hsi (Empress Dowager)
Emperor, Japanese, role and privileges of, 101, 103, 107, 108, 194, 226-227, 293, 294, 296, 297, 298, 531, 532, 533, 534, 536, 538, 548, 554, 565, 569, 831, 838; rising respect for, 193, 209, 210, 216; and the shogunate, 213-225; "restoration" of, 225-252; moved to Tōkyō, 229; advisers to, as political elite, 556-557; nationalism centered in, 588, 589;

position of, and World War II, 811, 815; Pl. 72
"Empirical research" (*k'ao-cheng hsüeh*), 122
Empress Dowager. *See* Tz'u-hsi
Encomienda, 25
Encouragement of Learning (*Gakumon no susume*) (Fukuzawa), 273
England, and East Asia, 27–29, 34, 43; diplomatic and trade relations of, with China, 53, 128, 133–136, 139, 151, 335–337, 355, 371–372; in India, 66, 67, 68–69, 426, 468, 746, 747, 800; sea power of, 68; and Chinese nationalism, 157; in China, 167, 340, 341, 390, 468, 469–474, 477, 647, 683; wars of, with China, 168–171, 175, 204–205; support of Ch'ing by, 175; larger role of, in China, 177–178, 316, 318; and Japan, 195, 204, 205, 207, 272, 303, 311, 478–479, 481; and France, relations of, in Asia, 316, 448, 449, 460, 471, 481; and Russia, relations of, in Asia, 316, 468, 469–473, 477, 478, 481, 800; two approaches to China of, 318; rejection of Alcock Convention by, 337; and Chefoo Agreement, 345, 371–372; during Sino-Japanese War, 382–383, 384; in Burma, 409, 446–449, 746, 747, 748, 772, 775; in Malay Peninsula, 409, 443–446, 455, 456, 775; foreign investments of, 413; and Siam, 429, 451, 457–458, 460; in Singapore, 441–442; in Borneo, 442–443; and Korea, 468; and Anglo-German agreement of 1900, 478; in World War II, 610, 806, 810; in banking consortium, 630, 645, 676; Chinese Republic recognized by, 647; and Washington Conference, 675; and Nationalist China, 689; in Philippines, 726; and Vietnam, 780; in Afghanistan and Kashmir, 793; in Tibet, 795–801; agreement of China and, on Tibet, 800; economic growth of, 822; in SEATO, 880; *see also* British East India Company *and* Imperialism
English Governess at the Siamese Court (Leonowens), 458n.
Enlightenment, the, 57, 58, 64
Enomoto Takeaki, 225, 237, 256, 271, 293
"Enrich the kingdom and increase its military power" (*fu-kuo ch'iang-ping*), 669
"*Ero, guro*, and *nansensu*," 522
Essay on Morals (Voltaire), 65
Eta (outcasts), 238, 239, 547
"Ethical policy," Dutch, in Indonesia, 731–732, 733, 736
Etō Shimpei, 242, 281, 288
Etorofu, 17, 256

Euclid, 36, 39, 42
Eugenics Protection Law, Japan, 827
Eunuchs, 352, 382; Pl. 51
Eurasians, 20, 733
Europe, ancient trade of, with East, 10, 11, 27–29, 73–75; expansion of, 10–15, 16–17; rivalry in, over East Asia, 24–29, 43, 468, 469–473, 478; *Ou-lo-pa*, 42; Chinese influence on, 64–66; and Japan, before and during World War II, 606, 608, 609; *see also various countries*
European envoys to Peking, early, 53 (table)
Evangelical movement, 152–153
Evangelization of the World in This Generation (Mott), 704
"Ever-normal" granary, 100, 102
Evolution and Ethics (Huxley), 619
Evolutions of Rites (*Li yün*), 389
Ewha Girls' School, Korea, 761
Ex Illa Die, 62
Ex Quo Singulari, 63
Examination system, in China, 84, (chart) 86, 87, 615, 616, 617; and gentry class, 88, 329–330; and mathematics, 362n.; as source of bureaucrats, 406; military, 620; Examination Yüan, 695
Examinations in Vietnam, 439, 440, 751; in Burma, 449; in Korea, 462; in Japan, 555
Exchange rates, 137–138, 210
Exclusion Act of 1924 (U.S.), 676
Executive Yüan, 695, 697
Exhortation to Study (*Ch'üan-hsüeh p'ien*) (Chang), 392–393
Existentialism, in Japan, 831
"Expel the barbarians" (*jōi*), 210, 211, 215, 218, 219, 221, 222, 267
Exports and imports, Chinese, 26, 93, 97, 155, 344, 345, 346, 469, 659, 797; Japanese, 210, 247, 248, 249, 260, 493, 494, 495, 497, 499, 500, 501, 502, 504, 583, 709, 823; Siamese, 456, 458, 738; in Dutch East Indies, 723, 724; Philippine, 726, 729, 737; in Burma, Indo-China, and Malaya, 738; Vietnamese, 751; in Taiwan, 759, 760; Korean, 762; in Tibet, 797; *see also* Economic conditions *and* Trade
"Extermination" campaigns of Chiang Kai-shek, 851
Extraterritoriality, 134, 409; in China, 145, 146, 154, 167, 177, 178, 340–342, 359, 616, 675, 676, 689; in Japan, 145, 204, 205, 311, 265, 291; in Siam, 145, 743–744; in Vietnam and Korea, 145; ending of, 303, 311; missionaries under, 333; in Burma, 448

"Face," 168
Factories. *See* "Thirteen Factories"
Factory Law, Japan, 575
Faint Smiles of the Gods (Akutagawa), 543
Falkenhausen, General von, 697
Family (Pa Chin), 702
"Family elders" (*karō*), 185
Family planning, Japan, 828
Family-state, concept of, Japan, 534–535, 536
Family system, Chinese, 82–84, 88, 325, 513–514, 660; extended, 88, 513–514; nuclear, 867; Japanese, 265, 507, 513–515, 523, 524, 532; Vietnamese, 436; branch, 514, 516, 524; conjugal-type, 514–515; generational changes in, 523; decline of, 660
Fang chün (Defense Army), 620
Far Eastern Bureau, of Comintern, 755
Far Eastern Commission, Occupation of Japan directed by, 812
Farmers' associations, 517, 705, 883
Farmers Bank of China, 699
Farming. *See* Agriculture
Fascism, 580, 582; in Germany, 597, 603, 604, 605, 606, 698; in Japan, 589, 597, 603, 606, 698; in Italy, 606, 678
Fast-boat, Pl. 16
Fatshan (Fo-shan), *133*
Favier, Bishop, 400
Federal Party, Philippines, 728
Federalist movement, China, 656
Federated Malay States, *444*, 445; *see also* Malaya
Feng Kuei-fen, 315, 316, 381, 386
Feng Kuo-chang, 650, 654, 655, 656n.
Feng Yü-hsiang, 656, 657, 678, 696; Pl. 78
Feng Yun-shan, 158
Feng-shui ("spirits of wind and water"), 335, 356, 357, 372, 396
Fengtien, *585*, 647
"Fengtien-Chekiang War," 657
Fengtien-Chihli Wars, 655, 657
Fengtien clique, 655, 657
Fenollosa, Ernest, 272
Ferghana. *See* Khokand
Feringhi (*Fo-lang-chi*), 21, 127
Ferry, Jules, 373, 374
Feudalism, Japan, 180, 181, 182, 183–184, 190, 191, 405, 816; end of, 210, 224, 238–243; "nomadic," 787; China, 870; *see also* Han
"Figurists," 58
Filial piety, Chinese, 82, 161, 405; Japanese, 532, 535, 537–538; *see also* Family system
Filibusterismo, El (The Subversive) (Rizal), 727n.

Finance, Ministry of, Chinese, 625, 626, 695; Japanese, 837
Finances, in Meiji Japan, 233–235, 257–259; of Ch'ing Restoration, 325–326, 327; and tax-farming, 349; and foreign exploitation, in China, 473–475; and the zaibatsu system, 505–511; reform in, in late Ch'ing, 624–625; and modern Chinese banking practices, 659–660; in Nationalist China, 698–700; *see also* Money and banking. Reforms, monetary, *and* Taxes
"Financial clique." *See* Zaibatsu
Fishing, Japan, 255, 257
"Five-anti" movement, 868
"Five Articles Oath," 228, 229, 230, 238, 271, 280
Five Classics, 360
"Five elements," 388n.
"Five Nations, Treaties with the," 204–211
"Five-power" (*five-yüan*) constitution, 627, 637, 695
Five Relationships or Bonds, 82, 667
"Five-Year Plan for the Production of War Material" (Japanese army), 597
Flint, James, 74–75
Floods, of Yellow River, 111–112, *156*, 873; *see also* Yellow River
Fo-lang-chi (Feringhi), 21, 127
Fontainebleau conference, 780
Foochow, 72, *95*, *105*, 120, 168, *339*, 374, 702n.; as treaty port, 144, 152; Customs Service in, 318; interpreters' schools and arsenal in, 319; naval academy at, 381; Pl. *57–58*
Foreign Affairs, ministry of (Wai-wu Pu), 623, 626, 695
Foreign exchange, nationalized control of, in China, 699
Foreign Inspectorate of Customs, 168, 317; *see also* Maritime Customs Service
Foreign investment, by Britain, 412, 449, 473; by France, 413, 751; by Germany, 413; in Japan, 496, 500, 826–827; in Manchuria, 584; in Southeast Asia, 738, 751
Foreign leased areas, *339*
Foreign legations in Peking, *401*; Boxer siege of, 400–402
"Foreign matters" (*yang-wu*), 320, 350, 354, 362n.
Formosa (Taiwan), *17*, 28, 29, 30, *40*, 67, 356, 366, *564*, *715*; and Japan, 241, 303, 312, 371, 383, 409, 481, 756–760; *see also* Taiwan
Four Books, 360
Four-Power Treaty, 570
Four Treasuries, 88

France, 43, 441, 478; and Catholic missions, 54, 437, 448, 450–451; role of, in Europe, 54; and China, 54, 128, 167, 316, 331, 337–338, *341*, 372–375, 390, 469, 470, 472, 477, 683; Society for the Propagation of the Faith in, 153; and Anglo-French War with China, 168–171, 204–205; Japanese treaties with, 169, 205, 481; support of Ch'ing by, 175; and Britain, in East Asia, 316, 448, 449, 460, 468, 471; after Sino-Japanese War, 384; in Cambodia, 409 (*see also* Cambodia); in Cochin China, 409, 438, 750, 733 (*see also* Cochin China); in Indo-China, 409, 450–455, 484, 485, 486, 738, 778–781, 879; foreign investments by, 413, 751; and Siam, 429–430, 452, 457; in Vietnam, 437, 438, 439, 451–455, 720, 750–751 (*see also* Vietnam); in Laos, 451–455, 486; and Korea, 464; *entente cordiale* of Britain and, 481; in international banking consortium, 630, 645, 676; Chinese worker-students in, 661, 671; and Washington treaties, 676; Communist Party in, 752; fall of, in World War II, 768; Vichy government of, 768, 778; recognition of Communist China by, 819; economic growth of, 822; in SEATO, 880; *see also* French East India Company

Franciscans, 26; in Japan, 33; in China, 43, 54, 60, 121, 331; in the Philippines, 725

Franco-Prussian War, 338

Franco-Russian alliance, 468, 481

Franco-Vietnamese treaty, 453

"Free Laotian" (Pathet Lao) movement, 780

Free trade, 77, 135, 146, 167, 413, 501

"Freedom Bloc," Burma, 749

French East India Company, 54, 68, 69, 75, 437

French Revolution, 68, 76, 280, 721

Friends of Constitutional Government (Rikken Seiyūkai), 307, 308, 309

Frontier, Treaty of the, 50–52

Fryer, John, 319

Fu (Viet. *phú*) (prefecture), 104, 232, 433

Fu-k'ang-an, Pl. 7

Fu Ssu-nien, 665n.

Fudai ("hereditary" lords), 183–184, 185, *187*, 188, 198, 199, 203, 221, 225; and the shogunate, 202, 206, 208, 217

Fu-jen University, Peiping, 702n.

Fuji, Mount, *201*

Fujita Tōko, 197

Fujiwara family, 227

Fukien, 22, 72, 92, *95*, 106, 113, 324; Taiwan made part of, 29; Catholic missionaries in, 36, 54, 60, 63, 121; pirates from, 118, 119; Triad Society in, 120; emigrants from, 430, 460

Fukien fleet, 374, 381

Fukoku kyōhei ("rich country and strong military"), 229, 266, 311, 895

Fukui, *187*, *825*

Fu-kuo ch'iang-ping ("enrich the kingdom and increase its military power"), title page, 669, 895

Fukuoka, *186*, 277, 295, *824*

Fukushima Prefecture, 290

Fukuzawa Yukichi, 279, 285, 287, 466, 634; educational program of, 273, 274, 275; and Constitutional Progressive Party, 289; on law, 566

Fu-nan, *419*, 420, 422

Fung Yu-lan, 665n.

Fur trade, 45

Furnivall, J. S., 746n.

Furukawa, 506

Fusan. *See* Pusan

Fushimi, *187*, 225

Fushun, *585*, 706

Gabet, 153, 799

Gadjah Mada; Gadjah Mada University, 422

Gakushūin University, 208, 540

Galdan, 46, 48, 49

Galleon trade, Mexico-Philippines, 25–26, 725, 726

Gama, Vasco da, 11, *16*, 18, 633

Gandhi, 747

Ganges River, *16*, *798*

Gangtok, 796, 797, *798*

Garnier, François, 452, 453

Gartok, 797, *798*

Gate (Natsume Sōseki), 541

Gate of Heavenly Peace (*T'ien-an men*), 666

Gendai Nihon no shisō, 548n.

General Conference of Protestant Missionaries, 363

General Council of Burmese Associations, 747

General Electric Company, 496

Generational change, in Japan, 523, 815

Geneva conference, 880

Genoa, 11

Genrō. *See* Elder Statesmen

Gentry, Chinese, 84–88, 158, 182, 661; and tax collectors, 110, 111; and Taiping movement, 162, 174; leadership of, 325, 326; and examination system, 329–330; hostility of, to Christians, 333–334, 338, 362; in late Ch'ing, 627–628, 629, 630, 631, 639, 874

Gentry (*shizoku*), Japanese, 238

Genyōsha (Black Ocean Society), 467

Geography, 42–43, 64; Chinese, *40–41, 148–149*, 150; Western, Chinese views of, 127; role of, in history, 460–461

Geological Survey of China, 702

George, Henry, 549, 637, 682

George III of England, 77

Gerbillon, Jean-François, 42, 48

Germany, influence of, in Japan, 272, 277, 292, 293, 294, 544, 553, 568; unification of, 365; and China, 372, 409, 469, 470, 471, 472, 473, 477, 620, 621, 697; after Sino-Japanese War, 384; imperialism of, 390, 413, 478; in Shantung, 390, 396; foreign investments of, 413; and Anglo-German agreement of 1900, 478; comparison of Japan and, 579, 603–606; Nazi, 580, 582, 597, 603, 604, 605, 606, 698; and Anti-Comintern Pact, 595, 711; Weimar, 603, 604; nonaggression pact of Soviet Union and, 607; in World War II, 608, 609, 810; in banking consortium, 630, 645, 676; in World War I, 648; and Rome-Berlin Axis, 711; and Tripartite Pact with Italy and Japan, 768

Ghantimur, 46, 48

Gia-Long, 438, 439

Gilbert Islands, 806, 807

Ginling College, Nanking, 660, 702n.

Ginza, Pl. 26–27

Globe Magazine (*Wan-kuo kung-pao*), 364, 385

Glover and Company, 223

Glynn, Commander, 196

Gneist, Rudolf von, 292

Goa, *16*, 22, 30, 31, 32, 36, 52

"God," transliteration of, 59, 154

"God Worshippers' Society" (*Pai Shang-ti hui*), 159

Goez, Benedict de, 43

Gold, discovered in California, 155; and silver exchange, 210, 344; outflow of, from Japan, 247; mining of, in Japan, 248

Gold standard, 344; in Japan, 480, 498, 499, 581, 583; in Taiwan, 759

Golovin, Fedor Alexeevich, 48, 52, 53

Golovkin, Count, 53

Good Hope, Cape of, 18, 28, 67, 70

Goodnow, F. J., 650

Gordon, Charles George ("Chinese"), 175

Gōshi ("rural samurai"), 212, 215, 253, 282

Goshimpei (Imperial Force), 237

Gospel Baptists in China, 332

Gotō Islands, *186, 824*

Gotō Shimpei, 758, 759

Gotō Shōjirō, 229, 281, 282, 289, 290, 291, 292, 294

Gottard, 53, 62

Government in China, Ch'ing, inertia of, 99–108; control system in, 102–103; corruption in, 108–116, 132, 167, 352, 381, 382 (*see also* Squeeze); declining power of, 116–122; and school of "statecraft," 123–125; administrative problems of, 156, 181; inadequacy of leadership of, in industrialization, 349–351; power structure in, 351–354; administrative reforms in, 622–625; parliamentary, 631–706; *see also* Constitution, constitutional government, Democracy in China, *and* "Statecraft"

Government in Japan, and industry, 245, 247–249, 250–252, 257–259; constitutional, 278, 297, 299–319; and experiments with representative institutions, 282–283; parliamentary, 283–288, 547, 548, 574–576, 816; strengthening authority of, 292–295; role of, in the economy, 495–496, 497, 503; and big business, 510–511; subsidies of, to agriculture, 517; political elites in, 554–559, 562, 568, 572, 579, 594; before World War II, 601–606; *see also* Constitution, constitutional government, Democracy in Japan, Emperor, Japanese, *and* Party government

Government in Southeast Asia, in Burma, 427–429; in Siam, 430, 456; in Vietnam, 432, 433–434; parliamentary, 748

"Government supervision and merchant operation" (*kuan-tu shang-pan*), 354–355, 356, 357

Governors, governors-general, China, 103, 351–352, 353 (table), 390, 615

Goyer, Pieter van, 53

Goyōkin (forced loans), 234

Gracey, Dr. S. L., Pl. 58

Grain tribute (*ts'ao-liang*), 109, 110, 111, 112, 354, 355, 625; *see also* Tribute system

Grand Canal, 92, *94*, 111–113, 124, 143, *156, 160, 176*, 337, 354

"Grand Constitutional Era" (*Hung-hsien*), 650

Grand Council (*Chün-chi-ch'u*), 107, 317, 373, 391, 403

Grand Council of Economic and Financial Interests, Vietnam, 750

Grand Prince. *See* Taewŏngun

Grand Secretariat (*Nei-ko*), 106, 107

Grant, U. S., 256, 280

Grass by the Road (Natsume [Sōseki]), 541

Great Camp, 174

Great Elder (*Tairō*), 208

Great Lake (Tonle Sap), 416–417, *428, 435*

"Great Leap Forward," 878, 881, 882

"Great Peace" (*T'ai-p'ing*), 159, 389
Great Peace and Great Unity (*ta-t'ung*), Age of, 389
Great Wall of China, *17*, 43, *94*, *785*
"Greater East Asia Co-Prosperity Sphere" (*Dai Tōa Kyōeiken*), 546, 765–767
"Greater East Asia War" (*Dai Tōa Sensō*), 767
"Green gang," Shanghai, 684
Green Standard, Army of the (*Lü-ying*), 116, 142, 392, 619–620
Grew, Joseph C., 805
Grimaldi, 57
Gros, Baron, 170, 171
"Groups of Ten for National Salvation," 666
Guadalcanal, 807
Guam, 476, 806
Guerrilla warfare, 449, 454, 710, 772, 774, 775, 776, 777, 854
"Guest merchants" (*k'o-shang*), 92
Guilds (*hui*), 73; regional (*t'ung-hsiang hui*), 347, 618, 684; pan-Chinese (*Chung-hua hui-kuan*), 734
Gujarat Peninsula, *16*, 18 67
Gurkhas, 796, 799
Gyantse, 797, *798*, 800

Hachisuka, *186*
Hague conferences, 482, 778
Hai lu (*A Maritime Record*), 127–128
Hai-chün ya-men ("Naval Yamen"), 381
Haikara ("high collar"), 264
Hai-kuo t'u-chih (*Illustrated Gazetteer of the Countries Overseas*) (Wei Yüan), 147, *148–149*
Hai-kuo wen-chien lu (*Record of Things Seen and Heard about the Overseas Countries*), 126, *148*, 149
Hainan Island, *17*, *95*, *339*, *435*, 459, *715*, *853*, 862, 881
Haiphong, *435*, 780
Haiphong-Kunming railroad, 768
Hakkas (*k'o-chia*), 158, 159
Hakodate, *187*, 204, 205, 225, 256, 269, *825*
Halde, J. B. du, 56, 57
Hall of Peaceful Seas (Hai Yen T'ang), Pl. 3
Hamaguchi, 573, 574, 577, 578, 581
Hami (Komul), *17*, 43, *47*, 366–367, *785*, 789
Ham-Nghi, 453
Han (feudal domains), 183–184, 185, *186–187*, 188; administration of, 189, 198, 405; role of, in struggle between shogunate and emperor, 207, 209, 210, 211–225; surrender of, to emperor,

231–232, 234; representatives of, in deliberative assemblies, 280–281; *see also* "Collateral" branches, "Hereditary" daimyo, *and* "Outer" daimyo
Han, Earlier or Western, 123, 388n.; Later or Eastern, 123, 173, 388n.
Han dynasty, 90, 431, 432
Han Learning, 123, 124, 164, 327, 388
Han River, China, 92, *94*, *113*, 117, *160*, 379; Korea, *465*, *585*
Hancock, W., Pl. 36
Handicraft industries, in Japan, 236, 247, 250; in China, 346
Hang (*merchants*). See Hong
Hangchow, *94*, *105*, 143, 175, *176*, 702n., 857n.
Han'gŭl (Korean writing system), 462, 467
Hankow, *94*, *113*, 177, 337, *339*, 379, 452, *564*, 636, *715*; Customs Service in, 318; foreign concessions at, 340; Japanese capture of, 600, 711; mass production in, 660; British concessions seized in, 689; Hua Chung University at, 702n.; CCP congress at, 857n.
Hankow-Canton, or -Peking, railroad, 393, 471, 472, 629, 630, 701
Hanlin Academy, 39, 399; in Vietnam, 438
Hanlin scholars, 63, 361, 373
Hanoi, 374, 432, 434, *435*, 436, 448, 471, 778; Mongols in, 433; taken by Tay-son brothers, 437; taken by Nguyen Anh, 438; French in, 453, 780; as capital of Vietnam, 455; Sun at, 638; University of, 750; l'École Française d'Extrême-Orient at, 751; Viet Minh in, 779; as capital of North Vietnam, 781
Hanyang, *94*, 379, 380, 393, 629
Han-Yeh-P'ing Coal and Iron Company, 629, 649
Hara Kei, 560, 562, 567, 568; and party government, 571–574; Pl. 64
Harbin, *339*, *585*
Harmony, ethic of, in China, 82; in Japan, 516, 518, 532
Harris, Townsend, 145, 205, 206, 211, 457–458; Japanese treaty negotiated by, 180, 207, 208, 216, 240; Siamese treaty negotiated by, 451
Hart, Robert, 319, 336, 370, 381, 400, 476, 627; and Chinese Customs Service, 317, 318, 343, 352; and postal service, 358, 359; and Sino-French negotiations, 373–374; Pl. 34
Hastings, Warren, 796
Ha-ta-men, Peking, *410*
Hatoyama Ichirō, 594, 837
Hatta, Mohammad, 736, 771, 777, 778

Index

Hausknecht, Emil, 277
Hawaii, 25, 154, 475, 476, 636
Hay, John, 476–477
Hayashi Razan, 59
Hayashi Senjūrō, 581, 595, 596
Hayashi Shihei, 199, 204
"Heaven" (T'ien), 59, 61
Heaven and Earth Society (T'ien-ti hui), 120
"Heavenly Chastising Force" (Tenchū-gumi), 216
Heavenly King (T'ien-wang), 159
"Heavenly Kingdom of Great Peace" (T'ai-p'ing t'ien-kuo), 159
Heavenly Reason Society (T'ien-li chiao), 120
"Heavenly Way, Society of the" (Ch'ŏndogyo), 467n., 762, 845
Hegel, 544, 545
Heilungkiang, 585, 647
Hemp, 726, 729
Heng-yang, 715
Henry the Navigator, of Portugal, 15–18
Henry (Prince) of Orleans, 799
Hepburn, J. C., 269
"Hereditary" daimyo (fudai), 183–184, 185, 187, 188, 198, 199, 203, 221, 225; and the shogunate, 202, 206, 208, 217
Heterodox sect, Christianity as, 62, 120–122, 463
Heung-shan. See Hsiang-shan
Heusken, 211
Hibbett, Howard, 540n.
Hideyoshi, 26, 32, 33, 34, 311, 462, 762
Higashikuni, Prince, 811
Hikone, 184, 186, 187, 203
Hinduism, 59, 420, 422, 731
Hippisley, A. E., 476
Hirado, 28, 29, 30, 34, 186, 824
Hiranuma Kiichirō, 581, 599, 607, 808
Hirata Tōsuke, 559
Hirohito, Emperor, Pl. 72
Hiroshige IV, Pl. 25
Hiroshima, 186, 224, 239, 810, 824
Hirota Kōki, 488, 581, 595
Hisamitsu, 212, 215, 217, 219, 227
Histoire générale de la Chine (de Mailla), 56
History of the Eclipse of Vietnam (Viet Nam vong quoc su) (Chau), 749
History of Great Japan (Dai Nihon shi), 193
Hitachi, 504
Hitotsubashi, 208
Hizen, 186, 235, 281, 288; schools in, 199; lord of, 203; returned to emperor, 232; revolt in, 242; coal and iron industry in, 246, 248
Hlutdaw, 427, 449

Ho Chi Minh, 752, 753, 768, 769, 773, 778, 779
Ho Ying-ch'in, 687, 697
Hoa Hao, 779
Hobbes, 534
Hobson, J. A., 414
Hodja (Khoja), 368
Ho-fei, 352
Hoihow, 459
Hokkaidō, 17, 187, 195, 204, 825; taken by revolutionaries, 225; development of, 255–257, 272; university of, 277
Hokkaidō Colliery and Shipping, 507
Hokkaidō Colonization Office, 256, 287
"Hokkien" language, 430
Holding companies, Japan, 507, 508; see also Zaibatsu
Holland. See Netherlands
Hollandia, 809
Holt, Alfred, 411
Home Ministry, Japan, 297, 519, 562–563, 813
Honam, 133
Honan, 94, 111, 120, 150, 159, 164, 657, 852, 853
Hong merchants (hang), 73, 74, 78, 144; decline of, 134, 136, 155; cooperation of, with foreign traders, 135, 141
Hong Kong, 17, 75, 95, 133, 154, 339, 341, 410, 459, 483, 564, 683, 715; British in, 141, 143, 144, 151, 409; Westernization of, 150; Perry in, 169; as treaty port, 331; smuggling from, 343; cable at, 344; as shipping and market center, 347, 348; missionary press in, 360; Chinese press in, 375; American Asiatic Squadron at, 476; strike and boycott against, 685, 686; area and population growth of, 741; Vietnamese Communist Party in, 752; Pl. 17–18
Hongkew, Shanghai, Pl. 56
Hongkong and Shanghai Banking Corporation, 347, 473, 698, 726
Honjō, General, 586
"Honor the emperor" (sonnō), 210, 214, 221, 223
"Honorable housemen," 183
Honshū, 17, 34, 184, 186–187, 190, 195, 585, 824–825
Hoorn, Pieter van, 53
Hoover, Herbert C., 356
Hopei, 598, 696, 709
Hopei-Honan border region, 582, 853
Hoppo, 73, 74, 133, 343
Hormuz, 16, 18
Ho-shen, 117
Hoshi Tōru, 302, 303, 307, 557
Hoshina, 186
Hoshino Naoki, 608

Hosokawa, *186*
Hotta Masayoshi, 206, 207, 208
"House," Japanese, 513–514
House of Peers, Japan, 292, 296, 297, 301, 307, 309, 556, 575–576
House of Representatives, Japan, 296, 297, 299, 301, 302
Howqua, 134, 141
Hozumi Yatsuka, 534–535, 536, 537
Hsi (West) River, *17*, *95*, *113*, *159*, *160*, *435*, *473*, *853*
Hsia-fang ("downward transfer"), 877
Hsia-men chih (gazetteer of Amoy), 127
Hsiang River, *95*, *113*
Hsiang-shan, *23*, *133*, 634, 635
Hsiang-yüeh (official lecturers), 102
Hsiao-k'ang (Small Tranquillity), 389
Hsiao-shuo yüeh-pao (*Short Story* magazine), 672
Hsiao-tao hui (Small Sword Society), 163, 167
Hsieh Ch'ing-kao, 128
Hsien (Viet. *huyen*) (district), 100, 104, 167, 433, 863
Hsien-feng, 108, 168, 174, 321, 351n., Pl. 32
Hsi-hsüeh ("Western Learning"), 463
Hsi-k'ang, *798*, 801
Hsin ch'ao (*New Tide*), 665
Hsin ch'ing-nien (*New Youth*), 663, 664, 670
Hsin-chiang (Sinkiang), 370, 696, 718, 719, 740, *785*, 789, 793–795, 797, *798*, 880, 881
Hsing-Chung hui ("Revive China Society"), 635, 637, 643
Hsing-i, chih-nan ("knowing is more difficult than doing"), 681
Hsin-hsüeh wei-ching k'ao (*Study of the Classics Forged during the Hsin Period*) (K'ang), 388
Hsin-k'o ("new guest"), 733
Hsin-min hui (New People's Association), 711, 766
Hsin-min ts'ung-pao ("Renovation of the People"), 633, 634
Hsin-wen chih (newsprints), 360
Hsi-pan-ya (Spain), 127
Hsiung Hsi-ling, 646
Hsiu-ts'ai degree, 439
Hsü Chi-yü, 150
Hsü Jun ("Ahyun"), 347, 348, 355
Hsü Kuang-ch'i (Paul Hsü), 39, 42, 56, 153; Pl. 1
Hsü Shih-ch'ang, 655, 656n.
Hsü Shu-tseng ("Little Hsü"), 790
Hsüan-t'ung (Henry Pu-yi), 587, 627, 641, 654, 707, 708
Hsü-chia-hui ("Hsü Family Village"), 39, 153 (Zikawei)

Hsuchow, 660, *853*
Hsüeh Fu-ch'eng, 387
Hsüeh-hai t'ang (academy), 138
Hsüeh-hui ("study societies"), 385, 639
Hsun-cheng ("tutelage"), 638
Hu Feng, 870
Hu Han-min, 638, 681, 693, 750
Hu Kuang-yung, 369
Hu Lin-i, 174
Hu Shih, 663–664, 667, 668–669, 671, 870; Pl. 75
Hua Chung University, Hankow, 702n.
Hua-chü ("speaking plays"), 855
Hua-hsing hui ("China Revival Society"), 636, 637, 643
Huai River and region, *94*, 112, 113, 124, *160*, 164, 321, *853*
Huang Hsing, 636, 637, 638, 639, 640, 643, 644, 645, 654; Pl. 73
Huang Tsun-hsien, 372, 390
Huang-ch'ao ching-shih wen-pien (*Collected Essays on Statecraft under the Reigning Dynasty*), 124
Huang-Ch'ing chih-kung t'u, 129
Hua-pei kuo ("North China-land"), 709
Huc, Évariste Régis, 153, 799
Hu-chou, *176*
Hué, 145, 434, *435*, 436, 437, 438, 453, 778
Hui (guilds), 618; *see also* Guilds
Hui (society or association), 119–120
Hui-chou (Waichow), *133*, 636
Hukbalahap (Anti-Japanese Resistance Army), 774
"Hukuang railways," 630
Hull, Cordell, 607, 608, 611, 612
Hulutao, *585*
Hu-men (Bogue, Boca Tigris, Tiger Gate), 135; treaty of, 145
Hunan, *95*, 114, 150, 157, 159, 164, 629; Reform Movement in, 390, 392; isolation of, 405; revolutionary movement in, 636, 637, 638, 639; federalism in, 656; peasant movement in, 686, 688
Hunan Army, 164, 174, 322, 620, 621
Hun-chun, *339*
Hundred Days of 1898, China, 392–394, 617
"Hundred Flowers" campaign, 876, 877
Hung Hsiu-ch'üan, 175, 463, 634; and Taiping rebellion, 158, 159, 160, 161, 162, 163
Hung League (*Hung-meng* or *Hung-men*) (Triad Society), 120, 159, 162–163, 443, 635, 636, 743
Hung Ta-ch'üan, 162
Hung-hsien ("Grand Constitutional Era"), 650
Huns, 12
Hupei, *94*, 114, 116, 159, 164, 174, 622, 629, *853*; mining in, 393; schools in

618; revolutionary movement in, 637, 639

Huxley, T. H., 387, 619, 749

Hydroelectric resources, Japan, 504

Hyōgo (Kōbe), *186*, 205, 216, 246, 521, *824*

Ibsen, 651

I ching (*Classic of Changes*), 316, 328

I-chan (mounted courier system), 105–106

Ichang, *94, 339*

Ides, Izbrandt, 49, 53

Ieyasu, 28, 32, 34, 59, 215

Ignatiev, Nikolai, 173

I-ho ch'üan or *I-ho t'uan*. *See* Boxer movement

I-hsin. *See* Kung, Prince

Ii, domain (Hikone), *186, 187*

Ii Naosuke, 184, 203, 206, 207, 208–210, 211, 214

Ikeda, *186*

Ikeda Hayato, 837, 838, 841

I-k'uang (Prince Ch'ing), 403, 621

I li, 388

Ildefonso, 53, 62

Ili region, *47*, 121, 172, *367*, 368, 469, *785*, 787, 789; Dzungars in, 46, 49, 367; Torguts in, 50; Russians in, 369, 370; combined with Tarim basin, 793; Kazakh and Kirghiz nomads of, 794; rebellion in, 795; Pl. 6

Illustrated Gazetteer of the Countries Overseas (*Hai-kuo t'u-chih*) (Wei Yüan), 147, 148–149

Ilocano, 724

Ilustrados, 726

Imamura, General, 593

Imperial Conferences, Japan, 601, 609, 610

Imperial Force (*Goshimpei*), 237

Imperial Guards (*Konoe*), 237, 242, 294

Imperial Headquarters, 601

Imperial House, 193, 226–227, 531, 534; *see also* Emperor, Japanese

Imperial Household Ministry, 293, 297, 304, 556, 593

Imperial Party (Teikokutō), 306

"Imperial Precept for the Military" ("Rescript to Soldiers and Sailors"), 295

Imperial Rescript on Education, 276, 294, 534, 536, 547

"Imperial restoration," 194, 224, 226–228, 231, 232, 268, 294, 296; *see also* Meiji period *and* Meiji Restoration

Imperial Rule Assistance Association, Japan, 602–603, 766, 808, 810, 835

Imperial system, Japan, 193–194; *see also* Emperor, Japanese

Imperial Telegraph Administration, China, 357

"Imperial troops," 216, 217, 225

Imperial Universities, Japan, 277

Imperial University, China, 617

Imperial Veterans Association, Japan, 602

Imperialism, economic and military, 13, 14, 15, 311–312; British, 136, 205, 365, 366, 369, 390, 413–414, 440–450, 460, 483–484; in China, 136, 205, 315, 384, 385, 390, 391, 396, 468–477; Japanese, 305, 311–312, 366, 409, 478–483, 488, 490, 499, 563–568, 613, 632, 649, 755, 765–767, 792; "cultural," of China, 334; French, 365, 366, 372, 390, 413, 450–455, 460; Chinese resistance to, 365–378, 670, 673, 683–686, 713; Russian, 366, 368–370, 390, 468–470, 471–473, 478–483, 484, 783–786, 789–790, 793; age of, 384, 385, 408–487; German, 390, 413, 478; late 19th century, 408–416; theories and attitudes concerning, 413–416; in Korea, 460–468; American, 475–477; sanction for, 475, 483–485; ideology of, 565–566; "secondary," 647, 789, 801; Lenin's theory of, 676–677; and world depression, 739; in Vietnam, 750–751, 752, 753; *see also* Colonialism *and various countries*

Imports. *See* Exports and imports

Inchon (Chemulpo), 376, *465, 585*, 848

Independence Club (*Tongnip Hyŏphoe*), 467, 761

"Independence Society" (*Tzu-li hui*), 636

Independent (*Tongnip Shinmun*), 467

"Independent self" (*shutaisei*), 831

India, *16*, 29, 43, *367*, 391, *428, 715, 785, 798*; European trade with, 10, 11, 28; Portuguese in, 18, 20, 30; French in, 54; Jesuits in, 59; British in, 66, 67, 68–69, 426, 468, 746, 747, 800; Dutch in, 67; "country" trade of, 69–71, 72, 76, 97, 129–130; agency houses in, 129, 130; and opium trade, 131, 137, 150–151, 326, 345; Sepoy Mutiny in, 170; tea from, 345; cotton from, 346; influence of, in Southeast Asia, 418–421, 422, 425; Lower Burma as province of, 447; and Burma, 450, 746, 747; Dalai Lama in (1910), 647; Japan's attempted invasion of, 773; in World War II, *809;* peace treaty of Japan and, after World War II, 819; and Communist China, 880

Indian Congress Party, 747, 749

"Indian National Army" (Japanese) in Malaya, 772, 773

Indian Ocean, 18, 43, 70

Indies, 20, 22, 28, 29, 66, 67; *see also* "East Indies"

Indigo, 726

"Indirect rule," French, in Indo-China, 454; Dutch, in Indonesia, 731, 733; British, in Burma, 746

Individualism, 12–13; and imperialism, 413; in Japan, 530, 538, 539, 540–541, 552–553, 569, 831; in China, 619, 651, 663, 664, 669; in new nations, 802, 803

Indo-china, *339*, 341, *410*, *435*, *444*, 471, *715*, 752; France in, 366, 409, *410*, 450–455, 484, 485, 486, 750–751, 778, 779; Japanese invasion of, 609, 610, 768–769, 778; economy of, 738; population growth in, 739, 742; Communist Party in, 752, 755, 779, 780; after World War II, 778–781; Chinese influence in, 879; French withdrawal from, 879; *see also* Cambodia, Laos, *and* Vietnam

Indochinese Federation and the French Union, 779–780

Indo-Chinese Union, 453

Indonesia, 11, 70, 179, 408–409, *410*, 422; Dutch in, 66–68, 426, 720, 721–724; Islam, in, 425, 766; united front in, 679; nationalism in, 730–737, 771; Japanese in, 734; communism in, 735–736, 755, 777, 778, 780; area and population growth of, 742; in and after World War II, 770–772, 776–778; independence of, 771–772, 773, 777, 778; Chinese in, 718, 781, 782; *see also* Netherlands East Indies

Indonesian Nationalist Party (*Partai Nasional Indonesia*), 736

Indonesians (*Proto-Malays*), 417

Indulgence, 540

Indus River, *16*, *367*, 797, *798*

Industrial Revolution, 77, 130, 483

Industrial Workers of the World, 550

Industrialization, 6, 7, 15; cottage industries, 6, 192; in China, 89, 319, 349–358, 380, 393, 658–659, 673, 684, 872, 875; in Japan, 190, 192, 244–250, 255, 259–261, 493–495, 499, 500–511, 512, 524–529; handicraft industries, 236, 247, 250, 346; government and, 245, 247–249, 258–259, 268; world, 411–412; zaibatsu system, 505–511, 512; in Manchuria, 708; Soviet, 784; in Mongolia, 792; *see also* Labor *and* Economic conditions and development

Industry, Ministry of, Japan, 247, 272

Inflation, in Japan, 257, 497, 498, 517, 822; in China, 708, 713, 858, 864–865

Inland Sea, *186*, *824*

Inner minister, Japan, 293, 297, 556, 557, 560

Inner Mongolia, 47, *94*, *564*, 600, 647, 649, *785*, 787, 788, 789, 792, 793; *see also* Mongolia *and* Outer Mongolia

Inner Mongolian Autonomous Region, 880, 881

"Inner" Tibet, 801

Inoue Junnosuke, 498

Inoue Kaoru, 219, 227, 251, 252, 254, 260, 282, 557; and modernization, 271; in new government, 288, 300; as foreign minister, 290, 291; as minister to Korea, 467

Inoue Kowashi (or Ki), 271, 288, 295

Inquisition, the, 61

Inspector General of Customs. *See* Hart, Lay, *and* Maritime Customs Service

Institute for the Investigation of Barbarian Books (*Bansho Shirabesho*), 199

Institute for the Study of Foreign Books, 274, 277

Intellectual currents, in China, 122–128, 319–320, 349–350, 405–406, 619, 658–672; in Japan, 182, 529–554, 568–569, 570, 830–835; and Marxism, 551–554, 570; liberalism in, 568–569; unorthodox, persecution of, 594–595, 605; economic and social background for, 658–662; *see also* Education *and* Literature

Interest rates, Japan, 248, 259

Interlocking directorates, Japan, 508; *see also* Corporations

Internal Affairs, Ministry of, China, 623, 626

International Commission of Bankers, Shanghai, 648

International Development of China (Sun), 681

International Relations of the Chinese Empire (Morse), 474

International Settlement, Shanghai, 167–168, 683, 689

International Trade and Industry, Ministry of, Japan, 837

Internationalism, in Japan, 568, 570–571, 589

Interpreters College (T'ung-wen Kuan), 318–319, 387, 617

Inukai family, 520–521

Inukai Tsuyoshi (or Ki), 288, 633; as leader of Kokumintō, 560; as prime minister, 573, 581, 583, 587; murder of, 592

Investment. *See* Foreign investment

Inventions, 10, 13, 14, 24, 36–37; *see also* Technology

Irkutsk, *367*, 764, *785*, 789

"Iron constituency," Okayama, 520–521

Iron and steel industry, 411; in Japan, 246, 248, 250, 261, 496, 503; in China, 393, 629, 706

Irrigation, 96, 516

Irrawaddy River, *17*, 416, *419*, 421, 422, *428*, 446, 447, 448, *715*, 737

Irtysh River, *16, 47*, 172, *785*
Ise Shrines, 277
Ishida Takeshi, 535n.
Ishikawa Takuboku, 529
Ishiwara, 586
Islam, 30; in Indonesia, 19, 20, 732, 733, 735, 736, 766, 771; in India and Egypt, 20, 735; spread of, 20, 425; in the Philippines, 25, 725; in Borneo, 485; in Malaya, 485, 766; in Sinkiang, 793, 794; *see also* Arab traders *and* Moslem rebellions
"Islamic Association" (*Sarekat Islam*), 735
Isolationism, Japanese, 33, 35, 78, 180, 182, 197–198, 202, 203, 208; American, 714
Itagaki, Colonel, 586
Itagaki Taisuke, 241, 290, 282, 283, 305; and democratic movement, 281, 284, 287, 288, 289; in Liberal Party, 300, 303, 561; in Kenseitō, 304
I-ta-li-ya (Italy), 127
Italy, and China, 342, 396, 474, 477, 683; unification of, 365; fascism in, 582, 606, 678; allied with Germany and Japan, 606, 711; and Anti-Comintern Pact, 711
Itō Hirobumi, 219, 227, 228, 240, 264, 282, 295, 311, 561, 568, 626; defiance of shogunate by, 220; and currency reform, 235; as minister of industry, 247; and modernization, 271; and Meiji constitution, 283, 289, 298, 299, 300; leadership of, in Meiji government, 286, 287, 288; and cabinet system, 292–294; as prime minister, 294, 301–302, 303, 304, 307, 309; and Yamagata, 305–306, 557; party government of, 307, 308; assassinated, 312; and Li-Itō Convention, 378; and Treaty of Shimonoseki, 383; and struggle with Russia over Korea, 478, 479, 482; view of the state taken by, 532–533, 536; Pl. 48–50
Itō Miyoji, 295, 303
Iwakura Tomomi, 224, 227, 228, 241, 288, 292; as emperor's minister of state, 231; as Meiji leader, 283, 286, 308
Iwakura Mission, 240, 269, 270, 271
Iwasaki Yatarō, 253, 254, 287, 289
Iwo Jima, 807, *809*
Izmailov, Lev Vasilevich, 49, 53
Izu Peninsula, *187, 201*, 204

Jaisohn, Philip (Sŏ Chae-p'il), 467
James, William, 545
Janes, Captain, 270
Jansen, Marius, 567n.
Japan, 3, 9, 11, *17*, 186–187, *585*, 824–825; central power in, 14–15; Portugal in, 22; and China, 22–24, 371, 372, 597–601, 606, 637, 648, 650, 665, 675, 706–717 (see *also* Sino-Japanese War); adventurers of, 26–27; Christian century in, 30–35; seclusion of, 33–35, 78, 180, 182, 197–198, 202, 203, 208; opening of, 169; and Russia, 171, 477–483, 792 (see *also* Russo-Japanese War); intellectual currents in, 182, 529–554, 568–569, 570, 830–835; social structure and change in, 191–193, 239–240, 513–529, 827–830; as world power, 312, 494, 497, 565, 632, 720; modernization of, 313, 350–351, 405, 407, 488–493; and Korea, 377, 409, 461, 462, 466, 467, 468, 485, 760–765; as model for China, 391; and Taiwan, 409, 756–760; and Siam (Thailand), 429, 745; and England, 195, 204, 205, 207, 272, 303, 311, 478–479, 481; and gold standard, 480, 498, 499, 581, 583; 20th-century, 493–612; party government in, 568–579; and Anti-Comintern Pact, 595, 711; in World War II, 606–612, 716, 720, 766, 768–773, 804–811, *809;* compared with Germany, 603–606; Chinese educated in, 617, 622, 661; influence of, in Chinese revolution, 631–633; and six-power banking consortium, 645, 676; in World War I, 648, 665; and Washington Conference, 675; relations of, with U.S., 676; area and population growth of, *564,* 740; "Greater East Asia Co-Prosperity Sphere" of, 765–767; American occupation of, 811–821; Bank of, 827; after World War II, 821–843; admitted to United Nations, 830; *see also* Meiji period *and* Tokugawa period
Japan Labor Unions Council, 602
Japan Mail Line (Nippon Yūsen Kaisha), 260, 261
Japan Teacher's Union, 832
Japan Women's University (Nihon Joshi Daigaku), 275
Japanese and Sun Yat-sen (Jansen), 567n.
Japanese conquests, chronology of, 766
Japanese Thrust into Siberia (Morley), 567n.
Jardine, Matheson and Company, 135, 345, 347, 355, 382, 659; Pl. 13, Pl. 42
Java, *17*, 29, 73, *149*, 423; Islam in, 19, 425, 732, 735; under the Dutch, 27, 28, 68, 70, 128, 442, 721–722, 723, 731, 736; early kingdom of, 421–422; English in, 441; area and population growth of, 723, 725, 742; after World War II, 776, 777; Chinese in, 782
Jayavarman VII, 420
Jebtsun-damba-hutukhtu (Living Buddha), 786, 787, 790, 791, 801
Jehangir, 368; Pl. 8
Jehol, *564, 585*, 587, 696, 708, *785*

Jen-ts'ai ("men of talent"), 328, 329, 330
Jesuits, in Japan, 30–32; in China, 35–43, 48–49, 50, 52–60, 63, 153, 331, 333, 450, 463; expelled from Japan and China, 59, 60–62; dissolution of order, 64, 121; in Vietnam, 437, 450; in Korea and Mongolia, 450; in Tibet, 450, 796; in the Philippines, 725; Pl. 1–3, Pl. 5
Jiga ishiki ("self-consciousness"), 831
Jiji Shimpō (*News of the Times*), 285
Jingikan ("Office of Deities"), 230, 268
Jinrikisha, 263, 342
Jiyū minken undō ("movement for freedom and people's rights"), 284, 286, 288
Jiyūtō (Liberty Party), 289, 290, 299, 300, 302, 303
Joffe, Adolph, 680
Jogjakarta, 422, 722, 778
Johore, 73, *444*, 445
Jōi ("expel the barbarians"), 210, 211, 215, 218, 219, 221, 222, 267
Joint Commission on Rural Reconstruction (J.C.R.R.), 883
Joint-stock companies, 66, 871
Jones Law, 728
Jordan, John, 649
Journalism, in Japan, 285, 286, 308, 560, 561, 569, 816, 828, 831, 834; in China, 359–361, 364, 385–386; *see also* Press
Juan Yüan, 125, 126, 127, 132, 138, 387
Judson, Adoniram, 448
Juichin, 851, *853*
Jung-lu, 351, 391, 393, 399, 402, 615, 621
Junk trade, 71, 72–73, 430; junk tracking, Pl. 41
Jürched, 462
Jūshin (Senior Statesmen), 556, 557, 808, 810
Justice, ministry, Japan, 297; Ministry of, China, 626, 695

Kabuki, 244
Kabul, *367*
Kachins, 446, 449, 747
Kaesŏng, *465*, *585*
Kaga, 184, *186*, *187*
Kagawa Toyohiko, 547, 569
Kageyama, Hideko, Pl. 26
Kagoshima, 31, *186*, 196, 219, 243, *824*
Kagoshima Bay, 611
Kaifeng, *94*, *105*, *156*, 159, *160*, *715*
Kaikoku hei dan (*Discussion of the Military Problems of a Maritime Nation*) (Hayashi), 199
Kailan Mining Administration, 356, 683
Kaiping Mining Company, 356
Kaishintō (Constitutional Progressive Party), 289, 290, 291, 299, 302, 303, 304, 562

Kaitakushi (Colonization Office), 256, 287
Kalgan, *94*, 785, 789
Kalgan-Peking railway, 647
Kalimantan, 742; *see also* Borneo
Kalmuks (Torguts), 50, 51, 787
Kamakura, *201*, *825*
Kamchatka, 195, *564*
Kamikaze, 807
Kampen, J. van, 53
Kan River, 92, *95*, *113*
Kanagawa, *201*, 203, 205; Treaty of, 145, 204, 207, 256
Kanazawa, 184, *187*, 212, *825*
Kan-pu ("cadre"), 855
Kanegafuchi Company (Kanebō), 260
Kaneko Kentarō, 295, 307
K'ang (brick bed), *804*, *856*
K'ang Yu-wei, 614, 636, 643, 654, 667, 734; and Reform Movement, 385, 632, 633, 743, 749; reinterpretation of Confucianism by, 388–390, 633; and Yüan Shih-k'ai, 621
K'ang-hsi, 42, 50, 56, 81, 88, 164, 439, 849; and the Russians, 46, 48; and Christianity, 49, 61, 62, 63, 66, 122; Sacred Edict of, 84, 85, 276, 333; Pl. 10–11
Kanghwa, *465*; Treaty of, 145, 242
Kang-i, 399
K'ang-te. *See* Pu-yi, Henry
K'ang-ting (Tachienlu), 797, *798*
Kansu, *94*, 323, 324, *367*, 369, 370, 785, 881
Kant, Immanuel, 634
Kantō Plain, 184, *187*, 290
Kao Kang, 851, 863
K'ao-cheng hsüeh ("empirical research"), 122
Karakhan, Leo, 671, 677, 678, 680
Karakoram Pass, *367*, 785, 797, *798*
Karakorum, 785, 795
Karens, 446, 447, 448, 747, 775
Karō ("family elders"), 185
Kashgar, 47, *367*, 368, 785, 789, 797, *798*; Pl. 8
Kashing, *176*
Kashmir, *367*, 785, 793, 797, *798*
Kataoka Kenkichi, 281, 284
Katayama Tetsu, 547, 597
Katipunan, 727
Katō Hiroyuki, 277, 282
Katō Kōmei, 558, 561, 562, 563, 573, 574–576, 580
Katō Tomosaburō, 572, 573
Katsu Awa, 225, 228
Katsura Tarō, 558, 562, 570; as prime minister, 302, 307–308, 309, 310, 311, 559–561; as army minister, 306; and Russia, 478; and Korea, 482; Pl. 63
Kawabata, 831

Index

Kawakami Hajime, 553, 597
Kawasaki, 506
Kazakhs, 47, 172, 793, 794, 795
Kedah, 441, 443, *444*, 445
Keelung, 757
Keene, Donald, 529n., 542n., 545n., 552n.
Keiki, 207, 208, 209, 214, 215, 217, 223-224, 225
Keiō-gijuku (Keiō University), 273, 275
Kelantan, 443, *444*, 445
Kemal Atatürk, 680
Kempeitai (military police), 767, 771, 772
Ken (prefecture), 232, 257, 297
Kenseihontō (Real Constitutional Party), 306, 307, 309
Kenseikai (Dōshikai), 556, 562, 573; name changed to Minseitō, 574, 579
Kenseitō (Constitutional Party), 304, 306, 307
Kerulen River, 47, *785*
Ketteler, von, 400, 403
Keyser, Jacob van, 53
Khabarov, 45
Khabarovsk, 47, 172, 763
Khalka (Eastern) Mongols, 47, 48, 49, 787
Khalkhyn Gol, 792
Khatmandu, 796, 797, *798*
Khiva, *16*, 172, *367*, 369
Khmers, 420, 421, 422
Khoja (Hodja or Khodja), 368; Pl. 8
Khokand, *367*, 368, 369
Khorat, *435*
Khotan, *367*, *785*, 797, *798*
Khrushchev, 882
Khuriltai (council of nobles), 790
Kiakhta, 47, 51, 172, *785*, 789
Kiangnan Arsenal, Shanghai, 319, 361
Kiangsi, 92, *95*, 104, 106, 114, 687, 705; communism in, 696
Kiangsi-Chekiang railroad, 701
Kiangsu, *94*, 104, 106, 110, 116, 124, 164, 174, 176, 330, 352, *853*
"Kiangsu-Chekiang Wars," 657
Kiangsu Education Association, 628
Kiangyin, *176*
Kiaochow (Tsingtao), *94*, *339*, 390, 471, 472, *564*, *585*, 648, 675
Kiaochow (Chiao-chou) Bay, 390
Kido Kōin, 215, 220, 222, 223, 227, 232, 240, 282, 283, 286; Pl. 29
Kiheitai, 218, 237
Kii, 184, *186*, *187*
Kim Ku, 764, 846, 847
Kim Il-sung, 845
Kim Ok-kyun, 377, 382, 466, 467
Kincheng Banking Corporation, 660
"Kingly Way" (Chinese: *Wang-tao;* Japanese: *Ōdō*), 708

Kinship, Chinese, chart of, 83
Kipling, Rudyard, 414
Kircher, 56
Kirghiz tribe, 172, 793, 794
Kirin, *585*, 647
Kishi Nobusuke, 837
Kiska, 806
Kita Ikki, 589, 593
Kiukiang, *95*, 318, *339*, 340, 689; Pl. 39
Kiyoura, 573, 574
Knox, Philander C., 630
Kobayashi Takiji, 594
Kobdo, *785*, 788, 789
Kōbe, *186*, 205, 246, 247, 521, *824*
Kōbu gattai ("union of court and shogunate"), 214, 215, 222, 223, 224
Kōchi, *186*, 216, *824*
K'o-chia (Hakkas), 158, 159
Kodama Gentarō, 758, 759
Koiso Kuniaki, 581, 810
Kōjin (Passers-by) (Natsume Sōseki), 541, 542
Kojong, 464, 466
Kokkai Kisei Dōmei (League for Establishing a National Assembly), 284, 289
Kokkashugi (statism), 830; see also Nationalism
Kokonor, *785*, 787
Kokoro (Mind) (Natsume Sōseki), 541
Koku (measure of rice yield), 184
Kokugaku (National Learning), 194
Kokumin Kyōkai (Nationalist Association), 306
Kokuminshugi (nationalism), 830; see also Nationalism
Kokumintō, 560, 561, 562
Kokutai ("national polity"), 531-538, 575, 589
Ko-lao hui (Society of Brothers and Elders), 396, 636, 638
Kolchak, Admiral, 784
Kōmei, 226
Komul (Hami), *17*, 43, 366-367, *785*, 789
Konbaung dynasty, 429, 446
Konoe (Imperial Guards), 237, 242
Konoe Fumimaro, 581, 597, 599, 600, 602, 608, 610, 611, 808
Kōnoike, 252
Koo, V. K. Wellington, 665
Koofunsing, 348
Koran, 426
Korea, 3, *17*, *41*, 145, 179, *339*, 366, 409, 486, 487, 718, *785*, 802; and Japan, 9, 240-242, 309, 311, 312, 376, 409, 468, 479, 480, 481, 482-483, 563, 564; as tributary of China, 72, 375-376; Sino-Japanese War over, 303, 382; "opening" of, 375, 376-378, 466; independence of, 383, 762-763; Tonghak rising

in, 398; comparison of Vietnam and, 431, 433, 437; missionaries in, 450; area and population growth of, 460, 740; response of, to outside world, 460–468; modern, 461–463, *465;* peasant rebellions in, 463, 466; division of, after World War II, *465, 585,* 844–848; revived Confucianism in, 485; China, Japan, and Russia in, 485; emigrants from, 763; relations of Japan and, after World War II, 820–821; Republic of, 847; Democratic People's Republic of, 847; Pl. 50; *see also* Korean War
Korean language, 462, 467, 764
Korean Repository (Reynolds), 761n.
Korean War, 819, 822, 847–848, 867, 871, 879
K'o-shang ("guest merchants"), 92
Kōtoku Shūsui, 549, 550
Kotow, 49, 51–52, 77, 78
Kowloon, *133,* 141, 171, *339,* 343, 472; Pl. 17
"Koxinga" (Cheng Ch'eng-kung), 28, 118, 758
Kra Isthmus, *428, 444*
Kropotkin, Peter, 550, 651, 662
Kropotov, Commissioner, 53
Ku Chieh-kang, 665n., 668
Ku Yen-wu, 63, 124
Kuala Lumpur, *444,* 445
Kuan Yü, 395
Kuang-fu hui ("Restoration Society"), 636
Kuang-hsü ("Glorious Succession") Emperor, 351, 380, 381, 390, 392, 403, 621, 627, 638; Pl. 33
Kuang-ya Shu-yüan (academy), Canton, 380
Kuan-tu shang-hsiao ("official supervision and merchant sales"), 114–115
Kuan-tu shang-pan ("government supervision and merchant operation"), 354–355, 356, 357
Kuan-yin (Kannon), 420
Kucha, *16,* 43, *367*
Ku-ch'eng, *785,* 789
Kuching, 442
Kuei-p'ing-hsien, 159
Kuhara, 506
Kuldja, *47,* 172, *367,* 369, *785,* 789
Kumamoto, *186,* 215, 242, 243, *824*
Kumamoto Band, 270
Kumsingmun, *133*
Kunashiri, *17,* 256
Kung, H. H., 693, 849
Kung, Prince, 171, 174, 317, 328, 373, 381, 621; and contacts with the West, 315, 316, 318, 337, 350, 387; and the Empress Dowager, 321, 351; Pl. 32

Kung Pu (Board of Works), 623
Kung-chin hui ("Common Advancement Society"), 639
Kung-hang (Cohong), 73–74, 134, 135, 144, 146, 155
Kung-ho tang (Republican Party), 643
Kung-sheng (degree-holders by purchase), 86, 87
K'ung-tzu kai-chih k'ao (Study of Confucius' Reform of Institutions) (K'ang), 389, 391
Kung-yang Commentary, 123, 389
Kunming (Yunnan-fu), *95,* 105, 323, *435, 471, 715, 853,* 859
K'un-shan, *176*
Kuo Mo-jo, 672
Kuo Sung-ling, 657
Kuo Sung-tao, 372
Kuo-feng pao ("National Spirit"), 633
Kuo-min chün ("Nationalist Army"), 657
Kuomintang (KMT), 584, 601, 645, 651, 752; and CCP, 597, 680–681, 685–686, 687, 688, 711–712, 716, 849, 850, 854, 857, 858–860; and Japanese aggression, 600, 709–710; Yüan Shih-k'ai and, 642–646; government by, 644, 691–706; decline and fall of, 646, 654, 716–717; reorganization of, 669–670, 678–681; rise to power of, 673, 683–691; and Comintern, 677, 678–682; structure of, 680; ideology of, 681–682; party army of, 682–683; National Congresses of, 694n.; "Orthodox," 711; and education, 713; *see also* Nationalist China
Kuo-yü ("national language"), 437, 734
Ku-pei-k'ou, *399*
Kuril Islands, *17,* 67, 195, 255, 256, *564,* 820
Kuroda domain, *186*
Kuroda Kiyotaka, 256, 286, 288, 293, 300, 302
Ku-wen ("ancient text") versions of classics, 123, 388
Kuznetsk Basin (Kuzbas), 784, *785*
Kwang-chow Bay, 471–473
Kwangsi, *41,* 72, *95, 113,* 157, 432, *435,* 696; Taiping revolt in, 158–164; and France, 374, 451, 471; revolutionary movement in, 638
Kwangsi clique, 655
Kwangtung, 26, 73, *95,* 106, 113, 119, 157, 432, 470n., 629, 686; gazetteer of, 126, 127; emigrants from, 430, 460; French sphere in, 471; revolutionary movement in, 638
Kwangtung fleet, 374
Kwangtung militarists, 655
Kwantung Army, 511, 577, 584, 586, 598, 600, 707, 708

Kwantung Civil Government, 706
Kwantung (Liaotung) Peninsula, 312, 383n., 470n., *585;* Japan in, 303, 309, 383, 481, 564, 683; given back to China, 384, 469, 474, 565; Russia in, 470
Kweichow, *95,* 121, 166, 323
Kweilin, *95, 105,* 159, *160,* 679, *715, 853*
Kweiyang, *95, 105,* 715, *853*
Kyŏngbok palace, 464
Kyōto, 31, 32, 184, *187,* 632, *825;* imperial government in, 183, 208, 209, 226; growth of, 190, 521; isolationism of, 203; terrorism in, 210; Edo and, 214; pro-imperialism in, 216; Chōshū and, 217, 218, 220, 223, 225; railroad to, 247; Dōshisha University at, 270
Kyōto University, 277, 594
Kyūshū, *17,* 184, *186,* 195, 196, *585,* 611, *824;* Christianity in, 31, 32; Yawata Iron Works in, 261; university at, 277

Labor, contract, 154–155, 501, 661; in modern Japan, 500–501; cheap, 501, 512, 513, 524–526, 660; industrial, in Japan, 525–529; legislation favoring, in Japan, 575; industrial, in China, 660; immigrant, in Southeast Asia, 733, 734, 738; forced, in Russia and China, 784, 868; *see also* Labor unions
Labor Disputes Mediation Law, Japan, 575
Labor Party, North Korea, 845
Labor Relations Adjustment Law, Labor Standards Law, Japan, 817
Labor unions, in Japan, 517, 518, 526–529, 547, 569, 817, 838–839; Marxism and, 551; and Chinese Communist Party, 678, 686; in China, 683, 684–685, 690, 863–864; "yellow," in China, 696; in Indonesia, 736
Ladakh, 797, *798*
Lamaism, 786–787, 788, 789, 791, 795–796
"Lampacau," 22
Lanchow, *47, 94, 105,* 367, 369, 797, *853*
Land reform, in Japan, 235–236, 519, 816; in China, 866, 873, 883
Land Reform in Japan (Dore), 519n.
Land-renters, Shanghai, 340, 341
Land tax, in China, 109–111, 325, 326, 327, 625, 700; in Japan, 254, 257, 259, 308; in Taiwan, 759
Land-and-capitation tax (*ti-ting*), 110
Landlordism, in China, 111, 851, 866; in Southeast Asia, 455; in Japan, 494, 517, 518, 553, 816; in the Philippines, 730; in Korea, 762, 765; *see also* Tenant farming
Lang, W. M., 381
Lang Shih-ning, Pl. 5

Lange, Lorentz, 49, 53
Langer, W. L., *472*
Langson, 374, *435*
Languages, Latin, 49; Chinese, romanization of, 153, 855; Sanskrit, 420–422; history of, in Southeast Asia, 433n.; Thai, 424, 432, 745; "Hokkien," Cantonese, and "Teochiu," 430; Vietnamese, 431–432, 436, 437; *kuo-yü* ("national"), 437, 734; Korean (*han'-gul*), 462, 467, 764; *pai-hua* (vernacular), 663, 664; Indonesian (*Bahasa*), 770; Altaic, 793; Mongolian, 793; Tungusic and Turkic, 793, 802; *see also* Writing systems
Lansing-Ishii Agreement, 571, 665
Lao Fo-yeh ("Old Buddha"), 627; *see also* Tz'u-hsi
Lao She, 702
Laos, 72, *95, 410,* 425, 426, *428, 435,* 802; as Chinese tributary, 72; Thai in, 423, 424, 431; Buddhism in, 432; French in, 454, 455, 486, area and population growth of, 742; after World War II, 780, 781; Chinese in, 782; influence of China in, 881
Lappa, 343
"Lascars," 70
Lashio, 714, *715*
Last Stand of Chinese Conservatism (Wright), 328n.
Later Han. *See* Han, Later
Later Le. *See* Le dynasty, Later
Later Li. *See* Li dynasty, Later
Latest News of China (*Novissima Sinica*) (Leibniz), 57
Latin, use of, in Ch'ing, 49
Latin-xua, 855
Laurel, José, 770
Law of Nations (Vattel), 140
Laxman, Lieutenant, 195
Lay, Horatio Nelson, 168, 317, 318
"Lay-Osborn Flotilla," 318, 381
Lazarists, in China, 64, 121, 153, 331; in Tibet, 799
Le dynasty, Later, 433, 434, 436, 438
Le Loi, 433
Le Thanh-ton, 433
Leaders, of Meiji Restoration, Pl. 28–31; of Imperial Japan, Pl. 62–65; of Chinese Republic, Pl. 73–78
League of Blood, Japan, 592
League for Establishing a National Assembly (*Kokkai Kisei Dōmei*), 284, 289
League for the Independence of Vietnam (Viet Nam Doc Lap Dong Minh Hoi), 768
League of Left-Wing Writers, China, 701

League of Nations, 587, 698, 707, 744
Ledo, Ledo Road, 715
Left Chamber (*Sa-in*), 230, 282, 283
"Left deviation" period, Mongolia, 791
Legal reform, in Japan, 265–266; in China, 623–624
Legaspi, 24–25
Legge, James, 360
Leh, 797, *798*
Lei I-hsien, 326
Leibniz, 57, 58
Lena River, *17*, 45, 784, *785*
Lend-Lease, 609, 714
Lenin, 550, 551, 676, 679, 680, 763, 791, 851; imperialism theory of, 553, 570, 676–677; death of, 678; and Sun, 681; *see also* Marxism-Leninism
Leonowens, Mrs. Anna, 458n.
"Letter hongs" (*min-hsin chü*), 359
Lettres édifiantes et curieuses, 56, 57
Leyte, 807, *809*
Lhasa, *17*, *47*, 54, *367*, 647, *715*, 793, 795, 796, 797, *798*, 799; Chinese in, 50, 801, 880; and Dalai Lama, 787, 800, 880
Li (miles), 105
Li (principles), 161, 327, 667–668
Li ("supplementary laws"), 624
Li chi (*Record of Rituals*), 389
Li Chih-tsao (Leo Li), 39
Li dynasty, Later, 433, 436
Li-Fournier convention, 373, 374
Li Hsiu-ch'eng, 163, 174, 175
Li Han-chang, 353
Li Hung-chang, 315, 319, 337, 350, 351, 353, 373, 384, 391, 469, 635; Anhwei Army of, 174–175, 620; and "self-strengthening," 175, 369; and Nien rebellion, 322, 324, 326; at Tientsin, 338, 351, 352–358, 380, 381; and "Chefoo Convention," 345, 372; and education, 361, 362; power of, 371; Korean policy of, 375, 376–377, 378; and Treaty of Shimonoseki, 383; as governor-general at Canton, 402; and Boxer Protocol, 403; and Russo-Chinese treaty, 470, 478; death of, 621; Pl. 43–44
Li-Itō Convention, 378, 382
Li Lien-ying, 352, 382; Pl. 51
Li Li-san, 850
Li Ma-tou (Matteo Ricci), *3*, 36–37, 38, 39, 42, 43, 55, 58, 59, 61, 62, 63, 64, 126; Pl. 1
Li Shih-tseng, 662
Li Ta-chao, 664, 670–671, 680, 688
Li Tsung-jen, 696
Li Yüan-hung, 640, 653, 654, 657
Li yün (*Evolutions of Rites*), 389
Liaison Council, Japan, 601, 607, 610
Liang A-fa, 153, 158

Liang Ch'i-ch'ao, 393, 636, 655, 658, 668, 861; as editor, 385, 390; as reform leader, 385, 389, 390, 392, 632, 633–634, 638; Progressive Party of, 643; and nationalism, 649; and Yüan Shih-k'ai, 650; "Research clique" of, 653–654, 694
Liang-Huai region, 113, 114, 116, 165, 175
Liang-Kiang provinces, 104
Liang Sou-ming, 668
Liao Chung-k'ai, 680, 682, 686
Liao River, *94*, *585*, *785*
Liaotung Peninsula, 312, 383n., 470n., *585*; Japanese acquisition of, 303, 309, 383, 481, 564, 683; restored to China, 384, 469, 474, 565; Russia in, 470
Liberal-Democratic Party, Japan, 836, 837, 838, 841–842; *see also* Conservative Party, Japan
Liberal Party, Japan, 289, 290, 299, 300, 302, 303, 561, 632, 835, 836; *see also* Constitutional Party and Seiyūkai
"Liberated Areas", 852, *853*
Liberty Party (*Jiyūto*). *See* Liberal Party
Li-chia system, 102
Lien Viet, 779
Lien-chün (Disciplined Forces), 620
Li-fan yüan (Mongolian Superintendency), 46, 49
Life (Tayama), 539, 540
Liga Filipina, 727
Light, Francis, 441
Ligor, 73, *444*
Likin (*li-chin*) system, 326, 327, 474, 625
Liliuokalani, 475
Lin Feng (Limahong), 26
Lin Shu, 619
Lin Tse-hsü, 139–141, 144, 147, 149, 152, 356
Lin Wei-hsi, 140
Lincoln, Abraham, 550
Linggadjati (Cheribon) agreement, 776
Linh, Dinh Bo, 433
Linschoten, J. H. van, 27; map by, *41*
Lintin Island, 21, 22, 132, *133*
Lisbon, 20, 32, 52, 69
Literacy, in Japan, 275, 523; in China, 363, 664; in the Philippines, 730
Literary Association (*Wen-hsüeh yen-chiu hui*), 672
Literature, Chinese, 334–335, 633–634, 663–665, 671–672, 701–702, 870; Japanese, 273–274, 522, 529–531, 533, 538–544, 545, 552, 831–832; and Marxism, 551–552; Philippine, 726; Mongolian, 790; *see also* Intellectual currents
Liu Feng-lu, 123
Liu K'un-i, 353, 384, 402, 615, 620, 621
Liu Ming-ch'uan, 379

Liu Shao-ch'i, 684, 869, 870
Liu Ssu-fu (Shih-fu), 662
Liu Yung-fu, 453
Liu-ch'iu. *See* Ryūkyū Islands
Livadia, Treaty of, 370
Living Buddha, 786, 787, 790, 791, 801
Living standard, in Japan, 190, 490, 495, 522, 821, 827–830; in Southeast Asia, 486, 751; in Korea, 762; in China, 877, 884
Lo Chia-lun, 665n.
Loans, to Japan, 234, 823; to China, 470, 472, 473–474, 629, 630, 645, 651, 655, 676
Lo-lang, 431
London, 67, 130, 344, 441, 458
London Disarmament treaty, 586
London Missionary Society, 152, 331, 360
London Naval Conference, 577, 581
Loneliness, 540
Long March of Chinese Communists, 163, 696n., 711, 851, *853*
"Lord of Heaven" (*T'ien-chu*), 61, 154
"Lord on High" (*Shang-ti*), 59, 61, 154
Louis XIV of France, 54, 58, 429
Louis XVI of France, 438
Lou-kuei (fees or "squeeze"), 101; *see also* Squeeze
Low, F. F., 375
Loyalty, in China, 84; in Japan, to company, 525; to state, 532, 535; transcendent, 546; *see also* Nationalism
Loyola, Ignatius de, 30
Lu Hsün (Chou Shu-jen), 664, 668, 672, 701
Lu K'un, 135
Luang Prabang, 424, *428,* 431, *435,* 452, 454
Lu-chün (New Army), 622, 640
Lu-chün Pu (Army Ministry), 623
Lun-ch'üan chao-shang chü, ("bureau for attracting merchants . . . steamships"), 354
Lunghai Railway, *853*
Lupin (Manchouli), *339, 585*
Luxemburg, Rosa, 550
Lü-ying ("Army of the Green Standard"), 116, 142, 392, 619–620
Luzon, *17, 148–149,* 462, 725, 774
Lytton Commission report, 587
Lyuh Woon-hyung, 845, 847

Ma Hua-lung, 323, 324
Ma Ju-lung, 323
Ma Te-hsin, 166
Mac family, 434, 436
Macao, *17, 23,* 26, 30, 31, *41,* 42, 52, 72, 74, 75, 79, *95,* 96, *133, 339;* Portuguese in, 22, 24, 36, 54, 127, 343, 436; Catholi-
cism in, 121; Napier in, 135; missionaries at, 139, 141, 331, 360; contract labor from, 154; Pl. 13
MacArthur, Douglas, 200, 769, 770; in World War II, 805, 807, 811; and Japanese Occupation, 812; and Korean War, 819, 847, 848; Pl. 72
Macartney, Lord, 53, 128, 133; mission of, to Peking, 76–78, 195
McClellan, Edwin, 543n.
Mackay treaty with China, 403, 404
Mackenzie, Robert, 388
McKinley, William, 728
Madras, *16,* 68, 441
Madrid, 32, 34, 726
Madura, 422, 742, 782
Maebara Issei, 242
Maeda domain, *186, 187;* daimyo of, 184, 212
Ma-fa (grandpa), 42
Magellan, Ferdinand, *17,* 24
Magellan, Straits of, 28
Magindanao confederacy, 724
Magsaysay, Ramon, 774–775
Mahan, A. T., 475
Mahommed, 166
Mailla, Father de, 56
Maillard de Tournon, T., 53
Mai-mai-ch'eng, 47, 171, *785,* 789
Majapahit, *419,* 422, 425, 732
Malabar, *16,* 18
Malacca, *17,* 22, *23, 41,* 44, *444;* Portuguese in, 18, 19, 24, 425; Christianity in, 20, 31; Dutch in, 28, 67, 429, 441, 442; Overseas Chinese in, 29; Anglo-Chinese College at, 139, 152; London Missionary Society press at, 360; British occupation of, 441; in Straits Settlement, 443
Malacca, Straits of, *17,* 19, 70–71, 73, *418, 419,* 421, *444*
Malay Peninsula, 73, 418, *419,* 421, 426, 430, 737; Islam in, 425; and Siam, 429, 430; and Britain, 455
Malay States, 409, *410, 428,* 443–446
Malaya, *17,* 26, 70, 128, 139, 154, *410,* 422, *444,* 486, 718; Islam in, 425, 485, 766; British in, 442, 443–446, 449, 456, 468; Chinese in, 450, 782; economy of, 737–738, 739; Indians in, 738; area and population growth of, 739, 741; communism in, 772, 776, 780; in World War II and after, 772, 775–776; Federation of, 775, 776; *see also* Straits Settlements
Malayan Chinese Association, 776
Malayan Indian Congress, 776
"Malayan National Liberation Army," 776
Malaysia, 741, 776, 782

Malebranche, 58
Malolos, 727
Mamiya Rinzō, 255–256
Manchouli (Lupin), *339, 585*
Manchus, 15, 35, 42, 174, 177, 350, 352, 367, 370, 381, 783; Dutch aid to, 29; contacts of, with Russia, 45–52; banner system of, 116, 121, 157, 165, 183, 351, 392, 619–620, 788; capitulation of, to British, 144; decline of, 157, 314, 328; reformers' threat to, 392; efforts to preserve power of, 393, 394, 627; support of Boxers by, 396, 397–400; in Korea, 462; in late Ch'ing, 621, 623, 626; hostility to, 636, 638, 640; and Mongolia, 787; in Tibet, 796; *see also* Ch'ing (Manchu) dynasty and empire
Manchukuo, *564*, 587, 707, 708, 766
Manchuria, 49, 92, 173, 303, 328, *339, 564, 585*, 718, *785*; Russia in, 44, 403, 478–479, 480, 481, 630, 689, 789–790; treaty ports in, 177; Japan in, 383, 481, 567, 570, 577, 584, 600, 629, 630, 649, 675, 683, 689, 696, 701, 706–709, 789–790; China in, 469, 470, 481, 881; railroads of, 470, 478, 480, 630, 701; European rivalry in, 473; Kwantung Army in, 511; Soviet withdrawal from, 671; Soviet interest in, 707; area and population growth of, 740; Koreans in, 763
Manchurian Affairs Board, 767
Manchurian Incident, 499, 580, 583–588, 592
Mandalay, *428*, 448, 449, *715*, 737
Mandarin Lessons, Pl. 37
Mandarin Road, *435*, 439
"Mandarin square", Pl. 2
"Mandarins," 101–102, 349, 357; Vietnamese, 455, 750
"Mandate of Heaven," 157, 161, 173, 463, 641, 860
Mandeville, Sir John, 64
"Manifest destiny," 196, 476
Manila, *17*, 27, 34, 73, 79, 341; and galleon trade, 25–26, 725; Chinese community in, 29, 96; Battle of, 476, 727; made an open port, 726; and World War II, 770
Manipur, *428*, 446, 447
Mao Tse-tung, 671, 713, 849, 854, 861, 872, 877, 879; and CCP-KMT cooperation, 681; and peasant risings, 686, 688; "New Democracy" of, 768, 779, 855, 857, 862; rise of, to leadership, 850–851; economic program of, 865; and thought reform, 870; and Soviet Union, 871, 880; and collectivization, 873, 874; and Policy of criticism, 876; and Great Leap Forward, 881; "cult of personality" around, 882; Pl. 77

Maoism, 855, 870
Mao Tun (Shen Yen-ping), 672, 701–702
Maps, 36–37, 42–43, 126
Marble Boat, 313, 382
March First (*Samil*) Movement, 762–763
Marcus Aurelius, 418
Margary, A. R., 371
Marianas Islands, 716, 807
Maring (Sneevliet), 671, 678, 679, 680, 735
Maritime Customs Service, China, 177, 317–318, 349, 799; revenues from, 175, 326, 327, 343, 352, 474, 625, 647, 648, 700; expansion of, 316, 318; and development of treaty ports, 342–343; postal department of, 359; and "compradors," 659; dominated by foreigners, 683; recovery of Chinese control over, 689; illustrations, Pl. 34–36. *See also* Alcock, Hart, *and* Lay
Maritime Province, *47*, 173, 783
Maritime Record (Hai lu), 127–128
Marriage in Japan, 513, 514, 515, 523; in China, *856*, 867; *see also* Family system
Marshall, George C., 857
Marshall Islands, 807
Martaban, 427, *428*
Martin, W. A. P., 319, 617
Maruyama Masao, 554n.
Marx, Karl, 550, 551, 553
Marxism, economic concepts of, 346; in Japan, 528, 548, 549–554, 570, 832–833, 834, 840, 842; in China, 669–672; European, 670; in Burma, 749; *see also* Communism
Marxism-Leninism, 677, 739, 752, 753, 754; China's slowness to modernize as explained by, 314; imperialism theory of, 414–415; in China, 870, 879, 881
Masjumi, 771, 778
Mass Education Movement, China, 705, *804*
Mass organizations, China, 863–864; Japan, 601–603, 604
Mateer, C. B., Pl. 37–38
Matheson, James, 129, 130, 140, 560
Matsudaira, *186*
Matsudaira Keiei, 206, 207, 215, 217, 227
Matsukata Masayoshi, 288, 312, 559; economic retrenchment under, 257–259, 272, 290, 505; as finance minister, 293; as prime minister, 294, 300, 301, 302, 303–304; in Privy Council, 308
Matsumae, *187*, 195, 255, 256
Matsuoka Yōsuke, 608, 609, 611
Matsushita Electric, 826
May Fourth incident (movement), 665–666, 678, 684, 762, 855
"May Thirtieth movement," 685

Mazaki, General, 591, 593
Meadows, Thomas Taylor, 168
Mecca, *16*, 731
Medhurst, W. H., Sr., 153
Medical Missionary Association of China, 363
Medical missions, 152
Mediocrity, 540
Mei-chou p'ing-lun (*Weekly Critic*), 664
Meiji constitution, 491, 492, 531–532, 536, 814, 815
Meiji Emperor, Pl. 28
Meiji Gakuin, 270
Meiji period, creation of new government in, 225–238; leadership in, 226–228, 266–267 (*see also* Chōshū *and* Satsuma); policies in, 228–229, centralization of government in, 229, 231–232; consolidation in, 232–238; industrialization in, 244–250, 255, 258, 259–261; farming in, 250; development of business community in, 250–255; growth of economy in, 255–261; transformation of society in, 261–266; thought and religion in, 266–270, 529–530; education in, 271–278; representative institutions in, 278–283; clamor for parliamentary government in, 283–288; preparation for constitution in, 289–298; constitutional government in, 299–310; modernization during, 313–314; Japan as model for China in, 391; problems of, 489–490; and transport, 503; colonial development during, 756–765; Pl. 23–31; *see also* "National polity"
Meiji Restoration (*Meiji ishin*), 194, 227, 394, 531, 554
Meiji seiji shisōshi kenkyū (Ishida), 535n.
Meirokusha ("Sixth Year of Meiji Society"), 273
Mekong River region, *17*, 26, 416, *419*, 420, 422, *428*, *435*, 737, 797, *798*; flooding of, 417; Thai in, 423, 424; Vietnam in, 434, 440; French in, 448, 454; exploration of, 452; rice production in, 738
Memel, 342
"Memorial of the Examination Candidates," 385
"Men of determination" (*shishi*), 185, 188, 229, 589, 632, 638
"Men of talent" (*jen-ts'ai*), 328, 329, 330
Menam (Chao Phraya) River and Valley, 416, *419*, 421, 423, *428*, 454, 458, 737
Mencius, 315
Mencius, Lo t'ien che, pao t'ien-hsia, 122; 393
Mendoza, Gonzales de, 55

Mengtze, *339*
Mercantilism, 25, 74, 75, 76
Merchant marine, Japan, 260, 497
Merchants, "guest," 92; Japanese, 184, 185, 190, 192, 193, 234, 252–253, 405; associations of, 190; Chinese, 346–347, 659; *see also* Hong merchants
"Merchants in oceanic trade" (*yang-hang*),73
Merdeka ("independence"), 736
Merrill, H. F., Pl. 35
Metello de Sousa y Menezas, A., 53, 62
Methodists, in China, 332; in Korea, 760–761
Metropolitan graduates (*chin-shih*), 39, 86, 87, 164, 439, 617
Mexico, 11, 25, 311; and galleon trade, 25–26, 725, 726; independence of, 726
Mezzabarba, Patriarch, 53, 62
Miao tribe, 117, 166, 323
Middle class, in Japan, 510, 604, 828, 839–840, 841; in China, 659; in Southeast Asia, 739
Middle Kingdom (Williams), 152
Midway, Battle of, 806
Mildew, 540
Military clique as political elite. See Army *and* Navy
Military techniques, Western, 150, 219; *see also* Technology
Militarism, Japanese, 490, 491, 492–493, 718; costs of, 495, 496, 499; and zaibatsu, 511; and military training, 576; growth of, 579–597, 695–698, 764; structure and nature of, 601–606; *see also* Army, in Japan
Militarism, Nationalist, in China, 695–698
Military academies, Chinese, 620, 622
Military Affairs Commission, China, 697, 712
"Military art" (*wu-shu*), 394
Military Cadets Academy, Japan, 622
Military expenditures, Japan, 237, 497, 500, 568, 576; Japan, U.S., and Western Europe, a comparison of, 822–823
Military Procurement Ministry, Japan, 602
Military strength, in Meiji Japan, 236–238; in China, 315, 619–622, 871
Military Staff Office, China, 626
Militia (*t'uan-lien*), 620
Mill, John Stuart, 267, 273, 387, 619, 749
Min, Queen, 466, 467
Min family, 466
Minami, General, 584, 586
Min-chu tang (Democratic Party), 643
Min-ch'üan ("people's rights"), 393, 637, 682
Min-chün ("people's army"), 651

Mindon Min, 447–448, 485

Mines, Bureau of, Japan, 248, 272

Ming dynasty and period, 42, 46, 63, 81, 123; decay of, 14–15, 39, 382; and voyages of discovery, 19, 35; and Portuguese trade, 21–24; and Japan, 26, 30, 462; and Dutch trade, 28–29; and Christianity, 38, 60; and tribute system, 72, 73; area of China during, 89; population during, 90; navy of, 118; examinations of, 122; lore inherited from, 126; and Southeast Asia, 426, 433; and Chinese resurgence, 423

Ming History, 22

Minh-Mang, 438, 439, 485

Min-hsin chü ("letter hongs"), 359

Mining, in Japan, 248, 250, 260, 504; in China, 356, 393, 471, 629, 706; in Southeast Asia, 455; in Dutch East Indies, 724; in Burma, 738; in Vietnam, 751; in Soviet Union, 784

Min-kuo ("the Republic"), 641

Minobe Tatsukichi, 533, 535, 536, 548, 569, 588, 594; Pl. 66

Minomura Rizaemon, 252

Min-pao ("The People"), 638

Minseitō (Progressive Party, Democratic Party), 573, 574, 577, 578, 581, 596, 604, 835; *see also* Kenseikai

Min-sheng ("people's livelihood"), 328, 350, 637, 682

Min-tsu chu-i ("nationalism"), 637; *see also* Nationalism

"Mission news" (*Chiao-hui hsin-pao*), 364

Missionaries, in China, 152–153, 154, 158, 166, 177, 330–332, 362–365, 395, 396, 450, 616, 702, 704–705; in Japan, 269, 270, 272, 275; hostility to, 332–335, 362, 395, 437, 439, 463, 451, 867; in Southeast Asia, 429, 437, 439, 450–451; in Burma, 448, 747; in Korea, 463, 466, 468, 761; and imperialism, 484–485; in Tibet, 796; in peripheral areas, 801; Pl. 37–39; *see also* Catholicism *and* Protestantism

Mito, 184, *186, 187, 825*; daimyo of, 193, 197, 198, 203, 208, 215; schools in, 199, 214; *ronin* of, 211; anti-shogunate feeling of, 212; pro-imperialist attitude in, 225; industry in, 246

Mitsubishi Company, 253, 287, 289, 557, 558, 561; growth of, 254, 506; and Japan Mail Line, 260, 261, 290; and "Mitsubishi cabinet," 578

Mitsui, house of, 234, 251, 261, 290, 557, 558, 583; origin and growth of, 190, 252, 254, 506; and Japan Mail Line, 260; structure of, 507–508; and "Mitsui cabinet," 578

Mitsukoshi, 252

Miura, General, 467

Mixed units, samurai and peasants, 218, 220, 221, 222, 242

Miyako (Kyōto), 40

Miyazaki Torazō, 637

Mizuno Tadakuni, 198

Mobo and *moga* (*modan boi* and *modan garu*), 522

Mocha, 16, 68

"Modern characters" (*chin-wen*), 388n.; *see also* "New text" movement

Modern Japanese Literature (Keene, ed.), 529n., 542n., 552n.

"Modern revisionism", 881, 882; Pl. 80

Modernization, historical view of, 4–6; and Westernization, 6–7, 321, 692; process of, 7–8; tradition and, 8–10; of Japan, 188–194, 244–245, 310–311, 313–314, 350–351, 405, 407, 488–493, 613; of China, 314–315, 321, 335–336, 352, 358–365, 378, 379–381, 392, 394, 404–407, 624, 641, 673, 692, 699–700; slow rate of, in China, 314–315, 321, 335–336, 358–365, 378, 379–381, 392, 394, 404–407; nationalism and, 409, 614; of Siam, 455–460; of Indonesia, 731; and colonialism, 720–721; of Southeast Asia, 754; and totalitarianism, 784; of China's neighbors, 801–803; and collectivization, 803; defined, 721, 801, 86in.

Moghuls, 368; Mogul empire, 16, 68, 69

Moluccas (Spice Islands), 11, 17, 18, 19, 24, 26, 27, 29, 31, 67, 73, 79, 149

Monaco, 342

Money and banking, in China, 96, 97–99, 347, 359, 470, 473, 630, 645, 648, 651, 676, 659–660, 698–700, 726; in Japan, 190, 210, 235, 252, 254, 259, 645, 676, 698–699, 827; international consortiums for, 630, 645, 651, 676; in the Philippines, 726; *see also* Deflation, Finances, Inflation, *and* Reforms, monetary

Moneylenders (Chettyars), 450, 775

Mongkut (Rama IV), 457, 458, 485, 486

Mongolia, 92, *94*, 367, 718, 786, 802; and Russia, 49, 50, 51, 171, 789, 790, 791, 792; missionaries in, 450; and China, 647, 786–788, 789, 790, 792; People's Republic of, *785*, 792–793; Buddhism in, 786–787; and Japan, 789–790, 792; opening of, 789; declared a republic, 791; nationalism in, 792; transport across, 795; *see also* Inner Mongolia *and* Outer Mongolia

Mongolian language, 793

"Mongolian-Manchurian Independence Movement," 584

Mongolian People's Revolutionary Party, 791

Mongolian Superintendency (*Li-fan yüan*), 46, 49
Mongolian and Tibetan Affairs Commission, Nanking, 792
Mongoloid peoples, 417, 422
Mongols, 38, 45, 60, 322, 368, 794; invasions of Persia, Russia, and Eastern Europe by, 10, 12, 367; Eastern, 46, 48, 49, 50, 787; Western, 46, 49, 50, 51, 52, 367, 783, 787, 788; banner forces of, 116; in Southeast Asia, 423, 433; relations of Russia and, 790, 791
Mōningu ("morning coat"), 264
Mons (Talaings), 421, 422, 426, 429, 446, 447
Montesquieu, 65, 619, 749
Montigny, 450, 451
Moors, 12, 15, 25; *see also* Arab traders *and* Islam
Mōri, 184, *186*; *see also* Chōshū
Mori Arinori, 271, 273, 275, 276, 277, 293
Morley, James, 567n.
Morrison, Robert, 121, 152
Morrison Education Society, 361
Morse, E. S., 272
Morse, H. B., 474
Moscow, Ch'ing mission in, 51; Jesuits in, 54; CCP congress at, 857n.; University for the Toilers of the East in, 752; Congress of the Toilers of the East in, 763
Moslem party (*Masjumi*), Indonesia, 771, 778
Moslem rebellions, China, 165–166, 177, 323–324, 368–369, 370, 448
Moslems. *See* Arab traders *and* Islam
Mosse, Albert, 292, 295
Most-favored-nation principle, 144, 145, 146, 169, 171, 204, 342, 384, 457, 475
Motoda Eifu, 276, 296, 534, 536
Mott, John R., 656, 704
Mo-tzu, 668
Moulmein, 427, *428*
"Movement for freedom and people's rights" (*jiyū minken undō*), 284, 286, 288
Movement for the Protection of the Constitution, Japan, 559, 560; Second, 574
Mu ("nothingness"), 545
Muang Thai ("Land of the Thai"), 745
Muhammadiyah, 735
Mukden, 72, *94*, *105*, *339*, 478, *564*, *585*, 598; battle for, 480; Japanese research center in, 632
Mukden incident, 587, 707
Mukyōkai ("No Church") movement, 270, 547
Mundy, Peter, 64

Muraviev, Nikolai, 172, 173, 256, 365, 468
Murray, David, 275
Mushakōji Saneatsu, 541, 569
Musso, 777
Mussolini, 678
Mutō, General, 593
Mutsu Munemitsu, 303, 557
Mutsuhito, 226–227; *see also* Emperor, Japanese
Muzart pass, *367*, 370

Nacionalista Party, Philippines, 728, 729, 769, 770, 774
Nagasaki, *17*, *186*, 195, 196, 197, 214, 344, *824*; Portuguese in, 22, 24; Chinese community at, 29, 182; Jesuits in, 32; Dutch trade with, 34, 67, 79, 96, 179; as open port, 204, 205; industry at, 246, 253; missionaries in, 269; atomic bombing of, 810; Pl. 19
Nagata Tetsuzan, 591, 593
Nagoya, 184, *186*, *187*, 220, 224, 521, *825*
Naha, *17*, 200, 820
Naidaijin, Japan. *See* Inner minister.
Nakae Chōmin, 285, 308, 554
Nakano Shigeharu, 552
Nakaoka Shintarō, 223
Nakayama (Sun Yat-sen), 635; *see also* Sun Yat-sen
Naktong River, *465*, 847
Namamugi, 219
Namoa Island, *95*, 132
Nam-viet (Nan-yüeh), 432; *see also* Vietnam
Nan Huai-jen (Ferdinand Verbiest), 42, 48, 54, 57, 61, 66
Nanchang, *17*, 37, *95*, *105*, *715*; Chiang's headquarters in, 687; civil war in, 688
Nan-chao, 166, *419*, 423
Nankai Middle School (University), Tientsin, 616
"Nankeens," 97, 346
Nanking, *17*, 26, *94*, 104, 105, 143, *176*, *339*, 374, *564*, 598, *853*; Christianity in, 54, 63, 121; textile industry in, 97; Treaty of, 144; Taiping capture of, 159, 160, 162, 163; Great Camp near, 174; seizure of, from Taipings, 175; arsenal at, 319, 352; naval academy at, 381; fall of, to Japan, 600, 710; Japan's puppet government in, 600–601, 711; Hunan Army at, 620; provisional Republican government at, 640–641; Ginling College in, 660, 702n.; Nationalist Chinese government at, 688, 689, 691–706, 716, 792; National Agricultural Research Institute at, 702–704
Nan-k'ou pass, 399
Nanning, *95*, *160*, *339*, *435*

Nantung, *176*, 628
Nan-yang ("Southern Ocean"), 72, 317, 423
Nanyang Brothers, 659
Nanyang fleet, 374, 381
Napier, Lord, 134–135
Naples, 66
Napoleon III, 169, 451, 452
Napoleonic wars, 195, 196
Nara, 216, *824*
Narai, 429, 430
Narcotics, 674
Nariaki, 197, 198, 203, 212
Nariakira, 198, 203, 206, 212
Narikin, 522
National Agricultural Research Institute, Nanking, 702–704
"National bourgeoisie," 677, 868
National Christian Council, China, 705
National Economic Council, Nationalist China, 698
National Health Insurance Law, Japan, 575
"National Humiliation Day," China, 666
"National language" (*kuo-yü*), 437, 734
National Learning (*Kokugaku*), 194
National Library of Peiping, 702
National Mayors Organization, Japan, 602
National Mobilization Law, Japan, 602
National Peking University. *See* Peita
National People's Congress, Peking, 862
"National People's Party." *See* Kuomintang
"National Police (Defense) Force," Japan, 820
"National polity" (*kokutai*), 531–538, 575, 589, 814–15, 830–31, 838
"National Salvation Association," China, 709–710
National socialism, Japan, 518, 529; *see also* Naziism
"National Spirit" (*Kuo-feng pao*), 633
Nationalism, rise of, 6, 7, 8, 15, 408–409, 481–482; and individualism, 12–13, 802, 803; in China, 143, 329, 334, 350, 365, 374–375, 378, 391, 553, 580, 584, 598, 614, 619, 626, 632, 637, 649, 667, 669, 674, 682, 733, 734, 854, 879, 881; in Japan, 181, 189, 193, 194, 197, 267, 291, 311, 313, 405, 406, 491–492, 605, 734, 830; in Korea, 466, 483, 760–765; and communism, 553; in peripheral areas, 719–720; and Westernization, 721, 801; in the Philippines, 726–728, 730, 737, 769, 770; in Indonesia, 730–737, 771–772; in Siam (Thailand), 739–745; in Burma, 746–749, 772, 773; in Vietnam, 749–754, 779, 780; in Taiwan, 760; and colonialism, **774**; and discrimination against

Overseas Chinese, 781; in Outer Mongolia, 788–793; in Sinkiang, 794; in Tibet, 799; *see also* Radical right
"Nationalist Army" (*Kuo-min chün*), 657
Nationalist Association (Kokumin Kyōkai), 306
Nationalist China, 598, 599, 600, 683–691, 795; foreign policy of, 689–690; government of, 691–706; and Japanese aggression, 707, 709–711, 712–717; and Communists, 711–712, 849, 850, 851, 852, 854, 858–860; in World War II, 768, 858; in Vietnam, 779; peace treaty of, with Japan, 819; on Taiwan, 860, 880, 882–884
Nationalist Party, in China, *see* Kuomintang; in Vietnam, 752
Nationalist Revolution, China, 657–658, 685, 687; background of, 673–683; and the foreign powers, 688–690
Natsume Sōseki, 530–531, 540–543, 835; Pl. 68
Naturalist writers, Japanese, 539–540
Nature, view of, in Japan, 532, 536–538, 541–543, 545, 552, 831
Naval strength and navigation, 13–14, 15, 24, 25, 246, 343, 412; British, 68; Chinese, 118–119, 164, 319, 344, 374; Japanese, 219, 272; in Sino-Japanese War, 383; and steam power, 411; importance of, 782
"Naval Yamen" (Hai-chün ya-men), 381
Navy, Japanese, 237, 480, 572; as political elite, 555–556, 559, 562, 568; limitation of, 577, 675; power of, in government, 601; and relations with U.S., 606
Naziism, 580, 582, 597, 603, 604, 605, 606, 698
Ne Win, 772, 775
Neesima, Joseph, 270, 546
Negri Sembilan, *444*, 445
Nei-ko (Grand Secretariat), 106, 107; Viet., Nôi-Các, 438
Nemesis, Pl. 15
Neng (administrative capacity), 682
Neo-Confucianism, 56; in Japan, 59, 181, 182, 193; *see also* Confucianism; in China, 84, 122, 124, 164, 327, 386, 388
Nepal, *16*, 78, *367*, 715, 796, 797, *798*
Nerchinsk, 45, 46, *47*; Treaty of, 48–49
Nestorianism, 38
Netherlands (Holland), in Indonesia, 66–68 (*see also* Netherlands East Indies); as Ch'ing tributary, 72; Japanese treaties with, 169, 204, 205, 206, 207; envoys to China from, 128; trade between Japan and, 179; Chinese treaty with, 342; and Britain and France, in

Southeast Asia, 441, 442; revolt of Belgium against, 722
Netherlands East Indies, 409, *410*, 426, 721–724, 755, 770; in World War II and after, 610, 776, 777, 778, 806, *809*; nationalism in, 730–737; *see also* Indonesia
Neutralism, 778
Neutrality Act, U.S., 600
New Army (Lu-chün), 622, 640
New Culture movement, China, 667–669, 670
"New Democracy," China, 768, 779, 855, 857, 862
"New Diplomacy" of Woodrow Wilson, 571
New Economic Policy, Soviet, 678, 679
New Fourth Army incident, 857
New Guinea, 806, 807, *809*
New Korea Society (*Shinganhoe*), 764
New Life movement, China, 706, 713, 868
"New Men's Association" (*Shinjinkai*), 550
New nations, emergence of, 720, 773–781
"New Order in East Asia," 600, 601, 606, 608, 711, 765, 773
New People's Association (*Hsin-min hui*), 711, 766
New Proposals (*Shinron*) (Aizawa), 197
New Teaching, China, 323
"New text" (*chin-wen*) movement, 122–123, 124, 388, 389, 634
New Tide (*Hsin ch'ao*), 664–665
New Youth (*Hsin ch'ing-nien*), 663, 664, 670
New Zealand, 67, 880
Newchwang (Yingkow), *339*, 340, *585*
News of the Times (*Jiji Shimpō*), 285
Newspapers. See Journalism *and* Press
Ngo Dinh Diem, 749n., 780, 781
Nguyen Ai Quoc (Ho Chi Minh), 752; *see also* Ho Chi Minh
Nguyen Anh, 437–438
Nguyen dynasty, 436, 438, 453, 454, 750
Nguyen family, 434, 436, 437, 749n.
Nichiren Buddhism, 833
Nicholas II of Russia, 469, 470, 480, 800
Nien rebellion, *160*, 164–165, 177, 321–322, 323, 335
Nihilism, in Japan, 831, 832, 834
Nihon Joshi Daigaku (Japan Women's University), 275
Nihon Kirisuto Kyōkai (Church of Christ in Japan), 270
Nihon no shisō (Maruyama), 554n.
Nihon no shisōka II, 545n., 549n.
Niigata, *187*, 205, 216, 253, *825*
Niishima Jō (Joseph Neesima), 270, 546
Nikkō, *187*

Nikolai, 269
Nine-Power Treaty, 570, 675, 679
Nineteenth Century — A History (Mackenzie), 388
Ning-hsia, 323
Ningpo, *17*, 22, *40*, 71, 92, *94*, *160*, *339*; French Jesuits in, 54; British in, 74, 77, 143, 144; banking in, 98; as treaty port, 144, 152, 175; Customs Service in, 318; Pl. 35
Nippon, Nihon, 830
Nippon Yūsen Kaisha (N. Y. K. or Japan Mail Line), 260, 261
Nishida Kitarō, 544–546
Nishida Zei, 593, 597
"Nishihara loans," 655, 676
Nishio faction, Socialist Party, 836
Nissan interests, 506
Nitobe Inazō, 270
"No Church" (Mukyōkai) movement, 270, 547
Nobel, C., 53
"Noble Endeavor" (*Boedi Oetomo*), 734–735
Nobunaga (surname: Oda), 31, 32, 33
Nom writing system, 436, 437
No-ma (Rome), *148*
Nomonhan (Nomynkhan) 607, *785*, 792
Noncooperation, in Indonesia, 736, 737; in India, 747; in Burma, 748; in Malaya, 772
Nonni River, 47
Nordic supremacy, 475, 481
Norodom Sihanouk, 452, 453, 781
North Borneo (Sabah), *410*, 741, 776, 782
North China, 3, 92; secret societies in, 119–120, 164–165; treaty ports in, 177; early railways in, 356; "Autonomous Political Council" of, 598, 599; resistance to Japan in, 852–854; *see also* Boxer movement, Nien rebellion, *and* Moslem rebellions
North China Army (Japanese), 598, 600, 710
North China Herald, 342, 360
"North China Incident," 598–599
"North China-land" (*Hua-pei kuo*), 709
North China Plain, 164
North Korea, 821, 844, 845, 847–848, 881
North Manchuria, 49, 51
North Vietnam (Tongking), *17*, 71, *410*, *428*, *435*, 452, 471, 737; Sino-French War in, 372–374; Chinese in, 418, 431, 432, 782; independence from China won in, 433; civil war in, 434; French missions to, 437; France in, 453, 455; Japanese invasion of, 609; area and population growth of, 742; Japanese bases in, 768; Viet Minh in, 769, 778;

after World War II, 779; as Democratic Republic of Vietnam, 781; and North Korea, 844; and Communist China, 881
Northern Expedition, 687–688, 689, 696, 707
"Northern Ocean" (*Pei-yang*), 317
"Nothingness" (*mu*), 545
Novissima Sinica (*Latest News of China*) (Leibniz), 57
Novosibirsk, *785*
Nu, Thakin, 749, 772, 775
Nung-kung-shang Pu (Ministry of Agriculture, Industry, and Commerce), 623
"Nurturing office," 213, 217

Ob River, *16*, 44, 45, *47*, *785*
Oberlin College, 363
Oc Eo, 418, *419*
Ōdō ("Kingly Way"), 708
Odoric, Friar, 64
"Office of Deities" (*Jingikan*), 230
"Office for General Management." *See* Tsungli Yamen
"Official supervision and merchant sales" (*Kuan-tu shang-hsiao*), 114–115
Oguri Tadamasa, 222
Oil production, in Borneo, 724; in Indonesia, 736; in Burma, 738
Okada, Admiral, 581, 588, 596
Ōkawa Shūmei, 592
Okayama, *186*, 520–521, *824*
Okhotsk, Sea of, 45, 195; city, *47*
Oki, *186*, *824*
Okinawa, *17*, 200, 241, *564*, 807, *809*, 810, 820
Ōkubo Toshimichi, 223, 224, 227, 232, 282, 283; as minister of finance, 231; on Iwakura mission, 240; assassination of, 284, 286; Pl. 30
Ōkuma Shigenobu, 241, 254, 257, 269, 271, 286, 291, 294, 302, 305, 307, 558, 566; monetary reforms of, 235, 236; Waseda University founded by, 275; liberalism of, 287, 288, 289, 296; as foreign minister, 292, 293; as prime minister, 302, 304, 562–563, 648, 649; and Progressive Party, 303, 561; and Real Constitutional Party, 309; and "Ōkuma doctrine," 632–633
Ōkura Kihachirō, 253
"Old characters" (*ku-wen*), 388n.
"Old China hands," 170, 342
Oligarchy, Japanese, 227–229, 295–298, 491, 506, 554, 556, 558, 559, 560, 579; *see also* Elder Statesmen; Thai, 769
Omsk, 784, *785*
Ōmura Masujirō, 237
On Liberty (Mill), 273, 619

On the New Democracy (Mao), 855
Ono, house of, 249, 252, 254
Open Door in China, 471, 472, 476–477, 481, 565, 608, 630, 675
"Opening" of East Asia (treaties), *145*
Opium, and British East India Company, 70, 76, 78; smuggling of, 343; raised in China, 346, 674; in Indonesia, 734; Pl. 55
Opium trade, 79, 130–132, 150–151, 166, 168, 326, 457, 674; legalized, 177, 345; decline and renewal of, 658
Opium War, 81, 136–146, 150, 166
Orenburg, *16*, 172
Organic Law, China, 862
"Organization clique," Kuomintang, 694
Oriental Free Press (*Tōyō Jiyū Shimbun*), 285, 308
Orphanage, missionary, Pl. 39
Ortelius' map, *40*
Orthodox Church missionaries, 269, 270
"Orthodox" Kuomintang, 711
Ōsaka, *186*, 225, 522, *824*; growth of, 190, 521; riot in, 192; opened to foreign residence, 205; movement of Western diplomats to, 218; shogun at, 221; mining at, 235; industry in, 246, 249, 255, 259–260; railroad to, 247; Society of Patriots in, 281
Ōsaka Spinning Mill, 255, 259–260
Osborn, Sherard, 318
Osmeña, Sergio, 728, 729, 769, 770
Ostend, 69
Ostrog (fortified outposts), 45
Ōtori, 467
Ottama, U, 747
Ottoman Empire, 12, *16*, 391
Ou-lo-pa ("Europe"), 42
Ōura, 562–563
"Outer" daimyo (*tozama*), 184, *186–187*, 202, 203, 206, 208, 209, 211, 212, 217, 224
Outer Mongolia, *47*, 51, 171, *564*, *585*, 719, *785*, *809*; and Soviet Union, 597, 793; independence of, 647, 790; Russian influence in, 647, 678; area and population growth of, 741; and Ch'ing Empire, 786–788; national revolution in, 788–793
"Outer" Tibet, 801
Outline and Details of the Comprehensive Mirror ... (*T'ung-chien kang-mu*) (Chu Hsi), 56
Overseas Chinese, 29–30, 718; Triad Society adherents among, 120; support of republican revolution by, 635, 637, 638–639; and Japanese expansion, 666; table of, in Southeast Asia, 782; *see also* Chinese overseas
Owari, 184, *186*, *187*

Ōyama Iwao, 293, 300
Ozaki Yukio, 288, 304, 560, 561, 563, 569

Pa Chin, 702
Pacheco Sampayo, F. X. Assis, 53
"Pacification of the South" (P'ing-nan), 166
Pacific War. *See* World War II, in the Pacific
Padroado, 20, 30, 54, 62
Paets, Vincent van, 53
Pagan, *419*, 421, 423, *428*, 429
Pagan Min, 447
Pagoda Anchorage, Foochow, 374
Pago Pago, 475, 476
Pahang, 73, *444*, 445
Pai Jai School, Seoul, 761
Pai Shang-ti hui ("God Worshippers' Society"), 159
Pai-hua (vernacular speech), 663, 664
Pai-lien chiao (White Lotus Society), 117, 119, 120, 164–165, 321
Pak Yŏng-hyo, 377, 466, 467
Pakhoi, *339*
Pakistan, 880
Pa-ku wen ("eight-legged essay"), 122, 392, 615
Pa-kua chiao (Eight Trigrams Society), 120, 394
Palanquin, Pl. 11, Pl. 51
Palembang, *17*, 19, *419*, 421
Palladius, Archimandrite, 172
Palmerston, Lord, 134, 135, 139, 143, 168, 169
Pamir Mountains, 43, *47*, *367*, 368, 793
Pan-Asianism, 589, 632, 654, 767
Panchen Lama, 796
Pan-Chinese society (*Chung-hua hui-kuan*), 734
Panmunjom, 848
Panthay Rebellion. *See* Moslem rebellions
Pao-chia system, 85, 89, 102, 325, 712, 756, 758
Pao-huang hui ("Protect-the-Emperor Society"), 633
Paoshan, *176*
Paoting, *94*, *105*, 622, 682
Papacy, 15, 52, 53, 61, 62, 128
Paper chase, Shanghai, Pl. 54
Parennin, Dominique, 42
Paris, Young China Communist Party in, 671
Paris Peace Conference (1919), 665, 668, 675
Park, Chung-hee, 848
Parker, Peter, 152
Parkes, Harry, 169, 170–171, 223, 365, 371, 457

Parliamentarism, in Japan, 283–288, 547, 548, 574–576, 816; in China, 631–706; in Burma, 748; *see also* Constitution
Parliamentary socialists, Japan, 528, 551
Parsees, 70
Partai Nasional Indonesia (Indonesian Nationalist Party), 736
"Particularistic" ethic, China, 82–84
Party government, in Japan, 306–307, 568–579, 580, 581–583; in China, 691–706, 883; in the Philippines, 728–729; *see also* Political parties
Passers-by (*Kōjin*) (Natsume Sōseki), 541, 542
Paternalism, in Japan, 517, 518, 525; in China, 628; Dutch, in Indonesia, 724, 732, 735; Japanese, in Korea, 762
Pathet Lao, 780
Patriotic societies, Japanese, 566–567, 588–594
Patriotism, Japanese, 251–252
Patriots, Society of (Aikokusha), 281, 283, 284
Pattani, 73, *428*, 430, *444*
Pax Britannica, 414
Peace Preservation Law, Japan, 291, 295, 575
Peak, the, Hong Kong, Pl. 17–18
Pearl Harbor, naval base at, 476; Japanese attack on, 610, 611, 612, 714, 805–807
Pearl River, 75, *133*
Peasant associations, Chinese, 686, 688, 696, 866–867
Peasant risings, in Japan, 192–193, 216, 239, 290–291, 294, 295; in Vietnam, 437; in Korea, 463, 466; in China, 639
Peasants, in Tokugawa class system, 184; rich, 185, 191, 192, 254, 284–285; included in military system, 218, 220, 221, 222, 237–238, 242, 243; tenancy of, 236 (*see also* Tenant farming); as entrepreneurs, 254–255
Peer's School (Gakushūin), 208, 540
Pegu, *419*, 421, 426, 427, *428*, 447
Peiping, 702, 704, 710; *see also* Peking
Peita (Pei-ching ta-hsüeh) (National Peking University), 617, 666, 668, 702; new thought at, 662–665
Pei-t'ang (North Church), Peking, 122, 331, 400, *401*
Pei-yang ("Northern Ocean"), 317
Peiyang Army, 621
Peiyang clique, 621, 623, 645, 646
Peiyang fleet, 374, 381–382, 383, 469
Peiyang *tu-chün*, 654, 655, 657
Peking, *17*, 22, 30, *40*, *47*, 73, 87, *94*, *105*, *113*, *156*, *160*, *339*, *399*, *401*, *564*, *785*, 789, 793, 795, *853*; early foreign embassies to, 29, 52, 53, 54, 76, 77, 78; Jesuits

at, 35, 37–39, 42, 52, 54, 55; and Russia, 46, 49, 50, 51, 54, 79, 172; role of missionaries in, 63; Yüan Ming Yüan at, 63, 171; Macartney mission to, 76–78, 195; licensing of banks by, 99; government at, 104, 105, 106–107, 109, 137; secret society attacks on, 120; Catholicism at, 121, 122; North Cathedral in, 122, 331, 400, *401*; opium revenues at, 132, 138; Anglo-French capture of, 170; foreign legations in, 170, 683; Sino-Russian Treaty of, 173; Ch'ing government restored at, 173–178; Japanese relations with, 241; T'ung-wen Kuan at, 318–319; Pei-t'ang in, 331; postal service from, 358; Board of Rites at, 375, 376; Self-Strengthening Society in, 385, 390; Boxers in, 399–402; Japan's North China Army in, 600; army mutiny at, 641; Yüan inaugurated president at, 641; Tsing Hua College at, 661; May Fourth incident in, 665–666, 762; World Student Christian Federation in, 668; Communist Party in, 671; Academy of Sciences at, 672; CCP congresses in, 857n.; in Communist hands, 860, 862; illustrations, Pl. 8–12, Pl. 51–52, Pl. 80
Peking cart, Pl. 10
Peking Field Force, 351, 620
Peking Gazette, 359
Peking-Hankow railway, 393, 471, 472
Peking-Kalgan railway, 647, 789
Peking Man, 704
Peking Union Medical College, 704
Penang, *17*, 70, 139, *410*, 441, 442, 443, *444*
Peninsular and Oriental Company, 411
"People, The" (*Min-pao*), 638
"People's army" (*min-chün*), 651
People's Assembly, People's Committee, North Korea, 845
People's Council (*Volksraad*), Indonesia, 735
"People's democratic dictatorship," Mao on the, 862
People's Liberation Army, China, *856*, 860
"People's livelihood" (*min-sheng*), 328, 350, 637, 682
"People's News," 549
People's Party, in Siam, 745; in Burma, 748
People's Political Consultative Conference, China, 862
People's Political Council, China, 712
People's Representative Congresses, China, 863

People's Republic of China, 862; of Mongolia, 792; of North Vietnam 778–780 "People's Republic" of South Korea, 845–846; of North Korea, 847
People's Revolutionary Party, Mongolia, 791
"People's rights" (*min-ch'üan*), 393, 637, 682
"People's rights" movement, Japan, 284–285, 286, 288, 549
Perak, *444*, 445
Peranakan, 733–734
Pereyra de Faria, Bento, 48, 53
Perlis, 443, *444*, 445
Perry, Matthew Calbraith, 169, 180, 182, 183, 200–202, 203–204, 207
Perserikaten Kommunist di India (Indonesian Communist Party), 735–736, 755, 777, 778
Persia, 10, *16*, 278, 342, 425, 481
Persian Gulf, *16*, 67
Peru, 11, 154
Pescadores Islands, 28, 303, 312, 379, 383, *564*, 757
Peter the Great of Russia, 50, 171, 172, 391
"Petition" (*ping*), 139
Phan Boi Chau, 749–750
Phan-Dinh-Phung, 454
Phaulkon, Constantine, 429, 430
Phibun Songgram, Luang, 745, 768, 769
Philip II of Spain, 32
Philippine Executive Commission, 728, 769
Philippine Islands, *17*, *41*, 54, 60, 128, *339*, 408–409, *410*, *564*, 718, 767; under Spain, 24–26, 724–727, 730; and U.S., 409, 476, 477, 727–728, 729–730; nationalism in, 726–728, 730, 737, 769, 770; preparation for independence of, 727–730; as Commonwealth, 730, 737; area and population growth of, 742; communism in, 755, 774, 780; in World War II, 769–770, 805, 807; Republic of, created, 770, 774; economy of, 774; postwar problems of, 774–775; Chinese in, 781, 782; in SEATO, 880
Philosophy, Japanese, 531–538, 544–546, 830–834; *see also* Confucianism, in Japan
Phraya Tak or Taksin, 430
Phya Bahol, 745
Physiocrats, 65
P'iao (ticket) system, 124
Pidgin English, 75
Pien-fa ("Change of method"), 387
Pigneau de Behaine, 437–438
Ping ("petition"), 139

Ping Pu (Board of War), 623, 695
P'ing-hsiang, 629, 638
P'ing-nan "(Pacification of the South")," 166
P'ing-yao, 98
"Pioneer," steam engine, Pl. 42
Piracy, 68, 112, 151; by Japanese, 21, 26, 30; by Chinese, 118, 119; suppression of, 157; in Southeast Asia, 442, 443, 445, 724
Pires, Tomé, 21–22, 53
"Plan for peace," association to (*Ch'ou-an hui*), 650
Planning Board, Japan, 601–602, 608; *see also* Economic Planning Agency
Plantations, Southeast Asia, 455, 722, 723
Plaskowitz, Gottard, 53, 62
Pnompenh, *17*, 26, *435*, 452
Po-erh-tu-chia-li-ya (Portugal), 127
Poiarkov, 45
Poland, 54
Police, in Japan, 297, 519; Ministry of, China, 623
Police Regulation Law, Japan, 526
Political associations, China, 385, 634, 655, 694
Political Bureau, China, 862
Political Council, Kuomintang, 694
Political Culture Association (*Cheng-wen she*), 634
Political parties, in Korea, 467; in China, 643, 644, 645 (*see also* Kuomintang); in the Philippines, 728–729; in Indonesia, 735–736, 778; in Burma, 748; in Vietnam, 752, 768, 780; in Mongolia, 791; *see also* Communist parties *and* Political parties in Japan
Political parties in Japan, democracy supported by, 281, 284, 596, 597; founding of, 289–290; in Diet, 299, 302, 303, 304, 309; government by, 306–307, 492, 568–579, 580, 581–583; influence of, in rural areas, 520; as government elite, 556, 558, 559, 562, 563; positions of, 567, 604; opposition of, to army, 596–597; before World War II, 602–603; since World War II, 835–843
Political Study clique (*Cheng-hsüeh hsi*), 655, 694
Polo, Marco, 10, *40*, 43, 55, 60, 64, 421
Pondichéry, *16*, 54, 438
Pongyi (nationalist-oriented monks), 747
Popular Account of People's Rights (*Tsūzoku minken ron*) (Fukuzawa), 285
Popular Front, in Vietnam, 753; in Indo-China, 779; *see also* United front

Population growth, in China, 89–91, 155–156, 673; in Japan, 190, 310, 489, 494, 512, 514, 583, 740; world, 411; in Java, 723, 725, 742; in Indonesia, 732, 742; in Burma, Malaya, and Siam, 739, 741; in Indo-China, 739, 742; in Korea, 740, 762; in Vietnam, 742, 751
Porcelain, 97
Port Arthur, *339*, *564*, *585*; naval base at, 381, 469; captured by Japan, 383, 480; Russians in, 470, 471, 472; Russian withdrawal from, 481
Port Hamilton, 469, *585*
Portsmouth, Treaty of, 481
Portugal, expansion of, *12*, 14, *15*–24, 27, 30–35, 36, 43, 54, 343, 426; and China, 52, 53, 62, 128; in Southeast Asia, 425, 429, 436
Postal service, China, 105–106, 358–359, 659, 683, 690, 788
Posts and Communications, Ministry of, China, 626, 695
Potsdam Conference, 810
Pottinger, Sir Henry, 143, 144
Poverty, in Southeast Asia, 754; in Korea, 762; in Vietnam, 779
Pradist Manudharm, Luang, 745
Pragmatism, in Japan, 182, 266–267; in China, 669
Prajadhipok, 745, 746
Prefectural assemblies, Japan, 283, 299
Prefectures (*fu* and *ken*), 104, 232, 257, 297, 433
Presbyterians, in China, 332; Pl. 37–38; in Korea, 760–761
Press, in Japan, 285, 515; in China, 342, 359–361, 364, 375, 380, 385–386, 631, 633, 636, 638, 664–665, 667–669; in Korea, 467; Mongolian, 790; *see also* Journalism
"Prester John," *12*, *40*
Pridi Banomyong, 745, 769
Private enterprise, Japan, 249–252
Private traders, 129–130, 134, 136
Privy Council (*Sūmitsu-in*), 293, 295, 297, 298, 301, 306, 307, 308, 556–557, 575
Prjevalski, 799
"Proclamation of Independence," Korea, 762–763
Progress, concept of, 350, 389, 413
Progressive Party, in Japan, 289, 290, 291, 299, 302, 303, 304, 561, 562, 632, 835; in China (*Chin-pu tang*), 643, 645, 646, 654; Philippine, 728
Proletarian Literary Federation, Japan, 552
Prome, *428*, 446, 737
Propaganda (Congregation of the Propagation of the Faith), 52, 54, 153

"Propaganda Movement," Philippines, 726
Prostitution, in Japan, 514–515, 547
"Protect-the-Emperor Society" (*Pao-huang hui*), 633
Protestant Reformation, 27
Protestantism, in China, 121, 152–153, 154, 158, 330, 331–332, 333, 360, 362, 363–364, 616, 660, 702, 704–705, 867; in Japan, 269, 270, 547; in Korea, 468, 760–761
Provincial assemblies, China, 627, 628–629, 631, 640
Provincial graduates (*chü-jen*), 86, 87, 385, 439, 617
Provisional constitution (*yüeh-fa*), 638
Provisional Government, of China, at Nanking, 640; at Peiping, 710; of Korea, in Chungking, 764, 846
Prussia, 342
Pu (ministries), 695
Public Party of Patriots (Aikoku Kōtō), 281
Public Peace Police Law, Japan, 575
Publishing, in China, 269, 363; in Japan, 831; *see also* Literature *and* Press
P'u-k'ou, *176*
Pulo Condore, *435*, 751
Puppet governments, Japanese, in China, 600–601, 707, 709, 710, 711
Pure Land (Shinshū) Buddhism, 269, 545
"Purification clique" (*ch'ing-liu tang*), 373
Pusan, 240, 242, 375, 376, *465*, *564*, *585*, 847
Pusat Tenaga Rakjat (*Putera*) ("Center of People's Power"), 771
Putiatin, 204
Putung, Shanghai, 341
Pu-yi (P'u-i), Henry (Hsüan-t'ung Emperor), 587, 627, 641, 654, 707, 708
P'yŏngyang, 431, *465*, *585*, 845

Quebec Conference, 806
Quemoy, 29, 880
Quesnay, 65
Quezon, Manuel, 728, 729, 730, 769, 770
Quoc-ngu, 437, 438n., 751

Radical reformers, China, 390–392, 404, 632
Radical right, Japan, 565–566, 583, 588–594, 599, 604, 842, 843
Raffles, Thomas Stamford, 441–442, 721, 722
"Raguzinski" (Sava Vladislavich), 49, 50–51, 53
Rahman, Abdul, 776
Railroads, in Japan, 234, 247, 251, 260, 261, *496*, 503, *824–825*; in China, 356, 393, 471, 473, 643, 647, 700–701, *853*; world, in 19th century, 411; American, 412; in Manchuria, 470, 478, 480, *585*, 647, 708; in Southeast Asia, 471, 473, 737; in Korea, *585*, 762; in Taiwan, 757; in Mongolia, 789, 795
Railway controversy, late Ch'ing, 629–630
"Railway protection" movement, China, 639
Rama I (Chakkri), 430
Rama III, 456
Rama IV (Mongkut), 457, 458, 485, 486
Rama V (Chulalongkorn), 458–459, 460, 485, 743
Rama VI (Maha Vajiravudh), 743, 744
Rama Kamheng, 423–424
Ramos, Benigno, 770
Rangaku ("Dutch learning"), 182, 189, 191, 198–200, 214, 272, 405
Rangoon, 416, 427, *428*, 446, 447, 448, 737, 772, 773; University of, 747, 748–749
Rapid Realization of Independence, Society for the, South Korea, 846–847
Rashōmon (Akutagawa), 543
Rayon, 502
Real Constitutional Party (Kenseihontō), 306, 307, 309
Realism ("socialist"), in Chinese literature, 701
Recollects, 725
"Reconstructionist" organizations, Japan, 569
Record of Imperial Military Exploits (*Sheng wu chi*), 125
Record of Rituals (*Li chi*), 389
Record of Things Seen and Heard about the Overseas Countries (*Hai-kuo wen-chien lu*), 126
"Rectification" drive, China, 877
Rebellion, rise of, in China, 155–166, 177; *see also* Taiping movement, Nien, Peasant risings, *and* Boxer movement
Red Army, Chinese, 851; *see also* Eighth Route Army *and* People's Liberation Army
"Red Flag" faction, Burma, 775
"Red gang," Shanghai, 684
Red River (Song Koi), *95*, *113*, 416, 418, *419*, *428*, 432, 433, *435*, 440, 448, 452, 461, 471, 737
Reform Movement, China, 328, 364, 384–394, 473, 613–631, 749, 801; background of, 366–384; ideology of, 386–390; and the radical reformers, 390–392, 404, 632; failure of, 392–394
Reforms, in Japan, 180, 197–199, 213, 222, 224, 235, 236, 237–238, 265–266, 548, 813–818; Tempō, 198, 213; military, 198–199, 222, 224, 237–238, 319, 620, 621,

622; land, 235–236, 519, 816, 866, 873; monetary, 236, 624–625, 699, 708, 759; legal, 265–266, 623–624; in China, 319, 336, 363, 624–625, 660, 699, 708, 854–855, 866, 873; thought, 854–855; in Siam, 457, 458–459, 744; in Korea, 464, 467; in the Philippines, 726–727, 775; in Taiwan, 759

Regional guilds (*t'ung-hsiang hui*), 347, 618, 684

Regionalism, Chinese, 324, 326, 352, 381, 623, 651, 653, 696

Religion, in Japan, 266–270, 492, 534–538; in Southeast Asia, 418, 420–421, 432, 485; in Korea, 463–464, 466–467; in Siam, 485, 744; in Indonesia, 731, 732, 735; in Communist China, 867–868; *see also* Buddhism, Christianity, Confucianism, Hinduism, Islam, Neo-Confucianism, Shintō, *and* Sōka Gakkai

Religious Instruction, Board of, Japan, 268

Renaissance, 31

"Renovation of the people" (*hsin-min*), 633, 634

Renville truce, 777

Reorganization Loan to China, 645

"Reorganized" National Government, Nanking, 711

Representative institutions, Japan, 278–288

"Republic" (*Min-kuo*), 641

Republican China, inauguration of, 640–642; decline of, into warlordism, 642–658; thought and culture in, 658–672; and Kuomintang, 673–706 (*see also* Kuomintang)

Republican Party (*Kung-ho tang*), 643

Republican revolutionary movement, China, 614, 617, 631–642

"Rescript to Soldiers and Sailors," Japan, 295

"Research clique" (*Yen-chiu hsi*), 654, 694

Resistance movements, World War II, 772, 773, 774; in Mongolia, to White Russians, 791

Restoration period in China, 173–178; reform movements in, 328; Christianity in, 330–338; economic development during, 338–348; industrialization in, 349–358; slow modernization in, 358–365; foreign imperialism during, 365–378; and war with Japan, 378–384; and reform Movement, 384–394; and Boxer rising, 394–404

"Restoration Society" (*Kuang-fu hui*), 636

Restoration of Vietnam, Society for the (Viet Nam Quang Phuc Hoi), 750

"Return of the *han* registers," 232

Returned students, *703*. See Students, "returned"

Revenue, Board of, China, 625

Revenues, Chinese, 325–326, 327 (table), 343, 349, 474, 624–625, 647–648, 683; Burmese, 427; Siamese, 456; *see also* Maritime Customs Service *and* Taxes

Review of the Times, China, 364

"Revive China Society" (*Hsing-Chung hui*), 635, 637, 643

Revolution, "bourgeois-democratic," in China, 676, 753, 857; in Indonesia, 736; "bloodless," in Siam, 745; "proletarian," in China, 753, 850, 855, 857

Revolutionary Army (Tsou), 636

Reynolds, W. D., 761n.

Rezanov, 195

Rhee, Syngman (Yi Sŭng-man), 761, 764, 846, 847, 848

Rhodes, Alexandre de, 437

Ricci, Matteo, *3*, 36–37, 38, 39, 42, 43, 58, 59, 61, 62, 63, 64, 126; "History . . ." by, 55; Pl. 1

"Rice Christians," 334

Rice culture, 416–417, 418, 432, 450, 458, 738, 760

Rice riots, 222, 527, 639

Rice trade, 190, 430, 498, 751, 762

"Rich country and strong military" (*fukoku kyōhei*), 229, 266, 311

Richard, Timothy, 364, 379, 386, 388

Ricksha, 263, 342; Pl. 27, Pl. 40, Pl. 47

Rickshaw Boy (Lao She), 702

Ridgway, Matthew, 819

Right Chamber (*U-in*), 230, 283

"Right deviation" period, Mongolia, 791

Rightists, Japan, 569, 842, 843; *see also* Radical right

"Rights recovery" movement, China, 629, 689, 691

Rikken Kaishintō, Rikken Seiyūkai, Rikken Teiseitō. See Kaishintō, Seiyūkai, Teiseitō

Rikkyō, 270

Risshisha ("Society to Establish One's Moral Will"), 281, 283–284

Rites, Ministry of, China, 626

Rites Controversy, 58–60, 63

Rituals of Chou (*Chou-li*), 161

Riverbird, Pl. 16

River War (Churchill), 413n.

Rizal, José, 726–727

Roberts, Edmund, 451, 456

Roberts, Issachar Jacox, 158

Robinson Crusoe, 273

Rochechouart, Julian de, 337

Roches, Léon, 222, 223, 225, 285
Rockefeller, John D., 704; Rockefeller Foundation, 705, 706
Rockhill, W. W., 476, 799
Rodjestvensky, Admiral, 480
Roessler, Hermann, 295
Rōjū (Elders), 198, 206, 209, 211
Rokumeikan, 264
Roman Catholic. *See* Catholicism
Romance of the Three Kingdoms, 395, 653
Romanization, 3, 437, 438n., 743n., 795n.
Rome, early contacts of, with Asia, 32, 34, 54, 418; Inquisition at, 61; Office of the Propaganda at, 153; Mussolini's march on, 678
Rome-Berlin Axis, 711
Rōnin, 185, 210, 211, 216, 223
Roosevelt, Franklin D., 611, 612, 844
Roosevelt, Theodore, 476, 481
Rosovsky, Henry, 496
Rousseau, Jean Jacques, 285, 550, 749
Roxas, Manuel, 770
Royal Dutch Shell, 659, 724
Royal Netherlands Trading Company, 722
Rubber production, in Malaya, 445, 446, 738; in Indonesia, 736; in Indo-China, 738; in Vietnam, 751
Rumania, 342
Rural life, in Japan, 515–521, 582, 604, 816, 829; in China, 661, 673, 699, 705–706; reconstruction of, in Taiwan, 760
"Rural samurai" (*gōshi*), 212, 215, 253, 282
Russell, Bertrand, 667
Russell and Company, 134, 141, 151, 348, 355
Russell, Sturgis and Company, 726
Russia, and China, 43–52, 53, 54–55, 79, 316, 390, 402, 470, 647, 680; and Japan, 169, 194–195, 204, 205, 206, 207, 256, 570, 575, 597, 606, 607, 608, 645, 676; in Manchuria, 171–173, 403, 409; in Sakhalin, 256; after Sino-Japanese War, 384; as model for China, 391, 670, 671, 676, 698; and Korea, 461, 467, 468, 485, 763–764; rivalry of Japan and, in Northeast Asia, 477–483; totalitarianism in, 580, 698, 784; aid to China by, in World War II, 607, 713–714; non-aggression pact of, with Germany, 607; in World War II, 609, 808, 809, 810; and Mongolia, 647, 789–791, 792, 793; foreign intervention in, after Revolution, 675; and Chinese revolution, 676–678, 682; and Nationalist China, 707, 795; and Vietnam, 780; and Sinkiang, 794–795; and Japan, after World War

II, 819; Kurils absorbed by, 820; and Communist China, 832, 843, 871–872, 881–882; in North Korea, 844, 845
Russian-American Company, 171
Russian Orthodox Church, in China, 50, 51, 54; in Japan, 269
Russian revolution, of 1905, 789; of 1917, 720, 784
Russian or Western Turkestan, 172, 367, 368, 784
Russo-Chinese Bank, 470, 472
Russo-Chinese treaty of alliance (1896), 470
Russo-Japanese War, 261, 307, 309, 312, 479–482, 563–564, 565, 566, 584, 719, 800
Ryūkyū (Liu-ch'iu) Islands, 72, 76, 179, 198, 212, *339,* 366, 462, *564;* Perry in, 200, 202; Japanese control over, 241; Japanese claims to, 312, 371; American take-over of, 820

Sabah (North Borneo), *410,* 741, 776, 782
Sacred Edict (Sheng Yü), 62, 84, 85, 87, 102, 276, 333
Sado, *187, 825*
Saga, *186,* 199, *824;* revolt in, 242
Saigō Takamori, 220, 223, 227, 228, 241, 242, 271, 282, 300; samurai army of, 243, 281; Pl. 31
Saigō Tsugumichi, 241, 271, 288, 293, 306
Saigon, 341, 416, 434, *435,* 437, 439, 779, 781; treaty of, 452; modernization of, 751; popular front in, 753
Sailendra dynasty, 19, 421–422
Sailing directions, 24, 27, 73
Sa-in (Left Chamber), 230, 282, 283
St. Jean ("Sancian") (Shang-ch'uan), 22
St. John's College, Shanghai, 363, 616, 702n.
St. Petersburg, 51, 256, 470; Treaty of, 370
Saionji Kimmochi, 560, 561, 562, 567, 588, 593, 597, 608n.; as prime minister, 302, 309–310, 559, 584; and parliamentary movement, 308; and decline of Elder Statesmen, 556; and Privy Council, 557; Pl. 62
Saipan, 807, 810
Saitō Makoto, 581, 588
Sakai, *186*
Sakai Toshihiko, 549
Sakamoto Ryōma, 223
Sakdal movement, Philippines, 730, 770
Sakhalin, 17, 47, 195, 255; division of, between Japan and Russia, 256, 784; Japanese control over southern half of, 309, 312, 481, *564*
Sakuma Shōzan, 199, 200, 214, 266
Saldanha, Manoel de, 53

Index

Salisbury, Lord, Pl. 44
Salt monopoly, *113–116*, 354, 700
Salt Revenue Administration, China, 648, 683, 690
Salt smuggling, 165, 343
Salt taxes, 109, 113–116, 175, 474, 496, 625, 645
Salween River, *17*, 416, *419*, 427, *428*, 797, *798*
Samarkand, *16*, 172, *367*, 369
Samil (March First) Movement, 762–763
Samoa, 475–476
Samqua (Wu Chien-chang), 167
Samurai, *179*, 184, 185, 188, 191, 192, 198; in imperial-shogunate struggle, 210, 211, 212, 215, 216, 218, 222, 223, 225; rural (*gōshi*), 212, 215, 253, 282; financial settlements for, 213, 233, 238–239, 247, 257; reorganization of, 222; in the new government, 226, 227, 230, 231, 237, 238, 257, 285; classified as gentry, 238; disaffection of, 240; revolt of, 242–243; as businessmen, 253–254; the Kumamoto Band, 270; education of, 274, 279; Pl. 22–23, Pl. 29–31, Pl. 70
San-min chu-i (Three Principles of the People), 636–637, 651, 681–682, 852
San-min chu-i Youth Corps, 712
Sangha, 446, 747
San-ho hui or *San-tien hui* (Triad Society), 120, 159, 162–163, 443, 635, 636, 743
Sanjō Sanetomi, 216, 217, 220, 227, 228, 241, 308; as minister of state, 231; as inner minister, 293
Sankin kōtai system, 182, 215, 221
Sanshoku ("three offices"), 230
Sanskrit, 420, 422
Santo Tomas, college of, Manila, 725
Santuao, *339*
San-tzu ching (*Three-character Classic*), 162
San'yo or *sangi* (Councilors), 230, 283, 286, 293
San-yüan-li, 143
Sapporo, 277, *825*; Sapporo Agricultural College (Hokkaidō University), 256, 270
Saragossa, Treaty of, 24
Sarawak, *410*, 442, 443, 456, 741, 776, 782
Sarekat Islam ("Islamic Association"), 735
Sasebo, *585*, *824*
"Sat-Chō clique," 288
Satsuma, 31, *186*, 198, 199, 203, 221, 237; and shogunate, 184, 206, 207, 210, 211–217, 220, 225; foreign attacks on, 218–219; coalition of Chōshū and, 222–223, 224; samurai control of, 226; surrender

of domains of, to emperor, 232; rebellion in, 242–243, 254, 257, 281; industry in, 246, 249, 250; dominance of, in new government, 282, 288, 293, 294, 302, 559, 560; Pl. 22, Pl. 30–31
Saya San, 748
Sayre, F. B., 145, 744
Scalapino, Robert, 572n.
Schall von Bell, Johannes Adam, 38, 39, 42, 61; Pl. 2
Schereschewsky, S. I. J., 616
Scholars, in Japan, 182, 198–200, 266–267; in China, 101, 122–128, 163, 164; *see also* Education
"School of Combined Learning" (T'ung-wen Kuan), 318–319
School system, Japanese, 274–275, 277, 278, 522–523, 530, 535, 818; late Ch'ing, 615–618; *see also* Education
"Scorched earth" in China, 710
Sea Dyaks, 442
Sebiro (business suit), 264
"Second revolution" (of provincial governments), China, 645
Secret society (societies), among Overseas Chinese, 29; Christianity as, 62, 120–122, 463; in China, 119–120, 132, 144, 154, 157, 164–165, 394–395, 396, 397, 635, 654, 684; in Malaya, 443; in the Philippines, 727; in Siam, 743
"Security merchants," 74
Seeckt, General von, 697
Seidensticker, Edward, 542n.
Sei-i tai shōgun ("Barbarian Subduing Generalissimo"), 202–203
Sei-in (Central Chamber), 230
Seiyō jijō (*Conditions in the West*) (Fukuzawa), 273
Seiyūkai, Rikken (Friends of Constitutional Government), 556, 557, 572, 573, 577, 586, 604, 835; in government, 307, 308, 309, 561, 583, 587, 596; and the Mitsui, 558, 578; and Taishō Crisis, 559, 560, 562; and demands for democracy, 563
Selangor, *444*, 445
Selenga River, 47, *785*, 789
"Self-consciousness" (*jiga ishiki*), 831
Self-criticism in China, 869, 870
Self-cultivation, Confucian, 870
Self-determination of peoples, 675, 720, 730, 752, 762, 844
Self-fulfillment. *See* Individualism
Self-Help (Smiles), 273, 281
"Self-strengthening" (*tzu-ch'iang*), 147, 175, 177, 369, 386, 392, 615; facets of, 316; limitations on, 350; attacked as appeasement, 373; in Korea, 377; fail-

ure of, against Japan, 378–384; and in-
dustrialization, 393; decline of, 404
Self-Strengthening Army, 380, 620–621
Self-Strengthening School, 380
Self-Strengthening Society (*Ch'iang-
hsüeh hui*), 385, 390, 391, 621, 643
Semi-colonialism, 409; in China, 683
Sendai, *187*, 277, *825*
Senggerinchin (Seng-ko-lin-ch'in), 170,
322
Senior Statesmen (*Jūshin*), 556, 557, 808,
810
Seoul, 377, 378, *465*, 466, 468, *564*, *585*,
761, 764, 845, 848
"Separationists," Burmese, 748
Sepoy Mutiny, 170
Setting Sun (Dazai), 831
Seven Years' War, 68
Seville, 34
Seymour, Admiral, 399, 400
Shaki bund, 685
Shameen, *133*
Shan people, 423, 426, 429, 446, 449, 747
Shan states, *428*, 449, 769
Shang dynasty, 704
Shang-ch'uan (St. Jean), 22
Shanghai, *17*, *94*, 104–105, 141, *156*, 157,
160, 174, *176*, *339*, 416, *564*, *715*, *853*,
860; Catholics in, 39, 153; occupied by
British, 143; as treaty port, 144, 151,
152; growth of, 154, 167–168, 340–342;
rebellion at, 163, 636; tariff treaties at,
171; defended by international forces,
175, 689; Japanese-English dictionary
published in, 269; Customs Service in,
317, 318, 473; interpreters' schools in,
319; Kiangnan Arsenal at, 319, 352;
foreign settlement at, 325, 340, *341;*
French concession in, 339, 450; newspapers and magazines in, 342, 360, 631;
cable at, 344; banking and finance in,
347, 473, 648, 660, 698, 726; as shipping
and market center, 347–348; telegraph
line to, 357; St. John's College in, 363,
616, 702n.; Nanyang fleet at, 381; Self-
Strengthening Society in, 385, 390;
Chinese-Japanese fighting in, 588, 600,
707, 710; boycott of American trade
in, 626; *Tōa Dōbun Shoin* in, 632; Sun
at, *655*, 681; American domination in,
659; mass production in, 660; strikes in,
666, 685; Communist organization in,
671, 857n.; Socialist Youth Corps in,
671; secret societies in, 684; anticommunist terror in, 688; pervasive foreign
interest in, 690; Aurora University at,
702n.; Comintern Far Eastern bureau
at, 755; inflation in, 865; Pl. 53–56
Shanghai Commercial and Savings Bank,
660
Shanghai Cotton Cloth Mill, 357
Shanghai Foreign Inspectorate system,
177
Shanghai Mixed Court, 341, 645, 648, 689
Shanghai Municipal Council, 683, 685,
689
Shanghai Volunteer Corps, 167
Shanghai-Wusung railroad, 356; Pl. 42
Shang-ti ("Lord on High"), 59, 61, 154
Shang-wu Pu (Ministry of Commerce),
623
Shanhaikuan, 72, *94*, 356, *399*, 470n., *585*
Shansi, *94*, *113*, 159, 399, 400, 657, 658,
696; banks in, 97–99, 359; salt produc-
tion in, 114; famine in, 364; Japanese
in, 709
Shansi-Hopei-Chahar border region, 852,
853
Shansi-Suiyuan border region, *853*
Shantung, *94*, 106, 111, 112, 124, *156*, 352,
381, *585*, *853;* salt production in, 113;
risings in, 120; secret societies in, 164,
397; Germany in, 390, 396, 409, 471,
473, 629, 659; famine in, 395; Japan in,
648, 649, 665, 675, 707, 709
Shen ("Divine spirit"), 154
Shen Chia-pen, 623–624
Shen Pao-chen, 356
Shen Yen-ping (Mao Tun), 672, 701–702
Sheng Hsüan-huai, 357, 358, 384, 393, 402,
629–630
Sheng Shih-ts'ai, 794, 795
Sheng wu chi (*Record of Imperial Mili-
tary Exploits*), 125
Sheng Yü (*Sacred Edict*), 62, 84, 85, 87,
102, 276, 333
Sheng-p'ing (Approaching Peace), 389
Sheng-yüan (government students), 86,
87
Shensi, *94*, 117; revolt in, 323, 324; Com-
munists in, 696
Shensi-Kansu-Ninghsia border region,
853
Shibaura Engineering Works, 504
Shibusawa Eiichi, 254–255, 259, 260, 506
Shidehara Kijūrō, 558, 571, 575, 577, 584
"Shidehara diplomacy," 571, 586
Shiga Naoya, 541
Shiga, Yoshio, 843
Shigatse, 796, *798*
Shih ching, 388
Shih Ta-k'ai, *160*, 163
Shih-fu (Liu Ssu-fu), 662
Shikoku, *186*, 199, 215, *824*
Shilka River, 45, 47, *785*
Shimabara, 34, *186*
Shimada, house of, 252
Shimazu, domain of, *186*
Shimazu Hisamitsu, 212, 215, 217, 219, 227
Shimazu Nariakira, 198, 203, 206, 212

Shimazu Shigehide, 198, 212

Shimoda, *187*, *201*, 204, 205, 256

Shimonoseki, 220, *585*, *824;* Straits of, *186*, 217, 218; Treaty of, 383, 758

Shimpan ("related *han*"). See "Collateral" branches

Shimpotō (Progressive Party), 303; *see also* Progressive Party

Shinagawa Yajirō, 301, 306

Shinganhoe (New Korea Society), 764

Shinjinkai ("New Men's Association"), 550

Shinron (*New Proposals*) (Aizawa), 197

Shinshū, or True (Pure Land) Sect, 269, 545

Shintō, 270, 492, 533, 543, 815; symbols of, 193–194; revived, 268, 274; history and, 536–538

Shintō Worship, Office of (*Jingikan*), 230, 268

Shipping, shipbuilding, in Japan, 246, 260, 261, 503; in China, 150, 381; revolutionized, 411; *see also* Transportation

Shishi ("men of determination"), 185, 188, 229, 589, 632, 638

Shiuhing (Chao-ch'ing), 36, *95*

Shizoku (gentry), 238

Shogunate, and emperor, 193, 197; changes in, 202; end of, 203, 217–225; controversies within, 206–208; movement for coalition of court and, 207, 213–217; efforts to maintain, 208–210; *see also* Tokugawa

Short Story magazine (*Hsiao-shuo yüeh-pao*), 672

Shōwa-kai, 596, 604

Shōya (village headmen), 215, 282

Shroffs, 155

Shuai-luan (Disorder), 389

Shu ching (*Classic of Documents; Book of History*), 123, 174

Shufeldt, R. W., 145, 377

Shui-hu-chuan (*All Men Are Brothers*), 395

Shun, 387

Shun Pao, 360, 631

Shun-chih, 42, 61

Shutaisei ("independent self"), 831

Shu-yüan (academies), 102, 329, 462, 615

Shwe Dagon pagoda, 427

Siam (Thailand), *17*, 72, 73, 76, *95*, 97, *339*, 424, 425, *428*, *435*, *444*, 462, 485, 737, 755; Western contacts with and exploitation of, 20, 26, 28, 29, 54, 67, 145, 409, *410*, 451, 454, 738; struggle of Burma and, 426–431, 446; rise of, 429–431; size and population of, 440, 460, 739, 741; opening and modernization of, 451, 455–460, 461, 486; compared with Japan, 458; Buddhism in, 485, 766;

Chinese in, 733, 781, 782; nationalism of, 739–745; constitutional revolution in, 745; Japan in, 766, 768, 769; *see also* Thailand

Sian, *17*, 38, *94*, *105*, *160*, 403; Chiang "kidnaped" at, 696n., 711

Siberia, 44–45, 46, *47*, 50, 54, 55, *367*, *585*, *785*, 789; Russian exploration of, 171; Japanese expedition in, 567–568; Allied forces in, 675, 784; civil war in, 790

Siemreap, *435*, 454

Sihanouk. *See* Norodom

Sikh policeman, *703*

Sikkim, *715*, 796, 797, *798*, 799

Silk trade, 70, 71, 74, 76; China to Europe, 10, 26, 76, 79, 93, 97, 151, 155, 168, 345, 346; Japan to Europe, 210, 247, 249, 493, 498, 499, 501–502

Silver, imported by China, 26, 70, 76, 79, 96–97, 98; "drain" of, from China, 137–138, 699; dumped on Japan, 210; foreign ownership of, in China, 698; mining of, in Burma, 738

Silver-copper exchange rate, China, 137–138

Silver-gold exchange rate, China, 137, 344; Japan, 210, 247

Simla, 797, *798*

Singapore, 120, 344, 360, *410*, 411, *444;* Chinese in, 154, 734, 775, 782; British control of, 442, 443; made a free port, 483; area and population growth of, 741; *T'ung-meng hui* in, 743; as part of Malaysia, 776; as self-governing state, 776; in World War II, 806

Singkeh (*hsin-k'o*), 733

Single-tax movement, 637, 682

Sining, *105*, 797, *798*

Sinkiang (*Hsin-chiang*), 370, 696, 718, 719, *785*, 789, 797, *798*, 881; area and population growth of, 740; Chinese government of, 793–795

Sinkiang Uighur Autonomous Region, 880

Sino-American Joint Commission on Rural Reconstruction, 883

Sino-American treaty of 1880, 361

Sino-British convention on Sikkim and Tibet, 799

Sino-French convention of 1860, 331

Sino-French War, 372–375, 453

Sino-Japanese treaties of 1915, 649

Sino-Japanese War of 1894–95, 244, 261, 303, 312, 358, 382–384, 474, 566

Sino-Russian-Mongolian agreement of 1915, 790

Sino-Russian treaties, 469, 784, 789, 790, 792, 794

Sino-Soviet alliance, 871

Sino-Soviet split, 832, 843, 881–882

Sinophilism, 64–66
Sisters of Charity, 335, 337
Siva, 420, 421, 422
Six Boards or Ministries (Liu Pu), 159, 391, 622, 623, 626
"Sixth Year of Meiji Society" (Meirokusha), 273
Sjahrir, Sutan, 736, 771, 776, 777
Skinner, G. W., 782
Slave trade, 18, 19, 20, 22, 154, 155
Small Sword Society (*Hsiao-tao hui*), 163, 167
Small Tranquillity (*hsiao-k'ang*), Age of, 389
Smiles, Samuel, 273, 281
Smith, Adam, 619, 749
Smith, Arthur H., 364–365
Smuggling, 75–76, 131, 137, 138, 144, 165, 343
Sneevliet, Hendrik (Maring), 671, 678, 679, 680, 735
Sō, *186*, 240
Sō Chae-p'il, 467
Social conditions and social change, in Japan, 191–193, 239–240, 513–529, 827–830; in China, 325, 335, 660–661, 706, 867–869; in Vietnam, 436; in Java, 723; in Siam, 744
Social Darwinism, 365, 391, 414, 475, 566, 619, 633, 668
Social democracy, Japan, 548, 549
Social gospel, China, 704–705
Social Mass Party, Japan, 551, 597, 601
Social science study groups, Japan, 550–551; *see also* Marxism, in Japan
Social services, missionary, in China, 363, 364
Social solidarity, in Japan, 515–517, 519, 525, 553, 580, 604, 829–830, 833
Socialism (*min-sheng chu-i*) in China, 637, 661–662, 667; *see also* Communism in China
Socialism in Japan, 492, 509, 514, 549, 550, 553, 570; and labor movement, 526, 528, 529, 575, 838–839; and Christianity, 547, 549; parliamentary, 548; 551; *see also* Christian socialism, Marxism, *and* National socialism
Socialist Party, in Japan, 547, 549, 597, 602, 836, 838–839, 840, 842; in China, 662
"Socialist transformation," Communist China, 873–879
Socialist Youth Corps, China, 671, 681
Société des Missions Étrangères, 54, 437
Society of Brothers and Elders (*Ko-lao hui*), 396
Society for the Diffusion of Christian and General Knowledge among the Chinese (SDK), 364

"Society to Establish One's Moral Will" (Risshisha), 281, 283–284
"Society of the Heavenly Way" (*Ch'ŏndogyo*), 467n., 762, 845
Society of Jesus. *See* Jesuits
Society for the Propagation of the Faith, 153
"Society for the Study of Self-Strengthening" (*Ch'iang-hsüeh hui*), 385, 390, 391, 621, 643
Sōdōmei, 528
Sōhak ("Western Learning"), 463
Sōhyō, 838, 840, 841
Sōka Gakkai (Value Creating Association), 833
Solidaridad, La, 726
Solomon Islands, 806, 807
Song Koi. *See* Red River
Songkhla (Sungora), 73, *428*, 430, *444*
Song-tsan Gam-po, 795
Sonnō ("honor the emperor"), 210, 214, 221, 223
Soochow (Su-chou), *94*, 97, 104, *105*, 113, 319, 702n.
Soong, T. V., 693, 698, 699, 849
Soong Ch'ing-ling (Madame Sun), 688; Pl. 74
Soong Mei-ling (Madame Chiang), 693, 705
Sōseki. *See* Natsume Sōseki
Sources of the Japanese Tradition, 545n.
South China. *See* Hunan, Kwangsi, Kwangtung, *etc.*
South Korea, 819, 821, 844, 845–848
South Manchurian Railway, 470, 584, *585*, 632, 683, 706, *785*
South Vietnam, 90, *410*, 781; French in, 438, 452; America rebuffed in, 451; area and population growth of, 742; Chinese in, 782, 881; and South Korea, 844; *see also* Cochin China *and* Annam
Southeast Asia, before colonial era, 416–417; types of livelihood and social organizations in, 416–417; invasions of, from the north, 422–425; linguistic history of, 423n.; influences brought to, by sea, 425–426, 430; Japanese designs and attack on, 606, 609, 610; population of, 719, 740–742; colonialism in, 737–765; economic growth of, 737–779; in World War II, 765–773; Allied reoccupation of, 773–774; emergence of independent nations in, 773–781; Sinocentric tradition in, 802; *see also* various countries
Southeast Asia Treaty Organization (SEATO), 879–880
Southern fleet. *See* Nanyang fleet
"Southern Ocean," 72, *149*, 317, *423*
Soviet Central Asia, 784, *785*

Soviet Union. *See* Russia

Sŏwŏn (academies), 462, 464

Spain (*Hsi-pan-ya*), 127; early conquests by, 11, 12, 14; Portugal united with, 21; expansion of, 24–26, 30–32, 33, 34, 36, 54; and galleon trade, 25–26, 725, 726; Dutch and, 27, 28; and China, 128, 342; Philippines ceded to U.S. by, 409; in Southeast Asia, 452; Philippines under, 724–727, 730; revolution of 1868 in, 726

Spanberg, 195

Spanish-American War, 476, 727

Spathar-Milescu, N. G., 46–48, 53, 54

Spencer, Herbert, 267, 387, 566, 619, 749

"Spheres of influence," in China, 471–473, 474, 476, 477, 481, 483, 630, 651; and international agreements, 586

Spice Islands, 11, *17*, 18, 19, 24, 26, 27, 29, 31, 67, 73, 79

Spice trade, 18–19, 20, 22, 28, 66, 67, 79

Spinoza, 58

Spirit of the Laws (Montesquieu), 65, 619

Spiritual Exercises (Loyola), 30

Spiritual mobilization movement, Japan, 602, 810

Spring (Pa Chin), 702

Spring and Autumn Annals (*Ch'un-ch'iu*), 123, 380; *Kung-yang Commentary on*, 389

Squeeze, 77, 99, 109, 110, 115, 137, 330, 352

Srivijaya, *419*, 421, 422, 432, 732

Stalin, 580, 677, 678, 686, 687, 688, 832, 858, 871

Stalinists, 753

Standard Oil, 659

State Council, China, 863

"Statecraft" (*ching-shih*), 123–125, 139, 150, 164, 315, 327, 329, 386

Status in Japan, 181, 191

Steamships, 411, 412; in China, 344, 348, 349, 354, 356, *408*, 701; in Dutch East Indies, 724; in Southeast Asia, 737; *see also* Naval strength *and* Transportation

Stein, Lorenz von, 292

Stepanov, 45

Sternberg, Ungern von ("Mad Baron"), 791

Stilwell, Joseph, 714, 716, 858

Stimson, Henry L., 707

Straits Settlements, 409, *410*, 443, *444*; *see also* Malay States

Stranger (Camus), 831

Strikes, 666, 684, 685, 747, 749

Stroganov family, 45

Student associations, in Japan, 550–551, 832; in China, 666, 668, 864

Student class, in Japan, 271, 273, 522, 529–530, 544; in China, 660–661

Student movement, in Japan, 550, 832; in China, *613*, 661 (*see also* May Fourth); in Burma, 748–749

Student Union, Burma, 748, 749

Student Volunteer Movement for Foreign Missions, 363, 704

Students, "returned" (from study abroad), to Japan, 271; to China, 361, 362, 616, 634, 643, 661, 689

Students' Social Science Federation, Japan, 550–551

Study of the Classics Forged during the Hsin Period (*Hsin-hsüeh wei-ching k'ao*) (K'ang), 388

Study of the Good (Nishida), 545

"Study societies" (*hsüeh-hui*), 385, 639

Suchow (Chia-yü-kuan), *17*, 43, *105*, 367, 370, *785*, 789

Suetsugu Nobumasa, 599, 600

Suez Canal, 344, 365, 411, 469

Suffrage, universal manhood, Japan, 528, 575, 578; universal, Japan, 569, 574; progressive extension of, 575, 576

Sugar, in "country" and junk trade, 70, 71; in Japan, 213; in Siam, 456; in the Philippines, 726, 729; in Indonesia, 736; in Taiwan, 759

Suifen, *339*

Suiyuan, 709, *785*, 789, 792

Sukarno (Soekarno), 736, 771, 773, 776, 777, 778

Sukebator, 791

Sukhothai, 423, 424, *428*

Sulu Islands, *17*, 25, 72, 425, 443, 724

Sumatra, *17*, 19, 154, *410*, 421, 432, *444*; British in, 28, 29, 70; Dutch in, 29, 724; spread of Islam to, 425; British withdrawal from, 442; risings in, 736; area and population growth of, 742; Japan in, 772; after World War II, 776, 777; Chinese in, 782

Sumitomo, 253, 506

Sūmitsu-in (Privy Council), 293, 295, 298, 301, 306, 307, 308, 556–557, 575

Summer Palace (Yüan Ming Yüan), 63, 171; Pl. 3; new (I Ho Yüan), 382; Pl. 51

Sun Ch'uan-fang, 657

Sun Goddess, 194

Sun Yat-sen (Sun Wen), 566, 645, 649, 743, 849, 855, 861; as leader of revolutionary movement, 614, 634–639, 640–642, 666, 669; "five-power" system of, 627, 695; and Liang, 633; Three Principles of, 636–637, 651, 681–682, 852; three-stage program of, 638; as president of Chinese Republic, 640; resignation of, from presidency, 641; as di-

Index

rector of railways, 643; at Canton, 654–655, 680; Kuomintang reorganized by, 678–680; and CCP, 680, 681; ideology of, 681; reverence for, 683; on "knowledge and action," 870; Pl. 73–74
Sunda, Straits of, *17*, 19, 67, *419*
Sung Chiao-jen, 643, 644, 645
Sung Learning, 327
Sung period, 10, 22, 84, 122, 124, 164, 181, 351; Southern, 118
Sungari River, 47
Sungkiang, *94*, 97, 104, *176* (Sung-chiang)
Sungora (Songkhla), 73, *428*, 430, *444*
Sun-Moon Lake, 757
Sun-tzu, 150, 386
Su-pao, 636
Supreme Commander for the Allied Powers (SCAP), 812, 816, 818
Supreme Court (*Daishin-in*), 283
Surat, *16*, 67, 70
Sutlej River, *16*, 367
Suzuki Bunji, 526, 527, 547, 569
Suzuki Kantarō, 581, 810, 811
Swatow, *95*, 318, *339*, 459, 688, *715*
Sweden, 128, *129*, *148*, 149
Swedish East India Company, 75
Swettenham, Frank, 445
Switzerland, *148*, 149
Symposium on the Development of Japanese Capitalism, 551
Syndicalism, Japanese, 549, 551
Syr Daria, *16*, 367, 785
System of Logic (Mill), 619
Szechwan, 92, *94*, 105, *113*, 150, 163, 651, 799; salt production in, 114; White Lotus Rebellion in, 116; Christianity in, 121, 334; isolation of, 405; Kuomintang in, 600; "railway protection" movement in, 630, 639; revolutionary movement in, 637; militarism in, 696; steamers to, 701; National Government in, 710; inflation in, 713
Szemao, *339*

Ta yüan-shuai (generalissimo), 655
Tabinshwehti, 426–427
Ta-ch'eng. *See* Chuguchak
Ta-Ch'ing hsien-hsing hsing-lü ("current criminal code"), 624
Tachienlu, 797, *798*
Taegu, *465*, *585*
Tael, 137, 344, 660, 699
Taewŏngun, 464, 466, 467
Taft, William Howard, 570, 630, 645, 728
Tagalog, 724
Tagore, Rabindranath, 667
Tai Chi-t'ao, 686
T'ai-ku, 98
Tainan, *95*, 757

Taipan (*tai-pan*), 135
Taipei, 379, 757, 758
T'ai-p'ing ("Great Peace"), 159, 389
Taiping movement, 158–164, *160*, 173, 323, 324, 340, 404; cooperation of, with Nien forces, 165, 322; and Christianity, 168, 333; end of, 173, 174–177, 315, 321
T'ai-p'ing t'ien-kuo ("Heavenly Kingdom of Great Peace"), 159
Tairō (Great Elder), 208
Taishō period (1912–1925), 535, 554
Taishō Political Crisis, 559–561, 562, 571, 584
T'ai-ts'ang, 104, *176*
Taiwan (Formosa), *17*, *95*, *149*, *160*, 410, 564, 718, 757, *809*, *853*; Dutch in, 28, 30; made part of Fukien, 29; piracy on, 30, 118, 119; revolt in, 120; treaty ports in, 177; Japan in, 241, 303, 312, 409, 481, 756–760; modernization of, 379; Japanese research center in, 632; area and population growth of, 740; "Republic of," 758; Nationalist China on, 819, 860, 880, 882–884; Pl. 7
Taiyuan, *94*, *105*
Takahashi Korekiyo, 499, 573
Takano Chōei, 199
Takashima Shūhan, 199, 200
Takasugi Shinsaku, 217–218, 220
Takeda Kiyoko, 549n.
Taklakot, 707, *798*
Taklamakan Desert, 367
Taksin, 459
Taku, *94*, 170, *399*, 400, 402
Talaings (Mons), 421, 422, 426, 429, 446, 447
Tali, 166, 323, *428*, 452
Tamerlane, 368, 793
Tamsui, *339*, 757
Tan Malaka, 736
Tan-Si degree, 439
T'an Ssu-t'ung, 393
Tanaka, 567, 571, 573, 577, 581; Pl. 65
Tanegashima, *186*, *824*
T'ang Chi-yao, 651
T'ang dynasty, 38, 174, 359, 431, 432
T'ang Jo-wang (Johannes Adam Schall von Bell), 38, 39, 42, 61
T'ang Shao-i, 643
T'ang Sheng-chih, 657
T'ang T'ing-shu. *See* Tong King-sing
T'ang Ts'ai-ch'ang, 636
T'ang-ku, *399*
Tang-pu (cells), 680
T'ang-shan, *399*
Tani Kanjō, 293
Tanizaki, 831
Tao (circuit), 104
T'ao Chu, 124

Taoism, 56, 61, 117
Tao-kuang, 108, 121, 138; Pl. 8–9
Taotai (*tao-t'ai*), 104, 318
Tarawa, 807
Tarbagatai, 789; *see also* Chuguchak
Tariff treaties, 144, 145, 146, 167, 171, 177, 234, 344
Tariffs, in China, 77, 138, 342–343, 689; in Japan, 218; in the West, against Japanese goods, 499; *see also* Maritime Customs Service *and* Revenues
Tarim River and Basin, *16*, *47*, *367*, 368, 369, 370, *785*, 793, 794, *798*
"Tartary," *40*
Taruc, Luis, 774
Tashi Lama. *See* Panchen Lama
Tashi-lhunpo, monastery of, 796
Tashiro, General, 598
Tashkent, *16*, *367*, 369, 784, *785*
Tasmania, Tasmania, 67
Ta-tao hui (Big Sword Society), 396
Tatekawa, General, 586, 592
Ta-t'ung (Great Unity), 389
Ta-t'ung shu (*Book of the Great Unity*), 389
Taxes, in China, 109–116, 325–326, 327, 344, 345, 349, 474, 624, 625, 700 (*see also* Salt taxes); in Japan, 235–236, 254, 259, 308, 496, 517; in Taiwan, 759–760
Tax-farming households, 111
Tax-farming system, 109, 354, 456
Tayama Katai, 539–540
Ta-yeh, 393, 629
Taylor, Hudson, 332, 337, 364
Tay-son brothers, 436, 437
Te Wang (Demchukdonggrub), 792
Tea, as England's national drink, 71; brick, 92, 345, 469, 799; Indian production of, 345; Indonesian production of, 736; Pl. 14
Tea trade, Chinese, 71, 75–76, 78, 79, 93, 97, 130, 141, 151, 155, 168, 345, 346, 797, 799; Japanese, 210, 249, 345; and Cohong merchants, 74; "Tea Road," in Tibet, *798*
Teak, 458, 738
Technology, modernization through, 5, 7, 8; and European expansion, 13–14; in China, 42, 91–96, 147–150, 175, 342, 380, 389, 628, 653; in Japan, 182, 188, 198–199, 246, 271–272, 826–827; military, 182, 653; agricultural, 254; world advances in, 411–412, *see also* Industrialization
Teikokutō (Imperial Party), 306
Teiseitō, Rikken (Constitutional Imperial Rule Party), 289
Telegraph and cables, 357, 412
"Temple schools" (*terakoya*), 274
"Tempō reforms," 198, 213

Ten Coming Disasters, 395
"Ten Thousand Word Memorial," 385
Tenant farming, in Japan, 192, 236, 490, 497, 517, 518, 519; in Burma, 450, 746; in China, 661, 673; in Korea, 764
Tenant unions, Japan, 517–518, 529, 569
Tenasserim coast, *17*, *28*, *428*, 429, 447
Tenchūgumi ("Heavenly Chastising Force"), 216
Tengchow, Pl. 37–38
Tengyueh, *339*
Tenrikyō, 268
"Teochiu," 430
Terakoya ("temple schools"), 274
Terauchi, 559, 562, 563, 567, 570, 571
"Term question," 154
Ternate, 19, 28
Textile industry, Indian, 70; English, 76, 77, 130, 151, 155; Chinese, 97, 346, 357–358, 628, 659; Japanese, 247, 248–249, 260, 261, 500–502, 526; mechanization and, 249, 254, 260, 345
Thai language, 424, 432, 745
Thai peoples, 423, 424; *see also* Shan people
Thailand, *410*, 422, 424, *444*, *715*, 718; Siam's name changed to, 745; after World War II, 774; in SEATO, 880; *see also* Siam
Thakin leaders, 749, 772, 775
Thanh Nien (*Youth*), 752
Tharrawaddy, 447
Tharrawaddy District, 748
Thibaw, 448–449, 485
Thieu-Tri, 439
Thinkers, of Japan, Pl. 66–68
Thirteen Classics, 125
"Thirteen Factories," 74, 75, *133*, 140; Pl. 16
Thought reform, 869–870; *see also Cheng-feng*
Three Ages, theory of, 389
"Three-anti" movement, 868
"Three bonds," 393, 667
Three-character Classic (*San-tzu ching*), 162
Three Feudatories, Rebellion of the, 42, 46
"Three Great Policies" of Sun Yat-sen, 682
"Three Houses," 184
"Three offices" (*sanshoku*), 230
Three Pagodas route, *419*, 426, *428*
Three Principles of the People, 636–637, 651, 681–682, 852
"Three sacred treasures," 826
"Three-self" movement, 761n., 867
"Three systems," Korean, 464
T'i ("substance"), 386

Index

Tibet, *94*, 366, *367*, 481, *715*, 718, 719, *785*, *798*; Ch'ing control over, 50, 52, 647; Jesuits in, 450; area and population growth of, 740; Britain and China in, 795–801; independence of, 801; Chinese invasions of, 871, 879, 880–881

Ticket (*p'iao*) system, 124

T'ien ("Heaven"), 59, 61

T'ien Shan ("Mountains of Heaven"), 367, 368, 370, 793

T'ien-an men (Gate of Heavenly Peace), *401*, 666; Pl. 80

T'ien-chu ("Lord of Heaven"), 61, 154

T'ien-chu shih-i (*True Disputation about the Lord of Heaven*), 55–56

T'ien-li chiao (Heavenly Reason Society), 120

T'ien-shan pei-lu, 369

Tien-shih-chai hua-pao, Pl. 53–56

T'ien-ti hui (Heaven and Earth Society), 120

Tientsin, *17*, 75, *94*, 98, 112, *113*, 124, 141, 143, *156*, 159, *160*, *339*; British embassy to, 77; treaties of, 170, 173; massacre at, 337–338; Customs Service in, 318; foreign concessions at, 340, 683; Li Hung-chang at, 351, 352–358, 377; Peiyang fleet at, 374; arsenal at, 381; naval academy at, 381; Boxers in, 400, 402; Provisional Government in, 402, 403; Nankai University at, 616; Anhwei Army at, 620; mass production in, 660; in Communist hands, 860

Tientsin-Shanghai telegraph line, 357

T'ien-wang (Heavenly King), 159

Tihwa (Urumchi), 367, 370, *785*, 789, 793

Tin, in Malaya, 443, 445, 446, 450, 737–738; in Indonesia, 724, 736

Ting, V. K., 668

Ting Ling, 870

Ting-hsien, 705

Tintoretto, 32

Tithsing, Isaac, 53

Ti-ting (land-and-capitation tax), 110

T'i-yung formula, 386–387, 391

Tōa Dōbun Kai (East Asian Common Culture Society), 632

Tōa Dōbun Shoin, Shanghai, 632

Toba, 225

Tobacco, 496, 726, 729

Tobolsk, 46, 47

Tōgō Heihachiro, 480

Tōgō Shigenori, 810, 811

Tōhoku University, 277

Toilers of the East, University for the, 752; Congress of the, 763

Tōjō Hideki, 593, 594; forced to retire, 557, 810; as prime minister, 581, 769,

772; in Konoe cabinet, 608; as chief of General Staff, 808; execution of, 813

T'o-ku kai-chih ("finding in antiquity the sanction for present-day changes"), 387

Tokugawa shogunate, coming to power of, 15, 27, 28, 32; seclusion under, 33–35; government by, 181, 182, 183; political structure of, 183–185, *186–187*; opposition to, 188; peace established by, 189; economic and social conditions under, 189–193; and the emperor, 193, 197; in 19th century, 202–203; fall of, 203, 217–226; secularism under, 267; Buddhism under, 268; and loyalty ethic, 491–492; and "national polity," 537; *see also* "Collateral" branches, "Hereditary" daimyo, "Outer" daimyo, *and individual Tokugawa shoguns listed by given names:* Ieyasu, Keiki, Nariaki, *etc.*

Tokushima, *186*, *824*

Tōkyō, *564*, *825*; as capital city, 229; new government at, 232; railway to Yokohama from, 234, 247; industry in, 246, 249; Mitsui headquarters in, 252; electricity in, 262; Rokumeikan at, 264; Russian Orthodox Church in, 269; missionary societies in, 270; rioting in, 309; earthquake of 1923 in, 498, 573; small business in, 511; size of, 521; "reconstructionist" organizations in, 569; rebellion of 1936 in, 593–594; Chinese educated in, 617; Chinese revolutionary movement in, 617; studies of China in, 632; Vietnamese in, 749–750; Greater East Asia Ministry in, 767; fall of Tōjō cabinet in, 769; and World War II, 808, 811; and American Occupation, 812, 813; in the 1960's, 821, 828; Pl. 25, Pl. 27, Pl. 47

Tōkyō Imperial University (Tōkyō University), 269, 274, 277, 530; Pl. 66–67

Tōkyō Women's University (Tōkyō Joshi Daigaku), 275

Tolstoi, 541

Tong King-sing (T'ang T'ing-shu), 347, 354–355, 356, 361, 634

Tonghak ("Eastern Learning"), movement, 398, 463–464, 466–467, 485

Tongking. See North Vietnam

Tongking, Gulf of, *95*, *435*

Tongnip Hyŏphoe (Independence Club), 467, 761

Tongnip Shinmun (*Independent*), 467

Tonle Sap (Great Lake), 416–417, *428*, *435*

Tordesillas, Treaty of, 24

Torguts (Kalmuks), 50, 51, 787

948

Torture, abolition of, as legal practice, 265

Tosa, *186*, 223, 253, 288; schools in, 199; daimyo of, 203, 209, 217, 224, 232; Chōshū supported by, 215, 216; men of, in Imperial Force, 237; democratic movement in, 281-282, 284, 289, 290

Tōshiba, 504

Totalitarianism, in Europe, 274, 580, 698; in Japan, 605, 698; Soviet, 698, 784; in China, 866, 868-870, 878-879

Totok, 733, 734

Toungoo, 427, *428*

Tourane (Da-Nang), *435*, 451, 452

Tournon, Maillard de, 61, 62

Tōyama Mitsuru, 632

Tōyō Jiyū Shimbun (*Oriental Free Press*), 285, 308

Tōyō keizai shimpō (*Eastern Economic News*), 567

Tozama. See "Outer" daimyo

Trade, early East-West, 10, 11-12, 18-30, 64, 71-78, 79, 92-97, 168, 177; and Christianity, 32; "country," 69-71, 72, 76, 97, 129-130; Canton system, 71-78, 79, 96-97, 128-136, 141, 168; free, 77, 135, 146, 167, 413, 501; private, 129-130, 134, 136; under the treaties, 150-152; coolie, 154-155; regulation of, 177; post-World War II, of China and Japan, 822-823, 872; *see also* East India Companies, Fur trade, Opium trade, Slave trade, Spice trade, Tea trade, *and various countries*

Trade taxes, 326

Trade Union Law, Japan, 817

Trade unions. *See* Labor unions

Trailok, 424

Tran dynasty, 433, 436

Translation, into Japanese, 270, 272-274, 544, 831; into Chinese, 319, 363, 619, 634, 667, 672; into Mongolian, 790

Transliteration. *See* Romanization

Transportation, in China, 344, 348, 349, 354, 356, 358-359, 411, 700-701; revolution in, 411-412; in Japan, 502-503, *824-825*, 828; in Korea, 762; *see also* Railroads *and* Steamships

Trans-Siberian Railway, 469, 480, 567, *585*, 763, 784, *785*, 789, 795

Travels (Mandeville), 64

Travels (Mundy), 64

Treaties, of Saragossa, 24; of Tordesillas, 24; of Nerchinsk, 48-49; of the Frontier, 50-52; of the Bogue, 144, 145; of Nanking, 144; opening Japan, 144, 169, 180, 200-211, 216, 311; Sino-American, 144, 146, 167, 169, 361; tariff, 144, 145, 146, 167, 171, 177, 234, 344; principal, in unequal treaty system, *145*; Western influence through, 146-155; trade under, 150-152; and missionary movement, 152-153; Franco-Japanese, 169, 205, 481; Japan-Netherlands, 169, 204, 205, 206, 207; Russo-Japanese, 169, 204, 205, 206, 207, 256, 570; of Tientsin, 170, 173; Sino-Russian, 171, 172, 173, 469, 470, 784, 789, 790, 792, 794; of Aigun, 173; Harris, 180, 207, 208, 216, 240, 451; British-Japanese, 204, 205, 207, 303, 311, 478-479, 481, 565, 675; with the Five Nations, 204-211; of Kanagawa, 207, 256; of Kanghwa, 242; Japanese, ending extraterritoriality, 303, 311; between China and Austria-Hungary, 342; China-Netherlands, 342; Sino-Spanish, 342; Sino-Turkish, 369; of Livadia, 370; of St. Petersburg, 370; in Southeast Asia, 376, 451, 457, 460; Japan-Korea, 383; of Shimonoseki, 383, 758; Mackay, 403, 404; Franco-Siamese, 452, 457; of Saigon, 452; Franco-Vietnamese, 453; Anglo-Siamese, 457; original principle of system of, 476; Anglo-Russian, 478, 481; of Portsmouth, 481; preservation of system of, 481; London Disarmament, 586; Sino-Japanese, 649; as phase of modernization, 801; *see also* Treaty system in China

Treaty ports, 166, 358, 406-407; business class in, 155; additional, 177, 345, 473; extraterritoriality and, 303, 311, 340-342; society in, 331; interport trade among, 347

Treaty system in China, 144-146, 166-173, 177, 178, 313, 349, 365, 472, 648, 673, 674, 683; attempted revision of, 335-337, 674-676; economic developments under, 338-348, 658-662; end of, 714

Trengganu, 73, 443, *444*, 445

Triad Society (*San-ho hui* or *San-tien hui*), 120, 159, 162-163, 443, 635, 636, 743

Tribute (*yasak*), 45

Tribute grain (*ts'ao-liang*), 109, 110, 111, 112, 354, 355, 625

Tribute system, Chinese, 72 (table), 73, 77, 129 (illustrations), 366, 881; and the Ryūkyūs, 76; and Siam, 76, 455; and Japan, 128; table of European envoys, 53; destruction of, 134, 143, 178, 375; British struggle against, 139; and Vietnam, 431, 433, 434, 439, 461; and Korea, 461; and Mongolia, 788; and Nepal, 796, 799

Trigault, N., 55, 56

Trinh family, 434, 436, 437

Tripartite Pact (Germany, Italy, Japan), 608, 609
Tripitaka, 448
Trotsky, 677, 678, 687, 850
Trotskyists, 752, 753
True Disputation about the Lord of Heaven (*T'ien-chu shih-i*), 55–56
Truman, Harry S., 819, 847, 848, 871
Truong Chinh, 780
Trusteeship, concept of, 441
Ts'ai Ao, 651
Ts'ai Yüan-p'ei, 636, 661, 662–663; Pl. 73
Tsangpo (Brahmaputra River), 17, 367, 428, 715, 796, 797, 798
Ts'ao K'un, 655, 656, 657
Ts'ao-liang (grain tribute), 109, 110, 111, 112, 354, 355, 625
Ts'en Yü-ying, 323
Tseng-Alexeiev agreement, 479
Tseng Chi-tse ("Marquis Tseng"), 370, 373
Tseng Kuo-ch'üan, 175, 353
Tseng Kuo-fan, 160, 164, 175, 315, 324, 327, 386, 393, 620; as governor-general, 174, 353; and suppression of rebellions, 174, 176, 322; and Lay, 318; and Kiangnan Arsenal, 319, 361; and Tientsin massacre, 337, 338, 397; economic views of, 350
Tsewang Araptan, 50
Tsinan, 94, 105, 660; Communist Party in, 671; Cheeloo University at, 702n.; Northern Expedition at, 707
Tsing Hua College (University), Peking, 661, 668, 702, 859
Tsingtao (Kiaochow), 94, 156, 339, 390, 471, 472, 564, 585, 648, 675
Tsitsihar, 585
Tso chuan, 388
Tso Tsung-t'ang, 142, 174, 175, 324, 337, 353, 374, 620; improvements at Foochow by, 319; campaigns of, in Central Asia, 354, 367, 369–370, 373, 793
Tsong-kha-pa, 796
Tsou Jung, 636
Tsuda Umeko, 275; Tsuda College, 275
Tsukiji Naval Ministry, Pl. 25
Tsungli Yamen ("Office for General Management"), 316–317, 319–320, 336, 366, 371, 372, 373, 376, 399, 401, 623, 625; Pl. 32
Ts'ung-shu (literary collections), 134
Tsung-ts'ai (Party Leader), 693, 694
Tsung-tu (governor-general), Viet. T'ông-Dôc, 438
Tsurumi Shunsuke, 548n.
Tsushima, 179, 186, 240, 256, 465, 824; Straits of, 480, 585

Tsūzoku minken ron (*Popular Account of People's Rights*) (Fukuzawa), 285
Tu Wen-hsiu, 323
Tuan, Prince, 399
Tuan Ch'i-jui, 650, 656n.; as minister of war, 646; as premier, 653, 654, 655; provisional government under, 657
T'uan-lien (militia), 620
Tu-ch'a Yüan (Censorate), 626
Tu-chün ("directors of armies"), 653, 654, 655, 657
"Tuchuns' parliament," 655
Tu-Duc, 439, 451, 452, 453, 485
Tulisen, 50, 51
Tumen River, 465, 585, 763
Tung Chung-shu, 388n.
T'ung-ch'eng school, 327
T'ung-chien kang-mu (*Outline and Details of the Comprehensive Mirror*) (Chu Hsi), 56
T'ung-chih ("Union for Order"), 174
T'ung-chih Emperor, 321, 351n., 371
T'ung-chou, 399
T'ung-hsiang hui (regional guilds), 347, 618, 684
Tung-hsueh ("Eastern Learning"), 398, 463–464, 466–467, 485
T'ung-meng hui ("United League"), 637–639, 640, 643, 644, 661, 662, 734, 743, 750
Tungus tribe, 45, 46, 47, 48
Tungusic language, 793
Tung-wang (Eastern King), 159
T'ung-wen Kuan ("School of Combined Learning" or Interpreters College), 318–319
Turfan, 367, 785, 789
Turkestan, 52; Chinese, 47, 172, 366, 367, 368, 370, 787, 793; Russian, 172, 367, 368, 784
Turkestan-Siberian (Turk-Sib) railroad, 784, 785, 794
Turkey, 151, 278, 369, 847
Turkic-speaking group, 793, 802
Turks, 12; Eastern, 793–794; *see also* Uighurs
Turner, Samuel, 796
Tu-Tai (*Hsiu-ts'ai*) degree, 439
"Tutelage" (*hsun-cheng, yüeh-fa*), 638, 678, 694, 883
"Tutenague," 71
Twenty-One Demands on China, by Japan, 566, 648–649, 666, 675
"Two J's," 547
Tydings-McDuffie Act, 730
Tzu-ch'iang ("self-strengthening"), 147; *see also* "Self-strengthening"
Tz'u-hsi (Empress Dowager), 370, 371; coming to power of, 174, 321; mainte-

nance of position of, 351, 352; nephew declared successor of, 352, 373; retirement of, 380, 381, 382; and radical reformers, 392, 393, 394, 614, 621, 626; and Boxer Rising, 396, 398-399, 400, 402; flight and return of, 403; death of, 627; Pl. 51-52

Tzu-li hui ("Independence Society"), 636

Tzu-liu-ching, *113*, 114

U Aung San, 749, 772, 773, 775

U Nu, 749, 772, 775

U Ottama, 747

Uchida Ryōhei, 467, 482, 632

Uchimura Kanzō, 270, 547

Uehara, General, 584, 591

Ueki Emori, 285

Uemura Masahisa, 270

Ueno Park, Edo, 225

Uesugi, *186*

Uesugi Shinkichi, 536, 569

Ueyama Shumpei, 545n.

Ugaki Kazushige, 576, 591, 592, 595, 596

Uighurs, 368, 369, 370, 793-794, 795

U-in (Right Chamber), 230, 283

Ukhtomskii, E. E., 469, 470

Ulan Bator (Urga), *47*, 49, 51, *367*, *785*, 786, 787, 788, 790, 791, 795, 801

Ulan-Ude (Verkhne Udinsk), *785*, 789

Uliasutai, *785*, 788, 789

Ultranationalism, Japanese, 566-567, 588-594 (*see also* Radical right); Burmese, 749

Ultrapatriotic societies, 632

Ume Kenjirō, 534

Underwood, Horace G., 761

Unequal treaty system, 145 (table), 180, 265, 303, 344, 346, 347, 376, 457, 460, 501; semi-colonial status through, 409; *see also* Treaties *and* Treaty system in China

Unfederated Malay States, *444*, 445

"Union of court and shogunate" (*kōbu gattai*), 214, 215, 222, 223, 224

"Union for Order" (*T'ung-chih*), 174

Unions. See Labor unions *and* Tenant unions

Unitarianism. Japan, 549

United front, in China, 677-681, 852, 881; in Indonesia, 679; in world communism, 753, 755; in Burma, 773; in Vietnam, 768

"United League" (*T'ung-meng hui*), 637-639, 640, 643, 644, 661, 662, 734, 743, 750

United Malays National Organization, 775, 776

United Nations, in Indonesia, 777; Mongolian People's Republic admitted to, 792; Japan admitted to, 819, 830; and Korean War, 819, 847; Communist China refused admission to, 882

United States, treaties of, with China, 144, 146, 167, 169; treaties of, with Japan, 180, 205-206, 207, 216, 311; interest of, in Japan, 195-196, 200-201, 203-204, 205-206, 272, 570-571; Iwakura mission to, 240, 271; technical aid to Japan from, 256; and China, 316, 340, *341*, 470, 472, 699, 702-704; exclusion of Orientals from, 361, 676; Christian colleges in, 363; Chinese diplomatic missions in, 372; and Korea, 375, 377, 378, 466, 468, 761; imperialism of, 409, 476-477; and the Philippines, 409, 727-728, 729-730, 774; and Southeast Asia, 451, 456, 457-458, 744; Alaska bought by, 468; Open Door policy of, 471, 472, 476-477, 481, 565, 608, 630, 675; war between Spain and, 476; in Northeast Asia, 478; during the depression, 496, 498; diplomatic relations of, with Soviet Union, resumed, 575; and Far East, before World War II, 600, 606, 607, 608-609, 610-612; discriminatory treatment of Chinese by, 626; "dollar diplomacy" of, 630; in international banking consortiums, 630, 645, 676; Chinese educated in, 661; and Washington Conference, 675; and Chinese civil war, 689, 859; and Nationalist China, 689, 859, 880, 883; aid to China by, in World War II, 713-717; in World War II, 716, 805-808, 810, 811; and Vietnam, 780, 781; occupation of Japan by, 811-821; retention of bases by, in Japan, 819; security treaty of, with Japan, 819-820, 822; Ryūkyūs taken over by, 820; aid of, to Japan, 822, 823; exports from Japan to, 823; influence of, in Japanese intellectual currents, 834; in South Korea, 844, 845-846; and Korean War, 847-848; relations of, with Communist China, 860-861, 867; in SEATO, 880

"Universalistic" vs. "particularistic" ethic, in China, 84, 870, 879; in Japan, 189, 524, 531-538, 546-547, 553-554, 833-834

Universities. See Colleges and universities

Uraga, *187*, 201, *201*, 203, 207

Urban society, Japan, 490, 514, 515, 521-525, 828-829

Urbanization, China, 660

Urga. See Ulan Bator

Urumchi (Tihwa), 367, 370, *785*, 789, 793
Ussuri River, *47*, 172, 173
Uzbeks, 793

Vajiravudh, Maha (Rama VI), 743, 744
Valignano, Alessandro, 32, 33, 36
Value Creating Association (Sōka Gakkai), 833
Vattel, 140
Veblen, Thorstein, 494
Venice, 11, 20, 32
Verbeck, Guido, 269
Verbiest, Ferdinand, 42, 48, 54, 57, 61, 66
Vereenigde Oostindische Compagnie. *See* Dutch East India Company
Verkhne Udinsk (Ulan-Ude), *785*, 789
Verne, Jules, 274
Versailles peace treaty, 312, 666, 675, 744
Victoria, city of, Hong Kong, Pl. 17–18
Victoria, Queen, of England, 140, 370
Vientiane (Vieng Chan), 424, *428*, 431, *435*, 452, 454
Viet Minh ("Viet League"), 768, 769, 778, 779, 780, 879
Vietnam (Annam), 3, *17*, 72, 73, *95*, 97, 145, 420, 425; Spanish in, 26; Dutch in, 28, 67; France in, 54, 372, 373, 437, 438, 439, 450, 451–453, 454, 455, 720, 750–751, 752, 753, 755; pirates based in, 119; and the West, 366, 409, *410*, 436–438, 486, 487, 718; Mongols in, 423; development of, 431–440; independence of, from China, 431–433; Chinese influence in, 438–440, 749, 778, 802; area and population of, 440, 460, 742; as tributary to China, 72, 461; Confucianism in, 485; nationalism in, 749–754, 779, 780; Japan in, 768; as independent nation, 769, 778, 779, 781
Viet Nam Doc Lap Dong Minh Hoi (League for the Independence of Vietnam), 768
Viet Nam Quang Phuc Hoi (Society for the Restoration of Vietnam), 750
Viet Nam Quoc Dan Dang (Vietnam Nationalist Party), 752
Vietnam Revolutionary Youth League, 752
Viet Nam vong quoc su (*History of the Eclipse of Vietnam*) (Chau), 749
Vietnam Workers (Viet Nam Lao Dong) Party, 780
Vietnamese language, 431–432, 436, 437
Village headmen (*shōya*), 215, 282
"Village samurai," 223; *see also* Rural samurai
Villages, Japan, 516, 518, 519; life in, since World War II, 829
Visayan, 724

Vishnu, 420, 422
Vladislavich, Sava ("Raguzinski"), 49, 50–51, 53
Vladivostok, *47*, 173, 341, 344, *585*, 763, 764, *785*
Vo Nguyen Giap, 768, 778, 781
Voitinsky, Gregory, 671, 678
Volga River, 50, 51
Volksraad (People's Council), Indonesia, 735
Voltaire, 58, 65
Voting, Japan, 299–302, 308, 520–521, 562–563, 575–576, 839

Wada Hiroo, 602
Wade, T. F., 336, 345, 371–372
Waichow (Hui-chou), *133*, 636
Wai-wu Pu (Ministry of Foreign Affairs), 623, 626, 695
Wakatsuki, 573, 574, 577, 581, 584, 587
Wakayama, 184, *186*, 303; lord of, 208, 209
Wake Island, 806
Waldersee, Alfred von, 403
Walled district (*hsien*), 100, 104, 167, 433
Wang (king), 159n.; (prince), 787
Wang, C. T., 665, 689
Wang An-shih, 161
Wang Ching-wei, 600, 638, 639, 683, 686, 693, 696, 711
Wang Mang, 161, 388
Wang T'ao, 360–361, 364, 387, 389
Wang Yang-ming, 634, 870
Wang-hsia, American Treaty of, 144, 145 (Wanghia)
Wang-tao ("Kingly Way"), 708
Wan-kuo kung-pao ("international gazette"; *Globe Magazine*), 364, 385
Wan-li, 37, 382
War, Board of (Ping Pu), 623, 626
War crimes trials, Tōkyō, 813
Ward, Frederick Townsend, 175
Warlordism, China, 621, 666, 696, 790; nature of, 649–653; struggle among the warlords, 653–658, 683
Warrior class. *See* Samurai
Waseda University, Tōkyō, 275
Washington Conference of 1922, 570, 573, 586, 674–676, 707
Watanabe Kazan, 199
Water forces, China, 118–119, 151; Pl. 15; *see also* Naval strength
Water gate, Peking, *401*
We Burmans Society (*Dobama Asiayone*), 749
Wealth of Nations (Smith), 619
Weddell, John, 64, 71
Weekly Critic (*Mei-chou p'ing-lun*), 664

Wei Ch'ang-hui, 163, 168
Wei River, *94*, *160*, *853*
Wei Yüan, 124–125, 128, 139, 147, 149, 150, 315, 316, 386, 388
Weihaiwei, *339*, 381, 383, 402, 472, 473, *585*, 675
Wellesley, Province, 443, *444*
Wen I-to, 860
Wenchow, *339*
Weng T'ung-ho, 380–381, 390–391, 392
Wen-hsiang, 328, 337, 350, 393
Wen-hsüeh yen-chiu hui (Literary Association), 672
Wen-yen (classical written style), 663
Wesleyan College, Pl. 74
Wesleyan Methodists in China, 332
West China Union University, Chengtu, 702n.
West Germany, 822
West New Guinea (West Irian), 742, 778
West (Hsi) River, *17*, *95*, *113*, 159, *160*, *435*, 473, *853*
"Western Learning" (Korean: *Sŏhak*; Chinese: *Hsi-hsüeh*), 463
"Western Ocean" country, 72, 127
Western world, Chinese image of, 125–128; disillusionment with "materialism" of, 668; *see also* Westernization
Westernization, and modernization, 5, 6–7; Christianity and, 33; in China, 150, 154–155, 313–320, 384–394, 404–407, 615, 619, 633–634, 651, 692, 801; revulsion against, 150, 264–265, 294; in Japan, 188, 262–264, 266, 291, 294, 492, 493, 522, 524, 801; and Japanese value system, 266; in self-defense, 313–320; sanction for, 386–387, 388; and Chinese Reform Movement, 384–394; and stability of civilization, 404–407; and colonialism, 720–721; in the Philippines, 724; in Siam, 744; *see also* "Foreign matters"
Whampoa, 75, *133*, 135, 381; French Treaty of, 144, 145
"Whampoa clique," 694, 859, 860
Whampoa Military Academy, 682, 752; Pl. 76
Whangpu River, 167
Wheaton, Henry, 319
White Birch school of novelists, 540–543, 551
"White Flag" faction, Burma, 775
White Lotus Rebellion, 115, 116–118
White Lotus Society (*Pai-lien chiao*), 117, 119, 120, 164–165, 321
"White man's burden," 365, 414
White Russians, 784, 790–791
White supremacy theory of Europeans, 754

Whitman, Walt, 540
Wild Tiger Scout Corps, 743
William II (Kaiser) of Germany, 471
Williams, S. Wells, 152, 200
Wilson, Woodrow, 571, 645, 665, 675
"Wind and water spirits" (*feng-shui*), 335, 356, 357, 372, 396
Witte, Sergei, 469, 470, 478, 479
Wo-jen, 320
Wo-k'ou ("dwarf pirates"), 350
Women, in Japan, 275, 278, 547, 830; education of, in Japan and China, 275, 278, 547, 660; in China, 660, 667, 867; in Korea, 761
Women's rights movement, Japan, 514, 547, 702n.
Wŏnsan, 376, *465*, *585*
Wood, Leonard, 729
Wool, Tibetan, 797
Woolen industry, Japan, 248, 502
Worker-students, Chinese, in France, 661, 671
Works, Board of (Kung Pu), 623
World Student Christian Federation, 668
World War I, 496–497, 720, 784; Japan in, 312, 561–563, 648; China and, 648, 655, 665; Siam in, 744
World War II, in the Pacific, 606–612, 720, 804–811, *809*; in Europe, 608, 609; in China, 710, 808, *809*; U.S. aid to China in, 713–717; Southeast Asia in, 765–773; chronology of, 776; peace treaty with Japan following, 818–820
Wright, Mary Clabaugh, 328n.
Writing systems, Vietnamese, 436, 437; Korean, 462, 467; Chinese, 663, 884; *see also* Languages
Wu Chien-chang (Samqua), 167
Wu Chih-hui, 662
Wu Hao-kuan, 134
Wu Men, Pl. 8
Wu P'ei-fu, 655, 656, 657, 678, 685
Wuchang, *94*, *105*, 159, *160*, 164, 379, 380, 640
Wuhan, 379, 380, 393, 640, 671, 683, 687
Wu-shu ("military art"), 394
Wusung, *176*, *339*, 356

Xavier, St. Francis, 22, 31, 36, 56
Xenophobia. *See* Antiforeignism

Ya-hang (licensed brokers), 73, 92
Ya-hsi-ya ("Asia"), 42
Yakub Beg, 369, 370
Yakutsk, 45, 47
Yalta Conference, 810
Yalu River, *149*, *465*, *585*, 844, 848
Yamada, *187*
Yamada Akiyoshi, 293, 300

Yamagata Aritomo, 237, 241, 243, 271, 286, 288, 302, 303, 311, 478, 554, 557, 559, 562, 568, 596; and the military, 291, 294–295, 298, 305; as home minister, 293; as prime minister, 299, 300, 301, 302, 306–307; and Itō, 305–306; in Privy Council, 308, 312; annexation of Korea favored by, 482; war predicted by, 563; and military expenditures, 566; and Trans-Siberian Railway, 567; theory of government of, 578, 633; Pl. 45–46

Yamaguchi, *186, 824*

Yamamoto Gombei, 559, 562, 573

Yamanouchi, domain of, *186*; daimyo, 215

Yamen, 100, 101, 104

Yanagawa Heisuke, 591, 599

Yandabo, 446

Yang Hsiu-ch'ing, 159, 160, 161, 163

Yang Kuang-hsien, 61, 334

Yang Ping-nan, 127–128

Yang Tseng-hsin, 794

Yangchow, *94, 113,* 116, 337

Yangban, 463, 464, 483

Yang-hang ("merchants in oceanic trade"), 73

Yangtze (River and) Valley, *17,* 37, *47,* 92, *94–95,* 104, 112, *113,* 117, *156, 160, 176,* 177, *367,* 379, 416, *428, 564, 715,* 797, *798, 853,* 860; land tax administration in, 110; and Grand Canal, 111, 143; Taipings in, 159, 162, 164; amphibious tactics in delta of, 175; rice-growing in, 321; cotton production in, 346; steamboating on, 348, 349; Garnier's expedition to, 452; British sphere of influence in, 471, 473, 476, 478; revolutionary movement in, 637; Pl. 41

Yang-wu ("foreign matters"), 320, 350, 354, 362n.

Yao, 387

Yao-k'ou (brokerage houses in opium trade), 131

Yarkand, *16,* 43, *367,* 368, 797, *798*

Yasak (tribute), 45

Yasuda Zenjirō, 255, 506

Yatung, *798,* 799

Yawata Iron and Steel Works, 261, 496, 503

"Year period," 198, 209, 227, 263

Yeh Ming-ch'en, 169, 170

Yellow River, *17, 47, 94, 113,* 114, *156, 160, 564, 715, 785, 798,* 852, *853*; transport services on, 111–113; shifts of, 156–157; flooding of, 164, 395; plan to control, 874

Yellow Sea, *156, 160, 465, 585*

Yellow sect of Lamaism, 786–787, 796

Yen, James Y. C., 661, 705

Yen-Bay, *435,* 752

Yen Fu, 387, 619, 650

Yen Hsi-shan ("the Model Governor"), 657, 658, 696; Pl. 78

Yen Jo-chü, 123

Yen Yang-ch'u (James Yen), 661, 705

Yenan, *853*; Yenan period, CCP, 851, 852–857; Pl. 77

Yenangyaung region, 738

Yenching University, Peiping, 702n.

Yen-chiu hsi ("research clique"), 654, 694

Yenisei River, *17,* 45, *47, 785*

Yeniseisk, 45, *47*

Yermak, 44

Yi dynasty, 433, 462, 464

Yi Ha-ŭng, 464

Yi Sŏng-gye, 464

Yi Sŭng-man (Syngman Rhee), 761, 764

Yi Tong-hwi, 763, 764

Yi Un, Pl. 50

Yin (certificate) system, 115, 124

Yin and *yang*, 388n.

Ying-huan chih-lueh (Brief Survey of the Maritime Circuit), 150

Yingkow (Newchwang), *339,* 340, *585*

Yochow, *95, 339*

Yokohama, *187,* 201, 210, 211, 521, *825*; Kanagawa now part of, 203; as chief port for foreign trade, 205–206; French school at, 222; railway to Tōkyō from, 234, 247; industry at, 246; gas lights in, 262; Christianity in, 269

Yokohama Daily Newspaper (Yokohama Mainichi Shimbun), 285

Yokohama Specie Bank, 698–699

Yokoi Shōnan, 215, 216

Yokosuka, *187,* 222, 246, *825*

Yonai Mitsumasa, 581, 607, 608, 808, 810, 811

Yoshida Shigeru, 595, 836

Yoshida Shōin, 214, 215, 218, 219, 237, 305; Pl. 21

Yoshino Sakuzō, 547–549, 550, 569, 815; Pl. 67

"Young China," 631

Young China Communist Party, Paris, 671

Young Communist League, Young Pioneers, China, 877

"Young Marshal" (Chang Hsüeh-liang), 587, 689, 696

Young Men's Buddhist Association (Y. M. B. A.), 747

Young Men's (and Young Women's) Christian Association, 705, 861

Younghusband, Francis, 800

Youth (Thanh Nien), 752

Youth Corps, CCP, 685, 712

Youth League, Mongolia, 791
Yü Ta-fu, 672
Yūaikai, 569
Yüan dynasty, 10, 646, 650; fleet, 118
Yüan Ming Yüan (Summer Palace), 63, 171, *399*
Yüan Shih-k'ai, 353, 384, 385, 402, 566, 654, 801; in Korea, 378, 382, 466; and Boxer rising, 398; and Provisional Government, 403; and abolition of examination system, 617; and Peiyang clique, 621, 623; dismissal of, 627; as premier and president (and dictator) of Chinese Republic, 640–646, 647, 649–650, 651, 652, 662; image of, on silver dollars, 660
Yüeh-fa (provisional constitution), 638, 678
Yü-hsien, 397, 398, 399, 400, 403
Yung ("braves"), 620
Yung ("function"), 386; (Western devices), 391
Yung Wing, 361, 362, 364, 616, 634, 643
Yung-an, 159, *160*

Yung-cheng, 50, 51, 62, 85, 120, 333, 334, 385
Yung-lo, 81
Yunnan, 72, *95*, *113*, *435*, 473, 696; mining in, 97, 114, 137; revolt in, 165, 166, 638; French explorers in, 448, 452; railroads in, 471, 629; declaration of independence by, 651; military academy in, 682
Yunnan-fu (Kunming), *95*, *105*, 323, *435*, 471, *715*, *853*, 859
Yurt, 789

Zaibatsu, 252, 253, 254, 255, 258, 505–513; concentration of wealth in, 494; as "modern" social organization, 512; as political elite, 557; in World War I, 565; and Planning Board, 602; reform of, 816–817
Zayton. *See* Chinchew
Zen Buddhism, 32, 541, 544–545
Zengakuren, 832; *see also* Student movement, in Japan
Zikawei (Hsü-chia-hui), 39, 153, *341*
Zinoviev, 763